THE WORLD IN 1997

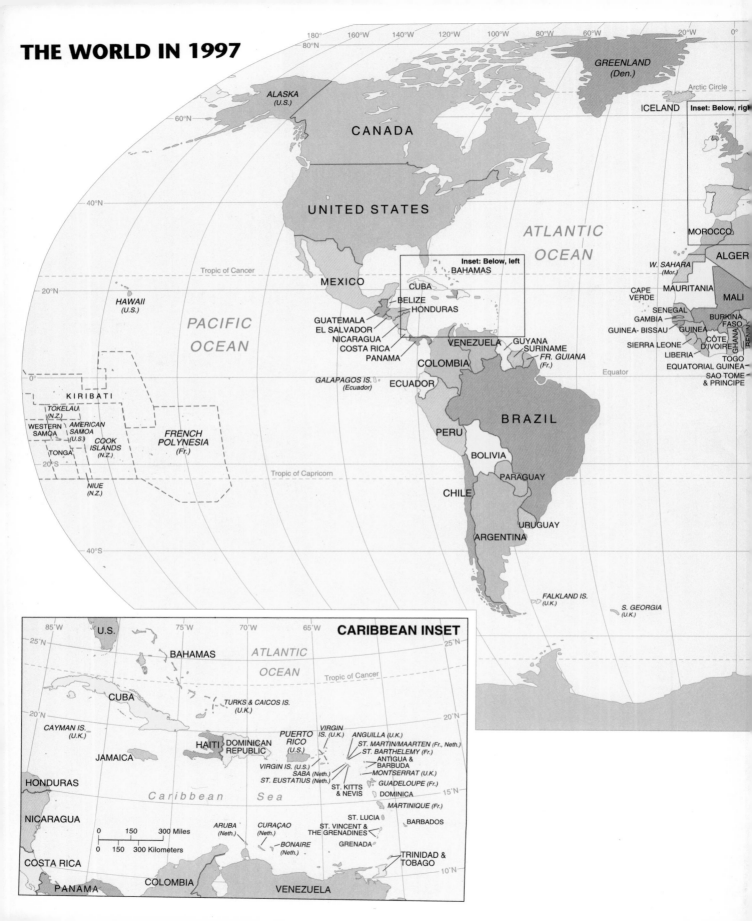

180° · **160°W** · **140°W** · **120°W** · **100°W** · **80°W** · **60°W** · **20°W** · **0°**

80°N

GREENLAND
(Den.)

Arctic Circle

ALASKA
(U.S.)

60°N

ICELAND

Inset: Below, right

CANADA

40°N

UNITED STATES

ATLANTIC
OCEAN

MOROCCO

ALGER

Tropic of Cancer

Inset: Below, left
BAHAMAS

W. SAHARA
(Mor.)

20°N

MEXICO

CUBA

CAPE
VERDE

MAURITANIA

MALI

HAWAII
(U.S.)

PACIFIC
OCEAN

BELIZE
HONDURAS

SENEGAL
GAMBIA
GUINEA-BISSAU

BURKINA
FASO
GUINEA

GUATEMALA
EL SALVADOR
NICARAGUA
COSTA RICA
PANAMA

VENEZUELA

GUYANA
SURINAME
FR. GUIANA
(Fr.)

SIERRA LEONE
LIBERIA

CÔTE
D'IVOIRE

GHANA

BENIN

TOGO

COLOMBIA

EQUATORIAL GUINEA
SAO TOME
& PRINCIPE

GALAPAGOS IS.
(Ecuador)

ECUADOR

Equator

0°

KIRIBATI

PERU

B R A Z I L

TOKELAU
(N.Z.)

WESTERN
SAMOA
AMERICAN
SAMOA
(U.S.)

COOK
ISLANDS
(N.Z.)

FRENCH
POLYNESIA
(Fr.)

BOLIVIA

TONGA

20°S

PARAGUAY

CHILE

NIUE
(N.Z.)

Tropic of Capricorn

URUGUAY

ARGENTINA

40°S

FALKLAND IS.
(U.K.)

S. GEORGIA
(U.K.)

CARIBBEAN INSET

85°W · **75°W** · **70°W** · **65°W**

25°N

U.S.

BAHAMAS

ATLANTIC

OCEAN

25°N

Tropic of Cancer

CUBA

TURKS & CAICOS IS.
(U.K.)

20°N

CAYMAN IS.
(U.K.)

HAITI
DOMINICAN
REPUBLIC

PUERTO
RICO
(U.S.)

VIRGIN
IS. (U.K.)

ANGUILLA *(U.K.)*
ST. MARTIN/MAARTEN (Fr., Neth.)
ST. BARTHELEMY (Fr.)

20°N

JAMAICA

VIRGIN IS. *(U.S.)*
SABA *(Neth.)*
ST. EUSTATIUS *(Neth.)*

ANTIGUA &
BARBUDA
MONTSERRAT *(U.K.)*

HONDURAS

Caribbean   Sea

ST. KITTS
& NEVIS

GUADELOUPE (Fr.)

DOMINICA

15°N

NICARAGUA

MARTINIQUE (Fr.)

ST. LUCIA

BARBADOS

0   150   300 Miles

ARUBA
(Neth.)

CURAÇAO
(Neth.)

ST. VINCENT &
THE GRENADINES

0   150   300 Kilometers

BONAIRE
(Neth.)

GRENADA

TRINIDAD &
TOBAGO

COSTA RICA

PANAMA

COLOMBIA

VENEZUELA

10°N

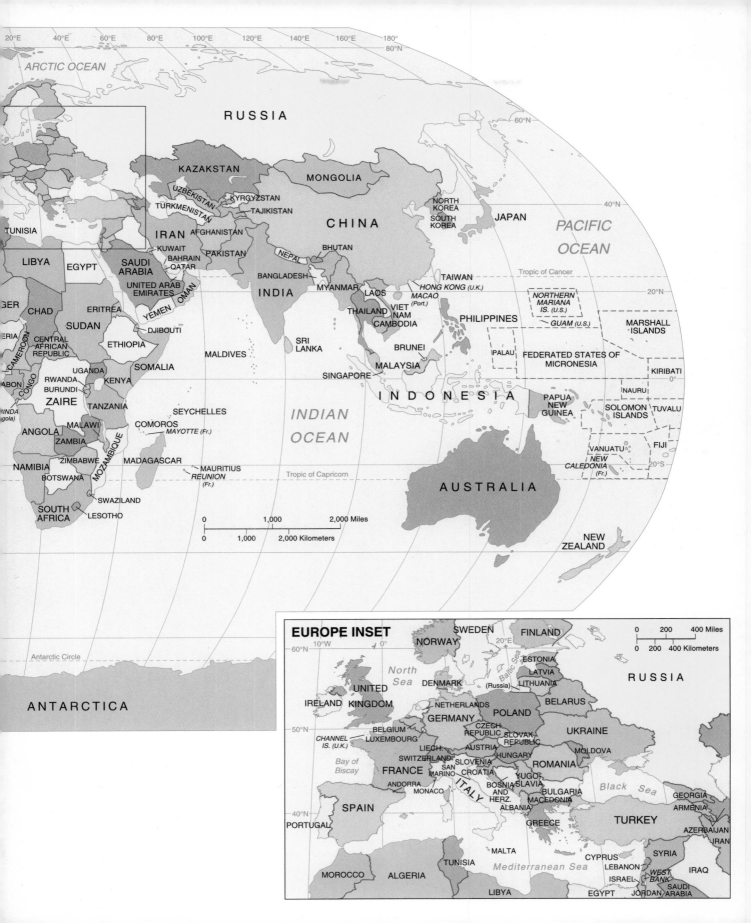

MARKETING

MANAGEMENT

ANALYSIS, PLANNING, IMPLEMENTATION, AND CONTROL

THE PRENTICE HALL INTERNATIONAL SERIES IN MARKETING

Philip Kotler, *Series Editor*

9TH EDITION

MARKETING MANAGEMENT

ANALYSIS, PLANNING, IMPLEMENTATION, AND CONTROL

PHILIP KOTLER

NORTHWESTERN UNIVERSITY

 Prentice Hall International, Inc., Upper Saddle River, New Jersey 07458

Ninth Edition
MARKETING MANAGEMENT
Analysis, Planning, Implementation, and Control
PHILIP KOTLER

Acquisitions Editor: David Borkowsky
Development Editor: Steven A. Rigolosi
Associate Editor: John Larkin
Editorial Assistant: Theresa Festa
Editor-in-Chief: James C. Boyd
Director of Development: Stephen Deitmer
Senior Project Manager: Linda M. DeLorenzo
Production Coordinator: David G. Cotugno
Managing Editor: Valerie Q. Lentz
Manufacturing Supervisor: Arnold Vila
Manufacturing Manager: Vincent Scelta
Design Director: Patricia H. Wosczyk
Interior Design: Ox & Company Inc
Cover Design: Patricia H. Wosczyk/Wendy Helft
Illustrator (Interior): Dartmouth Publishing, Inc.
Composition: Progressive Information Technologies

ISBN 0-13-261363-8

Prentice-Hall International (UK) Limited, London
Prentice-Hall of Australia Pty. Limited, Sydney
Prentice-Hall Canada, Inc., Toronto
Prentice-Hall Hispanoamericana, S.A., Mexico
Prentice-Hall of India Private Limited, New Delhi
Prentice-Hall of Japan, Inc., Tokyo
Simon & Schuster Asia Pte. Ltd., Singapore
Editora Prentice-Hall do Brasil, Ltda., Rio de Janeiro
Prentice-Hall, Upper Saddle River, New Jersey

Printed in the United States of America

10 9 8 7 6 5 4 3 2 1

This book is dedicated to my wife and best friend, Nancy, with love

ABOUT THE AUTHOR

Philip Kotler is one of the world's leading authorities on marketing. He is the S.C. Johnson & Son Distinguished Professor of International Marketing at the Kellogg Graduate School of Management, Northwestern University. He received his master's degree at the University of Chicago and his Ph.D at M.I.T., both in economics. He did postdoctoral work in mathematics at Harvard and behavioral science at the University of Chicago.

Dr. Kotler is the author of *Principles of Marketing* and *Marketing: An Introduction.* His *Strategic Marketing for Nonprofit Organizations,* now in its fifth edition, is the best seller in that specialized area. Dr. Kotler's other books include *The New Competition; Marketing Professional Services; Marketing for Health Care Organizations; Strategic Marketing for Educational Institutions; High Visibility; Social Marketing; Marketing Places; Marketing for Congregations; Marketing for Hospitality and Tourism; Standing Room Only: Strategies for Marketing the Performing Arts;* and *Marketing Models.*

In addition, he has written over 100 articles for leading journals, including *Harvard Business Review, Sloan Management Review, Business Horizons, California Management Review, Journal of Marketing, Journal of Marketing Research, Management Science, Journal of Business Strategy,* and *Futurist.* He is the only three-time winner of the coveted Alpha Kappa Psi award for the best annual article published in the *Journal of Marketing.*

Dr. Kotler has served as chairman of the College on Marketing of The Institute of Management Sciences (TIMS); a director of the American Marketing Association; a trustee of the Marketing Science Institute and the School of the Art Institute of Chicago; a director of The MAC Group (Gemini); and an advisory board member of The Peter Drucker Foundation and Copernicus. He has been a consultant to many major U.S. and foreign companies—AT&T, Bank of America, Ford, General Electric, IBM, Merck, Marriott, and Montedison among them—on marketing strategy.

In 1978, Dr. Kotler received the Paul D. Converse Award given by the American Marketing Association to honor "outstanding contributions to science in marketing." In 1983, he received the Steuart Henderson Britt Award as Marketer of the Year. In 1985, he was named the first recipient of the Distinguished Marketing Educator Award, a new award established by the American Marketing Association. In the same year, the Academy for Health Services Marketing established the Philip Kotler Award for Excellence in Health Care Marketing and nominated him as the first recipient. He also received the Prize for Marketing Excellence awarded by the European Association of Marketing Consultants and Sales Trainers. In 1989, he received the Charles Coolidge Parlin Award, which each year honors an outstanding leader in the field of marketing. In 1995, he received the Marketing Educator of the Year Award from Sales and Marketing Executives International. He has received honorary doctorate degrees from DePaul University, the University of Zurich, and the Athens University of Economics and Business.

BRIEF CONTENTS

TABLE OF CONTENTS

xi

Part IV
PLANNING MARKETING PROGRAMS

xvii

TECHNICAL APPENDIXES

FEATURES

MARKETING INSIGHT *Highlighting current research and findings in marketing management*

VISION 2000 *Looking ahead to marketing and marketing management in the twenty-first century*

MARKETING MEMO *Tips, procedures, and strategies for marketing managers*

THEMATIC EXAMPLES

MARKETING MANAGEMENT AND TECHNOLOGY

ETHICS AND SOCIAL RESPONSIBILITY

PREFACE

Toward the end of a century, let alone a millenium, people often feel a growing uneasiness about the future. Recent books such as *The End of Affluence*[1] and the *The End of Work*[2] foster a gloom about future incomes and job opportunities. Certainly many countries today suffer from chronic high unemployment, a persistent deficit, and deteriorating purchasing power. How justified is this pessimism?

Clearly, national economies are undergoing rapid and often wrenching transformations. Two forces underlie the dramatic changes. One is *globalization,* the explosive growth of global trade and international competition. No country today can remain isolated from the world economy. If it closes its markets to foreign competition, its citizens will pay much more for lower-quality goods. But if it opens its markets, it will face severe competition and many of its local businesses will suffer.

The other force is *technological change.* This decade has witnessed remarkable advances in the availability of information and the speed of communication; in new materials; in biogenetic advances and drugs; in electronic marvels. Anyone familiar with U.S. stores and catalogs will testify to the endless outpouring of new products. Some historians make the case that most historical change is technology-driven.

The paradox is that globalization and technological advances open up many new opportunities even as they threaten the status quo. Globalization has made it possible for Volvo to sells its automobiles to safety-conscious car buyers around the world, for McDonald's to cater to universal teen-age appetites, and for Boeing to source components for its 747s from producers in at least a dozen nations. Technology has created multibillion-dollar new companies such as Microsoft, Dell Computer, Sun Microsystems, and many others.

Yes, old businesses die and new ones appear. Companies operate in a Darwinian marketplace where the principles of natural selection lead to "survival of the fittest." Marketplace success goes to those companies best matched to the current environmental imperatives—those who can deliver what people are ready to buy. Individuals, businesses, cities, and even whole countries must discover how they can produce *marketable value*—namely, goods and services that others are willing to purchase.

Today's markets are changing at an incredible pace. In addition to globalization and technological change, we are witnessing a power shift from manufacturers to giant retailers, a rapid growth and acceptance of store brands, new retail forms, growing consumer price and value sensitivity, a diminishing role for mass marketing and advertising, and a disconcerting erosion of brand loyalty. These changes are throwing companies into a state

---

[1] Jeffrey G. Madrick, *The End of Affluence: The Causes and Consequences of America's Economic Dilemma* (New York: Random House, 1995).
[2] Jeremy Rivkin, *The End of Work: The Decline of the Global Labor Force and the Dawn of the Post-Market Era* (New York: G. P. Putnam's Sons, 1995).

of confusion regarding strategy. To protect their profits, companies have primarily responded by cutting their costs, reengineering their processes, and downsizing their work forces. Yet even companies that succeed in cutting their costs may fail to increase their revenue if they lack marketing vision and marketing know-how.

Unfortunately, the general public, and even many senior managers, do not understand marketing. The general public sees marketing as the vigorous and sometimes intrusive use (or abuse) of advertising and selling: "Oh, no, another commercial." Marketing, they think, attempts to make unwilling buyers purchase unwanted goods. Of course, companies often have to move surplus goods and can do so by cutting prices and resorting to hard-sell techniques. But this is a far cry from what marketing is and what marketing does.

Many managers think of marketing as a department consisting of several types of career people: marketing planners, marketing researchers, advertising and sales-promotion specialists, customer service personnel, new-product managers, product and brand managers, market-segment managers, and of course salespeople. Their collective job is to analyze the market, discern opportunities, formulate marketing strategies, develop specific tactics and actions, propose a budget, and establish a set of controls. But this view doesn't go far enough. Marketing is also responsible for driving the rest of the company to be customer-oriented and market-driven. Customers are scarce; without them, the company ceases to exist. Plans must be laid to acquire and keep customers. And because so many factors affect customer satisfaction, many of which lie outside the scope of the marketing department—such as delivery reliability, invoice clarity, and telephone manners—marketing must work hard to ensure that the rest of the company delivers on customers' expectations, and its own promises, consistently.

Marketing, however, is much more than a company "selling" department. Marketing is an orderly and insightful process for thinking about and planning for markets. The process starts with researching the marketplace to understand its dynamics. The marketer uses research to identify opportunities—that is, to find individuals or groups of people with unmet needs or a latent interest in some product or service. The marketing process involves segmenting the market and choosing those target markets that the company can satisfy in a superior way. The company must formulate a broad strategy and define a specific marketing mix and action plan to optimize its long-run performance. The company builds in a set of controls so that it can evaluate results and operate as a learning organization, constantly improving its marketing know-how.

The marketing process is applicable to more than just goods and services. Anything can be marketed, including ideas, events, organizations, places, and personalities. However, it is important to emphasize that marketing doesn't start so much with a product or offering, but with a search for opportunities in the marketplace.

TRENDS

Marketing is not like Euclidean geometry, a fixed system of concepts and axioms. Rather, marketing is one of the most dynamic fields within the management arena. The marketplace continually throws out fresh challenges, and companies must respond. Therefore it is not surprising that new marketing ideas keep surfacing to meet the new marketplace challenges.

Here are several emphases in current marketing thinking:

1. **A growing emphasis on quality, value, and customer satisfaction.** Different buying motivations (convenience, status, style, features, service, etc.) play a strong role at

different times and places. Today's customers are placing greater weight on quality and value in making their purchase decisions. Some remarkable companies are managing to increase their quality greatly while bringing down their costs. Their guiding principle is to continuously offer more for less.

2. **A growing emphasis on relationship building and customer retention.** Much marketing theory in the past has focused on how to "make a sale." But what good is it to make a sale and not know much about the customer and whether he or she will ever buy again? Today's marketers are focusing on creating lifelong customers. The shift is from transaction thinking to relationship building. Companies are now building customer databases containing customer demographics, lifestyles, levels of responsiveness to different marketing stimuli, past transactions—and orchestrating their offerings to produce pleased or delighted customers who will remain loyal to the company.

3. **A growing emphasis on managing business processes and integrating business functions.** Today's companies are shifting their thinking from managing a set of semi-independent departments, each with its own logic, to managing a set of fundamental business processes, all of which impact customer service and satisfaction. Companies are assigning cross-disciplinary personnel to manage each process. Marketing personnel are increasingly working on cross-disciplinary teams rather than only in the marketing department. This is a positive development that broadens marketers' perspectives on the business and gives them the greater opportunity to broaden the perspective of workers from other departments.

4. **A growing emphasis on global thinking and local market planning.** Companies are increasingly pursuing markets beyond their borders. As they enter these markets, they must drop their traditional assumptions about market behavior and adapt their offerings to other countries' cultural prerequisites. They must place decision-making power in the hands of their local representatives, who are much more aware of the local economic, political, legal, and social realities facing the firm. Companies must think globally, but plan and act locally.

5. **A growing emphasis on building strategic alliances and networks.** As companies globalize, they realize that no matter how large they are, they lack the total resources and requisites for success. Viewing the complete supply chain for producing value, they recognize the necessity of partnering with other organizations. Companies such as Ford, McDonald's, and Levi Strauss owe their success to having built a set of global partners who supply different requirements for success. Senior management is spending an increasing amount of time designing strategic alliances and networks that create a competitive advantage for the partnering firms.

6. **A growing emphasis on direct and online marketing.** The information and communication revolution promises to change the nature of buying and selling. People anywhere in the world can access the Internet and companies' home pages to scan offers and order goods. Via online services, they can give and get advice on products and services by chatting with other users, determine the best values, place orders, and get next-day delivery. As a result of advances in database technology, companies can do more direct marketing and rely less on wholesale and retail intermediaries. Beyond this, much company buying is now done automatically through electronic data interchange links among companies. All these trends portend greater buying and selling efficiency.

7. **A growing emphasis on services marketing.** The U.S. population today consists of only 2.5% farmers and about 15% factory workers. Most people are doing service work: field salespeople, retailers, craftspeople, and knowledge workers such as physi-

cians, engineers, accountants, and lawyers. Because services are intangible, perishable, variable, and inseparable, they pose additional challenges not found in tangible-goods marketing. Marketers are increasingly developing strategies for service firms that sell insurance, software, consulting services, and other services.

8. **A growing emphasis on high-tech industries.** Much economic growth is due to the emergence of high-tech firms, which differ from traditional firms. High-tech firms face higher risks, slower product acceptance, shorter product life cycles, and faster technological obsolescence. How many of today's thousands of software firms and biotech firms will survive in the face of these challenges? High-tech firms must master the art of marketing their venture to the financial community and convincing enough customers to adopt their new products.

9. **A growing emphasis on ethical marketing behavior.** The general public is wary of ads and sales approaches that distort or lie about product benefits or that manipulate people into hasty purchases. The marketplace is highly susceptible to abuse by those who lack scruples and are willing to prosper at the expense of others. Marketers, in particular, must hold to high standards in practicing their craft. The American Marketing Association has promulgated a code of ethical marketing behavior, and marketers need to act as watchdogs to preserve a trusted and efficient marketplace.

APPROACH AND ORGANIZATION

My goal in writing the ninth edition of *Marketing Management: Analysis, Planning, Implementation, and Control* was to capture these new challenges and propose fresh ways of thinking about them. At the same time, this edition continues to build on the fundamental features of past editions. These are:

1. *A managerial orientation:* This book focuses on the major decisions that marketing managers and top management face in their efforts to harmonize the organization's objectives, capabilities, and resources with marketplace needs and opportunities.

2. *An analytical approach:* This book presents a framework for analyzing recurrent problems in marketing management. Company cases and examples are introduced throughout the text to illustrate effective marketing principles, strategies, and practices.

3. *A basic disciplines perspective:* This book draws on the rich findings of various scientific disciplines. *Economics* provides fundamental concepts and tools for seeking optimal results in the use of scarce resources. *Behavioral science* provides fundamental concepts and tools for understanding consumer and organizational buying behavior. *Management theory* provides a framework for identifying the issues facing managers, as well as guidelines and tools for their satisfactory resolution. *Mathematics* provides an exact language for expressing relationships among important variables.

4. *Universal applications:* This book applies marketing thinking to the complete spectrum of marketing: products and services, consumer and business markets, profit and nonprofit organizations, domestic and foreign companies, small and large firms, manufacturing and intermediary businesses, and low-tech and high-tech industries.

5. *Comprehensive and balanced coverage:* This book covers all the topics that an informed marketing manager needs to know. It covers the main issues in strategic, tactical, and administrative marketing.

This ninth edition of *Marketing Management* is organized into five parts. *Part I, Understanding Marketing Management,* develops the societal, managerial, and strategic underpinnings of marketing theory and practice. *Part II, Analyzing Marketing Opportunities,* presents concepts and tools for analyzing any market and marketing environment to discern opportunities. *Part III, Developing Marketing Strategies,* examines issues in designing marketing strategies for companies in different market positions, global positions, and stages in the product life cycle. *Part IV, Planning Marketing Programs,* deals with tactical marketing and how companies should handle each element of the marketing mix—product, price, place, and promotion. Finally, *Part V, Managing the Marketing Effort,* examines the administrative side of marketing—how firms organize, implement, evaluate, and control marketing activities.

NEW TO THE NINTH EDITION

Readers will note the following new features of the ninth edition:

1. The book has been reduced from 27 to 24 chapters, by merging certain chapters where there was a natural fit. Also, some material less central to the interests of marketing managers has been pruned.
2. A new chapter has been added, *Chapter 23, Managing Direct and Online Marketing.* This chapter examines the burgeoning new channels of information, communication, and sales becoming available to marketers.
3. The ninth edition contains a great number of new materials and case examples from the 1990s, featuring such companies as Blockbuster Video, Starbucks, 3M, Proctor & Gamble, and many others. In addition, a high proportion of the book's research footnotes list the latest 1990s sources.
4. The ninth edition adds completely new end-of-chapter concept applications, many of them dealing with actual marketing challenges facing real companies.
5. Unlike earlier editions, the ninth edition includes illustrations of ads and other pictorial material to challenge and inform the reader.
6. Interesting material is featured in two kinds of boxes: *Marketing Insight* (which highlights current research work and findings in marketing management) and *Vision 2000* (which looks ahead at marketing and marketing management in the twenty-first century). In addition, *Marketing Memos* feature tips and suggestions for marketing managers at all phases of the marketing management process.
7. Expanded emphasis on the following themes: global marketing, marketing and technology, socially responsible/ethical marketing, and marketing's interaction with other departments. A listing of the examples associated with each of these themes can be found following the detailed table of contents.
8. New and expanded material on value marketing, brand building and equity, the war between national and store brands, geodemographics, database marketing, customer lifetime value, mass customization, integrated marketing communications, co-branding, major account management, marketing reengineering, category management, word-of-mouth marketing, market logistics, relationship marketing, loyalty marketing, competitive benchmarking, and imitation strategies.

THE TEACHING AND LEARNING PACKAGE

This edition of *Marketing Management* includes a number of ancillaries designed for teachers and students. Each ancillary is designed to make the marketing management course an exciting, interactive, dynamic experience.

INSTRUCTOR SUPPLEMENTS

The following supplements are available for instructors:

1. A comprehensive, extensively revised **Instructor's Resource Manual,** prepared by Dale Shook and Debra Rock of SUNY-Albany, Kenneth Schaefle of North Park College, and William F. Melberg, Jr., of the University of Illinois–Chicago, includes chapter summary/overviews, lists of key teaching objectives, answers to all end-of-chapter concept applications, detailed supplementary resource suggestions, applications exercises, and transparency lecture notes. Highly detailed lecture outlines integrate video material, cases, and transparency notes. The manual for this new edition also includes ordering information for Prentice Hall's Just-in-Time Marketing case program. Portions of the IRM may be downloaded as an electronic file from the Prentice Hall Web site at http://www.prenhall.com/~kotler.

2. The **Test Item File,** prepared by James V. Dupree of Grove City College, contains over 2,300 multiple-choice, true/false, and essay questions. Each question is rated by level of difficulty and includes a text page reference. It is available in both printed and electronic formats.

3. Based on the #1 best-selling, state-of-the-art software program developed by Engineering Software Associates (ESA), **Prentice Hall Custom Test** merges the Test Item File with a powerful software package. With Prentice Hall Custom Test's user-friendly test-creating abilities, you can create tailor-made, error-free tests quickly and easily. Whether you work in Macintosh, Windows, or DOS format, Custom Test allows you to create an exam, administer it traditionally or online, and evaluate and track students' results—all with a click of the mouse.

    Instructors without access to computers can use Prentice Hall's complimentary test preparation service. Just call 1-800-842-2958 and tell the customer service representative which questions from the test item file you want on the test. A ready-to-administer test will be faxed to you within 24 hours.

4. Nearly 150 **full-color transparencies** highlight key concepts for presentation. Each transparency is accompanied by a full page of teaching notes that include relevant key terms and discussion points from the chapters, as well as additional material from supplementary sources. (The transparency notes are located in the Instructor's Resource Manual.)

5. All transparency acetates and lecture notes, plus 50 more not included in the acetates, are available as **electronic transparencies** on PowerPoint 4.0. The PowerPoint disk, prepared by Robert W. Field of St. Mary's University of Minnesota, allows you to present the transparencies to your class electronically. In addition, the electronic transparencies may be downloaded as an electronic file from the Prentice Hall Web site at http://www.prenhall.com/~kotler.

6. Broadcast television and marketing education have joined forces to create the most exciting and valuable video series ever produced for business education—the **ON LOCATION! Custom Case Videos for Marketing.**

    Each of the six-to-eight-minute ON LOCATION! clips is issue-oriented. The clips grab and hold students' attention by linking video to all the text's major conceptual elements. They also expand on the written cases found in the Instructor's Resource Manual. Each clip interweaves facilities, advertisements, product shots, text illustrations, and interviews with marketing managers and customers to maximum effect. With On Location! you can take your class on the following marketing field trip without leaving the classroom:

    • Patagonia: Aiming for No Growth
    • Terra Chips: Eat Your Veggies!
    • The M/A/R/C Group: Talking to Customers

- DHL: Worldwide Express
- Rollerblade: The Asphalt is Calling
- MTV: Think Globally, Act Locally
- Mountain Travel Sobek: All Over the World
- Ritz-Carlton: Simply the Best
- Mall of America: The Ultimate Destination for Fun
- Lands' End: Enticing Millions of Customers to Shop "Out Our Way"

For more information regarding this exciting video series, please contact your local Prentice Hall representative.

7. **The New York Festivals International Advertising Awards** recognize the best advertising from around the world. Each year a distinguished panel of judges reviews nearly 10,000 campaign entries from over 50 countries and awards gold, silver, and bronze medals. Prentice Hall is the exclusive educational distributor of the gold medal winners in the television and cinema category; three videocassettes with nearly 200 of these award-winning spots are available upon adoption of this book. Instructor's Manuals accompanying the cassettes highlight key marketing concepts and provide discussion questions and teaching tips.

8. **Prentice Hall Presents** is a series of multimedia presentations for marketing and advertising. This CD-ROM, which organizes hundreds of media objects into simple-to-use presentations, is available free of charge to instructors who adopt this text. The CD-ROM includes:

- Approximately 300 illustrations taken from the text and other sources.
- Many EFFIE-award winning television and print advertisements.
- Key concept videos taken from the On Location! custom case video series.
- Lecture notes tying the media to each chapter in the textbook.

The media resources are built into Presentation Manager 2.0, a "point and click" lecture management software program. Presentation Manager allows instructors to use pre-packaged presentations with notes tied to the book or to create state-of-the-art presentations on their own.

9. Prentice Hall's **Just-in-Time Case Program** for marketing provides you with access to an on-demand database of material (cases, articles, and other material). More information, including a list of the available material, can be obtained by contacting your local Prentice Hall representative.

10. *The New York Times* and Prentice Hall offer **Themes of the Times,** a program designed to enhance student access to current information of relevance in the classroom. Through this program, the text's core subject matter is supplemented by a collection of time-sensitive articles from one of the world's most distinguished newspapers, *The New York Times.* These articles demonstrate the ongoing, vital connection between what is learned in the classroom and what is happening in the world around us. To enjoy the wealth of information in *The New York Times* daily, call 1-800-631-1222 for information on a reduced subscription rate.

STUDENT SUPPLEMENT
The following for-sale supplement is available for students:

11. Prentice Hall is proud to be the exclusive distributor of the **Career Paths in Marketing** interactive CD-ROM. Career Paths is a fun way for the students to discover

what career path is right for them, where the jobs are, what they pay, and how to succeed in marketing themselves in the information age. Also included are models for putting together effective resumes and tips on interviewing, networking, and negotiating.

For more information of any of these ancillaries, please speak to your Prentice Hall sales representative or visit the Kotler *Marketing Management* Web site at:

http://www.prenhall.com/~kotler

ACKNOWLEDGMENTS

The ninth edition bears the imprint of many people. My colleagues and associates at the Kellogg Graduate School of Management at Northwestern University continue to have an important impact on my thinking: James C. Anderson, Robert C. Blattberg, Bobby J. Calder, Gregory S. Carpenter, Richard M. Clewett, Anne T. Coughlan, Sachin Gupta, Dawn Iacobucci, Dipak C. Jain, Jill G. Klein, Lakshman Krishnamurthi (chairman), Sidney J. Levy, Ann L. McGill, Mohanbir S. Sawhney, John F. Sherry, Jr., Louis W. Stern, Brian Sternthal, Alice M. Tybout, and Andris A. Zoltners. I also want to thank the S. C. Johnson Family for the generous support of my chair at the Kellogg School. Completing the Northwestern team is my dean and longtime friend, Donald P. Jacobs, whom I want to thank for his continuous support of my research and writing efforts.

I am indebted to the following colleagues at other universities who reviewed this edition:

Owen Adikibi, South Bank University, London
David Andrus, Kansas State University
Bob Balderstone, Western Metropolitan College of Tafe
William O. Bearden, University of South Carolina
Chauncey Burke, Seattle University
Cephas Gbande, South Bank University, London
Tom Gillpatrick, Portland State University
Ted Mitchell, University of Nevada, Reno
Roger Sinclair, University of Witwatersrand
Susan Spiggle, University of Connecticut
Donna Tillman, California Sate Polytechnic University
Ugur Yucelt, Penn State, Harrisburg

Particular thanks must go to Kenneth R. Lord (State University of New York, Buffalo) and M. Krishna Erramilli (University of North Texas) for their many valuable insights and suggestions. I'm also greatly indebted to Richard D. Shaw and Alfred G. Hawkins, both of Rockhurst College, for their help in preparing each chapter's Concept Applications.

I would also like to thank all those who have reviewed previous editions:

Hiram Barksdale, University of Georgia
Boris Becker, Oregon State University
Sunil Bhatla, Case Western Reserve University
John Burnett, University of Denver
Surjit Chhabra, DePaul University
John Deighton, University of Chicago
Ralph Gaedeke, California State University, Sacramento
Dennis Gensch, University of Wisconsin, Milwaukee
David Georgoff, Florida Atlantic University
Arun Jain, State University of New York, Buffalo
H. Lee Matthews, Ohio State University
Mary Ann McGrath, Loyola University, Chicago
Pat Murphy, University of Notre Dame
Nicholas Nugent, Boston College
Donald Outland, University of Texas, Austin
Albert Page, University of Illinois, Chicago
Christopher Puto, Arizona State University
Robert Roe, University of Wyoming
Dean Siewers, Rochester Institute of Technology

My gratitude to all those who responded to our marketing research questionnaire on the World Wide Web:

Dennis E. Clayson, University of Northern Iowa
Lori S. Feldman, Purdue University, Calumet
Ralph Gaedeke, California State University, Sacramento
Kent N. Gourdin, University of North Carolina, Charlotte
Jon M. Hawes, University of Akron
Jim Hazeltine, Northeastern Illinois University
James M. Lattin, Stanford University
John Lowry, Humboldt State University
Henry Metzner, University of Missouri, Rolla
Steven Silverman, University of Pittsburgh
Leon Winer, Pace University

My thanks also go to my foreign-edition co-authors for their suggestions on the contents of the ninth edition:

Swee-Hoon Ang, Siew-Meng Leong, and Chin Tiong Tan—National University of Singapore (Singapore)
Friedhelm W. Bliemel—Universitat Kaiserslautern (Germany)
Peter Chandler, Linden Brown, and Stewart Adam—Monash and other Australian universities (Australia)
Bernard Dubois—Groupe HEC School of Management (France)
John Saunders and Veronica Wong—Loughborough University and Warwick University (United Kingdom)
Walter Giorgio Scott—Universita Cattolica del Sacro Cuore (Italy)
Ronald E. Turner—Queen's University (Canada)

The talented staff at Prentice Hall deserves praise for their roles in shaping this edition. My acquisitions editor, David Borkowsky, offered excellent advice and direction for the ninth edition. I benefitted greatly from the superb editorial help of Steven Rigolosi, who lent his considerable talents as a development editor to improve this edition. I also want to acknowledge the fine production assistance of Linda DeLorenzo, college senior project manager; the creative graphic design of Pat Wosczyk and Ann France; the editorial assistance of Theresa Festa; and the marketing research work of Patti Arneson. I'd also like to thank my marketing manager, John Chillingworth. Finally, many thanks to Nancy Brandwein for her hard work and tenacity in finding the many new examples included in this edition.

My overriding debt continues to be to my wife, Nancy, who provided me with the time, support, and inspiration needed to prepare this edition. It is truly our book.

Philip Kotler
S. C. Johnson Distinguished Professor of International Marketing
J. L. Kellogg Graduate School of Management
Northwestern University
Evanston, Illinois
July 1996

ASSESSING MARKETING'S CRITICAL ROLE IN ORGANIZATIONAL PERFORMANCE

Marketing is so basic that it cannot be considered a separate function. It is the whole business seen from the point of view of its final result, that is, from the customer's point of view. . . . Business success is not determined by the producer but by the customer.

PETER DRUCKER

❖

Marketing consists of all activities by which a company adapts itself to its environment—creatively and profitably.

RAY COREY

❖

Marketing's job is to convert societal needs into profitable opportunities.

ANONYMOUS

❖

Rapid changes can easily render yesterday's winning business principles obsolete. In the 1920s, Henry Ford kept producing black Model-T Fords even when car buyers started clamoring for more variety. General Motors responded and overtook Ford. Later, in the 1950s, GM kept producing large automobiles when customers started clamoring for smaller cars—a call that Volkswagen and the Japanese began to heed. Then, by the 1980s, customers began to insist on quality, and the Japanese responded with better cars.[1]

What challenges do companies confront as the 1990s come to a close? With the Cold War over, companies and countries are wrestling with increased global competition, a serious income gap, environmental deterioration, infrastructure neglect, economic stagnation, low labor skills, and a host of other economic, political, and social problems.

Yes, these are challenges; but they are also opportunities. The good news is that the global market means a much larger market for goods and services. The bad news is that these companies now face a greater number of competitors. Environmental deterioration presents many opportunities for companies that can create more effective means of protecting or cleaning up the environment. Infrastructure neglect provides huge opportunities for companies in the construction, transportation, and communication industries. Economic stagnation favors companies that are good at lean production and lean marketing. Low labor skills challenge educational and training companies to design more effective programs for upgrading human skills.

These challenges are only one source of business opportunities, however. Consider the opportunities presented by scientific and technological advances in genetic engineering, multisensory robotics, artificial intelligence, micromechanics, molecular designing, superconductors, and dozens of other scientific areas.

Marketing's role in helping companies take advantage of these opportunities is critical. One scholar has described *marketing* as "the creation and delivery of a standard of living." We take this as an inspired and insightful view of the purpose of marketing. In this chapter we present an overview of modern marketing thinking and practice. After we explore in detail the challenges facing business today, we address the following questions:

♦ **What core concepts underlie the discipline of marketing?**

♦ **What basic tasks do marketing managers perform?**

♦ **What is the marketing concept, and how does it contrast with other philosophies of doing business?**

♦ **What role does marketing play in different industries, in nonprofit organizations, and in different countries?**

Doing Business in the Global Economy

Let's look deeper at some specific challenges that are facing today's businesses.

The Global Economy

The world economy has undergone a radical transformation in the last two decades. Geographical and cultural distances have shrunk significantly with the advent of airplanes, fax machines, global computer and telephone linkups, and world television satellite broadcasting. These advances have permitted companies to widen substantially both their markets and their supplier sources. In the past, a U.S. company such as Chrysler would build its cars from components mostly purchased in the United States, and sell most of its cars in the United States. Today, Chrysler orders its components from suppliers in Japan, Korea, Germany, and a dozen other countries and also sells its cars throughout the world.

Companies in various industries are also developing their products using a global assembly line. Consider the following:[2]

> In the past, most U.S. clothing was made and sold in the United States. Much cutting and sewing were done in New York and New England sweatshops by immigrant laborers working long hours. The workers joined unions and raised wages. Searching for lower labor costs, many clothing manufacturers moved to Southern states. More recently, many U.S. companies moved their manufacturing operations to Asia. Today, Bill Blass, a top U.S. fashion designer, will examine woven cloth made from Australian wool with printed designs prepared in Italy. He will design a dress and fax the drawing to a Hong Kong agent who will place the order with a mainland China factory. The finished dresses will be airfreighted to New York, where they will be redistributed to department stores.

> Most books in U.S. bookstores used to be printed in the United States with U.S. equipment and supplies. Today, the author is probably typing on a computer made in Taiwan with software developed in California. The printing may be done on a German printing press with ink obtained from Korea and paper from Canada. The pages may have been shipped for binding in Mexico with the final books shipped back to the United States and other English-speaking markets. A good part of the book's price will have ended up as income paid to people in other countries.

In addition to sourcing their components, supplies, and goods from abroad, many U.S. companies are trying to sell their goods abroad. But they are recognizing that to do this well, they cannot do it alone. So they are forming strategic alliances with foreign companies—sometimes even with competitors—who serve as suppliers, distributors, technological partners, or joint venture partners. All of this means that we are seeing, and will continue to see, some surprising alliances between international competitors:

- Ford and Nissan successfully designed a minivan together, and Ford has also had a successful strategic alliance with Mazda for the past 20 years.
- General Electric and SNECMA, a French company, have been making jet engines together since 1971.
- Coca-Cola and Schweppes run a huge soft-drink bottling plant together that has brought both companies tremendous cost savings.

Furthermore, the revolution in telecommunications has spurred six of the world's leading players to join forces. Apple Computer, AT&T, Matsushita Electric Industrial, Motorola, Philips, and Sony have started General Magic to create two telecommunication standards for the next generation of computer technology: an independent operating system customized to interface with any existing computer

Assessing Marketing's Critical Role in Organizational Performance

application and a programming language for mobile computing. "We've come to the gradual realization that we can't afford to do everything ourselves," said AT&T's chairman, Robert E. Allen, of his company's involvement in General Magic. It's a realization that all forward-looking companies are making as they look across national boundaries for allies and partners.[3]

At the same time that global markets are expanding, regional trade blocs are emerging. The United States signed the North American Free Trade Agreement (NAFTA) with Canada and Mexico. Eventually the Western Hemisphere may act as one trading bloc, giving preferential treatment to goods made in the region. The European Union (EU) consists of 15 countries with 340 million consumers that is eliminating internal trade barriers and setting common standards and regulations. It now represents a larger market than the United States. Meanwhile, Japan and other Far Eastern nations are organizing a trade bloc in that region, which has the world's highest economic growth rate. Clearly, the world economic map is changing rapidly.

The Income Gap

A large part of the world has grown poorer in the last few decades. Although wages may have risen, real purchasing power has declined, especially for the less skilled members of the work force. In the United States, many households managed to maintain their purchasing power chiefly because women entered the work force. Many other workers lost their jobs as U.S. manufacturers downsized their work force to cut their costs. Company work forces in the computer, steel, auto, textile, and other industries have shrunk to a fraction of their former size.

In addition, the economies of several developing countries in Africa, South America, and other regions are stagnating. The gap between the rich and poor nations is growing. Many of the poorer nations pressure the richer nations to open their markets, but the rich nations maintain tariffs and quotas to protect their local industries and employment.

Two solutions can help close the income gap. The first is *countertrade,* in which poor nations pay for goods with other goods and services instead of money. In 1972 countertrade was used in only 15 countries; by 1993, 108 countries were conducting countertrade transactions. Gallo trades wine for airline seats, hotel rooms, and glass bottles. In exchange for a soft-drink concentrate, Pepsi accepts products ranging from sesame seeds to sisal for making rope, and General Motors trades automobiles for trainloads of strawberries.[4] Although countertrade is less efficient than hard cash transactions, it does permit consumers, companies, and countries lacking hard currency to obtain some of the goods they need.

The other solution is providing "more for less." America's largest retailer, Wal-Mart, rose to market leadership on two principles emblazoned in large letters on every Wal-Mart store: "Satisfaction Guaranteed" and "We Sell for Less." Customers enter Wal-Mart, are welcomed by a friendly greeter, and find a huge assortment of good quality merchandise at "everyday low prices." The same principle explains the rapid growth of factory outlet malls and discount chain stores.

The Environmental Imperative and Socially Responsible Marketing

In today's business climate, companies must accept increasing responsibility for the environment. In the past, a chemical company could belch out factory smoke and dispose of chemicals that polluted the water and soil without much accountability. Starting in the 1970s, environmental laws required companies to install pollution control equipment. As the air quality in major cities worsened, automobile manufacturers were held to increasingly stricter standards for catalytic converters. All these laws raised costs for U.S. manufacturers, who complain that they are being put at a disadvantage against global competitors who operate under weaker or nonexistent environmental regulations.

The environmental movement has continued to gather steam over time. The West was shocked not only by the Chernobyl nuclear disaster in 1986 but also by revelations about how negligently the former Eastern bloc governments had handled the environment. In many East European cities, the air is terrible, the water is polluted, and the soil is poisoned by chemical dumping.

In 1992, representatives from companies such as Johnson & Johnson, The Body Shop, Procter & Gamble, Pitney Bowes, IBM, and Colgate-Palmolive participated in a major conference on how to integrate environmental decision making into business with profitable results. These companies go beyond simply recognizing that companies must be held accountable for their effluents, packaging material, waste handling, and other activities that affect the environment; they see the establishment of "green policies" as providing a competitive advantage:

- Procter & Gamble has redesigned products, packages, and processes so that less material or less packaging is needed to achieve the same (if not better) profitability.

- When Pitney Bowes found itself spending over $16.3 million for such activities as hazardous waste disposal, it began a program to eliminate environmental problems even before products are created and placed on the market.[5]

Technological Advances

The boom in computer, telephone, and television technology, as well as the merging of these technologies, has had a major impact on the way businesses produce and market their products (Figure 1-1 on page 6). As technology has delivered new and better foods, clothing, housing, vehicles, and entertainment possibilities, our lives have changed dramatically. In 1954, two and a half hours were spent preparing the evening meal; by 1995 the main meal was prepared in 15 minutes as a result of convenience, frozen, snack, and fast foods. The food itself need not be purchased in person, because consumers today can sit down at their computers and walk the aisles, click on the foods they want, and receive delivery within a few hours. Through videoconferencing, marketing executives in Sydney, Tokyo, Paris, and New York meet in "real time" without ever stepping onto a plane. Direct marketers can know everything from what type of car you drive to what you read to what flavor of ice cream you prefer, all with the click of a mouse button. And a small business in Ann Arbor, Michigan, can advertise its products electronically to a worldwide audience of millions, 24 hours a day, for less than the cost of an ad in a neighborhood newspaper.

John Naisbitt, the author of *Megatrends* and *The Global Paradox,* says, "Telecommunications is the driving force that is simultaneously creating the huge global economy and making its parts smaller and more powerful."[6] At the heart of this phenomenon is the Information Superhighway and its backbone, the Internet (or "net," as it's called by users). The Internet, which has no ownership or central management, is a web of more than 2.2 million computers linked by telephone on more than 32,400 connected computer networks. Accessible in 135 countries and territories, its membership is growing at the rate of 10% to 15% a month.

Created a decade ago as a data link among a sprinkling of academic communities, the Internet is fast being embraced by businesses. Companies are using it to link employees in remote offices, stay in touch with customers and suppliers, and distribute sales information more quickly. The advent of a new, more user-friendly Internet application called the World Wide Web promises companies access to mil-

Assessing Marketing's Critical Role in Organizational Performance

(a) Videoconferencing allows people from around the globe to "meet" in real time without ever stepping onto a plane.

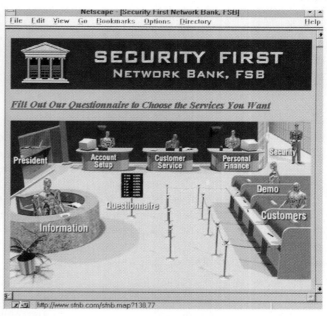

(b) The Internet is revolutionizing the delivery of banking services. People can now do all their personal banking and investing from their personal computers.

(c) Mini-computers strapped to inventory clerks' wrists have greatly increased warehousing and distribution efficiency.

(d) Technology under development at Anderson Consulting will soon allow consumers to do their grocery shopping from home.

FIGURE 1-1

The Information Technology Revolution

Technology is changing the way companies produce and market their products.

lions of new customers at a fraction of the cost of print or television advertising. The Web uses a technology called *hypertext,* which allows users to leap from one computer database to another by simply clicking on highlighted images or text. For a more detailed discussion of the Web and its implications for marketers, see the Vision 2000 box titled "Catching Consumers in the World Wide Web."

Alert marketers see technology as producing an endless stream of opportunities. Yet taking advantage of technology entails walking a thin line: Companies

Catching Consumers in the World Wide Web

Which is more effective at enticing a consumer to buy DeKuyper liquors: a print ad with a big picture of a bottle and a DeKuyper logo smack in the middle, or a virtual bar that allows computer users to click on drink recipes and talk to a "virtual bartender"? DeKuyper is betting on the latter and it's spending upward of $40,000 to put its "DeKuyper Room" in an online version of *Vibe*, the trendy LA-based magazine. But companies don't need to spend five figures to show their wares online. Scores of businesses are setting up shop on the Internet simply by creating a "home page" in the vast electronic publishing medium known as the World Wide Web. Garage-based startups and established companies like IBM, GE, Hyatt Hotels, and J. C. Penney are all racing to explore and exploit the Web's possibilities for marketing, shopping, and browsing for information. So-called browser software like Mosaic makes it easy for computer users to travel the world via the Web. Still, it's yet to be seen whether the millions of browsers will become buyers. The actuality is that few companies have made any money from their Web servers, and there are some drawbacks to consider:

♦ *Security:* When a company links its internal computer network to the outside world, it is exposed to possible unauthorized use or electronic attack by vandals. Companies may also be reluctant to use the Web to send price quotes or other financial information, which may be intercepted by competitors. Similarly, consumers are wary about sending their credit-card account numbers over the wires.

♦ *Legal issues:* The law of electronic commerce is still being defined, and there is plenty of confusion on such issues as the nature of electronic contracts and distribution of copyrighted material.

♦ *Technology:* While new software tools make the Internet more user-friendly, they also require more complex network connections.

♦ *Cost:* For companies to make the most of the Internet, they must pay hundreds or even thousands of dollars a month for leased telephone lines, powerful computers, and Internet specialists.

♦ *Cultural issues:* The Internet has an established culture that is not open to aggressive advertising. Early efforts to advertise on the Internet caused user outrage and retaliation. Smart advertisers are learning to be more low key, to make ads a positive option for the user, and to offer services along with their ads.

Given the lightning speed at which Internet technology and protocol develop, it's unlikely that these drawbacks will deter the millions of businesses and consumers who are logging onto the net each day. "Marketers aren't going to have a choice about being on Internet," says Midori Chan, vice president of creative services at Interse, which helped put Windham Hill Records and Digital Equipment Corp. on the Internet. "To not be on the Internet in the '90s is going to be like not having a phone."

Sources: Peter H. Lewis, "Getting Down to Business on the Net," *The New York Times,* June 19, 1994, C1:2; Peter H. Lewis, "Companies Rush to Set Up Shop in Cyberspace," *The New York Times,* November 2, 1994, D1:3; Cyndee Miller, "Marketers Find It's Hip to Be on the Internet," *Marketing News,* February 27, 1995, p. 2; Rick Tetzeli, "Electronic Storefronts on the Internet," *Fortune,* November 28, 1994, p. 191.

must avoid jumping in too soon (before the market is ready) or too late (after the market has been conquered). Thirty years passed between the time the microwave oven was invented and the time it became a feasible and popular household appliance. In the interim, many companies lost money. Every new technology requires much patience and investment, as well as the support of venture capital firms with vision.

Not all new technology is welcome. There are people who regard television sets, fast-food outlets, high-rise buildings, and birth-control devices as backward steps for humanity. Certainly the development of more powerful weapons of destruction must be looked upon as tragic. And, of course, there are the harmful effects of some technologies on the quality of our water, soil, and air—all of which must be taken into account in any evaluation of technological progress.

CHAPTER 1   **7**

Assessing Marketing's Critical Role in Organizational Performance

The Powerful Customer

The 1980s taught a humbling lesson to business firms everywhere. Domestic companies can no longer ignore foreign competitors, foreign markets, and foreign sources of supply. Companies cannot allow their wage and material costs to get far out of line with those in the rest of the world. Companies cannot ignore emerging technologies, materials, equipment, and new ways of organizing and marketing.

U.S. companies are a case in point. In the 1970s, the most powerful U.S. companies included General Motors, Sears, RCA, and IBM. Today, all four are struggling to remain profitable because they all failed at marketing. Each company did not understand its changing marketplace and customers and the need to provide competitive value. General Motors is still trying to figure out why German and Japanese cars are preferred more than GM cars in most of the world. Mighty Sears is caught between fashionable department stores and boutiques at one end and discount mass merchandisers at the other. RCA, inventor of so many new patents, never quite mastered the art of marketing and now puts its brand name on products largely imported from Japan and South Korea. IBM, one of the world's great sales-driven companies, experienced its first loss ever in 1992—$4.96 billion—because it continued to focus on selling mainframes while the market was moving toward microcomputing, computer networking, and computer workstations.

In view of all this "marketing myopia,"[7] it is not surprising that a flood of books have been published offering fresh perspectives on how to run a business in the new environment. In the 1960s, "Theory Y" called on companies to treat their employees not as cogs in a machine but as individuals whose creativity can be released through enlightened management practice. In the 1970s, "strategic planning" offered a way of thinking about building and managing a company's portfolio of businesses in a turbulent environment. In the 1980s, "excellence and quality" received major attention as the new formulas for success. All of these themes are valid and continue to inspire business thinking.

In the 1990s, many companies have acknowledged the critical importance of being customer-oriented and -driven in all their activities. It is not enough to be product-driven or technology-driven. Too many companies still design their products without customer input, only to find them rejected in the marketplace. And too many companies forget the customers after the sale, only to lose them to competitors later. Not surprisingly, we are witnessing a flood of books with such titles as *The Only Thing That Matters: Bringing the Power of the Customer into the Center of Your Business; Turning Lost Customers into Gold: And the Art of Achieving Zero Defections; Customer Bonding: The Five-Point System for Maximizing Customer Loyalty; The Customer-Driven Company;* and *Sustaining Knock Your Socks Off Service.*[8] All these books stress one theme: Success in the 1990s and beyond rests on a market- and customer-based view of business success.

Other Issues

Many other critical changes have occurred in consumer and business markets over the past decades. Consumer markets are often characterized by an aging population; an increasing number of working women; later marriage, more divorce, and smaller families; the emergence of distinct ethnic consumer groups and needs; and the proliferation of more varied consumer lifestyles. Business firms are demanding higher product quality from their suppliers, faster delivery, better service, and lower prices. Business firms need to speed up their product-development process because of shorter product life cycles. They also need to find better ways to distribute and promote their products at lower cost.

WHAT IS MARKETING? THE CORE CONCEPTS

Marketing has been defined in various ways. The definition that serves our purpose best is as follows:

❖ **MARKETING** is a social and managerial process by which individuals and groups obtain what they need and want through creating, offering, and exchanging products of value with others.

This definition of marketing rests on the following core concepts: *needs, wants,* and *demands; products (goods, services,* and *ideas); value, cost,* and *satisfaction; exchange* and *transactions; relationships* and *networks; markets;* and *marketers* and *prospects.* These concepts are illustrated in Figure 1-2.

Needs, Wants, and Demands

Marketing starts with human needs and wants. People need food, air, water, clothing, and shelter to survive. Beyond this, people have a strong desire for recreation, education, and other services. They have strong preferences for particular versions and brands of basic goods and services.

People's needs and wants today are staggering. In a given year, 261 million Americans might consume 67 billion eggs, 2 billion chickens, 5 million hair dryers, 133 billion domestic air travel passenger miles, and over 4 million lectures by college English professors. Together these consumer goods and services create a demand for more than 150 million tons of steel and 4 billion tons of cotton. These are just a few of the demands that get expressed in a $6.7 trillion economy.

It is important to distinguish among needs, wants, and demands. A *human need* is a state of deprivation of some basic satisfaction. People require food, clothing, shelter, safety, belonging, and esteem. These needs are not created by society or by marketers. They exist in the very texture of human biology and the human condition.

Wants are desires for specific satisfiers of needs. An American needs food and wants a hamburger, French fries, and a Coke. In another society these needs might be satisfied differently. A hungry person in Mauritius may want mangos, rice, lentils, and beans. Although people's needs are few, their wants are many. Human wants are continually shaped and reshaped by social forces and institutions, including churches, schools, families, and business corporations.[9]

Demands are wants for specific products that are backed by an ability and willingness to buy them. Wants become demands when supported by purchasing power. Many people want a Mercedes; only a few are able and willing to buy one. Companies must therefore measure not only how many people want their product but, more importantly, how many would actually be *willing and able* to buy it.

These distinctions shed light on the frequent criticism that "marketers create needs" or "marketers get people to buy things they don't want." Marketers do not create needs: Needs preexist marketers. Marketers, along with other societal influences, influence wants. Marketers might promote the idea that a Mercedes would satisfy a person's need for social status. They do not, however, create the need for social status. Marketers influence demand by making the product appropriate, attractive, affordable, and easily available to target consumers.

Products (Goods, Services, and Ideas)

People satisfy their needs and wants with products. A *product* is anything that can be offered to satisfy a need or want. Occasionally we will use other terms for *product,* such as *offering* or *solution.*

FIGURE 1-2
The Core Concepts of Marketing

Assessing Marketing's Critical Role in Organizational Performance

A product or offering can consist of as many as three components: physical good(s), service(s), and idea(s). For example, a fast-food restaurant is supplying goods (hamburgers, fries, soft drinks), services (purchasing, cooking, seating), and an idea ("saves me time"). A computer manufacturer is supplying goods (computer, monitor, printer), services (delivery, installation, training, maintenance, repair), and an idea ("computation power"). A church offers less in the way of physical goods (wine, wafer) and more in the way of services (sermon, singing, education, counseling) and ideas (community, salvation).[10]

The importance of physical products lies not so much in owning them as in obtaining the services they render. We buy a car because it supplies transportation service. We buy a microwave oven because it supplies a cooking service. Thus physical products are really vehicles that deliver services to us.

In fact, services are also supplied by other vehicles, such as people, places, activities, organizations, and ideas. If we are bored, we can attend a comedy club and watch a comedian (person); travel to a warm vacationland like Bermuda (place); go to the health club (activity); join a hiking club (organization); or adopt a different philosophy about life (idea). A major trend in the United States is the explosion of services and service organizations. In fact, over 70% of the nation's gross national product and employment occurs in the service sector.

Manufacturers often make the mistake of paying more attention to their physical products than to the services produced by those products. They see themselves as selling a product rather than providing a solution to a need. A carpenter isn't buying a drill; he is buying a hole. A physical object is a means of packaging a service. The marketer's job is to sell the benefits or services built into physical products rather than just describe their physical features. Sellers who concentrate their thinking on the physical product instead of the customer's need are said to suffer from *marketing myopia*.

Value, Cost, and Satisfaction

How do consumers choose among the many products that might satisfy a given need? Suppose Tom Moore needs to travel three miles to work each day. He could use a number of products to satisfy this need: roller skates, a bicycle, a motorcycle, a car, a taxicab, or a bus. These alternatives constitute his *product choice set*. Now assume that Moore would like to satisfy several additional needs in traveling to work: namely speed, safety, ease, and economy. Each product has a different capacity to satisfy his *need set*. A bicycle is slower, is less safe, and requires more effort than a car, but a bicycle is more economical. Somehow Tom Moore has to decide which product will deliver the most total satisfaction.

The guiding concepts here are value and satisfaction. *Value* is the consumer's estimate of the product's overall capacity to satisfy his or her needs. Suppose Tom is primarily interested in the speed and ease of getting to work. If he were offered any of these products at no cost, he would choose the automobile. But since each product involves a *cost,* he will not necessarily choose the car, which costs substantially more than a bicycle or cab ride. Tom will have to give up other things (called the *opportunity cost*) to obtain the car. Therefore, he will consider the product's value and price before making a choice. He will choose the product that produces the most value per dollar. According to DeRose, value is "the satisfaction of customer requirements at the lowest possible cost of acquisition, ownership, and use."[11]

We will look at current theories of consumer-choice behavior in Chapter 6.

Exchange and Transactions

People can obtain products in one of four ways. The first way is self-production. People can relieve hunger through hunting, fishing, or fruit gathering. In this case, there is no market and no marketing. The second way is coercion. Hungry people can wrest or steal food from others. No benefit is offered to the others except that of not being harmed. The third way is begging. Hungry people can approach others and beg for food. They have nothing tangible to offer except gratitude. The fourth way is *exchange*. Hungry people can offer a resource in return for food, such as money, a good, or a service. Marketing emerges when people decide to satisfy needs and wants through exchange.

Exchange is the act of obtaining a desired product from someone by offering something in return. For exchange potential to exist, five conditions must be satisfied:

1. There are at least two parties.
2. Each party has something that might be of value to the other party.
3. Each party is capable of communication and delivery.
4. Each party is free to accept or reject the exchange offer.
5. Each party believes it is appropriate or desirable to deal with the other party.

Whether exchange actually takes place depends upon whether the two parties can agree on terms of exchange that will leave them both better off (or at least not worse off) than they were before the exchange. Exchange is frequently described as a value-creating process because exchange normally leaves both parties better off.

Exchange must be seen as a process rather than as an event. Two parties are engaged in exchange if they are negotiating and moving toward an agreement. When an agreement is reached, we say that a transaction takes place. A *transaction* is a trade of values between two or more parties. We must be able to say: A gave X to B and received Y in return. Jones gave $400 to Smith and obtained a television set. This is a classic *monetary transaction*. Transactions, however, do not require money as one of the traded values. A *barter transaction* consists of the trading of goods or services for other goods or services, as when lawyer Jones writes a will for physician Smith in return for a medical examination.

A transaction involves several dimensions: at least two things of value, agreed-upon conditions, a time of agreement, and a place of agreement. Usually a legal system arises to support and enforce compliance on the part of the transactors. Without a law of contracts, people would approach transactions with some distrust, and everyone would lose.

A transaction differs from a transfer. In a *transfer,* A gives X to B but does not receive anything in return. Gifts, subsidies, and charitable contributions are all transfers. It might seem that marketing should be confined to the study of transactions only. However, transfer behavior can also be understood through the concept of exchange. Typically, the transferer expects to receive something in exchange for his or her gift—for example, gratitude or seeing good behavior in the recipient. Professional fund-raisers are acutely aware of this and try to provide benefits to the donors, such as thank-you notes, donor magazines, and special invitations to events. Marketers have recently broadened the concept of marketing to include the study of transfer behavior as well as transaction behavior.

In the most generic sense, marketers seek to elicit a *behavioral response* from another party. A business firm wants a response called buying, a political candidate wants a response called voting, a church or synagogue wants a response called joining, and a social-action group wants a response called adopting the

Assessing Marketing's Critical Role in Organizational Performance

idea. Marketing consists of the actions undertaken to elicit desired responses from a target audience.

To effect successful exchanges, marketers analyze what each party expects to give and get from the transaction. Simple exchange situations can be mapped by showing the two actors and the wants and offers flowing between them. Suppose Caterpillar, the world's largest manufacturer of earth-moving equipment, researches the benefits that a typical construction company wants when it buys earth-moving equipment. These benefits, listed at the top of the exchange map in Figure 1-3, include high-quality equipment, a fair price, on-time delivery, good financing terms, and good parts and service. All of the wants on this *want list* are not equally important and may vary from buyer to buyer. One of Caterpillar's tasks is to discover the relative importance of these different wants to the buyer.

Caterpillar also has a want list. It wants a good price for the equipment, on-time payment, and good word of mouth. If there is a sufficient match or overlap in the want lists, a basis for a transaction exists. Caterpillar's task is to formulate an offer that motivates the construction company to buy Caterpillar equipment. The construction company might in turn make a counteroffer. The process of trying to arrive at mutually agreeable terms is called *negotiation*. Negotiation leads to either mutually acceptable terms or a decision not to transact.

Relationships and Networks

So far, we have explained the nature of *transaction marketing*. Transaction marketing is part of a larger idea called relationship marketing. *Relationship marketing* is the practice of building long-term satisfying relations with key parties—customers, suppliers, distributors—in order to retain their long-term preference and business.[12] Smart marketers try to build up long-term, trusting, "win-win" relationships with valued customers, distributors, dealers, and suppliers. They accomplish this by promising and delivering high quality, good service, and fair prices to the other parties over time. Relationship marketing results in strong economic, technical, and social ties among the parties. It also cuts down on transaction costs and time. In the most successful cases, transactions move from being negotiated each time to being a matter of routine.

The ultimate outcome of relationship marketing is the building of a unique company asset called a marketing network. A *marketing network* consists of the company and all of its supporting stakeholders: customers, employees, suppliers, distributors, retailers, ad agencies, university scientists, and others with whom it has built mutually profitable business relationships. Increasingly, competition is

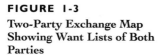

FIGURE 1-3
Two-Party Exchange Map Showing Want Lists of Both Parties

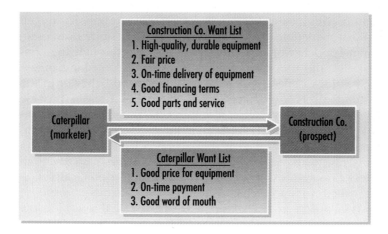

Understanding
Marketing
Management

not between companies but rather between whole networks, with the prize going to the company that has built the better network. The operating principle is simple: Build a good network of relationships with key stakeholders, and profits will follow.[13]

Markets

The concept of exchange leads to the concept of a market.

❖ A **MARKET** consists of all the potential customers sharing a particular need or want who might be willing and able to engage in exchange to satisfy that need or want.

Thus the size of the market depends on the number of people who exhibit the need or want, have resources that interest others, and are willing and able to offer these resources in exchange for what they want.

Traditionally, a "market" was the place where buyers and sellers gathered to exchange their goods, such as a village square. Economists use the term to refer to a collection of buyers and sellers who transact over a particular product or product class; hence the housing market, the grain market, and so on. Marketers, however, see the sellers as constituting the *industry* and the buyers as constituting the *market*. Figure 1-4 shows the relationship between the industry and the market. The sellers and the buyers are connected by four flows. The sellers send goods and services and communications (ads, direct mail, and so forth) to the market; in return they receive money and information (attitudes, sales data, and so forth). The inner loop shows an exchange of money for goods and services; the outer loop shows an exchange of information.

Businesspeople often use the term "markets" colloquially to cover various groupings of customers. They talk about need markets (such as the diet-seeking market); product markets (such as the shoe market); demographic markets (such as the youth market); and geographic markets (such as the French market). Or they extend the concept to cover noncustomer groupings as well, such as voter markets, labor markets, and donor markets.

All modern economies abound in markets. The five basic markets and the flows connecting them are shown in Figure 1-5 on page 14. Essentially, manufacturers go to *resource markets* (raw-material markets, labor markets, money markets, and so on), buy resources and turn them into goods and services, and then sell the finished products to intermediaries, who sell them to consumers. Consumers sell their labor, for which they receive money with which they pay for the goods and services they buy. The government uses tax revenues to buy goods from resource, manufacturer, and intermediary markets and uses these goods and services to provide public services. Each nation's economy and the whole world economy consist of complex interacting sets of markets that are linked through exchange processes.

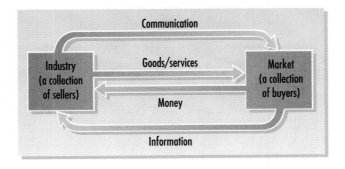

FIGURE 1-4
A Simple Marketing System

Assessing Marketing's Critical Role in Organizational Performance

FIGURE 1-5
Structure of Flows in a Modern Exchange Economy

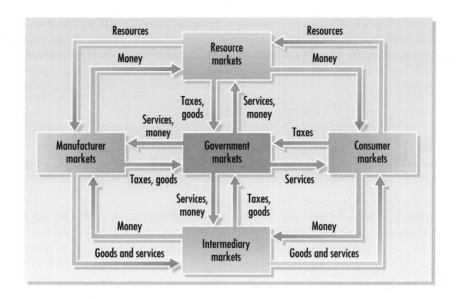

Marketers and Prospects

The concept of markets brings us full circle to the concept of marketing. Marketing means working with markets to actualize potential exchanges for the purpose of satisfying human needs and wants.

When one party is more actively seeking an exchange than the other party, we call the first party a marketer and the second party a prospect. A *marketer* is someone seeking one or more prospects who might engage in an exchange of values. A *prospect* is someone whom the marketer identifies as potentially willing and able to engage in an exchange of values.

The marketer can be a seller or a buyer. Suppose several people want to buy a house that has just become available. Each prospective buyer will try to market himself or herself to the seller. These buyers are actually doing the marketing! In the event that both parties actively seek an exchange, both are marketers and the situation is one of *reciprocal marketing*.

In the normal situation, the marketer is a company serving a market in the face of competitors (Figure 1-6). The company and the competitors send their respective products and messages directly and/or through marketing intermediaries to end users. Their relative effectiveness is influenced by their respective suppliers as well as major environmental forces (demographic, economic, physical, technological, political/legal, social/cultural). Thus Figure 1-6 represents the main elements in a modern marketing system.

Having reviewed these concepts, we can put all the pieces together to define marketing:

❖ **MARKETING** is a social and managerial process by which individuals and groups obtain what they need and want through creating, offering, and exchanging products of value with others.

MARKETING MANAGEMENT

Coping with exchange processes calls for a considerable amount of work and skill. *Marketing management* takes place when at least one party to a potential exchange thinks about the means of achieving desired responses from other parties. We will use the following definition of marketing (management) approved by the American Marketing Association:

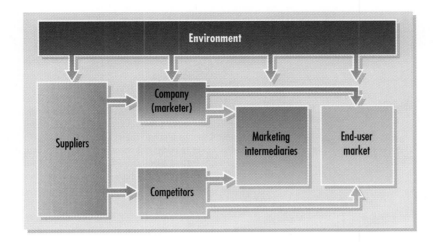

FIGURE 1-6
Main Actors and Forces in a
Modern Marketing System

❖ **MARKETING (MANAGEMENT)** Is the process of planning and executing the conception, pricing, promotion, and distribution of ideas, goods, and services to create exchanges that satisfy individual and organizational goals.[14]

This definition recognizes that marketing management is a process involving analysis, planning, implementation, and control; that it covers goods, services, and ideas; that it rests on the notion of exchange; and that the goal is to produce satisfaction for the parties involved.

Marketing management can be practiced in any market. Consider a food company. The vice-president of human resources deals in the labor market; the vice-president of purchasing, the raw-materials market. They must set objectives and develop strategies for achieving satisfactory results in these markets. Traditionally, however, these executives have not been called marketers, nor have they been trained in marketing. At best, they are "part-time" marketers.[15] Instead, marketing management has historically been identified with tasks and personnel dealing with the *customer market*. We will follow this tradition, although what we say about marketing applies to all markets.

Marketing work in the customer market is formally carried out by sales managers, salespeople, advertising and promotion managers, marketing researchers, customer-service managers, product and brand managers, market and industry managers, and the marketing vice-president. Each job carries well-defined tasks and responsibilities. Many of these jobs involve managing particular marketing resources such as advertising, salespeople, or marketing research. In contrast, product managers, market managers, and the marketing vice-president manage *programs*. Their job is to analyze, plan, and implement programs that will produce a desired level and mix of transactions with target markets.

The popular image of the marketing manager is someone whose task is primarily to stimulate demand for the company's products. However, this is too limited a view of the diversity of marketing tasks performed by marketing managers. *Marketing management has the task of influencing the level, timing, and composition of demand in a way that will help the organization achieve its objectives.* Marketing management is essentially *demand management*. Table 1-1 on page 16 distinguishes eight different states of demand and the corresponding tasks facing marketing managers.

Marketing managers manage demand by carrying out marketing research, planning, implementation, and control. Within *marketing planning,* marketers must make decisions on target markets, market positioning, product development, pricing, distribution channels, physical distribution, communication, and promotion. We will analyze all these marketing tasks in subsequent chapters.

TABLE 1-1	DEMAND STATES AND MARKETING TASKS
1. *Negative demand*	A market is in a state of negative demand if a major part of the market dislikes the product and may even pay a price to avoid it. People have a negative demand for vaccinations, dental work, vasectomies, and gall bladder operations. Employers feel a negative demand for ex-convicts and alcoholics as employees. The marketing task is to analyze why the market dislikes the product and whether a marketing program consisting of product redesign, lower prices, and more positive promotion can change the market's beliefs and attitudes.
2. *No demand*	Target consumers may be unaware of or uninterested in the product. Thus, farmers may not be interested in a new farming method, and college students may not be interested in foreign-language courses. The marketing task is to find ways to connect the benefits of the product with the person's natural needs and interests.
3. *Latent demand*	Many consumers may share a strong need that cannot be satisfied by any existing product. There is a strong latent demand for harmless cigarettes, safer neighborhoods, and more fuel-efficient cars. The marketing task is to measure the size of the potential market and develop effective goods and services that would satisfy the demand.
4. *Declining demand*	Every organization, sooner or later, faces declining demand for one or more of its products. Churches have seen their memberships decline, and private colleges have seen their applications fall. The marketer must analyze the causes of market decline and determine whether demand can be restimulated by finding new target markets, changing the product's features, or developing more effective communication. The marketing task is to reverse the declining demand through creative remarketing of the product.
5. *Irregular demand*	Many organizations face demand that varies on a seasonal, daily, or even hourly basis, causing problems of idle or overworked capacity. In mass transit, much of the equipment is idle during off-peak hours and insufficient during peak travel hours. Museums are undervisited on weekdays and overcrowded on weekends. Hospital operating rooms are overbooked early in the week and underbooked toward the end of the week. The marketing task, called *synchromarketing,* is to find ways to alter the same pattern of demand through flexible pricing, promotion, and other incentives.
6. *Full demand*	Organizations face full demand when they are pleased with their volume of business. The marketing task is to maintain the current level of demand in the face of changing consumer preferences and increasing competition. The organization must maintain or improve its quality and continually measure consumer satisfaction to make sure it is doing a good job.
7. *Overfull demand*	Some organizations face a demand level that is higher than they can or want to handle. Thus, the Golden Gate Bridge carries a higher amount of traffic than is safe, and Yosemite National Park is terribly overcrowded in the summertime. The marketing task, called *demarketing,* requires finding ways to reduce the demand temporarily or permanently. General demarketing seeks to discourage overall demand and consists of such steps as raising prices and reducing promotion and service. Selective demarketing consists of trying to reduce the demand coming from those parts of the market that are less profitable or less in need of the product. Demarketing aims not to destroy demand but only to reduce its level, temporarily or permanently.
8. *Unwholesome demand*	Unwholesome products will attract organized efforts to discourage their consumption. Unselling campaigns have been conducted against cigarettes, alcohol, hard drugs, handguns, and X-rated movies. The marketing task is to get people who like something to give it up, using such tools as fear messages, price hikes, and reduced availability.

Source: For a fuller discussion, see Philip Kotler, "The Major Tasks of Marketing Management," *Journal of Marketing,* October 1973, pp. 42–49; and Philip Kotler and Sidney J. Levy, "Demarketing, Yes, Demarketing," *Harvard Business Review,* November–December 1971, pp. 74–80.

COMPANY ORIENTATIONS TOWARD THE MARKETPLACE

We have defined marketing management as the conscious effort to achieve desired exchange outcomes with target markets. But what philosophy should guide marketing efforts? What relative weights should be given to the interests of the organization, the customers, and society? Very often these interests conflict. For instance, one of the most popular products at Dexter Corporation was a profitable grade of paper that prevented tea bags from disintegrating in hot water. Unfortunately, the materials used to produce the paper accounted for 98% of Dexter's annual hazardous wastes. Thus, while Dexter's product was extremely popular with customers, it was obviously detrimental to the environment.

Clearly, marketing activities should be carried out under a well-thought-out philosophy of efficient, effective, and socially responsible marketing. At Dexter, a task force of employees representing the company's environmental, legal, R&D, and marketing departments was formed to solve the hazardous-waste problem. The task force succeeded, and the company increased market share and virtually eliminated hazardous waste in the process.[16]

There are five competing concepts under which organizations can choose to conduct their marketing activities: the production concept, the product concept, the selling/sales concept, the marketing concept, and the societal marketing concept.

The Production Concept

The production concept is one of the oldest concepts in business.

❖ The **PRODUCTION CONCEPT** holds that consumers will favor those products that are widely available and low in cost. Managers of production-oriented organizations concentrate on achieving high production efficiency and wide distribution.

The assumption that consumers are primarily interested in product availability and low price holds in at least two situations. The first is where the demand for a product exceeds supply, as in many developing countries. Here consumers are more interested in obtaining the product than in its fine points, and suppliers will concentrate on finding ways to increase production. The second situation is where the product's cost is high and has to be decreased to expand the market. Texas Instruments provides an example. TI is one of the leading U.S. exponents of the "get-out-production, cut-the-price" philosophy that Henry Ford pioneered in the early 1900s to expand the automobile market. Texas Instruments puts all of its efforts in building production volume and improving technology in order to bring down costs. It uses its lower costs to cut prices and expand the market size. It strives to achieve the dominant position in its markets. This orientation has also been a key strategy of many Japanese companies.

Some service organizations also operate on the production concept. Many medical and dental practices are organized on assembly-line principles, as are some government agencies (such as unemployment offices and license bureaus). While this management orientation can handle many cases per hour, it is open to charges of impersonality and poor service quality.

The Product Concept

Other businesses are guided by the product concept.

❖ The **PRODUCT CONCEPT** holds that consumers will favor those products that offer the most quality, performance, or innovative features. Managers in product-

Assessing Marketing's Critical Role in Organizational Performance

oriented organizations focus their energy on making superior products and improving them over time.

Under the concept, managers assume that buyers admire well-made products and can appraise product quality and performance. However, these managers are sometimes caught up in a love affair with their product and do not realize that the market may be less "turned on." Marketing management becomes a victim of the "better-mousetrap" fallacy, believing that a better mousetrap will lead people to beat a path to its door. The story of Steven P. Jobs and his NeXT computer provides a cautionary tale:

JOBS AND THE NeXT COMPUTER   Jobs helped to create the PC industry with his Apple Macintosh, so expectations were running sky-high when he unveiled the sleek black NeXT desktop computer in the late 1980s. Yet after burning through $200 million in investment funds, NeXT stopped shipping the $10,000 computer early in 1993. What went wrong? The computer was attractive and user friendly. It featured a hi-fi speaker and the first CD-ROM reader ever included in a desktop computer. Yet it was never clear who NeXT's intended customers were or what the computer was supposed to do best. Jobs first introduced his dream machine as a scholar's workstation for the academic market, but few scholars could afford the hefty price tag. He then pushed it to engineers, but they preferred desktop workstations from Sun Microsystems and Silicon Graphics. There was also the major problem of software; NeXT was incompatible with IBM or Apple so there was not enough software available. By the time Jobs found the right marketing avenues for his computer, the technology had already slipped too far behind the competition.[17]

Product-oriented companies often design their products with little or no customer input. They trust that their engineers will know how to design or improve the product. Very often they will not even examine competitors' products. A General Motors executive said years ago: "How can the public know what kind of car they want until they see what is available?" GM's designers and engineers would develop plans for a new car. Then manufacturing would make it. Then the finance department would price it. Finally, marketing and sales would try to sell it. No wonder the car required such a hard sell! Fortunately, GM is today asking customers what they value in a car and bringing marketing people in at the very beginning stages of car design.

The product concept leads to the kind of marketing myopia we discussed earlier in this chapter. Railroad management thought that railroad users wanted trains rather than transportation and overlooked the growing challenge of airlines, buses, trucks, and automobiles. Slide-rule manufacturers thought that engineers wanted slide rules rather than calculating capacity and overlooked the challenge of pocket calculators. Churches, department stores, and the post office all assume that they are offering the public the right product and wonder why their sales falter. These organizations too often are looking into a mirror when they should be looking out of the window.

The Selling Concept/Sales Concept

The selling concept (or sales concept) is another common approach.

❖   The **SELLING CONCEPT** holds that consumers, if left alone, will ordinarily not buy enough of the organization's products. The organization must therefore undertake an aggressive selling and promotion effort.

This concept assumes that consumers typically show buying inertia or resistance and must be coaxed into buying. It also assumes that the company has available a whole battery of effective selling and promotion tools to stimulate more buying.

The selling concept is practiced most aggressively with unsought goods, those

Understanding
Marketing
Management

goods that buyers normally do not think of buying, such as insurance, encyclopedias, and funeral plots. These industries have perfected various sales techniques to locate prospects and hard-sell them on their product's benefits.

The selling concept is also practiced in the nonprofit area by fund-raisers, college admissions offices, and political parties. A political party vigorously "sells" its candidate to the voters. The candidate stomps through voting precincts from early morning to late evening, shaking hands, kissing babies, meeting donors, and making speeches. Countless dollars are spent on radio and television advertising, posters, and mailings. The candidate's flaws are concealed from the public because the aim is to make the sale, not to worry about postpurchase satisfaction. After the election, the new official continues to take a sales-oriented view toward the citizens. There is little research into what the public wants and a lot of selling to get the public to accept policies that the politician or party wants.[18]

Most firms practice the selling concept when they have overcapacity. *Their aim is to sell what they make rather than make what the market wants.* In modern industrial economies, productive capacity has been built up to a point where most markets are buyer markets (i.e., the buyers are dominant) and sellers have to scramble hard for customers. Prospects are bombarded with television commercials, newspaper ads, direct mail, and sales calls. At every turn, someone is trying to sell something. As a result, the public often identifies marketing with hard selling and advertising.

Therefore, people are surprised when they are told that the most important part of marketing is not selling! Selling is only the tip of the marketing iceberg. Peter Drucker, one of the leading management theorists, puts it this way:

> There will always, one can assume, be need for some selling. But the aim of marketing is to make selling superfluous. The aim of marketing is to know and understand the customer so well that the product or service fits him and sells itself. Ideally, marketing should result in a customer who is ready to buy. All that should be needed then is to make the product or service available. . . .[19]

When Sony designed its Walkman, when Nintendo designed a superior video game, and when Toyota introduced its Lexus automobile, these manufacturers were swamped with orders because they had designed the "right" product based on careful marketing homework.

Indeed, marketing based on hard selling carries high risks. It assumes that customers who are coaxed into buying the product will like it, and, if they don't, that they won't bad-mouth it or complain to consumer organizations. And they will possibly forget their disappointment and buy it again. These are indefensible assumptions to make about buyers. One study showed that dissatisfied customers may bad-mouth the product to 10 or more acquaintances; bad news travels fast.[20]

The Marketing Concept

The marketing concept is a business philosophy that challenges the three concepts we just discussed. Its central tenets crystallized in the mid-1950s.[21]

❖ The **MARKETING CONCEPT** holds that the key to achieving organizational goals consists of being more effective than competitors in integrating marketing activities toward determining and satisfying the needs and wants of target markets.

The marketing concept has been expressed in many colorful ways:

"Meeting needs profitably."
"Find wants and fill them."
"Love the customer, not the product."

"Have it your way." (Burger King)
"You're the boss." (United Airlines)
"Putting people first." (British Airways)
"Partners for profit." (Milliken Company)

Professor Theodore Levitt of Harvard drew a perceptive contrast between the selling and marketing concepts.

> *Selling focuses on the needs of the seller; marketing on the needs of the buyer. Selling is preoccupied with the seller's need to convert his product into cash; marketing with the idea of satisfying the needs of the customer by means of the product and the whole cluster of things associated with creating, delivering and finally consuming it.*[22]

The marketing concept rests on four pillars: *target market, customer needs, integrated marketing,* and *profitability.* These are discussed below and illustrated in Figure 1-7, where they are contrasted with a selling orientation. The selling concept takes an inside-out perspective. It starts with the factory, focuses on the company's existing products, and calls for heavy selling and promoting to produce profitable sales. The marketing concept takes an outside-in perspective. It starts with a well-defined market, focuses on customer needs, integrates all the activities that will affect customers, and produces profits by satisfying customers.

TARGET MARKET. No company can operate in every market and satisfy every need. Nor can it always do a good job within one broad market: Even Microsoft cannot offer the best solution for every information processing need. Companies do best when they define their target market(s) carefully and prepare a tailored marketing program. One example of successful target marketing came about after the 1990 census focused marketers' attention on minority groups' increasing buying power. Estee Lauder, Maybelline, and other cosmetic giants have begun to target African-Americans with special product lines designed for darker skin tones. In the fall of 1992, Prescriptives, a subsidiary of Estee Lauder, launched its "All Skins" line offering 115 different shades of foundation. The senior executive of creative marketing at Prescriptives credits All Skins for a 45% increase in Prescriptives' sales since the new line was launched. Sales of Maybelline's Shades of You,

FIGURE 1-7
The Selling and Marketing Concepts Contrasted

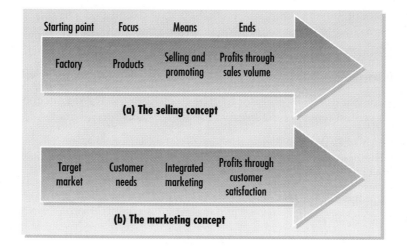

Starting point	Focus	Means	Ends
Factory	Products	Selling and promoting	Profits through sales volume

(a) The selling concept

Target market	Customer needs	Integrated marketing	Profits through customer satisfaction

(b) The marketing concept

Understanding
Marketing
Management

another line of cosmetics for African-American women, reached $15 million in its first 10 months on the market.[23]

CUSTOMER NEEDS. A company can define its target market but fail to fully understand the customers' needs. Consider the following example:

> A major chemical company invented a new substance that hardened into a marble-like material. Looking for an application, the marketing department decided to target the bathtub market. The company created a few model bathtubs and exhibited them at a bathroom trade show. They hoped to convince bathtub manufacturers to produce bathtubs with the new material. Although bathtub manufacturers thought the new bathtubs were attractive, none signed up. The reason soon became obvious. The bathtub would have to be priced at $2,000. For that price, consumers could buy bathtubs made out of real marble or onyx. In addition, the bathtubs were so heavy that homeowners would have to reinforce their floors. Furthermore, most bathtubs sold in the $500 range, and few people would spend $2,000. The chemical company found a target market but failed to understand the customers.

Although marketing is about meeting needs profitably, understanding customer needs and wants is not always a simple task. Some customers have needs of which they are not fully conscious. Or they cannot articulate these needs. Or they use words that require some interpretation. What does it mean when the customer asks for an "inexpensive" car, a "powerful" lawn mower, a "fast" lathe, an "attractive" bathing suit, or a "restful" hotel?

Consider the customer who says he wants an "inexpensive" car. The marketer must probe further. We can distinguish among five types of needs:

1. *Stated needs* (the customer wants an inexpensive car)
2. *Real needs* (the customer wants a car whose operating cost, not its initial price, is low)
3. *Unstated needs* (the customer expects good service from the dealer)
4. *Delight needs* (the customer buys the car and receives a complimentary U.S. road atlas)
5. *Secret needs* (the customer wants to be seen by friends as a value-oriented savvy consumer)

Responding only to the customer's stated need may shortchange the customer. Consider a customer who enters a hardware store and asks for a sealant to seal windows to frames. This customer is stating a *solution,* not a need. The need is to affix glass to a wooden frame. The hardware store salesperson might suggest a better solution than a sealant, namely using a tape. The tape has the additional advantage of zero curing time. In this case, the salesperson has aimed to meet the customer's real need, not the stated need.

Customer-oriented thinking requires the company to define customer needs from the customer's point of view. Every buying decision involves trade-offs, and management cannot know what these are without researching customers. Thus a car buyer would like a safe, attractive, reliable high-performance car that costs less than $10,000. Since all these features cannot be combined in one car, the car designers must make hard choices based on knowing customer trade-offs.

In general, a company can respond to customers' requests by giving customers what they want, or what they need, or what they really need. The key to professional marketing is to understand their customers' real needs and meet them better than any competitor can.

Some marketers draw a distinction between *responsive marketing* and *creative marketing*. A responsive marketer finds a stated need and fills it. A creative marketer discovers and produces solutions that customers did not ask for but to which they enthusiastically respond. Hamel and Prahalad believe that companies must go beyond just asking consumers what they want:

Assessing Marketing's Critical Role in Organizational Performance

Customers are notoriously lacking in foresight. Ten or 15 years ago, how many of us were asking for cellular telephones, fax machines, and copies at home, 24-hour discount brokerage accounts, multivalve automobile engines, compact disc players, cars with on-board navigation systems, hand-held global satellite positioning receivers, automated teller machines, MTV, or the Home Shopping Network?[24]

The Sony Corporation is a good example of a company that goes beyond "customer-led" marketing. Sony is a *marketing-driving* firm, not just a *market-driven* firm. Akio Morita, Sony's founder, proclaims that he doesn't serve markets; he creates markets.

Why is it supremely important to satisfy the target customer? Because a company's sales each period come from two groups: new customers and repeat customers. The Forum Company estimates that attracting a new customer can cost five times as much as pleasing an existing customer.[25] And it might cost sixteen times as much to bring the new customer to the same level of profitability as the lost customer. *Customer retention* is thus more important than *customer attraction.* The key to customer retention is *customer satisfaction.* A highly satisfied customer:

◆ Stays loyal longer

◆ Buys more as the company introduces new products and upgrades existing products

◆ Talks favorably about the company and its products

◆ Pays less attention to competing brands and advertising and is less sensitive to price

◆ Offers product/service ideas to the company

◆ Costs less to serve than new customers because transactions are routinized

One Japanese Lexus executive told the author: "My company's aim goes beyond satisfying the customer. Our aim is to *delight* the customer."

Thus a company would be wise to measure customer satisfaction regularly. For example, the company could phone a sample of recent buyers and inquire how many are highly satisfied, somewhat satisfied, indifferent, somewhat dissatisfied, and highly dissatisfied. It could also ask about the major factors in customer satisfaction and dissatisfaction, then use this information to improve its performance in the next period.

Some companies think that they are getting a measure of customer satisfaction by tallying the number and types of customer complaints they receive each period. But in fact, 95% of dissatisfied customers don't complain; many may just stop buying.[26] The best thing a company can do is to make it easy for the customer to complain. Suggestion forms found in hotel room and company "hot lines" such as those run by Procter & Gamble and General Electric serve this purpose. These companies hope that customers will call them with suggestions, inquiries, and even complaints. 3M claims that over two thirds of its product-improvement ideas come from listening to its customer complaints.

Listening is not enough, however. The company must respond constructively to the complaints:

> *Of the customers who register a complaint, between 54 and 70% will do business again with the organization if their complaint is resolved. The figure goes up to a staggering 95% if the customer feels that the complaint was resolved quickly. Customers who have complained to an organization and had their complaints satisfactorily resolved tell an average of five people about the treatment they received.*[27]

When a company realizes that a loyal customer may account for a substantial amount of revenue over the years, it also realizes how foolish it is to risk losing the customer by ignoring a grievance or quarreling over a small amount. IBM requires every salesperson to write a full report on each lost customer and all the steps taken to restore satisfaction. Reattracting lost customers is an important marketing activity and often costs less than attracting first-time customers.

One company long recognized for its emphasis on customer satisfaction is L. L. Bean, Inc., of Freeport, Maine, which runs a mail-order catalog business in clothing and equipment for rugged living. L. L. Bean has carefully blended its external and internal marketing programs. To its customers, it offers the following:[28]

100% GUARANTEE

All of our products are guaranteed to give 100% satisfaction in every way. Return anything purchased from us at any time if it proves otherwise. We will replace it, refund your purchase price or credit your credit card, as you wish. We do not want you to have anything from L. L. Bean that is not completely satisfactory.

To motivate its employees to serve the customers well, it displays the following poster prominently around its offices:[29]

What Is a Customer?

A Customer is the most important person ever in this office . . . in person or by mail.

A Customer is not dependent on us . . . we are dependent on him.

A Customer is not an interruption of our work . . . he is the purpose of it. We are not doing a favor by serving him . . . he is doing us a favor by giving us the opportunity to do so.

A Customer is not someone to argue or match wits with. Nobody ever won an argument with a Customer.

A Customer is a person who brings us his wants. It is our job to handle them profitably to him and to ourselves.

INTEGRATED MARKETING. When all the company's departments work together to serve the customer's interests, the result is *integrated marketing*. Unfortunately, not all employees are trained and motivated to work for the customer. An engineer complained that the salespeople were "always protecting the customer and not thinking of the company's interest"! He went on to blast customers for "asking for too much." The following example highlights the coordination problem:

> The marketing vice-president of a major airline wants to increase the airline's traffic share. Her strategy is to build up customer satisfaction through providing better food, cleaner cabins, and better trained cabin crews. Yet she has no authority in these matters. The catering department chooses food that keeps down food costs: the maintenance department uses cleaning services that keep down cleaning costs; and the human resources department hires people without regard to whether they are friendly and inclined to serve other people. Since these departments generally take a cost or production point of view, she is stymied in creating a high level of customer satisfaction.

Integrated marketing takes place on two levels. First, the various marketing functions—sales force, advertising, product management, marketing research, and so on—must work together. Too often the sales force is mad at the product managers for setting "too high a price" or "too high a volume target"; or the advertising director and a brand manager cannot agree on an advertising campaign. All these marketing functions must be coordinated from the customer's point of view.

Assessing Marketing's Critical Role in Organizational Performance

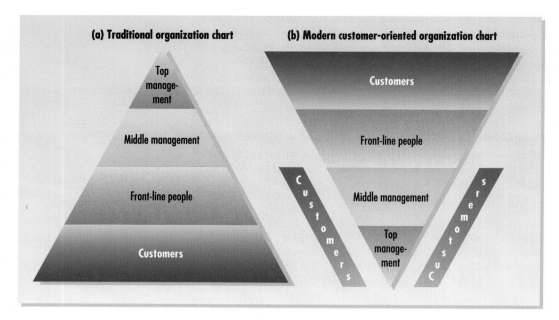

(a) Traditional organization chart

- Top management
- Middle management
- Front-line people
- Customers

(b) Modern customer-oriented organization chart

- Customers
- Front-line people
- Middle management
- Top management

Customers · Customers

FIGURE 1-8
Traditional Organization Chart versus Modern Customer-Oriented Company Organization Chart

Second, marketing must be well coordinated with other company departments. Marketing does not work when it is merely a department; it works only when all employees appreciate their impact on customer satisfaction. As David Packard of Hewlett Packard put it: "Marketing is too important to be left to the marketing department!" Xerox goes so far as to include in every one of its job descriptions an explanation of how that job impacts the customer. Xerox factory managers know that customer visits to the factory can help sell a potential customer if the factory is clean and efficient. Xerox accountants know that customer attitudes toward Xerox are affected by billing accuracy and their promptness in returning customer calls.

To foster teamwork among all departments, the company carries out internal marketing as well as external marketing. *External marketing* is marketing directed at people outside the company. *Internal marketing* is the task of successfully hiring, training, and motivating able employees who want to serve the customers well. In fact, internal marketing must precede external marketing. It makes no sense to promise excellent service before the company's staff is ready to provide excellent service.

Many managers who believe that the customer is the key to profitability consider the traditional organization chart in Figure 1-8(a)—a pyramid with the president at the top, management in the middle, and front-line people (sales and service people, telephone operators, receptionists) and customers at the bottom—to be obsolete. Master marketing companies know better; they invert the chart, as shown in Figure 1-8(b). At the top of the organization are the customers. Next in importance are the front-line people who meet, serve, and satisfy the customers. Under them are the middle managers, whose job is to support the front-line people so they can serve the customers well. Finally, at the base is top management, whose job is to support the middle managers. We have added customers along the sides of Figure 1-8(b) to indicate that all the company's managers are personally involved in knowing, meeting, and serving customers.

PROFITABILITY. The ultimate purpose of the marketing concept is to help organizations achieve their goals. In the case of private firms, the major goal is profit; in the case of nonprofit and public organizations, it is surviving and attracting enough funds to perform their work. In for-profit organizations, the key is not to aim for profits as such but to achieve them as a byproduct of doing the job well. A company makes money by satisfying customer needs better than its competitors do. Consider Frank Perdue's philosophy:

PERDUE CHICKEN FARMS   Perdue Farms is a $1.5 billion chicken business whose margins are substantially above the industry average and whose market shares in its major markets reach 50 percent. And the product is chicken—a commodity if there ever was one! Yet its colorful founder, Frank Perdue, does not believe that "a chicken is a chicken is a chicken," nor do his customers. His theme is, "It takes a tough man to make a tender chicken," and he offers a money-back guarantee to dissatisfied customers. He aims to produce tender-tasting chickens for which discriminating customers will pay a price premium. His attitude is that if one offers superior product quality and business integrity, high profits, market share, and growth will follow.

How many companies actually practice the marketing concept? Unfortunately, too few. Only a handful of companies stand out as master marketers: Procter & Gamble, Apple Computer, Disney, Nordstrom, Wal-Mart, Milliken, McDonald's, Marriott Hotels, American Airlines, and several Japanese companies (Sony, Toyota, Canon) and European companies (Ikea, Club Med, Ericsson, Bang & Olufsen, Marks & Spencer). These companies focus on the customer and are organized to respond effectively to changing customer needs. They all have well-staffed marketing departments, and all their other departments—manufacturing, finance, research and development, personnel, purchasing—also accept the concept that the customer is king.

Most companies do not embrace the marketing concept until driven to it by circumstances. Any of the following developments might prod them to take the marketing concept to heart:

- *Sales decline:* When companies experience falling sales, they panic and look for answers. For example, newspapers are experiencing declining circulation as more people turn to television and cable TV news. Some publishers now realize that they know little about why people read newspapers. These publishers are commissioning consumer research and attempting to redesign newspapers to be contemporary, relevant, and interesting to readers.

- *Slow growth:* Slow sales growth leads some companies to cast about for new markets. Many of these companies realize that they need marketing know-how to identify and select new opportunities. Wanting new sources of revenue, Dow Chemical decided to enter consumer markets and invested heavily in acquiring consumer marketing expertise to perform well in these markets.

- *Changing buying patterns:* Many companies operate in markets characterized by rapidly changing customer wants. These companies need more marketing know-how if they are to continue producing value for buyers.

- *Increasing competition:* Complacent companies may suddenly be attacked by powerful marketing companies and forced to meet the challenge. AT&T was a regulated, marketing-naive telephone company until the 1970s, when the government began allowing other companies to sell telecommunications equipment to AT&T's customers. AT&T plunged into the marketing waters and hired the best marketers it could find to help it compete.[30]

- *Increasing marketing expenditures:* Companies may find their expenditures for advertising, sales promotion, marketing research, and customer service getting out of hand. Management then decides it is time to undertake a marketing audit to improve its marketing.[31]

Assessing Marketing's Critical Role in Organizational Performance

FIGURE 1-9
Evolving Views of Marketing's Role in the Company

(a) Marketing as an equal function

(b) Marketing as a more important function

(c) Marketing as the major function

(d) The customer as the controlling function

(e) The customer as the controlling function and marketing as the integrative function

In the course of converting to a marketing-oriented company, a company faces three hurdles: organized resistance, slow learning, and fast forgetting.

Organized Resistance. Some company departments (often manufacturing, finance, and R&D) do not like to see marketing built up because they believe that a stronger marketing function threatens their power in the organization. The nature of the threat is illustrated in Figure 1-9. Initially, the marketing function is seen as one of several equally important business functions in a check-and-balance relationship (Figure 1-9[a]). A lack of demand then leads marketers to argue that their function is somewhat more important than the others (Figure 1-9[b]). A few marketing enthusiasts go further and say marketing is the major function of the enterprise, for without customers there would be no company. They put marketing at the center, with other business functions serving as support functions (Figure 1-9[c]). This view incenses the other managers, who do not want to think of themselves as working for marketing. Enlightened marketers clarify the issue by putting the customer rather than marketing at the center of the company (Figure 1-9[d]). They argue for a customer orientation in which all functions work together to sense, serve, and satisfy the customer. Finally, some marketers say that marketing still needs to command a central company position if customers' needs are to be correctly interpreted and efficiently satisfied (Figure 1-9[e]).

The marketer's argument for embracing the marketing concept is simple:

1. The company's assets have little value without the existence of customers.
2. The key company task is therefore to attract and retain customers.
3. Customers are attracted through competitively superior offers and retained through satisfaction.
4. Marketing's task is to develop a superior offer and deliver customer satisfaction.
5. Customer satisfaction is affected by the performance of the other departments.
6. Marketing needs to influence these other departments to cooperate in delivering customer satisfaction.

In spite of this argument, marketing is still resisted in many quarters. The resistance is especially strong in industries where marketing is being introduced for the first time—for instance, in law offices, colleges, hospitals, and government agencies. Colleges have to face the hostility of instructors and hospitals have to face the hostility of doctors; both groups often think that "marketing" their service would be degrading.

Slow Learning. In spite of resistance, many companies manage to introduce some marketing in their organization. The company president establishes a marketing department; marketing talent is hired; key managers attend marketing seminars; the marketing budget is substantially increased; marketing planning and control systems are introduced. Even with these steps, however, the learning of marketing comes slowly.

Fast Forgetting. Even after marketing has been installed, management must fight a strong tendency to forget basic marketing principles, especially in the wake of marketing success. For example, a number of major U.S. companies entered European markets in the 1950s and 1960s expecting to achieve outstanding success with their sophisticated products and marketing capabilities. A number of them failed because they forgot the marketing maxim: *Know your target market and how to satisfy it.* U.S. companies introduced their current products and advertising programs instead of adapting them. For example, General Mills introduced its Betty Crocker cake mixes in Britain only to withdraw them a short time later. Their angel food cake and devil's food cake sounded too exotic for British consumers. And many Britons felt that the perfect-looking cakes pictured on the Betty Crocker packages must be too hard to make. U.S. marketers failed to appreciate the major cultural variations between and even within European countries.

Companies face a particularly difficult task in adapting their ad slogans to international markets. When Coca-Cola tried to market to China in 1979, for instance, it discovered that Mao's simplification of Chinese characters had turned the literal meaning of Coca-Cola into "Bite the wax tadpole." Coca-Cola solved this problem by using four Mandarin characters meaning "Can Happy, Mouth Happy." Many people remember what happened when Frank Perdue's ad slogan—"It takes a tough man to make a tender chicken"—was rendered into Spanish for TV broadcasts to the U.S. Latino population. The garbled and offensive result was "It takes a sexually excited man to make a chick affectionate." And, even when the language is the same, the way words are used may differ from country to country: Electrolux's British ad line for its vacuum cleaners—"Nothing sucks like an Electrolux"—would certainly not lure customers in the United States![32]

The Societal Marketing Concept

In recent years, some have questioned whether the marketing concept is an appropriate philosophy in an age of environmental deterioration, resource shortages, explosive population growth, world hunger and poverty, and neglected social services.[33] Are companies that do an excellent job of satisfying consumer wants necessarily acting in the best long-run interests of consumers and society? The marketing concept sidesteps the potential conflicts among consumer wants, consumer interests, and long-run societal welfare.

Consider the following criticisms:

The fast-food hamburger industry offers tasty but unhealthy food. The hamburgers have a high fat content, and the restaurants promote fries and pies, two products high in starch and fat. The products are wrapped in convenient packaging, which leads to much waste. In satisfying consumer wants, these restaurants may be hurting consumer health and causing environmental problems.

The soft-drink industry has catered to the U.S. desire for convenience by increasing the share of one-way disposable bottles. However, the one-way bottle represents a great waste of resources; approximately 17 bottles are necessary where formerly one two-way bottle made 17 trips before it was damaged. In addition, many one-way bottles are not biodegradable; and these bottles often litter the environment.

The detergent industry caters to the U.S. passion for whiter clothes by offering a product that pollutes rivers and streams, kills fish, and injures recreational opportunities.

These situations call for a new concept that enlarges the marketing concept. Among the suggested names for the proposals are "humanistic marketing" and "ecological marketing." We propose calling it the societal marketing concept.

❖ The **SOCIETAL MARKETING CONCEPT** holds that the organization's task is to determine the needs, wants, and interests of target markets and to deliver the desired satisfactions more effectively and efficiently than competitors in a way that preserves or enhances the consumer's and the society's well-being.

Assessing Marketing's Critical Role in Organizational Performance

The societal marketing concept calls upon marketers to build social and ethical considerations into their marketing practices. They must balance and juggle the often conflicting criteria of company profits, consumer want satisfaction, and public interest. Yet a number of companies have achieved notable sales and profit gains through adopting and practicing the societal marketing concept. Two pioneers in putting the societal marketing concept to work are Ben & Jerry's and The Body Shop. But, as recent events show, even they have had difficulty keeping all the balls in the air at once:[34]

BEN & JERRY'S In 1978, two guys from Vermont—Ben Cohen and Jerry Greenfield— formed a company to produce a superpremium ice cream that they called Ben & Jerry's Homemade. Sixteen years after Ben & Jerry's Scoop Shop opened in Burlington, Vermont, sales have climbed to $150 million. The company now has more than 600 employees and 10 franchisees. Why the appeal? For one thing, Ben & Jerry are masters at creating innovative flavors such as Rainforest Crunch, Cherry Garcia, and Chocolate Chip Cookie Dough. For another, customers know that 7.5% of Ben & Jerry's pre-tax profits are donated to a variety of social and environmental causes. Ben & Jerry's was also noted for its egalitarian employer-employee relations; the company used to have a policy in which the highest-paid employee made no more than five times the lowest-paid worker. Business realities recently forced the company to modify this ratio to seven to one. In 1993, facing stiff competition in the superpremium ice cream category, the company suffered its first loss since going public in 1984, and it began to search for a new CEO to lead the company through its next stage of financial growth. To get a qualified CEO, the two founders felt they had to raise the compensation level. Of course, Ben & Jerry's still conducted the CEO search in their own iconoclastic style. An essay contest entitled "Yo, I'm Your C.E.O." garnered applications from 20,000 CEO hopefuls, but in the end the company made a rather conventional choice: corporate turnaround consultant Robert Holland, Jr.

THE BODY SHOP In 1976, Anita Roddick opened The Body Shop in Brighton, England, a tiny storefront selling beauty products out of urine-sample bottles. Now Roddick operates over 1,100 stores in 46 countries and The Body Shop's annual sales growth rate has been between 60% and 100%, with sales reaching $250 million in 1993. The company manufactures and sells natural-ingredient-based cosmetics in simple and appealing recyclable packaging. The ingredients are largely plant-based and are often sourced from developing countries. All the products are formulated without any animal testing, and The Body Shop donates a certain percentage of profits each year to animal rights groups, homeless shelters, Amnesty International, Save the Rainforest, and other social causes. To promote AIDS awareness, the company has handed out condoms and pamphlets about safe sex at its over 150 U.S. stores. The outspoken Roddick routinely speaks out against the mainstream beauty industry and promotes her company's brand of socially responsible capitalism. However, going out on a limb means facing closer scrutiny. In 1992 the company filed a libel suit over a television report that challenged its image as a company with social conscience. While The Body Shop won the suit in 1993, it is still besieged by critics who allege that the company does not live up to its reputation, and its profits have slipped slightly as copycat competitors enter the natural products market. Roddick, however, is unfazed, "Any company that is values-led can expect extreme responses. You're either raised above the angels or cast down with the demons, with a bull's-eye glued to your bum to boot."

These companies are practicing *cause-related marketing,* a version of the societal marketing concept, and it is one major factor in their success.[35]

A growing number of companies are using cause-related marketing on a more limited scale. When Continental Airlines wanted to reinstate flights to and from Hobby Airport in Houston, it promised to make a cash donation to renovate the air terminal for every customer boarding a Continental flight from Hobby. When money was being raised to refurbish the Statue of Liberty, American Express offered to contribute 1% of its credit card charges to the fundraising campaign, hoping that more people would charge their purchases on their American Express card. Several other companies have offered to contribute to a specific charity based on consumer purchases during a limited period. Companies run these cause-related marketing campaigns for several purposes: to enhance corporate image, thwart negative publicity, pacify consumer groups, launch a new product or brand, broaden their customer base, and generate incremental sales. Some critics complain that cause-related marketing exploits the cause's constituency and may make consumers feel that they have fulfilled their philanthropic duties by buying a product instead of donating directly.

THE RAPID ADOPTION OF MARKETING MANAGEMENT

Marketing management today is the subject of growing interest in all types of organizations, within and outside the business sector and in countries throughout the world.

In the Business Sector

In the business sector, marketing entered different companies' consciousness at different times. General Electric, General Motors, Procter & Gamble, and Coca-Cola were among the early leaders. Marketing spread most rapidly in consumer packaged-goods companies, consumer durables companies, and industrial-equipment companies—in that order. Producers of commodities like steel, chemicals, and paper came to marketing consciousness later, and many still have a long way to go. Within the past decade consumer-service firms, especially airlines and banks, have moved toward modern marketing. Marketing is beginning to attract the interest of insurance and stock-brokerage companies, although they also have a long way to go in applying marketing effectively. The Marketing Insight on page 30 titled "Five Stages in the Slow Learning of Bank Marketing" describes the stages through which bank marketing has passed.

The most recent business groups to take an interest in marketing are professional service providers, such as lawyers, accountants, physicians, and architects.[36] Professional societies used to prohibit their members from engaging in price competition, client solicitation, and advertising. But the U.S. antitrust division has ruled that these restraints are illegal. Accountants, lawyers, and other professional groups can now advertise and price aggressively. They call marketing "practice development," work on "positioning" their firms, and identify "hot prospects" for cultivation.

In the Nonprofit Sector

Marketing is increasingly attracting the interest of nonprofit organizations such as colleges, hospitals, churches, and performing arts groups.[37] Consider the following developments:

> Many performing arts groups need to attract larger audiences. Faced with declining ticket sales, the Colorado Symphony Orchestra realized that it needed to appeal to a new generation of music lovers for whom "classical music" is seen as either daunting or boring. One of the Orchestra's marketing innovations was to host a new weekend program called Casual Classics in which newcomers are invited to sip wine and beer with the orchestra and ask questions of the musicians before and after the program.[38]

Assessing Marketing's Critical Role in Organizational Performance

Five Stages in the Slow Learning of Bank Marketing

Years ago, bankers had little understanding or regard for marketing. Bankers did not have to make a case for checking accounts, savings, loans, or safe-deposit boxes. The bank building was created in the image of a Greek temple, calculated to impress the public with the bank's importance and solidity. The interior was austere, and the tellers rarely smiled. One lending officer arranged his office so that a prospective borrower would sit across from his massive desk on a lower chair. The office window was located behind the officer's back, and the sun would pour in on the hapless client, who tried to explain why he or she needed a loan. This was the bank's posture before the age of marketing.

1. *Marketing Is Advertising, Sales Promotion, and Publicity.* Marketing came into banks not in the form of the marketing concept but in the form of the "advertising and promotion concept." Banks were facing increased competition for savings. A few banks started to do heavy advertising and sales promotion. They offered umbrellas, radios, and other "come-ons" and attracted new customer accounts. Their competitors were forced to adopt the same measures and scurried out to hire advertising agencies and sales-promotion experts.

2. *Marketing Is Smiling and a Friendly Atmosphere.* The banks learned that attracting people to a bank is easy; converting them into loyal customers is hard. These banks began to formulate programs to please the customer. Bankers learned to smile. The bars were removed from the tellers' windows. The bank interior was redesigned to produce a warm, friendly atmosphere. Even the outside Greek-temple architecture was changed. Competitors quickly launched similar programs of friendliness training and decor improvement. Soon all banks were so friendly that friendliness lost its decisiveness as a factor in bank choice.

3. *Marketing Is Segmentation and Innovation.* Banks found a new competitive tool when they began to segment their markets and innovate new products for each target segment. Citibank, for example, today offers more than 500 financial products to customers. Financial services, however, are easily copied, and specific advantages are short-lived. But if the same bank invests in continuous innovation, it can stay ahead of the other banks. Bank One of Columbus, Ohio, is an example of a market leader whose rapid growth is based on an uncanny ability to continuously innovate new retail bank products.

4. *Marketing Is Positioning.* What happens when all banks advertise, smile, segment, and innovate? Clearly, they begin to look alike. They are forced to find a new basis for competition. They begin to realize that no bank can offer all products and be the best bank for all customers. A bank must examine its opportunities and "take a position" in the market.

   Positioning goes beyond image making. The image-making bank seeks to cultivate an image in the customer's mind as a large, friendly, or efficient bank. It often develops a symbol, such as a lion (Harris Bank in Chicago) or a kangaroo (Continental Bank in Chicago) to dramatize its personality in a distinctive way. Yet the customer may see the competing banks as basically alike, except for the chosen symbols. Positioning is an attempt to distinguish the bank from its competitors along real dimensions in order to be the preferred bank for certain market segments. Positioning aims to help customers know the real differences between competing banks, so that they can match themselves to the bank that can satisfy their needs best.

5. *Marketing Is Marketing Analysis, Planning, Implementation, and Control.* There is a higher concept of bank marketing. The issue is whether the bank has installed effective systems for marketing analysis, planning, implementation, and control. One large bank, which had achieved sophistication in advertising, friendliness, segmentation, innovation, and positioning, nevertheless lacked good systems of marketing planning and control. Each fiscal year, commercial loan officers submitted their volume goals, usually 10% higher than the previous year's goals. They also requested a budget increase of 10%. No rationale or plans accompanied these submissions. Top management was satisfied with the officers who achieved their goals. One loan officer, judged to be a good performer, retired and was replaced by a younger man, who proceeded to increase the loan volume 50% the following year! The bank painfully learned that it had failed to conduct marketing research to measure the potentials of its various markets, to require marketing plans, to set quotas, and to develop appropriate management incentive systems.

Faced with falling enrollments and rising costs, many private colleges are using marketing to compete for students and funds. They are defining their target markets better, improving their communication and promotion, and responding better to student wants and needs.[39]

As hospital costs soar, many hospitals have turned to marketing. They are developing product-line plans, improved emergency-room service, better physician services, advertising programs, and sales calls on corporations.[40]

Many of America's 300,000 churches are losing members and failing to attract enough financial support. Churches need to better understand member needs as well as competitive institutions and activities if they hope to revive their role in their communities.[41]

Many longstanding nonprofit organizations—the YMCA, the Salvation Army, the Girl Scouts, and the Woman's Christian Temperance Union—have lost members and are now modernizing their mission and "product" to attract more members and donors.[42]

To sustain their organizations in the face of rapidly changing consumer attitudes and diminishing financial resources, these organizations' administrators are turning to marketing. Over half of U.S. hospitals now have a marketing director. Even U.S. government agencies such as the U.S. Postal Service, Amtrak, and the U.S. Army have implemented marketing plans. Various government and private nonprofit agencies are also launching *social marketing campaigns* to discourage cigarette smoking, excessive drinking, hard-drug usage, and unsafe sex practices.[43]

In the Global Sector

Marketing theory and practice, at one time limited to certain Western countries, are rapidly spreading throughout the world. Part of the reason is that many large companies have gone global and brought their marketing practices with them. In competing for new markets, they have forced the local firms to defend their turf by learning and refining their own marketing practices. A small Indian soap company called Nirma bested the mighty Hindustan Lever Company of India (a subsidiary of Unilever), which had dominated the Indian soap market, by aggressively introducing a lower-priced value brand accompanied by a strong and memorable radio jingle campaign against Lever's more established brands.

Today high-quality marketing training seminars are being sponsored not only in industrialized countries but also in emerging countries such as Indonesia, Malaysia, Egypt, and Colombia. In the former Socialist countries, where marketing had a bad name, marketing is one of the hottest subjects in business: The translated version of this textbook became the number-one best-selling business book in Poland and can be obtained in Russia only on the black market. Clearly companies, both domestic and foreign, see their future as dependent on their ability to understand buyers and markets better than their competitors do. Global markets will only heat up in the future, and competitors will need to understand and apply the latest marketing concepts and strategies.

SUMMARY

1. Businesses today face several major challenges. Advances in technology and telecommunications have brought all the world's countries together into one global economy. At the same time, many nations remain poor, and the gap between rich and poor nations is growing. Companies must respond to marketplace trends while taking responsi-

bility for protecting the environment. They must also focus on the customer if they are to achieve success in the global marketplace.

2. *Marketing* is a social and managerial process by which individuals and groups obtain what they need and want through creating, offering, and exchanging products of value in the market. A *marketer* is someone seeking one or more prospects who might engage in an exchange of values. This definition carries several major insights: (1) Marketers do not create needs; needs preexist marketers. (2) Because a product provides a solution to a need, it is just a means of packaging a service. Thus a marketer's job is to sell the benefits or services built into a physical product rather than the product itself. (3) Marketers seek to elicit a behavioral response from another party. Thus marketing is not limited to consumer goods; it is also widely used to "sell" ideas and social programs.

3. Relationship marketing is the practice of building long-term satisfying relations with key parties—customers, suppliers, distributors—in order to retain their long-term preference and business. Good marketers build up long-term, "win-win" relationships by delivering high quality, good service, and fair prices to other parties over time.

4. *Marketing management* is the process of planning and executing the conception, pricing, promotion, and distribution of goods, services, and ideas to create exchanges with target groups that satisfy customer and organizational objectives. Marketing management is essentially demand management; its task is to influence the level, timing, and composition of demand.

5. There are five competing concepts under which organizations can choose to conduct their marketing activities: the production concept, the product concept, the selling/sales concept, the marketing concept, and the societal marketing concept. The first three concepts are of limited usefulness today. The *marketing concept* holds that the key to achieving organizational goals consists of determining the needs and wants of target markets and delivering the desired satisfactions more effectively and efficiently than competitors. It starts with a well-defined market, focuses on customer needs, integrates all the activities that will affect customers, and produces profits by satisfying customers.

   In recent years, some have questioned whether the marketing concept is an appropriate philosophy in a world faced with major demographic and environmental challenges. The *societal marketing concept* holds that the organization's task is to determine the needs, wants, and interests of target markets and to deliver the desired satisfactions more effectively and efficiently than competitors in a way that preserves or enhances the consumer's and the society's well-being. The concept calls upon marketers to balance three considerations: company profits, consumer want satisfaction, and public interest.

6. Because it makes such an important contribution to organizational objectives and/or profits, marketing management has rapidly been adopted in the business sector, the nonprofit sector, and the global sector.

CONCEPT APPLICATIONS

1. Compaq Computer Corporation made a name for itself in the early 1980s by becoming the first computer company to manufacture and market IBM "clones." Observers point to Compaq's ability to bring out products quickly and to work with other industry giants, such as Intel, as keys to its success.

   How would you expect Compaq to organize its operations if it chose to be guided by the production concept? The selling concept? The marketing concept?

2. The Marketing Insight box in this chapter uses the banking industry to discuss the five stages through which organizations pass as they develop an understanding of marketing. Discuss these same five stages in the context of four-year private liberal arts colleges that are facing declining enrollments.

3. Hospitals have been experiencing a dramatic increase in the hiring of marketing talent and the size of marketing budgets. Likewise, hospital administrators are stating that their hospitals must be "market-driven" institutions. What has caused this greater interest in marketing? What does it mean for a hospital to be "market-driven"?

4. Relationship marketing is one of the hottest trends in marketing today, and you will find this concept integrated throughout this book. Experts have defined the term in many ways—but the bottom line is always "getting to know your customers (clients, publics, etc.) better so you can meet their wants and needs better."

   Keep a record of the next four transactions in which you participate, and classify each one as very satisfying, satisfying, adequate, dissatisfying, or very dissatisfying. For those experiences that you found dissatisfying, what could the company or salesperson have done better? For those that you find satisfying, what specific factors led to your satisfaction?

5. Describe the marketing mixes used by each of the organizations listed below. For information, you might check general business publications like *Business Week, Advertising Age,* and *Fortune,* or specialty trade publications like *Restaurant News.* Specifically, what is each company's approach to product, price, place, and promotion?
   a. Burger King
   b. Canon Copiers
   c. Disneyland
   d. Jiffy Lube

6. Do all companies need to practice the marketing concept? Could you cite companies that do not need this orientation? Which companies need it most?

7. Russell Stover, a manufacturer of moderately priced chocolates sold in drugstores and discount chains, is looking to improve its market share. How might Russell Stover team with Hallmark to accomplish its goals? What benefits would Russell Stover receive? What benefits would Hallmark receive? If the two companies were to enter a strategic alliance, how might they develop advertisements that promote both their products?

8. "Marketing is not simply the job of a group of people in the company who are responsible for selling the company's products. Every member of the firm should function as a marketer." What does it mean for a company recruiter, for example, to function as a marketer?

9. Planter's is preparing to introduce honey-coated, fat-free nuts that retain the original flavor of nuts. The following information was gathered to help the management team analyze the marketing environment and decide which target market is most viable for the product introduction. What is the best market for the product, and why?

TABLE I

SEGMENT 1	SEGMENT 2	SEGMENT 3
Low income	Moderate income	High income
Blue collar	White collar	White collar
High school education	College education	Advanced degree
Urban residence	Suburbs	Suburbs
Socially active	Socially inactive	Active in community
Price sensitive	Price-value	Price-value
Heavy TV watcher	Heavy TV watcher	High magazine readership
Beer drinkers	Non-drinkers	Wine drinkers

10. A managing director of a large company made the following statement: "To be successful in business, all you need is a customer. You don't need any of those tight little academic concepts of how to manage. You don't even need to solve all your problems or to be efficient. All you need is to find out what you do right for the customer you've already got and do more of it." Assess the validity of this statement.

Assessing Marketing's Critical Role in Organizational Performance

1. Thomas Dudak, editor, *International Directory of Company Histories,* Vol. 1 (Chicago and London: St. James Press, 1988), pp. 135–215.

2. The following illustrations were reported in the television documentary, "Made in America?" narrated by Robert Reich and aired on public television channels on May 26–27, 1992.

3. Jordan D. Lewis, "Zen and the Art of an Alliance," *Management Review,* December 1994, pp. 17–19; John Naisbitt, *The Global Paradox* (New York: William Morrow, 1994), pp. 59–60; Catherine Arnst, "Phone Frenzy," *Business Week,* February 20, 1995, pp. 92–97.

4. Michael R. Czinkota, Ilkka A. Ronkainen, and John J. Tarrant, *The Global Marketing Imperative* (Chicago: NTC Business Books, 1995), p. 175.

5. Kathleen Dechant and Barbara Altman, "Environmental Leadership: From Compliance to Competitive Advantage," *Academy of Management Executive,* 8, no. 3 (1994), 7–19.

6. Naisbitt, *The Global Paradox,* pp. 59–60.

7. See Theodore Levitt's classic article, "Marketing Myopia," *Harvard Business Review,* July–August 1960, pp. 45–56.

8. Karl Albrecht, *The Only Thing That Matters: Bringing the Power of the Customer into the Center of Your Business* (New York: HarperBusiness, 1992); Joan K. Cannie, *Turning Lost Customers into Gold: And the Art of Achieving Zero Defections* (New York: Amacom, 1993); Richard Cross and Janet Smith, *Customer Bonding: The Five-Point System for Maximizing Customer Loyalty* (Chicago: NTC Business Books, 1994); Richard C. Whiteley, *The Customer-Driven Company* (Reading, MA: Addison-Wesley, 1991); and Ron Zemke and Thomas K. Connellan, *Sustaining Knock Your Socks Off Service* (New York: Amacom, 1993).

9. For more on the distinction between needs and wants, see Tibor Scitovsky, *The Joyless Economy: The Psychology of Human Satisfaction,* rev. ed. (New York: Oxford, 1992), pp. 107–8.

10. See Ian Bruce, *Meeting Needs: Successful Charity Marketing* (Hemel Hempstead, England: ICSA Publishing Ltd., 1994), pp. 75–78.

11. Louis J. DeRose, *The Value Network* (New York: Amacom, 1994), p. 12.

12. See Regis McKenna, *Relationship Marketing* (Reading, MA: Addison-Wesley, 1991); Martin Christopher, Adrian Payne, and David Ballantyne, *Relationship Marketing: Bringing Quality, Customer Service, and Marketing Together* (Oxford, England: Butterworth-Heinemann, 1991); and Jagdish N. Sheth and Atul Parvatiyar, eds., *Relationship Marketing: Theory, Methods, and Applications,* 1994 Research Conference Proceedings, Center for Relationship Marketing, Roberto C. Goizueta Business School, Emory University, Atlanta, GA.

13. See James C. Anderson, Hakan Hakansson, and Jan Johanson, "Dyadic Business Relationships Within a Business Network Context," *Journal of Marketing,* October 15, 1994, pp. 1–15.

14. *Dictionary of Marketing Terms,* 2d ed., ed. Peter D. Bennett (Chicago: American Marketing Association, 1995).

15. Evert Gummesson, "Marketing-Orientation Revisited: The Crucial Role of the Part-Time Marketer," *European Journal of Marketing,* 25, no. 2 (1991), 60–75.

16. Kathleen Dechant and Barbara Altman, "Environmental Leadership: From Compliance to Competitive Advantage," *Academy of Management Executive,* 8, no. 3 (1994), 7–19.

17. Kevin J. Clancy & Robert S. Shulman, *Marketing Myths That Are Killing Business: The Cure for Death Wish Marketing* (New York: McGraw-Hill, 1994), pp. 83–85; Christopher Power, "Flops," *Business Week,* August 16, 1993, pp. 76–82.

18. See Bruce I. Newman, *The Marketing of the President* (Thousand Oaks, CA: Sage Publications, 1993).

19. Peter Drucker, *Management: Tasks, Responsibilities, Practices* (New York: Harper & Row, 1973), pp. 64–65.

20. See Karl Albrecht and Ron Zemke, *Service America!* (Homewood, IL: Dow Jones-Irwin, 1985), pp. 6–7.

21. See John B. McKitterick, "What Is the Marketing Management Concept?" *The Frontiers of Marketing Thought and Action* (Chicago: American Marketing Association, 1957), pp. 71–82; Fred J. Borch, "The Marketing Philosophy as a Way of Business Life," *The Marketing Concept: Its Meaning to Management,* Marketing series, No. 99 (New York: American Management Association, 1957), pp. 3–5; and Robert J. Keith, "The Marketing Revolution," *Journal of Marketing,* January 1960, pp. 35–38.

22. Levitt, "Marketing Myopia," p. 50.

23. Maria Mallory, "Waking Up to a Major Market," *Business Week,* March 23, 1993, pp. 70, 73.

24. Gary Hamel and C. K. Prahalad, "Seeing the Future First," *Fortune,* September 5, 1994, pp. 64–70.

25. See Patricia Sellers, "Getting Customers to Love You," *Fortune,* March 13, 1989, pp. 38–49.

26. See *Technical Assistance Research Programs (TARP),* U.S. Office of Consumer Affairs Study on Complaint Handling in America, 1986.

27. Albrecht and Zemke, *Service America!,* pp. 6–7.

28. Courtesy L. L. Bean, Freeport, Maine.

29. Courtesy L. L. Bean, Freeport, Maine.

30. See Bro Uttal, "Selling Is No Longer Mickey Mouse at AT&T," *Fortune,* July 17, 1978, pp. 98–104.

31. See Thomas V. Bonoma and Bruce H. Clark, *Marketing Performance Assessment* (Boston: Harvard Business School Press, 1988).

32. Richard Barnet, *Global Dreams: Imperial Corporations and the New World Order* (New York: Simon & Schuster, 1994), pp. 170–71; Czinkota, Ronkainen, and Tarrant, *The Global Marketing Imperative,* p. 249.

33. See Marilyn Collins, "Global Corporate Philanthropy—Marketing Beyond the Call of Duty?", *European Journal of Marketing,* 27, no. 2 (1993), 46–58; Frederick E. Webster, Jr., "Defining the New Marketing Concept," *Marketing Management,* 2, no. 4 (1994), 22–31; Frederick E. Webster, Jr., "Executing the New Marketing Concept," *Marketing Management,* 3, no. 1 (1994), 8–16; Gregory R. Elliott, "The Marketing Concept—Necessary, but Sufficient?: An Environmental View," *European Journal of Marketing,* 24, no. 8 (1990), 20–30.

34. Glenn Collins, "Ben & Jerry's Talent Hunt Ends," *The New York Times,* February 2, 1995, D1:3; Claudia Dreifus, "Passing the Scoop," *The New York Times Magazine,* December 18, 1994, p. 6; Anita Roddick, *Body and Soul* (New York: Crown, 1991); Laura Zinn, "Anita Roddick: Body Shop International," *Business Week/Enterprise,* 1993, p. 120; Eric Utne, "Beyond the Body Shop Brouhaha," *Utne Reader,* January–February, 1995, pp. 101–2; Anita Roddick, "Who Judges the Judges?", *Utne Reader,* January–February 1995, p. 104.

35. See P. Rajan Varadarajan and Anil Menon, "Cause-Related

Marketing: A Coalignment of Marketing Strategy and Corporate Philanthropy," *Journal of Marketing,* July 1988, pp. 58–74; and L. Lawrence Embley, *Doing Well While Doing Good* (Englewood Cliffs, NJ: Prentice Hall, 1993).

36. See Philip Kotler and Paul Bloom, *Marketing Professional Services* (Englewood Cliffs, NJ: Prentice Hall, 1984).

37. See Philip Kotler and Alan R. Andreasen, *Strategic Marketing for Nonprofit Organizations,* 5th ed. (Englewood Cliffs, NJ: Prentice Hall, 1996).

38. Sandra D. Atchison, "Grand Ole Symphony?", *Business Week,* September 6, 1993, pp. 76–77.

39. See Philip Kotler and Karen Fox, *Strategic Marketing for Educational Institutions,* 2d ed. (Englewood Cliffs, NJ: Prentice Hall, 1995).

40. Philip Kotler and Roberta N. Clarke, *Marketing for Health Care Organizations* (Englewood Cliffs, NJ: Prentice Hall, 1987).

41. Norman Shawchuck, Philip Kotler, Bruce Wren, and Gustave Rath, *Marketing for Congregations: Choosing to Serve People More Effectively* (Nashville, TN: Abingdon Press, 1993).

42. Kotler and Andreasen, *Strategic Marketing for Nonprofit Organizations.*

43. Philip Kotler and Eduardo Roberto, *Social Marketing: Strategies for Changing Public Behavior* (New York: Free Press, 1990).

BUILDING CUSTOMER SATISFACTION THROUGH QUALITY, SERVICE, AND VALUE

Our goal as a company [Wal-Mart] is to have customer service that is not just the best, but legendary.

SAM WALTON

❖

The only job security anybody has in this company [Chrysler] comes from quality, productivity, and satisfied customers.

LEE IACOCCA

❖

Look at our balance sheet. On the asset side, you can see so-and-so many aircraft worth so-and-so many billions. But it's wrong; we are fooling ourselves. What we should put on the asset side is, last year SAS carried so-and-so many happy passengers. Because that's the only asset we've got—people who are happy with our service and willing to come back and pay for it again.

JAN CARLZON, SAS AIRLINES

❖

oday's companies are facing their toughest competition ever. We argued in Chapter 1 that companies can outdo their competition if they can move from a product and sales philosophy to a marketing philosophy. In this chapter, we spell out in detail how companies can go about winning customers and outperforming competitors. The answer lies in doing a better job of meeting and satisfying customer needs. Only customer-centered companies are adept at building customers, not just building products. They are skilled in market engineering, not just product engineering.

Too many companies think that it is the marketing/sales department's job to procure customers. If that department cannot, the company draws the conclusion that its marketing people aren't very good. But, in fact, marketing is only one factor in attracting and keeping customers. The best marketing department in the world cannot sell products that are poorly made or fail to meet anyone's need. The marketing department can be effective only in companies whose various departments and employees have designed and implemented a competitively superior customer value-delivery system.

Take McDonald's. People do not swarm to the world's 11,000 McDonald's outlets solely because they love the hamburger. Some other restaurants make better-tasting hamburgers. People are flocking to a system, not a hamburger. This fine-tuned system delivers throughout the world a high standard of what McDonald's calls QSCV—quality, service, cleanliness, and value. McDonald's is effective only to the extent that it works with its suppliers, franchise owners, employees, and others to deliver exceptionally high value to its customers.

In describing and illustrating the philosophy of the customer-focused firm and value marketing,[1] we will address the following questions:

- **What are customer value and satisfaction, and how do leading companies produce and deliver them?**
- **How can companies both attract and retain customers?**
- **How can companies improve customer profitability?**
- **How can companies practice total quality marketing?**

Building Customer
Satisfaction Through
Quality, Service, and Value

DEFINING CUSTOMER VALUE AND SATISFACTION

Over 35 years ago, Peter Drucker observed that a company's first task is "to create customers." But today's customers face a vast array of product and brand choices, prices, and suppliers. How do customers make their choices?

We believe that customers estimate which offer will deliver the most value. Customers are value-maximizers, within the bounds of search costs and limited knowledge, mobility, and income. They form an expectation of value and act on it. Whether or not the offer lives up to the value expectation affects customers' satisfaction and their repurchase probability.

Customer Value

Our premise is that buyers will buy from the firm that they perceive to offer the highest customer delivered value (Figure 2-1):

❖ **CUSTOMER DELIVERED VALUE** is the difference between total customer value and total customer cost. **TOTAL CUSTOMER VALUE** is the bundle of benefits customers expect from a given product or service. **TOTAL CUSTOMER COST** is the bundle of costs customers expect to incur in evaluating, obtaining, and using the product or service.

An example will help here. Suppose the buyer for a large construction company wants to buy a tractor. He will buy it from either Caterpillar or Komatsu. The competing salespeople carefully describe their respective offers to the buyer.

The buyer has a particular tractor application in mind: He wants to use the tractor in residential construction work. He would like the tractor to deliver certain levels of reliability, durability, and performance. He evaluates the two tractors and decides that Caterpillar has a higher product value based on perceived reliability, durability, and performance. He also perceives differences in the accompanying services—delivery, training, and maintenance—and decides that Caterpillar provides better service. He also perceives Caterpillar's personnel to be more knowledgeable and responsive. Finally, he places higher value on Caterpillar's corporate image. He adds all the values from these four sources—*product, services, personnel,* and *image*—and perceives Caterpillar as offering more total customer value.

Does he buy the Caterpillar tractor? Not necessarily. He also examines the total customer cost of transacting with Caterpillar versus Komatsu. The total customer cost consists of more than the monetary cost. As Adam Smith observed over two centuries ago, "The real price of anything is the toil and trouble of acquiring it." This total customer cost, in addition to *monetary cost,* includes the buyer's *time, energy,* and *psychic costs.* The buyer evaluates these costs along with the monetary cost to form a picture of total customer cost.

After calculating the costs, the buyer considers whether Caterpillar's total customer cost is too high in relation to the total customer value that Caterpillar delivers. If it is, the buyer might buy the Komatsu tractor. The buyer will buy from whoever offers the highest delivered value.

Now let's use this theory of buyer decision making to help Caterpillar succeed in selling its tractor to this buyer. Caterpillar can improve its offer in three ways. First, it can increase total customer value by improving product, services, personnel, and/or image benefits. Second, it can reduce the buyer's nonmonetary costs by lessening the buyer's time, energy, and psychic costs. Third, it can reduce its product's monetary cost to the buyer.

Suppose Caterpillar concludes that the buyer sees Caterpillar's offer as worth $20,000. Further, suppose Caterpillar's cost of producing the tractor is $14,000. This

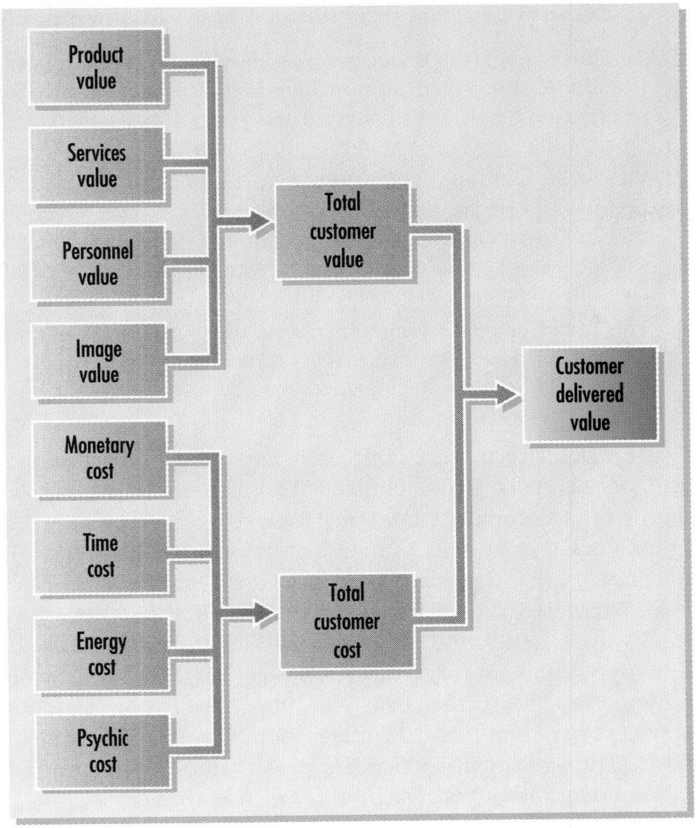

FIGURE 2-1
Determinants of Customer Delivered Value

means that Caterpillar's offer potentially generates $6,000 over the company's cost ($20,000 minus $14,000).

Caterpillar needs to charge a price between $14,000 and $20,000. If it charges less than $14,000, it won't cover its costs. If it charges more than $20,000, it will price itself out of the market. The price Caterpillar charges will determine how much value will be delivered to the buyer and how much will flow to Caterpillar. For example, if Caterpillar charges $19,000, it is granting $1,000 of customer delivered value and keeping $5,000 for itself. The lower Caterpillar sets its price, the higher is the delivered value and, therefore, the higher is the customer's incentive to purchase from Caterpillar.

Given that Caterpillar wants to win the sale, it must offer more delivered value than Komatsu does. Delivered value can be measured either as a difference or a ratio. If total customer value is $20,000 and total customer cost is $16,000, then the delivered value is $4,000 (measured as a difference) or 1.25 (measured as a ratio). Ratios that are used to compare offers are often called *value/price ratios*.[2]

Some marketers might argue that the theory we've just developed of how buyers choose suppliers is too rational. They cite examples where buyers did not choose the offer with the highest delivered value. Consider the following situation: The Caterpillar salesperson convinces the buyer that taking into account the purchase price and the benefits in use and disposal, Caterpillar's tractor offers a higher delivered value. The Caterpillar salesperson also points out that the Caterpillar tractor uses less fuel and has fewer breakdowns. Nonetheless, the buyer decides to buy the Komatsu tractor.

How can we explain this behavior? Here are three possible explanations:

1. The buyer might be under orders to buy at the lowest price. For this reason, the buyer is explicitly prevented from making a choice based on delivered value. The Caterpillar salesperson's task is to convince the buyer's manager that buying on price alone will damage the customer's long-run profitability.

2. The buyer will retire before the company realizes that the Komatsu tractor is more expensive to operate than the Caterpillar tractor. The buyer will look good in the short run; he is maximizing personal benefit and placing no weight on company benefit. The salesperson's task is to convince other people in the customer company that Caterpillar's offer delivers greater long-term value.

3. The buyer enjoys a long-term friendship with the Komatsu salesperson. In this case, Caterpillar's salesperson needs to show the buyer that the Komatsu tractor will draw complaints from the tractor operators when they discover its high fuel cost and need for frequent repairs.

The point of these examples is clear: Buyers operate under various constraints and occasionally make choices that give more weight to their personal benefit than to the company's benefit. However, delivered-value maximization is a useful framework that applies to many situations and yields rich insights. Here are its implications: First, the seller must assess the total customer value and total customer cost associated with each competitor's offer to know how his or her own offer stacks up. Second, the seller who is at a delivered-value disadvantage has two alternatives. She can try to either increase total customer value or decrease total customer cost. The former calls for strengthening or augmenting the offer's product, services, personnel, and/or image benefits. The latter calls for reducing the buyer's costs. The seller can reduce the price, simplify the ordering and delivery process, or absorb some buyer risk by offering a warranty.

Customer Satisfaction

Whether the buyer is satisfied after purchase depends on the offer's performance in relation to the buyer's expectations. In general:

❖ **SATISFACTION** is a person's feelings of pleasure or disappointment resulting from comparing a product's perceived performance (or outcome) in relation to his or her expectations.

As this definition makes clear, satisfaction is a function of *perceived performance* and *expectations*. If the performance falls short of expectations, the customer is dissatisfied. If the performance matches the expectations, the customer is satisfied. If the performance exceeds expectations, the customer is highly satisfied or delighted.

Many companies are aiming for high satisfaction because customers who are just satisfied still find it easy to switch when a better offer comes along. Those who are highly satisfied are much less ready to switch. High satisfaction or delight creates an emotional affinity with the brand, not just a rational preference. The result is high customer loyalty.

How do buyers form their expectations? Their expectations are influenced by their past buying experience, friends' and associates' advice, and marketers' and competitors' information and promises. If marketers raise expectations too high, the buyer is likely to be disappointed. For example, Holiday Inn ran a campaign a few years ago called "No Surprises." But hotel guests still encountered a host of problems and Holiday Inn had to withdraw the campaign. However, if the company sets expectations too low, it won't attract enough buyers (although it will satisfy those who do buy).

Some of today's most successful companies are raising expectations and delivering performances to match. These companies are aiming for *TCS—total customer satisfaction*. Xerox, for example, guarantees "total satisfaction" and will replace at its expense any dissatisfied customer's equipment for a period of three years after purchase. Cigna advertises "We'll never be 100% satisfied until you are, too." And one of Honda's ads says: "One reason our customers are so satisfied is that we aren't." Nissan invites potential Infiniti buyers to drop by for a "guest drive" (not a "test drive"), since the Japanese word for customer is "honored guest."

Look at what high satisfaction can do:

SATURN   In 1994, Saturn (General Motors' newest car division) invited all Saturn owners to a weekend party at its Tennessee headquarters to celebrate its fifth anniversary. It expected 1,000 owners to show up; to its amazement, 28,000 Saturn owners came to the plant from all over the country to celebrate. Skip LeFauve, president of Saturn, said at the festival: "Saturn is more than a car. It's an idea. It's a whole new way of doing things, of working with our customers and with one another. It's more of a cultural revolution than a product revolution."

Companies like Saturn realize that customers who are *just satisfied* will still find it easy to switch suppliers when a better offer comes along. In one consumer packaged-goods category, 44% of those reporting satisfaction subsequently switched brands. Those who are *highly satisfied* with the offer's quality and value are much less ready to switch. One study showed that 75% of Toyota buyers were highly satisfied, and about 75% of them said they intended to buy a Toyota again. The fact is that high satisfaction or delight creates an emotional affinity with the brand, not just a rational preference, and this creates high customer loyalty.

The challenge of implementing TCS is to create a company culture in which everyone within the company aims to delight the customer. Unisys, the information management company, recently introduced the term "customerize" in its ads, and defined it as follows: "to make a company more responsive to its customers and better able to attract new ones" (Figure 2-2 on the next page). Unisys sees customerizing as a matter of extending information system capabilities to field locations and other points of customer contact and support. But customerizing a company calls for more than providing good information and customer contact. Ultimately it may require linking staff pay to customer satisfaction. The company's staff must be "converted" to practicing a strong customer orientation. Anita Roddick, founder of The Body Shop, wisely observes: "Our people [employees] are my first line of customers."

In addition to tracking their customers' expectations, perceived company performance, and customer satisfaction, companies need to monitor their competitors' performance in these areas as well. For example, a company was pleased to find that 80% of its customers said they were satisfied. Then the CEO found out that its leading competitor attained a 90% customer satisfaction score. He was further dismayed when he learned that this competitor was aiming to reach a 95% satisfaction score.

Table 2–1 on page 43 describes a variety of methods that companies can use to track customer satisfaction.

For customer-centered companies, customer satisfaction is both a goal and a marketing tool. Companies that achieve high customer satisfaction ratings make sure that their target market knows it. The Honda Accord has received the number-one rating in customer satisfaction from J. D. Powers for several years, and Honda's advertising of this fact has helped sell more Accords. Dell Computer's meteoric growth in the personal computer industry can be partly attributed to achieving and advertising its number-one rank in customer satisfaction:

Building Customer
Satisfaction Through
Quality, Service, and Value

You have a reservoir of information.

How much is reaching your customer and how fast?

If your customer only knew you offer a product he wants. If your customer only knew you offer a service she needs. If your customer only knew what you know. And fast. Because what your customer doesn't know leaves revenue-generating potential untapped.

That's why Unisys has developed a powerful new initiative to help give business the advanced customer service crucial in an increasingly competitive environment—CUSTOMERIZE.℠

Unisys can help CUSTOMERIZE your enterprise by extending information technology out to the field locations, where a customer decides to do business with you—or not. And where your single most important influence over

that decision may be information. When the flow of information is comprehensive, you optimize customer satisfaction and increase sales content. With a timely flow of information, you not only boost the speed of transactions but also sharpen your competitive edge.

A CUSTOMERIZED enterprise draws information from customers even as it conveys information to them. Circulating through your organization, it all helps productivity, control and profitability.

Ask us about our CUSTOMERIZE assessment, which teams you with

experienced Unisys consultants to evaluate your organization's information flow. Ask, too, for a complimentary CUSTOMERIZE Information Kit.

cus·tom·er·ize \ kŭs'-tə-mə-rīze' \ *vt* **1:** to make a company more responsive to its customers and better able to attract new ones **2:** to customerize an organization's information strategy, e.g., to extend systems capabilities to field locations and other points of customer contact and support **3:** what Unisys Corporation does for a growing roster of companies, and government agencies, worldwide **syn** see CUSTOMER SERVICE, COMPETITIVE EDGE, BUSINESS-CRITICAL SOLUTIONS, REVENUE GENERATION

Call us at 1-800-874-8647, ext 13. Discover how Unisys can help you CUSTOMERIZE your enterprise and convert information into a stream of customers—and revenue.

UNISYS
We make it happen.

© 1993 Unisys Corporation

CUSTOMERIZE is a service mark of Unisys Corporation

DELL The first in the industry to offer manufacturer-direct technical support, Dell has institutionalized the delivery of customer satisfaction by focusing on service and support. The company has created a service capability based on "the Dell Vision," which states that a customer "must have a quality experience, and must be pleased, not just satisfied." In fact, the company ran into problems in 1993 when it began selling its personal computers through big retailers like Wal-Mart, which did not offer the same type of customer service. Once it returned to its mail-order roots, the company's profits began rising again.[3]

Although the customer-centered firm seeks to create high customer satisfaction, its main goal is not to maximize customer satisfaction. First, the company can increase customer satisfaction by lowering its price or increasing its services, but the result may be lower profits. Second, the company might be able to increase its profitability by means other than increased satisfaction (for example, by improving manufacturing processes or investing more in R&D). Third, the company has many stakeholders, including employees, dealers, suppliers, and stockholders. Spending

TABLE 2-1	TOOLS FOR TRACKING AND MEASURING CUSTOMER SATISFACTION
Complaint and suggestion systems	A customer-centered organization makes it easy for its customers to deliver suggestions and complaints. Many restaurants and hotels provide forms for guests to report their likes and dislikes. A hospital could place suggestion boxes in the corridors, supply comment cards to exiting patients, and hire a patient advocate to handle patient grievances. Some customer-centered companies—Procter & Gamble, General Electric, Whirlpool—establish customer hot lines with toll-free 800 telephone numbers to maximize the ease with which customers can inquire, make suggestions, or complain. These information flows provide these companies with many good ideas and enable them to act more rapidly to resolve problems.
Customer satisfaction surveys	Studies show that while customers are dissatisfied with one out of every four purchases, less than 5% of dissatisfied customers will complain. Most customers will buy less or switch suppliers rather than complain. Therefore, companies cannot use complaint levels as a measure of customer satisfaction. Responsive companies obtain a direct measure of customer satisfaction by conducting periodic surveys. They send questionnaires or make telephone calls to a random sample of their recent customers and ask if they were very satisfied, satisfied, indifferent, somewhat dissatisfied, or very dissatisfied with various aspects of the company's performance. They also solicit buyers' views on their competitors' performances. While collecting customer satisfaction data, it is also useful to ask additional questions to measure the customer's *repurchase intention;* this will normally be high if the customer's satisfaction is high. It is also useful to measure the customer's likelihood or willingness to recommend the company and brand to other persons. A high positive *word-of-mouth score* indicates that the company is producing high customer satisfaction.
Ghost shopping	Companies can hire persons to pose as potential buyers to report their findings on strong and weak points they experienced in buying the company's and competitors' products. These *ghost shoppers* can even pose certain problems to test whether the company's sales personnel handle the situation well. Thus, a ghost shopper can complain about a restaurant's food to test how the restaurant handles this complaint. Not only should companies hire ghost shoppers, but managers themselves should leave their office from time to time, enter company and competitor sales situations where they are unknown, and experience firsthand the treatment they receive as "customers." A variant of this is for managers to phone their own company with different questions and complaints to see how the call is handled.
Lost customer analysis	Companies should contact customers who have stopped buying or who have switched to another supplier to learn why this happened. When IBM loses a customer, it mounts a thorough effort to learn where it failed. Not only is it important to conduct *exit interviews* when customers first stop buying, but also to monitor the *customer loss rate,* which, if increasing, clearly indicates that the company is failing to satisfy its customers.

more to increase customer satisfaction might divert funds from increasing the satisfaction of other "partners." Ultimately, the company must operate on the philosophy that it is trying to deliver a high level of customer satisfaction subject to delivering at least acceptable levels of satisfaction to the other stakeholders within the constraints of its total resources.

SOME CAUTIONS IN MEASURING CUSTOMER SATISFACTION. When customers rate their satisfaction with an element of the company's performance—say, delivery—the company needs to recognize that customers vary in how they define good delivery. It could mean early delivery, on-time delivery, order completeness, and so on. Yet if the company had to spell out every element in detail, customers would face a huge questionnaire. The company must also realize

Building Customer
Satisfaction Through
Quality, Service, and Value

that two customers can report being "highly satisfied" for different reasons. One may be easily satisfied most of the time and the other might be hard to please but was pleased on this occasion.

Companies should also note that managers and salespeople can manipulate their ratings on customer satisfaction. They can be especially nice to customers just before the survey. They can also try to exclude unhappy customers from the survey. Another danger is that if customers know that the company will go out of its way to please customers, some customers may express high dissatisfaction (even if satisfied) in order to receive more concessions.

DELIVERING CUSTOMER VALUE AND SATISFACTION

Given the importance of customer value and satisfaction, what does it take to produce and deliver them? To answer this question, we need to discuss the concepts of a value chain and value-delivery systems.

Value Chain

Michael Porter of Harvard proposed the *value chain* as a tool for identifying ways to create more customer value (Figure 2-3).[4] Every firm is a collection of activities that are performed to design, produce, market, deliver, and support its product. The value chain identifies nine strategically relevant activities that create value and cost in a specific business. These nine value-creating activities consist of five primary activities and four support activities.

The primary activities represent the sequence of bringing materials into the business (inbound logistics), converting them into final products (operations), shipping out final products (outbound logistics), marketing them (marketing and sales), and servicing them (service). The support activities—procurement, technology development, human resource management, and firm infrastructure—are handled in certain specialized departments, but not only there. For example, other departments may do some purchasing and hiring of people. *Procurement* is the purchasing of various inputs for each primary activity. The firm's infrastructure covers the costs of general management, planning, finance, accounting, legal, and government affairs that are borne by all the primary and support activities.

FIGURE 2-3

The Generic Value Chain

Source: Reprinted with the permission of The Free Press, an imprint of Simon & Schuster from COMPETITIVE ADVANTAGE: Creating and Sustaining Superior Performance by Michael E. Porter. Copyright © 1985 by Michael E. Porter.

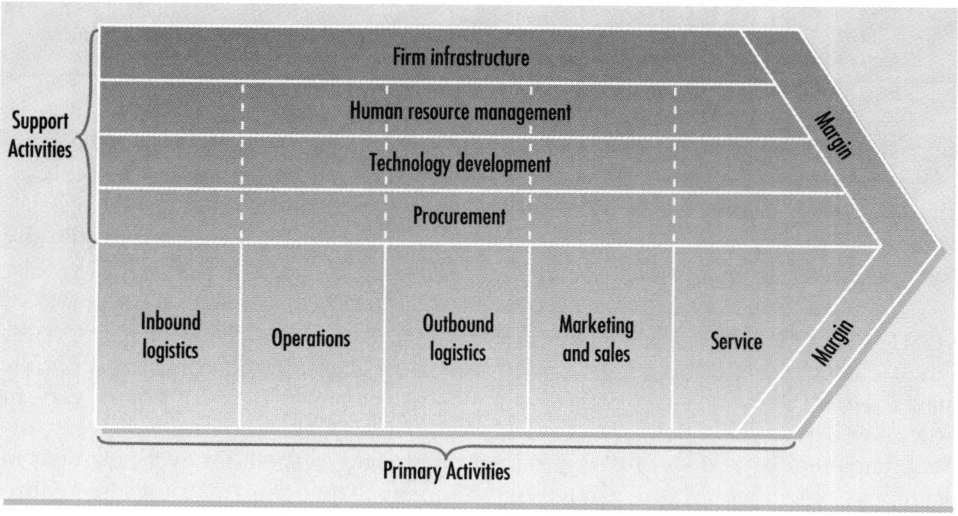

Understanding
Marketing
Management

The firm's task is to examine its costs and performance in each value-creating activity and to look for ways to improve it. The firm should estimate its competitors' costs and performances as *benchmarks* against which to compare its own costs and performances (see the discussion of benchmarking in Chapter 8). To the extent that it can perform certain activities better than its competitors, it can achieve a competitive advantage.

The firm's success depends not only on how well each department performs its work but also on how well the various departmental activities are coordinated. Too often, company departments act to maximize their interests rather than the company's and customers' interests. A credit department may take a long time to check a prospective customer's credit so as not to incur bad debts; meanwhile, the customer waits and the salesperson is frustrated. A traffic department chooses to ship the goods by rail to save money and again the customer waits. Each department has erected walls that slow down the delivery of quality customer service.

The solution to this problem is to place more emphasis on the smooth management of *core business processes*, most of which involve cross-functional inputs and cooperation. The core business processes include:

◆ *New-product realization process:* All the activities involved in researching, developing, and launching new high-quality products quickly and within budget.

◆ *Inventory management process:* All the activities involved in developing and managing the inventory levels of raw materials, semifinished materials, and finished goods so that adequate supplies are available and the costs of overstocks are low.

◆ *Order-to-remittance process:* All the activities involved in receiving and approving orders, shipping the goods on time, and collecting payment.

◆ *Customer service process:* All the activities involved in making it easy for customers to reach the right parties within the company and receive quick and satisfactory service, answers, and resolutions of problems.

Strong companies are those that develop superior capabilities in managing these core processes. For example, one of Wal-Mart's great strengths is its superefficiency in moving goods from its suppliers to its individual stores. As Wal-Mart stores sell their goods, sales information flows via computer not only to Wal-Mart's headquarters but also to Wal-Mart's suppliers, which ship replacement merchandise to the Wal-Mart stores almost at the rate it moves off the shelf.[5]

Value-Delivery Network

To be successful the firm also needs to look for competitive advantages beyond its own operations, into the value chains of its suppliers, distributors, and customers. Faced with intense competition, many companies today have partnered with specific suppliers and distributors to create a superior *value-delivery network*. For example:[6]

BAILEY CONTROLS An Ohio-headquartered $300-million-a-year manufacturer of control systems for big factories, Bailey Controls treats some of its suppliers as if they were departments within Bailey. The company recently plugged two of its suppliers directly into its inventory-management system. Every week Bailey electronically sends Montreal-based Future Electronics its latest forecasts of the materials it will need for the next six months so that Future can stock up. Whenever a bin of parts falls below a designated level, a Bailey employee passes a laser scanner over the bin's bar code, instantly alerting Future to send the parts at once. Although arrangements like this shift inventory costs to the suppliers, the suppliers expect those costs to be more than offset by the gain in volume. It's a win-win partnership.

Building Customer
Satisfaction Through
Quality, Service, and Value

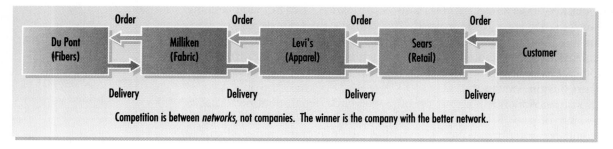

FIGURE 2-4
Levi Strauss' Value-Delivery Network

BETZ LABORATORIES Betz Laboratories, a Pennsylvania-based maker of industrial water-treatment chemicals, just used to sell chemicals to keep the water in its customers' plants from gunking up pipes or corroding machinery. Today Betz provides its large customers with both goods and expertise. High-level teams composed of Betz and its customers' engineers and managers preside over every inch of the water in the customers' plants. They ask and answer such questions as: Is the water as safe as possible for the equipment? Does it meet environmental standards? Is it being used in the least wasteful, most cost-effective way? In less than one year the Betz team in one AlliedSignal plant pinpointed $2.5 million in potential annual cost reductions.

Another excellent example of a value-delivery network is the one that connects Levi Strauss, the famous maker of blue jeans, with its suppliers and distributors (Figure 2-4). One of Levi's major retailers is Sears. Every night, thanks to electronic data interchange (EDI), Levi's learns the sizes and styles of its blue jeans that sold through Sears and other major outlets. Levi's then electronically orders more fabric for next-day delivery from the Milliken Company, its fabric supplier. Milliken, in turn, relays an order for more fiber to Du Pont, its fiber supplier. In this way, the partners in the supply chain use the most current sales information to manufacture what is selling, rather than to manufacture for a forecast that may be at variance with current demand. In this *quick response system,* the goods are pulled by demand rather than pushed by supply. Levi's performance against another jeans maker—say, Wrangler—depends on the quality of Levi's *marketing network* versus Wrangler's marketing network. Companies no longer compete—marketing networks do.

ATTRACTING AND RETAINING CUSTOMERS

In addition to improving their relations with their partners in the supply chain, many companies are intent on developing stronger bonds and loyalty with their ultimate customers. In the past, many companies took their customers for granted. Their customers may not have had many alternative sources of supply, or all suppliers were equally deficient in service, or the market was growing so fast that the company did not worry about satisfying its customers. Clearly, things have changed.

Computing the Cost of Lost Customers

Today's companies must pay closer attention to their *customer defection rate* (the rate at which they lose customers) and take steps to reduce it. There are four steps to this process.

First, the company must define and measure its retention rate. For a magazine, the renewal rate is a good measure of retention. For a college, it could be the first-to second-year retention rate or the class graduation rate.

Second, the company must distinguish the causes of customer attrition and identify those that can be managed better. (See the Marketing Memo titled, "Asking Questions When Customers Leave.") Not much can be done about customers who leave the region or go out of business. But much can be done about customers who leave because of poor service, shoddy products, high prices, and so on. The company needs to examine the percentages of customers who defect for different reasons.

Third, the company needs to estimate how much profit it loses when it loses customers. In the case of an individual customer, the lost profit is equal to the customer's *lifetime value*—that is, the present value of the profit stream that the company would have realized on a customer if the customer had not defected prematurely. For a group of lost customers, one major transportation carrier estimated its profit lost as follows:

◆ The company had 64,000 accounts.

◆ The company lost 5% of its accounts this year due to poor service: This was a loss of 3,200 accounts (.05 × 64,000).

◆ The average lost account represented a $40,000 loss in revenue. Therefore, the company lost $128,000,000 in revenue (3,200 × $40,000).

◆ The company's profit margin is 10 percent. Therefore, the company lost $12,800,000 (.10 × $128,000,000) this year. Since the customers left prematurely, the company's actual loss over time is much greater.

Fourth, the company needs to figure out how much it would cost to reduce the defection rate. As long as the cost is less than the lost profit, the company should spend that amount to reduce the defection rate.

The Need for Customer Retention

The cost of attracting a new customer is estimated to be five times the cost of keeping a current customer happy. It requires a great deal of effort to induce satisfied customers to switch away from their current suppliers.

Unfortunately, most marketing theory and practice center on the art of attracting new customers rather than retaining existing ones. The emphasis traditionally has been on making sales rather than building relationships. The focus has been on preselling and selling rather than on caring for the customer afterward. Today, however, more companies are recognizing the importance of satisfying and retaining current customers. One study indicated that companies can improve profits anywhere from 25% to 85% by reducing customer defections by 5 percent.[7] Sadly, companies' accounting systems fail to show the value of loyal customers.

We can work out an example to support the case for emphasizing customer retention. Suppose a company analyzes its new customer acquisition cost. It finds the following:

Cost of an average sales call (including salary, commission, benefits, and expenses)	$300
Average number of sales calls to convert an average prospect into a customer	× 4
Cost of attracting a new customer	$1,200

This is an underestimate because we are omitting the cost of advertising and promotion, operations, planning, and so on.

MARKETING MEMO

ASKING QUESTIONS WHEN CUSTOMERS LEAVE

To create effective retention programs, marketing managers need to identify patterns among customer defections. This analysis should start with internal records, such as sales logs, pricing records, and customer survey results. The next step is extending defection research to outside sources, such as benchmarking studies and statistics from trade associations. Some key questions to ask:

◆ Do customers defect at different rates during the year?

◆ Does retention vary by office, region, sales representative, or distributor?

◆ What is the relationship between retention rates and changes in prices?

◆ What happens to lost customers, and where do they usually go?

◆ What are the retention norms for your industry?

◆ Which company in your industry retains customers the longest?

Source: Reprinted from William A. Sherden, "When Customers Leave," *Small Business Reports,* November 1994, p. 45.

Building Customer Satisfaction Through Quality, Service, and Value

Now suppose the company estimates average customer lifetime value as follows:

Annual customer revenue	$5,000
Average number of loyal years	× 2
Company profit margin	× .10
Customer lifetime value	$1,000

Because the cost of attracting a new customer is higher than the customer's lifetime value, this company is clearly spending more to attract new customers than they are worth. Unless the company can sign up customers with fewer sales calls, spend less per sales call, stimulate higher new-customer annual spending, retain customers longer, or sell them higher-profit products, the company is headed for bankruptcy.

There are two ways to strengthen customer retention. One is to erect high switching barriers. Customers are less inclined to switch to another supplier when this would involve high capital costs, high search costs, the loss of loyal-customer discounts, and so on.

The better approach is to deliver high customer satisfaction. This makes it harder for competitors to overcome switching barriers by simply offering lower prices or switching inducements. The task of creating strong customer loyalty, as we saw in Chapter 1, is called *relationship marketing*. Relationship marketing embraces all those steps that companies undertake to know and serve better their valued individual customers.

Relationship Marketing: The Key

To understand customer relationship marketing, we must first examine the process involved in attracting and keeping customers. Figure 2-5 shows the main steps in the customer-development process. The starting point is *suspects,* everyone who might conceivably buy the product or service. The company looks hard at the suspects to determine who are the most likely *prospects*—the people who have a strong potential interest in the product and the ability to pay for it. *Disqualified prospects* are those whom the company rejects because they have poor credit or

FIGURE 2-5

The Customer-Development Process

Source: See Jill Griffin, *Customer Loyalty: How to Earn It, How to Keep It* (New York: Lexington Books, 1995), p. 36. Also see Murray Raphel and Neil Raphel, *Up the Loyalty Ladder: Turning Sometime Customers into Full-Time Advocates of Your Business* (New York: HarperBusiness, 1995).

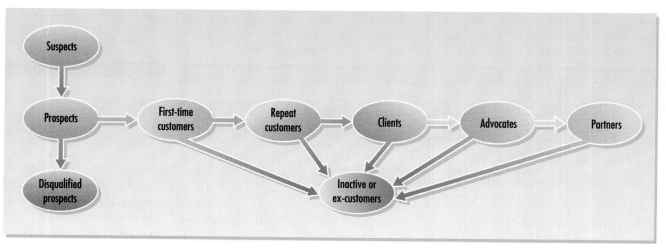

would be unprofitable. The company hopes to convert many of its *qualified prospects* into *first-time customers,* and to then convert those satisfied first-time customers into *repeat customers.* Both first-time and repeat customers may continue to buy from competitors as well. The company then acts to convert repeat customers into *clients*—people who buy only from the company in the relevant product categories. The next challenge is to turn clients into *advocates,* customers who praise the company and encourage others to buy from it. The ultimate challenge is to turn advocates into partners, where the customer and the company work actively together. At the same time, it must be recognized that some customers will inevitably become inactive or drop out, for reasons of bankruptcy, moves to other locations, dissatisfaction, and so on. The company's challenge is to reactivate dissatisfied customers through customer win-back strategies. It is often easier to reattract ex-customers than to find new ones.

Developing more loyal customers increases the company's revenue. However, the company has to spend more to build greater customer loyalty. Development of customer loyalty will be more profitable in some businesses than in others. How much should a company invest in customer-relationship building, so that the costs do not exceed the gains? We need to distinguish five different levels of company investment in customer-relationship building:

- *Basic marketing:* The salesperson simply sells the product.
- *Reactive marketing:* The salesperson sells the product and encourages the customer to call if he or she has any questions, comments, or complaints.
- *Accountable marketing:* The salesperson phones the customer a short time after the sale to check whether the product is meeting the customer's expectations. The salesperson also asks the customer for any product or service improvement suggestions and any specific disappointments. This information helps the company continuously improve its performance.
- *Proactive marketing:* The company salesperson contacts the customer from time to time with suggestions about improved product uses or helpful new products. (Kraft U.S.A.'s sales reps used to limit their customer efforts to devising promotions in supermarkets; now they are more proactive, offering research and tips for improving a store's profits.)
- *Partnership marketing:* The company works continuously with the customer to discover ways to effect customer savings or help the customer perform better. (General Electric has stationed some of its engineers full time at Praxair, Inc. to help boost Praxair's productivity.)

Most companies practice only basic marketing if their markets contain many customers and if their unit profit margins are small. Thus the Heinz Company is not going to phone each ketchup buyer to express appreciation. At best, Heinz will be reactive by setting up a customer hot line. At the other extreme, in markets with few customers and high profit margins, most sellers will move toward partnership marketing. Boeing, for example, works closely with United Airlines in designing Boeing airplanes and ensuring that they fully satisfy United's requirements. As Figure 2-6 on the next page shows, between these two extreme situations other levels of relationship marketing are appropriate.

What specific marketing tools can a company use to develop stronger customer bonding and satisfaction? Berry and Parasuraman have distinguished three customer value-building approaches:[8] adding financial benefits, adding social benefits, and adding structural ties.

ADDING FINANCIAL BENEFITS. Two financial benefits that companies can offer are frequency marketing programs and club marketing programs. *Frequency marketing programs (FMPs)* are designed to provide rewards to customers

FIGURE 2-6
Levels of Relationship
Marketing

	HIGH MARGIN	MEDIUM MARGIN	LOW MARGIN
Many customers/distributors	Accountable	Reactive	Basic or reactive
Medium number of customers/distributors	Proactive	Accountable	Reactive
Few customers/distributors	Partnership	Proactive	Accountable

who buy frequently and/or in substantial amounts. Frequency marketing is an acknowledgment of the fact that 20% of a company's customers might account for 80% of its business.

American Airlines was one of the first companies to pioneer a frequency marketing program when it decided to offer free mileage credit to its customers in the early 1980s. Hotels next adopted FMPs, with Marriott taking the lead with its Honored Guest Program. Frequent guests receive room upgrades or free rooms after earning so many points. Shortly thereafter, car rental firms sponsored FMPs. Then credit-card companies began to offer points based on their cards' usage level. For example, Sears offers rebates to its Discover card holders on charges made on the card. Today several supermarket chains offer "price club cards" that provide member customers with unadvertised discounts on particular items.

Typically, the first company to introduce an FMP gains the most benefit, especially if competitors are slow to respond. After competitors respond, FMPs can become a financial burden to all the offering companies.

One criticism of FMPs is that they might diminish the company's focus on delivering a superior level of customer service. That is, these programs attempt to produce repeat business on the basis of an economic incentive. European airlines, in contrast, claim to rely on offering superior service to attract repeat business.

Many companies have created *affinity* groups, or clubs, among their customers to bond them closer to the company. Club membership may be offered automatically upon purchase or promised purchase of a certain amount, or by paying a fee. Some clubs have been spectacularly successful:

SHISEIDO The Japanese cosmetics company Shiseido has enrolled over 10 million members in its Shiseido Club, which provides a Visa card, discounts at theaters, hotels, and retailers, and also "frequent buyer" points. Its members receive a free magazine containing articles on personal grooming.

NINTENDO The Japanese game company Nintendo has enrolled more than 2 million members in its Nintendo Club. For $16 a year, members receive a monthly magazine, *Nintendo Power,* previewing and reviewing Nintendo games, providing tips on winning, and so on. The company has also set up a "game counselor" phone number that kids and adults can call with questions or problems.

WALDEN BOOKS This bookstore chain sponsors a Preferred Reader Program that has attracted over 4 million members. Each member pays $10 a year and receives mailings about new books, a 10% discount on book purchases, toll-free ordering, and points toward $5 merchandise certificates redeemable in any Waldenbooks store.

TABLE 2-2 | SOCIAL ACTIONS AFFECTING BUYER-SELLER RELATIONSHIPS

GOOD THINGS	BAD THINGS
Initiate positive phone calls	Make only callbacks
Make recommendations	Make justifications
Candor in language	Accommodative language
Use phone	Use correspondence
Show appreciation	Wait for misunderstandings
Make service suggestions	Wait for service requests
Use "we" problem-solving language	Use "owe-us" legal language
Get to problems	Only respond to problems
Use jargon/shorthand	Use long-winded communications
Personality problems aired	Personality problems hidden
Talk of "our future together"	Talk about making good on the past
Routinize responses	Fire drill/emergency responsiveness
Accept responsibility	Shift blame
Plan the future	Rehash the past

Source: **Theodore Levitt,** *The Marketing Imagination* **(New York: Free Press, 1983), p. 119. Reprinted by permission of the** *Harvard Business Review.* **An exhibit from Theodore Levitt, "After the Sale is Over,"** *Harvard Business Review* **(September-October 1983, p. 119). Copyright © 1983 by the President and Fellows of Harvard College.**

HARLEY-DAVIDSON The world-famous motorcycle company sponsors the Harley Owners Group (HOG), which now numbers 127,000 members. The first-time buyer of a Harley-Davidson motorcycle gets a free one-year membership. HOG benefits include a magazine *(Hog Tales),* a touring handbook, emergency road service, a specially designed insurance program, theft reward service, discount hotel rates, and a Fly & Ride program enabling members to rent Harleys while on vacation.

LLADRO The Spanish maker of fine porcelain figurines, Lladro sponsors a "Collectors Society." For an annual membership fee of $35, members receive a free subscription to a quarterly magazine, a bisque plaque, free enrollment in the Lladro Museum of New York, and member-only tours to visit the company and the Lladro family in Valencia, Spain.

ADDING SOCIAL BENEFITS. Here company personnel work on increasing their social bonds with customers by individualizing and personalizing their customer relationships. Table 2–2 contrasts a socially sensitive approach to a socially insensitive approach to customers. In essence, thoughtful companies turn their customers into clients. Donnelly, Berry, and Thompson draw this distinction:

> *Customers may be nameless to the institution; clients cannot be nameless. Customers are served as part of the mass or as part of larger segments; clients are served on an individual basis. . . . Customers are served by anyone who happens to be available; clients are served by the professional assigned to them.[9]*

ADDING STRUCTURAL TIES. The company may supply customers with special equipment or computer linkages that help customers manage their orders, payroll, inventory, and so on. A good example is McKesson Corporation, a leading pharmaceutical wholesaler, which invested millions of dollars in EDI capabilities to help independent pharmacies manage their inventory, order entry processes, and shelf space. Another example is Milliken, which provides proprietary software programs, marketing research, sales training, and sales leads to its loyal customers. (For more on relationship marketing, see Chapter 22.)

CUSTOMER PROFITABILITY: THE ULTIMATE TEST

Ultimately, marketing is the art of attracting and keeping profitable customers. According to James V. Putten of American Express, the best customers outspend others by ratios of 16 to 1 in retailing, 13 to 1 in the restaurant business, 12 to 1 in the airline business, and 5 to 1 in the hotel/motel industry.[10] Carl Sewell, who runs one of the best-managed auto dealerships in the world, estimates that a typical auto buyer represents a potential lifetime value of over $300,000 in car purchases and services.[11]

Yet every company loses money on some of its customers. The well-known *80/20 rule* says that the top 20% of the customers may generate as much as 80% of the company's profits. William Sherden has suggested amending the rule to read 80/20/30, to reflect the idea that "the top 20% of customers generate 80% of the company's profits, half of which is lost serving the bottom 30% of unprofitable customers."[12] The implication is that a company could improve its profits by "firing" its worst customers.

Furthermore, it isn't necessarily the company's largest customers who are yielding the most profit. The largest customers demand considerable service and receive the deepest discounts, thus reducing the company's profit level. The smallest customers pay full price and receive minimal service, but the costs of transacting with small customers reduce their profitability. The mid-size customers receive good service and pay nearly full price and are often the most profitable. This fact helps explain why many large firms that formerly targeted only large customers are now invading the middle market. Major air express carriers, for instance, are finding that it doesn't pay to ignore the small and mid-size international shippers. Programs geared toward smaller customers are as simple as a network of drop boxes, which allow for substantial discounts over letters and packages picked up at the shipper's place of business. In addition to putting more drop boxes in place, United Parcel Service (UPS) conducts a series of seminars to instruct exporters in the finer points of shipping overseas.[13]

A company should not pursue and satisfy all customers. For example, if customers of Courtyard (Marriott Hotels' less-expensive chain of motels) start asking for Marriott-level business services, Courtyard will say "no." Granting these requests would only confuse the respective positioning of the Marriott and Courtyard systems. Lanning and Phillips make this point well:

> Some organizations try to do anything and everything customers suggest. . . . Yet, while customers often make many good suggestions, they also suggest many courses of action that are unactionable or unprofitable. Randomly following these suggestions is fundamentally different from market-focus— making a disciplined choice of which customers to serve and which specific combination of benefits and price to deliver to them (and which to deny them).[14]

What makes a customer profitable? We define a profitable customer as follows:

❖ **A PROFITABLE CUSTOMER** is a person, household, or company that over time yields a revenue stream that exceeds by an acceptable amount the company's cost stream of attracting, selling, and servicing that customer.

Note that the emphasis is on the lifetime stream of revenue and cost, not on the profit from a particular transaction. Here are two illustrations of customer lifetime value:

TACO BELL   When tacos cost less than a dollar each, you wouldn't think Taco Bell would fret over lost customers. However, executives at Taco Bell have determined that a repeat customer is worth as much as $11,000. By sharing such estimates

FIGURE 2-7
Customer/Product
Profitability Analysis

	Customers			
	C_1	C_2	C_3	
P_1	+	+	+	Highly profitable product
P_2	+			Profitable product
P_3		−	−	Losing product
P_4	+		−	Mixed-bag product
	High-profit customer	Mixed-bag customer	Losing customer	

Products

of customer lifetime value, Taco Bell's managers help employees understand the value of keeping customers satisfied.[15]

TOM PETERS The noted author of several books on managerial excellence, Tom Peters runs a business that spends $1,500 a month on Federal Express service. He spends this amount 12 months a year and expects to remain in business for another 10 years. Therefore, he expects to spend $180,000 on future Federal Express service. If Federal Express makes a 10% profit margin, his lifetime business will contribute $18,000 to Federal Express profits. All this is at risk if he starts getting poor service from the Federal Express driver or if a competitor offers better service.

Most companies fail to measure individual customer profitability. For example, banks claim that this is a difficult task because a customer uses different banking services and the transactions are logged in different departments. However, banks that have succeeded in linking customer transactions have been appalled by the number of unprofitable customers in their customer base. Some banks report losing money on over 45% of their customers. It is not surprising that banks are increasingly charging fees for various services that they supplied free in the past.

A useful type of profitability analysis is shown in Figure 2-7.[16] Customers are arrayed along the columns and products along the rows. Each cell contains a symbol for the profitability of selling that product to that customer. Customer 1 is very profitable; he buys three profit-making products (P_1, P_2, and P_4). Customer 2 yields a picture of mixed profitability; he buys one profitable product and one unprofitable product. Customer 3 is a losing customer because he buys one profitable product and two unprofitable products. What can the company do about Customers 2 and 3? It has two options: (1) It can raise the price of its less-profitable products or eliminate them, or (2) it can try to cross-sell its profit-making products to the unprofitable customers. Unprofitable customers who defect should not concern the company. In fact, the company would benefit by encouraging its unprofitable customers to switch to their competitors.

Ultimately, the company's profitability depends on the three elements shown in Figure 2-8.[17] Profit will be higher, the higher the company's value-creation ability, the more efficient its internal operations, and the greater its competitive advantage. Companies must not only be able to create high absolute value but also high value relative to competitors at a sufficiently low cost. *Competitive advantage* is a company's ability to perform in one or more ways that competitors cannot or will not

FIGURE 2-8
The Profit Triangle

match. Companies strive to build sustainable competitive advantages. Those that succeed deliver high customer value and satisfaction, which leads to high repeat purchases and therefore high company profitability. One of the major values that customers expect from vendors is high product and service quality, a subject to which we now turn.

IMPLEMENTING TOTAL QUALITY MARKETING

As we've seen, today's executives view the task of improving product and service quality as their top priority. The successes of many Japanese companies are due to the exceptional quality of their products. Most customers will no longer accept or tolerate average quality performance. If companies want to stay in the race, let alone be profitable, they have no choice but to adopt total quality management (TQM).

❖   **TOTAL QUALITY MANAGEMENT (TQM)** is an organization-wide approach to continuously improving the quality of all the organization's processes, products, and services.

According to G.E.'s Chairman, John F. Welch, Jr.: "Quality is our best assurance of customer allegiance, our strongest defense against foreign competition, and the only path to sustained growth and earnings."[18]

The drive to produce goods that are superior in world markets has led some countries—and groups of countries—to establish prizes that are awarded to companies that exemplify the best quality practices and improvements.

◆   *Japan:* In 1951, Japan became the first country to award a national quality prize, the Deming prize (named after W. Edwards Deming, the American statistician who taught the importance and methodology of quality improvement to postwar Japan). Deming's work formed the base on which many TQM practices were built.

◆   *United States:* In the mid-1980s, the United States established the Malcolm Baldrige National Quality Award in honor of the late Secretary of Commerce. The Baldrige award criteria consist of seven measures, each carrying a certain number of award points: customer focus and satisfaction (with the most points), quality and operational results, management of process quality, human resource development and management, strategic quality planning, information and analysis, and senior executive leadership. Xerox, Motorola, Federal Express, IBM, Texas Instruments, the Cadillac division of General Motors, and Ritz-Carlton hotels are some of the companies that have won a Baldrige.

◆   *Europe:* Not to be left out of the quality awards race, Europe developed the European Quality Award in 1993. The award was established by the European Foundation for Quality Management and the European Organization for Quality. Like the Baldrige, it is awarded to companies that have achieved high grades on certain criteria: leadership, people management, policy and strategy, resources, processes, people satisfaction, customer satisfaction, impact on society, and business results. While Europe was relatively late in developing a quality award, it was the initiator of an exacting set of international quality standards called *ISO 9000,* which has become a set of generally accepted principles for documenting quality. ISO 9000 provides a framework for showing customers how quality-oriented businesses around the world test products, train employees, keep records, and fix defects. Earning the ISO 9000 certification involves a quality audit every six months from a registered ISO (International Standards Organization) assessor.[19]

There is an intimate connection among product and service quality, customer satisfaction, and company profitability. Higher levels of quality result in higher levels of customer satisfaction while supporting higher prices and (often) lower costs. Therefore, *quality improvement programs (QIPs)* normally increase profitability. The well-known PIMS studies show a high correlation between relative product quality and company profitability.[20]

But what exactly is quality? Various experts have defined it as "fitness for use," "conformance to requirements," "freedom from variation," and so on.[21] We will use the American Society for Quality Control's definition, which has been adopted worldwide:[22]

❖   QUALITY is the totality of features and characteristics of a product or service that bear on its ability to satisfy stated or implied needs.

This is clearly a customer-centered definition of quality. We can say that the seller has delivered quality whenever the seller's product or service meets or exceeds the customers' expectations. A company that satisfies most of its customers' needs most of the time is called a *quality company*. The Marketing Memo on page 56 titled "Pursuing a Total Quality Marketing Strategy" spells out the assumptions that must underlie any total quality program.

It is important to distinguish between conformance quality and performance quality (or grade). A Mercedes provides higher *performance quality* than a Hyundai: The Mercedes rides smoother, goes faster, lasts longer, and so on. Yet both a Mercedes and a Hyundai can be said to deliver the same *conformance quality* if all the units deliver their respective promised quality.

Total quality is the key to value creation and customer satisfaction. Total quality is everyone's job, just as marketing is everyone's job. This idea was expressed well by Daniel Beckham:

> *Marketers who don't learn the language of quality improvement, manufacturing, and operations will become as obsolete as buggy whips. The days of functional marketing are gone. We can no longer afford to think of ourselves as market researchers, advertising people, direct marketers, strategists— we have to think of ourselves as customer satisfiers— customer advocates focused on whole processes.*[23]

Marketing managers have two responsibilities in a quality-centered company. First, they must participate in formulating strategies and policies designed to help the company win through total quality excellence. Second, they must deliver marketing quality alongside production quality. Each marketing activity—marketing research, sales training, advertising, customer service, and so on—must be performed to high standards.

Marketers play several roles in helping their company define and deliver high-quality goods and services to target customers. First, they bear the major responsibility for correctly identifying the customers' needs and requirements. Second, they must communicate customer expectations correctly to product designers. Third, they must make sure that the customers' orders are filled correctly and on time. Fourth, they must check that customers have received proper instructions, training, and technical assistance in the use of the product. Fifth, they must stay in touch with customers after the sale to ensure that they are satisfied and remain satisfied. Sixth, they must gather customer ideas for product and service improvements and convey them to the appropriate company departments. When marketers do all this, they are making their specific contributions to total quality management and customer satisfaction.

One implication of TQM is that marketing people must spend time and effort not only to improve external marketing but also to improve internal marketing. The marketer must complain like the customer complains when the product or the

MARKETING MEMO

PURSUING A TOTAL QUALITY MARKETING STRATEGY

A growing number of companies have appointed a "Vice President of Quality" to spearhead TQM efforts. TQM requires recognizing the following premises about quality improvement:

1. *Quality must be perceived by customers.* Quality work must begin with the customers' needs and end with the customers' perceptions. Quality improvements are only meaningful when they are perceived by customers.

2. *Quality must be reflected in every company activity, not just in company products.* Leonard A. Morgan of GE said: "We are not just concerned with the quality of the product, but with the quality of our advertising, service, product literature, delivery, after-sales support, and so on."[1]

3. *Quality requires total employee commitment.* Quality can be delivered only by companies in which all employees are committed to quality and motivated and trained to deliver quality. Employee teams are intent on satisfying their internal customers as well as external customers.

4. *Quality requires high-quality partners.* Quality can be delivered only by companies whose value-chain partners are also committed to quality. Therefore, the quality-driven company has a responsibility to find and work with high-quality suppliers and distributors.

5. *Quality can always be improved.* The best companies believe in *kaizen,* "continuous improvement of everything by everyone." The best way to improve quality is to benchmark the company's performance against the "best-of-class" competitors and strive to emulate them or even leapfrog over them.

6. *Quality improvement sometimes requires quantum leaps.* Although quality should be continuously improved, it sometimes pays for a company to target a quantum improvement. Small improvements are often obtainable through working harder. But large improvements call for fresh solutions, for working smarter. For example, former CEO John Young of Hewlett Packard did not ask for a 10% reduction in defects; he asked for a tenfold reduction, and got it.

7. *Quality does not cost more.* Philip Crosby argues that "quality is free."[2] The old idea was that achieving more quality would cost more and slow down production. But quality is really improved by learning ways to "do things right the first time." Quality is not inspected in; it must be designed in. When things are done right the first time, many costs are eliminated (such as salvage and repair). Motorola claims that its quality drive has saved the company over a billion dollars.

8. *Quality is necessary but may not be sufficient.* Improving a company's quality is absolutely necessary because buyers are becoming more demanding. But higher quality may not confer a winning advantage, especially as competitors increase their quality to more or less the same extent. For example, Singapore Airlines once enjoyed the reputation as the world's best airline. However, competitor airlines have recently been attracting a larger share of passengers as they have narrowed the perceived gap between their service quality and Singapore's service quality.

9. *A quality drive cannot save a poor product.* A quality drive cannot compensate for product deficiencies. Pontiac could not save its Fiero automobile simply by launching a quality drive since the car lacked a sports engine.

Sources: 1. Leonard A. Morgan, "The Importance of Quality," in *Perceived Quality of Products, Services and Stores,* ed. Jacob Jacobi and Jerry Olson (New York: Lexington Books, 1984), p. 61. 2. Philip B. Crosby, *Quality Is Free* (New York: McGraw-Hill, 1979).

Rubbermaid: Master of the Mundane, Master of Marketing

Nothing might seem less remarkable than the bin into which you toss your crumbled papers, the dustpan into which you sweep crumbs, or the plastic implement you use to scrape last night's dinner remains off of your plate. Yet Rubbermaid, the maker of mundane products such as these, has received top billing on *Fortune's* list of "America's Most Admired Companies" since 1985. Its sales and earnings have been phenomenal, with sales reaching over $1.8 billion in 1993. The Wooster, Ohio–based company doesn't depend on any one person or any one product for its success. Instead, it depends on making small improvements to some 5,000 unspectacular products.

How can a company that sells such unexciting products prosper in a mature market? How can it command a price premium, even though it is competing with more than 150 other companies making similar products? And how does it score a 90% success rate in introducing new products, *without* market testing? The components of Rubbermaid's stellar success could have come straight out of a marketing textbook:

- *Market and customer feedback:* Rubbermaid continuously monitors market trends to spot new customer needs. For instance, the trend toward smaller households led the company to introduce a successful line of space-saving products.

- *Focus on target markets:* Rubbermaid is organized into six divisions, each containing separate strategic business units that focus on specific product markets. It's smart about targeting promotions, too: The company promoted a new line of makeup organizers for teenage girls by giving away a free compact disc with every one.

- *Customer satisfaction orientation:* Rubbermaid makes good on every customer complaint by replacing its products for free—even when the complaint is about a product wrongly thought to be Rubbermaid's. Replacing the item with a Rubbermaid product is a simple way to illustrate the superiority of Rubbermaid products.

- *Quality obsession:* Rubbermaid workers sweat the smallest details of products others might not even take seriously: Trash-can engineers hunker down over blueprints of trash cans, making sure every detail is correct. Next to them, a designer of a bath duck—a tub for children—is intent on refining the tub's squirter unit, a little ducklike figurine that sucks up water from the bath and creates a spray.

- *Innovation:* Known as a new-product machine, Rubbermaid churns out new (not just improved) products at the rate of one a day. The company can bring a new product to market in an impressive 20 weeks. By obtaining customer input at the very start of the design process, Rubbermaid is able to ensure that 9 out of every 10 new products will be hits.

- *Process teamwork:* Rubbermaid decentralizes decision making by putting cross-functional teams, led by marketing, in charge of different products. Each unit has its own research, design, and manufacturing staffs. "Our business teams are as nimble as entrepreneurs," says CEO Wolfgang Schmitt.

- *Trade partnership:* Rubbermaid's customer center hosts some 110 major retail customers each year, including the biggies like Wal-Mart and Kmart. The company offers these retailers strong support in the form of jointly designed displays, merchandising plans, promotions, and logistics.

- *Strong communication programs:* Rubbermaid engages in extensive advertising and promotions to inform target customer segments about its new products and its high quality.

- *Green consciousness:* Rubbermaid's product line includes Litterless Lunchboxes (whose many containers make plastic wrap redundant) and Sip Saver drink bottles that can be used again and again, unlike disposable drink boxes.

- *Globalization:* While still heavily dependent upon domestic markets, Rubbermaid operates in several countries and is making a major push into global markets: Its goal is to receive 25% of revenues from markets outside the United States by the year 2000.

Sources: See Zachary Scheller, "At Rubbermaid, Little Things Mean a Lot," *Business Week,* November 11, 1991, p. 126; Seth Lubove, "Okay, Call Me a Predator," *Forbes,* February 15, 1993; Alan Farnham, "America's Most Admired Company," *Fortune,* February 7, 1994, pp. 50–54; and Rahul Jacob, "Corporate Reputations," *Fortune,* March 6, 1995, pp. 54–64.

service is not right. Marketing must be the customer's watchdog or guardian, and must constantly hold up the standard of "giving the customer the best solution." (See the Marketing Insight titled "Rubbermaid: Master of the Mundane, Master of Marketing.")

SUMMARY

1. Customers are value-maximizers. They form an expectation of value and act on it. Buyers will buy from the firm that they perceive to offer the highest *customer delivered value,* defined as the difference between total customer value and total customer cost. This means that sellers must assess the total customer value and total customer cost associated with each competitor's offer to know how their own offer stacks up. Sellers who are at a delivered-value disadvantage can either try to increase total customer value or decrease total customer cost. The former calls for strengthening or augmenting the offer's product, services, personnel, and/or image benefits. The latter calls for reducing the buyer's costs. The seller can reduce the price, simplify the ordering and delivery process, or absorb some buyer risk by offering a warranty.

2. A buyer's satisfaction is a function of the product's perceived performance and the buyer's expectations. Recognizing that high satisfaction leads to high customer loyalty, many companies today are aiming for TCS—total customer satisfaction. For customer-centered companies, customer satisfaction is both a goal and a marketing tool. However, a company's main goal should not be to maximize customer satisfaction. Spending more to increase customer satisfaction might divert funds from increasing the satisfaction of other business partners, including employees, dealers, suppliers, and stockholders.

3. Strong companies develop superior technological capabilities in managing the four core business processes: the new-product realization process, the inventory management process, the order-to-remittance process, and the customer service process. Managing these core processes effectively means creating a *marketing network* in which the company works closely with all the parties in the production and distribution chain, from suppliers of raw materials to retail distributors. Companies no longer compete—marketing networks do.

4. Losing profitable customers can dramatically impact a firm's profits. The cost of attracting a new customer is estimated to be five times the cost of keeping a current customer happy. Therefore, one of the marketer's main tasks is customer retention. The key to retaining customers is relationship marketing. To keep customers happy, marketers can add financial or social benefits to products, and/or create structural ties between themselves and their customers. However, marketers should avoid retaining unprofitable customers.

5. *Quality* is the totality of features and characteristics of a product or service that bear on its ability to satisfy stated or implied needs. Today's companies have no choice but to implement total quality management programs if they are to remain solvent and profitable. Total quality is the key to value creation and customer satisfaction.

6. Marketing managers have two responsibilities in a quality-centered company. First, they must participate in formulating strategies and policies designed to help the company win through total quality excellence. Second, they must deliver marketing quality alongside production quality. Each marketing activity—marketing research, sales training, advertising, customer service, and so on—must be performed to high standards. In all of these activities, marketers must work closely with the company's other departments.

CONCEPT APPLICATIONS

1. Peter Drucker has observed that a company's first task is "to create customers." Lee Iacocca emphasized the same idea when he said that "the only job security anybody has in this company [Chrysler] comes from quality, productivity and satisfied customers." What are some of the environmental factors that have contributed to the growing importance of satisfying the customer? Name some companies that have made "customer satisfaction" one of their main goals.

FIGURE 1

Courtesy of Hewlett Packard Company.

2. Hewlett Packard had the reputation for producing high-quality personal computers and electronic products, but its reputation began to slip when customers started finding problems with HP's products. Even though many of these have been solved, potential business customers still seem to be looking toward other competitors to fulfill their need for PCs.

   To pursue increased market share aggressively, HP produced the advertisement in Figure 1. But before it did so, it made some changes in other aspects of its business. What changes was HP likely to make in its manufacturing operations, and for what reasons? What kind of marketing strategy does the ad in Figure 1 imply?

3. The Japanese entered the car market in the United States by pursuing a quality strategy. Quality was a competitive weakness for the American car industry at the time, and the strategy proved very successful in securing a competitive advantage for the Japanese. Assume that Ford is looking for ways to compete against the Japanese in the U.S. market, but that it does not want to start a trade war with Japan by asking the government to impose quotas on Japanese imports. How could Ford use the value chain as an analytical tool to enhance its products' perceived value, knowing that value is currently a competitive weakness for the Japanese? On which of the five primary activities in the value chain do the Japanese compete best, and on which of the five activities should Ford focus?

4. Zeithaml, Parasuraman, and Berry have identified five dimensions of quality service. They are: (1) reliability—the ability to provide dependably and accurately what was promised, (2) assurance—the knowledge and courtesy of employees, and the ability to convey trust and confidence, (3) tangibles—the physical facilities and equipment and the professional appearance of personnel, (4) empathy—the degree of caring and indi-

Building Customer
Satisfaction Through
Quality, Service, and Value

vidual attention provided to customers, and (5) responsiveness—the willingness to help customers and provide prompt service. Describe how Xerox might deliver each of these dimensions to its customers. Is the company better at delivering some of these dimensions than others?

5. Unisys Corporation employs experienced business consultants to help companies evaluate the information flow between organizations and their customers, identify barriers to communication, and design technological solutions. Unisys has coined the word "customerize," which means "to make a company more responsive to its customer and better able to attract new ones" (see Figure 2-2). Design a short questionnaire that Unisys business consultants could use to determine whether or not a company is "customerized."

6. Define each of the following terms, then give an example of a company that has used each concept for competitive advantage:
   a. Value chain
   b Value-delivery network
   c. Relationship marketing
   d. Market-driven quality
   e. Customer satisfaction

7. A subcommittee of the board of directors of Hampton Inns has made a bold proposal that customers be given a guarantee of "complete satisfaction or your night's stay is free." Employees will be permitted to make good on this guarantee without the approval of managers. But although the proposed guarantee would show great confidence in the hotels' quality and would give Hampton Inns a competitive advantage, most of the hotel managers oppose the plan. Why would they not want to guarantee customer satisfaction? What are possible customer reactions to such a guarantee? What controls can be introduced to reduce customer abuse?

8. A sample of 500 customers who use Empire Satellite dishes were asked the following two questions. Their responses are summarized in the grid in Table 1.

SURVEY QUESTIONS:

Statement 1—I prefer to talk with an operator rather than a computerized voice recording when calling Empire Satellite about service.

Very Important	**Important**	**Neutral**	**Of Little Importance**	**Not at All Important**

Statement 2—I am satisfied with the computerized voice used by Empire Satellite.

Very Satisfied	**Satisfied**	**Neutral**	**Dissatisfied**	**Very Dissatisfied**

The company is considering changing from an electronic-voice system to a system in which customers will always speak to a human being when they call for service. From the data below, determine whether Empire should pursue this idea. If it does so, what are the implications of the survey for Empire's marketing program?

TABLE 1	**VERY IMPORTANT**	**IMPORTANT**	**NEUTRAL**	**OF LITTLE IMPORTANCE**	**NOT AT ALL IMPORTANT**	**TOTALS**
COMPUTERIZED VOICE RECORDINGS AND CUSTOMER SATISFACTION: DATA SUMMARY						
Very Satisfied	38	62	40	20	200	360
Satisfied	8	7	5	8	6	34
Neutral	5	5	7	7	20	44
Dissatisfied	3	3	6	7	8	27
Very Dissatisfied	3	5	7	9	11	35
Totals	57	82	65	51	245	500

1. See, for example, "Value Marketing: Quality, Service, and Fair Pricing Are the Keys to Selling in the '90s," *Business Week,* November 11, 1991, pp. 132–40.

2. See Irwin P. Levin and Richard D. Johnson, "Estimating Price-Quality Tradeoffs Using Comparative Judgments," *Journal of Consumer Research,* June 11, 1984, pp. 593–600.

3. Stephanie Forest Anderson, "Customers 'Must Be Pleased, Not Just Satisfied,'" *Business Week,* August 3, 1992, p. 52; Steve Lohr, "For Dell, A Tripling of Earnings," *The New York Times,* February 23, 1995, D4:4; Laura McDonald, "Setting New Standards for Customer Advocacy," *Journal of Business Strategy,* 14, no. 1 (1993), 11–15.

4. Michael E. Porter, *Competitive Advantage: Creating and Sustaining Superior Performance* (New York: Free Press, 1985).

5. See George Stalk, "Competing on Capability: The New Rules of Corporate Strategy," *Harvard Business Review,* March–April 1992, pp. 57–69; and Benson P. Shapiro, V. Kasturi Rangan, and John J. Sviokla, "Staple Yourself to an Order," *Harvard Business Review,* July–August 1992, pp. 113–22.

6. Myron Magnet, "The New Golden Rule of Business," *Fortune,* November 28, 1994, pp. 60–64.

7. Frederick F. Reichheld and W. Earl Sasser, Jr., "Zero Defections: Quality Comes to Services," *Harvard Business Review,* September–October 1990, pp. 301–7.

8. Leonard L. Berry and A. Parasuraman, *Marketing Services: Competing Through Quality* (New York: Free Press, 1991), pp. 136–42. See also Richard Cross and Janet Smith, *Customer Bonding: Pathways to Lasting Customer Loyalty* (Lincolnwood, IL: NTC Business Books, 1995).

9. James H. Donnelly, Jr., Leonard L. Berry, and Thomas W. Thompson, *Marketing Financial Services—A Strategic Vision* (Homewood, IL: Dow Jones-Irwin, 1985), p. 113.

10. Quoted in Don Peppers and Martha Rogers, *The One to One Future: Building Relationships One Customer at a Time* (New York: Currency Doubleday, 1993), p. 108.

11. Carl Sewell and Paul Brown, *Customers for Life* (New York: Pocket Books, 1990), p. 162.

12. William A. Sherden, *Market Ownership: The Art & Science of Becoming #1* (New York: Amacom, 1994), p. 77.

13. Robert J. Bowman, "Good Things, Smaller Packages," *World Trade,* 6, no. 9 (October 1993), 106–10.

14. Michael J. Lanning and Lynn W. Phillips, "Strategy Shifts Up a Gear," *Marketing,* October 1991, p. 9.

15. Lynn O'Rourke Hayes, "Quality Is Worth $11,000 in the Bank," *Restaurant Hospitality,* March 1993, p. 68.

16. See Thomas M. Petro, "Profitability: The Fifth 'P' of Marketing," *Bank Marketing,* September 1990, pp. 48–52; and Petro, "Who Are Your Best Customers?" *Bank Marketing,* October 1990, pp. 48–52.

17. In a memorandum published by the Boston Consulting Group, date unknown.

18. "Quality: The U.S. Drives to Catch Up," *Business Week,* November 1982, pp. 66–80, here p. 68. For a recent assessment of progress, see "Quality Programs Show Shoddy Results," *The Wall Street Journal,* May 14, 1992, B:1.

19. See "Quality in Europe," *Work Study,* January–February 1993, p. 30; Ronald Henkoff, "The Hot New Seal of Quality," *Fortune,* June 28, 1993, pp. 116–20; Amy Zukerman, "One Size Doesn't Fit All," *Industry Week,* January 9, 1995, pp. 37–40; and "The Sleeper Issue of the '90s," *Industry Week,* August 15, 1994, pp. 99–100, 108.

20. Robert D. Buzzell and Bradley T. Gale, *The PIMS Principles: Linking Strategy to Performance* (New York: Free Press, 1987), Chapter 6. *PIMS* stands for *P*rofit *I*mpact of *M*arket *S*trategy.

21. See "The Gurus of Quality: American Companies Are Hearing the Quality Gospel Preached by Deming, Juran, Crosby, and Taguchi," *Traffic Management,* July 1990, pp. 35–39.

22. See Cyndee Miller, "U.S. Firms Lag in Meeting Global Quality Standards," *Marketing News,* February 15, 1993.

23. J. Daniel Beckham, "Expect the Unexpected in Health Care Marketing Future," *The Academy Bulletin,* July 1992, p. 3.

WINNING MARKETS THROUGH MARKET-ORIENTED STRATEGIC PLANNING

There are five types of companies: those who make things happen; those who think they make things happen; those who watch things happen; those who wonder what happened; and those that did not know that anything had happened.

ANONYMOUS

Plans are nothing; planning is everything.

DWIGHT D. EISENHOWER

Marketing strategy is a series of integrated actions leading to a sustainable competitive advantage.

JOHN SCULLY

In Chapters 1 and 2, we asked the question: How do companies compete in a global marketplace? We found that one part of the answer is a commitment to creating and retaining satisfied customers. We can now add a second part to this answer: Successful companies and high-performance businesses know how to adapt to a continuously changing marketplace. They practice the art of market-oriented strategic planning.

❖ **MARKET-ORIENTED STRATEGIC PLANNING** is the managerial process of developing and maintaining a viable fit between the organization's objectives, skills, and resources and its changing market opportunities. The aim of strategic planning is to shape and reshape the company's businesses and products so that they yield target profits and growth.

The concepts that underlie strategic planning emerged in the 1970s as a result of a succession of shock waves that hit U.S. industry—the energy crisis, double-digit inflation, economic stagnation, Japanese competitive victories, deregulation of key industries. No longer could U.S. companies rely on simple growth projections in planning their production, sales, and profits. Strategic planning needed to replace conventional long-range planning. Today, the main goal of strategic planning is to help a company select and organize its businesses in a way that will keep the company healthy even when unexpected events upset any of its specific businesses or product lines.

Strategic planning calls for action in three key areas. The first calls for managing a company's businesses as an investment portfolio. Each business has a different profit potential, and the company's resources should be allocated accordingly.

The second key area involves assessing accurately each business by considering the market's growth rate and the company's position and fit in that market. It is not sufficient to use current sales or profits as a guide. For example, if the Ford Motor Company had used current profits as a guide to investment in the 1970s, it would have continued to pour money into large cars, since that was where it made its money at the time. But Ford's analysis showed that the profits on large cars would dry up. Therefore Ford needed to reallocate its funds to improving its compact cars, even though the company was losing money on compact cars at the time.

The third key area of strategic planning is *strategy*. For each of its businesses, the company must develop a game plan for achieving its long-run objectives. Because there is no one strategy that is optimal for all companies in that business, each company must determine what makes the most sense in the light of its industry position and its objectives, opportunities, skills, and resources. Thus, in the rubber-tire industry, Goodyear is pressing for cost reduction, Michelin is pursuing innovation, and Bridgestone is pressing for market share. Each strategy can be successful under the right circumstances.

Marketing plays a critical role in the company's strategic-planning process. According to a strategic-planning manager at General Electric:

> . . . the marketing manager is the most significant functional contributor to the strategic-planning process, with leadership roles in defining the business mission; analysis of the environmental, competitive, and business situations; developing objectives, goals, and strategies; and defining product, market, distribution, and quality plans to implement the business' strategies. This involvement extends to the development of programs and operating plans that are fully linked with the strategic plan.[1]

To understand marketing management, we must understand strategic planning. And to understand strategic planning, we need to recognize that most large companies consist of four organizational levels: the corporate level, division level, business unit level, and product level. Corporate headquarters is responsible for designing a *corporate strategic plan* to guide the whole enterprise into a profitable future; it makes decisions on how much resource support to allocate to each division, as well as which businesses to start or eliminate. Each division establishes a *division plan* covering the allocation of funds to each business unit within the division. Each business unit develops a *business unit strategic plan* to carry that business unit into a profitable future. Finally, each product level (product line, brand) within a business unit develops a *marketing plan* for achieving its objectives in its product market.

The marketing plan operates at two levels. The *strategic marketing plan* develops the broad marketing objectives and strategy based on an analysis of the current market situation and opportunities. The *tactical marketing plan* outlines specific marketing tactics, including advertising, merchandising, pricing, channels, service, and so on.

The marketing plan is the central instrument for directing and coordinating the marketing effort. In today's organizations the marketing department does not set the marketing plan by itself. Rather, today's plans are developed by teams, with inputs and signoffs from every important function. These plans are then implemented at the appropriate levels of the organization. Results are monitored, and corrective actions are taken when necessary. The complete planning, implementation, and control cycle is shown in Figure 3-1.

In this chapter, we examine the following questions:

- ◆ **What are the characteristics of a high-performance business?**
- ◆ **How is strategic planning carried out at the corporate and division levels?**
- ◆ **How is planning carried out at the business unit level?**
- ◆ **What are the major steps in the marketing process?**
- ◆ **How is planning carried out at the product level, and what does a marketing plan include?**

FIGURE 3-1

The Strategic Planning, Implementation, and Control Process

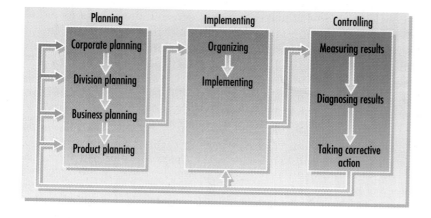

Understanding
Marketing
Management

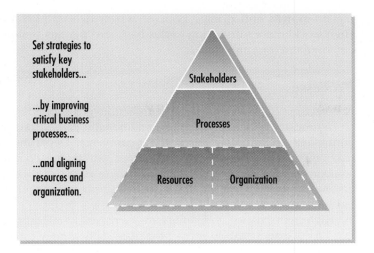

FIGURE 3-2
**The High-Performance
Business**

Source: P. Ranganath Nayak, Erica
Drazen, and George Kastner, "The
High-Performance Business: Accelerat-
ing Performance Improvement," *Prism,*
First Quarter 1992, p. 6. Reprinted by
permission of Arthur D. Little, Inc.

Set strategies to satisfy key stakeholders...

...by improving critical business processes...

...and aligning resources and organization.

Stakeholders

Processes

Resources   Organization

THE NATURE OF HIGH-PERFORMANCE BUSINESSES

One of the major challenges facing today's companies is how to build and main-tain viable businesses in a rapidly changing marketplace and business environ-ment. In the 1950s, the answer was thought to lie in increasing production effi-ciency. In the 1960s and 1970s, companies sought growth and profits through vigorous acquisition and diversification programs. They saw their businesses as constituting an investment portfolio to which they added promising businesses and removed faltering businesses. In the 1980s, companies decided to "stick to their knitting" and stay in businesses they knew well.

The consulting firm of Arthur D. Little proposed a model of the characteristics of a *high-performance business.* It pointed to the four factors shown in Figure 3-2 as keys to success: stakeholders, processes, resources, and organization.[2]

Stakeholders

As its first stop on the road to high performance, the business must define its stakeholders and their needs. Traditionally, most businesses paid greatest attention to their stockholders. Today's businesses, however, are increasingly recognizing that unless they nourish other *stakeholders*—customers, employees, suppliers, dis-tributors—the business may never earn sufficient profits for the stockholders. Thus, if General Motors' employees, customers, dealers, and suppliers are un-happy, GM is not likely to make any profits.

A business must strive to satisfy the minimum (threshold) expectations of each stakeholder group. At the same time, the company can aim to deliver satisfaction levels above the minimum for different stakeholders. For example, the company might aim to delight its customers, perform well for its employees, and deliver a threshold level of satisfaction to its suppliers. In setting these levels, the company must be careful not to violate the various stakeholder groups' sense of fairness about the relative treatment they are getting.

There is a dynamic relationship connecting the stakeholder groups. The pro-gressive company creates a high level of employee satisfaction, which leads em-ployees to work on continuous improvements as well as breakthrough innova-tions. The result is higher-quality products and services, which create high customers satisfaction. Customer satisfaction leads to repeat business and therefore higher growth and profits, both of which deliver high stockholder satisfaction. High stockholder satisfaction cycles back and permits building a still higher-quality environment for employees.

Processes

A company can accomplish its satisfaction goals only by managing and linking *work processes*. Company work is traditionally carried on in departments. But departmental organization poses some problems. Departments typically operate to maximize their own objectives, not necessarily the company's objectives. Walls sometimes separate departments, and there is usually less-than-ideal cooperation among departments. Work slows down and plans are altered as they pass from department to department.

High-performance companies are increasingly refocusing their attention on the need to manage core business processes such as new-product development, sales generation, and order fulfillment. They are *reengineering* the work flows and building *cross-functional teams* responsible for each process.[3] For example, at Xerox a customer operations group links sales, shipping, installation, service, and billing so that these activities flow smoothly into one another. Winning companies will be those that achieve excellent capabilities in managing core business processes.

AT&T, Polaroid, and Motorola are just some of the companies that have reorganized their workers into cross-functional teams. But cross-functional teams have become common in nonprofit and government organizations as well. For example:

SAN DIEGO ZOO As the San Diego Zoo's mission changed from simple exhibition to conservation through education, it changed its organization. The new revamped zoo consists of bioclimatic zones, exhibits that immerse zoogoers in an environment of predator and prey and flora and fauna from different parts of the world. Because the zones themselves are more interdependent, the employees who manage them must work together. Gardeners, groundskeepers, and animal care experts are no longer separated by traditional boundaries.[4]

INTERNAL REVENUE SERVICE At the IRS, customer service and employee involvement have improved since the agency has created a TQM environment. In its quest for total quality, the IRS urged regional offices to experiment with different team-based approaches. As a result, more than 400 cross-functional teams have been developed in the agency's seven regions.[5]

Resources

To carry out processes, a company needs *resources*—labor power, materials, machines, information, energy, and so on. These resources can be owned, leased, or rented. Traditionally, companies owned and controlled most of the resources that entered their business. But this situation is changing. Companies are finding that some resources under their control are not performing as well as those that they could obtain from outside the company. Many companies today have decided to *outsource* less-critical resources if they can be obtained at better quality and/or lower cost from outside the organization. Frequently outsourced resources include cleaning services, lawn care, and auto fleet management. Recently Kodak turned over the management of its data processing department to IBM. Another example of successful outsourcing:

TOPSYTAIL Some start-up businesses guarantee their success by skillful outsourcing. Tomima Edmark, inventor of the plastic hair-styling piece called Topsy-Tail, grew her company to sales of $80 million in 1993 with only two employees. Instead of hiring 50 or more employees, Edmark and her two employees set up a network of 20 vendors who handle everything from product manufacturing to servicing the retail accounts. Yet Edmark has been careful to follow the first rule of effective outsourcing: She keeps control of new-product development and marketing strategy, the core competencies that make up the heart of her company.[6]

The key, then, is to own and nurture the core resources and competences that make up the essence of the business. Nike, for example, does not manufacture its own shoes, because certain Asian manufacturers are more competent in this task. But Nike nurtures its superiority in shoe design and shoe merchandising, its two core competences. A *core competence* has three characteristics: (1) It is a source of competitive advantage, (2) it has a potential breadth of applications, and (3) it is difficult for competitors to imitate.[7]

Organization and Organizational Culture

A company's *organization* consists of its structures, policies, and corporate culture, all of which can become dysfunctional in a rapidly changing business environment. While structures and policies can be changed (with difficulty), the company's culture is very hard to change. Yet changing a corporate culture is often the key to implementing a new strategy successfully.

What exactly is a *corporate culture?* Most businesspeople would be hard pressed to find words to describe this elusive concept, which some define as "the shared experiences, stories, beliefs, and norms that characterize an organization." Yet, walk into any company and the first thing that strikes you is the corporate culture—the way people are dressed, how they talk to one another, and even how their offices are arranged. Even companies that do little conscious thinking about creating a culture can have a strong one. Microsoft is a case in point:

MICROSOFT "If this company were a car, it would not have a rear-view mirror," says Mike Murray, Microsoft's vice-president for human resources and administration. Rather than smugly looking back on past accomplishment, the corporate culture at Microsoft is forward looking and entrepreneurial. It therefore seems ironic that there has been no conscious attempt to shape this culture. With most of Microsoft's employees in their 30s, there is a strong generational influence on corporate culture. Indeed, Microsoft resembles a college campus where employees dress as they please, call each other by first name, and feel free to speak their mind. Yet Microsoft is not as free-wheeling as the shorts, sandals, and first names suggest. Everyone works extremely hard to get new products out and each employee is reviewed every six months to determine salary increases and bonuses. No other company has as many millionaires and billionaires on staff as Microsoft.[8]

What happens when entrepreneurial companies grow and need to create a tighter structure? What happens when a company with an entrepreneurial culture enters a joint venture with a more bureaucratic, hierarchical culture? Two computer giants had this experience recently:

IBM, APPLE, AND TALIGENT IBM and Apple Computer experienced corporate culture shock when the two companies joined forces to create Taligent, the software company charged with developing an operating system to compete with Microsoft and NeXT. Joe Guglielmi, the 30-year IBM veteran who is chief executive of Taligent, expressed the culture clash this way: "IBM is a very hierarchical company. Plans go up, are consolidated, and come back down as one world-wide strategy. Apple is a group of empowered individuals doing great things with great technology. Decisions are made at very low levels all the time."[9]

In situations like this one, it becomes clear that culture is intertwined with strategy.

The question of what accounts for the success of long-lasting high-performance companies was recently addressed in a six-year study by Collins and Porras called *Built to Last*.[10] The Stanford researchers identified two companies in each of 18 industries, one that they called a "visionary company" and one that they called a "comparison company." The visionary companies were acknowledged as the industry leaders and widely admired; they set ambitious goals, communicated them to their employees, and embraced a high purpose beyond making money. They also outperformed the comparison companies by a wide margin. The visionary companies included General Electric, Hewlett Packard, and Boeing; the corresponding comparison companies were Westinghouse, Texas Instruments, and McDonnell Douglas.

In searching for something common to the 18 market leaders, the authors concluded that each high-performance company had developed a core ideology from which it did not deviate. Thus IBM has held to the principles of respect for the individual, customer satisfaction, and continuous quality improvement throughout its history. And Johnson & Johnson holds to the principle that is first responsibility is to its customers, its second to its employees, its third to its community, and its fourth to its stockholders. The point is that while a company needs to change some elements of its culture and strategy in adapting to the changing environment, most market leaders have preserved their core ideology in navigating through the rough and changing waters.

CORPORATE AND DIVISION STRATEGIC PLANNING

Corporate headquarters has the responsibility for setting into motion the strategic planning process. By preparing statements of mission, policy, strategy, and goals, headquarters establishes the framework within which the divisions and business units prepare their plans. Some corporations give a lot of freedom to their business units to set their own sales and profit goals and strategies. Others set goals for their business units but let them develop their own strategies. Still others set the goals and get heavily involved in the individual business unit strategies.[11]

All corporate headquarters must undertake four planning activities:

♦ Defining the corporate mission

♦ Establishing strategic business units (SBUs)

♦ Assigning resources to each SBU

♦ Planning new businesses

Defining the Corporate Mission

An organization exists to accomplish something: to make cars, lend money, provide a night's lodging, and so on. Its specific mission or purpose is usually clear when the business starts. Over time some managers may lose interest in the mission, or the mission may lose its relevance because of changed market conditions. Or the mission may become unclear as the corporation adds new products and markets to its portfolio. American Can recently sold its original business, canning. Clearly, American Can is redefining its mission.

When management senses that the organization is drifting from its mission, it must renew its search for purpose. According to Peter Drucker, it is time to ask some fundamental questions.[12] *What is our business? Who is the customer? What is value to the customer? What will our business be? What should our business be?* These simple-sounding questions are among the most difficult the company will ever have to answer. Successful companies continuously raise these questions and answer them thoughtfully and thoroughly.

Each company's mission is shaped by five elements:

- *History:* Every company has a history of aims, policies; and achievements. The organization must not depart too radically from its past history. For example, it would not make sense for Harvard University to open two-year junior colleges, even if these colleges represented a growth opportunity.

- *Current preferences of the owners and management:* If Zenith's current management wants to get out of the television-receiver business, Zenith's mission statement is likely to be affected.

- *The market environment:* The Girl Scouts of America would not recruit successfully in today's market environment with their former purpose, "to prepare young girls for motherhood and wifely duties."

- *Resources:* The organization's resources determine which missions are possible. Singapore Airlines would be deluding itself if it adopted the mission of becoming the world's largest airline.

- *Distinctive competences.* The organization should base its mission on what it does best. For example, Japan's Honda has nurtured its major core competence—namely, making engines. Its skill at designing and improving engines has been the basis of its move into such products as motorcycles, automobiles, lawnmowers, snowmobiles, power tillers, and outboard motors. Similarly, Canon's skills in fine optics, precision mechanics, and microelectronics are the basis for its success with such products as copy machines, video cameras, printers, and fax machines. McDonald's could probably enter the solar energy business, but doing so would not use its core competence—providing low-cost food and quick service to large groups of customers.

Organizations develop mission statements to share them with their managers, employees, and (in many cases) customers. A well-worked-out mission statement provides company employees with a shared sense of purpose, direction, and opportunity. The company mission statement acts as an "invisible hand" that guides geographically dispersed employees to work independently and yet collectively toward realizing the organization's goals. Here are two examples of good mission statements:

AMOCO "Amoco is a worldwide integrated petroleum and chemical company. We find and develop petroleum resources and provide quality products and services for our customers. We conduct our business responsibly to achieve a superior financial return, balanced with our long-term growth, benefiting shareholders, and fulfilling our commitment to the community and the environment."

MOTOROLA "The purpose of Motorola is to honorably serve the needs of the community by providing products and services of superior quality at a fair price to our customers; to do this so as to earn an adequate profit which is required for the total enterprise to grow, and by so doing provide the opportunity for our employees and shareholders to achieve their reasonable personal objectives."

Good mission statements have three major characteristics. First, they focus on a limited number of goals. The statement, "We want to produce the highest-quality products, offer the most service, achieve the widest distribution, and sell at the lowest prices" claims too much. It fails to supply guidelines when management faces difficult decisions. Second, mission statements stress the major policies and values that the company wants to honor. *Policies* define how the company will deal with its stakeholders, employees, customers, suppliers, distributors, and other important groups. Policies narrow the range of individual discretion so that employees act consistently on important issues. Third, they define the major *competitive scopes* within which the company will operate:

Winning Markets
Through Market-Oriented
Strategic Planning

- *Industry scope:* The range of industries in which a company will operate. Some companies will operate in only one industry; some only in a set of related industries; some only in industrial goods, consumer goods, or services; and some in any industry. For example, Du Pont prefers to operate in the industrial market, while Dow is willing to operate in the industrial and consumer markets. 3M will get into almost any industry where it can make money.

- *Products and applications scope:* The range of products and applications that a company will supply. St. Jude Medical aims to "serve physicians worldwide with high-quality products for cardiovascular care."

- *Competence scope:* The range of technological and other core competences that a company will master and leverage. Thus, Japan's NEC has built its core competences in computing, communications, and components. These competences support its production of laptop computers, television receivers, hand-held telephones, and so on.

- *Market-segment scope:* The type of market or customers a company will serve. Some companies will serve only the upscale market. For example, Porsche makes only expensive cars, sunglasses, and other accessories. Gerber serves the baby market primarily.

- *Vertical scope:* The number of channel levels from raw material to final product and distribution in which a company will participate. At one extreme are companies with a large vertical scope; at one time Ford owned its own rubber plantations, sheep farms, glass manufacturing plants, and steel foundries. At the other extreme are corporations with low or no vertical integration. These "hollow corporations" or "pure marketing companies" consist of a person with a phone, fax, computer, and desk who contracts outside for every service including design, manufacture, marketing, and physical distribution.[13]

- *Geographical scope:* The range of regions, countries, or country groups in which a company will operate. At one extreme are companies that operate in a specific city or state. At the other extreme are multinationals like Unilever and Caterpillar, which operate in almost every one of the world's 180-plus countries.

Mission statements are at their best when they are guided by a vision, an almost "impossible dream" that provides a direction for the company for the next 10 to 20 years. Sony's former president, Akio Morita, wanted everyone to have access to "personal portable sound," so his company created the Walkman and portable CD player. Fred Smith wanted to deliver mail anywhere in the United States before 10:30 A.M. the next day, so he created Federal Express.

Mission statements should not be revised every few years in response to each new turn in the economy. However, a company must redefine its mission if that mission has lost credibility or no longer defines an optimal course for the company.[14] Mars Inc. modified its "Five Principles" in 1994 to incorporate references to the candy company's ambitions abroad; and Bell Atlantic has modified its vision— "to be the world's best communications and information management company"— to incorporate entertainment following its acquisition of cable giant Tele-Communications Inc.[15]

Establishing Strategic Business Units

Most companies operate several businesses. However, companies too often define their businesses in terms of products. They are in the "auto business" or the "slide-rule business." But Levitt argued that market definitions of a business are superior to product definitions.[16] A business must be viewed as a customer-satisfying process, not a goods-producing process. Products are transient, but basic needs and customer groups endure forever. A horse-carriage company will go out of business soon after the automobile is invented, unless it switches to making cars. Levitt encouraged companies to redefine their business in terms of needs, not products. Table 3-1 gives several examples of companies that moved from a product to a market definition of their business.

COMPANY	PRODUCT	MARKET DEFINITION	**TABLE 3-1**
Missouri-Pacific Railroad	We run a railroad.	We are a people-and-goods mover.	PRODUCT-ORIENTED VERSUS MARKET-ORIENTED DEFINITIONS OF A BUSINESS
Xerox	We make copying equipment.	We help improve office productivity.	
Standard Oil	We sell gasoline.	We supply energy.	
Columbia Pictures	We make movies.	We market entertainment.	
Encyclopedia Britannica	We sell encyclopedias.	We distribute information.	
Carrier	We make air conditioners and furnaces.	We provide climate control in the home.	

Management should avoid a market definition that is too narrow or too broad. Consider a lead-pencil manufacturer. If it sees itself as a writing-instruments company, it might expand into the production of pens. If it sees itself as a writing-equipment company, it might consider making computers. The broadest concept of its business is that it is a communication company, but this would be stretching things too far for a lead-pencil manufacturer.

In defining their businesses, many companies are thinking in terms of what their products accomplish instead of simply what they are. For instance, BMW talks of being a "transportation provider" rather than a "car maker." BMW sees its business as cars, motorcycles, traffic management systems, and auto recycling. This definition encompasses BMW's emphasis on leasing—the present rage in the auto business. Whirlpool defines itself as a fabric-care or a food-preservation enterprise rather than as a washing-machine or refrigerator maker.

A business can be defined in terms of three dimensions: *customer groups, customer needs,* and *technology.*[17] Consider, for example, a small company that defines its business as designing incandescent lighting systems for television studios. Its customer group is television studios; the customer need is lighting; and the technology is incandescent lighting. The company might want to expand into additional businesses. For example, it could make lighting for other customer groups, such as homes, factories, and offices. Or it could supply other services needed by television studios, such as heating, ventilation, or air conditioning. Or it could design other lighting technologies for television studios, such as infrared or ultraviolet lighting.

Large companies normally manage quite different businesses, each requiring its own strategy. General Electric classified its businesses into 49 *strategic business units* (SBUs). An SBU has three characteristics:

1. It is a single business or collection of related businesses that can be planned separately from the rest of the company.

2. It has its own set of competitors.

3. It has a manager who is responsible for strategic planning and profit performance and who controls most of the factors affecting profit.

Assigning Resources to Each SBU

The purpose of identifying the company's strategic business units is to develop separate strategies and assign appropriate funding. Senior management knows that its portfolio of businesses usually includes a number of "yesterday's has-beens" as well as "tomorrow's breadwinners." But it cannot rely just on impressions; it needs analytical tools for classifying its businesses by profit potential. Two of the best-known business portfolio evaluation models are the Boston Consulting Group model and the General Electric model.[18]

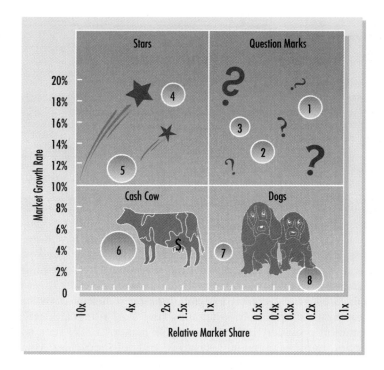

BOSTON CONSULTING GROUP MODEL. The Boston Consulting Group (BCG), a leading management consulting firm, developed and popularized the *growth-share matrix* shown in Figure 3-3. The eight circles represent the current sizes and positions of eight business units in a hypothetical company. The dollar-volume size of each business is proportional to the circle's area. Thus, the two largest businesses are 5 and 6. The location of each business unit indicates its market growth rate and relative market share.

Specifically, the *market growth rate* on the vertical axis indicates the annual growth rate of the market in which the business operates. In Figure 3-3, it ranges from 0% to 20%, although a larger range could be shown. A market growth rate above 10% is considered high. *Relative market share,* which is measured on the horizontal axis, refers to the SBU's market share relative to that of its largest competitor. It serves as a measure of the company's strength in the relevant market. A relative market share of 0.1 means that the company's sales volume is only 10% of the leader's sales volume; a relative share of 10 means that the company's SBU is the leader and has 10 times the sales of the next-strongest competitor in that market. Relative market share is divided into high and low share, using 1.0 as the dividing line. Relative market share is drawn in log scale, so that equal distances represent the same percentage increase.

The growth-share matrix is divided into four cells, each indicating a different type of business:

♦ *Question marks:* Question marks are businesses that operate in high-growth markets but have low relative market shares. Most businesses start off as question marks as the company tries to enter a high-growth market in which there is already a market leader. A question mark requires a lot of cash because the company has to spend money on plants, equipment, and personnel to keep up with the fast-growing market, and because it wants to overtake the leader. The term *question mark* is appropriate because the company has to think hard about whether to keep pouring money into this business. The company in Figure 3-3 operates three question-mark businesses, and this may be too many. The company might be better off investing more cash in one or two of these businesses instead of spreading its cash over all three businesses.

- *Stars:* If the question-mark business is successful, it becomes a star. A star is the market leader in a high-growth market. A star does not necessarily produce a positive cash flow for the company. The company must spend substantial funds to keep up with the high market growth and fight off competitors' attacks. In Figure 3-3, the company has two stars. The company would justifiably be concerned if it had no stars.

- *Cash cows:* When a market's annual growth rate falls to less than 10%, the star becomes a cash cow if it still has the largest relative market share. A cash cow produces a lot of cash for the company. The company does not have to finance a lot of capacity expansion because the market's growth rate has slowed down. And since the business is the market leader, it enjoys economies of scale and higher profit margins. The company uses its cash-cow businesses to pay its bills and support its other businesses. The company in Figure 3-3 has only one cash cow and is therefore highly vulnerable. If this cash cow starts losing relative market share, the company will have to pump enough money back into it to maintain market leadership. If it uses its cash to support its other businesses, its strong cash cow may devolve into a dog.

- *Dogs:* Dogs are businesses that have weak market shares in low-growth markets. They typically generate low profits or losses, although they may generate some cash. The company in Figure 3-3 holds two dogs, and this may be two too many. The company should consider whether it is holding on to these dog businesses for good reasons (such as an expected turnaround in the market growth rate or a new chance at market leadership) or for sentimental reasons. Dogs often consume more management time than they are worth and need to be phased down or out.

After plotting its various businesses in the growth-share matrix, a company must determine whether its portfolio is healthy. An unbalanced portfolio would have too many dogs or question marks and/or too few stars and cash cows.

The company's next task is to determine what objective, strategy, and budget to assign to each SBU. Four strategies can be pursued:

- *Build:* Here the objective is to increase the SBU's market share, even forgoing short-term earnings to achieve this objective if necessary. Building is appropriate for question marks whose market shares must grow if they are to become stars.

- *Hold:* Here the objective is to preserve the SBU's market share. This strategy is appropriate for strong cash cows if they are to continue yielding a large positive cash flow.

- *Harvest:* Here the objective is to increase the SBU's short-term cash flow regardless of long-term effect. Harvesting involves a decision to eventually withdraw from a business by implementing a program of continuous cost retrenchment. The company plans to cash in on its "crop," to "milk its business." Harvesting generally involves eliminating R&D expenditures, not replacing the physical plant as it wears out, not replacing salespeople, reducing advertising expenditures, and so on. The hope is to reduce costs at a faster rate than any potential drop in sales, thus resulting in an increase in the company's positive cash flow. This cost retrenchment must be done carefully and less visibly so that it doesn't become a disabling concern to the company's employees, customers, and distributors. This strategy is appropriate for weak cash cows whose future is dim and from which more cash flow is needed. Harvesting can also be used with question marks and dogs. The company carrying out a harvesting strategy faces prickly social and ethical questions over how much information to share with various stakeholders.

- *Divest:* Here the objective is to sell or liquidate the business because resources can be better used elsewhere. This strategy is appropriate for dogs and question marks that are acting as a drag on the company's profits.

  Companies must carefully decide whether harvesting or divestment is a better strategy for a weak business. Harvesting reduces the business's future value and therefore the price at which it could later be sold if divested. An early decision to divest, in contrast, is likely to produce fairly good bids if the business is in relatively good shape and of more value to another firm.

As time passes, SBUs change their position in the growth-share matrix. Successful SBUs have a life cycle. They start as question marks, become stars, then cash cows, and finally dogs at the end of their life cycle. For this reason, companies should examine not only their businesses' current positions in the growth-share matrix (as in a snapshot) but also their moving positions (as in a motion picture). Each business should be reviewed as to where it was in past years and where it will probably move in future years. If a given SBU's expected trajectory is not satisfactory, the corporation should ask its manager to propose a new strategy and the likely resulting trajectory.

The worst mistake a company could make would be to require all its SBUs to aim for the same growth rate or return level. The very point of SBU analysis is that each business has a different potential and requires its own objective. Other mistakes include: leaving cash cows with too little in retained funds (in which case they grow weak) or leaving them with too much in retained funds (in which case the company fails to invest enough in new businesses with growth potential); making major investments in dogs in hopes of turning them around but failing each time; and maintaining too many question marks and underinvesting in each. Question marks should either receive enough support to achieve segment dominance or be dropped.

THE GENERAL ELECTRIC MODEL. An SBU's appropriate objective cannot be determined solely by its position in the growth-share matrix. If additional factors are considered, the growth-share matrix can be seen as a special case of a multifactor portfolio matrix that General Electric (GE) pioneered. This model is shown in Figure 3-4(a), where one company's seven businesses are plotted. This time the size of each circle represents the size of the relevant market rather than the size of the company's business. The shaded part of the circle represents that business's market share. Thus, the company's clutch business operates in a moderate-size market and enjoys approximately a 30% market share.

Each business is rated in terms of two major dimensions, *market attractiveness* and *business strength* (Figure 3-4[b]). These two factors make excellent marketing sense for rating a business. Companies are successful to the extent that they enter attractive markets and possess the required business strengths to succeed in those markets. If one of these factors is missing, the business will not produce outstanding results. Neither a strong company operating in an unattractive market nor a weak company operating in an attractive market will do very well.

To measure these two dimensions, strategic planners must identify the factors underlying each dimension and find a way to measure them and combine them into an index. Table 3-2 on page 76 lists two possible sets of factors making up the two dimensions for the hydraulic-pumps business in Figure 3-4. (Each company has to decide on its own list of factors.) For the hydraulic-pumps business, market attractiveness varies with the market's size, annual market growth rate, historical profit margins, and so on. And business strength varies with the company's market share, share growth, product quality, and so on. Note that the two BCG factors—market growth rate and market share—are subsumed under the two major variables of the GE model. The GE model leads strategic planners to look at more factors in evaluating an actual or potential business than the BCG model does.

How does the company arrive at the data in Table 3-2 and the circles in Figure 3-4(a)? Management rates each factor from 1 (very unattractive) to 5 (very attractive). The hydraulic-pumps business is rated 4 on overall market size, indicating that the market size is pretty large (a 5 would be very large). Clearly, evaluating these factors requires data and assessment from marketing and other company personnel. The ratings are then multiplied by weights reflecting the factors' relative importance to arrive at the values, which are summed for each dimension. The hydraulic-pumps business scored a 3.70 on market attractiveness and a 3.40 on busi-

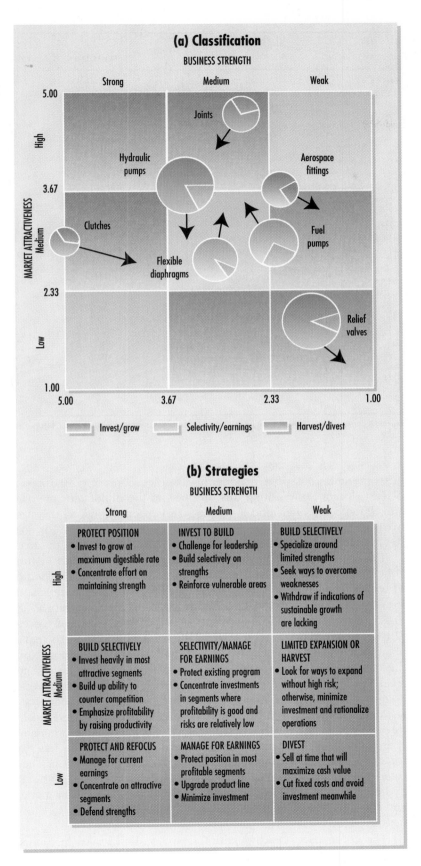

FIGURE 3-4
**Market Attractiveness —
Competitive-Position
Portfolio Classification
and Strategies**

Source: Reprinted by permission from
pages 202 and 204 of *Analysis for Strategic Marketing Decisions* by George S.
Day; Copyright © 1986 by West Publishing Company. All rights reserved.

Winning Markets
Through Market-Oriented
Strategic Planning

TABLE 3-2

FACTORS UNDERLYING
MARKET ATTRACTIVENESS
AND COMPETITIVE POSITION
IN GE MULTIFACTOR
PORTFOLIO MODEL:
HYDRAULIC-PUMPS MARKET

		WEIGHT	RATING = × (1–5)	VALUE
MARKET ATTRACTIVENESS	Overall market size	0.20	4	0.80
	Annual market growth rate	0.20	5	1.00
	Historical profit margin	0.15	4	0.60
	Competitive intensity	0.15	2	0.30
	Technological requirements	0.15	4	0.60
	Inflationary vulnerability	0.05	3	0.15
	Energy requirements	0.05	2	0.10
	Environmental impact	0.05	3	0.15
	Social/political/legal	Must be acceptable		
		1.00		3.70
BUSINESS STRENGTH	Market share	0.10	4	0.40
	Share growth	0.15	2	0.30
	Product quality	0.10	4	0.40
	Brand reputation	0.10	5	0.50
	Distribution network	0.05	4	0.20
	Promotional effectiveness	0.05	3	0.15
	Productive capacity	0.05	3	0.15
	Productive efficiency	0.05	2	0.10
	Unit costs	0.15	3	0.45
	Material supplies	0.05	5	0.25
	R&D performance	0.10	3	0.30
	Managerial personnel	0.05	4	0.20
		1.00		3.40

Source: Adapted from La Rue T. Hosmer, *Strategic Management* (Englewood Cliffs, NJ: Prentice Hall, 1982), p. 310.

ness strength, out of a maximum possible score of 5.00 for each. The analyst places a point representing this business in the multifactor matrix in Figure 3-4(a) and draws a circle around it whose size is proportional to the size of the relevant market. The company's market share of approximately 14% is shaded in. Clearly, the hydraulic-pumps business is in a fairly attractive part of the matrix.

In fact, the GE matrix is divided into nine cells, which in turn fall into three zones (Figure 3-4[b]). The three cells in the upper-left corner indicate strong SBUs in which the company should invest/grow. The diagonal cells stretching from the lower left to the upper right indicate SBUs that are medium in overall attractiveness. The company should pursue selectivity and manage for earnings in these SBUs. The three cells in the lower-right corner indicate SBUs that are low in overall attractiveness: The company should give serious thought to harvesting/divesting these companies. For example, the relief-valves business represents an SBU with a small market share in a fair-size market that is not very attractive and in which the company has a weak competitive position: It is a fit candidate for harvest/divest.[19]

Management should also forecast each SBU's expected position in the next three to five years, given current strategy. Making this determination involves analyzing where each product is in its product life cycle as well as expected competitor strategies, new technologies, economic events, and so on. The results are indicated by the length and direction of the arrows in Figure 3-4(a). For example, the hydraulic-pumps business is expected to decline slightly in market attractiveness, and the clutches business is expected to decline strongly in the company's business strength.

The company's objective is not always to build sales in each SBU. Rather, the objective might be to maintain the existing demand with fewer marketing dollars or to take cash out of the business and allow demand to fall. *Thus, the task of marketing management is to manage demand or revenue to the target level negotiated with the corporate management.* Marketing contributes to assessing each SBU's sales and profit potential, but once the SBU's objectives and budget are set, marketing's job is to carry out the plan efficiently and profitably.

CRITIQUE OF PORTFOLIO MODELS. In addition to the BCG and GE models, other portfolio models have been developed and used, particularly the Arthur D. Little model and the Shell directional-policy model.[20] Portfolio models have had a number of benefits. They have helped managers think more strategically, understand the economics of their businesses better, improve the quality of their plans, improve communication between business and corporate management, pinpoint information gaps and important issues, eliminate weaker businesses, and strengthen their investment in more promising businesses.

However, portfolio models must be used cautiously. They may lead the company to place too much emphasis on market-share growth and entry into high-growth businesses or to neglect its current businesses. The models' results are sensitive to the ratings and weights and can be manipulated to produce a desired location in the matrix. Furthermore, since these models use an averaging process, two or more businesses may end up in the same cell position but differ greatly in their underlying ratings and weights. Many businesses will end up in the middle of the matrix as a result of compromises in ratings, and this makes it hard to know what the appropriate strategy should be. Finally, the models fail to delineate the synergies between two or more businesses, which means that making decisions for one business at a time might be risky. There is a danger of terminating a losing business unit that actually provides an essential core competence needed by several other business units. Overall, though, portfolio models have improved managers' analytical and strategic capabilities and permitted them to make better decisions than they could with mere impressions.[21]

Planning New Businesses

The company's plans for its existing businesses allow it to project total sales and profits. Often, projected sales and profit are less than what corporate management wants them to be. If there is a strategic-planning gap between future desired sales and projected sales, corporate management will have to develop or acquire new businesses to fill it.

Figure 3-5 on the next page illustrates this strategic-planning gap for a major manufacturer of audiocassette tapes called Musicale (name disguised). The lowest curve projects the expected sales over the next 10 years from the company's current business portfolio. The highest curve describes the corporation's desired sales over the next 10 years. Evidently the company wants to grow much faster than its current businesses will permit. How can it fill the strategic-planning gap?

Three options are available. The first is to identify opportunities to achieve further growth within the company's current businesses *(intensive growth opportunities)*. The second is to identify opportunities to build or acquire businesses that are related to the company's current businesses *(integrative growth opportunities)*. The third is to identify opportunities to add attractive businesses that are unrelated to the company's current businesses *(diversification growth opportunities)*. The specific opportunities within each broad class are listed in Table 3-3.

INTENSIVE GROWTH. Corporate management's first course of action should be a review of whether any opportunities exist for improving its existing businesses' performance. Ansoff has proposed a useful framework for detecting new

Winning Markets
Through Market-Oriented
Strategic Planning

FIGURE 3-5

The Strategic-Planning Gap

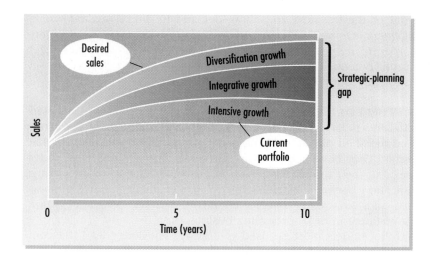

intensive growth opportunities called a *product/market expansion grid* (Figure 3-6).[22] The company first considers whether it could gain more market share with its current products in their current markets *(market-penetration strategy)*. Next it considers whether it can find or develop new markets for its current products *(market-development strategy)*. Then it considers whether it can develop new products of potential interest to its current markets *(product-development strategy)*. (Later it will also review opportunities to develop new products for new markets—*diversification strategy*.) How might Musicale use these three major intensive growth strategies to increase its sales?

Market-Penetration Strategy. There are three major approaches to increasing current products' market share in their current market. Musicale could try to encourage its current customers to buy more cassettes per period. This could work if its customers purchase cassettes infrequently and could be shown the benefits of using more cassettes for music recording or dictation. Or Musicale could try to attract the competitors' customers. This could work if Musicale noticed major weaknesses in the competitors' product or marketing program. Finally, Musicale could try to convince nonusers of cassettes to start using them. This could work if there are still many people who do not own cassette recorders or cassette players.

Market-Development Strategy. How can management look for new markets whose needs might be met by its current products? First, Musicale might try to identify potential user groups in the current sales areas whose interest in cassettes the company might stimulate. If Musicale has been selling cassette tapes only to consumer markets, it might go after office and factory markets. Second, Musicale might seek additional distribution channels in its present locations. If it has been selling its tapes only through stereo-equipment dealers, it might add mass-merchandising channels. Third, the company might consider selling in new locations in its home country or abroad. Thus, if Musicale sold only in the eastern part of the United States, it could consider entering the western states or Europe.

TABLE 3-3	MAJOR CLASSES OF GROWTH OPPORTUNITIES	
INTENSIVE GROWTH	**INTEGRATIVE GROWTH**	**DIVERSIFICATION GROWTH**
Market penetration	Backward integration	Concentric diversification
Market development	Forward integration	Horizontal diversification

FIGURE 3-6
Three Intensive Growth Strategies: Ansoff's Product/Market Expansion Grid

Source: Adapted from Igor Ansoff, "Strategies for Diversification," *Harvard Business Review,* September–October 1957, p. 114.

	Current Products	New Products
Current Markets	1. Market-penetration strategy	3. Product-development strategy
New Markets	2. Market-development strategy	(Diversification strategy)

Product-Development Strategy. In addition to penetrating and developing markets, management should consider new-product possibilities. Musicale could develop new cassette-tape features, such as a longer-playing tape and a tape that buzzes at the end of its play. It could develop different quality levels of tape, such as a higher-quality tape for fine-music listeners and a lower-quality tape for the mass market. Or it could research an alternative technology to cassette tape such as compact discs and digital audio tape.

By examining these three intensive growth strategies, management may discover several ways to grow. Still, that growth may not be enough, in which case management must also examine integrative growth opportunities.

INTEGRATIVE GROWTH. Often a business's sales and profits can be increased through backward, forward, or horizontal integration within its industry. Musicale might acquire one or more of its suppliers (such as plastic-material producers) to gain more control or generate more profit *(backward integration).* Or Musicale might acquire some wholesalers or retailers, especially if they are highly profitable *(forward integration).* Finally, Musicale might acquire one or more competitors, provided that the government does not bar this move *(horizontal integration).*

Through investigating possible integration moves, the company may discover additional sources of sales-volume increases over the next 10 years. These new sources may still not deliver the desired sales volume, however. In that case, the company must consider diversification.

DIVERSIFICATION GROWTH. Diversification growth makes sense when good opportunities can be found outside the present businesses. A good opportunity is one in which the industry is highly attractive and the company has the mix of business strengths to be successful. Three types of diversification are possible. The company could seek new products that have technological and/or marketing synergies with existing product lines, even though the new products themselves may appeal to a different group of customers *(concentric diversification strategy).* For example, Musicale might start a computer-tape manufacturing operation because it knows how to manufacture audiocassette tape. Second, the company might search for new products that could appeal to its current customers even though the new products are technologically unrelated to its current product line *(horizontal diversification strategy).* For example, Musicale might produce cassette-holding trays, even though producing them requires a different manufacturing process. Finally, the company might seek new businesses that have no relationship to the company's current technology, products, or markets *(conglomerate diversification strategy).* Musicale might want to consider such new business areas as fax machines, franchising, or diet products.

Downsizing Older Businesses

To pursue growth, companies must not only develop new businesses but also carefully divest tired old businesses in order to release needed resources and reduce costs. Weak businesses require a disproportionate amount of managerial attention. Because managers should focus on a company's growth opportunities, many companies have recently downsized and reengineered their businesses. They are pursuing three strategies: pruning, harvesting, and divesting. We discussed harvesting and divesting when we talked about the BCG matrix a few pages previously. The aim of *pruning* is to remove dead or dying parts of the business in order to improve its performance. For example, a hospital might find that it is devoting too much physical space to services that draw few patients—for example, an adult day-care program, a specialized burn unit, and so on. The space might be reallocated to other services that are in more demand. More generally, a company might decide to prune certain products, services, market segments, or specific customers. (For further discussion of marketing strategies during downsizing, see Chapter 12.)

BUSINESS STRATEGIC PLANNING

Having examined corporate management's strategic-planning tasks, we can now examine the strategic-planning tasks facing individual business unit managers. The business unit strategic-planning process consists of the eight steps shown in Figure 3-7. We examine each of these steps in the sections that follow.

Business Mission

Each business unit needs to define its specific mission within the broader company mission. Thus, the television-lighting-equipment company described earlier must define its business purpose more specifically—for example: "The company aims to target major television studios and become their vendor of choice for lighting technologies that represent the most advanced and reliable lighting arrangements." Notice that this mission does not attempt to win business from smaller television studios, win business on the basis of being lowest in price, or include plans to venture into non-lighting products.

FIGURE 3-7
The Business Strategic-Planning Process

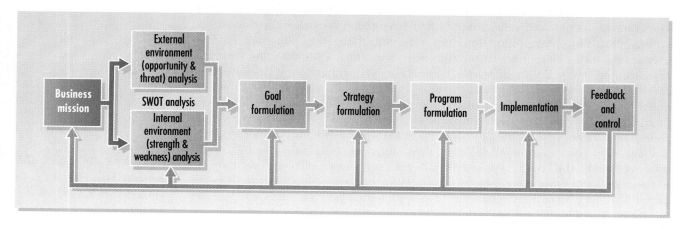

External Environment Analysis (Opportunity and Threat Analysis)

Once the business unit has formulated its mission statement, the business manager knows the parts of the environment it needs to monitor to achieve its goals. For example, the television-lighting-equipment company needs to watch the growth rate in the number of television studios, its own financial health, current and new competitors, new technological developments, laws and regulations that might affect equipment design or marketing, and distribution channels for selling lighting equipment.

In general, a business unit has to monitor key external *macroenvironment forces* (demographic/economic, technological, political/legal, and social/cultural) and significant *microenvironment actors* (customers, competitors, distribution channels, suppliers) that affect its ability to earn profits. The business unit should set up a *marketing intelligence system* to track trends and important developments. For each trend or development, management needs to identify the associated opportunities and threats.

OPPORTUNITIES.   A major purpose of environmental scanning is to discern new marketing opportunities.

❖   A MARKETING OPPORTUNITY is an area of buyer need in which a company can perform profitably.

Opportunities can be classified according to their *attractiveness* and their *success probability*. The company's success probability depends on whether its business strengths not only match the key success requirements for operating in the target market but also exceed those of its competitors. Mere competence does not constitute a competitive advantage. The best-performing company will be the one that can generate the greatest customer value and sustain it over time.

In the opportunity matrix in Figure 3-8(a) on page 82, the best marketing opportunities facing the TV-lighting-equipment company are listed in the upper-left cell (#1); management should pursue these opportunities. The opportunities in the lower-right cell (#4) are too minor to consider. The opportunities in the upper-right cell (#2) and lower-left cell (#3) should be monitored in the event that any of them improve in their attractiveness and success probability.

THREATS.   Some developments in the external environment represent threats.

❖   An ENVIRONMENTAL THREAT is a challenge posed by an unfavorable trend or development that would lead, in the absence of defensive marketing action, to deterioration in sales or profit.

Threats should be classified according to their *seriousness* and *probability of occurrence*. Figure 3-8(b) illustrates the threat matrix facing the TV-lighting-equipment company. The threats in the upper-left cell are major threats, since they can seriously hurt the company and have a high probability of occurrence. To deal with these threats, the company needs to prepare contingency plans that spell out what changes the company can make before or during the threat's occurrence. The threats in the lower-right cell are very minor and can be ignored. The threats in the upper-right and lower-left cells do not require contingency planning but need to be carefully monitored in the event that they grow more serious.

Once management has identified the major opportunities and threats facing a specific business unit, it can characterize that business's overall attractiveness. Four outcomes are possible:

♦   An *ideal business* is high in major opportunities and low in major threats.

♦   A *speculative business* is high in both major opportunities and threats.

FIGURE 3-8
Opportunity and Threat Ma-trixes

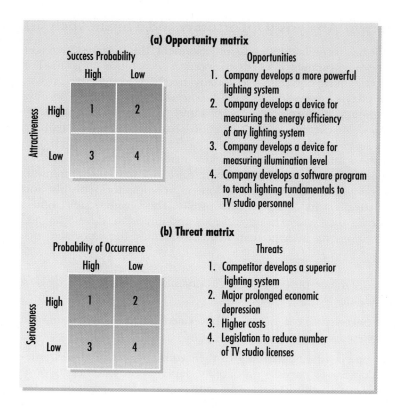

(a) Opportunity matrix

Success Probability

	High	Low
High	1	2
Low	3	4

Attractiveness

Opportunities

1. Company develops a more powerful lighting system
2. Company develops a device for measuring the energy efficiency of any lighting system
3. Company develops a device for measuring illumination level
4. Company develops a software program to teach lighting fundamentals to TV studio personnel

(b) Threat matrix

Probability of Occurrence

	High	Low
High	1	2
Low	3	4

Seriousness

Threats

1. Competitor develops a superior lighting system
2. Major prolonged economic depression
3. Higher costs
4. Legislation to reduce number of TV studio licenses

◆ A *mature business* is low in major opportunities and low in threats.

◆ A *troubled business* is low in opportunities and high in threats.

Internal Environment Analysis (Strengths/Weaknesses Analysis)

It is one thing to discern attractive opportunities in the environment; it is another to have the competencies needed to succeed in these opportunities. Thus each business needs to evaluate its internal strengths and weaknesses periodically. It can do so by using a form similar to the one shown in the Marketing Memo titled "Checklist for Performing Strengths/Weaknesses Analysis." Management—or an outside consultant—reviews the business's marketing, financial, manufacturing, and organizational competencies and rates each factor as a major strength, minor strength, neutral factor, minor weakness, or major weakness.

Clearly, the business does not have to correct all its weaknesses, nor should it gloat about all its strengths. The big question is whether the business should limit itself to those opportunities where it possesses the required strengths or should consider better opportunities where it might have to acquire or develop certain strengths. For example, managers at Texas Instruments (TI) split between those who wanted TI to stick to industrial electronics (where it had clear strength) and those who wanted the company to continue introducing consumer electronic products (where it lacked some required marketing strengths).

Sometimes a business does poorly not because its departments lack the required strengths but because they do not work together as a team. In one major electronics company the engineers look down on the salespeople as "engineers who couldn't make it" and the salespeople look down on the service people as "salespeople who couldn't make it." It is therefore critically important to assess in-

MARKETING MEMO

CHECKLIST FOR PERFORMING STRENGTHS/WEAKNESSES ANALYSIS

	PERFORMANCE					IMPORTANCE		
	MAJOR STRENGTH	MINOR STRENGTH	NEUTRAL	MINOR WEAK-NESS	MAJOR WEAK-NESS	HI	MED	LOW
MARKETING								
1. Company reputation	____	____	____	____	____	____	____	____
2. Market share	____	____	____	____	____	____	____	____
3. Product quality	____	____	____	____	____	____	____	____
4. Service quality	____	____	____	____	____	____	____	____
5. Pricing effectiveness	____	____	____	____	____	____	____	____
6. Distribution effectiveness	____	____	____	____	____	____	____	____
7. Promotion effectiveness	____	____	____	____	____	____	____	____
8. Sales force effectiveness	____	____	____	____	____	____	____	____
9. Innovation effectiveness	____	____	____	____	____	____	____	____
10. Geographical coverage	____	____	____	____	____	____	____	____
FINANCE								
11. Cost/availability of capital	____	____	____	____	____	____	____	____
12. Cash flow	____	____	____	____	____	____	____	____
13. Financial stability	____	____	____	____	____	____	____	____
MANUFACTURING								
14. Facilities	____	____	____	____	____	____	____	____
15. Economies of scale	____	____	____	____	____	____	____	____
16. Capacity	____	____	____	____	____	____	____	____
17. Able dedicated work force	____	____	____	____	____	____	____	____
18. Ability to produce on time	____	____	____	____	____	____	____	____
19. Technical manufacturing skill	____	____	____	____	____	____	____	____
ORGANIZATION								
20. Visionary capable leadership	____	____	____	____	____	____	____	____
21. Dedicated employees	____	____	____	____	____	____	____	____
22. Entrepreneurial orientation	____	____	____	____	____	____	____	____
23. Flexible/responsive	____	____	____	____	____	____	____	____

terdepartmental working relationships as part of the internal environmental audit. Honeywell does exactly this:

HONEYWELL Every year, Honeywell asks each of its departments to rate its own strengths and weaknesses and those of the other departments with which it interacts. The notion is that each department is a "supplier" to some departments and a "customer" of other departments. Thus, if Honeywell engineers frequently underestimate the cost and completion time of new products, their "internal customers" (manufacturing, finance, and sales) will all be hurt. Once each department's weaknesses are identified, work can be undertaken to correct them.

Winning Markets Through Market-Oriented Strategic Planning

George Stalk, a leading BCG consultant, suggests that winning companies are those that have achieved superior in-company capabilities, not just core competences.[23] Every company must manage some basic processes, such as new-product development, sales generation, and order fulfillment. Each process creates value and each process requires interdepartmental teamwork. Although each department may possess specific core competences, the challenge is to develop superior competitive capability in managing the company's key processes. Stalk calls this *capabilities-based competition*.

Goal Formulation

The overall evaluation of a company's strengths, weaknesses, opportunities, and threats is called *SWOT analysis*. Once the company has performed its SWOT analysis, it can proceed to develop specific goals for the planning period. This stage of the business strategic-planning process is called *goal formulation*. Managers use the term *goals* to describe objectives that are specific with respect to magnitude and time. Turning objectives into measurable goals facilitates management planning, implementation, and control.

Very few businesses pursue only one objective. Rather most business units pursue a mix of objectives including profitability, sales growth, market-share improvement, risk containment, innovativeness, reputation, and so on. The business unit sets these objectives and then *manages by objectives* (MBO). For an MBO system to work, the business unit's various objectives must meet four criteria:

◆ First, objectives must be arranged *hierarchically*, from the most to the least important. For example, the business unit's key objective for the period may be to increase the rate of return on investment. This can be accomplished by increasing the profit level and/or reducing the amount of invested capital. Profit itself can be increased by increasing revenue and/or reducing expenses. Revenue can be increased in turn by increasing market share and/or prices. By proceeding this way, the business can move from broad objectives to specific objectives for specific departments and individuals.

◆ Second, objectives should be stated *quantitatively* whenever possible. The objective "increase the return on investment (ROI)" is better stated as the goal "increase ROI to 15%" or, even better, "increase ROI to 15% within two years."

◆ Third, goals should be *realistic*. They should arise from an analysis of the business unit's opportunities and strengths, not from wishful thinking.

◆ Finally, the company's objectives must be *consistent*. It is not possible to maximize both sales and profits simultaneously.

Other important trade-offs include short-term profit versus long-term growth, deep penetration of existing markets versus developing new markets, profit goals versus nonprofit goals, and high growth versus low risk. Each choice in this set of goal trade-offs calls for a different marketing strategy.

Strategy Formulation

Goals indicate what a business unit wants to achieve; *strategy* is a game plan for how to get there. Every business must tailor a strategy for achieving its goals. Although many types of strategies are available, Michael Porter has condensed them into three generic types that provide a good starting point for strategic thinking: overall cost leadership, differentiation, and focus.[24]

◆ *Overall cost leadership:* Here the business works hard to achieve the lowest production and distribution costs so that it can price lower than its competitors and win a large

PART 1

Understanding
Marketing
Management

market share. Firms pursuing this strategy must be good at engineering, purchasing, manufacturing, and physical distribution. They need less skill in marketing. Texas Instruments is a leading practitioner of this strategy. The problem with this strategy is that other firms will usually emerge with still lower costs (from the Far East, for example) and hurt the firm that rested its whole future on being low cost. The real key is for the firm to achieve the lowest costs among those competitors adopting a similar differentiation or focus strategy.

- *Differentiation:* Here the business concentrates on achieving superior performance in an important customer benefit area valued by a large part of the market. It can strive to be the service leader, the quality leader, the style leader, the technology leader, and so on, but it is not possible to be all of these things. The firm cultivates those strengths that will give it a competitive advantage in one or more benefits. Thus the firm seeking quality leadership must make or buy the best components, put them together expertly, inspect them carefully, and so on. This has been Canon's strategy in the copy-machine field.

- *Focus:* Here the business focuses on one or more narrow market segments rather than going after a large market. The firm gets to know these segments' needs and pursues either cost leadership or a form of differentiation within the target segment. Armstrong Rubber has specialized in making superior tires for farm-equipment vehicles and recreational vehicles and keeps looking for new niches to serve.

According to Porter, those firms pursuing the same strategy directed to the same target market or segment constitute a *strategic group*. The firm that carries off that strategy best will make the most profits. Thus the lowest-cost firm among those pursuing a low-cost strategy will do the best. Firms that do not pursue a clear strategy—"middle-of-the-roaders"—do the worst. For example, International Harvester fell upon hard times because it did not stand out in its industry as lowest in cost, highest in perceived value, or best in serving some market segment. Middle-of-the-roaders try to be good on all strategic dimensions, but since strategic dimensions require different and often inconsistent ways of organizing the firm, these firms end up being not particularly excellent at anything.

Companies are also discovering that they might need to be strategic partners if they hope to be effective. Even giant companies—AT&T, IBM, Philips, Siemens— often cannot achieve leadership, either nationally or globally, without forming *strategic alliances* with domestic and/or multinational companies that complement or leverage their capabilities and resources. Just doing business in another country may require the firm to license its product, form a joint venture with a local firm, buy from local suppliers to meet "domestic content" requirements, and so on. As a result of these complexities, many firms are rapidly developing global strategic networks. And victory is going to those who build the better global network. For more details, see the Vision 2000 feature on page 86 titled "Strange Bedfellows: Pursuing Global Growth Through Strategic Alliances." [25]

Many strategic alliances take the form of *marketing alliances*. These fall into four major categories. [26]

- *Product and/or service alliances:* One company licenses another to produce its product, or two companies jointly market their complementary products or a new product. For instance, Apple joined with Digital Vax to co-design, co-manufacture, and co-market a new product. Sprint recently teamed up with RCA and Sony, offering long-distance callers a Sony Walkman or an RCA color TV in exchange for switching their telephone service to Sprint. H&R Block and Hyatt Legal Services—two service businesses—have also joined together in a marketing alliance.

- *Promotional alliances:* One company agrees to carry a promotion for another company's product or service. For example, Burger King teamed up with Disney to offer Lion King and Pocahontas figurines and other products to people buying its burgers. Similarly, a bank may agree to display paintings from a local art gallery on its walls.

Strange Bedfellows: Pursuing Global Growth Through Strategic Alliances

Open a newspaper's business pages on any given day and you might think you've flipped to the weddings listings. Except the names linked are those of companies—and often competing companies at that: "Northwest Airlines and KLM Link to Benefit Business Flier" or "IBM and Philips Electronics Join in Chip Venture." While the 1980s was the decade of mergers and takeovers, the 1990s are seeing a wave of strategic alliances and joint ventures.

Why the boom in alliances? First, they allow companies to gain added muscle without growing any bigger. Second, and perhaps more important in the global marketplace, many companies have discovered that they lack resources and access to newly opened markets. According to Jose Collazo, there are eight strategic reasons to enter into an alliance:

♦ Fill gaps in your current market and technological bases

♦ Turn excess manufacturing capacity into profits

♦ Reduce your risk and entry costs into new markets

♦ Accelerate product introductions

♦ Produce economies of scale

♦ Overcome legal and trade barriers

♦ Extend the scope of your existing operations

♦ Cut your exit costs when divesting operations

MCI's joint ventures with British Telecommunications (BT) and Mexico's Grupo Financiero Banamex-Accival (Banacci) are in sync with these reasons and fulfill the strategy outlined in its 1994 annual report: "MCI has become a major player in worldwide telecommunications by pursuing a clear, consistent strategy over the years: (1) grow market share profitably, (2) expand globally, and (3) leverage our core skills into new markets."

Despite the many good reasons for combining forces, a surprisingly high percentage of alliances end in failure. A study by McKinsey revealed that roughly one third of 49 alliances ended up as flops, failing to live up to the partners' expectations. But such painful lessons are teaching companies how to craft a winning alliance. Three keys seem to be:

♦ *Strategic fit:* Before even considering an alliance, companies need to assess their own core competencies. Then they need to find a partner that will complement them in business lines, geographic positions, or competencies. One good example of strategic fit is Northwest Airlines and KLM Royal Dutch Airlines' joint creation of a "World Business Class" service for the business flier. By joining together, the two airlines have been able to offer a new service for more routes than either could do alone.

♦ *A focus on the long term:* Rather than joining forces to save a few dollars, strategic partners should focus more on gains that can be harvested for years to come. Corning, the $3-billion-a-year glass and ceramics maker, is renowned for making partnerships work and even defines itself as "a network of organizations." That network includes German electronics giant Siemens and Mexico's biggest glassmaker, Vitro.

♦ *Flexibility:* Alliances can last only if they're flexible. One example of a flexible partnership is Merck's alliance with AB Astra of Sweden. Merck started out simply with U.S. rights to its partner's new drugs. For the next phase, Merck set up a new corporation to handle the partnership's $500-million-a-year business and sold half the equity to Astra.

Sources: Julie Cohen Mason, "Strategic Alliances: Partnering for Success," *Management Review*, May 1993, pp. 10–15; Stratford Sherman, "Are Strategic Alliances Working?" *Fortune*, September 21, 1992, pp. 77–78; Edwin Whenmouth, "Rivals Become Partners: Japan Seeks Links with U.S. and European Firms," *Industry Week*, February 1, 1993, pp. 11–12, 14; and John Naisbitt, *The Global Paradox* (New York: William Morrow, 1994), pp. 18–21.

♦ *Logistics alliances:* One company offers logistical support services for another company's product. For example, Abbott Laboratories warehouses and delivers all of 3M's medical and surgical products to hospitals across the United States.

♦ *Pricing collaborations:* One or more companies join in a special pricing collaboration. It is common for hotel and rental car companies to offer mutual price discounts.

Understanding
Marketing
Management

Companies need to give creative thought to finding partners who might complement their strengths and offset their weaknesses. When well-managed, alliances allow companies to obtain a greater sales impact at less cost.

Program Formulation

Once the business unit has developed its principal strategies, it must work out detailed supporting programs. Thus if the business has decided to attain technological leadership, it must plan programs to strengthen its R&D department, gather technological intelligence, develop leading-edge products, train the technical sales force, develop ads to communicate its technological leadership, and so on.

Once the programs are tentatively formulated, the marketing people must evaluate the program costs. Questions arise such as: Is participating in a particular trade show worth it? Will a specific sales contest pay for itself? Will hiring another salesperson contribute to the bottom line? Activity-based accounting should be applied to each marketing activity to determine whether the activity is likely to produce sufficient results to justify the cost.[27]

Implementation

A clear strategy and a well-thought-out supporting program may be useless if the firm fails to implement them carefully. Indeed, strategy is only one of seven elements, according to the McKinsey Consulting Firm, that the best-managed companies exhibit.[28] The McKinsey 7-S framework for business success is shown in Figure 3-9. The first three elements—strategy, structure, and systems—are considered the "hardware" of success. The next four—style, staff, skills, and shared values—are the "software."

The first "soft" element, *style,* means that company employees share a common way of thinking and behaving. Thus everyone at McDonald's smiles at the customer, and IBM employees are very professional in their customer dealings. The second, *staff,* means that the company has hired able people, trained them well, and assigned them to the right jobs. The third, *skills,* means that the employees have the skills needed to carry out the company's strategy. The fourth, *shared values,* means that the employees share the same guiding values. When these soft elements are present, companies are usually more successful at strategy implementation.[29]

Feedback and Control

As it implements its strategy, the firm needs to track the results and monitor new developments in the internal and external environments. Some environments are fairly stable from year to year. Other environments evolve slowly in a fairly predictable way. Still other environments change rapidly in major and unpredictable ways. Nonetheless, the company can count on one thing: The environment will eventually change. And when it does, the company will need to review and revise its implementation, programs, strategies, or even objectives. Consider what happened at computer-services giant Electronic Data Systems Corp. (EDS):

EDS, COMPUTER SCIENCES CORP., AND ANDERSEN CONSULTING For years EDS saw its base business—outsourcing—grow by 25% annually, but in 1993 that percentage dropped to a mere 7 percent. EDS's primary business had been managing the data processing operations of clients such as Continental Airlines and General Motors. But technological developments have led to a shift from mainframes to new platforms, including networks of personal computers. There was thus less demand for EDS's core talent: providing lots of software engineers and technicians to write programs and keep them running in giant data centers. Customers now want computer-services companies to act as management consultants to help reengineer key business processes. Computer Sciences Corp. and Andersen Consulting have already established themselves in this area, and EDS is undergoing a rocky transition as it attempts to respond

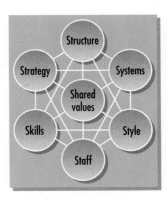

FIGURE 3-9
The McKinsey 7-S Framework

Source: McKinsey 7-S Framework from *In Search of Excellence: Lessons from America's Best Run Companies* by Thomas J. Peters and Robert H. Waterman, Jr. Copyright © 1982 by Thomas J. Peters and Robert H. Waterman, Jr. Reprinted by permission of HarperCollins Publishers, Inc.

to the changed environment. To counter loss of market share, EDS is cutting costs, expanding efforts in client-server setups, hiring more consultants for reengineering, and developing alliances with telecommunications partners.[30]

A company's strategic fit with the environment will inevitably erode because the market environment almost always changes faster than the company's 7-S's. Thus it is possible for a company to remain efficient while it loses effectiveness. Peter Drucker pointed out that it is more important to "do the right thing" (effectiveness) than "to do things right" (efficiency). The most successful companies excel at both.

Once an organization fails to respond to a changed environment, it becomes increasingly hard to restore its lost position. Consider what happened to Wang Laboratories:

WANG LABORATORIES When An Wang was running Wang Laboratories in the 1980s, the company's future couldn't have looked brighter. Its Wang computers were hot products among corporate customers, who used them for word processing. Yet, Wang's equipment couldn't communicate with machines made by other companies. This strategy locked in business at first, but customers eventually began asking for "open" systems, which would have made Wang hardware and software compatible with other systems. "Wang became addicted to the high margins of proprietary systems and wouldn't change," says John McCarthy. Wang's stubbornness crippled the company, which filed for bankruptcy in 1992. While the company managed to emerge unbloodied from Chapter 11 in 1993, the rapidly evolving PC technology had transformed its computers into high-tech relics. Now, with the help of new CEO Joseph Tucci, the company is racing into the software and high-tech consulting business. The challenges are formidable: Wang has to transform itself from a slow-moving hardware company into a fast-paced service provider; it must struggle to overcome the taint of its bankruptcy; and Tucci must persuade customers who own Wangs not to abandon their aging machines.[31]

Organizations, especially large ones, are subject to inertia. They are set up as efficient machines, and it is difficult to change one part without adjusting everything else. Yet organizations can be changed through leadership, preferably in advance of a crisis but certainly in the midst of one. The key to organizational health is the organization's willingness to examine the changing environment and to adopt appropriate new goals and behaviors. High-performance organizations continuously monitor the environment and attempt through flexible strategic planning to maintain a viable fit with the evolving environment.

THE MARKETING PROCESS

Planning at the corporate, division, and business levels is an integral part of the marketing process. To fully understand the marketing process, we must first look at how a company defines its business.

The task of any business is to deliver value to the market at a profit. There are at least two views of the *value-delivery process*.[32] The traditional view is that the firm makes something and then sells it (Figure 3-10[a]). For example, Thomas Edison invents the phonograph and then hires people to make and sell it. In this view, marketing takes place in the second half of the value-delivery process. The traditional view assumes that the company knows what to make and that the market will buy enough units to produce profits for the company.

Companies that subscribe to this traditional view have the best chance of succeeding in economies marked by goods shortages. For example, many consumers in Eastern Europe are desperate for goods and will buy whatever is made. They are generally not fussy about quality, features, or style. But the traditional view of

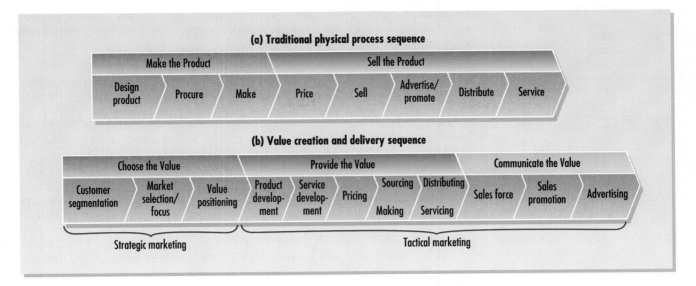

FIGURE 3-10

Two Views of the Value-Delivery Process

Source: Michael J. Lanning and Edward G. Michaels, "A Business Is a Value Delivery System," McKinsey staff paper No. 41, June 1988. © McKinsey & Co., Inc.

the business process will not work in more competitive economies where people face abundant choices. The "mass market" is actually splintering into many micromarkets, each with its own wants, perceptions, preferences, and buying criteria. The smart competitor therefore must design the offer for well-defined target markets.

This belief is at the core of the new view of business processes, which places marketing at the beginning of the business planning process. Instead of emphasizing making and selling, companies that take this view of the business process see themselves as part of a value creation and delivery sequence (Figure 3-10[b]). This sequence consists of three parts.

The first phase, choosing the value, represents the "homework" that marketing must do before any product exists. The marketing staff must segment the market, select the appropriate market target, and develop the offer's value positioning. The formula *segmentation, targeting, positioning (STP)* is the essence of strategic marketing.

Once the business unit has chosen the value, it is ready to provide the value. The tangible product's specifications and services must be detailed, a target price must be established, and the product must be made and distributed. Developing specific product features, prices, and distribution occur at this stage and are part of *tactical marketing,* the second phase of the value creation and delivery sequence.

The task in the third phase is communicating the value. Here further tactical marketing occurs in utilizing the sales force, sales promotion, advertising, and other promotional tasks to inform the market about the product. As Figure 3-10(b) shows, the marketing process begins before there is a product and continues while it is being developed and after it becomes available. The Japanese have further developed this view by promulgating the following concepts:

◆ *Zero customer feedback time:* Customer feedback should be continuously collected after purchase to learn how to improve the product and its marketing.

◆ *Zero product-improvement time:* The company should evaluate all the customers' and employees' improvement ideas and introduce the most valued and feasible improvements as soon as possible.

Winning Markets
Through Market-Oriented
Strategic Planning

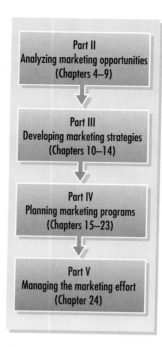

FIGURE 3-11

The Marketing Management Process

◆ *Zero purchasing time:* The company should receive the required parts and supplies continuously through just-in-time arrangements with suppliers. By lowering its inventories, the company can reduce its costs.

◆ *Zero setup time:* The company should be able to manufacture any of its products as soon as they are ordered, without facing high setup time or costs.

◆ *Zero defects:* The products should be of high quality and free of flaws.

To carry out their responsibilities, marketing managers—whether at the corporate, division, business, or product level—follow a marketing process. Working within the plans set by the levels above them, product managers come up with a marketing plan for individual products, lines, or brands.

❖ The **MARKETING PROCESS** consists of analyzing marketing opportunities, developing marketing strategies, planning marketing programs, and managing the marketing effort.

These steps are listed in Figure 3-11, along with the chapters in this book that describe each step in detail. We will illustrate each step here in connection with the following situation:

> *Zeus, Inc. (name disguised) operates in several industries, including chemicals, energy, typewriters, and consumer goods. The company is organized into SBUs. Corporate management is considering what to do with its Atlas typewriter division. At present, Atlas produces standard office electric typewriters. The market for standard electric typewriters is declining. On a growth-share matrix, this business would be a dog. Zeus's corporate management wants Atlas's marketing group to produce a strong turnaround plan. Marketing management has to come up with a convincing marketing plan, sell corporate management on the plan, and then implement and control it.*

The sections that follow apply to marketing planning at all levels of the organization. Later in this chapter, we will examine the components of a specific marketing plan developed to achieve the goals for a particular product line.

Analyzing Marketing Opportunities

The first task facing Atlas's marketing managers is to analyze the long-run opportunities in this market for improving the unit's performance. These managers recognize the abundance of opportunities in the burgeoning business-office-equipment field. The "office of the future" is fast becoming a reality, and high investment in this area is likely to continue in the coming decades. Even though the U.S. economy is increasingly becoming a service economy, offices are often poorly organized for such elementary tasks as typing, filing, storing, and transmitting information, especially in terms of the latest technologies. Many manufacturers are active in this market and are seeking to provide integrated systems of microcomputers, duplicating equipment, telecommunications equipment, and the like. Among them are IBM, Xerox, Olivetti, Canon, and NEC. All are engaged in developing office hardware and software that will increase office productivity.

Atlas's long-run goal is to become a complete office-equipment manufacturer. At present, however, it must come up with a plan for improving its product line. Even within typewriters, there are still some opportunities. Atlas can scale down its office typewriter to a version for the home market and advertise it as an "office-quality" home typewriter. It can design an electronic or "smart" typewriter. It can also consider designing a word processor, which would have more memory and text-editing capability than an electronic typewriter. Or it can develop a computer workstation that performs a large number of functions. Ultimately, Atlas can work on voice-activated typewriters.

To evaluate its opportunities, Atlas needs to operate a reliable marketing information system (Chapter 4). Marketing research is an indispensable marketing tool, because companies can serve their customers well only by researching their needs and wants, their locations, their buying practices, and so on. At the very least, Atlas needs a good internal accounting system that reports current sales by typewriter model, industry, location, salesperson, and distribution channel. In addition, Atlas's executives should continuously be collecting market intelligence on customers, competitors, dealers, and so on. The marketing people should conduct formal research in secondary sources, running focus groups and conducting telephone, mail, and personal surveys. By analyzing the collected data using advanced statistical methods and models, the company will gain useful information on how sales are influenced by various marketing forces.

The purpose of market research is to gather significant information about the marketing environment (Chapter 5). Atlas's *microenvironment* consists of all the players who affect the company's ability to produce and sell typewriters—namely, suppliers, marketing intermediaries, customers, and competitors. Atlas's *macroenvironment* consists of demographic, economic, physical, technological, political/legal, and social/cultural forces that affect its sales and profits. An important part of gathering environmental information includes measuring market potential and forecasting future demand.

To the extent that Atlas considers manufacturing typewriting equipment for the home, it needs to understand *consumer markets* (Chapter 6). It needs to know: How many households plan to buy typewriters or computers? Who buys and why do they buy? What are they looking for in the way of features and prices? Where do they shop? What are their images of different brands?

Atlas also sells to *business markets,* including large corporations, professional firms, retailers, and government agencies (Chapter 7). Large organizations use purchasing agents or buying committees who are skilled at evaluating equipment. Atlas needs to gain a full understanding of how organizational buyers buy. And, whether selling to consumers or organizations, Atlas needs a sales force that is well trained in presenting product benefits.

Atlas must also pay close attention to competitors (Chapter 8), anticipating its competitors' moves and knowing how to react quickly and decisively. It may want to initiate some surprise moves, in which case it needs to anticipate how its competitors will respond.

Once Atlas has analyzed its market opportunities, it is ready to select target markets. Modern marketing practice calls for dividing the market into major market segments, evaluating each segment, and selecting and targeting those market segments that the company can best serve (Chapter 9).

Developing Marketing Strategies

Suppose Atlas decides to target the home customer, electronic typewriter market. It needs to develop a *differentiating and positioning* strategy for that target market (Chapter 10). Should Atlas be the "Cadillac" of typewriters, offering a superior product at a premium price with excellent service that is well advertised and aimed at more affluent homeowners? Should it build a simple low-price electronic typewriter aimed at the more price-conscious homeowners? Or should it aim for a product of medium quality sold at a medium price?

Once Atlas decides on its product positioning, it must initiate new-product development, testing, and launching (Chapter 11). Different decision tools and controls are needed at different stages of the new-product development process.

Winning Markets
Through Market-Oriented
Strategic Planning

After launch, the product's strategy will have to be modified at the different stages in the product life cycle: introduction, growth, maturity, and decline (Chapter 12). Furthermore, strategy choice will depend on whether the firm plays the role of market leader, challenger, follower, or nicher (Chapter 13). Finally, strategy will have to take into account changing global opportunities and challenges (Chapter 14).

Planning Marketing Programs

To transform marketing strategy into marketing programs, marketing managers must make basic decisions on marketing expenditures, marketing mix, and marketing allocation. First, Atlas must decide what level of marketing expenditures is necessary to achieve its marketing objectives. Companies typically establish their marketing budget at a percentage of the sales goal. A particular company may spend more than the normal percentage ratio in the hope of achieving a higher market share.

Second, the company also has to decide how to divide the total marketing budget among the various tools in the marketing mix. Marketing mix is one of the key concepts in modern marketing theory.

❖ **MARKETING MIX** is the set of marketing tools that the firm uses to pursue its marketing objectives in the target market.

There are literally dozens of marketing-mix tools. McCarthy popularized a four-factor classification of these tools called the *four Ps:* product, price, place (i.e., distribution), and promotion.[33] The particular marketing variables under each *P* are shown in Figure 3-12. Marketing-mix decisions must be made for both distribution channels and final consumers. Figure 3-13 shows the company preparing an *offer mix* of products, services, and prices, and utilizing a *promotion mix* of sales promotion, advertising, sales force, public relations, direct mail, and telemarketing to reach the distribution channels and the target customers.

Not all marketing-mix variables can be adjusted in the short run. Typically, the firm can change its price, sales force size, and advertising expenditures in the short run. It can develop new products and modify its distribution channels only

FIGURE 3-12

The Four Ps of the Marketing Mix

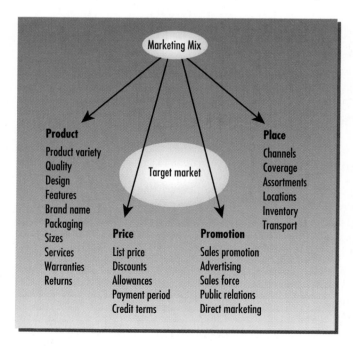

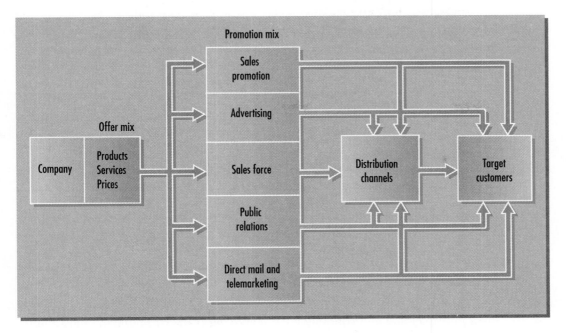

FIGURE 3-13
Marketing-Mix Strategy

in the long run. Thus the firm typically makes fewer period-to-period marketing-mix changes in the short run than the number of marketing-mix variables might suggest.

Finally, marketers must decide on the allocation of the marketing budget to the various products, channels, promotion media, and sales areas. How many dollars should support Atlas's electric versus electronic typewriters? Direct versus distributor sales? Direct-mail advertising versus trade-magazine advertising? East Coast markets versus West Coast markets? To make these allocations, marketing managers use *sales-response functions* that show how sales would be affected by the amount of money put into each possible application.

The most basic marketing-mix tool is *product*—the firm's tangible offer to the market, which includes the product quality, design, features, branding, and packaging (Chapter 15). As part of its product offering, Atlas provides various services, such as leasing, delivery, repair, and training (Chapter 16). Such support services can provide a competitive advantage in the globally competitive marketplace.

A critical marketing-mix tool is *price,* the amount of money that customers pay for the product (Chapter 17). Atlas has to decide on wholesale and retail prices, discounts, allowances, and credit terms. Its price should be commensurate with the offer's perceived value. If it is not, buyers will turn to competitors' products.

Place, another key marketing-mix tool, includes the various activities the company undertakes to make the product accessible and available to target customers (Chapters 18 and 19). Atlas must identify, recruit, and link various marketing facilitators to supply its products and services efficiently to the target market. It must understand the various types of retailers, wholesalers, and physical-distribution firms and how they make their decisions.

Promotion, the fourth marketing-mix tool, includes all the activities the company undertakes to communicate and promote its products to the target market (Chapters 20 to 23). Atlas has to hire, train, and motivate salespeople. It has to set up communication and promotion programs consisting of advertising, sales promotion, public relations, and direct and online marketing.

Winning Markets
Through Market-Oriented
Strategic Planning

Note that the 4Ps represent the sellers' view of the marketing tools available for influencing buyers. From a buyer's point of view, each marketing tool is designed to deliver a customer benefit. Robert Lauterborn suggested that the sellers' 4Ps correspond to the customers 4Cs.[34]

4PS	4CS
Product	Customer needs and wants
Price	Cost to the customer
Place	Convenience
Promotion	Communication

Thus, winning companies will be those who can meet customer needs economically and conveniently and with effective communication.

Managing the Marketing Effort

The final step in the marketing process is organizing the marketing resources and then implementing and controlling the marketing plan. The company must build a marketing organization that is capable of *implementing* the marketing plan (Chapter 24). In a small company, one person might carry out all the marketing tasks: marketing research, selling, advertising, customer servicing, and so on. Large companies (such as Atlas) will have several marketing specialists: salespeople, sales managers, marketing researchers, advertising personnel, product and brand managers, market-segment managers, and customer-service personnel.

Marketing departments are typically headed by a marketing vice-president who performs three tasks. The first is to coordinate the work of all of the marketing personnel. Atlas's marketing vice-president must ensure, for example, that the advertising manager works closely with the sales manager in timing promotions. The second task is to work closely with the other functional vice-presidents. If Atlas's marketing people advertise its new electronic typewriter as a quality product, but R&D does not design a quality product or manufacturing fails to manufacture it carefully, then marketing will not be able to deliver on its promise. The third task is selecting, training, directing, motivating, and evaluating personnel. Managers must meet with their subordinates periodically to review their performance, praise their strengths, point out their weaknesses, and suggest ways to improve.

There are likely to be surprises and disappointments as marketing plans are implemented. For this reason, the company needs feedback and control. There are three types of marketing control:

◆ *Annual-plan control* is the task of ensuring that the company is achieving its sales, profits, and other goals. First, management must state well-defined goals for each month or quarter. Second, management must measure its ongoing performance in the marketplace. Third, management must determine the underlying causes of any serious performance gaps. Fourth, management must choose corrective actions to close gaps between goals and performance.

◆ *Profitability control* is the task of measuring the actual profitability of products, customer groups, trade channels, and order sizes. This is not a simple task. A company's accounting system is seldom designed to report the real profitability of different marketing entities and activities. *Marketing profitability analysis* measures the profitability of different marketing activities. *Marketing efficiency studies* try to determine how various marketing activities could be carried out more efficiently.

◆ *Strategic control* is the task of evaluating whether the company's marketing strategy is appropriate to market conditions. Because of rapid changes in the marketing environ-

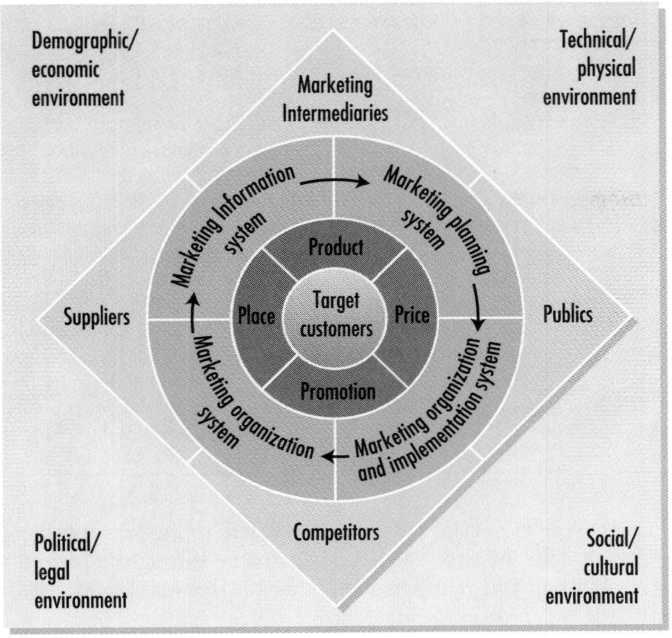

FIGURE 3-14
Factors Influencing Company Marketing Strategy

ment, each company needs to reassess periodically its marketing effectiveness through a control instrument known as the *marketing audit*.

Figure 3-14 presents a grand summary of the marketing process and the forces shaping the company's marketing strategy. Through the systems shown in Figure 3-14, the company monitors and adapts to the micro and macro marketing environments.

PRODUCT PLANNING: THE NATURE AND CONTENTS OF A MARKETING PLAN

As we've seen, each product level (product line, brand) within a business unit must develop a *marketing plan* for achieving its goals. The marketing plan is one of the most important outputs of the marketing process. But what does a marketing plan look like? What does it contain? Marketing plans have several sections, such as those listed in Table 3-4 on page 96. We will illustrate the plan's sections with the following example:

Jane Melody is the product manager of Zenith's line of modular stereo systems, called the Allegro line. Each system consists of an AM-FM tuner/amplifier, CD player, tape deck, and separate speakers. Zenith offers several different models that sell in the $150 to $400 range. Zenith's main goal is to increase its market share and profitability in the modular-stereo-system market. As product manager, Jane Melody has to prepare a marketing plan to improve the Allegro line's performance.

Executive Summary and Table of Contents

The marketing plan should open with a brief summary in a few pages of the plan's main goals and recommendations. Here is an abbreviated example:

The 1998 Allegro marketing plan seeks to generate a significant increase in company sales and profits over the preceding year. The profit target is $1.8 million. The sales-

TABLE 3-4   CONTENTS OF A MARKETING PLAN

I. Executive summary and table of contents	Presents a brief overview of the proposed plan
II. Current marketing situation	Presents relevant background data on the market, product, competition, distribution, and macro-environment
III. Opportunity and issue analysis	Identifies the main opportunities/threats, strengths/weaknesses, and issues facing the product line
IV. Objectives	Defines the plan's financial and marketing goals in terms of sales volume, market share, and profit
V. Marketing strategy	Presents the broad marketing approach that will be used to achieve the plan's objectives
VI. Action programs	Presents the special marketing programs designed to achieve the business objectives
VII. Projected profit-and-loss statement	Forecasts the plan's expected financial outcomes
VIII. Controls	Indicates how the plan will be monitored

revenue target is $18 million, which represents a planned 9% sales gain over last year. This increase is seen as attainable through improved pricing, advertising, and distribution. The required marketing budget will be $2,290,000, a 14% increase over last year. . . . [More details follow.]

The executive summary permits higher management to grasp quickly the plan's major thrust. A table of contents should follow the executive summary.

Current Marketing Situation

This section presents relevant background data on the market, product, competition, distribution, and macroenvironment. The data are drawn from a *product fact book* maintained by the product manager.

MARKET SITUATION. Here data are presented on the target market. The size and growth of the market (in units and/or dollars) are shown for several past years and by market and geographical segments. Data on customer needs, perceptions, and buying-behavior trends are also presented.

> The modular stereo market accounts for approximately $400 million, or 20% of the home stereo market. Sales are expected to be stable over the next few years. . . . The primary buyers are middle-income consumers, ages 20 to 40, who want to listen to good music but do not want to invest in expensive stereo component equipment. They want to buy a complete system produced by a name they can trust. They want a system with good sound and whose looks fit the decor primarily of family rooms.

PRODUCT SITUATION. Here the sales, prices, contribution margins, and net profits are shown for each major product in the line for several past years (Table 3-5).

> Row 1, in Table 3-5, shows the total industry sales in units growing at 5% annually until 1996, when demand declined slightly. Row 2 shows Zenith's market share hovering around 3%, although it reached 4% in 1995. Row 3 shows the average price for an Allegro stereo rising about 10% per year except the last year, when it rose 4%. Row 4 shows variable costs—materials, labor, energy—rising each year. Row 5 shows that the gross contribution margin per unit—the difference between price (row 3) and unit variable cost (row 4)—rose the first few years and remained at $100 in the latest year. Rows 6 and 7 show sales volume in units and dollars, and row 8 shows the total gross contribution margin, which rose until the latest year, when it fell. Row 9 shows that overhead remained constant during 1993 and 1994 and increased to a high level during 1995 and

TABLE 3-5 HISTORICAL PRODUCT DATA

VARIABLE	ROWS	1993	1994	1995	1996
1. Industry sales in units		2,000,000	2,100,000	2,205,000	2,200,000
2. Company market share		0.03	0.03	0.04	0.03
3. Average price per unit $		200	220	240	250
4. Variable cost per unit $		120	125	140	150
5. Gross contribution margin per unit ($)	(3 − 4)	80	95	100	100
6. Sales volume in units	(1 × 2)	60,000	63,000	88,200	66,000
7. Sales revenue ($)	(3 × 6)	12,000,000	13,860,000	21,168,000	16,500,000
8. Gross contribution margin ($)	(5 × 6)	4,800,000	5,985,000	8,820,000	6,600,000
9. Overhead ($)		2,000,000	2,000,000	3,500,000	3,500,000
10. Net contribution margin ($)	(8 − 9)	2,800,000	3,985,000	5,320,000	3,100,000
11. Advertising and promotion ($)		800,000	1,000,000	1,000,000	900,000
12. Sales force and distribution ($)		700,000	1,000,000	1,100,000	1,000,000
13. Marketing research ($)		100,000	120,000	150,000	100,000
14. Net operating profit ($)	(10 − 11 − 12 − 13)	1,200,000	1,865,000	3,070,000	1,100,000

1996, owing to an increase in manufacturing capacity. Row 10 shows net contribution margin—that is, gross contribution margin less overhead. Rows 11, 12, and 13 show marketing expenditures on advertising and promotion, sales force and distribution, and marketing research. Finally, row 14 shows net operating profit after marketing expenses. The picture is one of increasing profits until 1996, when they fell to about one third of the 1995 level. Clearly Zenith needs to find a strategy for 1997 that will restore healthy growth in sales and profits to the product line.

COMPETITIVE SITUATION. Here the major competitors are identified and described in terms of their size, goals, market share, product quality, marketing strategies, and other characteristics that are needed to understand their intentions and behavior.

Zenith's major competitors in the modular-stereo-system market are Panasonic, Sony, Magnavox, and General Electric. Each competitor has a specific strategy and niche in the market. Panasonic, for example, offers 33 models covering the whole price range, sells primarily in department stores and discount stores, and is a heavy advertising spender. It plans to dominate the market through product proliferation and price discounting. . . . [Similar descriptions are prepared for the other competitors.]

DISTRIBUTION SITUATION. This section presents data on the size and importance of each distribution channel.

Modular stereo sets are sold through department stores, radio/TV stores, appliance stores, discount stores, furniture stores, music stores, audio specialty stores, and mail order. Zenith sells 37% of its sets through appliance stores, 23% through radio/TV stores, 10% through furniture stores, 3% through department stores, and the remainder through other channels. Zenith dominates in channels that are declining in importance, while it is a weak competitor in the faster-growing channels, such as discount stores. Zenith gives about a 30% margin to its dealers, which is similar to what other competitors give.

MACROENVIRONMENT SITUATION. This section describes broad macro-environment trends—demographic, economic, technological, political/legal, social/cultural—that bear on the product line's future.

About 50% of U.S. households now have stereo equipment. As the market approaches saturation, effort must be turned to convincing consumers to upgrade their equipment. . . . The economy is expected to be weak, which means people will postpone consumer-durables purchases. . . . The Japanese have designed new and more compact audio systems that pose a challenge to conventional stereo systems.

Opportunity and Issue Analysis

After summarizing the current marketing situation, the product manager proceeds to identify the major opportunities/threats, strengths/weaknesses, and issues facing the product line.

OPPORTUNITIES/THREATS ANALYSIS. Here the product manager identifies the main opportunities and threats facing the business. The main opportunities facing Zenith's Allegro line are as follows:

◆ Consumers are showing increased interest in more compact modular stereo systems, so Zenith should consider designing one or more compact models.

◆ Two major national department store chains are willing to carry the Allegro line if we will give them extra advertising support.

◆ A major national discount chain is willing to carry the Allegro line if we will offer a special discount for its higher purchase volume.

The main threats facing Zenith's Allegro line are as follows:

◆ An increasing number of consumers are buying their sets in mass-merchandise and discount stores, in which Allegro has weak representation.

◆ An increasing number of upscale consumers are showing a preference for component systems, and we do not have an audio component line.

◆ Some of our competitors have introduced smaller speakers with excellent sound quality, and consumers are favoring these smaller speakers.

◆ The federal government is on the verge of passing a more stringent product-safety law, which would entail product redesign work.

STRENGTHS/WEAKNESSES ANALYSIS. The product manager needs to identify product strengths and weaknesses. The main strengths of Zenith's Allegro line are as follows:

◆ Zenith's name has excellent brand awareness and a high-quality image.

◆ Dealers who sell the Allegro line are knowledgeable and well trained in selling.

◆ Zenith has an excellent service network, and consumers know they will get quick repair service.

The main weaknesses of Zenith's Allegro line are as follows:

◆ Allegro's sound quality is not demonstrably better than that of competing sets. Sound quality can make a big difference in brand choice.

◆ Zenith is budgeting only 5% of its sales revenue for advertising and promotion, while some major competitors are spending twice that level.

- Zenith's Allegro line is not clearly positioned compared with Magnavox ("quality") and Sony ("innovation"). Zenith needs a unique selling proposition. The current advertising campaign is not particularly creative or exciting.

- Zenith's brand is priced higher than other brands, but this higher price is not being supported by a real perceived difference in quality. The pricing strategy should be reevaluated.

ISSUES ANALYSIS. In this section of the marketing plan, the product manager uses the strengths/weaknesses analysis to define the main issues that the plan must address. Zenith must consider the following basic issues:

- Should Zenith stay in the stereo-equipment business? Can it compete effectively? Or should it divest this product line?

- If Zenith stays in the business, should it continue with its present products, distribution channels, and price and promotion policies?

- Should Zenith switch to high-growth channels (such as discount stores)? Can it do this and yet retain the loyalty of its current channel partners?

- Should Zenith increase its advertising and promotion expenditures to match competitors' expenditures?

- Should Zenith pour money into R&D to develop advanced features, sound, and styling?

Objectives

After the product manager has summarized the issues involved with the product line, he or she must decide on the plan's objectives. Two types of objectives must be set: financial and marketing.

FINANCIAL OBJECTIVES. Zenith's management wants each business unit to deliver a good financial performance. The product manager sets the following financial objectives for the Allegro line:

- Earn an annual rate of return on investment over the next five years of 15% after taxes.
- Produce net profits of $1,800,000 in 1997.
- Produce a cash flow of $2,000,000 in 1997.

MARKETING OBJECTIVES. The financial objectives must be converted into marketing objectives. For example, if the company wants to earn $1,800,000 profit and its target profit margin is 10% on sales, then it must set a goal of $18 million in sales revenue. If the company sets an average price of $260, it must sell 69,230 units. If it expects total industry sales to reach 2.3 million units, it must gain 3% of the market share to achieve its goals. To maintain this market share, the company will have to set certain goals for consumer awareness, distribution coverage, and so on. Thus the marketing objectives might read:

- Achieve total sales revenue of $18,000,000 in 1997, which represents a 9% increase from last year. Therefore, achieve a unit sales volume of 69,230, which represents an expected market share of 3 percent.
- Expand consumer awareness of the Allegro brand from 15% to 30% over the planning period.
- Expand the number of dealers by 10 percent.
- Aim for an average price of $260.

Marketing Strategy

The product manager now outlines the broad marketing strategy or "game plan" that he or she will use to accomplish the plan's objectives. The marketing strategy is often presented in list form:

Target market:	Upscale households, with particular emphasis on female buyers
Positioning:	The best-sounding and most reliable modular stereo system
Product line:	Add one lower-priced model and two higher-priced models
Price:	Price somewhat above competitive brands
Distribution outlets:	Heavy in radio/TV stores and appliance stores; increased efforts to penetrate department stores
Sales force:	Expand by 10% and introduce a national account-management system
Service:	Widely available and quick service
Advertising:	Develop a new advertising campaign that supports the positioning strategy; emphasize higher-price units in the ads; increase the advertising budget by 20%
Sales promotion:	Increase the sales-promotion budget by 15% to develop a point-of-purchase display and to participate to a greater extent in dealer trade shows
Research and development:	Increase expenditures by 25% to develop better styling of Allegro line
Marketing research:	Increase expenditures by 10% to improve knowledge of consumer-choice process and to monitor competitor moves

In developing the strategy, the product manager needs to talk with the purchasing and manufacturing people to make sure they are able to buy enough material and produce enough units to meet the needed sales-volume levels. He or she also needs to talk to the sales manager to obtain the planned sales force support, and to the financial officer to make sure enough advertising and promotion funds will be available.

Action Programs

The marketing plan must specify the broad marketing programs designed to achieve the business objectives. Each marketing strategy element must now be elaborated to answer: What will be done? When will it be done? Who will do it? How much will it cost?

February. Zenith will advertise in the newspapers that a free Barbra Streisand CD will be given to everyone buying an Allegro unit this month. Ann Morris, consumer promotion director, will handle this project at a planned cost of $5,000.

April. Zenith will participate in the Consumer Electronics Trade Show in Chicago. Robert Jones, dealer promotion director, will make the arrangements. The expected cost is $14,000.

August. A sales contest will be conducted, which will award three Hawaiian vacations to the three dealers producing the greatest percentage increase in sales of Allegro units. The contest will be handled by Mary Tyler at a planned cost of $13,000.

September. A newspaper advertisement will announce that consumers who attend an Allegro store demonstration in the second week of September will have their names entered in a sweepstakes. Ten lucky winners will receive free Allegros. Ann Morris will handle this project at a planned cost of $6,000.

Projected Profit-and-Loss Statement

Action plans allow the product manager to build a supporting budget. On the revenue side, this budget shows the forecasted sales volume in units and the average price. On the expense side, it shows the cost of production, physical distribution, and marketing, broken down into finer categories. The difference between revenues and sales is projected profit.

Once the budget has been prepared, higher management will review it and approve or modify it. If the requested budget is too high, the product manager will have to make some cuts. Once approved, the budget is the basis for developing plans and schedules for material procurement, production scheduling, employee recruitment, and marketing operations.

Controls

The last section of the marketing plan outlines the controls for monitoring the plan's progress. Typically the goals and budget are spelled out for each month or quarter. Higher management can review the results each period and identify businesses that are not attaining their goals. Managers of lagging businesses must explain what is happening and the actions they will take to improve plan fulfillment.

Some control sections include contingency plans. A *contingency plan* outlines the steps that management would take in response to specific adverse developments, such as price wars or strikes. The purpose of contingency planning is to encourage managers to think about difficulties that might lie ahead.

Many of the tools that are used to develop marketing plans are mathematical. For an overview of these mathematical models, see Appendix 1 at the end of this book, "The Theory of Effective Resource Allocation."

THE SHAPE OF MARKETING PLANNING IN THE 1990s

Throughout this chapter, we've talked about the *theory* of modern marketing practices. It is therefore useful to conclude with the results of a survey that attempts to summarize the *practice* of marketing in the 1990s.

The Conference Board's comprehensive survey found that more companies have discovered the marketing concept and set their purpose as that of acquiring and satisfying customers rather than producing goods or services. Business plans are more customer- and competitor-oriented and better reasoned and more realistic than they were in the past. The plans draw more inputs from all the functions and are team-developed. Marketing executives increasingly see themselves as professional managers first and specialists second. Senior management is becoming more involved in making and/or approving marketing decisions. And planning is

Winning Markets
Through Market-Oriented
Strategic Planning

becoming a continual process throughout the year to respond to rapidly changing market conditions. In other words, the trends we've discussed in Chapters 1 to 3 are in full force in the world of marketing!

The survey did find, however, that marketing planning procedures and content vary considerably among companies. The plan is variously called a "business plan," a "marketing plan," and sometimes an "operating plan." Most marketing plans cover one year, but some cover a few years. The plans vary in their length from under 10 pages to over 50 pages. Some companies take their plans very seriously, while others see them as only a rough guide to action. According to marketing executives, the most frequently cited shortcomings of current marketing plans are lack of realism, insufficient competitive analysis, and a short-run focus.[35]

SUMMARY

1. *Market-oriented strategic planning* is the managerial process of developing and maintaining a viable fit between the organization's objectives, skills, and resources and its changing market opportunities. The aim of strategic planning is to shape and reshape the company's businesses and products so that they yield target profits and growth. Strategic planning takes place at four levels: corporate, division, business unit, and product.

2. High-performance companies consistently satisfy or exceed the expectations of their stakeholders, manage and link work processes, source and outsource efficiently, and develop a corporate organizational culture that is oriented toward success.

3. Corporate headquarters is responsible for setting into motion the strategic planning process. The corporate strategy establishes the framework within which the division and business units prepare their strategic plans. Setting out a corporate strategy entails four activities:
   a. Defining the corporate mission. Good mission statements focus on a limited number of goals, stress the company's major policies, and define the major competitive scopes in which the company will operate.
   b. Establishing *strategic business units (SBUs)*. An SBU is a business unit that can benefit from separate planning, faces specific competitors, and is managed as a profit center.
   c. Assigning resources to each SBU based on its market attractiveness and business strength. The tools used to decide whether to build, hold, harvest, or divest a business include the Boston Consulting Group's growth-share matrix and the General Electric model.
   d. Planning new businesses and expanding existing businesses. The company can identify several types of growth opportunities: *intensive growth opportunities* (market penetration, market development, and product development), *integrative growth opportunities* (backward, forward, and horizontal integration), and *diversification growth opportunities* (concentric, horizontal, and conglomerate diversification).

4. Strategic planning for individual businesses entails the following activities: defining the business mission, analyzing the business's external opportunities and threats, analyzing the business's internal strengths and weaknesses, formulating goals, formulating strategy (which may include joining strategic alliances), formulating supporting programs, implementing the programs, and gathering feedback and exercising control.

5. The marketing process consists of four steps: analyzing market opportunities; developing marketing strategies; planning marketing programs, which entails choosing the *marketing mix* (the four Ps of product, price, place, and promotion); and organizing, implementing, and controlling the marketing effort.

6. Each product level within a business unit must develop a *marketing plan* for achieving its goals. The marketing plan is one of the most important outputs of the marketing process, and it should contain the following elements: an executive summary and table of contents; an overview of the current marketing situation; an analysis of the opportu-

nities and issues facing the product; a summary of the plan's financial and marketing objectives; an overview of the marketing strategy to be used to achieve the plan's objectives; a description of the action programs to be implemented to achieve the plan's objectives; a projected profit-and-loss statement; and a summary of the controls to be used in monitoring the plan's progress.

CONCEPT APPLICATIONS

1. What competitive advantages have each of the following companies achieved in the marketplace? How has each company's marketing strategy communicated these competitive advantages to the marketplace?
   a. Wal-Mart
   b. Snap-on-Tools
   c. J. P. Morgan Investment Bankers
   d. Citicorp
   e. Kodak

2. Analyze the Lands' End advertisement in Figure 1 on page 104 and the following copy from another Lands' End ad.

   > When Lands' End first started selling 100% cotton Rugby shirts, we discovered to our horror that they shrank unmercifully. Sometimes as much as a full size. (We were getting back 16% of the shirts we sold. Unthinkable.)
   >
   > So, we went to work. First to locate a new manufacturer that pre-shrank his heavyweight, 100% cotton jersey knit so it eliminated virtually all shrinkage. . . .
   >
   > We've conquered the seam problems by going to a safety seam stitch. And on the placket problem we designed a continuously looped placket that leaves all stress with the placket itself, not the stitching. We've changed the rubber button we once had with one that won't melt under an iron that loses its way!
   >
   > Details, details, details! We fuss over them endlessly because they pay off in ever-improving quality—not just some standard once arrived at that is sacred forever more. Our quality standards keep going higher and higher. That's the Lands' End way. . . .
   >
   > On everything in our catalog we offer our short, sweet guarantee. In two words: GUARANTEED. PERIOD. As to service, when we get your order—by mail or phone—if we have it in stock, it's out the next day. (How many catalog companies can say that and mean it?)

   Name two competitive advantages that Lands' End is attempting to achieve in relation to its competitors. What business functions must be coordinated at Lands' End in order to achieve these advantages?

3. You have just been hired by Minnetonka—a small Minnesota company specializing in soaps and other products. You're new on the job, and you want to demonstrate to your boss all the training you've received in formal planning. You've heard through the grapevine that she thinks formal planning is an inefficient and ineffective mechanism for small companies. She believes that informal planning works best for a company Minnetonka's size. You are determined to change her attitude. Write a memo explaining how formal planning can be used in small companies too.

4. For several years a local community college has operated Communiversity, an adult education program, with only marginal success. Due to a recent tax referendum, the board of trustees has decided it must either significantly increase night-school enrollments or cancel the entire program. Develop a mission statement for Communiversity and a set of 10 objectives geared toward increasing enrollments.

5. As a member of a management consulting group, you have been retained by a business-to-business office-equipment manufacturer. The company's product line consists of the five strategic business units (SBUs) shown on the next page. Use the Boston Consulting Group portfolio analysis (as illustrated in Figure 3-3 on page 72) to determine

Winning Markets
Through Market-Oriented
Strategic Planning

FIGURE 1

We thought you'd like to know what's behind a Lands' End® label.

Some stores buy a sweater or a shirt off the shelf from a manufacturer, sew their names on the collar, and call it their "private label" merchandise.

Not us. At Lands' End, we don't put our label on *anything* unless we have a big hand in designing and manufacturing it – and then checking to make sure it's up to snuff.

We keep tinkering with it too, trying to make it a mite better. Often that involves putting back features and construction details that others have taken out over the years.

And we won't chintz on anything just to make an item cheaper.

Why not see for yourself? Pay a visit to our "store" on Stargazer. You'll find videos on some of our shirts and sweaters and other nice things. How to measure for the right size. And a few other items you'll find useful, or just plain fun.

Mind you, this is only a sample. To see the rest, call for our catalog – any time, 24 hours a day. And to look at the actual color or fabric of an item, ask for a swatch.

We stand foursquare behind everything that wears our label. It's – "Guaranteed. Period.®"

You see, where we come from – the sweet farm country of Dodgeville, Wisconsin – we still believe in doing an honest day's work. And we expect the same of the things we sell.

1·800·963·4818

each SBU's relative market share and whether the company as a whole is healthy. Describe the nature of the BCG Market Growth/Market Share matrix to top management and make recommendations as to future strategies.

STRATEGIC BUSINESS UNIT (SBU)	DOLLAR SALES (IN MILLIONS)	NUMBER OF COMPETITORS	DOLLAR SALES OF THE TOP 3 (IN MILLIONS)	MARKET GROWTH RATE
A	.5	8	.7, .7, .5	15%
B	1.6	22	1.6, 1.6, 1.0	18
C	1.8	14	1.8, 1.2, 1.0	7
D	3.2	5	3.2, .8, .7	4
E	.5	10	2.5, 1.8, 1.7	4

FIGURE 2

It's no longer a question of what to give, but which.

The new Cross Townsend Collection. A dramatic wide-diameter interpretation of the classic Cross silhouette. Fountain pen. Rolling Ball Selectip® Pen, ball-point pen, and 0.5mm pencil in seven distinctive finishes. Unquestioned lifetime mechanical guarantee.

DEALER NAME

6. Since the aim of strategic planning is to shape and reshape the company's businesses and products so that they yield target profits and growth, strategic game plans must be developed. Using the elements of the Strategic Planning, Implementation, and Control Process Model (Figure 3-1, page 64), analyze the process that company officials presumably went through to develop the strategy that resulted in the advertisement for Cross Pens in Figure 2 above and the accompanying radio ad, which ran as follows:

> *They were first admired in the cafes of Paris. In the board rooms of Geneva. Over tea in an English barrister's office. Cross Townsend writing instruments, now offered at (DEALER'S NAME). The Cross Townsend Collection is a dramatic wide-diameter interpretation of the classic Cross silhouette. It is offered in a choice of traditional and contemporary finishes, each with a lifetime mechanical guarantee. The new Cross Townsend Collection. See it now at (DEALER'S NAME AND ADDRESS).*

7. You are the CEO of a 500-bed Medical Center in a metropolitan area. Describe the factors influencing your company's marketing strategy, using Figure 3-14 as an outline. Who are the stakeholders and the players? How are your decisions affected by the environment in which you operate?

8. For years Greyhound Bus Lines has been faced with stiff competition from increased automobile ownership and discount airline tickets. In 1960 the bus industry accounted for 30% of interstate transportation, but by 1994 its share had dropped to 6 percent. Perform a SWOT analysis for the bus industry and make a recommendation based on your analysis to Greyhound Lines.

9. Joel Smith, Heinz's ketchup product manager, prepared the marketing plan on page 106. Critique the plan. What improvements can you suggest?

Winning Markets
Through Market-Oriented
Strategic Planning

1. Forecast of total market	25,000,000 cases*
This year's total market (23,600,000 cases) × recent growth rate (6%)	
2. Forecast of market share	28%
3. Forecast of sales volume (1 × 2)	7,000,000 cases
4. Price to distributor	$4.45 per case
5. Estimate of sales revenue (3 × 4)	$31,150,000
6. Estimate of variable costs	$2.75 per case
Tomatoes and spices ($0.50) + bottles and caps	
($1.00) + labor ($1.10) + physical distribution ($0.15)	
7. Estimate of contribution margin to cover fixed costs, profits, and marketing [3 × (4 − 6)]	$11,900,000
8. Estimate of fixed costs	$ 7,000,000
Fixed charge = $1 per case × 7 million cases	
9. Estimate of contribution margin to cover profits and marketing (7 − 8)	$ 4,900,000
10. Estimate of target profit goal	$ 1,900,000
11. Amount available for marketing (9 − 10)	$ 3,000,000
12. Split of the marketing budget:	
Advertising	$ 2,000,000
Sales promotion	900,000
Market research	100,000

* Note: Numbers are rounded.

10. "With more than 80% of the market already in its grasp, Campbell Soup Co. really doesn't need to increase its share of the $1.2 billion of condensed soup sold annually in food stores. What the company does need is to make folks hungrier for soup." What intensive growth strategy is being pursued here, and how might the company accomplish its objective?

NOTES

1. Steve Harrell, in a speech at the plenary session of the American Marketing Association's Educators' Meeting, Chicago, August 5, 1980.
2. See Tamara J. Erickson and C. Everett Shorey, "Business Strategy: New Thinking for the '90s," *Prism,* Fourth Quarter 1992, pp. 19–35.
3. See Jon R. Katzenbach and Douglas K. Smith, *The Wisdom of Teams: Creating the High-Performance Organization* (Boston: Harvard Business School Press, 1993); and Michael Hammer and James Champy, *Reengineering the Corporation* (New York: HarperBusiness, 1993).
4. David Glines, "Do You Work in a Zoo?" *Executive Excellence,* 11, no. 10 (October 1994), 12–13.
5. Matthew J. Ferrero, "Self-directed Work Teams Untax the IRS," *Personnel Journal,* July 1994, pp. 66–71.
6. Echo Montgomery Garrett, "Outsourcing to the Max," *Small Business Reports,* August 1994, pp. 9–14. The case for more outsourcing is ably spelled out in James Brian Quinn, *Intelligent Enterprise* (New York: Free Press, 1992).
7. C. K. Prahalad and Gary Hamel, "The Core Competence of the Corporation," *Harvard Business Review,* May–June 1990, pp. 79–91.
8. Andrea Mackiewicz and N. Caroline Daniels, *The Successful Corporation of the Year 2000* (New York and London: The Economist Intelligence Unit, 1994), pp. 33–43.
9. "Corporate Culture Shock: An IBM-Apple Computer Joint Venture," *Fortune,* April 5, 1993, p. 44.
10. James C. Collins and Jerry I. Porras, *Built to Last: Successful Habits of Visionary Companies* (New York: HarperBusiness, 1994).
11. See "The New Breed of Strategic Planning," *Business Week,* September 7, 1984, pp. 62–68.
12. See Drucker, *Management: Tasks, Responsibilities and Practices* (New York: Harper & Row, 1973), Chapter 7.
13. See "The Hollow Corporation," *Business Week,* March 3, 1986, pp. 57–59. Also see William H. Davidow and Michael S. Malone, *The Virtual Corporation* (New York: HarperBusiness, 1992).
14. For more discussion, see Laura Nash, "Mission Statements—Mirrors and Windows," *Harvard Business Review,* March–April 1988, pp. 155–56.
15. Gilbert Fuchsberg, "Visioning Missions Becomes its Own Mission," *The Wall Street Journal,* January 7, 1994, B1:3.
16. Theodore Levitt, "Marketing Myopia," *Harvard Business Review,* July–August 1960, pp. 45–56.
17. Derek Abell, *Defining the Business: The Starting Point of Strategic Planning* (Englewood Cliffs, NJ: Prentice Hall, 1980), Chapter 3.
18. See Roger A. Kerin, Vijay Mahajan, and P. Rajan Varadarajan, *Contemporary Perspectives on Strategic Planning* (Boston: Allyn & Bacon, 1990).
19. A hard decision must be made between harvesting and divesting a business. Harvesting a business will strip it of its long-run value, in which case it will be difficult to find a buyer. Divest-

ing, on the other hand, is facilitated by maintaining a business in a fit condition in order to attract a buyer.

20. See Peter Patel and Michael Younger, "A Frame of Reference for Strategy Development," *Long Range Planning,* April 1978, pp. 6–12; and S. J. Q. Robinson et al., "The Directional Policy Matrix—Tool for Strategic Planning," *Long Range Planning,* June 1978, pp. 8–15.

21. For a contrary view, however, see J. Scott Armstrong and Roderick J. Brodie, "Effects of Portfolio Planning Methods on Decision Making: Experimental Results," *International Journal of Research in Marketing,* 1994, pp. 73–84.

22. The same matrix can be expanded into nine cells by adding modified products and modified markets. See S. J. Johnson and Conrad Jones, "How to Organize for New Products," *Harvard Business Review,* May–June 1957, pp. 49–62.

23. George Stalk, Philip Evans, and Lawrence E. Shulman, "Competing Capabilities: The New Rules of Corporate Strategy," *Harvard Business Review,* March–April 1992, pp. 57–69.

24. See Michael E. Porter, *Competitive Strategy: Techniques for Analyzing Industries and Competitors* (New York: Free Press, 1980), Chapter 2.

25. For readings on strategic alliances, see Peter Lorange and Johan Roos, *Strategic Alliances: Formation, Implementation and Evolution* (Cambridge, MA: Blackwell, 1992), and Jordan D. Lewis, *Partnerships for Profit: Structuring and Managing Strategic Alliances* (New York: Free Press, 1990).

26. Adapted from Allan J. Magrath, *The 6 Imperatives of Marketing: Lessons from the World's Best Companies* (New York: Amacom, 1992), Chapter 4, with added examples.

27. See Robin Cooper and Robert S. Kaplan, "Profit Priorities from Activity-Based Costing," *Harvard Business Review,* May–June 1991, pp. 130–35.

28. See Thomas J. Peters and Robert H. Waterman, Jr., *In Search of Excellence: Lessons from America's Best-Run Companies* (New York: Harper & Row, 1982), pp. 9–12. The same framework is used in Richard Tanner Pascale and Anthony G. Athos, *The Art of Japanese Management: Applications for American Executives* (New York: Simon & Schuster, 1981).

29. See Terrence E. Deal and Allan A. Kennedy, *Corporate Cultures: The Rites and Rituals of Corporate Life* (Reading, MA: Addison-Wesley, 1982); "Corporate Culture," *Business Week,* October 27, 1980, pp. 148–60; Stanley M. Davis, *Managing Corporate Culture* (Cambridge, MA: Ballinger, 1984); and John P. Kotter and James L. Heskett, *Corporate Culture and Performance* (New York: Free Press, 1992).

30. Wendy Zellner, "Can EDS Shed Its Skin?" *Business Week,* November 15, 1993, pp. 56–57.

31. Andrew E. Serwer, "Can This Company Be Saved?" *Fortune,* April 19, 1993, pp. 89–90; Gary McWilliams, "Wang's Great Leap Out of Limbo," *Business Week,* March 7, 1994, pp. 68–69.

32. Michael J. Lanning and Edward G. Michaels, "A Business Is a Value Delivery System," McKinsey Staff Paper No. 41, June 1988 (McKinsey & Co., Inc.).

33. E. Jerome McCarthy, *Basic Marketing: A Managerial Approach,* 12th ed. (Homewood, IL: Irwin, 1996). Two alternative classifications are worth noting. Frey proposed that all marketing-decision variables could be categorized into two factors: the *offering* (product, packaging, brand, price, and service) and *methods and tools* (distribution channels, personal selling, advertising, sales promotion, and publicity). See Albert W. Frey, *Advertising,* 3d ed. (New York: Ronald Press, 1961), p. 30. Lazer and Kelly proposed a three-factor classification: *goods and service mix, distribution mix,* and *communications mix.* See William Lazer and Eugene J. Kelly, *Managerial Marketing: Perspectives and Viewpoints,* rev. ed. (Homewood, IL: Irwin, 1962), p. 413.

34. Robert Lautenborn, "New Marketing Litany: 4 P's Passe; C-Words Take Over," *Advertising Age,* October 1, 1990, p. 26.

35. Howard Sutton, *The Marketing Plan in the 1990s* (New York: The Conference Board, 1990).

Winning Markets
Through Market-Oriented
Strategic Planning

4

MANAGING MARKETING INFORMATION AND MEASURING MARKET DEMAND

A wise man recognizes the convenience of a general statement, but he bows to the authority of a particular fact.

OLIVER WENDELL HOLMES, JR.

To manage a business well is to manage its future; and to manage the future is to manage information.

MARION HARPER

Forecasting is like trying to drive a car blindfolded and following directions given by a person who is looking out of the back window.

ANONYMOUS

We have emphasized the importance of monitoring the marketing environment to keep products and marketing practices current. But how can management learn about changing customer wants, new competitor initiatives, changing distribution channels, and so on? The answer is clear: Management must develop and manage information. Three developments make the need for marketing information greater than at any time in the past:

From local to national to global marketing: As companies expand their geographical market coverage, their managers need more information more quickly than ever before.

From buyer needs to buyer wants: As buyers' incomes improve, they become more selective in their choice of goods. To predict buyers' response to different features, styles, and other attributes, sellers must turn to marketing research.

From price to nonprice competition: As sellers increase their use of branding, product differentiation, advertising, and sales promotion, they require information on these marketing tools' effectiveness.

Fortunately, the explosion of information requirements has been met by impressive new information technologies. The past 30 years have witnessed the emergence of the computer, microfilming, cable television, copy machines, fax machines, tape recorders, video recorders, videodisc players, CD-ROM drives, multimedia packages, and other devices that have revolutionized information handling. With respect to marketing management and marketing research, the single most important technological development has been the rise of computerized data capture systems.[1]

Some firms have developed advanced marketing information systems that provide company management with rapid and incredible detail about buyer wants, preferences, and behavior. For example, the Coca-Cola Company knows that we put 3.2 ice cubes in a glass, see 69 of its commercials every year, and prefer cans to pop out of vending machines at a temperature of 35 degrees. One million of us drink Coke with breakfast every day. Kimberly Clark, which makes Kleenex, has calculated that the average person blows his or her nose 256 times a year. Hoover hooked up timers and other equipment to vacuum cleaners in people's homes to learn that we spend about 35 minutes each week vacuuming, sucking up about 8 pounds of dust each year and using 6 bags to do so.[2] Marketers also have extensive information about consumption patterns in other countries. On a per capita basis within Western Europe, for example, the Swiss consume the most chocolate, the Greeks eat the most cheese, the Irish drink the most tea, and the Austrians smoke the most cigarettes.[3]

Nevertheless, many business firms lack information sophistication. Many do not have a marketing research department, and many others have small marketing research departments whose work is limited to routine forecasting, sales analysis, and occasional surveys. In addition, many managers are dissatisfied with the information available to them. Their complaints include not knowing where critical information is located in the company; getting too much information that they can't use and too little that they really need; getting important information too late; and doubting the accuracy of the information they receive.

In today's information-based society, development of good information can provide a company with a jump on its competitors. Once it has surveyed the market and obtained the information it requires, the company can carefully evaluate

Managing Marketing
Information and Measuring
Market Demand

its opportunities and choose its target markets to maximize profit. An important part of this evaluation entails forecasting current and future demand. In this chapter, we examine the following questions:

- ❖ **What is a marketing information system?**
- ❖ **What is involved in conducting marketing research?**
- ❖ **What factors distinguish good marketing research from poor marketing research?**
- ❖ **How are computerized decision support systems helping today's marketing managers make marketing decisions?**
- ❖ **What are the main concepts in forecasting and demand measurement? How can current and future demand be forecasted?**

WHAT IS A MARKETING INFORMATION SYSTEM?

Every firm must organize the flow of marketing information to its marketing managers. Companies are studying their managers' information needs and designing marketing information systems (MIS) to meet these needs.

> ❖ A MARKETING INFORMATION SYSTEM (MIS) consists of people, equipment, and procedures to gather, sort, analyze, evaluate, and distribute needed, timely, and accurate information to marketing decision makers.

The marketing-information-system concept is illustrated in Figure 4-1. To carry out their analysis, planning, implementation, and control responsibilities (shown at the far left), marketing managers need information about developments in the marketing environment (shown at the far right). The role of the MIS is to assess the manager's information needs, develop the needed information, and distribute the information in a timely fashion to the marketing managers. The needed information is developed through internal company records, marketing intelligence activities, marketing research, and marketing decision support analysis. In the sections that follow, we describe each of the components of the company's MIS.

INTERNAL RECORDS SYSTEM

The most basic information system used by marketing managers is the internal records system. Included in the internal system are reports on orders, sales, prices, inventory levels, receivables, payables, and so on. By analyzing this information, marketing managers can spot important opportunities and problems.

The Order-to-Payment Cycle

The heart of the internal records system is the *order-to-payment cycle*. Sales representatives, dealers, and customers dispatch orders to the firm. The order department prepares invoices and sends copies to various departments. Out-of-stock items are back ordered. Shipped items are accompanied by shipping and billing documents that are also multicopied and sent to various departments.

Today's companies need to perform these steps quickly and accurately. Customers favor those firms that can deliver their goods on time. Sales representatives need to send in their orders every evening, in some cases immediately. The order-fulfillment department must process these orders quickly. The warehouse must

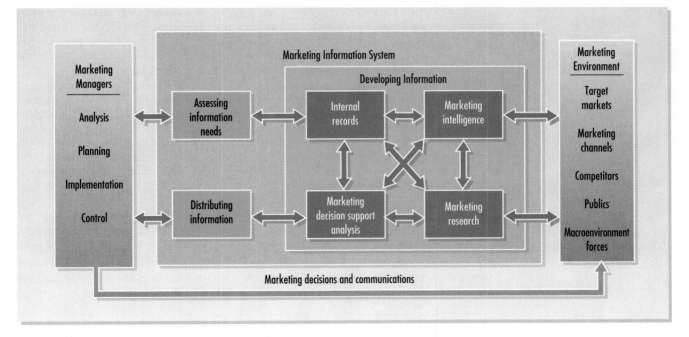

FIGURE 4-1
The Marketing Information System

send the goods out as soon as possible. And bills should go out promptly and be paid on time. Many companies are now using *electronic data interchange (EDI)* software to improve the speed, accuracy, and efficiency of the order-to-payment cycle. For example, retail giant Wal-Mart tracks and stores the stock levels of its products by computer. When a product's inventory drops to a certain point in a particular store, the computer electronically sends an electronic order to the vendor, which then automatically ships the merchandise to the store.[4]

Sales Reporting Systems

Marketing managers need up-to-date reports of their current sales. Computer technology has revolutionized sales representatives' jobs by turning the "art" of sales into an engineered business process. Armed with laptop computers, sales reps now have immediate access to information about their prospects and customers and can give their companies immediate feedback and sales reports. An ad for SalesCTRL, a sales automation software package, boasts, "Your salesperson in St. Louis knows what Customer Service in Chicago told their customer in Atlanta this morning. Sales managers can monitor everything in their territories and get current sales forecasts any time. Marketing managers know which lead sources produce the best results. . . . "

Here are three companies that have used computer technology to design fast and comprehensive sales reporting systems:

ASCOM TIMEPLEX, INC. Before heading out on a call, sales reps at this telecommunications equipment company use their Apple PowerBook computers to dial into the company's worldwide data network. They can retrieve the latest price lists, engineering and configuration notes, status reports on previous orders, and electronic mail from anywhere in the company. And when deals are struck, the laptop computers record each order, double-check them for errors, and send them electronically to Timeplex headquarters in Woodcliff Lake, New Jersey.[5]

Managing Marketing
Information and Measuring
Market Demand

BAXTER HEALTH CARE Baxter has supplied hospital purchasing departments with computers so that the hospitals can electronically transmit orders directly to Baxter. The timely arrival of orders enables Baxter to cut inventories, improve customer service, and obtain better terms from suppliers for higher volumes. Baxter has achieved a great advantage over competitors, and its market share has soared.

MEAD PAPER Mead sales representatives can obtain on-the-spot answers to customers' questions about paper availability by dialing Mead Paper's computer center. The computer determines whether paper is available at the nearest warehouse and when it can be shipped. If it is not in stock, the computer checks the inventory at nearby warehouses until the paper is located. If it is nowhere in stock, the computer determines where and when the paper can be produced. The sales representative gets an answer in seconds and thus has an advantage over competitors.

The company's marketing information system should represent a cross between what managers think they need, what managers really need, and what is economically feasible. A useful step is the appointment of an *internal MIS committee,* which interviews a cross-section of marketing executives—product managers, sales managers, sales representatives, and so on—to discover their information needs. Some useful questions that the committee should ask are:

1. What types of decisions are you regularly called upon to make?
2. What types of information do you need to make these decisions?
3. What types of information do you regularly get?
4. What types of special studies do you periodically request?
5. What types of information would you like to get that you are not getting now?
6. What information would you want daily? Weekly? Monthly? Yearly?
7. What magazines and trade reports would you like to see routed to you on a regular basis?
8. What specific topics would you like to be kept informed of?
9. What types of data analysis programs would you like to see made available?
10. What do you think would be the four most helpful improvements that could be made in the present marketing information system?

The MIS committee should evaluate the answers to these questions carefully, paying special attention to strong desires and complaints while discounting ideas that are quirky or unrealistic.

MARKETING INTELLIGENCE SYSTEM

While the internal records system supplies *results data,* the marketing intelligence system supplies *happenings data.*

❖ A **MARKETING INTELLIGENCE SYSTEM** is a set of procedures and sources used by managers to obtain their everyday information about pertinent developments in the marketing environment.

Marketing managers often carry on marketing intelligence by reading books, newspapers, and trade publications; talking to customers, suppliers, distributors, and other outsiders; and talking with other managers and personnel within the company. Yet if the system is too casual, valuable information could be lost or arrive too late. Managers might learn of a competitive move, a new-customer need, or a dealer problem too late to make the best response.

A well-run company takes four steps to improve the quality and quantity of marketing intelligence.

Analyzing
Marketing
Opportunities

First, it trains and motivates the sales force to spot and report new developments. Sales representatives are the company's "eyes and ears"; they are in an excellent position to pick up information missed by other means. Yet they are very busy and often fail to pass on significant information. For this reason, the company must "sell" its sales force on their importance as intelligence gatherers. Sales reps should know which types of information to send to which managers. For instance, the Prentice Hall sales reps who sell this textbook to college instructors are very important sources of information for the company. They let acquisitions editors know things like what is going on in each discipline, who is doing exciting research, and who wants to write cutting-edge books.

Second, the competitive company motivates distributors, retailers, and other intermediaries to pass along important intelligence. Consider the following example:[6]

PARKER HANNIFIN CORPORATION A major fluid-power-products manufacturer, Parker Hannifin has asked each of its distributors to forward to Parker's marketing research division a copy of all the invoices containing sales of their products. Parker analyzes these invoices to learn about end-user characteristics and to help its distributors improve their marketing programs.

Some companies even appoint specialists to gather marketing intelligence. Retailers may send "mystery shoppers" to pose as real shoppers at their stores, try out merchandise, and make purchases—all to assess how employees treat customers. For example, the city of Dallas recently hired Feedback Plus, a professional-shopper agency, to see how car-pound employees treat citizens picking up cars. Neiman Marcus employs the same agency to shop at its 26 stores nationwide. "Those stores that consistently score high on the shopping service," says a Neiman Marcus senior VP, "not so coincidentally have the best sales." After using a mystery shopper, the stores will tell salespeople that they've "been shopped" and give them copies of the mystery shopper's report. Typical questions on the report are: How long before a sales associate greeted you? Did the sales associate act as if he wanted your business? Was the sales associate knowledgeable about products in stock?[7] Companies also learn about competitors by purchasing their products; attending open houses and trade shows; reading competitors' published reports; attending their stockholders' meetings; talking to their former employees and present employees, dealers, distributors, suppliers, and freight agents; collecting competitors' ads; and reading *The Wall Street Journal, The New York Times,* and trade association papers.

Third, the company purchases information from outside suppliers such as the A. C. Nielsen Company and Information Resources, Inc. (see Table 4-3, part D). These research firms gather store and consumer-panel data at a much lower cost than the company could do on its own.

Fourth, some companies have established an internal *marketing information center* to collect and circulate marketing intelligence. The staff scans major publications, abstracts relevant news, and disseminates a news bulletin to marketing managers. It collects and files relevant information and assists managers in evaluating new information. These services greatly improve the quality of information available to marketing managers.

MARKETING RESEARCH SYSTEM

Marketing managers often commission marketing research, formal studies of specific problems and opportunities. They may request a market survey, a product-preference test, a sales forecast by region, or research on advertising effectiveness. We define *marketing research* as follows:

❖ **MARKETING RESEARCH** is the systematic design, collection, analysis, and reporting of data and findings relevant to a specific marketing situation facing the company.

Marketing research and market research should not be confused. *Market research*—research into a particular market—is just one component of marketing research.

Suppliers of Marketing Research

A company can obtain marketing research in a number of ways. Most large companies have their own marketing research departments.[8] The marketing research manager normally reports to the marketing vice-president and acts as a study director, administrator, company consultant, and advocate.

PROCTER & GAMBLE P&G assigns marketing researchers to each product operating division to conduct research for existing brands. There are two separate in-house research groups, one in charge of overall company advertising research and the other in charge of market testing. Each group's staff consists of marketing research managers, supporting specialists (survey designers, statisticians, behavioral scientists), and in-house field representatives to conduct and supervise interviewing. Each year, Procter & Gamble calls or visits over 1 million people in connection with about 1,000 research projects.

HEWLETT-PACKARD At HP, marketing research is handled by the Market Research & Information Center (MRIC), located at HP headquarters. The MRIC is a shared resource for all HP divisions worldwide and is divided into three groups. The Market Information Center provides background information on industries, markets, and competitors using syndicated and other information services. Decision Support Teams provide research consulting services. Regional Satellites are established in specific locales worldwide to support regional HP initiatives.[9]

While small companies may not have a separate marketing research department or be able to afford the services of a marketing research firm, they can conduct research in creative and affordable ways, such as:

- *Engaging students or professors to design and carry out marketing research projects:* In some of their marketing courses, faculty at Harvard and Boston Universities seek out marketing projects large and small within the community. One Boston University MBA project, designed to help American Express develop a campaign geared toward young professionals, led to one of the company's most successful advertising programs. The cost: $15,000. That's peanuts for American Express and eminently affordable for a small company.

- *Using online information services:* Online services such as America Online and CompuServe offer business information at a minimal cost. For example, small businesses can research potential customers using CompuServe at a cost of only $15 an hour.

- *Checking out rivals:* Many small companies routinely visit their competitors. Tom Coohill, a chef who owns two Atlanta restaurants, gives managers a food allowance to dine out and bring back ideas. Atlanta jeweler Frank Maier, Jr., who often visits out-of-town rivals, spotted and copied a dramatic way of lighting displays.[10]

Companies normally budget marketing research at 1% to 2% of company sales. Fifty percent to 80% of this money is spent directly by the marketing research department. The remainder is spent buying the services of outside marketing research firms. Marketing research firms fall into three categories:

- *Syndicated-service research firms:* These firms gather consumer and trade information, which they sell for a fee. Examples: A. C. Nielsen, SAMI/Burke.

- *Custom marketing research firms:* These firms are hired to carry out specific research projects. They participate in designing the study, and the report that results becomes the client's property.

- *Specialty-line marketing research firms:* These firms provide specialized research services to others. The best example is the field-service firm, which sells field interviewing services to other firms.

Marketing researchers have steadily expanded their activities and techniques over the years. Table 4-1 lists 36 marketing research activities and the percentage of companies performing each activity.

The Marketing Research Process

Effective marketing research involves the five steps shown in Figure 4-2 on the next page. We will illustrate these steps with the following situation:

American Airlines is constantly looking for new ways to serve the needs of air travelers. One manager came up with the idea of offering phone service to passengers. The other managers got excited about this idea and agreed that it should be researched further. The marketing manager volunteered to do some preliminary research. He contacted a major telecommunications company to find out the cost of providing this service on B-747 coast-to-coast flights. The telecommunications company said that the device would

TABLE 4-1	RESEARCH ACTIVITIES OF 435 COMPANIES		
TYPE OF RESEARCH	**PERCENT DOING**	**TYPE OF RESEARCH**	**PERCENT DOING**
A. Business/Economic and Corporate Research		D. Distribution *(continued)*	
1. Industry/market characteristics and trends	92	2. Channel performance studies	39
2. Acquisition/diversification studies	50	3. Channel coverage studies	31
3. Market-share analyses	85	4. Export and international studies	32
4. Internal employee studies (morale, communication, etc.)	72	E. Promotion	
		1. Motivation research	56
B. Pricing		2. Media research	70
1. Cost analysis	57	3. Copy research	68
2. Profit analysis	55	4. Advertising effectiveness	
3. Price elasticity	56	a. prior to marketplace airing	67
4. Demand analysis:		b. during marketplace airing	66
a. market potential	78	5. Competitive advertising studies	43
b. sales potential	75	6. Public image studies	65
c. sales forecasts	71	7. Sales force compensation studies	34
5. Competitive pricing analyses	71	8. Sales force quota studies	28
C. Product		9. Sales force territory structure	32
1. Concept development and testing	78	10. Studies of premiums, coupons, deals, etc.	47
2. Brand name generation and testing	55	F. Buying Behavior	
3. Test market	55	1. Brand preference	78
4. Product testing of existing products	63	2. Brand attitudes	76
5. Packaging design studies	48	3. Product satisfaction	87
6. Competitive product studies	54	4. Purchase behavior	80
D. Distribution		5. Purchase intentions	79
1. Plant/warehouse location studies	25	6. Brand awareness	80
		7. Segmentation studies	84

Source: Thomas C. Kinnear and Ann R. Root, ed., *1994 Survey of Marketing Research: Organization, Functions, Budget, Compensation* (Chicago: American Marketing Association, 1994), p. 49.

Managing Marketing Information and Measuring Market Demand

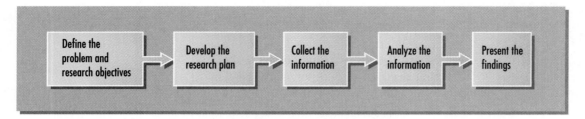

FIGURE 4-2
The Marketing Research
Process

cost the airline about $1,000 a flight. The airline could break even if it charged $25 a phone call and at least 40 passengers made calls during the flight. The marketing manager then asked the company's marketing research manager to find out how air travelers would respond to this new service.

STEP 1: DEFINE THE PROBLEM AND RESEARCH OBJECTIVES. The first step calls for the marketing manager and marketing researcher to define the problem carefully and agree on the research objectives. An old adage says, "A problem well defined is half solved."

Management must work at defining the problem neither too broadly nor too narrowly. A marketing manager who tells the marketing researcher, "Find out everything you can about air travelers' needs," will get a lot of unnecessary information. Similarly, a marketing manager who says, "Find out if enough passengers aboard a B-747 flying between the East Coast and West Coast would be willing to pay $25 to make a phone call so that American Airlines would break even on the cost of offering this service," is taking too narrow a view of the problem. To get the information she needs, the marketing researcher could say: "Why does a call have to be priced at $25? Why does American have to break even on the cost of the service? The new service might attract enough new passengers to American so that even if they don't make enough phone calls, American will make money on the extra tickets."

In discussing the problem, American's managers discovered another issue. If the new service were successful, how fast could other airlines copy it? Airline marketing competition is replete with examples of new services that were so quickly copied by competitors that no airline gained a sustainable competitive advantage. How important is it to be first and how long could the lead be sustained?

The marketing manager and marketing researcher agreed to define the problem as follows: "Will offering an in-flight phone service create enough incremental preference and profit for American Airlines to justify its cost against other possible investments that American might make?" They then agreed on the following specific research objectives:

1. What are the main reasons that airline passengers might place phone calls while flying?
2. What kinds of passengers would be the most likely to make phone calls?
3. How many passengers are likely to make phone calls, given different price levels?
4. How many extra passengers might choose American because of this new service?
5. How much long-term goodwill will this service add to American Airlines' image?
6. How important will phone service be relative to other factors such as flight schedules, food quality, and baggage handling?

Not all research projects can be this specific in their objectives. Some research is *exploratory*—its goal is to gather preliminary data to shed light on the real nature of the problem and to suggest possible solutions or new ideas. Some research

Analyzing
Marketing
Opportunities

is *descriptive*—it seeks to ascertain certain magnitudes, such as how many people would make an in-flight phone call at $25 a call. Some research is *causal*—its purpose is to test a cause-and-effect relationship. For example, would passengers make more calls if the phone were located next to their seat rather than in the aisle near the lavatory?

STEP 2: DEVELOPING THE RESEARCH PLAN.

The second stage of marketing research calls for developing the most efficient plan for gathering the needed information. The marketing manager needs to know the cost of the research plan before approving it. Suppose the company estimates that launching the in-flight phone service without doing any marketing research would yield a long-term profit of $50,000. The manager believes that doing the research would lead to an improved promotional plan and a long-term profit of $90,000. In this case, the manager should be willing to spend up to $40,000 on this research. If the research would cost more than $40,000, it is not worth doing.[11]

Designing a research plan calls for decisions on the data sources, research approaches, research instruments, sampling plan, and contact methods.

Data Sources. The research plan can call for gathering secondary data, primary data, or both. *Secondary data* are data that were collected for another purpose and already exist somewhere. *Primary data* are data gathered for a specific purpose or for a specific research project.

Researchers usually start their investigation by examining secondary data to see whether their problem can be partly or wholly solved without collecting costly primary data. (Table 4-2 on page 118 shows the rich variety of secondary-data sources available in the United States.[12]) Secondary data provide a starting point for research and offer the advantages of low cost and ready availability.

When the data needed by the researcher do not exist, or are dated, inaccurate, incomplete, or unreliable, the researcher will have to collect primary data. Most marketing research projects involve some primary-data collection. The normal procedure is to interview some people individually and/or in groups to get a preliminary sense of how people feel about the topic in question and then develop a formal research instrument, debug it, and carry it into the field.

When stored and used properly, the data collected in the field can form the backbone of later marketing campaigns. Direct marketers such as record clubs, credit-card companies, and catalog houses have long been wise to power of the database marketing.

❖ A **MARKETING DATABASE** is an organized collection of comprehensive data about individual customers, prospects, or suspects that is current, accessible, and actionable for marketing purposes such as lead generation, lead qualification, sale of a product or service, or maintenance of customer relationships.

Now companies with products ranging from packaged goods to automobiles are shifting their efforts from mass media to database marketing. Two examples:

BLOCKBUSTER The massive entertainment company is using its database of 36 million households and 2 million daily transactions to help its video-rental customers select movies and steer them to other Blockbuster subsidiaries.

KRAFT GENERAL FOODS KGF has amassed a list of more than 30 million users of its products who have provided their names when sending in coupons or responding to other KGF promotions. Based on their interests, KGF regularly send the respondents tips on such things as nutrition and exercise, as well as recipes and coupons for specific KGF brands.[13]

Chapter 23 discusses database marketing in more detail.

Managing Marketing
Information and Measuring
Market Demand

| **TABLE 4-2** | SECONDARY SOURCES OF DATA |

A. Internal Sources

Company profit-loss statements, balance sheets, sales figures, sales-call reports, invoices, inventory records, and prior research reports.

B. Government Publications

- *Statistical Abstract of the United States,* updated annually, provides summary data on demographic, economic, social, and other aspects of the U.S. economy and society.
- *County and City Data Book,* updated every three years, presents statistical information for counties, cities, and other geographical units on population, education, employment, aggregate and median income, housing, bank deposits, retail sales, and so on.
- *U.S. Industrial Outlook* provides projections of industrial activity by industry and includes data on production, sales, shipments, employment, and the like.
- *Marketing Information Guide* provides a monthly annotated bibliography of marketing information.
- Other government publications include the *Annual Survey of Manufacturers; Business Statistics; Census of Manufacturers; Census of Population; Census of Retail Trade, Wholesale Trade, and Selected Service Industries; Census of Transportation; Federal Reserve Bulletin; Monthly Labor Review; Survey of Current Business;* and *Vital Statistics Report.*

C. Periodicals and Books

- *Business Periodicals Index,* a monthly, lists business articles appearing in a wide variety of business publications.
- *Standard and Poor's Industry Surveys* provides updated statistics and analyses of industries.
- *Moody's Manuals* provide financial data and names of executives in major companies.
- *Encyclopedia of Associations* provides information on every major trade and professional association in the United States.
- Marketing journals include the *Journal of Marketing, Journal of Marketing Research,* and *Journal of Consumer Research.*
- Useful trade magazines include *Advertising Age, Chain Store Age, Progressive Grocer, Sales and Marketing Management,* and *Stores.*
- Useful general business magazines include *Business Week, Fortune, Forbes, The Economist, Inc.,* and *Harvard Business Review.*

D. Commercial Data

- *A. C. Nielsen Company* provides data on products and brands sold through retail outlets (Retail Index Services), supermarket scanner data (Scantrack), data on television audiences (Media Research Services), magazine circulation data (Neodata Services, Inc.), and others.
- *MRCA Information Services* provides data on weekly family purchases of consumer products (National Consumer Panel) and data on home food consumption (National Menu Census).
- *Information Resources, Inc.* provides supermarket scanner data (InfoScan) and data on the impact of supermarket promotions (PromotioScan).
- *SAMI/Burke* provides reports on warehouse withdrawals to food stores in selected market areas (SAMI reports) and supermarket scanner data (Samscam).
- *Simmons Market Research Bureau* (MRB Group) provides annual reports covering television markets, sporting goods, and proprietary drugs, giving demographic data by sex, income, age, and brand preferences (selective markets and media reaching them).
- Other commercial research houses selling data to subscribers include the *Audit Bureau of Circulation; Arbitron, Audits and Surveys; Dun and Bradstreet; National Family Opinion; Standard Rate & Data Service;* and *Starch.*

Research Approaches. Primary data can be collected in four ways: observation, focus groups, surveys, and experiments.

- ◆ *Observational research:* Fresh data can be gathered by observing the relevant actors and settings. The American Airlines researchers might meander around airports, airline offices, and travel agencies to hear how travelers talk about the different carriers. The researchers can fly on American and competitors' planes to observe the quality of in-flight service. This exploratory research might yield some useful hypotheses about how travelers choose their air carriers.

- ◆ *Focus-group research:* A *focus group* is a gathering of six to ten people who are invited to spend a few hours with a skilled moderator to discuss a product, service, organization, or other marketing entity (Figure 4-3). The moderator needs to be objective,

knowledgeable on the issue, and versed in group dynamics and consumer behavior. The participants are normally paid a small sum for attending the focus group. The meeting is typically held in pleasant surroundings (a home, for example), and refreshments are served.

In the American Airlines research, the moderator might start with a broad question, such as "How do you feel about air travel?" Questions then move to how people regard the different airlines, various services, and in-flight telephone service. The moderator encourages free and easy discussion, hoping that the group dynamics will reveal deep feelings and thoughts. At the same time, the moderator "focuses" the discussion. The discussion, recorded through note taking or on audio tape or videotape, is subsequently studied to understand consumer beliefs, attitudes, and behavior.

Focus-group research is a useful exploratory step to take before designing a large-scale survey. Consumer-goods companies have been using focus groups for many years, and an increasing number of newspapers, law firms, hospitals, and public-service organizations are discovering their value. However, researchers must avoid generalizing the reported feelings of the focus-group participants to the whole market, since the sample size is too small and the sample is not drawn randomly.[14]

- *Survey research:* While observation and focus groups are best suited for exploratory research, surveys are best suited for descriptive research. Companies undertake surveys to learn about people's knowledge, beliefs, preferences, satisfaction, and so on, and to measure these magnitudes in the general population. Thus American Airlines researchers might want to survey how many people know American, have flown it, prefer it, and so on. We will say more about survey research when we discuss research instruments, sampling plans, and contact methods in the next few pages.

- *Experimental research:* The most scientifically valid research is *experimental research*. Best suited for causal research, experimental research calls for selecting matched groups of subjects, subjecting them to different treatments, controlling extraneous variables, and checking whether observed response differences are statistically significant. To the extent that extraneous factors are eliminated or controlled, the observed effects can be related to the variations in the treatments. The purpose of experimental research is to capture cause-and-effect relationships by eliminating competing explanations of the observed findings.

For example, American Airlines might introduce in-flight phone service on one of its regular flights from New York to Los Angeles at a price of $25 a phone call. On the same flight the following day, it announces the availability of this service at $15 a phone

TABLE 4-3	TYPES OF QUESTIONS

A. CLOSED-END QUESTIONS		
NAME	**DESCRIPTION**	**EXAMPLE**
Dichotomous	A question with two possible answers.	In arranging this trip, did you personally phone American? Yes No
Multiple choice	A question with three or more answers.	With whom are you traveling on this flight? ☐ No one ☐ Spouse ☐ Spouse and children ☐ Children only ☐ Business associates/friends/relatives ☐ An organized tour group
Likert scale	A statement with which the respondent shows the amount of agreement/disagreement.	Small airlines generally give better service than large ones. Strongly Disagree Neither Agree Strongly disagree agree nor agree disagree 1__ 2__ 3__ 4__ 5__
Semantic differential	A scale connecting two bipolar words. The respondent selects the point that represents his or her opinion.	American Airlines Large _ _ _ _ _ _ _ _ _Small Experienced_ _ _ _ _ _ _Inexperienced Modern _ _ _ _ _ _ _ _ Old-fashioned

Importance scale	A scale that rates the importance of some attribute.	Airline food service to me is
		Extremely Very Some- Not very Not
		important impor- what impor- at all
		              tant impor- tant impor-
		                    tant tant
		1___ 2___ 3___ 4___ 5___

Rating scale	A scale that rates some attribute from "poor" to "excellent."	American's food service is Excellent Very Good Good Fair Poor 1___ 2___ 3___ 4___ 5___
Intention-to-buy scale	A scale that describes the respondent's intention to buy.	If an in-flight telephone were available on a long flight, I would Definitely Probably Not Probably Definitely buy buy sure not buy not buy 1___ 2___ 3___ 4___ 5___

call. If the plane carried the same number and type of passengers on each flight, and the day of the week made no difference, then any significant difference in the number of calls made could be related to the price charged. The experimental design could be elaborated further by trying other prices, replicating the same prices on a number of flights, and including other air routes in the experiment. To the extent that the design and execution of the experiment eliminate alternative hypotheses that might explain the results, the research and marketing managers can have confidence in the conclusions.

Research Instruments. Marketing researchers have a choice of two main research instruments in collecting primary data: questionnaires and mechanical devices.

◆ *Questionnaires:* A questionnaire consists of a set of questions presented to respondents for their answers. Because of its flexibility, the questionnaire is by far the most common instrument used to collect primary data. Questionnaires need to be carefully developed, tested, and debugged before they are administered on a large scale. One can usually spot several errors in a casually prepared questionnaire.

In preparing a questionnaire, the professional marketing researcher carefully

B. OPEN-END QUESTIONS

NAME	DESCRIPTION	EXAMPLE
Completely unstructured	A question that respondents can answer in an almost unlimited number of ways.	What is your opinion of American Airlines?
Word association	Words are presented, one at a time, and respondents mention the first word that comes to mind.	What is the first word that comes to your mind when you hear the following? Airline _____ American _____ Travel _____
Sentence completion	An incomplete sentence is presented and respondents complete the sentence.	When I choose an airline, the most important consideration in my decision is _____
Story completion	An incomplete story is presented, and respondents are asked to complete it.	"I flew American a few days ago. I noticed that the exterior and interior of the plane had very bright colors. This aroused in me the following thoughts and feelings. . . . Now complete the story."
Picture completion	A picture of two characters is presented, with one making a statement. Respondents are asked to identify with the other and fill in the empty balloon.	
Thematic Apperception Test (TAT)	A picture is presented and respondents are asked to make up a story about what they think is happening or may happen in the picture.	

chooses the questions and their form, wording, and sequence. A common error is including questions that cannot, would not, or need not be answered and omitting questions that should be answered. Questions that are merely interesting should be dropped because they may exhaust the respondent's patience.

In addition, the form of the question asked can influence the response. Marketing researchers distinguish between open-end and closed-end questions. *Closed-end questions* prespecify all the possible answers, and respondents make a choice among them. *Open-end questions* allow respondents to answer in their own words. Closed-end questions provide answers that are easier to interpret and tabulate. Open-end questions often reveal more because they do not constrain respondents' answers. Open-end questions are especially useful in the exploratory stage of research, where the researcher is looking for insight into how people think rather than in measuring how many people think a certain way. Table 4-3 provides examples of both types of questions.

Finally, the questionnaire designer should exercise care in the wording and sequencing of questions. The questionnaire should use simple, direct, unbiased wording and should be pretested with a sample of respondents before it is used. The lead question should attempt to create interest. Difficult or personal questions should be asked

Managing Marketing
Information and Measuring
Market Demand

toward the end of the questionnaire so that respondents do not become defensive early. Finally, the questions should flow in a logical order.

Recent research has shown that asking respondents to rate a brand on specific attributes early in a survey affects their responses when asked to give an overall rating later in the survey. A *carryover effect* occurs when an overall evaluation is consistent with a previous attribute rating, but a *backfire effect* occurs when the overall evaluation is inconsistent with previous responses. Market researchers need to be aware of these effects as they construct the sequence of questions in a questionnaire.[15]

♦ *Mechanical instruments:* Mechanical devices are used less frequently in marketing research. Galvanometers measure the subject's interest or emotions aroused by exposure to a specific ad or picture. The tachistoscope flashes an ad to a subject with an exposure interval that may range from less than one hundredth of a second to several seconds. After each exposure, the respondent describes everything he or she recalls. Eye cameras study respondents' eye movements to see where their eyes land first, how long they linger on a given item, and so on. The audiometer is attached to television sets in participating homes to record when the set is on and to which channel it is tuned.[16]

Sampling Plan. After deciding on the research approach and instruments, the marketing researcher must design a sampling plan. This plan calls for three decisions:

1. *Sampling unit: Who is to be surveyed?* The marketing researcher must define the target population that will be sampled. In the American Airlines survey, should the sampling unit be business travelers, vacation travelers, or both? Should travelers under age 21 be interviewed? Should both husbands and wives be interviewed? Once the sampling unit is determined, a sampling frame must be developed so that everyone in the target population has an equal chance of being sampled.

2. *Sample size: How many people should be surveyed?* Large samples give more reliable results than small samples. However, it is not necessary to sample the entire target population or even a substantial portion to achieve reliable results. Samples of less than 1% of a population can often provide good reliability, given a credible sampling procedure.

3. *Sampling procedure: How should the respondents be chosen?* To obtain a representative sample, a probability sample of the population should be drawn. *Probability sampling* allows the calculation of confidence limits for sampling error. Thus one could conclude after the sample is taken that "the interval five to seven trips per year has 95 chances in 100 of containing the true number of trips taken annually by air travelers in the Southwest." Three types of probability sampling are described in Table 4-4, section A. When the cost or time involved in probability sampling is too high, marketing researchers will take nonprobability samples. Table 4-4, section B describes three types of *nonprobabil-*

TABLE 4-4	PROBABILITY AND NONPROBABILITY SAMPLES
A. PROBABILITY SAMPLE	
Simple random sample	Every member of the population has an equal chance of selection.
Stratified random sample	The population is divided into mutually exclusive groups (such as age groups), and random samples are drawn from each group.
Cluster (area) sample	The population is divided into mutually exclusive groups (such as city blocks), and the researcher draws a sample of the groups to interview.
B. NONPROBABILITY SAMPLE	
Convenience sample	The researcher selects the most accessible population members from which to obtain information.
Judgment sample	The researcher uses judgment to select population members who are good prospects for accurate information.
Quota sample	The researcher finds and interviews a prescribed number of people in each of several categories.

Analyzing
Marketing
Opportunities

ity sampling. Some marketing researchers feel that nonprobability samples are very useful in many circumstances, even though they do not allow sampling error to be measured.

Contact Methods. Once the sampling plan has been determined, the marketing researcher must decide how the subject should be contacted. The choices are mail, telephone, or personal interviews.

The *mail questionnaire* is the best way to reach people who would not give personal interviews or whose responses might be biased or distorted by the interviewers. Mail questionnaires require simple and clearly worded questions, and the response rate is usually low and/or slow.

Telephone interviewing is the best method for gathering information quickly; the interviewer is also able to clarify questions if the respondents do not understand them. The response rate is typically higher than in the case of mailed questionnaires. The main drawback is that the interviews have to be short and not too personal.

Personal interviewing is the most versatile of the three methods. The interviewer can ask more questions and can record additional observations about the respondent, such as dress and body language. Personal interviewing is the most expensive method and requires more administrative planning and supervision than the other two methods. It is also subject to interviewer bias or distortion.

Personal interviewing takes two forms, arranged interviews and intercept interviews. In *arranged interviews,* respondents are randomly selected and are either telephoned or approached at their homes or offices and asked for an interview. Often a small payment or incentive is given to respondents in appreciation for their time. *Intercept interviews* involve stopping people at a shopping mall or busy street corner and requesting an interview. Intercept interviews have the drawback of being nonprobability samples, and the interviews must not require too much time from the interviewee.

Not all interviewers today are human. Some companies are now using toll-free telephone numbers to solicit marketing information via telephone. For example, in 1993 Pepsi-Cola sent a direct-mail piece to a million households that drank Diet Coke, offering them a chance to call an interactive 800-number, "talk" to Ray Charles, and possibly win a prize. But first they had to use their touch-tone phone to answer a series of market research questions designed to help Pepsi understand Diet Coke households. More than half a million people called and were greeted by Ray and the Uh-Huh Girls. Between questions, callers heard musical sound-bites and lots of "Uh-Huhs" to break the "teletedium" that can plague interactive calls. At the end of the 3½ minute survey Ray and the girls returned to award instant-win prizes, including a one-year supply of Diet Pepsi or a miniature Diet Pepsi vending machine. But Pepsi-Cola was the *real* winner here; the company received vital information on brand preference, consumption rates, and lifestyle activities from over 500,000 of their major competitor's customers.[17]

STEP 3: COLLECT THE INFORMATION. The data collection phase of marketing research is generally the most expensive and the most prone to error. In the case of surveys, four major problems arise. Some respondents will not be at home and must be recontacted or replaced. Other respondents will refuse to cooperate. Still others will give biased or dishonest answers. Finally, some interviewers will be biased or dishonest.

As we've seen, data collection methods are rapidly improving thanks to modern computers and telecommunications. Some research firms interview from a centralized location. Professional interviewers sit in booths and draw telephone numbers at random. When the phone is answered, the interviewer asks the person a

Managing Marketing
Information and Measuring
Market Demand

set of questions, reading them from a monitor and typing the respondents' answers into a computer. This procedure eliminates editing and coding, reduces the number of errors, saves time, and produces all the required statistics. Other research firms have set up interactive terminals in shopping centers. Persons willing to be interviewed sit at a terminal, read the questions from the monitor, and type in their answers. Most respondents enjoy this form of "robot" interviewing.[18]

Several recent technical advances have permitted marketers to test the sales impact of ads and sales promotion. Information Resources, Inc., recruits a panel of supermarkets equipped with optical scanners and electronic cash registers. These optical scanners read the universal product code on each product purchased, recording the brand, size, and price for inventory and ordering purposes. Meanwhile, the firm has also recruited a panel of these stores' customers who have agreed to charge their purchases with a special Shopper's Hotline ID card that holds information about their household characteristics, lifestyle, and income. These same customers have also agreed to let their television-viewing habits be monitored by a black box. All consumer panelists receive their programs through cable television, and Information Resources controls the advertising messages being sent to their houses. The firm can then capture through store purchases which ads led to more purchasing and by which kinds of customers.[19]

STEP 4: ANALYZE THE INFORMATION. The next-to-last step in the marketing research process is to extract pertinent findings from the collected data. The researcher tabulates the data and develops frequency distributions. Averages and measures of dispersion are computed for the major variables. The researcher will also apply some advanced statistical techniques and decision models in the hope of discovering additional findings. (We describe some of these techniques and models later in this chapter.)

STEP 5: PRESENT THE FINDINGS. As the last step in marketing research, the researcher presents his or her findings to the relevant parties. The researcher should not overwhelm management with lots of numbers and fancy statistical techniques, but rather should present major findings that are pertinent to the major marketing decisions facing management.

The main survey findings for the American Airlines case show that:

1. The chief reasons for using in-flight phone service are emergencies, urgent business deals, mix-ups in flight times, and so on. Making phone calls to pass the time would be rare. Most of the calls would be made by businesspeople on expense accounts.

2. About five passengers out of every 200 would make in-flight phone calls at a price of $25 a call; about 12 would make calls at $15. Thus a charge of $15 would produce more revenue ($12 \times \$15 = \$180$) than $25 a call ($5 \times \$25 = \$125$). Still, this is far below the in-flight break-even cost of $1,000.

3. The promotion of in-flight phone service would win American about two extra passengers on each flight. The net revenue from these two extra passengers would be about $620, but this still would not help meet the break-even cost.

4. Offering in-flight service would strengthen the public's image of American Airlines as an innovative and progressive airline. However, it would cost American about $200 per flight to create this extra goodwill.

Of course, these findings could suffer from a variety of errors, and management may want to study the issues further. However, it looks as if in-flight phone service would add more cost than long-term revenue and should not be implemented at the present time. Thus a well-defined marketing research project has helped American Airlines' managers make a better decision than they would have without research.

The Characteristics of Good Marketing Research

What is at the heart of good marketing research? We can pinpoint seven characteristics.

- *Scientific method:* Effective marketing research uses the principles of the scientific method: careful observation, formulation of hypotheses, prediction, and testing. For example, one mail-order house was suffering from a high rate (30%) of returned merchandise. Management asked the marketing research manager to investigate the causes. The marketing researcher examined the characteristics of returned orders, including the geographical locations of the customers, the sizes of the returned orders, and the merchandise categories. One hypothesis was that the longer the customer waited for ordered merchandise, the greater the probability of its return. Statistical analysis confirmed this hypothesis. The researcher estimated how much the return rate would drop for a specific speedup of service. The company did speed delivery time, and the return rate did drop.

- *Research creativity:* At its best, marketing research develops innovative ways to solve a problem. For example, many companies trying to get the scoop on teens and twentysomethings have found that traditional focus groups fail miserably. These often cynical youth are inured to sales pitches and just won't speak up in a conference room with two-way mirrors. Working with Chilton Research, clothing company Bugle Boy countered this problem by going a different research route. Researchers plucked four young men out of obscurity, handed each of them an 8 mm video camera, and told them to document their lives. The young auteurs were given only broad categories to work with: school, home, closet, and shopping. Bugle Boy then used the videos to prompt discussion of product and lifestyle issues in "free-form" focus groups held in unconventional locales, like restaurants. Says one Bugle Boy ad manager, "I think this really helped us to get a handle on what these kids do. It let us see what their lives are all about, their awareness of the Bugle Boy brand and how they perceived the brand."[20]

- *Multiple methods:* Good marketing researchers shy away from overreliance on any one method, preferring to adapt the method to the problem rather than the other way around. They also recognize that using multiple sources leads to better information.

- *Interdependence of models and data:* Good marketing researchers recognize that data are interpreted from underlying models. These models guide the type of information sought and therefore should be made as explicit as possible.

- *Value and cost of information:* Good marketing researchers show concern for estimating the value of information against its cost. Value/cost considerations help the marketing research department determine which research projects to conduct, which research designs to use, and whether to gather more information after the initial results are in. Research costs are typically easy to determine, but the value of research is harder to quantify. The value depends on the reliability and validity of the research findings and management's willingness to accept and act on those findings.

- *Healthy skepticism:* Good marketing researchers show a healthy skepticism toward glib assumptions made by managers about how a market works. (For more on this topic, see the Marketing Insight titled "Marketing Researchers Challenge Conventional Marketing Wisdom.")

- *Ethical marketing:* Good marketing research benefits both the sponsoring company and its consumers. Through marketing research, companies learn more about consumers' needs and are able to supply more satisfying products and services. However, the misuse of marketing research can also harm or annoy consumers. Many consumers see marketing research as an intrusion of their privacy or misperceive it as an attempt to sell them something. Indeed, many research studies appear to be little more than vehicles for pitching the sponsor's products. For example, two studies sponsored by the cloth-diaper industry concluded that cloth diapers are more environmentally friendly. Not surprisingly, two other studies sponsored by the disposable-diaper industry concluded just the opposite. Increasing consumer resentment at such self-serving research has become a major problem for the research industry. This resentment has led to lower survey re-

Managing Marketing
Information and Measuring
Market Demand

Marketing Researchers Challenge Conventional Marketing Wisdom

Kevin Clancy and Robert Shulman—chairman and CEO, respectively, of Copernicus, a leading marketing research company—charge that too many companies build their marketing plans on "marketing myths." Webster's dictionary defines a *myth* as "an ill-founded belief held uncritically, especially by an interested group." Clancy and Shulman list the following myths that have led marketing managers down the wrong path:

1. *A brand's best prospects are the heavy buyers in the category.* Although most companies pursue heavy buyers, these people may not be the best target of marketing efforts. Many heavy users are highly committed to specific competitors, and those who are not are often willing to switch products when a competitor offers them a better deal.

2. *The more appealing a new product is, the more likely it will be a success.* This philosophy can lead the company to give away too much to the customer and result in lower profitability.

3. *The effectiveness of advertising is revealed by how memorable and persuasive it is.* Actually, the best ads, when measured by recall and persuasion scores, are not necessarily the most effective ads. A much better predictor of an ad's effectiveness is the buyer's attitude toward the advertising— specifically, whether the buyer feels he or she received useful information and whether the buyer liked the advertising.

4. *A company is wise to spend the major portion of its research budget on focus groups and qualitative research.* Focus groups and qualitative research are useful but the major part of the research budget should be spent on quantitative research and surveys.

Some marketers will undoubtedly present counter-examples where these "myths" have actually yielded positive results. Nevertheless, the authors deserve credit for forcing marketers to rethink some of their basic assumptions.

Source: Kevin J. Clancy and Robert S. Shulman, *The Marketing Revolution: A Radical Manifesto for Dominating the Marketplace* (New York: HarperBusiness, 1991).

---

sponse rates in recent years. One study found that 36% of Americans now refuse to be interviewed in an average study.[21]

Overcoming Barriers to the Use of Marketing Research

In spite of the rapid growth of marketing research, many companies still fail to use it sufficiently or correctly. Several factors stand in the way of its greater utilization.

- ◆ *A narrow conception of marketing research:* Many managers see marketing research as only a fact-finding operation. They expect the marketing researcher to design a questionnaire, choose a sample, conduct interviews, and report results, often without giving him or her a careful definition of the problem or of the decision alternatives facing management. Then, when fact finding fails to be useful, management's idea of the limited usefulness of marketing research is reinforced.

- ◆ *Uneven caliber of marketing researchers:* Some managers view marketing research as little more than a clerical activity and reward it as such. Less competent marketing researchers are hired, and their weak training and deficient creativity lead to unimpressive results. The disappointing results reinforce management's prejudice against marketing research. Management continues to pay low salaries to its market researchers, thus perpetuating the basic problem.

- ◆ *Late and occasionally erroneous findings by marketing research:* Managers want quick results that are accurate and conclusive. But good marketing research takes time and money. Managers become disappointed when marketing research costs too much or takes too much time, and they lower their opinion of marketing research. This is especially a problem in conducting marketing research in foreign countries, where data are often nonexistent, unreliable, or very costly to collect. For example, Mexico is an important market for U.S. companies, but learning which products Mexicans want has been difficult because of the problems firms have encountered in conducting marketing research. Telephone surveys, for instance, are an unreliable means of collecting data since relatively few people in Mexico have telephones—in Mexico City only 55% to 60% of the population have telephones. In other Mexican cities, the number is as low as 35 percent. The only way to conduct reliable research is through house-to-house surveys, but researchers must be careful in crafting questionnaires, using words that are not difficult to translate. Companies must also bear in mind that many Mexicans have never been exposed to marketing research.[22]

◆ *Personality and presentational differences:* Differences between the styles of line managers and marketing researchers often get in the way of productive relationships. To a manager who wants concreteness, simplicity, and certainty, a marketing researcher's report may seem abstract, complicated, and tentative. Yet in the more progressive companies, marketing researchers are increasingly being included as members of the product management team, and their influence on marketing strategy is growing.

MARKETING DECISION SUPPORT SYSTEM

A growing number of organizations are using a marketing decision support system to help their marketing managers make better decisions. Little defines an *MDSS* as follows:

❖ A MARKETING DECISION SUPPORT SYSTEM (MDSS) is a coordinated collection of data, systems, tools and techniques with supporting software and hardware by which an organization gathers and interprets relevant information from business and environment and turns it into a basis for marketing action.[23]

Here is how an MDSS works. Suppose a marketing manager needs to analyze a problem and take action. The manager puts questions to the appropriate model located in the MDSS. The model draws up data, which are then analyzed statistically. The manager can then use a program to determine the optimal course of action. The manager takes this action, which (along with other forces) affects the environment and results in new data. All of these actions take place, of course, in the computer. (Table 4-5 on pages 128–129 describes the major statistical tools, models, and optimization routines that comprise a modern MDSS.)

MDSS are often found in computer marketing workstations. These workstations are to marketing managers what cockpit controls are to airline pilots—they arm managers with the tools to "fly" the business in the right direction.

New software programs regularly appear to help marketing managers analyze, plan, and control their operations. For example, the introduction of the free market in Eastern Europe has brought an increased need for timely and relevant information to businesses marketing their products and services there. So a team of researchers at Michigan State University has developed a new decision support tool to provide this information. MSU's "Country Consultant" incorporates judgments and guidelines pertaining to various aspects of the countries included in the package. Its ultimate purpose is to aid companies in making intelligent decisions when selecting countries in which to market their products.[24]

Marketing News, April 11, 1994, lists over 100 current marketing and sales software programs that assist in designing marketing research studies, segmenting markets, setting prices and advertising budgets, analyzing media, planning sales force activity, and so on. Here are examples of decision models that have been used by marketing managers:

TABLE 4-5

STATISTICAL TOOLS

1. **Multiple regression.** A statistical technique for estimating a "best fitting" equation showing how the value of a dependent variable varies with changing values in a number of independent variables.

   Example: A company can estimate how unit sales are influenced by changes in the level of company advertising expenditures, sales force size, and price.

2. **Discriminant analysis.** A statistical technique for classifying an object or persons into two or more categories.

   Example: A large retail chain store can determine the variables that discriminate between successful and unsuccessful store locations.[1]

3. **Factor analysis.** A statistical technique used to determine the few underlying dimensions of a larger set of intercorrelated variables.

   Example: A broadcast network can reduce a large set of TV programs down to a small set of basic program types.[2]

4. **Cluster analysis.** A statistical technique for separating objects into a specified number of mutually exclusive groups such that the groups are relatively homogeneous.

   Example: A marketing researcher might want to classify a miscellaneous set of cities into four groups of similar cities.

5. **Conjoint analysis.** A statistical technique whereby respondents' ranked preferences for different offers are decomposed to determine the person's inferred utility function for each attribute and the relative importance of each attribute.

   Example: An airline can determine the total utility delivered by different combinations of passenger services.

6. **Multidimensional scaling.** A variety of techniques for producing perceptual maps of competitive products or brands. Objects are represented as points in a multidimensional space of attributes where their distance from each other is a measure of dissimilarity.

   Example: A computer manufacturer wants to see where his brand is positioned in relation to competitive brands.

MODELS

1. **Markov-process model.** This model shows the probability of moving from a current state to any future state.

   Example: A branded packaged-goods manufacturer can determine the period-to-period switching and staying rates for her brand and, if the probabilities are stable, the brand's ultimate brand share.

BRANDAID: A flexible marketing-mix model focused on consumer packaged goods whose elements are a manufacturer, competitors, retailers, consumers, and the general environment. The model contains submodels for advertising, pricing, and competition. The model is calibrated with a creative blending of judgment, historical analysis, tracking, field experimentation, and adaptive control.[25]

CALLPLAN: A model to help salespeople determine the number of calls to make per period to each prospect and current client. The model takes into account travel time as well as selling time. The model was tested at United Airlines with an experimental group that managed to increase its sales over a matched control group by 8 percentage points.[26]

DETAILER: A model to help salespeople determine which customers to call on and which products to represent on each call. This model was largely developed for pharmaceutical detail people calling on physicians where they could represent no more than three products on a call. In two applications, the model yielded strong profit improvements.[27]

GEOLINE: A model for designing sales and service territories that satisfies three principles: The territories equalize sales workloads; each territory consists of adjacent areas; and the territories are compact. Several successful applications were reported.[28]

2. **Queuing model.** This model shows the waiting times and queue lengths that can be expected in any system, given the arrival and service times and the number of service channels.

Example: A supermarket can use the model to predict queue lengths at different times of the day given the number of service channels and service speed.

3. **New-product pretest models.** This model involves estimating functional relations between buyer states of awareness, trial, and repurchase based on consumer preferences and actions in a pretest situation of the marketing offer and campaign. Among the well-known models are ASSESSOR, COMP, DEMON, NEWS, and SPRINTER.[3]

4. **Sales-response models.** This is a set of models that estimate functional relations between one or more marketing variables—such as sales force size, advertising expenditure, sales-promotion expenditure, etc.—and the resulting demand level.

5. **Discrete choice models (Logit and Probit).** These models compute the probability of choosing an alternative (e.g., a particular brand within a product category) as a function of the attributes of all the alternatives available. They have been widely applied to household panel data for evaluating the effects of various marketing instruments (e.g., price, end-of-aisle display, feature advertising) on brand choice behavior.

OPTIMIZATION ROUTINES

1. **Differential calculus.** This technique allows finding the maximum or minimum value along a well-behaved function.

2. **Mathematical programming.** This technique allows finding the values that would optimize some objective function that is subject to a set of constraints.

3. **Statistical decision theory.** This technique allows determining the course of action that produces the maximum expected value.

4. **Game theory.** This technique allows determining the course of action that will minimize the decision maker's maximum loss in the face of the uncertain behavior of one or more competitors.

5. **Heuristics.** This involves using a set of rules of thumb that shorten the time or work required to find a reasonably good solution in a complex system.

1. S. Sands, "Store Site Selection by Discriminant Analysis," *Journal of the Market Research Society*, 1981, pp. 40–51.

2. V. R. Rao, "Taxonomy of Television Programs Based on Viewing Behavior," *Journal of Marketing Research*, August 1975, pp. 355–58.

3. See Kevin J. Clancy, Robert Shulman, and Marianne Wolf, *Simulated Test Marketing* (New York: Lexington Books, 1994).

MEDIAC: A model to help an advertiser buy media for a year. The media planning model includes market-segment delineation, sales potential estimation, diminishing marginal returns, forgetting, timing issues, and competitor media schedules.[29]

Some of these programs now claim to duplicate the way expert marketers normally make their decisions. Some recent expert system models include:

PROMOTER evaluates sales promotions by determining baseline sales (what sales would have been without promotion) and measuring the increase over baseline associated with the promotion.[30]

ADCAD recommends the type of ad (humorous, slice of life, and so on) to use given the marketing goals and characteristics of the product, target market, and competitive situation.[31]

COVERSTORY examines a mass of syndicated sales data and writes an English-language memo reporting the highlights.[32]

The late 1990s will undoubtedly usher in further software programs and decision models.[33] For more on this topic, see the Vision 2000 feature titled "Neural Networks and Artificial Intelligence Come to Marketing."

Managing Marketing
Information and Measuring
Market Demand

Neural Networks and Artificial Intelligence Come to Marketing

With the advent of neural networking technology, marketing and sales professionals can now access the knowledge of experts with only a few taps on their computer keyboard. By the beginning of the twenty-first century, it is widely believed, expert systems will be the primary force in segmenting, targeting, and making marketing and sales more efficient.

Neural networking software, designed after the patterns of cells in the human brain, can actually "learn" from large sets of data. By scanning thousands of data records again and again, the software can build a strong statistical model describing important relationships and patterns in the data—not something a human marketing researcher has the time (or eye power) to do accurately and consistently. IBM developed a set of six computer programs called Data Mining that can analyze large data sets and reveal clusters, relationships, rules, and so on. Using Data Mining, the catalog company Lands' End was able to identify over 5,200 customer segments based on different purchase patterns. As a result, Lands' End could better target its mailings to those customer segments most likely to be interested in its changing offers.

The beauty of today's expert systems is that most do not require a powerful (and expensive) supercomputer. Within the past five years neural networking and other artificial intelligence technology have finally become adaptable to PCs. Nielson is one of the marketing research giants developing its own expert system for use on the PC. One of its newest products, "Spotlight," helps companies determine their market share in a fraction of the time it used to take. "We're talking a matter of minutes instead of days," says Nielson's director of client sales and service.

Sales reps, who have reaped huge benefits from sales automation in recent years, have also shaved whole weeks from the sales process using the power of expert systems. At Wells Fargo Alarm Services, it used to take sales reps up to 10 days to close a deal, including preparation of all of the pre- and post-sales paperwork. Today, each of Wells Fargo's 50 managers and 185 sales reps use an IBM ThinkPad 700c equipped with a sales support system that includes an expert system. Instead of going back to the office after a call, Wells Fargo reps now turn on their computer and press a button. A program in the computer begins asking questions regarding the customer's needs. Based on the answers the sales rep gives, the system automatically builds a bill of materials, prepares a printed pricing proposal, and sets up contracts for the sale—all in less than 20 minutes.

Sources: Beverly Cramp, "It's Not That Clever," *Marketing,* July 28, 1994, pp. 36, 38; Howard Schlossberg, "Real Hopes for Research Placed in Artificial Intelligence," *Marketing News,* January 3, 1994, p. 8; Melissa Campanelli, "Sound the Alarm!" *Sales and Marketing Management,* Part 2, December 1994, pp. 20–25; and "Data Mining—An IBM Overview," a paper by Dr. Michael J. Rothman, Hudson Valley Research Park, Zip 47A, 1580 Route 52, Hopewell Junction, NY.

AN OVERVIEW OF FORECASTING AND DEMAND MEASUREMENT

One of a company's major reasons for undertaking marketing research is to identify market opportunities. Once the research is complete, the company must carefully evaluate each opportunity before choosing its target markets. Specifically, the company needs to measure and forecast the size, growth, and profit potential of each opportunity. Sales forecasts are used by finance to raise the needed cash for investment and operations; by the manufacturing department to establish capacity and output levels; by purchasing to acquire the right amount of supplies; and by human resources to hire the needed number of workers. Marketing is responsible for preparing the sales forecasts. If its forecast is far off the mark, the company either will be saddled with excess capacity and inventory or will lose money because of inadequate inventories.

Sales forecasts are based on estimates of demand. Managers need to define carefully what they mean by market demand.

FIGURE 4-4
Ninety Types of Demand
Measurement (6 × 5 × 3)

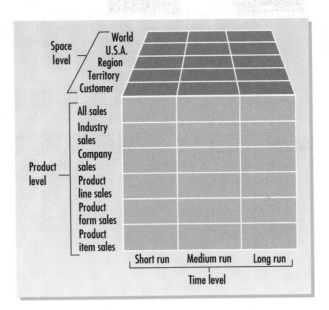

Measures of Market Demand

As part of their ongoing planning, companies prepare many estimates of market size. Figure 4-4 shows 90 different types of demand estimates that a company can make. Demand can be measured for six different *product levels,* five different *space levels,* and three different *time levels.*

Each demand measure serves a specific purpose. A company might forecast short-run demand for a particular product for the purpose of ordering raw materials, planning production, and borrowing cash. It might forecast regional demand for its major product line to decide whether to set up regional distribution.

Which Market to Measure?

Marketers talk about potential markets, available markets, served markets, and penetrated markets. To clarify these terms, let us start with the definition of *market:*

❖   A **MARKET** is the set of all actual and potential buyers of a product.

Given this definition, the size of a market hinges on the number of buyers who might exist for a particular market offer. The *potential market* is the set of consumers who profess a sufficient level of interest in a defined market offer.

Consumer interest is not enough to define a market, however. Potential consumers must have enough income for the product, and they must have access to the product offer. If the product is not distributed in certain areas, potential consumers in those areas are not available to marketers. The *available market* is the set of consumers who have interest, income, and access to a particular market offer.

For some market offers, the company or government may restrict sales to certain groups. For example, a particular state might ban motorcycle sales to anyone under 21 years of age. The remaining adults constitute the *qualified available market*—the set of consumers who have interest, income, access, and qualifications for the particular market offer.

Once the company has identified the available market, it has the choice of going after the whole available market or concentrating on certain segments. The *target market* (also called the *served market*) is the part of the qualified available market the company decides to pursue. A company, for example, might decide to concentrate its marketing and distribution effort on the East Coast. The East Coast becomes its target market.

The company and its competitors will end up selling to a certain number of buyers in its target market. The *penetrated market* is the set of consumers who have already bought the company's product.

These market definitions are a useful tool for market planning. If the company is not satisfied with its current sales, it can take a number of actions. It can try to attract a larger percentage of buyers from its target market. It can lower the qualifications of potential buyers. It can expand its available market by opening distribution on the West Coast or lowering its price. Ultimately, the company can try to expand the potential market by advertising the product to less interested consumers or ones not previously targeted. Some liquor companies have been successful at expanding their market with new ad campaigns. Consider the case of Dewar's:

DEWAR'S   For years Dewar's ran its classic "Profile" ads in which relatively famous middle-aged achievers coyly listed their "small" accomplishments—winning a Pulitzer, performing brain surgery, or composing a sonata in G minor—along with their favorite Dewar's drink. While these Dewar's Profile ads lent prestige to the brand for the past quarter century, Dewar's scotch sales began slipping drastically as a new generation of drinkers was clearly not impressed. In 1994 Dewar's launched new ads with the aim of turning Generation X on to the pleasures of drinking scotch. "You finally have a real job, a real place, a real girlfriend," reads the award-winning Leo Burnett ad. "How about a real drink?"[34]

A Vocabulary for Demand Measurement

The major concepts in demand measurement are *market demand* and *company demand*. Within each, we distinguish among a demand function, a sales forecast, and a potential.

MARKET DEMAND.   As we've seen, the marketer's first step in evaluating marketing opportunities is to estimate total market demand.

FIGURE 4-5
Market Demand Functions

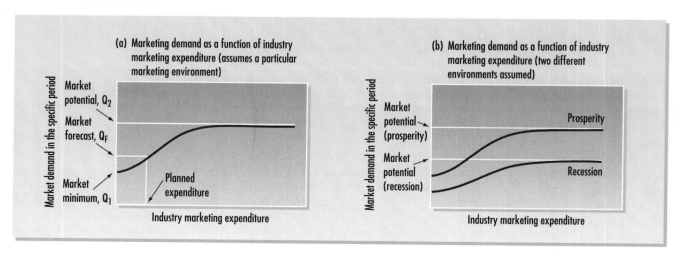

❖ **MARKET DEMAND** for a product is the total volume that would be bought by a defined customer group in a defined geographical area in a defined time period in a defined marketing environment under a defined marketing program.

Market demand is not a fixed number but rather a function of the stated conditions. For this reason, it can be called the *market demand function*. The dependence of total market demand on underlying conditions is illustrated in Figure 4-5(a). The horizontal axis shows different possible levels of industry marketing expenditure in a given time period. The vertical axis shows the resulting demand level. The curve represents the estimated market demand associated with varying levels of industry marketing expenditure. Some base sales (called the *market minimum* labeled Q_1 in the figure) would take place without any demand-stimulating expenditures. Higher levels of industry marketing expenditures would yield higher levels of demand, first at an increasing rate, then at a decreasing rate. Marketing expenditures beyond a certain level would not stimulate much further demand, thus suggesting an upper limit to market demand called the *market potential* (labeled Q_2 in the figure).

The distance between the market minimum and the market potential shows the overall *marketing sensitivity of demand*. We can think of two extreme types of markets, the expansible and the nonexpansible. An *expansible* market, such as the market for racquetball playing, is very much affected in its total size by the level of industry marketing expenditures. In terms of Figure 4-5(a), the distance between Q_1 and Q_2 is relatively large. A *nonexpansible* market—for example, the market for eyeglasses—is not much affected by the level of marketing expenditures; the distance between Q_1 and Q_2 is relatively small. Organizations selling in a nonexpansible market must accept the market's size (the level of *primary demand* for the product class) and direct their marketing efforts to winning a larger market share for their product (the level of *selective demand* for the company's product).

It is important to emphasize that the market demand function is *not* a picture of market demand over time. Rather, the curve shows alternative current forecasts of market demand associated with alternative possible levels of industry marketing effort in the current period.

MARKET FORECAST.   Only one level of industry marketing expenditure will actually occur. The market demand corresponding to this level is called the *market forecast*.

MARKET POTENTIAL.   The market forecast shows expected market demand, not maximum market demand. For the latter, we have to visualize the level of market demand for a "very high" level of industry marketing expenditure, where further increases in marketing effort would have little effect in stimulating further demand.

❖ **MARKET POTENTIAL** is the limit approached by market demand as industry marketing expenditures approach infinity, for a given environment.

The phrase "for a given environment" is crucial in the concept of market potential. Consider the market potential for automobiles in a period of recession versus a period of prosperity. The market potential is higher during prosperity. The dependence of market potential on the environment is illustrated in Figure 4-5(b). Market analysts distinguish between the position of the market demand function and movement along it. Companies cannot do anything about the position of the market demand function, which is determined by the marketing environment (discussed in detail in Chapter 5). However, companies influence their particular location on the function when they decide how much to spend on marketing.

Managing Marketing
Information and Measuring
Market Demand

COMPANY DEMAND. We are now ready to define *company demand.*

❖ **COMPANY DEMAND** is the company's estimated share of market demand at alternative levels of company marketing effort.

In symbols:

$$Q_i = s_i Q \tag{4-1}$$

where:

$$Q_i = \text{company } i\text{'s demand}$$
$$s_i = \text{company } i\text{'s market share}$$
$$Q = \text{total market demand}$$

The company's share of market demand depends on how its products, services, prices, communications, and so on are perceived relative to its competitors'. If other things are equal, the company's market share would depend on the size and effectiveness of its market expenditures relative to competitors. Marketing model builders have developed *sales-response functions* to measure how a company's sales are affected by its marketing expenditure level, marketing mix, and marketing effectiveness.[35]

COMPANY SALES FORECAST. Once marketers have estimated company demand, their next task is to choose a level of marketing effort. The chosen level will produce an expected level of sales.

❖ The **COMPANY SALES FORECAST** is the expected level of company sales based on a chosen marketing plan and an assumed marketing environment.

The company sales forecast is represented graphically with company sales on the vertical axis and company marketing effort on the horizontal axis, as in Figure 4-5.

Too often the sequential relationship between the company forecast and the company marketing plan is confused. One frequently hears that the company should develop its marketing plan on the basis of its sales forecast. This forecast-to-plan sequence is valid if "forecast" means an estimate of national economic activity or if company demand is nonexpansible. The sequence is not valid, however, where market demand is expansible or where "forecast" means an estimate of company sales. The company sales forecast does not establish a basis for deciding what to spend on marketing. On the contrary, the sales forecast is the *result* of an assumed marketing expenditure plan.

Two other concepts are worth mentioning in relation to the company sales forecast.

❖ A **SALES QUOTA** is the sales goal set for a product line, company division, or sales representative. It is primarily a managerial device for defining and stimulating sales effort.

Management sets sales quotas on the basis of the company sales forecast and the psychology of stimulating its achievement. Generally, sales quotas are set slightly higher than estimated sales to stretch the sales force's effort.

❖ A **SALES BUDGET** is a conservative estimate of the expected volume of sales and is used primarily for making current purchasing, production, and cash-flow decisions.

Analyzing
Marketing
Opportunities

The sales budget considers the sales forecast and the need to avoid excessive risk. Sales budgets are generally set slightly lower than the sales forecast.

COMPANY SALES POTENTIAL. *Company sales potential* is the sales limit approached by company demand as company marketing effort increases relative to competitors. The absolute limit of company demand is, of course, the market potential. The two would be equal if the company achieved 100% of the market. In most cases, company sales potential is less than market potential, even when company marketing expenditures increase considerably relative to competitors'. The reason is that each competitor has a hard core of loyal buyers who are not very responsive to other companies' efforts to woo them.

Estimating Current Demand

We are now ready to examine practical methods for estimating current market demand. The planning and execution of marketing strategy requires marketing executives to estimate total market potential, area market potential, and total industry sales and market shares.

TOTAL MARKET POTENTIAL. *Total market potential* is the maximum amount of sales that might be available to all the firms in an industry during a given period under a given level of industry marketing effort and given environmental conditions. A common way to estimate total market potential is as follows:

$$Q = nqp \qquad (4\text{-}2)$$

where:

Q = total market potential
n = number of buyers in the specific product/market under the given
  assumptions
q = quantity purchased by an average buyer
p = price of an average unit

Thus if 100 million people buy books each year, and the average book buyer buys three books a year, and the average price of a book is $10, then the total market potential for books is $3 billion (= 100,000,000 × 3 × $10). The most difficult component to estimate in formula (4-2) is n, the number of buyers in the specific product/market. One can always start with the total population in the nation, say 261 million people. The next step is to eliminate groups that obviously would not buy the product. Let us assume that illiterate people and children under 12 do not buy books, and they constitute 20% of the population. This means that only 80% of the population, or approximately 209 million people, would be in the *suspect pool*. We might do further research and find that people of low income and low education do not read books, and they constitute over 30% of the suspect pool. Eliminating them, we arrive at a *prospect pool* of approximately 146,300,000 book buyers. We would use this number of potential buyers in formula (4-2) to calculate total market potential.

A variation on formula (4-2) is the *chain-ratio method*. This method involves multiplying a base number by several adjusting percentages. Suppose a brewery is interested in estimating the market potential for a new light beer. An estimate can be made by the following calculation.[36]

Demand for the new light beer = *Population* × *personal discretionary income per capita* × *average percentage of discretionary income spent on food* × *average percentage of amount spent on food that is spent on beverages* × *average percentage of amount spent on beverages that is spent on alcoholic beverages* × *average percentage of amount spent on alcoholic beverages that is spent on beer* × *expected percentage of amount spent on beer that will be spent on light beer*

Managing Marketing
Information and Measuring
Market Demand

AREA MARKET POTENTIAL. Companies face the problem of selecting the best territories and allocating their marketing budget optimally among these territories. Therefore they need to estimate the market potential of different cities, states, and nations. Two major methods of assessing area market potential are available: the market-buildup method, which is used primarily by business marketers, and the multiple-factor index method, which is used primarily by consumer marketers.

Market-Buildup Method. The *market-buildup method* calls for identifying all the potential buyers in each market and estimating their potential purchases. This method produces accurate results if we have a list of all potential buyers *and* a good estimate of what each will buy. Unfortunately, this information is not always easy to gather.

Consider a machine-tool company that wants to estimate the area market potential for its wood lathe in the Boston area. Its first step is to identify all potential buyers of wood lathes in the Boston area. The buyers consist primarily of manufacturing establishments that have to shape or ream wood as part of their operation, so the company could compile a list from a directory of all manufacturing establishments in the Boston area. Then it could estimate the number of lathes each industry might purchase based on the number of lathes per thousand employees or per $1 million of sales in that industry.

An efficient method of estimating area market potentials makes use of the *Standard Industrial Classification (SIC) System* developed by the U.S. Bureau of the Census. The SIC classifies all manufacturing into 20 major industry groups, each with a two-digit code. Thus number 25 is furniture and fixtures, and number 35 is machinery except electrical. Each major industry group is further subdivided into about 150 industry groups designated by a three-digit code (number 251 is household furniture, and number 252 is office furniture). Each industry is further subdivided into approximately 450 product categories designated by a four-digit code (number 2521 is wood office furniture, and number 2522 is metal office furniture). For each four-digit SIC number, the Census of Manufacturers provides the number of establishments subclassified by location, number of employees, annual sales, and net worth.

To use the SIC, the lathe manufacturer must first determine the four-digit SIC codes that represent products whose manufacturers are likely to require lathe machines. For example, lathes will be used by manufacturers in SIC number 2511 (wood household furniture), number 2521 (wood office furniture), and so on. To get a full picture of all four-digit SIC industries that might use lathes, the company can use three methods: (1) It can determine past customers' SIC codes; (2) it can go through the SIC manual and check off all the four-digit industries that, in its

			(3)	
TABLE 4-6		(2)	**POTENTIAL**	
		NUMBER	**NUMBER OF**	
MARKET-BUILDUP METHOD	(1)	**OF**	**LATHE SALES**	
USING SIC CODES	**ANNUAL**	**ESTABLISH-**	**PER $1 MILLION**	**MARKET**
(HYPOTHETICAL LATHE	**SALES**	**MENTS**	**CUSTOMER**	**POTENTIAL**
MANUFACTURER — BOSTON	**IN MILLIONS OF $**		**SALES**	**(1 × 2 × 3)**
AREA) SIC				
2511	1	6	10	60
	5	2	10	100
2521	1	3	5	15
	5	1	5	25
				200

judgment, would have an interest in lathes; and/or (3) it can mail questionnaires to a wide range of companies inquiring about their interest in wood lathes.

The company's next task is to determine an appropriate base for estimating the number of lathes that will be used in each industry. Suppose customer industry sales are the most appropriate base. For example, in SIC number 2511, 10 lathes may be used for every $1 million worth of sales. Once the company estimates the rate of lathe ownership relative to the customer industry's sales, it can compute the market potential.

Table 4-6 shows a hypothetical computation for the Boston area involving two SIC codes. In number 2511 (wood household furniture), there are six establishments with annual sales of $1 million and two establishments with annual sales of $5 million. It is estimated that 10 lathes can be sold in this SIC code for every $1 million in customer sales. The six establishments with annual sales of $1 million account for $6 million in sales, which is a potential of 60 lathes (6 × 10). Altogether, it appears that the Boston area has a market potential for 200 lathes.

The company can use the same method to estimate the market potential for other areas in the country. Suppose the market potentials for all the markets add up to 2,000 lathes. This means that the Boston market contains 10% of the total market potential, which might warrant the company's allocating 10% of its marketing expenditures to the Boston market. In practice, SIC information is not enough. The lathe manufacturer also needs additional information about each market, such as the extent of market saturation, the number of competitors, the market growth rate, and the average age of existing equipment.

If the company decides to sell lathes in Boston, it must know how to identify the best-prospect companies. In the old days, sales reps called on companies door to door; this was called *bird-dogging* or *smokestacking.* Cold calls are far too costly today. The company should get a list of Boston companies and qualify them by direct mail or telemarketing to identify the best prospects. The lathe manufacturer can access *Dun's Market Identifiers,* which lists 27 key facts for over 9,300,000 business locations in the United States and Canada.

Multiple-Factor Index Method. Like business marketers, consumer companies also have to estimate area market potentials. But the customers of consumer companies are too numerous to be listed. Thus the method most commonly used in consumer markets is a straightforward index method. A drug manufacturer, for example, might assume that the market potential for drugs is directly related to population size. If the state of Virginia has 2.28% of the U.S. population, the company might assume that Virginia will be a market for 2.28% of total drugs sold.

A single factor, however, is rarely a complete indicator of sales opportunity. Regional drug sales are also influenced by per capita income and the number of physicians per 10,000 people. Thus it makes sense to develop a *multiple-factor index* with each factor assigned a specific weight. Consider the following buying-power index used in the "Annual Survey of Buying Power" published by *Sales and Marketing Management:*

$$B_i = 0.5y_i + 0.3r_i + 0.2p_i \qquad (4\text{-}3)$$

where:

B_i = percentage of total national buying power found in area i
y_i = percentage of national effective buying income originating in area i
r_i = percentage of national retail sales in area i
p_i = percentage of national population of ages 18 and over per household located in area i

Managing Marketing
Information and Measuring
Market Demand

	(1)	(2)	
TABLE 4-7	CALCULATING THE BRAND DEVELOPMENT INDEX (BDI)		
TERRITORY	PERCENT OF U.S. BRAND SALES	PERCENT OF U.S. CATEGORY SALES	BDI (1 ÷ 2) × 100
Seattle	3.09	2.71	114
Portland	6.74	10.41	65
Boston	3.49	3.85	91
Toledo	.97	.81	120
Chicago	1.13	.81	140
Baltimore	3.12	3.00	104

The numbers are the weights attached to each variable. For example, suppose Virginia has 2.00% of the U.S. disposable personal income, 1.96% of U.S. retail sales, and 2.28% of U.S. population. The buying-power index for Virginia would be

$$0.5\ (2.00) + 0.3\ (1.96) + 0.2\ (2.28) = 2.04$$

Thus 2.04% of the nation's drug sales might be expected to take place in Virginia.

The weights used in the buying-power index are somewhat arbitrary. Other weights can be assigned if appropriate. Furthermore, a manufacturer would want to adjust the market potential for additional factors, such as competitors' presence in that market, local promotional costs, seasonal factors, and local market idiosyncrasies.

Many companies compute other area indexes as a guide to allocating marketing resources. Suppose the drug company is reviewing the six cities listed in Table 4-7. The first two columns show its percentage of U.S. brand and category sales in these six cities. Column 3 shows the *brand development index (BDI),* which is the index of brand sales to category sales. Seattle, for example, has a BDI of 114 because the brand is relatively more developed than the category in Seattle. Portland has a BDI of 65, which means that the brand in Portland is relatively underdeveloped. Normally, the lower the BDI, the higher the market opportunity, in that there is room to grow the brand. However, other marketers would argue the opposite, that marketing funds should go into the brand's strongest markets—where it might be easy to capture more brand share. Clearly, other factors have to be considered.[37]

After the company decides on the city-by-city allocation of its budget, it can refine each city allocation down to census tracts or ZIP+4-code centers. *Census tracts* are small, locally defined statistical areas in metropolitan areas and some other counties. They generally have stable boundaries and a population of about 4,000. *ZIP+4-code centers* (which were designed by the U.S. Post Office) are a little larger than neighborhoods. Data on population size, median family income, and other characteristics are available for these geographical units. Marketers have found these data extremely useful for identifying high-potential retail areas within large cities or for buying mailing lists to use in direct-mail campaigns.

INDUSTRY SALES AND MARKET SHARES. Besides estimating total potential and area potential, a company needs to know the actual industry sales taking place in its market. This means identifying its competitors and estimating their sales.

The industry's trade association will often collect and publish total industry sales, although it usually does not list individual company sales separately. Using

Analyzing
Marketing
Opportunities

this information, each company can evaluate its performance against the whole industry. Suppose a company's sales are increasing 5% a year, and industry sales are increasing 10 percent. This company is actually losing its relative standing in the industry.

Another way to estimate sales is to buy reports from a marketing research firm that audits total sales and brand sales. For example, A. C. Nielsen Company audits retail sales in various product categories in supermarkets and drugstores and sells this information to interested companies. These audits can give a company valuable information about its total product-category sales as well as brand sales. It can compare its performance to the total industry and/or any particular competitor to see whether it is gaining or losing share.

Business-goods marketers typically have a harder time estimating industry sales and market shares than consumer-goods manufacturers. Business marketers have no Nielsens to rely on. Distributors typically will not supply information about how much of competitors' products they are selling. Business-goods marketers therefore operate with less knowledge of their market share results.

Estimating Future Demand

We are now ready to examine methods of estimating future demand. Very few products or services lend themselves to easy forecasting. Cases of easy forecasting generally involve a product whose absolute level or trend is fairly constant and where competition is nonexistent (public utilities) or stable (pure oligopolies). In most markets, total demand and company demand are not stable, and good forecasting becomes a key factor in company success. The more unstable the demand, the more critical is forecast accuracy, and the more elaborate is forecasting procedure.

Companies commonly use a three-stage procedure to prepare a sales forecast. They prepare a macroeconomic forecast first, followed by an industry forecast, followed by a company sales forecast. The macroeconomic forecast calls for projecting inflation, unemployment, interest rates, consumer spending, business investment, government expenditures, net exports, and other variables. The end result is a forecast of gross national product, which is then used, along with other environmental indicators, to forecast industry sales. Then the company derives its sales forecast by assuming that it will win a certain market share.

How exactly do firms develop their macroeconomic forecasts? Many large firms have planning departments that use sophisticated mathematical techniques to carry out this task. (For a detailed discussion of these methods, see Appendix 2, "Statistical Methods for Future Demand Projection.") Smaller firms can buy forecasts from three sources:

- *Marketing research firms,* which develop a forecast by interviewing customers, distributors, and other knowledgeable parties.
- *Specialized forecasting firms,* which produce long-range forecasts of particular macroenvironmental components, such as population, natural resources, and technology. Among the best-known of these firms are Data Resources, Wharton Econometric, and Chase Econometric.
- *Futurist research firms,* which produce speculative scenarios. Among the most well-known of these firms are the Hudson Institute, the Futures Group, and the Institute for the Future.

All forecasts are built on one of three information bases: what people say, what people do, or what people have done. The first basis—what people say—involves surveying the opinions of buyers or those close to them, such as salespeople or outside experts. It encompasses three methods: surveys of buyer's intentions, composites of sales force opinions, and expert opinion. Building a forecast on what people do involves another method, that of putting the product into a test market to measure buyer response. The final basis—what people have done—involves analyzing records of past buying behavior or using time-series analysis or statistical demand analysis.

SURVEY OF BUYERS' INTENTIONS. Forecasting is the art of anticipating what buyers are likely to do under a given set of conditions. Because buyers' behavior is so important, buyers should be surveyed. Surveys are especially valuable if the buyers have clearly formulated intentions, will carry them out, and will describe them to interviewers.

In regard to large consumer durables (for example, major appliances), several research organizations conduct periodic surveys of consumer buying intentions. These organizations ask questions like the following:

DO YOU INTEND TO BUY AN AUTOMOBILE WITHIN THE NEXT SIX MONTHS?					
0.00	0.20	0.40	0.60	0.80	1.00
No chance	Slight possibility	Fair possibility	Good possibility	High probability	Certain

This is called a *purchase probability scale.* The various surveys also inquire into the consumers' present and future personal finances and their expectations about the economy. The various bits of information are then combined into a consumer sentiment measure (Survey Research Center of the University of Michigan) or a consumer confidence measure (Sindlinger and Company). Consumer durable-goods producers subscribe to these indexes in the hope of anticipating major shifts in consumer buying intentions so that they can adjust their production and marketing plans accordingly.

Some surveys measuring purchase probability are geared toward getting feedback on specific new products before they are released in the marketplace:

NABISCO　　　Each month Richard Saunders Inc.'s AcuPOLL research system tests 35 new-product concepts in person on 100 nationally representative primary grocery store shoppers. The poll rates participants' interest in buying a given new product, their perceptions of how new and different the product idea is, and their judgment of the product's value compared with its price. In a recent poll Nabisco's Oreo Chocolate Cones received a rare A+ rating, meaning consumers think it is an outstanding concept that they would try and buy. Other products didn't fare so well. Nubrush Anti-bacterial Toothbrush spray disinfectant, from Applied Microdontics, is one new product concept that received an F on its "report card." AcuPOLL found Nubrush to be overpriced and overzealous: Most consumers don't think they have a problem with "infected" toothbrushes.[38]

In the realm of business buying, various agencies carry out buyer-intention surveys regarding plant, equipment, and materials. The better-known agencies are McGraw-Hill Research and Opinion Research Corporation. Their estimates tend to fall within a 10% error band of the actual outcomes. Buyer-intention surveys are particularly useful in estimating demand for industrial products, consumer durables, product purchases where advanced planning is required, and new products. The value of a buyer-intention survey increases to the extent that the cost of reaching buyers is small, the buyers are few, they have clear intentions, they implement their intentions, and they willingly disclose their intentions.[39]

COMPOSITE OF SALES FORCE OPINIONS. Where buyer interviewing is impractical, the company may ask its sales representatives to estimate their future sales. Each sales representative estimates how much each current and prospective customer will buy of each of the company's products.

Few companies use their sales force's estimates without making some adjustments. Sales representatives might be pessimistic or optimistic, or they might go from one extreme to another because of a recent sales setback or success. Furthermore, they are often unaware of larger economic developments and do not know how their company's marketing plans will influence future sales in their territory. They might deliberately underestimate demand so that the company will set a low sales quota. Or they might lack the time to prepare careful estimates or might not consider the effort worthwhile.

To encourage better estimating, the company could supply certain aids or incentives to the sales force. For example, the sales reps might receive a record of their past forecasts compared with their actual sales and also a description of company assumptions on the business outlook, competitor behavior, marketing plans, and so on.

A number of benefits can be gained by involving the sales force in forecasting. Sales representatives might have better insight into developing trends than any other single group. After participating in the forecasting process, the sales representatives might have greater confidence in their sales quotas and more incentive to achieve them.[40] Also, a "grass-roots" forecasting procedure provides very detailed estimates broken down by product, territory, customer, and sales representatives.

EXPERT OPINION. Companies can also obtain forecasts from experts. Experts include dealers, distributors, suppliers, marketing consultants, and trade associations. Large appliance companies survey their dealers periodically for their forecasts of short-term demand, as do car companies. Dealer estimates are subject to the same strengths and weaknesses as sales force estimates. Many companies buy economic and industry forecasts from well-known economic-forecasting firms. These forecasting specialists are able to prepare better economic forecasts than the company because they have more data available and more forecasting expertise.

Occasionally companies will invite a group of experts to prepare a forecast. The experts exchange views and produce a group estimate *(group-discussion methods)*. Or the experts supply their estimates individually, and an analyst combines them into a single estimate *(pooling of individual estimates)*. Alternatively, the experts supply individual estimates and assumptions that are reviewed by the company, then revised. Further rounds of estimating and refining follow *(Delphi method)*.[41]

MARKET-TEST METHOD. Where buyers do not plan their purchases carefully or experts are not available or reliable, a direct market test is desirable. A direct market test is especially desirable in forecasting new-product sales or established product sales in a new distribution channel or territory. We discuss market testing in detail in Chapter 11.

SUMMARY

1. Three developments make the need for marketing information greater now than at any time in the past: the rise of global marketing, the new emphasis on buyers' wants, and the trend toward nonprice competition.

2. To carry out their analysis, planning, implementation, and control responsibilities, marketing managers need a *marketing information system (MIS)*. The MIS's role is to assess the managers' information needs, develop the needed information, and distribute the information to marketing managers in a timely manner.

3. An MIS has four components: (1) an internal records system, which includes information on the order-to-payment cycle and sales reporting systems; (2) a marketing intelligence system, a set of procedures and sources used by managers to obtain everyday information about pertinent developments in the marketing environment; (3) a marketing research system that allows for the systematic design, collection, analysis, and reporting of data and findings relevant to a specific marketing situation; and (4) a computerized marketing decision support system that helps managers interpret relevant data and information and turn them into a basis for marketing action.

4. Companies can conduct their own marketing research or hire other companies to do the research for them. The marketing research process consists of defining the problem and research objectives, developing the research plan, collecting the information, analyzing the information, and presenting the findings to management. In conducting research, firms must decide whether to collect their own data or use data that already exist. They must also decide which research approach (observational, focus group, survey, experimental) and which research instrument (questionnaires or mechanical instruments) to use. In addition, they must decide on a sampling plan and contact methods. Good marketing research is characterized by the scientific method, creativity, multiple research methods, accurate model building, cost/benefit analysis, healthy skepticism, and an ethical focus. A growing number of companies are now using *marketing decision support systems* to help their marketing managers make better decisions.

5. One of a company's major reasons for undertaking marketing research is to discover market opportunities. Once the research is complete, the company must carefully evaluate its opportunities and decide which markets to enter. Once in the market, it must prepare sales forecasts. These forecasts are based on estimates of demand.

6. There are two types of demand: market demand and company demand. To estimate current demand, companies attempt to determine total market potential, area market potential, industry sales, and market share. To estimate future demand, companies can survey buyers' intentions, solicit their sales force's input, gather expert opinions, and/or engage in market testing. Mathematical models, advanced statistical techniques, and computerized data collection procedures are essential to all types of demand and sales forecasting.

CONCEPT APPLICATIONS

1. Seaquist Closures, a manufacturer of screw-on plastic caps for shampoo bottles, tried unsuccessfully to obtain from its customers (shampoo manufacturers) product information that it needed to make continuous product improvements. What steps could Seaquist take to obtain the information it needs? What consumer problems might its research uncover?

2. A client of your marketing research firm has just made the following statement to you: "You guys are always creating new terms to describe the same old concepts. MIS is just an expensive word for marketing research!" Explain to your client how MIS differs from marketing research.

3. You are the marketing director for a manufacturer of canned food products. Your boss wants to know how many stores carry your picante sauce. Since you sell through food brokers, you don't know the answer. Your boss wants an answer in two days. How will you find it?

4. A researcher wishes to evaluate the effects of three alternative shelf arrangements (referred to as A, B, and C). The researcher plans to do this by observing the sales gener-

ated by each variation in each of three stores during three time periods. What kind of experimental design might the researcher use?

5. FabuLooks is a company that manufacturers women's hair care products (shampoos, conditioners, gels, sprays, spritzes, hair coloring/highlighting, home permanents). FabuLooks presently distributes its products nationwide, and top management thinks the company should add a number of products to each of its lines. Why might the company want to expand its product line? What are some factors that FabuLooks' management should consider and weigh before making the decision to expand its line? What factors should the company consider in designing its new products? What types of market research might the company conduct to get answers to these questions?

6. Evaluate the following questions found in a consumer survey. How well will each question elicit the information desired? How is the consumer likely to respond to each question?
   a. What is your husband's favorite brand of golf ball?
   b. What TV programs did you watch last Monday?
   c. How many times did you eat pizza last year?
   d. What was the total income you reported on your federal tax return last year?
   e. What are the food and nonfood products that you typically buy at the supermarket each month?

7. Each of the following questions appears on a paper questionnaire that respondents fill out and return to a research firm. Rephrase and/or reformat each question so that the respondent is more likely to provide the research firm with the information it needs.
   a. Which brand do you like best?
   b. Can you tell me how many children you have, whether they are girls or boys, and how old they are?
   c. How much say do you have regarding the charities that your church contributes to?
   d. With what frequency have you experienced this phenomenon of late?
   e. Are auto manufacturers making satisfactory progress in controlling auto emissions?

8. Levi Strauss is interested in developing a new line of dress suits that would appeal to young, independent, professional men who usually shop in specialty stores. The marketing team has determined that the men who buy Levi's jeans fall into five categories:

   ◆ *Utilitarian jeans customer:* The Levi loyalist who wears jeans for work and play
   ◆ *Trendy casual:* High-fashion customers who come to life at night
   ◆ *Price shopper:* Buys on the basis of price at department stores and discount stores
   ◆ *Mainstream traditionalist:* Over 45 years old and shops in a department store accompanied by his wife
   ◆ *Classic independent:* Independent buyer, shops alone in specialty stores, and wants clothes that make him "look right" (the target in this case)

   The marketing team's task is to determine (1) whether the Levi name should be used on the new product and (2) whether this product could be successfully marketed through Levi's current channels of distribution. How could the team "get the ball rolling" in terms of answering these questions and generating a plan for conducting more intensive research into the preferences of the "classic independent" segment? What kinds of formal market research should the company conduct to help it make a decision whether or not to pursue this segment? If it does go after classic independents, what challenges might Levi's face?

9. A mail panel consists of large and nationally representative samples of households that have agreed to participate periodically in mail questionnaires, product tests, and telephone surveys. Under what circumstances would you use mail panels as part of the marketing research process described in this chapter?

10. Suggest creative ways to help companies research the following issues:
   a. A liquor company needs to estimate liquor consumption in a legally dry town.
   b. A magazine distribution house wants to know how many people read a specific magazine in doctors' offices.

Managing Marketing
Information and Measuring
Market Demand

TABLE I	SALES FORECASTS		
	HIGH MARKETING BUDGET	MEDIUM MARKETING BUDGET	LOW MARKETING BUDGET
Recession	15	12	10
Normal	20	16	14

    c. A men's hair tonic producer wants to know at least four ways it can find and interview the men who use its products.

11. A chemical company wants to estimate the demand for sulfur next year. One use of sulfur is in manufacturing sulfuric acid. Another use of sulfur is in polishing new cars. General Motors (which produces new cars and therefore needs sulfur to polish them with) is a customer of this chemical company. How could the chemical company determine how GM's new-car production next year might affect its sulfur sales?

12. A children's toy manufacturer is developing its sales forecast for next year. The company's forecaster has estimated sales for six different environment/strategy combinations in Table 1. The forecaster believes that there is an 0.20 probability of recession and an 0.80 probability of normal times. He also believes the probabilities of a high, medium, and low company market budget are 0.30, 0.50, and 0.20, respectively. How might he arrive at a single-point sales forecast? What assumptions are being made?

NOTES

1. William D. Perreault, Jr., Paul E. Green, and Naresh K. Malhotra, "The Shifting Paradigm in Marketing Research," *Journal of the Academy of Marketing Science,* 20, no. 4 (Fall 1992), 367–87.
2. John Koten, "You Aren't Paranoid if You Feel Someone Eyes You Constantly," *The Wall Street Journal,* March 29, 1985, pp. 1, 22; "Offbeat Marketing," *Sales and Marketing Management,* January 1990, p. 35; and Erik Larson, "Attention Shoppers: Don't Look Now but You Are Being Tailed," *Smithsonian Magazine,* January 1993, pp. 70–79.
3. From *Consumer Europe 1993,* a publication of Euromonitor, pnc. London: Tel +4471 251 8021; U.S. offices: (312) 541–8024.
4. Donna DeEulio, "Should Catalogers Travel the EDI Highway?", *Catalog Age,* 11, no. 2 (February 1994), 99.
5. John W. Verity, "Taking a Laptop on a Call," Business Week, October 25, 1993, pp. 124–25.
6. James A. Narus and James C. Anderson, "Turn Your Industrial Distributors into Partners," *Harvard Business Review,* March–April 1986, pp. 66–71.
7. Kevin Helliker, "Smile: That Cranky Shopper May Be a Store Spy," *The Wall Street Journal,* November 30, 1994, B1:3, 6:6.
8. See *1994 Survey of Market Research: Organization, Functions, Budget, Compensation,* ed. Thomas Kinnear and Ann Root (Chicago: American Marketing Association, 1994).
9. See William R. BonDurant, "Research: The 'HP Way,'" *Marketing Research,* June 1992, pp. 28–33.
10. Kevin J. Clancy and Robert S. Shulman, *Marketing Myths That Are Killing Business* (New York: McGraw-Hill, 1994), p. 58; Phaedra Hise, "Comprehensive CompuServe," *Inc.,* June 1994, p. 109; "Business Bulletin: Studying the Competition," *The Wall Street Journal,* A1:5.
11. For a discussion of the decision-theory approach to the value of research, see Donald R. Lehmann, *Market Research and Analysis,* 3d ed. (Homewood, IL: Irwin, 1989), Chapter 2.
12. For an excellent annotated reference to major secondary sources of business and marketing data, see Gilbert A. Churchill, Jr., *Marketing Research: Methodological Foundations,* 6th ed. (Fort Worth, TX: Dryden, 1994).
13. Jonathan Berry, "A Potent New Tool for Selling: Database Marketing," *Business Week,* September 4, 1994, pp. 56–62.
14. Thomas L. Greenbaum, *The Handbook for Focus Group Research* (New York: Lexington Books, 1993).
15. Barbara A. Bickart, "Carryover and Backfire Effects in Marketing Research," *Journal of Marketing Research,* 30, no. 1, (February 1993), 52–62.
16. An overview of mechanical devices is presented in Roger D. Blackwell, James S. Hensel, Michael B. Phillips, and Brian Sternthal, *Laboratory Equipment for Marketing Research* (Dubuque, IA: Kendall/Hunt, 1970), pp. 7–8. For newer devices, see Wally Wood, "The Race to Replace Memory," *Marketing and Media Decisions,* July 1986, pp. 166–67.
17. Debra Aho, "Pepsi Puts Callers in Touch with Ray," *Advertising Age,* November 15, 1993, p. 20.
18. Selwyn Feinstein, "Computers Replacing Interviewers for Personnel and Marketing Tasks," *The Wall Street Journal,* October 9, 1986, p. 35.
19. For further reading see Joanne Lipman, "Single-Source Ad Research Heralds Detailed Look at Household Habits," *The Wall Street Journal,* February 16, 1988, p. 39; Joe Schwartz, "Back to the Source," *American Demographics,* January 1989, pp. 22–26; and Magid H. Abraham and Leonard M. Lodish, "Getting the Most Out of Advertising and Promotions," *Harvard Business Review,* May–June 1990, pp. 50–60.

20. Cyndee Miller, "Sometimes a Researcher Has No Choice but to Hang Out in a Bar," *Marketing News,* January 3, 1994, pp. 16, 26.

21. Cynthia Crossen, "Studies Galore Support Products and Positions, but Are They Reliable?" *The Wall Street Journal,* November 14, 1991, A:1, 9. Also see Betsey Spethmann, "Cautious Consumers Have Surveyors Wary," *Advertising Age,* June 10, 1991, p. 34.

22. Naghi Namakforoosh, "Data Collection Methods Hold Key to Research in Mexico," *Marketing News,* August 29, 1994, p. 28.

23. John D. C. Little, "Decision Support Systems for Marketing Managers," *Journal of Marketing,* Summer 1979, p. 11.

24. S. Tamer Mitri Cavusgil, Michel Evirgen, and T. Cuneyt, "A Decision Support System for Doing Business with Eastern Bloc Countries: The Country Consultant," *European Business Review,* 92, no. 4 (1992), 24–34.

25. John D. C. Little, "BRANDAID: A Marketing Mix Model, Part I: Structure; Part II: Implementation," *Operations Research,* Vol. 23 (1975), 628–73.

26. Leonard M. Lodish, "CALLPLAN: An Interactive Salesman's Call Planning System," *Management Science,* December 1971, pp. 25–40.

27. David B. Montgomery, Alvin J. Silk, and C. E. Zaragoza, "A Multiple-Product Sales-Force Allocation Model," *Management Science,* December 1971, pp. 3–24.

28. S. W. Hess and S. A. Samuels, "Experiences with a Sales Districting Model: Criteria and Implementation," *Management Science,* December 1971, pp. 41–54.

29. John D. C. Little and Leonard M. Lodish, "A Media Planning Calculus," *Operations Research,* January–February 1969, pp. 1–35.

30. Magid M. Abraham and Leonard M. Lodish, "PROMOTER: An Automated Promotion Evaluation System," *Marketing Science,* Spring 1987, pp. 101–23.

31. Raymond R. Burke, Arvind Rangaswamy, Jerry Wind, and Jehoshua Eliashberg, "A Knowledge-Based System for Advertising Design," *Marketing Science,* 9, no. 3 (1990), 212–29.

32. John D. C. Little, "Cover Story: An Expert System to Find the News in Scanner Data," Sloan School, MIT Working Paper, 1988.

33. For further reading, see Gary Lilien, Philip Kotler, and K. Sridhar Moorthy, *Marketing Models* (Englewood Cliffs, NJ: Prentice Hall, 1992).

34. Judy Quinn, "Dewar's," *Incentive,* July 1994, pp. 38–39.

35. For further discussion, see Gary L. Lilien, Philip Kotler, and K. Sridhar Moorthy, *Marketing Models* (Englewood Cliffs, NJ: Prentice-Hall, 1992).

36. See Russell L. Ackoff, *A Concept of Corporate Planning* (New York: Wiley-Interscience, 1970), pp. 36–37.

37. For suggested strategies related to the market area's *BDI* standing, see Don E. Schultz, Dennis Martin, and William P. Brown, *Strategic Advertising Campaigns* (Chicago: Crain Books, 1984), p. 338.

38. Adrienne Ward Fawcett, "Oreo Cones Make Top Grade in Poll," *Advertising Age,* June 14, 1993, p. 30.

39. Marketing researchers have indicated that measuring buyer intention may have an effect on subsequent buying behavior. Repurchase rates increase if researchers ask consumers *once* about intent to buy. However, repeatedly asking those with low levels of interest about purchase intent prompts a decreased propensity to buy. See Vicki G. Morwitz, Eric Johnson, and David Schmittlein, "Does Measuring Intent Change Behavior?" *Journal of Consumer Research,* 20, no. 1 (June 1993), 46–61.

40. See Jacob Gonik, "Tie Salesmen's Bonuses to Their Forecasts," *Harvard Business Review,* May–June 1978, pp. 116–23.

41. See Norman Dalkey and Olaf Helmer, "An Experimental Application of the Delphi Method to the Use of Experts," *Management Science,* April 1963, pp. 458–67. Also see Roger J. Best, "An Experiment in Delphi Estimation in Marketing Decision Making," *Journal of Marketing Research,* November 1974, pp. 447–52.

Managing Marketing
Information and Measuring
Market Demand

SCANNING THE MARKETING ENVIRONMENT

It is useless to tell a river to stop running; the best thing is to learn how to swim in the direction it is flowing.

ANONYMOUS

The future ain't what it used to be.

YOGI BERRA

We have repeatedly emphasized that successful companies take an outside-inside view of their business. They recognize that the marketing environment is constantly spinning new opportunities and threats and understand the importance of continuously monitoring and adapting to the changing environment. One of the companies most lauded for knowing when, what, and how to sell in emerging markets is Microsoft.

MICROSOFT Always several steps ahead of the competition, Microsoft's CEO Bill Gates has taken the company from computer languages to operating systems, and then from business applications like the Word word processor to consumer products like the Encarta CD-ROM encyclopedia. Gates is constantly analyzing the marketing environment, spending a third of his time talking to customers and prospective customers. By keeping his ears open he's able to craft products that will see the company well into the next millennium. At a recent Comdex Computer Show, Gates delivered the keynote address to a packed house, showing a film of gadgets he says will be in use by 2005—from dashboard PC's that handle videoconferencing to wallet-size computers for electronic shopping. At the press conference later that day Gates introduced Microsoft Network, an ambitious online service that allows families around the globe to communicate easily through electronic mail. "The PC industry has come a long way, but that's nothing compared with what's going to happen," predicts Gates.[1]

Unlike Microsoft, many companies fail to see change as opportunity. They ignore or resist changes until it is too late. Their strategies, structures, systems, and organizational culture grow increasingly obsolete and dysfunctional. Corporations as mighty as General Motors, IBM, and Sears have been brought to their knees for ignoring macroenvironmental changes too long.

The major responsibility for identifying significant changes in the environment falls to a company's marketers. More than any other group in the company, they must be the trend trackers and opportunity seekers. Although every manager in an organization needs to observe the outside environment, marketers have two advantages here. They have disciplined methods—marketing intelligence and marketing research—for collecting information about the marketing environment. They also spend more time with customers and more time watching competitors.

In this and the next four chapters, we examine the firm's *external environment*—the macroenvironment forces that affect it, its consumer markets, its business markets, and its competitors. In this chapter, we focus on the macroenvironment and address two questions:

♦ **What are the key methods for tracking and identifying opportunities in the macroenvironment?**

♦ **What are the key demographic, economic, natural, technological, political, and cultural developments worth noting?**

Scanning
the Marketing
Environment

Faith Popcorn Points to 10 Trends in the Economy

Faith Popcorn runs a marketing consultancy firm called BrainReserve, which she started in 1974. Her clients include AT&T, Citibank, Black & Decker, Hoffman-LaRoche, Nissan, Rubbermaid, and many others. Her firm offers several services: Brand Renewal, which attempts to breathe new life into fading brands; Brain-Jam, which uses a list of trends to generate new ideas; FutureFocus, which develops marketing strategies and concepts that create long-term competitive advantages; and TrendBank, a proprietary database made up of culture monitoring and consumer interviews. Popcorn and her associates have identified 10 major trends in the U.S. economy:

1. *Cashing out:* Cashing out is the impulse to change one's life to a slower but more rewarding pace. It is manifested by career persons who suddenly quit their hectic urban jobs and turn up in Vermont or Montana running a small newspaper, managing a bed-and-breakfast establishment, or joining a band. They don't think the office stress is worth it. There is a nostalgic return to small-town values with clean air, safe schools, and plain-speaking neighbors.

2. *Cocooning:* Cocooning is the impulse to stay inside when the outside gets too tough and scary. More people are turning their home into a nest. They are becoming "couch potatoes," glued to watching TV movies, ordering goods from catalogs, redecorating their homes, and using their answering machine to filter out the outside world. In reaction to increased crime and other social problems, Armored Cocoon people are burrowing in, building bunkers. Self-preservation is the underlying theme. Also manifest are Wandering Cocoons, people eating in their cars and phoning from their cars. Socialized Cocooning describes the forming of a small group of friends who frequently get together for conversation, for "saloning."

3. *Down-aging:* Down-aging is the tendency to act and feel younger than one's age. The sexy heroes today are Cher (over 45), Paul Newman (over 65), Elizabeth Taylor (over 60). Older people are spending more on youthful clothes, hair coloring, and facial plastic surgery. They are engaging in more playful behavior, willing to act in ways not normally found in their age group. They buy adult toys, attend adult camps, and sign up for adventurous vacations.

4. *Egonomics:* Egonomics is people's desire to develop an individuality so that they are seen and treated as different than anyone else. It is not egomania but simply the wish to individualize oneself through one's possessions and experiences. People are increasingly subscribing to narrow-interest magazines; joining small groups with a narrow mission; and buying customized clothing, cars, and cosmetics. Egonomics provides marketers with a competitive opportunity to succeed by offering customized goods, services, and experiences.

5. *Fantasy adventure:* Fantasy adventure meets people's

ANALYZING NEEDS AND TRENDS IN THE MACROENVIRONMENT

Successful companies recognize and respond profitably to unmet needs and trends in the macroenvironment. Unmet needs always exist. Companies could make a fortune if they could solve any of these problems: a cure for cancer, chemical cures for mental diseases, desalinization of sea water, nonfattening tasty nutritious food, practical electric cars, voice-controlled computers, and affordable housing.

Even in slow-growth economies, some enterprising individuals and companies manage to create new solutions to unmet needs. Club Mediterranee emerged to meet the needs of single people for exotic vacations; the Walkman and CD Man were created for active people who wanted to listen to music; Nautilus was created for men and women who wanted to tone their bodies; and Federal Express was created to meet the need for next-day mail delivery.

Many opportunities are found by identifying *trends*.

❖ A **TREND** is a direction or sequence of events that have some momentum and durability.

For example, one major trend is the increasing participation of women in the work force, which has spawned the child day-care business, increased consumption of

growing needs for emotional escapes to offset their daily routines. People express this need through taking vacations, eating exotic foods, going to Disneyland and other fantasy parks, redecorating their homes with a Santa Fe look, and so on. For marketers, the desire for adventure is an opportunity to create new fantasy products and services or add fantasy touches to their current products and services.

6. *99 Lives:* 99 Lives is the desperate state of people who must juggle many roles and responsibilities—think of SuperMom, who has a full-time career, must manage the home and the children, do the shopping, and so on. People feel time-poor and attempt to save time by using fax machines and car phones, eating at fast-food restaurants, and so on. Marketers can address this need by creating *cluster marketing enterprises*—all-in-one service stops, such as "Video Town Laundrette," which includes laundry facilities, a tanning room, an exercise bike, copying and fax machines, and 6,000 video titles to rent.

7. *S.O.S. (Save Our Society):* S.O.S. is the drive of a growing number of people to make society more socially responsible along the three critical Es: Environment, Education, and Ethics. These individuals are joining groups to promote more social responsibility on the part of companies and other citizens. Marketers are urging their own companies to practice more socially responsible marketing, along the lines of The Body Shop, Ben & Jerry's, Levi Strauss, and other socially concerned companies.

8. *Small indulgences:* Stressed-out consumers need occa-sional emotional fixes. They might not be able to afford a BMW car but might buy a BMW motorcycle. They might eat healthfully during the week and then indulge themselves with a pint of superpremium Haagen-Dazs ice cream on the weekend. They won't take a two-week vacation to Europe but instead a three-day minicruise in the Caribbean. Marketers should be aware of the deprivations many consumers feel and the opportunity to offer them small indulgences for an emotional lift.

9. *Staying alive:* Staying alive is about people's drive to live longer and better lives. They now know that their lifestyle can kill them—eating the wrong foods, smoking, breathing bad air, using hard drugs. People are ready to take responsibility for their own health and choose better foods, exercise more regularly, and relax more often. Marketers can meet this need by designing healthier products and services for consumers.

10. *The vigilante consumer:* Vigilante consumers are those who will no longer tolerate shoddy products and inept service. They want companies to be more human. They want automobile companies to take back "lemons" and fully refund their money. They subscribe to the *National Boycott News* and *Consumer Reports,* join MADD (Mothers Against Drunk Driving), and look for lists of good companies and bad companies. Marketers must be the conscience of their company in bringing about higher standards in the goods and services they provide.

Source: This summary is drawn from various pages of Faith Popcorn's *The Popcorn Report* (New York: HarperBusiness, 1992).

microwavable foods, office-oriented clothing lines for women, and other business opportunities. Identifying a trend, ferreting out the likely consequences, and determining opportunities are critical marketing skills.

We need to draw distinctions among fads, trends, and megatrends. Unlike a trend, a *fad* is "unpredictable, short-lived, and without social, economic, and political significance." [2] A company can cash in on a fad such as Pet Rocks or Cabbage Patch dolls, but this is more a matter of luck and good timing than anything else.

Trends are more predictable and durable than fads. A trend reveals the shape of the future. Friedrich von Schiller said: "In today already walks tomorrow." According to futurist Faith Popcorn, a trend has longevity, is observable across several market areas and consumer activities, and is consistent with other significant indicators occurring or emerging at the same time. [3] Popcorn has identified 10 major trends in the 1990s and their implications for business decision making. (For more on this topic, see the Marketing Insight titled "Faith Popcorn Points to 10 Trends in the Economy.")

John Naisbitt, another futurist, prefers to talk about *megatrends,* which are "large social, economic, political and technological changes [that] are slow to form, and once in place, they influence us for some time—between seven and ten years, or longer." [4] Naisbitt and his staff spot these trends by counting the number of times hard-news items bearing on different topics appear in major newspapers. Popcorn's trends are more psychological and mood-oriented; Naisbitt's megatrends are more societal in their scope. The 10 megatrends Naisbitt has identified for the 1990s are:

1. The booming global economy
2. A renaissance in the arts
3. The emergence of free-market socialism
4. Global lifestyles and cultural nationalism
5. The privatization of the welfare state
6. The rise of the Pacific Rim
7. The decade of women in leadership
8. The age of biology
9. The religious revival of the new millennium
10. The triumph of the individual

Both trends and megatrends merit marketers' close attention. A new product or marketing program is likely to be more successful if it is in line with strong trends rather than opposed to them. But detecting a new market opportunity does not guarantee its success, even if it is technically feasible. For example, it is possible to offer people a customized daily newspaper that will appear on their computer and cover only items they are interested in. But there may not be a sufficient number of people interested in such a product or willing to pay the required price. This is why market research must be undertaken to determine an opportunity's profit potential.

IDENTIFYING AND RESPONDING TO THE MAJOR MACROENVIRONMENT FORCES

Companies and their suppliers, marketing intermediaries, customers, competitors, and publics all operate in a macroenvironment of forces and trends that shape opportunities and pose threats. These forces represent "noncontrollables," which the company must monitor and respond to. In the economic arena, companies and consumers are increasingly affected by global forces. These include:

♦ The substantial speedup of international transportation, communication, and financial transactions, leading to the rapid growth of world trade and investment, especially tri-polar trade (North America, Western Europe, Far East).

♦ The gradual erosion of U.S. international dominance and competitiveness and the rising economic power of Japan and several Far Eastern countries in world markets.

♦ The rise of trade blocs such as the European Union and the NAFTA signatories to foster economic cooperation within regions.

♦ The severe debt problems of several Latin American and Eastern European countries, along with the increasing fragility of the international financial system.

♦ The increasing use of barter and countertrade to support international transactions. (*Countertrade* is a form of barter in which a country requires that a foreign company buy products in that nation in exchange for the privilege of selling its good there.)

♦ The move toward market economies in formerly Socialist countries along with rapid privatization of publicly owned companies.

♦ The rapid dissemination of global lifestyles resulting from the growth of global communications.

- The gradual opening of major new markets, namely China, India, Eastern Europe, and the Arab countries.

- The increasing tendency of multinationals to transcend their locational and national characteristics and become transnational firms.

- The increasing number of cross-border corporate strategic alliances—for example, MCI and British Telecom, Texas Instruments and Hitachi, and Coca-Cola and Cadbury Schweppes.

- The increasing regional tensions and conflicts resulting from the ending of the Cold War.

- The growth of global brands in autos, food, clothing, electronics, and so on. For example, Colgate-Palmolive is well known for crafting global brands that sell as well in Manila as they do in Manchester. When the company began preparing for the 1991 global launch of Total, its antibacterial plaque-fighting toothpaste, it took no chances. Colgate test marketed Total in six separate countries, each representing a different cultural profile: the Philippines, Australia, Colombia, Greece, Portugal, and the United Kingdom. The team in charge of the global launch was a veritable corporate United Nations of operations, logistics, and marketing strategists. Their efforts paid off handsomely: In 1994 Total was a $150 million brand worldwide, selling in 75 countries, with virtually identical packaging, positioning, and advertising (Figure 5-1).[5]

Within the rapidly changing global picture, the firm must monitor six major forces: demographic, economic, natural, technological, political/legal, and social/cultural forces. Although these forces will be described separately, marketers must pay attention to their causal interactions, since these set the stage for new opportunities as well as threats. For example, the explosive population growth (demographic) leads to more resource depletion and pollution (natural environment), which leads consumers to call for more laws (political/legal). The imposed restrictions stimulate new technological solutions and products (technology), which if they are affordable (economic forces) may actually change people's attitudes and behavior (social/cultural).

Demographic Environment

The first macroenvironmental force that marketers monitor is population because people make up markets. Marketers are keenly interested in the size and growth rate of population in different cities, regions, and nations; age distribution and ethnic mix; educational levels; household patterns; and regional characteristics and movements.

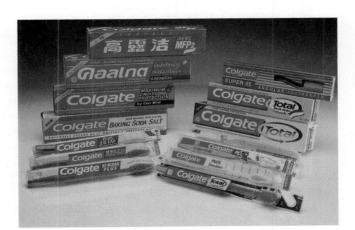

FIGURE 5-1

Colgate-Palmolive's Total Global Branding Strategy
Colgate-Palmolive has had global success with its Colgate line of tooth-care products. The products and their packaging design do not vary from country to country; the only thing that changes is the language on the packages.

Source: Brandweek, October 31, 1994.

WORLDWIDE POPULATION GROWTH. The world population is showing "explosive" growth. It totaled 5.4 billion in 1991 and is growing at 1.7% per year. At this rate, the world's population will reach 6.2 billion by the year 2000.[6]

The world population explosion has been a source of major concern, for two reasons. The first is the fact that the resources needed to support this much human life (fuel, foods, and so forth) are limited and are likely to run out at some point. First published in 1972, *The Limits to Growth* presented an impressive array of evidence that unchecked population growth and consumption would eventually result in insufficient food supply, depletion of key minerals, overcrowding, pollution, and an overall deterioration in the quality of life.[7] One of the study's strong recommendations is the worldwide social marketing of family planning.[8]

The second cause for concern is that population growth is highest in countries and communities that can least afford it. The less developed regions of the world currently account for 76% of the world population and are growing at 2% per year, while the population in the more developed countries is growing at only 0.6% per year. In the developing countries, the death rate has been falling as a result of modern medicine, but the birth rate has remained fairly stable. Feeding, clothing, and educating their children while also providing a rising standard of living is out of the question in these countries.

The explosive world population growth has major implications for business. A growing population means growing human needs, but it does not mean growing markets unless these markets have sufficient purchasing power. If the growing population presses too hard against the available food supply and resources, costs will shoot up and profit margins will decline.

Nonetheless, companies that carefully analyze their markets can find major opportunities. For example, to curb its skyrocketing population, the Chinese government has passed regulations limiting Chinese families to one child per family. Toy marketers, in particular, are paying attention to one consequence of these regulations: Chinese children are spoiled and fussed over as never before. Known in China as "little emperors," Chinese children are being showered with everything from candy to computers as a result of what's known as the "six pocket syndrome." As many as six adults—parents, grandparents, great-grandparents, and aunts and uncles—may be indulging the whims of each child. This trend has encouraged such companies as Japan's Bandai Co. (famous for its Mighty Morphin Power Rangers), Denmark's Lego Group, and Mattel to enter the Chinese market.[9]

POPULATION AGE MIX. National populations vary in their age mix. At one extreme is Mexico, a country with a very young population and rapid population growth. At the other extreme is Japan, a country with one of the world's oldest populations. Products of high importance in Mexico would be milk, diapers, school supplies, and toys. Japan's population will consume many more adult products.

A population can be subdivided into six age groups: preschool, school-age children, teens, young adults age 25 to 40, middle-aged adults age 40 to 65; and older adults age 65 and up. The age groups that will experience the most rapid growth in the United States in the coming decades will be teens, middle-aged adults, and older adults. For marketers, this age mix signals the kinds of products and services that will be in high demand. For example, the increasing segment of older adults will lead to increased demand for assisted living communities, small-portion items, and medical equipment and appliances. Stores catering to senior citizens will need stronger lighting, larger print signs, and safe restrooms. And companies that have focused on one age group will have to split their marketing approaches as the populations of other age groups begin increasing. For example, with the 13- to 19-year-old population on the rise for the first time since the 1950s,

Pepsi Co is finding it has to reach out to teens in addition to its primary market of baby boomers. "We have to keep the original Pepsi Generation involved with the franchise," says Pepsi's senior vice-president of brands, "and we have to enroll the new generation."[10]

Marketers are increasingly identifying age groups within age groups as possible target markets. They bear such acronyms as:

- SKIPPIES: School Kids with Income and Purchasing Power
- MOBYS: Mother Older, Baby Younger
- DINKS: Double Income, No Kids
- DEWKS: Dual Earners with Kids
- PUPPIES: Poor Urban Professionals
- WOOFS: Well-Off Older Folks

Each group has a known range of product and service needs and media and retail preferences, which helps marketers fine-tune their market offers.

ETHNIC MARKETS. Countries vary in their ethnic and racial makeup. At one extreme is Japan, where almost everyone is Japanese; at the other extreme is the United States, with people from virtually all nations. The United States was originally called a "melting pot" but there are increasing signs that the melting didn't occur. Now people call the United States a "salad bowl" society with ethnic groups maintaining their ethnic differences, neighborhoods, and cultures. The U.S. population (261 million in 1994) is 76% white, African-Americans constitute another 12%, and Latinos another 9 percent. The Latino population has been growing fast, with the largest subgroups of Mexican (5.4%), Puerto Rican (1.1%), and Cuban (0.4%) descent. Asian-Americans constitute 3% of the U.S. population, with the Chinese constituting the largest group, followed by the Filipinos, Japanese, Asian Indians, and Koreans, in that order. Latino and Asian-American consumers are concentrated in the far western and southern parts of the country, although some dispersal is taking place. Finally, there are 5 million practicing Muslims in the United States.

Each population group has certain specific wants and buying habits. Several food, clothing, and furniture companies have directed their products and promotions to one or more of these groups.[11] For instance, Sears is taking note of the preferences of different ethnic groups:

SEARS If a Sears & Roebuck store has a shopping base that is at least 20% Latino, it is designated as a Hispanic store for the purpose of Sears' Hispanic marketing program. More than 130 stores in Southern California, Texas, Florida, and New York have earned this label. "We make a special effort to staff those stores with bilingual sales personnel, to use bilingual signage, and to support community programs," says a Sears spokesperson. Choosing merchandise for the Latino marketplace is primarily a color and size issue. "What we find in Hispanic communities is that people tend to be smaller than the general market, and that there is a greater demand for special-occasion clothing and a preference for bright colors. In hardlines, there isn't much difference from the mainstream market."

Yet marketers must be careful not to overgeneralize about ethnic groups. Within each ethnic group are consumers who are as different from each other as they are from Americans of European background. "There is really no such thing as an Asian market," says Greg Macabenta, whose ethnic advertising agency specializes in the Filipino market. Macabenta emphasizes that the five major Asian-American groups have their own very specific market characteristics, speak different languages, consume different cuisines, practice different religions, and represent very distinct national cultures.[12]

EDUCATIONAL GROUPS. The population in any society falls into five educational groups: illiterates, high school dropouts, high school degrees, college degrees, and professional degrees. In Japan, 99% of the population is literate, while in the United States 10% to 15% of the population may be functionally illiterate. However, the United States has one of the world's highest percentages of college-educated citizenry, around 36 percent. The high number of educated people in the United States spells a high demand for quality books, magazines, and travel.

HOUSEHOLD PATTERNS. The "traditional household" consists of a husband, wife, and children (and sometimes grandparents). In the United States today, the traditional household is no longer the dominant household pattern. Today's households also include single live-alones, adult live-togethers of one or both sexes, single-parent families, childless married couples, and empty nesters. More people are divorcing or separating, choosing not to marry, marrying later, or marrying without the intention to have children. Each group has a distinctive set of needs and buying habits. For example, people in the SSWD group (single, separated, widowed, divorced) need smaller apartments; inexpensive and smaller appliances, furniture, and furnishings; and food packaged in smaller sizes. Marketers must increasingly consider the special needs of nontraditional households, since they are now growing more rapidly than traditional households.

GEOGRAPHICAL SHIFTS IN POPULATION. The 1990s is a period of great migratory movements between countries and within countries. As a result of the collapse of Soviet Eastern Europe, nationalities are reasserting themselves and forming independent countries. The new countries are making certain ethnic groups unwelcome (such as Russians in Latvia, or Muslims in Serbia), and many of these groups are migrating to safer areas. As foreign groups enter other countries for political sanctuary, some local groups start protesting. In the United States, there has been opposition to the influx of immigrants from Mexico, the Caribbean, and certain Asian nations.

Population movement also occurs as people migrate from rural to urban areas, and then to suburban areas. People's location makes a difference in their goods-and-service preferences. For example, the movement to the Sunbelt states has lessened the demand for warm clothing and home heating equipment and increased the demand for air conditioning. Those who live in large cities such as New York, Chicago, and San Francisco account for most of the sales of expensive furs, perfumes, luggage, and works of art. These cities also support the opera, ballet, and other forms of culture. Americans living in the suburbs lead more casual lives, do more outdoor living, and have greater neighbor interaction, higher incomes, and younger families. Suburbanites buy station wagons, home workshop equipment, outdoor furniture, lawn and gardening tools, and outdoor cooking equipment. There are also regional differences: For example, people in Seattle buy more toothbrushes per capita than people in any other U.S. city; people in Salt Lake City eat more candy bars; people from New Orleans use more ketchup; and people in Miami drink more prune juice.

SHIFT FROM A MASS MARKET TO MICROMARKETS. The effect of all these changes is fragmentation of the mass market into numerous *micromarkets* differentiated by age, sex, ethnic background, education, lifestyle, geography, and so on. Each group has strong preferences and consumer characteristics and is reached through increasingly targeted communication and distribution channels. Companies are abandoning the "shotgun approach" that aimed at a mythical "average" consumer and are increasingly designing their products and marketing programs for specific micromarkets (Figure 5-2).

Demographic trends are highly reliable for the short and intermediate run. There is little excuse for a company's being suddenly surprised by demographic developments. The Singer Company should have known for years that its sewing machine business would be hurt by smaller families and more working wives, yet it was slow in responding. In contrast, think of the rewards marketers reap when they monitor the major demographic trends, their probable impacts, and plot what actions they should take. Some marketers, for example, are actively courting the so-called "bridge" generation that preceded the baby boomers. Jeff Ostroff, director of the Data Group's Over 40 Marketing division, considers the 50- to 64-year-old "Eisenhower Generation" a harbinger of what is to come with the baby boomers. "If a company does well marketing to this pre-boomer group," he says, "they'll be in a good position to reach the baby boomers when they enter the mature market." Two examples:

- Ocean Spray has been quick on the draw with its first print ad aimed directly at the over 50 consumer, pitching Ocean Spray cranberry juice cocktail as a "good for you" drink and featuring an older model.
- Kellogg's aired a new TV spot for All-Bran cereal in which individuals ranging in age from 53 to 81 are featured playing ice hockey, water skiing, running hurdles, and playing baseball, all to the tune of "Wild Thing."[13]

FIGURE 5-2

Microtargeting: Sears Advertisements to the Latino Community

Source: Jacquelyn Lynn, "Tapping the Riches of Bilingual Markets," *AMA Management Review*, March 1995, pp. 56–57.
Courtesy of Sears Roebuck & Company and Mendoza, Dillion & Associates, Inc.

Economic Environment

Markets require purchasing power as well as people. The available purchasing power in an economy depends on current income, prices, savings, debt, and credit availability. Marketers must pay close attention to major trends in income and consumer-spending patterns.

INCOME DISTRIBUTION. Nations vary greatly in their level and distribution of income. A major determinant is the nation's industrial structure. There are four types of industrial structures:

1. *Subsistence economies:* In a subsistence economy, the vast majority of people engage in simple agriculture. They consume most of their output and barter the rest for simple goods and services. These economies offer few opportunities for marketers.

2. *Raw-material-exporting economies:* These economies are rich in one or more natural resources but poor in other respects. Much of their revenue comes from exporting these resources. Examples are Zaire (copper) and Saudi Arabia (oil). These countries are good markets for extractive equipment, tools and supplies, materials-handling equipment, and trucks. Depending on the number of foreign residents and wealthy native rulers and landholders, they are also a market for Western-style commodities and luxury goods.

3. *Industrializing economies:* In an industrializing economy, manufacturing begins to account for 10% to 20% of the country's gross domestic product. Examples include India, Egypt, and the Philippines. As manufacturing increases, the country relies more on imports of raw materials, steel, and heavy machinery and less on imports of finished textiles, paper products, and processed foods. The industrialization creates a new rich class and a small but growing middle class, both demanding new types of goods, some of which can be satisfied only by imports.

4. *Industrial economies:* Industrial economies are major exporters of manufactured goods and investment funds. They buy manufactured goods from each other and also export them to other types of economies in exchange for raw materials and semifinished goods. The large and varied manufacturing activities of these industrial nations and their sizable middle class make them rich markets for all sorts of goods.

Income distribution is related to a country's industrial structure but is also affected by the political system. Marketers often distinguish countries with five different income-distribution patterns: (1) very low incomes, (2) mostly low incomes, (3) very low, very high incomes, (4) low, medium, high incomes, and (5) mostly medium incomes. Consider the market for Lamborghinis, an automobile costing more than $100,000. The market would be very small in countries with type 1 or 2 income patterns. One of the largest single markets for Lamborghinis turns out to be Portugal (income pattern 3)—one of the poorest countries in Western Europe, but one with enough wealthy families to afford expensive cars.

In the United States, there is some evidence that the rich have grown richer, the middle class has shrunk, and the poor have remained poor. This is leading to a two-tier U.S. market with affluent people buying expensive goods and working-class people spending more carefully, shopping at discount stores and factory outlet malls, and selecting less expensive store brands. Conventional retailers who offer medium-price goods are the most vulnerable to these changes.

SAVINGS, DEBT, AND CREDIT AVAILABILITY. Consumer expenditures are affected by consumer savings, debt, and credit availability. The Japanese, for example, save about 18% of their income, while U.S. consumers save about 6 percent. The result is that Japanese banks have been able to loan out money to Japanese companies at a much lower interest rate than U.S. banks could offer to U.S. companies. Access to lower interest rates has helped Japanese companies expand faster. U.S. consumers also have a high debt-to-income ratio, which retards further expenditures on housing and large-ticket items. Credit is very available in

PART 2

Analyzing
Marketing
Opportunities

the United States but at fairly high interest rates, especially to lower-income borrowers. Marketers must pay careful attention to any major changes in incomes, cost of living, interest rates, savings, and borrowing patterns because they can have a high impact on business, especially in companies whose products have high income and price sensitivity.

Natural Environment

As we saw in Chapter 1, the deterioration of the natural environment is one of the major issues of the 1990s. In many world cities, air and water pollution have reached dangerous levels. There is great concern about certain chemicals causing air, soil, and water pollution. In Western Europe, "green" parties have vigorously pressed for public action to reduce industrial pollution. In the United States, several thought leaders—including Kenneth Boulding, the Erlichs, the Meadowses, and Rachel Carson—have documented the amount of ecological deterioration, while watchdog groups such as the Sierra Club and Friends of the Earth have carried these concerns into political and social action.

New legislation passed as a result of environmentalism has hit certain industries very hard. Steel companies and public utilities have had to invest billions of dollars in pollution-control equipment and more environmentally friendly fuels. The auto industry has had to introduce expensive emission controls in cars. The soap industry has had to increase its products' biodegradability.

Marketers need to be aware of the threats and opportunities associated with four trends in the natural environment: the shortage of raw materials, the increased cost of energy, the increased levels of pollution, and the changing role of governments.

SHORTAGE OF RAW MATERIALS. The earth's raw materials consist of the infinite, the finite renewable, and the finite nonrenewable. Infinite resources, such as air and water, pose no immediate problem, although some groups see a long-run danger. Environmental groups have lobbied for a ban on certain propellants used in aerosol cans because of the potential damage they can cause to the ozone layer. Water shortages and pollution are already major problems in some parts of the world.

Finite renewable resources, such as forests and food, must be used wisely. Forestry companies are required to reforest timberlands in order to protect the soil and to ensure sufficient wood to meet future demand. Because the amount of arable land is fixed and urban areas are constantly encroaching on farmland, food supply can also be a major problem.

Finite nonrenewable resources—oil, coal, platinum, zinc, silver—will pose a serious problem as their time of depletion approaches. Firms making products that require these increasingly scarce minerals face substantial cost increases. They may not find it easy to pass these cost increases on to customers. Firms engaged in research and development face an excellent opportunity to develop new substitute materials.

INCREASED ENERGY COSTS. One finite nonrenewable resource, oil, has created serious problems for the world economy. Oil prices shot up from $2.23 a barrel in 1970 to $34.00 a barrel in 1982, creating a frantic search for alternative energy forms. Coal became popular again, and companies searched for practical means to harness solar, nuclear, wind, and other forms of energy. In the solar energy field alone, hundreds of firms introduced first-generation products to harness solar energy for heating homes and other uses. Other firms looked for ways to

Scanning
the Marketing
Environment

make a practical electric automobile, with a potential prize of billions going to the winner.

The development of alternative sources of energy and more efficient ways to use energy and the weakening of the oil cartel led to a decline in oil prices by 1986. Lower prices had an adverse effect on the oil-exploration industry but considerably improved the income of oil-using industries and consumers. In the meantime, the search continues for alternative sources of energy. Geothermal heat pumps (which harness energy from the earth itself) look particularly promising. A consortium that includes the U.S. Department of Energy and 71 utilities has pledged $100 million toward the ambitious goal of raising the sales of pumps to 400,000 annually by the year 2000.[14]

INCREASED POLLUTION LEVELS. Some industrial activity will inevitably damage the natural environment. Consider the dangerous mercury levels in the ocean, the quantity of DDT and other chemical pollutants in the soil and food supply, and the littering of the environment with nonbiodegradable bottles, plastics, and other packaging materials.

Research has shown that about 42% of U.S. consumers are willing to pay higher prices for "green" products. This willingness creates a marketing opportunity for alert companies. It creates a large market for pollution-control solutions, such as scrubbers, recycling centers, and landfill systems. It leads to a search for alternative ways to produce and package goods that do not cause environmental damage. Smart companies, instead of dragging their feet, are initiating environment-friendly moves to show their concern for the environment. 3M runs a Pollution Prevention Pays program that has led to a substantial reduction in pollution and costs. Dow built a new ethylene plant in Alberta that uses 40% less energy and releases 97% less waste water. AT&T uses a special software package to choose the least harmful materials, cut hazardous waste, reduce energy use, and improve product recycling in its operations. McDonald's and Burger King eliminated their polystyrene cartons and now use smaller, recyclable paper wrappings and paper napkins.[15]

CHANGING ROLE OF GOVERNMENTS IN ENVIRONMENTAL PROTECTION. Governments vary in their concern and efforts to promote a clean environment. For example, the German government is vigorous in its pursuit of environmental quality, partly because of the strong green movement in that country and partly because of the ecological devastation in former East Germany. Meanwhile, many poor nations are doing little about pollution, largely because they lack funds or the political will. It is in the richer nations' interest to help the poorer nations control their pollution, but even the richer nations today lack the necessary funds. The major hopes are that companies around the world will accept more social responsibility and that less expensive devices will be invented to control and reduce pollution.

Technological Environment

One of the most dramatic forces shaping people's lives is technology. Technology has released such wonders as penicillin, open-heart surgery, and the birth-control pill. It has released such horrors as the hydrogen bomb, nerve gas, and the submachine gun. It has also released such mixed blessings as the automobile and video games.

Every new technology is a force for "creative destruction." Transistors hurt the vacuum-tube industry, xerography hurt the carbon-paper business, autos hurt the railroads, and television hurt the newspapers. Instead of moving into the new business, many old industries fought or ignored them, and their businesses declined.

New technologies that provide superior value in satisfying needs stimulate investment and economic activity. Unfortunately, technological discoveries do not arise evenly through time—the railroad industry created a lot of investment, and then investment petered out until the auto industry emerged. Later, radio created a lot of investment, which then petered out until television appeared. In the time between major innovations, the economy can stagnate.

In the meantime, minor innovations fill the gap: freeze-dried coffee, Hamburger Helper, antiperspirant/deodorants, and the like. Minor innovations involve less risk, but critics argue that too much research effort is going into producing minor improvements rather than major breakthroughs.

New technology creates major long-run consequences that are not always foreseeable. The contraceptive pill, for example, led to smaller families, more working wives, and larger discretionary incomes—resulting in higher expenditures on vacation travel, durable goods, and luxury items.

The marketer should watch the following trends in technology.

ACCELERATING PACE OF TECHNOLOGICAL CHANGE. Many of today's common products were not available 30 years ago. John F. Kennedy did not know personal computers, digital wristwatches, video recorders, or fax machines. More ideas are being worked on; the time lag between new ideas and their successful implementation is decreasing rapidly; and the time between introduction and peak production is shortening considerably. Ninety percent of all the scientists who ever lived are alive today, and technology feeds upon itself.

The advent of personal computers and fax machines has made it possible for people to *telecommute*—that is, work at home instead of traveling to offices that may be 30 or more minutes away. Some hope that this trend will reduce auto pollution, bring the family closer together, and create more home-centered entertainment and activity. It will also have substantial impact on shopping behavior and marketing performance. (We will discuss the effects of new technologies on buying and selling behavior in Chapter 23, "Managing Direct and Online Marketing.")

UNLIMITED OPPORTUNITIES FOR INNOVATION. Scientists today are working on a startling range of new technologies that will revolutionize products and production processes. Some of the most exciting work is being done in biotechnology, solid-state electronics, robotics, and materials sciences.[16] Scientists today are working on AIDS cures, happiness pills, painkillers, totally safe contraceptives, and nonfattening tasty nutritious foods. They are designing robots for firefighting, underwater exploration, and home nursing. In addition, scientists also speculate on fantasy products, such as small flying cars, three-dimensional television, and space colonies. The challenge in each case is not only technical but also commercial—namely, to develop affordable versions of these products.

Companies are already harnessing the power of *virtual reality (VR),* the combination of technologies that allows users to experience three-dimensional, computer-generated environments through sound, sight, and touch (Figure 5-3 on page 160). Virtual reality has already been applied in medicine, entertainment, defense training, and architecture, and now pioneering companies are using it both to research and test products and to advertise and sell their wares. For a closer look at the marketing applications of virtual reality, see the Vision 2000 feature on page 161 titled "Virtual Reality Comes to Marketing."

VARYING R&D BUDGETS. The United States leads the world in annual R&D expenditures ($74 billion), but nearly 60% of these funds are still earmarked for defense. There is a need to transfer more of this money into research on material science, biotechnology, and micromechanics. Currently, Japan is increasing its R&D expenditures much faster than the United States and is now spending $30 billion a year, mostly on nondefense-related research in physics, biophysics, and computer science.[17]

A growing portion of U.S. R&D expenditures is going into the development side of R&D, raising concerns about whether the United States can maintain its lead in basic science. Many companies are pursuing minor product improvements rather than gambling on major innovations. Even basic-research companies such as Du Pont, Bell Laboratories, and Pfizer are proceeding cautiously. Many companies are content to put their money into copying competitors' products and making minor feature and style improvements. Much of the research is defensive rather than offensive. And, increasingly, research directed toward major breakthroughs is being conducted by consortiums of companies rather than by single companies.

INCREASED REGULATION OF TECHNOLOGICAL CHANGE. As products become more complex, the public needs to be assured of their safety. Consequently, government agencies' powers to investigate and ban potentially unsafe products have been expanded. In the United States the Federal Food and Drug Administration must approve all drugs before they can be sold. Safety and health regulations have also increased in the areas of food, automobiles, clothing, electrical appliances, and construction. Marketers must be aware of these regulations when proposing, developing, and launching new products.

Political/Legal Environment

Marketing decisions are strongly affected by developments in the political and legal environment. This environment is composed of laws, government agencies, and pressure groups that influence and limit various organizations and individuals. Sometimes these laws also create new opportunities for business. For example, mandatory recycling laws have given the recycling industry a major boost. A discussion of the main political trends and their implications for marketing management follows.

FIGURE 5-3

Virtual Reality Applications in Marketing
Virtual reality technology lets users interact with computer-generated worlds through sight, sound, and touch. A handset and some sort of handheld input device are necessary for many current VR applications. (left) CyberSim's VR program allows prospective home buyers to simulate their future homes and move around inside as if they were actually living in the as-yet unbuilt house. (right) Another VR program allows prospective car buyers to simulate driving around town in the car of their choice.

Virtual Reality Comes to Marketing

It sounds like a new computer game that's destined to be a flop: The customer puts on a virtual reality headset, grips the joystick, and plays the part of a cold-sore virus trying to escape from a cold-sore cream. Yet, Warner Wellcome Consumer Healthcare is successfully using this virtual reality simulation to promote Zovirax, its new over-the-counter cold-sore cream. Warner Wellcome first used the VR system at its sales conference in 1993—before the Zovirax launch—to motivate the sales force and impress upon them how much their product differs from the competition. It then used VR to launch the product to the media and at trade shows to promote the cream to pharmacists. Finally, consumers were exposed to a modified version of the VR simulation at a *London Daily Mail* ski show, where they learned how ultraviolet light can cause cold sores.

The benefits of VR to consumers are obvious. Customers like to try before they buy, and, of course, they also like being entertained. VR does both. In fact, it's often hard to tell whether some of the new VR promotions are advertising or entertainment. Using a virtual reality promotion for its Bubble Yum brand, Nabisco's LifeSavers division was able to get some 18,000 kids in malls across the United States to don an electronic headset and handgear and travel to Planet Bubble Yum. This is a world where chunks of gum fly through the air in 3-D animation, and the object of the game is to capture more Bubble Yum than your competitors.

In addition to using VR to raise brand awareness, marketers are using it to test brand preferences and other variables before products even hit the shelves. Atlanta-based MarketWare Corp. has created virtual reality software that lets companies conduct very real marketing research. Called Visionary Shopper, the system runs on PC's and allows consumers to stroll through store aisles on a computer screen and examine packages as though the shelf were really in front of them. Consumers can even rotate the package, seemingly by hand. A multitude of marketing variables can be measured through the process, ranging from pricing and promotional considerations to shelf-layout changes. MarketWare's director, Stephen Needel, says that a VR system is more appealing to consumers who are weary of market research phone calls and mailings. In addition, it may prove to be more accurate than market surveys. For instance, a consumer might not think twice about "removing" two six-packs of beer from the virtual shelves yet underreport the amount of beer he consumes on a traditional marketing survey, for fear of being seen as a heavy drinker. What's more, consumers who provide companies with data by strolling through virtual stores may be honing skills that will come in quite handy in the future. "This *is* how people will shop someday," says Needel.

Sources: Carrie Goerne, "Visionary Marketers Hope for Concrete Gains from the Fantasy of Virtual Reality," *Marketing News,* December 7, 1992, p. 2; Sue Norris, "Being Is Believing," *Marketing Week,* November 11, 1994, pp. 63–64; Andrew Jaffe, "Not Leaving Soon: Virtual Reality," *Adweek,* September 12, 1994, p. 9; Howard Schlossberg, "Shoppers Virtually Stroll Through Store Aisles to Examine Packages," *Marketing News,* June 7, 1993, p. 2.

LEGISLATION REGULATING BUSINESS. Business legislation has three main purposes: to protect companies from unfair competition, to protect consumers from unfair business practices, and to protect the interests of society from unbridled business behavior. A major purpose of business legislation and/or enforcement is to charge businesses with the social costs created by their products or production processes.

Legislation affecting business has steadily increased over the years. The European Commission has been active in establishing a new framework of laws covering competitive behavior, product standards, product liability, and commercial transactions for the 15 member nations of the European Union. With the demise of the Soviet Union, ex-Soviet nations are rapidly passing laws to promote and regulate an open market economy. The United States has many laws on its books covering such issues as competition, product safety and liability, fair trade and credit practices, packaging and labeling, and so on (Table 5-1).[18] Several countries have gone further than the United States in passing strong consumer-protection legisla-

TABLE 5-1	MILESTONE U.S. LEGISLATION AFFECTING MARKETING
Sherman Antitrust Act (1890)	Prohibits (a) "monopolies or attempts to monopolize" and (b) "contracts, combinations, or conspiracies in restraint of trade" in interstate and foreign commerce.
Federal Food and Drug Act (1906)	Forbids the manufacture, sale, or transport of adulterated or fraudulently labeled foods and drugs in interstate commerce. Supplanted by the Food, Drug, and Cosmetic Act, 1938; amended by Food Additives Amendment, 1958, and the Kefauver-Harris Amendment, 1962. The 1962 amendments deal with pretesting of drugs for safety and effectiveness and labeling of drugs by generic name.
Meat Inspection Act (1906)	Provides for the enforcement of sanitary regulations in meatpacking establishments and for federal inspection of all companies selling meats in interstate commerce.
Federal Trade Commission Act (1914)	Establishes the Federal Trade Commission (FTC), a body of specialists with broad powers to investigate and to issue cease-and-desist orders to enforce Section 5, which declares that "unfair methods of competition in commerce are unlawful."
Clayton Act (1914)	Supplements the Sherman Act by prohibiting certain specific practices (certain types of price discrimination, tying clauses and exclusive dealing, intercorporate stockholdings, and interlocking directorates) "where the effect . . . may be to substantially lessen competition or tend to create a monopoly in any line of commerce." Provides that corporate officials who violate the Act can be held individually responsible; exempts labor and agricultural organizations from its provisions.
Robinson-Patman Act (1936)	Amends the Clayton Act. Adds the phrase "to injure, destroy, or prevent competition." Defines price discrimination as unlawful (subject to certain defenses) and provides the FTC with the right to establish limits on quantity discounts, to forbid brokerage allowances except to independent brokers, and to prohibit promotional allowances or the furnishing of services or facilities except where made available to all "on proportionately equal terms."
Miller-Tydings Act (1937)	Amends the Sherman Act to exempt fair-trade (price-fixing) agreements from antitrust prosecution. (The McGuire Act, 1952, reinstates the legality of the nonsigner clause.)
Wheeler-Lea Act (1938)	Prohibits unfair and deceptive acts and practices regardless of whether competition is injured; places advertising of foods and drugs under FTC jurisdiction.
Antimerger Act (1950)	Amends Section 7 of the Clayton Act by broadening the government's power to prevent intercorporate acquisitions where the acquisition may have a substantially adverse effect on competition.
Automobile Information Disclosure Act (1958)	Prohibits car dealers from inflating the factory price of new cars.

tion. Norway bans several forms of sales promotion—trading stamps, contests, premiums—as inappropriate or "unfair" instruments for promoting products. Thailand requires food processors selling national brands to market low-price brands also so that low-income consumers can find economy brands. In India, food companies need special approval to launch brands that duplicate what already exists on the market, such as another cola drink or brand of rice.

A central concern about business legislation is: At what point do the costs of regulation exceed the benefits? The laws are not always administered fairly by those responsible for enforcing them. Regulators and enforcers may be overzealous and capricious; the agencies are dominated by lawyers and economists who often lack a practical sense of how business and marketing work. Tough antitrust laws have been criticized as hampering U.S. firms' ability to enter new markets and compete internationally. Although each new law may have a legitimate ratio-

PART 2

Analyzing
Marketing
Opportunities

National Traffic and Safety Act (1958)	Provides for the creation of compulsory safety standards for automobiles and tires.
Fair Packaging and Labeling Act (1966)	Provides for the regulation of the packaging and labeling of consumer goods. Requires manufacturers to state what the package contains, who made it, and how much it contains. Permits industries' voluntary adoption of uniform packaging standards.
Child Protection Act (1966)	Bans sale of hazardous toys and articles. Amended in 1969 to include articles that pose electrical, mechanical, or thermal hazards.
Federal Cigarette Labeling and Advertising Act (1967)	Requires that cigarette packages contain the statement: "Warning: The Surgeon General Has Determined That Cigarette Smoking Is Dangerous to Your Health."
Truth-in-Lending Act (1968)	Requires lenders to state the true costs of a credit transaction, outlaws the use of actual or threatened violence in collecting loans, and restricts the amount of garnishments. Establishes a National Commission on Consumer Finance.
National Environmental Policy Act (1969)	Establishes a national policy on the environment and provides for the establishment of the Council on Environmental Quality. The Environmental Protection Agency was established by "Reorganization Plan No. 3 of 1970."
Fair Credit Reporting Act (1970)	Ensures that a consumer's credit report will contain only accurate, relevant, and recent information and will be confidential unless requested for an appropriate reason by a proper party.
Consumer Product Safety Act (1972)	Establishes the Consumer Product Safety Commission and authorizes it to set safety standards for consumer products as well as exact penalties for failure to uphold the standards.
Consumer Goods Pricing Act (1975)	Prohibits the use of price maintenance agreements among manufacturers and resellers in interstate commerce.
Magnuson-Moss Warranty/FTC Improvement Act (1975)	Authorizes the FTC to determine rules concerning consumer warranties and provides for consumer access to means of redress, such as the class-action suit. Also expands FTC regulatory powers over unfair or deceptive acts or practices.
Equal Credit Opportunity Act (1975)	Prohibits discrimination in a credit transaction because of sex, marital status, race, national origin, religion, age, or receipt of public assistance.
Fair Debt Collection Practice Act (1978)	Makes it illegal to harass or abuse any person and make false statements or use unfair methods when collecting a debt.
Toy Safety Act (1984)	Gives the government the power to recall dangerous toys quickly when they are found.

nale, it may have the unintended effect of sapping initiative and retarding economic growth.

It is the marketer's responsibility to have a good working knowledge of the major laws protecting competition, consumers, and society. Companies generally establish legal review procedures and promulgate ethical standards to guide their marketing managers. Here's how one company got tough on ethics:

NYNEX In 1991 Nynex appointed Graydon Wood to the new position of vice-president of ethics and gave him a dozen full-time staff people and a million-dollar annual budget. Wood's department has trained some 95,000 Nynex employees since then. Such training includes sending 22,000 managers to full-day workshops that include case studies on ethical actions in marketing, finance, and other business functions. One workshop deals with the inappropriateness of using wrongly obtained competitive data.[19]

GROWTH OF SPECIAL-INTEREST GROUPS. The number and power of special-interest groups have increased over the past three decades. Political-action committees (PACs) lobby government officials and pressure business executives to pay more attention to consumer rights, women's rights, senior citizen rights, minority rights, gay rights, and so on. Many companies have established public-affairs departments to deal with these groups and issues.

An important force affecting business is the *consumerist movement*—an organized movement of citizens and government to strengthen the rights and powers of buyers in relation to sellers. Consumerists have advocated and won the right to know the true interest cost of a loan, the true cost per standard unit of competing brands (unit pricing), the basic ingredients in a product, the nutritional quality of food, the freshness of products, and the true benefits of a product. In response to consumerism, several companies have established consumer-affairs departments to help formulate policies and respond to consumers' complaints. Whirlpool Corporation is just one of the companies that have installed toll-free phone numbers for consumers to use if they are dissatisfied with their products or services. Whirlpool even expanded the coverage of its product warranties and rewrote them in basic English.

Clearly, new laws and growing numbers of pressure groups have put more restraints on marketers. Marketers have to clear their plans with the company's legal, public-relations, public-affairs, and consumer-affairs departments. Insurance companies directly or indirectly affect the design of smoke detectors; scientific groups affect the design of spray products by condemning aerosols. In essence, many private marketing transactions have moved into the public domain.

Social/Cultural Environment

The society in which people grow up shapes their beliefs, values, and norms. People absorb, almost unconsciously, a world view that defines their relationship to themselves, to others, to nature, and to the universe.

- *People's views of themselves:* People vary in the relative emphasis they place on self-gratification. The move toward self-gratification was especially strong in the United States during the 1960s and 1970s. "Pleasure seekers" sought fun, change, and escape. Others sought "self-realization" and joined therapeutic or religious groups. The marketing implications of a "me society" were many. People bought products, brands, and services as a means of self-expression. They bought dream cars and dream vacations. They spent more time in health activities (jogging, tennis), in introspection, and in arts and crafts. The leisure industry (camping, boating, arts and crafts, sports) benefited from the growing number of self-gratifiers. Today, in contrast, people are adopting more conservative behaviors and ambitions. They have witnessed harder times and cannot rely on continuous employment and rising real income. They are more cautious in their spending pattern and more value-driven in their purchases.

- *People's views of others:* Some observers have pointed to a countermovement from a "me society" to a "we society." People are concerned about the homeless, about crime and victims, and other social problems. They would like to live in a more humane society. At the same time, people are seeking out their "own kind" and avoiding strangers. People hunger for serious and long-lasting relationships with a few others. These trends portend a growing market for social-support products and services that promote direct relations between human beings, such as health clubs, cruises, and religious activity. They also suggest a growing market for "social surrogates," things that allow people who are alone to feel that they are not, such as television, home video games, and computers.

- *People's views of organizations:* People vary in their attitudes toward corporations, government agencies, trade unions, and other organizations. Most people are willing to work for these organizations, although they may be critical of particular ones. But there has been an overall decline in organizational loyalty. The massive wave of company downsizings and delayerings has bred cynicism and distrust of companies. Many people today see work not as a source of satisfaction but as a necessary evil to earn money to enjoy their nonwork hours.

This outlook has several marketing implications. Companies need to find new ways to win back consumer and employee confidence. They need to review their various activities to make sure they are good corporate citizens. They need to review their advertising communications to make sure their consumer messages are honest. More companies are turning to social audits and public relations to improve their image performance with their publics (see Chapter 21).

♦ *People's views of society:* People vary in their attitudes toward their society. Some defend it (preservers), some run it (makers), some take what they can from it (takers), some want to change it (changers), some are looking for something deeper (seekers), and some want to leave it (escapers).[20] Often peoples' consumption patterns reflect their social attitude. Makers tend to be high achievers who eat, dress, and live well. Changers usually live more frugally, drive smaller cars, wear simpler clothes, and so on. Escapers and seekers are a major market for movies, music, surfing, and camping.

♦ *People's views of nature:* People vary in their attitude toward nature. Some feel subjugated by it, others feel harmony with it, and still others seek mastery over it. A long-term trend has been people's growing mastery over nature through technology. More recently, however, people have awakened to nature's fragility and finite supplies. People recognize that nature can be destroyed by human activities.

People's love of nature is leading to more camping, hiking, boating, and fishing. Business has responded with hiking boots, tenting equipment, and other gear for nature enthusiasts. Tour operators are packaging more tours to wilderness areas. Marketing communicators are using more scenic backgrounds in advertising their products. Food producers have found growing markets for "natural" products, such as natural cereal, natural ice cream, and health foods. For example, natural-food grocery stores such as Whole Foods Markets and Fresh Fields had sales of $4.2 million in 1993, up 17% over the previous year.[21]

♦ *People's views of the universe:* People vary in their beliefs about the origin of the universe and their place in it. Most Americans are monotheistic, although their religious conviction and practice have been waning through the years. Church attendance has fallen steadily, with the exception of certain evangelical movements that reach out to bring people back into organized religion. Some of the religious impulse has been redirected into an interest in Eastern religions, mysticism, the occult, and the human-potential movement.

As people lose their religious orientation, they seek self-fulfillment and immediate gratification. At the same time, every trend seems to breed a countertrend, as indicated by a worldwide rise in religious fundamentalism.

Here are some of the other cultural characteristics of interest to marketers:

HIGH PERSISTENCE OF CORE CULTURAL VALUES.

The people living in a particular society hold many *core beliefs* and values that tend to persist. Thus most Americans still believe in work, in getting married, in giving to charity, and in being honest. Core beliefs and values are passed on from parents to children and are reinforced by major social institutions—schools, churches, business, and government.

People's *secondary beliefs* and values are more open to change. Believing in the institution of marriage is a core belief; believing that people ought to get married early is a secondary belief. Thus family-planning marketers could make some headway arguing that people should get married later than that they should not get married at all. Marketers have some chance of changing secondary values but little chance of changing core values. For instance, the nonprofit organization

Scanning
the Marketing
Environment

Mothers Against Drunk Drivers (MADD) does not try to take away from the U.S. culture's freedom to drink, but it does promote the idea of using a designated driver if one is too intoxicated to get behind the wheel. The group also lobbies to raise the legal drinking age.

EXISTENCE OF SUBCULTURES. Each society contains *subcultures,* various groups with shared values emerging from their special life experiences or circumstances. Episcopalians, teen-agers, and Hell's Angels all represent subcultures whose members share common beliefs, preferences, and behaviors. To the extent that subcultural groups exhibit different wants and consumption behavior, marketers can choose subcultures as their target markets.

Marketers sometimes reap unexpected rewards in targeting subcultures. For instance, marketers have always loved teens because they're society's trend setters in fashion, music, entertainment, ideas, and attitudes. And marketers also know that if they attract someone as a teen, there's a good chance they'll keep her as a customer in the years ahead. Frito-Lay, which draws 15% of its sales from teens, says it has seen a rise in chip snacking by grown-ups. "We think it's because we brought them in as teen-agers," says a Frito-Lay marketing director.[22]

SHIFTS OF SECONDARY CULTURAL VALUES THROUGH TIME. Although core values are fairly persistent, cultural swings do take place. The advent in the 1960s of hippies, the Beatles, Elvis Presley, and other cultural phenomena had a major impact on young people's hairstyles, clothing, sexual norms, and life goals. Today's young people are influenced by new heroes and fads: Pearl Jam's Eddie Vedder, Michael Jordan, and rollerblading.

Marketers have a keen interest in spotting cultural shifts that might augur new marketing opportunities or threats. Several firms offer social/cultural forecasts in this connection. One of the best known is the Yankelovich Monitor. The Monitor interviews 2,500 people each year and tracks 35 social trends, such as "antibigness," "mysticism," "living for today," "away from possessions," and "sensuousness." It describes the percentage of the population who share the attitude as well as the percentage who are antitrend. For example, the percentage of people who value physical fitness and well-being has risen steadily over the years, especially in the under-thirty group, the young women and upscale group, and people living in the West. Marketers of health foods and exercise equipment cater to this trend with appropriate products and communications. This trend plays itself out even in the fast-food industry, where companies are now racing to see who can come up with the healthiest new products. Taco Bell has been a pioneer in catering to the new health-conscious consumers. In 1995 the company unveiled its new lower-fat "Border Lights" menu. The Center for Science in the Public Interest, a consumer advocacy group in Washington, praised the new menu as being "more than a marketing gimmick"[23]

SUMMARY

1. Successful companies realize that the marketing environment presents a never-ending series of opportunities and threats. The major responsibility for identifying significant changes in the macroenvironment falls to a company's marketers. More than any other group in the company, marketing managers must be the trend trackers and opportunity seekers.

2. Many opportunities are found by identifying *trends* (directions or sequences of events that have some momentum and durability) and *megatrends* (large social, economic, po-

litical, and technological changes that are slow to form, and once in place have long-lasting influence).

3. Within the rapidly changing global picture, marketers must monitor six major environmental forces: demographic, economic, natural, technological, political/legal, and social/cultural. In the *demographic* environment, marketers must be aware of worldwide population growth; changing mixes of age, ethnic composition, and educational levels; the rise of nontraditional families; large geographic shifts in population; and the move to micromarketing and away from mass marketing. In the *economic* arena, they need to focus on income distribution and levels of savings, debt, and credit availability. In the *natural* environment, marketers need to be aware of raw-materials shortages, increased energy costs and pollution levels, and the changing role of governments in environmental protection. In the *technological* arena, they should take account of the accelerating pace of technological change, opportunities for innovation, varying R&D budgets, and the increased governmental regulation brought about by technological change. In the *political/legal* environment, marketers must work within the many laws regulating business practices and with various special-interest groups. Finally, in the *social/cultural* arena, they must understand people's views of themselves, others, organizations, society, nature, and the universe; market products that correspond to society's core and secondary values; and address the needs of different subcultures within a society.

CONCEPT APPLICATIONS

1. Kentucky Fried Chicken's success in Asia dramatizes the case for becoming a global firm. While KFC's market share in the United States has fallen because of Americans' interest in reducing their consumption of fried foods, KFC has become the fast-food leader in China, South Korea, Malaysia, Thailand, and Indonesia. In Japan and Singapore, it is second only to McDonald's. Its more than 1,470 foreign outlets average $1.2 million in revenue per store, about 60% more than its average U.S. store. In Tiananmen Square, KFC operates its busiest outlet—a 701-seat restaurant serving 2.5 million customers a year. In general, KFC's Asian outlets appeal to young, middle-class, urban workers with rising incomes.

   KFC's Asian restaurants serve basically its standard fried chicken, mashed potatoes, and cole slaw but have also offered a few adaptations, such as a spicier chicken in Thailand and chicken curry in Japan. KFC offers no beef or pork products, which are not generally consumed by the people in Asian countries.

   What other U.S. companies in the food business do you think would appeal to the markets that KFC is serving? Why? What are some of the cultural, linguistic, or technological barriers that U.S. exporters would have to overcome to be successful in these markets?

2. Business definition (see Chapter 3) can also play an important role in environmental analysis. A business definition that is too narrow can prevent the company from understanding how technological change can affect its ability to respond to changes in the environment. The railroad industry encountered this problem, stubbornly refusing to change its business definition even as the United States grew, the auto took over the road, and interstate highways were built. How did the railroad industry's narrow business definition keep it from responding to changes in the technological environment?

3. Every country has its own set of core values and beliefs. For example, if you were born and grew up in the United States, you hold a number of core values and beliefs that are distinctively American. Identify ten of these core values and beliefs and clip magazine ads that attempt to appeal to at least three of them. Explain how the ads weave core values into the message.

4. One of the changes in the demographic environment is the increasing proportion of older adults, who comprise many markets for certain products. Discuss how this demographic trend could affect the product features and/ or distribution arrangements of the following:

Scanning
the Marketing
Environment

a. Minute Maid orange juice
b. Mail-order businesses
c. the Social Security Office

5. The Whirlpool Corporation sells kitchen and other household appliances in the global marketplace. One of its newer products is the VIP Crispwave Microwave Oven, which was invented in Europe for European markets but which has now been introduced in the United States and other parts of the world. This microwave actually cooks food crisp, is easy to operate, and provides consistent cooking performance. Discuss some of the forces and trends in the global marketing environment that will face Whirlpool as it markets this product around the world.

6. NordicTrack markets an exercise machine to men and women who are into fitness. Which demographic segment is the ad in Figure 1 targeting? How can you tell? Do you think that this demographic segment has enough potential to warrant the cost of promotion? What benefits does the product have for this targeted group? Explain.

FIGURE 1
NordicTrack Ad

7. You are a product manager at Minolta. Your boss has just received a copy of *The Popcorn Report* (see the Marketing Insight on pages 148–49 for a review of Faith Popcorn's work). Although her background is in engineering, she has always been interested in the sensory appeal of product features and this book has aroused her curiosity about this phenomenon. Prepare a report summarizing the potential impact of each of Popcorn's 10 trends on Minolta's product (cameras). Specifically, how will each trend affect product development, features, and marketing?

8. On April 23, 1985, Roberto C. Goizueta, chairman of Coca-Cola, announced that "the best has been made even better." Coke's 99-year-old formula had been abandoned, and a new, sweeter tasting Coke would replace the old Coke. By July 11, 1985, Coca-Cola admitted that it had made a mistake and that it was bringing back the old Coke under

the name "Coca-Cola Classic." Business schools will dissect this case for years to come and wonder how the Coca-Cola Company (known for years as an astute marketer) could have made such a blunder.

But that was then. This is now, and you are part of a marketing team at Coca-Cola charged with taking the company into the twenty-first century. Before you make any further decisions, discuss in some depth how the six macroenvironmental forces discussed in this chapter may affect the marketing of Coca-Cola by the year 2002.

9. Budweiser, Calvin Klein, McDonald's, Coca-Cola, and Chevrolet are examples of brands that have become cultural symbols for the United States. Name some brand names and products that are cultural symbols for the following countries:

a. Japan
b. Germany
c. Russia
d. France
e. Italy
f. Ireland
g. Colombia
h. Mexico
i. England
j. Switzerland
k. the Middle Eastern nations
l. Australia

10. Lifestyle studies have shown a positive trend in the attitude that "meal preparation should take as little time as possible." How might this attitude affect the sales of frozen vegetables? (Think very carefully before you answer. . . .)

NOTES

1. Bradley Johnson, "Marketer of the Year: Bill Gates' Vision of Microsoft in Every Home," *Advertising Age,* December 19, 1994, pp. 14–15; Richard Brandt, "Microsoft Wants to Move into Your Family Room," *Business Week,* November 28, 1994, pp. 92–93.
2. Gerald Celente, *Trend Tracking* (New York: Warner Books, 1991).
3. See Faith Popcorn, *The Popcorn Report* (New York: HarperBusiness, 1992).
4. John Naisbitt and Patricia Aburdene, *Megatrends 2000* (New York: Avon Books, 1990).
5. Pam Weisz, "Border Crossings: Brands Unify Image to Counter Cult of Culture," *Brandweek,* October 31, 1994, pp. 24–28.
6. Many of the statistical data in this chapter are drawn from the *World Almanac and Book of Facts,* 1994 and the *Statistical Abstract of the United States,* 1994 (Washington, DC: U.S. Bureau of the Census, 1995).
7. Donella H. Meadows, Dennis L. Meadows, Jorgen Randers, and William W. Behrens III, *The Limits to Growth* (New York: New American Library, 1972), p. 41.
8. Philip Kotler and Eduardo Roberto, *Social Marketing: Strategies for Changing Public Attitudes* (New York: Free Press, 1989).
9. Sally D. Goll, "Marketing: China's (Only) Children Get the Royal Treatment," *The Wall Street Journal,* February 8, 1995, B1:3.
10. Laura Zinn, "Teens: Here Comes the Biggest Wave Yet," *Business Week,* April 11, 1994, pp. 76–86.
11. For descriptions on the buying habits and marketing approaches to African-Americans and Latinos, see Chester A. Swenson, *Selling to a Segmented Market: The Lifestyle Approach* (Lincolnwood, IL: NTC Business Books, 1992).
12. Jacquelyn Lynn, "Tapping the Riches of Bilingual Markets," *Management Review,* March 1995, pp. 56–61.
13. Laurie Freeman, "Completing the Span of 'Bridge' to Boomers," *Advertising Age,* November 7, 1994, p. S-8.
14. John Wyatt, "Solar Power Comes Back: No, Really," *Fortune,* February 20, 1995, p. 20.
15. Francoise L. Simon, "Marketing Green Products in the Triad," *The Columbia Journal of World Business,* Fall & Winter 1992, pp. 268–85; Jacquelyn A. Ottman, *Green Marketing: Responding to Environmental Consumer Demands* (Lincolnwood, IL: NTC Business Books, 1993); Patrick Carson and Julia Moulden, *Green Is Gold: Business Talking to Business About the Environmental Revolution* (Toronto: HarperBusiness, 1991); and Edward Woolard, Jr., "Environmental Stewardship," *Chemical and Engineering News,* May 29, 1989.
16. See "White House to Name 22 Technologies It Says Are Crucial to Prosperity, Security," *The Wall Street Journal,* April 26, 1991, p. 2.
17. See "R&D Scoreboard: On a Clear Day You Can See Progress," *Business Week,* June 29, 1992, pp. 104–25.
18. For an explanation of the legal terminology and current information on U.S. legislation affecting businesses and consumers, see Dorothy Cohen, *Legal Issues on Marketing Decision Making* (Cincinnati: South-Western, 1995). For a discussion of the interaction between antitrust concerns and market competition, see Oliver P. Heil and Arlen W. Langvardt, "The Interface Between Competitive Market Signaling and Antitrust Law," *Journal of Marketing,* 58, no. 3 (July 1994), 81–96.
19. Mark Henricks, "Ethics in Action," *Management Review,* January 1995, pp. 53–55.
20. Arnold Mitchell of the Stanford Research Institute, private publication.
21. Laura Loro, "Doing What Comes Naturally," *Advertising Age,* August 8, 1994, p. 22.
22. Zinn, "Teens: Here Comes the Biggest Wave Yet."
23. Glenn Collins, "From Taco Bell, a Healthier Option," *The New York Times,* February 9, 1995, D4:3.

ANALYZING CONSUMER MARKETS AND BUYER BEHAVIOR

There is an old saying in Spain: To be a bullfighter,
you must first learn to be a bull.

ANONYMOUS

❖

You never really understand a person until you consider things from his point
of view— until you climb into his skin and walk around in it.

ATTICUS FINCH IN HARPER LEE'S *TO KILL A MOCKINGBIRD*

❖

The aim of marketing is to meet and satisfy target customers' needs and wants. The field of *consumer behavior* studies how individuals, groups, and organizations select, buy, use, and dispose of goods, services, ideas, or experiences to satisfy their needs and desires.

Understanding consumer behavior and "knowing customers" are never simple. Customers may state their needs and wants but act otherwise. They may not be in touch with their deeper motivations. They may respond to influences that change their mind at the last minute. Nevertheless, marketers must study their target customers' wants, perceptions, preferences, and shopping and buying behavior:

SEGA Sega of America, the scrappy little company that overtook Nintendo in the U.S. video game market, spends a tremendous amount of time trying to understand the needs and wants of its major market: teens. Says Sega's senior vice president of marketing, "Kids' No. 1 desire is to be up on new stuff all the time and know things that their parents don't know." The company has gathered this information by conducting focus groups two or three times a week, and researchers at Sega's ad agency find out how kids buy by hanging around some 150 kids' bedrooms and shopping with them in malls. They've discovered that the typical teen is surprisingly price-conscious and shops for video games with the same attentiveness that an adult shops for a new car. Teens read consumer guidebooks, talk to friends, and even rent games before buying. Above all, they want everything to be fast. And Sega complies by introducing new video games at a relentless pace (about 65 new games a year), and wooing kids with hip and frenetic TV ads that clock in at 15 seconds.[1]

Studying consumers, as Sega does, provides clues for developing new products, product features, prices, channels, messages, and other marketing-mix elements. This chapter explores consumers' buying dynamics; the next chapter explores the buying dynamics of business buyers.

A MODEL OF CONSUMER BEHAVIOR

At one time, marketers could understand consumers through the daily experience of selling to them. But the growth of companies and markets has removed many marketing managers from direct contact with customers. Increasingly, managers have had to rely on the 7 O's framework for consumer research to answer the following key questions about any market:

Who constitutes the market?	Occupants
What does the market buy?	Objects
Why does the market buy?	Objectives
Who participates in the buying?	Organizations
How does the market buy?	Operations
When does the market buy?	Occasions
Where does the market buy?	Outlets

The starting point for understanding buyer behavior is the stimulus-response model shown in Figure 6-1 on the next page. Marketing and environmental stimuli enter the buyer's consciousness. The buyer's characteristics and decision process lead to certain purchase decisions. The marketer's task is to understand what happens in the buyer's consciousness between the arrival of outside stimuli and the buyer's purchase decisions. They must answer two questions:

◆ **How do the buyer's characteristics—cultural, social, personal, and psychological—influence buying behavior?**

◆ **How does the buyer make purchasing decisions?**

MAJOR FACTORS INFLUENCING BUYING BEHAVIOR

Figure 6-2 summarizes the factors influencing a consumer's buying behavior. We will illustrate these influences for a hypothetical consumer named Linda Brown, who is 35, married, and a regional sales manager in a leading chemical company. She travels a lot and wants to acquire a laptop computer. She faces a great number of brand choices: IBM, Apple, Dell, Compaq, and so on. Her choice will be influenced by many cultural, social, personal, and psychological factors.

Cultural Factors

Cultural factors exert the broadest and deepest influence on consumer behavior. The roles played by the buyer's culture, subculture, and social class are particularly important.

CULTURE. *Culture* is the most fundamental determinant of a person's wants and behavior. The growing child acquires a set of values, perceptions, preferences, and behaviors through his or her family and other key institutions. A child growing up in the United States is exposed to the following values: achievement and success, activity, efficiency and practicality, progress, material comfort, individualism, freedom, external comfort, humanitarianism, and youthfulness.[2]

Linda Brown's interest in computers reflects her upbringing in a technological society. Linda knows what computers are and she knows that the society values computer expertise. In another culture, say a remote tribe in central Africa, a computer would mean nothing. It would simply be a curious piece of hardware, and there would be no buyers.

FIGURE 6-1
Model of Buyer Behavior

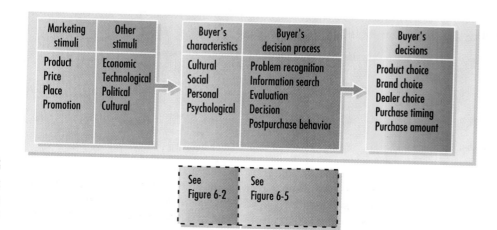

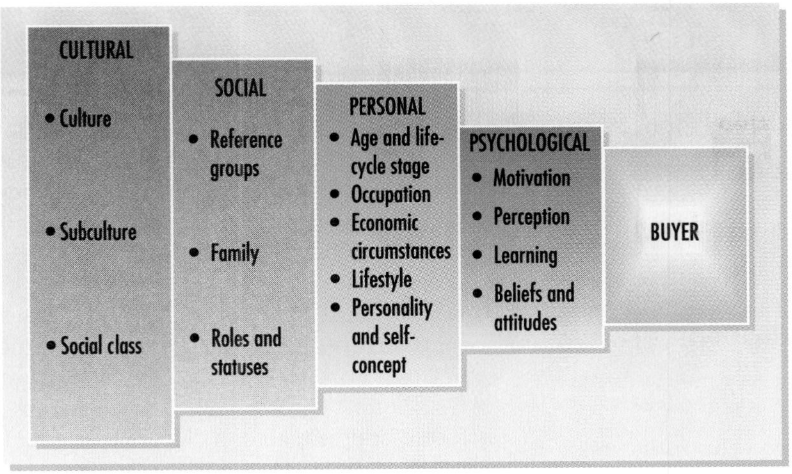

FIGURE 6-2
Factors Influencing Behavior

CULTURAL	SOCIAL	PERSONAL	PSYCHOLOGICAL	BUYER
• Culture	• Reference groups	• Age and life-cycle stage	• Motivation	
• Subculture	• Family	• Occupation	• Perception	
		• Economic circumstances	• Learning	
		• Lifestyle	• Beliefs and attitudes	
• Social class	• Roles and statuses	• Personality and self-concept		

SUBCULTURE. As we saw in the previous chapter, each culture consists of smaller subcultures that provide more specific identification and socialization for its members. Subcultures include nationalities, religions, racial groups, and geographical regions. Many subcultures make up important market segments, and marketers often design products and marketing programs tailored to their needs. (For more on this topic, see the Marketing Insight titled "Marketing to Latinos, African-Americans, and Seniors.") Linda Brown's buying behavior will be influenced by her subculture identifications. They will influence her food preferences, clothing choices, recreation, and career aspirations. She may come from a subculture that places a high value on being an "educated person," and this helps explain her interest in computers.

SOCIAL CLASS. Virtually all human societies exhibit social stratification. Stratification sometimes takes the form of a caste system where the members of different castes are reared for certain roles and cannot change their caste membership. More frequently, stratification takes the form of social classes.

❖ **SOCIAL CLASSES** are relatively homogeneous and enduring divisions in a society, which are hierarchically ordered and whose members share similar values, interests, and behavior.

Social classes do not reflect income alone but also other indicators such as occupation, education, and area of residence. Social classes differ in their dress, speech patterns, recreational preferences, and many other characteristics. Table 6-1 describes the seven social classes identified by social scientists.

Social classes have several characteristics. First, persons within each social class tend to behave more alike than persons from two different social classes. Second, persons are perceived as occupying inferior or superior positions according to their social class. Third, a person's social class is indicated by a cluster of variables—for example, occupation, income, wealth, education, and value orientation—rather than by any single variable. Fourth, individuals can move from one social class to another—up or down—during their lifetime. The extent of this mobility varies according to the rigidity of social stratification in a given society.

Social classes show distinct product and brand preferences in many areas, including clothing, home furnishings, leisure activities, and automobiles. Some marketers focus their efforts on one social class. Thus the Four Seasons restaurant in upper Manhattan focuses on upper-class customers, while Joe's Diner in lower

Marketing to Latinos, African-Americans, and Seniors

When subcultures grow large and affluent enough, companies often design special marketing programs to serve them. Here are examples of three important subculture groups.

Latinos

For years, marketers have viewed the Latino market—Americans of Mexican, Cuban, Puerto Rican, and Central and South American descent—as small and having low purchasing power, but these perceptions are badly out of date. Expected to account for 11% of the U.S. population by the year 2020, Latinos (sometimes called Hispanic-Americans) are the second largest and fastest-growing U.S. minority. Annual Latino purchasing power exceeds $134 billion. Over half of all Latinos live in one of six metropolitan areas—Los Angeles, New York, Miami, San Antonio, San Francisco, and Chicago. Latinos have long been a target for marketers of food, beverages, and household care products. But as the segment's buying power increases, Latinos are emerging as an attractive market for pricier products such as computers, financial services, photography equipment, large appliances, life insurance, and automobiles. Many companies are devoting larger ad budgets and preparing special appeals and media to woo Latinos. Smart companies are also recognizing the differences that exist among Latino communities with respect to country of origin, culture, social class, and stage in the family life cycle.

As a result of the Latino market's growing clout, many companies (including Colgate-Palmolive, Nestlé, PepsiCo, and Procter & Gamble) are increasing the number of products they're shipping from Latin Amer-ica. This trend has accelerated since the passage of the North American Free Trade Agreement (NAFTA). For instance, Nestlé began rolling out Nido, a powdered milk it sells in Mexico; Wal-Mart stores started carrying Maizoro, one of the big Mexican cereal brands; and Colgate-Palmolive began marketing its Mexican household cleaner, Fabuloso, in Los Angeles and Miami. The biggest revenue producer of Latin American products is Goya Foods, the Secaucus, New Jersey, ethnic-foods distributor. By tapping Latinos' desires for "comfort foods" like nopalitos (sliced cactus) and tostones (fried green plantains), Goya's sales have risen from $300 million to $480 million since 1990.

African-Americans

If the U.S. population of over 31 million black Americans—with a total purchasing power of more than $218 billion annually—were a separate nation, their buying power would rank twelfth in the world. The African-American population is growing in affluence. African-Americans spend relatively more than whites on clothing, personal care, home furnishings, and fragrances; and relatively less on food, transportation, and recreation. They tend to be strongly motivated by quality and selection and shop more at neighborhood stores.

To tap the African-American market, KFC (formerly Kentucky Fried Chicken) is giving some of its restaurants an African-American flavor, outfitting employees in traditional African-oriented uniforms, providing rhythm and blues music, and offering menu additions that reflect local tastes, such as "soul sides" of red beans, rice, or greens. Large companies including Quaker Oats, McDonald's, Procter & Gamble, Coca-Cola, and Clorox are forging promotional ties with the black community and its institutions. Quaker Oats shows its respect and concern for black families by running sweepstakes in which winners can enjoy an

Manhattan focuses on lower-class customers. The social classes differ in their media preferences, with upper-class consumers preferring magazines and books and lower-class consumers preferring television. Even within a media category such as TV, upper-class consumers prefer news and drama, and lower-class consumers prefer soap operas and quiz shows. There are also language differences among the social classes. The advertiser has to compose copy and dialogue that ring true to the targeted social class.

Linda Brown comes from a middle-class background. Her family places high value on education and becoming a professional. As a result, Linda has acquired good verbal and mathematical skills and is not intimidated by computers, as someone from a less-educated background might be.

PART 2

Analyzing
Marketing
Opportunities

all-expense-paid "family reunion" at Chicago's Gospelfest, the city's largest free outdoor gospel music event, which Quaker sponsors. Clorox ran the Pine Sol Clean Start campaign, in which Pine Sol consumers in minority communities were entered into a scholarship sweepstakes.

Spike Lee, the African-American filmmaker who is a master at tapping black purchasing power, advises marketers to "use the black press, spend a lot of your promotional dollars with black institutions. And don't just do it on a . . . product-by-product basis. You have to be in it for the long run." Another caveat for those who are marketing to the black or other minority communities: Hire the consumers you are trying to target. When department store giant J. C. Penney began marketing merchandise to African-American and Latino consumers, it was blasted by minority leaders who said the company should concentrate on increasing the number of minority employees.

Mature Consumers

As the U.S. population ages, mature consumers—those 65 and older—are becoming a very attractive market. The seniors market will grow to over 40 million consumers by the year 2000. Seniors are better off financially, spending about $200 billion each year, and they average twice the disposable income of consumers in the under-35 group. Mature consumers have long been the target of the makers of laxatives, tonics, and denture products. But smart marketers know that many seniors are healthy and active, and they have many of the same needs and wants as younger consumers. Their buying decisions are based not on age but on lifestyle—a distinction that is sometimes missed. Today's seniors want to stay fit and healthy so they can maintain their lifestyle. This interest in health and fitness has fueled the popularity of events such as the Senior Sports Classic, which gives seniors an opportunity to compete and corporate sponsors like AT&T, Johnson & Johnson, and the Medicine Shoppe (a pharmacy chain) a chance to get their message across. Surprisingly, seniors spend more on personal-care products than any other age group, and consume more fast-food meals than teen-agers. Too few marketers really understand this and fail to take aim at this huge market.

Despite some belief to the contrary, seniors certainly don't spend all their time shopping. Because today's seniors consume 80% of luxury travel, many airlines and hotel chains offer discounts to this market. For instance, Choice Hotels International introduced "Prime Rate," which gives a 30% room discount to people over the age of 50, subject to availability. Some travel companies do "cross-generational" marketing to appeal to grandparents and their grandchildren. And GrandTravel of Chevy Chase, Maryland, sponsors barge trips through Holland, safaris to Kenya, and other exotic vacations for grandparents and their grandchildren.

Sources: For more on marketing to Latinos, African-Americans, mature consumers, as well as Asian-Americans, see Jon Berry, "Special Report: Hispanic Marketing," *Adweek*, July 9, 1990, pp. 28–34; Gary L. Berman, "The Hispanic Market: Getting Down to Cases," *Sales and Marketing Management*, October 1991, pp. 65–74; Laura Zinn, "Run to the Supermart and Pick Me Up Some Cactus," *Business Week*, June 20, 1994, pp. 70–71; Judith Waldrop, "Shades of Black," *American Demographics*, September 1990, pp. 30–34; Melissa Campanelli, "The African-American Market: Community, Growth, and Change," *Sales and Marketing Management*, May 1991, pp. 75–81; Geoffrey Brewer, "Spike Speaks," *Incentive*, 167, no. 2 (February 1993), 26–34; "Minority Leaders Blast J. C. Penney Plan to Target Blacks, Hispanics," *Marketing News*, 27, no. 21 (October 11, 1993), 1, 15; Milinda Beck, "The Geezer Boom," in "The 21st Century American Family," a special issue of *Newsweek*, Winter–Spring 1990, pp. 62–67; Melissa Campanelli, "The Senior Market: Rewriting the Demographics and Definitions," *Sales and Marketing Management*, February 1991, pp. 63–70; Regina Eisman, "Young at Heart," *Incentive*, 167, no. 4 (April 1993), 33–38; and Maria Shao, "Suddenly, Asian-Americans Are a Marketer's Dream," *Business Week*, June 17, 1991, pp. 54–55.

Social Factors

In addition to cultural factors, a consumer's behavior is influenced by such social factors as reference groups, family, and roles and statuses.

REFERENCE GROUPS.

Many groups influence a person's behavior.

❖   A person's **REFERENCE GROUPS** consist of all the groups that have a direct (face-to-face) or indirect influence on the person's attitudes or behavior. Groups having a direct influence on a person are called **MEMBERSHIP GROUPS**.

Analyzing Consumer Markets and Buying Behavior

TABLE 6-1	CHARACTERISTICS OF SEVEN MAJOR U. S. SOCIAL CLASSES
1. **Upper Uppers** (less than 1%)	The social elite who live on inherited wealth and have well-known families. They give large sums to charity, run the debutante balls, maintain more than one home, and send their children to the finest schools. They are a market for jewelry, antiques, homes, and vacations. They often buy and dress conservatively, not being interested in ostentation. While small as a group, they serve as a reference group for others to the extent that their consumption decisions trickle down and are imitated by the other social classes.
2. **Lower Uppers** (about 2%)	Persons who have earned high income or wealth through exceptional ability in the professions or business. They usually come from the middle class. They tend to be active in social and civic affairs and seek to buy the symbols of status for themselves and their children, such as expensive homes, schools, yachts, swimming pools, and automobiles. They include the nouveau riche, whose pattern of conspicuous consumption is designed to impress those below them. The ambition of lower uppers is to be accepted in the upper-upper stratum, a status that is more likely to be achieved by their children than themselves.
3. **Upper Middles** (12%)	Possess neither family status nor unusual wealth. They are primarily concerned with "career." They have attained positions as professionals, independent businesspersons, and corporate managers. They believe in education and want their children to develop professional or administrative skills so that they will not drop into a lower stratum. Members of this class like to deal in ideas and "high culture." They are highly civic minded. They are the quality market for good homes, clothes, furniture, and appliances. They are home-oriented and enjoy entertaining friends and clients.
4. **Middle Class** (32%)	Average-pay white- and blue-collar workers who live on "the better side of town" and try to "do the proper things." Often, they buy products that are popular to keep up with the trends. Twenty-five percent own imported cars, and most are concerned with fashion, seeking "one of the better brand names." Better living means a nicer home in "a nice neighborhood on the better side of town" with "good schools." The middle class believes in spending more money on "worthwhile experiences" for their children and aiming them toward a college education.
5. **Working Class** (38%)	Average-pay blue-collar workers and those who lead a working-class lifestyle, whatever their income, school background, or job. The working class depends heavily on relatives for economic and emotional support, for tips on job opportunities, for advice on purchases, and for assistance in times of trouble. A working-class vacation means staying in town, and "going away" means to a lake or resort no more than two hours away. The working class tends to maintain sharp sex-role division and stereotyping. Car preferences include standard size and larger cars, rejecting domestic and foreign compacts.
6. **Upper Lowers** (9%)	Upper lowers are working, not on welfare, although their living standard is just above poverty. They perform unskilled work and are very poorly paid, although they are striving toward a higher class. Often, upper lowers are educationally deficient.
7. **Lower Lowers** (7%)	Lower lowers are on welfare, visibly poverty stricken, and usually out of work. Some are not interested in finding a permanent job and most are dependent on public aid or charity for income. Their homes, clothes, and possessions are often viewed as "dirty," "raggedy," and "broken-down."

Sources: Richard P. Coleman, "The Continuing Significance of Social Class to Marketing," *Journal of Consumer Research,* December 1983, pp. 265–80; and Richard P. Coleman and Lee P. Rainwater, *Social Standing in America: New Dimension of Class* (New York: Basic Books, 1978).

Some membership groups are *primary groups,* such as family, friends, neighbors, and co-workers, with whom the person interacts fairly continuously and informally. People also belong to *secondary groups,* such as religious, professional, and trade-union groups, which tend to be more formal and require less continuous interaction.

People are significantly influenced by their reference groups in at least three ways. Reference groups expose an individual to new behaviors and lifestyles. They also influence the person's attitudes and self-concept. And they create pressures for conformity that may affect the person's actual product and brand choices.

People are also influenced by groups in which they are not members. Groups to which a person would like to belong are called *aspirational groups.* For example, a teen-ager may hope one day to play basketball for the Chicago Bulls. A *dissociative group* is one whose values or behavior an individual rejects. The same teen-ager may want to avoid any relationship with the Hare Krishna group.

Marketers try to identify their target customers' reference groups. However, the level of reference-group influence varies among products and brands. Reference groups appear to strongly influence both product and brand choice only in the case of automobiles and color televisions; mainly brand choice in such items as furniture and clothing; and mainly product choice in such items as beer and cigarettes.

Manufacturers of products and brands where group influence is strong must determine how to reach and influence the opinion leaders in these reference groups. An *opinion leader* is the person in informal product-related communications who offers advice or information about a specific product or product category, such as which of several brands is best or how a particular product may be used.[3] Opinion leaders are found in all strata of society, and a person can be an opinion leader in certain product areas and an opinion follower in other areas. Marketers try to reach opinion leaders by identifying demographic and psychographic characteristics associated with opinion leadership, identifying the media read by opinion leaders, and directing messages at the opinion leaders. This is exactly what San Francisco–based The Gap Inc. is trying to do since it has begun to lose its edge with opinion leaders in its most important market: shoppers under the age of 30:

THE GAP   In 1992, about 90% of teens said Gap clothes were "cool," in Leo Burnett Co.'s annual "What's hot among kids" survey. That number fell to 83% the next summer and plummeted to 63% in two 1995 polls. In fact, Gap attire and advertising have become the butt of jokes and the target of resentment by teens and Generation Xers. "Their clothes promote a straight, white, lame lifestyle, which is just how THEY want us to be," writes Hugh Galagher in a satire in Los Angeles's *Grand Royal* magazine. While the company is hardly in trouble, Gap is trying to get a more interesting and targeted assortment of merchandise in appealing colors, and the monitors of "cool" at corporate headquarters are busily working up campaigns directed at opinion leaders.[4]

Group influence is strong for products that are visible to others whom the buyer respects. Linda Brown's interest in a laptop computer and her attitudes toward various brands will be strongly influenced by some of her membership groups. Her co-workers' attitudes and brand choices will influence her. The more cohesive the group, the more effective the group's communication process, and the higher the person esteems the group, the more the group will shape the person's product and brand choices.

FAMILY.   The family is the most important consumer-buying organization in society, and it has been researched extensively.[5] Family members constitute the most influential primary reference group. We can distinguish between two families in

Analyzing Consumer
Markets and Buying
Behavior

the buyer's life. The *family of orientation* consists of one's parents and siblings. From parents a person acquires an orientation toward religion, politics, and economics and a sense of personal ambition, self-worth, and love.[6] Even if the buyer no longer interacts very much with his or her parents, the parents' influence on the buyer's behavior can be significant. In countries where parents live with their grown children, their influence can be substantial. A more direct influence on everyday buying behavior is one's *family of procreation*—namely, one's spouse and children.

Marketers are interested in the roles and relative influence of the husband, wife, and children in the purchase of a large variety of products and services. These roles vary widely in different countries and social classes. In the United States, husband-wife involvement has traditionally varied widely by product category. The wife has traditionally acted as the family's main purchasing agent, especially for food, sundries, and staple-clothing items. In the case of expensive products and services, husbands and wives have engaged in more joint decision making. Marketers need to determine which member normally has the greater influence in choosing various products. Often it is a matter of who has more power or expertise. Here are the traditional product patterns:

♦ *Husband dominant:* Life insurance, automobiles, television

♦ *Wife dominant:* Washing machines, carpeting, furniture, kitchenware

♦ *Equal:* Vacation, housing, outside entertainment

These patterns are gradually changing, however, due to the rise in employment of women, especially in nontraditional jobs. Shifts in social values regarding the division of domestic labor have also weakened such standard conceptions as "women buy all the household goods." Recent research has shown that while traditional buying patterns still hold, baby boomer husband and wives are more willing to shop jointly for products traditionally thought to be under the separate control of one spouse or the other.[7] Hence, convenience-goods marketers are making a mistake if they think of women as the main or only purchasers of their products. Similarly, marketers of products traditionally purchased by men may need to start thinking of women as possible purchasers. This is already happening in the hardware business:

BUILDERS SQUARE In 1993 hardware outlets in the United States saw sales rise 9.8% to $104.4 billion. According to the National Retail Hardware Association/ Home Center Institute, women account for 49.6% of all hardware-store purchases. The rise in women's tool ownership is due to more divorced women being forced to handle minor home emergencies, and more married and single women buying less-expensive homes that need repairs. One retailer that spotted the trend early and has capitalized on it is Builders Square. In 1991 the San Antonio–based company turned what had been an intimidating warehouse into a user-friendly retail outlet. The new Builders Square II outlets feature decorator design centers toward the front of the store. To draw more women into the more appealing stores, Builders Square began running ads targeting women in *Home, House Beautiful, Woman's Day,* and *Better Homes and Gardens.* Builders Square now even offers bridal registries. Says a marketing director at Builders Square, "It's more meaningful to them to have a great patio set or gas grill than to have fine china."[8]

Another shift in buying patterns is the increasing amount of influence wielded by children and teens. Children aged 4 to 12 years old spent $11.2 billion on their wants and needs in 1993, and influenced additional purchases totaling $154.4 billion. Spending is also growing faster among children than in other demographic groups at close to 20% a year.[9]

In the case of Linda Brown's purchase of a laptop computer, her husband and children may play influencer roles. Her husband may have initiated the suggestion, and he may offer advice on the brand and features. His influence will depend on the strength of his opinion and how much Linda values his opinion. Her children may hope that Linda will purchase software programs that can help them with their homework or play games.

ROLES AND STATUSES. A person participates in many groups throughout life—family, clubs, organizations. The person's position in each group can be defined in terms of role and status. A *role* consists of the activities that a person is expected to perform. With her parents, Linda Brown plays the role of daughter; in her family, she plays wife and mother; in her company, she plays sales manager. Each of Linda's roles will influence some of her buying behavior.

Each role carries a *status*. A Supreme Court justice has more status than a sales manager, and a sales manager has more status than an office clerk. People choose products that communicate their role and status in society. Thus company presidents often drive Mercedes, wear expensive suits, and drink Chivas Regal Scotch. Marketers are aware of the *status symbol* potential of products and brands.

Personal Factors

A buyer's decisions are also influenced by personal characteristics. These include the buyer's age and stage in the life cycle, occupation, economic circumstances, lifestyle, and personality and self-concept.

AGE AND STAGE IN THE LIFE CYCLE. People buy different goods and services over their lifetime. They eat baby food in the early years, most foods in the growing and mature years, and special diets in the later years. People's taste in clothes, furniture, and recreation is also age related.

Consumption is also shaped by the *family life cycle*. Nine stages of the family life cycle are listed in Table 6-2 on the next page, along with the financial situation and typical product interests of each group. Marketers often choose life-cycle groups as their target market. But it should be added that target households are not always family based. Marketers are also targeting single households, gay households, and cohabitor households.

Some recent work has identified *psychological life-cycle stages*. Adults experience certain "passages" or "transformations" as they go through life.[10] Marketers pay close attention to changing life circumstances—divorce, widowhood, remarriage—and their effect on consumption behavior.

OCCUPATION. A person's occupation also influences his or her consumption pattern. A blue-collar worker will buy work clothes, work shoes, and lunch boxes. A company president will buy expensive suits, air travel, country club membership, and a large sailboat. Marketers try to identify the occupational groups that have above-average interest in their products and services. A company can even specialize its products for certain occupational groups. Thus computer software companies will design different computer software for brand managers, engineers, lawyers, and physicians.

ECONOMIC CIRCUMSTANCES. Product choice is greatly affected by one's economic circumstances. People's economic circumstances consist of their spendable income (its level, stability, and time pattern), savings and assets (including the percentage that is liquid), debts, borrowing power, and attitude toward spending versus saving. Linda Brown can consider buying a laptop computer if she has enough spendable income, savings, or borrowing power and prefers spending to saving.

TABLE 6-2	THE FAMILY LIFE CYCLE AND BUYING BEHAVIOR
STAGE IN FAMILY LIFE CYCLE	**BUYING OR BEHAVIORAL PATTERN**
1. Bachelor stage: young, single people not living at home.	Few financial burdens. Fashion opinion leaders. Recreation oriented. Buy: basic kitchen equipment, basic furniture, cars, equipment for the mating game, vacations.
2. Newly married couples: young, no children.	Better off financially than they will be in near future. Highest purchase rate and highest average purchase of durables. Buy: cars, refrigerators, stoves, sensible and durable furniture, vacations.
3. Full nest I: youngest child under six.	Home purchasing at peak. Liquid assets low. Dissatisfied with financial position and amount of money saved. Interested in new products. Like advertised products. Buy: washers, dryers, TV, baby food, chest rubs and cough medicines, vitamins, dolls, wagons, sleds, skates.
4. Full nest II: youngest child six or over.	Financial position better. Less influenced by advertising. Buy larger-size packages, multiple-unit deals. Buy: many foods, cleaning materials, bicycles, music lessons, pianos.
5. Full nest III: older married couples with dependent children	Financial position still better. Some children get jobs. Hard to influence with advertising. High average purchase of durables. Buy: new, more tasteful furniture, auto travel, unnecessary appliances, boats, dental services, magazines.
6. Empty nest I: older married couples, no children living with them, head of household in labor force.	Home ownership at peak. Most satisfied with financial position and money saved. Interested in travel, recreation, self-education. Make gifts and contributions. Not interested in new products. Buy: vacations, luxuries, home improvements.
7. Empty nest II: older married. No children living at home, head of household retired.	Drastic cut in income. Keep home. Buy: medical appliances, medical-care products that aid health, sleep, and digestion.
8. Solitary survivor, in labor force.	Income still good but likely to sell home.
9. Solitary survivor, retired.	Same medical and product needs as other retired group; drastic cut in income. Special need for attention, affection, and security.

Sources: **William D. Wells and George Gubar, "Life-Cycle Concepts in Marketing Research,"** *Journal of Marketing Research,* **November 1996, pp. 355–63, here p. 362. Also see Patrick E. Murphy and William A. Staples, " A Modernized Family Life Cycle,"** *Journal of Consumer Research,* **June 1979, pp 12–22; and Frederick W. Derrick and Alane E. Linfield, "The Family Life Cycle: An Alternative Approach,"** *Journal of Consumer Research,* **September 1980, pp. 214–17.**

Marketers of income-sensitive goods pay constant attention to trends in personal income, savings, and interest rates. If economic indicators point to a recession, marketers can take steps to redesign, reposition, and reprice their products so they continue to offer value to target customers.

LIFESTYLE. People coming from the same subculture, social class, and occupation may lead quite different lifestyles.

❖ A person's **LIFESTYLE** is the person's pattern of living in the world as expressed in the person's activities, interests, and opinions. Lifestyle portrays the "whole person" interacting with his or her environment.

Linda Brown, for example, can choose to live a "belonging" lifestyle by wearing conservative clothes, spending a lot of time with her family, and helping her church. Or she can choose an "achiever" lifestyle by working long hours on major projects and playing hard at travel and sports.

Marketers search for relationships between their products and lifestyle groups. For example, a computer manufacturer might find that most computer buyers are achievement-oriented. The marketer may then aim the brand more clearly at the achiever lifestyle. Ad copywriters can then employ words and symbols that appeal to achievers.

Two frameworks that have been used to develop lifestyle classification are described in the Marketing Insight titled "How Lifestyles Are Identified." But lifestyle segmentation schemes are by no means universal. McCann-Erickson London, for example, identified the following British lifestyles: Avant-Gardians (interested in change), Pontificators (traditionalists, very British), Chameleons (follow the crowd), and Sleepwalkers (contented underachievers). In 1992 the advertising agency D'Arcy, Masius, Benton & Bowles published *The Russian Consumer: A New Perspective and a Marketing Approach,* which revealed five categories of Russian consumers: "Kuptsi" (merchants), "Cossacks," "Students," "Business Executives," and "Russian Souls." For example, Cossacks are characterized as ambitious, independent, and status seeking, while Russian Souls are passive, fearful of choices, and hopeful. While Cossacks would drive a BMW, smoke Dunhill cigarettes, and drink Remy Martin liquor, Russian Souls would drive a Lada, smoke Marlboros, and drink Smirnoff vodka.[11]

PERSONALITY AND SELF-CONCEPT. Each person has a distinct personality that influences his or her buying behavior.

❖   By **PERSONALITY,** we mean a person's distinguishing psychological characteristics that lead to relatively consistent and enduring responses to his or her environment.

Personality is usually described in terms of such traits as self-confidence, dominance, autonomy, deference, sociability, defensiveness, and adaptability.[12] Personality can be a useful variable in analyzing consumer behavior, provided that personality types can be classified accurately and that strong correlations exist between certain personality types and product or brand choices. For example, a computer company might discover that many prospects have high self-confidence, dominance, and autonomy. This suggests designing computer advertisements to appeal to these traits.

Related to personality is a person's *self-concept* (or self-image). Linda Brown may see herself as highly accomplished and deserving the best, in which case she will favor a computer that projects the same qualities. If the IBM laptop computer is promoted and priced for those who want the best, then its brand image will match her self-image. Marketers try to develop brand images that match the target market's self-image.

It is possible that Linda's *actual self-concept* (how she views herself) differs from her *ideal self-concept* (how she would like to view herself) and from her *others-self-concept* (how she thinks others see her). Which self will she try to satisfy in choosing a computer? Because it is difficult to answer this question, self-concept theory has had a mixed record of success in predicting consumer responses to brand images.[13]

Psychological Factors

A person's buying choices are influenced by four major psychological factors— motivation, perception, learning, and beliefs and attitudes.

MOTIVATION. A person has many needs at any given time. Some needs are *biogenic;* they arise from physiological states of tension such as hunger, thirst, discomfort. Other needs are *psychogenic;* they arise from psychological states of ten-

Analyzing Consumer
Markets and Buying
Behavior

How Lifestyles Are Identified

For marketers in the 1990s, the critical question is: "What is going on in the consumer's head?" *Psychographics*—the science of measuring and categorizing consumer lifestyles—offers insight into this question. By identifying different consumer lifestyles, marketers can achieve more precision in their targeting. Two of the most popular lifestyle classifications based on psychographic measurements are the AIO framework and the VALS 2 framework.

The AIO Framework

In this approach, respondents are presented with long questionnaires designed to measure their activities, interests, and opinions (AIO). The following table shows the major dimensions used to measure the AIO elements, as well as respondents' demographics.

ACTIVITIES	INTERESTS	OPINIONS	DEMOGRAPHICS
Work	Family	Themselves	Age
Hobbies	Home	Social issues	Education
Social events	Job	Politics	Income
Vacation	Community	Business	Occupation
Entertainment	Recreation	Economics	Family size
Clubs	Fashion	Education	Dwelling
Community	Food	Products	Geography
Shopping	Media	Future	City size
Sports	Achievements	Culture	Stage in cycle

Source: From Joseph T. Plummer, "The Concept and Application of Life-Style Segmentation," *Journal of Marketing,* January 1974, p. 34. Reprinted with permission of the American Marketing Association.

Many of the questions are in the form of agreeing or disagreeing with such statements as:

♦ I would like to become an actor.

♦ I enjoy going to concerts.

♦ I usually dress for fashion, not for comfort.

Once collected, the data are analyzed on a computer to find distinctive lifestyle groups. Using this approach, the Chicago-based advertising agency of Needham, Harper and Steers identified several major lifestyle groups. Here are the five male groups:

♦ Self-made businessman

♦ Successful professional

♦ Devoted family man

♦ Frustrated factory worker

♦ Retiring homebody

When developing an advertising campaign, the marketers state the target lifestyle group, and the ad people develop an ad appealing to the AIO characteristics of the group(s).

VALS™

Introduced in 1978, SRI International's Values and Lifestyles (VALS) framework has been the only commercially available psychographic segmentation to gain widespread acceptance. Through a proprietary research program initiated in 1960, SRI designed its original VALS system to yield insights into why people believe and act as they do; how internal values and attitudes are expressed as external lifestyles. The VALS system was revised in 1989 (VALS 2, Figure 1) to focus more explicitly on explaining and understanding consumer behavior. VALS 2 classifies all U.S. adults into eight consumer groups based on their answers to 35 attitudinal and 4 demographic questions. In 1996, the smallest two groups, Fulfilleds and Strugglers, each account for about 10% of the adult population, while the other segments each represent from 12% to 16% of the population. The major tendencies of the four groups with greater resources are:

♦ **Actualizers:** Successful, sophisticated, active, "take-charge" people. Purchases often reflect cultivated tastes for relatively upscale, niche-oriented products.

♦ **Fulfilleds:** Mature, satisfied, comfortable, reflective. Favor durability, functionality and value in products.

♦ **Achievers:** Successful, career- and work-oriented. Favor established, prestige products that demonstrate success to their peers.

♦ **Experiencers:** Young, vital, enthusiastic, impulsive, and rebellious. Spend a comparatively high proportion of their income on clothing, fast food, music, movies, and video.

The major tendencies of the four groups with fewer resources are:

♦ **Believers:** Conservative, conventional, and traditional. Favor familiar products and established brands.

FIGURE 1
The VALS™ 2 Framework

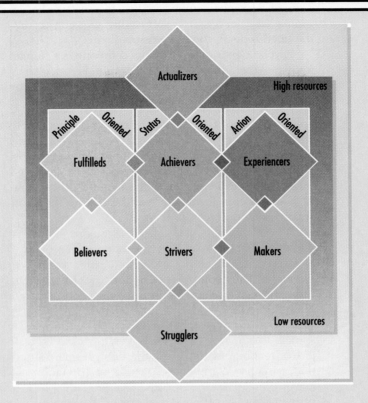

Actualizers

High resources

Principle Oriented Status Oriented Action Oriented

Fulfilleds   Achievers   Experiencers

Believers   Strivers   Makers

Low resources

Strugglers

Source: SRI International, Menlo Park, CA. VALS™ 2 is a trademark of SRI International.

- **Strivers:** Uncertain, insecure, approval-seeking, resource constrained. Favor stylish products that emulate the purchases of those with greater material wealth.
- **Makers:** Practical, self-sufficient, traditional, family oriented. Favor only products with a practical or functional purpose such as tools, utility vehicles, fishing equipment.
- **Strugglers:** Elderly, resigned, passive, concerned, resource constrained. Cautious consumers who are loyal to favorite brands.

Arnold Mitchell, the developer of the original VALS system, relied heavily on the research of personality theorists working in the area of developmental psychology. Mitchell's goal was to better explain the dynamics of societal change, and he postulated that individual's values, developing and changing over a lifetime, are crucial determinants of social change. Despite its broad focus on society, VALS was widely used in the marketing community as a way to better understand product acceptance and to design target advertising. However, its usefulness in marketing diminished in the late 1980s with an increasing diversity of products, of distribution, and of media. Consequently, SRI developed and released VALS 2 in 1989 to segment Americans into groups exhibiting distinctive consumer behaviors. VALS 2 combines general personality theory with research on product diffusion. The system identifies persons' VALS 2 types by scoring responses to the VALS 2 questionnaire, which asks them to agree or disagree with statements such as "I like my life to be pretty much the same from week to week," "I often crave excitement," and "I would rather make something than buy it" in contrast to original VALS items asking people, for example, about their attitudes toward abortion or legalizing marijuana.

Sources: Arnold Mitchell, *The Nine American Lifestyles* (New York: Warner Books), pp. viii–x, 25–31; Personal Communication from the VALS™ Program, Business Intelligence Center, SRI Consulting, Menlo Park, CA, February 1, 1996.

sion such as the need for recognition, esteem, or belonging. Most psychogenic needs are not intense enough to motivate the person to act on them immediately. A need becomes a motive when it is aroused to a sufficient level of intensity. A *motive* is a need that is sufficiently pressing to drive the person to act. Satisfying the need reduces the felt tension.

Psychologists have developed theories of human motivation. Three of the best known—the theories of Sigmund Freud, Abraham Maslow, and Frederick Herzberg—carry quite different implications for consumer analysis and marketing strategy.

Freud's Theory of Motivation. Freud assumed that the real psychological forces shaping people's behavior are largely unconscious. Thus a person cannot fully understand his or her own motivations. If Linda Brown wants to purchase a laptop computer, she may describe her motive as wanting to work more efficiently when traveling. At a deeper level, she may be purchasing a computer to impress others. At a still deeper level, she may be buying the computer because it helps her feel smart and sophisticated.[14]

When Linda examines specific brands, she will react not only to their stated capabilities but also to other, less conscious cues. Each computer's shape, size, weight, material, color, and brand name can all trigger certain associations and emotions. Thus computer designers should be aware of the impact of visual, auditory, and tactile elements in triggering consumer emotions that could stimulate or inhibit purchase.

Motivation researchers collect "in-depth interviews" with a few dozen consumers to uncover deeper motives triggered by a product. They use various "projective techniques" to throw the ego off guard—techniques such as word association, sentence completion, picture interpretation, and role playing. Their research has produced interesting and occasionally bizarre hypotheses: Consumers resist prunes because prunes are wrinkled looking and remind people of old age, men smoke cigars as an adult version of thumb sucking, and women prefer vegetable shortening to animal fats because the latter arouse a sense of guilt over killing animals.

More recent practicing motivational researchers hold that each product is capable of arousing a unique set of motives in consumers. For example, whisky can draw someone who seeks social relaxation, or status, or fun. Therefore it is not surprising that different whisky brands have specialized in one of these three different appeals. Jan Callebaut calls this approach "motivational positioning."[15]

Maslow's Theory of Motivation. Abraham Maslow sought to explain why people are driven by particular needs at particular times.[16] Why does one person spend considerable time and energy on personal safety and another on pursuing the high opinion of others? Maslow's answer is that human needs are arranged in a hierarchy, from the most pressing to the least pressing. In their order of importance, they are physiological needs, safety needs, social needs, esteem needs, and self-actualization needs (Figure 6-3). People will try to satisfy their most important needs first. When a person succeeds in satisfying an important need, that need will cease being a current motivator, and the person will try to satisfy the next-most-important need. For example, a starving man (need 1) will not take an interest in the latest happenings in the art world (need 5), nor in how he is viewed by others (need 3 or 4), nor even in whether he is breathing clean air (need 2). But when he has enough food and water, the next-most-important need will become salient.

Maslow's theory helps marketers understand how various products fit into the plans, goals, and lives of potential consumers. What light does Maslow's theory shed on Linda Brown's interest in buying a computer? We can guess that Linda has satisfied her physiological, safety, and social needs. Her computer interest might

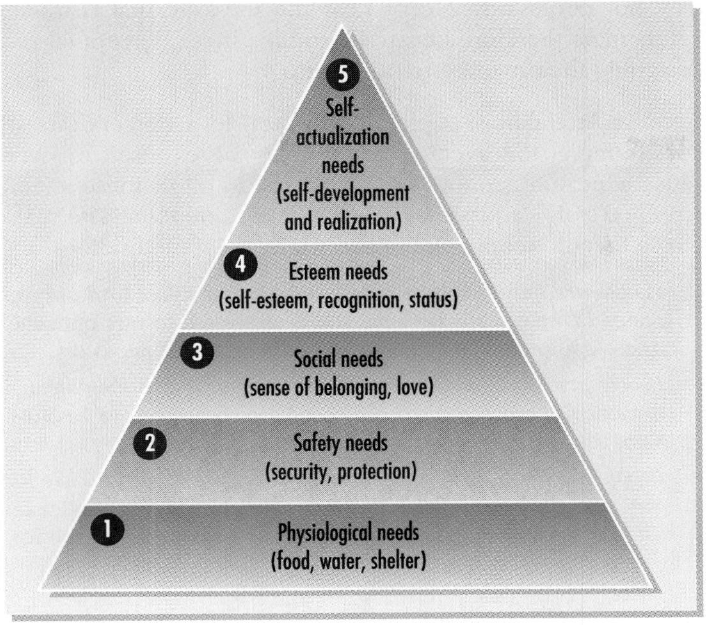

FIGURE 6-3
Maslow's Hierarchy of Needs

5
Self-
actualization
needs
(self-development
and realization)

4 Esteem needs
(self-esteem, recognition, status)

3 Social needs
(sense of belonging, love)

2 Safety needs
(security, protection)

1 Physiological needs
(food, water, shelter)

come from a strong need for more esteem from others or from a higher need for self-actualization.

Herzberg's Theory of Motivation. Frederick Herzberg developed a *two-factor theory* of motivation that distinguishes dissatisfiers (factors that cause dissatisfaction) and satisfiers (factor that cause satisfaction).[17] The absence of dissatisfiers is not enough; rather, satisfiers must be actively present to motivate a purchase. For example, an Apple computer that does not come with a warranty would be a dissatisfier. Yet the presence of a product warranty would not act as a satisfier or motivator of Linda's purchase, since it is not a source of intrinsic satisfaction with the Apple computer. The Apple computer's ease of use would be a satisfier and enhance Linda's enjoyment of the computer.

Herzberg's theory of motivation has two implications. First, sellers should do their best to avoid dissatisfiers (for example, a poor training manual or a poor service policy). While these things will not sell the computer, they might easily unsell the computer. Second, the manufacturer should identify the major satisfiers or motivators of purchase in the market and then supply them. These satisfiers will make the major difference as to which computer brand the customer buys.

PERCEPTION. A motivated person is ready to act. How the motivated person actually acts is influenced by his or her perception of the situation.

❖   **PERCEPTION** is the process by which an individual selects, organizes, and interprets information inputs to create a meaningful picture of the world.[18]

Perception depends not only on the physical stimuli but also on the stimuli's relation to the surrounding field and on conditions within the individual.

The key word in the definition of perception is "individual." Linda Brown might perceive a fast-talking computer salesperson as aggressive and insincere. Another shopper might perceive the same salesperson as intelligent and helpful. Why do people perceive the same situation differently? People can emerge with different perceptions of the same object because of three perceptual processes: selective attention, selective distortion, and selective retention. As a result, people may not necessarily see or hear the message that marketers want to send. Marketers must therefore be careful to take these perceptual processes into account in designing their marketing campaigns.

Selective Attention. People are exposed to a tremendous amount of daily stimuli. For example, the average person may be exposed to over 1,500 ads a day. Because a person cannot possibly attend to all of these stimuli, most stimuli will be screened out—a process called *selective attention*. The real challenge is to explain which stimuli people will notice. Here are some findings:

◆ *People are more likely to notice stimuli that relate to a current need.* Linda Brown will notice computer ads because she is motivated to buy one; she will probably not notice stereo-equipment ads when a computer tops her needs list.

◆ *People are more likely to notice stimuli that they anticipate.* Linda Brown is more likely to notice computers than radios in a computer store because she did not expect the store to carry radios.

◆ *People are more likely to notice stimuli whose deviations are large in relation to the normal size of the stimuli.* Linda Brown is more likely to notice an ad offering $100 off the list price of an Apple computer than one offering $5 off the list price.

Selective attention means that marketers have to work hard to attract consumers' notice. Their messages will be lost on most people who are not in the market for the product. Even people who are in the market may not notice a message unless it stands out from the surrounding sea of stimuli. Ads that are novel or larger in size, use bold colors, or provide contrast to their surroundings are more likely to be noticed.

Selective Distortion. Even noted stimuli do not always come across in the way their creators intended. *Selective distortion* is people's tendency to twist information into personal meanings and interpret information in a way that will support rather than challenge their preconceptions. Thus Linda Brown may hear the salesperson mention good and bad points about an IBM computer. If Linda has a strong leaning toward IBM, she is likely to discount the negative statements to justify buying an IBM. Unfortunately, there is not much that marketers can do about selective distortion.

Selective Retention. People will forget much that they learn but will tend to retain information that supports their attitudes and beliefs. Because of *selective retention,* Linda is likely to remember good points mentioned about the IBM and forget good points mentioned about competing computers. She remembers IBM's good points because she "rehearses" them more (that is, she "talks to herself" more about IBM's good points) whenever she thinks about choosing a computer. Selective retention explains why marketers use drama and repetition in sending messages to their target market.

LEARNING. When people act, they learn.

❖   **LEARNING** involves changes in an individual's behavior arising from experience.

Most human behavior is learned. Learning theorists believe that learning is produced through the interplay of drives, stimuli, cues, responses, and reinforcement.

A *drive* is a strong internal stimulus impelling action. Presumably Linda Brown has a drive toward self-actualization. Her drive becomes a motive when it is directed toward a particular drive-reducing *stimulus,* in this case a computer. Linda's response to the idea of buying a computer is conditioned by the surrounding cues. *Cues* are minor stimuli that determine when, where, and how the person responds. Her husband's support, seeing a computer in a friend's home, seeing computer ads and articles, and hearing about a special sales price are all cues that can influence Linda's interest in buying a computer.

Suppose Linda buys a computer and chooses an IBM. If her experience is rewarding, her response to computers will be positively reinforced. Later on, when Linda wants to buy a copier, she may notice several brands, including one by IBM. Since she knows that IBM makes good computers, she may assume that IBM also makes good copiers. In other words, she *generalizes* her response to similar stimuli.

A counter-tendency to generalization is *discrimination*. When Linda examines a copier made by Sharp, she sees that it is lighter and more compact than IBM's copier. Discrimination means that Linda has learned to recognize differences in sets of similar stimuli and can adjust her responses accordingly.

Learning theory teaches marketers that they can build up demand for a product by associating it with strong drives, using motivating cues, and providing positive reinforcement. A new company can enter the market by appealing to the same drives that competitors use and providing similar cue configurations because buyers are more likely to transfer loyalty to similar brands than to dissimilar brands (generalization). Or the company might design its brand to appeal to a different set of drives and offer strong cue inducements to switch (discrimination).

Companies that produce commodity products can take advantage of consumers' ability to discriminate. Consider what has happened in the poultry industry, where you'd think that one chicken is pretty much like the next:

PERDUE   Perdue, Holly Farms, and other poultry companies maintain that their breeding methods, manufacturing equipment, and overall quality control processes distinguish their chickens from the rest. For example, Perdue controls the breeding operation as the first step toward producing a quality bird with distinct characteristics. Its chickens are raised on a chemical-free and steroid-free diet. Perdue has also differentiated itself through advertising that features Frank Perdue and the slogan, "It takes a tough man to make a tender chicken."[19]

BELIEFS AND ATTITUDES.   Through doing and learning, people acquire beliefs and attitudes. These in turn influence their buying behavior.

❖   A **BELIEF** is a descriptive thought that a person holds about something.

Linda Brown may believe that an IBM computer has a large memory, stands up well under rugged usage, and costs $2,000. These beliefs may be based on knowledge, opinion, or faith. They may or may not carry an emotional charge. For example, Linda Brown's belief that an IBM laptop computer is heavier than an Apple might not matter to her decision.

Of course, manufacturers are very interested in the beliefs that people carry in their heads about their products and services. These beliefs make up product and brand images, and people act on their images. If some beliefs are wrong and inhibit purchase, the manufacturer will want to launch a campaign to correct these beliefs.[20]

Particularly important to global marketers is the fact that buyers often hold distinct beliefs about brands or products based on their country of origin. Several country-of-origin studies have found the following:

◆   The impact of country of origin varies with the type of product. Consumers would want to know where a car was made but not where the lubricating oil came from.

◆   Certain countries enjoy a reputation for certain goods: Japan for automobiles and consumer electronics; the United States for high-tech innovations, soft drinks, toys, cigarettes, and jeans; and France for wine, perfume, and luxury goods.

Analyzing Consumer
Markets and Buying
Behavior

- The more favorable a country's image, the more prominently the "Made in . . . " label should be displayed in promoting the brand.

- Attitudes toward country of origin can change over time. Note how Japan has greatly improved its quality image in comparison to pre–World War II days.

A company has several options when its products are competitively priced but their place of origin turns off consumers. The company can consider co-production with a foreign company that has a better name. Thus South Korea could make a fine leather jacket that it sends to Italy for finishing. Or the company can adopt a strategy to achieve world-class quality in the local industry, as is the case with Belgian chocolates, Polish ham, and Colombian coffee. Finally, the company can hire a well-known celebrity to endorse the product. Nike has had a great deal of success using basketball star Michael Jordan to promote its footware in Europe.[21]

Just as important as beliefs are attitudes.

- ❖ An **ATTITUDE** is a person's enduring favorable or unfavorable evaluations, emotional feelings, and action tendencies toward some object or idea.[22]

People have attitudes toward almost everything: religion, politics, clothes, music, food, and so on. Attitudes put them into a frame of mind of liking or disliking an object, moving toward or away from it. Thus Linda Brown may hold such attitudes as, "Computers are an essential tool for professional workers," "Buy the best," and "IBM makes the best computers in the world." The IBM computer is therefore relevant to Linda because it fits well into her preexisting attitudes. A computer company can benefit greatly from researching the attitudes people hold toward the company, the product, and the brand.

Attitudes lead people to behave in a fairly consistent way toward similar objects. People do not have to interpret and react to every object in a fresh way. Attitudes economize on energy and thought. For this reason, attitudes are very difficult to change. A person's attitudes settle into a consistent pattern, and to change a single attitude may require major adjustments in other attitudes.

Thus a company would be well advised to fit its product into existing attitudes rather than to try to change people's attitudes. Of course, there are exceptions where the great cost of trying to change attitudes might pay off. Here are two example of food organizations that used ad campaigns to change consumer attitudes, with handsome results:

CALIFORNIA RAISINS When California raisin growers found themselves with a huge surplus, they faced a major obstacle in consumer attitudes toward the wrinkled little snack. Research showed that consumers were aware that raisins are nutritious, they thought they were "boring." Enter the California Raisin Advisory Board and its dancing raisin ads. The campaign, featuring Claymation raisins dancing to Marvin Gaye's "Heard It Through the Grapevine," had emotional appeal and is credited with wiping out the state's raisin surplus.[23]

THE NATIONAL PORK COUNCIL By 1985 pork consumption had dropped to 59 pounds per capita from a high of 68 pounds in 1980. The nation was on an anti-beef and anti-pork kick, favoring leaner, less cholesterol-laden poultry. While pork products were actually improved as a result of new feeding and breeding methods, the public still considered pork an unhealthy choice. The National Pork Producers Council called in ad agency Bozell Inc. to change the image of pork, and it put some $12 million a year into a national marketing campaign. The new campaign centered on the slogan, "Pork. The Other White Meat" (Figure 6-4). Between 1986, when the campaign began, and 1988, pork sales rose 11%—about equal to the gain for chicken, and far ahead of the 2% increase for beef in the same period.[24]

Try stir-frying pork strips with some sesame oil and julienne veggies for an oriental-style dish.

AFTER CHOPS AND ROASTS

Peachy Pork Picante
Coat one pound cubed boneless **pork loin** with **taco seasoning**, brown in a little **oil** in a skillet. Add an 8-ounce jar of **salsa** and 4 tablespoons **peach preserves** to skillet, stir to mix well, cover and lower heat. Simmer gently for 15 minutes. Preparation Time: 25 minutes. Serves four.

Nutrient Information, Approximately, per Serving: Calories: 263, Protein: 24 gm., Fat: 9 gm., Sodium: 762 mg., Cholesterol: 70 mg.

Nutrient analysis done by The Food Processor II Diet Analysis Software. Pork data from USDA Handbook 8-10 (1991).

Pork is more than you remember.
Cut up some boneless pork loin, and the options are endless. Slice strips for stir-fry or fajitas, cut cubes for kabobs or a quick stew. Go wild with fruits, vegetables, sauces and condiments. Pork will go as far as your imagination. *Boneless pork—chops, strips, cubes—absorbs flavor or a marinade in just 30 minutes.*

TASTE
WHAT'S
NEXT™
 The Other White Meat.

Pork and fruit are a natural pair. Try simmering cutlets in your favorite jam, mixed with a little vinegar or water.
For recipes, send a self-addressed, stamped, business-size envelope to: Recipes-Ad, Box 10383, Des Moines, IA 50306.
America's Pork Producers ©1995 National Pork Producers Council in cooperation with the National Pork Board

THE BUYING PROCESS

To be successful, marketers have to go beyond the various influences on buyers and develop an understanding of how consumers actually make their buying decisions. Specifically, marketers must identify who makes the buying decision, the types of buying decisions, and the steps in the buying process.

Buying Roles

It is easy to identify the buyer for many products. Men normally choose their shaving equipment, and women choose their pantyhose. But even here marketers must be careful in making their targeting decisions, because buying roles change. ICI, the giant British chemical company, discovered to its surprise that women made 60% of the decisions on the brand of household paint; ICI therefore decided to advertise its DeLux brand to women.

We can distinguish five roles people might play in a buying decision:

- *Initiator:* A person who first suggests the idea of buying the product or service
- *Influencer:* A person whose view or advice influences the decision
- *Decider:* A person who decides on any component of a buying decision—whether to buy, what to buy, how to buy, or where to buy
- *Buyer:* The person who makes the actual purchase
- *User:* A person who consumes or uses the product or service

Consider Linda Brown's interest in buying a laptop computer. Her interest might have been initially stimulated by a co-worker (initiator). In searching for a brand, she may have consulted with the head of her company's data processing department, who made some suggestions (influencer). Linda made the final decision (decider). Her husband said that he would purchase it for her as a birthday gift (buyer). Linda will be the computer's primary user (user).

Buying Behavior

Consumer decision making varies with the type of buying decision. The decisions to buy toothpaste, a tennis racket, a personal computer, and a new car are all very different. Complex and expensive purchases are likely to involve more buyer deliberation and more participants. Assael distinguished four types of consumer buying behavior based on the degree of buyer involvement and the degree of differences among brands[25] (Table 6-3).

COMPLEX BUYING BEHAVIOR. Consumers engage in *complex buying behavior* when they are highly involved in a purchase and aware of significant differences among brands. This is usually the case when the product is expensive, bought infrequently, risky, and highly self-expressive. Typically the consumer does not know much about the product category and has much to learn. For example, a person buying a personal computer may not know what attributes to look for. Many of the product features carry no meaning unless the buyer has done some research: "16K memory," "disk storage," "screen resolution," and so on.

Complex buying behavior involves a three-step process. First, the buyer develops beliefs about the product. Second, he or she develops attitudes about the product. Third, he or she makes a thoughtful purchase choice. The marketer of a high-involvement product must understand high-involvement consumers' information-gathering and evaluation behavior. The marketer needs to develop strategies

TABLE 6-3	FOUR TYPES OF BUYING BEHAVIOR	
	HIGH INVOLVEMENT	**LOW INVOLVEMENT**
Significant Differences Between Brands	Complex buying behavior	Variety-seeking buying behavior
Few Differences Between Brands	Dissonance-reducing buying behavior	Habitual buying behavior

Source: **Reproduced from Henry Assael, *Consumer Behavior and Marketing Action.* p. 87, with the permission of South-Western College Publishing, a division of International Thomson Publishing Inc. Copyright © 1987 Kent Publishing Company. All rights reserved.**

Analyzing
Marketing
Opportunities

that assist the buyer in learning about the product's attributes and their relative importance, and that call attention to the high standing of the company's brand on the more important attributes. The marketer needs to differentiate the brand's features, use print media to describe the brand's benefits, and motivate store sales personnel and the buyer's acquaintances to influence the final brand choice.

DISSONANCE-REDUCING BUYER BEHAVIOR. Sometimes the consumer is highly involved in a purchase but sees little difference in the brands. The high involvement is based on the fact that the purchase is expensive, infrequent, and risky. In this case, the buyer will shop around to learn what is available but will buy fairly quickly, perhaps responding primarily to a good price or to purchase convenience. For example, carpet buying is a high-involvement decision because carpeting is expensive and self-expressive, yet the buyer may consider most carpet brands in a given price range to be the same.

After the purchase, the consumer might experience dissonance that stems from noticing certain disquieting features of the carpet or hearing favorable things about other carpets. The consumer will be alert to information that justifies his or her decision. In this example, the consumer first acted, then acquired new beliefs, then ended up with a set of attitudes. Thus marketing communications should aim at supplying beliefs and evaluations that help the consumer feel good about his or her brand choice.

HABITUAL BUYING BEHAVIOR. Many products are bought under conditions of low consumer involvement and the absence of significant brand differences. Consider salt. Consumers have little involvement in this product category. They go to the store and reach for the brand. If they keep reaching for the same brand, it is out of habit, not strong brand loyalty. There is good evidence that consumers have low involvement with most low-cost, frequently purchased products.

With low-involvement products, consumer behavior does not pass through the normal belief/attitude/behavior sequence. Consumers do not search extensively for information about the brands, evaluate their characteristics, and make a weighty decision on which brand to buy. Instead, they are passive recipients of information as they watch television or see print ads. Ad repetition creates *brand familiarity* rather than *brand conviction*. Consumers do not form a strong attitude toward a brand; rather, they select it because it is familiar. After purchase, they may not even evaluate the choice because they are not highly involved with the product. Thus for low-involvement products the buying process begins with brand beliefs formed by passive learning and is followed by purchase behavior, which may be followed by evaluation.

Marketers of low-involvement products with few brand differences find it effective to use price and sales promotions to stimulate product trial, since buyers are not highly committed to any brand. The ad copy should stress only a few key points and use visual symbols and imagery that can be easily remembered and associated with the brand. The ad campaigns should aim for high repetition with short-duration messages. Television is more effective than print media because it is a low-involvement medium that is suitable for passive learning.[26]

Marketers use four techniques to try to convert low-involvement product into one of higher involvement. First, they can link the product to some involving issue, as when Crest toothpaste is linked to avoiding cavities. Second, they can link the product to some involving personal situation—for instance, by advertising a coffee brand early in the morning when the consumer wants to shake off sleepiness. Third, they might design their advertising to trigger strong emotions related to personal values or ego defense. Fourth, they might add an important product

Analyzing Consumer
Markets and Buying
Behavior

FIGURE 6-5
Five-Stage Model of the Consumer Buying Process

feature to a low-involvement product (for example, fortifying a plain drink with vitamins). These strategies at best raise consumer involvement from a low to a moderate level; they do not propel the consumer into highly involved buying behavior.

VARIETY-SEEKING BUYING BEHAVIOR. Some buying situations are characterized by low consumer involvement but significant brand differences. Here consumers often do a lot of brand switching. Think about cookies. The consumer has some beliefs about cookies, chooses a brand of cookies without much evaluation, and evaluates the product during consumption. But next time, the consumer may reach for another brand out of boredom or a wish for a different taste. Brand switching occurs for the sake of variety rather than dissatisfaction.

The market leader and the minor brands in this product category have different marketing strategies. The market leader will try to encourage habitual buying behavior by dominating the shelf space, avoiding out-of-stock conditions, and sponsoring frequent reminder advertising. Challenger firms will encourage variety seeking by offering lower prices, deals, coupons, free samples, and advertising that presents reasons for trying something new.

The Stages of the Buying Decision Process

Smart companies research the buying decision process involved in their product category. They ask consumers when they first became acquainted with the product category and brands, what their brand beliefs are, how involved they are with the product, how they make their brand choices, and how satisfied they are after purchase.

How can marketers learn about the stages in the buying process for their product? They can think about how they themselves would act *(introspective method)*. They can interview a small number of recent purchasers, asking them to recall the events leading to their purchase *(retrospective method)*. They can locate consumers who plan to buy the product and ask them to think out loud about going through the buying process *(prospective method)*. Or they can ask consumers to describe the ideal way to buy the product *(prescriptive method)*. Each method yields a picture of the steps in the consumer buying process.

Figure 6-5 shows a "stage model" of the typical buying process. The consumer passes through five stages: problem recognition, information search, evaluation of alternatives, purchase decision, and postpurchase behavior. Clearly the buying process starts long before the actual purchase and has consequences long afterward.[27]

The model in Figure 6-5 implies that consumers pass sequentially through all five stages in buying a product. But this is not the case, especially with low-involvement purchases. Consumers may skip or reverse some stages. Thus a woman buying her regular brand of toothpaste goes directly from the need for toothpaste to the purchase decision, skipping information search and evaluation. However, we will use the model in Figure 6-5 because it captures the full range of considerations that arise when a consumer faces a highly involving new purchase. Let's look once again at Linda Brown and try to understand how she became interested in buying a laptop computer and the stages she went through to make her final choice.[28]

PROBLEM RECOGNITION. The buying process starts when the buyer recognizes a problem or need. The buyer senses a difference between his or her actual state and a desired state. The need can be triggered by internal or external stimuli. In the former case, one of the person's normal needs—hunger, thirst, sex—rises to a threshold level and becomes a drive. In the latter case, a need is aroused by an external stimulus. A person passes a bakery and sees freshly baked bread that stimulates her hunger; she admires a neighbor's new car; or she watches a television commercial advertising a Hawaiian vacation.

Marketers need to identify the circumstances that trigger a particular need. Linda Brown's need might be triggered by the fact that her "busy season" is peaking or that she was impressed with a co-worker's laptop. By gathering information from a number of consumers, marketers can identify the most frequent stimuli that spark an interest in a product category. The marketer can then develop marketing strategies that trigger consumer interest.

INFORMATION SEARCH.   An aroused consumer will be inclined to search for more information. We can distinguish between two levels of arousal. The milder search state is called *heightened attention*. At this level Linda Brown simply becomes more receptive to information about computers. She pays attention to computer ads, computers purchased by friends, and conversation about computers.

At the next level, Linda may enter *active information search*. She actually looks for reading material, phones friends, and engages in other activities to learn about computers. How much search she undertakes depends on the strength of her drive, the amount of information she initially has, the ease of obtaining additional information, the value she places on additional information, and the satisfaction she gets from search.

Of key interest to the marketer are the major information sources to which the consumer will turn and the relative influence each will have on the subsequent purchase decision. Consumer information sources fall into four groups:

- *Personal sources:* Family, friends, neighbors, acquaintances
- *Commercial sources:* Advertising, salespersons, dealers, packaging, displays
- *Public sources:* Mass media, consumer-rating organizations
- *Experiential sources:* Handling, examining, using the product

The relative amount and influence of these information sources vary with the product category and the buyer's characteristics. Generally speaking, the consumer receives the most information about a product from commercial sources—that is, marketer-dominated sources. But the most effective information comes from personal sources. Each information source performs a different function in influencing the buying decision. Commercial information normally performs an informing function, and personal sources perform a legitimizing and/or evaluation function. For example, physicians often learn of new drugs from commercial sources but turn to other doctors for evaluation information.

Through gathering information, the consumer learns about competing sets of brands and their features. The first box in Figure 6-6 on the next page shows the *total set* of brands available to the consumer. Linda Brown will come to know only a subset of these brands *(awareness set)*. Some brands will meet Linda's initial buying criteria *(consideration set)*. As Linda gathers more information, only a few will remain as strong contenders *(choice set)*. The brands in the choice set might all be acceptable. Linda makes her final choice from this set.[29]

Figure 6-6 makes it clear that a company must strategize to get its brand into the prospect's awareness set, consideration set, and choice set. The company must also identify the other brands in the consumer's choice set so that it can plan its competitive appeals. In addition, the company should identify the consumer's information sources and evaluate their relative importance. Consumers should be asked how they first heard about the brand, what information came in later, and the relative importance of the different information sources. The answers will help the company prepare effective communications for the target market.

FIGURE 6-6

Successive Sets Involved in
Consumer Decision Making

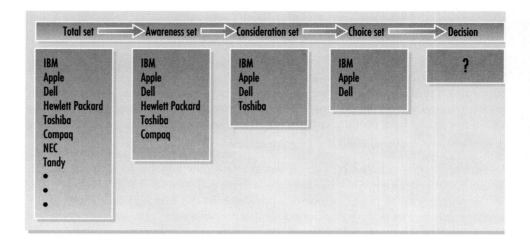

EVALUATION OF ALTERNATIVES. How does the consumer process competitive brand information and make a final judgment of value? There is no simple and single evaluation process used by all consumers or by one consumer in all buying situations. There are several decision evaluation processes, the most current models of which see the consumer evaluation process as cognitively oriented. That is, they see the consumer as forming product judgments largely on a conscious and rational basis.

Some basic concepts will help us understand consumer evaluation processes: First, the consumer is trying to satisfy a *need*. Second, the consumer is looking for certain *benefits* from the product solution. Third, the consumer sees each product as a *bundle of attributes* with varying abilities of delivering the benefits sought to satisfy this need. The attributes of interest to buyers vary by product:

- *Cameras:* Picture sharpness, camera speeds, camera size, price
- *Hotels:* Location, cleanliness, atmosphere, price
- *Mouthwash:* Color, effectiveness, germ-killing capacity, price, taste/flavor
- *Tires:* Safety, tread life, ride quality, price

Consumers differ as to which product attributes they see as most relevant as well as on the importance of weights they attach to each attribute. They will pay the most attention to the attributes that deliver the sought benefits. The market for a product can often be segmented according to the attributes that are salient to different consumer groups.

The consumer develops a set of *brand beliefs* about where each brand stands on each attribute. The set of beliefs about a brand make up the *brand image*. The consumer's brand image will vary with his or her experiences as filtered by the effects of selective perception, selective distortion, and selective retention.

The consumer arrives at attitudes (judgments, preferences) toward the various brands through an attribute evaluation procedure.[30] Suppose that Linda Brown has narrowed her choice set to four computers (A, B, C, D). Assume that she is interested in four attributes: memory capacity, graphics capability, size and weight, and price. Table 6-4 shows her beliefs about how each brand rates on the four attributes. Linda rates brand A as follows: memory capacity, 10 on a 10-point scale; graphics capability, 8; size and weight, 6; and price, 4 (somewhat expensive). She also has beliefs about how the other three computers rate on these attributes. Clearly, if one computer dominated the others on all the criteria, we could predict that Linda would choose it. But her choice set consists of brands that vary in their appeal. If Linda wants the best memory capacity, she should buy A; if she wants the best graphics capability, she should buy B; and so on.

| | ATTRIBUTE | | | |
COMPUTER	MEMORY CAPACITY	GRAPHICS CAPABILITY	SIZE AND WEIGHT	PRICE
A	10	8	6	4
B	8	9	8	3
C	6	8	10	5
D	4	3	7	8

Note: Each attribute is rated from 0 to 10, where 10 represents the highest level on that attribute. Price, however, is indexed in a reverse manner, with a 10 representing the lowest price, since a consumer prefers a low price to high price. Reproduced from Henry Assael, *Consumer Behavior and Marketing Action,* 1987, p. 87, with the permission of South-Western College Publishing, A division of International Thomson Publishing Inc. Copyright © 1987 Kent Publishing Company. All rights reserved.

However, most buyers consider several attributes in their purchase decision. If we knew the weight that Linda Brown attaches to each of the four attributes, we could more reliably predict her computer choice. Suppose Linda assigned 40% of the importance to the computer's memory capacity, 30% to its graphics capability, 20% to its size and weight, and 10% to its price. To find Linda's perceived value for each computer, we multiply her weights by her beliefs about each computer's attributes. This computation leads to the following perceived values:

Computer A = 0.4(10) + 0.3(8) + 0.2(6) + 0.1(4) = 8.0

Computer B = 0.4(8) + 0.3(9) + 0.2(8) + 0.1(3) = 7.8

Computer C = 0.4(6) + 0.3(8) + 0.2(10) + 0.1(5) = 7.3

Computer D = 0.4(4) + 0.3(3) + 0.2(7) + 0.1(8) = 4.7

We would predict that Linda will favor computer A, which (at 8.0) has the highest perceived value.[31]

Suppose most computer buyers form their preferences the same way Linda does. Knowing this, a computer manufacturer can do a number of things to influence buyer decisions. The marketer of computer C, for example, could apply the following strategies to stimulate greater interest in brand C:

♦ *Modify the computer:* The marketer could redesign brand C so that it offers more memory or other characteristics that the buyer desires. This technique is called *real repositioning.*

♦ *Alter beliefs about the brand:* The marketer could try to alter buyers' beliefs about where the brand stands on key attributes. This tactic is especially useful if buyers underestimate brand C's qualities. It is not recommended if buyers are accurately evaluating brand C; exaggerated claims would lead to buyer dissatisfaction and bad word-of-mouth. Attempting to alter beliefs about the brand is called *psychological repositioning.*

♦ *Alter beliefs about the competitors' brands:* The marketer could try to change buyers' beliefs about where competitive brands stand on different attributes. This strategy, called *competitive depositioning,* makes sense when buyers mistakenly believe a competitor's brand has more quality than it actually has. It is often accomplished by running a comparison ad.

♦ *Alter the importance weights:* The marketer could try to persuade buyers to attach more importance to the attributes in which the brand excels. The marketer of brand C can tout the benefits of choosing a laptop computer with an ideal size and weight, since C is superior in this attribute.

♦ *Call attention to neglected attributes:* The marketer could draw the buyer's attention to neglected attributes. If brand C is a more ruggedly made computer, the market might tout the benefits of ruggedness.

◆ *Shift the buyer's ideals:* The marketer could try to persuade buyers to change their ideal levels for one or more attributes. The marketer of brand C might try to convince buyers that computers with a large memory are more likely to jam and that a moderate-size memory is more desirable.[32]

In using these strategies, marketers are trying to influence the consumer's buying decision. But many consumers today are very knowledgeable about attempts by advertisers and salespeople to influence their behavior. Hence, marketers may want to take into account how consumers' own knowledge of persuasion techniques may guide their weighing of certain aspects of an advertising campaign or sales presentation.[33]

PURCHASE DECISION.   In the evaluation stage, the consumer forms preferences among the brands in the choice set. The consumer may also form an intention to buy the most preferred brand. However, two factors can intervene between the purchase intention and the purchase decision (Figure 6-7).[34]

The first factor is the *attitudes of others.* Suppose Linda Brown's close colleague recommends strongly that Linda buy the lowest-priced computer (D). As a result, Linda's purchase probability will be somewhat reduced for computer A and somewhat increased for computer D. The extent to which another person's attitude reduces one's preferred alternative depends on two things: (1) the intensity of the other person's negative attitude toward the consumer's preferred alternative and (2) the consumer's motivation to comply with the other person's wishes.[35] The more intense the other person's negativism and the closer the other person is to the consumer, the more the consumer will adjust his or her purchase intention. The converse is also true: A buyer's preference for a brand will increase if someone he or she likes favors the same brand strongly. The influence of others becomes complex when several people close to the buyer hold contradictory opinions and the buyer would like to please them all.

The second factor is *unanticipated situational factors.* These may erupt to change the purchase intention. Linda Brown might lose her job, some other purchase might become more urgent, or a store salesperson may turn her off. Thus preferences and even purchase intentions are not completely reliable predictors of purchase behavior.

A consumer's decision to modify, postpone, or avoid a purchase decision is heavily influenced by *perceived risk.*[36] The amount of perceived risk varies with the amount of money at stake, the amount of attribute uncertainty, and the amount of consumer self-confidence. Consumers develop routines for reducing risk, such as decision avoidance, information gathering from friends, and preference for national brand names and warranties. Marketers must understand the factors that provoke a feeling of risk in consumers and provide information and support to reduce the perceived risk.

In executing a purchase intention, the consumer may make up to five purchase subdecisions. Thus Linda Brown will make a *brand decision* (brand A), *vendor decision* (dealer 2), *quantity decision* (one computer), *timing decision* (weekend),

FIGURE 6-7
Steps Between Evaluation of Alternatives and a Purchase Decision

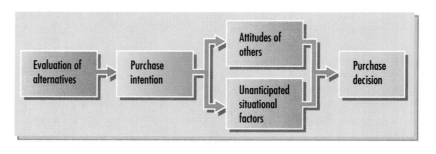

Analyzing
Marketing
Opportunities

and *payment-method decision* (credit card). Purchases of everyday products involve fewer decisions and less deliberation. For example, in buying sugar, Linda gives little thought to the vendor or payment method.

POSTPURCHASE BEHAVIOR. After purchasing the product, the consumer will experience some level of satisfaction or dissatisfaction. The marketer's job does not end when the product is bought but continues into the postpurchase period. Marketers must monitor postpurchase satisfaction, postpurchase actions, and postpurchase product use and disposal.

Postpurchase Satisfaction. After purchasing a product, a consumer may detect a flaw. Some buyers will no longer want the flawed product, others will be indifferent to the flaw, and some may even see the flaw as enhancing the product's value.[37] For instance, an upside-down page in the first edition of a famous author's book might make the book become a collectible item worth many times its original purchase price. Some flaws can be dangerous to consumers. Companies making automobiles, toys, and pharmaceuticals must quickly recall any product that has the slightest chance of injuring users.

What determines whether the buyer will be highly satisfied, somewhat satisfied, or dissatisfied with a purchase? The buyer's satisfaction is a function of the closeness between the buyer's product expectations and the product's perceived performance.[38] If the product's performance falls short of customer expectations, the customer is disappointed; if it meets expectations, the customer is satisfied; if it exceeds expectations, the customer is delighted. These feelings make a difference in whether the customer buys the product again and talks favorably or unfavorably about the product to others.

Consumers form their expectations on the basis of messages received from sellers, friends, and other information sources. If the seller exaggerates the benefits, consumers will experience disconfirmed expectations, which lead to dissatisfaction. The larger the gap between expectations and performance, the greater the consumer's dissatisfaction. Here the consumer's coping style comes into play. Some consumers magnify the gap when the product is not perfect, and they are highly dissatisfied. Other consumers minimize the gap and are less dissatisfied.[39]

The importance of postpurchase satisfaction suggests that sellers must make product claims that truthfully represent the product's likely performance. Some sellers might even understate performance levels so that consumers experience higher-than-expected satisfaction with the product. For example, a seller may create more satisfaction by promising delivery by 4 P.M. and actually delivering by 2 P.M. than if the seller promised delivery by 11 A.M. and didn't deliver until 12 noon.

Postpurchase Actions. The consumer's satisfaction or dissatisfaction with the product will influence subsequent behavior. If the consumer is satisfied, he or she will exhibit a higher probability of purchasing the product again. For example, data on automobile brand choice show a high correlation between being highly satisfied with the last brand bought and the intention to rebuy the brand. One survey showed that 75% of Toyota buyers were highly satisfied and about 75% intended to buy a Toyota again; 35% of Chevrolet buyers were highly satisfied and about 35% intended to buy a Chevrolet again. The satisfied customer will also tend to say good things about the brand to others. Marketers say: "Our best advertisement is a satisfied customer."[40]

Dissatisfied consumers respond differently. They may abandon or return the product. They may seek information that confirms its high value. They may take public action such as by complaining to the company, going to a lawyer, or complaining to other groups (such as business, private, or government agencies). Private actions include making a decision to stop buying the product *(exit option)* or warning friends *(voice option).*[41] In all these cases, the seller has done a poor job of satisfying the customer.[42]

Marketers can and should take steps to minimize the amount of consumer postpurchase dissatisfaction. Postpurchase communications to buyers have been shown to result in fewer product returns and order cancellations.[43] Computer companies can send a letter to new computer owners congratulating them on having selected a fine computer. They can place ads showing satisfied brand owners. They can solicit customer suggestions for improvements and list the location of available services. They can write instruction booklets that are intelligible. They can send owners a magazine containing articles describing new computer applications. In addition, they can provide good channels for speedy redress of customer grievances.

Postpurchase Use and Disposal. Marketers should also monitor how the buyers use and dispose of the product (Figure 6-8). If consumers store the product in their closet, the product is probably not very satisfying, and word-of-mouth will not be strong. If they sell or trade the product, new-product sales will be depressed. If consumers find new uses for the product, marketers should advertise these uses:

AVON For years Avon's customers have been spreading the word that Skin-So-Soft bath oil and moisturizer is a terrific bug repellent. While some consumers simply bathed in water scented with the fragrant oil, others carried it in their backpacks to mosquito-infested campsites or kept a bottle on the deck of their beach houses. Now, after receiving approval by the Environmental Protection Agency, Avon is touting Skin-So-Soft Moisturizing Suncare Plus as a triple-action product, providing insect repellent and waterproof SPF 15 sunscreen as well as moisturizers.[44]

If consumers throw the product away, the marketer needs to know how they dispose of it, especially if it can hurt the environment (as in the case with beverage containers and disposable diapers). Increased public awareness of recycling

FIGURE 6-8

How Customers Use or Dispose of Products

Source: From Jacob Jacoby, Carol K. Berning, and Thomas F. Dietvorst, "What about Disposition?" *Journal of Marketing,* July 1977, p. 23. Reprinted with permission of the American Marketing Association.

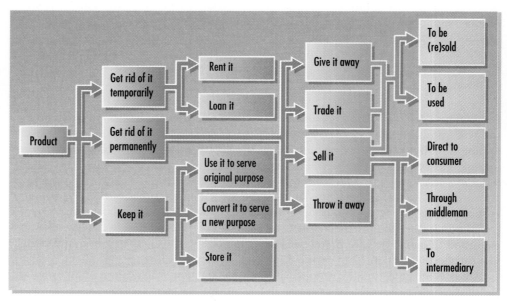

Analyzing
Marketing
Opportunities

and ecological concerns as well as consumer complaints about having to throw away beautiful bottles led French perfume maker Rochas to think about introducing a new refillable fragrance line. The company's new fragrance for women, Tocade, was introduced worldwide in 1994 in refillable Eau de Toilette sprays in 30, 50, and 100 milliliter sizes. Another French perfumer, Parfums Thierry Mugler, launched Angel in 1992 in a star-shaped bottled designed with an innovative refill system. Customers are offered the choice between refilling the bottle themselves by purchasing a prepackaged "recharge" or returning to one of the 800 outlets in France at which a salesperson refills the bottle.[45]

SUMMARY

1. Before developing their marketing plans, marketers need to study consumer markets and consumer behavior. In analyzing consumer markets, firms need to research who constitutes the market (occupants), what the market buys (objects), why the market buys (objectives), who participates in the buying (organizations), how the market buys (operations), when the market buys (occasions), and where the market buys (outlets).

2. Consumer behavior is influenced by four factors: cultural (culture, subculture, and social class), social (reference groups, family, and roles and statuses), personal (age, stage in the life cycle, occupation, economic circumstances, lifestyle, personality, and self-concept), and psychological (motivation, perception, learning, beliefs, and attitudes). Research into all these factors can provide clues as to how to reach and serve consumers more effectively.

3. To understand how consumers actually make their buying decisions, marketers must identify who makes and has input into the buying decision; people can be initiators, influencers, deciders, buyers, or users, and different marketing campaigns might be targeted to each type of person. Marketers must also examine buyers' levels of involvement and the number of brands available to determine whether consumers are engaging in complex buying behavior, dissonance-reducing buying behavior, habitual buying behavior, or variety-seeking buying behavior.

4. The typical buying process consists of the following sequence of events: problem recognition, information search, evaluation of alternatives, purchase decision, and postpurchase behavior. The marketers' job is to understand the buyer's behavior at each stage and what influences are operating. The attitudes of others, unanticipated situational factors, and perceived risk may all affect the decision to buy, as will consumers' levels of postpurchase satisfaction and postpurchase actions on the part of the company. Satisfied customers will continue to purchase; dissatisfied customers will stop purchasing the product and are likely to spread the word among their friends. For this reason, companies must work to ensure customer satisfaction at all levels of the buying process.

CONCEPT APPLICATIONS

1. Savvy retailers use a variety of marketing techniques to capture the shopper's attention. How do retailers appeal to each of the five senses to attract the consumer's attention?

2. Use the appropriate components of the model of buyer behavior in the chapter (Figure 6-1) to explain the following consumer behaviors:
   a. Bird's nest soup (which is made from dried bird spittle) is not generally viewed as a

Analyzing Consumer
Markets and Buying
Behavior

delicacy in the United States, but honey (which is regurgitated nectar) is highly esteemed.
   b. Some consumers shop in a broad variety of stores while other stick to a few known stores.
   c. Some products are purchased after extensive searching, while others are bought at a moment's notice.
   d. Two people are exposed to the same ad—one notices and processes the ad, while the other is unaware of its existence.

3. How could a marketing manager for each of the following organizations use Maslow's needs hierarchy to develop marketing strategy?
   a. American Cancer Society
   b. Revlon cosmetics
   c. Colonial Penn Life Insurance
   d. the Girl Scouts
   e. Calvin Klein jeans

4. Which of the following products are susceptible to the most postpurchase dissonance by consumers? Why? How might retailers reduce postpurchase dissonance for those products?
   a. Jaguar
   b. Tide detergent
   c. Sony CD player
   d. Encyclopaedia Britannica
   e. Suave shampoo

5. You are the brand manager responsible for marketing Dissolve mouthwash, which was recently introduced to the market. It is targeted toward the "extremely bad breath" segment and is especially effective for people who need to remove garlic from their breath. Your boss is not pleased with the current market penetration. He has asked you to look into the possibility of a coupon offer. Given your understanding of modifying behavior from the chapter, develop a free sample and progressive coupon program designed to achieve an increase in sales. How large should the free samples be? Where should coupons be placed—in newspapers, with the free samples, with the product, or a combination of all these? How should the value of the coupon vary with the place the coupon is found?

6. Develop a description of the different types of restaurants that people tend to frequent during the different family life cycle stages. What marketing strategies and tactics should the owners/managers of each of these establishments employ to appeal to their selected markets?

7. Select a low-involvement brand name product (e.g., Morton's salt, Hunt's ketchup) that is frequently purchased by consumers and assume that your company is its competitive challenger. What actions can you recommend to convince consumers to switch to your brand? What counteractions would you recommend to the original company to persuade their customers not to switch brands?

8. Although technological advances have resulted in "better sound for less money" for home audio equipment, the fastest-growing segment of the market is the high end—the most expensive equipment. What might explain this phenomenon?

9. A friend of yours plans to buy a new car. She prefers foreign makes and has narrowed her choices to a Volkswagen, Toyota, and Volvo. She looks for three things in a car: economy, quality, and roominess, and she values these attributes' importance at .5, .3, and .2, respectively. On a scale of 1 to 10 (10 being the best), she rates Volkswagen at 8, 8, and 2 on the three attributes; Toyota 3, 5, and 9; and Volvo 5, 8, and 7. Predict the car she is most likely to buy and least likely to buy. How might the latter company influence consumers to choose its car?

10. Describe the consumer market for briefcases, using the "Seven O's" framework described in this chapter.

Analyzing
Marketing
Opportunities

NOTES

1. Patricia Sellers, "They Understand Your Kids," *Fortune,* Autumn–Winter 1993, p. 29.

2. See Leon G. Schiffman and Leslie Lazar Kanuk, *Consumer Behavior,* 6th ed. (Upper Saddle River, NJ: Prentice Hall, 1997).

3. Schiffman and Kanuk, *Consumer Behavior.*

4. Christina Duff, " 'Bobby Short Wore Khakis'—Who's He, and Who Cares?" *The Wall Street Journal,* February 16, 1995, A1:4.

5. See Rosann L. Spiro, "Persuasion in Family Decision Making," *Journal of Consumer Research,* March 1983, pp. 393–402; Lawrence H. Wortzel, "Marital Roles and Typologies as Predictors of Purchase Decision Making for Everyday Household Products: Suggestions for Research," in *Advances in Consumer Research,* Vol. 7, ed. Jerry C. Olson (Provo, UT: Association for Consumer Research, 1980), pp. 212–15; David J. Burns, "Husband-Wife Innovative Consumer Decision Making: Exploring the Effect of Family Power," *Psychology and Marketing,* May–June 1992, pp. 175–89; Robert Boutilier, "Pulling the Family's Strings," *American Demographics,* August 1993, pp. 44–48. For cross-cultural comparisons of husband-wife buying roles, see John B. Ford, Michael S. LaTour, and Tony L. Henthorne, "Perception of Marital Roles in Purchase-Decision Processes: A Cross-Cultural Study," *Journal of the Academy of Marketing Science,* Spring 1995, pp. 120–31.

6. George Moschis, "The Role of Family Communication in Consumer Socialization of Children and Adolescents," *Journal of Consumer Research,* March 1985, pp. 898–913.

7. Marilyn Lavin, "Husband-Dominant, Wife-Dominant, Joint: A Shopping Typology for Baby Boom Couples?" *Journal of Consumer Marketing,* 10, no. 3 (1993), pp. 33–42.

8. Jeffery Zbar, "Hardware Builds Awareness Among Women," *Advertising Age,* July 11, 1994, p. 18.

9. Malia Boyd, "Look Who's Buying," *Incentive,* September 1994, pp. 76–79.

10. See Lawrence Lepisto, "A Life Span Perspective of Consumer Behavior," in *Advances in Consumer Research,* Vol. 12, ed. Elizabeth Hirshman and Morris Holbrook (Provo, UT: Association for Consumer Research, 1985), p. 47. Also see Gail Sheehy, *New Passages: Mapping Your Life Across Time* (New York: Random House, 1995).

11. Stuart Elliott, "Sampling Tastes of a Changing Russia," *The New York Times,* April 1, 1992, D:1, 19.

12. See Harold H. Kassarjian and Mary Jane Sheffet, "Personality and Consumer Behavior: An Update," in *Perspectives in Consumer Behavior,* ed. Harold H. Kassarjian and Thomas S. Robertson (Glenview, IL: Scott, Foresman, 1981), pp. 160–80.

13. See M. Joseph Sirgy, "Self-Concept in Consumer Behavior: A Critical Review," *Journal of Consumer Research,* December 1982, pp. 287–300.

14. A technique called *laddering* can be used to trace a person's motivations from the stated instrumental ones to the more terminal ones. Then the marketer can decide at what level to develop the message and appeal. See Thomas J. Reynolds and Jonathan Gutman, "Laddering Theory, Method, Analysis, and Interpretation," *Journal of Advertising Research,* February–March 1988, pp. 11–34.

15. See Jan Callebaut et al., *The Naked Consumer: The Secret of Motivational Research in Global Marketing* (Antwerp, Belgium: Censydiam Institute, 1994).

16. Abraham Maslow, *Motivation and Personality* (New York: Harper & Row, 1954), pp. 80–106.

17. See Frederick Herzberg, *Work and the Nature of Man* (Cleveland: William Collins, 1966); and Henk Thierry and Agnes M. Koopman-Iwerna, "Motivation and Satisfaction," in *Handbook of Work and Organizational Psychology,* ed. P. J. Drenth (New York: John Wiley, 1984), pp. 141–42.

18. Bernard Berelson and Gary A. Steiner, *Human Behavior: An Inventory of Scientific Findings* (New York: Harcourt Brace Jovanovich, 1964), p. 88.

19. Diane Feldman, "Building a Better Bird," *Management Review,* May 1989, pp. 10–14.

20. See Alice M. Tybout, Bobby J. Calder, and Brian Sternthal, "Using Information Processing Theory to Design Marketing Strategies," *Journal of Marketing Research,* February 1981, pp. 73–79.

21. Johnny K. Johansson, "Determinants and Effects of the Use of 'Made In' Labels," *International Marketing Review* (UK), 6, iss. 1 (1989), 47–58; Warren J. Bilkey and Erik Nes, "Country-of-Origin Effects on Product Evaluations," *Journal of International Business Studies,* Spring–Summer 1982, pp. 89–99; and P. J. Cattin et al., "A Cross-Cultural Study of 'Made-In' Concepts," *Journal of International Business Studies,* Winter 1982, pp. 131–41.

22. See David Krech, Richard S. Crutchfield, and Egerton L. Ballachey, *Individual in Society* (New York: McGraw-Hill, 1962), Chapter 2.

23. Cathy Curtis, "Grocery Marketing—Growers See Ads as Precious Commodity," *Advertising Age,* October 12, 1987, pp. S20–S22; Diane Schneidman, "Perception-Altering Ads for Generic Foods Are Spread on the Grapevine," *Marketing News,* June 5, 1987, pp. 15, 19.

24. Joshua Levin, "Cluck, Cluck, Oink," *Forbes,* April 16, 1990, pp. 126, 128.

25. See Henry Assael, *Consumer Behavior and Marketing Action* (Boston: Kent, 1987), Chapter 4.

26. Herbert E. Krugman, "The Impact of Television Advertising: Learning without Involvement," *Public Opinion Quarterly,* Fall 1965, pp. 349–56.

27. Marketing scholars have developed several models of the consumer buying process. See John A. Howard and Jagdish N. Sheth, *The Theory of Buyer Behavior* (New York: John Wiley, 1969); and James F. Engel, Roger D. Blackwell, and Paul W. Miniard, *Consumer Behavior,* 8th ed. (Fort Worth, TX: Dryden, 1994).

28. See William P. Putsis, Jr. and Narasimhan Srinivasan, "Buying or Just Browsing? The Duration of Purchase Deliberation," *Journal of Marketing Research,* August 1994, pp. 393–402.

29. See Chem L. Narayana and Rom J. Markin, "Consumer Behavior and Product Performance: An Alternative Conceptualization," *Journal of Marketing,* October 1975, pp. 1–6.

30. See Paul E. Green and Yoram Wind, *Multiattribute Decisions in Marketing: A Measurement Approach* (Hinsdale, IL: Dryden Press, 1973), Chapter 2; Leigh McAlister, "Choosing Multiple Items from a Product Class," *Journal of Consumer Research,* December 1979, pp. 213–24.

31. This expectancy-value model was developed by Martin Fishbein in "Attitudes and Prediction of Behavior," in *Readings in Attitude Theory and Measurement,* ed. Martin Fishbein (New York: John Wiley, 1967), pp. 477–92. For a critical review, see Paul W. Miniard and Joel B. Cohen, "An Examination of the Fishbein-Ajzen Behavioral-Intentions Model's Concepts and Measures," *Journal of Experimental Social Psychology,* May 1981, pp. 309–39.

Other models of consumer evaluation include the *ideal-*

brand model, which assumes that a consumer compares actual brands to her ideal brand and chooses the brand that comes closest to her ideal brand; the *conjunctive model,* which assumes that a consumer sets minimum acceptable levels on all the attributes and considers only the brands that meet all the minimum requirements; and the *disjunctive model,* which assumes that a consumer sets minimum acceptable levels on only a few attributes and eliminates those brands falling short. For a discussion of these and other models, see Green and Wind, *Multiattribute Decisions in Marketing.*

32. See Harper W. Boyd, Jr., Michael L. Ray, and Edward C. Strong, "An Attitudinal Framework for Advertising Strategy," *Journal of Marketing,* April 1972, pp. 27–33.

33. Marian Friestad and Peter Wright, "The Persuasion Knowledge Model: How People Cope with Persuasion Attempts," *Journal of Consumer Research,* June 1994, pp. 1–31.

34. See Jagdish N. Sheth, "An Investigation of Relationships among Evaluative Beliefs, Affect, Behavioral Intention, and Behavior," in *Consumer Behavior: Theory and Application,* ed. John U. Farley, John A. Howard, and L. Winston Ring (Boston: Allyn & Bacon, 1974), pp. 89–114.

35 See Fishbein, "Attitudes and Prediction."

36. See Raymond A. Bauer, "Consumer Behavior as Risk Taking," in *Risk Taking and Information Handling in Consumer Behavior,* ed. Donald F. Cox (Boston: Division of Research, Harvard Business School, 1967); and James W. Taylor, "The Role of Risk in Consumer Behavior," *Journal of Marketing,* April 1974, pp. 54–60.

37. See Philip Kotler and Murali K. Mantrala, "Flawed Products: Consumer Responses and Marketer Strategies," *Journal of Consumer Marketing,* Summer 1985, pp. 27–36.

38. See Priscilla A. La Barbera and David Mazursky, "A Longitudinal Assessment of Consumer Satisfaction/Dissatisfaction: The Dynamic Aspect of the Cognitive Process," *Journal of Marketing Research,* November 1983, pp. 393–404.

39. See Ralph L. Day, "Modeling Choices among Alternative Responses to Dissatisfaction," in *Advances in Consumer Research,* Vol. 11 (Provo, UT: Association for Consumer Research, 1984), 496–99.

40. See Barry L. Bayus, "Word of Mouth: The Indirect Effects of Marketing Efforts," *Journal of Advertising Research,* June–July 1985, pp. 31–39.

41. See Albert O. Hirschman, *Exit, Voice, and Loyalty* (Cambridge, MA: Harvard University Press, 1970).

42. See Mary C. Gilly and Richard W. Hansen, "Consumer Complaint Handling as a Strategic Marketing Tool," *Journal of Consumer Marketing,* Fall 1985, pp. 5–16.

43. See James H. Donnelly, Jr., and John M. Ivancevich, "Post-Purchase Reinforcement and Back-Out Behavior," *Journal of Marketing Research,* August 1970, pp. 399–400.

44. Pam Weisz, "Avon's Skin-So-Soft Bugs Out," *Brandweek,* June 6, 1994, p. 4.

45. Alev Aktar, "Refillable Fragrances," *Drug and Cosmetic Industry,* December 1994, pp. 16–19.

ANALYZING BUSINESS MARKETS AND BUSINESS BUYING BEHAVIOR

Companies don't make purchases; they establish relationships.

CHARLES S. GOODMAN

Treat the customer as an appreciating asset.

TOM PETERS

❖

Business organizations do not only sell. They also buy vast quantities of raw materials, manufactured parts, plant and equipment, supplies, and business services. There are 13 million buying organizations in the United States alone. Companies such as GE, Xerox, and AT&T that sell aircraft engines, office equipment, and telecommunication services to buying organizations need to understand those organizations' needs, resources, policies, and buying procedures.

In this chapter, we look at business markets and at institutional and government markets. We will examine six questions:

♦ **What is the business market, and how does it differ from the consumer market?**

♦ **What buying situations do organizational buyers face?**

♦ **Who participates in the business buying process?**

♦ **What are the major influences on organizational buyers?**

♦ **How do business buyers make their buying decisions?**

♦ **How are institutional and government markets similar to business markets?**

WHAT IS ORGANIZATIONAL BUYING?

Webster and Wind define *organizational buying* as follows:

❖ ORGANIZATIONAL BUYING is the decision-making process by which formal organizations establish the need for purchased products and services and identify, evaluate, and choose among alternative brands and suppliers.[1]

Although no two companies buy in the same way, the seller hopes to identify clusters of business firms that buy in similar ways to permit marketing strategy targeting.

The Business Market versus the Consumer Market

The *business market* consists of all the organizations that acquire goods and services used in the production of other products or services that are sold, rented, or supplied to others. The major industries making up the business market are agriculture, forestry, and fisheries; mining; manufacturing; construction; transportation; communication; public utilities; banking, finance, and insurance; distribution; and services.

More dollars and items are involved in sales to business buyers than to consumers. Consider the process of producing and selling a simple pair of shoes. Hide dealers must sell hides to tanners, who sell leather to shoe manufacturers, who sell shoes to wholesalers, who sell shoes to retailers, who finally sell them to consumers. Each party in the supply chain also has to buy many other goods and services.

Business markets have several characteristics that contrast sharply with consumer markets.

♦ *Fewer buyers:* The business marketer normally deals with far fewer buyers than the consumer marketer does. Goodyear Tire Company's fate depends critically on getting an order from one of the big three U.S. automakers. But when Goodyear sells replacement tires to consumers, it faces a potential domestic market of 176 million U.S. car owners, as well as a global market of millions of other car owners.

♦ *Larger buyers:* Many business markets are characterized by a high buyer-concentration ratio. A few large buyers do most of the purchasing in such industries as aircraft engines and defense weapons.

♦ *Close supplier-customer relationship:* Because of the smaller customer base and the importance and power of the larger customers, we observe close relationships between customers and suppliers in business markets. Suppliers are frequently expected to customize their offerings to individual business customer needs. Contracts go to those suppliers who cooperate with the buyer on technical specifications and delivery requirements. Suppliers are expected to attend special seminars held by the business customer to become familiar with the buyer's quality and procurement requirements. Sometimes these seminars go well beyond introductory material and into efforts at educating and even reorganizing. For example, Honda developed a mini-reengineering program aimed at strengthening its suppliers. One of its first graduates was Donnelly Corp., which supplies all of the mirrors for Honda's U.S.-manufactured cars. Early in the partnership, Honda sent engineers to two Donnelly plants to scrutinize operations for kinks in the work flow. Based on the program's recommendations, Honda hopes Donnelly will reduce costs about 2% a year, with the two companies splitting the savings. Actions like this are light-years away from a conventional supply contract. They mark a commitment between two entire corporations, not between a salesperson and a purchasing agent.[2]

♦ *Geographically concentrated buyers:* More than half of U.S. business buyers are concentrated in seven states: New York, California, Pennsylvania, Illinois, Ohio, New Jersey, and Michigan. Industries such as petroleum, rubber, and steel show an even greater geographical concentration. Most agricultural output comes from relatively few states. This geographical concentration of producers helps to reduce selling costs. At the same time, business marketers need to monitor regional shifts of certain industries, as when textiles and shoes moved out of New England to the southern states.

♦ *Derived demand:* The demand for business goods is ultimately derived from the demand for consumer goods. Thus animal hides are purchased because consumers want to buy shoes, purses, and other leather goods. If the demand for these consumer goods slackens, so will the demand for all the business goods entering into their production.[3] For this reason, the business marketer must closely monitor the buying patterns of ultimate consumers. For instance, a 1995 report in *Purchasing* magazine indicated that the Big Three automakers in Detroit are driving the boom in demand for steel-bar products. Much of that demand is derived from consumers' continued love affair with minivans and other light trucks, which consume far more steel than cars.[4]

♦ *Inelastic demand:* The total demand for many business goods and services is inelastic—that is, not much affected by price changes. Shoe manufacturers are not going to buy much more leather if the price of leather falls. Nor are they going to buy much less leather if the price of leather rises unless they can find satisfactory leather substitutes. Demand is especially inelastic in the short run because producers cannot make quick changes in their production methods. Demand is also inelastic for business goods that represent a small percentage of the item's total cost. For example, an increase in the price of metal eyelets for shoes will barely affect the total demand for metal eyelets. However, producers may switch their eyelets supplier in response to price differences.

♦ *Fluctuating demand:* The demand for business goods and services tends to be more volatile than the demand for consumer goods and services. This is especially true of the demand for new plant and equipment. A given percentage increase in consumer demand can lead to a much larger percentage increase in the demand for plant and equipment necessary to produce the additional output. Economists refer to this effect as the *acceleration effect*. Sometimes a rise of only 10% in consumer demand can cause as

Analyzing Business
Markets and Business
Buying Behavior

much as a 200% rise in businesses' demand for products in the next period; and a 10% fall in consumer demand may cause a complete collapse in businesses' demand. This sales volatility has led many business marketers to diversify their products and markets to achieve more balanced sales over the business cycle.

◆ *Professional purchasing:* Business goods are purchased by trained purchasing agents, who must follow the organization's purchasing policies, constraints, and requirements. Many of the buying instruments—for example, requests for quotations, proposals, and purchase contracts—are not typically found in consumer buying.

Professional buyers spend their professional lives learning how to buy better. Many belong to the National Association of Purchasing Managers (NAPM), which seeks to improve professional buyers' effectiveness and status. Professional Buyers' greater ability to evaluate technical information leads to more cost-effective buying. This means that business marketers have to provide greater technical data about their product and its advantages over competitors' products. For example, SPS Technologies' ad for Unbrako fasteners (Figure 7-1) appeals directly to purchasing agents and offers a toll-free number they can call to get the complete facts on the division's line of fasteners.

◆ *Several buying influences:* More people typically influence business buying decisions than consumer buying decisions. Buying committees consisting of technical experts and even senior management are common in the purchase of major goods. Consequently, business marketers have to send well-trained sales representatives and often sales teams to deal with the well-trained buyers. Although advertising, sales promotion, and publicity play an important role in the business promotional mix, personal selling usually serves as the main marketing tool. For example, Phelps Dodge (a metal supplier) is currently pursuing an "account management approach" in its attempt to reach all the people who influence their customers' buying decisions. "We're trying to encourage a direct dialogue between appropriate departments at Phelps Dodge and its clients," says a regional sales rep for the company.[5]

Business marketers also need to remember that women and minorities now account for a significant share of purchase decision makers. A study by Penton Publishing shows that women and minorities now account for 42% of all managers, engineers, and purchasing agents, up from 31% ten years ago. Recognizing this change, many companies are rewriting marketing communications programs to appeal to a broader range of buyers. Still, some companies are slow to adapt: A recent ad for AutoStrip Model 9800, a wire stripper from Eubanks, pictures a woman posed suggestively over the machinery with the headline reading, "Eubanks re-invents the wire stripper." An ad like this is more likely to offend than appeal to women buyers.[6]

◆ *Direct purchasing:* Business buyers often buy directly from manufacturers rather than through intermediaries, especially those items that are technically complex and/or expensive (such as mainframes or aircraft).

◆ *Reciprocity:* Business buyers often select suppliers who also buy from them. An example would be a paper manufacturer that buys chemicals from a chemical company that buys a considerable amount of its paper.

◆ *Leasing:* Many industrial buyers lease their equipment instead of buying it. Leasing is common with computers, shoe machinery, packaging equipment, heavy-construction equipment, delivery trucks, machine tools, and company automobiles. The lessee gains a number of advantages: conserving capital, getting the seller's latest products, receiving better service, and gaining some tax advantages. The lessor often ends up with a larger net income and the chance to sell to customers who could not afford outright purchase.

Buying Situations

The business buyer faces many decisions in making a purchase. The number of decisions depends on the type of buying situation. Robinson and others distinguish three types of buying situations: the straight rebuy, the modified rebuy, and the new task.[7]

FIGURE 7-1

Appealing to Professional Purchasers with Product Information: Unbrako Advertisement

Source: SPS Technologies Inc.

Who gets blamed when an industrial fastener fails?

A failed industrial fastener can destroy a costly machine. A production schedule. Even a customer relationship.

All of which can come back to haunt The Person Responsible. The purchaser who ordered that fastener.

Wherever, whenever fastener failure occurs, in an estimated 85% of cases the cause is fatigue. Although the new Fastener Quality Act requires compliance to industry standards, none of those standards, repeat **none**, includes requirements for fatigue strength.

Unbrako Division, SPS Technologies, offers more unique fatigue failure safeguards to protect your product than any other line of industrial fasteners, period.

Order UNBRAKO® fasteners. Get more assurance you'll be a hero...and not the goat. For full facts, call the Unbrako Division, SPS Technologies, 1-800-241-6221 or FAX 1-800-225-5777

© 1992 SPS Technologies, Inc. All rights reserved.

SPS TECHNOLOGIES

Unbrako

◆ *Straight rebuy:* The *straight rebuy* is a buying situation in which the purchasing department reorders on a routine basis (e.g., office supplies, bulk chemicals). The buyer chooses from suppliers on its "approved list," giving weight to its past buying satisfaction with the various suppliers. The "in-suppliers" make an effort to maintain product and service quality. They often propose automatic reordering systems so that the purchasing agent will save reordering time. The "out-suppliers" attempt to offer something new or to exploit dissatisfaction with a current supplier. Out-suppliers try to get a small order and then enlarge their purchase share over time.

◆ *Modified rebuy:* The *modified rebuy* is a situation in which the buyer wants to modify product specifications, prices, delivery requirements, or other terms. The modified rebuy usually involves additional decision participants on both the buyer and seller sides. The in-suppliers become nervous and have to protect the account. The out-suppliers see an opportunity to propose a better offer to gain some business.

Analyzing Business
Markets and Business
Buying Behavior

- *New task:* The *new task* is a buying situation in which a purchaser buys a product or service for the first time (e.g., office building, new security system). The greater the cost and/or risk, the larger the number of decision participants and the greater their information gathering—and therefore the longer the time to decision completion.[8] The new-task situation is the marketer's greatest opportunity and challenge. The marketer tries to reach as many key buying influencers as possible and provide helpful information and assistance. Because of the complicated selling involved in the new task, many companies use a *missionary sales force* consisting of their best salespeople.

    New-task buying passes through several stages: awareness, interest, evaluation, trial, and adoption.[9] Communication tools' effectiveness varies at each stage. Mass media are most important during the initial awareness stage; salespeople have their greatest impact at the interest stage; and technical sources are the most important during the evaluation stage.

The business buyer makes the fewest decisions in the straight-rebuy situation and the most in the new-task situation. In the latter, the buyer has to determine product specifications, price limits, delivery terms and times, service terms, payment terms, order quantities, acceptable suppliers, and the selected supplier. Different decision participants influence each decision, and the order varies in which these decisions are made.

SYSTEMS BUYING AND SELLING. Many business buyers prefer to buy a total solution to their problem from one seller. Called *systems buying,* this practice originated with government purchases of major weapons and communication systems. The government would solicit bids from prime contractors, who would assemble the package or system. The contractor who was awarded the contract would be responsible for bidding out and assembling the system's subcomponents from second-tier contractors. The prime contractor would thus provide a "turnkey solution," so called because the buyer simply had to turn one key to get the job done.

Sellers have increasingly recognized that buyers like to purchase in this way and many have adopted *systems selling* as a marketing tool. Systems selling can take different forms. For example, the supplier might sell a set of interlocking products; thus a glue supplier sells not only glue but glue applicators and dryers as well. Or the supplier might sell a system of production, inventory control, distribution, and other services to meet the buyer's need for a smooth-running operation. A variant on systems selling is *systems contracting,* where a single supply source provides the buyer with his or her entire requirement of MRO (maintenance, repair, operating) supplies. The customer benefits from reduced costs because the seller maintains the inventory. Savings also result from reduced time spent on supplier selection and from price protection over the term of the contract. The seller benefits from lower operating costs because of a steady demand and reduced paperwork.

Systems selling is a key industrial marketing strategy in bidding to build large-scale industrial projects, such as dams, steel factories, irrigation systems, sanitation systems, pipelines, utilities, and even new towns. Project engineering firms such as Bechtel and Fluor must compete on price, quality, reliability, and other attributes to win contracts. Consider the following example:

JAPAN AND INDONESIA   The Indonesian government requested bids to build a cement factory near Jakarta. A U.S. firm made a proposal that included choosing the site, designing the cement factory, hiring the construction crews, assembling the materials and equipment, and turning over the finished factory to the Indonesian government. A Japanese firm, in outlining its proposal, included all of these services, plus hiring and training the workers to run the factory, exporting the cement through their trading companies, and using the cement to build needed roads out of Jakarta and new office buildings in Jakarta. Although the Japanese proposal involved more money, its appeal was

Analyzing
Marketing
Opportunities

greater, and they won the contract. Clearly, the Japanese viewed the problem not just as one of building a cement factory (the narrow view of systems selling) but as one of contributing to Indonesia's economic development. They saw themselves not as an engineering project firm but as an economic development agency. They took the broadest view of the customer's needs. This is true systems selling.

Participants in the Business Buying Process

Who does the buying of the trillions of dollars' worth of goods and services needed by business organizations? Purchasing agents are influential in straight-rebuy and modified-rebuy situations, while other department personnel are more influential in new-buy situations. Engineering personnel usually have major influence in selecting product components, and purchasing agents dominate in selecting suppliers.[10] Thus in new-buy situations, the business marketer must first direct product information to the engineering personnel. In rebuy situations and at supplier-selection time, communications should be directed primarily to the purchasing agent.

Webster and Wind call the decision-making unit of a buying organization the *buying center.* The buying center is composed of "all those individuals and groups who participate in the purchasing decision-making process, who share some common goals and the risks arising from the decisions."[11] The buying center includes all members of the organization who play any of seven roles in the purchase decision process.[12]

- ◆ *Initiators:* Those who request that something be purchased. They may be users or others in the organization.
- ◆ *Users:* Those who will use the product or service. In many cases, the users initiate the buying proposal and help define the product requirements.
- ◆ *Influencers:* People who influence the buying decision. They often help define specifications and also provide information for evaluating alternatives. Technical personnel are particularly important influencers.
- ◆ *Deciders:* People who decide on product requirements and/or on suppliers.
- ◆ *Approvers:* People who authorize the proposed actions of deciders or buyers.
- ◆ *Buyers:* People who have formal authority to select the supplier and arrange the purchase terms. Buyers may help shape product specifications, but they play their major role in selecting vendors and negotiating. In more complex purchases, the buyers might include high-level managers participating in the negotiations.
- ◆ *Gatekeepers:* People who have the power to prevent sellers or information from reaching members of the buying center. For example, purchasing agents, receptionists, and telephone operators may prevent salespersons from contacting users or deciders.

Within any organization, the buying center will vary in the number and type of participants for different classes of products. According to a Penton Research Services survey, the average number of people involved in a buying decision ranges from about three (for services and items used in day-to-day operations) to almost five (for such high-ticket purchases as construction work and machinery). There is also a trend toward team-based buying; another Penton survey found that 87% of the purchasing executives at Fortune 1000 companies expect teams of people from different departments and functions to be making buying decisions in the year 2000.[13]

To target their efforts properly, business marketers have to figure out: Who are the major decision participants? What decisions do they influence? What is their level of influence? What evaluation criteria do they use? Consider the following example:

BAXTER HEALTHCARE Baxter sells nonwoven disposable surgical gowns to hospitals. It tries to identify the hospital personnel who participate in this buying decision. They include the vice-president of purchasing, the operating-room administrator, and the surgeons. Each participant plays a different role. The vice-president of purchasing analyzes whether the hospital should buy disposable gowns or reusable gowns. If the findings favor disposable gowns, then the operating-room administrator compares various competitors' products and prices and makes a choice. This administrator considers the gown's absorbency, antiseptic quality, design, and cost and normally buys the brand that meets the functional requirements at the lowest cost. Finally, surgeons influence the decision retroactively by reporting their satisfaction with the particular brand.

When a buying center includes many participants, the business marketer will not have the time or resources to reach all of them. Small sellers concentrate on reaching the key buying influencers. Larger sellers go for multilevel in-depth selling to reach as many buying participants as possible. Their salespeople virtually "live" with their high-volume customers. As buying teams become more prevalent, however, salespeople will find it increasingly difficult to locate, much less call on, all of the individuals involved in the purchase decision. Rather, companies will have to rely more heavily on their communications program to reach hidden buying influences and keep their current customers sold.[14]

Business marketers must periodically review their assumptions of the roles and influence of different decision participants. For years, Kodak's strategy for selling X-ray film to hospitals was to sell to lab technicians. The company did not notice that the decision was increasingly being made by professional administrators. As its sales declined, Kodak finally grasped the change in buying practices and hurriedly revised its market targeting strategy.

Business marketers who work in global markets must also be aware of business buying practices internationally. For example, while business buyers in the United States are definitely leaning toward a team-based approach and expect more team decision-making in the future, U.S. purchasers are lone eagles when compared to their counterparts in other countries. A recent study compared purchasing decision-making processes in the United States, Sweden, France, and Southeast Asia, with 236 firms providing data on buying center influences and supplier search criteria. The survey found that buying decisions in Sweden had the highest team effort while the United States had the lowest, even though the U.S. and Swedish firms had very similar demographics. In making purchasing decisions, Swedish companies depended on technical staff, both their own and suppliers', much more than the firms in other countries.[15]

Major Influences on Business Buyers

Business buyers are subject to many influences when they make their buying decisions. Some marketers assume that the most important influences are economic; others see buyers as responding to personal factors such as favors, attention, or risk avoidance. In reality, business buyers respond to both economic and personal factors. Where there is substantial similarity in supplier offers, business buyers have little basis for rational choice. Since they can satisfy the purchasing requirements with any supplier, they will place more weight on the personal treatment they receive. Where competing offers differ substantially, business buyers are more accountable for their choice and pay more attention to economic factors.

In general, the influences on business buyers can be classified into four main groups: environmental, organizational, interpersonal, and individual (Figure 7-2).[16]

ENVIRONMENTAL FACTORS. Business buyers are heavily influenced by factors in the current and expected economic environment, such as the level of

Analyzing
Marketing
Opportunities

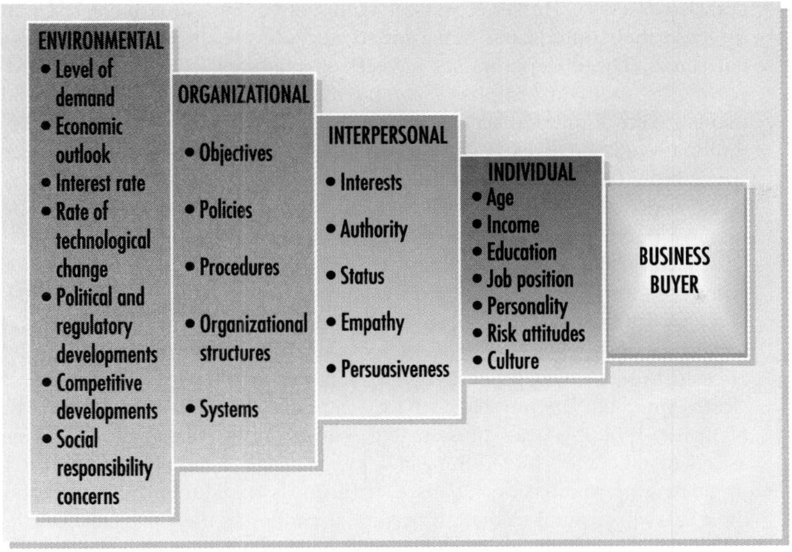

FIGURE 7-2

Major Influences on Industrial Buying Behavior

demand for their product, the economic outlook, and the interest rate. In a recession economy, business buyers reduce their investment in plant, equipment, and inventories. Business marketers can do little to stimulate total demand in this environment. They can only fight harder to increase or maintain their share of demand.

Companies that fear a shortage of key materials are willing to buy and hold large inventories. They will sign long-term contracts with suppliers to ensure a steady flow of materials. Du Pont, Ford, Chrysler, and several other major companies regard long-term *supply planning* as a major responsibility of their purchasing managers.

Business buyers are also affected by technological, political/regulatory, and competitive developments in the environment. The business marketer has to monitor all of these forces, determine how they will affect buyers, and try to turn problems into opportunities. For example, the greening of corporate America has added a new criterion to some organizational buying decisions: that a product or service must not damage the environment. Thus a printer might favor paper suppliers that have a wide selection of recycled papers or ink vendors who use chemicals that are made through environmentally sensitive processes. Interestingly, socially responsible buying is rarely initiated by purchasing departments but rather comes about either through the actions of a policy entrepreneur (a person who plays a key role in putting social issues on the corporate agenda) or because the organization is already dedicated to being socially responsible. Buyers in socially responsible organizations will put pressure on suppliers to be socially responsible as well. One manager explains, "We push suppliers with technical expertise to be more socially conscious. We say, 'You're a successful company. Tell us why we should continue to do business with you. Tell us what difference you're going to make.' We don't tell them how to make a difference."[17]

ORGANIZATIONAL FACTORS. Each buying organization has specific objectives, policies, procedures, organizational structures, and systems. The business marketer has to be familiar with all of these. Business marketers should be particularly aware of the following organizational trends in the purchasing area:

◆ *Purchasing-department upgrading:* Purchasing departments commonly occupy a low position in the management hierarchy, in spite of managing often more than half of the

Analyzing Business
Markets and Business
Buying Behavior

company's costs. However, recent competitive pressures have led many companies to upgrade their purchasing departments and elevate their administrators to vice-presidential status. These departments have been changed from old-fashioned "purchasing departments" with an emphasis on buying at the lowest cost to "procurement departments" with a mission to seek the best value from fewer and better suppliers. Some multinationals have even elevated them into "strategic materials departments" with responsibility for sourcing around the world and working with strategic partners. At Caterpillar, functions such as purchasing, inventory control, production scheduling, and traffic have been combined into one department.

In addition, many companies are looking for top buying talent and offering higher compensation. Once considered a corporate backwater, purchasing has begun to attract some of the best young executives. At General Motors, for instance, G. Richard Wagoner served as both CFO and head of worldwide purchasing in 1993 and 1994. His experience in procurement helped elevate Wagoner to the top post in GM's $90-billion-a-year North American operations. At AT&T, purchasing chief Daniel Caroll was a former CEO of the $6-billion-a-year division that manufactures switching equipment. When he was asked to take the chief purchasing job in 1993, it was considered a promotion.[18] The upgrading of purchasing means that business marketers must correspondingly upgrade their sales personnel to match the higher caliber of the business buyers.

◆ *Centralized purchasing:* In multidivisional companies, most purchasing is carried out by separate divisions because of their differing needs. Recently, however, some companies have started to recentralize some of the purchasing. Headquarters identifies materials purchased by several divisions and buys them centrally, thereby gaining more purchasing clout. The individual divisions can buy from another source if they can get a better deal, but in general centralized purchasing produces substantial savings for the company. For the business marketer, this development means dealing with fewer and higher-level buyers. Instead of the business marketer's sales forces selling at separate plant locations, the marketer may use a national account sales force to deal with large corporate buyers. National account selling is challenging and demands a sophisticated sales force and marketing planning effort.

◆ *Decentralized purchasing of small ticket items:* At the same time that many companies are centralizing their purchasing processes, they are also decentralizing some purchasing operations by empowering employees to purchase small-ticket items such as duplicate keys, coffee makers, or Christmas trees. This revolution has come about through the availability of corporate purchasing cards issued by credit-card organizations. Companies distribute the cards to foremen, clerks, and secretaries; the cards incorporate codes that set credit limits and restrict where they can be used. A factory worker, for example, might carry a card limited to the local hardware emporium. National Semiconductor and AlliedSignal are two companies that are using Visa and American Express purchasing cards, with great cost-cutting effect. National Semiconductor's purchasing chief has noted that the cards have cut processing costs from $30 an order to a few cents. The additional benefit, for both buyers and suppliers, is that with less time to spend on paperwork, purchasing departments have more time for building partnerships.[19]

◆ *Long-term contracts:* Business buyers are increasingly initiating or accepting long-term contracts with reliable suppliers. For example, General Motors wants to buy from fewer suppliers, who are willing to locate close to its plants and produce high-quality components. In addition, business marketers are supplying electronic data interchange (EDI) systems to their customers. The customer can enter orders directly on the computer, and the orders are automatically transmitted to the supplier. Many hospitals order directly from Baxter in this way, and many bookstores order from Follett's in this way.

◆ *Purchasing-performance evaluation and buyers' professional development:* Many companies have set up incentive systems to reward purchasing managers for good buying performance, in much the same way that sales personnel receive bonuses for good selling performance. These systems are leading purchasing managers to increase their pressure on sellers for the best terms.

Purchasing managers are also spurred by competition within their field. In 1992 *Purchasing* magazine started the first annual Cost Savers' Hall of Fame competition. The winners included two purchasing managers at General Binding Corp. who investigated recycled paper as a means of cost reduction. Their efforts resulted in an estimated annual savings of $733,450 on paper, not to mention the marketing leverage of offering recycled goods.[20]

The emergence of just-in-time production systems promises to have a major impact on organizational purchasing policies. Its ramifications are described in the Marketing Insight on pages 214–215 titled "Lean Production Changes the Face of Business Buying."

INTERPERSONAL FACTORS. The buying center usually includes several participants with differing interests, authority, status, empathy, and persuasiveness. The business marketer is not likely to know what kind of group dynamics take place during the buying decision process, although whatever information he or she can discover about the personalities and interpersonal factors would be useful. Particularly important can be information about customers' relationships with other companies' sales reps.

INDIVIDUAL FACTORS. Each participant in the buying process has personal motivations, perceptions, and preferences. These are influenced by the participant's age, income, education, job position, personality, attitudes toward risk, and culture. Buyers definitely exhibit different buying styles. There are "keep-it-simple" buyers, "own-expert" buyers, "want-the-best" buyers, and "want-everything done" buyers. Some younger, highly educated buyers are computer experts who conduct rigorous analyses of competitive proposals before choosing a supplier. Other buyers are "toughies" from the old school and pit the competing sellers against one another.

Even factors that seem consistent across one country or culture can vary drastically in another country or culture. Because international business requires businesspeople to understand and adapt to the local business culture and norms, here are some rules of social and business etiquette that marketers should understand when doing business in other countries:[21]

France	Dress conservatively, except in the south where more casual clothes are worn. Do not refer to people by their first names—the French are formal with strangers.
Germany	Be especially punctual. A U.S. businessperson invited to someone's home should present flowers, preferably unwrapped, to the hostess. During introductions, greet women first and wait until, or if, they extend their hands before extending yours.
Italy	Italian businesspeople tend to be style conscious. Make appointments well in advance. Prepare for and be patient with Italian bureaucracies.
United Kingdom	Toasts are often given at formal dinners. If the host honors you with a toast, be prepared to reciprocate. Business entertaining is done more often at lunch than at dinner.
Saudi Arabia	Although men will kiss each other in greeting, they will never kiss a woman in public. An American woman should wait for a man to extend his hand before offering hers. If a Saudi offers refreshment, accept—it is an insult to decline it.
Japan	Don't imitate Japanese bowing customs unless you understand them thoroughly—who bows to whom, how many times, and when. It's a complicated ritual. Presenting business cards is another ritual. Carry many cards, present them with

Analyzing Business
Markets and Business
Buying Behavior

Lean Production Changes the Face of Business Buying

Many manufacturers today are moving toward a whole new way of manufacturing called *lean production*. Lean production enables a company to produce a greater variety of high-quality products at lower cost, in less time, using less labor. It permits more rapid model changes and performance improvements, and allows companies to enter new markets.

Lean production is changing business customers' attitude toward the selection and management of suppliers. It is imperative that business-to-business marketers recognize and adapt to the changes implied by lean production. The major elements of lean production that companies are now adopting include:

1. *Just-in-time (JIT) production:* JIT is a production method that brings together all materials and parts needed at each stage of production at the precise moment that they are required. The goal of JIT is zero inventory with 100% quality. JIT means that materials arrive at the customer's factory exactly when needed. This calls for a synchronization between supplier and customer production schedules so that inventory buffers are unnecessary.

   Some companies are now going beyond JIT and pursuing JIT II—empowerment of suppliers. For instance, at

Foxboro Company in Foxboro, Massachusetts, orders for personal computing equipment are satisfied by a full-time on-site representative from supplier Computopia, and Honeywell has empowered suppliers on-site in such diverse areas as printing services, printed wiring boards, and waste management.

2. *Strict quality control:* Maximum cost savings from JIT and JIT II are achieved if the buyer receives perfect goods from the supplier. This means that the suppliers must apply strict quality-control procedures before shipping their products. Motorola teams tour suppliers' plants every two years, grading them on how well they stack up against their competitors on both quality and timeliness. Motorola's suppliers welcome these ratings, which often help the companies find ways to cut costs anywhere from 12 to 20 percent.

3. *Frequent and reliable delivery:* Daily delivery is frequently the only way to avoid inventory buildup. Increasingly, customers are specifying delivery dates rather than shipping dates with penalties for not meeting them. This means that suppliers must develop reliable transportation arrangements. 3M has speeded delivery of its office products to Boise Cascade (which distributes office products), while Kasle Steel makes around-the-clock deliveries to General Motors.

4. *Closer location:* Suppliers should locate close to their important customers because closeness means more reliable delivery. This means that suppliers must make large commitments to major customers. Kasle Steel set up its blanking mill within Buick City to serve the General Motors

---

Japan (cont'd)

both hands so your name can be easily read, and hand them to others in descending rank. Examine carefully each business card you receive to show interest. Expect Japanese business executives to take time making decisions and to work through all of the details before making a commitment.

The Purchasing/Procurement Process

Business buyers do not buy goods and services for personal consumption. They buy goods and services to make money, or to reduce operating costs, or to satisfy a social or legal obligation. A steel company will add another furnace if it sees a chance to make more money. It will computerize its accounting system to reduce the costs of doing business. It will add pollution-control equipment to meet legal requirements.

To buy the needed goods, business buyers move through a purchasing/procurement process. Robinson et al. have identified eight stages of the industrial buying process and called them *buyphases*.[22] These stages are shown in Table 7-1 on page 216. This model is called the *buygrid* framework. The eight steps for the typical new-task buying situation are as follows.

plant there. Sometimes distributors must even be prepared to move their plants onto the customer's premises. Arrow Electronics, once headquartered in Long Island, New York, now has a warehouse in the factory of Ohio-based Bailey Controls. Bailey provides the space, and the warehouse is stocked with Arrow inventory according to Bailey's twice-monthly forecasts.

5. *Telecommunication:* New communication technologies permit suppliers to establish computerized purchasing systems with their customers. Such systems allow for just-in-time online ordering at the lowest prices. These technologies reduce transaction costs but put pressure on business marketers to keep their prices competitive.

6. *Stable production schedules:* Customers provide their production schedule to the supplier so that the delivery is made on the day the materials are required. Navistar provides one of its suppliers a six-month forecast and a firm 20-day order. If any last-minute changes are made, the supplier bills Navistar for the additional costs. This system helps reduce the uncertainty and costs faced by the suppliers.

7. *Single sourcing and early supplier involvement:* JIT and JIT II imply that the buying and selling organizations work closely together to reduce costs. Business buyers realize that suppliers are experts in their field and should be brought into the design process. Business customers often award a long-term contract to only one supplier. The payoff is high for the winning supplier, and it is very difficult for other competitors to subsequently get the contract.

Contracts are almost automatically renewed, provided the supplier has met delivery schedules and quality standards. In 1993, for instance, AlliedSignal's 150 plants bought valves, pipes, and fittings from no fewer than 400 suppliers. In 1994 the company packed all that business into a $10-million-a-year contract with Van Leeuwan, a Dutch-owned manufacturer and distributor. The endless paperwork associated with pipe orders disappeared.

All these elements of lean production add up to a closer relationship between the business customer and the business marketer. "It's like a marriage," says one big-league purchasing agent. A less sentimental top industrial manager says, "It's like committing to one relationship instead of sleeping around." Because of the time invested by the parties, joint location decisions, and telecommunications hookups, the costs of switching partners are high. A major implication is that business marketers must improve their skill in relationship marketing as compared with transaction marketing. Business marketers must plan for profit maximization over the entire relationship period rather than over each transaction.

Sources: See "JIT II Comes of Age," *Purchasing,* October 20, 1994, pp. 41–44; Myron Magnet, "The New Golden Rule of Business," *Fortune,* February 21, 1994, pp. 60–64; Shawn Tully, "Purchasing's New Muscle," *Fortune,* February 20, 1995, pp. 75–79, 82–83; Rahul Jacob, "Why Some Customers Are More Equal Than Others," *Fortune,* September 19, 1994, pp. 215–16+; John E. Murray, "The EDI Explosion," *Purchasing,* February 16, 1995, pp. 28–30; and James P. Womack, Daniel T. Jones, and Daniel Roos, *The Machine That Changed the World* (New York: Macmillan, 1990).

PROBLEM RECOGNITION. The buying process begins when someone in the company recognizes a problem or need that can be met by acquiring a good or a service. Problem recognition can occur as a result of internal or external stimuli. Internally, the most common events leading to problem recognition are the following:

◆ The company decides to develop a new product and needs new equipment and materials to produce this product.

◆ A machine breaks down and requires replacement or new parts.

◆ Purchased material turns out to be unsatisfactory, and the company searches for another supplier.

◆ A purchasing manager senses an opportunity to obtain lower prices or better quality.

Externally, the buyer may get new ideas at a trade show, see an ad, or receive a call from a sales representative who offers a better product or a lower price. Business marketers can stimulate problem recognition by direct mail, telemarketing, and calling on prospects.

GENERAL NEED DESCRIPTION. Once a need is recognized, the buyer proceeds to determine the needed item's general characteristics and quantity

TABLE 7-1

BUYGRID FRAMEWORK:
MAJOR STAGES (BUYPHASES)
OF THE INDUSTRIAL BUYING
PROCESS IN RELATION TO
MAJOR BUYING SITUATIONS
(BUYCLASSES)

		BUYCLASSES		
		NEW TASK	MODIFIED REBUY	STRAIGHT REBUY
Buyphases	1. Problem recognition	Yes	Maybe	No
	2. General need description	Yes	Maybe	No
	3. Product specification	Yes	Yes	Yes
	4. Supplier search	Yes	Maybe	No
	5. Proposal solicitation	Yes	Maybe	No
	6. Supplier selection	Yes	Maybe	No
	7. Order-routine specification	Yes	Maybe	No
	8. Performance review	Yes	Yes	Yes

Source: Adapted from Patrick J. Robinson, Charles W. Faris, and Yoram Wind, *Industrial Buying and Creative Marketing,* 1967, p.14. Reprinted with permission of Allyn & Bacon.

needed. For standard items, this is not a very involved process. For complex items, the buyer will work with others—engineers, users, and so on—to define the general characteristics that the product must have. These may include reliability, durability, price, and/or other attributes. The business marketer can assist the buyer in this phase by describing how his or her products fit the organization's general needs.

PRODUCT SPECIFICATION.   After general needs are identified, the buying organization must develop the item's technical specifications. Often, the company will assign a product-value-analysis (PVA) engineering team to the project.

❖   **PRODUCT VALUE ANALYSIS** is an approach to cost reduction in which components are carefully studied to determine if they can be redesigned or standardized or made by cheaper methods of production.

The PVA team will examine the high-cost components in a given product—usually 20% of the parts account for 80% of the costs of manufacturing it. The team will also identify overdesigned product components that last longer than the product itself, then decide on the optimal product characteristics. Tightly written specifications will allow the buyer to refuse components that are too expensive or that fail to meet the specified standards.

Suppliers, too, can use product value analysis as a tool for positioning themselves to win an account. By getting in early and influencing buyer specifications, the supplier increases its chances of being chosen in the supplier-selection stage.

SUPPLIER SEARCH.   Once the product has been specified, the buyer tries to identify the most appropriate suppliers. The buyer can examine trade directories, do a computer search, phone other companies for recommendations, watch trade advertisements, and attend trade shows.[23] The supplier's task is to get listed in major directories, develop a strong advertising and promotion program, and build a good reputation in the marketplace. Suppliers who lack the required production capacity or suffer from a poor reputation will be rejected. Those who qualify may be visited by the buyer's agents, who will examine the suppliers' manufacturing facilities and meet their personnel. After evaluating each company, the buyer will end up with a short list of qualified suppliers.

PROPOSAL SOLICITATION.   The buyer will now invite qualified suppliers to submit proposals. Where the item is complex or expensive, the buyer will require a detailed written proposal from each qualified supplier. After evaluating the pro-

MARKETING MEMO

ASKING THE RIGHT QUESTIONS AT SALES PRESENTATIONS

Sales and Marketing Management recently asked purchasing managers what they think are the worst and best questions salespeople can ask. Here's what they said:

1. Worst question: **"What does your company do?"**

   "The worst thing salespeople can ask is for information they already know. Salespeople should do a background check on a company they plan to approach. There are plenty of sources for that kind of information. I don't have time to educate them on our products."

   Best question: **"What kind of added value are you looking for?"**

   "To me, added value—such as just-in-time delivery or providing us with a full-time specialist—is more important than price alone."

2. Worst question: **"Can we do something for you?"**

   "Salespeople should never hint at perks or gifts they can offer in exchange for closing a deal. Ethics are very important to me, so it's of paramount importance that they treat me professionally."

   Best question: **"How can we help improve your product or process?"**

   "I want to know that a salesperson is interested in how his company can add value to my company—in ways such as R&D or other services. It's important to know what value both sides of the desk can bring to the equation."

3. Worst question: **"Are you the person who is going to make the buying decision?"**

   "Why are you there and why is the salesperson there if you're not the one who is going to make that decision? It's a question that's asked too often."

   Best question: **"If you're interested in my product, how do you plan to use it?**

   "Salespeople should be interested to know how their product or service fits into your business; what its application will be. Too many salespeople don't ask that question."

4. Worst question: **"Who are you buying from now?**

   "This question makes it seem that the salesperson is putting a narrow focus on price, trying to outbid a competitor instead of presenting his company's product or service and showing how it can add value to my company."

   Best question: **"What can I do to add value to your process?"**

   "Simply put, today, customers are looking for added-value."

Source: Reprinted from "Purchasing Managers Sound Off," *Sales and Marketing Management,* February 1995, pp. 84–85.

posals, the buyer will eliminate some suppliers and invite the remaining suppliers to make formal presentations.

Business marketers must thus be skilled in researching, writing, and presenting proposals. Their written proposals should be marketing documents, not just technical documents. Their oral presentations should inspire confidence, positioning their company's capabilities and resources so that they stand out from the competition. An important part of any presentation involves not only giving information but also asking questions. For more on the kinds of questions to ask—and the kinds of questions *not* to ask—during a presentation, see the Marketing Memo titled "Asking the Right Questions at Sales Presentations."

Consider the hurdles that the Campbell Soup Company and Xerox have set up in qualifying suppliers:

Analyzing Business
Markets and Business
Buying Behavior

CAMPBELL'S SOUP COMPANY   The Campbell Qualified Supplier Program requires would-be suppliers to pass through three stages: that of a qualified supplier, an approved supplier, and a select supplier. To become qualified, the supplier has to demonstrate technical capabilities, financial health, cost effectiveness, high quality standards, and innovativeness. A supplier that satisfies these criteria then applies for approval, which is granted only after the supplier has attended a Campbell Vendor seminar, accepted an implementation team visit, agreed to make certain changes and commitments, and so forth. Once approved, the supplier becomes a select supplier when it demonstrates high product uniformity, continuous quality improvement, and just-in-time delivery capabilities.

XEROX   Xerox qualifies only suppliers who meet the ISO 9000 quality standards (see Chapter 2). But to win the company's top award—certification status—a supplier must first complete the Xerox Multinational Supplier Quality Survey. The survey requires the supplier to issue a quality assurance manual, to adhere to continuous improvement principles, and to demonstrate effective systems implementation. Once a supplier has been qualified, it must participate in Xerox's Continuous Supplier Involvement process, in which the two companies work together to create specifications for quality, cost, delivery times, and process capability. The final step toward certification requires a supplier to undergo additional rigorous quality training and an evaluation based on the same criteria as the Malcolm Baldrige National Quality Award. Not surprisingly, only 176 suppliers worldwide have achieved the 95% rating required for certification as a Xerox supplier.[24]

SUPPLIER SELECTION.   Before selecting a supplier, the buying center will specify desired supplier attributes and indicate their relative importance. It will then rate suppliers on these attributes and identify the most attractive suppliers. They often use a supplier-evaluation model such as the one shown in Table 7-2.

The choice and importance of different attributes varies with the type of buying situation.[25] Delivery reliability, price, and supplier reputation are highly important for *routine-order products*. For *procedural-problem products,* such as a copying machine, the three most important attributes are technical service, supplier flexibility, and product reliability. For *political-problem products* that stir rivalries in the organization (such as the choice of a computer system) the most important attributes are price, supplier reputation, product reliability, service reliability, and supplier flexibility.

The buying center may attempt to negotiate with its preferred suppliers for better prices and terms before making the final selection. Marketers can counter the request for a lower price in a number of ways. They may be able to show evidence that the "life-cycle cost" of using its product is lower than that of competitors' products. They can also cite the value of the services the buyer now receives, especially where those services are superior to those offered by competitors. "Value-added" services have become as important to suppliers as price. (For more on this topic, see the Vision 2000 feature titled "The Value of Added Value.") Other

TABLE 7-2	AN EXAMPLE OF VENDOR ANALYSIS				
		RATING SCALE			
ATTRIBUTES	**IMPORTANCE WEIGHTS**	**(1) POOR**	**(2) FAIR**	**(3) GOOD**	**(4) EXCELLENT**
Price	.30				x
Supplier reputation	.20			x	
Product reliabilty	.30				x
Service reliabilty	.10		x		
Supplier flexibility	.10			x	

Total score: .30(4) + .20(3) + .30(4) + .10(2) + .10(3) = 3.5.

The Value of Added Value

To counter pressure to lower their prices, suppliers used to rely on wining and dining their customers. "It's all a matter of how many lunches and dinners and ball games you take them to," says a cement sales veteran on the way things used to be. But today, wining and dining is no longer enough. Winning suppliers are increasingly those who are able to reduce cost while providing value-added services for their business customers. Here are some examples of how suppliers, both small and large, are using value-added services to give them a competitive edge:

♦ *Thomas Industrial Products Co.* Voted Number One in *Industrial Distribution*'s list of the Top 25 small distributors in 1992, Thomas Industrial Products Co. credits the lion's share of its success to its value-added services, which make up 50% of its business. The hose and accessory distributor has beat out larger competitors in the mid-Atlantic area by offering customers such services as application assistance, technical engineering, product testing, and custom crimping, coupling, and cutting. Today Thomas is one of the few companies in the area that performs these services. The company's employees even passed a stringent examination so that Thomas could become a "certified coupler" for several types of hose.

♦ *Jefferson Smurfit Corp.* When General Electric expanded a no-frost refrigerator line in 1990, it needed more shipping boxes, and fast. Jefferson Smurfit Corp., a $4.5 billion packaging supplier, assigned a coordinator to juggle production from three of its plants—and sometimes even divert product intended for other customers—to keep the GE's Decatur plant humming. This kind of value-added hustling helped Jefferson Smurfit win the GE appliance unit's "Distinguished Supplier Award." It has also sheltered Smurfit from the bruising struggle of competing only on price. "Today, it's not just getting the best price but getting the best value—and there are a lot of pieces to value," says a vice president for procurement at Emerson Electric Co., a major Smurfit customer that has cut its supplier count by 65 percent.

♦ *Essroc Materials.* Essroc operates on the principle that helping clients sell to their customers can make a huge difference in securing a relationship, even if the services offered have little to do with the actual product. Essroc, a French building materials company, helps its customers with their marketing efforts. It keeps them informed both on what the competition is doing and about the industry itself.

Sources: "Value-Added Services Gain Momentum," *Purchasing,* March 16, 1995, p. 63; Minda Zetlin, "It's All the Same to Me," *Sales and Marketing Management,* February 1994, pp. 71–75; Richard A. Melcher, "The Middlemen Stay on the March," *Business Week,* January 9, 1995, p. 87; Christine Forbes, "Top 25 Small Distributors," *Industrial Distribution,* January 15, 1992, pp. 30–36; James E. Ellis, "There's Even a Science to Selling Boxes," *Business Week,* August 3, 1992, pp. 51–52.

approaches may also be used to counter intense price pressure. Consider the following example:

LINCOLN ELECTRIC Lincoln Electric has instituted a Guaranteed Cost Reduction Program for its distributors. When a customer insists that a Lincoln distributor lower prices on Lincoln's equipment to match Lincoln's competitors, the company and the particular distributor may guarantee that, during the coming year, they will find cost reductions in the customer's plant that meet or exceed the price difference between Lincoln's products and the competition's. If they fail, they will rebate the difference. Lincoln then sends in its expert production team to identify and propose specific customer cost savings. If an independent audit at the end of the year does not reveal the promised cost savings, Lincoln Electric and the distributor compensate the customer for the difference, with Lincoln paying 70% and the distributor paying the rest.[26]

As part of the buyer selection process, buying centers must also decide how many suppliers to use. In the past, many companies preferred a large supplier base to ensure adequate supplies and to obtain price concessions. These companies would insist on annual negotiations for contract renewal and would often shift the amount of business they gave to each supplier from year to year. The company would normally place most of the year's order with a prime supplier, and the rest with secondary suppliers. The prime supplier would make an effort to protect its prime position, while the secondary suppliers would try to expand their share. Out-suppliers would meanwhile try to get their foot in the door by offering an especially low price.

Increasingly, however, companies are reducing the number of suppliers. Companies such as Ford, Motorola, and AlliedSignal have cut the number of suppliers anywhere from 20 to 80 percent. Furthermore, these companies want each chosen supplier to be responsible for a larger component system. They also often require the chosen suppliers to achieve continuous quality and performance improvement while at the same time lowering the supply price each year by a given percentage. These companies rely on their suppliers to work closely with them during product development and value their suggestions.

ORDER-ROUTINE SPECIFICATION. After the suppliers have been selected, the buyer negotiates the final order, listing the technical specifications, the quantity needed, the expected time of delivery, return policies, warranties, and so on. In the case of maintenance, repair, and operating items, buyers are increasingly moving toward blanket contracts rather than periodic purchase orders. Writing a new purchase order each time stock is needed is expensive and time-consuming. Nor does the buyer want to write fewer and larger purchase orders because that means carrying more inventory. A *blanket contract* establishes a long-term relationship in which the supplier promises to resupply the buyer as needed at agreed-upon prices over a specified period of time. Because the stock is held by the seller, blanket contracts are sometimes called *stockless purchase plans*. The buyer's computer automatically sends an order to the seller when stock is needed.

Blanket contracting leads to more single-source buying and ordering of more items from that single source. This system locks the supplier in tighter with the buyer and makes it difficult for out-suppliers to break in unless the buyer becomes dissatisfied with the in-supplier's prices, quality, or service.

PERFORMANCE REVIEW. When all is said and done, the buyer reviews the performance of the chosen supplier(s). Three methods are commonly used. The buyer may contact the end users and ask for their evaluations. Or the buyer may rate the supplier on several criteria using a weighted score method. Or the buyer might aggregate the cost of poor supplier performance to come up with adjusted costs of purchase, including price. The performance review may lead the buyer to continue, modify, or drop his relationship with the supplier. The supplier should monitor the same variables that are monitored by the product's buyers and end users.

We have described the buying stages involved in a new-task buying situation. In modified-rebuy or straight-rebuy situations, some of these stages would be compressed or bypassed. For example, in a straight-rebuy situation, the buyer normally has a favorite supplier or a ranked list of suppliers. Thus the supplier search and proposal solicitation stages would be skipped.

Buyflow Maps. The eight-stage buyphase model we've just described represents the major steps in the business buying process. Tracing out a *buyflow map* can provide many clues to the business marketer. A buyflow map for the purchase of a packaging machine in Japan is shown in Figure 7-3. The numbers within the icons are defined at the right. The italicized numbers between icons show the flow of events. Over 20 people in the purchasing company were involved, including the production manager and staff, the new-product committee, the company laboratory, the marketing department, and the department for market development. The entire decision-making process took 121 days.

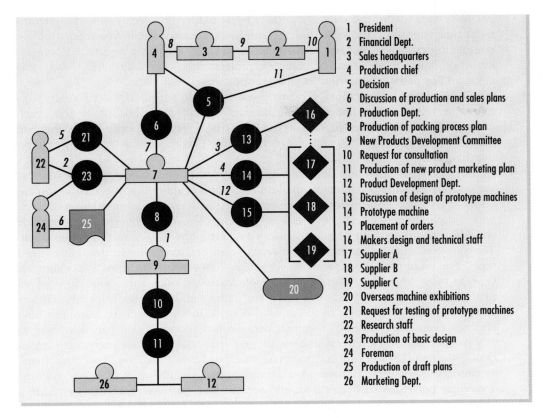

1	President
2	Financial Dept.
3	Sales headquarters
4	Production chief
5	Decision
6	Discussion of production and sales plans
7	Production Dept.
8	Production of packing process plan
9	New Products Development Committee
10	Request for consultation
11	Production of new product marketing plan
12	Product Development Dept.
13	Discussion of design of prototype machines
14	Prototype machine
15	Placement of orders
16	Makers design and technical staff
17	Supplier A
18	Supplier B
19	Supplier C
20	Overseas machine exhibitions
21	Request for testing of prototype machines
22	Research staff
23	Production of basic design
24	Foreman
25	Production of draft plans
26	Marketing Dept.

FIGURE 7-3

Organizational Buying Behavior in Japan: Packaging-Machine Purchase Process

Source: "Japanese Firms Use Unique Buying Behavior," *The Japan Economic Journal*, December 23, 1980, p. 29. Reprinted by permission.

INSTITUTIONAL AND GOVERNMENT MARKETS

Our discussion has concentrated largely on the buying behavior of profit-seeking companies. Much of what we said also applies to the buying practices of institutional and government organizations. However, we want to highlight certain special features found in these markets.

The *institutional market* consists of schools, hospitals, nursing homes, prisons, and other institutions that must provide goods and services to people in their care. Many of these organizations are characterized by low budgets and captive clienteles. For example, hospitals have to decide what quality of food to buy for the patients. The buying objective here is not profit, since the food is provided to the patients as part of the total service package. Nor is cost minimization the sole objective because poor food will cause patients to complain and hurt the hospital's reputation. The hospital purchasing agent has to search for institutional-food vendors whose quality meets or exceeds a certain minimum standard and whose prices are low. In fact, many food vendors set up a separate division to sell to institutional buyers because of these buyers' special buying needs and characteristics. Thus Heinz will produce, package, and price its ketchup differently to meet the different requirements of hospitals, colleges, and prisons.

In most countries, government organizations are a major buyer of goods and services. Government organizations typically require suppliers to submit bids, and normally they award the contract to the lowest bidder. In some cases, the government unit will make allowance for the supplier's superior quality or reputation for completing contracts on time. Governments will also buy on a negotiated contract basis, primarily in the case of complex projects involving major R&D costs and risks, and in cases where there is little competition.

Government organizations tend to favor domestic suppliers over foreign suppliers. A major complaint of multinationals operating in Europe is that each country shows favoritism toward its nationals in spite of superior offers that are made by foreign firms. The European Economic Commission is gradually removing this bias.

Because their spending decisions are subject to public review, government organizations require considerable paperwork from suppliers, who often complain about excessive paperwork, bureaucracy, regulations, decision-making delays, and frequent shifts in procurement personnel. Most governments provide would-be suppliers with detailed guides describing how to sell to the government. Yet suppliers still have to master the system and find ways to cut through the red tape. For example, the federal government has always been ADI Technology Corp.'s most important client—federal contracts account for about 90% of its nearly $6 million in annual revenues. Yet managers at this professional services company often shake their heads at all the work that goes into winning the coveted government contracts. A comprehensive bid proposal will run from 500 to 700 pages because of federal paperwork requirements. And, the company's president estimates that the firm has spent as much as $20,000, mostly in worker hours, to prepare a single bid proposal. Fortunately for businesses of all sizes, reforms are being put in place that will simplify contracting procedure and make bidding more attractive, particularly to smaller vendors. Some of these reforms are more emphasis on buying commercial off-the-shelf items instead of items built to the government's specs, online communication with vendors to eliminate the massive paperwork, and a "debriefing" from the appropriate government agency for vendors who lose a bid, enabling them to increase their chances of winning the next time around.[27]

Many companies that sell to the government have not manifested a marketing orientation—for a number of reasons. The government's procurement policies have traditionally emphasized price, leading the suppliers to invest considerable effort in bringing their costs down. Where the product's characteristics are carefully specified, product differentiation is not a marketing factor. Nor are advertising and personal selling of much consequence in winning bids.

Several companies, however, have established separate government marketing departments. Rockwell, Kodak, and Goodyear are examples. These companies anticipate government needs and projects, participate in the product specification phase, gather competitive intelligence, prepare bids carefully, and produce stronger communications to describe and enhance their companies' reputations.[28]

SUMMARY

1. *Organizational buying* is the decision-making process by which formal organizations establish the need for purchased products and services, then identify, evaluate, and choose among alternative brands and suppliers. The *business market* consists of all the organizations that acquire goods and services used in the production of other products or services that are sold, rented, or supplied to others.

2. Compared to consumer markets, business markets generally have fewer and larger buyers, a closer customer-supplier relationship, and more geographically concentrated buyers. Demand in the business market is derived from demand in the consumer market and fluctuates with the business cycle. Nonetheless, the total demand for many business goods and services is quite price-inelastic. Business marketers need to be aware of the role of professional purchasers and their influencers, as well as the importance of direct purchasing, reciprocity, and leasing.

3. The buying center is the decision-making unit of a buying organization. It consists of initiators, users, influencers, deciders, approvers, buyers, and gatekeepers. To sell to each of these parties, marketers must be aware of environmental, organizational, interpersonal, and individual factors. Environmental factors include the level of demand for the product, the economic outlook, interest rate, rate of technological change, political and regulatory developments, competitive developments, and social responsibility concerns. At the organizational level, marketers must be aware of their clients' objectives, policies, procedures, organizational structures, and systems, as well as trends toward purchasing-department upgrading, centralized purchasing in multidivisional companies, decentralized purchasing of small ticket items, long-term contracts, and increasing incentives for purchasing agents. At the interpersonal level, the buying center includes participants with different interests, authority, status, empathy, and persuasiveness. An individual's approach to the buying process is affected by his or her age, income, education, job position, personality, attitudes toward risk, and culture.

4. The buying process consists of eight stages called *buyphases:* (1) problem recognition, (2) general need description, (3) product specification, (4) supplier search, (5) proposal solicitation, (6) supplier selection, (7) order-routine specification, and (8) performance review. As business buyers become more sophisticated, business-to-business marketers must upgrade their marketing capabilities.

5. The *institutional market* consists of schools, hospitals, nursing homes, prisons, and other institutions that must provide goods and services to people in their care. Institutional buyers tend to be less concerned with profit or cost minimization than industrial buyers. Buyers for government organizations tend to require a great deal of paperwork from their vendors and tend to favor open bidding and domestic companies. Suppliers must be prepared to adapt their offers to the special needs and procedures found in institutional and government markets.

CONCEPT APPLICATIONS

1. City Hall in Zenobia, Michigan—a city with a population of 45,000—is planning to buy a new mainframe computer to assist in all areas of running the city, from public-works administration to tax collection. The people who will make the decision regarding which computer to buy (the deciders) are City Hall's computer center and the city manager. Who are the other participants in the buying process? Assess the amount of influence each participant or group would have in the decision process.

2. The emphasis on relationship marketing is gaining momentum in business-to-business marketing. Before adopting relationship marketing, top management should have a good understanding of what the term means. Offer a definition of relationship marketing. What key elements must exist for it to be successful? Before adopting this long-term marketing management philosophy, what questions should a company ask about itself and the companies with which it will form relationships? What outcomes should each party in the relationship expect from the long-term relationship?

3. Caterpillar has decided to focus more of its marketing efforts on international markets. Top management realizes that there are cultural differences between Asian companies and U.S. companies and that these differences influence business buying behavior. However, they are not sure which areas of behavior are most likely to affect marketing communications. Evaluate U.S. versus Japanese approaches to the following topics, and

Analyzing Business
Markets and Business
Buying Behavior

discuss how these differences might affect how a U.S. sales negotiator for Caterpillar should attempt to sell to a Japanese customer:

a. Individual decision making versus majority rule (How are decisions made in each country—individually or as a group?)

b. Time orientation (How does each culture feel about time?)

c. Achievement orientation (How focused on results is each culture?)

d. Action orientation (How much emphasis does each culture place on action? How much does each culture value silence?)

e. Length and depth of business relationships (How important are relationships between companies in each nation?)

4. How do the buying influences on the government buyer differ from those on the producer or reseller buyer? How do these differences affect those companies attempting to sell to the government?

5. A professional purchasing agent's decision process is more elaborate when greater risk is involved. How would a purchasing agent be likely to behave in each of the following buying situations? For each situation, how likely is the buyer to get other people in the organization involved? Which situation is likely to take the most time for the buyer to reach a decision? Which situation is a new task, which is a modified rebuy, and which is a straight rebuy?

a. The agent needs to purchase a custom-designed machine to manufacture steering columns for vehicles.

b. The agent is purchasing brake systems from a regular supplier. The buyer has bought brake systems from this supplier before.

c. The agent is purchasing improved and updated motherboards for PCs from a recognized and well-respected supplier. However, this supplier did not supply the current motherboards.

6. The market for prescription drugs is unique in many ways. Prescription drug makers must convince a third party—a physician—to "sell" their product to the ultimate consumer, the patient. In other words, the decider in this business-to-business transaction is the physician, and drug manufacturers' promotional efforts have traditionally been directed toward this member of the buying center. Today drug firms are appealing directly to buyers and encouraging them to ask their doctors about specific drugs. Using the outline in Figure 7-2 on page 211, analyze the four major influences (environmental, organizational, interpersonal, and individual) that affect the sales efforts of a pharmaceutical manufacturer like Hoechst Marion Roussel.

7. You are the leader of a sales team for an industrial seller of rubber hoses. Next week you are scheduled to meet with the buying team for Saturn. You have observed the following buyer behavior on the part of members on this buying team.

Dan Beavens	Bill Smith	Cathy Jones	Phil Hazard
critical	pushy	supportive	enthusiastic
picky	tough	respectful	egotistical
serious	dominating	dependable	ambitious
orderly	efficient	agreeable	excitable
exacting	decisive	conferring	dramatic
persistent	practical	pliable	undisciplined

Prepare a sales strategy for dealing with each member of Saturn's buying team.

8. You are the marketing manager for a wholesale distributor of chemicals. What kinds of concerns would you have in distributing products for manufacturer-suppliers like Celanese and Dow?

9. Over the years, the steel industry witnessed the erosion of its market as aluminum-can manufacturers took the beverage-container market away from steel manufacturers. The

FIGURE I

Source: Used by permission of the American Iron and Steel Institute.

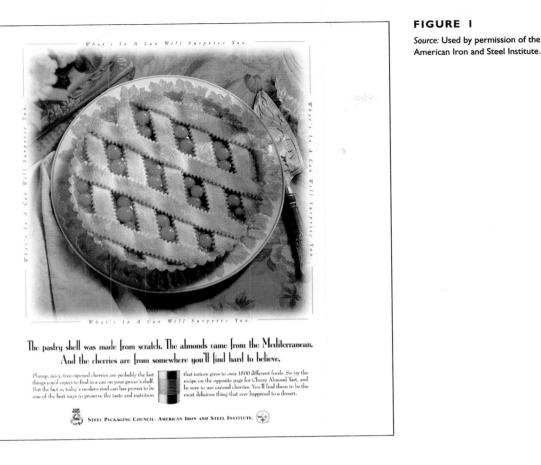

steel industry does not want to see the same thing happen in the canned-food industry and has produced the advertisement shown in Figure 1. Where should ads like this be placed? What other methods might the steel industry use to convince its markets of the value of packaging food in cans?

NOTES

1. Frederick E. Webster, Jr., and Yoram Wind, *Organizational Buying Behavior* (Englewood Cliffs, NJ: Prentice Hall, 1972), p. 2.
2. Myron Magnet, "The New Golden Rule of Business," *Fortune,* February 21, 1994, pp. 60–64.
3. For more on derived demand, see Karl E. Case and Ray C. Fair, *Principles of Economics,* 4th ed. (Upper Saddle River, NJ: Prentice Hall, 1996).
4. Tom Stundza, "Still on a Roll!" *Purchasing,* February 16, 1995, pp. 32B1–32B5.
5. Minda Zetlin, "It's All the Same to Me," *Sales and Marketing Management,* February 1994, pp. 71–75.
6. Weld F. Royal, "Good-Bye, Good Ol' Boys," *Sales and Marketing Management,* December 1994, p. 12.
7. Patrick J. Robinson, Charles W. Faris, and Yoram Wind, *Industrial Buying and Creative Marketing* (Boston: Allyn & Bacon, 1967).
8. See Daniel H. McQuiston, "Novelty, Complexity, and Importance as Causal Determinants of Industrial Buyer Behavior," *Journal of Marketing,* April 1989, pp. 66–79, and Peter Doyle, Arch G. Woodside, and Paul Mitchell, "Organizational Buying in New Task and Rebuy Situations," *Industrial Marketing Management,* February 1979, pp. 7–11.
9. Urban B. Ozanne and Gilbert A. Churchill, Jr., "Five Dimensions of the Industrial Adoption Process," *Journal of Marketing Research,* 1971, pp. 322–28.
10. See Donald W. Jackson, Jr., Janet E. Keith, and Richard K. Burdick, "Purchasing Agents' Perceptions of Industrial Buying Center Influence: A Situational Approach," *Journal of Marketing,* Fall 1984, pp. 75–83.
11. Webster and Wind, *Organizational Buying Behavior,* p. 6.
12. Webster and Wind, *Organizational Buying Behavior,* pp. 78–80.
13. See " 'I Think You Have a Great Product, But It's Not My Decision,' " *American Salesman,* April 1994, pp. 11–13.
14. " 'I Think You Have a Great Product.' "

15. Melvin R. Mattson and Esmail Salshi-Sangari, "Decision Making in Purchases of Equipment and Materials: A Four-Country Comparison," *International Journal of Physical Distribution and Logistics Management,* 23, no. 8 (1993), 16–30.

16. Webster and Wind, *Organizational Buying Behavior,* pp. 33–37.

17. Minette E. Drumwright, "Socially Responsible Organizational Buying: Environmental Concern as a Noneconomic Buying Criterion," *Journal of Marketing,* July 1994, pp. 1–19.

18. Shawn Tully, "Purchasing's New Muscle," *Fortune,* February 20, 1995, pp. 75–79, 82–83.

19. Tully, "Purchasing's New Muscle," Mark Fitzgerald, "Decentralizing Control of Purchasing," *Editor and Publisher,* June 18, 1994, pp. 8, 10.

20. See "*Purchasing* Honors First Hall-of-Fame Inductees," *Purchasing,* January 14, 1993, pp. 25–28.

21. Adapted from Susan Harte, "When in Rome, You Should Learn to Do What the Romans Do," *The Atlanta Journal-Constitution,* January 22, 1990, pp. D1, D6. Also see Lufthansa's *Business Travel Guide/Europe.*

22. Robinson, Faris, and Wind, *Industrial Buying.*

23. See Allen M. Weiss and Jan B. Heide, "The Nature of Organizational Search in High Technology Markets," *Journal of Marketing Research,* May 1993, pp. 220–33, and William A. Dempsey, "Vendor Selection and the Buying Process," *Industrial Marketing Management,* Vol. 7 (1978), 257–67.

24. See "Xerox Multinational Supplier Quality Survey," *Purchasing,* January 12, 1995, p. 112.

25. See Donald R. Lehmann and John O'Shaughnessy, "Differences in Attribute Importance for Different Industrial Products," *Journal of Marketing,* April 1974, pp. 36–42.

26. See James A. Narus and James C. Anderson, "Turn Your Industrial Distributors into Partners," *Harvard Business Review,* March–April 1986, pp. 66–71.

27. Laura M. Litvan, "Selling to Uncle Sam: New, Easier Rules," *Nation's Business,* March 1995, pp. 46–48.

28. See Warren H. Suss, "How to Sell to Uncle Sam," *Harvard Business Review,* November–December 1984, pp. 136–44; and Don Hill, "Who Says Uncle Sam's a Tough Sell?" *Sales and Marketing Management,* July 1988, pp. 56–60.

ANALYZING INDUSTRIES AND COMPETITORS

Marketing is merely a civilized form of warfare in which most battles are won with words, ideas, and disciplined thinking.

ALBERT W. EMERY

An opponent is our helper.

EDMUND BURKE

The previous two chapters examined the dynamics of consumer and business markets. The question facing any company is whether to invest in a particular market given its dynamics. Much depends on the nature and intensity of competition in that market. This chapter examines the role that competition plays in determining a market's attractiveness.

Michael Porter of Harvard identified five forces that determine the intrinsic long-run profit attractiveness of a market or market segment. His model is shown in Figure 8-1. The five forces are industry competitors, potential entrants, substitutes, buyers, and suppliers. The five threats they pose are as follows:

1. *Threat of intense segment rivalry:* A segment is unattractive if it already contains numerous, strong, or aggressive competitors. It is even more unattractive if the segment is stable or declining, if plant capacity additions are done in large increments, if fixed costs are high, if exit barriers are high, or if competitors have high stakes in staying in the segment. These conditions will lead to frequent price wars, advertising battles, and new-product introductions and will make it expensive for the companies to compete.

2. *Threat of new entrants:* A segment's attractiveness varies with the height of its entry and exit barriers.[1] The most attractive segment is one in which entry barriers are high and exit barriers are low (Figure 8-2, page 230). Few new firms can enter the industry, and poor-performing firms can easily exit. When both entry and exit barriers are high, profit potential is high, but firms face more risk because poorer-performing firms stay in and fight it out. When entry and exit barriers are both low, firms easily enter and leave the industry, and the returns are stable and low. The worst case is when entry barriers are low and exit barriers are high: Here firms enter during good times but find it hard to leave during bad times. The result is chronic overcapacity and depressed earnings for all.

3. *Threat of substitute products:* A segment is unattractive when there are actual or potential substitutes for the product. Substitutes place a limit on prices and on the profits that a segment can earn. The company has to watch closely the price trends in the substitutes. If technology advances or competition increases in these substitute industries, prices and profits in the segment are likely to fall.

4. *Threat of buyers' growing bargaining power:* A segment is unattractive if the buyers possess strong or growing bargaining power. Buyers will try to force prices down, demand more quality or services, and set competitors against one another, all at the expense of seller profitability. Buyers' bargaining power grows when they become more concentrated or organized, when the product represents a significant fraction of the buyers' costs, when the product is undifferentiated, when the buyers' switching costs are low, when buyers are price sensitive because of low profits, or when buyers can integrate upstream. To protect themselves, sellers might select buyers who have the least power to negotiate or switch suppliers. A better defense consists of developing superior offers that strong buyers cannot refuse.

5. *Threat of suppliers' growing bargaining power:* A segment is unattractive if the company's suppliers are able to raise prices or reduce quantity supplied. Suppliers tend to be powerful when they are concentrated or organized, when there are few substitutes, when the supplied product is an important input, when the costs of switching suppliers are high, and when the suppliers can integrate downstream. The best defenses are to build win-win relations with suppliers or use multiple supply sources.

The first three forces in Porter's model allude explicitly to competitors. Clearly, competition is not only rife but growing more intense every year. Many companies are setting up production in Eastern Europe to bring cheaper goods into the West. To compete more effectively, the European Union is removing trade barriers among Western European countries, while NAFTA is removing trade barriers among the United States, Canada, and Mexico.

These developments go a long way toward explaining the current talk about "marketing warfare," "competitive intelligence systems," and similar themes.[2] Because markets have become so competitive, understanding customers is no longer enough. The result is that companies must start paying as much attention to their competitors as to their target customers. Successful companies design and operate systems for gathering continuous intelligence about their competitors.[3]

Knowing one's competitors is critical to effective marketing planning. A company must constantly compare its products, prices, channels, and promotion with those of its competitors. In this way, it can identify areas of competitive advantage and disadvantage. The company can launch more precise attacks on its competitors as well as prepare stronger defenses against attacks.

Companies need to know five things about competitors:

- **Who are our competitors?**
- **What are their strategies?**
- **What are their objectives?**
- **What are their strengths and weaknesses?**
- **What are their reaction patterns?**

Companies also need to know how to design a competitive intelligence system, which competitors to attack and which to avoid, and how to balance customer and competitor orientations.

IDENTIFYING COMPETITORS

It would seem a simple task for a company to identify its competitors. Coca-Cola knows that Pepsi-Cola is its major competitor, and Sony knows that Matsushita is a major competitor.[4] But the range of a company's actual and potential competitors is actually much broader. A company is more likely to be outdone by its emerging competitors or new technologies than by its current competitors. Here are two vivid examples:

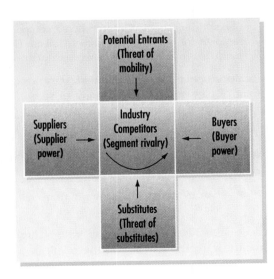

FIGURE 8-1

Five Forces Determining Segment Structural Attractiveness

Source: Reprinted with the permission of The Free Press, an imprint of Simon & Schuster from *Competitive Advantage: Creating and Sustaining Superior Performance* by Michael E. Porter. Copyright © 1985 by Michael E. Porter.

CHAPTER 8   **229**

Analyzing
Industries and
Competitors

FIGURE 8-2
Barriers and Profitability

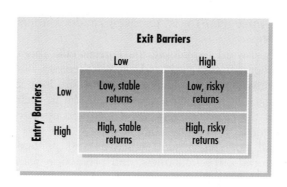

Eastman Kodak In its film business, Kodak has been worrying about the growing competition from Fuji, the Japanese film maker. But Kodak faces a much greater long-term threat from the recent invention of the filmless camera. This camera, sold by Canon and Sony, takes video still pictures that can be shown on a TV, turned into hard copy, and even erased. What greater threat is there to a film business than a filmless camera?

Unilever Along with other detergent manufacturers, Unilever is nervous about research being done on an ultrasonic washing machine. If perfected, this machine would wash clothes in water with little or no detergent. So far, it can clean only certain kinds of dirt and fabrics. What greater threat is there to the detergent business than an ultrasonic washing machine?

We can distinguish four levels of competition, based on the degree of product substitutability:

1. *Brand competition:* Occurs when a company sees its competitors as other companies offering a similar product and services to the same customers at similar prices. Thus Buick might see its major competitors as Ford, Toyota, Honda, Renault, and other manufacturers of moderate-price automobiles. But it would not see itself as competing with Mercedes on the one hand, or with Hyundai on the other.

2. *Industry competition:* Occurs when a company sees its competitors as all companies making the same product or class of products. Here Buick would see itself as competing against all other automobile manufacturers.

3. *Form competition:* Occurs when a company sees its competitors as all companies manufacturing products that supply the same service. Here Buick would see itself competing against not only other automobile manufacturers but also manufacturers of motorcycles, bicycles, and trucks.

4. *Generic competition:* Occurs when a company sees its competitors as all companies that compete for the same consumer dollars. Here Buick would see itself competing with companies that sell major consumer durables, foreign vacations, and new homes.

More specifically, we can identify a company's competitors from an industry point of view and a market point of view.

Industry Concept of Competition

We talk about the auto industry, the oil industry, the pharmaceutical industry, and so on. But what exactly is an industry?

❖ An **Industry** is a group of firms that offer a product or class of products that are close substitutes for each other.

Analyzing
Marketing
Opportunities

Close substitutes are products with a high *cross-elasticity of demand:* If the demand for a product rises as the result of a price increase for another product, the two products are close substitutes. For example, if the price of Japanese cars rises and people switch to American cars, then American cars and Japanese cars are close substitutes.

Industries are classified according to number of sellers, degree of product differentiation; presence or absence of entry, mobility, exit, and shrinkage barriers; cost structure; degree of vertical integration; and degree of globalization.

NUMBER OF SELLERS AND DEGREE OF DIFFERENTIATION. The starting point for describing an industry is to specify whether there are one, few, or many sellers of the product and whether the product is homogeneous or highly differentiated. These characteristics give rise to four well-known industry structure types:

- *Pure monopoly:* Exists when only one firm provides a certain product or service in a certain country or area (U.S. Post Office, local electricity company). This monopoly might be the result of a regulatory edict, patent, license, scale economies, or other factors. An unregulated monopolist that seeks to maximize profits would charge a high price, do little or no advertising, and offer minimal service, since customers have to buy its product in the absence of close substitutes. If partial substitutes are available and there is some danger of imminent competition, the pure monopolist might invest in more service and technology to preserve its market share. A regulated monopoly is required to charge a lower price and provide more service as a matter of public interest.

- *Oligopoly:* An industry structure in which a small number of (usually) large firms produce products that range from highly differentiated to standardized. There are two forms of oligopoly, pure and differentiated. *Pure oligopoly* consists of a few companies producing essentially the same commodity (oil, steel, and so on). A company in a purely oligopolistic industry would find it hard to charge anything more than the going price unless it can differentiate its services. If the competitors match on services, then the only way to gain a competitive advantage is through lower costs. Lower costs can be achieved by pursuing a higher volume strategy. *Differentiated oligopoly* consists of a few companies producing partially differentiated products (autos, cameras, and so on). The differentiation can occur along lines of quality, features, styling, or services. Each competitor may seek leadership in one of these major attributes, attract the customers favoring that attribute, and charge a price premium for that attribute.

- *Monopolistic competition:* Consists of many competitors able to differentiate their offers in whole or part (restaurants, beauty shops). Many of the competitors focus on market segments where they can meet customer needs in a superior way and command a price premium.

- *Pure competition:* Consists of many competitors offering the same product and service (stock market, commodity market). Since there is no basis for differentiation, competitors' prices will be the same. No competitor will advertise unless advertising can create psychological differentiation (cigarettes, beer), in which case it would be more proper to describe the industry as monopolistically competitive. Sellers will enjoy different profit rates only to the extent that they achieve lower costs of production or distribution.

An industry's competitive structure can change over time. Consider the case when Sony innovated the Walkman. Sony started as a monopolist, but soon a few other companies entered the market, turning the industry into an oligopoly. As more competitors began to offer their version of a Walkman, the industry took on a monopolistically competitive structure. When demand growth slowed down, some competitors exited from the industry, returning it to an oligopoly.

ENTRY AND MOBILITY BARRIERS. Industries differ greatly in their ease of entry—that is, how easy it is for a new firm to enter a market that is showing attractive profits. It is easy to open a new restaurant but difficult to enter the aircraft industry. The major *entry barriers* include high capital requirements; economies of scale; patents and licensing requirements; scarce locations, raw materials, or distributors; and reputational requirements. Some barriers are intrinsic to certain industries, and others are erected by the single or combined actions of the incumbent firms. Even after a firm enters an industry, it might face *mobility barriers* when it tries to enter more attractive market segments. This is what happened in the early 1980s when PepsiCo tried to move its Grandma's brand cookies from their niche in the vending machine market to the supermarket shelves. The small brand was not able to fight the big-time marketing muscle of cookie market kings Nabisco and Keebler.

EXIT AND SHRINKAGE BARRIERS. Ideally, firms should be free to leave industries in which profits are unattractive, but they often face *exit barriers*.[5] Among the most common exit barriers are legal or moral obligations to customers, creditors, and employees; government restrictions; low asset salvage value due to overspecialization or obsolescence; lack of alternative opportunities; high vertical integration; and emotional barriers. Many firms persevere in an industry as long as they cover their variable costs and some or all of their fixed costs. Their continued presence, however, dampens profits for everyone. Companies that want to stay in the industry should lower the exit barriers for others. They can offer to buy competitors' assets, meet customer obligations, and so on.

Even if some firms do not want to exit the industry, they might want to decrease their size. Here, companies should try to reduce the *shrinkage barriers* to help their ailing competitors get smaller gracefully.[6] Two of the most common shrinkage barriers are contract commitments and stubborn management.

COST STRUCTURE. Each industry has a certain cost mix that drives much of its strategic conduct. For example, steelmaking involves heavy manufacturing and raw-material costs, while toy manufacturing involves heavy distribution and marketing costs. Firms will pay the greatest attention to their greatest costs and will strategize to reduce these costs. Thus the steel company with the most modern (i.e., most cost-efficient) plant will have a great advantage over other steel companies.

DEGREE OF VERTICAL INTEGRATION. In some industries, companies find it advantageous to integrate backward and/or forward *(vertical integration)*. A good example is the oil industry, where major oil producers carry on oil exploration, oil drilling, oil refining, chemical manufacture, and service-station operation. Vertical integration often lowers costs and gives the company more control over the value-added stream. In addition, vertically integrated firms can manipulate their prices and costs in different segments of their business to earn profits where taxes are lowest. However, vertical integration can create certain disadvantages, such as being stuck with high costs in certain parts of the value chain and a certain lack of flexibility.

DEGREE OF GLOBALIZATION. Some industries are highly local (such as lawn care); others are global (such as oil, aircraft engines, cameras). Companies in global industries need to compete on a global basis if they are to achieve economies of scale and keep up with the latest advances in technology.[7] Consider, for example, how U.S. forklift manufacturers lost their market leadership:

THE FORKLIFT INDUSTRY Less than 20 years ago, five companies dominated the U.S. forklift market—Clark Equipment, Caterpillar, Allis and Chalmers, Hyster, and Yale. By 1992, debt-burdened Clark prepared to sell its assets for a mere $95 million, and Caterpillar was the minor partner in an 80%–20% venture with Mitsubishi. Only Hyster held on to its market share while Japanese manufacturers ate into the forklift market. By speeding up product development, concentrating on low-end models, and moving some production to job-hungry Ireland, Hyster was able to compete against Nissan, Toyota, and Komatsu. Hyster also filed an antidumping suit against Japanese models, claiming that these were priced below cost, and won the case. Meanwhile, Clark invested in some expensive features on new models that buyers did not want. Caterpillar made the mistake of trying to sell its forklifts through its heavy earth-moving equipment dealers, who did not have any enthusiasm for selling the low-margin forklifts. Clark and Caterpillar moved some production to South Korea but encountered even higher costs because Korean labor costs rose sharply and because of the need to carry larger inventories at home due to shipment delays.

Market Concept of Competition

In addition to looking at companies making the same product (the industry approach), we can look at companies that satisfy the same customer need (the market approach). For example, a manufacturer of word processing software normally sees its competition as other word processing software manufacturers. From a customer-need point of view, however, a customer who buys a word processing package really wants "writing ability." This need can be satisfied by pencils, pens, typewriters, and so on. In general, the market concept of competition opens the company's eyes to a broader set of actual and potential competitors and stimulates more long-run strategic market planning.

The key to identifying competitors is to link industry analysis with market analysis by mapping out the *product/market battlefield*. Figure 8-3 illustrates the product/market battlefield map in the toothpaste market according to product types and customer age groups. We see that P&G and Colgate-Palmolive occupy nine segments; Lever Brothers, three; Beecham, two; and Topol, two. If Topol wanted to enter other segments, it would need to estimate each segment's market size; competitors' market shares in each segment; competitors' capabilities, objectives, and strategies; and the entry barriers in each segment.

IDENTIFYING COMPETITORS' STRATEGIES

A company's closest competitors are those pursuing the same target markets with the same strategy. A group of firms following the same strategy in a given target market is called a *strategic group*.[8] A company needs to identify the strategic group in which it competes.

FIGURE 8-3
Product/Market Battlefield Map for Toothpaste

Source: William A. Cohen, *Winning on the Marketing Front: The Corporate Manager's Game* (New York: John Wiley, 1986), p. 63.

Product segmentation	Customer segmentation		
	Children/Teens	Age 19–35	Age 36+
Plain toothpaste	Colgate-Palmolive Procter & Gamble	Colgate-Palmolive Procter & Gamble	Colgate-Palmolive Procter & Gamble
Toothpaste with fluoride	Colgate-Palmolive Procter & Gamble	Colgate-Palmolive Procter & Gamble	Colgate-Palmolive Procter & Gamble
Gel	Colgate-Palmolive Procter & Gamble Lever Bros.	Colgate-Palmolive Procter & Gamble Lever Bros.	Colgate-Palmolive Procter & Gamble Lever Bros.
Striped	Beecham	Beecham	
Smoker's toothpaste		Topol	Topol

FIGURE 8-4
Strategic Groups in the
Major Appliance Industry

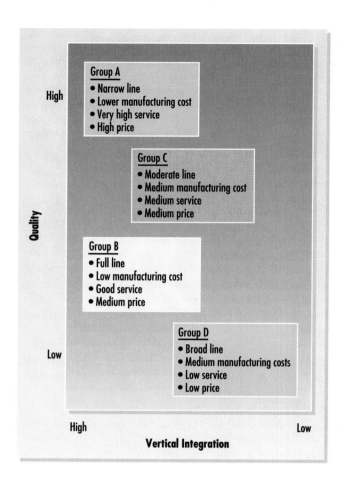

Suppose a company wants to enter the major appliance industry, and two important strategic dimensions of this industry are quality image and vertical integration. The company develops the chart shown in Figure 8-4 and discovers that there are four strategic groups. Strategic group A consists of one competitor (Maytag). Strategic group B consists of three major competitors (General Electric, Whirlpool, and Sears). Strategic group C consists of four competitors, and strategic group D consists of two competitors.

Important insights emerge from this strategic-group identification. First, the height of the entry barriers differs for each strategic group. A new company would find it easiest to enter group D because doing so requires minimal investment in vertical integration and in quality components and reputation. The company would find it hardest to enter group A or group B because both require high investment in quality and vertical integration. Second, if the company successfully enters one of the groups, the members of that group become its key competitors. Thus if the company enters group B, it will need strength primarily against General Electric, Whirlpool, and Sears. It will need to possess some competitive advantage if it hopes to succeed.

Although competition is most intense within a strategic group, there is often rivalry between the groups as well, for several reasons. First, some strategic groups may appeal to overlapping customer groups. For example, major appliance manufacturers with different strategies might nevertheless all go after high-rise apartment builders. Second, customers might not see much difference in the different strategic groups' offers. Third, each group might want to expand its market share, especially if the companies are fairly equal in size and power and the mobility barriers between groups are low.

Figure 8-4 uses only two dimensions to identify strategic groups within an industry. Other dimensions include level of technological sophistication, geographical scope, manufacturing methods, and so on. In fact, each competitor should be more fully profiled than Figure 8-4 suggests. A company needs detailed information on each competitor's business, marketing, manufacturing, R&D, financial, and human resource strategies; product quality, features, and mix; customer services; pricing policy; distribution coverage; sales force strategy; and advertising and sales-promotion programs.

A company must continuously monitor its competitors' strategies. Resourceful competitors revise their strategy through time. For example, Ford was an early winner because it was successful in producing cars at low cost. Then GM surpassed Ford because it responded to the market's new wish for variety. Later, Japanese companies took leadership because they supplied cars with fuel economy. The Japanese next moved into producing cars with high reliability. When U.S. automakers just about caught up in quality, the Japanese automakers shifted to sensory qualities, namely the look and feel of the car and its various components. A former Ford engineer explained: "It's the turn-signal lever that doesn't wobble . . . the speed of the power window up and down . . . the feel of a climate-control knob . . . this is the next nuance of customer competition."[9]

Clearly, companies must be alert to changes in what customers want and to how competitors are revising their strategy to meet these emerging desires.

Determining Competitors' Objectives

Once a company has identified its main competitors and their strategies, it must ask: What is each competitor seeking in the marketplace? What drives each competitor's behavior?

A useful initial assumption is that competitors strive to maximize their profits. However, companies differ in the weights they put on short-term versus long-term profits. Furthermore, some companies orient their thinking around "satisficing" rather than maximizing—they set target profit goals and are satisfied when they achieve them, even if they could have produced more profits with other strategies or more effort.

An alternative assumption is that each competitor pursues a mix of objectives: current profitability, market share growth, cash flow, technological leadership, service leadership, and so on. Knowing how a competitor weighs each objective helps us figure out whether the competitor is satisfied with its current financial results, how it might react to different types of competitive attack, and so on. For example, a competitor pursuing low-cost leadership will react more strongly to a competitor that has reduced costs significantly than to an advertising budget increase by the same competitor.

The fact that competitors' goals can differ sharply is well illustrated by contrasting U.S. and Japanese firms. Most U.S. firms operate on a short-run profit-maximization model, largely because their current performance is judged by stockholders, who might lose confidence, sell their stock, and cause the company's cost of capital to rise. In contrast, Japanese firms operate largely on a market-share-maximization model. They receive much of their funds from banks at a lower interest rate and are satisfied with earning lower profits.

A competitor's objectives are shaped by many things, including its size, history, current management, financial situation, and place in the larger organization. If the competitor is part of a larger company, it is important to know whether the parent

Analyzing
Industries and
Competitors

company is running it for growth or milking it. If the competitor is not critical to its parent company, it could be attacked more readily. Rothschild contends that the worst competitor to attack is the one for whom this is the only business and who has a global operation.[10]

Finally, a company must also monitor its competitors' expansion plans. Figure 8-5 shows a product/market battlefield map for the personal computer industry. It appears that Dell, which is a strong force in selling personal computers to individual users, is adding hardware accessories and also pursuing commercial and industrial buyers. The other incumbents in these segments (not shown) are therefore forewarned and may want to set up mobility barriers to Dell's expansion.

ASSESSING COMPETITORS' STRENGTHS AND WEAKNESSES

Whether a company's competitors can carry out their strategies and reach their goals depends on each competitor's resources and capabilities. As the first step in identifying its competitors' strengths and weaknesses, a company should gather recent information on each competitor's business, including data on sales, market share, profit margin, return on investment, cash flow, new investment, and capacity utilization. Some of this information will be difficult to collect. For example, industrial-goods companies find it hard to estimate competitors' market shares because no syndicated data services serve that industry.

Companies normally learn about their competitors' strengths and weaknesses through secondary data, personal experience, and hearsay. They can augment their knowledge by conducting primary marketing research with customers, suppliers, and dealers. All these sources helped a company decide whom to attack in the programmable-controls market:

> A company made a decision to enter the programmable-controls market. It faced three entrenched competitors: Allen Bradley, Texas Instruments, and Gould. Its research showed that Allen Bradley had an excellent reputation for technological leadership; Texas Instruments had low costs and engaged in bloody battles for market share; and Gould did a good job but not a distinguished job. The company concluded that its best target was Gould.

Table 8-1 shows the results of a company survey that asked customers to rate its three competitors, A, B, and C, on five attributes. Competitor A turns out to be well known and respected for producing high-quality products sold by a good sales force. However, competitor A is poor at providing product availability and technical assistance. Competitor B is good across the board and excellent in product availability and sales force. Competitor C rates poor to fair on most attributes. This information suggests that our company could attack competitor A on product

FIGURE 8-5
A Competitor's Expansion Plans

236   PART 2

Analyzing
Marketing
Opportunities

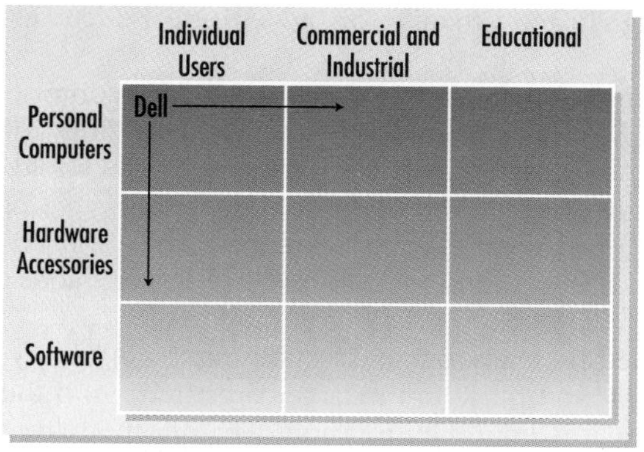

TABLE 8-1

	CUSTOMER AWARENESS	PRODUCT QUALITY	PRODUCT AVAILABILITY	TECHNICAL ASSISTANCE	SELLING STAFF
Competitor A	E	E	P	P	G
Competitor B	G	G	E	G	E
Competitor C	F	P	G	F	F

CUSTOMER'S RATINGS OF COMPETITORS ON KEY SUCCESS FACTORS

Note: E = excellent, G = good, F = Fair, P = poor.

availability and technical assistance and competitor C on almost anything, but should not attack competitor B, which has no glaring weakness.

In general, every company should monitor three variables when analyzing its competitors:

- *Share of market:* The competitor's share of the target market.
- *Share of mind:* The percentage of customers who named the competitor in responding to the statement, "Name the first company that comes to mind in this industry."
- *Share of heart:* The percentage of customers who named the competitor in responding to the statement, "Name the company from whom you would prefer to buy the product."

There is an interesting relationship among these three measures. Table 8-2 shows the numbers for these three measures for the three competitors listed in Table 8-1. Competitor A enjoys the highest market share, but it is falling. A partial explanation is provided by the fact that its mind share and heart share are also falling. This slip in customer awareness and preference is probably because competitor A, although providing a good product, is not providing good product availability and technical assistance. Competitor B is steadily gaining market share, probably due to strategies that are increasing its mind share and heart share. Competitor C seems to be stuck at a low level of market share, mind share, and heart share, given its poor product and marketing attributes. We could generalize as follows: *Companies that make steady gains in mind share and heart share will inevitably make gains in market share and profitability.*

In an attempt to improve their market share, many companies have begun *benchmarking* their most successful competitors. This technique, and the benefits that it brings, are described in the Marketing Insight titled "How Benchmarking Helps Improve Competitive Performance."

A final word: In searching for competitors' weaknesses, we should identify any assumptions they make about their business and the market that are no longer valid. Some companies believe they produce the best quality in the industry when they do not. Many companies mistakenly subscribe to conventional wisdom like "Customers prefer full-line companies," "The sales force is the only important marketing tool," and "Customers value service more than price." If we know that a competitor is operating on a major wrong assumption, we can take advantage of it.

TABLE 8-2   MARKET SHARE, MIND SHARE, AND HEART SHARE

	MARKET SHARE			MIND SHARE			HEART SHARE		
	1994	1995	1996	1994	1995	1996	1994	1995	1996
Competitor A	50%	47%	44%	60%	58%	54%	45%	42%	39%
Competitor B	30	34	37	30	31	35	44	47	53
Competitor C	20	19	19	10	11	11	11	11	8

How Benchmarking Helps Improve Competitive Performance

Benchmarking is the art of finding out how and why some companies can perform tasks much better than other companies. There can be as much as a tenfold difference in the quality, speed, and cost performance of an average company versus a world-class company.

The aim of benchmarking a company is to copy or improve upon its best practices. The Japanese used benchmarking assiduously in the post–World War II period, copying many U.S. products and practices. Xerox in 1979 undertook one of the first U.S. major benchmarking projects. Xerox wanted to learn how Japanese competitors were able to produce more reliable copiers and charge a price below Xerox's production costs. By buying Japanese copiers and analyzing them through "reverse engineering," Xerox learned how to greatly improve its own copiers' reliability and costs.

Another early benchmarking pioneer was Ford. Ford was losing sales to Japanese and European automakers. Don Peterson, then chairman of Ford, instructed his engineers and designers to build a new car that combined the 400 features that Ford customers said were the most important. If Saab made the best seats, then Ford should copy Saab's seats, and so on. Peterson went further: He asked his engineers to "better the best" where possible. When the new car (the highly successful Taurus) was finished, Peterson claimed that his engineers had improved upon, not just copied, most of the best features found in competitive automobiles.

Today many companies (including AT&T, IBM, Kodak, Du Pont, and Motorola) use benchmarking. Some companies benchmark only the best companies in their industry. Others choose to benchmark the "best practices" in the world. In this sense, benchmarking

goes beyond standard competitive analysis. Motorola, for example, starts each benchmarking project with a search for "best of breed" in the world. According to one Motorola executive, "The further away from our industry we reach for comparisons, the happier we are. We are seeking competitive superiority, after all, not just competitive parity."

As an example of seeking best of breed, Robert C. Camp, Xerox's benchmarking expert, flew to Freeport, Maine, to visit L. L. Bean to find out how Bean's warehouse workers managed to "pick and pack" items three times as fast as Xerox workers. On later occasions, Xerox benchmarked American Express for its billing expertise and Cummins Engine for its production scheduling expertise.

Benchmarking involves the following seven steps: (1) Determine which functions to benchmark; (2) identify the key performance variables to measure; (3) identify the best-in-class companies; (4) measure performance of best-in-class companies; (5) measure the company's performance; (6) specify programs and actions to close the gap; and (7) implement and monitor results.

How can a company identify "best-practice" companies? A good starting point is asking customers, suppliers, and distributors whom they rate as doing the best job. In addition, major consulting firms can be contacted because they have built voluminous files of best practices. To keep costs under control, a company should focus primarily on benchmarking those critical tasks that deeply affect customer satisfaction and company cost and where substantially better performance is known to exist.

Sources: Robert C. Camp, *Benchmarking: The Search for Industry-Best Practices That Lead to Superior Performance* (White Plains, NY: Quality Resources, 1989); Michael J. Spendolini, *The Benchmarking Book* (New York: Amacom, 1992); Jeremy Main, "How to Steal the Best Ideas Around," *Fortune,* October 19, 1992; A. Steven Walleck et al., "Benchmarking World Class Performance," *McKinsey Quarterly,* No. 1 (1990), 3–24; Otis Port, "Beg, Borrow—and Benchmark," *Business Week,* November 30, 1992, pp. 74–75; and Stanley Brown, "Don't Innovate—Imitate!" *Sales and Marketing Management,* January 1995, pp. 24–25.

ESTIMATING COMPETITORS' REACTION PATTERNS

Identifying a competitor's objectives and strengths/weaknesses goes a long way toward helping managers anticipate its likely reactions to other companies' strategies (for example, a price cut, a promotion step-up, or a new-product introduction). In addition, each competitor has a certain philosophy of doing business, a certain internal culture, and certain guiding beliefs. One needs a deep understanding of a competitor's mind-set to have hope of anticipating how it might act or react.

Most competitors fall into one of four categories:

1. *The laid-back competitor:* A competitor that does not react quickly or strongly to a rival's move. For example, when Miller introduced its Lite beer in the late 1970s, Anheuser-Busch rested on its laurels as beer-industry leader. Later, as Miller became more aggressive in its marketing and its Lite beer claimed a 60% market share, Anheuser-Busch roused itself to develop its own light beer.

   Reasons for a lack of response to competitive moves vary. Laid-back competitors may feel their customers are loyal; they may be milking the business; they may be slow in noticing the move; they may lack the funds to react. Rivals must try to assess the reasons for the competitors' laid-back behavior.

2. *The selective competitor:* A competitor that reacts only to certain types of attacks and not to others. It might respond to price cuts but not to advertising expenditure increases. Oil companies such as Shell and Exxon are selective competitors, responding only to competitors' price cuts but not to promotions, for instance. Knowing what a key competitor reacts to gives its rivals a clue as to the most feasible lines of attack.

3. *The tiger competitor:* A competitor that reacts swiftly and strongly to any assault on its terrain. Thus P&G does not let a new detergent come easily into the market. A tiger competitor is signaling that another firm had better not attack because the defender will fight to the finish. It is always better to attack a sheep than a tiger. Lever Brothers found this out during its first foray into the "ultra" detergent market pioneered by Proctor & Gamble. Ultras are more concentrated detergents that come in smaller bottles. Retailers like them because they take up less shelf space, yet when Lever introduced its Ultra versions of Wisk and Surf, it couldn't get shelf space for long. P&G vastly overspent Lever to support its own detergent brands.[11]

4. *The stochastic competitor:* A competitor that does not exhibit a predictable reaction pattern. Such a competitor might or might not retaliate on a particular occasion; there is no way of predicting this decision on the basis of its economic situation, history, or anything else. Many small businesses are stochastic competitors, competing on certain fronts when they can afford to wage a battle and holding back when competition is too costly.

Some industries are characterized by relative accord among the competitors, and others by constant fighting. Bruce Henderson thinks that much depends on the industry's "competitive equilibrium." Here are some of his observations about the likely state of competitive relations.[12]

1. *If competitors are nearly identical and make their living in the same way, then their competitive equilibrium is unstable.* There is likely to be perpetual conflict in industries where competitive differentiation is hard to maintain. This is the case in commodity industries such as steel or newsprint, where sellers have not found any major way to differentiate their costs or their offers. In such cases, the competitive equilibrium would be upset if any firm lowers its price—a strong temptation, especially for a competitor with overcapacity. This explains why price wars frequently break out in these industries.

2. *If a single major factor is the critical factor, then competitive equilibrium is unstable.* This is the case in industries where cost-differentiation opportunities exist through economies of scale, advanced technology, experience, or some other factor. In such industries, any company that achieves a cost breakthrough can cut its price and win market share at the expense of other firms, which can defend their market shares only at great cost. Price wars frequently break out in these industries as a result of cost breakthroughs.

3. *If multiple factors may be critical factors, then it is possible for each competitor to have some advantage and be differentially attractive to some customers. The more factors that may provide an advantage, the more competitors who can coexist. Competitors all have their competitive segment, defined by the preference for the factor trade-offs that they offer.* Multiple factors exist in industries where many opportunities exist to differentiate

quality, service, convenience, and so on. If customers place different values on these factors, then many firms can coexist through niching.

4. *The fewer the number of critical competitive variables, the fewer the number of competitors.* If only one factor is critical, then no more than two or three competitors are likely to coexist. Conversely, the more competitive variables, the more competitors.

5. *A ratio of 2 to 1 in market share between any two competitors seems to be the equilibrium point at which it is neither practical nor advantageous for either competitor to increase or decrease share.* At this level, the costs of extra promotion, distribution, and so forth would outweigh the gains in market share.

DESIGNING THE COMPETITIVE INTELLIGENCE SYSTEM

Gathering competitive information should not be a haphazard process. Rather, each company should carefully design its competitive intelligence system to be cost effective. Everyone in the company must not only sense, serve, and satisfy the customer but also be given an incentive to spot competitive information and pass it on to the relevant parties in the company. Sometimes cross-disciplinary teams are formed specifically for this purpose.

There are four main steps involved in designing a competitive intelligence system.

1. *Setting up the system:* The first step calls for identifying vital types of competitive information, identifying the best sources of this information, and assigning a person who will manage the system and its services.

2. *Collecting the data:* The data are collected on a continuous basis from the field (sales force, channels, suppliers, market research firms, trade associations), from recruits and competitors' employees, from people who do business with competitors, from observing competitors or analyzing physical evidence, and from published data (government publications, speeches, articles). In addition, a vast store of data on both domestic and overseas companies is available via CD-ROM and online services. (For more on this topic, see the Vision 2000 feature titled "CD-ROM and Online Services: Global Information at Your Fingertips.")

   Although most techniques of gathering information are legal, some involve questionable ethics. For example, companies have been known to advertise and hold interviews for jobs that don't exist in order to pump competitors' employees for information. Although it is illegal for a company to photograph a competitor's plant from the air, aerial photos are often on file with the U.S. Geological Survey or Environmental Protection Agency. Some companies even buy their competitors' garbage. Once it has left the competitor's premise, refuse is legally considered abandoned property.[13] Clearly, the company has to develop effective ways of acquiring needed information about competitors without violating legal or ethical standards. For some of the most effective of these techniques, see the Marketing Memo on page 242 titled "Outsmarting the Competition with Guerrilla Marketing Research."

3. *Evaluating and analyzing the data:* The data are checked for validity and reliability, interpreted, and organized.

4. *Disseminating information and responding:* Key information is sent to relevant decision makers, and managers' inquiries about competitors are answered.

With a well-designed system, company managers receive timely information about competitors via phone calls, bulletins, newsletters, and reports. Managers can also contact the market intelligence department when they need help interpreting a competitor's sudden move, when they need to know a competitor's weaknesses and strengths, or when they want to discuss a competitor's likely response to a contemplated company move.

CD-ROM and Online Services: Global Information at Your Fingertips

Where do marketers look if they need information on what their competitors are doing in Sweden or Singapore? Thanks to advances in technology, companies can now gather accurate and timely marketplace intelligence with CD-ROMs and electronic services such as America Online and CompuServe. Virtual libraries, which will allow the user to tap into online catalogs and call up texts, are also a possibility for the near future. Today, marketers are using the following global databases:

Europe
Globalbase is the new and revamped version of the former Infomat International business database. Now with abstracts from 800 current business periodicals from around the world (especially the United Kingdom and Europe), Globalbase has moved into new regions, namely Scandinavia and the Pacific Rim. Even Brunei and Papua New Guinea are included. The database concentrates on trade publications with special attention to several sectors: transportation; food and hospitality; electronics; health care; packaging, paper, and plastics; cosmetics; and chemicals.

Russia
Access Russia is a database that delivers business, scientific, and legal information in both English and Cyrillic. The database offers information that is not currently available on any other online or CD-ROM-based product, and provides timely, hard-to-find data that have previously been unavailable due to political, economic, or linguistic constraints. Databases included on the Access Russia CD-ROM, which premiered in 1993, are legislation and regulations, business and economics, and science and technology.

Japan
Although U.S. reports on Japanese business have long been available online, the emergence of English-language electronic data from Japanese sources has opened a new door to the Far East. Two of the leading providers of Japanese business information in the United States are Nihon Keizai Shimbun America and Teikoku Databank America. The former company's Nikkei Telecom offers a variety of business-related information, including timely English-language access to Japanese news reports. Teikoku Databank is particularly useful for gaining crucial business and financial information about Japanese companies. However, the real power of this database lies in its ability to search its 200,000 company files according to most of the key information fields contained in each company report.

Sources: Mick O'Leary, "Globalbase Reaches New Global Markets," *Information Today*, June 1994, pp. 11–12; Linda Rosen, "Access Russia," *Information Today*, June 1994, pp. 22–24; and David A. Fryxell, "Japan Is Only a Keystroke Away . . . When You Tap into Its Databases," *Link-Up*, July–August 1994, pp. 8–9.

In smaller companies that cannot afford to set up a formal competitive intelligence office, specific executives should be assigned to watch specific competitors. Thus a manager who used to work for a competitor would closely follow that competitor and act as the in-house expert on that competitor. In this way, any manager who needs to know what a specific competitor is thinking could contact the corresponding in-house expert.[14]

SELECTING COMPETITORS TO ATTACK AND AVOID

With good competitive intelligence, managers will find it easier to formulate their competitive strategies. They will have a better sense of whom they can effectively compete with in the market. Very often, managers conduct a *customer value*

MARKETING MEMO

OUTSMARTING THE COMPETITION WITH GUERRILLA MARKETING RESEARCH

Directories, annual reports, brochures, and press releases are good sources of historical information, but they're often not good enough if a company hopes to compete against a recently introduced new product. Experts point to the following eight techniques that could give a company a lead of two or more years on the competition:

1. *Watch the small companies in your industry and related industries.* True innovation often comes from small, inconspicuous companies. Who would have thought, for instance, that Arizona Iced Tea from Ferolito Vultagio & Sons of Brooklyn would make serious inroads in the soft-drink and fruit juice markets?

2. *Follow patent applications.* Not all applications lead to products. Still, patent filings indicate a company's direction. Patent application information can be found in various online and CD-ROM databases.

3. *Track the job changes and other activities of industry experts.* Seek the answers to such questions as: Whom have the competitors hired? Have the new hires written papers or made presentations at conferences? What is the value of their expertise to the competitor? If the company gains this expertise, will it affect your firm's competitive position? For instance, when a pulp and paper company hires a marketing director with significant experience in Eastern Europe, the company could be looking toward that market.

4. *Be aware of licensing agreements.* These provide useful information about where, how, and when a company can sell a new product.

5. *Monitor the formation of business contracts and alliances.*

6. *Find out about new business practices that are saving your competitors money.* What does it mean if a competing insurance company has bought thousands of laptops and portable printers? It is very likely that its claims adjusters soon will be writing estimates and generating checks on the spot, saving time and overhead.

7. *Follow changes in pricing.* For instance, when luxury items become cheap enough for the mass market, they supplant some of the more expensive equipment, as when camcorders supplanted home movie cameras in the late 1980s.

8. *Be aware of social changes and changes in consumer tastes and preferences that could alter the business environment.* Consumers are fickle. During the past 15 years, jogging has given way to aerobics, and now walking is the preferred leisure activity. By anticipating changing fads, some shoe companies were able to introduce new types of athletic shoes.

Source: Adapted from Ruth Winett, "Guerrilla Marketing Research Outsmarts the Competition," *Marketing News*, January 2, 1995, p. 33. Reprinted with permission of the American Marketing Association.

analysis to reveal the company's strengths and weaknesses relative to various competitors.

The aim of a customer value analysis is to determine the benefits that customers in a target market segment want and how they perceive the relative value of competing suppliers' offers. The major steps in customer value analysis are:

1. *Identify the major attributes that customers value.* Customers are asked what functions and performance levels they look for in choosing a product and vendors. Different customers will mention different features/benefits.

2. *Assess the quantitative importance of the different attributes.* Customers are asked to supply their ratings or rankings of the importance of the different attributes. If the cus-

tomers diverge too much in their ratings, they should be clustered into different customer segments.

3. *Assess the company's and competitors' performances on the different customer values against their rated importance.* The customers are asked where they see the company's and each competitor's performance on each attribute. Ideally, the company's performance should be rated higher on the attributes the customers value most and lower on the attributes customers value least.

4. *Examine how customers in a specific segment rate the company's performance against a specific major competitor on an attribute-by-attribute basis.* The key to gaining competitive advantage is to take each customer segment and examine how the company's offer compares to that of its major competitor. If the company's offer exceeds the competitor's offer on all important attributes, the company can charge a higher price (thereby earning higher profits), or it can charge the same price and gain more market share.

5. *Monitor customer values over time.* Although customer values are fairly stable in the short run, they will most probably change as technologies and features change and as customers face different economic climates. The company must periodically redo its studies of customer values and competitors' standings if it wants to be strategically effective.

After the company has done its customer value analysis, it can focus its attack on one of the following classes of competitors: strong versus weak competitors, close versus distant competitors, and "good" versus "bad" competitors.

STRONG VERSUS WEAK COMPETITORS. Most companies aim their shots at their weak competitors. This strategy requires fewer resources and time per share point gained. But in the process of attacking weak competitors, the firm may achieve little in the way of improved capabilities. The firm should also compete with strong competitors to keep up with the state of the art. Furthermore, even strong competitors have some weaknesses, and the firm may prove to be a worthy competitor.

CLOSE VERSUS DISTANT COMPETITORS. Most companies compete with competitors who resemble them the most. Thus Chevrolet competes with Ford, not with Jaguar. At the same time, the company should avoid trying to destroy the close competitor. Porter cites two examples of counterproductive "victories":

> Bausch and Lomb in the late 1970s moved aggressively against other soft contact lens manufacturers with great success. However, this led each weak competitor to sell out to larger firms, such as Revlon, Johnson & Johnson, and Schering-Plough, with the result that Bausch and Lomb now faced much larger competitors.

> A specialty rubber manufacturer attacked another specialty rubber manufacturer and took away share. The damage to the other company allowed the specialty divisions of the large tire companies to move more quickly into specialty rubber markets, using them as a dumping ground for excess capacity.[15]

In both cases, the company's success in hurting its close rivals brought in tougher competitors.

"GOOD" VERSUS "BAD" COMPETITORS. Porter argues that every industry contains "good" and "bad" competitors.[16] A company should support its good competitors and attack its bad competitors. Good competitors have a number of characteristics: They play by the industry's rules; they make realistic assumptions about the industry's growth potential; they set prices in a reasonable relation to costs; they favor a healthy industry; they limit themselves to a portion or segment of the industry; they motivate others to lower costs or improve differentiation; and they accept the general level of their share and profits. Bad competitors violate the rules: They try to buy share rather than earn it; they take large risks; they invest in overcapacity; and in general, they upset the industrial equilibrium. For example, IBM finds Cray Research to be a good competitor because it plays by the rules, sticks to its segment, and does not attack IBM's core markets; but IBM finds Fujitsu a bad competitor because it attacks IBM in its core markets with subsidized prices and little differentiation. The implication is that the "good" companies should try to configure their industry to consist of only good competitors. Through careful licensing, selective retaliation, and coalitions, they can shape the industry so that the competitors are not seeking to destroy each other. They can create an industry in which each firm follows the rules, each differentiates somewhat, and each tries to earn share rather than buy it.

A company benefits in several ways from good competitors. Competitors confer several strategic benefits: They lower the antitrust risk; they increase total demand; they lead to more differentiation; they share the cost of market development and legitimatize a new technology; they improve bargaining power vis-à-vis labor unions or regulators; and they may serve less attractive segments.

BALANCING CUSTOMER AND COMPETITOR ORIENTATIONS

We have stressed the importance of a company's watching its competitors closely. Is it possible to spend too much time and energy tracing competitors? The answer is yes! A company can become so competitor-centered that it loses its customer focus.[17]

A *competitor-centered company* is one whose moves are basically dictated by competitors' actions and reactions. The company tracks competitors' moves and market shares on a market-by-market basis. It sets its course as follows:

Competitor-Centered Company

Situation

- ◆ Competitor W is going all out to crush us in Miami.
- ◆ Competitor X is improving its distribution coverage in Houston and hurting our sales.
- ◆ Competitor Y has cut its price in Denver, and we lost three share points.
- ◆ Competitor Z has introduced a new service feature in New Orleans, and we are losing sales.

Reactions

- ◆ We will withdraw from the Miami market because we cannot afford to fight this battle.
- ◆ We will increase our advertising expenditure level in Houston.
- ◆ We will meet competitor Y's price cut in Denver.
- ◆ We will increase our sales-promotion budget in New Orleans.

This mode of strategy planning has some pluses and minuses. On the positive side, the company develops a fighter orientation. It trains its marketers to be on constant alert, watching for weaknesses in its competitors' and its own position. On the negative side, the company is too reactive. Rather than formulating and executing a consistent customer-oriented strategy, it determines its moves based on its competitors' moves. It does not move toward its own goal. It does not know where it will end up, since so much depends on what the competitors do.

A *customer-centered company* focuses more on customer developments in formulating its strategies. It would pay attention to the following developments:

Customer-Centered Company

Situation

- The total market is growing at 4% annually.

- The quality-sensitive segment is growing at 8% annually.

- The deal-prone customer segment is also growing fast, but these customers do not stay with any supplier very long.

- A growing number of customers have expressed an interest in a 24-hour hot line, which no one in the industry offers.

Reactions

- We will focus more effort on reaching and satisfying the quality segment of the market. We will buy better components, improve quality control, and shift our advertising theme to quality.

- We will avoid cutting prices and making deals because we do not want the kind of customer that buys this way.

- We will install a 24-hour hot line if it looks promising.

Clearly, the customer-centered company is in a better position to identify new opportunities and set a strategy course that makes long-run sense. By monitoring customer needs, it can decide which customer groups and emerging needs are the most important to serve, given its resources and objectives.

In practice, today's companies must carefully monitor both customers and competitors.

SUMMARY

1. To prepare an effective marketing strategy, a company must study its competitors as well as its actual and potential customers. Companies need to identify their competitors' strategies, objectives, strengths, weaknesses, and reaction patterns. They also need to know how to design an effective competitive intelligence system, which competitors to attack and which to avoid, and how to balance a competitor orientation with a customer orientation.

2. A company's closest competitors are those seeking to satisfy the same customers and needs and making similar offers. A company should also pay attention to its latent competitors, who may offer new or other ways to satisfy the same needs. The company should identify its competitors by using both industry and market-based analyses.

3. Competitive intelligence needs to be collected, interpreted, and disseminated continuously. Managers should be able to receive timely information about competitors and contact the marketing intelligence department when they need competitive information. With good competitive intelligence, managers can more easily formulate their strategies.

4. Managers need to conduct a customer value analysis to reveal the company's strengths and weaknesses relative to competitors. The aim of this analysis is to determine the benefits that customers want and how they perceive the relative value of competitors' offers.

5. As important as a competitive orientation is in today's global markets, companies should not overdo their emphasis on competitors. Companies should manage a good balance of consumer and competitor monitoring.

CONCEPT APPLICATIONS

1. Why is the concept of "strategic groups" useful to marketing strategists?

2. The following products have had tremendous market success and redefined their industries: Tekna's high-tech flashlights, Ingersoll-Rand's ergonomic power tools, Ciba Corning's diagnostic equipment, Oxo's kitchen tools, Gillette's Sensor razor, and Boeing's 777 airplane. In one word, what is it that makes these products special?

Analyzing
Industries and
Competitors

3. Funny Bone, a comedy club in Overland Park, Kansas, is experiencing declining attendance. Overland Park is an affluent suburb located just outside of Kansas City, Missouri. Disposable income is above the national average. Jim Haney, Funny Bone's owner, is perplexed. He doesn't understand the recent decrease in attendance and would like to do some competitive analysis. What product does the Funny Bone sell? Who are its competitors at the brand, industry, form, and generic levels?

4. Twenty-five years ago, it seemed a safe bet that either a U.S. or German producer of bias-belted tires would become the world leader in the global tire market. Instead, Michelin, a French company that produces radial tires, has won the honor. What accounts for the fact that Michelin grew while the former market leaders like Uniroyal, Goodrich, and Firestone lost market share? What questions should U.S. tire companies have asked themselves 25 years ago?

5. Procter & Gamble has enjoyed considerable success in the detergent market by being a customer-centered company. Its products have been in the mature stage of the product life cycle for years—for some products, decades. But lately, private and dealer brands have made some inroads into P&G's market share. Using the concepts of competition from the chapter, provide some possible explanations for the decline in market share of some of P&G's products.

6. Three variables that every company should monitor when assessing the strengths and weaknesses of its competition are share of market, share of mind, and share of heart. Who are the leaders in each of these categories in the following industries?
   a. Personal computers
   b. Automobile models
   c. Fast food
   d. Income-tax preparation
   e. Discount stores

7. What is benchmarking? Describe the steps involved in carrying out benchmarking.

8. In the medical field, there is a battle between old and new technologies. Traditionally, a surgeon would make large incisions in patients, but in endoscopic surgery the doctor makes a tiny cut and inserts a slender, tubular instrument called a trochar into the body to perform the surgery. Both United States Surgical Corporation (USSC) and Ethicon Endo-Surgery, a Johnson & Johnson company, supply endoscopic equipment for surgery. USSC was the first to enter the market in the late 1980s, when Leon Hirsh pioneered the endoscopic procedure for gallbladder removal. In the early 1990s, Ethicon Endo-Surgery was formed to compete in global markets. The following table summarizes the customer-value research conducted by J&J into endoscopic versus traditional surgery.

TABLE 1		**PERFORMANCE**				
QUALITY PROFILE: GALLBLADDER OPERATIONS ENDOSCOPIC VERSUS TRADITIONAL SURGERY	**QUALITY ATTRIBUTES**	**(1) ENDO METHOD**	**(2) TRADITIONAL METHOD**	**(3) RATIO***	**(4) RELATIVE WEIGHT**	**(5) WEIGHT TIMES RATIO**
	At-home recovery	1–2 weeks	6–8 weeks	3.0	40	120
	Hospital stay	1–2 days	3–7 days	2.0	30	60
	Operation time	1/2–1 hour	1–2 hours	2.0	15	30
	Complication rate	5%	10%	1.5	10	15
	Postoperative scar	0.5–1 inch	3–5 inches	1.4	05	07
			Sum of quality weights:		100	
			Market-perceived quality score:			232
			Market-perceived quality ratio:			2.32

* In this example the ratios are not calculated directly from performance measures shown in columns one and two. They are based on performance scores from 1 to 10 that are linked to the performance data shown.

Assuming that the surgeons charge the same amount for both kinds of surgery, which form of surgery is better—endoscopic or traditional? How can J&J's Ethicon Endo-Surgery business gain a competitive advantage over USSC—which already has the first-to-market advantage?

9. Listed below are several company strengths noted by top management of an office-supply company like Office Max after conducting an internal audit.
   a. Innovative product features
   b. Broad distribution
   c. Lower costs and prices
   d. Broad product line
   e. Strong technical service

   How could each of these business strengths be translated into customer benefits that would give Office Max a competitive advantage?

NOTES

1. Michael E. Porter, *Competitive Strategy* (New York: Free Press, 1980), pp. 22–23.
2. See Al Ries and Jack Trout, *Marketing Warfare* (New York: McGraw-Hill, 1986).
3. See Leonard M. Fuld, *The New Competitor Intelligence: The Complete Resource for Finding, Analyzing, and Using Information About Your Competitors* (New York: John Wiley, 1995); John A. Czepiel, *Competitive Marketing Strategy* (Englewood Cliffs, NJ: Prentice Hall, 1992).
4. See Hans Katayama, "Fated to Feud: Sony versus Matsushita," *Business Tokyo,* November 1991, pp. 28–32.
5. See Kathryn Rudie Harrigan, "The Effect of Exit Barriers upon Strategic Flexibility," *Strategic Management Journal,* Vol. 1 (1980), 165–76.
6. See Michael E. Porter, *Competitive Advantage* (New York: Free Press, 1985), pp. 225, 485.
7. Porter, *Competitive Strategy,* Chapter 13.
8. Porter, *Competitive Strategy,* Chapter 7.
9. "The Hardest Sell," *Newsweek,* March 30, 1992, p. 41.
10. William E. Rothschild, *How to Gain (and Maintain) the Competitive Advantage* (New York: McGraw-Hill, 1989), Chapter 5.
11. Pam Weisz, "Surrender! Lever Cedes Ultra Detergent Market to P&G," *Brandweek,* October 10, 1994, pp. 1, 6; "Lever to Re-enter Ultras, P&G's Way," *Brandweek,* April 10, 1995, pp. 1, 6.
12. The following has been drawn from various Bruce Henderson writings, including "The Unanswered Questions, The Unsolved Problems" (paper delivered in a speech at Northwestern University in 1986); *Henderson on Corporate Strategy* (New York: Mentor, 1982); and "Understanding the Forces of Strategic and Natural Competition," *Journal of Business Strategy,* Winter 1981, pp. 11–15.
13. Steven Flax, "How to Snoop on Your Competitors," *Fortune,* May 14, 1984, pp. 29–33.
14. For more discussion, see Leonard M. Fuld, *Monitoring the Competition* (New York: John Wiley, 1988).
15. Porter, *Competitive Advantage,* pp. 226–27.
16. Porter, *Competitive Advantage,* Chapter 6.
17. See Alfred R. Oxenfeldt and William L. Moore, "Customer or Competitor: Which Guidelines for Marketing?" *Management Review,* August 1978, pp. 43–48.

IDENTIFYING MARKET SEGMENTS AND SELECTING TARGET MARKETS

The mythological homogeneous America is gone.
We are a mosaic of minorities.

JOEL WEINER

Small opportunities are often the beginning of great enterprises.

DEMOSTHENES

❖

A company that decides to operate in a broad market recognizes that it normally cannot serve all customers in that market. The customers are too numerous and diverse in their buying requirements. Instead of competing everywhere, the company needs to identify the market segments that it can serve most effectively.

To choose its markets and serve them well, many companies are embracing target marketing. In *target marketing*, sellers distinguish the major market segments, target one or more of those segments, and develop products and marketing programs tailored to each segment. Instead of scattering their marketing effort (a "shotgun" approach), they can focus on the buyers whom they have the greatest chance of satisfying (a "rifle" approach).

Target marketing requires marketers to take three major steps (Figure 9-1):

1. *Market segmentation:* Identify and profile distinct groups of buyers who might require separate products and/or marketing mixes.
2. *Market targeting:* Select one or more market segments to enter.
3. *Market positioning:* Establish and communicate the products' key distinctive benefits in the market.

This chapter will describe the first two steps and answer the following questions:

◆ **How can a company identify the segments that make up a market?**

◆ **What criteria can a company use to choose the most attractive target markets?**

The next chapter will discuss market positioning.

MARKET SEGMENTATION

Markets consist of buyers, and buyers differ in many ways. Markets can be segmented in a number of ways. Here we will examine levels of segmentation, patterns of segmentation, market-segmentation procedure, bases for segmenting consumer and business markets, and requirements for effective segmentation.

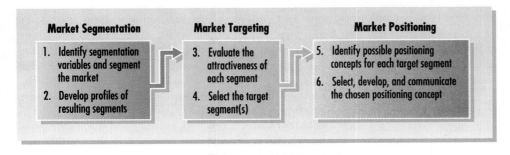

Market Segmentation	Market Targeting	Market Positioning
1. Identify segmentation variables and segment the market	3. Evaluate the attractiveness of each segment	5. Identify possible positioning concepts for each target segment
2. Develop profiles of resulting segments	4. Select the target segment(s)	6. Select, develop, and communicate the chosen positioning concept

FIGURE 9-1

Steps in Market Segmentation, Targeting, and Positioning

Identifying Market Segments and Selecting Target Markets

Levels of Market Segmentation

Market segmentation represents an effort to increase a company's targeting precision. It can be carried out at four levels: segments, niches, local areas, and individuals. Before we discuss these levels, however, we need to say a word about mass marketing.

MASS MARKETING. In *mass marketing,* the seller engages in the mass production, mass distribution, and mass promotion of one product for all buyers. Henry Ford epitomized this marketing strategy when he offered the Model-T Ford to all buyers; they could have the car "in any color as long as it is black." Coca-Cola also practiced mass marketing for many years when it sold only one size Coke in a 6.5-ounce bottle.

The traditional argument for mass marketing is that it creates the largest potential market, which leads to the lowest costs, which in turn can translate into either lower prices or higher margins. However, many critics point to the increasing splintering of the market, which makes mass marketing more difficult. According to Regis McKenna:

> [Consumers] . . . have more ways to shop: at giant malls, specialty shops, and superstores; through mail-order catalogs, home shopping networks, and virtual stores on the Internet. And they are bombarded with messages pitched through a growing number of channels: broadcast and narrow-cast television, radio, on-line computer networks, the Internet, telephone services such as fax and telemarketing, and niche magazines and other print media.[1]

The proliferation of advertising media and distribution channels is making it difficult to practice "one size fits all" marketing. No wonder some have claimed that mass marketing is dying. Not surprisingly, many companies are retreating from mass marketing and turning to micromarketing at one of four levels.

SEGMENT MARKETING. A *market segment* consists of a large identifiable group within a market. A company that practices segment marketing recognizes that buyers differ in their wants, purchasing power, geographical locations, buying attitudes, and buying habits. At the same time, though, the company is not willing to customize its offer/communication bundle to each individual customer. The company instead tries to isolate some broad segments that make up a market. For example, an auto company may identify four broad segments: car buyers seeking basic transportation, those seeking high performance, those seeking luxury, and those seeking safety.

Thus segmentation is a midpoint between mass marketing and individual marketing. The consumers belonging to a segment are assumed to be quite similar in their wants and needs. Yet they are not identical. Some segment members will want additional features and benefits not included in the offer, while others would gladly give up something that they don't want very much. For example, Ritz-Carlton Hotels target affluent guests and provide many amenities in their rooms. Yet some guests may want to find more items in their room, such as a fax machine, while others may prefer fewer amenities and a lower price. Thus segment marketing is not as precise as individual marketing but is much more precise than mass marketing.[2]

Segment marketing offers several benefits over mass marketing. The company can create a more fine-tuned product/service offer and price it appropriately for the target audience. The choice of distribution channels and communications channels becomes much easier. And the company may face fewer competitors if fewer competitors are focusing on this market segment.

NICHE MARKETING. Market segments are normally large identifiable groups within a market—for example, nonsmokers, occasional smokers, regular smokers, and heavy smokers. A *niche* is a more narrowly defined group, typically a small market whose needs are not being well served. Marketers usually identify niches by dividing a segment into subsegments or by defining a group with a distinctive set of traits who may seek a special combination of benefits. For example, the heavy-smoker segment may include subsegments of heavy smokers with emphysema, and heavy smokers with emphysema who are overweight.

While segments are fairly large and thus normally attract several competitors, niches are fairly small and normally attract only one or a few competitors. Niches typically attract smaller companies. Larger companies, such as IBM, whose lose pieces of their market to nichers; Dalgic labeled this confrontation as "guerrillas against gorillas."[2a] As a defense, some larger companies have turned to niche marketing, which has required more decentralization and some changes in the way they do business. For example, Johnson & Johnson consists of 170 affiliates (business units), most of which pursue niche markets.

Niche marketers presumably understand their niches' needs so well that their customers willingly pay a price premium. For example, Ferrari gets a high price for its cars because its loyal buyers feel that no other automobile comes close to offering the product-service-membership benefit bundle that Ferrari does.

An attractive niche is characterized as follows: The customers in the niche have a distinct and complete set of needs; they will pay a premium to the firm best satisfying their needs; the "nicher" has the required skills to serve the niche in a superior fashion; the nicher gains certain economies through specialization; the niche is not likely to attract other competitors or the nicher can depend on itself; and the niche has sufficient size, profit, and growth potential.

Here are some examples of companies that have moved into niche marketing:

RAMADA Ramada Franchises Enterprises offers lodgings in a variety of niches: Ramada Limited for economy travelers; Ramada Inn for those seeking a mid-priced full-service hotel; Ramada Plaza, a new offering in the upper-mid-priced niche; Ramada Hotels offering three-star service; and Ramada Renaissance hotels, offering four-star service.[3]

AMERICAN EXPRESS American Express offers not only its traditional green cards but also gold cards, corporate cards, and even platinum cards aimed at different customer groups.

PROGRESSIVE CORP. Progressive Corp., a Cleveland auto insurer, grew rapidly as a result of filling a niche: The company sells "nonstandard" auto insurance to risky drivers with a record of auto accidents or drunkenness. Progressive charges a high price for coverage, has made a lot of money, and had the field to itself for several years.

An advertising agency executive wrote: "There will be no market for products that everybody likes a little, only for products that somebody likes a lot."[4] A chemical company executive predicted that chemical companies that succeed in the future will be those that can identify niches and specialize their chemicals to serve each niche's needs.[5] According to Linneman and Stanton, niche-pickers will find riches in niches and companies will have to niche or be niched.[6] Blattberg and Deighton claim that "niches too small to be served profitably today will become viable as marketing efficiency improves."[7] In many markets today, niches are the norm.

LOCAL MARKETING. Target marketing is increasingly taking on the character of regional and local marketing, with marketing programs being tailored to the needs and wants of local customer groups (trading areas, neighborhoods, even individual stores). Thus Citibank provides different mixes of banking services in its branches depending on the bank's neighborhood demographics. And Kraft helps supermarket chains identify the cheese assortment and shelf positioning that will optimize cheese sales in low-income, middle-income, and high-income stores, and in different ethnic communities.

Those in favor of localizing a company's marketing point to the pronounced regional differences in communities' demographics and lifestyles. They see national advertising as wasteful because it fails to address local target groups. They also see powerful local and regional retailers who are demanding more fine-tuned product assortments for their neighborhoods.

Those against local marketing argue that it drives up manufacturing and marketing costs by reducing economies of scale. Logistical problems (see Chapter 19) become magnified when companies try to meet different regional and local markets' requirements. And a brand's overall image might be diluted if the product and message differ in different localities.

INDIVIDUAL MARKETING.   The ultimate level of segmentation leads to "segments of one," "customized marketing," or "one-to-one marketing."[8] The prevalence of mass marketing has obscured the fact that for centuries consumers were served as individuals: The clothier tailor-made the suit, the cobbler designed shoes for the individual, and so on. And much business-to-business marketing today is customized, in that a manufacturer will customize the offer, logistics, and financial terms for each major account. It is the new technologies—specifically computers, databases, robotic production, and instant communication media such as e-mail and fax—that are permitting companies to consider a return to customized marketing, or what is called "mass customization."[9] *Mass customization* is the ability to prepare on a mass basis individually designed products and communications to meet each customer's requirements.

Consumer marketers are now experimenting with new systems of providing custom-made products in such areas as textbooks, greeting cards, vacations, and cosmetics. Here are some examples:

SUITED FOR SUN AND LEVI STRAUSS   Suited for Sun, a Maryland swimwear manufacturer, has installed in several retail stores a computer/camera system that makes it possible to design a woman's custom-tailored swimsuit. The customer puts on an "off the rack" garment, and the system's digital camera captures her image on the computer screen. The store clerk applies a stylus to the screen to create a garment with perfect fit. The customer than selects from more than 150 patterns and styles, which are re-imaged over her body on the computer screen until she finds the one that she likes best. The measurements are then transmitted to the factory for production, and the unique swimming suit is mailed to the delighted customer in a matter of days. Using a similar system, Levi Strauss has started to market custom-made women's jeans in selected retail locations for a charge of only $10 more than its mass-produced jeans.

NATIONAL BICYCLE   The National Bicycle Industrial Company of Japan operates the Panasonic Order System, which manufactures custom-made bikes fitted to the preferences and anatomies of individual buyers. Customers sit on a special frame that is adjusted to their comfort level and specify the frame size, gearshift system, saddle, pedals, color, and other features they want. This information is then faxed to the factory, where the measurements are punched into a computer that creates blueprints in three minutes (Figure 9-2). The computer than guides robots and workers through the production process. The factory can produce any of 11,231,862 variations on 18 bicycle models in 199 color patterns and about as many sizes as there are people. Prices range from $700 to $1,220—but within two weeks the buyer is riding a custom-made, one-of-a-kind bicycle.[10]

FIGURE 9-2
Customized Manufacturing
Japan's National Bicycle
Industrial Company practices
the ultimate in individual
marketing: It custom-makes
bikes fitted to the
preferences and anatomies of
individual buyers.

Photo credit: Louis Psihoyos/Matrix
International.

PERSONICS   Personics developed a system that allows music buyers to customize their own tape by choosing from over 5,000 songs (at $1.10 per song). The machine produces the tape in about 10 minutes and prints out a label listing the selections and the customer's name.

Business marketers are also pursuing mass customization:

MOTOROLA   Motorola salespeople are able to custom-design pagers for a company customer and deliver them in an unbelievably short time. The Motorola salesperson transmits the design to Motorola's factory, and production starts within 17 minutes. The factory ships the pagers within two hours to arrive on the customer's desk the next day.

JOHN DEERE   John Deere's Moline, Illinois, plant manufactures seeders that can be configured in more than 2 million versions to customer specifications. The seeders are produced one at a time, in any sequence, on a single production line.

BECTON-DICKINSON   Becton-Dickinson, a major medical supplier, offers a great number of options to its hospital customers: custom-designed labeling, bulk or individual packaging, customized quality control, customized computer software, and customized billing.

According to Arnold Ostle, chief designer for Mazda, "Customers will want to express their individuality with the products they buy." The opportunities offered by these technologies promise to turn marketing from "a broadcast medium to a dialog medium," where the customer participates actively in the design of the product and offer.[11] This move toward individual marketing is so important that we will examine it further in Chapter 23.

SELF-MARKETING. *Self-marketing* is a form of individual marketing in which the individual consumer takes more responsibility for determining which products and brands to buy. Consider two purchasing agents with two different purchasing

Identifying Market
Segments and Selecting
Target Markets

styles. The first may see several salespeople who each try to persuade him to buy their product. The second sees no salespeople but rather logs onto the Internet; looks up information about and evaluations of the available product/service offers; dialogs electronically with the various suppliers, users, and product critics; and in the end makes up his own mind about the best offer. The second purchasing agent is taking more responsibility for the marketing decision process, and traditional marketers have less influence over his final decision.

As the trend toward more interactive dialogue and less advertising monologue continues, self-marketing will grow in importance. We will see a growing number of shoppers who look up consumer reports, who join electronic product-discussion forums, and who place orders via phone or computer. Marketers will still influence the process but in new ways. They will need to set up toll-free phone numbers (clearly listed in ads and on their products) to enable potential and actual customers to easily reach them with questions, suggestions, and complaints. They will involve customers more in the product-development process so that new products are virtually co-designed by the producer and representatives from the target group. They will place their company on an Internet home page that provides full information about their company, product, guarantees, and so on. These steps will increase individual buyers' ability to practice self-marketing—that is, to carry on their own search for the best product offer.

Patterns of Market Segmentation

Market segments can be built up in many ways. Instead of looking at demographic or lifestyle segments, we can distinguish *preference segments*. Suppose ice cream buyers are asked how much they value sweetness and creaminess as two product attributes. Three different patterns can emerge.

- *Homogeneous preferences:* Figure 9-3(a) shows a market where all the consumers have roughly the same preference. The market shows no natural segments. We would predict that existing brands would be similar and cluster around the middle of the scale in both sweetness and creaminess.

- *Diffused preferences:* At the other extreme, consumer preferences may be scattered throughout the space (Figure 9-3[b]), indicating that consumers vary greatly in their preferences. The first brand to enter the market is likely to position in the center to appeal to the most people. A brand in the center minimizes the sum of total consumer dissatisfaction. A second competitor could locate next to the first brand and fight for market share. Or it could locate in a corner to attract a customer group that was not satisfied with the center brand. If several brands are in the market, they are likely to position throughout the space and show real differences to match consumer-preference differences.

FIGURE 9-3
Basic Market-Preference Patterns

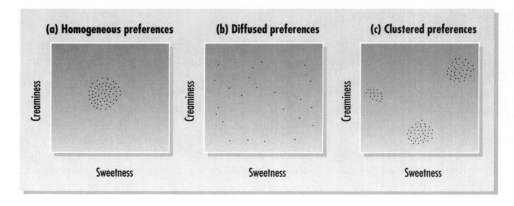

Analyzing
Marketing
Opportunities

- *Clustered preferences:* The market might reveal distinct preference clusters, called *natural market segments* (Figure 9-3[c]). The first firm in this market has three options. It might position in the center, hoping to appeal to all groups. It might position in the largest market segment (*concentrated marketing*). It might develop several brands, each positioned in a different segment. If the first firm developed only one brand, competitors would enter and introduce brands in the other segments.

Market-Segmentation Procedure

We have seen that market segments and niches can be identified by applying successive variables to subdivide a market. For example:

An airline is interested in attracting nonflyers (segmentation variable: user status). Nonflyers consist of those who fear flying, those who are indifferent, and those who are positive toward flying (segmentation variable: attitude). Among those who feel positive are people with higher incomes who can afford to fly (segmentation variable: income). The airline may decide to target higher-income people who have a positive attitude toward flying but simply have not flown.

Is there a formal procedure to identifying the major segments in a market? Here is one common three-step approach used by marketing research firms:

STEP ONE: SURVEY STAGE. The researcher conducts exploratory interviews and focus groups to gain insight into consumer motivations, attitudes, and behavior. Using these findings, the researcher prepares a formal questionnaire to collect data on:
- Attributes and their importance ratings
- Brand awareness and brand ratings
- Product-usage patterns
- Attitudes toward the product category
- Demographics, geographics, psychographics, and mediagraphics of the respondents (discussed later in this chapter)

STEP TWO: ANALYSIS STAGE. The researcher applies *factor analysis* to the data to remove highly correlated variables, then applies *cluster analysis* to create a specified number of maximally different segments. (For a review of these terms, see Table 4-5.)

STEP THREE: PROFILING STAGE. Each cluster is profiled in terms of its distinguishing attitudes, behavior, demographics, psychographics, and media patterns. Each segment can be given a name based on a dominant distinguishing characteristic. Thus in a study of the leisure market, Andreasen and Belk found six segments and their corresponding profiles:[12] passive homebody, active sports enthusiast, inner-directed self-sufficient, culture patron, active homebody, and socially active. They found that performing arts organizations could sell the most tickets by targeting culture patrons and socially active people.

Market segmentation must be redone periodically because market segments change. At one time the personal computing industry segmented its products purely on speed and power, thus appealing to two broad swathes of the PC market (high-end users and low-end users) but missing out on the prosperous middle. In the beginning of the 1990s, PC marketers began to see the power of the emerging "SoHo" market, so-named for "small office and home office." Mail-order companies like Dell and Gateway appealed to this market's requirement for high per-

Identifying Market
Segments and Selecting
Target Markets

formance coupled with low price and user-friendliness. Only a year after PC makers raced to target this lucrative market, many companies were beginning to see SoHo as comprised of smaller, very lucrative segments. "Small office needs might be very different from home-office needs," says one Dell executive. "So we've got to get beyond that target segmentation." Compaq Computer is doing exactly that with its Presario line, which is targeted to a subgroup of the SoHo market: first-time home-computer buyers with computer experience, customers with a mix of sophistication and naiveté.[13]

One way to discover new segments is to investigate the hierarchy of attributes that consumers examine in choosing a brand. This process is called *market partitioning*. In the 1960s, most car buyers first decided on the manufacturer and then on one of its car divisions (*brand-dominant hierarchy*). Thus a buyer might favor General Motors cars and, within this set, Pontiac. Today, many buyers decide first on the nation from which they want to buy a car (*nation-dominant hierarchy*). Thus a growing number of buyers may first decide that they want to buy a Japanese car. They then may have a second-level preference for, say, Toyota followed by a third-level preference for the Corolla model of Toyota. The lesson is that a company must monitor potential shifts in the consumers' hierarchy of attributes and adjust to changing consumer priorities.

The hierarchy of attributes can also be used to reveal customer segments. Those buyers who first decide on price are price dominant; those who first decide on the type of car (e.g., sports, passenger, station wagon) are type dominant; those who first decide on the car brand are brand dominant; and so on. One can go further and identify those who are type/price/brand dominant, in that order, as making up a segment; those who are quality/service/type dominant as making up another segment; and so on. Each segment may have distinct demographics, psychographics, and mediagraphics.[14]

Bases for Segmenting Consumer Markets

Two broad groups of variables are used to segment consumer markets. Some researchers try to form segments by looking at *consumer characteristics*. They commonly use geographic, demographic, and psychographic characteristics. Then they examine whether these customer segments exhibit different needs or product responses. For example, they might examine the differing attitudes of "professionals," "blue collars," and other groups toward "safety" as a car benefit.

Other researchers try to form segments by looking at *consumer responses* to benefits sought, use occasions, or brands. Once the segments are formed, the researcher sees whether different consumer characteristics are associated with each consumer-response segment. For example, the researcher might examine whether people who want "quality" versus "low price" in buying an automobile differ in their geographic, demographic, and psychographic makeup.

The major segmentation variables—geographics, demographics, psychographics, and behavioral segmentation—are summarized in Table 9-1. These segmentation variables can be used singly or in combination.

GEOGRAPHIC SEGMENTATION. *Geographic segmentation* calls for dividing the market into different geographical units such as nations, states, regions, counties, cities, or neighborhoods. The company can decide to operate in one or a few geographic areas or operate in all but pay attention to local variations in geographic needs and preferences. For example, Kraft General Foods' Maxwell House ground coffee is sold nationally but flavored regionally. Its coffee is flavored stronger in the West than in the East. Campbell's Soup Company

GEOGRAPHIC

Region	Pacific, Mountain, West North Central, West South Central, East North Central, East South Central, South Atlantic, Middle Atlantic, New England
City or Metro size	Under 4,999; 5,000–19,999; 20,000–49,999; 50,000–99,999; 100,000–249,999; 250,000–499,999; 500,000–999,999; 1,000,000–3,999,999; 4,000,000 or over
Density	Urban, suburban, rural
Climate	Northern, southern

DEMOGRAPHIC

Age	Under 6, 6–11, 12–19, 20–34, 35–49, 50–64, 65+
Family size	1–2, 3–4, 5+
Family life cycle	Young, single; young, married, no children; young, married, youngest child under 6; young, married, youngest child 6 or over; older, married, with children; older, married, no children under 18; older, single; other
Gender	Male, female
Income	Under $9,999; $10,000–$14,999; $15,000–$19,999; $20,000–$29,999; $30,000–$49,999; $50,000–$99,999; $100,000 and over
Occupation	Professional and technical; managers, officials, and proprietors; clerical, sales; craftspeople; forepersons; operatives; farmers; retired; students; homemakers; unemployed
Education	Grade school or less; some high school; high school graduate; some college; college graduate
Religion	Catholic, Protestant, Jewish, Muslim, Hindu, other
Race	White, black, Asian
Generation	Baby boomers, Generation X
Nationality	North American, South American, British, French, German, Italian, Japanese
Social class	Lower lowers, upper lowers, working class, middle class, upper middles, lower uppers, upper uppers

PSYCHOGRAPHIC

Lifestyle	Straights, Swingers, longhairs
Personality	Compulsive, gregarious, authoritarian, ambitious

BEHAVIORAL

Occasions	Regular occasion, special occasion
Benefits	Quality, service, economy, speed
User status	Nonuser, ex-user, potential user, first-time user, regular user
Usage rate	Light user, medium user, heavy user
Loyalty status	None, medium, strong, absolute
Buyer-readiness stage	Unaware, aware, informed, interested, desirous, intending to buy
Attitude toward product	Enthusiastic, positive, indifferent, negative, hostile

recently appointed local area market managers and gave them budgets to study local markets and to adapt Campbell's products and promotions to local conditions.[15] Some companies even subdivide major cities into smaller geographic areas:

R. J. REYNOLDS   RJR has subdivided Chicago into three distinct submarkets. In the North Shore area, Reynolds promotes its low-tar brands because residents are better educated and concerned about health. In the blue-collar southeast area, Reynolds promotes Winston because this area is conservative. In the black South Side, Reynolds promotes the high menthol content of Salem, using the African-American press and billboards heavily.

DEMOGRAPHIC SEGMENTATION. In *demographic segmentation,* the market is divided into groups on the basis of demographic variables such as age, family size, family life cycle, gender, income, occupation, education, religion, race, generation, nationality, or social class. Demographic variables are the most popular bases for distinguishing customer groups. One reason is that consumer wants, preferences, and usage rates are often highly associated with demographic variables. Another is that demographic variables are easier to measure than most other types of variables. Even when the target market is described in nondemographic terms (say, a personality type), the link back to demographic characteristics is needed in order to know the size of the target market and the media that should be used to reach it efficiently.

Here is how certain demographic variables have been used to segment markets.

Age and Life-Cycle Stage. Consumer wants and abilities change with age. Gerber realized this and began expanding beyond its traditional baby foods line. Its new "Graduates" line is geared for the one- to three-year old. One of the reasons for Gerber's expansion into this new segment is that the baby food category's growth is declining, due to factors including the declining birth rate, babies staying on formula longer, and children moving to solid foods sooner. The company is hoping that the parents who buy Gerber's baby food for their infants will be receptive to Gerber's Graduates line as their baby grows.[16]

Photo companies are now applying age and life-cycle segmentation to the film market. With film sales down, filmmakers are working hard to exploit promising niche markets: moms, kids, and older people. Konica markets 400-speed "baby film," which is designed "to bring out the very delicate skin tones of young children's faces," as the promotional literature claims. Eastman Kodak, the U.S. filmmaker, has begun shipping children's photo hobby kits to Kmart and Wal-Mart stores and other mass merchandisers. In an innovative attempt to reach the older market, Kodak is training its own retirees to teach photography to members of their retirement homes and churches. And Polaroid promotes some of its products through the American Association of Retired Persons.[17]

Nevertheless, age and life cycle can be tricky variables. For example, the Ford Motor Company used buyers' ages in developing its target market for its Mustang automobile. The car was designed to appeal to young people who wanted an inexpensive sporty automobile. But Ford found that the car was being purchased by all age groups. It then realized that its target market was not the chronologically young but the psychologically young.

The Neugartens' research indicates that age stereotypes need to be guarded against:

> *Age has become a poor predictor of the timing of life events, as well as a poor predictor of a person's health, work status, family status, and therefore, also, of a person's interests, preoccupations, and needs. We have multiple images of persons of the same age: there is the 70-year-old in a wheelchair and the 70-year-old on the tennis court. Likewise, there are 35-year-olds sending children off to college and 35-year-olds furnishing the nursery for newborns, producing in turn, first-time grandparenthood for persons who range in age from 35 to 75.[18]*

Gender. Gender segmentation has long been applied in clothing, hairstyling, cosmetics, and magazines. Occasionally other marketers notice an opportunity for gender segmentation. Consider the cigarette market, where most brands are smoked by both men and women. But brands like Eve and Virginia Slims have been introduced, accompanied by appropriate flavor, packaging, and advertising cues to reinforce a female image. Today it is unlikely that men will smoke Virginia Slims.

Another industry that is beginning to recognize gender segmentation is the automobile industry. In the past, cars primarily were designed to appeal to men. With more women car owners, however, some manufacturers are designing certain cars to appeal to women, although stopping short of advertising them explicitly as women's cars.

Income. Income segmentation is another longstanding practice in such product and service categories as automobiles, boats, clothing, cosmetics, and travel. However, income does not always predict the best customers for a given product. Blue-collar workers were among the first purchasers of color television sets; it was cheaper for them to buy these sets than to go to movies and restaurants. The most economical cars are not bought by the really poor, but rather by those who think of themselves as poor relative to their status aspirations and to their needs for a certain level of clothing, furniture, and housing which they could not afford if they bought a more expensive car. Medium-price and expensive cars tend to be purchased by the overprivileged segments of each social class.

Generation. Many researchers are now turning to generation segmentation. The idea is that each generation is profoundly influenced by the milieu in which it grows up—the music, movies, politics, and events of the time. Some marketers target baby boomers (those born between 1946 and 1964) using communications and symbols that appeal to the optimism of that generation. Other marketers are targeting Generation X (those born between 1964 and 1984), aware that the members of this generation grew up distrustful of society, politicans, and slick advertising and merchandising. Generation X'ers are more sophisticated in evaluating products and many are turned off by advertising that has too much hype or takes itself too seriously.[19]

Social Class. Social class has a strong influence on a person's preference in cars, clothing, home furnishings, leisure activities, reading habits, retailers, and so on. Many companies design products and/or services for specific social classes. (We described the seven U.S. social classes in Table 6-1.)

Like most other segmentation variables, the tastes of social classes can change with the years. For instance, the 1980s were about greed and ostentation for the upper classes, but the nineties are about values and self-fulfillment. Experts observe that affluent tastes now run more toward the utilitarian, a Range Rover or Ford Explorer rather than a Mercedes, for instance.[20]

PSYCHOGRAPHIC SEGMENTATION. In *psychographic segmentation,* buyers are divided into different groups on the basis of lifestyle and/or personality. People within the same demographic group can exhibit very different psychographic profiles.

Lifestyle. People exhibit many more lifestyles than are suggested by the seven social classes. People's product interests are influenced by their lifestyles. In fact, the goods they consume express their lifestyles. Marketers are increasingly segmenting their markets by consumer lifestyles. For example:

> Seeking to market to upscale people with active lifestyles, Oldsmobile goes after golfers. Demographics show that the average golf player is a 43-year-old man who makes $50,000 a year. And research reveals that people who play golf are 143% more likely to buy a new car than the average person. With these data in mind, Oldsmobile holds its Oldsmobile Scramble golf tournament for Olds dealers and prospective buyers at country clubs across the United States.[21]

Identifying Market Segments and Selecting Target Markets

Demographics and psychographics have recently revealed a growing affinity for a "country lifestyle." Magazines covering the country lifestyle have experienced increased circulation, and more radio listeners are tuning into country stations. The rise of the country lifestyle gave Van den Bergh Foods extra leverage in marketing its Shedd's Spread Country Crock margarine. With advertisements promoting a country image, Shedd's Spread Country Crock and its line extension, Churn Style, have become the top-selling margarine spreads.[22]

The President's Commission on American Outdoors divided Americans into five recreational lifestyle clusters: "health-conscious sociables," "get-away actives," "excitement-seeking competitives," "fitness driven," and "unstressed and unmotivated."

Companies making cosmetics, alcoholic beverages, and furniture are always seeking opportunities in lifestyle segmentation. But lifestyle segmentation does not always work. Nestlé introduced a special brand of decaffeinated coffee for "late nighters," and it failed.

Personality. Marketers have used personality variables to segment markets. They endow their products with *brand personalities* that correspond to consumer personalities. In the late fifties, Fords and Chevrolets were promoted as having different personalities. Ford buyers were identified as independent, impulsive, masculine, alert to change, and self-confident, while Chevrolet owners were conservative, thrifty, prestige-conscious, less masculine, and seeking to avoid extremes.[23]

BEHAVIORAL SEGMENTATION.

In *behavioral segmentation,* buyers are divided into groups on the basis of their knowledge of, attitude toward, use of, or response to a product. Many marketers believe that behavioral variables—occasions, benefits, user status, usage rate, loyalty status, buyer-readiness stage, and attitude—are the best starting points for constructing market segments.

Occasions. Buyers can be distinguished according to the occasions they develop a need, purchase a product, or use a product. For example, air travel is triggered by occasions related to business, vacation, or family. An airline can specialize in serving people for whom one of these occasions dominates. Thus charter airlines serve groups of people who fly for vacation.

Occasion segmentation can help firms expand product usage. For example, orange juice is usually consumed at breakfast. An orange juice company can try to promote drinking orange juice on other occasions—lunch, dinner, midday. Certain holidays—Mother's Day and Father's Day, for example—were promoted partly to increase the sale of candy and flowers. The Curtis Candy Company promoted the trick-or-treat custom at Halloween, with every home ready to dispense candy to eager little callers knocking at the door.

In addition to product-specific occasions, a company can consider critical events that mark life's passages to see whether they are accompanied by certain needs that can be met by product and/or service bundles. These occasions include: marriage, separation, divorce; acquisition of a home; injury or illness; change in employment or career; retirement; and death of a family member. Among the providers that have emerged to offer services on these critical occasions are marriage, employment, and bereavement counselors.

Benefits. A powerful form of segmentation involves classifying buyers according to the benefits they seek from the product. For example, one study of the benefits derived from travel uncovered three major market segments: those who travel to get away and be with family, those who travel for adventure or educational purposes, and people who enjoy the "gambling" and "fun" aspects of travel.[24]

One of the most successful benefit segmentations was reported by Haley, who studied the toothpaste market (Table 9-2). Haley's research uncovered four benefit segments: economy, medicinal, cosmetic, and taste. Each benefit-seeking group had particular demographic, behavioral, and psychographic characteristics. For example, decay-prevention seekers had large families, were heavy toothpaste users, and were conservative. Each segment also favored certain brands. A toothpaste company can use these findings to focus its current brand better and to launch new brands. Thus Procter & Gamble launched Crest toothpaste offering the benefit of anticavity protection and became extremely successful. "Anticavity protection" became its unique selling proposition. A *unique selling proposition (USP)* is stronger than just a unique proposition (UP). For example, a purple toothpaste is unique, but it probably won't sell.

User Status. Markets can be segmented into groups of nonusers, ex-users, potential users, first-time users, and regular users of a product. Thus blood banks must not rely only on regular donors to supply blood. They must recruit new first-time donors and contact ex-donors, and each will require a different marketing strategy. The company's position in the market will also influence its focus. Market-share leaders will focus on attracting potential users, while smaller firms will often focus on attracting current users away from the market leader.

To a certain extent, the state of the economy determines which user groups a company will focus on. In a slow growth economy, companies will concentrate their efforts on first-time users in emerging markets (such as young people and immigrants) or those who are going through a life stage for the first time (such as newly married or first-time moms). To maintain market share, they will also work on maintaining brand awareness and discouraging loyal users from switching to another brand.

Usage Rate. Markets can be segmented into light, medium, and heavy product users. Heavy users are often a small percentage of the market but account for a high percentage of total consumption. Marketers usually prefer to attract one heavy user to their product or service rather than several light users. For example, a travel industry study showed that frequent users of travel agents for vacation travel are more involved, more innovative, more knowledgeable, and more likely to be opinion leaders than less frequent users. Heavy users take more trips and gather more information about vacation travel from newspapers, magazines,

TABLE 9-2	**BENEFIT SEGMENTATION OF THE TOOTHPASTE MARKET**			
BENEFIT SEGMENTS	**DEMOGRAPHICS**	**BEHAVIORISTICS**	**PSYCHOGRAPHICS**	**FAVORED BRANDS**
Economy (low price)	Men	Heavy users	High autonomy, value oriented	Brands on sale
Medicinal (decay prevention)	Large families	Heavy users	Hypochondriac, conservative	Crest
Cosmetic (bright teeth)	Teens, young adults	Smokers	High sociability, active	Maclean's, Ultra Brite
Taste (good tasting)	Children	Spearmint lovers	High self-involvement, hedonistic	Colgate, Aim

Source: **Adapted from Russell J. Haley, "Benefit Segmentation: A Decision Oriented Research Tool,"** *Journal of Marketing,* **July 1963, pp. 30–35. Reprinted with permission of the American Marketing Association.**

Identifying Market
Segments and Selecting
Target Markets

books, and travel shows.[25] Clearly, a travel agency would benefit by directing its marketing efforts toward heavy users, perhaps using telemarketing and special parties and promotions.

Figure 9-4 shows usage rates for some popular consumer products. For example, 41% of the sampled households buy beer. But the heavy users accounted for 87% of the beer consumed—almost seven times as much as the light users. Clearly, a beer company would prefer to attract one heavy user to its brand rather than several light users. Thus, most beer companies target the heavy beer drinker, using appeals such as Miller Lite's "tastes great, less filling." A product's heavy users often have common demographics, psychographics, and media habits. The profile of heavy beer drinkers shows the following characteristics: working class; ages 25 to 50; heavy viewers of television, particularly sports programs. These profiles can assist marketers in developing price, message, and media strategies.

Social marketing agencies face a heavy-user dilemma. A family-planning agency would normally target poor families who have many children, but these families are usually the most resistant to birth-control messages. In addition, some may charge discrimination. The National Safety Council would target unsafe drivers, but these drivers are the most resistant to safe-driving appeals. The agencies must consider whether to go after a few highly resistant heavy offenders or many less-resistant light offenders.

Loyalty Status. A market can be segmented by consumer-loyalty patterns. Consumers can have varying degrees of loyalty to brands (Coca-Cola), stores (Sears), and other entities. Suppose there are five brands: A, B, C, D, and E. Buyers can be divided into four groups according to their brand-loyalty status:

◆ *Hard-core loyals:* Consumers who buy one brand all the time. Thus a buying pattern of A, A, A, A, A, A might represent a consumer with undivided loyalty to brand A.

◆ *Split loyals:* Consumers who are loyal to two or three brands. The buying pattern A, A, B, B, A, B represents a consumer with a divided loyalty between A and B. This group of people is rapidly increasing. More people now buy from a small set of acceptable brands that are equivalent in their minds.

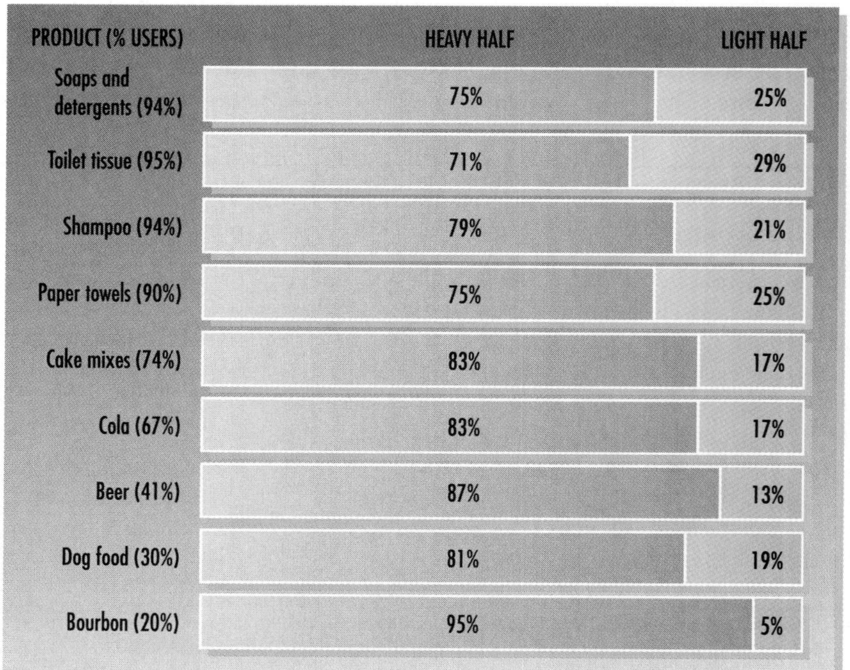

Analyzing
Marketing
Opportunities

FIGURE 9-4
Heavy and Light Users of Common Consumer Products

Source: See Victor J. Cook and William Mindak, "A Search for Constants: The 'Heavy User' Revisited," *Journal of Consumer Marketing,* Spring 1984, p. 80.

PRODUCT (% USERS)	HEAVY HALF	LIGHT HALF
Soaps and detergents (94%)	75%	25%
Toilet tissue (95%)	71%	29%
Shampoo (94%)	79%	21%
Paper towels (90%)	75%	25%
Cake mixes (74%)	83%	17%
Cola (67%)	83%	17%
Beer (41%)	87%	13%
Dog food (30%)	81%	19%
Bourbon (20%)	95%	5%

- *Shifting loyals:* Consumers who shift from favoring one brand to another. The buying pattern A, A, A, B, B, B would suggest a consumer who has shifted brand loyalty from A to B.

- *Switchers:* Consumers who show no loyalty to any brand. The buying pattern A, C, E, B, D, B would suggest a nonloyal consumer who is either *deal prone* (buys the brand on sale) or *variety prone* (wants something different each time).[26]

Each market consists of different numbers of the four types of buyers. A *brand-loyal market* is one with a high percentage of hardcore brand-loyal buyers. The toothpaste market and the beer market are fairly high brand-loyal markets. Companies selling in a brand-loyal market have a hard time gaining more market share, and companies that enter such a market have a hard time getting in.

A company can learn a great deal by analyzing the degrees of brand loyalty:

- By studying its hard-core loyals, the company can identify its products' strengths. Colgate, for example, finds that its hard-core loyals are more middle class, have larger families, and are more health conscious. These characteristics pinpoint the target market for Colgate.

- By studying its split loyals, the company can pinpoint which brands are most competitive with its own. If many Colgate buyers also buy Crest, Colgate can attempt to improve its positioning against Crest, possibly using direct-comparison advertising.

- By looking at customers who are shifting away from its brand, the company can learn about its marketing weaknesses and attempt to correct them. The company can also attract switchers by running frequent sales; however, these consumers may not be worth attracting.

One caution: What appear to be brand-loyal purchase patterns may reflect habit, indifference, a low price, a high switching cost, or the nonavailability of other brands. Thus a company must carefully interpret what is behind the observed purchase patterns. It must determine whether users are loyal, switchers, or emergent, and it must craft its marketing campaigns accordingly. For more on this topic, see the Marketing Insight on page 264 titled "Targeting Consumers in a Slow-Growth Economy."

Buyer-Readiness Stage. A market consists of people in different stages of readiness to buy a product. Some are unaware of the product, some are aware, some are informed, some are interested, some desire the product, and some intend to buy. The relative numbers make a big difference in designing the marketing program.

Suppose a health agency wants women to take an annual Pap test to detect possible cervical cancer. At the beginning, most women are unaware of the Pap test. The marketing effort should go into high-awareness-building advertising using a simple message. Later, to move more women into desiring the test, the advertising should dramatize the benefits of the Pap test and the risks of not taking it. A special offer of a free health examination might be made to motivate women into actually signing up for the test. In general, the marketing program should be adapted to the different stages of buyer readiness.

Attitude. Five attitude groups can be found in a market: enthusiastic, positive, indifferent, negative, and hostile. Door-to-door workers in a political campaign use the voter's attitude to determine how much time to spend with that voter. They thank enthusiastic voters and remind them to vote; they reinforce those who are positively disposed; they try to win the votes of indifferent voters; they spend no time trying to change the attitudes of negative and hostile voters. To the extent that attitudes are correlated with demographic descriptors, the political party can more efficiently locate the best prospects.

The Strategic Directions Group divided its sample of mature Americans (age 50 and up) into categories based on their attitudes toward three topics: health care,

Identifying Market
Segments and Selecting
Target Markets

Targeting Consumers in a Slow-Growth Economy

Companies today are faced with a wide variety of economic conditions. Even as new markets open up in Central and Eastern Europe, population growth and disposable income in the United States, Western Europe, and Japan have settled into a slow-growth mode. In high-growth areas, simply making consumers aware of products will stimulate demand. But in slow-growth (mature) markets, companies can be effective only if they design their marketing strategy to appeal to the four kinds of product users.

- *Nonusers* may be aware of a product but have rejected it. Unless marketers can identify new uses for the product, marketing efforts directed at this group will have little effect. The well-known Arm and Hammer Baking Soda campaign is an example of how to attract nonusers by promoting new uses for an established product: deodorizing carpets and refrigerators, freshening drains, and cleaning toilet bowls. Each new use became the focus of an ad campaign designed to revitalize the product. Yet nonusers are relatively unimportant when compared with the other three groups of consumers.

- *Loyal customers* are already using and loyal to the product. In a market with a very high proportion of loyal consumers, marketing may not produce big increases in awareness or in sales. Yet advertising can still do the important job of reinforcing brand loyalty. The primary goal of marketing to loyals should be to discourage switching.

- *Switchers* have little or no brand loyalty, and their purchase decisions are based on some other factor (such as price, variety seeking, and so on). When price is the determining factor, price promotions are likely to be the most effective vehicle for inducing brand switching. But this group may not be an attractive target, since they will switch again.

- *Emergent consumers* are entering the market for the first time and may be the most valuable group. Two groups of particular importance for a wide range of consumer products are young people and immigrants. Both groups are forming preferences for numerous products and services, and both will support the market for decades after they make their initial choices. Advertising directed at emergents should be similar to advertising for new products. The ads must create awareness and build brand image. They must create a sense of identity with the product and reinforce trial and preference. Yet emergents may also need to be reached with messages and media unique to their age and culture. A Latino immigrant in Texas will use different media and respond to different types of appeals than will a native-born 16-year-old in Boise, Idaho.

The best marketing campaigns take all these groups into account, reinforcing the preferences of loyal consumers while also influencing consumers who could switch brands and creating product awareness in emergent markets.

Source: American Demographics magazine, © 1994. Reprinted with permission.

food consumption, and self regard. In the self-regard category, SDG found the following types of people:[27]

- *Upbeat enjoyers* feel that the best years are now and in the future. Looking good and staying active are high priorities for them.

- *Insecures* feel that they haven't been successful in life and that the best years are over. They are afraid of not having enough money, invest conservatively, shop for value, and worry about crime.

- *Threatened actives* worry about crime but have a more positive outlook on life. They are resistant to change and want to keep living in their own homes, working, and driving their own cars.

- *Financial positives* are more open to change and more concerned about looking good. They feel financially secure, successful, and optimistic.

MULTI-ATTRIBUTE SEGMENTATION (GEOCLUSTERING). Marketers no longer talk about the average consumer, or even limit their analysis to only a few market segments. Rather, they are increasingly crossing several variables in an effort to identify smaller, better defined target groups. Thus a bank may not only identify a group of wealthy retired adults but also within that group distinguish several segments depending on their current income, assets, and savings and risk preferences.

One of the most promising developments in multi-attribute segmentation is called *geoclustering.* Geoclustering yields richer descriptions of consumers and neighborhoods than traditional demographics because it reflects the socioeconomic status and lifestyle of a neighborhood's inhabitants. Claritas Inc. has developed a geoclustering approach called PRIZM (Potential Rating Index by Zip Markets) that classifies over 500,000 U.S. residential neighborhoods into 62 distinct lifestyle groupings called PRIZM Clusters.[28] The groupings take into consideration 39 factors in five broad categories: (1) education and affluence, (2) family life cycle, (3) urbanization, (4) race and ethnicity, and (5) mobility. The neighborhoods are broken down by ZIP code, ZIP+4, or census tract and block group. The clusters have descriptive titles that convey their essence, such as *Blue Blood Estates, Winner's Circle, Hometown Retired, Latino America, Shotguns and Pickups,* and *Back Country Folks.*

PRIZM is based on the maxim that "birds of a feather flock together." The inhabitants in a cluster tend to lead similar lives, drive similar cars, have similar jobs, and read similar magazines. Here are three of PRIZM's clusters:

American Dreams: This segment represents the emerging, upscale, ethnic, big-city mosaic. People in this segment are likely to buy import cars, *Elle* magazine, Mueslix cereal, tennis weekends, and designer jeans. Their annual median household income is $46,000.

Rural Industria: This cluster includes young families in heartland offices and factories. Their lifestyle is typified by trucks, *True Story* magazine, Shake n' Bake, fishing trips, and tropical fish. Annual median household income is $22,900.

Cashmere and Country Club: These aging baby boomers live the good life in the suburbs. They're likely to buy Mercedes, *Golf Digest,* salt substitutes, European getaways, and high-end TVs. Annual median household income is $68,600.

Other PRIZM clusters include *Kids & Cul-de-Sacs,* which points to baby boomer migration to the suburbs; *Young Literati,* which taps Generation X; and *New Ecotopia,* which represents the country's aging hippies.[29]

Marketers can use PRIZM to answer such questions as: Which clusters (neighborhoods or ZIP codes) produce our most valuable customers? How deeply have we already penetrated these segments? Which markets, performance sites, and promotional media provide us with the best opportunities for growth? Direct marketers, such as Spiegel, use geoclustering information to do customized searches for where to mail their catalogs. The Helene Curtis Company, in marketing its Suave shampoo, used PRIZM to identify neighborhoods with high concentrations of young working women; these women responded best to advertising messages that Suave is inexpensive, yet will make their hair "look like a million."

Geoclustering's importance as a segmentation tool is growing for several reasons. First, the diversity of the U.S. population is growing daily, with faster population growth among certain ethnic groups, more women in the work force, changing household structures, and changing sizes of age groups. Second, marketing to microsegments has become accessible to even small organizations as database costs decline, PC's proliferate, software becomes easier to use, and data integration increases.[30]

TARGETING MULTIPLE SEGMENTS. Very often, companies may begin their marketing with one targeted segment, then expand into other segments. Consider the experiences of one small technology company:

PAGING NETWORK INC. PageNet is a small developer of paging systems that has used segmentation to outflank such major competitors as the paging subsidiaries of Southwestern Bell and Pacific Telesis. Segmentation was crucial to PageNet because the company couldn't differentiate itself from competitors by boasting unique technology, and the company was already competing on price, setting its prices about 20% below those of its competitors. PageNet took the following steps to boost its competitive advantage:

1. Targeting what it considered easily accessible markets in Ohio and the company's home state of Texas, PageNet initially used geographic segmentation. In both areas, local competitors were vulnerable to PageNet's aggressive pricing. Once these markets were secure, the company rolled out its products into 13 geographically dispersed market segments that represented the most growth potential.

2. PageNet's segmenting strategy didn't end with geography. The managers developed a profile of users for paging services. Among the primary groups targeted were salespeople, messengers, and service people. PageNet then set out to capture the largest possible percentage of the total market for pagers. To reach its objective of 75% market penetration by 1993 (up from 45% in 1992), the company's managers used lifestyle segmentation to target additional consumer groups, such as parents who leave their baby with a sitter and elderly people living alone whose families want to keep an eye on them.

3. Looking to broaden its segments even further by reaching larger audiences, PageNet decided to distribute its products through the electronics departments of Kmart, Wal-Mart, and Home Depot. It gave these outlets very attractive discounts in return for the right to keep the revenue from the monthly service charges on any pagers sold. With a sales forecast of 80,000 new users, PageNet's managers calculated that the enormous potential revenue from service charges would more than make up for the smaller up-front profits from the discounted products.

The results of this strategy: PageNet is continuing to add new customers at the rate of 50% a year.[31]

Bases for Segmenting Business Markets

Business markets can be segmented with many of the same variables employed in consumer market segmentation, such as geography, benefits sought, and usage rate. Yet business marketers can also use several other variables. Bonoma and Shapiro proposed segmenting the business market with the variables shown in Table 9-3. The demographic variables are the most important, followed by the operating variables—down to the personal characteristics of the buyer.

The table lists major questions that business marketers should ask in determining which segments and customers to serve. Thus a rubber-tire company should first decide which industries it wants to serve, noting the following differences: Automobile manufacturers vary in their requirements, with luxury car manufacturers wanting a much higher-grade tire than standard car manufacturers. And the tires needed by aircraft manufacturers have to meet much higher safety standards than tires needed by farm tractor manufacturers.

Within a chosen target industry, a company can further segment by company size. The company might set up separate programs for dealing with large and small customers. For example, Steelcase, a major manufacturer of office furniture, divides its customers into three groups: national (large) accounts, field (medium-sized) accounts, and dealer (small) accounts.

Within a given target industry and customer size, the company can segment by purchase criteria. For example, laboratories typically differ in their purchase criteria for scientific instruments. Government laboratories need low prices and service contracts. University laboratories need equipment that requires little service. Industrial laboratories need equipment that is highly reliable and accurate.

TABLE 9-3 | MAJOR SEGMENTATION VARIABLES FOR BUSINESS MARKETS

DEMOGRAPHIC

1. *Industry:* Which industries should we serve?
2. *Company size:* What size companies should we serve?
3. *Location:* Which geographical areas should we serve?

OPERATING VARIABLES

4. *Technology:* What customer technologies should we focus on?
5. *User/nonuser status:* Should we serve heavy users, medium users, light users, or nonusers?
6. *Customer capabilities:* Should we serve customers needing many or few services?

PURCHASING APPROACHES

7. *Purchasing-function organization:* Should we serve companies with highly centralized or decentralized purchasing organizations?
8. *Power structure:* Should we serve companies that are engineering dominated, financially dominated, and so forth?
9. *Nature of existing relationships:* Should we serve companies with which we have strong relationships or simply go after the most desirable companies?
10. *General purchase policies:* Should we serve companies that prefer leasing? Service contracts? Systems purchases? Sealed bidding?
11. *Purchasing criteria:* Should we serve companies that are seeking quality? Service? Price?

SITUATIONAL FACTORS

12. *Urgency:* Should we serve companies that need quick and sudden delivery or service?
13. *Specific application:* Should we focus on certain applications of our product rather than all applications?
14. *Size of order:* Should we focus on large or small orders?

PERSONAL CHARACTERISTICS

15. *Buyer-seller similarity:* Should we serve companies whose people and values are similar to ours?
16. *Attitudes toward risk:* Should we serve risk-taking or risk-avoiding customers?
17. *Loyalty:* Should we serve companies that show high loyalty to their suppliers?

Source: Adapted from Thomas V. Bonoma and Benson P. Shapiro, *Segmenting the Industrial Market,* 1983. Reprinted by permission of Benson P. Shapiro.

Business marketers generally identify segments through a sequential segmentation process. Consider an aluminum company:

> The aluminum company first undertook macrosegmentation consisting of three steps.[32] It looked at which end-use market to serve: automobile, residential, or beverage containers. Choosing the residential market, it needed to determine the most attractive product application: semifinished material, building components, or aluminum mobile homes. Deciding to focus on building components, it considered the best customer size and chose large customers. The second stage consisted of microsegmentation. The company distinguished among customers buying on price, service, or quality. Because the aluminum company had a high-service profile, it decided to concentrate on the service-motivated segment of the market.

The aluminum company's segmentation scheme postulates a single benefit as driving product choice within each segment. Yet business buyers may seek different benefit bundles. Robertson and Barich identified three business segments based on their stage in the purchase decision process:[33]

1. *First-time prospects:* Customers who have not yet purchased. They want to buy from a salesperson or vendor who understands their business, who explains things well, and whom they can trust.

2. *Novices:* Customers who have already purchased the product. They want easy-to-read manuals, hot lines, a high level of training, and knowledgeable sales reps.

3. *Sophisticates:* Customers who want speed in maintenance and repair, product customization, and high technical support.

Robertson and Barich suggest that these segments may have different channel preferences. For example, first-time prospects would prefer to deal with a company salesperson instead of a catalog/direct-mail channel, since the latter provides too little information. But as the market matures, more buyers become sophisticated and may prefer different channels. Thus companies that have committed themselves to channels that were effective in the market's early stage will lose flexibility in keeping and satisfying sophisticates.

Rangan, Moriarty, and Swartz studied a mature commodity market, steel strapping, to test the normal occurrence of two business segments: buyers who prefer a low price and little service and buyers who are willing to pay a higher price for more service.[34] To their surprise, they found four business segments:

1. *Programmed buyers:* Buyers who view the product as not very important to their operation. They buy it as a routine purchase item, usually paying full price and receiving below-average service. Clearly this is a highly profitable segment for the vendor.

2. *Relationship buyers:* Buyers who regard the product as moderately important and are knowledgeable about competitive offerings. They get a small discount and a modest amount of service and prefer the vendor as long as the price is not far out of line. They are the second most profitable group.

3. *Transaction buyers:* Buyers who see the product as very important to their operations. They are price- and service-sensitive. They receive about a 10% discount and above-average service. They are knowledgeable about competitive offerings and are ready to switch for a better price, even at the sacrifice of some service.

4. *Bargain hunters:* Buyers who see the product as very important and demand the deepest discount and the highest service. They know the alternative suppliers, bargain hard, and are ready to switch at the slightest dissatisfaction. The company needs these buyers for volume purposes, but they are not very profitable.

This segmentation scheme can help a company in a mature commodity industry do a better job of figuring out where to apply price and service increases and decreases, since each segment would react differently.[35]

Finally, in attempting to develop an effective segmentation scheme, it is important to recognize that many shoppers cannot be neatly pigeonholed into one segment. Many consumers are cross-shoppers. Consider the "cross-dresser" who buys an expensive Bill Blass suit but shops at Wal-Mart for underwear. Or the "cross-eater" who eats a Healthy Choice frozen dinner followed by rich Ben & Jerry's ice cream for dessert. It is dangerous to interpret someone's segment membership by observing one purchase. Segmentation ignores the whole customer profile, which becomes clear only with individual customer profiling.

Requirements for Effective Segmentation

As we've seen, there are many ways to segment a market. Not all segmentations, however, are effective. For example, buyers of table salt could be divided into blond and brunet customers. But hair color is not relevant to the purchase of salt. Furthermore, if all salt buyers buy the same amount of salt each month, believe all salt is the same, and would pay only one price for salt, this market would be minimally segmentable from a marketing point of view.

To be useful, market segments must be:

- *Measurable:* The size, purchasing power, and characteristics of the segments can be measured.

- *Substantial:* The segments are large and profitable enough to serve. A segment should be the largest possible homogeneous group worth going after with a tailored marketing program. It would not pay, for example, for an automobile manufacturer to develop cars for people who are shorter than four feet.

- *Accessible:* The segments can be effectively reached and served.

- *Differentiable:* The segments are conceptually distinguishable and respond differently to different marketing-mix elements and programs. If married and unmarried women respond similarly to a sale on perfume, they do not constitute separate segments.

- *Actionable:* Effective programs can be formulated for attracting and serving the segments.

MARKET TARGETING

Once the firm has identified its market-segment opportunities, it has to evaluate the various segments and decide how many and which ones to target. We will now examine the process of evaluating and selecting marketing segments.

Evaluating the Market Segments

In evaluating different market segments, the firm must look at two factors: the overall attractiveness of the segment, and company's objectives and resources. First, the firm must ask whether a potential segment has the characteristics that make it generally attractive, such as size, growth, profitability, scale economies, low risk, and so on. We mentioned several desirable characteristics earlier in Chapter 3 in connection with the GE model (see Figure 3-4). To these we should add other considerations. For example, how easy will it be to persuade the members of the segment to shift their purchases? (The company should avoid targeting loyals of other brands or deal-prone shoppers; rather, it should go after dissatisfied shoppers and those who have not become firmly brand loyal.) How much is their business worth? (The company should target consumers who will spend a lot on the category, stay loyal, and influence others.)

Second, the firm must consider whether investing in the segment makes sense given the firm's objectives and resources. Some attractive segments could be dismissed because they do not mesh with the company's long-run objectives. Even if the segment fits the company's objectives, the company must consider whether it possesses the skills and resources it needs to succeed in that segment. The segment should be dismissed if the company lacks one or more necessary competences and is in no position to acquire them. But even if the company possesses the requisite competences, it needs to develop some superior advantages. It should enter only market segments in which it can offer superior value.

Selecting the Market Segments

Having evaluated different segments, the company must decide which and how many segments to serve. In other words, it must decide which segments to *target*. The company can consider the five patterns of target market selection shown in Figure 9-5 on the next page.

SINGLE-SEGMENT CONCENTRATION. In the simplest case, the company selects a single segment. Volkswagen concentrates on the small-car market, and Richard D. Irwin on the economics and business texts market. Through concen-

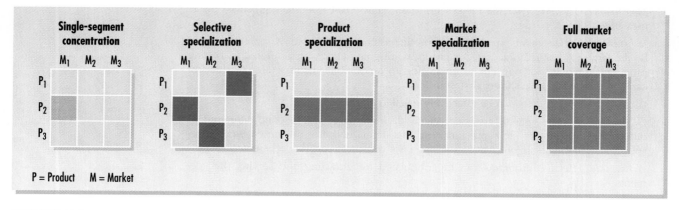

FIGURE 9-5

Five Patterns of Target Market Selection

Source: Adapted from Derek F. Abell, *Defining the Business: The Starting Point of Strategic Planning* (Englewood Cliffs, NJ: Prentice Hall, 1980), Chapter 8, pp. 192–96.

trated marketing, the firm gains a strong knowledge of the segment's needs and achieves a strong market position in the segment. Furthermore, the firm enjoys operating economies through specializing its production, distribution, and promotion. If it captures leadership in the segment, the firm can earn a high return on its investment.

However, concentrated marketing involves higher than normal risks. A particular market segment can turn sour; for example, when young women suddenly stopped buying sportswear, Bobbie Brooks's earnings fell sharply. Or a competitor may invade the segment. For these reasons, many companies prefer to operate in more than one segment.

SELECTIVE SPECIALIZATION. Here the firm selects a number of segments, each objectively attractive and appropriate, given the firm's objectives and resources. There may be little or no synergy among the segments, but each segment promises to be a money maker. This multi-segment coverage strategy has the advantage of diversifying the firm's risk. Even if one segment becomes unattractive, the firm can continue to earn money in other segments.

Selective specialization is becoming quite popular in radio broadcasting. Radio broadcasters that want to appeal both to younger and older listeners (and thus to a broader range of advertisers) can do so by having two different stations in the same market. For example, Emmis Broadcasting owns New York's KISS-FM, which describes itself as "smooth R&B [rhythm and blues] and classic soul" and appeals to older listeners, and WQHT-FM ("Hot 97"), which plays hip-hop (urban street music) for listeners in the under-25 crowd.[36]

PRODUCT SPECIALIZATION. Here the firm concentrates on making a certain product that it sells to several segments. An example would be a microscope manufacturer that sells microscopes to university laboratories, government laboratories, and commercial laboratories. The firm makes different microscopes for these different customer groups, but does not manufacture other instruments that laboratories might use. Through a product specialization strategy, the firm builds a strong reputation in the specific product area. The downside risk is that the product may be supplanted by an entirely new technology.

MARKET SPECIALIZATION. Here the firm concentrates on serving many needs of a particular customer group. An example would be a firm that sells an assortment of products for university laboratories, including microscopes, oscillo-

Analyzing
Marketing
Opportunities

scopes, Bunsen burners, and chemical flasks. The firm gains a strong reputation for specializing in serving this customer group and becomes a channel for all new products that the customer group could feasibly use. The down-side risk is that the customer group may have its budgets cut.

FULL MARKET COVERAGE. Here a firm attempts to serve all customer groups with all the products that they might need. Only very large firms can undertake a full market coverage strategy. Examples include IBM (computer market), General Motors (vehicle market), and Coca-Cola (drink market).

Large firms can cover a whole market in two broad ways: through undifferentiated marketing or differentiated marketing.

Undifferentiated Marketing. In *undifferentiated marketing,* the firm ignores market-segment differences and goes after the whole market with one market offer.[37] It focuses on buyers' needs rather than differences among buyers. It designs a product and a marketing program that will appeal to the broadest number of buyers. It relies on mass distribution and mass advertising. It aims to endow the product with a superior image in people's minds. An example of undifferentiated marketing is the Coca-Cola Company's early marketing of only one drink in one bottle size in one taste to suit everyone. A current example in Japan is the popular *fukubukoro* ("lucky bag"), a sealed bag of miscellaneous goods that people buy because they believe the store manager's assertion that what is contained in the bag is a good buy for the price.[38]

Undifferentiated marketing is often seen as "the marketing counterpart to standardization and mass production in manufacturing."[39] The narrow product line keeps down production, inventory, and transportation costs. The undifferentiated advertising program keeps down advertising costs. The absence of segment research and planning lowers the costs of marketing research and product management. Presumably, the company can turn its lower costs into lower prices to win the price-sensitive segment of the market.

Nevertheless, many marketers have expressed strong doubts about this strategy. Gardner and Levy, while acknowledging that "some brands have very skillfully built up reputations of being suitable for a wide variety of people," noted that "it is not easy for a brand to appeal to stable lower-middle-class people and at the same time to be interesting to sophisticated, intellectual upper-middle-class buyers. . . . It is rarely possible for a product or brand to be all things to all people."[40] This is true even for seemingly simple products like horseshoes and horseshoe nails. There are more than 600 types of horseshoes and 50 kinds of horseshoe nails.[41]

When several competitors practice undifferentiated marketing, the result is intense competition in the largest market segments and undersatisfaction of the smaller ones. Kuehn and Day have called this tendency to chase the largest market segment the "majority fallacy."[42] The recognition of this fallacy has led firms to increase their interest in entering smaller neglected market segments.

Differentiated Marketing. In *differentiated marketing,* the firm operates in several market segments and designs different programs for each segment. General Motors does this when it says that it produces a car for every "purse, purpose, and personality." IBM offers many hardware and software packages for different segments in the computer market. Also consider the cases of American Drug and Edison Brothers:

AMERICAN DRUG   The number-two chain in U.S. drugstore retailing, American Drug is pursuing a strategy of differentiated marketing. The company's marketing team assesses shopping patterns at hundreds of Osco and Sav-on Drug

Stores on a market-by-market basis. Using volumes of scanned data, along with a handful of other tools, the company has been fine-tuning the stores' product mix, revamping store layout, and refocusing marketing efforts to be more closely aligned with real consumer demand. Depending on its demographics, each store unit varies the amount and type of merchandise in such categories as hardware, electrical supplies, automotive, cookware, over-the-counter drugs, convenience goods, and so on. "We have a number of stores located in urban markets, for example, where Afro-Americans or Hispanics make up 85 percent to 95 percent of our customers. Their purchasing preferences and motivations can be very different from another urban market. . . . Our stores are now beginning to reflect those differences," says the chain's director of sales and marketing.[43]

EDISON BROTHERS This large retail organization operates 900 shoe stores that fall into four different chain categories, each appealing to a different market segment. Chandler's sells higher-priced shoes. Baker's sells moderate-priced shoes, Burt's sells shoes for budget shoppers, and Wild Pair is oriented to the shopper who wants very stylish shoes. Within three blocks on State Street in Chicago are found Burt's, Chandler's, and Baker's. Putting the stores near each other does not hurt them because they are aimed at different segments of the women's shoe market. This strategy has made Edison Brothers the country's largest retailer of women's shoes.

Differentiated marketing typically creates more total sales than undifferentiated marketing. However, it also increases the costs of doing business. The following costs are likely to be higher:

- *Product modification costs:* Modifying a product to meet different market-segment requirements usually involves some R&D, engineering, and/or special tooling costs.

- *Manufacturing costs:* It is usually more expensive to produce 10 units of 10 different products than 100 units of one product. The longer the production setup time and the smaller the sales volume of each product, the more expensive the product becomes. However, if each model is sold in sufficiently large volume, the higher costs of setup time may be quite small per unit.

- *Administrative costs:* The company has to develop separate marketing plans for each market segment. This requires extra marketing research, forecasting, sales analysis, promotion, planning, and channel management.

- *Inventory costs:* It is more costly to manage inventories containing many products than inventories containing few products.

- *Promotion costs:* The company has to reach different market segments with different promotion programs. The result is increased promotion-planning costs and media costs.

Since differentiated marketing leads to both higher sales and higher costs, nothing general can be said regarding this strategy's profitability. Companies should be cautious about oversegmenting their market. If this happens, they may want to turn to countersegmentation to broaden the customer base.[44] Johnson & Johnson, for example, broadened its target market for its baby shampoo to include adults. And Smith Kline Beecham launched its Aquafresh toothpaste to attract three benefit segments simultaneously: those seeking fresh breath, whiter teeth, and cavity protection.

Additional Considerations in Evaluating and Selecting Segments

Four other considerations must be taken into account in evaluating and selecting segments: ethical choice of market targets, segment interrelationships and supersegments, segment-by-segment invasion plans, and intersegment cooperation.

ETHICAL CHOICE OF MARKET TARGETS. Market targeting sometimes generates controversy.[45] The public is concerned when marketers take unfair advantage of vulnerable groups (such as children) or disadvantaged groups (such as inner-city poor people), or promote potentially harmful products. For example, the cereal industry has been heavily criticized for its marketing efforts directed toward children. Critics worry that sophisticated advertising, in which high-powered appeals are presented through the mouths of lovable animated characters, will overwhelm children's defenses. Children will be enticed to gobble too much sugared cereal or to eat poorly balanced breakfasts. The marketers of toys and other children's products have been similarly criticized.

Cigarette, beer, and fast-food marketers have also generated much controversy in recent years by their attempts to target inner-city minority consumers. For example, McDonald's and other chains have drawn criticism for pitching their high-fat, salt-laden fare to low-income inner-city residents, who are much more likely than suburbanites to be heavy consumers. R. J. Reynolds took heavy flak in 1990 when it announced plans to market Uptown, a menthol cigarette targeted toward low-income African-Americans.

Not all attempts to target children, minorities, or other special segments draw such criticism. For example, Colgate-Palmolive's Colgate Junior toothpaste has special features designed to get children to brush longer and more often. Golden Ribbon Playthings has developed a highly acclaimed and very successful black character doll named "Huggy Bean" targeted toward minority consumers to connect them with their African heritage.

Thus, in market targeting, the issue is not *who* is targeted but rather *how* and for *what*. Socially responsible marketing calls for segmentation and targeting that serve not just the interests of the company but also the interests of those targeted.[46]

SEGMENT INTERRELATIONSHIPS AND SUPERSEGMENTS.

In selecting more than one segment to serve, the company should pay close attention to segment interrelationships on the cost, performance, and technology side. A company carrying a fixed cost (its sales force, store outlets, and so on) can add products to absorb and share some of the cost. Thus a sales force will be given additional products to sell, and a fast-food outlet will offer additional menu items. This is a search for economies of scope, which can be just as important as economies of scale.

Companies should also identify and try to operate in supersegments rather than in isolated segments. A *supersegment* is a set of segments sharing some exploitable similarity. For example, Aquafresh toothpaste is targeted toward a supersegment that wants three benefits in one (anticavity protection, whiter teeth, and fresh breath). The firm would be wise to target supersegments when possible; otherwise, it might be at a competitive disadvantage with firms that have locked into that supersegment.

SEGMENT-BY-SEGMENT INVASION PLANS.

Even if the firm plans to target a supersegment, it is wise to enter one segment at a time and conceal its grand plan. The competitors must not know to what segment(s) the firm will move next. This need for segment-by-segment invasion plans is illustrated in Figure 9-6 on page 274. Three firms, A, B, and C, have specialized in adapting computer systems to the needs of airlines, railroads, and trucking companies. Company A has specialized in meeting all the computer needs of airlines. Company B has specialized in selling large computer systems to all three transportation sectors. Company C recently entered this market and has specialized in selling personal computers to trucking companies. The question is: Where should company C move next? The arrows have been added to the chart to show the planned sequence of market-segment invasions unknown to company C's competitors. Company C will next offer mid-size computers to trucking companies. Then, to allay company B's concern

Identifying Market
Segments and Selecting
Target Markets

FIGURE 9-6
**Segment-by-Segment
Invasion Plan**

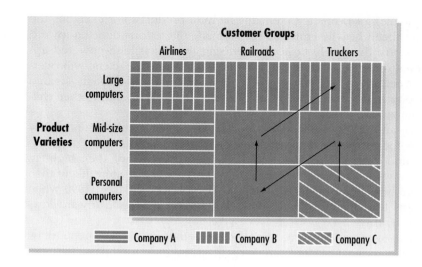

about its large computer business with trucking companies, company C will move into offering personal computers tailored to railroad needs. Later, it will offer mid-size computers to railroads. Finally, it will launch a full-scale attack on company B's large computer position in trucking companies. Of course, C's planned sequence is provisional in that much depends on the competitors' segment moves over time.

Unfortunately, too many companies fail to develop a long-term invasion plan in which they have plotted the sequence and timing of market-segment entries. Pepsi-Cola is an exception. In its attack on Coca-Cola, Pepsi thought everything through in grand-plan terms, first attacking Coca-Cola in the grocery market, then in the vending-machine market, then in the fast-food market, and so on. Japanese firms are also known for plotting their invasion sequence. They first gain a foothold in a market, then add new products as their earlier products become successful. For example, Toyota began by introducing small cars (e.g., Tercel, Corolla) into the market, then expanded into mid-size cars (Camry, Cressida) and finally into luxury cars (Lexus). U.S. firms usually turn blue when a Japanese firm enters the market, knowing that the Japanese firm will not stop at the first segment but will use it as a launching pad for successive invasions.

A company's invasion plans can be thwarted when it confronts blocked markets. The invader must then figure out a way to break into a blocked market. The problem of entering *blocked markets* calls for a megamarketing approach.

❖ **MEGAMARKETING** is the strategic coordination of economic, psychological, political, and public-relations skills to gain the cooperation of a number of parties in order to enter and/or operate in a given market.

Pepsi used megamarketing to enter the Indian market:

PEPSICO   After Coca-Cola was asked to leave India, Pepsi began to lay plans to enter this huge market. Pepsi worked with an Indian business group to seek government approval for its entry over the objections of both domestic soft-drink companies and anti-multinational legislators. Pepsi saw the solution to lie in making an offer that the Indian government would find hard to refuse. Pepsi offered to help India export some of its agricultural products in a volume that would more than cover the cost of importing soft-drink concentrate. Pepsi also promised to focus considerable selling effort on rural areas to help in their economic development. Pepsi further offered to transfer food-processing, packaging, and water-treatment technology to India. Clearly, Pepsi's strategy was to bundle a set of benefits that would win the support of various interest groups in India.

Thus Pepsi's marketing problem went beyond the normal four Ps of operating effectively in a market. To enter India, Pepsi faced a six-P marketing problem, with politics and public opinion constituting the two additional Ps.

Once in, a multinational must be on its best behavior, since it is under great critical scrutiny. This calls for well-thought-out *civic positioning*. Olivetti, for example, enters new markets by building housing for workers, generously supporting local arts and charities, and hiring and training indigenous managers.[47]

INTERSEGMENT COOPERATION. The best way to manage segments is to appoint segment managers with sufficient authority and responsibility for building their segment's business. At the same time, segment managers should not be so segment-focused as to resist cooperation with other company personnel to improve overall company performance. Consider the following situations calling for cross-departmental cooperation:

BAXTER   Baxter operates several divisions selling different products and services to hospitals. Each division sends out its own invoices. Some hospitals complain about receiving as many as seven different invoices from Baxter each month. Baxter's marketers finally convinced the separate divisions to send the invoices to Baxter's headquarters so that Baxter could send just one invoice a month to its customers.

ARTHUR ANDERSEN   Certified public accounting firms operate three divisions: auditing, taxes, and business consulting. Auditing staffs are loath to provide leads to the consulting staff for fear that clients will change auditors if Andersen consultants do a poor job for them.

CHASE   Like most banks, Chase originally kept separate customer records by department—loans, deposits, trust work, and so on. Thus it was difficult for a Chase officer to gain a picture of a customer's overall bank activity. Finally, several of Chase's departments agreed to work closely with accounting and information systems specialists to build one seamless customer information system.

SUMMARY

1. To choose its markets and serve them well, companies must target their markets. Target marketing involves three activities: market segmentation, market targeting, and market positioning.

   Because the proliferation of advertising media and distribution channels is making it difficult for marketers to engage in mass marketing, companies are increasingly turning to micromarketing at four levels: segments, niches, local areas, and individuals. *Market segments* are large identifiable groups within a market. A *niche* is a more narrowly defined group, usually identified by dividing a segment into subsegments or by defining a group with a distinctive set of traits who may seek a special combination of benefits. At the local level, marketers are customizing their campaigns for trading areas, neighborhoods, and even individual stores. At the individual level, companies are practicing both individual and mass customization. The future is likely to see more *self-marketing,* a form of individual marketing in which individual consumers take more responsibility for determining which products and brands to buy.

2. There are two bases for segmenting consumer markets: consumer characteristics and consumer responses. The major segmentation variables for consumer markets are geographic (nation, state, region, county, city, neighborhood), demographic (age, family

size, family life cycle, gender, income, occupation, education, religion, race, generation, nationality, social class), psychographic (lifestyle, personality), and behavioral (occasions, benefits, user status, usage rate, loyalty status, buyer-readiness stage, attitude). These variables can be used singly or in combination. Business marketers use all these variables as well, along with operating variables, purchasing approaches, and situational factors. To be useful, market segments must be measurable, substantial, accessible, differentiable, and actionable.

3. Once a firm has identified its market-segment opportunities, it has to evaluate the various segments and decide how many and which ones to target. In evaluating segments, it must look at the segment's attractiveness indicators and the company's objectives and resources. In choosing which segments to target, the company can choose to focus on a single segment, several segments, a specific product, a specific market, or the full market. If it decides to serve the full market, it must choose between undifferentiated and differentiated marketing. Differentiated marketing typically creates more total sales than undifferentiated marketing, but it also increases the costs of doing business.

4. Marketers must choose target markets in a socially responsible manner. The issue is not who is targeted but rather how and for what. Marketers must also monitor segment interrelationships, seeking out economies of scope and the potential for marketing to supersegments. Marketers should develop segment-by-segment invasion plans, entering one segment at a time and concealing the grand plan. Finally, market segment managers should be prepared to cooperate in the interest of overall company performance.

CONCEPT APPLICATIONS

1. Two Swiss leaders in the watchmaking industry in the early 1980s were SSIH, which manufactured the Omega watch, and ASUAG, which manufactured both the Rado and Longines watches. As the decade progressed, both companies found themselves in trouble. Omega had become a highly diluted brand, while ASUAG held several small, mismanaged companies. In addition, the market was being flooded by inexpensive Japanese quartz watches, a development that the Swiss chose to ignore. Swiss banks kept the industry alive by allowing SSIH and ASUAG to merge and form SMH. SMH chose to segment the market into three distinct areas: low end, middle, and high end. Suggest the type of watch that might appeal to each segment. Into which segment does the famous Swatch watch fall?

2. For many years if you wanted a Coke, you had one choice: a 6.5-ounce refreshment that was available only in a greenish "Coke bottle." And until the early 1980s, the Coca-Cola company did not allow its name to be associated with any product other than its flagship beverage—Coca-Cola. Considering both the container and the beverage, how many different kinds of Coke are now available? What other brands of soft drinks does the company now sell? What types of non-soft-drink products are now available from the Coca-Cola Company?

3. The Nestlé Company is considering introducing its coffee product in Thailand. Market research has revealed the following information about Thai society and culture: People in the traffic-congested urban areas of Thailand tend to experience high levels of stress. Temperatures in the country are often above 80 degrees. Given this information, should Nestlé use traditional advertising promoting the coffee's taste, aroma, and stimulative properties, or should it choose other factors?

4. Suggest a useful way to segment the markets for the following products:
   a. Household detergents
   b. Animal feeds
   c. Household coffee
   d. Automobile tires

5. A clock manufacturer recognizes that it is basically in the time-measurement business. It wants to segment the time-measurement market in order to identify new opportunities. Identify the major segments in this market.

6. Psychographic segmentation attempts to divide buyers into groups based on lifestyle and/or personality. The use of psychographics can help marketers fine-tune their marketing mixes in targeting certain groups. The following list is an example of the activities, interests, and opinions (AIOs) associated with the buying behaviors of users and nonusers of shotgun ammunition. Examine the AIOs and try to determine which are associated with heavy users of ammunition and which are associated with nonusers of ammunition:

   a. I like fishing.
   b. I like danger.
   c. I would like to be on the police force.
   d. I like hunting.
   e. There is too much violence on television.
   f. I like to play poker.
   g. I love the out-of-doors.
   h. I love to eat.
   i. There should be a gun in every home.
   j. I would like to be a professional football player.
   k. I like war stories.
   l. I like to work outdoors.
   m. I would do better than average in a fist fight.
   n. I read the newspaper every day.
   o. If given a chance, most men would cheat on their wives.

7. Ordinarily, a monopolist would find no advantage in segmenting the market. Name three other instances in which segmentation would not be a viable alternative for a company.

8. You work for a marketing research company specializing in the development of new and innovative market segments. The Prudential Insurance company has contacted your organization because it is interested in developing new segmentation approaches to the insurance field. Life insurance has been traditionally a husband-dominated decision. However, the decision to purchase life insurance is becoming increasingly *syncratic* (i.e., involving both husband and wife). Prudential wants to know how its life-insurance division can use lifestyles to understand buyer behavior in syncratic decision making. Name some lifestyles categories that Prudential might target as potential customers.

9. For each of the following product categories, choose a specific product. Name (1) the brand, (2) the size, (3) the manufacturer, and (4) the product's market-segment/positioning strategy. In each case, why do you think the manufacturer chose to target this particular segment? How is each product's segmentation strategy obvious from its packaging or promotion?

   a. Dry breakfast cereal
   b. Facial tissue
   c. Bar soap
   d. Toothpaste
   e. Dry dog food
   f. Laundry detergent

10. Evaluate the pros and cons of regionalized marketing, or segmenting markets on a geographic basis. What impact might increased use of regionalized marketing have on marketers?

NOTES

1. Regis McKenna, "Real-Time Marketing," *Harvard Business Review,* July–August 1995, pp. 87–95, here p. 87.

2. See James C. Anderson and James A. Narus, "Capturing the Value of Supplementary Services," *Harvard Business Review,* January–February 1995, pp. 75–83.

2a. See Tevfik Dalgic and Maarten Leeuw, "Niche Marketing Revisited: Concept, Applications, and Some European Cases," *European Journal of Marketing,* 28, no. 4 (1994), 39–55.

3. Robert A. Nozar, "Ramada Three-Tier Plan Wins Kudos," *Hotel and Motel Management,* May 8, 1995, pp. 1, 25; and Laura Koss, "Upper Midpriced Niche Entices Ramada," *Hotel and Motel Management,* August 16, 1993, pp. 6, 44.

4. Laurel Cutler, quoted in "Stars of the 1980s Cast Their Light," *Fortune,* July 3, 1989, p. 76.

5. Andrew A. Boccone, "Speciality Chemicals: In Pursuit of Fast-Growth Niche Markets," *Chemical Week,* April 12, 1989, pp. 32–34.

6. Robert E. Linneman and John L. Stanton, Jr., *Making Niche Marketing Work: How to Grow Bigger by Acting Smaller* (New York: McGraw-Hill, 1991).

7. Robert Blattberg and John Deighton, "Interactive Marketing: Exploiting the Age of Addressibility," *Sloan Management Review,* 33, no. 1 (1991), 5–14.

8. See Don Peppers and Martha Rogers, *The One to One Future: Building Relationships One Customer at a Time* (New York: Currency/Doubleday, 1993).

9. B. Joseph Pine II, *Mass Customization* (Boston: Harvard Business School Press, 1993); and B. Joseph Pine II, Don Peppers, and Martha Rogers, "Do You Want to Keep Your Customers Forever?" *Harvard Business Review,* March–April 1995, pp. 103–14.

10. Susan Moffat, "Japan's New Personalized Production," *Fortune,* October 22, 1990, pp. 132–35.

11. McKenna, "Real-Time Marketing."

12. Alan R. Andreasen and Russell W. Belk, "Predictors of Attendance at the Performing Arts," *Journal of Consumer Research,* September 1980, pp. 112–20.

13. Catherine Arns, "PC Makers Head for 'SoHo,'" *Business Week,* September 28, 1992, pp. 125–26; Gerry Khermouch, "The Marketers Take Over," *Brandweek,* September 27, 1993, pp. 29–35.

14. For a market-structure study of the hierarchy of attributes in the coffee market, see Dipak Jain, Frank M. Bass, and Yu-Min Chen, "Estimation of Latent Class Models with Heterogeneous Choice Probabilities: An Application to Market Structuring," *Journal of Marketing Research,* February 1990, pp. 94–101.

15. See "Marketing's New Look: Campbell Leads a Revolution in the Way Consumer Products Are Sold," *Business Week,* January 26, 1987, pp. 64–69.

16. Leah Rickard, "Gerber Trots Out New Ads Backing Toddler Food Line," *Advertising Age,* April 11, 1994, pp. 1, 48.

17. Joan E. Rigdon, "Marketing: Photography Companies Focus on Niches," *The Wall Street Journal,* March 12, 1993, B1:4.

18. *American Demographics,* August 1986.

19. For more on generations, see Michael R. Solomon, *Consumer Behavior,* 3d ed. (Upper Saddle River, NJ: Prentice Hall, 1996), Chapter 14; and Frank Feather, *The Future Consumer* (Toronto: Warwick Publishing, 1994), pp. 69–75.

20. Andrew E. Serwer, "42,496 Secrets Bared," *Fortune,* January 24, 1994, pp. 13–14; Kenneth Labich, "Class in America," *Fortune,* February 7, 1994, pp. 114–26.

21. Geoffrey Brewer, "Bringing Buyers to the Fore," *Incentive,* May 1992, pp. 77–79.

22. Junu Bryan Kim, "Taking Comfort in Country: After Decade of '80s Excess, Marketers Tap Easy Lifestyle as Part of Ad Messages," *Advertising Age,* January 11, 1993, pp. S1–S4.

23. Quoted in Franklin B. Evans, "Psychological and Objective Factors in the Prediction of Brand Choice: Ford versus Chevrolet," *Journal of Business,* October 1959, pp. 340–69.

24. Stowe Shoemaker, "Segmenting the U.S. Travel Market According to Benefits Realized," *Journal of Travel Research,* Winter 1994, pp. 8–21.

25. Ronald E. Goldsmith, Leisa Reinecke Flynn, and Mark Bonn, "An Empirical Study of Heavy Users of Travel Agencies," *Journal of Travel Research,* Summer 1994, pp. 38–43.

26. This classification was adapted from George H. Brown, "Brand Loyalty—Fact or Fiction?" *Advertising Age,* June 1952–January 1953, a series.

27. Gabrielle Sandor, "Attitude (Not Age) Defines the Mature Market," *American Demographics,* January 1994, pp. 18–21.

28. Other leading suppliers of geodemographic data are ClusterPlus (by Donnelly Marketing Information Services) and Acord (C.A.C.I., Inc.).

29. Christina Del Valle, "They Know Where You Live—and How You Buy," *Business Week,* February 7, 1994, p. 89.

30. See Michael J. Weiss, *The Clustering of America* (New York: Harper & Row, 1988).

31. See Norton Paley, "Cut Out for Success," *Sales and Marketing Management,* April 1994, pp. 43–44.

32. See Yoram Wind and Richard Cardozo, "Industrial Market Segmentation," *Industrial Marketing Management,* Vol. 3 (1974), 153–66; and James D. Hlavacek and B. C. Ames, "Segmenting Industrial and High-Tech Markets," *Journal of Business Strategy,* Fall 1986, pp. 39–50.

33. Thomas S. Robertson and Howard Barich, "A Successful Approach to Segmenting Industrial Markets," *Planning Forum,* November–December 1992, pp. 5–11.

34. V. Kasturi Rangan, Rowland T. Moriarty, and Gordon S. Swartz, "Segmenting Customers in Mature Industrial Markets," *Journal of Marketing,* October 1992, pp. 72–82.

35. For another interesting approach to segmenting the business market, see John Berrigan and Carl Finkbeiner, *Segmentation Marketing: New Methods for Capturing Business* (New York: HarperBusiness, 1992).

36. Wendy Brandes, "Advertising: Black-Oriented Radio Tunes into Narrower Segments," *The Wall Street Journal,* February 13, 1995, B5:1.

37. See Wendell R. Smith, "Product Differentiation and Market Segmentation as Alternative Marketing Strategies," *Journal of Marketing,* July 1956, pp. 3–8; and Alan A. Roberts, "Applying the Strategy of Market Segmentation," *Business Horizons,* Fall 1961, pp. 65–72.

38. Norihiko Shimizu, "Bacon and Eggs, Hold the Eggs," *Tokyo Business,* September 1994, p. 35.

39. Smith, "Product Differentiation," p. 4.

40. Burleigh Gardner and Sidney Levy, "The Product and the Brand," *Harvard Business Review,* March–April 1955, p. 37.

41. Mark D. Fefer, "Job Tip: Horses Need Shoes Too," *Fortune,* December 27, 1993, pp. 14–18.

42. Alfred A. Kuehn and Ralph L. Day, "Strategy of Product Quality," *Harvard Business Review,* November–December 1962, pp. 101–2.

43. Susan Reda, "American Drug Stores Custom-Fits Each Market," *Stores,* September 1994, pp. 22–24.

44. Alan J. Resnik, Peter B. B. Turney, and J. Barry Mason, "Marketers Turn to 'Countersegmentation,'" *Harvard Business Review,* September–October, 1979, pp. 100–6.

45. See Bart Macchiette and Roy Abhijit, "Sensitive Groups and Social Issues," *Journal of Consumer Marketing,* 11, no. 4 (1994), 55–64.

46. See "Selling Sin to Blacks," *Fortune,* October 21, 1991, p. 100; Martha T. Moore, "Putting on a Fresh Face," *USA Today,* January 3, 1992, pp. B1, B2; Dorothy J. Gaiter, "Black-Owned Firms Are Catching an Afrocentric Wave," *The Wall Street Journal,* January 8, 1992, B:2; and Maria Mallory, "Waking Up to a Major Market," *Business Week,* March 23, 1992, pp. 70–73.

47. See Philip Kotler, "Megamarketing," *Harvard Business Review,* March–April 1986, pp. 117–24.

DIFFERENTIATING AND POSITIONING THE MARKET OFFERING

You should never go into battle before you win the war.

ANONYMOUS

All men can see the tactics whereby I conquer, but what none can see is the strategy out of which victory is evolved.

ANONYMOUS

I n an industry known for intense competition, how can a small company compete against industry leaders? One answer: by differentiating its product and service and avoiding direct competition. Consider the case of Southwest Airlines, which has become an expert at avoiding competition with larger airlines like United and American:

SOUTHWEST AIRLINES Differentiation has been the key to Southwest's two decades of profitability. The small Dallas-based airline has carved its niche in short-haul flights with low prices and no frills. Starting in 1973 with three Boeing 737s connecting three Texas cities, by 1993 the company had grown to 157 planes, a route network to 37 cities, and annual revenues of $2 billion. Flying from smaller airports and avoiding the major airport hubs, it avoids direct competition from other airlines. In California, for instance, Southwest operates between Oakland and Burbank rather than San Francisco and Los Angeles. And by offering point-to-point short flights at an affordable price, it has been able to lure motorists who normally drove these short distances. Southwest is consistent at keeping fares low because it operates only one type of plane, the 737, thus eliminating the expense of maintaining different types of planes, and it offers strictly no frills services: a bag of peanuts is all you get and you carry on your luggage. As a result Southwest can fly one passenger one mile for 6.8 cents while a passenger mile costs American 8.8 cents and United 9.6 cents.[1]

Southwest offers cheaper flights, and "cheaper" is one of the broad ways a company can differentiate its offering. The firm can also create value by offering something that is better, newer, or faster. "Better" means that the company's offering outperforms its rivals' offers; it usually involves improving an existing product in a minor way. "Newer" means developing a solution that didn't exist before; it usually involves higher risk than a simple improvement but also the chance of a higher gain. "Faster" means reducing the performance or delivery time involved in using or buying a product or service.

Companies that differentiate their offering solely by cutting their costs and price may be making a mistake, for several reasons. First, "cheaper" products are often viewed as inferior in quality. Second, the firm may cut services to keep the price down, and this action may alienate buyers. Third, a competitor will usually find a lower-cost production site and offer an even cheaper version. If the firm did not distinguish its offering in any other way than price, it will be soundly beaten by this competitor.

Southwest understands this, and that's why it does not compete on price alone. Rather, it has one of the best on-time flight records in the industry because it bypasses most congested hubs. For the same reason, it can offer more flights—a boon to business travelers with busy schedules. Above all, Southwest has distinguished itself as a "fun" airline that breaks rules but doesn't break promises. What other passenger airline has planes painted like Shamu the Killer Whale or has a CEO who dresses up like Elvis Presley and greets the passengers? At what other airline would a pilot turn the plane back to the gate for a passenger who missed the last boarding call?

Companies are constantly trying to differentiate their market offering or value package from competitors'. They dream up new guarantees, special rewards for loyal users, new conveniences and enjoyments, and so on. Even when they succeed, competitors may copy their value package. As a result, most competitive advantages last only a short time. Companies therefore need to constantly think up new features and benefits to win the attention and interest of choice-rich, price-prone consumers. Consider the following example:

VIRGIN AIR There is intense competition between two British air carriers, Virgin Air and British Air. Richard Branson, who runs Virgin Air, is a master at publicizing his airline. Some Virgin flights from London to Hong Kong feature a tailor or beauty therapist. The tailor will fax passengers' measurements to Hong Kong so that suits can be ready almost upon arrival. The beautician offers massages and manicures. On many flights, Virgin serves ice cream during the movies. The airline makes special arrangements for birthday cakes, champagne for newlyweds, and mid-flight marriage announcements. The airline also offers motorcycle or limousine rides to Heathrow Airport for Upper Class passengers.

Should British Air (BA) compete along the same lines as Branson? No, for two reasons. First, Branson is more creative. Second, British Air has too dignified an image for Virgin's "cute" style of competition. BA needs to differentiate its airline by developing more fundamental benefits for its target market, and this is what it has been doing. For example, BA offers its first-class passengers on long flights something approaching bedroom comfort, including pajamas and seats that lay flatter. In addition, BA has created an arrival lounge at Heathrow where arriving passengers can shower, press their clothes, and have breakfast before taxiing to Central London. Many business travelers perceive these as more substantial benefits than those offered by Virgin Air (see Figure 20-6).

Sony is a good example of a company that constantly comes up with new benefits for its customers. As soon as Sony develops a new product, it assembles three teams that are asked to view the new product as if it were a competitor's product. The first team thinks of minor improvements, the second team thinks of major improvements, and the third team thinks of ways to make the product completely obsolete. Sony recognizes that products evolve and that the best thing a company can do is to be the first in improving its own product.

Good improvement ideas often come out of brainstorming sessions. Recently a major chemical company held a brainstorming session and came up with over a dozen ways to create extra value for its customers (Table 10-1). In choosing among the possible value-adds, the company would need to estimate the cost of

TABLE 10-1	BUSINESS-TO-BUSINESS VALUE-ADDING

Help customer reduce process costs
  Improve yields
  Reduce waste (through recycling, etc.)
  Reduce rework
  Reduce direct labor
  Reduce indirect labor (inspection, handling)
  Reduce energy costs
Help customer reduce inventory
  Consignment
  Just-in-time delivery
  Reduce cycle time
Help customer reduce administrative costs
  Simplify billing
  Improve traceability
  Use electronic data interchange
Improve safety for customer and his employees
Reduce price to the customer
  Substitute certain product components
  Improve company processes and supplier processes

Differentiating
and Positioning
the Market Offering

offering each potential benefit, how much the customers would value it, and how the competitors are likely to respond.

Crego and Schiffrin have proposed that customer-centered organizations should study what customers value and then prepare an offering that exceeds their expectations.[2] They see this process as involving three steps:

1. *Defining the customer value model.* The company first lists all the product and service factors that might influence the target customers' perception of value.

2. *Building the customer value hierarchy.* The company now assigns each factor to one of four groups: basic, expected, desired, and unanticipated. Consider the set of factors at a fine restaurant:

   - *Basic:* The food is edible and accurately delivered. (If this is all the restaurant does right, however, the customer would normally not be satisfied.)

   - *Expected:* There is good china and tableware, a linen tablecloth and napkin, flowers, discreet services, and well-prepared food. (These factors make the offering acceptable, but not exceptional.)

   - *Desired:* The restaurant is pleasant and quiet, and the food is especially good and interesting.

   - *Unanticipated:* The restaurant serves an unexpected complimentary sorbet between the courses, and places candy on the table after the last course is served.

3. *Deciding on the customer value package.* Now the company chooses that combination of tangible and intangible items, experiences, and outcomes designed to outperform competitors and win the customers' delight and loyalty.

This chapter explores specific ways a company can effectively differentiate and position its offering to achieve competitive advantage. We will address the following questions:

- **What are the major differentiating attributes available to firms?**
- **How can the firm choose an effective positioning in the market?**
- **How can the firm communicate its positioning to the market?**

FIGURE 10-1
The BCG Competitive Advantage Matrix

TOOLS FOR COMPETITIVE DIFFERENTIATION

A company must try to identify the specific ways it can differentiate its products to obtain a competitive advantage.

❖ **DIFFERENTIATION** is the act of designing a set of meaningful differences to distinguish the company's offering from competitors' offerings.

The number of differentiation opportunities vary with the type of industry. The Boston Consulting Group has distinguished four types of industries based on the number of available competitive advantages and their size (Figure 10-1):

- *Volume industry:* A volume industry is one in which companies can gain only a few, but rather large, competitive advantages. An example is the construction-equipment industry, where a company can strive for the low-cost position or the highly differentiated position and win big on either basis. Here profitability is correlated with company size and market share.

- *Stalemated industry:* A stalemated industry is one in which there are few potential competitive advantages and each is small. An example is the steel industry, where it is hard to differentiate the product or decrease its manufacturing cost. The companies can try to hire better salespeople, entertain more lavishly, and the like, but these are small advantages. Here profitability is unrelated to company market share.

- *Fragmented industry:* A fragmented industry is one in which companies face many opportunities for differentiation, but each opportunity for competitive advantage is small. A restaurant, for example, can differentiate in many ways but end up not gaining a large market share. Profitability is not related to restaurant size: Both small and large restaurants can be profitable or unprofitable.

- *Specialized industry:* A specialized industry is one in which companies face many differentiation opportunities, and each differentiation can have a high payoff. An example is companies making specialized machinery for selected market segments. In this market, some small companies can be as profitable as some large companies.

In a similar vein, Milind Lele observed that companies differ in their potential "maneuverability" along five dimensions: their target market, product, place (channels), promotion, and price. The company's freedom of maneuver is affected by the industry structure and the firm's position in the industry. For each potential maneuver, the company needs to estimate the return. Those maneuvers that promise the highest return define the company's strategic leverage. Companies in a stalemated industry have by definition very little maneuverability and strategic leverage, and those in specialized industries have great scope for maneuverability and strategic leverage.

How exactly can a company differentiate its market offering from competitors'? Here we will examine how a market offering can be differentiated along five dimensions: product, services, personnel, channel, or image (Table 10-2). Let us look at these tools more closely.

Product Differentiation

Differentiation of physical products takes place along a continuum. At one extreme we find highly standardized products that allow little variation: chicken, steel, aspirin. Yet even here, genuine variation is possible. Frank Perdue claims that his chickens are better because they are more tender—and he gets a 10% price premium based on this claim. Steel can vary in its consistency and properties. Bayer claims that its aspirin "gets into the bloodstream faster." P&G makes nine brands of laundry detergent (Tide, Cheer, Gain, Dash, Bold, Dreft, Ivory Snow, Oxydol, and Era) and has created a separate brand identity for each. Its strategy consists of selling different benefits that people might want from a laundry detergent. For example, Tide is "so powerful, it cleans down to the fiber." Ivory Snow is "99 and 44/100 percent pure" and therefore mild for diapers and baby clothes. Bold is the detergent with fabric softener; it "cleans, softens, and controls static." Dash is P&G's value entry; it "attacks tough dirt," and does it "for a great low price."

At the other extreme are products capable of high differentiation, such as automobiles, commercial buildings, and furniture. Here the seller faces an abundance

TABLE 10-2	DIFFERENTIATION VARIABLES			
PRODUCT	**SERVICES**	**PERSONNEL**	**CHANNEL**	**IMAGE**
Features	Ordering ease	Competence	Coverage	Symbol
Performance	Delivery	Courtesy	Expertise	Written and
Conformance	Installation	Credibility	Performance	audiovisual
Durability	Customer training	Reliability		media
Reliability	Customer consulting	Responsiveness		Atmosphere
Repairability	Maintenance and	Communication		Events
Style	repair			
Design	Miscellaneous			

Differentiating
and Positioning
the Market Offering

of design parameters. The main product differentiators are features, performance, conformance, durability, reliability, repairability, style, and design.[3]

FEATURES. Most products can be offered with varying features.

❖   FEATURES are characteristics that supplement the product's basic function.

The starting point of feature differentiation is a stripped-down, or "bare-bones," version of the product. The company can create additional versions by adding extra features. Thus an automobile manufacturer can offer optional features, such as electric windows, air bags, automatic transmission, and air conditioning. Each feature has a chance of capturing the fancy of additional buyers.

Some companies are extremely innovative in adding new features to their product. One of the key factors in the success of Japanese companies is their continuous enhancement of the features in their watches, cameras, automobiles, motorcycles, calculators, VCRs, and so on. Being the first to introduce valued new features is one of the most effective ways to compete.

How can a company identify and select appropriate new features? One answer is for the company to contact recent buyers and ask them a series of questions: How do you like the product? Any bad features? Good features? Are there any features that could be added that would improve your satisfaction? What are they? How much would you pay for each feature? How do you feel about each of several features that other customers suggested?

This research will provide the company with a long list of potential features. The next task is to decide which features are worth adding. For each potential feature, the company should calculate customer value versus company cost. Suppose an auto manufacturer is considering the three possible improvements shown in Table 10-3. Rear window defrosting would cost the company $100 per car to add at the factory level. The average customer said this feature was worth $200. The company could therefore generate $2 of incremental customer satisfaction for every $1 increase in company cost. Looking at the other two features, it appears that automatic transmission would create the most customer satisfaction per dollar of company cost.

These criteria are only a starting point, of course. The company also needs to consider how many people want each feature, how long it would take to introduce each feature, whether competitors could easily copy the feature, and so on.

Companies must also think in terms of feature bundles or packages. Japanese car companies, for example, often manufacture cars at three "trim levels" rather than allowing the customer to specify all the individual options. This lowers the companies' manufacturing and inventory costs. Companies must decide whether to offer feature customization to customers at a higher cost or more standardization to customers at a lower cost.

PERFORMANCE QUALITY. Most products are established initially at one of four performance levels: low, average, high, and superior.

TABLE 10-3	MEASURING CUSTOMER EFFECTIVENESS VALUE		
FEATURE	**COMPANY COST (1)**	**CUSTOMER VALUE (2)**	**CUSTOMER EFFECTIVENESS (3 = 2 ÷ 1)**
Rear window defrosting	$100	$200	2
Cruise control	600	600	1
Automatic transmission	800	2400	3

❖ **PERFORMANCE QUALITY** refers to the level at which the product's primary characteristics operate.

The important question here is: Does higher product performance produce higher profitability? The Strategic Planning Institute studied the impact of higher relative product quality (which is a surrogate for performance and other value-adding factors) and found a significantly positive correlation between relative product quality and return on investment (ROI). In a subsample of 525 mid-size business units, those with low relative product quality earned about 17% ROI; medium quality, 20%; and high quality, 27 percent. Thus the high-quality business units earned nearly 59% more than the low-quality business units. They earned more because their premium quality allowed them to charge a premium price; they benefited from more repeat purchasing, consumer loyalty, and positive word of mouth; and their costs of delivering more quality were not much higher than for business units producing low quality.

Quality's link to profitability does not mean that the firm should always design the highest performance level possible. There are diminishing returns to ever-increasing performance, in that fewer buyers are willing to pay for it. The manufacturer must design a performance level appropriate to the target market and competitors' performance levels. A person who drives 10 blocks to work each day does not need a Rolls-Royce.

A company must also decide how to manage performance quality through time. Three strategies are available here. The first, where the manufacturer continuously improves the product, often produces the highest return and market share. Procter & Gamble is a major practitioner of product-improvement strategy. The second strategy is to maintain product quality at a given level. Many companies leave their quality unaltered after its initial formulation unless glaring faults or opportunities occur. The third strategy is to reduce product quality through time. Some companies cut quality to offset rising costs, hoping the buyers will not notice any difference. Others reduce the quality deliberately in order to increase their current profits, although this course of action often hurts their long-run profitability.

CONFORMANCE QUALITY. Buyers expect products to have a high conformance quality.

❖ **CONFORMANCE QUALITY** is the degree to which all the produced units are identical and meet the promised target specifications.

Suppose a Porsche 944 is designed to accelerate to 60 miles an hour within 10 seconds. If every Porsche 944 coming off the assembly line does this, the model is said to have high conformance quality. However, if 944s vary greatly in their acceleration time, they have low conformance on this criterion. The problem with low conformance is that the product will fail to deliver on its promises to many buyers, who will be disappointed. One of the major reasons for the high-quality reputation enjoyed by Japanese manufacturers is that their products have high conformance quality. Their automobiles are praised for having good "fit and finish"—two attributes for which people gladly pay.

DURABILITY. Durability is a very important product attribute to most buyers.

❖ **DURABILITY** is a measure of the product's expected operating life under natural and/or stressful conditions.

Buyers will generally pay more for products that have more durability. However, this rule is subject to some qualifications. The extra price must not be excessive. Furthermore, the product must not be subject to technological obsolescence, in

Differentiating
and Positioning
the Market Offering

which case the buyer may not pay more for longer-lived products. Thus advertising that a particular brand of personal computer or videocamera has the highest durability may have little appeal because these products' features and performance levels are undergoing rapid change.

In contrast, wristwatches (which are "timeless" products whose underlying technology changes little) are often marketed on the basis of their durability:

TIMEX CORP Timex's early television ads promoting its wristwatches' durability are legendary. Timex watches have survived such tests as being crushed under car wheels, being thrown off cliffs, and being stepped on by an elephant. Though the company moved away from the durability theme for a while, it returned to it in 1992 with a series of award-winning and humorous ads featuring watch-wearing people and animals who had survived various accidents. The tag line: "It Takes a Licking and Keeps on Ticking."

RELIABILITY. Buyers normally will pay a premium for products with more reliability.

❖ RELIABILITY is a measure of the probability that a product will not malfunction or fail within a specified time period.

Buyers want to avoid the high costs of product breakdowns and repair time. The U.S. manufacturer Maytag, which manufactures major home appliances, has an outstanding reputation for creating reliable appliances. Japanese companies have been especially successful in improving the reliability of their products. For example:

MATSUSHITA The Matsushita company acquired Motorola's Quasar division, which manufactured television receivers. Motorola had experienced 141 defects in every 100 sets; Matsushita reduced this to 6 per 100. Buyer complaints fell to one-tenth their previous level and the company's warranty liability also dropped to one tenth.

REPAIRABILITY. Buyers prefer products that are easy to repair.

❖ REPAIRABILITY is a measure of the ease of fixing a product that malfunctions or fails.

Thus an automobile made with standard parts that are easily replaced has high repairability. Ideal repairability would exist if users could fix the product themselves with little or no cost or time lost. The buyer might simply remove the defective part and insert a replacement part. As the next best thing, some products include a diagnostic feature that allows servicepeople to correct a problem over the telephone or advise the user how to correct it. For example, before GE sends a repairperson to fix a home appliance, it tries to solve the problem over the phone. In over 50% of the cases, the problem is solved, and the customer has saved money and feels good about GE. Similarly, many computer hardware and software companies offer toll-free technical support to their customers. The availability of such support is often an important component of the consumer's decision to purchase.

STYLE. Buyers are normally willing to pay a premium for products that are attractively styled.

❖ STYLE describes the product's looks and feel to the buyer.

Many car buyers pay a premium for Jaguar automobiles because of their extraordinary look, even though Jaguar had in the past a poor record of reliability. General Motors' Cadillac division hired Pininfarina, a famous Italian automobile-design firm, to design its high-priced Allanté with European styling. Some companies have outstanding reputations for styling, such as Olivetti in office machines, Nissan and Mazda in sports cars, and Swatch in watches.

Style has the advantage of creating product distinctiveness that is difficult to copy. Therefore it is surprising that more companies have not invested in better styling. Many products are yawn-producing rather than eye-catching. For example, most small kitchen appliances lack styling distinctiveness, with the exceptions of some coffee makers and other small appliances made by Italian and German firms. On the negative side, a strong style does not always mean high performance. A chair may look sensational but be extremely uncomfortable.

Under style differentiation, we must include packaging as a styling weapon, especially in food products, cosmetics, toiletries, and small consumer appliances. The package provides the buyer's first encounter with the product and is capable of turning the buyer on or off. Packaging is discussed in detail in Chapter 15.

DESIGN: THE INTEGRATING FORCE. As competition intensifies, design will offer one of the most potent ways to differentiate and position a company's products and services.[4]

❖   **DESIGN** is the totality of features that affect how a product looks and functions in terms of customer requirements.

Design is particularly important in making and marketing durable equipment, apparel, retail services, and packaged goods. All of the qualities we've discussed under the heading "Product Differentiation" are design parameters. They suggest how difficult the product-design task is, given all the trade-offs that can be made. The designer has to figure out how much to invest in feature development, performance, conformance, reliability, repairability, style, and so forth. From the company's point of view, a well-designed product would be easy to manufacture and distribute. From the customer's point of view, a well-designed product would be pleasant to look at and easy to open, install, use, repair, and dispose of. The designer has to take all these factors into account and follow the maxim "Form follows function." A chair would be designed differently depending upon whether it is for buyers who are seeking comfort, posture, or elegance, or some combination thereof. The designer may have to compromise some of the desirable characteristics; much depends on knowing how the target market perceives and weighs the different benefits and costs.

Two gold medalists in the Industrial Design Excellence Awards (IDEA) exemplify the form-follows-function maxim:

TUPPERWARE   Tupperware used to tout its plastic containers' ability to "lock in freshness." But that market positioning strategy eventually went stale, and the company's new aim is to provide "extraordinary design for everyday living." Tupperware's colander is a perfect example of what the new slogan means. It features a curved thumb grip, different-sized holes for maximum drainage, and a locking lid. "It is exceptionally functional and it looks really cool," says a Tupperware marketing VP.[5]

BLACK & DECKER   What could be handier than a flashlight that you don't have to hold while you're probing under the sink for the cause of a leaky faucet? Black & Decker's flexible snakelight looks just like its namesake and attaches itself to almost anything, leaving your hands free. It can also stand up like an illuminated cobra to light your work space. In a market where the average price is just $6, consumers are paying $30 for this flexible flashlight.[6]

Unfortunately, too many companies fail to invest in good design. Some companies confuse design with styling and think that design is a matter of enclosing a product in a fancy casing. Or they think that reliability is something to catch during inspections rather than designing it into the manufacturing process. They may think of designers as people who pay insufficient attention to cost or who produce designs that are too novel for the market to accept. A design audit instrument to

Differentiating
and Positioning
the Market Offering

measure a company's design sensitivity and effectiveness would help management gauge whether design is adding sufficient value.

Certain countries have established themselves as design leaders: Italian design in apparel and furniture; Scandinavian design for functionality, aesthetics, and environmental consciousness; German design for austerity and robustness. Japanese companies currently outspend many other industrial countries in the amount they spend on design.

Does design investment pay off? Both anecdotal evidence and research suggest it does. Braun, a German division of Gillette, has elevated design to a high art and has had much success with its various small appliances—electric shavers, coffee makers, hair dryers, food processors, and so forth. The company's design department enjoys equal status with engineering and manufacturing. Braun's designers know the latest materials and design and test their products for consumer acceptance and easy "manufacturability" (see the Marketing Memo titled "Braun's 10 Principles of Good Design"). The Danish firm Bang & Olufsen has received many kudos for the design of its stereo and TV equipment. Herman Miller, the American office furniture company, has won much admiration for its furniture's ergonomic and aesthetic distinctiveness. As for research study evidence, consider the following: The Design Innovation Group in Great Britain carried out a three-year research study surveying 221 product, engineering, industrial, and graphic design projects. These design projects took place in medium and small U.K. manufacturing companies and were partly supported by government subsidies. The study found that 90% of the projects made a profit with an average payback period of 15 months from product launch. The average design project cost about $100,000 and produced an average sales increase of 41 percent.

MARKETING MEMO

BRAUN'S 10 PRINCIPLES OF GOOD DESIGN

Dieter Rams is Braun's chief designer, and he has developed the following 10 commandments of good design for his company:

1. Good design is innovative.
2. Good design enhances the usefulness of a product.
3. Good design is aesthetic.
4. Good design displays the logical structure of a product; its form follows its function.
5. Good design is unobtrusive.
6. Good design is honest.
7. Good design is enduring.
8. Good design is consistent right down to details.
9. Good design is ecologically conscious.
10. Good design is minimal design.

Note: Not all designers accept all of these principles. Some critics think they lead to designs that are too austere and functionalist. But it is precisely these principles that have given Braun products their distinctive identity.

Services Differentiation

In addition to differentiating its physical product, a firm can also differentiate its services. When the physical product cannot easily be differentiated, the key to competitive success often lies in adding more value-adding services and improving their quality. The main service differentiators are ordering ease, delivery, installation, customer training, customer consulting, maintenance and repair, and a few others.

ORDERING EASE. *Ordering ease* refers to how easy it is for the customer to place an order with the company. Baxter Healthcare, for example, has eased the ordering process by supplying hospitals with computer terminals through which they send orders directly to Baxter. The Jewel supermarket chain in Chicago provides willing customers with computer software that allows them to click on the grocery items they want delivered to their homes. Many banks are now providing home banking software to help customers get information and transact with the bank more efficiently.

DELIVERY. *Delivery* refers to how well the product or service is delivered to the customer. It includes the speed, accuracy, and care attending the delivery process. Deluxe Check Printers, Inc., for example, has built an impressive reputation for shipping out its checks one day after receiving an order—without being late once in 15 years. Buyers will often choose the supplier with a better reputation for on-time delivery. The choice among rail carriers often hinges on their perceived differences in delivery speed and reliability. (For more on this topic, see the Marketing Insight on page 290 titled "Turbomarketing: Using Quick Response Time as a Competitive Tool.")

INSTALLATION. *Installation* refers to the work done to make a product operational in its planned location. Buyers of heavy equipment expect good installation service from the vendor. IBM, for example, delivers all of the purchased equipment to the site at the same time rather than sending in different components at different times. When IBM is asked to move IBM equipment to another location, it is willing to move competitors' equipment and furniture as well.

CUSTOMER TRAINING. *Customer training* refers to training the customer's employees to use the vendor's equipment properly and efficiently. Thus General Electric not only sells and installs expensive X-ray equipment in hospitals but also takes on the responsibility for training the users of this equipment. McDonald's requires its new franchisees to attend Hamburger University in Oakbrook, Illinois, for two weeks to learn how to manage their franchise properly.

CUSTOMER CONSULTING. *Customer consulting* refers to data, information systems, and advising services that the seller offers free or for a price to buyers. McKesson Corporation, a major drug wholesaler, helps its 12,000 independent pharmacists set up accounting and inventory systems, computer ordering systems, and so forth. McKesson believes that helping its customers compete better will make them more loyal to McKesson. One of the best providers of value-adding consulting service is Milliken & Company:

MILLIKEN & COMPANY Milliken sells shop towels to industrial launderers, who rent them to factories. These towels are physically similar to competitors' towels. Yet Milliken charges a higher price for its towels and enjoys the leading market share. How can it charge more? The answer is that Milliken continuously "decommoditizes"

Turbomarketing: Using Quick Response Time as a Competitive Tool

Many companies are trying to establish a competitive advantage by being faster. They are becoming *turbomarketers,* learning the art of cycle-time compression and speed to market. They are applying turbomarketing to four areas: innovation, manufacturing, logistics, and retailing.

Speeding up innovation time is essential in an age of shortening product life cycles. Competitors in many industries learn about new technologies and new market opportunities at about the same time. Those companies that first reach practical solutions will enjoy "first-mover" advantages in the market. Being early rather than late pays off. One study found that products that came out six months late but on budget earned an average of 33% less profit in their first five years; products that came out on time but 50% over budget cut their profits by only 4 percent.

Manufacturing is a second area in which great strides have been made in reducing cycle time. Toyota can design and introduce a new car in three years; it used to take five or more years. Toyota used to take five weeks to build a special-order car. Now it can do this in three days.

Logistics is a third area where alert manufacturers are working hard to develop faster resupply systems. Apparel manufacturers such as Levi Strauss, Benetton, and The Limited have adopted computerized "quick response systems" that link the information systems of their suppliers, manufacturing plants, distribution centers, and retailing outlets.

Retailing speedup is a fourth frontier for competitive advantage. Today, film is developed in one hour, and a new pair of glasses can be produced in an hour. The key concept has been to convert retail stores into minifactories. Today's photo stores operate film-developing equipment, and optician retailers operate mini-laboratories in their stores. The same factory principle is applied by Mrs. Fields, Dunkin Donuts, and others who bake the goods as needed in their stores.

Services are also being speeded up. Mortgage loans typically take several weeks to process before approval. Traditionally, "We take your life story, and you take Rolaids for the next 30 days until we tell you you're approved," according to one mortgage broker. But things are changing. Today's applicant simply goes to Citibank, supplies a simple statement of finances, and a CitiQuik software program lets the bank determine within a matter of minutes whether to approve the mortgage. Auto damage insurance claims are also being settled faster. Progressive Insurance dispatches a Ford Explorer equipped with a PC, modem, printer, and fax to an accident scene or shortly thereafter to the insured's home. The claims adjuster can assess damages, issue a check, and arrange for a loaner car on the spot. Policyholders with other companies normally wait several business days before a claims adjuster contacts the policyholder and starts the paperwork.

All it takes is one company in the industry to find a way to serve customers faster and better to force the others to reexamine their speed of performance in innovation, manufacturing, logistics, and retailing.

Sources: For further reading, see Brian Dumaine, "Speed," *Fortune,* February 17, 1989, pp. 54–59; George Stalk, Jr., and Thomas M. Hout, *Competing Against Time* (New York: Free Press, 1990); Joseph D. Blackburn, *Time-Based Competition* (Homewood, IL: Irwin, 1991); Christopher Meyer, *Fast Cycle Time* (New York: Free Press, 1993); "The Computer Liked Us," *U.S. News & World Report,* August 14, 1995, pp. 71–72; and Carol J. Loomis, "Sex, Reefer? And Auto Insurance!," *Fortune,* August 7, 1995, p. 88.

its product through continuous service enhancements for its launderer customers. Milliken trains its customers' salespeople; supplies prospect leads and sales-promotional material to them; supplies online computer-order-entry and route-optimization systems; carries on marketing research for customers; sponsors quality-improvement workshops; and sends its salespeople to work with customers on customer action teams. Launderers are more than willing to buy Milliken shop towels and pay a price premium because the extra services improve their profitability.[7]

MAINTENANCE AND REPAIR. *Maintenance and repair* describes the company's service program for helping customers keep their purchased products in good working order. Caterpillar claims to offer better and faster maintenance and repair service for its heavy-construction equipment than any other dealer in the world. Automobile buyers are especially concerned with the quality of repair service that they can expect from their dealer.

MISCELLANEOUS SERVICES. Companies can find many other ways to add value by differentiating their customer services. They can offer a better product warranty or maintenance contract than their competitors. They can establish patronage awards, as the airlines have done with their frequent-flyer programs. Here are two creative company examples:

VALLEY VIEW CENTER MALL The Valley View Center Mall in Dallas recently unveiled its Smart Shoppers Club, a program that rewards customers who tap onto their computerized interactive touch-screen kiosks. To obtain a membership and personal identification number, mallgoers fill out a short application that asks simple demographic and psychographic questions. Then, each time members visit the mall, they input their ID number into one of the mall's three touch-screen kiosks and receive daily discount retail coupons, prizes awarded randomly each week, and a calendar of events. While customers reap discounts and prizes, Valley View retailers get valuable marketing information about their customers. The shopping center is one of only about 10 of the nation's 35,000 malls to use this high-tech consumer loyalty program.[8]

MCI In its battle to compete with AT&T, MCI crafted its unique "Friends and Family" program. MCI customers can identify up to 20 phone numbers for inclusion on a private "mini-network" that entitles them to a 20% discount on all long-distance calls made to anyone in that group. The discount applies on top of MCI's usual rates as well as any other discount calling plans that might be in place when the customer signs up. The catch—and the bonus for MCI—is that people on *both* ends of the line must be MCI customers for the discount to apply.

There are a virtually unlimited number of specific services and benefits that companies can offer to differentiate themselves from their competitors.

Personnel Differentiation

Companies can gain a strong competitive advantage through hiring and training better people than their competitors do. Thus Singapore Airlines enjoys an excellent reputation in large part because of its flight attendants. The McDonald's people are courteous, the IBM people are professional, and the Disney people are upbeat. The sales forces of such companies as Connecticut General Life and Merck enjoy an excellent reputation.[9] Wal-Mart has differentiated its superstores by assigning an employee at each store to be a "people greeter" who welcomes shoppers, gives advice on where to find items, marks merchandise carried in for returns or exchanges, and gives small gifts to children.

Better-trained personnel exhibit six characteristics:

- *Competence:* The employees possess the required skill and knowledge.
- *Courtesy:* The employees are friendly, respectful, and considerate.
- *Credibility:* The employees are trustworthy.
- *Reliability:* The employees perform the service consistently and accurately.
- *Responsiveness:* The employees respond quickly to customers' requests and problems.
- *Communication:* The employees make an effort to understand the customer and communicate clearly.[10]

Differentiating
and Positioning
the Market Offering

Channel Differentiation

Companies can achieve differentiation through the way they shape their distribution channels, particularly these channels' coverage, expertise, and performance. For example, Caterpillar's success in the construction-equipment industry is based partly on its superior channel development. Its dealers are found in more locations than competitors' dealers, and Caterpillar's dealers are typically better trained and perform more reliably. Companies such as Dell in computers and Avon in cosmetics distinguish themselves by developing and managing direct marketing channels of high quality. Dell, for example, managed to achieve the number-one rating in customer satisfaction even though it dealt with its customers only over the phone. (We discuss marketing channels in detail in Chapter 18 and direct marketing fully in Chapter 23.)

Image Differentiation

Even when competing offers look the same, buyers may respond differently to the company image or brand image. Consider the success of Marlboro cigarettes. The primary way to account for Marlboro's extraordinary worldwide market share (around 30%) is that Marlboro's "macho cowboy" image has struck a responsive chord with much of the cigarette-smoking public. Marlboro has developed a distinctive "personality." But competitors have begun to attack this image. In a 1994 ad blitz, R. J. Reynolds pitted Camel's whimsical, irreverent Joe Camel character directly against Marlboro's venerable cowboy. In the ad Joe Camel bursts through a billboard with the tagline "Genuine Taste. Never Boring" blaring above him. In the background there's a Western sunset and a riderless horse stands next to a seated cowboy.[11]

IDENTITY VERSUS IMAGE. It is important to distinguish between identity and image. *Identity* comprises the ways that a company aims to identify itself or position its product. *Image* is the way the public perceives the company or its products. The company designs an identity or positioning to shape the public's image, but other factors may intervene to determine each person's resulting image.

An effective image does three things for a product. First, it conveys a singular message that establishes the product's character and value proposition. Second, it conveys this message in a distinctive way so that it is not confused with similar messages from competitors. Third, it delivers emotional power so that it stirs the hearts as well as the minds of buyers.

Developing a strong image calls for creativity and hard work. The image cannot be implanted in the public's mind overnight nor seeded by one media vehicle alone. Rather, the image must be conveyed through every available communication vehicle and disseminated continuously. If "IBM means service," this message must be expressed in symbols, written and audiovisual media, atmosphere, and behavior. Companies that are inconsistent in conveying a message leave customers confused and more vulnerable to campaigns of competitors with stronger messages. For example, Burger King has had some difficulties in this area. When the company created Herb, a hapless nerd who had never been to Burger King, consumers began thinking that only nerds went there. Then a Burger King campaign suggesting that "sometimes you gotta break the rules" was not greeted with enthusiasm by parents. "None of the campaigns dealt with the issue of why a consumer should go to Burger King rather than McDonalds," says marketing guru Al Ries.[12]

SYMBOLS. A strong image consists of one or more symbols that trigger company or brand recognition. The company and brand *logos* should be designed for instant recognition. The company might choose some object such as the lion (Harris Bank), apple (Apple Computer), or doughboy (Pillsbury) to symbolize the organization. The company might build a brand around a famous person, as with new perfumes—Passion (Elizabeth Taylor) and Uninhibited (Cher). Companies may also choose a color identifier such as blue (IBM) or red (Campbell soup) or a specific piece of sound/music. Figure 10-2 reproduces the logos of America's most admired companies.

WRITTEN AND AUDIOVISUAL MEDIA. The chosen symbols must be worked into advertisements that convey the company or brand personality. The ads should convey a storyline, a mood, a performance level—something distinctive. The message should be replicated in other publications, such as annual reports, brochures, and catalogs. The company's stationery and business cards should reflect the same image that the company wants to convey.

ATMOSPHERE. The physical space in which the organization produces or delivers its products and services is another powerful image generator. Hyatt Regency hotels developed a distinctive image through its atrium lobbies. A bank that wants to look friendly must choose the right building design, interior design, layout, colors, materials, and furnishings.

EVENTS. A company can build an identity through the type of events it sponsors. Perrier, the bottled water company, came into prominence by laying out exercise tracks and sponsoring health sports events. AT&T and IBM identify them-

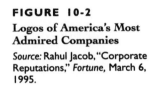

FIGURE 10-2
Logos of America's Most Admired Companies
Source: Rahul Jacob, "Corporate Reputations," *Fortune*, March 6, 1995.

Differentiating
and Positioning
the Market Offering

selves as sponsors of cultural events such as symphony performances and art exhibits. Other organizations identify themselves with popular causes: Heinz gives money to hospitals, and Kraft General Foods makes donations to MADD (Mothers against Drunk Drivers).

One of the best examples of a product that has used a multitude of image-building techniques to etch a singular image on the public mind is the Swatch watch from Switzerland.

SWATCH   Swatch is a lightweight, water-resistant, shock-proof electronic analog watch with a colorful plastic band. It is issued in many different faces and bands, all very colorful and sporty. Prices range from $40 to $100. The watch is designed to appeal as a fashion item to young, active, and trendy people.

Swatch watches are sold today in more than 30 countries. They are sold in jewelry stores, fashion outlets, and upscale department stores but not in mass-merchandise outlets. One of Swatch's chief strengths has been its promotional and merchandising skill. Here are some examples:

◆ Swatch issues new watches during the year and people eagerly await the new arrivals. Many people own more than one Swatch watch, since they want to wear different colors on different days or occasions.

◆ Swatch launches limited editions of "snazzy" watch designs twice a year. Swatch watch collectors have the privilege of bidding to buy one of the limited edition. The catch is that Swatch may produce only 40,000 units and yet receive orders from 100,000 or more collectors. The company will sponsor a drawing to choose the 40,000 lucky collectors who can buy the watch.

◆ Christie's, the auction house, holds periodic auctions of early Swatch watches. One collector paid $60,000 for one of the rarer Swatch watches. Given that Swatches appeared only in the last 18 years, they have achieved the status of "classics of our time."

◆ In a Lisbon museum, there is an exhibit of rare Swatch watches protected behind bullet-proof glass.

◆ Swatch operates some of its own retail stores. On the famous Via Monte Napoleone fashion street in Milan, the Swatch store attracts more visitors than any of the other stores that line the street. Sometimes crowds will form outside of the store and a voice on a loudspeaker will read four digits and only persons whose passport numbers contain the four digits will be allowed into the store to buy watches.

◆ Many companies have approached Swatch to issue a Swatch with their company logo. Swatch acceded only once to Coca-Cola but has refused to do this for other companies.

Swatch clearly has written the marketing book on how to build a cult following by applying superior styling, merchandising, and promotion.[13]

DEVELOPING A POSITIONING STRATEGY

We have seen how companies, products, and brands can be differentiated. Even in the case of a commodity product, the company must see its task as that of converting an undifferentiated product into a differentiated offering. Levitt and others have pointed out dozens of ways to differentiate an offering.[14]

But not all brand differences are meaningful or worthwhile. Not every difference is a differentiator. Each difference has the potential to create company costs as well as customer benefits. Therefore the company must carefully select the ways in which it will distinguish itself from competitors. A difference is worth establishing to the extent that it satisfies the following criteria:

◆ *Important:* The difference delivers a highly valued benefit to a sufficient number of buyers.

◆ *Distinctive:* The difference either isn't offered by others or is offered in a more distinctive way by the company.

- *Superior:* The difference is superior to other ways of obtaining the same benefit.
- *Communicable:* The difference is communicable and visible to buyers.
- *Preemptive:* The difference cannot be easily copied by competitors.
- *Affordable:* The buyer can afford to pay for the difference.
- *Profitable:* The company will find it profitable to introduce the difference.

Many companies have introduced differentiations that failed on one or more of these tests. The Westin Stamford hotel in Singapore advertises that it is the world's tallest hotel. Actually, this isn't important to many tourists and in fact turns many off. Polaroid's Polarvision, which produced instantly developed film, bombed too. Although Polarvision was distinctive and even preemptive, it was inferior to another way of capturing motion—namely, videocameras. When the Turner Broadcasting System installed TV monitors to beam Cable News Network (CNN) to bored shoppers in store checkout lines, it thought it had a winner in its Checkout Channel. Yet, even though this product was both distinctive and even preemptive, it didn't pass the "superior" test. Customers weren't looking for a new source of entertainment in supermarkets. Turner took a $16 million tax write-down to pull the plug on Checkout Channel.[15]

These examples notwithstanding, Carpenter, Glazer, and Nakamoto posit that brands can sometimes successfully differentiate on attributes that *appear* to create a meaningful product difference but are actually irrelevant to creating that benefit. They argue that buyers may infer that a distinctive but irrelevant attribute is actually relevant and valuable. For instance, Procter & Gamble differentiates its Folger's instant coffee by its "flaked coffee crystals" created through a "unique patented process." The advertising implies that the process improves the coffee's taste. In reality, the shape of the coffee particle is irrelevant because the crystal immediately dissolves in the hot water and its surface area doesn't affect flavor (as it would do if the coffee were brewed). Another example is Alberto Culver's Alberto Natural Silk shampoo. Alberto Culver differentiates this product by putting silk in the shampoo and advertising it with the slogan "We put silk in a bottle" to suggest that the shampoo will make the user's hair silky. However, a company spokesman conceded that silk doesn't really do anything for hair. These campaigns can successfully attach value to the differences they promote because customers infer the attributes' value and have no way of knowing if flaked coffee crystals really improve taste or if actual silk makes hair softer. However, this strategy could be damaging in the long run if competitors introduce stronger or more authentic benefits. There is also the danger that consumer groups will point out the misleading qualities of the attribute. Marketers should give serious consideration to the ethics of this practice.[16]

Each firm will want to promote those few differences that will appeal most strongly to its target market. In other words, the firm will want to develop a focused positioning strategy.

❖ **POSITIONING** is the act of designing the company's offering and image so that they occupy a meaningful and distinct competitive position in the target customers' minds.

For example, one auto company might choose to differentiate its cars on durability, while its competitors may choose to emphasize fuel economy, comfort, or smoothness of ride. The end result of positioning is the successful creation of a market-focused value proposition, a simple clear statement of why the target market should buy the product. Table 10-4 on the next page shows how three companies—Perdue, Volvo, and Domino's—defined their value proposition given their target customers, benefits, and prices. (Domino's has since changed its promise of 30-minute delivery.)

Differentiating
and Positioning
the Market Offering

TABLE 10-4   EXAMPLES OF VALUE PROPOSITIONS

COMPANY/ PRODUCT	TARGET CUSTOMERS	BENEFITS	PRICE	VALUE PROPOSITION
Perdue (chicken)	Quality-conscious consumers of chicken	Tenderness	10% premium	More tender golden chicken at a moderate premium price
Volvo (station wagon)	Safety-conscious "upscale" families	Durability and safety	20% premium	The safest, most durable wagon in which your family can ride
Domino's (pizza)	Convenience-minded pizza lovers	Delivery speed and good quality	15% premium	A good hot pizza, delivered to your door within 30 minutes of ordering, at a moderate price

To do focused positioning, the company must decide how many and which differences (e.g., benefits, features) to promote to its target customers.

How Many Differences to Promote?

Many marketers advocate promoting only one benefit to the target market. Rosser Reeves said a company should develop a *unique selling proposition (USP)* for each brand and stick to it.[17] Thus Crest toothpaste consistently promotes its anticavity protection, and Mercedes promotes its great automotive engineering. Ries and Trout also favor one consistent positioning message.[18] Each brand should pick an attribute and tout itself as "number one" on that attribute. Buyers tend to remember "number-one" messages, especially in a society that suffers from information overload. For more on this topic, see the Marketing Insight titled " 'Positioning' According to Ries and Trout."

The most commonly promoted number-one positionings are "best quality," "best service," "lowest price," "best value," "safest," "fastest," "most customized," "most convenient," and "most advanced technology." If a company hammers away at one of these positionings and convincingly delivers on it, it will probably be best known and recalled for this strength. For example, Home Depot has gained a reputation for "best service" among home-improvement product retailers. The company has created a culture of service that has won the hearts and minds of consumers:

HOME DEPOT   Home Depot's founder and CEO, Bernard Marcus, preaches the service gospel to its salespeople in cheerleading sessions known as "Breakfast with Bernie." Legend has it that Marcus once walked into the back office of one of his stores and noticed a Sears Craftsman wrench lying in a pile of items that customers had returned. When Marcus called the store's customer-service people together, he held up the wrench and asked who had accepted it as a return, since Home Depot doesn't sell Sears wrenches. One nervous employee admitted guilt, but Marcus broke into a grin and cited the incident as a great example of someone doing the unorthodox to please a customer. Yet instances of salespeople going out of their way for customers are not isolated occurrences at Home Depot. Its sales staff is trained to offer on-the-spot lessons in tile laying, electrical installations, and other projects. The chain also is the only large building products retailer to place experienced tradespeople—such as plumbers, electricians, and carpenters—on its floor to help customers.[19]

Not everyone agrees that single-benefit positioning is always best. *Double-benefit positioning* may be necessary if two or more firms are claiming to be best on

"Positioning" According to Ries and Trout

The word *positioning* was popularized by two advertising executives, Al Ries and Jack Trout. They see positioning as a creative exercise done with an existing product:

Positioning starts with a product. A piece of merchandise, a service, a company, an institution, or even a person. . . . But positioning is not what you do to a product. Positioning is what you do to the mind of the prospect. That is, you position the product in the mind of the prospect.

Ries and Trout argue that well-known products generally have a distinctive position in consumers' minds. Thus Hertz is thought of as the world's largest auto-rental agency, Coca-Cola as the world's largest soft-drink company, Porsche as one of the world's best sports cars, and so on. These brands own those positions and it would be hard for a competitor to steal them. A competitor has only three strategy options.

The first strategy is to strengthen its own current position in the consumer's mind. Thus Avis took its second position in the auto rental business and made a strong point about it: "We're number two. We try harder." And 7-Up capitalizes on the fact that it is not a cola soft drink by advertising itself as the Uncola.

The second strategy is to search for and grab a new unoccupied position that is valued by enough consumers. Thus the Three Musketeers chocolate bar began advertising itself as having 45% less fat than most of the other chocolate bars on the market. United Jersey Bank was searching for a way to compete against the giant New York banks such as Citibank and Chase. Its marketers noticed that giant banks were usually slower in arranging loans. They positioned United Jersey as "the fast-moving bank."

The third strategy is to deposition or reposition the competition. Most U.S. buyers of dinnerware thought that Lenox and Royal Doulton china both come from England. Royal Doulton put out ads showing that Lenox china is made in New Jersey, but that Royal Doulton comes from England. In a similar vein, Stolichnaya vodka attacked Smirnoff and Wolfschmidt vodka by pointing out that these brands are made, respectively, in Hartford (Connecticut) and Lawrenceburg (Indiana), but "Stolichnaya is different. It is Russian." Wendy's famous commercial, where a 70-year-old woman named Clara looks at a competitor's hamburger and says "Where's the beef?" showed how an attack could destabilize the consumer's confidence in the leader.

Ries and Trout outline how similar brands can acquire some distinctiveness in a society in which there is so much advertising that consumers screen out most of the messages. A consumer may know only about seven soft drinks even though there are many more on the market. Even then, the mind often knows them in the form of a *product ladder*, such as Coke/Pepsi/RC Cola or Hertz/Avis/National. The top firm is remembered best. The second firm may achieve only half the sales volume of the first firm, and the third firm may achieve half the sales volume of the second firm.

People tend to remember *number one*. For example, when asked, "Who was the first person to successfully fly alone over the Atlantic Ocean?" we will answer "Charles Lindbergh." When asked, "Who was the second person to do it?" we draw a blank. This is why companies fight for the number-one position. Ries and Trout point out that the "largest in the total market" position can be held by only one brand. But a company can achieve the largest size within a segment. Thus 7-Up is the number-one Uncola, Porsche is the number-one small sports car, and Dial is the number-one deodorant soap. The marketer should identify an important attribute or benefit that a brand can convincingly own.

A fourth strategy, not mentioned by Ries and Trout, is the exclusive-club strategy. It can be developed by a company when a number-one position along some meaningful attribute cannot be achieved. For example, a company can promote the idea that it is one of the Big Three. The Big Three idea was invented by the third-largest auto firm, Chrysler. (The market leader never invents this concept.) The implication is that those in the club are the "best."

Ries and Trout essentially deal with communication strategies for positioning or repositioning a brand in the consumer's mind. Yet they would add that positioning requires the company to work up every tangible aspect of product, price, place, and promotion to support the chosen positioning strategy.

Source: Al Ries and Jack Trout, *Positioning: The Battle for Your Mind* (New York: Warner Books, 1982).

the same attribute. The intention is to find a special niche within the target segment. For example, Steelcase, Inc., a leading office-furniture-systems company, differentiates itself from its competitors on two benefits: best on-time delivery and best installation support. Volvo positions its automobiles as "safest" and "most durable." Fortunately, these two benefits are compatible. One expects that a very safe car would also be very durable.

There are even cases of successful triple-benefit positioning. Smith Kline Beecham promotes its Aquafresh toothpaste as offering three benefits: anticavity protection, better breath, and whiter teeth. Clearly, many people want all three benefits, and the challenge is to convince them that the brand delivers all three. Smith Kline's solution was to create a toothpaste that squeezed out of the tube in three colors, thus visually confirming the three benefits. In doing this, Beecham "countersegmented"; that is, it attracted three segments instead of one.

As companies increase the number of claims for their brand, they risk disbelief and a loss of clear positioning. In general, a company must avoid four major positioning errors:

◆ *Underpositioning:* Some companies discover that buyers have only a vague idea of the brand. Buyers don't really sense anything special about it. The brand is seen as just another entry in a crowded marketplace. When Pepsi introduced its clear Crystal Pepsi in 1993, customers were distinctly unimpressed. They didn't see "clarity" as an important benefit in a soft drink.[20]

◆ *Overpositioning:* Buyers may have too narrow an image of the brand. Thus a consumer might think that diamond rings at Tiffany start at $5,000 when in fact Tiffany now offers affordable diamond rings starting at $900.

◆ *Confused positioning:* Buyers might have a confused image of the brand resulting from the company's making too many claims or changing the brand's positioning too frequently. This was the case with Stephen Jobs's sleek and powerful NeXT desktop computer, which was positioned first for students, then for engineers, and then for businesspeople, all unsuccessfully.[21]

◆ *Doubtful positioning:* Buyers may find it hard to believe the brand claims in view of the product's features, price, or manufacturer. When GM's Cadillac division introduced the Cimarron, it positioned the car as a luxury competitor with BMW, Mercedes, and Audi. While the car featured leather seats, a luggage rack, lots of chrome, and a Cadillac logo stamped on the chassis, customers saw the car as merely a dolled-up version of Chevy's Cavalier and Oldsmobile's Firenza. While the car was positioned as "more for more," the customers saw it as "less for more."[22]

The advantage of solving the positioning problem is that it enables the company to solve the marketing-mix problem. The marketing mix—product, price, place, and promotion—is essentially the working out of the tactical details of the positioning strategy. Thus a firm that seizes upon the "high-quality position" knows that it must produce high-quality products, charge a high price, distribute through high-class dealers, and advertise in high-quality magazines. This is the primary way to project a consistent and believable high-quality image.

How do companies go about selecting a position? We will answer this question by way of the following example:

A theme park company wants to build a new theme park in the Los Angeles area to take advantage of the large number of tourists who come to Los Angeles to see Disneyland and other tourist attractions. Seven theme parks now operate in the Los Angeles area: Disneyland, Magic Mountain, Knott's Berry Farm, Busch Gardens, Japanese Deer Park, Marineland of the Pacific, and Lion Country Safari. Management of all the existing theme parks need to know how to position themselves against each other and the new competitor.

The new competitor used the following procedure to decide on its positioning. It presented consumers with a series of triads (for example, Busch Gardens, the

PART 3

Developing
Marketing
Strategies

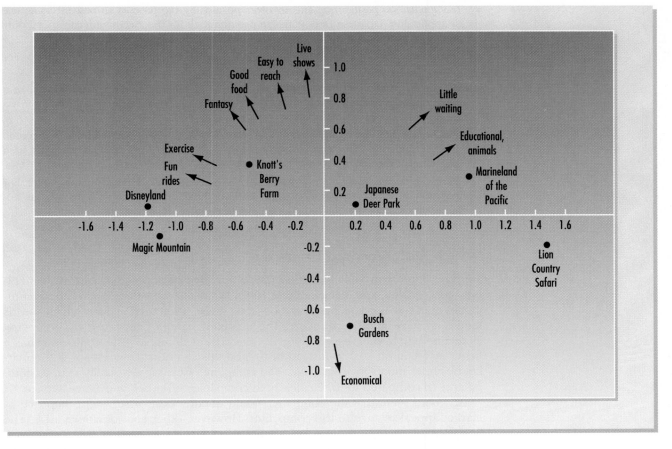

FIGURE 10-3
Perceptual Map

Japanese Deer Park, and Disneyland) and asked them to choose the two most similar attractions and the two least similar attractions in each triad. A statistical analysis led to the *perceptual map* in Figure 10-3.

The map contains two features. The seven dots represent the seven tourist attractions. The closer any two attractions are, the more similar they are in tourists' minds. Thus Disneyland and Magic Mountain are perceived as similar, while Disneyland and Lion Country Safari are perceived as very different.

The map also shows nine satisfactions that people look for in tourist attractions. These are indicated by arrows. Marineland of the Pacific is perceived as involving the "least waiting time," so it is farthest along the imaginary line of the "little waiting" arrow. Consumers think of Busch Gardens as the most economical choice.[23]

Using the information in the perceptual map, the theme park company can recognize the different positioning strategies that theme park competitors in Los Angeles can pursue:[24]

◆ *Attribute positioning:* This occurs when a company positions itself on an attribute, such as size, number of years in existence, and so forth. For example, Disneyland can advertise itself as the largest theme park in the world.

◆ *Benefit positioning:* Here the product is positioned as the leader in a certain benefit. For example, Knott's Berry Farm may try to position itself as a theme park for people seeking a fantasy experience, such as living in the Old West of cowboy fame.

- *Use/application positioning:* This involves positioning the product as best for some use or application. Japanese Deer Park can position itself for the tourist who can spend only an hour and wants to catch some quick entertainment.
- *User positioning:* This involves positioning the product as best for some user group. For example, Magic Mountain can advertise itself as the theme park for "thrill seekers."
- *Competitor positioning:* Here the product positions itself as better in some way than a named or implied competitor. For example, Lion Country Safari can advertise that it has a greater variety of animals than the Japanese Deer Park.
- *Product category positioning:* Here the product is positioned as the leader in a certain product category. For example, Marineland of the Pacific can position itself not as a "recreational theme park" but as an "educational institution."
- *Quality/price positioning:* Here the product is positioned as offering the best value. For example, Busch Gardens can position itself as the "best value" for the money (as opposed to such positionings as "high quality/high price" or "lowest price").

Which Differences to Promote?

Suppose a company has identified four alternative positioning platforms: technology, cost, quality, and service (Table 10-5). It has one major competitor. Both companies stand at 8 on technology (1 = low score, 10 = high score), which means they both have good technology. The company cannot gain much by improving its technology further, especially given the cost of doing so. The competitor has a better standing on cost (8 instead of 6), and this can hurt the company if the market becomes more price-sensitive. The company offers higher quality than its competitors (8 compared to 6). Finally, both companies offer below-average service.

It would seem that the company should go after cost or service to improve its market appeal relative to the competitor. However, other considerations arise. The first is how target customers feel about improvements in each of these attributes. Column 4 indicates that improvements in cost and service would be of high importance to customers. But can the company afford to make the improvements in cost and service, and how fast can it complete them? Column 5 shows that improving service would have high affordability and speed. But would the competitor also be able to improve service if the company started to do so? Column 6 shows that the competitor's ability to improve service is low, perhaps because the competitor does not believe in service or is strapped for funds. Based on the information in Columns 1 through 6, Column 7 shows the appropriate actions to take with respect to each attribute. The one that make the most sense is for the company to improve its service and promote this improvement. This was the conclusion that

TABLE 10-5	METHOD FOR COMPETITIVE-ADVANTAGE SELECTION					
1 COMPETITIVE ADVANTAGE	**2** COMPANY STANDING	**3** COMPETITOR STANDING	**4** IMPORTANCE OF IMPROVING STANDING (H-M-L)*	**5** AFFORDABILITY AND SPEED (H-M-L)	**6** COMPETITOR'S ABILITY TO IMPROVE STANDING (H-M-L)	**7** RECOM-MENDED ACTION
Technology	8	8	L	L	M	Hold
Cost	6	8	H	M	M	Monitor
Quality	8	6	L	L	H	Monitor
Service	4	3	H	H	L	Invest

* H = High; M = Medium; L = Low.

Monsanto reached in one of its chemical markets. Monsanto immediately hired additional technical service people. When they were trained and ready, Monsanto promoted itself as the "technical service leader."

COMMUNICATING THE COMPANY'S POSITIONING

Once the company has developed a clear positioning strategy, it must communicate that positioning effectively. Suppose a company chooses the "best-in-quality" strategy. Quality is communicated by choosing those physical signs and cues that people normally use to judge quality. Here are some examples:

A lawn-mower manufacturer claims its lawn mower is "powerful" and uses a noisy motor because buyers think noisy lawn mowers are more powerful.

A truck manufacturer undercoats the chassis not because it needs undercoating but because undercoating suggests concern for quality.

A car manufacturer makes cars with good-slamming doors because many buyers slam the doors in the showroom to test how well the car is built.

Ritz Carlton Hotels signal high quality in the way they handle phone calls. Employees are trained to answer within three rings, to answer with a genuine "smile" in their voices, to eliminate call transfers when possible, and to be extremely knowledgeable about all hotel information.[25]

Quality is also communicated through other marketing elements. A high price usually signals a premium-quality product to buyers. The product's quality image is also affected by the packaging, distribution, advertising, and promotion. Here are some cases where a brand's quality image was hurt:

A well-known frozen-food brand lost its prestige image by being on sale too often.

A premium beer's image was hurt when it switched from bottles to cans.

A highly regarded television receiver lost its quality image when mass-merchandise outlets began to carry it.

Kraft General Foods used lower-quality beans in its "good to the last drop" Maxwell House coffee, leading once-loyal customers to look elsewhere for their coffee fix.

A manufacturer's reputation also contributes to the perception of quality. Certain companies are sticklers for quality; consumers expect Nestlé products and IBM products to be well made. Smart companies communicate their quality to buyers and guarantee that this quality will be delivered or their money will be refunded.

SUMMARY

1. In a competitive industry, the key to competitive advantage is product differentiation. A market offering can be differentiated along five dimensions: product (features, performance quality, conformance quality, durability, reliability, repairability, style, design), services (ordering ease, delivery, installation, customer training, customer consulting, maintenance and repair, miscellaneous services), personnel, channel, or image (symbols, written and audiovisual media, atmosphere, and events). A difference is worth establishing to the extent that it is important, distinctive, superior, communicable, preemptive, affordable, and profitable.

Differentiating
and Positioning
the Market Offering

2. Many marketers advocate promoting only one product benefit, thus creating a unique selling proposition as they position their product. People tend to remember "number one." But double-benefit position and triple-benefit positioning can also be successful, as long as marketers take steps to ensure that they do not underposition, overposition, or create confused or doubtful positioning.

3. Once the company has developed a clear positioning strategy, it must communicate that positioning effectively via the marketing mix.

CONCEPT APPLICATIONS

1. What types of "atmospherics" do restaurants use to project a desired image? Select three restaurants in your community that appeal to different market segments. What positioning strategies do they use to attract their target clientele? How do they employ atmospherics to enhance the image they want to project? Do you observe any inconsistencies between the positioning strategies they are trying to project and their actual operations?

2. Positioning is not so much what the product actually is, but rather how a company wants its target consumers to perceive the product. A company can choose from a number of different positioning strategies. Match the positioning strategy in column (I) with an example of that positioning strategy from column (II).

(I) POSITIONING STRATEGY	(II) EXAMPLE
1. *Positioning by attribute:* Associating a product with a particular feature	a. "Master Card is accepted at more restaurants than any other card."
2. *Positioning by benefit:* Associating a product with a special customer benefit	b. "Head & Shoulders is the best shampoo for people with dandruff."
3. *Positioning by use/application:* Associating the product with a use or application	c. "Chevy trucks outperform Ford trucks."
4. *Positioning by user:* Associating a product with a user or class of user	d. "Timex watches 'take a licking and keep on ticking.'"
5. *Positioning by competitor:* Identifying the product by using a competitor as a reference point	e. "Preference by L'Oreal. It costs a little more, but I'm worth it."
6. *Positioning by product category:* Associating the product with others in a similar product class	f. "7-Up is the Uncola. It's lighter and more refreshing."
7. *Positioning by quality/price:* Using price as a cue to higher quality, with higher quality being reflected in more features and/or services	g. "A box of Arm & Hammer baking soda in your refrigerator will keep it clean-smelling."

3. Define the following concepts and describe their relationship to one another:
   a. Image
   b. Position
   c. Customer perception
   d. Product features
   e. Competitive advantage
   f. Positioning strategy

4. Examine the following clusters of U.S. magazine titles. For each cluster, suggest the market niche to which the magazines appeal. Be as specific as possible in your answer.

a. *Car and Driver*
   Road and Track
   Motor Trend
b. *Ebony*
   Jet
   Essence
c. *New York Woman*
   Sassy
   Cosmopolitan
d. *Financial World*
   Forbes
   Fortune
e. *Savvy*
   Worth
   Success

f. *Billboard*
   Rolling Stone
   Spin
g. *Details*
   GQ
   Esquire
h. *Mother Jones*
   Village Voice
   Utne Reader
i. *Guitar Player*
   Musician

In addition, name some publications targeted toward the following groups:
a. Suburban dwellers
b. The gay population
c. Sports enthusiasts

5. The following are four examples of positioning errors: underpositioning, overpositioning, confused positioning, and doubtful positioning. Which example corresponds to each positioning error? Give another example of each type of error.
   a. Buyers do not believe Ford's ads that its LTD is as quiet as a Rolls Royce, and they do not believe that Jacqueline Smith wears clothes sold by Kmart.
   b. People don't really have an idea of what Royal Crown Cola's attributes are.
   c. Dr. Pepper's ad campaigns have changed so much over the years that the company has never really established an image for its soft drink in the consumers' minds.
   d. Levi Strauss, which is known for its jeans, encountered some problems when trying to add three-piece suits to its product line.

6. Analyze the following perceptual map and decide how you would reposition Lever 2000 bar soap based on competitive positioning. This map profiles the bar and hand soap industry. (Data created for demonstration purposes only.) How does your brand awareness compare to that of the competition? What positioning error might your brand be suffering from?

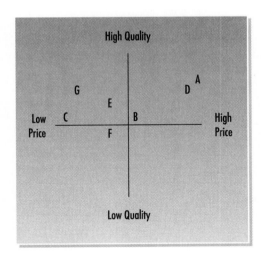

BRAND	BRAND AWARENESS
A = Dove	77%
B = Lever 2000	35
C = Dial	60
D = Camay	68
E = Ivory	74
F = Caress	52
G = Safeguard	59

7. A new-product development team at Colgate-Palmolive is developing a new dry bleach. The team is considering each of the seven positioning options utilized by the theme park company on pages 299–300. For each option, describe how the company might

develop the product and communicate its positioning to the market. Once you've determined the position, try to come up with a name for the product.

8. In conducting market research, the R. J. Reynolds Tobacco Company found that African-Americans tend to prefer a lighter menthol flavor in their cigarettes. As a result, RJR began developing a product for this niche. When the new cigarette (called Uptown) was ready for the test market, the furor began. Various civil rights groups and the Secretary of Health and Human Services, Louis W. Sullivan, contended that the new cigarette—which would be specifically targeted at African-Americans—would bring more disease, suffering, and death to a group that already has too many health problems. However, many cigarette ads, particularly ads for menthol cigarettes, already used African-American models (see Figure 1), and RJR was surprised that it had been singled out for criticism. In response to the outcry, RJR withdrew the new product from the market.

Discuss the ethical and social implications of this case. What implications does the withdrawal of Uptown from the market have for Virginia Slims cigarettes? Since magazines that are targeted toward the African-American community stood to gain large sums from advertising revenues if the product were marketed, what reaction would you anticipate from them? Are there circumstances where targeted advertising of a legal product to an adult group should be restricted?

FIGURE 1

9. Four brands of washing machines have been compared on the following seven dimensions. The highest possible rating on a given dimension is $+5$; the lowest possible rating is -5. Create a two-dimensional perceptual map for brands A, B, C, and D. (You will need to collapse the dimensions into two categories, "washing effectiveness" and "service quality.")

ATTRIBUTE	BRAND			
	A	B	C	D
Variable wash and spin	−2	2	2	3
Variable water temperature control	−1	2	1	3
Frequency-of-repair record	2	3	2	−1
Detergent requirement	−3	2	1	2
Repair-service availability	1	2	1	−2
Guarantee	1.5	2.5	2	−1
Maximum load capacity	−2	3	1	2

NOTES

1. Gail C. Rigler, "Case Study: Southwest Airlines," *Across the Board,* March 1995, p. 56; "ATW Awards Twenty Years of Excellence: . . . In Short-Haul Airline Service: Southwest Airlines," *Air Transport World,* February 1994, pp. 44–45; Richard S. Teitelbaum, "Keeping Promises," *Fortune,* Autumn–Winter 1993, pp. 32, 34; Don Reynolds, Jr., *Crackerjack Positioning: Niche Marketing Strategy for the Entrepreneur* (Tulsa, OK: Atwood Publishing, 1993), pp. 160–61.

2. Edwin T. Crego, Jr., and Peter D. Schiffrin, *Customer Centered Reengineering* (Homewood, IL: Irwin, 1995).

3. Some of these bases are discussed in David A. Garvin, "Competing on the Eight Dimensions of Quality," *Harvard Business Review,* November–December 1987, pp. 101–9.

4. See Philip Kotler, "Design: A Powerful but Neglected Strategic Tool," *Journal of Business Strategy,* Fall 1984, pp. 16–21. Also see Christopher Lorenz, *The Design Dimension* (New York: Basil Blackwell, 1986).

5. Pam Weisz, "Times Sure Have Changed When Tupperware Is Cool," *Brandweek,* July 11, 1994, p. 28.

6. Joseph Weber, "A Better Grip on Hawking Tools," *Business Week,* June 5, 1995, p. 99.

7. Adapted from Tom Peters's description in *Thriving on Chaos* (New York: Alfred Knopf, 1987), pp. 56–57.

8. See "Club for the Smart," *Marketing News,* May 23, 1994, p. 1.

9. See M. D. Harkavay, *100 Best Companies to Sell For* (New York: John Wiley, 1989).

10. For a similar list, see Leonard L. Berry and A. Parasuraman, *Marketing Services: Competing Through Quality* (New York: Free Press, 1991), p. 16.

11. Fara Warner, "Cowpokin' Joe: New Cam Ads Dis the Marlboro Man," *Brandweek,* 35, no. 31 (August 1, 1994), 1, 6.

12. See "Big Flops," *American Demographics,* February 1995, p. 8.

13. See "Swatch: Ambitious," *The Economist,* April 18, 1992, pp. 74–75.

14. Theodore Levitt, "Marketing Success through Differentiation—of Anything," *Harvard Business Review,* January–February 1980.

15. Tim Triplett, "Consumers Show Little Taste for Clear Beverages," *Marketing News,* May 23, 1994, pp. 1, 11; Ronald Grover, "Big Brother Is Grocery Shopping with You," *Business Week,* March 29, 1993, p. 60.

16. Gregory S. Carpenter, Rashi Glazer, and Kent Nakamoto, "Meaningful Brands from Meaningless Differentiation: The Dependence on Irrelevant Attributes," *Journal of Marketing Research,* August 1994, pp. 339–50.

17. Rosser Reeves, *Reality in Advertising* (New York: Alfred Knopf, 1960).

18. See Al Ries and Jack Trout, *Positioning: The Battle for Your Mind* (New York: Warner Books, 1982).

19. Michael Treacy and Fred Wiersema, *The Discipline of Market Leaders* (Reading, MA: Addison-Wesley, 1994), p. 181; Walecia Konrad, "Cheerleading, and Clerks Who Know Awls from Augers," *Business Week,* August 3, 1992, p. 51.

20. Kevin J. Clancy and Robert S. Shulman, *Marketing Myths That Are Killing Business: The Cure for Death Wish Marketing* (New York: McGraw-Hill, 1994), pp. 83–85; Christopher Power, "Flops," *Business Week,* August 16, 1993, pp. 76–82.

21. See Clancy and Shulman, *Marketing Myths;* Power, "Flops."

22. Robert B. Tucker, *Win the Value Revolution* (Franklin Lakes, NJ: Career Press, 1995), pp. 159–60.

23. See Robert V. Stumpf, "The Market Structure of the Major Tourist Attractions in Southern California," *Proceedings of the 1976 Sperry Business Conference* (Chicago: American Marketing Association), pp. 101–6.

24. See Yoram J. Wind, *Product Policy: Concepts, Methods and Strategy* (Reading, MA: Addison-Wesley, 1982), pp. 79–81; and David Aaker and J. Gary Shansby, "Positioning Your Product," *Business Horizons,* May–June 1982, pp. 56–62.

25. Patricia Galagan, "Putting on the Ritz," *Training and Development,* December 1993, pp. 41–45.

DEVELOPING NEW PRODUCTS

While great devices are invented in the laboratory, great products are invented in the Marketing Department.

WILLIAM H. DAVIDOW

❖

Great ideas need landing gear as well as wings.

ANONYMOUS

O nce a company has carefully segmented the market, chosen its target customer groups, identified their needs, and determined its desired market positioning, it is ready to develop and launch appropriate new products. Marketing management plays a key role in the new-product-development process. Rather than leave it to the R&D department to develop new products on its own, marketing actively participates with other departments in every stage of product development.

Every company must carry on new-product development. Replacement products must be created to maintain or build sales. Furthermore, customers want new products, and competitors will do their best to supply them. Each year over 16,000 new products (including line extensions and new brands) are introduced into groceries and drugstores.

A company can add new products through acquisition and/or new-product development. The acquisition route can take three forms. The company can buy other companies, it can acquire patents from other companies, or it can buy a license or franchise from another company.

The new-product development route can take two forms. The company can develop new products in its own laboratories. Or it can contract with independent researchers or new-product-development firms to develop specific products for the company.

The consulting firm Booz, Allen & Hamilton has identified six categories of new products in terms of their newness to the company and to the marketplace:[1]

- *New-to-the-world products:* New products that create an entirely new market
- *New product lines:* New products that allow a company to enter an established market for the first time
- *Additions to existing product lines:* New products that supplement a company's established product lines (package sizes, flavors, and so on)
- *Improvements and revisions of existing products:* New products that provide improved performance or greater perceived value and replace existing products
- *Repositionings:* Existing products that are targeted to new markets or market segments
- *Cost reductions:* New products that provide similar performance at lower cost

Only 10% of all new products are truly innovative and new to the world. These products involve the greatest cost and risk because they are new to both the company and the marketplace. Thus most company new-product activity is devoted to improving existing products. At Sony, over 80% of new-product activity is undertaken to modify and improve existing Sony products.

Because new-product development is the life source of the company's future, this chapter examines the following questions:

- **What challenges does a company face in developing new products?**
- **What organizational structures are used to manage new-product development?**
- **What are the main stages in developing new products, and how can they be managed better?**
- **What factors affect the rate of diffusion and consumer adoption of newly launched products?**

Developing
New
Products

CHALLENGES IN NEW-PRODUCT DEVELOPMENT

Given today's intense competition, companies that fail to develop new products are putting themselves at great risk. Their existing products are vulnerable to changing consumer needs and tastes, new technologies, shortened product life cycles, and increased domestic and foreign competition.

At the same time, new-product development is risky. Texas Instruments lost $660 million before withdrawing from the home computer business, RCA lost $500 million on its ill-fated videodisc players, Ford lost $250 million on its ill-fated Edsel, Du Pont lost an estimated $100 million on its synthetic leather called Corfam, and the French Concorde aircraft will never recover its investment.[2]

New products continue to fail at a disturbing rate. The new-product failure rate in packaged goods (consisting mostly of line extensions) is estimated at 80 percent.[3] Clancy and Shulman believe that the same high failure rate befalls new financial products and services, such as credit cards, insurance plans, and brokerage services.[4] Cooper and Kleinschmidt estimate that about 75% of new products fail at launch.[5]

Why do new products fail? Several factors may be responsible:

♦ A high-level executive might push a favorite idea through in spite of negative market research findings.

♦ The idea is good, but the market size is overestimated.

♦ The actual product is not well designed.

♦ The new product is incorrectly positioned in the market, not advertised effectively, or overpriced.

♦ Development costs are higher than expected.

♦ Competitors fight back harder than expected.

In addition, several other factors hinder new-product development:

♦ *Shortage of important new-product ideas in certain areas:* There may be few ways left to improve some basic products (such as steel, detergents, and so forth).

♦ *Fragmented markets:* Keen competition is leading to market fragmentation. Companies have to aim their new products at smaller market segments, and this can mean lower sales and profits for each product.

♦ *Social and governmental constraints:* New products have to satisfy such criteria as consumer safety and ecological compatibility. Government requirements have slowed down innovation in the drug industry and have complicated product-design and advertising decisions in industries such as industrial equipment, chemicals, automobiles, and toys.

♦ *Costliness of the new-product-development process:* A company typically has to generate many new-product ideas to find just one worthy of development. Furthermore, the company often faces high R&D, manufacturing, and marketing costs.

♦ *Capital shortages:* Some companies with good ideas cannot raise the funds needed to research them.

♦ *Faster development time:* Many competitors are likely to get the same idea at the same time, and the victory often goes to the swiftest. Alert companies compress development time by using computer-aided design and manufacturing techniques (see the Vision 2000 feature later in this chapter), strategic partners, early concept tests, and advanced marketing planning. They are also using a new type of product development called *concurrent new-product development,* in which cross-functional teams work together to push new products through development and onto the market. If one functional area hits a snag, it works to resolve the problem while the rest of the team moves on. Concurrent product development resembles a rugby match rather than a relay race, with team members passing the new product back and forth as they head toward the goal. For example, the Allen-Bradley Company (a maker of industrial controls) recently developed a new electrical control device in just two years. Under its old system, the process would have taken six years. (For more details on the importance of speed to market, see the discussion of turbomarketing in the previous chapter.)

◆ *Shorter product life cycles:* When a new product is successful, rivals are quick to copy it. Sony used to enjoy a three-year lead on its new products before competitors could successfully copy them. Now Matsushita and other rivals will copy the product within six months, leaving hardly enough time for Sony to recoup its investment.

Given these challenges, what can a company do to ensure the success of its new products? Cooper and Kleinschmidt found that the number-one success factor is a unique superior product (for example, higher quality, new features, higher value in use, and so forth). Products with a high product advantage succeed 98% of the time, compared to products with a moderate advantage (58% success) or minimal advantage (18% success). Another key success factor is a well-defined product concept prior to development, where the company carefully defined and assessed the target market, product requirements, and benefits before proceeding. Other success factors are technological and marketing synergy, quality of execution in all stages, and market attractiveness.[6]

Madique and Zirger, in a separate study of successful product launches in the electronics industry, found eight factors accounting for new-product success. They found new-product success to be greater the deeper the company's understanding of customer needs, the higher the performance-to-cost ratio, the earlier the product is introduced ahead of competition, the greater the expected contribution margin, the more spent on announcing and launching the product, the greater the top management support, and the greater the cross-functional teamwork.[7]

The teamwork aspect is particularly important. New-product development is most effective when there is teamwork among R&D, engineering, manufacturing, purchasing, marketing, and finance from the beginning. The product idea must be researched from a marketing point of view, and a specific cross-functional team must guide the project throughout its development. Studies of Japanese companies show that the success of their new products is due in large part to utilizing cross-functional teamwork. Also of great importance is the fact that Japanese companies bring customers in at an early stage to get their views.

EFFECTIVE ORGANIZATIONAL ARRANGEMENTS

Successful new-product development requires the company to establish an effective organization for managing the new-product-development process. An effective organization begins with its top management.

Top management is ultimately accountable for the success of new products. New-product development requires management to define the business domains and product categories that the company wants to emphasize. Thus top management must establish specific criteria for acceptance of new-product ideas, especially in large multidivisional companies. For example, the Gould Corporation established the following acceptance criteria.

◆ The product can be introduced within five years.
◆ The product has a market potential of at least $50 million and a 15% growth rate.
◆ The product will provide at least 30% return on sales and 40% on investment.
◆ The product will achieve technical or market leadership.

A major decision facing top management is how much to budget for new-product development. R&D outcomes are so uncertain that it is difficult to use normal investment criteria for budgeting. Some companies solve this problem by encouraging and financing as many projects as possible, hoping to achieve a few winners. Other companies set their R&D budget by applying a conventional percentage of sales figures or by spending what the competition spends. Still other companies decide how many successful new products they need and work backward to estimate the required R&D investment.

The U.S. company best known for its commitment to new-product research and development is Minneapolis-based 3M Company:

3M Minnesota Mining and Manufacturing (3M) makes more than 60,000 products, including sandpaper, adhesives, computer diskettes, contact lenses, and Post-It Notes. Each year, 3M launches more than 200 new products. This $13 billion company's immodest goal is to have each of its 40 divisions generate at least 25% of its income from products introduced within the last five years. And it generally succeeds! Here are major features of 3M's approach to innovation:

- 3M encourages everyone, not just its engineers, to become "product champions." The company's 15% rule allows all employees to spend up to 15% of their time working on projects of personal interest.

- Each promising new idea is put in the hands of a multidisciplinary venture team headed by an "executive champion."

- 3M expects some failures and learns from them. Its slogan is "You have to kiss a lot of frogs to find a prince."

- 3M hands out its Golden Step awards each year to the venture teams whose new product earned more than $2 million in U.S. sales or $4 million in worldwide sales within three years of its commercial introduction.

Table 11-1 shows how a company might calculate the cost of new-product development. The new-products manager at a large consumer packaged-goods company reviewed the results of 64 new-product ideas. Only one in four ideas, or 16, passed the idea-screening stage. It cost $1,000 to review each idea at this stage. Half of these ideas, or eight, survived the concept-testing stage, at a cost of $20,000 each. Half of these, or four, survived the product-development stage, at a cost of $200,000 each. Half of these, or two, did well in the test market, at a cost of $500,000 each. When these two ideas were launched, at a cost of $5,000,000 each, only one was highly successful. Thus the one successful idea had cost the company $5,721,000 to develop. In the process, 63 other ideas fell by the wayside. Therefore the total cost for developing one successful new product was $13,984,400. Unless the company can improve the pass ratios and reduce the costs at each stage, it will have to budget nearly $14,000,000 for each successful new

TABLE 11-1				
ESTIMATED COST OF FINDING ONE SUCCESSFUL NEW PRODUCT (STARTING WITH 64 NEW IDEAS)	**STAGE**	**NUMBER OF IDEAS**	**PASS RATIO**	**COST PER PRODUCT IDEA**	**TOTAL COST**
	1. Idea screening	64	1:4	$ 1,000	$ 64,000
	2. Concept testing	16	1:2	20,000	320,000
	3. Product development	8	1:2	200,000	1,600,000
	4. Test marketing	4	1:2	500,000	2,000,000
	5. National launch	2	1:2	5,000,000	10,000,000
				$5,721,000	$13,984,000

idea it hopes to find. If top management wants four successful new products in the next few years, it will have to budget at least $56,000,000 (= 4 × $14,000,000) for new-product development.

Companies handle the organizational aspect of new-product development in several ways.[8] The most common of these are:

- *Product managers:* Many companies assign responsibility for new-product ideas to their product managers. In practice, this system has several faults. Product managers are usually so busy managing their existing product lines that they give little thought to new products other than line extensions. They also lack the specific skills and knowledge needed to develop and critique new products.

- *New-product managers:* Kraft General Foods and Johnson & Johnson have new-product managers who report to group product managers. This position professionalizes the new-product function. However, like product managers, new-product managers tend to think in terms of product modifications and line extensions limited to their product market.

- *New-product committees:* Many companies have a high-level management committee charged with reviewing and approving new-product proposals.

- *New-product departments:* Large companies often establish a new-product department headed by a manager who has substantial authority and access to top management. The department's major responsibilities include generating and screening new ideas, working with the R&D department, and carrying out field testing and commercialization.

- *New-product venture teams:* 3M, Dow, Westinghouse, and General Mills often assign new-product development work to venture teams. A *venture team* is a group brought together from various operating departments and charged with developing a specific product or business. They are "intrapreneurs" relieved of their other duties and given a budget, a time frame, and a "skunkworks" setting. *Intrapreneurs* are company employees charged with building new businesses or products. *Skunkworks* are informal workplaces, sometimes garages, where intrapreneurial teams attempt to develop new products.

The most sophisticated tool for managing the innovation process is the *stage-gate system.*[9] It is used by 3M and a number of other companies. The basic idea is to divide the innovation process into several distinct stages. At the end of each stage is a gate or checkpoint. The project leader, working with a cross-functional team, must bring a set of known deliverables to each gate before the project can pass to the next stage. For example, to move from the business plan stage into product development requires a convincing market research study of consumer needs and interest, a competitive analysis, and a technical appraisal. Senior managers review the criteria at each gate to judge whether the project deserves to move to the next stage, which always involves higher cost. The gatekeepers make one of four decisions: go, kill, hold, or recycle. The project leader and team know the criteria they must meet at each stage. Stage-gate systems put strong discipline into the innovation process, making its steps visible to all involved and clarifying the project leader's and team's responsibilities at each point.

MANAGING THE NEW-PRODUCT DEVELOPMENT PROCESS

We are now ready to look at the major marketing challenges at each stage of the new-product-development process. Eight stages are involved: idea generation, idea screening, concept development and testing, marketing strategy development, business analysis, product development, market testing, and commercialization. A

Developing
New
Products

preview of the various steps and decisions in the new-product development process is presented in Figure 11-1.

Idea Generation

The new-product development process starts with the search for ideas. Top managers should define the products and markets to emphasize and should state the new products' objectives. They should also state how much effort should be devoted to developing breakthrough products, modifying existing products, and copying competitors' products.

New-product ideas can come from many sources: customers, scientists, employees, competitors, channel members, and top management.

◆ The marketing concept holds that *customers' needs and wants* are the logical place to start the search for new-product ideas. Hippel has shown that the highest percentage of ideas for new industrial products originate with customers.[10] Technical companies can learn a great deal by studying their *lead users*—namely, those customers who make the most advanced use of the company's products and who recognize the need for improvements before other customers do. Companies can identify customers' needs and wants through surveys, projective (association) tests, focused group discussion, and suggestion and complaint letters from customers. Many of the best ideas come from asking

FIGURE 11-1

The New-Product-Development Decision Process

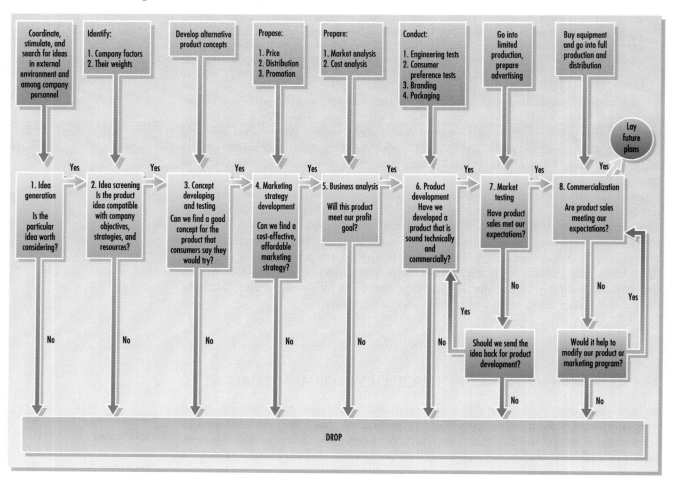

customers to describe their problems with current products. Chrysler, for example, asks recent buyers what they like and dislike about their minivans, what improvements could be made, and how much they would be willing to pay for each improvement.

◆ Companies also rely on their *scientists, engineers, designers, and other employees* for new-product ideas. Successful companies have established a company culture that encourages every employee to seek new ways of improving the company's production, products, and services. Toyota claims that its employees submit 2 million ideas annually (about 35 suggestions per employee), over 85% of which are implemented. Kodak and other firms give monetary and recognition awards to their employees who submit the best ideas.

◆ Companies can also find good ideas by examining their *competitors' products and services*. They can learn from distributors, suppliers, and sales representatives what competitors are doing. They can find out what customers like and dislike in their competitors' new products. They can buy their competitors' products, take them apart, and build better ones. The Japanese are masters of this product imitation and improvement strategy; they have licensed or copied many Western products and found ways to improve them.

◆ Company *sales representatives* and *intermediaries* are a particularly good source of new-product ideas. These groups have firsthand exposure to customers' needs and complaints. They are often the first to learn about competitive developments. An increasing number of companies train and reward their sales representatives, distributors, and dealers for finding new ideas. For example: Bill Keefer, chairman of Warner Electric Brake and Clutch, requires his sales force to list on each monthly call report the three best product ideas they heard on customer visits. He reads these ideas each month and pens notes to his engineers and manufacturing executives to follow up the better ideas.

◆ *Top management* can be another major source of new-product ideas. Some company leaders, like Edwin H. Land, former CEO of Polaroid, took personal responsibility for technological innovation in their companies. This is not always in the company's best interests. Land pushed forward his Polavision project (instantly developed movies), but the product was a major failure. The market was more interested in videotapes as a way to film action.

In companies that are known for innovation, it's more likely that the top manager's role is not inventing products but making it possible for others to come up with new ideas and set them in motion. For instance, Lewis Platt, CEO of Hewlett Packard, believes that senior management's role is to create an environment that encourages business managers to take risks and create new growth opportunities. Under Platt's leadership, HP has been structured as a collection of highly autonomous entrepreneurial businesses.[11]

New-product ideas can come from other sources as well, including inventors, patent attorneys, university and commercial laboratories, industrial consultants, advertising agencies, marketing research firms, industrial publications, and other "idea people." For instance, two idea men named John and Anthony Gentile pitched an idea for a flying doll to San Francisco–based Lewis Galoob toys. The Gentiles got the idea by watching children play with twirling maple seedlings. They routinely look at the world for ideas that will turn into successful products, dreaming up shapes and functions and the stories to go with them.

Although ideas can flow from many sources, their chance of receiving serious attention often depends on someone in the organization taking the role of *product champion*. The product idea is not likely to receive serious consideration unless it has a strong advocate.

IDEA-GENERATING TECHNIQUES. A number of creative idea-generating techniques can help individuals and groups generate ideas.

Attribute Listing. The *attribute listing technique* calls for listing an existing product's major attributes and then modifying each attribute in the search for an improved product. Consider a screwdriver.[12] Its attributes are a round, steel shank; a wooden handle, manually operated; and torque provided by twisting action. After listing these attributes, a group considers ways to improve product performance or appeal. The round shank could be made hexagonal so that a wrench could be applied to increase the torque; electric power could replace manual power; the torque could be produced by pushing rather than twisting. Osborn suggested that useful ideas can be found by addressing the following questions to an object and its attributes: put to other uses? adapt? magnify? minify (make smaller)? substitute? rearrange? reverse? combine?[13]

Forced Relationships. In the *forced relationships technique,* several objects are considered in relation to one another to create a new product. An office-equipment manufacturer decided to combine a fax machine, telephone answering machine, and copy machine into one unit.

Morphological Analysis. The *morphological analysis* method calls for identifying the structural dimensions of a problem and examining the relationships among them. The hope is to find some novel combinations.[14] Suppose the problem is that of "getting something from one place to another via a powered vehicle." The important dimensions are the type of vehicle (cart, chair, bed); the medium (air, water, snow, hard surface, rollers, rails); the power source (pressed air, internal-combustion engine, electric motor). Thus a cart-type vehicle powered by an internal-combustion engine and moving through snow is the snowmobile.

Need/Problem Identification. The preceding creativity techniques do not require consumer input. *Need/problem identification,* in contrast, starts with consumers. Consumers are asked about needs, problems, and ideas. For example, they can be asked about their problems in using a particular product or product category.

The Landis Group, a marketing research firm, uses this technique. For a given product category, it interviews about 1,000 respondents and asks whether they are completely satisfied, slightly dissatisfied, moderately dissatisfied, or extremely dissatisfied. If they have any degree of dissatisfaction, the respondents describe their problems and complaints in their own words. For example, in a study of consumers of English muffins, 15% expressed some dissatisfaction, and the largest problems were muffins that were not precut, were too dry or soft, or had poor taste. The demographics revealed that the most dissatisfied users were in the 19-to-29 age group with low incomes. An existing competitor or a new entrant can use this information to improve the product and target the most dissatisfied groups. To determine which product improvements to make, the company would rate the various problems on their seriousness, incidence, and cost of remedying.

This technique can also be used in reverse. Consumers receive a list of problems and report which products come to mind as having each problem.[15] Thus the problem: "The package of _____ doesn't fit well on the shelf" might lead consumers to name dog foods and dry breakfast cereals. A food or pet-products marketer might think of entering these markets with a smaller-size package.

Brainstorming. Group creativity can be stimulated through *brainstorming* techniques developed by Alex Osborn. The usual brainstorming group consists of six to ten people discussing a specific problem. The chair starts each discussion by saying, "Remember, we want as many ideas as possible—the wilder the better—and remember, no evaluation." The ideas start flowing, one idea sparks another, and within an hour over a hundred or more new ideas may find their way into the

PART 3

Developing
Marketing
Strategies

tape recorder. Osborn laid down four guidelines for the brainstorming conference to be maximally effective:

- *Criticism is ruled out:* Negative comments on ideas must be withheld until later.
- *Freewheeling is welcomed:* The wilder the idea, the better; it is easier to tame down than to think up.
- *Quantity is encouraged:* The greater the number of ideas generated, the greater the likelihood of finding an idea worth pursuing.
- *Combining and improving ideas is encouraged:* Participants should suggest how other people's ideas can be joined into more ideas.[16]

Synectics. William J. J. Gordon felt that Osborn's brainstorming sessions tend to produce solutions too quickly, before a sufficient number of perspectives have been developed. Thus Gordon has espoused a very different technique: Define the problem so broadly that the group will have no inkling of the specific problem. For example, one company needed to design a method of closing vaporproof suits worn by workers who handle high-powered fuels.[17] Gordon kept the specific problem a secret and led a discussion on the general problem of "closure," which led to images of different closure mechanisms, such as birds' nests, mouths, or thread. As the group exhausted the initial perspectives, Gordon gradually introduced facts that refined the problem further. When the group was getting close to a good solution, Gordon described the problem. Then the group started to refine the solution. These sessions would last a minimum of three hours, for Gordon believed that fatigue played an important role in unlocking ideas.

Gordon described five principles underlying this *synectics* method:

- *Deferment:* Look first for viewpoint rather than solutions.
- *Autonomy of object:* Let the problem take on a life of its own.
- *Use of the commonplace:* Take advantage of the familiar as a springboard to the strange.
- *Involvement/detachment:* Alternate between entering into the particulars of the problem and standing back from them.
- *Use of metaphor:* Let apparently irrelevant, accidental things suggest analogies that are sources of new viewpoints.[18]

Idea Screening

Any company can attract good ideas by organizing itself properly. The company should motivate its employees to submit their ideas to an *idea chairman* whose name and phone number are widely circulated. The ideas should be written down and reviewed each week by an *idea committee,* which should sort the ideas into three groups: promising ideas, marginal ideas, and rejects. Each promising idea should be researched by a committee member, who then reports back to the committee. The surviving promising ideas then move into a full-scale screening process. The company should offer payments or recognition to the employees submitting the best ideas.

In screening ideas, the company must avoid two types of errors. A *DROP-error* occurs when the company dismisses an otherwise good idea. It is extremely easy to find fault with other people's ideas (Figure 11-2). Some companies shudder when they look back at some ideas they dismissed: Xerox saw the novel promise of Chester Carlson's copying machine; IBM and Eastman Kodak did not see it at all. IBM thought the market for personal computers was minuscule; Compaq did not. RCA was able to envision the innovative opportunity of radio; the Victor Talking Machine Company could not. Henry Ford recognized the promise of the automobile; yet only General Motors realized the need to segment

FIGURE 11-2
Forces Fighting New Ideas
Source: With permission of Jerold Panas, Linzy & Partners, Inc.

315

the automobile market into price and performance categories. Marshall Field understood the unique market development possibilities of installment buying; Endicott Johnson did not, calling it "the vilest system yet devised to create trouble." Sears dismissed the importance of discounting; Wal-Mart and Kmart did not.[19] If a company makes too many DROP-errors, its standards are too conservative.

A *GO-error* occurs when the company permits a poor idea to move into development and commercialization. We can distinguish three types of product failures. An *absolute product failure* loses money; its sales do not cover variable costs. A *partial product failure* loses money, but its sales cover all its variable costs and some of its fixed costs. A *relative product failure* yields a profit that is less than the company's target rate of return.

The purpose of screening is to drop poor ideas as early as possible. The rationale is that product-development costs rise substantially with each successive development stage (see again Table 11-1).

PRODUCT-IDEA RATING DEVICES.

Most companies require new-product ideas to be described on a standard form that can be reviewed by a new-product committee. The description states the product idea, the target market, and the competition, and it roughly estimates the market size, product price, development time and costs, manufacturing costs, and rate of return.

The executive committee then reviews each new-product idea against a set of criteria. In the case of the Kao Company of Japan, the committee considers such questions as: Does the product meet a need? Would it offer superior price performance? Can it be distinctively advertised? Figure 11-3 shows a detailed set of questions about whether a product idea meshes well with the company's objectives, strategies, and resources. Ideas that do not satisfy one or more of these questions are dropped.

The surviving ideas can then be rated using the weighted-index method shown in Table 11-2. The first column lists factors required for successful product launches. In the next column, management assigns weights to these factors to reflect their relative importance. The next task is to score the product on each factor on a scale from .0 to 1.0, with 1.0 the highest score. The final step is to multiply each factor's importance by the product scores to obtain an overall rating of the company's ability to launch the product successfully. In this example, the product idea scores .69, which places it in the "good idea" level.

This basic rating device can be refined further. Its purpose is to promote systematic product-idea evaluation and discussion—it is not supposed to make the decision for management.

As the new-product idea moves through development, the company will need to constantly revise its estimate of the product's overall probability of success, using the following formula:

$$
\begin{array}{c}
\text{Overall} \\
\text{probability} \\
\text{of success}
\end{array}
=
\begin{array}{c}
\text{Probability} \\
\text{of technical} \\
\text{completion}
\end{array}
\times
\begin{array}{c}
\text{Probability of} \\
\text{commercialization} \\
\text{given technical} \\
\text{completion}
\end{array}
\times
\begin{array}{c}
\text{Probability of} \\
\text{economic} \\
\text{success given} \\
\text{commercialization}
\end{array}
$$

For example, if the three probabilities are estimated as .50, .65, and .74 respectively, the company would conclude that the overall probability of success is .24. The company then has to judge whether this probability is high enough to warrant continued development of the new product.

Concept Development and Testing

Attractive ideas must be refined into testable product concepts. We can distinguish among a product idea, a product concept, and a product image. A *product idea* is a possible product that the company might offer to the market. A *product concept* is an elaborated version of the idea expressed in meaningful consumer terms. A *product image* is the particular picture that consumers acquire of an actual or potential product.

TABLE 11-2	PRODUCT-IDEA RATING DEVICE		
PRODUCT SUCCESS REQUIREMENTS	(1) RELATIVE WEIGHT	(2) PRODUCT SCORE	(3 = 1 × 2) PRODUCT RATING
Unique or superior product	.40	.8	.32
High performance-to-cost ratio	.30	.6	.18
High marketing dollar support	.20	.7	.14
Lack of strong competition	.10	.5	.05
Total	1.00		.69*

* Rating scale: .00–.30 poor; .31–.60 fair; .61–.80 good. Minimum acceptance rate: .61.

CONCEPT DEVELOPMENT. We shall illustrate concept development with the following situation: A large food processing company gets the idea of producing a powder to add to milk to increase its nutritional value and taste. This is a product idea. But consumers do not buy product ideas; they buy product concepts.

Any product idea can be turned into several product concepts. The first question is: Who will use this product? The powder can be aimed at infants, children, teen-agers, young or middle-aged adults, or older adults. Second, what primary benefit should this product provide? Taste, nutrition, refreshment, energy? Third, when will people consume this drink? Breakfast, mid-morning, lunch, mid-afternoon, dinner, late evening? By answering these questions, a company can form several concepts:

- *Concept 1:* An instant breakfast drink for adults who want a quick nutritious breakfast without preparing a breakfast.
- *Concept 2:* A tasty snack drink for children to drink as a midday refreshment.
- *Concept 3:* A health supplement for older adults to drink in the late evening before they go to bed.

Each of these concepts represents a *category concept*—that is, each positions the idea within a category. It is the category concept, not the product concept, that defines the product's competition. An instant breakfast drink would compete against bacon and eggs, breakfast cereals, coffee and pastry, and other breakfast alternatives. A tasty snack drink would compete against soft drinks, fruit juices, and other thirst quenchers.

Suppose the instant-breakfast-drink concept looks best. The next task is to show where this powdered product would stand in relation to other breakfast products. Figure 11-4(a) uses the two dimensions of cost and preparation time to create a *product-positioning map* for the breakfast drink. An instant breakfast drink offers the buyer low cost and quick preparation. Its nearest competitor is cold cereal; its most distant competitor is bacon and eggs. These contrasts can be utilized in communicating and promoting the concept to the market.

Next, the product concept has to be turned into a *brand concept*. Figure 11-4(b) is a *brand-positioning map* showing the current positions of three existing brands of instant breakfast drinks. The company needs to decide how much to charge and how caloric to make its drink. The new brand would be distinctive in the medium-price, medium-calorie market or in the high-price, high-calorie market. The company would not want to position it next to an existing brand, where it would have to fight for market share.

CONCEPT TESTING. Concept testing calls for testing product concepts with an appropriate group of target consumers, then getting those consumers' reactions. The concepts can be presented symbolically or physically. At this stage, a word and/or picture description can suffice. However, the more the tested concepts resemble the final product or experience, the more dependable concept testing is. In the past, creating physical prototypes was costly and time-consuming, but computer-aided design and manufacturing programs have changed that. Today firms can design alternative physical products (for example, small appliances or toys) on a computer, and then produce plastic molds of each. This makes it easy for potential consumers to view the plastic molds and give their reactions.[20]

Some companies are also using virtual reality to test product concepts. Virtual reality programs use computers and sensory devices (such as gloves or goggles) to simulate reality. For example, a designer of kitchen cabinets can use a virtual reality program to help a customer "see" how his or her kitchen would look remodeled with the company's products. Though virtual reality is still in its infancy, its applications are increasing daily.[21]

FIGURE 11-4
Product and Brand Positioning

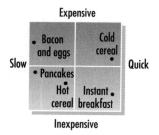

(a) Product-positioning map (breakfast market)

(b) Brand-positioning map (instant breakfast market)

Developing
Marketing
Strategies

Many companies today are using an approach called customer-driven engineering to design new products. *Customer-driven engineering* is engineering effort that attaches high importance to incorporating customer preferences in the final design. Suppose a major auto company decides to design a car for middle- to high-income people who drive a long distance to work. Using focus groups, the auto researchers find that these drivers want the following: a comfortable seat, a tray for beverages, a coin slot for toll-road charges, fast acceleration, and good mirrors for lane switching. These desires are called the *customer attributes (CAs)*. The marketing department turns the CAs over to engineers, who convert them into *engineering attributes (EAs),* such as horsepower, weight, gear ratios, and wind drag. *Customer-driven engineering* involves turning the CAs into EAs and determining the best trade-offs given the attributes and their costs.[22]

An important part of concept testing entails presenting consumers with an elaborated version of the concept. Here is the elaboration of Concept 1 in our milk example:

> Our product is a powdered mixture that is added to milk to make an instant breakfast that gives the person all the needed breakfast nutrition along with good taste and high convenience. The product would be offered in three flavors (chocolate, vanilla, and strawberry) and would come in individual packets, six to a box, at $2.49 a box.

After receiving this information, consumers are asked to respond to the following questions:

QUESTION	PRODUCT DIMENSION MEASURED
1. Are the benefits clear to you and believable?	*Communicability* and *believability*. If the scores on these dimensions are low, the concept must be refined or revised.
2. Do you see this product as solving a problem or filling a need for you?	*Need level*. The stronger the need, the higher the expected consumer interest.
3. Do other products currently meet this need and satisfy you?	*Gap level* between the new product and existing products. The greater the gap, the higher the expected consumer interest. The need level can be multiplied by the gap level to produce a *need-gap score*. A high need-gap score means that the consumer sees the product as filling a strong need that is not satisfied by available alternatives.
4. Is the price reasonable in relation to the value?	*Perceived value*. The higher the perceived value, the higher the expected consumer interest.
5. Would you (definitely, probably, probably not, definitely not) buy the product?	*Purchase intention*. This would be high for consumers who answered the previous three questions positively.
6. Who would use this product, and when and how often would the product be used?	*User targets, purchase occasions,* and *purchasing frequency*.

The marketer summarizes the respondents' answers to judge whether the concept has a broad and strong consumer appeal. This information also tells the company what products this new product competes against and which consumers are the best targets. The need-gap levels and purchase-intention levels can be checked against norms for the product category to see whether the concept appears to be a winner, a long shot, or a loser. One food manufacturer rejects any concepts that draw a definitely-would-buy score of less than 40 percent.

FIGURE 11-5
Samples for Conjoint Analysis

Conjoint Analysis. Consumer preferences for alternative product concepts can be measured through a popular research technique called *conjoint analysis,* a method for deriving the utility values that consumers attach to varying levels of a product's attributes. Respondents are shown different hypothetical offers formed by combining varying levels of the attributes, then asked to rank the various offers. Management can use the results to determine the most appealing offer and the estimated market share and profit the company might realize.

Green and Wind have illustrated this approach in connection with developing a new spot-removing carpet-cleaning agent for home use.[23] Suppose the new-product marketer is considering the following five design elements:

◆ Three package designs (A, B, C—Figure 11-5)

◆ Three brand names (K2R, Glory, Bissell)

◆ Three prices ($1.19, $1.39, $1.59)

◆ A possible Good Housekeeping seal (yes, no)

◆ A possible money-back guarantee (yes, no)

Although the researcher can form 108 possible product concepts ($3 \times 3 \times 3 \times 2 \times 2$), it would be too much to ask consumers to rank all of these concepts. A sample of, say, 18 contrasting product concepts can be chosen, and consumers would find it easy enough to rank them from the most preferred to the least preferred. Table 11-3 shows how one consumer ranked the 18 product concepts. This consumer ranked product concept 18 the highest, thus preferring package design C, the name Bissell, a price of $1.19, a Good Housekeeping seal, and a money-back guarantee.

By compiling and analyzing the consumer's responses, a statistical program can derive the individual consumer's utility functions for the five attributes (Figure 11-6). Utility is measured by a number that ranges between zero and one; the higher the utility, the stronger the consumer's preference for that level of the at-

TABLE 11-3	ONE CONSUMER'S RANKING OF 18 STIMULUS COMBINATIONS					
CARD	**PACKAGE DESIGN**	**BRAND NAME**	**PRICE**	**GOODHOUSE-KEEPING SEAL**	**MONEY-BACK GUARANTEE?**	**RESPONDENT'S EVALUATION (RANK NUMBER)**
1	A	K2R	$1.19	No	No	13
2	A	Glory	1.39	No	Yes	11
3	A	Bissell	1.59	Yes	No	17
4	B	K2R	1.39	Yes	Yes	2
5	B	Glory	1.59	No	No	14
6	B	Bissell	1.19	No	No	3
7	C	K2R	1.59	No	Yes	12
8	C	Glory	1.19	Yes	No	7
9	C	Bissell	1.39	No	No	9
10	A	K2R	1.59	Yes	No	18
11	A	Glory	1.19	No	Yes	8
12	A	Bissell	1.39	No	No	15
13	B	K2R	1.19	No	No	4
14	B	Glory	1.39	Yes	No	6
15	B	Bissell	1.59	No	Yes	5
16	C	K2R	1.39	No	No	10
17	C	Glory	1.59	No	No	16
18	C	Bissell	1.19	Yes	Yes	1*

* Highest rank.

FIGURE 11-6
**Utility Functions Based on
Conjoint Analysis**

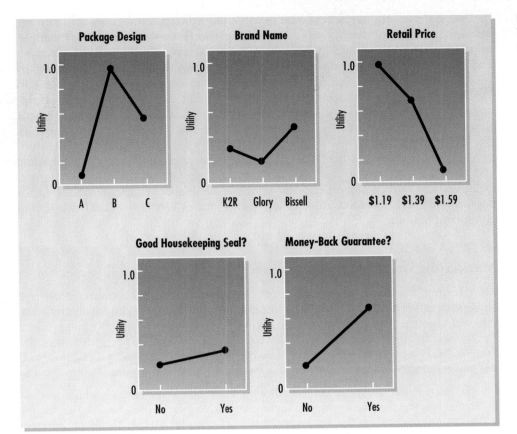

tribute. Looking at packaging, for example, we see that Package B is the most fa-vored, followed by C and then A (A hardly has any utility). The preferred names are Bissell, K2R, and Glory, in that order. The consumer's utility varies inversely with price. A Good Housekeeping seal is preferred, but it does not add that much utility and may not be worth the effort to obtain it. A money-back guarantee is strongly preferred. Putting these results together, we can see that the consumer's most desired offer would be package design B, with the brand name Bissell, sell-ing at the price of $1.19, with a Good Housekeeping seal and a money-back guar-antee.

We can also determine the relative importance of each attribute to this con-sumer. An attribute's relative importance is given by the difference between the highest and lowest utility level for that attribute. The greater the difference, the more important the attribute. Clearly, this consumer sees price and package design as the most important attributes followed by money-back guarantee, brand name, and last, a Good Housekeeping seal.

When preference data are collected from a large sample of target consumers, the data can be used to estimate the market share that any specific offer is likely to achieve, given any assumptions about competitive response. The company, how-ever, may not launch the market offer that promises to gain the greatest market share because of cost considerations. For example, it may decide that package C, although it adds less utility than package B, might cost considerably less and be more profitable. The most appealing offer is not always the most profitable offer to make.

Under some conditions, researchers will collect the data not using a full-profile description of each offer but rather presenting two factors at a time. For example, respondents may be shown a table with three price levels and three package types and asked which of the nine combinations they would like most, followed by which one they would prefer next, and so on. They would then be shown a further table consisting of trade-offs between two other variables. The trade-off approach may be easier to use when there are many variables and possible offers. However, it is less realistic in that respondents are focusing on only two variables at a time.

Conjoint analysis has become one of the most popular concept development and testing tools, having had several thousand commercial applications. Marriott designed its Courtyard hotel concept with the benefit of conjoint analysis. Other applications have included auto styling, airline travel services, ethical drugs, and credit-card features.

Marketing Strategy Development

After testing, the new-product manager must develop a preliminary marketing strategy plan for introducing the new product into the market. The marketing strategy will undergo further refinement in subsequent stages.

The marketing strategy plan consists of three parts. The first part describes the target market's size, structure, and behavior; the planned product positioning; and the sales, market share, and profit goals sought in the first few years:

> The target market for the instant breakfast drink is families with children who are receptive to a new, convenient, nutritious, and inexpensive form of breakfast. The company's brand will be positioned at the higher-price, higher-quality end of the instant breakfast drink category. The company will aim initially to sell 500,000 cases or 10% of the market, with a loss in the first year not exceeding $1.3 million. The second year will aim for 700,000 cases or 14% of the market, with a planned profit of $2.2 million.

The second part of the marketing strategy outlines the product's planned price, distribution strategy, and marketing budget for the first year:

> The product will be offered in chocolate, vanilla, and strawberry in individual packets of six to a box at a retail price of $2.49 a box. There will be 48 boxes per case, and the case's price to distributors will be $24. For the first two months, dealers will be offered one case free for every four cases bought, plus cooperative-advertising allowances. Free samples will be distributed door to door. Coupons for 20¢ off will appear in newspapers. The total sales-promotional budget will be $2,900,000. An advertising budget of $6,000,000 will be split 50/50 between national and local. Two thirds will go into television and one third into newspapers. Advertising copy will emphasize the benefit concepts of nutrition and convenience. The advertising-execution concept will revolve around a small boy who drinks instant breakfast and grows strong. During the first year, $100,000 will be spent on marketing research to buy store audits and consumer-panel information to monitor the market's reaction and buying rates.

The third part of the marketing strategy plan describes the long-run sales and profit goals and marketing-mix strategy over time:

> The company intends to win a 25% market share and realize an after-tax return on investment of 12 percent. To achieve this return, product quality will start high and be improved over time through technical research. Price will initially be set at a high level and lowered gradually to expand the market and meet competition. The total promotion budget will be boosted each year about 20%, with the initial advertising/sales promotion split of 65:35 evolving eventually to 50:50. Marketing research will be reduced to $60,000 per year after the first year.

Business Analysis

After management develops the product concept and marketing strategy, it can evaluate the proposal's business attractiveness. Management needs to prepare sales, cost, and profit projections to determine whether they satisfy the company's objectives. If they do, the product concept can move to the product-development stage. As new information comes in, the business analysis will undergo revision and expansion.

ESTIMATING TOTAL SALES. Management needs to estimate whether sales will be high enough to yield a satisfactory profit. Total estimated sales are the sum of estimated first-time sales, estimated replacement sales, and estimated repeat sales. Sales-estimation methods depend on whether the product is a one-time-purchase product (such as an engagement ring or retirement home), an infrequently purchased product, or a frequently purchased product. For one-time purchased products, sales rise at the beginning (when the product is introduced), peak, and later approach zero as the number of potential buyers is exhausted (Figure 11-7[a]). If new buyers keep entering the market, the curve will not go down to zero.

Infrequently purchased products—such as automobiles, toasters, and industrial equipment—exhibit replacement cycles dictated either by their physical wearing out or by obsolescence associated with changing styles, features, and performance. Sales forecasting for this product category calls for estimating first-time sales and replacement sales separately (Figure 11-7[b]).

Frequently purchased products, such as consumer and industrial nondurables, have product life-cycle sales resembling Figure 11-7(c). The number of first-time buyers initially increases and then decreases as fewer buyers are left (assuming a fixed population). Repeat purchases occur soon, providing that the product satisfies some buyers. The sales curve eventually falls to a plateau representing a level of steady repeat-purchase volume; by this time, the product is no longer a new product.

Estimating First-Time Sales.

In estimating a new product's sales, the manager's first task is to estimate first-time purchases of the new product in each period. A variety of techniques are available. For example, one medical equipment manufacturer developed a new instrument for analyzing blood specimens. The company identified three market segments: hospitals, clinics, and unaffiliated laboratories. It then

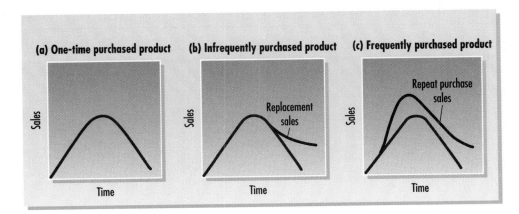

(a) One-time purchased product **(b) Infrequently purchased product** **(c) Frequently purchased product**

Replacement sales

Repeat purchase sales

Sales Sales Sales

Time Time Time

FIGURE 11-7
Product Life-Cycle Sales for Three Types of Products

Developing
New
Products

used a three-step process to estimate new-product sales. First, for each segment, management defined the minimum-size facility that would buy the instrument, then estimated the number of facilities in each segment. It reduced this estimate by the estimated purchase probability, which varied from segment to segment, then summed the remaining number of potential customers and called this the "market potential." Second, it estimated the new product's "market penetration" on the basis of a number of factors, including planned advertising expenditures and competitors' activity. Finally, it multiplied market potential by market penetration to estimate new-product sales.

Estimating Replacement Sales. To estimate replacement sales, management has to research the product's *survival-age distribution*—that is, the number of units that fail in year one, two, three, and so on. The low end of the distribution indicates when the first replacement sales will take place. The actual timing of replacement will be influenced by the customer's economic situation, cash flow, and product alternatives as well as the company's prices, financing terms, and sales effort. Because replacement sales are difficult to estimate before the product is in use, some manufacturers base their decision to launch a new product solely on their estimate of first-time sales.

Estimating Repeat Sales. For a frequently purchased new product, the seller has to estimate repeat sales as well as first-time sales. A high rate of repeat purchasing means that customers are satisfied; sales are likely to stay high even after all first-time purchases take place. The seller should note the percentage of repeat purchases that take place in each repeat-purchase class: those who rebuy once, twice, three times, and so on. Some products and brands are bought a few times and dropped. It is important to estimate whether the repeat-purchase ratio is likely to rise or fall, and at what rate, for each repeat-purchase class.[24]

ESTIMATING COSTS AND PROFITS. After preparing the sales forecast, management should estimate the expected costs and profits. The costs are estimated by the R&D, manufacturing, marketing, and finance departments. Table 11-4

TABLE 11-4	PROJECTED FIVE-YEAR CASH-FLOW STATEMENT (IN THOUSANDS OF DOLLARS)					
	YEAR 0	YEAR 1	YEAR 2	YEAR 3	YEAR 4	YEAR 5
1. Sales revenue	$ 0	$11,889	$15,381	$19,654	$28,253	$32,491
2. Cost of goods sold	0	3,981	5,150	6,581	9,461	10,880
3. Gross margin	0	7,908	10,231	13,073	18,792	21,611
4. Development costs	−3,500	0	0	0	0	0
5. Marketing costs	0	8,000	6,460	8,255	11,866	13,646
6. Allocated overhead	0	1,189	1,538	1,965	2,825	3,249
7. Gross contribution	−3,500	−1,281	2,233	2,853	4,101	4,716
8. Supplementary contribution	0	0	0	0	0	0
9. Net contribution	−3,500	−1,281	2,233	2,853	4,101	4,716
10. Discounted contribution (15%)	−3,500	−1,113	1,691	1,877	2,343	2,346
11. Cumulative discounted cash flow	−3,500	−4,613	−2,922	−1,045	−1,298	3,644

illustrates a five-year projection of sales, costs, and profits for the instant breakfast drink.

Row 1 shows the projected sales revenue over the five-year period. The company expects to sell $11,889,000 (approximately 500,000 cases at $24 per case) in the first year. Behind this sales projection is a set of assumptions about the rate of market growth, the company's market share, and the factory-realized price.

Row 2 shows the *cost of goods sold,* which hovers around 33% of sales revenue. This cost is found by estimating the average cost of labor, ingredients, and packaging per case.

Row 3 shows the expected *gross margin,* which is the difference between sales revenue and cost of goods sold.

Row 4 shows anticipated development costs of $3.5 million, which include product-development cost, marketing research costs, and manufacturing-development costs.

Row 5 shows the estimated marketing costs over the five-year period to cover advertising, sales promotion, and marketing research and an amount allocated for sales force coverage and marketing administration.

Row 6 shows the allocated overhead to this new product to cover its share of the cost of executive salaries, heat, light, and so on.

Row 7, the *gross contribution,* is found by subtracting the preceding three costs from the gross margin.

Row 8, *supplementary contribution,* lists any change in income from other company products caused by the introduction of the new product. It has two components. *Dragalong income* is additional income on other company products resulting from adding this product to the line. *Cannibalized income* is the reduced income on other company products resulting from adding this product to the line.[25] Table 11-4 assumes no supplementary contributions.

Row 9 shows the *net contribution,* which in this case is the same as the gross contribution.

Row 10 shows the *discounted contribution*—that is, the present value of each future contribution discounted at 15% per annum. For example, the company will not receive $4,716,000 until the fifth year. This amount is worth only $2,346,000 today if the company can earn 15% on its money through other investments.[26]

Finally, row 11 shows the *cumulative discounted cash flow,* which is the cumulation of the annual contributions in row 10. Two things are of central interest. The first is the *maximum investment exposure,* which is the highest loss that the project can create. We see that the company will be in a maximum loss position of $4,613,000 in year 1. The second is the *payback period,* which is the time when the company recovers all of its investment including the built-in return of 15 percent. The payback period here is approximately three and a half years. Management therefore has to decide whether to risk a maximum investment loss of $4.6 million and a possible payback period of three and a half years.

Companies use other financial measures to evaluate the merit of a new-product proposal. The simplest is *break-even analysis,* in which management estimates how many units of the product the company would have to sell to break even with the given price and cost structure. If management believes that the company could easily reach the break-even number, it is likely to move the project into product development.

The most complex method of estimating profit is *risk analysis.* Here three estimates (optimistic, pessimistic, and most likely) are obtained for each uncertain variable affecting profitability under an assumed marketing environment and marketing strategy for the planning period. The computer simulates possible outcomes and computes a rate-of-return probability distribution, showing the range of possible rates of returns and their probabilities.[27]

Product Development

If the product concept passes the business test, it moves to R&D and/or engineering to be developed into a physical product. Up to now it has existed only as a word description, a drawing, or a prototype. This step calls for a large jump in investment that dwarfs the idea-evaluation costs incurred in the earlier stages. At this stage the company will determine whether the product idea can be translated into a technically and commercially feasible product. If it cannot, the company's accumulated project cost will be lost except for any useful information gained in the process.

The R&D department will develop one or more physical versions of the product concept. Its goal is to find a prototype that the consumers see as embodying the key attributes described in the product-concept statement, that performs safely under normal use and conditions, and that can be produced within the budgeted manufacturing costs.

Developing and manufacturing a successful prototype can take days, weeks, months, or even years. Designing a new commercial aircraft takes several years of development work, even with sophisticated computer technology. (For more on this topic, see the Vision 2000 feature titled "Using CAD, CAM, and 3-D in New-Product Development.") Even developing a new taste formula can take time. For example, the Maxwell House Division of Kraft General Foods discovered that consumers wanted a brand of coffee that was "bold, vigorous, and deep tasting." Its laboratory technicians spent over four months working with various coffee blends and flavors to formulate a corresponding taste. It turned out to be too expensive to produce, and the company cost-reduced the blend to meet the target manufacturing cost. The change compromised the taste, however, and the new coffee brand did not sell well in the market.

Lab scientists must not only design the product's required functional characteristics but also know how to communicate its psychological aspects through physical cues. How will consumers react to different colors, sizes, weights, and other physical cues? In the case of a mouthwash, a yellow color supports an "antiseptic" claim (Listerine), a red color supports a "refreshing" claim (Lavoris), and a green or blue color supports a "cool" claim (Scope). Marketers need to supply lab people with information on what attributes consumers seek and how consumers judge whether these attributes are present.

When the prototypes are ready, they must be put through rigorous functional and consumer tests. The *functional tests* are conducted under laboratory and field conditions to make sure that the product performs safely and effectively. The new aircraft must fly; the new snack food must have a long shelf life; the new drug must not create dangerous side effects. Functional product testing of new drugs now takes years of laboratory work with animal subjects and then human subjects before the drugs obtain Federal Drug Administration approval. Here are some of the functional tests that products go through before they enter the marketplace:

SHAW INDUSTRIES At Shaw Industries, temps are paid $5 an hour to pace up and down five long rows of sample carpets for up to eight hours a day, logging an average of 14 miles each. One regular reads three mysteries a week while pacing and shed 40 pounds in two years. Shaw Industries counts walkers' steps and figures that 20,000 steps equal several years of average carpet wear.

APPLE COMPUTER Apple Computer assumes the worst for its PowerBook customers and submits the computers to a battery of indignities: It drenches the computers in Pepsi and other sodas, smears them with mayonnaise, and bakes them in ovens at temperatures of 140 degrees or more to simulate conditions in a car trunk.

GILLETTE At Gillette, 200 volunteers from various departments come to work unshaven each day, troop to the second floor of the company's South

Using CAD, CAM, and 3-D in New-Product Development

At Chrysler's development lab in Auburn Hills, Michigan, viewers stare expectantly at an eight- by ten-inch picture frame containing a seemingly black sheet. Presto! When the frame is held up and white light hits it, a hologram of a miniature red Dodge Viper sports car appears to leap a foot in front of the frame, almost close enough for the audience to touch. Working with firms specializing in holography, Chrysler is now trying to figure out how to use the same types of holograms to design cars and trucks and thus eliminate the costly, time-consuming full-size clay models of new-car designs.

As enticing as holography is, the technology is still several years away from accomplishing what car makers have in mind: holograms measuring 22- by 12-feet that arise at the click of a button after engineers type data into a computer—and that can be modified at another click of a button. In the meantime, automakers and other manufacturers are reaping benefits from *computer-aided design (CAD)* and *computer-aided manufacturing (CAM),* two technologies introduced in the 1960s but only now enjoying widespread use. CAD software allows engineers to produce electronic 2-D sketches that they turn into 3-D designs by inputting mathematical data. CAM, which is used to control the automated equipment used in manufacturing a product, is the technology underlying robotics.

One of the main benefits of using CAD-CAM tech-nology is that it allows companies to speed up the product-development process significantly for everything from tiny pieces of jewelry to automobiles and hulking airlines. For instance, RPD productions of Plymouth, Minnesota, used CAD-CAM to help its jewelry manufacturer customers go from "art to part" in five days as opposed to the usual one month using traditional methods. Once jewelry designers draw the shape of, say, a charm pendant with CAD software, RPD can use another type of software to manipulate the new product's look and texture so that customers can see several different versions.

Meanwhile, Chrysler used CAD-CAM technology to develop its new compact car, the Neon, in only 31 months at a cost of $1.3 billion. (The U.S. automotive industry typically takes more than four years and spends billions of dollars to bring a new car to market.) Working in tandem with the CAD-CAM technology was the company's new organizational structure. Chrysler formed development teams that put everyone—including key people from engineering, manufacturing, and marketing—in the same place to speed up the product development process. CAD-CAM facilitated communication by allowing the development team in Michigan to pull up drawings on the screen and hold online communications with the Belvedere, Illinois, assembly staff to get immediate feedback on their ideas' feasibility.

Sources: Nichole M. Christian, "Detroit in 3-D: Car Design Gets New Dimension," *The Wall Street Journal,* March 24, 1995, B1:3; Gene Bylinsky, "The Digital Factory," *Fortune,* November 14, 1994, pp. 92–110; "High-Tech Jewelry Design," *Industry Week,* July 18, 1994, p. 18S; "Chrysler Team Drives Neon Success," *Industry Week,* July 18, 1994, p. 7S.

Boston manufacturing and research plant, and enter small booths with a sink and mirror. There they take instructions from technicians on the other side of a small window as to which razor, shaving cream, or aftershave to use, and then they fill out questionnaires. "We bleed so you'll get a good shave at home," says one Gillette employee.[28]

Consumer testing can take a variety of forms, from bringing consumers into a laboratory to giving them samples to use in their homes. In-home product placement tests are common with products ranging from ice cream flavors to new appliances. When Du Pont developed its new synthetic carpeting, it installed free carpeting in several homes in exchange for the homeowners' willingness to report their likes and dislikes about synthetic carpeting.

When testing cutting-edge products such as electric cars, marketers must be as creative as the product designers and engineers: Ruegen, a small island in the Baltic sea, has become the testing ground for the cars of the future. Fifty-eight residents of the former East German island have gone from driving decrepit gas-guzzling cars to sleek new electric models manufactured by BMW, Mercedes Benz, and Audi. Ironically, these cars are designed for sale in California, which is requiring that 2% of all vehicles sold be emission-free starting in 1998. The Ruegen tests have made the auto manufacturers aware of several problems: Ruegen residents with electric cars have found that trips of any length must be carefully mapped out because of the batteries' limited life. And recharging the batteries is not easy, consuming anywhere from a half hour to an entire evening.[29]

TECHNIQUES FOR MEASURING CONSUMER PREFERENCES. Consumer-preference testing draws on a variety of techniques. The three most common are simple ranking, paired comparisons, and rating scales. Each has its advantages and limitations.

Suppose a consumer is shown three items—*A, B,* and *C.* They might be three cameras, three insurance plans, or three advertisements.

- The *simple-rank-order* method asks the consumer to rank the three items in order of preference. The consumer might respond with $A > B > C$. Although this method has the advantage of simplicity, it does not reveal how intensely the consumer feels about each item. Indeed, the consumer may not like any one of them very much. Nor does it indicate how much the consumer prefers one object to another. Also, it is difficult to use this method when there are many objects to be evaluated.

- The *paired-comparison* method calls for presenting pairs of items to the consumer, then asking which one is preferred in each pair. Thus the consumer could be presented with the pairs *AB, AC,* and *BC* and say that she prefers *A* to *B, A* to *C,* and *B* to *C.* Then we could conclude that $A > B > C$. Paired comparisons offer two major advantages. First, people find it easy to state their preference between items taken two at a time. Second, the paired-comparison method allows the consumer to concentrate intensely on the two items, noting their differences and similarities.

- The *monadic-rating* method asks the consumer to rate his or her liking of each product on a scale. Suppose a seven-point scale is used, where 1 = intense dislike, 4 = indifference, and 7 = intense like. Suppose the consumer returns the following ratings: $A = 6$, $B = 5$, $C = 3$. This rating yields more information than the other methods. We can derive the individual's preference order (i.e., $A > B > C$) and even know the qualitative levels of her preference for each and the rough distance between preferences. This method is also easy for respondents to use, especially when a large set of objects is to be evaluated.

Market Testing

After management is satisfied with the product's functional and psychological performance, the product is ready to be dressed up with a brand name, packaging, and a preliminary marketing program. The goals are to test the new product in more authentic consumer settings and to learn how large the market is and how consumers and dealers react to handling, using, and repurchasing the actual product.

Not all companies choose the route of market testing. For example, a company officer at Revlon, Inc., stated: "In our field—primarily higher-priced cosmetics not geared for mass distribution—it would be unnecessary for us to market test. When we develop a new product, say an improved liquid makeup, we know it's going to sell because we're familiar with the field. And we've got 1,500 demonstrators in department stores to promote it." Most companies, however, know that market testing can yield valuable information about buyers, dealers, marketing program effectiveness, market potential, and other matters. The main issues are: How much market testing should be done, and what kind(s)?

The amount of market testing is influenced by the investment cost and risk on the one hand, and the time pressure and research cost on the other. High-investment/high-risk products, where the chance of failure is high, must be market

PART 3

Developing
Marketing
Strategies

tested; the cost of the market tests will be an insignificant percentage of the total project cost. High-risk products—those that create new-product categories (first instant breakfast drink) or have novel features (first fluoride toothpaste)—warrant more market testing than modified products (another toothpaste brand). But the amount of market testing may be severely reduced if the company is under great time pressure because the season is just starting or because competitors are about to launch their brands. The company may therefore prefer the risk of a product failure to the risk of losing distribution or market penetration on a highly successful product. The cost of market testing will also affect how much is done and what kind.

CONSUMER-GOODS MARKET TESTING. In testing consumer products, the company seeks to estimate four variables: trial, first repeat, adoption, and purchase frequency. The company hopes to find all these variables at high levels. In some cases, it will find many consumers trying the product but few rebuying it. Or it might find high permanent adoption but low purchase frequency (as with gourmet frozen foods) because the buyers use the product only on special occasions.

A discussion of the major methods of consumer-goods market testing, from the least to the most costly, follows.

Sales-Wave Research. In *sales-wave research,* consumers who initially try the product at no cost are reoffered the product, or a competitor's product, at slightly reduced prices. They might be reoffered the product as many as three to five times (sales waves), with the company noting how many customers selected that company's product again and their reported level of satisfaction. Sales-wave research can also include exposing consumers to one or more advertising concepts in rough form to see the impact of that advertising on repeat purchase.

Sales-wave research can be implemented quickly, conducted with a fair amount of security, and carried out without final packaging and advertising. However, sales-wave research does not indicate the trial rates that would be achieved with different sales-promotion incentives, since the consumers are preselected to try the product. Nor does it indicate the brand's power to gain distribution and favorable shelf position.

Simulated Test Marketing. *Simulated test marketing* calls for finding 30 to 40 qualified shoppers (at a shopping center or elsewhere) and questioning them about their brand familiarity and preferences in a specific product category. These people are then invited to a brief screening of both well-known and new commercials or print ads. One ad advertises the new product, but it is not singled out for attention. The consumers receive a small amount of money and are invited into a store where they may buy any items. The company notes how many consumers buy the new brand and competing brands. This provides a measure of the ad's relative effectiveness against competing ads in stimulating trial. The consumers are asked the reasons for their purchases or nonpurchases. Those who did not buy the new brand are given a free sample. Some weeks later, they are reinterviewed by phone to determine product attitudes, usage, satisfaction, and repurchase intention and are offered an opportunity to repurchase any products.

The simulated test marketing method has several advantages. It gives accurate, secure results on advertising effectiveness and trial rates (and repeat rates if extended) in a much shorter time and at a fraction of the cost of using real test markets. Pretests often take only three months and may cost only $250,000.[30] The results are usually incorporated into new-product forecasting models to project ultimate sales levels. Marketing research firms report surprisingly accurate predictions of sales levels of products that are subsequently launched in the market.[31]

Controlled Test Marketing. In this method, a research firm manages a panel of stores that will carry new products for a fee. The company with the new product specifies the number of stores and geographical locations it wants to test. The research firm delivers the product to the participating stores and controls shelf position; number of facings, displays, and point-of-purchase promotions; and pricing. Sales results can be measured through electronic scanners at the checkouts. The company can also evaluate the impact of local advertising and promotions during the test.

Controlled test marketing allows the company to test the impact of in-store factor and limited advertising on consumer's buying behavior without involving consumers directly. A sample of consumers can be interviewed later to give their impressions of the product. The company does not have to use its own sales force, give trade allowances, or "buy" distribution. However, controlled test marketing provides no information on how to sell the trade on carrying the new product. This technique also exposes the product and its features to competitors' scrutiny.

Test Markets. *Test markets* are the ultimate way to test a new consumer product. The company usually works with an outside research firm to locate a few representative test cities in which the company's sales force will try to sell the trade on carrying the product and giving it good shelf exposure. The company will put on a full advertising and promotion campaign in these markets similar to the one that it would use in national marketing. A full-scale test can cost the company over $1 million, depending on the number of cities tested, the duration of the test, and the amount of data the company wants to collect.

In deciding to do test marketing, management faces several questions:

1. *How many test cities?* Most tests use between two and six cities, with an average of four. The greater the maximum possible loss, the greater the number of contending marketing strategies, the greater the regional differences, and the greater the chance of calculated test-market interference by competitors, the larger the number of cities that should be used.

2. *Which cities?* In a recent study, *American Demographics* discovered that the towns and cities most selected as test sites are not the places that most accurately represent the U.S. average demographically and psychographically. The study revealed that researchers are likely to choose test market cities by gut feelings rather than hard psychographic and demographic data. For instance, despite Baltimore's consistently high rankings as a typically American city, researchers seem to shy away from it.[32]

   Nonetheless, each company must develop its own test-city selection criteria. One company looks for test cities that have diversified industry, good media coverage, cooperative chain stores, average competitive activity, and no evidence of being overtested.

3. *Length of test?* Market tests last anywhere from a few months to several years. The longer the product's average repurchase period, the longer the test period necessary to observe repeat-purchase rates. This period should be cut down if competitors are rushing to the market.

4. *What information?* Management must decide on the type of information to collect in relation to its value and cost. Warehouse shipment data will show gross inventory buying but will not indicate weekly sales at the retail level. *Store audits* will show actual retail sales and competitors' market shares but will not reveal the characteristics of the buyers of the different brands. *Consumer panels* will indicate which people are buying which brands and their loyalty and switching rates. *Buyer surveys* will yield in-depth information about consumer attitudes, usage, and satisfaction. Among other things that can be researched are trade attitudes, retail distribution, and the effectiveness of advertising, promotion, and point-of-sale material.

Developing
Marketing
Strategies

5. *What action to take?* If the test markets show high trial and high repurchase rates, the product should be launched nationally. But if the test markets show a high trial rate and a low repurchase rate, customers are not satisfied and the product should be redesigned or dropped. If the test markets show a low trial rate and a high repurchase rate, the product is satisfying but more people have to try it. This means increasing advertising and sales promotion. If the trial and repurchase rates are both low, then the product should be dropped.

Test marketing yields several benefits. Its primary benefit is a more reliable forecast of future sales. If product sales fall below target levels in the test market, the company must drop or modify the product or change the marketing program.

A second benefit of test marketing is the pretesting of alternative marketing plans. For example, Colgate-Palmolive used a different marketing mix in each of four cities to market a new soap product. The four approaches were (1) an average amount of advertising coupled with free samples distributed door to door, (2) heavy advertising plus samples, (3) an average amount of advertising linked with mailed redeemable coupons, and (4) an average amount of advertising with no special introductory offer. The third alternative generated the best profit level, although not the highest sales level.

In spite of the benefits of test marketing, many companies question its value today. In this fast-changing marketplace, companies that have spotted an unfulfilled need are eager to get to the market first. Test marketing would slow them down and reveal their plans to competitors, who will rush to develop their own rival products. This happened to Procter & Gamble several years ago when it began testing a ready-to-spread Duncan Hines frosting. General Mills immediately took note and rushed out its own Betty Crocker brand, which now dominates the category.[33] Furthermore, aggressive competitors increasingly take steps to spoil the test markets, making the test results less reliable. For instance, when Pepsi tested its Mountain Dew Sport drink in Minneapolis in 1990, Gatorade counterattacked furiously with coupons and ads.[34]

Many large companies today are skipping the test-marketing stage and relying on other market-testing methods.[35] For example, General Mills now prefers to launch new products in perhaps 25% of the country, an area too large for rivals to disrupt. The company's managers review scanner data, which tell them within days how the product is doing and what corrective fine-tuning actions they should take. And Colgate-Palmolive often launches a new product in a set of small "lead countries" and keeps rolling it out if it proves successful.[36]

Nonetheless, managers should consider all the angles before deciding to dispense with market testing. Consider what happened at Unilever:

UNILEVER London-based Unilever learned a costly lesson when it decided to skip formal test marketing in favor of a full-blown rollout of its Power laundry detergent. It was so excited about Power's patented manganese-based catalyst, the Accelerator, that it forged ahead with a $300 million Power introduction across Europe. The company rolled out its product despite a warning from arch-rival Procter & Gamble that the new stain-annihilating detergent also annihilated customers' clothing. When Unilever was on the brink of launching Power, P&G CEO Edwin Artz paid a secret visit to Unilever vice chairman Niall Fitzgerald, telling him that Power actually damaged clothes. Unilever ignored him, and the new Power brand was a disaster. Of course, P&G was not motivated by altruism but by its own hidden agenda: It was secretly preparing to relaunch its flagship European brand Ariel as Ariel Future, a stain-fighting concentrated detergent. P&G ended up bombarding journalists across Europe with color photos of tattered rags washed in Power next to pristine garments laundered with its own Ariel.[37]

BUSINESS-GOODS MARKET TESTING. Business goods can also benefit from market testing, the tests varying with the type of goods. Expensive industrial goods and new technologies will normally undergo alpha testing and beta testing.

Alpha testing refers to in-company product testing to measure and improve product performance, reliability, design, and operating cost. Following satisfactory results, companies will initiate *beta testing,* which involves inviting potential adopters to conduct confidential testing at their sites. Beta testing provides benefits to both the vendors and the test sites. The vendor's technical people observe how these test sites use the product, a practice that often exposes unanticipated problems of safety and servicing and clues the vendor about customer training and servicing requirements. The vendor can also observe how much value the equipment adds to the customer's operation as a clue to subsequent pricing. The vendor will ask the test sites to express their purchase intention and other reactions after the test.

The test sites also benefit in several ways: They can influence the vendor's product design, gain experience with the new product ahead of competitors, receive a price break in return for their cooperation, and enhance their reputation as technological pioneers. Vendors must carefully interpret the beta test results because only a small number of test sites are used, they are not randomly drawn, and the tests are somewhat customized to each site, therefore limiting generalizability. Another risk is that test sites that are unimpressed with the product may leak unfavorable reports about it.

A second common market-test method for business goods is to introduce the new product at trade shows. Trade shows draw a large number of buyers, who view new products in a few concentrated days. The vendor can observe how much interest buyers show in the new product, how they react to various features and terms, and how many express purchase intentions or place orders. Book publishers, for instance, regularly launch their forthcoming fall titles at the American Booksellers Association convention each Spring. There they display galleys, or "proofs" of steamy new novels or groundbreaking reference books on CD-ROM, all wrapped in dummy book covers. If a big customer, such as bookstore chain Barnes & Noble, objects to a cover design or title of a promising new book, the publisher will often come up with a new title or commission a new cover. The disadvantage of trade shows is that they reveal the product to competitors; therefore, the vendor should be ready to launch the product soon after the trade show.

New industrial products can also be tested in distributor and dealer display rooms, where they may stand next to the manufacturer's other products and possibly competitors' products. This method yields preference and pricing information in the product's normal selling atmosphere. The disadvantages are that the customers might want to place orders that cannot be filled, and those customers who come in might not represent the target market.

Although test marketing is most often used for consumer goods, it has been used by some manufacturers. They produce a limited supply of the product and give it to the sales force to sell in a limited set of geographical areas that receive promotional support, printed catalog sheets, and so on. In this way, management can learn what might happen under full-scale marketing and make a more informed decision about commercializing the product.

Commercialization

Market testing presumably gives management enough information to decide whether to launch the new product. If the company goes ahead with commercialization, it will face its largest costs to date. The company will have to contract for manufacture or build or rent a full-scale manufacturing facility. The size of the plant will be a critical decision variable. The company can build a plant smaller than called for by the sales forecast, to be on the safe side. That is what Quaker Oats did when it launched its 100 Percent Natural breakfast cereal. The demand so exceeded the company's sales forecast that for about a year it could not supply enough product to the stores. Although Quaker Oats was gratified with the response, the low forecast cost it a considerable amount of profit.

Another major cost is marketing. To introduce a major new consumer packaged good into the national market, the company may have to spend between $20 million and $80 million in advertising and promotion in the first year. In the introduction of new food products, marketing expenditures typically represent 57% of sales during the first year.

WHEN (TIMING). In commercializing a new product, market-entry timing is critical. Suppose a company has almost completed the development work on its new product and hears about a competitor nearing the end of its development work. The company faces three choices:

1. *First entry:* The first firm entering a market usually enjoys the "first mover advantages" of locking up key distributors and customers and gaining reputational leadership. A McKinsey study showed that being first to introduce a new product, even if it is over budget, is better than coming in later but on budget. However, if the product is rushed to the market before it is thoroughly debugged, the product can acquire a flawed image.
2. *Parallel entry:* The firm might time its entry to coincide with the competitor's entry. If the competitor rushes to launch, the company does the same. If the competitor takes its time, the company also takes time, using the extra time to refine its product.
3. *Late entry:* The firm might delay its launch until after the competitor has entered. This strategy has three potential advantages. The competitor will have borne the cost of educating the market. The competitor's product may reveal fault that the late entrant can avoid. And the company can learn the size of the market. For example, the British company EMI pioneered the CAT scan, but GE took over the market because of greater manufacturing excellence and hospital distribution strength.

The timing decision involves additional considerations. If the new product replaces the company's older product, the company might delay the introduction until the old product's stock is drawn down. If the product is highly seasonal, it might be held back until the right season.[38]

WHERE (GEOGRAPHICAL STRATEGY). The company must decide whether to launch the new product in a single locality, a region, several regions, the national market, or the international market. Few companies have the confidence, capital, and capacity to launch new products into full national or global distribution. Rather, they will develop a planned market rollout over time. Company size is an important factor here. Small companies, in particular, will select an attractive city and put on a blitz campaign to enter the market. They will enter other cities one at a time. Large companies will introduce their product into a whole region and then move to the next region. Companies with national distribution networks, such as auto companies, will launch their new models in the national market.

It is interesting to note that most companies design their new products to sell primarily in the domestic market. Then, if the product does well, the company considers exporting the product to neighboring countries or the world market, redesigning it if necessary. Yet Cooper and Kleinschmidt, in their study of industrial products, found that domestic products designed solely for the domestic market tend to show a high failure rate, low market share, and low growth. In contrast, products that are designed for the world market—or at least to include neighboring countries—achieve significantly more profits, both at home and abroad. Yet only 17% of the products in the Cooper/Kleinschmidt study were designed with this orientation.[39] The implication is clear. Companies would achieve a higher rate of new-product success if they adopted an international focus in designing and developing their new products. They would be more careful in naming the product, choosing materials, designing features, and so on, and subsequent alterations would be less costly.

Before proceeding with rollout marketing, the company must rate alternative markets for their attractiveness. The candidate markets can be listed as rows, and rollout attractiveness criteria can be listed as columns. The major rating criteria are market potential, company's local reputation, cost of filling the pipeline, cost of communication media, influence of area on other areas, and competitive penetration.

Competitive presence is particularly important to geographical strategy. Suppose McDonald's wants to launch a new chain of fast-food pizza parlors. Also suppose that Pizza Hut, a formidable competitor, is strongly entrenched on the East Coast. Another pizza chain is entrenched on the East Coast but is weak. The Midwest is the battleground between two other chains. The South is open, but Shakey's is planning to move in. We can see that McDonald's faces quite a complex decision in choosing a market rollout strategy.

TO WHOM (TARGET-MARKET PROSPECTS). Within the rollout markets, the company must target its distribution and promotion to the best prospect groups. Presumably, the company has already profiled the prime prospects. Prime prospects for a new consumer product would ideally have the following characteristics:

◆ They would be early adopters.

◆ They would be heavy users.

◆ They would be opinion leaders.

◆ They could be reached at a low cost.[40]

Few groups have all of these characteristics. The company should rate the various prospect groups on these characteristics and target the best prospect group. The aim is to generate strong sales as soon as possible to motivate the sales force and attract further prospects.

Many companies are surprised to learn who really buys their product and why. Microwave ovens began to enjoy explosive growth only after microwave-oven popcorn was developed. Households dramatically increased their purchase of computers when the CD-ROM multimedia feature was introduced.

HOW (INTRODUCTORY MARKET STRATEGY). The company must develop an action plan for introducing the new product into the rollout markets. Notices of product launches regularly appear in *Brandweek* magazine, and here's the kind of introduction one company gave its product:

> Fila USA bumped its marketing budget 25% to some $40 million in 1995 to introduce the new Grant Hill line of basketball shoes (named for NBA rookie sensation) and Fila Sport, a line of fashionable menswear. The signature shoes hit the shelves March 1, 1995, but Fila heralded the new line with a teaser campaign, "A Rookie's Journal," shot by the directors of the film *Hoop Dreams* and broadcast nationally for the first time on February 1 on ESPN, MTV, and BET. Key retailers Foot Locker and FootAction provided co-op radio ads to support their limited-time rights to exclusive shoe styles. Fila is also underwriting FootAction's new sponsorship of the AVP beach volleyball tour—two top stars of which wear Fila apparel—as co-op sponsor.[41]

To sequence and coordinate the many activities involved in launching a new product, management can use network-planning techniques such as critical path scheduling. *Critical path scheduling (CPS)* calls for developing a master chart showing the simultaneous and sequential activities that must take place to launch the product. By estimating how much time each activity takes, the planners estimate completion time for the entire project. Any delay in any activity on the critical path will cause the project to be delayed. If the launch must be completed earlier, the planner searches for the least time-consuming critical path and seeks ways of reducing time along it.[42]

THE CONSUMER-ADOPTION PROCESS

How do potential customers learn about new products, try them, and adopt or reject them? Management must understand this *consumer-adoption process* to build an effective strategy for early market penetration. (*Adoption* is an individual's decision to become a regular user of a product.) The consumer-adoption process is later followed by the *consumer-loyalty process,* which is the concern of the established producer.

Years ago, new-product marketers used a *mass-market approach* in launching their product. They would distribute the product everywhere and advertise it to everyone on the assumption that most people are potential buyers. This approach has two main drawbacks: It calls for heavy marketing expenditures, and it involves many wasted exposures to people who are not potential consumers. These drawbacks led to a second approach, *heavy-user target marketing,* where the product is initially aimed at the heavy users. This approach makes sense, provided that heavy users are identifiable and are early adopters. But even within the heavy-user group, consumers differ in their interest in new products and brands; many heavy users are loyal to their existing brands. Many new-product marketers now aim at those consumers who are early adopters. According to *early-adopter theory:*

- Persons within a target market differ in the amount of elapsed time between their exposure to a new product and their trying it.
- Early adopters share some traits that differentiate them from late adopters.
- Efficient media exist for reaching early adopters.
- Early adopters tend to be opinion leaders and helpful in "advertising" the new product to other potential buyers.

We now turn to the theory of innovation diffusion and consumer adoption, which help marketers identify early adopters.

Stages in the Adoption Process

An *innovation* refers to any good, service, or idea that is *perceived* by someone as new. The idea may have a long history, but it is an innovation to the person who sees it as new. Innovations take time to spread through the social system. Rogers defines the *innovation diffusion process* as "the spread of a new idea from its source of invention or creation to its ultimate users or adopters."[43] The consumer-adoption process focuses on the mental process through which an individual passes from first hearing about an innovation to final adoption.

Adopters of new products have been observed to move through the following five stages:

- *Awareness:* The consumer becomes aware of the innovation but lacks information about it.
- *Interest:* The consumer is stimulated to seek information about the innovation.
- *Evaluation:* The consumer considers whether to try the innovation.
- *Trial:* The consumer tries the innovation to improve his or her estimate of its value.
- *Adoption:* The consumer decides to make full and regular use of the innovation.

This progression suggests that the new-product marketer should aim to facilitate consumer movement through these stages. A portable electric-dishwasher manufacturer might discover that many consumers are stuck in the interest stage; they do not buy because of their uncertainty and the large investment cost. But these same consumers would be willing to use an electric dishwasher on a trial basis for a small monthly fee. The manufacturer should consider offering a trial-use plan with option to buy.

Factors Influencing the Adoption Process

It is sometimes hard to generalize about consumers. However, marketers recognize a few basic truths about the adoption process.

PEOPLE DIFFER MARKEDLY IN THEIR READINESS TO TRY NEW PRODUCTS. Rogers defines a person's innovativeness as "the degree to which an individual is relatively earlier in adopting new ideas than the other members of his social system." In each product area, there are consumption pioneers and early adopters. Some people are the first to adopt new clothing fashions or new appliances; some doctors are the first to prescribe new medicines; and some farmers are the first to adopt new farming methods. Other individuals adopt new products much later. People can be classified into the adopter categories shown in Figure 11-8. After a slow start, an increasing number of people adopt the innovation, the number reaches a peak, and then it diminishes as fewer nonadopters remain.

Rogers sees the five adopter groups as differing in their value orientations. Innovators are venturesome; they are willing to try new ideas at some risk. Early adopters are guided by respect; they are opinion leaders in their community and adopt new ideas early but carefully. The early majority are deliberate; they adopt new ideas before the average person, although they rarely are leaders. The late majority are skeptical; they adopt an innovation only after a majority of people have tried it. Finally, laggards are tradition bound; they are suspicious of changes, mix with other tradition-bound people, and adopt the innovation only when it takes on a measure of tradition itself.

This adopter classification suggests that an innovating firm should research the demographic, psychographic, and media characteristics of innovators and early adopters and direct communications specifically to them. Identifying early adopters

FIGURE 11-8

Adopter Categorization on the Basis of Relative Time of Adoption of Innovations

Source: Redrawn from Everett M. Rogers, *Diffusion of Innovations* (New York: Free Press, 1983).

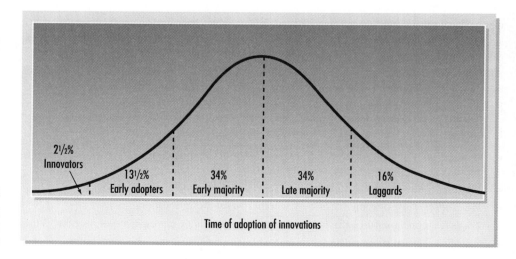

2½% Innovators

13½% Early adopters

34% Early majority

34% Late majority

16% Laggards

Time of adoption of innovations

is not always easy. For example, innovative farmers are likely to be better educated and more efficient than noninnovative farmers. The marketer's challenge is to identify the characteristics of early adopters in its product area. Innovative homemakers are more gregarious and usually higher in social status than noninnovative homemakers. Certain communities have a high share of early adopters. According to Rogers, earlier adopters tend to be younger in age, have higher social status, and a more favorable financial position. They utilize a greater number of more cosmopolitan information sources than do later adopters.[44]

PERSONAL INFLUENCE PLAYS A LARGE ROLE IN THE ADOPTION OF NEW PRODUCTS. *Personal influence* is the effect one person has on another's attitude or purchase probability. Although personal influence is an important factor, its significance is greater in some situations and for some individuals than for others. Personal influence is more important in the evaluation stage of the adoption process than in the other stages. It has more influence on late adopters than early adopters. And it is more important in risky situations than in safe situations.

THE CHARACTERISTICS OF THE INNOVATION AFFECT ITS RATE OF ADOPTION. Some products catch on immediately (e.g., Frisbees), while others take a long time to gain acceptance (e.g., diesel-engine autos). Five characteristics are especially important in influencing the rate of adoption of an innovation. We will consider each of these with respect to the adoption of personal computers for home use.

The first is the innovation's *relative advantage*—the degree to which it appears superior to existing products. The greater the perceived relative advantage of using a personal computer, say, in preparing income taxes and keeping financial records, the more quickly personal computers will be adopted.

The second is the innovation's *compatibility*—the degree to which it matches the values and experiences of the individuals in the community. Personal computers, for example, are highly compatible with the lifestyles found in upper-middle-class homes.

Third is the innovation's *complexity*—the degree to which it is relatively difficult to understand or use. Personal computers are complex and will therefore take a longer time to penetrate into home use.

Fourth is the innovation's *divisibility*—the degree to which it can be tried on a limited basis. The availability of rentals of personal computers with an option to buy increases their rate of adoption.

The fifth characteristic is the innovation's *communicability*—the degree to which the beneficial results of its use are observable or describable to others. The fact that personal computers lend themselves to demonstration and description helps them diffuse faster in the social system.

Other characteristics that influence the rate of adoption are cost, risk and uncertainty, scientific credibility, and social approval. The new-product marketer has to research all these factors and give the key ones maximum attention in designing the new-product and marketing program.[45]

LIKE PEOPLE, ORGANIZATIONS VARY IN THEIR READINESS TO ADOPT AN INNOVATION. Thus the creator of a new teaching method would want to identify innovative schools. The producer of a new piece of medical equipment would want to identify innovative hospitals. Adoption is associated with variables in the organization's environment (community progressiveness, community income), the organization itself (size, profits, pressure to change), and

Developing
New
Products

the administrators (education level, age, sophistication). Once useful indicators are found, they can be used to identify the best target organizations.

SUMMARY

1. Once a company has segmented the market, chosen its target customer groups, identified their needs, and determined its desired market positioning, it is ready to develop and launch appropriate new products. Marketing should actively participate with other departments in every stage of new-product development.

2. Successful new-product development requires the company to establish an effective organization for managing the development process. Companies can choose to use product managers, new-product managers, new-product committees, new-product departments, or new-product venture teams.

3. Eight stages are involved in the new-product development process: idea generation, idea screening, concept development and testing, marketing strategy development, business analysis, product development, market testing, and commercialization. The purpose of each stage is to determine whether the new-product idea should be dropped or moved to the next stage. The company wants to minimize the chances that good ideas will be dropped or that bad ideas will be developed.

4. The consumer-adoption process is the process by which customers learn about new products, try them, and adopt or reject them. Today many marketers are targeting heavy users and early adopters of new products, recognizing that both groups can be reached by specific media and tend to be opinion leaders. The consumer-adoption process is influenced by many factors beyond the marketer's control, including consumers' and organizations' willingness to try new products, personal influences, and the characteristics of the new product or innovation.

CONCEPT APPLICATIONS

1. To generate really good new-product ideas you need inspiration, perspiration, and good techniques. Some companies struggle with trying to develop new-product ideas because they place more emphasis on inspiration and perspiration than they do on technique. Attribute listing, Alex Osborn's powerful creative tool, can activate the creative juices in just about everyone. Identify a product or service that you are familiar with and list its attributes. Then modify each attribute in search of an improved product. The following form will be useful in your deliberations.

Attribute Listing Worksheet

Attributes	Magnify	Minify	Substitute	Adapt	Rearrange	Reverse	Combine	New Uses	Replace

If you are having trouble getting started, consider a famous example of attribute alteration and expansion: that of Oreo cookies. From the simple, black-and-white Oreo, Nabisco has developed double-stuff Oreos, chocolate-covered Oreos, giant-size Oreos, mini-size Oreos, low-fat Oreos, lower-calorie Oreos, different packaging and package sizes, Oreo cookie ice cream, Oreo cookie ice cream cones, Oreo granola bars, and Oreo snack treats.

2. Prepare a list of questions that management should answer prior to developing a new product or service. Organize the questions according to the following categories: (1) market opportunity, (2) competition, (3) production, (4) patentable features, (5) distribution (for products) or delivery (for services), and (6) finance. Then answer each question for a new-product idea you have. Would the development and testing of a new service differ from those of a new product?

3. A food company wants to develops a new salad-dressing powder. The consumer mixes the powder with water, shakes the bottle, and *voilà*—fresh dressing. The company is trying to compete against another company that has a powdered dressing that is mixed with oil and vinegar. The company plans to conduct blindfold taste tests, asking consumers to compare the new product with a variety of alternative dressings currently marketed. But the new-product development team fears that the results from this test may not be fully reliable, and it wants to test its concept in at least three other ways. It also wants to test alternative formulations of the dressing, including one that is sweeter and one that is spicier. Suggest some additional concept-test formats to the development team.

4. Scenario: A couple of your friends drop by, and as the conversation continues into the evening you realize that you would all like a bite to eat. So you call Domino's and order pizza and chicken wings. Then it occurs to you: Why is a pizza place selling chicken?

   Although chicken has been one of the perennial best sellers in fast-food restaurants, today Pizza Hut, Little Caesar's, and Domino's—all of which have a deep line of pizza—have added buffalo wings to their menus. (Buffalo wings are simply chicken wings drenched in hot sauce.) Assume that you were working for Domino's (or one of the other major pizza chains) at the time it was considering the introduction of buffalo wings. Take the buffalo wings idea through the eight-step new-product development process, spelling out the questions that will arise at each step of the process. How are pizza and buffalo wings similar? What problems might the chains encounter if the wings are *too* successful? Do you think buffalo wings will continue to be commercially successful for the pizza chains?

5. Screening new ideas in the new-product development process requires the ability to think critically and in an unbiased manner. However, many barriers may impede the product-development team's progress, and ultimately the success of the new product. One of these barriers is *groupthink,* a phenomenon in which people in groups tend to conform to the opinions or feelings prevailing in the group rather than question assumptions or challenge conventional wisdom. Another barrier is *rationalization,* the tendency for the group to discount its earlier bad decisions. Rationalization allows individuals in the group to diffuse their own responsibility by sharing their failures with the group.

   Reflecting back on the groups in which you have been involved, suggest some other barriers to success that were operating in your idea-generating environment.

6. Table 1 on page 340 reports the results of an in-home-use test of Odor-Eater socks. Before beginning the test, each consumer participant selected the Odor-Eaters sock style he or she preferred. At the end of the test, the participants summarized how likely they would be to purchase Odor-Eaters in the future. These are the data reported in Table 1. What conclusions can you draw from these data? What type of sock is most popular with consumers? Assuming that the consumer testers are representative of the market, how price-sensitive is this market? Should the company package Odor-Eaters one to the box (columns 6 and 7), or would multiple packs (columns 8 and 9) be preferable?

TABLE I	LIKELIHOOD OF PURCHASING ODOR-EATERS								
		TYPE OF SOCK					PACKAGE SIZE AND PRICE		
	(1) TOTAL RESPON- DENTS	(2) 24-INCH TUBE SOCK	(3) 18-INCH TUBE SOCK	(4) ATHLETIC SOCK	(5) CREW SOCK	(6) 1 PAIR AT $1.79– $1.99	(7) 1 PAIR AT $1.99– $2.49	(8) 3 PAIRS AT $4.99– $5.99	(9) 3 PAIRS AT $5.99– $6.49
Respondent base*	(185)	(60)	(22)	(34)	(69)	(53)	(42)	(42)	(48)
Definitely would buy	38%	43%	45%	42%	29%	42%	45%	31%	33%
Probably would buy	44	47	27	35	51	38	40	48	50
Might or might not buy	14	7	23	15	16	13	20	19	13
Probably would not but	3	3	5	6	1	4	5	—	4
Definitely would not buy	2	—	—	3	3	4	—	2	—

* Based on four-week consumer home-use test.
Source: **CU Market Research.**

7. Procter & Gamble wants to enter the healthy-soup market. The new soup will consist of vegetables, protein, and fiber and will be positioned as a "complete meal." Evaluate this product in terms of both product-market fit and product-company fit.

8. You are the leader of a new-product committee at Nestlé. Your task is to extend Nestlé Quik by altering the product's image so that it will appeal to new market segments. Suggest new marketing strategies to reposition the product in the minds of the consumer. Quik is used most conventionally as a chocolate-milk mix, but it has many other uses. What are some of these other uses? When deciding to extend the product's image by promoting its other uses, what challenges does the company face?

9. Analyze the following conjoint analysis for computers. What implications does it have for new product development and design in the Southeast region? What attributes are the major determinants of buying behavior in this market? What combination of the six attributes would hold the greatest value for the consumer? What challenges is the product-design team likely to meet in attempting to design a computer that delivers maximum value to customers?

	ATTRIBUTES	SOUTHEAST REGION
Relative Importance	RAM	12.3%
	Megahertz	19.7
	Processing speed	25.0
	Storage	4.4
	Warranty	7.4
	Retail price	23.5
Attribute #1 RAM	Level #1 (2mb)	16.7%
	Level #2 (4mb)	51.1
	Level #3 (6mb)	45.5
	Level #4 (8mb)	10.5

Developing
Marketing
Strategies

ATTRIBUTES		SOUTHEAST REGION
Attribute #2 Megahertz	Level #1 (25mh)	67.9%
	Level #2 (33mh)	65.5
	Level #3 (50mh)	34.6
	Level #4 (75mh)	3.0
Attribute #3 Processing Speed	Level #1 (286)	0.0%
	Level #2 (386)	30.3
	Level #3 (486)	72.7
	Level #4 (586)	82.2
Attribute #4 Storage	Level #1 (100mb)	41.0%
	Level #2 (150mb)	55.3
	Level #3 (200mb)	53.2
	Level #4 (300mb)	43.1
Attribute #5 Warranty	Level #1 (6 mos.)	26.7%
	Level #2 (1 yr.)	49.6
	Level #3 (2 yrs.)	51.1
	Level #4 (3 yrs.)	30.6
Attribute #6 Retail Price	Level #1 ($1500)	100.0%
	Level #2 ($1800)	72.7
	Level #3 ($2100)	40.4
	Level #4 ($2400)	22.7

10. A company president asked the new-product manager what a proposed new product would earn if launched. "Profits of three million dollars in five years," was the answer. Then the president asked whether the product might fail. "Yes." "What would we lose if the product fails?" "One million dollars." "Forget it," said the president. Do you agree with his decision?

NOTES

1. *New Products Management for the 1980s* (New York: Booz, Allen & Hamilton, 1982).
2. Christopher Power, "Flops," *Business Week,* August 16, 1993, pp. 76–82.
3. Cited in Kevin J. Clancy and Robert S. Shulman, *The Marketing Revolution: A Radical Manifesto for Dominating the Marketplace* (New York: Harper Business, 1991), p. 6.
4. Clancy and Shulman, *The Marketing Revolution.*
5. Robert G. Cooper and Elko J. Kleinschmidt, "New Product Processes at Leading Industrial Firms," Industrial Marketing Management, May 1991, pp. 137–47.
6. Robert G. Cooper and Elko J. Kleinschmidt, *New Products: The Key Factors in Success* (Chicago: American Marketing Association, 1990).
7. Modesto A. Madique and Billie Jo Zirger, "A Study of Success and Failure in Product Innovation: The Case of the U.S. Electronics Industry," *IEEE Transactions on Engineering Management,* November 1984, pp. 192–203.
8. See David S. Hopkins, *Options in New-Product Organization* (New York: Conference Board, 1974).
9. See Robert G. Cooper, "Stage-Gate Systems: A New Tool for Managing New Products," *Business Horizons,* May–June 1990, pp. 44–54. See also his "The New Prod System: The Industry Experience," *Journal of Product Innovation Management,* Vol. 9 (1992), pp. 113–27.
10. Eric von Hippel, "Lead Users: A Source of Novel Product Concepts," *Management Science,* July 1986, pp. 791–805. Also see his *The Sources of Innovation* (New York: Oxford University Press, 1988); and "Learning from Lead Users," in *Marketing in an Electronic Age,* ed. Robert D. Buzzell (Cambridge, MA: Harvard Business School Press, 1985), pp. 308–17.
11. John H. Sheridan, "Lew Platt: Creating a Culture for Innovation," *Industry Week,* December 19, 1994, pp. 26–30.
12. See John E. Arnold, "Useful Creative Techniques," in *Source Book for Creative Thinking,* ed. Sidney J. Parnes and Harold F. Harding (New York: Scribner's, 1962), p. 255.
13. See Alex F. Osborn, *Applied Imagination,* 3d ed. (New York: Scribner's, 1963), pp. 286–87.
14. See Edward M. Tauber, "HIT: Heuristic Ideation Technique—A Systematic Procedure for New Product Search," *Journal of Marketing,* January 1972, pp. 58–70; and Charles L. Alford and Joseph Barry Mason, "Generating New Product Ideas," *Journal of Advertising Research,* December 1975, pp. 27–32.
15. See Edward M. Tauber, "Discovering New Product Opportunities with Problem Inventory Analysis," *Journal of Marketing,* January 1975, pp. 67–70.

16. Osborn, *Applied Imagination*, p. 156.

17. John W. Lincoln, "Defining a Creativeness in People," in *Source Book for Creative Thinking*, pp. 274–75.

18. Lincoln, "Defining a Creativeness in People," p. 274.

19. Mark Hanan, "Corporate Growth through Venture Management," *Harvard Business Review*, January–February 1969, p. 44. See also Carol J. Loomis, "Dinosaurs?" *Fortune*, May 3, 1993, pp. 36–42.

20. "The Ultimate Widget: 3-D 'Printing' May Revolutionize Product Design and Manufacturing," *U.S. News & World Report*, July 20, 1992, p. 55.

21. Benjamin Wooley, *Virtual Worlds* (London: Blackwell, 1992).

22. See John Hauser, "House of Quality," *Harvard Business Review*, May–June 1988, pp. 63–73. Customer-driven engineering is also called "quality function deployment." See Lawrence R. Guinta and Nancy C. Praizler, *The QFD Book: The Team Approach to Solving Problems and Satisfying Customers through Quality Function Deployment* (New York: Amacom, 1993).

23. The full-profile example was taken from Paul E. Green and Yoram Wind, "New Ways to Measure Consumers' Judgments," *Harvard Business Review* (July–August, 1975), pp. 107–17. Copyright © 1975 by the President and Fellows of Harvard College; all rights reserved. Also see Paul E. Green and V. Srinivasan, "Conjoint Analysis in Marketing: New Developments with Implications for Research and Practice," *Journal of Marketing*, October 1990, pp. 3–19; Jonathan Weiner, "Forecasting Demand: Consumer Electronics Marketer Uses a Conjoint Approach to Configure Its New Product and Set the Right Price," *Marketing Research: A Magazine of Management & Applications*, Summer 1994, pp. 6–11; Dick R. Wittnick, Marco Vriens, and Wim Burhenne, "Commercial Uses of Conjoint Analysis in Europe: Results and Critical Reflections," *International Journal of Research in Marketing*, January 1994, pp. 41–52.

24. See Robert Blattberg and John Golanty, "Tracker: An Early Test Market Forecasting and Diagnostic Model for New Product Planning," *Journal of Marketing Research*, May 1978, pp. 192–202.

25. See Roger A. Kerin, Michael G. Harvey, and James T. Rothe, "Cannibalism and New Product Development," *Business Horizons*, October 1978, pp. 25–31.

26. The present value (V) of a future sum (I) to be received t years from today and discounted at the interest rate (r) is given by $V = I^t/(1 + r)^t$. Thus $\$4,761/(1.15)^5 = \$2,346$.

27. See David B. Hertz, "Risk Analysis in Capital Investment," *Harvard Business Review*, January–February 1964, pp. 96–106.

28. Faye Rice, "Secrets of Product Testing," *Fortune*, November 28, 1994, pp. 172–74; Lawrence Ingrassia, "Taming the Monster: How Big Companies Can Change: Keeping Sharp: Gillette Holds Its Edge by Endlessly Searching for a Better Shave," *The Wall Street Journal*, December 10, 1992, A1:6.

29. Audrey Choi and Gabriella Stern, "The Lessons of Reugen: Electric Cars Are Slow, Temperamental and Exasperating," *The Wall Street Journal*, March 30, 1995, B1:3.

30. Christopher Power, "Will It Sell in Podunk? Hard to Say," *Business Week*, August 10, 1992, pp. 46–47.

31. See Kevin J. Clancy, Robert S. Shulman, and Marianne Wolf, *Simulated Test Marketing: Technology for Launching Successful New Products* (New York: Lexington Books, 1994); and V. Mahajan and Jerry Wind, "New Product Models: Practice, Shortcomings, and Desired Improvements," *Journal of Product Innovation Management*, Vol. 9 (1992), 128–39.

32. Judith Waldrop, "Markets with Attitude," *American Demographics*, July 1994, pp. 22–32.

33. Christopher Power, "Will It Sell in Podunk?" *Business Week*, August 10, 1992, pp. 46–47.

34. *Ibid.*

35. "Spotting Competitive Edges Begets New Product Success," *Marketing News*, December 21, 1984, p. 4; "Testing Time for Test Marketing," *Fortune*, October 29, 1984, pp. 75–76; and Jay E. Klompmaker, G. David Hughes, and Russell I. Haley, "Test Marketing in New Product Development," *Harvard Business Review*, May–June 1976, pp. 128–38.

36. *Ibid.*

37. Laurel Wentz, "Unilever's Power Failure a Wasteful Use of Haste," *Advertising Age*, March 6, 1995, p. 42.

38. For further discussion, see Frank H. Alpert and Michael A. Kamins, "Pioneer Brand Advantages and Consumer Behavior: A Conceptual Framework and Propositional Inventory," *Journal of the Academy of Marketing Science*, Summer 1994, pp. 244–53.

39. See Cooper and Kleinschmidt, *New Products: The Key Factors*, pp. 35–38.

40. Philip Kotler and Gerald Zaltman, "Targeting Prospects for a New Product," *Journal of Advertising Research*, February 1976, pp. 7–20.

41. Elaine Underwood, "Fila Budgets $40M on Hill, AVP, Upscale Apparel Line," *Brandweek*, January 16, 1995, p. 4.

42. For details, see Keith G. Lockyer, *Critical Path Analysis and Other Project Network Techniques* (London: Pitman, 1984).

43. The following discussion leans heavily on Everett M. Rogers, *Diffusion of Innovations* (New York: Free Press, 1962). Also see his third edition, published in 1983.

44. Rogers, *Diffusion of Innovations*, p. 192. Also see S. Ram and Hyung-Shik Jung, "Innovativeness in Product Usage: A Comparison of Early Adopters and Early Majority," *Psychology and Marketing*, January–February 1994, pp. 57–68.

45. For another summary of the literature, see Hubert Gatignon and Thomas S. Robertson, "A Propositional Inventory for New Diffusion Research," *Journal of Consumer Research*, March 1985, pp. 849–67.

MANAGING LIFE-CYCLE

STRATEGIES

Profit is the payment you get when you take advantage of change.

JOSEPH SCHUMPETER

❖

This is one of the saddest days of my life, a sad one for me, for our employees,
officers, and directors; indeed, it is sad for the American public.
Apparently, there is just not the need for our product in today's scheme
of living.

MARTIN ACKERMAN, PRESIDENT OF *THE SATURDAY EVENING POST*

❖

C ompanies normally reformulate their marketing strategy several times during a product's life. Economic conditions change, competitors launch new assaults, and the product passes through new stages of buyer interest and requirements. Consequently, a company must plan strategies appropriate to each stage in the product's life cycle. The company hopes to extend the product's life and profitability, keeping in mind that the product will not last forever.

We will answer three questions in this chapter:

- **What is a product life cycle?**
- **What marketing strategies are appropriate at each stage of the product life cycle?**
- **How do markets evolve, and what marketing strategies are appropriate at each stage of market evolution?**

THE PRODUCT LIFE CYCLE

The *product life cycle (PLC)* is an important concept that provides insights into a product's competitive dynamics. To fully explain the PLC, we will first describe its parent concept, the demand/technology life cycle.[1]

Demand/Technology Life Cycle

Remember that most products exist as one solution among many to meet a need. For example, the human race has a need for "calculating power," and this need has grown over the centuries. The changing need level is described by a *demand life-cycle curve*, the highest curve shown in Figure 12-1(a). For each need, there is a stage of *emergence (E)*, followed by stages of *accelerating growth* (G_1), *decelerating growth* (G_2), *maturity (M)*, and *decline (D)*. In the case of calculating power,

FIGURE 12-1

Demand/Technology Product Life Cycles

Source: H. Igor Ansoff, *Implanting Strategic Management*, 2d ed (Englewood Cliffs, NJ: Prentice Hall, 1991).

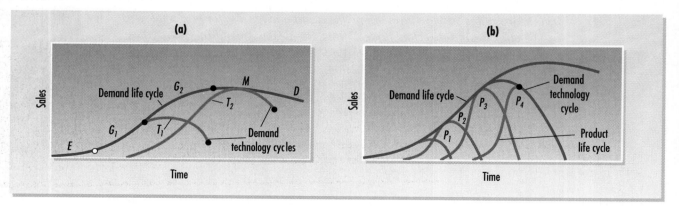

the maturity and decline stages have not set in yet. Indeed, the need for calculating power today seems greater than ever.

Once the need is identified, it is satisfied by some technology. The need for calculating power was first satisfied by finger counting; then by abacuses; still later by slide rules, adding machines, hand calculators, and computers. Each new technology normally satisfies the need in a better way than the previous technology. Each exhibits a *demand/technology life cycle,* shown by the curves T_1 and T_2 under the demand life-cycle curve in Figure 12-1(a). Each demand/technology life cycle shows an emergence, rapid growth, slower growth, maturity, and then decline.

Within a given demand/technology life cycle, there will appear a succession of product forms that satisfy the specific need. Thus the hand calculator initially took the product form of a large plastic box with a small screen and numerical keys, and it could perform only four tasks: adding, subtracting, multiplying, and dividing. This form lasted a few years and was succeeded by smaller hand calculators that could perform additional mathematical operations. Today's product forms include hand calculators the size of a business card. Figure 12-1(b) shows a succession of *product-form life cycles, P_1, P_2, P_3, P_4.* Later we will show that each product form contains a set of brands with their own *brand life cycles.*

If a company concentrates only on its own brand life cycle, it is missing the bigger picture of what is happening to the product life cycle. Thus a manufacturer of slide rules might have paid attention to the slide-rule brands, but it should actually have worried about a new technology (hand calculators) destroying the slide-rule market.

Companies must decide what demand technology to invest in and when to move to a new demand technology. Ansoff calls a demand technology a *strategic business area (SBA),* "a distinctive segment of the environment in which the firm does or may want to do business."[2] Today's companies face many changing technologies but cannot invest in all of them. They have to bet on which demand technology will win. They can bet heavily on one new technology or bet lightly on several. If they do the latter, they are not likely to become the industry leader. The pioneering firm that bets heavily on the winning technology is likely to capture leadership. Thus firms must carefully choose the strategic business areas in which they will operate:

FORE SYSTEMS Four researchers put $100,000 of their combined savings into developing a simple notion. They saw that the high-speed networking switches being developed for telephone companies could also be used to increase the capacity of smaller computer networks that link workstations and PCs. The company they created, Fore Systems Inc., used the new technology, called asynchronous transfer mode (ATM), to build a big lead in the market for switches and the accompanying software that helps run high-speed, flexible local area networks. Fore's ability to capitalize on this technology brought it 60% of the $100 million market for ATM switches.[3]

Stages in the Product Life Cycle

We can now focus on the product life cycle. To say that a product has a life cycle is to assert four things:

- Products have a limited life.
- Product sales pass through distinct stages, each posing different challenges, opportunities, and problems to the seller.
- Profits rise and fall at different stages of the product life cycle.
- Products require different marketing, financial, manufacturing, purchasing, and human resource strategies in each stage of their life cycle.

FIGURE 12-2
Sales and Profit Life Cycles

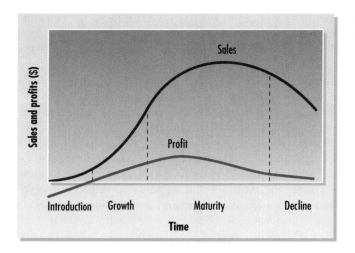

Most discussions of product life cycle portray the sales history of a typical product as following a bell-shaped curve (Figure 12-2). This curve is typically divided into four stages: introduction, growth, maturity, and decline.[4]

♦ *Introduction:* A period of slow sales growth as the product is introduced in the market. Profits are nonexistent in this stage because of the heavy expenses incurred with product introduction.

♦ *Growth:* A period of rapid market acceptance and substantial profit improvement.

♦ *Maturity:* A period of a slowdown in sales growth because the product has achieved acceptance by most potential buyers. Profits stabilize or decline because of increased marketing outlays to defend the product against competition.

♦ *Decline:* The period when sales show a downward drift and profits erode.

It is often difficult to designate where each stage begins and ends. Usually the stages are marked where the rates of sales growth or decline become pronounced. Nonetheless, marketers should check the normal sequence of stages in their industry and the average duration of each stage. Cox found that a typical ethical drug spanned an introductory period of one month, a growth stage of six months, a maturity stage of fifteen months, and a very long decline stage—the last because of manufacturers' reluctance to drop drugs from their catalogs.[5] These stage lengths must be reviewed periodically. Intensifying competition is leading to shorter PLCs over time, which means that products must earn their profits in a shorter period.

Product-Category, Product-Form, Product, and Brand Life Cycles

The PLC concept can be used to analyze a product category (liquor), a product form (white liquor), a product (vodka), or a brand (Smirnoff).

♦ *Product categories* have the longest life cycles. Many product categories stay in the mature stage indefinitely, since they grow only at the population growth rate. Some major product categories—cigars, newspapers—seem to have entered the decline stage of the PLC. Meanwhile some others—fax machines, cellular telephones, bottled water—are clearly in the growth stage.

♦ *Product forms* follow the standard PLC more faithfully than do product categories. Thus manual typewriters passed through the stages of introduction, growth, maturity, and decline; their successors—electric typewriters and electronic typewriters—passed through these same stages.

♦ *Products* follow either the standard PLC or one of several variant shapes.

- *Branded products* can have a short or long PLC. Although many new brands die an early death, some brand names—such as Ivory, Jell-O, Hershey's—have a very long PLC and are used to name and launch new products. For instance, while we might think of Hershey's Kisses, Hershey's has also successfully introduced Hershey's Hugs, Hershey's Kisses with Almonds, and Hershey's Cookies & Mint candy bar. P&G believes that it can keep a strong brand name going forever.

Other Shapes of the Product Life Cycle

Not all products exhibit a bell-shaped PLC. Researchers have identified from six to seventeen different PLC patterns.[6] Three common alternate patterns are shown in Figure 12-3. Figure 12-3(a) shows a *growth-slump-maturity pattern*, often characteristic of small kitchen appliances. For example, the sales of electric knives grew rapidly when first introduced and then fell to a "petrified" level. The petrified level is sustained by late adopters buying the product for the first time and early adopters replacing the product.

The *cycle-recycle pattern* in Figure 12-3(b) often describes the sales of new drugs. The pharmaceutical company aggressively promotes its new drug, and this produces the first cycle. Later, sales start declining and the company gives the drug another promotion push, which produces a second cycle (usually of smaller magnitude and duration).

Another common pattern is the *scalloped PLC* in Figure 12-3(c). Here sales pass through a succession of life cycles based on the discovery of new-product characteristics, uses, or users. Nylon's sales, for example, show a scalloped pattern because of the many new uses—parachutes, hosiery, shirts, carpeting—discovered over time. The Marketing Insight titled "Forecasting the Shape and Duration of the Product Life Cycle" describes some ways a firm can shape the PLC for a specific product.

STYLE, FASHION, AND FAD LIFE CYCLES. There are three special categories of product life cycles that should be distinguished—those pertaining to styles, fashions, and fads (Figure 12-4 on page 349).

A *style* is a basic and distinctive mode of expression appearing in a field of human endeavor. For example, styles appear in homes (colonial, ranch, Cape Cod); clothing (formal, casual, funky); and art (realistic, surrealistic, abstract). Once a style is invented, it can last for generations, going in and out of vogue.

A *fashion* is a currently accepted or popular style in a given field. For example, jeans are a fashion in today's clothing, and "grunge" is a fashion in today's popular music. Fashions pass through four stages:[7]

FIGURE 12-3
Common Product Life-Cycle Patterns

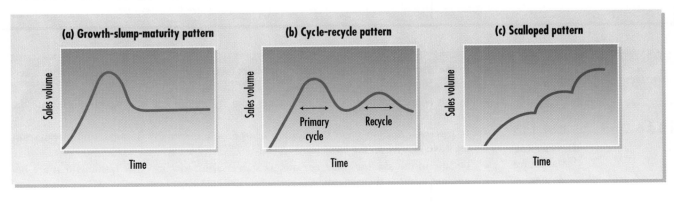

Forecasting the Shape and Duration of the Product Life Cycle

Goldman and Muller have presented interesting observations on factors influencing the shape and duration of product life cycles. First consider the shape of an ideal PLC:

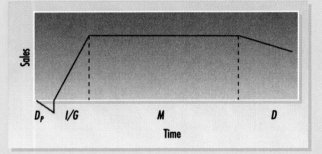

The product-development period (D_p) is short, and therefore the product-development costs are low. The introduction/growth period (I/G) is short, so sales reach their peak quite soon, which means early maximum revenue. The maturity period (M) lasts a long time, which means the company enjoys an extended period of profits. The decline (D) is very slow, which means that profits fall only gradually.

A firm considering the launch of a new product should keep several things in mind:

♦ *Development time* is shorter and less costly for routine products than for high-tech products.

♦ *Introduction and growth time* will be short under the following conditions: (1) The product does not require setting up a new infrastructure of distribution channels, transportation, services, or communication. (2) The dealers will readily accept and promote the new product. (3) Consumers have an interest in the product, will adopt it early, and will give it favorable word of mouth.

♦ *Maturity time* will last long to the extent that consumer tastes and product technology are fairly stable and the company maintains leadership in the market. Companies make the most money by riding out a long maturity period. If the maturity period is short, the company might not recover its full investment.

♦ *Decline time* is long if consumer tastes and product technology change only slowly. The more brand loyal the consumers, the slower the rate of decline. The lower the exit barriers in the industry, the faster some firms will exit, and the slower the rate of decline for the remaining firms.

Given these factors, we can see why many high-tech firms fail. They face highly unattractive PLCs. The worst type of PLC would look like this:

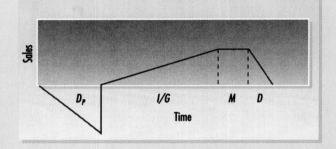

The development time is long, and the development cost is steep; the introduction/growth time is long; the maturity period is short; and the decline is fast. Many high-tech firms must invest a great amount of time and cost to develop their product; they find that it takes a long time to introduce it to the market; the market does not last long; and the decline is steep, owing to the rapid technological change.

Source: Arieh Goldman and Eitan Muller, "Measuring Shape Patterns of Product Life Cycles: Implications for Marketing Strategy," paper, Hebrew University of Jerusalem, Jerusalem School of Business Administration, August 1982.

♦ In the *distinctiveness stage,* some consumers take an interest in something new that sets them apart from other consumers.

♦ In the *emulation stage,* other consumers take an interest out of a desire to emulate the fashion leaders.

♦ In the *mass-fashion stage,* the fashion has become extremely popular, and manufacturers have geared up for mass production.

♦ Finally, in the *decline stage,* consumers start moving toward other fashions that are beginning to catch their attention.

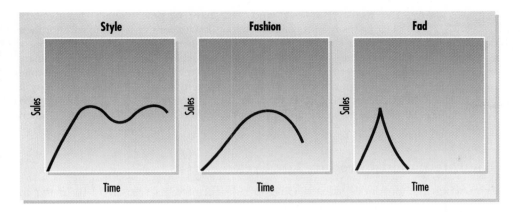

FIGURE 12-4
Style, Fashion, and Fad Life Cycles

Thus fashions tend to grow slowly, remain popular for a while, and decline slowly. The length of a fashion cycle is hard to predict. Wasson believes that fashions come to an end because they represent a purchase compromise, and consumers start looking for missing attributes.[8] For example, as automobiles become smaller, they become less comfortable, and then a growing number of buyers start wanting larger cars. Furthermore, too many consumers adopt the fashion, thus turning others away. Reynolds suggests that the length of a particular fashion cycle depends on the extent to which the fashion meets a genuine need, is consistent with other trends in the society, satisfies societal norms and values, and does not exceed technological limits as it develops.[9]

Fads are fashions that come quickly into the public eye, are adopted with great zeal, peak early, and decline very fast. Their acceptance cycle is short, and they tend to attract only a limited following. They often have a novel or capricious aspect, such as body piercing and body tattooing. Fads appeal to people who are searching for excitement or who want to distinguish themselves from others. Fads do not survive because they do not normally satisfy a strong need or do not satisfy it well. It is difficult to predict whether something will be only a fad or how long a fad will last. The amount of media attention, along with other factors, will influence the fad's duration.

The real winners in the fad wars are those who recognize them early and can leverage those fads into products with staying power. Here are two success stories of companies that managed to extend a fad's life span and one story of a huge short-term success that didn't have staying power:[10]

THE WACKY WALLWALKER It was a tacky-to-the-touch rubber octopus that you could throw at walls and watch as it "walked" down. When Ken Hakuta's "Wacky Wallwalker" was a must-have item in 1983, 350 people worked night and day in a Korean factory to turn them out. To extend the life of his fad, Hakuta stopped production in 1985 and then milked the fad by selling millions more to the Kellogg Co., which included them as premiums in cereal boxes as recently as 1991. But don't expect the Wallwalkers to disappear yet. "Maybe only 25% of third to sixth graders know what a Wacky Wallwalker is," says Hakuta. "When that percentage falls a bit lower I might consider bringing them back as a nostalgia item."

TRIVIAL PURSUIT In the mid-1980s, the board game Trivial Pursuit was part of the furniture in almost every living room and dormitory. The creation of three Canadian buddies, Trivial Pursuit sold about 20 million copies in 1984 alone. Yet, even with the fad long over, the game and its offshoots—travel packs, a children's version, and annual year-in-review editions—continue to sell more than 1.5 million units each year in 19 languages. The game's inventors were also smart to give the product new life with new technology and have had a hand in developing a CD-ROM version of the game.

THE PET ROCK The words "Pet Rock" and "fad" have become virtually synonymous. Hearing his friends complain about how expensive it was to care for their dogs, advertising copywriter Gary Dahl joked about his pet rock and was soon writing a spoof of a dog-training manual for it. Soon Dahl was selling some 1.5 million ordinary beach pebbles at $4 each. Yet the fad, which broke in October 1975, had sunk like a stone by the next February. Dahl's advice to those who want to succeed with a fad: "Enjoy it while it lasts. The Pet Rock was fun, but I let it go on a year too long. I wanted that next year. I believed my own publicity, and I think my ego got in the way of my common sense."

The International Product Life Cycle

Even when the product's sales decline in one country, its sales may be rising in another country. Product adoption occurs throughout the world at different rates. Often a late-adopting country may end up producing the product more economically and become a leader in diffusing the product to other countries. Thus, in addition to a domestic PLC many products have an *international product life cycle.* The four stages of the international product life cycle are:

- *U.S. manufacturers export product:* An innovation is launched in the United States and succeeds because of the country's huge market and the highly developed infrastructure. Eventually, U.S. producers start exporting the product to other countries.

- *Foreign production starts:* As foreign manufacturers become familiar with the product, some of them start producing it for their home market. They do this under a licensing or joint venture arrangement or simply by copying the product. Their government often aids their efforts by imposing tariffs or quotas on imports of the product.

- *Foreign production becomes competitive in export markets:* Foreign manufacturers have gained production experience, and, with their lower costs, they start exporting the product to other countries.

- *Import competition begins:* The foreign manufacturers' growing volume and lower costs enable them to export the product to the United States in direct competition with U.S. producers.

The main implication of the international PLC is that a U.S. manufacturer's sales in the home market will eventually decline as foreign markets start producing the product and exporting it to the United States. For example, Taiwan now manufactures more baseball gloves and basketballs than the United States does. The U.S. manufacturers' best defense is to become global marketers. U.S. firms should open production and distribution facilities in other countries with large markets and/or lower costs. Global marketers are able to extend the product life cycle by moving the product into countries that are getting ready to use it.[11]

MARKETING STRATEGIES THROUGHOUT THE PLC

We now turn to each stage of the PLC and consider the appropriate marketing strategies.

Introduction Stage

The introduction stage starts when the new product is launched. Because it takes time to roll out the product in several markets and to fill the dealer pipelines, sales growth is apt to be slow at this stage. Such well-known products as instant coffee, frozen orange juice, and powdered coffee creamers lingered for many years before they entered a stage of rapid growth. Buzzell identified several causes for the slow growth of many new products: delays in the expansion of production capacity;

technical problems ("working out the bugs"); delays in obtaining adequate distribution through retail outlets; and customer reluctance to change established behaviors.[12] In the case of expensive new products such as high-definition TV, sales growth is retarded by additional factors, including the small number of buyers who can afford the new product.

Profits are negative or low in the introduction stage because of the low sales and heavy distribution and promotion expenses. Much money is needed to attract distributors. Promotional expenditures are at their highest ratio to sales because of the need for a high level of promotional effort to (1) inform potential consumers of the new and unknown product, (2) induce trial of the product, and (3) secure distribution in retail outlets.[13] The firms focus their selling on those buyers who are the readiest to buy, usually higher-income groups. In addition, prices tend to be on the high side because (1) costs are high due to relatively low output rates, (2) technological problems in production may have not yet been fully mastered, and (3) high margins are required to support the heavy promotional expenditures that are necessary to achieve growth.[14]

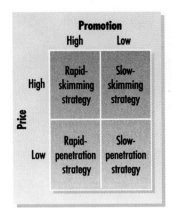

FIGURE 12-5
Four Introductory Marketing Strategies

MARKETING STRATEGIES IN THE INTRODUCTION STAGE. In launching a new product, marketing management can set a high or a low level for each marketing variable (price, promotion, distribution, product quality). Considering only price and promotion, management can pursue one of the four strategies shown in Figure 12-5.

◆ A *rapid-skimming strategy* consists of launching the new product at a high price and a high promotion level. The firm charges a high price in order to recover as much profit per unit as possible. It spends heavily on promotion to convince the market of the product's merits even at the high price. The high promotion acts to accelerate the rate of market penetration. This strategy makes sense under the following assumptions: a large part of the potential market is unaware of the product; those who become aware of the product are eager to have it and can pay the asking price; and the firm faces potential competition and wants to build brand preference.

◆ A *slow-skimming strategy* consists of launching the new product at a high price and low promotion. The high price helps recover as much profit per unit as possible, and the low level of promotion keeps marketing expenses down. This combination is expected to skim a lot of profit from the market. This strategy makes sense when the market is limited in size; most of the market is aware of the product; buyers are willing to pay a high price; and potential competition is not imminent.

◆ A *rapid-penetration strategy* consists of launching the product at a low price and spending heavily on promotion. This strategy promises to bring about the fastest market penetration and the largest market share. This strategy makes sense when the market is large, the market is unaware of the product, most buyers are price-sensitive, there is strong potential competition, and the company's unit manufacturing costs fall with the company's scale of production and accumulated manufacturing experience.

◆ A *slow-penetration strategy* consists of launching the new product at a low price and low level of promotion. The low price will encourage rapid product acceptance, and low promotion costs bring profits up. The company believes that market demand is highly sensitive to price but minimally sensitive to promotion. This strategy makes sense when the market is large, the market is highly aware of the product, the market is price-sensitive, and there is some potential competition.

We discuss skimming and penetration strategies in more detail in Chapter 17.

MARKET PIONEERS. Companies that plan to introduce a new product must decide on when they will enter the market. To be first in the market can be highly rewarding, but risky and expensive. To come in later would make sense if the firm can bring superior technology, quality, or brand strength.

Managing
Life-Cycle
Strategies

Most studies indicate that the market pioneer gains the most advantage. Clearly such pioneering companies as Campbell's, Coca-Cola, Eastman Kodak, Hallmark, and Xerox developed sustained market dominance. Robinson and Fornell studied a broad range of mature consumer and industrial-goods businesses, and found that market pioneers generally enjoy a substantially higher market share than do early followers and late entrants:[15]

| | AVERAGE MARKET SHARE (%) | |
	CONSUMER GOODS	INDUSTRIAL GOODS
Pioneer	29	29
Early follower	17	21
Late entrant	13	15

Urban's study also found a pioneer advantage: It appears that the second entrant obtained only 71% of the pioneer's market share, and the third entrant obtained only 58 percent.[16] And Carpenter and Nakamoto found that 19 out of 25 companies who were market leaders in 1923 were still the market leaders in 1983, fifty years later.[17]

What are the sources of the pioneer's advantage? Some advantages are consumer based. Research has shown that consumers often prefer pioneering brands to other brands.[18] Early users will favor the pioneer's brand because they tried it and it satisfied them. The pioneer's brand also establishes the attributes that the product class should possess. Because the pioneer's brand normally aims at the middle of the market, it captures more users. There are also producer advantages stemming from economies of scale, technological leadership, ownership of scarce assets, and other barriers to entry.

However, doubts can be raised about the strength or inevitability of the pioneer advantage. One only has to reflect on the fate of Bowmar (hand calculators), Reynolds (ballpoint pens), and Osborne (portable computers), market pioneers who were overtaken by later entrants. Schnaars studied 28 industries where the imitators surpassed the innovators.[19] He found several weaknesses among the failing pioneers, including new products that were too crude, were improperly positioned, or appeared before there was strong demand; product development costs that exhausted the innovator's resources; a lack of resources to compete against entering larger firms; and managerial incompetence or unhealthy complacency. Successful imitators thrived by offering lower prices, improving the product more continuously, or using brute market power to overtake the pioneer.

In another paper, Golder and Tellis raise further doubts about the pioneer advantage.[20] They distinguish between an *inventor* (first to develop patents in a new-product category), *product pioneer* (first to develop a working model), and a *market pioneer* (first to sell in the new-product category). They also include nonsurviving pioneers in their sample, who were omitted in other studies. With these refinements they conclude that while pioneers may still have an advantage, it is less pronounced than claimed. A larger number of market pioneers fail than has been reported and a larger number of early market leaders (though not pioneers) succeed, especially if they enter decisively and commit substantial resources to obtaining market leadership. Examples of later entrants overtaking market pioneers are IBM over Sperry in mainframe computers, Matsushita over Sony in VCRs, Texas Instruments over Bowmar in hand calculators, and GE over EMI in CAT scan equipment. At a minimum, this suggests that under the right circumstances the late entrant can overcome the pioneer advantage. Yet an alert pioneer, according to

Robertson and Gatignon, can pursue various strategies to prevent later market entrants from wresting away leadership.[21]

Market pioneers must choose a launch strategy that is consistent with their intended product positioning. The launch strategy should be the first step in a grand plan for life-cycle marketing.

The pioneer should visualize the various product markets it could initially enter, knowing that it cannot enter all of them at once. Suppose market-segmentation analysis reveals the product market segments shown in Figure 12-6. The pioneer should analyze the profit potential of each product market singly and in combination and decide on a market expansion strategy. Thus the pioneer in Figure 12-6 plans first to enter product market P_1M_1, then move the product into a second market (P_1M_2), then surprise competition by developing a second product for the second market (P_2M_2), then take the second product back into the first market (P_2M_1), and then launch a third product for the first market (P_3M_1). If this game plan works, the pioneer firm will own a good part of the first two segments and serve them with two or three products. Naturally, this game plan may be altered as time passes and new factors emerge.

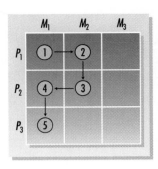

FIGURE 12-6
Long-Range Product Market Expansion Strategy (P_i = product i; M_j = Market j)

THE COMPETITIVE CYCLE. By looking ahead, the pioneer knows that competition will eventually enter and cause prices and its market share to fall. The questions are: When will this happen? What should the pioneer do at each stage? Frey has described five stages of the *competitive cycle* that the pioneer has to anticipate (Figure 12-7).[22]

- Initially the pioneer is the *sole supplier,* with 100% of the production capacity and sales. The second stage, *competitive penetration,* starts when a new competitor has built production capacity and begins commercial sales. Other competitors enter as well, and the leader's share of production capacity and share of sales fall. As subsequent competitors enter the market and charge a lower price than the leader, the perceived relative value of the leader's offer declines, forcing a reduction in the leader's price premium.

FIGURE 12-7

Stages of the Competitive Cycle

Source: John B. Frey, "Pricing Over the Competitive Cycle," speech at the 1982 Marketing Conference. © 1982, The Conference Board, New York.

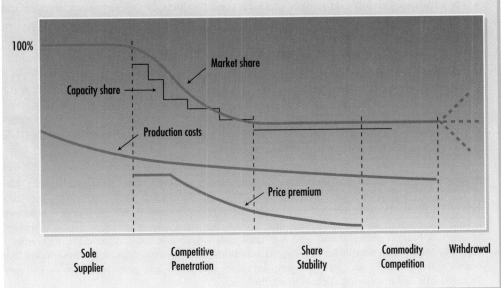

Managing
Life-Cycle
Strategies

- Capacity tends to be overbuilt during the rapid growth stage, so that when a cyclical slowdown occurs, industry overcapacity drives down margins to lower levels. New competitors decide not to enter, and existing competitors try to solidify their positions. This leads to the third stage, *share stability,* in which capacity shares and market shares stabilize.

- This period is followed by a stage of *commodity competition.* The product is viewed as a commodity, buyers no longer pay a price premium, and the suppliers earn only an average rate of return. At this point, the *withdrawal* stage begins. The pioneer might decide to build share further as other firms withdraw. As the pioneer moves through the various stages of this competitive cycle, it must continuously formulate new pricing and marketing strategies.

Growth Stage

The growth stage is marked by a rapid climb in sales. The early adopters like the product, and additional consumers start buying the product. New competitors enter the market, attracted by the opportunities for large-scale production and profit. They introduce new product features and expand the distribution chain.

Prices remain where they are or fall slightly, depending on how fast demand is increasing. Companies maintain their promotional expenditures at the same or a slightly increased level to meet competition and to continue to educate the market. Sales rise much faster than promotional expenditures do, causing a decline in the promotion-sales ratio.

Profits increase during the growth stage as (1) promotion costs are spread over a larger volume and (2) unit manufacturing costs fall faster than price declines owing to the producer learning effect.

The rate of growth eventually changes from an accelerating rate to a decelerating rate. Firms have to watch for the onset of the decelerating rate in order to prepare new strategies.

MARKETING STRATEGIES IN THE GROWTH STAGE. During the growth stage, the firm uses several strategies to sustain rapid market growth as long as possible:

- It improves product quality and adds new product features and improved styling.

- It adds new models and flanker products (i.e., products of different sizes, flavors, and so forth that protect the main product).

- It enters new market segments.

- It increases its distribution coverage and enters new distribution channels.

- It shifts from product-awareness advertising to product-preference advertising.

- It lowers prices to attract the next layer of price-sensitive buyers.

The firm that pursues these market expansion strategies will strengthen its competitive position. For example, Starbucks has emerged as the leader in the U.S. market for gourmet coffee and espresso bars:[23]

STARBUCKS From its initial nine Seattle stores in 1987, CEO Howard Schultz has grown the company to 425 stores. Starbucks' premium coffees are also being sold now in such venues as airport vending stands and Barnes & Noble bookstore cafes. Not content to sell only steaming brews, the company is offering a new "flanker" product, a bottled coffee drink, and it is taking its winning formula abroad. However, as a result of its success Starbucks is facing competition in a variety of guises, from chains like Seattle's Best Coffee, to mom-and-pop espresso stands, to big players (such as Dunkin' Donuts) that are improving their coffee offerings.

The firm in the growth stage faces a trade-off between high market share and high current profit. By spending money on product improvement, promotion, and distribution, it can capture a dominant position. It forgoes maximum current profit in the hope of making even greater profits in the next stage.

Maturity Stage

At some point, a product's rate of sales growth will slow down, and the product will enter a stage of relative maturity. This stage normally lasts longer than the previous stages, and it poses formidable challenges to marketing management. *Most products are in the maturity stage of the life cycle, and therefore most of marketing management deals with the mature product.*

The maturity stage can be divided into three phases. In the first phase, *growth maturity,* the sales growth rate starts to decline. There are no new distribution channels to fill, although some laggard buyers still enter the market. In the second phase, *stable maturity,* sales flatten on a per capita basis because of market saturation. Most potential consumers have tried the product, and future sales are governed by population growth and replacement demand. In the third phase, *decaying maturity,* the absolute level of sales starts to decline, and customers start switching to other products and substitutes.

The slowdown in the rate of sales growth creates overcapacity in the industry. This overcapacity leads to intensified competition. Competitors scramble to find and enter niches. They engage in frequent markdowns. They increase their advertising and trade and consumer deals. They increase their R&D budgets to develop product improvements and line extensions. They make deals to supply private brands. These steps spell some profit erosion. A shakeout period begins, and weaker competitors withdraw. The industry eventually consists of well-entrenched competitors whose basic drive is to gain competitive advantage.

These competitors are of two types. Dominating the industry are a few giant firms that produce a large proportion of the industry's output. These firms serve the whole market and make their profits mainly through high volume and lower costs. These volume leaders may include a quality leader, a service leader, and a cost leader. Surrounding these dominant firms are a multitude of market nichers. The nichers include market specialists, product specialists, and customizing firms. The nichers serve and satisfy their small target markets very well and command a price premium. The issue facing a firm in a mature market is whether to struggle to become one of the "big three" and achieve profits through high volume and low cost or to pursue a niching strategy and achieve profits through high margin.

MARKETING STRATEGIES IN THE MATURITY STAGE. In the maturity stage, some companies abandon their weaker products. They prefer to concentrate their resources on their more profitable products and on new products. Yet by doing so they may be ignoring the high potential that many old products still have. Many industries widely thought to be mature—autos, motorcycles, television, watches, cameras—were proved otherwise by the Japanese, who found ways to offer new values to customers. Seemingly moribund brands like Jell-O, Ovaltine, and Arm & Hammer baking soda have achieved major sales revivals several times through the exercise of marketing imagination (more details on this in the next chapter). Marketers should systematically consider strategies of market, product, and marketing-mix modification.

Market Modification. The company might try to expand the market for its mature brand by working with the two factors that make up sales volume:

$$Volume = number\ of\ brand\ users \times usage\ rate\ per\ user$$

The company can try to expand the number of brand users in three ways:

◆ *Convert nonusers:* The company can try to attract nonusers to the product. For example, the key to the growth of air freight service is the constant search for new users to whom air carriers can demonstrate the benefits of using air freight rather than ground transportation.

◆ *Enter new market segments:* The company can try to enter new market segments—geographic, demographic, and so on—that use the product but not the brand. For example, Johnson & Johnson successfully promoted its baby shampoo to adult users.

◆ *Win competitors' customers:* The company can attract competitors' customers to try or adopt the brand. For example, Pepsi-Cola is constantly tempting Coca-Cola users to switch to Pepsi-Cola, throwing out one challenge after another.

Volume can also be increased by convincing current brand users to increase their annual usage of the brand. Here are three strategies:

◆ *More frequent use:* The company can try to get customers to use the product more frequently. For example, orange juice marketers try to get people to drink orange juice at occasions other than breakfast time.

◆ *More usage per occasion:* The company can try to interest users in using more of the product on each occasion. Thus a shampoo manufacturer might indicate that the shampoo is more effective with two rinsings than one.

◆ *New and more varied uses:* The company can try to discover new product uses and convince people to use the product in more varied ways. Food manufacturers, for example, list several recipes on their packages to broaden the consumers' uses of the product.

Product Modification. Managers also try to stimulate sales by modifying the product's characteristics through quality improvement, feature improvement, or style improvement.

A strategy of *quality improvement* aims at increasing the product's functional performance—its durability, reliability, speed, taste. A manufacturer can often overtake its competition by launching a "new and improved" machine tool, automobile, television set, or detergent. Grocery manufacturers call this a "plus launch" and promote a new additive or advertise something as "stronger," "bigger," or "better." This strategy is effective to the extent that the quality is improved, buyers accept the claim of improved quality, and a sufficient number of buyers will pay for higher quality. But customers are not always willing to accept an "improved" product, as the classic tale of New Coke illustrates:

COCA-COLA   Battered by competition from the sweeter Pepsi-Cola, Coca Cola decided to put its old formula away and give the Pepsi Generation a sweeter drink, dubbed the New Coke. While blind taste tests showed that Coke drinkers preferred the company's new sweeter formula, the birth of New Coke provoked a national uproar. Market researchers hadn't counted on the emotional attachment that consumers had to Coca-Cola. There were angry letters, formal protests, and even lawsuit threats, all to force the retention of "The Real Thing." Eventually, the New Coke debacle worked in Coca-Cola's favor. Two months after announcing the demise of New Coke, the company reintroduced its century-old formula as "Coca-Cola Classic," giving the old formula new status in the marketplace.

A strategy of *feature improvement* aims at adding new features (for example, size, weight, materials, additives, accessories) that expand the product's versatility, safety, or convenience. For example, adding electric power to hand lawn mowers increased the speed and ease of cutting grass. Lawn-mower manufacturers then worked on designing better safety features. Some manufacturers have added conversion features so that a power lawn mower doubles as a snow plow.

A feature-improvement strategy has several advantages. New features build company image of innovativeness and win the loyalty of certain market segments who value these features. Some features can be adopted or dropped quickly or made optional to the buyer. They provide an opportunity for free publicity and they generate sales force and distributor enthusiasm. The chief disadvantage is that feature improvements are easily imitated; unless there is a permanent gain from being first, the feature improvement might not pay off in the long run.

A strategy of *style improvement* aims at increasing the product's aesthetic appeal. The periodic introduction of new car models amounts to style competition rather than quality or feature competition. In the case of packaged-food and household products, companies introduce color and texture variations and often restyle the package, treating it as an extension of the product. The advantage of a style strategy is that it might give the product a unique market identity and win a loyal following. Yet style competition has some problems. First, it is difficult to predict whether people—and which people—will like a new style. Second, a style change usually requires discontinuing the old style, and the company risks losing customers who liked the old style. For example, consumers may become attached to something as seemingly insignificant as a peanut shell. In the United States, eating unshelled peanuts at baseball games is a time-honored tradition. The peanuts have traditionally come in shells, and spectators discard the shells on the stadium's floor. During the 1986 major league baseball season at New York's Shea Stadium, where the Mets play their home games, the concessionaire tampered with tradition and began selling preshelled peanuts in cellophane packages. Sales fell 15 percent and consumers complained strongly.[24]

Marketing-Mix Modification. Product managers might also try to stimulate sales by modifying other marketing-mix elements. They should ask the following questions:

◆ *Prices:* Would a price cut attract new triers and users? If so, should the list price be lowered, or should prices be lowered through price specials, volume or early-purchase discounts, freight cost absorption, or easier credit terms? Or would it be better to raise the price to signal higher quality?

◆ *Distribution:* Can the company obtain more product support and display in the existing outlets? Can more outlets be penetrated? Can the company introduce the product into new distribution channels? When Goodyear decided to sell its tires via Wal-Mart, Sears, and Discount Tire, it boosted market share from 14% to 16% in the first year of the arrangement. Moving beyond the confines of its tire-dealer distribution channel made all the difference to this mature product's growth.[25]

◆ *Advertising:* Should advertising expenditures be increased? Should the advertising message or copy be changed? Should the media mix be changed? Should the timing, frequency, or size of ads be changed?

◆ *Sales promotion:* Should the company step up sales promotion—trade deals, cents-off coupons, rebates, warranties, gifts, and contests?

◆ *Personal selling:* Should the number or quality of salespeople be increased? Should the basis for sales force specialization be changed? Should sales territories be revised? Should sales force incentives be revised? Can sales-call planning be improved?

◆ *Services:* Can the company speed up delivery? Can it extend more technical assistance to customers? Can it extend more credit?

Marketers often debate which tools are most effective in the mature stage. For example, would the company gain more by increasing its advertising or sales-promotion budget? Some say that sales promotion has more impact at this stage because consumers have reached an equilibrium in their buying habits and preferences, and psychological persuasion (advertising) is not as effective as financial persuasion (sales-promotion deals). In fact, many consumer-packaged-goods companies spend over 60% of their total promotion budget on sales promotion to support

Managing
Life-Cycle
Strategies

Breaking Through the Mature-Product Syndrome

Managers of mature products need a systematic framework for identifying possible "breakthrough" ideas. Professor John A. Weber of Notre Dame developed the following framework, which he calls *gap analysis,* to guide the search for growth opportunities.

The key idea is to identify possible gaps in the product line, distribution, usage, competition, and so on. Market-structure analysis would prompt the following questions about a mature beverage product such as Kool-Aid:

1. *Natural changes in the size of industry market potential:* Will current birth rates and demographics favor more consumption of Kool-Aid? How will the economic outlook affect Kool-Aid consumption?

2. *New uses or new user segments:* Can Kool-Aid be made to appeal to teen-agers, young adult singles, young adult parents, and so on?

3. *Innovative product differentiations:* Can Kool-Aid be made in different versions such as low calorie or super-sweet?

4. *Add new product lines:* Can the Kool-Aid name be used to launch a new soft-drink line?

5. *Stimulate nonusers:* Can elderly people be persuaded to try Kool-Aid?

6. *Stimulate light users:* Can children be reminded to drink Kool-Aid daily?

7. *Increase amount used on each use occasion:* Can more Kool-Aid be put in each package at a higher price?

8. *Close existing product and price gaps:* Should new sizes of Kool-Aid be introduced?

9. *Create new product-line elements:* Should Kool-Aid introduce new flavors?

10. *Expand distribution coverage:* Can Kool-Aid distribution coverage be expanded to Europe and the Far East?

11. *Expand distribution intensity:* Can the percentage of convenience stores in the Midwest that carry Kool-Aid be increased from 70 to 90 percent?

12. *Expand distribution exposure:* Can offers to the trade get more shelf space for Kool-Aid?

13. *Penetrate substitutes' positions:* Can consumers be convinced that Kool-Aid is a better drink than other types of soft drinks (e.g., soda, milk)?

14. *Penetrate direct competitors' position(s):* Can consumers of other brands be convinced to switch to Kool-Aid?

15. *Defend firm's present position:* Can Kool-Aid satisfy the current users more so that they remain loyal?

Source: John A. Weber, *Identifying and Solving Marketing Problems with Gap Analysis* (Notre Dame, IN: Strategic Business Systems, 1986).

mature products. Other marketers argue that brands should be managed as capital assets and supported by advertising. Advertising expenditures should be treated as a capital investment, not a current expense. Brand managers, however, use sales promotion because its effects are quicker and more visible to their superiors, but excessive sales-promotion activity can hurt the brand's image and long-run profit performance.

A major problem with marketing-mix modifications, especially price reductions and additional services, is that they are easily imitated by competitors. The firm may not gain as much as expected, and all firms might experience profit erosion as they step up their marketing attacks on one another.

The Marketing Insight titled "Breaking Through the Mature-Product Syndrome" presents a framework for finding ideas for rebuilding the sales of mature products.

Decline Stage

The sales of most product forms and brands eventually decline. The sales decline might be slow, as in the case of oatmeal; or rapid, as in the case of the Edsel automobile. Sales may plunge to zero, or they may petrify at a low level.

Sales decline for a number of reasons, including technological advances, shifts in consumer tastes, and increased domestic and foreign competition. All lead to overcapacity, increased price cutting, and profit erosion.

As sales and profits decline, some firms withdraw from the market. Those remaining may reduce the number of products they offer. They may withdraw from smaller market segments and weaker trade channels, and they may cut their promotion budget and reduce their prices further.

Unfortunately, most companies have not developed a well-thought-out policy for handling their aging products. Sentiment often plays a role:

> [P]utting products to death—or letting them die—is a drab business, and often engenders much of the sadness of a final parting with old and tried friends. The portable, six-sided pretzel was the first product The Company ever made. Our line will no longer be our line without it.[26]

Logic may also play a role. Management believes that product sales will improve when the economy improves, or when the marketing strategy is revised, or when the product is improved. Or the weak product may be retained because of its alleged contribution to the sales of the company's other products. Or its revenue may cover out-of-pocket costs, even if it is not turning a profit.

Unless strong reasons for retention exist, carrying a weak product is very costly to the firm. The cost is not just the amount of uncovered overhead and profit. Financial accounting cannot adequately convey all the hidden costs. Weak products often consume a disproportionate amount of management's time, require frequent price and inventory adjustments, generally involve short production runs in spite of expensive setup times, require both advertising and sales force attention that might be better used to make the healthy products more profitable, and can cause customer misgivings and cast a shadow on the company's image. The biggest cost might well lie in the future. Failing to eliminate weak products delays the aggressive search for replacement products. The weak products create a lopsided product mix, long on yesterday's breadwinners and short on tomorrow's breadwinners; they depress current profitability and weaken the company's foothold on the future.

MARKETING STRATEGIES DURING THE DECLINE STAGE. In handling its aging products, a company faces a number of tasks and decisions.

Identifying the Weak Products. The first task is to establish a system for identifying weak products. To do this, many companies appoint a product-review committee with representatives from marketing, R&D, manufacturing, and finance. This committee develops a system for identifying weak products. The controller's office supplies data for each product showing trends in market size, market share, prices, costs, and profits. A computer program then analyzes this information to help managers decide which products are dubious. The managers responsible for dubious products fill out rating forms showing where they think sales and profits will go, with and without any changes in marketing strategy. The product-review committee examines this information and makes a recommendation for each dubious product—leave it alone, modify its marketing strategy, or drop it.[27]

Determining Marketing Strategies. Some firms will abandon declining markets earlier than others. Much depends on the presence and height of exit barriers in the industry.[28] The lower the exit barriers, the easier it is for firms to leave the industry, and the more tempting it is for the remaining firms to stay and attract the withdrawing firms' customers. The remaining firms will enjoy increased sales and profits. For example, Procter & Gamble stayed in the declining liquid-soap business and improved its profits as the others withdrew.

In a study of company strategies in declining industries, Harrigan identified five decline strategies available to the firm:

♦ Increasing the firm's investment (to dominate the market or strengthen its competitive position)

♦ Maintaining the firm's investment level until the uncertainties about the industry are resolved

♦ Decreasing the firm's investment level selectively, by dropping unprofitable customer groups, while simultaneously strengthening the firm's investment in lucrative niches

♦ Harvesting ("milking") the firm's investment to recover cash quickly

♦ Divesting the business quickly by disposing of its assets as advantageously as possible[29]

The appropriate decline strategy depends on the industry's relative attractiveness and the company's competitive strength in that industry. For example, a company that is in an unattractive industry but possesses competitive strength should consider shrinking selectively. A company that is in an attractive industry and has competitive strength should consider strengthening its investment. Procter & Gamble on a number of occasions has taken disappointing brands that were in strong markets and restaged them.

PROCTER & GAMBLE P&G launched a "not oily" hand cream called Wondra that was packaged in an inverted bottle so the cream would flow out from the bottom. Although initial sales were high, repeat purchases were disappointing. Consumers complained that the bottom got sticky and that "not oily" suggested it wouldn't work well. P&G carried out two restagings: First, it reintroduced Wondra in an upright bottle, and later reformulated the ingredients so they would work better. Sales then picked up.

P&G prefers restaging to abandoning brand names. P&G spokespersons like to claim that there is no such thing as a product life cycle, and they point to Ivory, Camay, and many other "dowager" brands that are still thriving.

If the company were choosing between harvesting and divesting, its strategies would be quite different. As we saw in Chapter 3, *harvesting* calls for gradually reducing a product or business's costs while trying to maintain its sales. The first costs to cut are R&D costs and plant and equipment investment. The company might also reduce product quality, sales force size, marginal services, and advertising expenditures. It would try to cut these costs without tipping off customers, competitors, and employees that it is slowly pulling out of the business. If customers knew that, they would switch suppliers; if competitors knew it, they would tell customers; if employees knew it, they would seek new jobs elsewhere. Thus harvesting is an ethically ambivalent strategy, and it is also difficult to execute. Yet many mature products warrant this strategy. Harvesting can substantially increase the company's current cash flow, provided that sales do not collapse.[30]

Harvesting eventually makes a business worthless. In contrast, if the firm had decided instead to divest the business, it would have first looked for a buyer. It would have tried to increase the attractiveness of the business, not run it down. Therefore the company must think carefully about whether to harvest or divest the weakening business unit.

Companies that successfully restage or rejuvenate a mature product often do so by adding value to the original, declining product. Consider the experience of Yamaha, a maker of pianos, motorcycles, and many other products:[31]

YAMAHA When Yamaha controlled 40% of the global piano market, total demand was sliding by 10% a year. Rather than giving up on pianos, managers took a close look at customers and the product and found that the majority of pianos sit around idle and neglected—and out of tune most of the time. It seemed that many people owned pianos, but that few were playing them. People do not want to invest the time that it takes to master the instrument. So Yamaha decided to add value to the millions of pianos already on the market by developing a sophisticated advanced combination of digital and optical technology that can record professional pianists' live performances and play compositions on the piano. The advent of this new technology has revived the piano industry.

For additional information on how to mastermind a successful product rejuvenation, see the Marketing Memo titled "Five Steps to Product Rejuvenation."

The Drop Decision. When a company decides to drop a product, it faces further decisions. If the product has strong distribution and residual goodwill, the company can probably sell it to another firm.

MARKETING MEMO

FIVE STEPS TO PRODUCT REJUVENATION

Rejuvenation strategies for mature products vary widely. Reintroducing abandoned products or reviving seriously declining ones requires managers to learn how to recognize an opportunity for injecting new life into a product. Five steps can minimize potential problems and increase the revamped product's chances of success.

1. *Determine the reasons for the product's abandonment or decline.* Was the product abandoned because of resource constraints? Poor management? Did the product decline because it delivered only limited value to customers?

2. *Examine whether the forces in the macroenvironment support a rejuvenation strategy.* Products today are not necessarily perceived in the same manner as in the past. Thus managers must explore whether and how the product altered with changing circumstances. For example, Lucazade, a product promoted years ago as a "get-well drink" ("Lucazade aids recovery"), could not be promoted as such today, given the current political and legal environment.

3. *Examine what the product name communicates to consumers.* A brand name communicates product attributes—not by an advertising message, but simply by its appearance on the product. The manner in which the brand name is used and its relation to competitive products also communicate something.

4. *Explore whether there is a potential segment to be reached, as well as competitors' strengths and weaknesses in that potential segment.* An abandoned product can be reintroduced to previous users, if there are some who miss it. Competitors cannot compete effectively if the product has nostalgic value. Given the new market niche for the product, competitive analysis ought to reveal exactly how it relates to competition.

5. *Examine the possibilities of creating value for customers.* By monitoring the changing environment, the firm may see an opportunity for rejuvenation. The forces and megatrends of the macroenvironment—demographic, economic, physical, technological, political, legal, and sociocultural—may offer opportunities for rejuvenation.

Managers tend to place considerable importance on developing new products. But given the pitfalls of new-product introduction (discussed in the previous chapter), they might also consider rejuvenating abandoned or declining products. Product rejuvenation strategies are often simpler, cheaper, and faster, and can offer handsome returns.

Source: Reprinted from *Business Horizons*, November–December 1994. Copyright © 1994 by the Foundation for the School of Business at Indiana University. Used with permission.

Managing
Life-Cycle
Strategies

COLECO, HASBRO, AND CABBAGE PATCH KIDS

In the mid-1980s, Cabbage Patch dolls caught the nation's fancy and enjoyed three years as the nation's best-selling toys. Sales in 1984 and 1985 exceeded half a billion dollars before the dolls lost popularity and nearly vanished. Yet, in the summer of 1989, Hasbro Industries bought the production and marketing rights to Cabbage Patch from Coleco Industries. By advertising the doll heavily and increasing shipments to big toy stores, Hasbro managed to tap into the lingering strength of the Cabbage Patch name. The dolls are now on most toy industry lists of top sellers.[32]

If the company can't find any buyers, it must decide whether to liquidate the brand quickly or slowly. It must also decide on how much parts inventory and service to maintain for past customers.

Summary and Critique of the Product Life-Cycle Concept

The PLC concept is best used to interpret product and market dynamics. As a planning tool, the PLC concept helps managers characterize the main marketing challenges in each stage of a product's life and develop major alternative marketing strategies. As a control tool, the PLC concept helps the company measure product performance against similar products launched in the past. The PLC concept is less useful as a forecasting tool because sales histories exhibit diverse patterns, and the stages vary in duration.

PLC theory has its share of critics who claim that life-cycle patterns are too variable in their shape and duration. PLCs lack what living organisms have—namely, a fixed sequence of stages and a fixed length of each stage. Critics also charge that marketers can seldom tell what stage the product is in. A product may appear to be mature when actually it has only reached a temporary plateau prior to another upsurge. They charge that the PLC pattern is the result of marketing strategies rather than an inevitable course that sales must follow:

> Suppose a brand is acceptable to consumers but has a few bad years because of other factors—for instance, poor advertising, delisting by a major chain, or entry of a "me-too" competitive product backed by massive sampling. Instead of thinking in terms of corrective measures, management begins to feel that its brand has entered a declining stage. It therefore withdraws funds from the promotion budget to finance R&D on new items. The next year the brand does even worse, panic increases. . . . Clearly, the PLC is a dependent variable which is determined by marketing actions; it is not an independent variable to which companies should adapt their marketing programs.[33]

Figure 12-8 summarizes the characteristics, marketing objectives, and marketing strategies of the four stages of the PLC. Figure 12-9 on page 364 displays the life-cycle strategies that might be used for grocery-product marketing.

MARKET EVOLUTION

Because the PLC focuses on what is happening to a particular product or brand rather than on what is happening to the overall market, it yields a product-oriented picture rather than a market-oriented picture. The demand/technology life cycle we mentioned earlier reminds us to take a broader look at the whole market. Consider what happened at Quarterdeck Office Systems, a small computer software firm:

Developing
Marketing
Strategies

FIGURE 12-8

Summary of Product Life-Cycle Characteristics, Objectives, and Strategies

Source: This figure was assembled from several sources: Chester R. Wasson, *Dynamic Competitive Strategy and Product Life Cycles* (Austin, TX: Austin Press, 1978); John A. Weber, "Planning Corporate Growth with Inverted Product Life Cycles," *Long Range Planning,* October 1976, pp. 12–29; and Peter Doyle, "The Realities of the Product Life Cycle," *Quarterly Review of Marketing,* Summer 1976, pp. 1–6.

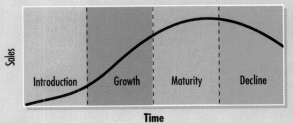

CHARACTERISTICS

	Introduction	Growth	Maturity	Decline
Sales	Low sales	Rapidly rising sales	Peak sales	Declining sales
Costs	High cost per customer	Average cost per customer	Low cost per customer	Low cost per customer
Profits	Negative	Rising profits	High profits	Declining profits
Customers	Innovators	Early adopters	Middle majority	Laggards
Competitors	Few	Growing number	Stable number beginning to decline	Declining number

MARKETING OBJECTIVES

	Introduction	Growth	Maturity	Decline
	Create product awareness and trial	Maximize market share	Maximize profit while defending market share	Reduce expenditure and milk the brand

STRATEGIES

	Introduction	Growth	Maturity	Decline
Product	Offer a basic product	Offer product extensions, service, warranty	Diversify brands and models	Phase out weak items
Price	Charge cost-plus	Price to penetrate market	Price to match or best competitors	Cut price
Distribution	Build selective distribution	Build intensive distribution	Build more intensive distribution	Go selective: phase out unprofitable outlets
Advertising	Build product awareness among early adopters and dealers	Build awareness and interest in the mass market	Stress brand differences and benefits	Reduce to level needed to retain hard-core loyals
Sales Promotion	Use heavy sales promotion to entice trial	Reduce to take advantage of heavy consumer demand	Increase to encourage brand switching	Reduce to minimal level

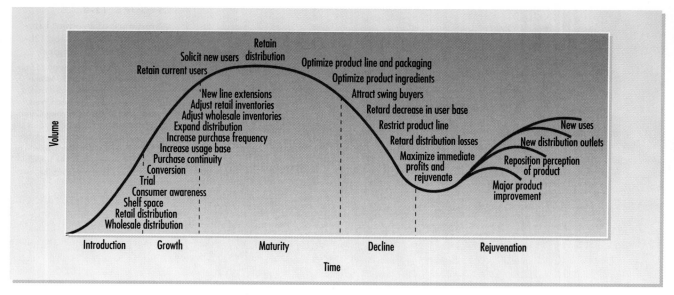

FIGURE 12-9
PLC Marketing for Grocery Products

QUARTERDECK OFFICE SYSTEMS Quarterdeck used to turn a tidy profit serving a niche created solely by Microsoft. It sold software enhancements to Microsoft's DOS systems. So when Microsoft launched its Windows 3.0, which incorporated features of Quarterdeck's software, the smaller company could have gone belly up. Instead, Quarterdeck thought long and hard about the technology life cycle. While Microsoft was aiming Windows at the introductory and growth stages of the computer life cycle, Quarterdeck found that it could aim its software at products in the mature and declining stages. For instance, Quarterdeck managers observed that its software worked more efficiently with older computer models that run DOS and for users who struggle to learn new programs and who resist trading up to new hardware. They also found that these segments were substantial—large enough enough to fuel the continued success of their business.[34]

Firms need to anticipate a market's evolutionary path as it is affected by new needs, competitors, technology, channels, and other developments.

Stages in Market Evolution

Like products, markets evolve through four stages: emergence, growth, maturity, and decline.

EMERGENCE STAGE. Before a market materializes, it exists as a latent market. A *latent market* consists of people who share a similar need or want for something that does not yet exist. For example, for centuries people have wanted a means of more rapid calculation than can be provided by a paper and pencil. Until fairly recently, this need was imperfectly satisfied through abacuses, slide rules, and large adding machines.

Suppose an entrepreneur recognizes this need and imagines a technological solution in the form of a small, hand-size electronic calculator. He now has to determine the product attributes, including the calculator's physical size and the number of mathematical functions it will perform. Because he is market-oriented,

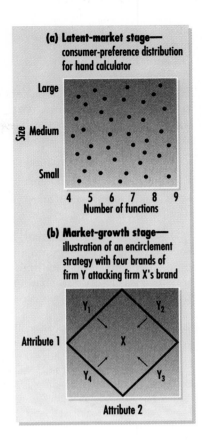

FIGURE 12-10
Market-Space Diagrams

(a) Latent-market stage— consumer-preference distribution for hand calculator

Large

Medium

Small

Size

4   5   6   7   8   9
Number of functions

(b) Market-growth stage— illustration of an encirclement strategy with four brands of firm Y attacking firm X's brand

Y_1 Y_2

Attribute 1   X

Y_4 Y_3

Attribute 2

he interviews potential buyers and asks them to state their preferred levels on each attribute.

Assume that consumer preferences are represented by the dots in Figure 12-10(a). Each dot represents one person's preferences. Evidently target customers vary greatly in their preferences. Some want a four-function calculator (adding, subtracting, multiplying, and dividing) and others want more functions (calculating percentages, square roots, logs, and so forth). Some want a small hand calculator and others want a large one. This type of market, in which buyer preferences scatter evenly in a market, is called a *diffused-preference market*.

The entrepreneur's problem is to design an optimal product for this market.[35] He has three options:

◆ The new product can be designed to meet the preferences of one of the corners of the market (a *single-niche strategy*).

◆ Two or more products can be simultaneously launched to capture two or more parts of the market (a *multiple-niche strategy*).

◆ The new product can be designed for the middle of the market (a *mass-market strategy*).

For small firms, a single-niche market strategy makes the most sense. A small firm has insufficient resources for capturing and holding the mass market. Therefore its best bet is to develop a specialized product and capture a corner of the market that will not attract competitors for a long time.

A large firm might go after the mass market by designing a product that is medium in size and number of functions. A product in the center minimizes the sum of the distances of existing preferences from the actual product. A hand calcu-

Managing
Life-Cycle
Strategies

lator designed for the mass market will minimize total dissatisfaction. We will assume that the pioneer firm is large and designs its product for the mass market. On launching the product, the *emergence stage* begins.

GROWTH STAGE. If sales of the new product are good, new firms will enter the market, ushering in a *market-growth stage*. An interesting question is: Where will a second firm enter the market, assuming that the first firm established itself in the center? The second firm has three options:

◆ It can position its brand in one of the corners (single-niche strategy).

◆ It can position its brand next to the first competitor (mass-market strategy).

◆ It can launch two or more products in different unoccupied corners (multiple-niche strategy).

If the second firm is small, it is likely to avoid head-on competition with the pioneer and launch its brand in one of the market corners. If the second firm is large, it might launch its brand in the center against the pioneer firm. The two firms can easily end up sharing the mass market almost equally. Or a large second firm can implement a multiple-niche strategy.

PROCTER & GAMBLE P&G occasionally will enter a market containing a large, entrenched competitor. Instead of launching a me-too product or a single-segment product, it introduces a succession of products aimed at different segments. Each entry creates a loyal following and takes some business away from the major competitor. Soon the major competitor is surrounded, its revenue is weakened, and it is too late to launch new brands in outlying segments. P&G, in a moment of triumph, then launches a brand against the major segment. This is called an *encirclement strategy* and is illustrated in Figure 12-10(b).

MATURITY STAGE. Each firm entering the market will go after some position, locating either next to a competitor or in an unoccupied segment. Eventually, the competitors cover and serve all the major market segments and the market will enter the *maturity stage*. In fact, they go further and invade each other's segments, reducing everyone's profits in the process. As the market's growth slows down, the market splits into finer segments and a condition of high *market fragmentation* occurs. This situation is illustrated in Figure 12-11(a), where the letters represent different companies supplying various segments. Note that two segments are unserved because they are too small to yield a profit.[36]

Market fragmentation is often followed by a *market consolidation* caused by the emergence of a new attribute that has strong market appeal. Market consolidation took place in the toothpaste market when P&G introduced its new fluoride toothpaste, Crest, which effectively retarded dental decay. Suddenly toothpaste brands that claimed whitening power, cleaning power, sex appeal, taste, or mouthwash effectiveness were pushed into the corners because consumers primarily wanted a dental-protection toothpaste. P&G's Crest won a lion's share of the market, as shown by the X territory in Figure 12-11(b).

But even a consolidated market condition will not last. Other companies will copy a successful brand such as P&G's Crest, and the market will eventually splinter again. Mature markets swing between market fragmentation and market consolidation. The fragmentation is brought about by competition, and the consolidation is brought about by innovation.

DECLINE STAGE. Eventually, the market demand for the present products will begin to decrease, and the market will enter the *decline stage*. Either society's total need level declines or a new technology starts replacing the old. Thus an entrepre-

FIGURE 12-11
Market-Fragmentation and Market-Consolidation Strategies

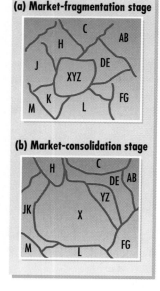

(a) Market-fragmentation stage

(b) Market-consolidation stage

neur might invent a mouth-spray substitute that is superior to toothpaste. In this case, the old technology will eventually disappear and a new demand/technology life cycle will emerge.

AN EXAMPLE: THE PAPER-TOWEL MARKET. To see how markets emerge and evolve through several stages, consider the evolution of the paper-towel market. Originally, homemakers used cotton and linen dish cloths and towels in their kitchens. A paper company, looking for new markets, developed paper towels to compete with cloth towels. This development crystallized a latent market. Other paper manufacturers entered and expanded the market. The number of brands proliferated and created market fragmentation. Industry overcapacity led manufacturers to search for new features. One manufacturer, hearing consumers complain that paper towels were not absorbent, introduced "absorbent" paper towels and increased its market share. This market consolidation did not last long because competitors came out with their own versions of absorbent paper towels. The market became fragmented again. Then another manufacturer heard consumers express a wish for a "superstrength" paper towel and introduced one. It was soon copied by other manufacturers. Another manufacturer introduced a "lint-free" paper towel, which was subsequently copied. Thus paper towels evolved from a single product to one with various absorbencies, strengths, and applications. Market evolution was driven by the forces of innovation and competition. The latest jag in the paper-towel market is paper towels whose size can be "customized," an innovation that will undoubtedly soon be copied.

Dynamics of Attribute Competition

Competition produces a continuous round of newly discovered product attributes. If a new attribute succeeds, then several competitors soon offer it. To the extent that most banks are now "friendly," friendliness no longer influences consumer choice of a bank. To the extent that most airlines serve in-flight meals on long flights, meals are no longer a basis for air-carrier choice. *Customer expectations are progressive.* This fact underlines the strategic importance of a company's maintaining the lead in introducing new attributes. Each new attribute, if successful, creates a competitive advantage for the firm, leading to temporarily higher-than-average market share and profits. The implication for marketers is clear: The market leader must learn to routinize the innovation process.

A crucial question is: Can a firm look ahead and anticipate the succession of attributes that are likely to win favor and be technologically feasible? How can the firm discover new attributes? There are four approaches.

♦ The first approach employs a *customer-survey process* to identify new attributes. The company asks consumers what benefits they would like added to the product and their desire level for each. The firm also examines the cost of developing each new attribute and likely competitive responses. It chooses those attributes promising the highest profit.

♦ The second approach uses an *intuitive process.* Entrepreneurs get hunches and undertake product development without much marketing research. Natural selection determines winners and losers. If a manufacturer has intuited an attribute that the market wants, that manufacturer is considered smart (although from another perspective, it was only luck).

♦ A third approach says that new attributes emerge through a *dialectical process.* Dialectical theory says that innovators should not march with the crowd but rather in the opposite direction toward market segments that are suffering from increasing neglect. Thus blue jeans, starting out as an inexpensive clothing article, over time became fashionable and more expensive. This unidirectional movement, however, contains the seeds of its own destruction. Eventually the price falls again or some manufacturer introduces a cheaper material for pants, and consumers flock to buy it.

♦ A fourth approach holds that new attributes emerge through a *needs-hierarchy process* (see the discussion of Maslow's theory in Chapter 6). On this theory, we would predict that the first automobiles would provide basic transportation and be designed for safety. At a later time, automobiles would start appealing to social acceptance and status needs. Still later, automobiles would be designed to help people "fulfill" themselves. The innovator's task is to assess when the market is ready to satisfy a higher-order need.

The actual unfolding of new attributes in a market is more complex than any simple theories would suggest. We should not underestimate the role of technological and societal processes in influencing the emergence of new attributes. For example, the strong consumer interest in compact-size television sets remained unmet until miniaturization technology was sufficiently developed. Developments such as inflation, shortages, environmentalism, consumerism, and new lifestyles create consumer disequilibrium and lead consumers to reevaluate product attributes. For example, inflation increases the desire for a smaller car, and a desire for car safety increases the desire for a heavier car. The innovator must use marketing research to gauge the demand potency of different attributes in order to determine the company's best move with respect to competition.

SUMMARY

1. Because economic conditions change and competitive activity varies, companies normally find it necessary to reformulate their marketing strategy several times during a product's life cycle. Technologies, product forms, and brands also exhibit life cycles with distinct stages. The general sequence of stages in any life cycle is introduction, growth, maturity, and decline. The majority of products today are in the maturity stage.

2. Although many products exhibit a bell-shaped product life cycle (PLC), there are many other patterns, including the growth-slump-maturity pattern, the cycle-recycle pattern, and the scalloped pattern. The PLCs of styles, fashions, and fads can be erratic; the key to success in these areas lies in creating products with staying power.

3. In addition to a domestic product life cycle, there is an international product life cycle: Domestic firms produce and export, foreign production starts, foreign production becomes competitive in export markets, and import competition begins.

4. Each stage of the PLC calls for different marketing strategies. The *introduction* stage is marked by slow growth and minimal profits as the product is pushed into distribution. During this stage, the company has to decide among strategies of rapid skimming, slow skimming, rapid penetration, or slow penetration. It must also decide when to enter the market; market pioneers may have a strong advantage. If successful, the product enters a *growth* stage marked by rapid sales growth and increasing profits. The company attempts to improve the product, enter new market segments and distribution channels, and reduce its prices slightly. There follows a *maturity* stage in which sales growth slows and profits stabilize. The company seeks innovative strategies to renew sales growth, including market, product, and marketing-mix modification. Finally, the product enters a *decline* stage in which little can be done to halt the deterioration of sales and profits. The company's task is to identify the truly weak products; develop for each one a strategy of continuation, focusing, or milking; and finally phase out weak products in a way that minimizes the hardship to company profits, employees, and customers.

5. Like products, markets evolve through four stages: emergence, growth, maturity, and decline. A new market emerges when a new product is created to serve the needs of a latent market. Competitors enter the market, leading to market growth. Growth eventually slows down and the market enters maturity; in this stage the market undergoes in-

creasing fragmentation until some firm introduces a powerful new attribute that consolidates the market into fewer and larger segments. This stage does not last, because competitors copy the new attributes. There is a cycling back and forth between fragmentation and consolidation. The market for the present technology will ultimately decline upon the discovery of superior technologies.

6. Companies must try to anticipate new attributes that the market wants. Profits go to those who introduce new and valued benefits early. The search for new attributes can be based on customer survey work, intuition, dialectical reasoning, or needs-hierarchy reasoning. Successful marketing comes through creatively visualizing the market's evolutionary potential.

CONCEPT APPLICATIONS

1. General Mills bought the U.S. rights to the Lacoste brand, which had a $400 million business in the United States, predominantly from sales of its classic polo shirt with its famous alligator logo. By the mid-1980s, however, sales of the Lacoste brand were declining rapidly and the competition was singing, "See you later, alligator." Although General Mills heavily promoted the alligator logo, it started manufacturing the shirts in the Far East and changed the all-cotton construction to a cheaper synthetic blend. Consequently, the brand lost its prestige and U.S. retailers stopped ordering Lacoste products. In 1992 Devanlay S.A. bought back the U.S. license from General Mills for $31.5 million. What strategies could Devanlay employ to regain the prestige of products displaying the alligator logo?

2. When there is a downward trend in demand, many companies lower price to stimulate consumer demand. However, when production costs are primarily fixed and a company's capital is specialized to a particular market like the automobile-tire industry, the effects of market decline are more burdensome. Companies might try to increase cash flow by lowering prices, but tire customers seldom buy extra tires just because tires are on sale, preferring to postpone purchase until they actually need the new tires.

   In response to the declining market in the 1970s, the three major tire companies pursued different strategies. Firestone chose retrenchment, B. F. Goodrich chose harvesting, and Goodyear chose consolidation. What did each of these strategies entail? How have the fortunes of these companies changed following the adoption of these strategies?

3. A stroll through any retail store will reveal that new packaging is replacing old packaging at an accelerating rate. How might packaging strategies coincide with each of the four PLC stages? At what stage will packaging be the flashiest? At which stage will packaging be the most basic, with the most attention paid to costs? In what stage might the package be redesigned the most radically?

   Examine the Jergens advertisement in Figure 1. What stage of the PLC is Jergens lotion in? How might the packaging strategy seen in the advertisement help Jergen's face the challenges of this stage?

4. Schick has patented a new "wet" razor for women. The razor is used in the shower or bathtub, has microfine wire wraps over pivoting twin blades, and has a handle that fits easily into a woman's hand. Discuss the changes in the promotion level and promotion mix (including trade deals) that Schick should consider for this product as it moves through the four stages of the PLC.

5. Research and various articles have suggested that MBA programs across the country were going to face declining enrollments in the 1990s. They concluded that the PLC for MBA programs was entering the decline stage. However, the latest statistics lead to an entirely different conclusion. MBA programs are in fact reversing the expected trend by reporting increasing enrollments. What factors may explain this phenomenon?

6. The product life cycle as a managerial tool has been criticized since its introduction as a "mere theory." One of the sharpest criticisms is that it proves itself—in other words, that you can tell that a product is in the growth stage because it is growing, in the de-

FIGURE 1

Source: Reprinted by permission of The Andrew Jergens Company.

369

cline stage because it is declining, and in the maturity stage because it is neither declining or growing. If these criticisms are indeed valid, then it may be the case that other managerial tools may be more valuable than the PLC concept. For example, demographics have a major impact on some product categories. As people age, their need for products changes; thus studying demographics may be as valuable as studying PLC theory. Name four other factors that influence product or market evolution that managers should study.

7. What investment strategy should each of the following companies pursue in the short run and the long run?

COMPANY	INDUSTRY ATTRACTIVENESS	COMPANY'S COMPETITIVE POSITION
A	Relatively attractive	Company has a competitive strength
B	Unattractive	Company has no competitive strength
C	Uncertain	Company has a competitive strength
D	Unattractive	Company has a competitive strength

8. Tupperware, which arranges home parties to sell kitchen and other products, is in the mature stage of the product life cycle. Based on your understanding of the concepts in the chapter, brainstorm with a group some possible strategies for reviving this product.

9. Examine the data in Table 1, which summarizes selected results from a fabric-softener-usage monitoring study. The study was commissioned by a fabric-softener manufacturer whose product is in the mature stage of the product life cycle. What product and promotional suggestions would you make to this manufacturer? What type of brand extension might be warranted?

TABLE 1 SELECTED RESULTS FROM FABRIC-SOFTENER-USAGE MONITORING STUDIES		JUNE 1993	FEBRUARY 1995
Percentage of respondents who were:			
Fabric-softener users[a]		60.0%	60.0%
Nonusers		40.0	40.0
Homemakers aware that fabric softeners allegedly harm the environment:			
Fabric-softener users		55.0%	74.0%
Nonusers		66.0	70.0
Fabric-softener users claiming to:[b]			
Use less fabric softener per load		18.0%	24.0%
Soften fewer loads		16.0	14.0
Total (unduplicated)		26.0	27.0
Reasons nonusers never used/stopped using softener:			
Environmental reasons		42.0%	48.0%
Softness dissatisfaction		26.0	13.0
Effects on skin		29.0	23.0
Drying on clothesline		20.0	29.0

[a] Fabric-softener users had used the product at least once in the previous three months before the interview: nonusers had not.
[b] Seventy-two percent of the users who used less softener or softened fewer loads claimed to be doing so for environmental reasons.
Source: Adapted from Harvard Case Study—9-592-016.

10. Discuss the products that have made up the demand/technology life cycle for home entertainment over the last 100 years.

Developing
Marketing
Strategies

1. This discussion of demand/technology cycles is drawn from H. Igor Ansoff, *Implanting Strategic Management,* 2d ed. (Englewood Cliffs, NJ: Prentice Hall, 1991).

2. Ansoff, *Implanting Strategic Management.*

3. Amy Barrett, "Hot Growth Companies," *Business Week,* May 22, 1995, pp. 68–70.

4. Some authors distinguished additional stages. Wasson suggested a stage of competitive turbulence between growth and maturity. See Chester R. Wasson, *Dynamic Competitive Strategy and Product Life Cycles* (Austin, TX: Austin Press, 1978). *Maturity* describes a stage of sales growth slowdown and *saturation,* a stage of flat sales after sales have peaked.

5. See William E. Cox, Jr., "Product Life Cycles as Marketing Models," *Journal of Business,* October 1967, pp. 375–84.

6. John E. Swan and David R. Rink, "Fitting Market Strategy to Varying Product Life Cycles,"*Business Horizons,* January–February 1982, pp. 72–76; and Gerald J. Tellis and C. Merle Crawford, "An Evolutionary Approach to Product Growth Theory," *Journal of Marketing,* Fall 1981, pp. 125–34.

7. Chester R. Wasson, "How Predictable Are Fashion and Other Product Life Cycles?" *Journal of Marketing,* July 1968, pp. 36–43.

8. Wasson, "How Predictable."

9. William H. Reynolds, "Cars and Clothing: Understanding Fashion Trends," *Journal of Marketing,* July 1968, pp. 44–49.

10. John Grossmann, "A Follow-Up on Four Fabled Frenzies," *Inc.,* October 1994, pp. 66–67.

11. Some critics feel that the international PLC has less validity today because multinational enterprises now operate vast global networks through which they might innovate new products anywhere in the world and move them through various countries not necessarily in the sequence predicted by the original formulation of the international PLC. See Louis T. Wells, Jr., "A Product Life Cycle for International Trade?" *Journal of Marketing,* July 1968, pp. 1–6; Sak Onkvisit and John J. Shaw, "An Examination of the International Product Life Cycle and Its Applications Within Marketing," *Columbia Journal of World Business,* Fall 1983, pp. 73–79; and Warren J. Keegan, *Global Marketing Management,* 5th ed. (Englewood Cliffs, NJ: Prentice Hall, 1995), pp. 37–43.

12. Robert D. Buzzell, "Competitive Behavior and Product Life Cycles," in *New Ideas for Successful Marketing,* ed. John S. Wright and Jack Goldstucker (Chicago: American Marketing Association, 1956), p. 51.

13. Buzzell, "Competitive Behavior."

14. Buzzell, "Competitive Behavior."

15. William T. Robinson and Claes Fornell, "Sources of Market Pioneer Advantages in Consumer Goods Industries," *Journal of Marketing Research,* August 1985, pp. 305–17.

16. Glen L. Urban et al., "Market Share Rewards to Pioneering Brands: An Empirical Analysis and Strategic Implications," *Management Science,* June 1986, pp. 645–59.

17. Gregory S. Carpenter and Kent Nakamoto, "Consumer Preference Formation and Pioneering Advantage," *Journal of Marketing Research,* August 1989, pp. 285–98.

18. Frank R. Kardes, Gurumurthy Kalyanaram, Murali Chankdrashekaran, and Ronald J. Dornoff, "Brand Retrieval, Consideration Set Composition, Consumer Choice, and the Pioneering Advantage," *Journal of Consumer Research,* June 1993, pp. 62–75. See also Frank H. Alpert and Michael A. Kamins, "Pioneer Brand Advantage and Consumer Behavior: A Conceptual Framework and Propositional Inventory," *Journal of the Academy of Marketing Science,* Summer 1994, pp. 244–53.

19. Steven P. Schnaars, *Managing Imitation Strategies* (New York: Free Press, 1994).

20. Peter N. Golder and Gerald J. Tellis, "Pioneer Advantage: Marketing Logic or Marketing Legend?" *Journal of Marketing Research,* May 1992, pp. 34–46.

21. Thomas S. Robertson and Hubert Gatignon, "How Innovators Thwart New Entrants into Their Market," *Planning Review,* September–October 1991, pp. 4–11, 48. Also see David M. Szymanski, Lisa C. Troy, and Sundar G. Bharadwaj, "Order of Entry and Business Performance: An Empirical Reexamination," *Journal of Marketing,* October, 1995, pp. 17–33.

22. John B. Frey, "Pricing Over the Competitive Cycle," speech presented at the 1982 Marketing Conference, Conference Board, New York.

23. Dori Jones Yang, "The Starbucks Enterprise Shifts into Warp Speed," *Business Week,* October 24, 1994, pp 76–79.

24. Donald W. Hendon, *Classic Failures in Product Marketing* (New York: Quorum Books, 1989), p. 29.

25. Allen J. McGrath, "Growth Strategies with a '90s Twist," *Across the Board,* March 1995, pp. 43–46.

26. R. S. Alexander, "The Death and Burial of 'Sick Products,'"*Journal of Marketing,* April 1964, p. 1.

27. See Philip Kotler, "Phasing Out Weak Products," *Harvard Business Review,* March–April 1965, pp. 107–18; Richard T. Hise, A. Parasuraman, and R. Viswanathan, "Product Elimination: The Neglected Management Responsibility," *Journal of Business Strategy,* Spring 1984, pp. 56–63; and George J. Avlonitis, "Product Elimination Decision Making: Does Formality Matter?" *Journal of Marketing,* Winter 1985, pp. 41–52.

28. See Kathryn Rudie Harrigan, "The Effect of Exit Barriers upon Strategic Flexibility," *Strategic Management Journal,* Vol. 1 (1980), 165–76.

29. Kathryn Rudie Harrigan, "Strategies for Declining Industries," *Journal of Business Strategy,* Fall 1980, p. 27.

30. See Philip Kotler, "Harvesting Strategies for Weak Products," *Business Horizons,* August 1978, pp. 15–22; and Laurence P. Feldman and Albert L. Page, "Harvesting: The Misunderstood Market Exit Strategy," *Journal of Business Strategy,* Spring 1985, pp. 79–85.

31. Conrad Berenson and Iris Mohr-Jackson, "Product Rejuvenation: A Less Risky Alternative to Product Innovation," *Business Horizons,* November–December 1994, pp. 51–56.

32. Grossmann, "A Follow-Up," pp. 66–67; Berenson and Mohr-Jackson, "Product Rejuvenation," pp. 51–56.

33. Nariman K. Dhalla and Sonia Yuspeh, "Forget the Product Life Cycle Concept!" *Harvard Business Review,* January–February 1976, pp. 102–12, here p. 105.

34. Norton Paley, "A Strategy for All Ages," *Sales and Marketing Management,* January 1994, pp. 51–52.

35. This problem is trivial if consumers' preferences are concentrated at one point. If there are distinct clusters of preference, the entrepreneur can design a product for the largest cluster or for the cluster that the company can serve best.

36. The product space is drawn with two attributes for simplicity. Actually, more attributes come into being as the market evolves.

DESIGNING MARKETING STRATEGIES FOR MARKET LEADERS, CHALLENGERS, FOLLOWERS, AND NICHERS

*"Cheshire Puss," she [Alice] began . . . "would you please tell me
which way I ought to go from here?"
"That depends on where you want to get to," said the cat.*

LEWIS CARROLL, ALICE'S ADVENTURES IN WONDERLAND

It takes a rough sea to make a great captain.

ANONYMOUS

In the last chapter, we examined the marketing strategies relevant at different stages of the product life cycle. We will now examine the problem of designing marketing strategies that take into account competitors' strategies. Some competitors will be large, others small. Some will have many resources, others will be strapped for funds. According to the Arthur D. Little consulting firm, a firm will occupy one of six competitive positions in the target market:[1]

- *Dominant:* This firm controls the behavior of other competitors and has a wide choice of strategic options.
- *Strong:* This firm can take independent action without endangering its long-term position and can maintain its long-term position regardless of competitors' actions.
- *Favorable:* This firm has an exploitable strength and a better-than-average opportunity to improve its position.
- *Tenable:* This firm is performing at a sufficiently satisfactory level to warrant continuing in business, but it exists at the sufferance of the dominant company and has a less-than-average opportunity to improve its position.
- *Weak:* This firm has unsatisfactory performance but an opportunity exists for improvement. The firm must change or else exit.
- *Nonviable:* This firm has unsatisfactory performance and no opportunity for improvement.

We can gain further insight into the competitive arena by classifying firms by the role they play in the target market: that of leader, challenger, follower, or nicher. Suppose a market is occupied by the firms shown in Figure 13-1. Forty percent of the market is in the hands of a *market leader,* the firm with the largest market share. Another 30% is in the hands of a *market challenger,* a runner-up firm that is fighting hard for increased market share. Another 20% is in the hands of a *market follower,* another runner-up firm that is willing to maintain its market share and not rock the boat. The remaining 10% is in the hands of *market nichers,* firms that serve small market segments not being served by larger firms.

In this chapter we will explore these questions:

- **What steps can a market leader take to expand, defend, and prolong its market leadership?**
- **What are the key attacks available to a market challenger in trying to wrest market share from the market leader?**
- **How can a market follower perform profitably without attacking the market leaders?**
- **What are the major opportunities and strategies available to market nichers?**

FIGURE 13-1
Hypothetical Market Structure

Designing Strategies for
Leaders, Challengers,
Followers, and Nichers

MARKET-LEADER STRATEGIES

Many industries contain one firm that is the acknowledged market leader. This firm has the largest market share in the relevant product market. It usually leads the other firms in price changes, new-product introductions, distribution coverage, and promotional intensity. The leader may or may not be admired or respected, but other firms acknowledge its dominance. The leader is an orientation point for competitors, a company to either challenge, imitate, or avoid. Some of the best-known market leaders are General Motors (autos), Kodak (photography), IBM (mainframe computers), Xerox (copying), Procter & Gamble (consumer packaged goods), Caterpillar (earth-moving equipment), Coca-Cola (soft drinks), McDonald's (fast food), and Gillette (razor blades).

Unless a dominant firm enjoys a legal monopoly, its life is not altogether easy. It must maintain constant vigilance because other firms keep challenging its strengths or trying to take advantage of its weaknesses. The market leader can easily miss a turn in the road and plunge into second or third place. A product innovation may come along and hurt the leader (for example, Tylenol's nonaspirin painkiller taking over the lead from Bayer Aspirin, and JVC and Matsushita's video-cassette recorders taking over Sony's Betamax). The leader might spend conservatively, expecting hard times, while a challenger spends liberally (Montgomery Ward's loss of its retail dominance to Sears after World War II). The leader might misjudge its competition and find itself left behind (as Sears did when it underestimated Kmart and Wal-Mart as serious competitors). The dominant firm might look old-fashioned against new and peppier rivals (Hallmark has been losing market share to flashier products from rivals like Chicago Recyled Paper Greetings). The dominant firm's costs might rise excessively and hurt its profits (Food Fair's decline, resulting from poor cost control).

Dominant firms want to remain number one. This calls for action on three fronts. First, the firm must find ways to expand total market demand. Second, the firm must defend its current market share through good defensive and offensive actions. Third, the firm can try to increase its market share further, even if market size remains constant.

Expanding the Total Market

The dominant firm normally gains the most when the total market expands. If Americans increase their picture taking, Kodak stands to gain the most because it sells over 80% of the country's film. If Kodak can convince more Americans to buy cameras and take pictures, or to take pictures on other occasions besides holidays, or to take more pictures on each occasion, Kodak will benefit considerably. In general, the market leader should look for new users, new uses, and more usage of its products.

NEW USERS. Every product class has the potential of attracting buyers who are unaware of the product or who are resisting it because of its price or lack of certain features. A manufacturer can search for new users among three groups. For example, a perfume manufacturer can try to convince women who do not use perfume to use perfume (*market-penetration strategy,* see Chapter 3), or convince men to start using perfume (*new-market strategy*), or sell perfume in other countries (*geographical-expansion strategy*).

Johnson & Johnson accomplished one of the great successes in developing a new class of users with its baby shampoo. The company became concerned about future sales growth when the birth rate slowed down. Their marketers noticed that other family members occasionally used the baby shampoo for their own hair. Management decided to develop an advertising campaign aimed at adults. In a short time, Johnson & Johnson baby shampoo became the leading brand in the total shampoo market. Another example: Oil of Olay—which for years targeted exclusively older women—is now running ads in teen magazines.

NEW USES. Markets can be expanded through discovering and promoting new uses for the product. For example, the average American eats dry breakfast cereal three mornings a week. Cereal manufacturers would gain if they could promote cereal eating on other occasions during the day—perhaps as a late-night or mid-morning snack.

Du Pont's nylon provides a classic story of new-use expansion. Every time nylon became a mature product, Du Pont discovered a new use. Nylon was first used in parachutes; then as a fiber for women's stockings; later, as a major material in women's blouses and men's shirts. Still later, it entered automobile tires, seat upholstery, and carpeting.[2] Each new use started the product on a new life cycle. Credit goes to Du Pont's continuous R&D program to find new uses.

In many cases, customers deserve credit for discovering new uses. Vaseline petroleum jelly started out as a lubricant in machine shops. Over the years, consumers have reported many new uses for the product, including use as a skin ointment, a healing agent, and a hair dressing.

Arm & Hammer, the baking-soda manufacturer, had a product whose sales had been drifting downward for 125 years. Baking soda had a number of uses, but no single use was advertised. Then the company discovered some consumers who used it as a refrigerator deodorant. It launched a heavy advertising and publicity campaign focusing on this single use and succeeded in getting half of the homes in America to place an open box of baking soda in their refrigerator. A few years later, Arm & Hammer discovered consumers who used its product to quell kitchen grease fires, and it promoted this use with great results.

The company's task is to monitor customers' uses of the product. This applies to industrial products as well as consumer products. Von Hippel's studies show that most new industrial products were originally suggested by customers rather than by company R&D laboratories.[3]

MORE USAGE. A third market expansion strategy is to convince people to use more of the product per use occasion. If a cereal manufacturer convinces consumers to eat a full bowl of cereal instead of half a bowl, total sales will increase. Procter & Gamble advises users that its Head & Shoulders shampoo is more effective with two applications instead of one per shampoo.

A creative example of a company that stimulated higher usage per occasion is the Michelin Tire Company (French). Michelin wanted to encourage French car owners to drive their cars more miles per year—thus leading to more tire replacement. It conceived the idea of rating French restaurants on a three-star system. They promoted the names of many of the best restaurants in the South of France, leading many Parisians to take weekend drives to Provence and the Riviera. Michelin also published guidebooks with maps and sights along the way to encourage additional driving.

Designing Strategies for Leaders, Challengers, Followers, and Nichers

Defending Market Share

While trying to expand total market size, the dominant firm must continuously defend its current business against rival attacks. The leader is like a large elephant being attacked by a swarm of bees. The largest and nastiest bee keeps buzzing around the leader. Coca-Cola must constantly guard against Pepsi-Cola; Gillette against Bic; Hertz against Avis; McDonald's against Burger King; General Motors against Ford; and Kodak against Fuji.[4] Sometimes the competitor is domestic; sometimes it is foreign:

KODAK AND FUJI

For more than 100 years, Eastman Kodak has been known for its easy-to-use cameras, high-quality film, and solid profits. But during the past decade, Kodak's sales have flattened and its profits have declined. Kodak has been outpaced by more innovative competitors, many of whom are Japanese, who introduced or improved upon 35-mm cameras, video cameras, and one-hour film-processing labs. However, when Fuji Photo Film Company moved in on Kodak's bread-and-butter color film business, Kodak took the challenge seriously.

Fuji entered the U.S. film market offering high-quality color films at 10% lower prices than Kodak. It also beat Kodak to the market with high-speed films. Fuji pulled off a major marketing coup by outbidding Kodak to become the official film of the 1984 Los Angeles Summer Olympic Games. Fuji's share of the huge U.S. color film market grew to more than 8% in 1984, and it aimed at winning a 15% market share. Fuji's U.S. sales were growing at a rate of 20% a year—much faster than the overall market-growth rate.

Kodak fought back fiercely to protect its U.S. market share. It matched Fuji's lower prices and unleashed a series of film improvements. Kodak outspent Fuji by 20 to 1 on advertising and promotion, paid $10 million to obtain sponsorship of the 1988 Summer Olympics in Seoul, South Korea, and snapped up the rights to the 1992 Olympics in Barcelona. Kodak successfully defended its U.S. market position; by the early 1990s, Kodak's share of the U.S. market had stabilized at a whopping 80 percent.

But Kodak took the battle a step further—it took several aggressive steps to increase its presence and sales in Japan. It set up a separate subsidiary—Kodak Japan—and tripled its Japanese staff. It bought out a Japanese distributor and set up its own Japanese marketing and sales staff. It invested in a new technology center and a large Japanese research facility. Finally, Kodak greatly increased its Japanese promotion and publicity. Kodak Japan now sponsors everything from Japanese television talk shows to sumo wrestling tournaments.

Kodak will gain several benefits from its stepped-up attack on Japan. First, Japan offers big opportunities for increased sales and profits—its $1.5 billion film and photo paper market is second only to that of the United States. Second, much of today's new photographic technology originates in Japan, so a greater presence in Japan will help Kodak keep up with the latest developments. Third, ownership and joint ventures in Japan will help Kodak better understand Japanese manufacturing and obtain new products for the United States and other world markets. Kodak reaps one more important benefit from its attack on the Japanese market: If Fuji must devote heavy resources to defending its Japanese home turf against Kodak's attacks, it will have fewer resources to use against Kodak in the United States.

Sometimes there are several large, dangerous bees. AT&T has to defend its telecommunications business against the former Bell regional companies, the connect companies (MCI, Sprint), domestic and foreign equipment producers (Northern Telecom, Siemens), and computer firms moving into telecommunications (IBM, Apple, and so on). Clearly, it cannot defend all of its territory and needs to decide where to draw the battle lines.

What can the market leader do to defend its terrain? Twenty centuries ago, Sun Tsu told his warriors: "One does not rely on the enemy not attacking, but relies on the fact that he himself is unassailable." The most constructive response is *continuous innovation*. The leader refuses to be content with the way things are and leads the industry in developing new product and customer services, distribution effectiveness, and cost cutting. It keeps increasing its competitive effectiveness and value to customers. The leader applies the military principle of the offensive: *The commander exercises initiative, sets the pace, and exploits enemy weaknesses.* The best defense is a good offense.

Even when it does not launch offensives, the market leader must guard all fronts and not leave any major flanks exposed. It must keep its costs down, and its prices must be consonant with the value the customers see in the brand. The leader must "plug holes" so that attackers do not jump in. Thus a consumer-packaged-goods leader will produce its brands in several sizes and forms to meet varying consumer preferences and hold on to as much dealer shelf space as possible.

The cost of plugging holes can be high. But the cost of abandoning an unprofitable product/market segment can be higher! General Motors did not want to lose money by making small cars, but it is losing more now because it allowed Japanese car makers to invade the U.S. market. Xerox felt it would lose money making small copier machines, but now it has lost much more by allowing the Japanese to enter and grow in the market.

Clearly, the market leader must consider carefully which terrains are important to defend even at a loss and which can be given up with little risk. The aim of defensive strategy is to reduce the probability of attack, divert attacks to less threatening areas, and lessen the intensity of attack. Any attack is likely to hurt profits. But the defender's form and speed of response can make an important difference in the profit consequences. Researchers are currently exploring the most appropriate forms of response to price and their attacks (for more on this topic, see the Marketing Insight on page 378 titled "Defense Strategies").

The intensified competition that has taken place worldwide in recent years has sparked management's interest in models of military warfare, particularly as described in the writings of Sun-Tsu, Mushashi, von Clausewitz, and Liddell-Hart.[5] Leading companies, like leading nations, have been advised to protect their interest with such strategies as "brinkmanship," "massive retaliation," "limited warfare," "graduated response," "diplomacy of violence," and "threat systems." There are, in fact, six defense strategies that a dominant firm can use. These are summarized in Figure 13-2 on page 379 and described in the following paragraphs.[6]

POSITION DEFENSE.   The most basic idea of defense is to build an impregnable fortification around one's territory. The French built the famous Maginot line in peacetime to protect their territory against possible future German invasion. But this fortification, like all static defense maneuvers, failed. Simply defending one's current position or products is a form of marketing myopia. Henry Ford's myopia about his Model-T brought an enviably healthy company with $1 billion in cash reserves to the brink of financial ruin. Even such strong brands as Coca-Cola and Bayer aspirin cannot be relied on as the main sources of future growth and profitability. Coca-Cola today, in spite of selling nearly half the soft drinks of the world, has acquired fruit-drink companies and diversified into desalinization equipment and plastics. While defense is important, leaders under attack would be foolish to put all their resources into building fortifications around their current product.

FLANK DEFENSE.   The market leader should not only guard its territory but also erect outposts to protect a weak front or possibly serve as an invasion base for counterattacking. Here are two good examples of a flanking defense:

JEWEL FOOD STORES   Jewel is a leading supermarket food chain store in Chicago. The company believes that supermarkets will continue to remain a dominant force but is flanking its position by strengthening its food-retailing-assortment mix. Jewel is meeting the fast-food boom by offering a wide assortment of instant and frozen meals, and it is meeting the discount-food challenge by promoting generic lines.

Defense Strategies

Professors Hauser, Shugan, and Gaskin have developed a market defense model called Defender. Their model makes the following assumptions about consumers:

1. Consumers share the same perceptions of each brand's product attributes.

2. Consumers differ in their preferences for various product characteristics.

3. Consumers vary in the number of brands they know and will consider.

4. Consumers' choices are affected by product features, price, distribution, advertising, and promotion.

They illustrate the Defender model with the history of battle between two headache remedies, Tylenol and Datril. Tylenol had gained a large market share based on its perceived gentleness (no stomach upsets) and was achieving outstanding profits. Bristol-Myers then introduced the same product, Datril, and advertised it as "just as good as Tylenol, only cheaper." If consumers believed this, Datril would make deep inroads into Tylenol's market share. How should Tylenol defend itself?

Using the Defender model, the researchers came to the following conclusions about Tylenol's best defense:

1. Tylenol should lower its prices, especially if the market is unsegmented. If the market is segmented, the price might be raised in some of the less vulnerable segments.

2. Tylenol should reduce its expenditures on distribution; specifically, it should drop marginal retailers who no longer are profitable to serve.

3. Tylenol should improve its strong product features even more rather than try to improve along the lines of the attacker's strong product features.

4. Tylenol should spend less on awareness-building advertising and direct more on repositioning-building advertising.

What did Tylenol actually do to defend itself from Datril's attack? Tylenol quickly cut its price to match Datril's, and later added the Extra Strength Tylenol brand to capture consumers' interest in greater effectiveness. Through these steps, Tylenol preserved its market leadership position and prevented Datril from gaining much ground.

Sources: John R. Hauser and Steve M. Shugan, "Defensive Marketing Strategy," *Marketing Science,* Fall 1983, pp. 319–60; John R. Hauser and S. P. Gaskin, "Application of the 'DEFENDER' Consumer Model," *Marketing Science,* Fall 1984, pp. 327–51.

Jewel is tailoring its various stores to suit local demands for such items as fresh bakery products and ethnic foods. Jewel has set up the Jewel-T division, a network of small food discount stores patterned after pioneer Aldi. To fight "combination stores," Jewel integrated a large number of its supermarkets with its Osco Drug Stores.

NABISCO The market leader in cookies, Nabisco created a highly successful flanking defense with the introduction of its low-fat cookie line, SnackWells. Tapping the U.S. low-fat obsession, SnackWells rocketed to a $400 million megabrand in the space of two years. As competitors scrambled to launch their own fat-free lines, Nabisco shored up its SnackWells flank by extending into new territories such as ice cream and frozen novelties, bakery pies, and a line of chocolate yogurt.[7]

The flanking defense is of little value unless it is seriously mounted. This was precisely General Motors' and Ford's mistake when they halfheartedly designed the Vega and Pinto compact cars years ago to ward off the small-car attacks launched by the Japanese and European car makers. The American compacts were poorly made, and they failed to retard the sale of the foreign compact cars.

PREEMPTIVE DEFENSE. A more aggressive defense maneuver is to launch an attack on the enemy *before* the enemy starts its offense against the leader. Pre-

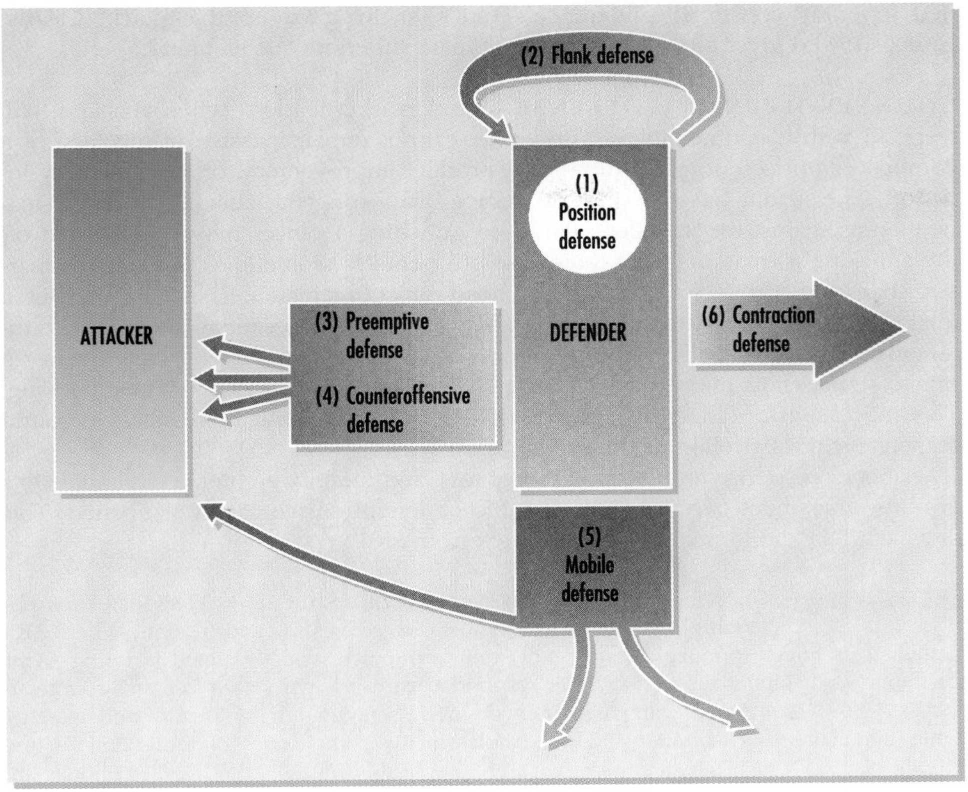

FIGURE 13-2
Defense Strategies

emptive defense assumes that an ounce of prevention is worth more than a pound of cure. When Chrysler's market share began rising from 12% to 18% some years ago, one rival marketing executive was overheard to say, "If they [Chrysler] go to 20%, it will be over our dead bodies."

A company can launch a preemptive defense in several ways. It could wage guerrilla action across the market—hitting one competitor here, another there—and keep everyone off balance. Or it could try to achieve a grand market envelopment, as Seiko has done with its 2,300 watch models distributed worldwide. Or it could begin sustained price attacks, as Texas Instruments often initiated. Sustained, high-pressure strategies aim at retaining the initiative at all times and keeping the competition always on the defensive.

Sometimes the preemptive strike is waged psychologically. The market leader sends out market signals to dissuade competitors from attacking.[8] A major U.S. pharmaceutical firm is the leader in a certain drug category. Every time it learns that a competitor might build a factory to produce that drug, the company leaks the news that it is considering cutting the drug price and building another plant. This news intimidates the competitor, who decides against entering that product arena. Meanwhile the leader never does cut its price or add another plant. Of course, this bluff can work only a few times.

Market leaders with strong resources have the capacity to withstand some attacks and may even choose to entice the opponents into costly attacks. Heinz let Hunt's carry out its massive attack in the ketchup market without much counteroffensive. Hunt's attacked Heinz with two new flavors of ketchup; it lowered its price to 70% of Heinz's price; it offered heavy trade allowances to retailers; it raised its advertising budget to over twice the level of Heinz's. Hunt's was willing to lose money during the attack. The strategy failed and the Heinz brand continued to enjoy consumer preference. Hunt's finally gave up the attack. Clearly, Heinz showed great confidence in the ultimate superiority of its brand.

COUNTEROFFENSIVE DEFENSE. Most market leaders, when attacked, will respond with a counterattack. The leader cannot remain passive in the face of a competitor's price cut, promotion blitz, product improvement, or sales-territory invasion. The leader has the strategic choice of meeting the attacker frontally, maneuvering against the attacker's flank, or launching a pincer movement to cut off the attacking formations from their base of operation. Sometimes the leader's market share erosion is so rapid that a head-on counterattack is necessary. But a leader enjoying some strategic depth can often weather the initial attack and counterattack effectively at the opportune moment. In many situations, it may be worth minor setbacks to allow the offensive to develop fully before counterattacking. This may seem a dangerous strategy of "wait and see," but there may be sound reasons for not barreling into a counteroffensive.

A better response to an attack is to pause and identify a chink in the attacker's armor—a segment gap in which a viable counteroffensive can be launched. This is what AT&T did in response to an attack from MCI:

AT&T AND MCI Since the phone industry was deregulated in 1984, AT&T has been defending itself against competitors like MCI and Sprint. When MCI launched its hugely popular Friends and Family campaign, directly aimed at luring AT&T customers with higher discounts, AT&T responded with its own very successful counterattack. AT&T's "True Voice" campaign built on AT&T's reputation for quality and integrity while simultaneously attempting to poke holes in the complexities of MCI's Friends and Family plan, in which maximum savings aren't applicable unless an MCI caller phones another MCI customer within his or her designated "calling circle" (Figure 13-3). Nine months from the start of its True campaign, AT&T had gained anywhere from .5% to a full point of market share.[9]

When a market leader's territory is attacked, an effective counterattack is to invade the attacker's main territory so that it will have to pull back some of its troops to defend its territory. One of Northwest Airlines' most profitable routes is

FIGURE 13-3
AT&T True Campaign

MCI Math, Part II.
40% = 13%

40% = The discount on calls to MCI customers in your Friends & Family II calling circle.

13% = The average discount that shows up on your MCI Friends & Family II Basic bill.

Friends & Family II. Big claims. Big disappointments.

Friends & Family II advertises 40% off on calls to other MCI customers in your calling circle. But on calls to non-MCI customers in your circle, the savings is only 20%. And on calls to numbers outside your calling circle—that's any number you don't give them in advance—**the savings**

is a nice round 0%. Then there's the small matter of the $36 a year in monthly fees. In the end, the total Friends & Family II discount is a far cry from the 40% you might expect. It's more like 13%.* No wonder 4 out of 5 Friends & Family II Basic customers will save more with...

AT&T True Math.
20% = 20%

20% = The discount you get on calls to everyone.

20% = The discount you see on your AT&T bill with AT&T True USA™ Savings.

AT&T True USA™ Savings. We say 20%. You save 20%.

AT&T True USA™ Savings. Just spend $25 a month on long distance, and we'll subtract 20% off your AT&T bill.** That's 20% off on calls to anyone, anytime, anywhere in the USA. Guaranteed. To sign up, just call *1 800-TRUE-USA.*

AT&T. Your True Voice.™

AT&T

Minneapolis to Atlanta. A smaller air carrier launched a deep fare cut and advertised it heavily to expand its share in this market. Northwest retaliated by cutting its fares on the Minneapolis/Chicago route, which the attacking airline depended on for its major revenue. With its major revenue source hurting, the attacking airline restored its Minneapolis/Atlanta fare to a normal level.

Another common form of counteroffensive defense is the exercise of economic or political clout to deter the attacker. The leader may try to crush a competitor by subsidizing lower prices for the vulnerable product with revenue from its more profitable products. Or the leader may prematurely announce that a product upgrade will be available to delay customers from buying the competitor's product, even though the upgrade is far from ready. Or the leader may lobby legislators to take political actions that would inhibit or cripple the competition.

MOBILE DEFENSE. Mobile defense involves more than the leader aggressively defending its territory. In mobile defense, the leader stretches its domain over new territories that can serve as future centers for defense and offense. It spreads to these new territories not so much through normal brand proliferation as through market broadening and market diversification. These moves generate strategic depth for the firm, enabling it to weather continual attacks and launch retaliatory strikes.

Market broadening calls upon a company to shift its focus from the current product to the underlying generic need and get involved in R&D across the whole range of technology associated with that need. Thus "petroleum" companies sought to recast themselves into "energy" companies. Implicitly, this change demanded that they dip their research fingers into the oil, coal, nuclear, hydroelectric, and chemical industries.

A market-broadening strategy should not be carried too far, lest it fault two fundamental military principles—the *principle of the objective* (pursue a clearly defined, decisive, and attainable objective) and the *principle of mass* (concentrate your efforts at a point of the enemy's weakness). The objective of being in the energy business is too broad. The energy business is not a single need but rather a whole range of needs (heating, lighting, propelling, and so on). Furthermore, too much broadening would dilute the company's mass in the current competitive theater, and survival today surely must take precedence over the grand battles imagined for tomorrow. In such a situation, marketing myopia would be replaced by *marketing hyperopia,* where there is too much focus on the future at the expense of the present.

Reasonable broadening, however, makes sense. Armstrong World Industries carried out a successful market-broadening strategy by redefining its domain from "floor covering" to "decorative room covering" (including walls and ceilings). By recognizing the customer's need to create a pleasant interior through various covering materials, Armstrong expanded into neighboring businesses that were synergistically balanced for growth and defense.

Market diversification into unrelated industries (which we first discussed in Chapter 3) is the other alternative to generating strategic depth. When U.S. tobacco companies like Reynolds and Philip Morris acknowledged the growing curbs on cigarette smoking, they were not content with position defense or even with looking for new substitutes for the cigarette. Instead they moved quickly into new industries, such as beer, liquor, soft drinks, and frozen foods.

CONTRACTION DEFENSE. Large companies sometimes recognize that they can no longer defend all of their territory. Their forces are spread too thin, and competitors are nibbling away on several fronts. The best course of action then appears to be *planned contraction* (also called *strategic withdrawal*). Planned contraction is not market abandonment but rather giving up the weaker territories and reassigning resources to stronger territories. Planned contraction is a move to consolidate one's competitive strength in the market and concentrate mass at pivotal positions. Heinz, General Mills, Del Monte, General Electric, and Georgia-Pacific are among those companies that have significantly pruned their product lines in recent years.

Expanding Market Share

Market leaders can improve their profitability by increasing their market share. In many markets, one share point is worth tens of millions of dollars. A one-share-point gain in coffee is worth $48 million and in soft drinks, $120 million! No wonder normal competition has turned into marketing warfare.

Some years ago, the Strategic Planning Institute launched a study called *Profit Impact of Market Strategy (PIMS),* which sought to identify the most important variables affecting profits. Data were collected from hundreds of business units in a variety of industries to identify the most important variables associated with profitability. The key variables included market share, product quality, and several others.

The study found that a company's profitability, measured by pre-tax return on investment (ROI), rises with its *relative market share* of its served market,[10] as shown in Figure 13-4(a).[11] According to a PIMS report, the average ROI for businesses with under 10% market share was about 11 percent. On the average, a difference of ten percentage points in market share is accompanied by a difference of about five points in pre-tax ROI. The PIMS study shows that businesses with market shares above 40% earn an average ROI of 38.5%, more than three times that of those with shares under 10 percent.[12]

These findings have led many companies to pursue market share expansion and leadership as their objective. General Electric, for example, has decided that it must be number one or two in each market or else get out. GE divested its computer business and its air-conditioning business because it could not achieve the top position in these industries.

Various critics have attacked the PIMS study as either weak or spurious. Hamermesh reported finding many profitable companies with low market shares.[13]

FIGURE 13-4

Relationship Between Market Share and Profitability

Figure (a) from Strategic Planning Institute (The PIMS Program), 1030 Massachusetts Avenue, Cambridge, MA 02138.

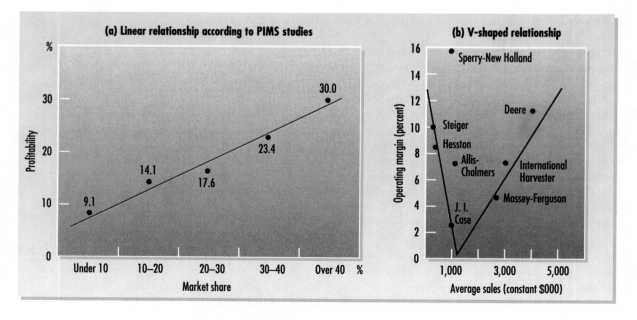

Woo and Cooper identified 40 low-share businesses that enjoyed pretax ROIs of 20% or more; they characterized these businesses as having high relative product quality, medium to low prices, narrow product lines, and low total costs.[14] Most of these companies produced industrial components or supplies.

Some industry studies have yielded a **V**-shaped relationship between market share and profitability. Figure 13-4(b) shows a **V**-curve for agricultural-equipment firms. The industry leader, Deere & Company, earns a high return. However, Hesston and Steiger, two small specialty firms, also earn high returns. J. I. Case and Massey-Ferguson are trapped in the valley, and International Harvester commands substantial market share but earns lower returns. Thus such industries have one or a few highly profitable large firms, several profitable small and more-focused firms, and several medium-sized firms with poorer profit performance. According to Roach:

> *The large firms on the **V**-curve tend to address the entire market, achieving cost advantages and high market share by realizing economies of scale. The small competitors reap high profits by focusing on some narrower segment of the business and by developing specialized approaches to production, marketing, and distribution for that segment. Ironically, the medium-sized competitors at the trough of the **V**-curve are unable to realize any competitive advantage and often show the poorest profit performance. Trapped in a strategic "No Man's Land," they are too large to reap the benefits of more focused competition, yet too small to benefit from the economies of scale that their larger competitors enjoy.[15]*

How can the two graphs in Figure 13-4 be reconciled? The PIMS findings argue that profitability increases as a business gains share relative to its competitors in its *served (target) market*. The **V**-shaped curve ignores market segments and looks at a business's profitability relative to its size in the *total market*. Thus Mercedes earns high profit because it is a high-share company in its served market of luxury cars even though it is a low-share company in the total auto market. And it has achieved this high share in its served market because it does many things right, such as producing high relative product quality and achieving high asset turnover and good cost control.

Companies must not think, however, that gaining increased market share in their served market will automatically improve their profitability. Much depends on their strategy for gaining increased market share. Because the cost of buying higher market share may far exceed its revenue value, the company should consider three factors before pursuing increased market share:

♦ The first factor is the possibility of provoking antitrust action. Jealous competitors are likely to cry "monopolization" if a dominant firm makes further inroads on market share. This rise in risk would cut down the attractiveness of pushing market share gains too far. This is why Microsoft walked away from a potential $2 billion merger with rival software company Intuit in 1995. Microsoft wanted to purchase Intuit so that it could corner the market on personal finance software. (Intuit owns the best-selling Quicken software.) When the justice department challenged Microsoft with an antitrust suit, the software giant backed down rather than confronting the challenge.[16]

♦ The second factor is economic cost. Figure 13-5 on page 384 shows the possibility that profitability might begin to fall with further market share gains after some level. In the illustration, the firm's *optimal market share* is 50 percent. A larger share might come at the expense of profitability. This conclusion is consistent with the PIMS findings in that PIMS did not show what happens to profitability for different levels within the over-40% category. Basically, the cost of gaining further market share might exceed the value. A company that has, say, 60% of the market must recognize that the "holdout" customers may dislike the company, be loyal to competitive suppliers, have unique needs, or prefer dealing with smaller suppliers. The cost of legal work, public relations, and lobbying

Designing Strategies for
Leaders, Challengers,
Followers, and Nichers

FIGURE 13-5

The Concept of Optimal
Market Share

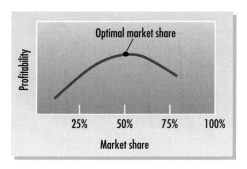

rises with market share. In general, pushing for higher market share is less justified when there are few scale or experience economies, unattractive market segments exist, buyers want multiple sources of supply, and exit barriers are high. The leader might be better off concentrating on expanding market size rather than fighting for further increases in market share. Some market leaders have even increased their profitability by selectively decreasing their market share in weaker areas.[17]

♦ The third factor is that companies might pursue the wrong marketing-mix strategy in their bid for higher market share and therefore not increase their profit. While certain marketing-mix variables are effective in building market share, not all lead to higher profits. Higher shares tend to produce higher profits when unit costs fall with increased market share and when the company offers a superior-quality product and charges a premium price that more than covers the cost of offering higher quality.

Buzzell and Wiersema found that share-gaining companies typically outperformed their competitors in three areas: new-product activity, relative product quality, and marketing expenditures.[18] Specifically:

1. Share-gaining companies typically developed and added more new products to their line.

2. Companies that increased their product quality relative to competitors enjoyed greater share gains than those whose quality ratings remained constant or declined.

3. Companies that increased their marketing expenditures faster than the rate of market growth typically achieved share gains. Increases in sales force expenditures were effective in producing share gains for both industrial and consumer markets. Increased advertising expenditures produced share gains mainly for consumer-goods companies. Increased sales-promotion expenditures were effective in producing share gains for all kinds of companies.

4. Companies that cut their prices more deeply than competitors did not achieve significant market share gains. Presumably, enough rivals met the price cuts partly, and others offered other values to the buyers, so that buyers did not switch as much to the price cutter.

Two Case Studies: Procter & Gamble and Caterpillar

All said, market leaders who stay on top have learned the art of expanding the total market, defending their current territory, and increasing their market share profitably. Two companies that have had the most success in these arenas are Procter & Gamble and Caterpillar. Both these companies have shown a remarkable ability to protect their market shares against repeated attacks by able challengers. They do not allow any weaknesses to develop.[19]

PROCTER & GAMBLE. Procter & Gamble (P&G) is widely regarded as the United States' most skilled marketer of consumer packaged goods. It markets the leading brand in 19 of the 39 categories in which it competes, and one of the top three brands in 34 of its categories. Its average market share is close to 25 percent. Its market leadership rests on several principles:

- *Customer knowledge:* P&G studies its customers—both final consumers and the trade—through continuous marketing research and intelligence gathering. It provides a toll-free 800 number so consumers can call P&G directly with any inquiries, suggestions, or complaints about P&G products.

- *Long-term outlook:* P&G takes its time to analyze an opportunity and prepare the best product, then commits itself for the long run to make this product a success. It struggled with Pringles potato chips for almost a decade before achieving market success.

- *Product innovation:* P&G is an active product innovator and benefit segmenter, and it spent almost a billion dollars on R&D in 1994. It launches brands offering new consumer benefits rather than "me-too" brands backed by heavy advertising. P&G spent 10 years researching and developing the first effective anticavity toothpaste, Crest. It spent several years researching the first effective over-the-counter antidandruff shampoo, Head & Shoulders. P&G found that new parents wanted relief from handling and washing diapers and innovated Pampers, an affordable disposable paper diaper. The company thoroughly tests its new products with consumers, and only when real preference is indicated does it launch them in the national market.

- *Quality strategy:* P&G designs products of above-average quality. Once launched, the product is continuously improved. When P&G announces "new and improved," it means it. This is in contrast to some companies that establish a quality level then rarely improve it, and to other companies that reduce the quality in an effort to squeeze out more profit.

- *Line-extension strategy:* P&G produces its brands in several sizes and forms to satisfy varying consumer preferences. This strategy gives its brand more shelf space and prevents competitors from moving in to satisfy unmet market needs.

- *Brand-extension strategy:* P&G often uses its strong brand names to launch new products. For example, the Ivory brand has been extended from a soap to include liquid soap, a dishwashing detergent, and a shampoo. Launching a new product under a strong existing brand name gives the new brand instant recognition and credibility with much less advertising outlay.

- *Multibrand strategy:* P&G originated the art of marketing several brands in the same product category. For example, it produces eight brands of hand soap and six shampoo brands. The aim is to design brands that meet different consumer wants and that compete against specific competitors' brands. Each brand manager runs the brand independently and competes for company resources. However, as part of its response to the growing consumer demand for value, P&G has begun to simplify its vast array of products. Since 1991, the company has eliminated almost a quarter of the different sizes, flavors, and other varieties of its brands. It also keeps close tabs on which brands are not performing to expectations. Some products, such as White Cloud toilet tissue, have been eliminated and combined with stronger products.[20]

- *Heavy advertising:* P&G is the nation's second largest consumer-packaged-goods advertiser, spending over $3 billion on advertising in fiscal year 1994. It never stints on spending money to create strong consumer awareness and preference.

- *Aggressive sales force:* P&G has a top-flight field sales force that is very effective in working with key retail customers to gain shelf space and cooperation in point-of-purchase displays and promotions.

- *Effective sales promotion:* P&G has a sales-promotion department to counsel its brand managers on the most effective promotions to achieve particular objectives. The department studies the results of consumer and trade deals and develops an expert sense of these deals' effectiveness under varying circumstances. At the same time, P&G tries to minimize the use of sales promotion, preferring to rely on advertising to build long-term consumer preference.

- *Competitive toughness:* P&G carries a big stick when it comes to constraining aggressors. P&G is willing to spend large sums of money to outpromote new competitive brands and prevent them from gaining a foothold in the market.

Designing Strategies for
Leaders, Challengers,
Followers, and Nichers

- *Manufacturing efficiency and cost cutting:* P&G's reputation as a great marketing company is matched by its excellence as a manufacturing company. P&G spends large sums of money developing and improving production operations to keep its costs among the lowest in the industry. And P&G has recently begun slashing its costs even further, allowing it to reduce the premium prices at which some of its goods sell.

- *Brand-management system:* P&G originated the brand-management system, in which one executive is responsible for each brand. The system has been copied by many competitors but frequently without the success that P&G has achieved by perfecting its system over the years. In a recent development, P&G modified its general management structure so that each product category is now run by a general manager with volume and profit responsibility. While this new organization does not replace the brand-management system, it helps to sharpen strategic focus on the key consumer needs and competition in the category.

Thus P&G's market leadership is not based on doing one thing well but on the successful orchestration of myriad factors that contribute to market leadership. Both in the United States and abroad, P&G has boosted its market share in most of its businesses over the past five years.

CATERPILLAR. Since the 1940s, Caterpillar has dominated the construction-equipment industry. Its tractors, crawlers, and loaders, painted in the familiar yellow, are a common sight at any construction area and account for 50% of the world's sales of heavy construction equipment. Caterpillar has managed to retain leadership in spite of charging a premium price for its equipment and being challenged by a number of able competitors, including John Deere, Massey-Ferguson, J. I. Case, and Komatsu. Several principles combine to explain Caterpillar's success:

- *Premium product quality:* Caterpillar produces high-quality equipment known for its reliability. Reliability is a key buyer consideration in the purchase of heavy industrial equipment. To convince buyers of its superior quality, Caterpillar designs its equipment with a heavier gauge of steel than necessary.

- *Extensive and efficient dealership system:* Caterpillar maintains the largest number of independent construction-equipment dealers in the industry. Its 260 dealers throughout the world carry a complete line of Caterpillar equipment and do not carry other lines. Competitors' dealers, in contrast, normally lack a full line and carry complementary, noncompeting lines. Caterpillar can choose the best dealers (a new Caterpillar dealership costs the franchisee $5 million) and spends the most money in training, servicing, and motivating them.

- *Superior service:* Caterpillar has built a worldwide parts and service system second to none in the industry. Caterpillar can deliver replacement parts and service anywhere in the world within 24 hours of equipment breakdown. Competitors cannot match this ability without making a substantial investment. Any competitor duplicating this service level would only neutralize Caterpillar's advantage rather than score a new advantage.

- *Superior parts management:* Thirty percent of Caterpillar's sales volume and over 50% of its profit come from the sale of replacement parts. Caterpillar has developed a superior parts-management system to keep margins high in this end of the business.

- *Premium price:* Caterpillar charges a 10% to 15% premium over comparable competitors' equipment because of the extra value perceived by buyers.

- *Full-line strategy:* Caterpillar produces a full line of construction equipment to enable customers to do one-stop buying.

- *Good financing:* Caterpillar arranges generous financial terms for customers who buy its equipment. Such terms are important because of the high purchase cost.

Recently Caterpillar experienced difficulties because of the depressed global construction-equipment market and cutthroat competition. Its biggest headache has been Komatsu, Japan's number-one construction firm, which adopted the internal slogan "Encircle Caterpillar." Komatsu studies and attacks market niches, continuously enlarges its product line and improves its product quality, and prices its equipment sometimes as much as 40% lower. Caterpillar tells buyers that Komatsu's lower prices reflect lower quality, but not all buyers accept this or are willing to pay more for higher quality.

Caterpillar has fought back by cutting its costs and meeting Komatsu's prices and sometimes even initiating price cutting. The price wars drove competitors like International Harvester and Clark Equipment near the brink of ruin. Komatsu, in the meantime, has had to raise its prices several times and its market share has dropped. The long and damaging price wars appear to be coming to an end, with both sides settling for peaceful coexistence and improved profits.

MARKET-CHALLENGER STRATEGIES

Firms that occupy second, third, and lower ranks in an industry are often called runner-up, or trailing, firms. Some, such as Colgate, Ford, Montgomery Ward, Avis, Westinghouse, and Pepsi-Cola, are quite large in their own right. These runner-up firms can adopt one of two postures. They can attack the leader and other competitors in an aggressive bid for further market share (market challengers). Or they can play ball and not "rock the boat" (market followers).

There are many cases of market challengers that gained ground on the market leader or even overtook the leader. Canon, which was only one-tenth the size of Xerox in the mid-1970s, today produces more copier machines than Xerox. Toyota today produces more cars than General Motors, Nikon produces more fine cameras than Leica, and British Airways flies more international passengers than the former leader, Pan Am. These challengers set high aspirations and leveraged their smaller resources while the market leaders ran their businesses as usual.

Dolan found that competitive rivalry and price cutting are most intense in industries with high fixed costs, high inventory costs, and stagnant primary demand, such as steel, auto, paper, and chemicals.[21] We will now examine the competitive attack strategies available to market challengers.

Defining the Strategic Objective and Opponent(s)

A market challenger must first define its strategic objective. Most market challengers' strategic objective is to increase their market shares. These decisions to attack interact with the decision of whom to attack:

- *It can attack the market leader.* This is a high-risk but potentially high-payoff strategy and makes good sense if the leader is a "false leader" who is not serving the market well. The terrain to examine is consumer need or dissatisfaction. A substantial segment that is unserved or poorly served provides an excellent strategic target. Miller's "lite beer" campaign was successful because it pivoted on discovering many consumers who wanted a less caloric, less filling beer. The alternative strategy is to out-innovate the leader across the whole segment. Thus Xerox wrested the copy market from 3M by developing a better copying process (dry instead of wet copying). Later Canon grabbed a large chunk of Xerox's market by introducing desk copiers.

- *It can attack firms of its own size that are not doing the job and are underfinanced.* It can attack firms that have aging products, are charging excessive prices, or are not satisfying customers in other ways.

- *It can attack small local and regional firms that are not doing the job and are underfinanced.* Several of the major beer companies grew to their present size not by stealing each other's customers but by gobbling up the smaller firms, or "guppies."

Designing Strategies for Leaders, Challengers, Followers, and Nichers

If the attacking company goes after the market leader, its objective might be to wrest a certain share. Thus Bic is under no illusion that it could topple Gillette in the razor market—it is simply seeking a larger share. If the attacking company goes after a small local company, its objective might be to drive that company out of existence.

Choosing a General Attack Strategy

Given clear opponents and objectives, what options are available in attacking an enemy? We can make progress by imagining an opponent who occupies a certain market territory. We distinguish among five attack strategies shown in Figure 13-6.

FRONTAL ATTACK. An aggressor is said to launch a frontal (or "head-on") attack when it masses its forces right up against its opponent. It attacks the opponent's strengths rather than its weaknesses. The outcome depends on who has more strength and endurance. In a pure frontal attack, the attacker matches its opponent's product, advertising, price, and so on. The *principle of force* says that *the side with the greater manpower (resources) will win the engagement*. This rule is modified if the defender has greater firing efficiency through enjoying a terrain advantage (such as holding a mountaintop). The military dogma is that for a frontal attack to succeed against a well-entrenched opponent or one controlling the "high ground," the attacking forces must deploy at least a 3:1 advantage in combat firepower. If the aggressor has a smaller force or poorer firepower than the defender, a frontal attack amounts to a suicide mission and makes no sense. The runner-up

FIGURE 13-6
Attack Strategies

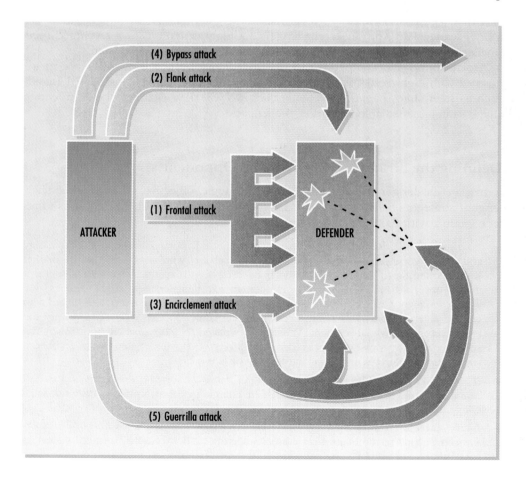

razor-blade manufacturer in Brazil attacked Gillette, the market leader. The attacker was asked if it was offering the consumer a better razor blade. "No," was the reply. "A lower price?" "No." "A better package?" "No." "A more clever advertising campaign?" "No." "Better allowances to the trade?" "No." "Then how do you expect to take share away from Gillette?" "Sheer determination" was the reply. Needless to say, the competitor's offensive failed.

A frontal attacker needs to add strength to back up its determination, and this is precisely what IBM has been trying to do since Microsoft has reduced it to a challenger position in the software industry:

IBM AND MICROSOFT   In 1995 IBM made a hostile takeover bid—Big Blue's first ever—for Lotus Development Corp. The takeover—the biggest in IBM's history—made IBM a serious challenger to Microsoft, which owns 80% of the market for the operating systems and applications suites that run on PC's. IBM wanted Lotus because Lotus Notes is the market leader in networking software. The combination of IBM's marketing muscle and Lotus's technological advantage put Microsoft on the defensive.[22]

As an alternative to a pure frontal attack, the aggressor can launch a modified frontal attack, the most common of which involves cutting its price vis-à-vis the opponent's. Such attacks can take two forms. The more usual ploy is to match the leader's offer on other counts and beat it on price. This can work (1) if the market leader does not retaliate by cutting price and (2) if the competitor convinces the market that its product is equal to the competitor's, but better because it is sold at a lower price. Helene Curtis is a master practitioner of the strategy of convincing the market that its brands—such as Suave and Finesse—are equal in quality but a better value than higher-priced competitors' brands. Curtis makes low-budget imitations of leading high-priced brands and promotes them sometimes with a blatant competitive advertising campaign: "We do what theirs does for less than half the price."

The other form of price-aggressive strategy involves a heavy investment by the attacker to achieve lower production costs and then an attack on competitors on a price basis. Texas Instruments and several Japanese firms had success in launching modified frontal attacks involving price and cost cutting.

FLANK ATTACK. An enemy's army is strongest where it expects to be attacked. It is necessarily less secure in its flanks and rear. Its weak spots (blind sides), therefore, are natural targets for attack. The major principle of modern offensive warfare is *concentration of strength against weakness*. The aggressor may attack the strong side to tie up the defender's troops but will launch the real attack at the side or rear. This maneuver catches the defending army off guard. Flank attacks make excellent marketing sense and are particularly attractive to an aggressor with fewer resources than the opponent. If the aggressor cannot overwhelm the defender with brute strength, it can outmaneuver the defender with subterfuge.

A flank attack can be directed along two strategic dimensions—geographical and segmental. In a geographical attack, the aggressor spots areas where the opponent is underperforming. For example, some of IBM's rivals chose to set up strong sales branches in medium- and smaller-size cities that were relatively neglected by IBM. For example, Honeywell pursued businesses in smaller cities and towns where it did not have to battle against large numbers of IBM salespeople.

The other flanking strategy is to spot uncovered market needs not being served by the leaders, as Japanese automakers did when choosing to serve the growing consumer market for fuel-efficient cars, and as Miller Brewing Company did when it discovered the consumer market for light beer.

A flanking strategy is another name for identifying shifts in market segments

Designing Strategies for Leaders, Challengers, Followers, and Nichers

that are causing gaps to develop, then rushing in to fill the gaps and develop them into strong segments. Instead of a bloody battle between two or more companies trying to serve the same market, flanking leads to a fuller coverage of the market's varied needs. Flanking is in the best tradition of modern marketing philosophy, which holds that the purpose of marketing is to discover needs and satisfy them. Flank attacks are much more likely to be successful than frontal attacks.

ENCIRCLEMENT ATTACK. The encirclement maneuver is an attempt to capture a wide slice of the enemy's territory through a comprehensive "blitz" attack. Encirclement involves launching a grand offensive on several fronts, so that the enemy must protect its front, sides, and rear simultaneously. The aggressor may offer the market everything the opponent offers and more, so that the offer is unrefusable. Encirclement makes sense where the aggressor commands superior resources and believes that a swift encirclement will break the opponent's will. Here is an example:

SEIKO Seiko, the Japanese watch manufacturer, expanded distribution in every major watch market and overwhelmed its competitors with an enormous variety of models. In the United States, it offers 400 watch models; globally it makes and sells 2,300 models. "They hit the mark on fashion, features, user preferences, and everything else that might motivate the consumer," said an admiring vice-president of a U.S. competitor.

BYPASS ATTACK. The bypass is the most indirect of assault strategies. It means bypassing the enemy and attacking easier markets to broaden one's resource base. This strategy offers three lines of approach: diversifying into unrelated products, diversifying into new geographical markets, and leapfrogging into new technologies to supplant existing products.

COLGATE At one time, Colgate had the reputation as a stodgy marketer of soap and detergent. Its CEO, David Foster, recognized that any head-on battles with P&G were futile. "They outgunned us three to one at the store level and had three research people to our one." Foster's strategy was simple—increase Colgate's lead abroad and bypass P&G at home by diversifying into non-P&G markets. A string of acquisitions followed in textile and hospital products, cosmetics, and a range of sporting goods and food products. The result: Colgate could comfortably face P&G in several markets and not face it at all in other markets.

Technological leapfrogging is a bypass strategy practiced typically in high-tech industries. Instead of copying the competitor's product and waging a costly frontal attack, the challenger patiently researches and develops the next technology and launches an attack, shifting the battleground to its territory, where it has an advantage. Nintendo's successful attack in the video-game market was precisely about wresting market share by introducing a superior technology and redefining the "competitive space." Now Sega/Genesis is doing the same with more advanced technology, as are the creators of virtual-reality-based entertainment.

GUERRILLA ATTACK. Guerrilla warfare consists of waging small, intermittent attacks on an opponent's different territories. The aim is to harass and demoralize the opponent and eventually secure permanent footholds. Liddell-Hart stated the military rationale:

> *The more usual reason for adopting a strategy of limited aim is that of awaiting a change in the balance of force—a change often sought and achieved by draining the enemy's force, weakening him by pricks instead of risking blows. The essential condition of such a strategy is that the drain on him should be disproportionately greater than on oneself. The object may be sought by raiding his supplies; by local attacks which annihilate or inflict disproportionate loss on parts of his force; by*

bringing him into unprofitable attacks; by causing an excessively wide distribution of his force; and, not least, by exhausting his moral and physical energy.[23]

The guerrilla aggressor uses both conventional and unconventional means to attack the opponent. These include selective price cuts, intense promotional blitzes, and occasional legal actions. Here's an example of a very successful guerrilla strategy:

THE PRINCETON REVIEW Founded by Stanley H. Kaplan in 1938, Kaplan Educational Centers spent nearly half a century developing the market for its test-coaching services and building a national chain. By the 1980s, Kaplan had become the largest test-prep business in the United States. Then a young Princeton graduate named John Katzman burst on the scene with a competing company, The Princeton Review, and a spate of guerrilla marketing actions. Most of the attacks were levied against Kaplan's image, which was, as one former student put it, "dull as dirt." The Princeton Review's ads were brash, to say the least: "Stanley's a wimp," some proclaimed. Others said, "Friends don't let friends take Kaplan," while touting the Princeton Review's smaller, livelier classes. Katzman himself appropriated Kaplan's name on the Internet so he could post horror stories about his competitor. The company even picked fights with the Educational Testing Service (ETS), which administers the standardized tests that test-prep companies coach students to take, and earned a reputation as a champion of students' rights. By the 1990s, Princeton Review's guerrilla warfare had paid off. The company was no longer an upstart but rather the market leader, at least in the SAT market (Kaplan still holds a 60% share in the grad-school exam market).

The guerrilla attack by Princeton Review turned out to be a badly needed wake-up call for Kaplan. Determined to abolish its stodgy image and earn back its market share, Kaplan hired a young marketing director and was soon plastering hip-looking ads all over buses, billboards, and subway posters. Now, with such fierce and focused competition, both Stanley Kaplan and the Princeton Review are compelled to innovate constantly and seek competitive advantages and opportunities outside the current market. For a look at some of the other benefits of an intense rivalry, see the Marketing Memo on page 392 titled "The Spoils of War."[24]

Normally, guerrilla warfare is practiced by a smaller firm against a larger one. It is a case of David attacking Goliath. Unable to mount an effective frontal or flank attack, the smaller firm launches a barrage of short promotional and price attacks in random corners of the larger opponent's market in a manner calculated to gradually weaken the opponent's market power. Even here, the attacker has to decide between launching a few major attacks or a continual stream of minor attacks. Military dogma holds that a continual stream of minor attacks usually creates more cumulative impact, disorganization, and confusion in the enemy than a few major attacks. Thus the guerrilla attacker would find it more effective to attack small, isolated, weakly defended markets rather than major stronghold markets like New York, Chicago, and Los Angeles, where the defender is better entrenched and more willing to retaliate quickly and decisively.

It would be a mistake to think of a guerrilla campaign as only a "low-resource" strategy alternative available to financially weak challengers. Conducting a continual guerrilla campaign can be expensive, although admittedly less expensive than a frontal, flank, or encirclement attack. Furthermore, guerrilla war is more a preparation for war than a war itself. Ultimately it must be backed by a stronger attack if the aggressor hopes to beat the opponent.

Choosing a Specific Attack Strategy

The five attack strategies we just discussed are very broad. The challenger must put together a total strategy consisting of several specific strategies. Market challengers can choose from several specific attack strategies:

Designing Strategies for Leaders, Challengers, Followers, and Nichers

◆ *Price-discount strategy:* The challenger can sell a comparable product at a lower price. This is the essential strategy of discount retailers, such as Best Buy and Office Depot. For a price-discount strategy to work, three conditions must be fulfilled. First, the challenger must convince buyers that its product and service are comparable to the leader's. Second, the buyers must be sensitive to the price difference and feel comfortable about shifting their suppliers. Third, the market leader must refuse to cut its price in spite of the competitor's attack.

◆ *Cheaper-goods strategy:* The challenger can offer an average- or low-quality product at a much lower price. For example, Little Debbie snack cakes are lower in quality than Drake's but sell at less than half the price. This strategy works when there is a sufficient segment of buyers who are interested only in price. Firms that establish themselves through this strategy, however, can be attacked by "cheaper-goods" firms whose prices are even lower. In defense, they can try to upgrade their quality over time.

◆ *Prestige-goods strategy:* A market challenger can launch a higher-quality product and charge a higher price than the leader. Mercedes gained on Cadillac in the U.S. market by offering a car of higher quality and higher price. Some prestige-goods firms later roll out lower-price products to take advantage of their charisma.

◆ *Product-proliferation strategy:* The challenger can attack the leader by launching a larger product variety, thus giving buyers more choice. Baskin-Robbins achieved its growth in the fountain ice cream business by promoting more ice cream flavors—31— than its larger competitors.

◆ *Product-innovation strategy:* The challenger might pursue product innovation to attack the leader's position. 3M typically enters new markets by introducing a product improvement or breakthrough. The public often gains most from challenger strategies oriented toward product innovation.

◆ *Improved-services strategy:* The challenger can try to offer new or better services to customers. IBM achieved its early success by recognizing that customers were more interested in software and service than in hardware. Avis's famous attack on Hertz, "We're only second. We try harder," was based on promising and delivering cleaner cars and faster service than Hertz.

◆ *Distribution-innovation strategy:* A challenger might discover or develop a new channel of distribution. Avon became a major cosmetics company by perfecting door-to-door selling instead of battling other cosmetic firms in conventional stores. U.S. Time Company achieved great success by selling its low-price Timex watches through mass-merchandise channels instead of jewelry stores.

◆ *Manufacturing-cost-reduction strategy:* The challenger might pursue lower manufacturing costs than its competitors through more efficient purchasing, lower labor costs, and/or more modern production equipment. The company can use its lower costs to price more aggressively to gain market share. This strategy has been critical to the successful Japanese invasion of world markets.

◆ *Intensive advertising promotion:* Some challengers attack the leader by increasing their expenditures on advertising and promotion. Miller Beer outspent Budweiser in its attempt to increase its market share of the U.S. beer market. Substantial promotional spending, however, is usually not a sensible strategy unless the challenger's product or advertising message exhibits superiority over competition.

A challenger rarely improves its market share by relying on only one strategy. Its success depends on combining several principles to improve its position over time.

MARKET-FOLLOWER STRATEGIES

Some years ago, Theodore Levitt wrote an article titled "Innovative Imitation," in which he argued that a strategy of *product imitation* might be as profitable as a strategy of *product innovation.*[25] An innovator, such as Sony, bears the huge expense of developing new products, getting them into distribution, and informing and educating the market. The reward for all this work and risk is normally market leadership. However, other firms can copy or improve on the new products. For example, Panasonic rarely innovates. Rather, it copies Sony's new products, then sells them at lower prices. Panasonic turns a higher profit than Sony because it did not bear the innovation and education expense. Sony regards Panasonic as a bitter enemy.

Many runner-up/follower companies prefer to follow rather than challenge the market leader. But leaders never take lightly any effort to draw away their customers. If the runner-up's lure is lower prices, improved service, or additional product features, the leader can quickly match these to diffuse the attack. The leader probably has more staying power in an all-out battle. Because a hard fight might leave both firms worse off, the runner-up firm must think carefully before attacking. Unless the runner-up can launch a preemptive strike—in the form of a substantial product innovation or distribution breakthrough—it will often prefer to follow rather than attack the leader.

Patterns of "conscious parallelism" are common in capital-intensive homogeneous-product industries, such as steel, fertilizers, and chemicals. The opportunities for product differentiation and image differentiation are low; service quality is often comparable; and price sensitivity runs high. Price wars can erupt at any time. The mood in these industries is against short-run grabs for market share because

Designing Strategies for
Leaders, Challengers,
Followers, and Nichers

that strategy only provokes retaliation. Most firms decide against stealing each other's customers. Instead, they present similar offers to buyers, usually by copying the leader. Market shares show a high stability.

This is not to say that market followers lack strategies. A market follower must know how to hold current customers and win a fair share of new customers. Each follower tries to bring distinctive advantages to its target market—location, services, financing. And, because the follower is often a major target of attack by challengers, it must keep its manufacturing costs low and its product quality and services high. It must also enter new markets as they open up.

Followership is usually not the same as being passive or a carbon copy of the leader. The follower has to define a growth path, but one that does not invite competitive retaliation. Four broad followership strategies can be distinguished:

◆ *Counterfeiter:* The counterfeiter duplicates the leader's product and package and sells it on the black market or through disreputable dealers. Firms such as Apple Computer and Rolex are plagued with the counterfeiter problem, especially in the Far East, and are seeking ways to defeat counterfeiters.

◆ *Cloner:* The cloner emulates the leader's products, distribution, advertising, and so on. The cloner's product and packaging may resemble the leader's, while the brand name might be slightly different, such as "Coko-Cola" instead of "Coca-Cola." The cloner parasitically lives off the market leader's investments. For example, Ralcorp Holding Inc. sells imitations of name-brand cereals in lookalike boxes. Its Tasteeos, Fruit Rings, and Corn Flakes (Figure 13-7) sell for nearly a $1 a box less than the leading name brands. In the computer business, clones are a fact of life. Most IBM competitors in the PC market began by cloning IBM PC's.[26]

◆ *Imitator:* The imitator copies some things from the leader but maintains differentiation in terms of packaging, advertising, pricing, and so on. The leader doesn't mind the imitator as long as the imitator doesn't attack the leader aggressively. The imitator even helps the leader avoid the charge of monopoly.

◆ *Adapter:* The adapter takes the leader's products and adapts or improves them. The adapter may choose to sell to different markets to avoid direct confrontation with the leader. But often the adapter grows into the future challenger, as many Japanese firms have done after adapting and improving products developed elsewhere.

What does a follower firm earn? Although a follower doesn't bear innovation expenses, it normally earns less than the leader. For example, a study of food processing companies showed the largest firm averaging a 16% return on investment;

FIGURE 13-7

Cloned Brands

Source: Rob Doyle, *Business Week*, June 26, 1995.

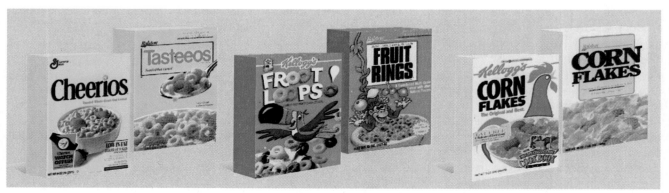

the number-two firm, 6%; the number-three firm, − 1%; and number-four firm, − 6 percent. In this case, only the top two firms have profits, and the number-two firm's profits are nothing to brag about. No wonder Jack Welch, CEO of GE, told his business units that each must reach the number-one or -two position in its market or else! Thus followership is not often a rewarding path to pursue.

MARKET-NICHER STRATEGIES

An alternative to being a follower in a large market is to be a leader in a small market, or niche (see the discussion of niches in Chapter 9). Smaller firms normally avoid competing with larger firms by targeting small markets of little or no interest to the larger firms. Here are two examples:

LOGITECH INTER-NATIONAL   Logitech has become a $300 million global success story by making every variation of computer mouse imaginable. Producing a mouse every 1.6 seconds, the company turns out mice for left- and right-handed people, cordless mice that use radio waves, mice shaped like real mice for children, and 3-D mice that let the user appear to move behind screen objects. Breeding only computer mice has been so successful that Logitech dominates the world market, with Microsoft as its runner-up.[27]

TECNOL MEDICAL PRODUCTS   By focusing on hospital face masks, Tecnol Medical Products competes against two giants: Johnson & Johnson and 3M. Tecnol has transformed an ordinary face mask into a lucrative line of specialty masks that shield health-care workers from infection. Now the little-known company has surpassed J&J and 3M to become the top mask supplier to U.S. hospitals.[28]

Yet cultivating a niche is only one facet of these companies' success. For instance, Tecnol's ultimate success in market niching can be attributed to its ability to (1) pick its fight carefully (surgical masks are small potatoes to J&J and 3M), (2) keep costs down by developing and producing its product in-house, (3) innovate constantly by bringing out a dozen new products a year, and (4) acquire smaller rivals to help stretch and expand its product offering.

Increasingly, even large firms are setting up business units, or companies, to serve niches. Here are some examples of large profitable companies that have pursued niching strategies:

THE BEER INDUSTRY   Microbrewers' specialty beers—such as Pyramid Ale and Pete's Wicked Ale—are the only beer market showing any growth potential in the late 1990s. This fact has prompted the Big Four brewers—Anheuser Busch, Miller, Adolph Coors, and Stroh Brewery—to launch their own specialty beers. For instance, there's Anheuser's Elk Mountain ale, Miller's Red Dog and Icehouse beers, and Coors's George Killian. But because consumers don't want to buy their specialty beers from the big players in the market, some of these companies keep their names off the label. Miller even advertises its Red Dog and Icehouse beers as coming from Plank Road Brewery. Consumers in the know might figure out that Plank Road was the name of a 19th-century Milwaukee brewery that has long since faded away.[29]

ILLINOIS TOOL WORKS   Illinois Tool Works (ITW) manufactures thousands of products, including nails, screws, plastic six-pack holders for soda cans, bicycle helmets, backpacks, plastic buckles for pet collars, resealable food packages, and so on. ITW has 90 highly autonomous divisions. When one division commercializes a new product, the product and personnel are spun off into a new entity.

The main point is that firms with low shares of the total market can be highly profitable through smart niching. Clifford and Cavanagh identified over two dozen highly successful mid-size companies and studied their success factors.[30] They

Designing Strategies for Leaders, Challengers, Followers, and Nichers

Strategies for Entering Markets Held by Incumbent Firms

What marketing strategies can companies use to enter a market held by incumbent firms? Biggadike examined the strategies of 40 invading firms. He found that 10 firms entered at a lower price, 9 matched the incumbents' prices, and 21 entered at a higher price. While 28 claimed superior quality, 5 matched incumbents' quality, and 7 reported inferior product quality. Most entrants offered a specialist product line and served a narrower market segment. Less than 20% managed to innovate a new channel of distribution. Over half the entrants offered a higher level of customer service. Over half the entrants spent less than incumbents on sales force, advertising, and promotion. Thus, the winning marketing mix of entrants was (1) higher prices and higher quality, (2) narrower product line, (3) narrower market segment, (4) similar distribution channels, (5) superior service, and (6) lower expenditure on sales force, advertising, and promotion.

Carpenter and Nakamoto examined strategies for launching a new product into a market dominated by one brand such as Jell-O or Federal Express. (These brands, which include many market pioneers, are particularly difficult to attack because many are the standard against which others are judged. A slightly different new brand, therefore, can be perceived as less attractive, and a similar one can be seen as offering nothing unique.) They identified four strategies that have good profit potential in this situation:

- *Differentiation*—positioning away from the dominant brand with a comparable or premium price and heavy advertising spending to establish the new brand as a credible alternative to the dominant brand. Example: Honda's motorcycle challenges Harley Davidson.

- *Challenger*—positioning close to the dominant brand with heavy advertising spending and comparable or premium price to challenge the dominant brand as the category standard. Examples: Pepsi competing against Coke, Avis competing against Hertz.

- *Niche*—positioning away from the dominant brand with a high price and a low advertising budget to exploit a profitable, remaining niche. Example: Tom's of Maine all-natural toothpaste competing against Crest.

- *Premium*—positioning near the dominant brand with little advertising spending but a premium price to move "up market" relative to the dominant brand. Examples: Godiva chocolate and Haagen-Dazs ice cream competing against standard brands.

Schnaars examined the strategies of successful invading firms that entered incumbent-occupied markets and eventually overtook leadership. He detailed more than 30 cases in which the imitator displaced the innovator, including:

Product	*Innovator*	*Imitator*
Word processing software	Word Star	WordPerfect
Spreadsheet software	Unicalc	Lotus 1-2-3
Credit cards	Diners' Club	Visa and MasterCard
Ball-point pens	Reynolds	Parker
CAT scanners	EMI	General Electric
Hand calculators	Bowmar	Texas Instruments
Food processors	Cuisinart	Black & Decker

The imitators captured the market by offering lower prices, selling an improved product, or using superior market power and resources. The innovators often failed because of complacency, poor management, poor product quality, or inadequate resources to compete with the invaders.

Sources: See Ralph Biggadike, *Entering New Markets: Strategies and Performance* (Cambridge, MA: Marketing Science Institute, 1977), pp. 12–20; Gregory S. Carpenter and Kent Nakamoto, "Competitive Strategies for Late Entry into a Market with a Dominant Brand," *Management Science,* October 1990, pp. 1268–78; Gregory S. Carpenter and Kent Nakamoto, "Competitive Late Mover Strategies," working paper, Northwestern University, 1993; and Steven P. Schnaars, *Managing Imitation Strategies: How Later Entrants Seize Markets from Pioneers* (New York: Free Press, 1994).

found that virtually all these companies were nichers. One example is A. T. Cross, which niched itself in the high-price pen-and-pencil market with its famous gold writing instruments that many executives, managers, and professionals own. Instead of manufacturing all types of writing instruments, A. T. Cross has stuck to the high-price niche and enjoyed great sales growth and profit. Other factors shared by successful niche companies include offering high value, charging a premium price, achieving lower manufacturing costs, and shaping a strong corporate culture and vision.

In a study of hundreds of business units, the Strategic Planning Institute found that the return on investment averaged 27% in smaller markets, but only 11% in larger markets.[31] Why is niching so profitable? The main reason is that the market nicher ends up knowing the target customers so well that it meets their needs better than other firms that are selling to this niche casually. As a result, the nicher can charge a substantial markup over costs because of the perceived added value. The nicher achieves *high margin,* while the mass marketer achieves *high volume.*

Nichers have three tasks: creating niches, expanding niches, and protecting niches. For example, Nike, the athletic shoe company, is constantly creating new niches by designing shoes for different sports and exercises such as hiking, walking, cycling, cheerleading, windsurfing, and so on. After creating a market for a particular use, Nike then expands the niche by designing different versions (for example, walking shoes specialized for those who walk fast versus slow, and for those who are thin versus heavy) and brands (for example, Nike Air Jordans versus Nike Airwalkers). Finally, Nike must protect its leadership position as new competitors enter the niche.

Niching carries a major risk in that the market niche might dry up or be attacked. The company is then stuck with highly specialized resources that may not have high-value alternative uses. For example, Minnetonka, a small Minnesota company, developed a liquid soap in a dispenser that provided aesthetics and convenience in the bathroom. The soap was purchased by some households as a specialty item. But when the larger firms noticed this niche, they invaded it and turned it from a niche into a supersegment, and Minnetonka's share suffered.

Niche Specialization

The key idea in nichemanship is specialization. The following specialist roles are open to nichers:

- *End-user specialist:* The firm specializes in serving one type of end-use customer. For example, a law firm can specialize in the criminal, civil, or business law markets. Computer companies are among the newest converts to end-user specialization, except they call it *vertical marketing.* For years, computer companies sold general hardware and software systems across many markets and the price battles got rough. Smaller companies started to specialize by vertical slices—law firms, medical practices, banks, and the like—studying the specific hardware and software needs of their target group and designing high value-added products that had a competitive advantage over more general products. Their sales forces were trained to understand and service the particular vertical market. Computer companies also worked with independent *value-added resellers (VARs)* who customized the computer hardware and software for individual clients or customer segments and earned a price premium in the process.[32]

- *Vertical-level specialist:* The firm specializes at some vertical level of the production-distribution value chain. For example, a copper firm may concentrate on producing raw copper, copper components, or finished copper products.

- *Customer-size specialist:* The firm concentrates on selling to either small, medium-size, or large customers. Many nichers specialize in serving small customers who are neglected by the majors.

- *Specific-customer specialist:* The firm limits its selling to one or a few major customers. Many firms sell their entire output to a single company, such as Sears or General Motors.

- *Geographic specialist:* The firm sells only in a certain locality, region, or area of the world.

- *Product or product-line specialist:* The firm carries or produces only one product or product line. For example, a firm may specialize in producing lenses for microscopes. A retailer may carry only ties or socks, as the British chains Tie Rack and Socks-Box do.

- *Product-feature specialist:* The firm specializes in producing a certain type of product feature. Rent-a-Wreck, for example, is a car-rental agency that rents only "beat-up" cars.
- *Job-shop specialist:* The firm customizes its products for individual customers.
- *Quality/price specialist:* The firm operates at the low- or high- quality ends of the market. For example, Hewlett Packard specializes in the high-quality, high-price end of the hand-calculator market.
- *Service specialist:* The firm offers one or more services not available from other firms. An example would be a bank that takes loan requests over the phone and hand delivers the money to the customer.
- *Channel specialist:* The firm specializes in serving only one channel of distribution. For example, a soft-drink company decides to make a very large-size soft drink available only at gas stations.

Because niches can weaken, the firm must continually create new niches. The firm should "stick to its niching" but not necessarily to its niche. That is why *multiple niching* is preferable to *single niching*. By developing strength in two or more niches the company increases its chances for survival.

Firms entering a market should aim at a niche initially rather than the whole market. The Marketing Insight on page 396 titled "Strategies for Entering Markets Held by Incumbent Firms" describes the major strategies used by several firms that entered occupied markets. Most of them chose a niching strategy.

SUMMARY

1. Marketing strategies are highly dependent on whether the company is a market leader, challenger, follower, or nicher.

2. A market leader has the largest market share in the relevant product market. To remain the dominant firm, the leader engages in three activities. First, it looks for ways to expand total market demand by seeking new users, new uses, and more usage of its products. Second, it attempts to protect its current market share through a position, flank, preemptive, counteroffensive, mobile, or contraction defense strategy. The most sophisticated leaders cover themselves by doing everything right, leaving no openings for competitive attack. Third, it may try to increase its market share. Such a strategy makes sense if profitability increases at higher market share levels and if the company does not have to worry about antitrust action.

3. A market challenger attacks the market leader and other competitors in an aggressive bid for more market share. Challengers can choose from five types of general attack: frontal, flank, encirclement, bypass, guerrilla, or any combination of these. In terms of specific attack strategies, challengers can discount prices, produce cheaper goods, produce prestige goods, produce a wide variety of goods, innovate widely in products or distribution, improve services, reduce manufacturing costs, or engage in intensive advertising.

4. A market follower is a runner-up firm (behind the market leader) that is willing to maintain its market share and not rock the boat. However, even market followers must have strategies aimed at maintaining and increasing market share and expanding the market. A follower can play the role of counterfeiter, cloner, imitator, or adapter.

5. A market nicher is a firm that serves small market segments not being served by larger firms. While nichers have traditionally been smaller firms, several larger firms today are pursuing niche strategies. The key to nichemanship is specialization. Nichers can select one or more of the following areas of specialization: end user, vertical level, customer size, specific customer, geographic, product or product line, product feature, job shop, quality/price, service, or channel. Multiple niching is generally preferable to single niching.

1. Over the last decade the cola wars have been waged between the two major cola companies, but now it looks like a new kid is vying for a larger market share. In its recent acquisition of the Dr. Pepper-7Up companies, Cadbury-Schweppes increased its U.S. market share from 4% to 16% and paved the way for Dr. Pepper-7Up's overseas expansion. Who is the market leader in the cola and soft-drink market? Who is the challenger? Suggest a course of action for Cadbury-Schweppes to follow in a market that consists of only these two other major players.

2. In 1986 a headline in *Business Week* proclaimed, "How Ford Hit the Bull's-Eye with Taurus." A subheadline read, "A Team Approach Borrowed from Japan Has Produced the Hottest U.S. Car in Years."

   Before designing the Taurus, Ford bought a Honda Accord and a Toyota Corolla, trying to find things that it could copy or make better than its target competition. Ford also conducted customer-preference studies to discover what "little things" its potential customers would like to have on their cars. All this research has paid off—by the early 1990s the Ford Taurus was America's number-one selling car, replacing the Honda Accord, which had held the number-one position for a number of years. What are some strategies that the challenger, Honda Accord, could now employ to take the market back from Ford?

3. As markets mature, they tend to acquire a fixed set of suppliers, competitors, distributors, and customers. A closed system seems to develop in which these groups of players join forces to protect themselves from intruders. This situation is often supported by outside groups such as government regulatory boards, labor unions, business associations, lending institutions, and the like.

   Roger Billings has invented a hydrogen-powered automobile that makes use of nuclear energy. What are some of the challenges Billings is likely to face in bringing this product to the market? Do you think the market leaders or challengers in the auto industry would be interested in partnering with Billings to produce a hydrogen car? Could a market niche be developed? How might Billings proceed?

4. When personal computers were first introduced, IBM chose not to enter the market. IBM was already the market leader in the mainframe computer industry. It saw the personal computer primarily as a "toy" and did not want to risk its solid reputation on what could prove to be a fad.

   Of course, IBM is now a major player in the PC industry. Identify the market leaders, challengers, followers, and nichers in the personal computer industry. What are some of the strategies they employ? What additional strategies would you recommend?

5. Burger King has had its share of problems in finding a strategy it is comfortable with—it dumped four major ad campaigns from 1985 to 1987. Its "Best Food in Fast Times" campaign was not received well by either customers or franchisees, and the "Battle of the Burgers" and "Herb" campaigns were equally unpopular. It has been Burger King's inability to find a successful market-challenger strategy that has kept its market share relatively stagnant.

   Which market-challenger strategies might Burger King use to improve its market share? Keep in mind that the company's attempts to generate growth through new-product introductions have not set it apart from McDonald's or Wendy's. Thus, BK has not found a frontal attack (the "Battle of the Burgers" campaign) or flank attack (the introduction of mini-hamburgers called Burger Bundles) to work effectively. An improved-services strategy has not worked either; table service was scrapped shortly after it was introduced.

6. Comment on the following statements made about the appropriate marketing strategy of smaller firms:
   a. "The smaller firm should concentrate on pulling away the larger firm's customers, while the larger firm should concentrate on stimulating new customers to enter the market."
   b. "Larger firms should pioneer new products, and smaller ones should copy them."

Designing Strategies for
Leaders, Challengers,
Followers, and Nichers

7. You are part of a product-management team for a Lever Brothers laundry-detergent line. Your group's objective is to challenge P&G's laundry-detergent line and to become the market leader, but you are not sure how you should proceed. Discuss the pros and cons of each of the following strategies in this market: (a) frontal attack, (b) flank attack, (c) encirclement attack, (d) bypass attack, and (e) guerrilla attack.

8. Using the list of market-nicher strategies from the text (end-user specialist, vertical-level specialist, customer-size specialist, specific-customer specialist, geographic specialist, product or product-line specialist, product-feature specialist, job-shop specialist, quality/price specialist, service specialist, channel specialist), identify a company (other than one identified in the chapter) that employs each strategy, and describe briefly how the company has implemented this strategy.

9. In Chapter 11, we discussed the challenges of bringing new products to market. Development costs are generally very high. For this reason, a strategy of product imitation might be as profitable as (or more profitable than) a strategy of product innovation. In addition to the costs of developing a new product, what other challenges arise for a company that has pioneered a new product?

NOTES

1. See Robert V. L. Wright, *A System For Managing Diversity* (Cambridge, MA: Arthur D. Little, 1974).
2. See Jordan P. Yale, "The Strategy of Nylon's Growth," *Modern Textiles Magazine,* February 1964, pp. 32 ff. Also see Theodore Levitt, "Exploit the Product Life Cycle," *Harvard Business Review,* November—December 1965, pp. 81–94.
3. See Eric von Hippel, "A Customer-Active Paradigm for Industrial Product Idea Generation," working paper, Sloan School of Management, MIT, Cambridge, MA, May 1977.
4. See Carla Rapoport, "You Can Make Money in Japan," *Fortune,* February 12, 1990, pp. 85–92; Keith H. Hammonds, "A Moment Kodak Wants to Capture," *Business Week,* August 27, 1990, pp. 52–53; Alison Fahey, "Polaroid, Kodak, Fuji Get Clicking," *Advertising Age,* May 20, 1991, p. 18; and Peter Nulty, "The New Look of Photography," *Fortune,* July 1, 1991, pp. 36–41.
5. Sun Tsu, *The Art of War* (London: Oxford University Press, 1963); Miyamoto Mushashi, *A Book of Five Rings* (Woodstock, NY: Overlook Press, 1974); Carl von Clausewitz, *On War* (London: Routledge & Kegan Paul, 1908); and B. H. Liddell-Hart, *Strategy* (New York: Praeger, 1967).
6. These six defense strategies, as well as the five attack strategies, are taken from Philip Kotler and Ravi Singh, "Marketing Warfare in the 1980s," *Journal of Business Strategy,* Winter 1981, pp. 30–41. For additional reading, see Gerald A. Michaelson, *Winning the Marketing War: A Field Manual for Business Leaders,* 2d ed. (Knoxville, TN: Pressmark, 1993); Al Ries and Jack Trout, *Marketing Warfare* (New York: McGraw-Hill, 1986); Jay Conrad Levinson, *Guerrilla Marketing* (Boston, MA: Houghton-Mifflin, 1984); and Barrie G. James, *Business Wargames* (Harmondsworth, England: Penguin Books, 1984).
7. Betsy Spethmann, "Nabisco Leverage: SnackWell's Push," *Brandweek,* March 27, 1995, pp. 1, 6.
8. See Michael E. Porter, *Competitive Strategy* (New York: Free Press, 1980), Chapter 4.
9. Terry Lefton, "Truth Hurts AT&T's Rivals," *Adweek (Eastern Ed.) Superbrands 1995 Supplement,* 1995, pp. 128–32.
10. *Relative market share* is the business's market share in its served market relative to the combined market share of its three leading competitors, expressed as a percentage. For example, if this business has 30% of the market and its three largest competitors have 20%, 10%, and 10%: 30/(20 + 10 + 10) = 75% relative market share.
11. Sidney Schoeffler, Robert D. Buzzell, and Donald F. Heany, "Impact of Strategic Planning on Profit Performance," *Harvard Business Review,* March–April 1974, pp. 137–45; and Robert D. Buzzell, Bradley T. Gale, and Ralph G. M. Sultan, "Market Share—A Key to Profitability," *Harvard Business Review,* January–February 1975, pp. 97–106.
12. See Buzzell et al., "Market Share," pp. 97, 100. The results held up in later PIMS studies, where the database included 2,600 business units in a wide range of industries. See Robert D. Buzzell and Bradley T. Gale, *The PIMS Principles: Linking Strategy to Performance* (New York: Free Press, 1987).
13. Richard G. Hamermesh, M. J. Anderson, Jr., and J. E. Harris, "Strategies for Low Market Share Businesses," *Harvard Business Review,* May–June 1978, pp. 95–102.
14. Carolyn Y. Woo and Arnold C. Cooper, "The Surprising Case for Low Market Share," *Harvard Business Review,* November–December 1982, pp. 106–13; also see their "Market-Share Leadership—Not Always So Good," *Harvard Business Review,* January–February 1984, pp. 2–4.
15. John D. C. Roach, "From Strategic Planning to Strategic Performance: Closing the Achievement Gap," *Outlook,* (New York: Booz, Allen & Hamilton, 1981), p. 21. This curve assumes that pre-tax return on sales is highly correlated with profitability and that company revenue is a surrogate for market share. Michael Porter, in his *Competitive Strategy,* page 43, shows a similar **V**-shaped curve.
16. Steve Lohr, "Gates, the Pragmatist, Walked Away," *The New York Times,* May 22, 1995, D1:2.
17. Philip Kotler and Paul N. Bloom, "Strategies for High Market-Share Companies," *Harvard Business Review,* November–December 1975, pp. 63–72. Also see Michael E. Porter, *Competitive Advantage* (New York: Free Press, 1985), pp. 221–26.
18. Robert D. Buzzell and Frederick D. Wiersema, "Successful Share-Building Strategies," *Harvard Business Review,* January–February, 1981, pp. 135–44.
19. Faye Rice, "The King of Suds Reigns Again," *Fortune,* August 4, 1986, pp. 120–34; Bill Kelley, "Komatsu in Cat Fight," *Sales*

and *Marketing Management,* April 1986, pp. 50–53; and Ronald Henkoff, "This Cat Is Acting Like a Tiger," *Fortune,* December 19, 1988, pp. 71–76.

20. Zachary Schiller, "Ed Artzt's Elbow Grease Has P&G Shining," *Business Week,* October 10, 1994, pp. 84–85.

21. See Robert J. Dolan, "Models of Competition: A Review of Theory and Empirical Evidence," in *Review of Marketing,* ed. Ben M. Enis and Kenneth J. Roering (Chicago: American Marketing Association, 1981), pp. 224–34.

22. Amy Cortese, "Gerstner at the Gates," *Business Week,* June 19, 1995, pp. 36–38.

23. Liddell-Hart, *Strategy,* p. 335.

24. Anne Murphy, "Enemies, a Love Story," *Inc.,* April 1995, pp. 77–81.

25. Theodore Levitt, "Innovative Imitation," *Harvard Business Review,* September–October 1966, pp. 63 ff. Also see Steven P. Schnaars, *Managing Imitation Strategies: How Later Entrants Seize Markets from Pioneers* (New York: Free Press, 1994).

26. Greg Burns, "A Fruit Loop by Any Other Name," *Business Week,* June 26, 1995, pp. 72, 76.

27. Allen J. McGrath, "Growth Strategies with a '90s Twist," *Across the Board,* March 1995, pp. 43–46.

28. Stephanie Anderson, "Who's Afraid of J&J and 3M?" *Business Week,* December 5, 1994, pp. 66–68.

29. Richard A. Melcher, "From the Microbrewers Who Brought You Bud, Coors. . . ," *Business Week,* April 24, 1995, pp. 66–70.

30. Donald K. Clifford and Richard E. Cavanagh, *The Winning Performance: How America's High- and Midsize Growth Companies Succeed* (New York: Bantam Books, 1985).

31. Reported in E. R. Linneman and L. J. Stanton, *Making Niche Marketing Work* (New York: McGraw-Hill, 1991).

32. See Bro Uttal, "Pitching Computers to Small Businesses," *Fortune,* April 1, 1985, pp. 95–104; also see Stuart Gannes, "The Riches in Market Niches," *Fortune,* April 27, 1987, pp. 227–30.

Designing Strategies for
Leaders, Challengers,
Followers, and Nichers

DESIGNING AND MANAGING GLOBAL MARKETING STRATEGIES

A traveler without knowledge is like a bird without wings.

SA'DI, GULISTAN (1258)

❖

We strategize and resource globally, manufacture regionally, and market locally. . . . We leverage brand strengths while keeping a tight focus on local customer preferences.

HERBERT BAUM, FORMER PRESIDENT, CAMPBELL'S SOUP

❖

The world is rapidly shrinking with the advent of faster communication, transportation, and financial flows. Products developed in one country—Gucci purses, Monte Blanc pens, McDonald's hamburgers, Japanese sushi, Pierre Cardin suits, German BMWs—are finding enthusiastic acceptance in other countries. We would not be surprised to hear about a German businessman wearing an Italian suit meeting an English friend at a Japanese restaurant who later returns home to drink Russian vodka and watch *Melrose Place* on TV.

True, many companies have been conducting international marketing for decades. Nestlé, Shell, Bayer, and Toshiba are familiar to most consumers around the world. But today global competition is intensifying. Domestic companies that never thought about foreign competitors suddenly find these competitors in their backyard. Newspaper headlines report on Japanese victories over U.S. producers in consumer electronics, motorcycles, copying machines, cameras, and watches; the gains of Japanese, German, Swedish, and Korean car imports in the U.S. market; and the loss of textile and shoe markets to Third World imports. Many companies that are thought to be American firms are really foreign firms: Bantam Books, Baskin-Robbins Ice Cream, Capitol Records, Kiwi Shoe Polish, and Lipton Tea.

Although some want to eliminate foreign competition through protective legislation, protectionism in the long run only raises costs and protects inefficient domestic firms. The better way for companies to compete is to continuously improve their products at home and expand into foreign markets.

Ironically, while companies need to enter and compete in foreign markets, the risks are high. There are many challenges here, including shifting borders, unstable governments, foreign-exchange problems, corruption, and technological pirating (Table 14-1, page 404).[1] For this reason, one might conclude that companies are doomed whether they stay at home or go abroad. We would argue that companies selling in global industries have no choice but to internationalize.

❖ A **GLOBAL INDUSTRY** is an industry in which the strategic positions of competitors in major geographic or national markets are fundamentally affected by their overall global positions.[2] A *global firm* is a firm that operates in more than one country and captures R&D, production, logistical, marketing, and financial advantages in its costs and reputation that are not available to purely domestic competitors.

Global firms plan, operate, and coordinate their activities on a worldwide basis. For example, Ford's "world truck" has a European-made cab and a North American–built chassis, is assembled in Brazil, and is imported into the United States for sale. Otis Elevator gets its elevators' door systems from France, small geared parts from Spain, electronics from Germany, and special motor drives from Japan, and uses the United States for systems integration. A company need not be large to sell globally. Small and medium-size firms can practice global nichemanship, as many Scandinavian and Benelux companies do.

In this chapter, we will examine the following questions (Figure 14-1):

♦ **What factors should a company review before deciding to go abroad?**

♦ **How can companies evaluate and select specific foreign markets to enter?**

♦ **What are the major ways of entering a foreign market?**

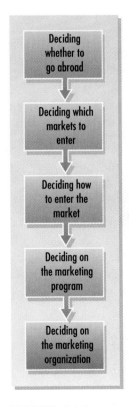

FIGURE 14-1
Major Decisions in International Marketing

DECIDING WHETHER TO GO ABROAD

Most companies would prefer to remain domestic if their domestic market were large enough. Managers would not need to learn another country's language and laws, deal with volatile currencies, face political and legal uncertainties, or redesign their products to suit different customer needs and expectations. Business would be easier and safer.

Yet there are several factors that might draw a company into the international arena:

♦ Global firms offering better products or lower prices might attack the company's domestic market. The company might want to counterattack these competitors in their home markets to tie up their resources.

TABLE 14-1	**CHALLENGES IN INTERNATIONAL MARKETING**

1. *Huge foreign indebtedness:* Many countries have accumulated huge foreign debts on which it is difficult to pay even the interest. Among these countries are Brazil, Poland, and Mexico.
2. *Unstable governments:* High indebtedness, high inflation, and high unemployment in several countries have resulted in high unstable governments that expose foreign firms to the risks of expropriation, nationalization, and limits on profit repatriation. To help guard against these risks, many companies buy political-risk-assessment reports such as Business International's (BI) Country Assessment Service, BERI, or Frost & Sullivan's World Political Risk Forecasts. Using different models and measurement techniques, these services come up with numerical ratings showing each country's current risk level and, in some cases, their expected risk levels three years from now.
3. *Foreign-exchange problems:* High indebtedness and economic and political instability decrease the value of a country's currency. Foreign firms want payment in hard currency with profit-repatriation rights, but these options are not available in many markets.
4. *Foreign-government entry requirements and bureaucracy:* Governments place many regulations on foreign firms. For example, they might require joint ventures with the majority share going to the domestic partner, a high number of nationals to be hired, transfer of technology know-how, and limits on profit repatriation.
5. *Tariffs and other trade barriers:* Governments often impose high tariffs to protect their industries. They also resort to invisible trade barriers such as slowing down important approvals, requiring costly product adjustments, and slowing down inspection or clearance of arriving goods.
6. *Corruption:* Officials in several countries require bribes to cooperate. They award business to the highest briber rather than the lowest bidder. U.S. managers are prohibited by the Foreign Corrupt Practices Act of 1977 from paying bribes, but competitors from other countries operate under no such limitation.
7. *Technological pirating:* A company locating its plant abroad worries about foreign managers learning how to make its product and breaking away to compete openly or clandestinely. This has happened in such diverse areas as machinery, electronics, chemicals, and pharmaceuticals.
8. *High cost of product and communication adaptation:* A company going abroad must study each foreign market carefully; become sensitive to its economics, laws, politics, and culture; and adapt its products and communications to each market's tastes. Otherwise, it might make serious blunders.
9. *Shifting borders:* Many international boundaries are in a state of flux for the first time since 1945. National borders are fundamental to marketing because they dominate and shape economic behavior within the country's borders. Changing boundaries may mean moving targets for marketers.

- The company might discover that some foreign markets present higher profit opportunities than the domestic market.
- The company might need a larger customer base to achieve economies of scale.
- The company might want to reduce its dependence on any one market so as to reduce its risk.
- The company's customers might be going abroad and require international servicing.

Before making a decision to go abroad, the company must weigh several risks:

- The company might not understand foreign customer preferences and fail to offer a competitively attractive product (Table 14-2 lists some famous blunders in this arena).
- The company might not understand the foreign country's business culture or know how to deal effectively with foreign nationals.
- The company might underestimate foreign regulations and incur unexpected costs.
- The company might realize that it lacks managers with international experience.
- The foreign country might change its commercial laws, devalue its currency, or undergo a political revolution and expropriate foreign property.

Because of the competing advantages and risks, companies often don't act until some event thrusts them into the international arena. Someone—a domestic exporter, a foreign importer, a foreign government—solicits the company to sell abroad. Or the company is saddled with overcapacity and must find additional markets for its goods.

DECIDING WHICH MARKETS TO ENTER

In deciding to go abroad, the company needs to define its international marketing objectives and policies. What proportion of foreign to total sales will it seek? Most companies start small when they venture abroad. Some plan to stay small, viewing

TABLE 14-2	**BLUNDERS IN INTERNATIONAL MARKETING**
Hallmark cards bombed when they were introduced in France. The French dislike syrupy sentiment and prefer writing their own cards.	Coca-Cola had to withdraw the two-liter bottle in Spain after discovering that few Spaniards owned refrigerators with large enough compartments.
Philips began to earn a profit in Japan only after it reduced the size of its coffee makers to fit into the smaller Japanese kitchens and its shavers to fit the smaller Japanese hands.	General Foods' Tang initially failed in France because it was positioned as a substitute for orange juice at breakfast. The French drink little orange juice and almost none at breakfast.
Kellogg's Pop-Tarts failed in Britain because the percentage of British homes with toasters was significantly lower than in the United States, and the product was too sweet for British tastes.	General Foods squandered millions trying to introduce packaged cake mixes to Japanese consumers. The company failed to note that only 3% of Japanese homes were equipped with ovens. Then they promoted the idea of baking cakes in Japanese rice cookers, overlooking the fact that the Japanese use their rice cookers throughout the day to keep rice warm and ready.
P&G's Crest toothpaste initially failed in Mexico when it used the U.S. campaign. Mexicans did not care as much for the decay-prevention benefit, nor did scientifically oriented advertising appeal to them.	S. C. Johnson's wax floor polish initially failed in Japan. The wax made the floors too slippery and Johnson had overlooked the fact that Japanese do not wear shoes in their homes.

Designing and
Managing Global
Marketing Strategies

The Last Marketing Frontiers: China, Vietnam, and Cuba

Within hours of the lifting of the 19-year-long U.S. trade embargo against Vietnam, a giant Pepsi can was placed on a main Ho Chi Minh City square. Not to be outdone, Coca-Cola flew in a 30-foot inflatable Coke bottle for a celebration at the city's concert hall. What could be more potent symbols of the United States' entry into one of the world's last Communist countries?

As formerly Communist countries reform their markets, multinational companies are eagerly anticipating the profits that await them. Here are snapshots of three of the world's global marketing frontiers, and the opportunities and challenges that marketers face in these regions.

China: 1.2 Billion Consumers

In Guangdong province, Chinese "yuppies" walk department store aisles to buy $95 Nike or Reebok sneakers or think nothing of spending $4 on a jar of Skippy peanut butter in the supermarket section. While consumers here might make as little as $130 a month, they still have plenty of spending money because of subsidized housing and health care, and lots of savings under the mattress. In Shenzen, Guangdong's second-largest city, consumers have the highest disposable income in all of China—$3,900 annually. With purchasing power like this, a population of 1.2 billion, and the fastest growing economy in the world, China is encouraging foreign companies to set up shop there. Procter & Gamble was one of the first major U.S. companies to enter China; its 1993 sales in China were about $130 million, up 50% from the previous year.

Yet multinationals face a number of hurdles. For one, China is not one market, but many, and regional blockades effectively discriminate against certain goods. Distribution channels are undeveloped and an abysmal infrastructure can turn a rail shipment traveling from Guanzhou to Beijing into a month-long odyssey. Then there's the logistics of supplying thousands of tiny mom-and-pop stores that can afford to stock only a few bottles or packages at a time. Smart firms, such as AlliedSignal, try to jump these hurdles by partnering with Chinese government bodies (in some regions doing so is a prerequisite for establishing a business). Chinese business partners can also be invaluable in penetrating distribution channels and hiring experienced personnel.

A major concern to some U.S. businesses has been China's distressing human-rights record. Levi Strauss, the world's largest brand-name apparel manufacturer, has turned its back on China's vast market for blue jeans because of human-rights concerns. But many U.S. firms counter that industry can be part of the solution. "Supporting the business sector will result in economic and political freedoms for the Chinese people," says a 3M spokesman. 3M established the first wholly owned foreign company in Shanghai in 1984. Today it has a local work force of 400 and estimates its sales will rise to as high as $1 billion by the year 2000.

Vietnam: A Virgin Market

Vietnam seems like a marketer's dream: a country with 72 million consumers, 80% of whom are younger than 40; loads of natural resources, including oil, gold, gas, and timber; and a coastline of pristine beaches that could turn out to be the hot new tourist locale. With the ending of the U.S. trade embargo against Vietnam, this dream has become a reality for U.S. companies. While European and Asian companies have been tak-

foreign operations as a small part of their business. Others have bigger plans, believing that their foreign business will eventually be equal to, or even more important than, their domestic business.

The company must decide whether to market in a few countries or many countries. The Bulova Watch Company made the latter choice and expanded into over 100 countries. It spread itself too thin, made profits in only two countries, and lost around $40 million. In contrast, consumer-product company Amway is breaking into markets at a furious pace but only after decades of gradually building up its overseas presence. Known for its neighbor-to-neighbor direct-selling networks, Amway expanded into Australia in 1971, a country far away from but similar to the U.S. market. Then, in the 1980s, Amway expanded into 10 more countries, and the

ing advantage of the Vietnamese market reforms that began in 1986, their foothold doesn't faze many U.S. marketers, who are banking on the popularity of American brands. "Vietnam promises to be a significant battleground for the rival colas," Pepsi said in a statement after the embargo was lifted.

Amid all the excitement, however, there are some notes of caution. The per capita income of most Vietnamese is $200 a year, and as in China, Vietnam's infrastructure is in a dismal state, with one of the world's worst transportation and communication systems. Vietnam has a long, long way to go before it will be in the same league as some of the Southeast Asian "tigers" such as Singapore or South Korea. While the markets and the country develop, marketers are spending their money cautiously. The invested dollars tend to go toward very simple advertising campaigns, because most consumers are seeing products for the first time ever. For this reason radio and billboards are fruitful venues for advertising. A billboard in Ho Chi Minh City boasts a single word: Sony.

Cuba: Watching and Waiting

While the United States is tightening the screws on Havana by extending its Cuban trade embargo even to foreign subsidiaries of U.S. companies, other countries are tightening their grip on the Cuban market. U.S. policy makers hope the embargo will pressure Fidel Castro to liberalize his repressive regime. The drawback, however, is that other nations have refused to participate in the embargo. For example, Mexico's businesses have been the beneficiaries of their country's hands-off policy. At Havana In-Bound, a quasi free-trade zone on the capital's outskirts, warehouses are packed with Mexican goods entering Cuba, often destined for the hotels and other businesses Cubans are setting up with foreign partners.

Cuba is one of the most lush Caribbean islands, so the biggest influx has been the boom in hotels built or managed by Spanish, Canadian, and Mexican operators. Tourist revenues totaled about $900 million in 1994, overtaking sugar exports as Cuba's top hard-currency earner.

While U.S. companies are losing out on a potentially lucrative market, they may not have long to wait. Many U.S. marketers are banking on Castro's imminent fall or death and the subsequent lifting of the embargo. "Here we have a consumer market of 11 million that is a 32-minute flight away with 30 years of pent-up demand. Is that not exciting?" says Ana Maria Fernandez Haar, a Cuban-American who is president of the IAC Advertising Group. Procter & Gamble, United Airlines, American Airlines, and Sprint are just a few of the marketers interested in serving a free Cuban market.

Cuba's infrastructure needs years of rebuilding. In some places there is no running water, gasoline, sewer systems, and energy sources. "They'll have to take care of the basic concept of survival before they can think about pizza and Pepsi," says Joe Zubizarreta, another Cuban-born advertising executive. Then, too, there's the added concern of political unrest. The Castro regime may not go gently, and violence in Cuba would certainly keep marketers away. For now, though, foreign companies will continue to make inroads in Cuba and U.S. marketers will simply watch and wait.

Sources: Marlene Piturro, "Capitalist China?" Brandweek, May 16, 1994, pp. 22–27; Bryan Batson, "Chinese Fortunes," Sales and Marketing Management, March 1994, pp. 93–98; Valerie Reitman, "Enticed by Visions of Enormous Numbers, More Western Marketers Move into China," The Wall Street Journal, July 12, 1993, B1:3; Cyndee Miller, "U.S. Firms Rush to Claim Share of Newly Opened Vietnam Market," Marketing News, March 14, 1994, p. 11; Geoffrey Brewer, "American Businesses Bank On," Sales and Marketing Management, April 1994, p. 15; and Christy Fisher, "U.S. Marketers Wait for Opening in Cuba," Advertising Age, August 29, 1994, pp. 1, 6.

pace increased rapidly from then on. By 1994 Amway was firmly established in 60 countries, including Hungary, Poland, and the Czech Republic, and boasted worldwide sales of $5 billion.[3]

Generally speaking, it makes sense to operate in fewer countries with a deeper commitment and penetration in each. Ayal and Zif have argued that a company should enter fewer countries when

- ◆ Market entry and market control costs are high;
- ◆ Product and communication adaptation costs are high;
- ◆ Population and income size and growth are high in the initial countries chosen; and
- ◆ Dominant foreign firms can establish high barriers to entry.[4]

The company must also decide on the types of countries to consider. Country attractiveness is influenced by the product, geographical factors, income and population, political climate, and other factors. The seller might have a predilection for certain groups of countries or parts of the world. Kenichi Ohmae recommends that companies concentrate on selling in the "triad markets"—the United States, Western Europe, and Japan—because these markets account for a large percent of all international trade.[5]

While Ohmae's position makes short-run sense—that is, profits are likely to be higher in the triad regions—it can spell a disastrous policy for the world economy in the long run. The triad markets are rich but mature: Companies have to strain their creativity to find growth opportunities in these markets. In contrast, the unmet needs of the developing world represent an ocean of opportunity. They are huge potential markets for food, clothing, shelter, consumer electronics, appliances, and other goods. Unless purchasing power is somehow put into the Third World, the industrial world will remain saddled with excess productive capacity and a very slow growth rate; and the developing economies will be stuck with excess consumer needs that they are unable to satisfy.

Furthermore, companies today don't seem to be heeding Ohmae's recommendations. Rather, many market leaders are rushing headlong into formerly Communist markets in Eastern Europe and into the last remaining Communist strongholds, such as China and Vietnam, where there are many unmet needs for technology and quality consumer products. (For more on this topic, see the Vision 2000 feature on pages 406–407 titled "The Last Marketing Frontiers: China, Vietnam, and Cuba.")

Suppose a company has assembled a list of potential export markets. How does it choose among them? Many companies prefer to sell to neighboring countries because they understand these countries better, and they can control their costs better because of the proximity. Thus it is not surprising that the United States's largest market is Canada, or that Swedish companies first sold their goods to their Scandinavian neighbors. At other times, *psychic proximity* rather than *geographical proximity* determines choices. Many U.S. firms prefer to sell in Canada, England, and Australia—rather than in larger markets such as Germany and France—because they feel more comfortable with the language, laws, and culture.

In general, the candidate countries should be rated initially on three major criteria: market attractiveness, competitive advantage, and risk. Here is an example of this rating system in action:

INTERNATIONAL HOUGH The International Hough Company manufactures mining equipment and is evaluating China and four Eastern European countries as possible market opportunities. It first rates the *market attractiveness* of each country, looking at such indicators as GDP/capita, work force in mining, imports of machinery, and population growth. It then rates its own potential *competitive advantage* in each country, looking at such indicators as prior business dealings, whether it would be a low-cost producer, and whether its senior management can work comfortably in that country. Finally it rates the *risk level* of each country, looking at such indicators as political stability, currency stability, and repatriation rules. By indexing, weighing, and combining the various numbers, it arrives at the picture shown in Figure 14-2. China appears to present the best opportunity because it rates high on market attractiveness and competitive advantage, and low on risk. Romania, in contrast, ranks low on market attractiveness, medium on competitive advantage, and high on risk.

Developing
Marketing
Strategies

Next International Hough would have to prepare a financial analysis to see whether it could earn enough on its investment in any country to cover the risk.

FIGURE 14-2
Evaluating Which Markets
to Enter

	Market attractiveness				
	High (H)	Medium (M)	Low (L)		
H	China				
M		Czech Republic		L	
L	Germany				Risk
H		Poland			
M			Romania	H	
L					

(Competitive advantage — rows labeled H, M, L, H, M, L)

DECIDING HOW TO ENTER THE MARKET

Once a company decides to target a particular country, it has to determine the best mode of entry. Its broad choices are *indirect exporting, direct exporting, licensing, joint ventures,* and *direct investment.* These five market-entry strategies are shown in Figure 14-3 and examined in the following pages. Each succeeding strategy involves more commitment, risk, control, and profit potential.

Indirect Export

The normal way to get involved in a foreign market is through export. Since 1986 total U.S. exports have been growing four times as fast as GDP—at a 9% annual rate, adjusted for inflation. Exports in 1994 totaled nearly $700 billion, more than 10% of GDP, up from 7.5% in 1986.[6]

Occasional exporting is a passive level of involvement in which the company exports from time to time, either on its own initiative or in response to unsolicited orders from abroad. *Active exporting* takes place when the company makes a commitment to expand its exports to a particular market. In either case, the company produces all of its goods in the home country. It might or might not adapt them to the foreign market. Exporting involves the least change in the company's product lines, organization, investments, and mission.

Companies typically start with *indirect exporting*—that is, they work through independent intermediaries to export their product. There are four types of intermediaries:

◆ *Domestic-based export merchant:* Buys the manufacturer's products and then sells them abroad.

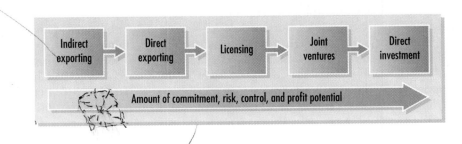

FIGURE 14-3
Five Modes of Entry into
Foreign Markets

CHAPTER 14   **409**

Designing and
Managing Global
Marketing Strategies

- *Domestic-based export agent:* Seeks and negotiates foreign purchases and is paid a commission. Included in this group are trading companies.

- *Cooperative organization:* Carries on exporting activities on behalf of several producers and is partly under their administrative control. Often used by producers of primary products—fruits, nuts, and so on.

- *Export-management company:* Agrees to manage a company's export activities for a fee.

Indirect export has two advantages. First, it involves less investment. The firm does not have to develop an export department, an overseas sales force, or a set of foreign contacts. Second, it involves less risk. Because international marketing intermediaries bring know-how and services to the relationship, the seller will normally make fewer mistakes.

Direct Export

Companies eventually may decide to handle their own exports. The investment and risk are somewhat greater, but so is the potential return as a result of not paying an intermediary. The company can carry on direct exporting in several ways:

- *Domestic-based export department or division:* An export sales manager carries on the actual selling and draws on market assistance as needed. The department might evolve into a self-contained export department performing all the activities involved in export and operating as a profit center.

- *Overseas sales branch or subsidiary:* An overseas sales branch allows the manufacturer to achieve greater presence and program control in the foreign market. The sales branch handles sales and distribution and might handle warehousing and promotion as well. It often serves as a display center and customer-service center also.

- *Traveling export sales representatives:* The company can send home-based sales representatives abroad to find business.

- *Foreign-based distributors or agents:* The company can hire foreign-based distributors or agents to sell the company's goods. These distributors and agents might be given exclusive rights to represent the manufacturer in that country or only limited rights.

Whether companies decide to enter foreign markets through direct or indirect exporting, one of the best ways to initiate or extend export activities is by exhibiting at an overseas trade show. A U.S. software firm might test the waters by showing its wares at an international software expo in Hong Kong, for instance. See the Marketing Memo titled "Making the Most of Trade Shows" for some tips on preparing for an international trade show.

Licensing

Licensing is a simple way for a manufacturer to become involved in international marketing. The licensor licenses a foreign company to use a manufacturing process, trademark, patent, trade secret, or other item of value for a fee or royalty. The licensor thus gains entry into the foreign market at little risk; the licensee gains production expertise or a well-known product or name without having to start from scratch. Gerber introduced its baby foods in the Japanese market through a licensing arrangement. Coca-Cola carries out its international marketing by licensing bottlers around the world—or, more technically, franchising bottlers—and supplying them with the syrup and the training needed to produce, distribute, and sell the product. Acucobol, a San Diego software firm whose product is now more widely used abroad than in the United States, began its international operations by licensing the Acucobol name to a German entrepreneur and taking a 20% equity stake in his company. The company entered into similar minority partnerships in Italy, Britain, and Scandinavia.[7]

Licensing has several potential disadvantages. The firm has less control over the licensee than if it had set up its own production facilities. Furthermore, if the licensee is very successful, the firm has given up profits; and if and when the contract ends, the company might find that it has created a competitor. To avoid creating a future competitor, the licensor usually supplies some proprietary ingredients or components needed in the product (as Coca-Cola does). But the best strategy is for the licensor to lead in innovation so that the licensee will continue to depend on the licensor.

There are several variations on a licensing arrangement. A company can sell a *management contract* to the owners of a foreign hotel, airport, hospital, or other organization to manage these businesses for a fee. In this case, the firm is exporting management services instead of a product. Management contracting is a low-risk method of getting into a foreign market, and it yields income from the beginning. The arrangement is especially attractive if the contracting firm is given an option to purchase some share in the managed company within a stated period. The arrangement is not sensible if the company can put its scarce management talent to better uses or if there are greater profits to be made by undertaking the whole venture. Management contracting prevents the company from competing with its clients.

Another entry method is *contract manufacturing,* in which the firm engages local manufacturers to produce the product. When Sears opened department stores in Mexico and Spain, Sears found qualified local manufacturers to produce many of its products. Contract manufacturing has the drawback of giving the company less control over the manufacturing process and the loss of potential profits on manufacturing. However, it offers the company a chance to start faster, with less risk and with the opportunity to form a partnership or to buy out the local manufacturer later.

Finally, a company can enter a foreign market through *franchising,* which is a more complete form of licensing. Here the franchiser offers a franchisee a complete brand concept and operating system. In return, the franchisee invests in and pays certain fees to the franchiser. Companies such as McDonald's, KFC, and Avis have entered scores of foreign markets by franchising their retail concepts.

Joint Ventures

Foreign investors may join with local investors to create a joint venture in which they share ownership and control. Many companies have announced joint ventures in recent years. For instance:[8]

♦ Coca-Cola and the Swiss company Nestlé are joining forces to develop the international market for "ready to drink" tea and coffee, which currently sell in significant amounts only in Japan.

♦ Procter & Gamble has formed a joint venture with its Italian arch-rival Fater to cover babies' bottoms in the United Kingdom and Italy. Their diaper joint venture will give the combined group almost 60% of the U.K. market and up to 90% of the Italian market.

♦ Domestic appliance manufacturer Whirlpool has taken a 53% stake in the Dutch electronics group Philips' white-goods business to leapfrog into the European market.

Forming a joint venture might be necessary or desirable for economic or political reasons. The foreign firm might lack the financial, physical, or managerial resources to undertake the venture alone. Or the foreign government might require joint ownership as a condition for entry. Even corporate giants need joint ventures to crack the toughest markets. When it wanted to enter China's ice cream market, Anglo-Dutch giant Unilever joined forces with Sumstar, a state-owned Chinese investment company. The venture's general manager says Sumstar's help with the formidable Chinese bureaucracy was crucial in getting a high-tech ice cream plant up and running in just 12 months.[9]

Joint ownership has certain drawbacks. The partners might disagree over investment, marketing, or other policies. One partner might want to reinvest earnings for growth, and the other partner might want to withdraw these earnings. The failure of the joint venture between AT&T and the Italian computer maker Olivetti collapsed due to the companies' inability to formulate a clear, mutually agreeable strategy. Furthermore, joint ownership can hamper a multinational company from carrying out specific manufacturing and marketing policies on a worldwide basis.[10]

Direct Investment

The ultimate form of foreign involvement is direct ownership of foreign-based assembly or manufacturing facilities. The foreign company can buy part or full interest in a local company or build its own facilities. As a company gains experience in export, and if the foreign market appears large enough, foreign production facilities offer distinct advantages. First, the firm could secure cost economies in the form of cheaper labor or raw materials, foreign-government investment incentives, freight savings, and so on. Second, the firm will gain a better image in the host country because it creates jobs. Third, the firm develops a deeper relationship with government, customers, local suppliers, and distributors, enabling it to adapt its products better to the local marketing environment. Fourth, the firm retains full control over its investment and therefore can develop manufacturing and marketing policies that serve its long-term international objectives. Fifth, the firm assures itself access to the market in case the host country starts insisting that purchased goods have domestic content.

The main disadvantage of direct investment is that the firm exposes its large investment to risks such as blocked or devalued currencies, worsening markets, or expropriation. The firm will find it expensive to reduce or close down its operations, since the host country might require substantial severance pay to the employees. The firm has no choice but to accept these risks if it wants to operate on its own in the host country.

The Internationalization Process

The problem facing most countries is that too few of their companies participate in foreign trade. This keeps the country from earning sufficient foreign exchange to pay for needed imports. Consequently, many governments sponsor aggressive export promotion programs to get the foreign exchange they need. These programs should be based on a deep understanding of how companies become internationalized.

Johanson and his associates have studied the *internationalization process* among Swedish companies.[11] They see firms moving through four stages:

1. No regular export activities
2. Export via independent representatives (agents)
3. Establishment of one or more sales subsidiaries
4. Establishment of production facilities abroad

The first task is to get companies to move from stage 1 to stage 2. This move is helped by studying how firms made their first export decisions.[12] Most firms work with an independent agent, usually in a country posing low psychic barriers to entry. A company then engages further agents to enter additional countries. Later, it establishes an export department to manage its agent relationships. Still later, the company replaces its agents with sales subsidiaries in its larger export markets. This increases the company's investment and risk but also increases its earning potential. To manage these sales subsidiaries, the company replaces the export department with an international department. If certain markets continue to be large and stable, or if the host country insists on local production, the company takes the next step of locating production facilities in those markets, representing a still larger commitment and still larger potential earnings. By this time, the company is operating as a multinational company and reconsidering the best way to organize and manage its global operations.

DECIDING ON THE MARKETING PROGRAM

Companies that operate in one or more foreign markets must decide how much to adapt their marketing-strategy mix to local conditions. At one extreme are companies that use a *standardized marketing mix* worldwide. Standardization of the product, advertising, and distribution channels promises the lowest costs because it involves no major changes to the current marketing mix. At the other extreme is an *adapted marketing mix,* where the producer adjusts the marketing-mix elements to each target market. The Marketing Insight on page 414 titled "Global Standardization or Adaptation?" discusses the main issues.

Global Standardization or Adaptation?

The marketing concept holds that consumers' needs vary and that marketing programs will be more effective when tailored to each customer target group. Since this concept applies within a country, it should also apply in foreign markets, where economic, political, and cultural conditions vary widely.

Yet many multinationals are bothered by what they see as an excessive amount of adaptation. Consider Gillette:

GILLETTE Gillette sells over 800 products in more than 200 countries. It has fallen into a situation where different brand names are used for the same product in different countries, and where the same brand is formulated differently in different countries. Gillette's Silkience shampoo is called Soyance in France, Sientel in Italy, and Silience in Germany; its formula is the same in some cases but varies in others. Its advertising messages and copy are also varied because each Gillette country manager proposes several changes that he or she thinks will increase sales.

Gillette would like to impose more standardization, globally or at least regionally. So would Lever Europe, which is trying to standardize its detergent lineup. Both companies see this as a way to save costs and to build up global brand power.

They take inspiration from the British advertising firm of Saatchi & Saatchi and Professor Theodore Levitt of Harvard. Saatchi & Saatchi won several advertising accounts on the strength of their claim that they can build single advertising campaigns that will work globally. Meanwhile, Professor Levitt supplied the intellectual rationale for global standardization. He wrote:

> The world is becoming a common marketplace in which people—no matter where they live—desire the same products and lifestyles. Global companies must forget the idiosyncratic differences between countries and cultures and instead concentrate on satisfying universal drives.

Levitt believes that new communication and transportation technologies have created a more homogeneous world market. People around the world want the same basic things—things that make life easier and increase their discretionary time and buying power. This convergence of needs and wants has created global markets for standardized products.

According to Levitt, traditional multinational corporations focus on differences between specific markets. They cater to superficial preference differences and produce a proliferation of highly adapted products. Adaptation results in less efficiency and higher prices to consumers.

In contrast, according to Levitt, the global corporation sells the same product the same way to all consumers. It focuses on similarities across world markets and aggressively works to "sensibly force suitably standardized products and services on the entire globe." These global marketers realize substantial economies through standardization of production, distribution, marketing, and management. They translate their efficiency into greater value for consumers by offering high quality and more reliable products at lower prices.

Levitt would advise an auto company to make a world car, a shampoo company to make a world shampoo, and a construction company to make a world tractor. In fact, some companies have successfully marketed global products: Coca-Cola, McDonald's hamburgers, Marlboro cigarettes. Ford took a step in this direction with the Mondeo, its latest try at a "world car." Some products are more global and require less adaptation on the whole. Yet even in these cases, some adaptation takes place. Coca-Cola is less sweet or less carbonated in certain countries; McDonald's uses chili sauce instead of ketchup on its hamburgers in Mexico. The Mondeo has U.S. adaptations called the Ford Contour and the Mercury Mystique.

When thinking of adaptation versus standardization, a company needs to think in terms of incremental revenue versus incremental cost. Consider the following example:

FRITO-LAY Frito-Lay had successfully sold its Cheetos brand of cheese snack in dozens of countries with little modification, but the company was stymied when it came to China. How do you sell a cheese-based product in a country where cheese is not a dietary staple? Frito-Lay brand managers at Guangzhou Frito-Lay would not be deterred. After consumer tests of 600 different flavors, the company launched an oxymoronic cheeseless version of Cheetos in "Savory American Cream" flavor and teriyaki-tasting "Zesty Japanese Steak" (see photo). The flexibility paid off; after six months the brand was selling out across China, and plant capacity shifted into overdrive to meet demand.

Rather than assuming that the company's domestic product can be introduced as is in another country, the company should review all possible adaptation elements and determine which adaptations would add more revenue than cost. The adaptation elements include the following:

- Product features
- Brand name
- Labeling
- Packaging
- Colors
- Materials
- Prices
- Advertising themes
- Advertising media
- Advertising execution
- Sales promotion

One study showed that companies made one or more marketing-mix adaptations in 80% of their foreign-directed products and that the average number of adapted elements was four. It should also be recognized that some host countries require adaptations, independent of whether the company wants to make them. The French do not allow children to be used in ads; the Germans ban the use of the word *best* to describe a product.

Thus global standardization is not an all-or-nothing proposition but a matter of degree. Companies are certainly justified in looking for more standardization, regionally if not globally. Goodyear, for example, is trying to bring regional uniformity into its logos, corporate advertising, and product lines in continental Europe so that it will have a more recognizable presence. Resistance typically arises from country managers because regional standardization puts more power into the hands of the regional manager and less in the hands of each country manager. Yet, companies must remember that while standardization might save some costs, competitors are always ready to offer more of what the customers in each country want. Global marketing, yes; global standardization, not necessarily.

To sell Cheetos in China, Frito-Lay had to remove all the cheese from its product.

Source: Wayne Simpson, *Brandweek*, March 27, 1995, p. 32.

Sources: Theodore Levitt, "The Globalization of Markets," *Harvard Business Review*, May–June 1983, pp. 92–102; Shari Caudron, "The Myth of the European Consumer," *Industry Week*, February 21, 1994, pp. 28–36. For an example of the work involved in building a single global campaign, see Pam Weisz, "Border Crossings: Brands Unify Image to Countercult of Culture," *Brandweek*, October 31, 1994, pp. 24–28; and Karen Benezra, "Fritos 'Round the World," *Brandweek*, March 27, 1995, pp. 32, 35. For findings and approaches regarding the standardization versus adaptation quandary, see Subhash C. Jain, "Standardization of International Marketing Strategy: Some Research Hypotheses," *Journal of Marketing*, 53, no. 1, (January 1989), 70–79; Johann P. Du Preez, Adamantios Diamantopoulos, and Bodo B. Schlegelmilch, "Product Standardization and Attribute Salience: A Three-Country Empirical Comparison," *Journal of International Marketing*, 2, no. 1, (1994), 7–28; David M. Szymanski, Sundar G. Bharadwaj, and P. Rajan Varadarajan, "Standardization versus Adaptation of International Marketing Strategy: An Empirical Investigation," *Journal of Marketing*, October 1993, pp. 1–17; and John A. Quelch and Edward J. Hoff, "Customizing Global Marketing," *Harvard Business Review*, May–June 1986, pp. 59–68.

FIGURE 14-4
Five International Product
and Promotion Strategies

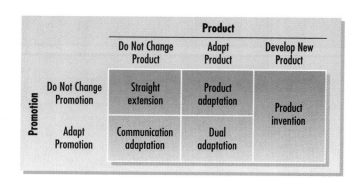

Between the two extremes, many possibilities exist. Here we will examine potential adaptations that firms might make of their product, promotion, price, and distribution as they enter foreign markets.

Product

Keegan has distinguished five adaptation strategies of product and promotion to a foreign market (Figure 14-4).[13]

Straight extension means introducing the product in the foreign market without any change. Top management instructs its salespeople: "Find customers for the product as it is." Before giving this order, however, the company must determine whether foreign consumers use that product. Deodorant usage among men ranges from 80% in the United States to 55% in Sweden to 28% in Italy to 8% in the Philippines. In interviewing women in one country about how often they used a deodorant, a typical response was "I use it when I go dancing once a year," which is hardly grounds for introducing the product.

Straight extension has been successful with cameras, consumer electronics, many machine tools, and so on. In other cases, it has been a disaster. General Foods introduced its standard powdered Jell-O in the British market only to find that British consumers prefer the solid wafer or cake form. Campbell's Soup lost an estimated $30 million in introducing its condensed soups in England; the consumers saw the small-size cans and did not realize that water needed to be added. Straight extension is tempting because it involves no additional R&D expense, manufacturing retooling, or promotional modification. But it can be costly in the long run.

Product adaptation involves altering the product to meet local conditions or preferences. There are several levels of adaptation. A company can produce a *regional version* of its product, such as a Western European version, a North American version, and so on. Or it can produce a *country version*. In Japan, Mister Donut's coffee cup is smaller and lighter to fit the hand of the average Japanese consumer; even the doughnuts are a little smaller. In Australia, Heinz sells a baby food made from strained lamb brains; and in the Netherlands, a baby food made from strained brown beans. Kraft General Foods blends different coffees for the British (who drink their coffee with milk), the French (who drink their coffee black), and Latin Americans (who want a chicory taste). Unilever provides 85 flavors of chicken soup in the European market alone. A company can produce a *city version* of its product—for instance, a beer to meet Munich tastes or Tokyo tastes. Finally, a company can produce different *retailer versions* of its product, such as one coffee brew for the Migros chain store and another for the Cooperative chain store, both in Switzerland.

While products are frequently adapted to local tastes and preferences, in some instances they must be adapted to local superstitions or beliefs, too. In Asia, the supernatural world is directly related to sales. The concept of *feng shui* is a good example:

HYATT HOTELS A practice widely followed in China, Hong Kong, and Singapore (and which has spread to Japan, Vietnam, and Korea), *feng shui* means "wind and water." Practitioners of *feng shui,* or geomancers, will recommend the most favorable conditions for any venture, particularly the placement of office buildings and the arrangement of desk, doors, and other items within. To have good *feng shui,* a building should face the water and be flanked by mountains. It also should not block the view of the mountain spirits. The Hyatt Hotel in Singapore was designed without *feng shui* in mind, and, as a result, had to be redesigned to boost business. Originally the front desk was parallel to the doors and road, and this was thought to lead to wealth flowing out. Furthermore, the doors were facing northwest, which easily let undesirable spirits in. The geomancer recommended design alterations so that wealth could be retained and undesirable spirits kept out.[14]

Product invention consists of creating something new. It can take two forms, *Backward invention* is reintroducing earlier product forms that are well adapted to a foreign country's needs. The National Cash Register Company reintroduced its crank-operated cash register at half the price of a modern cash register and sold substantial numbers in Latin America and Africa. (This illustrates a good understanding of the international product life cycle, where countries stand at different stages of readiness to accept a particular product.) *Forward invention* is creating a new product to meet a need in another country. There is an enormous need in less-developed countries for low-cost, high-protein foods. Companies like Quaker Oats, Swift, and Monsanto are researching these countries' nutrition needs, formulating new foods, and developing advertising campaigns to gain product trial and acceptance. Product invention is a costly strategy, but the payoffs can be great.

A growing part of international trade is taking place in services. In fact, the world market for services is growing at double the rate of world merchandise trade. The largest firms in accounting, advertising, banking, communications, construction, insurance, law, management consulting, and retailing are pursuing global expansion. Arthur Andersen, American Express, Citicorp, Club Med, Hilton, and Thomas Cook are known worldwide; many retailers are trying to make similar inroads. Armed with the latest in technology and operational know-how, Wal-Mart and its Mexican partner Cifra now operate 67 discount stores and Sam's Clubs in Mexico. In addition, Wal-Mart is opening three stores in Brazil and two in Argentina and already has three joint venture stores in Hong Kong with plans for a store in China.

At the same time that retailers and other service providers are expanding overseas, many countries have erected entry barriers or regulations that make the going difficult. Brazil requires all accountants to possess a professional degree from a Brazilian university. Many Western European countries want to limit the number of U.S. television programs televised in those countries. Many U.S. states bar foreign bank branches, and at the same time, the United States is pressuring South Korea to open its markets to U.S. banks. GATT is pressing for more free trade in international services, but the progress is slow.

Promotion

Companies can run the same advertising and promotion campaigns used in the home market or change them for each local market, a process called *communication adaptation.* If it adapts both the product and the communication, the company engages in *dual adaptation.*

Consider the message. The company can change the message at four different levels. The company can use one message everywhere, varying only the language, name, and colors. Exxon used "Put a tiger in your tank" with minor variations and gained international recognition. Colors might be changed to avoid taboos in some countries. Purple is associated with death in Burma and some Latin American nations; white is a mourning color in Japan; and green is associated with disease in Malaysia. Even names and headlines may have to be modified. In Germany, *mist* means "manure," *scotch* (Scotch tape) means "schmuck," and Pepsi's "Come Alive with Pepsi" was translated as "Come Out of the Grave with Pepsi." In Spain, Chevrolet's *Nova* translates as "it doesn't go." An Electrolux vacuum cleaner ad, translated from Swedish into English, was run in a Korean magazine reading "Nothing sucks like Electrolux." And a laundry soap ad claiming to wash "really dirty parts" was translated in French-speaking Quebec to read "a soap for washing private parts."

The second possibility is to use the same theme globally but adapt the copy to each local market. For example, a Camay soap commercial showed a beautiful woman bathing. In Venezuela, a man was seen in the bathroom; in Italy and France, only a man's hand was seen; and in Japan, the man waited outside.

The third approach consists of developing a global pool of ads, from which each country selects the most appropriate one. Coca-Cola and Goodyear use this approach.

Finally, some companies allow their country managers to invest in creating country-specific ads—within guidelines, of course. Consider the following two examples:

KRAFT   Kraft uses different ads for Cheez Whiz in different countries, given that household penetration is 95% in Puerto Rico, where the cheese is put on everything; 65% in Canada, where it is spread on toast in the morning breakfast; and 35% in the United States, where it is considered a junk food.

RENAULT   Renault advertises its car differently in different countries. In France, Renault is described as a little "supercar," which is fun to drive on highways and in the city. In Germany Renault emphasizes safety, modern engineering, and interior comfort. In Italy, Renault emphasizes road handling and acceleration. And in Finland, Renault emphasizes solid construction and reliability.

The use of media also requires international adaptation because media availability varies from country to country. Norway and Sweden do not permit television advertising. Belgium and France do not allow cigarettes and alcohol to be advertised on TV. Austria and Italy regulate TV advertising to children. Saudi Arabia does not want advertisers to use women in ads. India taxes advertising. Magazines vary in their availability and effectiveness; they play a major role in Italy and a minor one in Austria. Newspapers have a national reach in the United Kingdom, but the advertiser can buy only local newspaper coverage in Spain.

Marketers must also adapt their sales-promotion techniques to different markets. For example, Greece prohibits coupons and France prohibits games of chance and limits premiums and gifts to 5% of product value. People in Europe and Japan tend to make inquiries via the mail rather than the phone—which may have ramifications for direct-mail and other sales-promotion campaigns. The result of these varying preferences and restrictions is that international companies generally assign sales promotion as a responsibility of local management.

Price

Multinationals face several specific pricing problems when selling abroad. They must deal with price escalation, transfer prices, dumping charges, and gray markets.

When companies sell their goods abroad, they face a *price escalation* problem. A Gucci handbag may sell for $120 in Italy and $240 in the United States. Why? Gucci has to add the cost of transportation, tariffs, importer margin, wholesaler margin, and retailer margin to its factory price. Depending on these added costs, as well as the currency-fluctuation risk, the product might have to sell for two to five times as much in another country to make the same profit for the manufacturer. Because the cost escalation varies from country to country, the question is how to set the prices in different countries. Companies have three choices:

1. *Setting a uniform price everywhere:* Thus Coca-Cola might want to charge 60 cents for a can of Coke everywhere in the world. But then Coca-Cola would earn quite different profit rates in different countries because of varying escalation costs. Also, this strategy would result in the price being too high in poor countries and not high enough in rich countries.

2. *Setting a market-based price in each country:* Here Coca-Cola would charge what each country could afford. But this strategy ignores differences in the actual cost from country to country. Also, it could lead to a situation in which intermediaries in low-price countries re-ship their Coca-Cola to high-price countries.

3. *Setting a cost-based price in each country:* Here Coca-Cola would use a standard markup of its costs everywhere. But this strategy might price Coca-Cola out of the market in countries where its costs are high.

Another problem arises when a company sets a *transfer price* (i.e., the price that it charges to another unit in the company) for goods that it ships to its foreign subsidiaries. Consider the following:

HOFFMAN-LaROCHE The Swiss pharmaceutical company Hoffman-LaRoche charged its Italian subsidiary only $22 a kilo for Librium so that it could make high profits in Italy, where corporate taxes were lower. It charged its British subsidiary $925 per kilo for the same Librium so that it could make high profits at home instead of in Britain, where corporate taxes were high. The British Monopoly Commission sued Hoffman-LaRoche for back taxes and won.

If the company charges too high a price to a subsidiary, it may end up paying higher tariff duties, although it may pay lower income taxes in the foreign country. If the company charges too low a price to its subsidiary, it can be charged with *dumping*. Dumping occurs when a company either charges less than its costs or less than it charges in its home market, in order to enter or win a market. Thus Zenith accused Japanese television manufacturers of dumping their TV sets on the U.S. market. When the U.S. Customs Bureau finds evidence of dumping, it can levy a dumping tariff on the guilty company. Various governments are watching for abuses and often force companies to charge the *arm's-length price*—that is, the price charged by other competitors for the same or a similar product.

Many multinationals are plagued by the gray-market problem. A *gray market* occurs when the same product sells at different prices geographically. Dealers in the low-price country find ways to sell some of their products in higher-price countries, thus earning more. For example:

MINOLTA Because of lower transportation costs and tariffs, Minolta sold its cameras to dealers in Hong Kong for a lower price than it sold the same cameras to dealers in Germany. The Hong Kong dealers worked on smaller margins than the German retailers, who preferred high markups to high volume. Minolta's cameras ended up selling at retail for $174 in Hong Kong and $270 in Germany. Some Hong Kong wholesalers noticed this price difference and shipped Minolta cameras to German dealers for less than they were paying the German distributor. The German distributor couldn't sell his stock and complained to Minolta.

Very often a company finds some enterprising distributors buying more than they can sell in their own country and reshipping goods to another country to take advantage of price differences. Multinationals try to prevent gray markets by policing the distributors, by raising their prices to lower-cost distributors, or by altering the product characteristics or service warranties for different countries.

Place (Distribution Channels)

Too many U.S. manufacturers think their job is done once the product leaves their factory. They should pay attention to how the product moves within the foreign country. In other words, the international company must take a whole-channel view of the problem of distributing its products to the final users. Figure 14-5 shows the three major links between the seller and the ultimate user. In the first link, *seller's international marketing headquarters,* the export department or international division makes decisions on channels and other marketing-mix elements. The second link, *channels between nations,* gets the products to the borders of the foreign nations. The decisions made in this link include the types of intermediaries (agents, trading companies, and the like) that will be used, the type of transportation (air, sea, and so on), and the financing and risk arrangements. The third link, *channels within foreign nations,* gets the products from their foreign entry point to the final buyers and users.

Within-country channels of distribution vary considerably among countries. There are striking differences in the number and types of intermediaries serving each foreign market. To sell soap in Japan, Procter & Gamble has to work through what is probably the most complicated distribution system in the world. It must sell to a general wholesaler, who sells to a product wholesaler, who sells to a product-specialty wholesaler, who sells to a regional wholesaler, who sells to a local wholesaler, who finally sells to retailers. All these distribution levels can mean that the consumers' price ends up double or triple the importer's price.[15] If P&G takes the same soap to tropical Africa, the company might sell to an import wholesaler, who sells to several jobbers, who sell to petty traders (mostly women) working in local markets.

Another difference lies in the size and character of retail units abroad. While large-scale retail chains dominate the U.S. scene, much foreign retailing is in the hands of many small independent retailers. In India, millions of retailers operate

FIGURE 14-5

Whole-Channel Concept for International Marketing

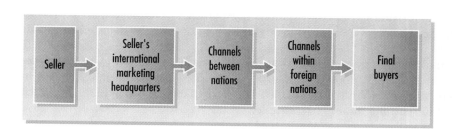

tiny shops or sell in open markets. Their markups are high, but the real price is brought down through price haggling. People's incomes are low, and they must shop daily for small amounts and are limited to whatever quantity can be carried home on foot or on a bicycle. Also, most homes lack storage and refrigeration space to keep food fresh for several days. Packaging costs are kept low in order to keep the prices low. In India, cigarettes are often bought singly. Breaking bulk remains an important function of intermediaries and helps perpetuate the long channels of distribution, which are a major obstacle to the expansion of large-scale retailing in developing countries.

The Marketing Insight on pages 422–423 titled "The World's Champion Marketers: The Japanese" brings together many of the factors underlying effective international marketing.

DECIDING ON THE MARKETING ORGANIZATION

Depending on their level of involvement in the international arena, companies manage their international marketing activities in three ways: through export departments, international divisions, or a global organization.

Export Department

A firm normally gets into international marketing by simply shipping out its goods. If its international sales expand, the company organizes an export department consisting of a sales manager and a few assistants. As sales increase further, the export department is expanded to include various marketing services so that the company can go after business more aggressively. If the firm moves into joint ventures or direct investment, the export department will no longer be adequate to manage international operations.

International Division

Many companies become involved in several international markets and ventures. A company might export to one country, license to another, have a joint venture in a third, and own a subsidiary in a fourth. Sooner or later it will create an international division to handle all its international activity. The international division is headed by an international-division president, who sets goals and budgets and is responsible for the company's growth in the international market.

International divisions are organized in a variety of ways. The international division's corporate staff consists of specialists in marketing, manufacturing, research, finance, planning, and human resources; they plan for and provide services to various operating units. The operating units can be organized in several ways. First, they can be *geographical organizations*. Reporting to the international-division president might be regional vice-presidents for North America, Latin America, Europe, Africa, the Middle East, and the Far East. Reporting to the regional vice-presidents are country managers who are responsible for a sales force, sales branches, distributors, and licensees in the respective countries. Or the operating units may be *world product groups*, each with an international vice-president responsible for worldwide sales of each product group. The vice-presidents may draw on corporate-staff area specialists for expertise on different geographical areas. Finally, the operating units may be *international subsidiaries*, each headed by a president. The various subsidiary presidents report to the president of the international division.

The World's Champion Marketers: The Japanese

Few dispute that the Japanese have performed an economic miracle since World War II. In a relatively short time, they have achieved global market leadership in industries thought to be mature and dominated by impregnable giants: autos, motorcycles, watches, cameras, optical instruments, steel, shipbuilding, musical instruments, zippers, radios, television, video recorders, hand calculators, and so on. Japanese firms are currently moving into the number-two position in computers and construction equipment and making strong inroads into the chemical, rubber tires, pharmaceutical, and machine-tool industries. They are building a stronger position in designer clothing and cosmetics and slowly moving into aircraft manufacture.

Many theories have been offered to explain Japan's global successes. Some point to its unique business practices, such as consensus management and just-in-time production. Others point to the supportive role of government policies and subsidies, the existence of powerful trading companies, and businesses' access to low-cost bank financing. Still others view Japan's success as based on unfair dumping practices, protected markets, and almost-zero defense industry costs.

One of the main keys to Japan's performance is its skill in marketing strategy formulation and implementation. The Japanese came to the United States to study marketing and went home understanding its principles better than many U.S. companies did. The Japanese know how to select a market, enter it, build their market share, and protect their leadership position against competitors' attacks.

Selecting Markets

The Japanese government and companies work hard to identify attractive global markets. They favor global industries that are capital intensive and knowledge intensive but that require only small quantities of natural resources. Candidates include consumer electronics, cameras, watches, motorcycles, and pharmaceuticals. They prefer product markets that are in a state of technological evolution. They identify product markets where consumers are dissatisfied. They look for industries where the market leaders are complacent or underfinanced. They adopt a strategic intent to dominate these industries and reduce or destroy competition.

Entering Markets

The Japanese send study teams into the target country to spend several weeks or months evaluating the market and figuring out a strategy. They study and license existing technology from abroad. They manufacture first in Japan and build their base, discouraging foreign competitors from selling in Japan through a variety of tariff and nontariff barriers. They often enter a foreign market by selling their products to a private brander, such as an American department store or manufacturer. Later, they will introduce their own brand—a low-price, stripped-down product, or a product as good as

---

Many multinationals shift among these three types of organizations because each creates problems. The history of Westinghouse's international operations is illustrative:

WESTING-HOUSE   Before 1960, Westinghouse had several foreign subsidiaries that were loosely linked through an international division. To achieve more coordination, Westinghouse established in 1960 a strong international division with regional and country managers. However, several of Westinghouse's product groups found it frustrating to work through the international division, and they pressed for global control over planning and implementation. The corporation acceded in 1971 and disbanded the international division and gave 125 division managers worldwide responsibility. However, the results were not uniformly good. Many product groups did not pay sufficient attention to the international opportunities, since most of their business was domestic; they lacked international expertise; and they failed to coordinate their international operations with each other. Not surprisingly, in 1979 Westinghouse established a matrix organization consisting of an international vice-president who managed four regional managers, who in turn managed country managers, along with an overlay of international product managers from the various product groups. The matrix solution promised to be sensitive both to local

the competition's but priced lower, or a product exhibiting higher quality or new features or designs. The Japanese proceed to line up good distribution in order to provide reliable service to their customers. They rely on advertising to bring their products to the public's attention. A key characteristic of their entry strategy is to build market share rather than early profits. The Japanese are patient capitalists who will wait a decade to realize their profits.

Building Market Share

Once Japanese firms gain a market foothold, they direct their energies toward expanding their market share. They rely on product-development strategies and market-development strategies. They pour money into product improvement, product upgrading, and product proliferation, so that they can offer more and better things than the competition. They spot new opportunities through market segmentation and sequence market development across a number of countries, with the aim of building a network of world markets and production locations. They gain further volume through an aggressive program of buying up competitors or joint venturing with them.

Protecting Market Share

Once the Japanese achieve market domination, they find themselves in the role of defenders rather than attackers. The Japanese defense strategy is a good offense through continuous product development and refined market segmentation. Japanese firms use two market-oriented principles to maintain their leadership.

The first is zero-customer-feedback time, whereby they survey recent customers to find out how they like the product and what improvements they would want. The second is zero-product-improvement time, whereby they add worthwhile product improvements continuously, so that the product remains the leader. The Japanese also protect themselves by hiring U.S. lawyers, public relations people, and former public officials to defend their U.S. interests and improve their image.

Responding to the Japanese Competitors

Although U.S. and European firms were at first slow to respond to Japanese inroads, most of them are now mounting counteroffensives. IBM is adding new products, automatizing its factories, sourcing components from abroad, and entering strategic partnerships with others. Black & Decker is closing product-line gaps, increasing product quality, streamlining manufacturing, and pricing more aggressively. More companies are copying Japanese practices that work—quality control, consensus management, just-in-time production—when they fit the company culture. And more companies are entering the Japanese market to compete on their soil. Although getting in and operating successfully in Japan takes a considerable amount of money and patience, several companies have done an outstanding job, including Coca-Cola, McDonald's, Max Factor, Xerox, IBM, and Warner-Lambert.

Source: For further discussion, see Philip Kotler, Liam Fahey, and Somkid Jatusripitak, *The New Competition* (Englewood Cliffs, NJ: Prentice Hall, 1985).

area needs and to global product strategy but at greater cost and greater management conflict along the way.

In recent years, the matrix model has been widely criticized. Some companies are getting frustrated with the greater potential for both conflict and inaction as regional managers and product managers struggle for consensus. Digital Equipment Corp. blames the matrix for delaying its shift from minicomputers to PC's by several years. While DEC's manufacturing, engineering, marketing and other groups debated the move, competitors moved ahead.

While companies are not eliminating the matrix completely, they are modifying it. A pioneer in this area has been IBM:

IBM Part of IBM's massive reorganization strategy has been to put 235,000 employees into 14 customer-focused groups such as oil and gas, entertainment, and financial services. This way a big customer will be able to cut one deal with a central sales office to have IBM computers installed worldwide. Under the old system, a corporate customer with operations in 20 countries had to contract, in effect, with 20 little Big Blues, each with its own pricing structure and service standards.[16]

Designing and
Managing Global
Marketing Strategies

Global Organization

Several firms have passed beyond the international-division stage and have become truly global organizations. They have stopped thinking of themselves as national marketers who have ventured abroad and now think of themselves as global marketers. Their top corporate management and staff plan worldwide manufacturing facilities, marketing policies, financial flows, and logistical systems. The global operating units report directly to the chief executive or executive committee, not to the head of an international division. Executives are trained in worldwide operations, not just domestic or international ones. Management is recruited from many countries; components and supplies are purchased where they can be obtained at the least cost; and investments are made where the anticipated returns are greatest.

Companies that operate in many countries face several organizational complexities. For example, when it comes to pricing a company's mainframe computers to a large banking system in Germany, how much influence should be wielded by the product manager, by the company's market manager for the banking sector, and by the company's German country manager? The answer partly boils down to whether the decisions should be made globally with a high degree of standardization or whether the decisions should be made locally.

Bartlett and Ghoshal have proposed the circumstances under which each approach works best. In their *Managing Across Borders,* they describe a number of forces that favor "global integration" (e.g., capital-intensive production, homogeneous demand, and so on) versus "national responsiveness" (e.g., local standards and barriers, strong local preferences). They distinguish three organizational strategies:[17]

1. A *global strategy* treats the world as a single market. This strategy is warranted when the forces for global integration are strong and the forces for national responsiveness are weak. This is true of the consumer electronics market, for example, where most buyers around the world will accept a fairly standardized pocket radio, CD player, TV, and so on. Matsushita has performed better than GE and Philips in the consumer electronics market because Matsushita operates in a more globally coordinated and standardized way.

2. A *multinational strategy* treats the world as a portfolio of national opportunities. This strategy is warranted when the forces favoring national responsiveness are strong and the forces favoring global integration are weak. This is the situation in the branded packaged-goods business (food products, cleaning products, and so on). Bartlett and Ghoshal cite Unilever as a better performer than Kao and P&G because Unilever grants more autonomy in decision making to its local branches.

3. A *"glocal" strategy* standardizes certain core elements and localizes other elements. This strategy makes sense for an industry (such as telecommunications) where each nation requires some adaptation of its equipment but the providing company can also standardize some of the core components. Bartlett and Ghoshal cite Ericsson as balancing these considerations better than NEC (which is too globally oriented) and ITT (which is too locally oriented).

One of the most successful "glocal" companies is ABB, formed by a merger between the Swedish company ASEA and the Swiss company Brown Boveri.

ABB   ABB's products are industrial, including power transformers, electrical installations, instrumentation, auto components, air-conditioning equipment, railroad equipment, and so on. With annual revenues of $32 billion and 210,000 employees, ABB is headed by Percy Barnevik, one of Europe's most dynamic CEOs. The company's motto is "ABB is a global company local everywhere." Barnevik established English as the company's official language (all ABB managers must be conversant in English) and all financial results must be reported in dollars. ABB is organized with the aim of reconciling three contradictions: to be global and local; to be big and small; and to be radically decentralized with centralized reporting and control. ABB has only 170 staff people at headquarters (with about 19 nationalities among them), compared to the 3,000 who populate Siemens headquarters. The company's many product lines are organized into 8 business segments, 65 business areas, 1,300 companies, and 5,000 profit centers, with the average employee belonging to a profit center of around 50 employees. Managers are regularly rotated among countries and mixed-nationality teams are encouraged. Depending on the type of business, some are treated as superlocal businesses with lots of autonomy and others as global businesses with major central control. Barnevik uses a proprietary software system called Abacus that allows him to review performance data each month in each of the 5,000 profit centers. When the system flags exceptional and deficient performances, he contacts the appropriate country managers, business area managers, and local company presidents. He wants his managers to be locally knowledgeable but also attuned to global considerations in making their decisions.[18]

SUMMARY

1. Most companies can no longer focus solely on the domestic market. Despite the many challenges in the international arena (shifting borders, unstable governments, foreign-exchange problems, corruption, and technological pirating), companies selling in global industries have no choice but to internationalize their operations. Companies cannot simply stay domestic and expect to maintain their markets.

2. In deciding to go abroad, a company needs to define its international marketing objectives and policies. First, the company must determine whether to market in a few countries or many countries. Then it must decide on which types of country to consider. Often psychic proximity is more important than geographical proximity. In general, the candidate countries should be rated on three criteria: market attractiveness, competitive advantage, and risk.

3. Once a company decides to enter a particular country, it must determine the best mode of entry. Its broad choices here are indirect exporting, direct exporting, licensing, joint ventures, and direct investment. Each succeeding strategy involves more commitment, risk, control, and profit potential. Companies generally begin with indirect exporting, then proceed through later stages as they gain more experience in the international arena.

4. In deciding on the marketing program, a company must decide how much to adapt its marketing mix (product, promotion, price, and place) to local conditions. At the two ends of the spectrum are standardized and adapted marketing mixes, with many steps in between them.

    At the product level, firms can pursue a strategy of straight extension, product adaptation, or product invention. At the promotion level, firms may choose communication adaptation or dual adaptation. At the price level, firms may encounter price escalation and gray markets, and it may be very difficult to set standard prices. At the distribution level, firms need to take a whole-channel view of the challenge of distributing its products to the final users. In creating all elements of the marketing mix, firms must be aware of the cultural, social, political, technological, environmental, and legal limitations they face in other countries.

5. Depending on their level of international involvement, companies manage their international marketing activity in three ways: through export departments, international divisions, or a global organization. Most firms start with an export department and graduate to an international division. A few become global companies in which the top management plans and organizes on a global basis.

1. Before introducing its infant formula into Third World countries, Nestlé failed to analyze the marketing environment properly, ignoring three major macroenvironmental forces:

   ♦ First, Nestlé ignored the cultural environment. Nestlé did not take into account the cultural norms of Third World countries, where breast feeding is the norm. Pamphlets discouraged breast feeding and portrayed it as "primitive." Once the mothers stopped breast feeding their infants, their milk dried up and they were forced to buy formula.

   ♦ Second, Nestlé ignored the infrastructure of the developing nations. Third World countries have problems with contaminated water due to undeveloped water transport and filtering systems. Since many families were too poor to buy the right amount of formula, mothers diluted the formula with contaminated water, which made the infants sick.

   ♦ Third, Nestlé ignored the educational environment. Because the product represented a new technology in Third World countries, the company should have trained mothers on how to use the product. Proper sterilization of bottles and nipples did not occur, and many children became sick as a result.

   Suppose that Nestlé is now preparing to introduce a new line of powdered soft drinks into the developing nations. The powders will be added to milk or to water to create a refreshing, healthy drink. How might the company take into account the environmental forces discussed above in its new marketing programs, before introducing the products?

2. Many marketers now believe that teen-agers are becoming "global consumers." That is, teen-agers around the world are increasingly wearing the same clothes, drinking the same drinks, and listening to the same music. What has caused the global teen-ager phenomenon, which originated in the United States? What other types of products have this kind of universal appeal? How might a company whose target market is the global teen-ager reach this group?

3. Because of shrinking domestic markets due to competition, a moderate-size company in the salad-dressing industry is trying to decide "whether to go abroad" (see Figure 14-1). What are some questions concerning political, religious, and cultural factors that the company should ask itself before it decides to engage in international business? Choose a country and answer each of these questions for that country, then decide whether or not to market salad dressing in that country.

4. "While cigarettes sales decline or stagnate in many industrialized nations . . . the Third World is where the growth is. Tobacco companies operate unburdened by many of the restraints they face in the West." Discuss the pros and cons of this "marketing opportunity."

5. Select one of the following foreign nations or regions and prepare a brief (two- to five-page) report on its marketing institutions and practices. Also discuss the challenges that face domestic marketers within those countries, as well as the challenges faced by U.S. marketers who want to do business there.
   a. Mexico
   b. the European Union
   c. Poland
   d. Mainland China
   e. Japan
   f. Developing nations/Third World countries

6. Suppose that Microsoft is preparing to launch Microsoft Integrator, a hypothetical medium- to low-priced software product that provides a complete group of software packages (including spreadsheet, word processing, database, graphics, and communications) in the United States and in the countries listed in Table 1. The question is whether to introduce only one version of Integrator or to create a differentiated product for each country. If the product must be differentiated, there will be a delay in getting Integrator to market. If undifferentiated, the launch will be immediate. Analyze Table 1

COMPARATIVE CRITERIA	FRANCE	GERMANY	NETHERLANDS	ITALY
(Leading IBM-compatible hardware manufacturers ranked roughly in descending order of 1986 units sales of low-end PC clones)	1. IBM 2. Bull 3. Goupil 4. Olivetti	1. IBM 2. Schneider/ Amstrand 3. Olivetti 4. Siemens	1. IBM 2. Olivetti 3. Tulip 4. Phillip	1. Olivetti 2. IBM 3. Sperry 4. Commodore
Estimated position of Microsoft products: Multiplan Spreadsheet* Microsoft Word*	 Leader Leader	 Leader Leader	 In the top 4 In the top 5	 In the top 3 Tied for #2
Microsoft corporate advertising theme	"The software of the simple life"	"Software with a future"	"Pioneers in compatibility"	"Power and simplicity together"

* Note: Multiplan and Word are both customized for each of the four countries listed.
Sources: Information on leading hardware manufacturers is from International Data Corporation. All other information is from Microsoft internal records. *Harvard Business Case 9-588-028.*

and suggest which strategy Microsoft should pursue. Should it introduce the product in all four countries? Should it differentiate or not? On which market segments might Microsoft choose to focus?

7. Cuisinart, the famous manufacturer of upscale food processors, has decided to enter the international market. Top management is having trouble deciding how to develop the market. Brainstorm some market-entry options for the company.

8. Dentsu, Inc. issued a recent report stating that "self-searching" has become a very important consumer movement in Japan. In fact, for the last 10 years businesses have seen the Japanese consumer move from valuing the tangible to valuing the intangible. As a result of self-searching, Japanese consumers are becoming more interested in products and services that provide qualitatively richer lives and a greater sense of fulfillment. The key phrase that Dentsu uses to describe this phenomenon is "taking care." "Taking care" means that consumers are increasingly concerned with quality of life and a sense of fulfillment. Consumers are seeking products and services to enhance their lives in three categories: taking care of body and soul, taking care of relationships, and taking care of their daily lives.

   In groups of five or six, determine how you would define these three categories for U.S. companies interested in exporting goods to Japan. What broad classifications of products would fit into each category? What are some specific products that seem to have potential for success in Japan?

9. A large U.S. company decided to enter the French tire market some years ago. The company produced tires for medium-sized trucks designed to meet the official rear-axle weight. Its subsequent experience was bad, with many of its tires blowing out. The company acquired a poor image in France as a result. What went wrong?

10. A U.S. heavy equipment manufacturer operating in Western Europe has been using Americans as salespeople. The company feels that it could reduce its costs by hiring and training nationals as salespeople. What are the advantages and disadvantages to using Americans versus nationals for selling abroad?

NOTES

1. For more on shifting borders, see Terry Clark, "National Boundaries, Border Zones, and Marketing Strategy: A Conceptual Framework and Theoretical Model of Secondary Boundary Effects," *Journal of Marketing,* July 1994, pp. 67–80.
2. Michael E. Porter, *Competitive Strategy* (New York: Free Press, 1980), p. 275.
3. Charles A. Coulombe, "Global Expansion: The Unstoppable Crusade," *Success,* September 1994, pp. 18–20.
4. Igal Ayal and Jehiel Zif, "Market Expansion Strategies in Multinational Marketing," *Journal of Marketing,* Spring 1979, pp. 84–94.
5. See Kenichi Ohmae, *Triad Power* (New York: Free Press, 1985);

and Philip Kotler and Nikhilesh Dholakia, "Ending Global Stagnation: Linking the Fortunes of the Industrial and Developing Countries," *Business in the Contemporary World,* Spring 1989, pp. 86–97.

6. Rob Norton, "Strategies for the New Export Boom," *Fortune,* August 22, 1994, pp. 124–130.

7. Norton, "Strategies."

8. Laura Mazur and Annik Hogg, *The Marketing Challenge* (Wokingham, England: Addison-Wesley, 1993), pp. 42–44; Jan Willem Karel, "Brand Strategy Positions Products Worldwide," *Journal of Business Strategy,* 12, no. 3 (May–June 1991), 16–19.

9. Paula Dwyer, "Tearing Up Today's Organization Chart," *Business Week,* November 18, 1994, pp. 80–90.

10. However, see J. Peter Killing, "How to Make a Global Joint Venture Work," *Harvard Business Review,* May–June 1982, pp. 120–27.

11. See Jan Johanson and Finn Wiedersheim-Paul, "The Internationalization of the Firm," *Journal of Management Studies,* October 1975, pp. 305–22.

12. See Stan Reid, "The Decision Maker and Export Entry and Expansion," *Journal of International Business Studies,* Fall 1981, pp. 101–12; Igal Ayal, "Industry Export Performance: Assessment and Prediction," *Journal of Marketing,* Summer 1982, pp. 54–61; and Somkid Jatusripitak, *The Exporting Behavior of Manufacturing Firms* (Ann Arbor, MI: University of Michigan Press, 1986).

13. Warren J. Keegan, *Multinational Marketing Management,* 5th ed. (Englewood Cliffs, NJ: Prentice Hall, 1995), pp. 378–81.

14. J. S. Perry Hobson, "*Feng Shui:* Its Impacts on the Asian Hospitality Industry," *International Journal of Contemporary Hospitality Management,* 6, no. 6 (1994), 21–26; Bernd H. Schmitt and Yigang Pan, "In Asia, the Supernatural Means Sales," *The New York Times,* February 19, 1995, 3, 11:2.

15. See William D. Hartley, "How Not to Do It: Cumbersome Japanese Distribution System Stumps U.S. Concerns," *The Wall Street Journal,* March 2, 1972.

16. Dwyer, "Tearing Up Today's Organization Chart," pp. 80–90.

17. See Christopher A. Bartlett and Sumantra Ghoshal, *Managing Across Borders* (Cambridge, MA: Harvard Business School Press, 1989).

18. See William Taylor, "The Logic of Global Business: An Interview with ABB's Percy Barnevik," *Harvard Business Review,* March–April 1991, pp. 91–105; and Gail E. Schares, "Percy Barnevik's Global Crusade," *Business Week,* Special Enterprise Issue, October 22, 1993, pp. 204–11.

Developing
Marketing
Strategies

MANAGING PRODUCT LINES, BRANDS, AND PACKAGING

*Any damn fool can put on a deal, but it takes genius, faith,
and perseverance to create a brand.*

Dᴀᴠɪᴅ Oɢɪʟᴠʏ

*A product is something that is made in a factory: a brand is something that is
bought by a customer. A product can be copied by a competitor: a brand
is unique. A product can be quickly outdated: a successful brand is timeless.*

Sᴛᴇᴘʜᴇɴ Kɪɴɢ

I ced tea in a bottle. It doesn't sound that exciting, but Snapple's real brewed teas have revolutionized the beverage world.

SNAPPLE   Snapple Beverage Corp. was virtually unknown in 1982 when it began producing its Snapple Line of natural beverages, distributed through health food and convenience stores. But in 1987, when the company launched its ready-to-drink teas without any additives or preservatives, it sparked a nationwide tea party. Consumers found that Snapple really tastes *good,* unlike the tinny, artificial taste of canned iced teas, and they were willing to pay a premium price for it. By 1992, the company's first year of national distribution, Snapple's 59 beverage varieties produced revenues of more than $200 million. As the company moved further into the limelight, it has even faced intense competition from the beverage behemoths, Pepsi- and Coca-Cola. Banking on the grass roots enthusiasm for its product, Snapple began airing snappy national television commercials starring real customers reading testimonials endorsing Snapple. Now the company's goals are to increase the trial and cross-trial of other flavors by adding new ones and dropping ones that don't sell. This testing is a result of the following statistic: While only one out of every three people in the United States has tried a Snapple, two out of every three of those people are regular users.[1]

Snapple's success story underscores the importance of the first and most important element of the marketing mix: the *product.* All the advertising and promotion in the world won't make a beverage fly off the supermarket shelves if people don't like its taste.

Product is a key element in the *market offering.* Marketing-mix planning begins with formulating an offering to meet target customers' needs or wants. The customer will judge the offering by three basic elements: the product features and quality, the services mix and quality, and the offering's price appropriateness (Figure 15-1). In this chapter, we examine product; in the next chapter, services; and in the following chapter, prices. All three elements must be meshed into a competitively attractive offering.

Here, we will address the following questions about products:

♦   **What is a product?**

♦   **How can a company build and manage its product mix and product lines?**

♦   **How can a company make better brand decisions?**

♦   **How can packaging and labeling be used as marketing tools?**

FIGURE 15-1

Components of the Market Offering

WHAT IS A PRODUCT?

Recall the definition of *product* from Chapter 1:

❖   A **PRODUCT** is anything that can be offered to a market to satisfy a want or need.

Products that are marketed include *physical goods* (automobiles, books), *services* (haircuts, concerts), *persons* (Michael Jordan, Barbra Streisand), *places* (Hawaii, Venice), *organizations* (American Heart Association, Girl Scouts), and *ideas* (family planning, safe driving).

Five Levels of a Product

In planning its market offering, the marketer needs to think through five levels of the product (Figure 15-2).[2] Each level adds more customer value, and the five constitute a *customer value hierarchy*. The most fundamental level is the *core benefit:* the fundamental service or benefit that the customer is really buying. A hotel guest is buying "rest and sleep." The purchaser of a drill is buying "holes." Marketers must see themselves as benefit providers.

At the second level, the marketer has to turn the core benefit into a *basic product*. Thus a hotel room includes a bed, bathroom, towels, desk, dresser, and closet.

At the third level, the marketer prepares an *expected product,* a set of attributes and conditions that buyers normally expect and agree to when they purchase this product. For example, hotel guests expect a clean bed, fresh towels, working lamps, and a relative degree of quiet. Since most hotels can meet this minimum expectation, the traveler normally will have no preference and will settle for whichever hotel is most convenient or least expensive.

At the fourth level, the marketer prepares an *augmented product* that meets the customers' desires beyond their expectations. A hotel can augment its product by including a remote-control television set, fresh flowers, rapid check-in, express checkout, fine dining and room service, and so on. Elmer Wheeler once observed, "Don't sell the steak—sell the sizzle."

Today's competition essentially takes place at the product-augmentation level. (In less developed countries, competition takes place mostly at the expected product level.) Product augmentation leads the marketer to look at the buyer's total *consumption system:* the way a purchaser of a product performs the total task of whatever it is that he or she is trying to accomplish when using the product.[3] In this way, the marketer will recognize many opportunities for augmenting its offer in a competitively effective way. According to Levitt:

> The new competition *is not between what companies produce in their factories, but between what they add to their factory output in the form of packaging, services, advertising, customer advice, financing, delivery arrangements, warehousing, and other things that people value.*[4]

However, some things should be noted about product-augmentation strategy. First, each augmentation costs the company money. The marketer has to ask whether customers will pay enough to cover the extra cost. Second, augmented

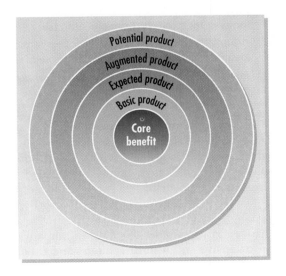

FIGURE 15-2
Five Product Levels

Managing Product
Lines, Brands,
and Packaging

benefits soon become expected benefits. Thus hotel guests today expect a remote-control television set and other amenities in their room. This means that competitors will have to search for still further features and benefits to add to their offer. Third, as companies raise the price of their augmented product, some competitors can revert to offering a "stripped-down" product at a much lower price. Thus alongside the growth of fine hotels like Four Seasons, Westin, and Hyatt we see the emergence of lower-cost hotels and motels (like Motel Six and Comfort Inn) catering to clients who simply want the basic product.

At the fifth level stands the *potential product,* which encompasses all the augmentations and transformations that the product might ultimately undergo in the future. While the augmented product describes what is included in the product today, the potential product points to its possible evolution. Here is where companies search aggressively for new ways to satisfy customers and distinguish their offer. The recent emergence of all-suite hotels where the guest occupies a set of rooms represents an innovative transformation of the traditional hotel product.

Some of the most successful companies add benefits to their offering that not only *satisfy* customers but also surprise and *delight* them. Delighting is a matter of exceeding the normal expectations and desires with unanticipated benefits. Thus the hotel guest finds candy on the pillow, or a bowl of fruit, or a video recorder with optional videotapes. Guests of the Ritz-Carleton hotels, for example, often report surprise and delight at the attention and service they receive.

Product Hierarchy

Each product is related to certain other products. The product hierarchy stretches from basic needs to particular items that satisfy those needs. We can identify seven levels of the product hierarchy. Here we define and illustrate them for life insurance:

1. *Need family:* The core need that underlies the existence of a product family. Example: security.

2. *Product family:* All the product classes that can satisfy a core need with reasonable effectiveness. Example: savings and income.

3. *Product class:* A group of products within the product family recognized as having a certain functional coherence. Example: financial instruments.

4. *Product line:* A group of products within a product class that are closely related because they perform a similar function, are sold to the same customer groups, are marketed through the same channels, or fall within given price ranges. Example: life insurance.

5. *Product type:* A group of items within a product line that share one of several possible forms of the product. Example: term life.

6. *Brand:* The name, associated with one or more items in the product line, that is used to identify the source or character of the item(s). Example: Prudential.

7. *Item* (also called *stockkeeping unit* or *product variant*): A distinct unit within a brand or product line that is distinguishable by size, price, appearance, or some other attribute. Example: Prudential renewable term life insurance.

Another example: The need "to look and feel better" gives rise to a product family called toiletries and a product class within that family called cosmetics, of which one line is lipstick, which has different product types, such as tube lipstick, which is offered as a brand called Revlon, in a particular item type, such as "frosted tube lipstick."

Two other terms are frequently used with respect to the product hierarchy. A *product system* is a group of diverse but related items that function in a compatible manner. For example, the Nikon Company sells a basic 35-mm camera along with an extensive set of lenses, filters, and other options that constitute a product system. A *product mix* (or product assortment) is the set of all products and items that a particular seller offers for sale to buyers.

Product Classifications

Marketers have traditionally classified products on the basis of varying product characteristics: durability, tangibility, and use (consumer or industrial). Each product type has an appropriate marketing-mix strategy.[5]

DURABILITY AND TANGIBILITY. Products can be classified into three groups, according to their durability and tangibility:

- *Nondurable goods:* Nondurable goods are tangible goods that normally are consumed in one or a few uses. Examples are beer, soap, and salt. Since these goods are consumed quickly and purchased frequently, the appropriate strategy is to make them available in many locations, charge only a small markup, and advertise heavily to induce trial and build preference.
- *Durable goods:* Durable goods are tangible goods that normally survive many uses. Examples include refrigerators, machine tools, and clothing. Durable products normally require more personal selling and service, command a higher margin, and require more seller guarantees.
- *Services:* Services are intangible, inseparable, variable, and perishable. As a result, they normally require more quality control, supplier credibility, and adaptability. Examples include haircuts and repairs.

CONSUMER-GOODS CLASSIFICATION. Consumers buy a vast array of goods. These goods can be classified on the basis of consumer shopping habits. We can distinguish among convenience, shopping, specialty, and unsought goods.

- ❖ **CONVENIENCE GOODS** are goods that the customer usually purchases frequently, immediately, and with a minimum of effort. Examples include tobacco products, soaps, and newspapers.

Convenience goods can be further divided into staples, impulse goods, and emergency goods. *Staples* are goods that consumers purchase on a regular basis. For example, one buyer might routinely purchase Heinz ketchup, Crest toothpaste, and Ritz crackers. *Impulse goods* are purchased on impulse, without any planning or search effort. These goods are usually displayed widely. Thus candy bars and magazines are placed next to checkout counters because shoppers may not have thought of buying them until they spot them. *Emergency goods* are purchased when a need is urgent—umbrellas during a rainstorm, boots and shovels during the first winter snowstorm. Manufacturers of emergency goods will place them in many outlets so as to capture the sale when the customer needs them.

- ❖ **SHOPPING GOODS** are goods that the customer, in the process of selection and purchase, characteristically compares on such bases as suitability, quality, price, and style. Examples include furniture, clothing, used cars, and major appliances.

Shopping goods can be divided into homogeneous goods and heterogeneous goods. The buyer sees *homogeneous shopping goods* as similar in quality but different enough in price to justify shopping comparisons. The seller has to "talk price" with the buyer. But in shopping for clothing, furniture, and other *heterogeneous shopping goods,* product features are often more important to the consumer than the price. The seller of heterogeneous shopping goods must therefore carry a wide assortment to satisfy individual tastes and must have well-trained salespeople to provide information and advice to customers.

❖ SPECIALTY GOODS are goods with unique characteristics and/or brand identification for which a significant group of buyers is habitually willing to make a special purchasing effort. Examples include specific brands and types of fancy goods, cars, stereo components, photographic equipment, and men's suits.

A Mercedes, for example, is a specialty good because interested buyers will travel far to buy one. Specialty goods do not involve the buyer in making comparisons; buyers invest time only to reach dealers carrying the wanted products. The dealers do not need convenient locations; however, they must let prospective buyers know their locations.

❖ UNSOUGHT GOODS are goods that the consumer does not know about or knows about but does not normally think of buying. New products, such as smoke detectors and food processors, are unsought goods until the consumer is made aware of them through advertising. The classic examples of known but unsought goods are life insurance, cemetery plots, gravestones, and encyclopedias.

Unsought goods require substantial marketing effort in the form of advertising and personal selling. Some of the most sophisticated personal-selling techniques have developed from the challenges involved in selling unsought goods.

INDUSTRIAL-GOODS CLASSIFICATION. Organizations buy a vast variety of goods and services. Industrial goods can be classified in terms of how they enter the production process and their relative costliness. We can distinguish three groups of industrial goods: materials and parts, capital items, and supplies and business services.

❖ MATERIALS AND PARTS are goods that enter the manufacturer's product completely. They fall into two classes: raw materials and manufactured materials and parts.

Raw materials fall into two major classes: *farm products* (e.g., wheat, cotton, livestock, fruits, and vegetables) and *natural products* (e.g., fish, lumber, crude petroleum, iron ore). Each is marketed somewhat differently. Farm products are supplied by many producers, who turn them over to marketing intermediaries, who provide assembly, grading, storage, transportation, and selling services. Their perishable and seasonal nature gives rise to special marketing practices. Their commodity character results in relatively little advertising and promotional activity, with some exceptions. From time to time, commodity groups will launch campaigns to promote the consumption of their product—potatoes, prunes, milk. And some producers brand their product—Sunkist oranges, Chiquita bananas.

Natural products are highly limited in supply. They usually have great bulk and low unit value and require substantial transportation to move them from producer to user. Natural products have fewer and larger producers, who often market them directly to industrial users. Because the users depend on these materials, long-term-supply contracts are common. The homogeneity of natural materials limits the amount of demand-creation activity. Price and delivery reliability are the major factors influencing the selection of suppliers.

Manufactured materials and parts are divided into two categories: component materials (e.g., iron, yarn, cement, wires) and component parts (e.g., small motors, tires, castings). *Component materials* are usually fabricated further—for example, pig iron is made into steel, and yarn is woven into cloth. The standardized nature of component materials usually means that price and supplier reliability are the most important purchase factors. *Component parts* enter the finished product completely with no further change in form, as when small motors are put into vacuum cleaners, and tires are put on automobiles. Most manufactured materials and parts are sold directly to industrial users, with orders often placed a year or more in advance. Price and services are the major marketing considerations, and branding and advertising tend to be less important.

❖   **Capital Items** are long-lasting goods that facilitate developing and/or managing the finished product. They include two groups: installations and equipment.

Installations consist of buildings (e.g., factories and offices) and equipment (e.g., generators, drill presses, mainframe computers, elevators). Installations are major purchases. They are usually bought directly from the producer, with the typical sale preceded by a long negotiation period. The producers use a top-notch sales force, which often includes technical personnel. The producers have to be willing to design to specification and to supply postsale services. Advertising is used but is much less important than personal selling.

Equipment comprises portable factory equipment and tools (e.g., hand tools, lift trucks) and office equipment (e.g., personal computers, desks). These types of equipment do not become part of the finished product. They simply help in the production process. They have a shorter life than installations but a longer life than operating supplies (discussed below). Although some equipment manufacturers sell direct, more often they use intermediaries, because the market is geographically dispersed, the buyers are numerous, and the orders are small. Quality, features, price, and service are major considerations in vendor selection. The sales force tends to be more important than advertising, although the latter can be used effectively.

❖   **Supplies and Business Services** are short-lasting goods and services that facilitate developing and/or managing the finished product.

Supplies are of two kinds: *operating supplies* (e.g., lubricants, coal, writing paper, pencils) and *maintenance and repair items* (paint, nails, brooms). Supplies are the equivalent of convenience goods in the industrial field; they are usually purchased with a minimum effort on a straight rebuy basis. They are normally marketed through intermediaries because of their low unit value and the great number and geographical dispersion of customers. Price and service are important considerations, since suppliers are quite standardized, and brand preference is not high.

Business services include *maintenance and repair services* (e.g., window cleaning, typewriter repair) and *business advisory services* (e.g., legal, management consulting, advertising). Maintenance and repair services are usually supplied under contract. Maintenance services are often provided by small producers, and repair services are often available from the manufacturers of the original equipment. Business advisory services are usually purchased in new task-buying situations, and the industrial buyer will choose the supplier on the basis of the supplier's reputation and people.

With this background, we are ready to examine company decisions regarding the product mix, product lines, and individual products.

Product-Mix Decisions

We will first consider product-mix decisions.

❖   A **Product Mix** (also called **Product Assortment**) is the set of all products and items that a particular seller offers for sale to buyers.

For example, Kodak's product mix consists of two strong product lines: information products and image products. NEC's (of Japan) basic product mix consists of communication products and computer products. Michelin has three product lines: tires, maps, and restaurant-rating services.

| | PRODUCT-MIX WIDTH | | | | |
	DETERGENTS	TOOTHPASTE	BAR SOAP	DISPOSABLE DIAPERS	PAPER TISSUE
Product-Line Length	Ivory Snow 1930 Dreft 1933 Tide 1946 Cheer 1950 Oxydol 1914 Dash 1954 Bold 1965 Gain 1966 Era 1972	Gleem 1952 Crest 1955	Ivory 1879 Kirk's 1885 Lava 1893 Camay 1926 Zest 1952 Safeguard 1963 Coast 1974 Oil of Olay 1993	Pampers 1961 Luvs 1976	Charmin 1928 Puffs 1960 Banner 1982 Summit 1100's 1992

A company's product mix has a certain width, length, depth, and consistency. These concepts are illustrated in Table 15-1 for selected Procter & Gamble consumer products.

♦ The *width* of P&G's product mix refers to how many different product lines the company carries. Table 15-1 shows a product-mix width of five lines. (In fact, P&G produces many additional lines—hair care products, health care products, personal-hygiene products, beverages, food, and so on.)

♦ The *length* of P&G's product mix refers to the total number of items in its product mix. In Table 15-1, it is 25. We can also talk about the average length of a line at P&G. This is obtained by dividing the total length (here 25) by the number of lines (here 5), or an average product length of 5.

♦ The *depth* of P&G's product mix refers to how many variants are offered of each product in the line. Thus if Crest comes in three sizes and two formulations (regular and mint), Crest has a depth of six. The average depth of P&G's product mix can be calculated by averaging the number of variants within the brand groups.

♦ The *consistency* of the product mix refers to how closely related the various product lines are in end use, production requirements, distribution channels, or some other way. P&G's product lines are consistent insofar as they are consumer goods that go through the same distribution channels. The lines are less consistent insofar as they perform different functions for the buyers.

These four dimensions of the product mix provide the handles for defining the company's product strategy. The company can expand its business in four ways. The company can add new product lines, thus widening its product mix. The company can lengthen each product line. The company can add more product variants to each product and deepen its product mix. Finally, the company can pursue more product-line consistency or less, depending upon whether it wants to acquire a strong reputation in a single field or participate in several fields.

Product-mix planning is largely the responsibility of the company's strategic planners. They must assess, with information supplied by the company marketers, which product lines to grow, maintain, harvest, and divest (see Chapter 3).

PRODUCT-LINE DECISIONS

A product mix consists of various product lines. Recall that

❖ A **PRODUCT LINE** is a group of products that are closely related because they perform a similar function, are sold to the same customer groups, are marketed through the same channels, or fall within given price ranges.

Each product line is usually managed by a different executive. In General Electric's Consumer Appliance Division, there are product-line managers for refrigerators, stoves, washing machines, and other appliances. At Northwestern University, there are separate academic deans for the medical school, law school, business school, engineering school, music school, speech school, journalism school, and school of liberal arts.

Product-Line Analysis

Product-line managers need to know the sales and profits of each item in their line in order to determine which items to build, maintain, harvest, or divest. They also need to understand each product's market profile.

PRODUCT-LINE SALES AND PROFITS. The product-line manager needs to know the percentage of total sales and profits contributed by each item in the line. Figure 15-3 shows a sales/profit report for a five-item product line.

The first item accounts for 50% of total sales and 30% of total profits. The first two items account for 80% of total sales and 60% of total profits. If these two items were suddenly hurt by a competitor, the product line's sales and profitability could collapse. A high concentration of sales in a few items means line vulnerability. These items must be carefully monitored and protected.

At the other end, the last item constitutes only 5% of the product line's sales and profits. The product-line manager may consider dropping this slow-selling item from the line unless it has strong growth potential.

PRODUCT-LINE MARKET PROFILE. The product-line manager must also review how the product line is positioned against competitors' product lines. Consider Paper Company X with a product line consisting of paper board.[6] Two of the major attributes of paper board are paper weight and finish quality. Paper weight is usually offered at standard levels of 90, 120, 150, and 180 weight. Finish quality is offered at three standard levels: low, medium, and high. The product map in Figure 15-4 on the next page shows the location of the various product-line items of company X and four competitors, A, B, C, and D. Competitor A sells two product items in the extra-high weight class ranging from medium to low finish quality. Competitor B sells four items that vary in weight and finish quality. Competitor C sells three items in which the greater their weight, the greater their finish quality. Competitor D sells three items, all lightweight but varying in finish quality. Finally, company X offers three items that vary in weight and finish quality.

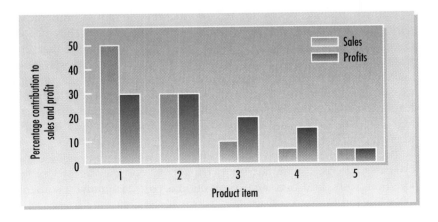

CHAPTER 15   **437**

Managing Product Lines, Brands, and Packaging

FIGURE 15-4

Product Map for a Paper-Product Line

Source: Industrial Product Policy: Managing the Existing Product Line by Benson P. Shapiro. Cambridge, MA: Marketing Science Institute Report No. 77-110.

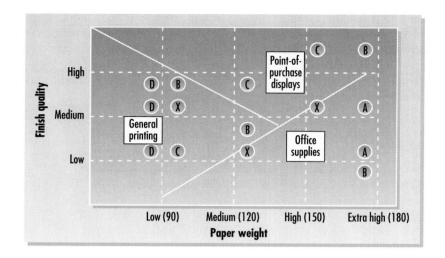

This product map is useful for designing product-line marketing strategy. It shows which competitors' items are competing against company X's items. For example, company X's low-weight/medium-quality paper competes against competitor D's and B's papers. But its high-weight/medium-quality paper has no direct competitor. The map also reveals possible locations for new-product items. For example, no manufacturer offers a high-weight/low-quality paper. If company X estimates a strong unmet demand and can produce and price this paper at low cost, it could consider adding this item to its line.

Another benefit of product mapping is that it identifies market segments. Figure 15-4 shows the types of paper, by weight and quality, preferred by the general printing industry, the point-of-purchase display industry, and the office-supply industry. The map shows that company X is well positioned to serve the needs of the general printing industry but is less effective in serving the other two industries and might consider bringing out more paper types that meet their needs.

After performing a product-line analysis, the product-line manager has to consider decisions on product-line length, line modernization, line featuring, and line pruning.

Product-Line Length

An issue facing product-line managers is optimal product-line length. A product line is too short if the manager can increase profits by adding items; the line is too long if the manager can increase profits by dropping items.

Company objectives influence product-line length. Companies seeking high market share and market growth will carry longer lines. They are less concerned when some items fail to contribute to profits. Companies that emphasize high profitability will carry shorter lines consisting of carefully chosen items.

Product lines tend to lengthen over time. Excess manufacturing capacity puts pressure on the product-line manager to develop new items. The sales force and distributors also pressure the company for a more complete product line to satisfy their customers. The product-line manager will add items in pursuit of greater sales and profits.

But as items are added, several costs rise: design and engineering costs, inventory-carrying costs, manufacturing-changeover costs, order-processing costs, transportation costs, and new-item promotional costs. Eventually someone calls a halt to the mushrooming product line. Top management may freeze things because of insufficient funds or manufacturing capacity. The controller may question the line's profitability and call for a study, which will probably show a large number of money-losing items. A pattern of product-line growth followed by massive product pruning may repeat itself many times.

A company can enlarge the length of its product line in two ways: by line stretching and line filling.

LINE STRETCHING. Every company's product line covers a certain part of the total possible range. For example, BMW automobiles are located in the upper price range of the automobile market. *Line stretching* occurs when a company lengthens its product line beyond its current range. The company can stretch its line downward, upward, or both ways.

Downward Stretch. Many companies initially locate at the upper end of the market and subsequently stretch their line downward.

GODIVA Godiva Chocolates, in their signature gold boxes, have always been considered the ultimate in luxury products. Yet while the chocolatier flourished in the 1980s, the company experienced some difficulties in the 1990s, when a recession seriously affected the sales of super-premium goods like chocolate that sells for $45 a pound. In the mid-1990s, Godiva underwent a makeover and downward stretch by exchanging the black lacquer and pink marble of its intimidating stores (where customers had to stand on tiptoe to see a sales clerk) for warm bleached wood floors and displays of chocolates that weren't under glass. In the redesigned stores, customers can serve themselves and find prices from lists, and on the list they'll even find a new line of Godiva chocolates that retail for as little as $3.00 per pound.[7]

Companies often add models to the lower end of their line in order to advertise their brand as starting at a low price. Thus Sears may advertise room air conditioners "starting at $240," and General Motors may advertise a new Chevrolet at $9,000. These "fighter" or "promotional" models are used to draw customers in. Upon seeing the better models, customers often trade up. This strategy must be used carefully. The promotional brand, although stripped, must support the brand's quality image. The seller must also stock the promotional model when it is advertised. Consumers must not feel they were "baited and switched."

A company might stretch downward for any of the following reasons:

- The company is attacked by a competitor at the high end and decides to counterattack by invading the competitor's low end.
- The company finds that slower growth is taking place at the high end (as Godiva did).
- The company initially entered the high end to establish a quality image and intended to roll downward.
- The company adds a low-end unit to plug a market hole that would otherwise attract a new competitor.

In making a downward stretch, the company faces risks. The new low-end item might *cannibalize* higher-end items—that is, sales of the lower-priced items might take away from sales of the higher-priced item. Consider the following:

GENERAL ELECTRIC General Electric's Medical Systems Division is the market leader in CAT scanners, those expensive diagnostic machines used in hospitals. GE learned that a Japanese competitor was planning to attack its market. GE's guess was that the Japanese model would be smaller, more electronic, and less expensive. The best GE defense would be to introduce a similar machine before the Japanese model entered the market. But some GE executives were concerned that this lower-price version would hurt the sales and higher profit margin on their large CAT scanner. But one manager settled the issue by saying: "Aren't we better off to cannibalize ourselves than to let the Japanese do it?"

Managing Product
Lines, Brands,
and Packaging

In addition, the low-end item might provoke competitors to move into the higher end. Or the company's dealers may not be willing or able to handle the lower-end products because they are less profitable or dilute their image. Harley Davidson's dealers neglected the small motorcycles that Harley designed to compete with the Japanese.

A major miscalculation of several U.S. companies has been their failure to plug holes in the lower end of their markets. General Motors resisted building smaller cars, and Xerox resisted building smaller copying machines. Japanese companies spotted a major opening and moved in quickly.

Upward Stretch. Companies in the lower end of the market might contemplate entering the higher end. They might be attracted by a higher growth rate, higher margins, or simply the chance to position themselves as full-line manufacturers. Avon and Mary Kay cosmetics, both traditionally middlebrow companies that sell products through direct-sales networks, have reached into the upscale market with new products and advertising aimed at the department-store shopper. Avon launched its Natori fragrance in 1995, in cooperation with high-end lingerie designer Josie Natori. Natori gives Avon a chance to improve its image in fragrance, a category where most of its offerings are lower-priced, mass market products. Mary Kay is counting on alpha hydroxy acids, the popular skin-care ingredient, to lure department-store shoppers to its new Triple Action Eye Enhancer. Like Avon, it is advertising in the upscale fashion magazine *Vogue* for the first time ever.

An upward-stretch decision can be risky. The higher-end competitors may be well entrenched and may counterattack by going downmarket. Prospective customers may not believe that the lower-end company can produce high-quality products. Finally, the company's sales representatives and distributors may lack the talent and training to serve the higher end of the market. Toyota and Nissan took steps to prevent this from happening when they introduced their first luxury cars, the Lexus and the Infiniti, in 1990. The companies have set up programs to ensure that everyone involved with the product understands the need for a customer focus in the luxury-car market. They also have empowered dealers to do anything necessary to keep car buyers pleased. The results have been remarkable: The Lexus has achieved the highest marks in J. D. Power & Associates' customer satisfaction survey every year since 1992.

Two-Way Stretch. Companies serving the middle market might decide to stretch their line in both directions. Texas Instruments (TI) introduced its first calculators in the medium-price/medium-quality end of the market. Gradually, it added calculators at the lower end, taking market shares away from Bowmar; and it introduced high-quality calculators selling at lower prices than Hewlett-Packard calculators, which had dominated the high end. This two-way stretch won TI early market leadership in the hand-calculator market.

The Marriott Hotel group also has performed a two-way stretch of its hotel product line (Figure 15-5). Alongside its medium-price hotels, it added the Marriott Marquis line to serve the upper end of the market, the Courtyard line to serve a lower end of the market, and Fairfield Inns to serve the economy end of the market. Each branded hotel line is aimed at a different target market. Marriott Marquis aims to attract and please top executives; Marriotts, middle managers; Courtyards, salespeople; and Fairfield Inns, vacationers and others on a low travel budget. The major risk with this strategy is that some travelers will trade down after finding the lower-price hotels in the Marriott chain have pretty much everything they want. But it is still better for Marriott to capture its customers who move downward than to lose them to competitors.

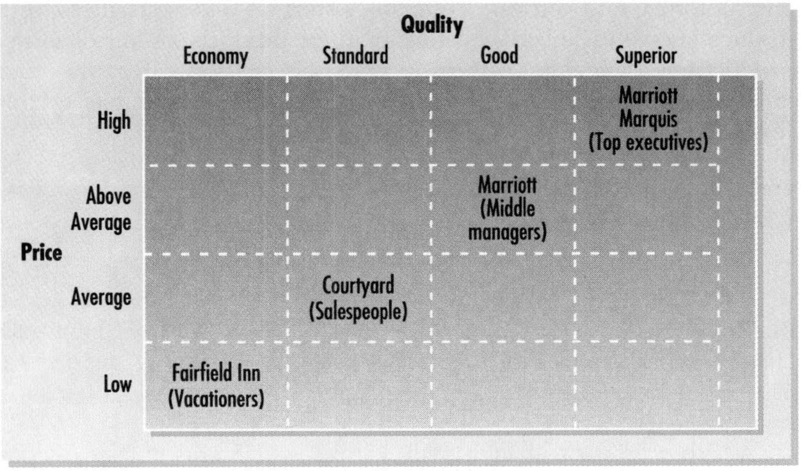

FIGURE 15-5
Two-Way Product-Line Stretch: Marriott Hotels

Figure 15-5: Two-Way Product-Line Stretch: Marriott Hotels

Price \ Quality	Economy	Standard	Good	Superior
High				Marriott Marquis (Top executives)
Above Average			Marriott (Middle managers)	
Average		Courtyard (Salespeople)		
Low	Fairfield Inn (Vacationers)			

LINE FILLING. A product line can also be lengthened by adding more items within the line's present range. There are several motives for *line filling:* reaching for incremental profits, trying to satisfy dealers who complain about lost sales because of missing items in the line, trying to utilize excess capacity, trying to be the leading full-line company, and trying to plug holes to keep out competitors.

Line filling is overdone if it results in cannibalization and customer confusion. The company needs to differentiate each item in the consumer's mind. Each item should possess a *just-noticeable difference.* According to Weber's law, customers are more attuned to relative than to absolute difference.[8] They will perceive the difference between boards 2 and 3 feet long and boards 20 and 30 feet long but not between boards 29 and 30 feet long. The company should make sure that new-product items have a noticeable difference.

The company should also check that the proposed item meets a market need and is not being added simply to satisfy an internal need. The famous Edsel automobile, on which Ford lost $350 million, met Ford's internal positioning needs but not the market's needs. Ford noticed that Ford owners would trade up to General Motors cars like Oldsmobile or Buick rather than step up to Ford's Mercury or Lincoln. Ford decided to create a steppingstone car to fill its line. The Edsel was created, but it failed to meet a market need because many similar cars were available, and many buyers were turning to smaller cars.

Once the product-line manager decides to add another item to sell at a certain price, the design task is turned over to the company engineers. The planned price will dictate how the item is designed, rather than the design dictating the price that will be charged.

Line Modernization

Even when product-line length is adequate, the line might need to be modernized. For example, a company's machine tools might have a 1950s look and lose out to newer-styled competitors' lines.

The issue is whether to overhaul the line piecemeal or all at once. A piecemeal approach allows the company to see how customers and dealers take to the new style. It is also less draining on the company's cash flow, but it allows competitors to see changes and to start redesigning their own lines.

In rapidly changing product markets, product modernization is carried on continuously. Companies plan product improvements to encourage *customer migration* to higher-valued, higher-priced items. Microprocessor companies such as Intel and Motorola, and software companies such as Microsoft and Lotus, continually introduce more advanced versions of their products. A major issue is timing the product improvements so they do not come out too early (thus damaging sales of the current product line) or too late (after competition has established a strong reputation for more advanced equipment).

Line Featuring

The product-line manager typically selects one or a few items in the line to feature. Managers might feature low-end promotional models to serve as traffic builders. Thus Sears will announce a special low-price washing machine to attract customers. And Rolls Royce announced an economy model selling for only $178,000—in contrast to its high-end model selling for $310,000—to attract new buyers.

At other times, managers will feature a high-end item to lend prestige to the product line. Stetson promotes a man's hat selling for $150, which few men buy but which acts as a "flagship" or "crown jewel" to enhance the line's image.

Sometimes a company finds one end of its line selling well and the other end selling poorly. The company may try to boost demand for the slower sellers, especially if they are produced in a factory that is idled by the lack of demand. This situation faced Honeywell when its medium-size computers were not selling as well as its large computers. But things are not always this simple. It could be argued that the company should promote the items that sell well rather than trying to prop up weak demand.

Line Pruning

Product-line managers must periodically review items for pruning. There are two occasions for pruning. One is when the product line includes deadwood that is depressing profits. The weak items can be identified through sales and cost analysis. RCA cut down its color television sets from 69 to 44 models. A chemical company cut down its products from 217 to the 93 with the largest volume, the largest contribution to profits, and the greatest long-term potential.

The other occasion for product pruning is when the company is short of production capacity. The manager should concentrate on producing the higher-margin items. Companies typically shorten their lines in periods of tight demand and lengthen their lines in periods of slow demand.

BRAND DECISIONS

In developing a marketing strategy for individual products, the seller has to confront the branding decision. Branding is a major issue in product strategy. On the one hand, developing a branded product requires a great deal of long-term investment spending, especially for advertising, promotion, and packaging. Many brand-oriented companies subcontract manufacturing to other companies. For example, Taiwanese manufacturers make a great amount of the world's clothing, consumer electronics, and computers, but not under Taiwanese brand names.

On the other hand, manufacturers eventually learn that market power lies with the brand-name companies. Brand-name companies can replace their Taiwanese manufacturing sources with cheaper sources in Malaysia and elsewhere. Japanese and South Korean companies realized this and spent liberally to build up brand names such as Sony, Toyota, Goldstar, and Samsung. Even when these companies can no longer afford to manufacture their products in their homeland, the brand names continue to command customer loyalty.

What Is a Brand?

Perhaps the most distinctive skill of professional marketers is their ability to create, maintain, protect, and enhance brands. Marketers say that "branding is the art and cornerstone of marketing." The American Marketing Association defines a brand as follows:

> ❖ A BRAND is a name, term, sign, symbol, or design, or a combination of them, intended to identify the goods or services of one seller or group of sellers and to differentiate them from those of competitors.

In essence, a brand identifies the seller or maker. It can be a name, trademark, logo, or other symbol. Under trademark law, the seller is granted exclusive rights to the use of the brand name in perpetuity. Thus brands differ from other assets such as patents and copyrights, which have expiration dates.

A brand is essentially a seller's promise to consistently deliver a specific set of features, benefits, and services to the buyers. The best brands convey a warranty of quality. But a brand is even a more complex symbol.[9] A brand can convey up to six levels of meaning:

- *Attributes:* A brand first brings to mind certain attributes. Thus, Mercedes suggests expensive, well built, well engineered, durable, high prestige, high resale value, fast, and so on. The company may use one or more of these attributes to advertise the car. For years Mercedes advertised, "Engineered like no other car in the world." This tagline served as the positioning platform for projecting the car's other attributes.

- *Benefits:* A brand is more than a set of attributes. Customers are not buying attributes; they are buying benefits. Attributes need to be translated into functional and/or emotional benefits. The attribute "durable" could translate into the functional benefit, "I won't have to buy a new car every few years." The attribute "expensive" might translate into the emotional benefit, "The car helps me feel important and admired." The attribute "well built" might translate into the functional and emotional benefit, "I am safe in case of an accident."

- *Values:* The brand also says something about the producer's values. Thus, Mercedes stands for high performance, safety, prestige, and so on. The brand marketer must figure out the specific groups of car buyers who are seeking these values.

- *Culture:* The brand may represent a certain culture. The Mercedes represents German culture: organized, efficient, high quality.

- *Personality:* The brand can also project a certain personality. If the brand were a person, an animal, or an object, what would come to mind? Mercedes may suggest a no-nonsense boss (person), a reigning lion (animal), or an austere palace (object). Sometimes it might take on the personality of an actual well-known person or spokesperson.

- *User:* The brand suggests the kind of consumer who buys or uses the product. We would be surprised to see a 20-year-old secretary driving a Mercedes. We would expect instead to see a 55-year-old top executive behind the wheel. The users will be those who respect the product's values, culture, and personality.

If a company treats a brand only as a name, it misses the point of branding. The challenge in branding is to develop a deep set of meanings for the brand. When the audience can visualize all six dimensions of a brand, the brand is *deep;* otherwise it is *shallow.* A Mercedes is a deep brand because we understand its meaning along all six dimensions. An Audi is a brand with less depth, since we may not grasp as easily its specific benefits, personality, and user profile.

Given the six levels of a brand's meanings, marketers must decide at which level(s) to deeply anchor the brand's identity. One mistake would be to promote only the brand's attributes. First, the buyer is not interested in the brand attributes as much as the brand benefits. Second, competitors can easily copy the attributes. Third, the current attributes may become less valuable later, hurting a brand that is too tied to specific attributes.

Promoting the brand solely on one or more of its benefits can also be risky. Suppose Mercedes touts its main benefit as "high performance." Suppose several competitive brands emerge with high or higher performance. Or suppose car buyers start placing less importance on high performance as compared to other benefits. Mercedes needs the freedom to maneuver into a new benefit positioning.

The most enduring meanings of a brand are its values, culture, and personality. They define the brand's essence. The Mercedes stands for high technology, performance, success, and so on. This is what Mercedes must project in its brand strategy. It would be a mistake for Mercedes to market an inexpensive car bearing the name Mercedes. Doing so would dilute the value and personality that Mercedes has built up over the years.

The Concept and Measurement of Brand Equity

Brands vary in the amount of power and value they have in the marketplace. At one extreme are brands that are not known by most buyers in the marketplace. Then there are brands for which buyers have a fairly high degree of *brand awareness* (measured either by brand recall or recognition). Beyond this are brands with a high degree of *brand acceptability*—in other words, brands that most customers would not resist buying. Then there are brands that enjoy a high degree of *brand preference*. These are brands that are selected over the others. Finally there are brands that command a high degree of *brand loyalty*. Tony O'Reilly, CEO of H. J. Heinz, proposed this test of brand loyalty: "My acid test . . . is whether a housewife, intending to buy Heinz tomato ketchup in a store, finding it to be out of stock, will walk out of the store to buy it elsewhere or switch to an alternative product."

Few customers are as brand-loyal as O'Reilly hopes Heinz's customers will be. Aaker distinguished five levels of customer attitude toward their brand, from lowest to highest:

1. Customer will change brands, especially for price reasons. No brand loyalty.
2. Customer is satisfied. No reason to change the brand.
3. Customer is satisfied and would incur costs by changing brand.
4. Customer values the brand and sees it as a friend.
5. Customer is devoted to the brand.

Brand equity is highly related to how many of a brand's customers are in classes 3, 4, or 5. It is also related, according to Aaker, to the degree of brand-name recognition, perceived brand quality, strong mental and emotional associations, and other assets such as patents, trademarks, and channel relationships.[10]

Certain companies are basing their growth on acquiring and building rich *brand portfolios*. Grand Metropolitan acquired various Pillsbury brands, Green Giant vegetables, Haagen-Dazs ice cream, and Burger King. Nestlé acquired Rowntree (U.K.), Carnation (U.S.), Stouffer (U.S.), Buitoni-Perugina (Italy), and Perrier (France), making it the world's largest food company. In fact, Nestlé paid $4.5 billion to buy Rowntree, five times its book value. These companies do not normally list brand equity on their balance sheet because of the somewhat arbitrariness of the estimate. (For example, one measure of brand equity value is the price premium the brand commands times the extra volume it moves over what an average brand would command.[11])

The world's 10 most valuable brands, according to the 1994 *Financial World* survey of brand value, are (in rank order): Coca-Cola, Marlboro, Nescafe, Kodak, Microsoft, Budweiser, Kellogg's, Motorola, Gillette, and Bacardi. According to the survey, Coca-Cola's brand equity is $36 billion, Marlboro's is $33 billion, and Nescafe's is $11.5 billion.[12]

High brand equity provides a number of competitive advantages:

♦ The company will enjoy reduced marketing costs because of the high level of consumer brand awareness and loyalty.

♦ The company will have more trade leverage in bargaining with distributors and retailers since customers expect them to carry the brand.

♦ The company can charge a higher price than its competitors because the brand has higher perceived quality.

♦ The company can more easily launch brand extensions since the brand name carries high credibility.

♦ The brand offers the company some defense against fierce price competition.

A brand name needs to be carefully managed so that its brand equity doesn't depreciate. This requires maintaining or improving over time brand awareness, brand perceived quality and functionality, positive brand associations, and so on. These tasks require continuous R&D investment, skillful advertising, and excellent trade and consumer service. Some companies, such as Canada Dry and Colgate-Palmolive, have appointed "brand equity managers" to guard the brand's image, associations, and quality—especially when the brand name is extended over other products—and to prevent short-term tactical actions by overzealous brand managers from hurting the brand.

P&G believes that well-managed brands are not subject to a brand life cycle. Many brand leaders of 70 years ago are still today's brand leaders: Kodak, Wrigley's, Gillette, Coca-Cola, Heinz, and Campbell's Soup.

Some analysts see brands as outlasting a company's specific products and facilities. They see brands as the company's major enduring asset. Yet every powerful brand really represents a set of loyal customers. Therefore, the fundamental asset underlying brand equity is *customer equity*. This suggests that the proper focus of marketing planning is that of extending *loyal customer lifetime value,* with brand management serving as a major marketing tool.

Unfortunately, many companies have mismanaged their greatest asset—their brands—by not making an effort to manage brand equity. In Kuczmarski and Associates' nationwide study of companies in a wide range of industries, only 43% of companies indicated that they were even measuring brand equity. And while 72% of companies were confident enough in their brand equity to project that it would last two years with no financial support, over two thirds of the respondents had no formal long-term brand strategy.[13]

Challenges in Branding

Branding poses several challenges to the marketer. The key decisions are shown in Figure 15-6 on page 446 and discussed in the following sections.

BRANDING DECISION: TO BRAND OR NOT TO BRAND? The first decision is whether the company should develop a brand name for its product. In the past, most products went unbranded. Producers and intermediaries sold their goods out of barrels, bins, and cases, without any supplier identification. Buyers depended on the seller's integrity. The earliest signs of branding were the medieval guilds' efforts to require craftspeople to put trademarks on their products to

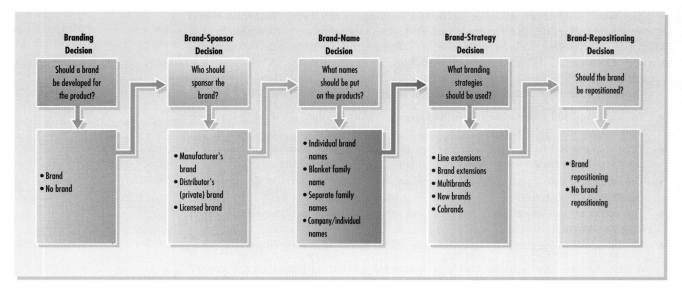

FIGURE 15-6
An Overview of Branding Decisions

protect themselves and consumers against inferior quality. In the fine arts, too, branding began with artists signing their works.

Today, branding is such a strong force that hardly anything goes unbranded. Salt is packaged in distinctive manufacturers' containers, oranges are stamped with growers' names, common nuts and bolts are packaged in cellophane with a distributor's label, and automobile components—spark plugs, tires, filters—bear separate brand names from the automakers'. Fresh food products—such as chicken, turkey, and salmon—are increasingly being sold under strongly advertised brand names.

In some cases, there has been a return to "no branding" of certain staple consumer goods and pharmaceuticals. Correfours, the originator of the French hypermarket (see Chapter 19), introduced a line of "no brands" in its stores in the early 1970s. In 1977, the Jewel Food Stores in Chicago introduced a 40-item "generic" line. *Generics* are unbranded, plainly packaged, less expensive versions of common products such as spaghetti, paper towels, and canned peaches. They offer standard or lower quality at a price that may be as much as 20% to 40% lower than nationally advertised brands and 10% to 20% lower than retailer private-label brands. The lower price is made possible by lower-quality ingredients, lower-cost labeling and packaging, and minimal advertising. Nevertheless, generics are sufficiently satisfying; over 70% of consumers who have purchased generics say they would buy them again. Generic products in the food, household goods, and pharmaceutical industries present a major challenge to high-priced brands and weaker brands.

National brands have fought generics in a number of ways. Ralston-Purina increased its quality and targeted pet owners who identified strongly with their pets and cared most about quality. Procter & Gamble introduced its Banner paper products, a line offering lower quality than its higher lines but greater quality than generics and at a competitive price. Other companies simply have cut their prices to compete with generics.[14]

Why do sellers brand their products when doing so clearly involves costs—packaging, labeling, advertising, legal protection—and the risk that the product may prove unsatisfying to the user? Branding gives the seller several advantages:

- The brand name makes it easier for the seller to process orders and track down problems. Thus Anheuser-Busch receives an order for a hundred cases of Michelob eight-ounce beer instead of an order for "some of your better beer." Furthermore, the seller finds it easier to trace the order if it is misshipped, or to determine why the beer was rancid if consumers complain.

- The seller's brand name and trademark provide legal protection of unique product features, which competitors would otherwise be likely to copy.

- Branding gives the seller the opportunity to attract a loyal and profitable set of customers. Brand loyalty gives sellers some protection from competition and greater control in planning their marketing program.

- Branding helps the seller segment markets. Instead of P&G's selling a simple detergent, it can offer eight detergent brands, each formulated differently and aimed at specific benefit-seeking segments.

- Strong brands help build the corporate image, making it easier to launch new brands and gain acceptance by distributors and consumers.

There is evidence that distributors want manufacturers' brand names because brands make the product easier to handle, hold production to certain quality standards, strengthen buyer preferences, and make it easier to identify suppliers. Consumers want brand names to help them identify quality differences and shop more efficiently.

BRAND-SPONSOR DECISION. A manufacturer has several options with respect to brand sponsorship. The product may be launched as a *manufacturer's brand* (sometimes called a national brand), a *distributor's brand* (also called retailer, store, house, or private brand), or a *licensed brand name* (for more on this topic, see the Marketing Insight on page 448 titled "What's in a Name? Billions"). Or the manufacturer may produce some output under its own name and some under distributor labels. Kellogg's, John Deere & Company, and IBM sell virtually all of their output under their own brand names. Hart Schaffner & Marx sells some of its manufactured clothes under licensed names such as Christian Dior, Pierre Cardin, and Johnny Carson. Whirlpool produces output both under its own name and under distributors' names (for example, Sears Kenmore appliances).

The Battle Between Manufacturers' Brands and Store Brands. Although manufacturers' brands tend to dominate, large retailers and wholesalers have been rapidly developing their own brands. Sears has created several names—Diehard batteries, Craftsman tools, Kenmore appliances—that command brand preference and even brand loyalty. Retailers such as The Limited, Benetton, The Body Shop, The Gap, and Marks & Spencer carry mostly own-brand merchandise. An increasing number of department stores, supermarkets, and drugstores feature store brands. In Britain, for example, two large supermarket chains have developed popular store-brand colas—Sainsbury Cola (from Sainsbury) and Classic Cola (from Tesco). The products stocked in Sainsbury, Britain's largest food chain, are 50% private label; the chain's operating margins are six times as high as U.S. retailer operating margins. U.S. supermarkets average 19.7% private-brand sales, and some marketers think that this number is heading toward 25% to 30% by the year 2000. Some experts believe that 50% is the natural limit for carrying private brands because (1) consumers prefer certain national brands, and (2) many product categories are not attractive on a private-brand basis.

Why do intermediaries bother sponsoring their own brands? They have to hunt down qualified suppliers who can deliver consistent quality, order large quantities and tie up their capital in inventories, and spend money promoting their private label. In spite of these potential disadvantages, private brands offer two advantages. First, they are more profitable. Intermediaries search for manufacturers with

Managing Product
Lines, Brands,
and Packaging

What's In a Name? Billions

Manufacturers or retailers may take years and spend millions to develop consumer preference for their brands. An alternative is to "rent" names that hold magic for consumers. The names or symbols previously created by other manufacturers, the names of well-known celebrities, the characters introduced in popular movies and books—for a fee, any of these can provide a manufacturer's product with an instant and proven brand name. Nowadays a children's feature film, like Disney's *The Lion King* or *Pocahontas,* is much more than an hour or two of entertainment—it's also a vehicle for selling hundreds of products: stuffed animals, chocolates, backpacks, notebooks, lunch boxes, hairbrushes, and so on—all things that children will crave if the film's a hit. In fact, *The Lion King* has so far turned out to be the king of the licensing jungle. It topped $1 billion in merchandise sales in 1994 and is Disney's most global marketing effort, with more than 5,000 different Lion King products introduced across 80 countries.

Due in part to the popularity of merchandise linked to entertainment properties like *The Lion King,* the TV series *Mighty Morphin' Power Rangers,* and the many reincarnations of Batman, retail sales of licensed merchandise in North America reached $70 billion in 1994, up from $4 billion in 1977. And while some big brand names will be licensing history by the time you read this, classic names such as Mickey Mouse, Peanuts, and Barbie continue to be printed on clothing, toys, and school supplies, year after year after year.

Apparel and accessories sellers are the largest licensers, accounting for about 35% of all licensing. Producers and retailers pay sizable royalties to adorn their products with the names of such fashion innovators as Christian Dior, Bill Blass, Calvin Klein, Pierre Cardin, Gucci, and Halston, all of whom license their names or initials for everything from blouses to ties and linens to luggage. In recent years, designer labels have become so common that some retailers are discarding them in favor of their own store brands in order to regain exclusivity, pricing freedom, and higher margins. Even less fashionable names can bring astounding success. Coca-Cola clothes by Murjani rang up $100 million in retail sales in just two years. Other consumer-products companies jumped quickly into corporate fashion licensing—Hershey, Jell-O, Burger King, McDonald's, and others.

The newest form of licensing is corporate licensing—renting a corporate trademark or logo made famous in one category and using it in a related or unrelated category. Currently successful examples include Singer sewing supplies, Caterpillar work clothes, Fabergé costume jewelry, Winnebago camping equipment, and Coppertone swimwear and sunglasses. London-based Virgin Group, parent of Virgin Atlantic Airlines, has aggressively extended its airline brand name, allowing a multimedia personal computer to be marketed under the Virgin name. American Airlines and United Airlines are putting their corporate logos on products like kid's pajamas, hair dryers, and computer software.

Such deals are very good business. As one United executive said, "Whatever proceeds are generated from the use of our trademark names is pure owner's profit."

Sources: See John A. Quelch, "How to Build a Product Licensing Program," *Harvard Business Review,* May–June 1985, pp. 186 ff; Cyndee Miller, "Corporate Licensing Grows as Firms Seek 'Risk-Free' Products," *Marketing News,* April 29, 1991, pp. 1, 8; Kate Fitzgerald, "Licensing: Safe Bet in Recession," *Advertising Age,* June 17, 1991, p. 46; Fitzgerald, " 'Lion' Is New King of Licensing Jungle," *Advertising Age,* July 4, 1994, p. 4; Lois Sloane, "Not Just for Selling T-Shirts, Licensing Is Brand-Building," *Brandweek,* June 13, 1994, p. 43; and Jennifer Lawrence, "United, American License Brands," *Advertising Age,* December 19, 1994, p. 38.

excess capacity who will produce the private label at a low cost. Other costs, such as research and development, advertising, sales promotion, and physical distribution are also much lower for the intermediary. This means that the private brander is often able to charge a lower price and still make a higher profit margin. Second, the retailers develop strong exclusive store brands to differentiate themselves from competitors. Many consumers don't distinguish between national and store brands.

In the confrontation between manufacturers' and private brands, the retailers have many advantages and increasing market power. Because retail shelf space is scarce, many supermarkets now charge a *slotting fee* as a condition for accepting a new brand, to cover the cost of listing it and stocking it. Thus Safeway, the giant supermarket chain, required a payment of $25,000 from a small pizza-roll manufacturer to stock its product. Retailers also charge for special display space and in-store advertising space. They typically give more prominent display to their own brands and make sure they are well stocked. Retailers are now building better quality in their store brands. Consider the following case:

LOBLAW Loblaw, the Canadian supermarket chain, is increasing the number of its store brands. Loblaw now sells the leading cookie brand in Canada, its President's Choice Decadent Chocolate Chip Cookie, which tastes better and costs less than Nabisco's Chips Ahoy brand. It has captured 14% of the market, mostly from Nabisco. Loblaw also introduced its private-label cola, called President's Choice Cola, which racked up 50% of Loblaw's canned cola sales. Loblaw's store brands have become so successful that Loblaw is licensing them to noncompetitive retailers in other countries, thus turning a local store brand into—believe it or not—a global brand!

One interesting fact about Loblaw is that it turned the development of its private-brand programs over to Cott. Cott is a "virtual company"—it owns little—but is able to assemble the necessary suppliers. Thus for President's Choice Cola, Cott chose a syrup supplier (Royal Crown), bottlers, advertising and merchandising agencies, and transportation companies—thus painlessly putting the private-brand program together for Loblaw, the retailer.

Manufacturers of national brands are very frustrated by the growing power of retailer brands. Kevin Price put it well: "A decade ago, the retailer was a chihuahua nipping at the manufacturer's heels—a nuisance, yes, but only a minor irritant; you fed it and it went away. Today it's a pit bull and it wants to rip your arms and legs off. You'd like to see it roll over, but you're too busy defending yourself to even try."[15] Some marketing commentators predict that private brands will eventually knock out all but the strongest manufacturers' brands.

In years past, consumers saw the brands in any category arranged as a *brand ladder,* with their favorite brand at the top and remaining brands in descending order of preference. There are now increasing signs that this ladder is disappearing and being replaced with a consumer perception of *brand parity*—that many brands are equivalent.[16] Instead of a strongly preferred brand, they buy from a set of acceptable brands, choosing whichever is sale-priced that day. As Joel D. Weiner, a former Kraft executive, said: "People don't think the world will come to a screeching halt if they use Tide instead of Cheer." A 1990 study by DDB Needham Worldwide reported that the percentage of packaged-goods consumers saying that they bought only well-known brands fell from 77% to 62% between 1975 and 1990. A Grey Advertising Inc. study reported that 66% of consumers said they were trading down to lower-priced brands, particularly store brands.

This weakening in brand preeminence is due to many factors. Consumers, hard pressed to spend more wisely, are more sensitive to quality, price, and value. They are noting more quality equivalence as competing manufacturers and national retailers copy and duplicate the qualities of the best brands. The continuous barrage of coupons and price specials is training a generation of consumers to buy on price. The fact that companies have reduced their advertising to 30% of their total promotion budget has weakened their brand equity. The endless stream of brand extensions and line extensions has blurred brand identity and led to a confusing amount of product proliferation. Store brands have been improving in quality, posing a strong challenge to manufacturer-owned brands. In the United States, the shares of the top three manufacturer-owned grocery brands have dropped precipitously in some categories.[17]

Manufacturers have reacted by spending substantial amounts of money on consumer-directed advertising and promotion to maintain strong brand preference. Their price has to be somewhat higher to cover the higher promotion cost. At the

Managing Product
Lines, Brands,
and Packaging

same time, the mass distributors pressure the manufacturers to put more promotional money into trade allowances and deals if they want adequate shelf space. Once manufacturers start giving in, they have less to spend on advertising and consumer promotion, and their brand leadership starts spiraling down. This is the national brand manufacturers' dilemma.

To maintain their power vis-à-vis the trade, leading brand marketers need to apply the following strategies. They must invest in heavy and continuous R&D to bring out new brands, line extensions, features, and quality improvements. They must sustain a strong "pull" advertising program to maintain high consumer brand awareness and preference. They must find ways to "partner" with major mass distributors in a joint search for logistical economies and competitive strategies that produce joint savings. Here are two examples:

PROCTER & GAMBLE P&G has assigned 20 of its managers to work alongside Wal-Mart managers at Wal-Mart headquarters in Bentonville, Arkansas, in a search for ways to reduce their joint cost and produce joint savings. As a result, P&G has established customized ordering and automatic stock replenishment programs that result in retail partners' carrying far less inventory. Because of more predictable deliveries, P&G has achieved better production scheduling and spends less time on promotion dealing.

KRAFT Kraft holds so much category expertise in cheese that retailers need Kraft's help to optimize profits from the cheese section in their stores. Kraft uses a proprietary software expert system to advise retail chains what mix of cheeses to carry in each branch neighborhood store (depending on the neighborhood's characteristics) and how to lay it out on the shelves. The Kraft trade marketing team at headquarters manages a database on each store and chain, and has trained and empowered the local sales forces to use this database to provide each store with the optimal Kraft product mix.

BRAND-NAME DECISION. Manufacturers who decide to brand their products must choose which brand names to use. Four strategies are available here:

1. *Individual brand names:* This policy is followed by General Mills (Bisquick, Gold Medal, Betty Crocker, Nature Valley).
2. *Blanket family name for all products:* This policy is followed by Heinz and General Electric.
3. *Separate family names for all products:* This policy is followed by Sears (Kenmore for appliances, Craftsman for tools, and Homart for major home installations).
4. *Company trade name combined with individual product names:* This policy is followed by Kellogg's (Kellogg's Rice Krispies, Kellogg's Raisin Bran, and Kellogg's Corn Flakes).

What are the advantages of an individual-brand-names strategy? A major advantage is that the company does not tie its reputation to the product's acceptance. If the product fails or appears to have low quality, the company's name or image is not likely to be hurt. A manufacturer of good-quality watches, such as Seiko, can introduce a lower-quality line of watches (called Pulsar) without diluting the Seiko name. The individual-brand-names strategy permits the firm to search for the best name for each new product. A new name permits the building of new excitement and conviction.

A blanket family name also has advantages. The development cost is less because there is no need for "name" research or heavy advertising expenditures to create brand-name recognition. Furthermore, sales of the new product are likely to be strong if the manufacturer's name is good. Thus Campbell's introduces new soups under its brand name with extreme simplicity and achieves instant recognition.

Where a company produces quite different products, it is not desirable to use one blanket family name. Swift and Company developed separate family names for its hams (Premium) and fertilizers (Vigoro). When Mead Johnson developed a diet supplement for gaining weight, it created a new family name, Nutriment, to avoid confusion with its weight-reducing family products, Metrecal. Companies often invent different family names for different quality lines within the same product class. Thus A&P food stores sold a first-grade, second-grade, and third-grade set of brands—Ann Page, Sultana, and Iona, respectively.

Finally, some manufacturers tie their company name to an individual brand name for each product. The company name legitimizes, and the individual name individualizes, the new product. Thus Quaker Oats in *Quaker Oats Cap'n Crunch* taps the company's reputation in the breakfast-cereal field, and Cap'n Crunch individualizes and dramatizes the new product.

Once a company decides on its brand-name strategy, it faces the task of choosing a specific brand name. The company could choose the name of a person (Honda, Estée Lauder), location (American Airlines, Kentucky Fried Chicken), quality (Safeway stores, Duracell), lifestyle (Weight Watchers, Healthy Choice), or artificial name (Exxon, Kodak). Among the desirable qualities for a brand name are the following:[18]

1. *It should suggest something about the product's benefits.* Examples: Beauty-rest, Craftsman, Accutron.

2. *It should suggest product qualities such as action or color.* Examples: Sunkist, Spic and Span, Firebird.

3. *It should be easy to pronounce, recognize, and remember.* Short names help. Examples: Tide, Crest, Puffs.

4. *It should be distinctive.* Examples: Mustang, Kodak, Exxon.

5. *It should not carry poor meanings in other countries and languages.* Example: *Nova* is a poor name for a car to be sold in Spanish-speaking countries; it means "doesn't go."

Normally, companies choose brand names by developing a list, debating the merits of different names, and making a choice. Today many companies hire a marketing research firm to develop names and test them. Name-research procedures include *association tests* (What images come to mind?), *learning tests* (How easily is the name pronounced?), *memory tests* (How well is the name remembered?), and *preference tests* (Which names are preferred?). One of the best-known specialists in the "name game" is NameLab, Inc., which is responsible for such brand names as Acura, Compaq, and Zapmail.

Many firms strive to build a unique brand name that eventually will become intimately identified with the product category. A number of brand names have succeeded in this way: Frigidaire, Kleenex, Kitty Litter, Levis, Jell-O, Popsicle, Scotch Tape, Xerox, and Fiberglas. In 1994 Federal Express officially shortened its marketing identity to FedEx, a term that has become a synonym for "to ship overnight."

Unfortunately, success at identifying a brand name with a product category may threaten the company's exclusive rights to the name. Cellophane and shredded wheat are now names in the common domain. The Xerox name now represents a product category (copier machines), not a single product or the company that makes it. For this reason, top executives at Xerox decided in 1994 to seek a new marketing identity that would better communicate Xerox's leadership as an office-systems marketer, not just a copier manufacturer. As a result, the company changed its marketing identity to "The Document Company Xerox." While ads feature "The Document Company" first and "Xerox" in a secondary position, a stylized red "X" features prominently on all advertising, marketing materials, and products.[19]

Given the rapid growth of the global marketplace, companies should choose brand names with an eye to their global reach. These names should be meaningful and pronounceable in other languages. Otherwise companies will find that they cannot use well-known local brand names as they expand geographically. (For

Managing Product
Lines, Brands,
and Packaging

more on this topic, see the Marketing Insight titled "How Far Should Global Branding Be Pushed?")

BRAND-STRATEGY DECISION. A company has five choices when it comes to brand strategy. The company can introduce *line extensions* (existing brand name extended to new sizes, flavors, and so on in the existing product category), *brand extensions* (brand names extended to new-product categories), *multibrands* (new brand names introduced in the same product category), *new brands* (new brand name for a new category product), and *cobrands* (brands bearing two or more well-known brand names). According to Marketing Intelligence Services, of the 17,363 new consumer packaged goods introduced in calendar year 1993, only a handful—794 to be exact—could truly be considered innovative. The rest were line extensions and product enhancements.[20]

Line Extensions. Line extensions occur when a company introduces additional items in the same product category under the same brand name, usually with new features, such as new flavors, forms, colors, added ingredients, package sizes, and so on. Thus, Dannon Company recently introduced several Dannon yogurt line extensions, including fat-free "light" yogurt, dessert flavors like "mint chocolate cream pie" and "caramel apple crunch," a Sprinkle-ins line containing everything from crunchy granola and chocolate graham crackers in a clear covered lid, and "creamy" versions of yogurt specially formulated to appeal to children. The line extensions may be *innovative* (dessert flavors), *"me-too"* (Sprinkle-ins), or *filling-in* (another package size, such as a yogurt four-pack in a cardboard container).

The vast majority of new-product introductions consist of line extensions, as much as 89% in the case of grocery products. The company might be trying to utilize excess manufacturing capacity, meet new consumer needs, match a competitor's new offering, or lock up more retail shelf space.

Many companies are now introducing *branded variants,* which are specific brand lines that are supplied to specific retailers or distribution channels. They result from the pressure that retailers put on manufacturers to enable the retailers to provide distinctive offerings to their customers. Thus, a camera company may supply its low-end cameras to mass merchandisers while limiting its higher-priced items to specialty camera shops. Or Valentino may design and supply different lines of its suits and jackets to different department stores.[21]

Line extension involves risks and has provoked heated debate among marketing professionals.[22] On the down side, extensions may lead to the brand name losing its specific meaning; Ries and Trout call this the "line-extension trap."[23] When a person asked for a Coke in the past, she received a six-and-a-half-ounce bottle. Today the seller will have to ask: New, Classic, or Cherry Coke? Regular or diet? Caffeine or caffeine-free? Bottle or can? Sometimes the original brand identity is so strong that its line extensions only serve to confuse and don't sell enough to cover their development and promotion costs. For example, A-1 poultry sauce flopped because people identify A-1 with beef, and Clorox detergent was doomed from the start because people think of "bleach" and don't want all their clothes to come out colorless. Consider the following misfires:

BAYER   Bayer Select, a line of nonaspirin pain relievers, was introduced in 1992 by Kodak's Sterling Winthrop drug unit to combat the rapid growth of Tylenol and Advil. Bayer Select has 11 products, each for extremely specific ailments, ranging from menstrual cramps to sinus pain to backaches. But the Bayer name has been clearly linked with aspirin for almost a century, so the ailment-specific line is confusing to customers. "They have not done well in relationship to what they spent," commented one senior buyer for Walgreens, the retail drugstore giant. Despite an estimated $100 million marketing budget, the Bayer Select painkillers accounted for less than 2% of the $2.46 billion analgesic market over a year after its introduction.

How Far Should Global Branding Be Pushed?

In the past, most companies established new brand names that made sense in their country. When they later attempted to introduce their brand into foreign markets, some companies discovered that the existing brand name was not appropriate. The name was difficult to pronounce, offensive, funny, meaningless, or already co-opted by someone else. The company would be forced to develop a new brand name for the same product when it was introduced in other countries. P&G had to create a different brand name for its Pert Plus shampoo when it introduced it in Japan (called Rejoy) and the United Kingdom (called Vidal Sassoon). Using different brand names for the same product comes at a high cost, however. The company has to prepare different labels, packaging, and advertising.

The trend today is toward a "borderless world." In Europe, custom duties, border delays, and other impediments to inter-European trade are rapidly diminishing. Companies are eager to launch new brands as Eurobrands. P&G launched its detergent Ariel as a Eurobrand. Mars has replaced its Treets and Bonitas brand names with M&M's worldwide and changed its third largest United Kingdom brand—Marathon—to the Snickers name that it uses in the United States.

Sara Lee's successful line of Eurobrands.

Source: Sara Lee Company.

Unilever is now seeking to market its various detergent brands—All, Omo, Persil, Presto, Skip, and Via—under fewer labels.

Clearly some brand names have gained worldwide acceptance. Such companies as Kodak, McDonald's, IBM, Sony, and Coca-Cola would not think of using different brand names as they enter additional countries.

What are the advantages of a global brand name? One main advantage is economy of scale in preparing standard packaging, labels, promotions, and advertising. Advertising economies result from using standardized ads and the fact that media coverage increasingly overlaps between countries. Another advantage is that sales may increase because travelers will see their favorite brands advertised and distributed in other markets. Third, trade channels are more ready to accept a global brand that has been advertised in their market. Finally, a worldwide recognized brand name is a power in itself, especially when the country-of-origin associations are highly respected. Japanese companies have developed a global reputation for high technology and quality and their names on products give buyers instant confidence that they are getting good value.

But there are also costs and risks to global branding. A single brand name may not be as appealing as locally chosen names. If the company replaces a well-regarded local name with a global name, the changeover cost can be substantial. The company will have to inform millions of people that its brand still exists but under another name. Even the company's local managers may resist the name change ordered from headquarters. The overcentralization of brand planning and programming may dissipate local creativity that might have produced even better ideas for marketing the product.

Even when a company has promoted its global brand name worldwide, it is difficult to standardize its brand associations in all countries. Heineken beer, for example, is viewed as a high-quality beer in the United States and France; a grocery beer in the United Kingdom; and a cheap beer in Belgium. Cheez Whiz, a Kraft General Foods company cheese spread, is viewed as a "junk food" in the United States; a toast spread in Canada; and a coffee flavorer in Puerto Rico.

The major inference to draw from all of this is that wise companies will globalize those elements that make or save substantial sums of money and localize those that competitive positioning and success require.

Even when line extensions sell well, the sales may come at the expense of other items in the line. Sometimes that expense may be more psychological than financial. While Fig Newtons' cousins Cranberry Newtons, Blueberry Newtons, and Apple Newtons are all doing well for Nabisco, the original Fig Newton brand—an innovative product when introduced—now seems like just another flavor. A line extension works best when it takes sales away from competing brands, not when it cannibalizes the company's other items.

However, line extensions can and often do have a positive side. They have a higher chance of survival than new products, which have a 80% to 90% failure rate. Some marketing executives defend line extensions as the best way to build a business. Kimberly-Clark's Kleenex unit has had great success with line extensions. "We try to get facial tissue in every room of the home," says one Kimberly-Clark executive. "If it is there, it will get used." This philosophy has led to 20 varieties of Kleenex facial tissues, including lotion-impregnated tissues, boxes with nursery-rhyme drawings for children's rooms, and a "man-sized" box with tissues 60% larger than regular Kleenex. Sales of the entire Doritos line of corn chips rose to more than $1 billion on the success of the Cool Ranch Doritos extension.

In addition, Hardle and Lodish contend that the need to come up with line extensions is fueled by fierce competition in the marketplace: "In many markets, the development of product-line extensions is a competitive reality. As product categories evolve, a company must continuously adapt its product lines. . . . Could Crest and Colgate have ignored the threat from Arm & Hammer's baking-soda toothpaste?" Nabisco's line of Fat Free Fruit Bars and its immensely popular Snackwell line illustrate this point. These fat-free new offerings have so appealed to U.S. consumers that Nabisco's sales have increased three times as fast as the overall market. Clearly, Nabisco's competitors must start thinking about extending their product lines to compete with Nabisco.

What factors lead to the success or failure of a line extension? The Marketing Memo titled, "The Bottom Line on Line Extensions" discusses some current findings in this area.

Brand Extensions. A company may decide to use an existing brand name to launch a product in a new category. Armour used its Dial brand name to launch a variety of new products that would not easily have obtained distribution without the strength of the Dial name. Honda uses its company name to cover such different products as its automobiles, motorcycles, snowblowers, lawnmowers, marine engines, and snowmobiles. This allows Honda to advertise that it can fit "six Hondas in a two-car garage." Several specialty clothing retailers, such as The Gap and Ann Taylor, are extending their brands into the bath- and body-products arena. Gap stores throughout the United States now feature soap, lotion, shampoo, conditioner, shower gel, bath salts, and perfume spray. Ann Taylor's brand equity is so strong among its core consumers that women bought its new fragrance, Destination, out of the company's catalog without any idea what it smelled like.

Brand-extension strategy offers a number of advantages. A well-regarded brand name gives the new product instant recognition and earlier acceptance. It enables the company to enter new-product categories more easily. Sony puts its name on most of its new electronic products and instantly establishes a conviction of the new product's high quality. Brand extension saves considerable advertising cost that would normally be required to familiarize consumers with a new brand name.

Like line extension, brand extension also involves risks. The new product might disappoint buyers and damage their respect for the company's other products. The brand name may be inappropriate to the new product—consider buying Standard Oil ketchup, Drano milk, or Boeing cologne. The brand name may lose its special positioning in the consumer's mind through overextension. *Brand dilu-*

tion occurs when consumers no longer associate a brand with a specific product or highly similar products. Competitors benefit from brand dilution. Consider the contrast between how Hyatt and Marriott hotels are named:

HYATT AND MARRIOTT Hyatt practices a brand-extension strategy. Hyatt's name appears in every hotel variation: that is, Hyatt Resorts, Hyatt Regency, Hyatt Suites, and Park Hyatt. Marriott, in contrast, practices multibranding. Its various types of hotels are called Marriott Marquis, Marriott, Residence Inn, Courtyard, and Fairfield Inns. It is harder for Hyatt guests to know the differences between Hyatt hotel types, while Marriott more clearly aims its hotels at different segments and builds distinct brand names and images for each.

Transferring an existing brand name to a new category requires great care. For example, S. C. Johnson's popular shaving cream is called Edge. This name was successfully extended to an aftershave lotion. The name Edge probably could also be used to introduce a brand of razor blades. However, the risk would increase in using the name Edge to launch a new shampoo or toothpaste. Then Edge would lose its meaning as a name for a line of shaving products.

Companies that are tempted to transfer their brand name must research how well the brand's associations fit the new product. The best result would occur when the brand name builds the sales of both the new product and the existing product. An acceptable result would be where the new product sells well without affecting the sales of the existing product. The worst result would be where the new product fails and hurts the sales of the existing product.[24]

Multibrands. A company will often introduce additional brands in the same product category. There are various motives for doing this. Sometimes the company is trying to establish different features and/or appeal to different buying motives. Thus, P&G produces nine different brands of detergents. A multibranding strategy also enables the company to lock up more distributor shelf space and to protect its major brand by setting up *flanker brands*. For example, Seiko establishes different brand names for its higher-priced (Seiko Lasalle) and lower-priced watches (Pulsar) to protect its flanks. Sometimes the company inherits different brand names, each with a loyal following, in the process of acquiring competitors. Thus, Electrolux, the Swedish multinational, owns a stable of acquired brand names (Frigidaire, Kelvinator, Westinghouse, Zanussi, White, Gibson) for its appliance lines.

A major pitfall in introducing multibrand entries is that each might obtain only a small market share, and none may be particularly profitable. The company will have dissipated its resources over several brands instead of building a few brands to a highly profitable level. These companies should weed out the weaker brands and establish tighter screening procedures for choosing new brands. Ideally, a company's brands should cannibalize the competitors' brands and not each other. At the very least, the net profits with the multibrand strategy should be larger even if some cannibalism occurs.[25]

New Brands. When a company launches products in a new category, it may find that none of its current brand names are appropriate. Thus, if Timex decides to make toothbrushes, it is not likely to call them Timex toothbrushes. When the present brand image is not likely to help the new product, companies are better off creating new brand names.

In deciding whether to introduce a new brand name, the manufacturer should consider several questions. For example, the 3M Company asks: Is the venture large enough? Will the product last long enough? Is it best to avoid using the 3M name in case the product fails? Does the product need the boost power of the 3M name? Will the cost of establishing a new brand name be covered by the probable sales and profits? Companies are naturally wary about the high cost of imprinting a new brand name in the public's mind. Establishing a new brand name in the U.S. marketplace for a mass-consumer-packaged good can cost anywhere from $50 million to $100 million.

Cobrands. A rising phenomenon is the appearance of *cobranding* (also called *dual branding*), in which two or more well-known brands are combined in an offer. Each brand sponsor expects that the other brand name will strengthen brand preference or purchase intention. In the case of co-packaged products, each brand hopes it might be reaching a new audience by associating with the other brand.

Cobranding takes a variety of forms. One is *component cobranding,* as when Volvo advertises that it uses Michelin tires or Betty Crocker's brownie mix includes a can of Hershey's chocolate syrup. Another form is *same-company cobranding,* as when General Mills advertises Trix/Yoplait yogurt. Still another form is *joint venture cobranding,* as in the case of General Electric/Hitachi lightbulbs in Japan and the Citibank AAdvantage credit card cosponsored by Citibank and American Airlines. Finally, there is *multiple-sponsor cobranding,* as in the case of Taligent, which is a technological alliance among Apple, IBM, and Motorola.

With regard to component branding, many manufacturers make components—motors, computer chips, carpet fibers—that enter into final branded products, and whose individual identity normally gets lost. These component manufacturers hope that their brand will be featured as part of the final product. Among the few component branders that have succeeded in building a separate identity are Intel,

Nutrasweet, and Gortex. Intel's consumer-directed brand campaign has convinced many personal computer buyers to buy only computer brands with "Intel Inside." As a result, major PC manufacturers—IBM, Dell, Compaq—have had to purchase their chips from Intel at a higher price rather than buy equivalent chips from another supplier. Similarly, Searle has convinced many beverage consumers to look for Nutrasweet as an ingredient. And manufacturers of outerware can charge a higher price if their garments include Gortex. Despite these success stories, most component manufacturers do not find it easy to convince consumers to insist on a certain component, material, or ingredient in the final product. The consumer is not likely to choose a car because it features Champion spark plugs or Stainmaster upholstery.

Brand-Repositioning Decision

However well a brand is positioned in a market, the company may have to reposition it later. A competitor may launch a brand next to the company's brand and cut into its market share. Or customer preferences may shift, leaving the company's brand with less demand.

A classic story of successful brand repositioning is the Seven-Up campaign. Seven-Up was one of several soft drinks bought primarily by older people who wanted a bland, lemon-flavored drink. Research indicated that while a majority of soft-drink consumers preferred a cola, they did not prefer it all the time, and many other consumers were noncola drinkers. Seven-Up went for leadership in the noncola market by executing a brilliant campaign, calling itself the Uncola. The campaign featured the Uncola as a youthful and refreshing drink, the one to reach for instead of a cola. Seven-Up created a new way for consumers to view the soft-drink market, as consisting of colas and uncolas, with Seven-Up leading the uncolas. It thus repositioned Seven-Up as an *alternative* to the traditional soft drink, not just another soft drink.

Another exciting story of brand repositioning is PepsiCo's campaign to reincarnate its flagging 30-year-old Mountain Dew brand.

PEPSICO AND MOUNTAIN DEW When the citrus soft drink was originally launched in 1964 it was marketed as "zero-proof hillbilly moonshine that will tickle yer innards." The company used hillbilly characters in its ads and featured an unforgettable slogan: "Ya-hooo! Mountain Dew!" yelped by Willy the Hillbilly. But hillbillies certainly wouldn't make the brand appealing for today's Generation Xers, so Pepsi dropped the country image and began positioning Mountain Dew as the drink of daredevil "Dew Dudes," a bungee-jumping, sky-surfing, mountain-biking gang of guys. Instead of positioning the drink for everyone of all ages, men and women alike, PepsiCo repositioned the product to tap the taste buds of a very narrowly defined group: 12- to 24-year-old males. These consumers aren't concerned with calories or caffeine, which "Dew" has aplenty. The campaign has been a fantastic success: With $2.7 billion in sales in 1995, Mountain Dew has been the fastest growing soft drink in the fastest growing segment of a $50 billion national industry.

PACKAGING AND LABELING DECISIONS

Many physical products going to the market have to be packaged and labeled. Packaging can play a minor role (e.g., inexpensive hardware items) or a major role (e.g., cosmetics). Some packages—such as the Coke bottle and the L'eggs container—are world famous. Many marketers have called packaging a fifth P, along with price, product, place, and promotion. Most marketers, however, treat packaging and labeling as an element of product strategy.

Packaging

We define *packaging* as follows:

❖ **PACKAGING** includes the activities of designing and producing the container or wrapper for a product.

The container or wrapper is called the *package*. The package might include up to three levels of material. Thus, Old Spice After-Shave Lotion is in a bottle *(primary package)* that is in a cardboard box *(secondary package)* that is in a corrugated box *(shipping package)* containing six dozen boxes of Old Spice.

In recent times, packaging has become a potent marketing tool. Well-designed packages can create convenience value for the consumer and promotional value for the producer. Various factors have contributed to packaging's growing use as a marketing tool:

◆ *Self-service:* An increasing number of products are sold on a self-service basis in supermarkets and discount houses. In an average supermarket, which stocks 15,000 items, the typical shopper passes by some 300 items per minute. Given that 53% of all purchases are made on impulse, the effective package operates as a "five-second commercial." The package must perform many of the sales tasks. It must attract attention, describe the product's features, create consumer confidence, and make a favorable overall impression.

◆ *Consumer affluence:* Rising consumer affluence means consumers are willing to pay a little more for the convenience, appearance, dependability, and prestige of better packages.

◆ *Company and brand image:* Companies are recognizing the power of well-designed packages to contribute to instant recognition of the company or brand. The Campbell Soup Company estimates that the average shopper sees its familiar red and white can 76 times a year, creating the equivalent of $26 million worth of advertising.

◆ *Innovation opportunity:* Innovative packaging can bring large benefits to consumers and profits to producers. Toothpaste pump dispensers have captured 12% of the toothpaste market because for many consumers they are more convenient and less messy. Chesebrough-Pond's increased its overall nail-polish sales by 22% after introducing its novel Aziza Polishing Pen for fingernails. The first companies to put their soft drinks in pop-top cans and their liquid sprays in aerosol cans attracted many new customers.

Developing an effective package for a new product requires several decisions. The first task is to establish the *packaging concept.* The packaging concept defines what the package should basically *be* or *do* for the particular product. Should the package's main function(s) be to offer superior product protection, introduce a novel dispensing method, suggest certain qualities about the product or the company, or something else? Consider one example from Kraft General Foods:

KRAFT GENERAL FOODS Kraft General Foods developed a new dog-food product in the form of meatlike patties. Management decided that the unique and palatable appearance of these patties demanded maximum visibility. *Visibility* was defined as the basic packaging concept. Management considered various alternatives and finally chose a tray with a film covering.

Once the packaging concept has been determined, decisions must be made on additional packaging elements—size, shape, materials, color, text, and brand mark. Decisions must be made on how much or little text, cellophane or other transparent films, a plastic or a laminate tray, and so on. Where a product safety issue is involved, decisions must be made on "tamperproof" devices. The various packaging elements must be harmonized. Size interacts with materials, colors, and so on. The packaging elements must also be harmonized with decisions on pricing, advertising, and other marketing elements.

After the packaging is designed, it must be tested. *Engineering tests* are conducted to ensure that the package stands up under normal conditions; *visual tests,* to ensure that the script is legible and the colors harmonious; *dealer tests,* to ensure that dealers find the packages attractive and easy to handle; and *consumer tests,* to ensure favorable consumer response.

In spite of these precautions, a packaging design occasionally gets through with some basic flaw:

> *Sizzl-Spray, a pressurized can of barbecue sauce developed by Heublein . . . had a potential packaging disaster that was discovered in the market tests. . . . "We thought we had a good can, but fortunately we first test marketed the product in stores in Texas and California. It appears as soon as the cans got warm they began to explode. Because we hadn't gotten into national distribution, our loss was only $150,000 instead of a couple of million.*[26]

Developing effective packaging may cost several hundred thousand dollars and take from a few months to a year. The importance of packaging cannot be overemphasized, considering the functions it performs in attracting and satisfying customers. Companies must pay attention, however, to the growing environmental and safety concerns about packaging. Shortages of paper, aluminum, and other materials suggest that marketers should try to reduce their packaging. The growth of nonreturnable glass containers has resulted in using up to 17 times as much glass as with returnable containers. Many packages end up as broken bottles and crumpled cans littering the streets and countryside. All of this packaging creates a major problem in solid waste disposal, requiring huge amounts of labor and energy. Fortunately, many companies have gone "green" in their packaging: S. C. Johnson repackaged Agree Plus shampoo in a stand-up pouch using 80% less plastic, and P&G eliminated outer cartons from its Secret and Sure deodorants, saving 3.4 million pounds of paperboard per year. Companies must make decisions that serve society's interests as well as immediate customer and company objectives.[27]

Labeling

Labeling is a subset of packaging. Sellers must label their products. The label may be a simple tag attached to the product or an elaborately designed graphic that is part of the package. The label might carry only the brand name or a great deal of information. Even if the seller prefers a simple label, the law may require additional information.

Labels perform several functions. First, the label *identifies* the product or brand—for instance, the name Sunkist stamped on oranges. The label might also *grade* the product; thus canned peaches are grade labeled A, B, and C. The label might *describe* the product: who made it, where it was made, when it was made, what it contains, how it is to be used, and how to use it safely. Finally, the label might *promote* the product through its attractive graphics.

Labels eventually become outmoded and need freshening up. The label on Ivory soap has been redone 18 times since the 1890s, with gradual changes in the size and design of the letters. The label on Orange Crush soft drink was substantially changed when its competitors' labels began to picture fresh fruits, thereby pulling in more sales. Orange Crush developed a label with new symbols to suggest freshness and with much stronger and deeper colors.

There is a long history of legal concerns surrounding labels, as well as packaging and products in general. In 1914, the Federal Trade Commission Act held that false, misleading, or deceptive labels or packages constitute unfair competition. The Fair Packaging and Labeling Act, passed by Congress in 1967, set mandatory labeling requirements, encouraged voluntary industry packaging standards, and allowed federal agencies to set packaging regulations in specific industries. The

Food and Drug Administration has required processed-food producers to include nutritional labeling that clearly states the amounts of protein, fat, carbohydrates, and calories contained in products, as well as their vitamin and mineral content as a percentage of the recommended daily allowance. The FDA recently launched a drive to control health claims in food labeling by taking action against the potentially misleading use of such descriptions as "light," "high fiber," and "no cholesterol." Consumerists have lobbied for additional labeling laws to require *open dating* (to describe product freshness), *unit pricing* (to state the product cost in standard measurement units), *grade labeling* (to rate the quality level of certain consumer goods), and *percentage labeling* (to show the percentage of each important ingredient).

SUMMARY

1. Product is the first and most important element of the marketing mix. Product strategy calls for making coordinated decisions on product mixes, product lines, brands, and packaging and labeling.

2. In planning its market offer or product, the marketer needs to think through the five levels of the product. The most fundamental level is the core benefit, the fundamental benefit or service that the customer is really buying. At the second level, the marketer has to turn the core benefit into a basic product. At the third level, the marketer prepares an expected product, a set of attributes that buyers normally expect and agree to when they buy the product. At the fourth level, the marketer prepares an augmented product, one that includes additional services and benefits that distinguish the company's offer from that of competitors. At the fifth and final level, the marketer prepares a potential product, which encompasses all the augmentations and transformations that the product might ultimately undergo.

3. Products can be classified in several ways. In terms of durability and tangibility, products can be nondurable goods, durable goods, or services. In the consumer-goods category, products are either convenience goods (staples, impulse goods, emergency goods); shopping goods (homogeneous and heterogeneous); specialty goods; or unsought goods. In the industrial-goods category, products fall into one of three categories: materials and parts (raw materials—i.e., farm products and natural products—and manufactured materials and parts—i.e., component materials and component parts); capital items (installations and equipment); or supplies and business services (operating supplies, maintenance and repair items, maintenance and repair services, business advisory services).

4. Most companies sell more than one product. Their product mix can be classified according to width, length, depth, and consistency. These four dimensions are the tools for developing the company's marketing strategy and deciding which product lines to grow, maintain, harvest, and divest. Strong products should be grown or maintained; weak and/or unprofitable lines should be harvested or divested. To analyze a product line and decide how many resources should be invested in that line, product-line managers need to look at the line's sales and profits and market profile.

5. A company can change the product component of its marketing mix by lengthening its product via line stretching (downward, upward, or two-way) or line filling; by modernizing its products; by featuring certain products; and by pruning its products to eliminate the least profitable.

6. Branding is a major issue in product strategy. Branding is expensive and time-consuming, and can make or break a product. The most valuable brands have a brand equity that is considered an important company asset. In thinking about branding strategy, companies must decide whether or not to brand, whether to produce manufacturer brands or distributor/private brands, which brand name to use, and whether to use line

extensions, brand extensions, multibrands, new brands, or cobrands. The best brand names suggest something about the product's benefits; suggest product qualities; are easy to pronounce, recognize, and remember; are distinctive; and do not carry negative meanings or connotations in other countries or languages.

7. Many physical products going to the market have to be packaged and labeled. Well-designed packages can create convenience value for customers and promotional value for producers. In effect, they can act as "five-second commercials" for the product. Marketers have to develop a packaging concept and test it functionally and psychologically to make sure it achieves its desired objectives and is compatible with public policy and social-responsibility concerns. Physical products also require labeling for identification and possible grading, description, and product promotion. Sellers may be required by law to present certain information on the label to protect and inform consumers.

CONCEPT APPLICATIONS

1. Suppose that Wal-Mart approaches 3M Company and asks it to develop a cellophane tape that it can sell in its stores under the Wal-Mart name. Wal-Mart wants the product to be of the same quality as 3M's Scotch brand tape. 3M is willing to produce a good-quality tape but is not willing to produce an excellent tape that would compete head-to-head with its own Scotch tape. Evaluate the dilemma facing 3M. What are the advantages and disadvantages to 3M of producing cellophane tape for Wal-Mart?

2. Consumers today are very interested in getting the best value for their money. As a result, many companies are looking to find ways to keep their customers from abandoning their brands in favor of lower-cost, nonbranded equivalents. As one solution to this problem, some companies are turning to *cobranding*—forming alliances with other companies to produce more value for the consumer. However, a poorly planned cobranding strategy can confuse customers and devalue a company's brand. What safeguards should be taken to avoid this costly mistake?

3. Using the levels of the product concept (Figure 15-2), compare the following vehicles: a Porsche, a Ford pickup truck, and a Toyota Tercel.

4. Offer a definition of the basic business of each of the following large companies. In other words, what basic needs does each company seek to satisfy?
   a. General Motors
   b. Bayer (maker of aspirin)
   c. Twentieth Century Mutual Funds
   d. Sears
   e. *U.S. News & World Report* (magazine)

5. Most firms prefer to develop a diversified product line to avoid overdependence on a single product. Yet there are certain advantages that accrue to a firm that produces and sells one product. What are some of these advantages?

6. Celestial Seasonings teas originally made a name for themselves in health food stores before moving into the mass market. Whether in small shops or larger supermarkets, Celestial Seasonings teas command a price premium. Analyze the Celestial Seasonings ad in Figure 1 on page 462, and briefly explain what elements of product and packaging strategy are incorporated into the ad's theme and copy.

7. An experienced product manager and a new product manager at Sunbeam were engaged in a heated discussion. Bob Adams, the new product manager, contends that a product should be dropped as soon as it becomes troubled and that a new product should be introduced to replace the troubled product. Shirley Cheswick, the experienced product manager, insists that products can be rejuvenated and do not necessarily have to be replaced. Present arguments that will help Shirley win this debate.

Managing Product
Lines, Brands,
and Packaging

8. The American Marketing Association established the Edison Award Program in 1986 to recognize excellence in innovation in consumer products. The winners (which are the products themselves) are chosen on the basis of the following criteria:

   ◆ Marketplace innovativeness—innovative strategy, positioning, advertising, and sales promotion, all of which translate into marketplace success

   ◆ Profitability and staying power

   ◆ Technological innovativeness

   ◆ Market-structure innovativeness—innovation in pioneering a new market or restructuring a present market by creating a new segment or dominating an existing one

   ◆ Lasting value

   ◆ Societal impact—the product improves the consumer's lifestyle and/or increases the consumer's freedom of choice.

   Some products that have won awards in the past are Kellogg's Healthy Choice cereals, Nabisco's Reduced Fat Oreos, Frito-Lay's Baked Tostitos, and Ferolito's Arizona Iced Tea.

   Select five products that you believe meet the criteria listed above, and explain why you identified these products as winners.

9. Although we sometimes talk about *companies* as being market leaders, market challengers, market followers, or market nichers, very often it is the company's individual *product lines* that fit these categories rather than the company itself. A company may have a mixture of products—some leaders, some challengers, some followers, and some nichers. The following is a list of some AT&T businesses. Into which of the four categories does each business fall?

   a. video telephones
   b. McCaw cellular phones
   c. long-distance telephone service

d. AT&T Submarine Systems (produces undersea fiber-optic cables)

e. the AT&T Universal Card (credit card)

f. NCR (personal computers and business computer systems)

g. AT&T Network Systems (provides phone switches to modernize phone systems around the world)

h. AT&T Credit Corp. (supplies credit to businesses)

10. Several companies are planning to put their brand names on fresh food, and many of their initial forays will be in produce. (For example, Dole recently introduced freshly packaged salads with croutons and dressing.) Discuss the challenges that the companies might face, and suggest how these challenges might be overcome.

NOTES

1. Greg W. Prince, "Snapple Comes of Age," *Beverage World,* February 1993, pp. 24–30; Melissa Campanelli, "Profiles in Marketing: Arnold Greenberg," *Sales and Marketing Management,* August 1993, p. 12.

2. This discussion is adapted from Theodore Levitt, "Marketing Success through Differentiation—of Anything," *Harvard Business Review,* January–February 1980, pp. 83–91. The first level, core benefit, has been added to Levitt's discussion.

3. See Harper W. Boyd, Jr., and Sidney Levy, "New Dimensions in Consumer Analysis," *Harvard Business Review,* November–December 1963, pp. 129–40.

4. Theodore Levitt, *The Marketing Mode* (New York: McGraw-Hill, 1969), p. 2.

5. For some definitions, see *Dictionary of Marketing Terms,* ed. Peter D. Bennett (Chicago: American Marketing Association, 1995). Also see Patrick E. Murphy and Ben M. Enis, "Classifying Products Strategically," *Journal of Marketing,* July 1986, pp. 24–42.

6. This illustration is found in Benson P. Shapiro, *Industrial Product Policy: Managing the Existing Product Line* (Cambridge, MA: Marketing Science Institute, 1977), pp. 3–5, 98–101.

7. Fara Warner, "Upscale Chocolate's Not Hot, so Godiva Does a Makeover," *Brandweek,* July 4, 1994, p. 21.

8. See Steuart Henderson Britt, "How Weber's Law Can Be Applied to Marketing," *Business Horizons,* February 1975, pp. 21–29.

9. The following scheme benefitted from a presentation by Larry Light, former international division chairman of Ted Bates Advertising, at the Kellogg School, Northwestern University, where he spoke of four dimensions: attributes, benefits, values, and personality; and the scheme of Jean-Noel Kapferer called the *prism of identity* in which he outlined six dimensions of a brand, though not all the same six dimensions described here. See Jean-Noel Kapferer, *Strategic Brand Management: New Approaches to Creating and Evaluating Brand Equity* (London: Kogan Page, 1992), pp. 38 ff.

10. David A. Aaker, *Managing Brand Equity* (New York: Free Press, 1991). Also see Kevin Lane Keller, "Conceptualizing, Measuring, and Managing Customer-Based Brand Equity," *Journal of Marketing,* January 1993, pp. 1–23.

11. Aaker, *Managing Brand Equity,* pp. 21–30. Also see Patrick Barwise et al., *Accounting for Brands* (London: Institute of Chartered Accountants in England and Wales, 1990); and Peter H. Farquhar, Julia Y. Han, and Yuji Ijiri, "Brands on the Balance Sheet," *Marketing Management,* Winter 1992, pp. 16–22. Brand equity should reflect not only the capitalized value of the incremental profits from the current use of the brand name but also the value of its potential extensions to other products.

12. Alexandra Ourusoff, "Brands: What's Hot. What's Not, " *Financial World,* August 2, 1994, pp. 40–54.

13. Scott Davis and Darrell Douglass, "Holistic Approach to Brand Equity Management," *Marketing News,* January 16, 1995, pp. 4–5.

14. For further reading, see Brian F. Harris and Roger A. Strang, "Marketing Strategies in the Age of Generics," *Journal of Marketing,* Fall 1985, pp. 70–81.

15. Quoted in "Trade Promotion: Much Ado About Nothing," *Promo,* October 1991, p. 37.

16. For a more detailed discussion on consumers' perceptions of store brand quality, see Paul S. Richardson, Alan S. Dick, and Arun K. Jain, "Extrinsic and Intrinsic Cue Effects on Perceptions of Store Brand Quality," *Journal of Marketing,* October, 1994, pp. 28–36.

17. See Gretchen Morgenson, "The Trend Is Not Their Friend," *Forbes,* September 16, 1991; and "What's in a Name? Less and Less," *Business Week,* July 8, 1991.

18. See Kim Robertson, "Strategically Desirable Brand Name Characteristics," *Journal of Consumer Marketing,* Fall 1989, pp. 61–70.

19. Tim Triplett, "Generic Fear to Xerox Is Brand Equity to FedEx," *Marketing News,* August 15, 1994, pp. 12–13; "Xerox Changes Identity," *Marketing News,* August 29, 1994, p. 1.

20. Robert McMath, "Product Proliferation," *Adweek (Eastern Ed.) Superbrands 1995 Supplement,* 1995, pp. 34–40.

21. See Steven M. Shugan, "Branded Variants," *1989 AMA Educators' Proceedings* (Chicago: American Marketing Association, 1989), pp. 33–38.

22. McMath, "Product Proliferation," pp. 34–40; John A. Quelch and David Kenny, "Extend Profits, Not Product Lines," *Harvard Business Review,* September–October 1994, pp. 153–60; and Bruce G. S. Hardle, Leonard M. Lodish, James V. Kilmer, David R. Beatty, et al., "The Logic of Product-Line Extensions," *Harvard Business Review,* November–December 1994, pp. 53–62.

23. Al Ries and Jack Trout, *Positioning: The Battle for Your Mind* (New York: McGraw-Hill, 1981).

24. Barbara Loken and Deborah Roedder John, "Diluting Brand Beliefs: When Do Brand Extensions Have a Negative Impact?" *Journal of Marketing,* July 1993, pp. 71–84; Susan M. Broniarcyzk and Joseph W. Alba, "The Importance of the Brand in Brand Extension," *Journal of Marketing Research,* May 1994,

pp. 214–28 (this entire issue of *JMR* is devoted to brands and brand equity).

25. See Mark B. Taylor, "Cannibalism in Multibrand Firms," *Journal of Business Strategy,* Spring 1986, pp. 69–75.

26. "Product Tryouts: Sales Tests in Selected Cities Help Trim Risks of National Marketing," *The Wall Street Journal,* August 10, 1962.

27. See Alicia Swasy, "Sales Lost Their Vim? Try Repackaging," *The Wall Street Journal,* October 11, 1989, B1; Marisa Manley, "Product Liability: You're More Exposed Than You Think," *Harvard Business Review,* September–October 1987, pp. 28–40; and John E. Calfee, "FDA's Ugly Package," *Advertising Age,* March 16, 1992, p. 25.

MANAGING
SERVICE BUSINESSES
AND PRODUCT
SUPPORT SERVICES

*There are no such things as service industries. There are only
industries whose service components are greater
or less than those of other industries. Everybody is in service.*

THEODORE LEVITT

❖

*I am sick and tired of visitng plants to hear nothing but great things
about quality and cycle time . . .
and then to visit customers who tell me of problems.*

JOHN AKERS, FORMER CEO, IBM

❖

*Customer service isn't a stand-alone department . . . it is a strategic tool for
managing the entire customer relationship.*

AN AT&T MANAGER

❖

M

arketing theory and practice developed initially in connection with physical products such as toothpaste, cars, and steel. Yet one of the major megatrends (see Chapter 6) has been the phenomenal growth of services. In the United States, service jobs now account for 79% of all jobs and 74% of gross domestic product. And according to the Bureau of Labor Statistics, service occupations will be responsible for all net job growth through the year 2005.[1] These numbers have led to a growing interest in the special problems of marketing services.[2]

Service industries are quite varied. The *government sector,* with its courts, employment services, hospitals, loan agencies, military services, police and fire departments, post office, regulatory agencies, and schools, is in the service business. The *private nonprofit sector,* with its museums, charities, churches, colleges, foundations, and hospitals, is in the service business. A good part of the *business sector,* with its airlines, banks, computer-service bureaus, hotels, insurance companies, law firms, management consulting firms, medical practices, motion-picture companies, plumbing-repair companies, and real-estate firms, is in the service business. Many workers in the *manufacturing sector,* such as the computer operators, accountants, and legal staff, are really service providers. In fact, they make up a "service factory" providing services to the "goods factory."

Not only are there traditional service businesses, but new types keep popping up to serve the needs of a changing population:

> With more and more companies trimming their support staffs, the use of "corporate concierges" is on the rise. These people are on call for time-consuming or unusual assignments like repairing a briefcase, shopping for a hard-to-find gift, or finding a hotel room in a booked-up city. For people who want to hose down the dog without messing up their homes, there are self-service pet grooming centers. And, for your average stressed-out person, there are massage-therapy outfits that offer everything from sensory deprivation tanks to enzyme treatments.

Manufacturing companies can use a service strategy to differentiate themselves. In the 1980s Caterpillar started up such service units as Caterpillar Insurance Company to arrange insurance programs for its dealers. And former Caterpillar employees started Advanced Technology Services to provide computer maintenance and repair services to both their former company and other businesses.

In this chapter, we examine the following questions:

+ **How are services defined and classified?**
+ **How do services differ from goods?**
+ **How can service firms improve their differentiation, quality, and productivity?**
+ **How can goods-producing companies improve their product support services?**

THE NATURE AND CLASSIFICATION OF SERVICES

We define a service as follows:

❖ A **SERVICE** is any act or performance that one party can offer to another that is essentially intangible and does not result in the ownership of anything. Its production may or may not be tied to a physical product.

A company's offer to the marketplace often includes some services. The service component can be a minor or a major part of the total offer. Five categories of offer can be distinguished:

1. *Pure tangible good:* The offer consists primarily of a tangible good such as soap, toothpaste, or salt. No services accompany the product.

2. Tangible good with accompanying services: The offer consists of a tangible good accompanied by one or more services to enhance its consumer appeal. For example, an automobile manufacturer must sell more than an automobile. Levitt observes that "the more technologically sophisticated the generic product (e.g., cars and computers), the more dependent are its sales on the quality and availability of its accompanying customer services (e.g., display rooms, delivery, repairs and maintenance, application aids, operator training, installation advice, warranty fulfillment). In this sense, General Motors is probably more service intensive than manufacturing intensive. Without its services, its sales would shrivel."[3] In fact, many manufacturers are now discovering opportunities to sell their services as a separate profit center. (For more on this topic, see the Marketing Insight box on page 468 titled "Selling Services for Profit.")

3. *Hybrid:* The offer consists of equal parts of goods and services. For example, people patronize restaurants for both their food and their service.

4. *Major service with accompanying minor goods and services:* The offer consists of a major service along with additional services and/or supporting goods. For example, airline passengers are buying transportation service. They arrive at their destinations without anything tangible to show for their expenditure. However, the trip includes some tangibles, such as food and drinks, a ticket stub, and an airline magazine. The service requires a capital-intensive good—an airplane—for its realization, but the primary item is a service.

5. *Pure service:* The offer consists primarily of a service. Examples include baby-sitting, psychotherapy, and massages.

As a consequence of this varying goods-to-service mix, it is difficult to generalize about services unless further distinctions are made. However, some generalizations seem safe:

First, services vary as to whether they are *equipment based* (automated car washes, vending machines) or *people based* (window washing, accounting services). People-based services vary by whether they are provided by unskilled, skilled, or professional workers.

Second, some services require the *client's presence.* Thus brain surgery involves the client's presence, but a car repair does not. If the client must be present, the service provider has to be considerate of his or her needs. Thus beauty shop operators will invest in their shop's decor, play background music, and engage in light conversation with the client.

Third, services differ as to whether they meet a *personal need* (personal services) or a *business need* (business services). Physicians will price physical examinations differently for private patients versus employees on a prepaid company health plan. Service providers typically develop different marketing programs for personal and business markets.

Fourth, service providers differ in their *objectives* (profit or nonprofit) and *ownership* (private or public). These two characteristics, when crossed, produce four quite different types of service organizations. Clearly, the marketing programs of a

Selling Services for Profit

As many companies experience shrinking profit margins on the products they sell, they are trying to make more money on the services they provide. They sometimes charge fees for services that they formerly provided free with the product. In other cases, they are pricing their services higher. Auto dealers today make most of their profit on financing, insurance, and repair services, not on automobiles. In still other cases, companies are creating service businesses alongside their product businesses. In some cases, these service businesses are growing faster and are more profitable than the company's product businesses.

Here are six ways that manufacturers can create service businesses:

1. *Repackaging its product into a system solution:* Rather than selling only its products—chemicals, computers, machine tools—the company can embed these products into service programs that meet more of the customers' needs. Thus, a service-minded fertilizer company can offer to customize the fertilizer for each individual farm and even spread the fertilizer with its own equipment. Fanuc Robotics of North America has changed itself from an assembler of robots into a designer and installer of customized manufacturing systems.

2. *Packaging the company's internal services into saleable external services:* Some companies, in developing an internal competence, recognize that they can sell this competence to other companies. For example, Xerox developed a highly effective internal sales force training program and subsequently decided to launch Xerox Learning Systems to sell its sales training system to other companies.

3. *Servicing other companies from the company's physical facilities:* Companies that manage a physical facility often find that they can sell the facility's services to other companies. Kimberly-Clark, located in Neenah, Wisconsin, operates and maintains its own fleet of corporate aircraft. It has expanded its ability to provide and sell maintenance and overhaul services to other companies operating corporate aircraft.

4. *Offering to manage other companies' physical facilities:* A major growth area is contract management of such facilities as lawns, cafeterias, data processing centers, and so on. Thus Scott, the seed company, also operates a lawn maintenance business. S. C. Johnson, which sells insect sprays, also manages a major extermination service business called BBBK. At Johnson Controls, a manufacturer of thermostats and energy systems, design engineers who were once confined to their cubicles and harnessed to their computers now are out in their customers' buildings, managing the heating and cooling systems they helped to create.

5. *Selling financial services:* Equipment companies often discover that they can profit from financing the customers' purchases. GE Credit Corporation originally financed only GE customers and dealers but today finances commercial and home loans, auto leases, and dealer inventories.

6. *Moving into distribution services.* Manufacturers can own and operate retailing outlets for their products. Hart Schaffner and Marx is essentially a clothing manufacturer that also operates a series of retail clothing chains. Quaker Oats, the cereal manufacturer, manages several restaurant chains. Many manufacturers also operate factory outlet stores, and some manufacturers have opened up their own flagship stores that sell only their own products. These brand-name showcases include Speedo Authentic Fitness stores, Nike Town, OshKosh B'Gosh Inc., and Original Levi's Stores and Dockers Shops.

Sources: See Irving D. Canton, "Learning to Love the Service Economy," *Harvard Business Review,* May–June 1984, pp. 89–97; Mack Hanan, *Profits Without Products: How to Transform Your Product Business into a Service* (New York: Amacom, 1992); and Ronald Henkoff, "Service Is Everybody's Business," *Fortune,* June 27, 1994, pp. 48–60.

private investor hospital will differ from those of a private charity hospital or a Veterans' Administration hospital.[4]

CHARACTERISTICS OF SERVICES AND THEIR MARKETING IMPLICATIONS

Services have four major characteristics that greatly affect the design of marketing programs: intangibility, inseparability, variability, and perishability.

Intangibility

Services are intangible. Unlike physical products, they cannot be seen, tasted, felt, heard, or smelled before they are bought. The person getting a face lift cannot see the exact results before the purchase, and the patient in the psychiatrist's office cannot know the exact outcome.

To reduce uncertainty, buyers will look for signs or evidence of the service quality. They will draw inferences about service quality from the place, people, equipment, communication material, symbols, and price that they see. Therefore, the service provider's task is to "manage the evidence," to "tangibilize the intangible."[5] Whereas product marketers are challenged to add abstract ideas, service marketers are challenged to put physical evidence and imagery on their abstract offers. Consider the following tangible images: "You are in good *hands* with Allstate"; "I've got a piece of the *rock*" (Prudential).

Suppose a bank wants to position itself as the "fast" bank. It could make this positioning strategy tangible through a number of marketing tools:

1. *Place:* The bank's physical setting must connote quick service. The bank's exterior and interior should have clean lines. The layout of the desks and the traffic flow should be planned carefully. Lines should not get overly long.
2. *People:* The bank's personnel should be busy. There should be a sufficient number of employees to manage the workload.
3. *Equipment:* The bank's equipment—computers, copying machines, desks—should be and look "state of the art."
4. *Communication material:* The bank's communication material—text and photos—should suggest efficiency and speed.
5. *Symbols:* The bank should choose a name and symbol suggesting its fast service. It could adopt the Greek god Mercury as a pictorial symbol.
6. *Price:* The bank could advertise that it will deposit $5 in the account of any customer who waits in line for more than five minutes.

Inseparability

Services are typically produced and consumed simultaneously. This is not true of physical goods, which are manufactured, put into inventory, distributed through multiple resellers, and consumed still later. If a person renders the service, then the provider is part of the service. Since the client is also present as the service is produced, provider-client interaction is a special feature of services marketing. Both the provider and the client affect the service outcome.

In the case of entertainment and professional services, buyers are highly interested in the specific provider. It is not the same concert if Pearl Jam is indisposed and replaced by Marie Osmond, or if a legal defense will be supplied by John Nobody because F. Lee Bailey is unavailable. When clients have strong provider preferences, price is raised to ration the preferred provider's limited time.

Several strategies exist for getting around this limitation. The service provider can learn to work with larger groups. Psychotherapists have moved from one-on-one therapy to small-group therapy to groups of over 300 people in a large hotel ballroom. The service provider can learn to work faster—the psychotherapist can spend 30 minutes with each patient instead of 50 minutes and can see more patients. The service organization can train more service providers and build up client confidence, as H&R Block has done with its national network of trained tax consultants.

Managing Service
Businesses and Product
Support Services

Variability

Because they depend on who provides them and when and where they are provided, services are highly variable. Some doctors have an excellent bedside manner and are very good with children; other are more gruff and have less patience with children. Some surgeons have a track record of success in performing a certain type of operation; other surgeons are less successful in this area. Service buyers are aware of this high variability and frequently talk to others before selecting a service provider.

Service firms can take three steps toward quality control. The first is investing in good human resources selection and training. Airlines, banks, and hotels spend substantial sums to train their employees in providing good service. Thus one should find the same friendly and helpful personnel in every Hyatt Hotel.

The second step is standardizing the service-performance process throughout the organization. This is helped by preparing a *service blueprint* that depicts the service events and processes in a flow chart, with the objective of recognizing potential service fail points. Figure 16-1 shows a service blueprint for a nationwide floral-delivery organization.[6] The customer's experience is limited to dialing

FIGURE 16-1

A Service-Performance-Process Map: Nationwide Floral Delivery

Source: G. Lynn Shostack, "Service Positioning Through Structural Change," *Journal of Marketing*, January 1987, p. 39. Reprinted with permission of the American Marketing Association.

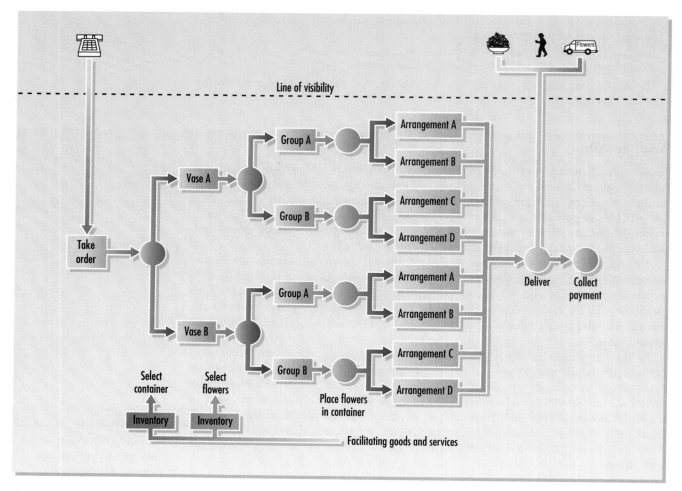

the phone, making choices, and placing an order. Behind the scenes, the floral organization gathers the flowers, places them in a vase, delivers them, and collects payment.

The third step is monitoring customer satisfaction through suggestion and complaint systems, customer surveys, and comparison shopping, so that poor service can be detected and corrected.

Perishability

Services cannot be stored. Some doctors charge patients for missed appointments because the service value existed only at that point. The perishability of services is not a problem when demand is steady because it is easy to staff the services in advance. When demand fluctuates, service firms have difficult problems. For example, public-transportation companies have to own much more equipment because of rush-hour demand than they would if demand were even throughout the day.

Sasser has described several strategies for producing a better match between demand and supply in a service business.[7]

On the demand side:

♦ *Differential pricing* will shift some demand from peak to off-peak periods. Examples include low early-evening movie prices and weekend discount prices for car rentals.

♦ *Nonpeak demand can be cultivated.* McDonald's opened a breakfast service, and hotels developed their minivacation weekends.

♦ *Complementary services* can be developed during peak time to provide alternatives to waiting customers, such as cocktail lounges to sit in while waiting for a table and automatic tellers in banks.

♦ *Reservation systems* are a way to manage the demand level. Airlines, hotels, and physicians employ them extensively.

On the supply side:

♦ *Part-time employees* can be hired to serve peak demand. Colleges add part-time teachers when enrollment goes up, and restaurants call in part-time servers when needed.

♦ *Peak-time efficiency routines* can be introduced. Employees perform only essential tasks during peak periods. Paramedics assist physicians during busy periods.

♦ *Increased consumer participation* in the tasks can be encouraged. Example: consumers fill out their own medical records or bag their own groceries.

♦ *Shared services* can be developed. Example: several hospitals share medical-equipment purchases.

♦ *Facilities for future expansion* can be developed. Example: an amusement park buys surrounding land for later development.

MARKETING STRATEGIES FOR SERVICE FIRMS

Until recently, service firms lagged behind manufacturing firms in their use of marketing. Many service businesses are small (shoe repair, barbershops) and do not use formal management or marketing techniques. There are also professional service businesses (law and accounting firms) that formerly believed it was unprofessional to use marketing. Other service businesses (colleges, hospitals) faced so much demand or so little competition until recently that they saw no need for marketing. But all of this is changing. Consider the case of the U.S. Postal Service:

Managing Service
Businesses and Product
Support Services

In 1992, Marvin Runyon was hired as Postmaster General to overhaul the U.S. Postal Service. One of his key priorities was to increase mail volume and revenues by making the USPS more marketing oriented—a new goal for a government service that had never had to market itself to U.S. consumers. However, with private overnight delivery services (such as Federal Express and Airborne Express) and new technology products (such as fax machines and computer e-mail) eroding market share, the USPS had no choice. In 1994 a marketing executive finally joined the USPS's highest ranks and put the focus on priority mail, residential package delivery, and mailed advertisements. As part of its marketing campaign, the USPS is striving to improve the service of its priority-mail product so that it can truly fulfill its promise of two-day delivery. "Overnight is overkill" is the 2-day delivery slogan, devised to pit the $3.00 per two-pound service against more expensive private overnight services.[8]

Traditional 4P marketing approaches often work well for goods, but additional elements require attention in service businesses. Booms and Bitner suggested the addition of three Ps involved in service marketing: people, physical evidence, and process.[9] Because most services are provided by *people,* the selection, training, and motivation of employees can make a huge difference in customer satisfaction. Ideally, employees should exhibit competence, a caring attitude, responsiveness, initiative, problem solving ability, and goodwill. Service companies such as Federal Express and Marriott trust their people enough to empower their front-line personnel to spend up to $100 to resolve a customer problem. Companies also try to demonstrate their service quality through *physical evidence* and presentation. Thus a hotel will develop a look and observable style of dealing with customers that carries out its intended customer-value proposition, whether it is cleanliness, speed, or some other benefit. Finally, service companies can choose among different *processes* to deliver their service. Thus restaurants have developed such different formats as cafeteria-style, fast-food, buffet, and candlelight service.

Service encounters are affected by more elements than product encounters (Figure 16-2). Consider a customer visiting a bank to get a loan (service X). The customer sees other customers waiting for this and other services. The customer

FIGURE 16-2

Elements in a Service Encounter

Source: Slightly modified from P. Eiglier and E. Langeard, "A Conceptual Approach to the Service Offering," in *Proceedings of the EAARM X Annual Conference,* ed. H. Hartvig Larsen and S. Heede (Copenhagen: Copenhagen School of Economics and Business Administration, 1981).

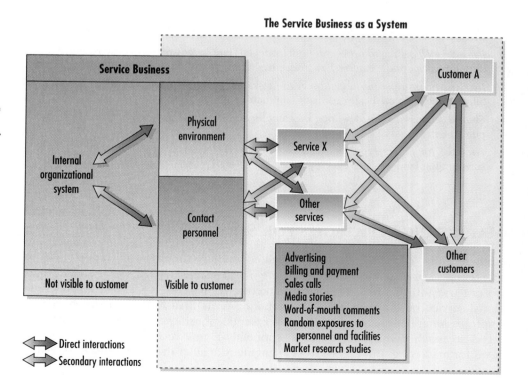

also sees a physical environment consisting of a building, interior, equipment, and furniture. In addition, the customer sees contact personnel and deals with a loan officer. All this is visible to the customer. Not visible is a whole "back-room" production process and organization system that supports the visible service business. Thus the service outcome, and whether or not people will remain loyal to a service provider, is influenced by a host of variable elements.[10]

In view of this complexity, Gronroos has argued that service marketing requires not only external marketing but also internal and interactive marketing (Figure 16-3).[11] *External marketing* describes the normal work done by the company to prepare, price, distribute, and promote the service to customers. *Internal marketing* describes the work done by the company to train and motivate its employees to serve customers well. Berry has argued that the most important contribution the marketing department can make is to be "exceptionally clever in getting everyone else in the organization to practice marketing."[12] For example, Radford (Illinois) Community Hospital set up a fund of $10,000 out of which it pays patients who have a justified complaint ranging from cold food to overlong waits in the emergency room. The "hook" is that any money not paid out of the fund at the end of the year is divided among the hospital's employees. This plan has added a tremendous incentive for the staff to treat the patients well. If there are 100 employees, and no patients have to be paid by the end of the year, each employee gets a $100 bonus. In the first six months, the hospital had to pay out only $300 to patients.

Interactive marketing describes the employees' skill in serving the client. Because the client judges service quality not only by its *technical quality* (e.g., Was the surgery successful?) but also by its *functional quality* (e.g., Did the surgeon show concern and inspire confidence?),[13] service providers must deliver "high touch" as well as "high tech."[14] Consider the cases of two companies that have been successful at delivering a combination of high touch and high tech:

CHARLES SCHWAB Charles Schwab, the premier U.S. discount broker, uses an innovative combination of high-tech and high-touch services. Two Schwab high-tech options that eliminate customers' reliance on brokers and that save them time and money are tele-broker (an automated telephone touch-pad order entry system) and StreetSmart (a software package that allows customers to trade through Schwab using a PC). At the same time, customers who crave high-touch contact can drop in at any of the company's big-city or local branches and enjoy a one-on-one customer/broker relationship. Four regional call centers also offer front-line customer/broker contact via telephone.[15]

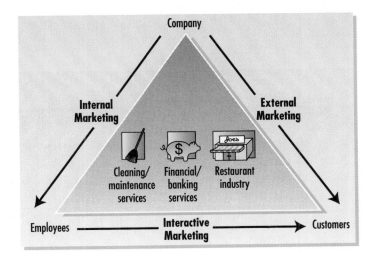

FIGURE 16-3
Three Types of Marketing in Service Industries

Managing Service
Businesses and Product
Support Services

When a client calls this insurance company, the service representative pulls up a complete computerized client profile within seconds. The company is able to settle death claims in four days (versus the industry norm of twenty-one days) and respond to general inquiries within four hours (versus the industry norm of five days). Equally impressive, the company is accomplishing these tasks with 20% fewer employees and 35% higher productivity.

There are some services where the customers cannot judge the service's technical quality even after they have received the service. Figure 16-4 arrays various products and services according to their difficulty of evaluation.[16] At the left are goods high in *search qualities*—that is, characteristics that the buyer can evaluate before purchase. In the middle are goods and services high in *experience qualities*—characteristics that the buyer can evaluate after purchase. At the right are goods and services high in *credence qualities*—characteristics that the buyer normally finds hard to evaluate even after consumption.[17]

Because services are generally higher in experience and credence qualities than goods are, consumers feel more risk in their purchase. This fact has several consequences. First, service consumers generally rely more on word of mouth than on service-firm advertising. Second, they rely heavily on price, personnel, and physical cues to judge the service quality. Third, they are highly loyal to the service provider when satisfied.

Service companies face three tasks—increasing their *competitive differentiation,* their *service quality,* and their *productivity.* Although these interact to some extent, we will examine each separately.

Managing Differentiation

Service marketers frequently complain about the difficulty of differentiating their services from those of competitors. The deregulation of several major service industries—communications, transportation, energy, banking—precipitated intense price competition. The success of the budget-priced Southwest Airlines has shown that many fliers care more about travel costs than service. The early and continued success of Charles Schwab in the discount brokerage service showed that many

FIGURE 16-4

Continuum of Evaluation for Different Types of Products

Source: Valarie A. Zeithaml, "How Consumer Evaluation Processes Differ between Goods and Services," in *Marketing of Services*, ed. James H. Donnelly and William R. George Reprinted with permission of the American Marketing Association, 1981.

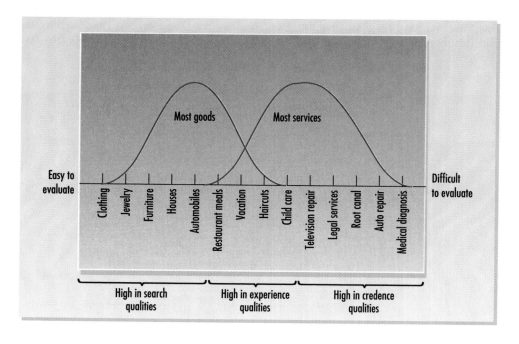

customers had little loyalty to the more established brokerage houses when they could save money. To the extent that customers view a service as fairly homogeneous, they care less about the provider than the price.

The alternative to price competition is to develop a differentiated offer, delivery, and/or image.

OFFER. The offer can include innovative features to distinguish it from competitors' offers. What the customer expects is called the *primary service package,* and to this can be added *secondary service features.* In the airline industry, for example, various carriers have introduced such secondary service features as movies, advanced seating, merchandise for sale, air-to-ground telephone service, and frequent-flyer award programs. Marriott is setting up hotel rooms for high-tech travelers who need accommodations that will support computers, fax machines, and e-mail. Hertz recently added an innovative secondary service feature to differentiate its auto rental service—namely, its #1 Club Gold service for its Club Gold members:

HERTZ   At the airport, the Hertz customer is picked up by a Hertz courtesy shuttle bus and taken directly to the preassigned car. The keys will be in the ignition and the trunk open, ready to receive the luggage. The preprinted invoice will be hanging from the rear-view mirror, and the customer simply shows his or her driver's license to the security guard on the way out.

The major challenge in service differentiation is that most service innovations are easily copied. Few of them are preemptive in the long run. Still, the service company that regularly researches and introduces service innovations will gain a succession of temporary advantages over its competitors. And, through earning a reputation for innovation, it may retain customers who want to go with the best. Thus Citicorp enjoys the reputation of being a lead innovator in the banking industry for aggressively creating or furthering such innovations as automatic teller machines, nationwide banking, broad-spectrum financial accounts and credit cards, and floating prime rates.

DELIVERY. A service company can distinguish its service delivery quality by having more able and reliable customer-contact people than its competitors (Home Depot, Nordstrom). It can develop a more attractive physical environment in which the service is delivered (Borders Book & Music Stores, Cineplex Odeon movie theaters). Or it can design a superior delivery process (Citicorp, the first bank to introduce automatic teller machines on a wide scale).

IMAGE. Service companies can also work on differentiating their image. They often do this through symbols and branding. The Harris Bank of Chicago adopted the lion as its symbol and uses it on its stationery, on its advertising, and even on the stuffed animals it offers to new depositors. As a result, the Harris lion is well known and confers an image of strength to the bank. Several hospitals have attained "megabrand" reputations for being the best in their field, such as the Mayo Clinic, Massachusetts General, and Sloane-Kettering. Any of these hospitals could open clinics in other cities and attract patients on the strength of its brand power.

Several highly branded service companies have developed successful international operations. For example, Club Med (a subsidiary of the French firm, Club Méditerranée, S.A.) has managed to achieve exceptional marketing and financial success in its short 40-year history. Gilbert Trigano opened the first Club Med "village" in Greece in 1955, and today Club Med operates more than 114 villages in 36 countries:

CLUB MED   The Club Med formula is simple: provide a vacation that removes people from everyday pressures; where they don't have to make many decisions; where they can dress casually, meet, play, and dine with other people; and where they enjoy beautiful warm weather. For a few memorable weeks, the vacationers escape from the competitive world and enter into a simpler, more cooperative existence in a Club Med village.

Guests prepay for their whole stay and use beads instead of money in the village. The guests, called GMs (gentils membres) are assisted by the staff members, called GOs (gentils organisateurs). The GOs, of whom there may be 100 in a village, work long hours and act as the guests' instructors, entertainers, and friends. The villages are located in picturesque settings and are fully equipped with tennis courts, discotheques, and excellent food service.

Club Med turns an attractive profit stemming from the guests' fees, earning millions in interest by receiving and depositing guests' prepayments weeks in advance of the guests' visits. In addition, Club Med is able to buy air transportation at wholesale rates because of its large volume, while charging retail rates to the guests. In addition, substantial money for building new villages comes from the host countries, which are eager to build their tourism industry.

Until recently, Club Med applied a standard approach to the design and operation of its villages. Today it is introducing more adaptations in the effort to attract and satisfy more target markets. Club Med has created some villages to appeal to more mature customers who are married and have children. The Club has established computer workshops in some villages to appeal to more business-oriented guests. The Club has increased the number of non-French GOs as a way to further internationalize the villages. New villages have been located more conveniently to guests traveling from the northeastern United States. In other words, Club Med is moving from standardized global marketing to adaptive global marketing.[18]

Managing Service Quality

One of the major ways to differentiate a service firm is to deliver consistently higher-quality service than competitors. The key is to meet or exceed the target customers' service-quality expectations. Customers' expectations are formed by their past experiences, word of mouth, and service-firm advertising. The customers choose providers on these bases and, after receiving the service, compare the *perceived service* with the *expected service*. If the perceived service falls below the expected service, customers lose interest in the provider. If the perceived service meets or exceeds their expectations, they are apt to use the provider again. For a checklist of questions that marketers should ask themselves when trying to exceed customer expectations, see the Marketing Memo titled "Exceeding Customers' Highest Hopes: A Service Marketing Checklist."

Parasuraman, Zeithaml, and Berry formulated a service-quality model that highlights the main requirements for delivering high service quality.[19] The model, shown in Figure 16-5 on page 478, identifies five gaps that cause unsuccessful service delivery:

1. *Gap between consumer expectation and management perception:* Management does not always perceive correctly what customers want. Hospital administrators may think that patients want better food, but patients may be more concerned with nurse responsiveness.

2. *Gap between management perception and service-quality specifications:* Management might correctly perceive the customers' wants but not set a specified performance standard. Hospital administrators may tell the nurses to give "fast" service without specifying it quantitatively.

MARKETING MEMO

EXCEEDING CUSTOMERS' HIGHEST HOPES: A SERVICE MARKETING CHECKLIST

Customers' expectations are the true standards for judging service quality. Understanding the nature and determinants of expectations is essential to ensuring that service performance meets or exceeds expectations.

Effectively managing expectations sets the stage for surpassing them—which, in turn, contributes to cultivating a customer franchise. Berry and Parasuraman propose that marketing managers ask themselves the following questions as they seek to manage and exceed expectations:

1. **Do we strive to present a realistic picture of our service to customers?** Do we always check the accuracy of our promotional messages prior to customers' exposure to them? Is there regular communication between employees who serve customers and those who make promises to customers? Do we assess the impact on customer expectations on cues such as price?

2. **Is performing the service right the first time a top priority in our company?** Do we stress to our employees that providing reliable service is an effective way of managing customers' expectations? Are our employees trained and rewarded for delivering error-free service? Do we regularly evaluate our service designs to identify and correct potential flaws?

3. **Do we communicate effectively with customers?** Do we periodically contact customers to ascertain their needs and appreciate their business? Do we train and require employees to demonstrate to customers we care about and value them?

4. **Do we surprise customers during the service process?** Are our employees aware that the process of service delivery represents the prime opportunity to exceed customers' expectations? Do we take specific steps to encourage excellence during service delivery?

5. **Do our employees regard service problems as opportunities to impress customers, or as annoyances?** Do we prepare and encourage employees to excel in the service recovery process? Do we reward them for providing exceptional recovery service?

6. **Do we continuously evaluate and improve our performance against customers' expectations?** Do we perform consistently above the adequate service level? Do we capitalize on opportunities to exceed the desired service level?

Sources: Reprinted with the permission of The Free Press, an imprint of Simon & Schuster from *Marketing Services: Competing Through Quality* by Leonard L. Berry and A. Parasuraman. Copyright © 1991 by The Free Press. Also see Leonard L. Berry, *On Great Service: A Framework for Action* (New York: Free Press, 1995).

3. *Gap between service-quality specifications and service delivery:* The personnel might be poorly trained or incapable of or unwilling to meet the standard. Or they may be held to conflicting standards, such as taking time to listen to customers and serving them quickly.

4. *Gap between service delivery and external communications:* Consumer expectations are affected by statements made by company representatives and ads. If a hospital brochure shows a beautiful room but the patient arrives and finds the room to be cheap and tacky looking, then the external communications have distorted the customer's expectations.

FIGURE 16-5

Service-Quality Model

Source: A. Parasuraman, Valarie A. Zeithaml, and Leonard L. Berry, "A Conceptual Model of Service Quality and Its Implications for Future Research," *Journal of Marketing*, Fall 1985, p. 44. Reprinted with permission of the American Marketing Association.

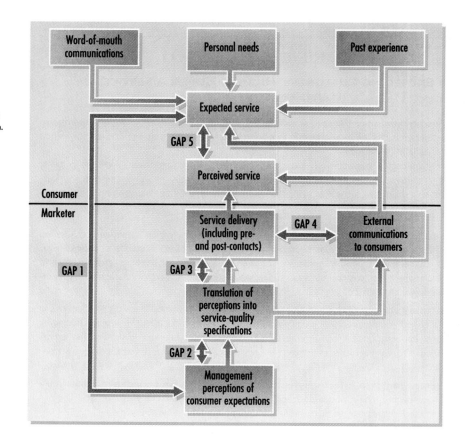

5. *Gap between perceived service and expected service:* This gap occurs when the consumer misperceives the service quality. The physician may keep visiting the patient to show care, but the patient may interpret this as an indication that something really is wrong.

The same researchers found that there are five determinants of service quality. These are presented in the order of their importance as rated by customers (an allocation of 100 points):[20]

1. *Reliability:* The ability to perform the promised service dependably and accurately. (32 points)

2. *Responsiveness:* The willingness to help customers and to provide prompt service. (22)

3. *Assurance:* The knowledge and courtesy of employees and their ability to convey trust and confidence. (19)

4. *Empathy:* The provision of caring, individualized attention to customers. (16)

5. *Tangibles:* The appearance of physical facilities, equipment, personnel, and communication materials. (11)

Various studies have shown that excellently managed service companies share the following common practices: a strategic concept, a history of top-management commitment to quality, high standards, systems for monitoring service performance, systems for satisfying customers' complaints, and an emphasis on employee and customer satisfaction.

STRATEGIC CONCEPT. Top service companies are "customer obsessed." They have a clear sense of their target customers and the customer needs they are trying to satisfy. They have developed a distinctive strategy for satisfying these needs that wins enduring customer loyalty.

HISTORY OF TOP-MANAGEMENT COMMITMENT TO QUALITY. Companies such as Marriott, Disney, Delta, and McDonald's have thorough commitments to quality. Their management looks not only at financial performance on a monthly basis but also at service performance. Ray Kroc of McDonald's insisted on continually measuring each McDonald's outlet on its conformance to QSCV: quality, service, cleanliness, and value. Franchises that failed to conform were dropped.

HIGH STANDARDS. The best service providers set high service-quality standards. Swissair, for example, aims at having 96% or more of its passengers rate its service as good or superior. Citibank aims to answer phone calls within ten seconds and customer letters within two days. The standards must be set *appropriately* high. A 98% accuracy standard may sound good but it would result in Federal Express losing 64,000 packages a day, 10 misspelled words on each page, 400,000 misfilled prescriptions daily, and unsafe drinking water eight days a year. Companies can be distinguished between those offering "merely good" service and those offering "breakthrough" service aiming at 100% defect-free service.[21]

SYSTEMS FOR MONITORING SERVICE PERFORMANCE. The top service firms audit service performance, both their own and competitors', on a regular basis. They use a number of devices to measure performance: comparison shopping, ghost shopping (see Chapter 2), customer surveys, suggestion and complaint forms, service-audit teams, and letters to the president. General Electric sends out 700,000 response cards a year asking households to rate its servicepeople's performance. Citibank checks continuously on measures of ART (accuracy, responsiveness, and timeliness). It does ghost shopping to find out if its employees deliver good service. The First Chicago Bank employs a weekly Performance Measurement Program charting its performance on a large number of customer-sensitive issues. Figure 16-6 on the next page shows a typical chart used by the bank to track its speed in answering customer-service phone inquiries. It will take action whenever its performance falls below the minimum acceptable performance level. It also raises its performance goal over time.

When designing customer feedback mechanisms such as surveys, marketers may need to reevaluate cherished beliefs and assumptions. If they do not, the survey's results may steer them down the wrong road to quality, as United Parcel Service (UPS) discovered:

UNITED PARCEL SERVICE UPS always assumed that on-time delivery was its customers' paramount concern, and it even based its definition of quality on the results of time-and-motion studies. To get packages to customers faster, UPS would factor in such details as how long it took elevators to open on certain city apartment blocks and how long it took people to answer their doorbells. Accordingly, UPS's surveys barraged customers with questions about whether they were pleased with UPS's delivery time and whether they thought the company could be any speedier. Yet, it turned out that UPS was not asking the right questions. When the company began asking broader questions regarding how it could improve its service, it discovered that what customers wanted most was more face-to-face contact with drivers. If drivers were less harried and more willing to stay and chat, customers might come away with practical advice on shipping.[22]

Managing Service Businesses and Product Support Services

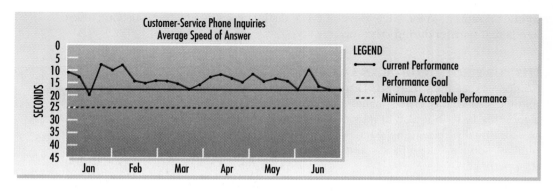

FIGURE 16-6
Tracking Customer-Service Performance

Services can be usefully rated according to their *customer importance* and *company performance*. *Importance-performance analysis* can be used to rate the various elements of the service bundle and identify what actions are required. For example, Table 16-1 shows how customers rated 14 service elements (attributes) of an automobile dealer's service department on importance and performance. Importance was rated on a four-point scale of "extremely important," "important," "slightly important," and "not important." Dealer performance was rated on a four-point scale of "excellent," "good," "fair," and "poor." For example, "Job done right the first time" (attribute #1) received a mean importance rating of 3.83 and a mean performance rating of 2.63, indicating that customers felt it was highly important but was not being performed well.

The ratings of the 14 elements are displayed in Figure 16-7 and are divided into four sections. Quadrant A shows important service elements that are not being performed at the desired levels; they include elements 1, 2, and 9. The dealer

TABLE 16-1	ATTRIBUTE NUMBER	ATTRIBUTE DESCRIPTION	MEAN IMPORTANCE RATING*	MEAN PERFORMANCE RATING†
CUSTOMER IMPORTANCE AND PERFORMANCE RATINGS FOR AN AUTO DEALERSHIP	1	Job done right the first time	3.83	2.63
	2	Fast action on complaints	3.63	2.73
	3	Prompt warranty work	3.60	3.15
	4	Able to do any job needed	3.56	3.00
	5	Service available when needed	3.41	3.05
	6	Courteous and friendly service	3.41	3.29
	7	Car ready when promised	3.38	3.03
	8	Perform only necessary work	3.37	3.11
	9	Low prices on service	3.29	2.00
	10	Clean up after service work	3.27	3.02
	11	Convenient to home	2.52	2.25
	12	Convenient to work	2.43	2.49
	13	Courtesy buses and cars	2.37	2.35
	14	Send out maintenance notices	2.05	3.33

* Ratings obtained from a four-point scale of "extremely important" (4), "important" (3), "slightly important" (2), and "not important" (1).
† Ratings obtained from a four-point scale of "excellent" (4), "good" (3), "fair" (2), and "poor" (1). A "no basis for judgment" category was also provided.

should concentrate on improving the service department's performance on these elements. Quadrant B shows important service elements where the department is performing well; its job is to maintain the high performance. Quadrant C shows minor service elements that are being delivered in a mediocre way but do not need any attention, since they are not very important. Quadrant D shows that a minor service element, "Send out maintenance notices," is being performed in an excellent manner, a case of possible overkill. Perhaps the company should spend less on sending out maintenance notices and reallocate the savings toward improving the company's performance on important elements where it is weak. The analysis can be enhanced further by checking on the competitors' performance levels on each element. The worst case is where a close competitor is performing much better than the company on a very important element.[23]

SYSTEMS FOR SATISFYING CUSTOMERS' COMPLAINTS.

Studies of customer dissatisfaction show that customers are dissatisfied with their purchases about 25% of the time, but that only about 5% complain. The other 95% either feel that complaining is not worth the effort or that they don't know how or to whom to complain.

Of the 5% of customers who complain, only about 50% report a satisfactory problem resolution. Yet the need to resolve a customer problem in a satisfactory manner is critical. Whereas, on average, a satisfied customer tells three people about a good product experience, the average dissatisfied customer gripes to eleven people. If each of them tells still other people, the number of people exposed to bad word of mouth may grow exponentially.

Nonetheless, customers whose complaints are satisfactorily resolved often become more company-loyal than customers who were never dissatisfied. About 34% of customers who register major complaints will buy again from the company if their complaint is resolved, and this number rises to 52% for minor complaints. If the complaint is resolved quickly, between 52% (major complaints) and 95% (minor complaints) will buy again from the company.[24]

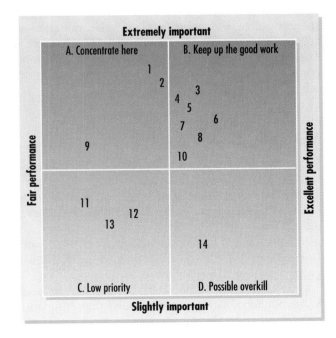

FIGURE 16-7
Importance-Performance Analysis

For all these reasons, companies need to develop a *service recovery program*. As a first step, companies should make it easy for dissatisfied customers to complain. They should not be like the Spanish hotel that tells guests that it will accept complaints at the front desk only from 9 to 11 A.M. Businesses instead should maximize the ease with which customers can complain. They should provide suggestion and complaint forms and a toll-free telephone number. Pizza Hut prints its toll-free number on all pizza boxes. When a customer complains, Pizza Hut sends voice mail to the store manager, who must call the customer within 48 hours and resolve the complaint.

Second, the company's employees who receive complaints must be trained and empowered to resolve customer problems speedily and satisfactorily. Studies show that the faster the company responds to the complaint, the higher the customer's satisfaction with the company. Third, the company should go beyond satisfying particular customers to discovering and correcting the root causes of frequent problems. By studying the pattern of complaints, the company can correct system failures that give rise to these complaints. Timothy Firnstahl, who runs a Seattle restaurant chain called Satisfaction Guaranteed Eateries, Inc., set down these service recovery guidelines: "When guests have to wait more than ten minutes beyond their reservation time, but less than twenty, we suggest free drinks. If they wait more than twenty minutes, the entire meal may be free. If the bread arrives more than five minutes after the guests sit down, we suggest free chowder."[25]

SATISFYING BOTH EMPLOYEES AND CUSTOMERS. Excellently managed service companies believe that employee relations will reflect on customer relations. Management carries out internal marketing and creates an environment of employee support and rewards for good service performance. Management regularly audits employees' satisfaction with their jobs. Karl Albrecht observed that unhappy employees can be "terrorists." Rosenbluth and Peters, in *The Customer Comes Second,* go so far as to say that the company's employees, not the company's customers, have to be made number one if the company hopes to truly satisfy its customers.[26]

An important part of satisfying employees is helping them cope with the demands on their lives outside the office. As employees put a higher premium on spending time with their families, smart companies are going out of their way to accommodate employees' needs with flexible work schedules. Connecticut's Union Trust Bank is able to hire—and retain—more mothers of young children by accommodating their desire not to work when their children are home from school.[27]

Managing Productivity

Service firms are under great pressure to keep costs down and increase productivity. There are seven approaches to improving service productivity.

The first is to have service providers work more skillfully. The company can hire and foster more skillful workers through better selection and training procedures.

The second is to increase the quantity of service by surrendering some quality. Doctors working for some HMOs have moved toward handling more patients and giving less time to each patient.

The third is to "industrialize the service" by adding equipment and standardizing production. Levitt recommended that companies adopt a "manufacturing attitude" toward producing services as represented by McDonald's assembly-line approach to fast-food retailing, culminating in the "technological hamburger."[28] Hyatt is testing self-service machines to facilitate guest check-in and checkout. Southwest Airlines uses ATM-like machines to allow self-service for ticket purchasing and boarding passes. Shouldice Hospital near Toronto, Canada, operates only on patients with hernias and has reduced patient stay from the typical seven days to half that time by industrializing the service. Although its doctors are paid less than in private practice and its nurses attend more patients than in a normal hospital, patient satisfaction is unbelievably high.[29]

The fourth is to reduce or make obsolete the need for a service by inventing a product solution, the way television substituted for out-of-home entertainment, the wash-and-wear shirt reduced the need for commercial laundries, and certain antibiotics reduced the need for tuberculosis sanitariums.

The fifth is to design a more effective service. How-to-quit-smoking clinics may reduce the need for expensive medical services later on. Hiring relatively inexpensive paralegal workers reduces the need for more expensive legal professionals.

The sixth is to present customers with incentives to substitute their own labor for company labor. For example, business firms that are willing to sort their own mail before delivering it to the post office pay lower postal rates. A restaurant that features a self-service salad bar is replacing "serving" work with customer work.

The seventh is to harness the power of technology. While we often think of technology's power to save time and costs in manufacturing companies, it also has great—and often untapped—potential to make service workers more productive. Consider these examples:[30]

SAN DIEGO MEDICAL CENTER Respiratory therapists at the University of California at San Diego Medical Center now carry miniature computers in their lab pockets. In the past, therapists had to wait at the nurses' station for patients' records. Today, therapists call up the information on hand-held computers, which pluck the data from a central computer. As a result, they can spend more time working directly with patients.

STORAGE DIMENSIONS Using a computerized system called Apriori, Storage Dimensions operators can answer customer service questions on the spot. When a customer calls with a problem, the operator inputs key words. If the customer's question has been asked and answered before, a solution document "bubbles up" to the top of the PC screen. Since installing Apriori, SD has reduced problem resolution time from an average of two hours to twenty minutes. As an added bonus, the company has also used information gleaned during the "help" conversations to generate sales leads and product-development ideas.

Companies must avoid pushing productivity so hard that they reduce perceived quality. Some methods for increasing productivity increase customer satisfaction by standardizing quality. Other methods lead to too much standardization and rob the customer of customized service; "high touch" is replaced by "high tech." Burger King challenged McDonald's by running a "Have it your way" campaign, where customers could get a "customized" hamburger sandwich even though this offer reduced Burger King's productivity somewhat. In addition, many college publishers today are offering customized textbooks, rearranging some chapters and eliminating others to suit professors' classroom needs.

MANAGING PRODUCT SUPPORT SERVICES

Thus far we have focused our attention on service industries. No less important are product-based industries that must provide a service bundle to their customers. Manufacturers of equipment—small appliances, office machines, tractors, mainframes, airplanes—all have to provide the buyers with *product support services*. In fact, product support service is becoming a major battleground for competitive advantage. Some equipment companies, such as Caterpillar Tractor and John Deere, make more than 50% of their profits from product support services. In the global marketplace, companies that make a good product but provide poor local product support are seriously disadvantaged. When Subaru entered the Australian market, it avoided the product support problem by contracting to use the Australian Volkswagen dealer network to provide parts and service.

Firms that provide high-quality service will undoubtedly outperform their less service-oriented competitors. Table 16-2 provides evidence. The Strategic Planning Institute sorted out the top third and the bottom third of 3,000 business units according to ratings of "relative perceived service quality." The table shows that the high-service businesses managed to charge more, grow faster, and make more profits on the strength of their superior service quality.

The company must define customer needs carefully in designing both the product and the product support system. Customers are most concerned about an interruption of the service that they expect from the product. They have three specific worries:[31]

◆   First, they worry about reliability and *failure frequency,* how often the product is likely to break down in a given period. A farmer may tolerate a combine that will break down once a year, but not two or three times.

◆   Second, customers worry about *downtime duration*. The longer the downtime, the higher the cost, especially if a crew cannot work when the product is idle. A construction manager, for example, can tolerate a few hours downtime for an excavator, but her impatience is likely to rise at an increasing rate as more hours pass. The customer counts on the seller's *service dependability*—that is, the seller's ability to fix the machine quickly, or at least provide a loaner so that work can resume.[32]

◆   Third, customers worry about *out-of-pocket costs of maintenance and repair service*. How much does the customer have to spend on regular maintenance, repair costs, and so on?

An intelligent buyer takes all of these factors into consideration in choosing a vendor. The buyer wants to estimate the offer's expected *life-cycle cost,* which is the product's purchase cost plus the discounted cost of maintenance and repair less the discounted salvage value. Buyers have a right to ask for hard data in choosing among vendors.

The importance of reliability, service dependability, and maintenance vary among different products and product users. A one-computer office will need higher product reliability and faster repair service than an office where there are other computers available if one breaks down. An airline needs 100% reliability in

TABLE 16-2	CONTRIBUTION OF SERVICE QUALITY TO RELATIVE PERFORMANCE		
	HIGH THIRD IN SERVICE QUALITY	**LOW THIRD IN SERVICE QUALITY**	**DIFFERENCE IN % POINTS**
Price index relative to competition	7%	−2%	+9%
Change in market share per annum	6%	−2%	+8%
Sales growth per annum	17%	8%	+9%
Return on sales	12%	1%	+11%

Source: **Phillip Thompson, Glenn Desourza, and Bradley T. Gale, "The Strategic Management of Service and Quality,"** *Quality Progress,* **June 1985, p. 24. Reprinted with permission of American Society for Quality Control.**

the air. Where reliability is important, manufacturers or service providers can offer guarantees to promote sales. For more on this topic, see the Marketing Insight on pages 486–487 titled "Offering Guarantees to Promote Sales."

To provide the best support, a manufacturer must identify the services that customers value most and their relative importance. In the case of expensive equipment, such as medical imaging equipment, manufacturers offer *facilitating services,* such as equipment installation, staff training, maintenance and repair services, and financing. They may also add *value-augmenting services.* Herman Miller, a major office-furniture company, offers the Herman Miller promise to buyers: (1) five-year product warranties, (2) quality audits after project installation, (3) guaranteed move-in dates, and (4) trade-in allowances on systems products.

Companies need to plan their product design and service-mix decisions in tandem. Design and quality-assurance managers should be part of the new-product development team. Good product design will reduce the amount of subsequent servicing needed. The Canon home copier uses a disposable toner cartridge that greatly reduces the need for service calls. Kodak and 3M are designing equipment allowing the user to "plug in" to a central diagnostic facility that performs tests, locates the trouble, and fixes the equipment over the telephone lines.

Postsale Service Strategy

Companies must decide how they want to offer after-sales service (e.g., maintenance and repair services, training services) to customers. Most companies operate customer service departments. The quality of these customer service departments varies greatly. At one extreme are customer service departments that simply turn over customer calls to the appropriate person or department for action, with little follow-up as to whether the customer's request was satisfied. At the other extreme are customer service departments eager to receive customer requests, suggestions, and even complaints and handle them expeditiously. For example:[33]

♦ P&G prints a toll-free number on every product and receives nearly a million calls a year. Included are calls requesting information on how to use a product, or suggestions on how to improve a product, or complaints about a defective product. P&G welcomes these calls as a basis for constantly improving its operations.

♦ GE spends $10 million annually to operate the GE Answer Center 24 hours a day, 365 days a year. It handles 3 million calls a year. Customer Representatives (CRs) have instant access to 750,000 answers concerning 8,500 models in 120 product lines. GE has discovered that when it handles a complaint in a satisfactory manner, over 80% of the complainers will buy again from GE.

♦ Merck runs a Medical Question Answering Service for physicians. A physician can call Merck for information about a certain illness and Merck's librarians will mail or fax important articles clarifying that illness. Although this service is expensive to operate, it builds a strong image of Merck in the physician's mind.

STAGES IN POSTSALE SERVICE STRATEGY. Most companies progress through a series of service-provision stages as they gain more success in a market. Manufacturers usually start out by running their own parts and service department. They want to stay close to the equipment and know its problems. They also find it expensive and time-consuming to train others, and discover that they can make good money running the parts-and-service business. As long as they are the only supplier of the needed parts, they can charge a premium price. In fact, many equipment manufacturers price their equipment low and compensate by charging high prices for parts and service. (This explains why competitors emerge who manufacture the same or similar parts and sell them to customers or intermediaries

Managing Service
Businesses and Product
Support Services

Offering Guarantees to Promote Sales

All sellers are legally responsible for fulfilling a buyer's normal or reasonable expectations. *Warranties* are formal statements of expected product performance by the manufacturer. Products under warranty can be returned to the manufacturer or a designated repair center for repair, replacement, or refund. Warranties, whether expressed or implied, are legally enforceable.

Many sellers go further and offer *guarantees,* general assurances that the product can be returned if its performance is unsatisfactory. (An example would be a "money-back" guarantee.) Guarantees work best when the terms are clearly stated and without loopholes. The customer should find them easy to act upon, and the company's redress should be swift. Otherwise, buyers will be dissatisfied. This dissatisfaction can lead to no further purchases, bad word of mouth, and a potential lawsuit. Consider what happened at Domino's Pizza, which underwent phenomenal growth when it guaranteed 30-minute delivery on all telephone orders for its pizzas. The guarantee originally stated that late-arriving pizzas would be free (later amended to $3 off the order). But the company was forced to cancel its guarantee when a St. Louis court awarded $78 million to a woman who had been struck by a Domino's driver in 1989.

Today many companies promise "general or complete satisfaction" without being more specific. Thus, Procter & Gamble advertises: "If you are not satisfied for any reason, return for replacement, exchange, or refund." Some companies go beyond a general guarantee of satisfaction to a special or extraordinary promise that sets them apart from their competition and acts as an effective sales tool. Here are examples of the creative use of guarantees:

- L. L. Bean, the outdoors furnishings company, promises its customers "100% satisfaction in every way, forever." For example, if a customer buys a pair of boots and two months later finds that they scuff easily, L. L. Bean will take them back and refund the money or replace them with another brand.

- A. T. Cross guarantees its Cross pens and pencils for life. Thus, the customer whose pen stops working simply mails it to A. T. Cross (mailing envelopes are provided at stores selling Cross writing instruments) and the pen is repaired or replaced at no charge.

- Federal Express won its place in the minds and hearts of mailers by promising next-day delivery "absolutely, positively by 10:30 A.M."

- Oakley Millwork, a Chicago supplier of construction in-

for less. Manufacturers warn customers of the danger of using competitor-made parts, but they are not always convincing. Meanwhile, in Australia, the Prices Surveillance Authority has held inquiries into the prices charged for car parts.)

Over time, manufacturers switch more of the maintenance and repair service to authorized distributors and dealers. These intermediaries are closer to the customers, operate in more locations, and can offer quicker (if not better) service. Manufacturers still make a profit on selling the parts but leave the servicing profit to their intermediaries.

Still later, independent service firms emerge. Over 40% of auto service work is now done outside franchised automobile dealerships, by independent garages and chains such as Midas Muffler, Sears, and J. C. Penney. Independent service organizations have emerged to handle mainframes, telecommunications equipment, and a variety of other equipment lines. They typically offer lower price and/or faster service than the manufacturer or authorized intermediaries.

Ultimately, some large customers take over responsibility for handling their own maintenance and repair services. Thus a company with several hundred personal computers, printers, and related equipment might find it cheaper to have its own service personnel on site. These companies typically press the manufacturer for a lower price, since they are providing their own services.

dustry products, made the following guarantee: If any item in its catalog was out of stock and unavailable for immediate delivery, the customer would get the item free. This customer-pleasing guarantee helped push company sales up 33% between 1988 and 1991—a time when housing starts in its area fell 41 percent.

♦ BBBK, a pest extermination company, offers the following guarantee: (1) no payment until all pests are eradicated; (2) if the effort fails, the customer receives a full refund and fees to pay the next exterminator; (3) if guests on the client's premises spot a pest, BBBK will pay for the guest's room and send an apology letter; and (4) if the client's facility is closed down, BBBK will pay all fines, lost profits, and $5,000. For this high level of guarantee, BBBK is able to charge up to five times more than its competitors, enjoys a high market share, and has paid out only 0.4% of sales in guarantees.

♦ At ScrubaDub Auto Wash in Natick, Massachusetts, customers who purchase the basic wash can get a rewash if they're not satisfied, and ScrubaDub club members (who spend $5.95 for a membership pass that entitles them to certain specials) will get a free replacement wash if it rains or snows within 24 hours after they've left the lot.

Guarantees are most effective in two situations. The first is where the company and/or the product is not well known. For example, a company might develop and offer a liquid that claims to remove the toughest spots from carpeting. A "money-back guarantee if not satisfied" would provide buyers with some confidence in purchasing the product. The second situation is where the product's quality is superior to competition. Here the company can gain by guaranteeing superior performance because it knows that competitors cannot offer the same guarantee.

In a final twist on the guarantee, some companies are now offering "internal" guarantees, in which one division or segment of the company guarantees its product or service to another division. For example, GTE's management executive training operations in Norwalk, Connecticut, train about 18,000 GTE management personnel annually. If these seminars don't live up to attendees' expectations, the training division will refund their tuition or find some other way to satisfy them. While the seminars are paid for by company funds, each attendee "pays" with its department's money. The refund comes out of the seminar operations and is reflected in its budget. Companies like GTE are finding that internal guarantees are a great way to carry out their goals of total quality management.

For additional reading, see "More Firms Pledge Guaranteed Service," *The Wall Street Journal*, July 17, 1991, B:1, B:6; and Barbara Ettore, "Phenomenal Promises Mean Business," *Management Review*, March 1994, pp. 18–23. For a list of pointers on deciding whether or not a company should offer an unconditional guarantee, see Christopher W. L. Hart, *Extraordinary Guarantees* (New York: Amacom, 1993).

Lele has noted the following major trends in the product support area:[34]

1. Equipment manufacturers are building more reliable and more easily fixable equipment. One reason is the shift from electromechanical equipment to electronic equipment, which has fewer breakdowns and is more repairable. Also, companies are adding modularity and disposability to facilitate self-servicing.

2. Customers are becoming more sophisticated about buying product support services and are pressing for "services unbundling." They want separate prices quoted for each service element and the right to shop for the service elements they want.

3. Customers increasingly dislike having to deal with a multitude of service providers handling their different types of equipment. Some third-party service organizations now service a greater range of equipment.[35]

4. *Service contracts* (also called *extended warranties*), in which sellers agree to provide free maintenance and repair services for a specified period of time at a specified contract price, are an endangered species. Because of the increase in disposable and/or never-fail equipment, customers are less inclined to pay anywhere from 2% to 10% of the purchase price every year for a service.

5. Customer service choices are increasing rapidly, and this is holding down prices and profits on service. Equipment manufacturers increasingly have to figure out how to make money on pricing their equipment independent of service contracts.

Managing Service
Businesses and Product
Support Services

SUMMARY

1. A *service* is any act or performance that one party can offer to another that is essentially intangible and does not result in the ownership of anything. Its production may or may not be tied to a physical product. As the United States has moved increasingly toward a service economy, marketers have become increasingly interested in the special challenges involved in marketing services.

2. Services are intangible, inseparable, variable, and perishable. Each characteristic poses challenges and requires certain strategies. Marketers must find ways to give tangibility to intangibles; to increase the productivity of service providers; to increase and standardize the quality of the service provided; and to match the supply of services during peak and nonpeak periods with market demand.

3. Service industries have lagged behind manufacturing firms in adopting and using marketing concepts and tools, but this situation is now changing. Service marketing strategy calls not only for external marketing but also for internal marketing to motivate employees and interactive marketing to emphasize the importance of both "high tech" and "high touch."

4. The service organization faces three tasks in marketing. (1) It must differentiate its offer, delivery, and/or image. (2) It must manage service quality in order to meet or exceed customers' expectations. The most customer-oriented companies have a strategic concept, a history of top-management commitment to service quality, high standards, systems for monitoring service performance, systems for satisfying customers' complaints, and an internal environment that focuses on satisfying employees as well as customers. (3) It must manage its workers' productivity by getting its employees to work more skillfully, increasing the quantity of service by surrendering some quality, industrializing the service, inventing new-product solutions, designing more effective services, presenting customers with the incentive to substitute their own labor for company labor, or using technology to save time and money.

5. Even product-based companies must provide a service bundle for their customers. To provide the best support, a manufacturer must identify the services that customers value most and their relative importance. The service mix includes both presale services (facilitating and value-augmenting services) and postsale services (customer-service departments, repair and maintenance services).

CONCEPT APPLICATIONS

1. Service companies like hotels, hospitals, colleges, banks, restaurants, and theme parks have recognized the importance of a fifth P: people.* The employees of service companies are in constant contact with the customers, and these customers judge the establishment based on their impressions of the employees with whom they've dealt. Describe five steps you would take to teach the employees of Fantasy Enterprises, a theme park similar to Disneyland, to develop "positive customer attitudes."

2. When a service is completed, the customer is not left with a tangible product but rather with feelings—elation, delight, satisfaction, frustration, disappointment, anger, and so on. Providers of services must therefore clearly identify the feelings that they want the customer to experience as a result of the service. Think of three companies that have recently supplied services to you, and consider both the services that pleased you and those that displeased you. Using these thoughts as a starting point, design some procedures for a small medical center to follow to increase customer (patient) delight.

3. In an era in which many customers consider airflights just another commodity, the airline with the lowest fare often wins. However, if the airline fails to cover expenses, it

* As we saw in the text, there are two additional Ps in service marketing: physical evidence and process.

loses. While the customer is elated to book a flight with a two-for-one price and frequent-flier mileage, many airlines will post losses. However, Southwest Airlines, a low-fare provider, has been showing good profits since 1987, as the following data indicate:

Sales (1992)	$1.5 billion (up 22.1% over 1991)
Net profit	$74.1 billion (up 256% over 1991)
Return on equity	9.3%
Total return to investors	26.5%
Price/earnings multiple	25.8
Dividend yield	0.2%

Source: Richard S. Teitelbaum, "Where Service Flies Right," *Fortune,* August 24, 1992, pp. 115–16. Reprinted with permission from *Fortune.*

Southwest Airlines is profitable while other airlines operate in the red for two reasons: (1) it spends money wisely and cuts costs whenever possible; and (2) it goes out of its way to meet customers' needs and exceed their expectations. For example, frequent fliers sit in with HR managers to interview and evaluate prospective flight attendants. They also participate in focus groups to evaluate new services.

Prepare a brief report (two to five pages) explaining at least ten other ways in which Southwest Airlines services its customers.

4. A CPA firm based in Cleveland, Ohio, has grown from billings of $315,000 to over $5 million since 1987—an annual growth rate of 22 percent. Amazingly, the growth has been accomplished without mergers, acquisitions, or even a large marketing budget. The firm's managing partner, Gary Shamis, admits that the firm's service is excellent but not particularly better than hundreds of good competitors. What, then, is the secret to success for this CPA firm?

The firm uses a multidimensional marketing strategy that began with the drafting of a road map—a list of specific objectives that the firm wanted to achieve. The road map is a working tool that is used and reinforced daily to keep the goals visualized in the minds of the firm's partners and associates. In addition, Shamis believes that clients buy perception and end up with reality. Creating a positive perception requires constant attention and reinforcement. The following marketing tools can help create this perception:
a. publicity
b. advertising
c. seminars
d. printed materials

For each of these marketing tools, suggest ways that a CPA firm can differentiate its services from those of its competitors, keeping in mind that most CPA firms offer the same types of services. Who should be responsible for implementing the firm's multidimensional success strategy?

5. Identify the core need, service characteristics (quality level, features, styling, brand name, and packaging), and augmented product* provided by the customers of the following service businesses:
a. the U.S. Navy
b. organized religion
c. a life insurance company

---

* For a review of these terms, see Chapter 15.

6. Does a service organization need a marketing department to be market-oriented? Discuss.

7. Figure 1 outlines the GUEST program at Liberty National Bank and Trust Company. The program is designed to emphasize the quality of service at the bank.

FIGURE 1

THE QUALITY SERVICE CONNECTION

"Every Customer Is Our GUEST"

*G*reet the customer:

- Acknowledge customer immediately
- Stand and show respect
- Smile to show friendliness
- Introduce self and use customer's name
- Establish eye contact
- Shake hands
- Offer assistance by saying "May I help you?"
- Offer the customer a seat

*U*nderstand the customer's feelings:

- Listen attentively
- Ask questions to probe and clarify
- Rephrase so that understanding occurs
- Maintain a friendly tone of voice
- Maintain confidentiality

*E*mpathize with the customer:

- Put yourself into the customer's shoes
- If the customer complains, seek out something to agree with
- Demonstrate genuine concern

*S*olve the customer's needs yourself:

- Take responsibility
- Offer additional support, if needed

*T*hank the customer:

- Offer business card
- Thank the customer
- Invite the customer back

Remember, every customer is our GUEST. Be a professional at all times in appearance and dress. Always keep your work area neat. Be cautious not to eat, smoke, or chew gum in front of the customer because to the customer, YOU ARE THE BANK!

How does a program like GUEST contribute to the development of a service culture?

Choose another service business (for example, a business in the restaurant industry or the housekeeping industry). Assume that you are the CEO of that business and adapt the GUEST program to it. Which elements of Figure 1 will remain the same? Which will differ? What additional guidelines can you offer your employees? What is your role in maintaining the GUEST program and motivating your employees to do the same?

8. Individually or with a group, develop a set of written guidelines for measuring and rewarding service performance in organizations.

9. Theodore R. Cunningham of the Chrysler Corporation recently remarked, "In a recent survey, new-car buyers said they'd rather visit the dentist for a root canal than have to go through the process of buying a car again." In other words, most new-car buyers expect the following scenario: They enter the showroom and are approached immediately by an enthusiastic salesperson who seems to know everything but the answers to their questions. If they ask what the price is, then the salesperson will go in search of someone who can deal. Once it looks like they are about to sign the contract, the salesperson starts selling more options or option packages, rustproofing, extended warranties, and so forth. After the car is delivered and if something goes wrong, it is extremely difficult to get in touch with the salesperson.

Individually or with a group, list some of the underlying reasons for the consumer-perception problems facing car dealerships. Then design a new system that would change the dealership culture by introducing the concept of relationship marketing into the process.

NOTES

1. Ronald Henkoff, "Service Is Everybody's Business," *Fortune,* June 27, 1994, pp. 48–60.
2. See G. Lynn Shostack, "Breaking Free from Product Marketing," *Journal of Marketing,* April 1977, pp. 73–80; Leonard L. Berry, "Services Marketing Is Different," *Business,* May–June 1980, pp. 24–30; Eric Langeard, John E. G. Bateson, Christopher H. Lovelock, and Pierre Eiglier, *Services Marketing: New Insights from Consumers and Managers* (Cambridge, MA: Marketing Science Institute, 1981); Karl Albrecht and Ron Zemke, *Service America! Doing Business in the New Economy* (Homewood, IL: Dow Jones-Irwin, 1986); Karl Albrecht, *At America's Service* (Homewood, IL: Dow Jones-Irwin, 1988); and Benjamin Scheider and David E. Bowen, *Winning the Service Game* (Boston: Harvard Business School Press, 1995).
3. Theodore Levitt, "Production-Line Approach to Service," *Harvard Business Review,* September–October 1972, pp. 41–42.
4. Further classifications of services are described in Christopher H. Lovelock, *Services Marketing,* 3d ed. (Upper Saddle River, NJ: Prentice Hall, 1996). Also see John E. Bateson, *Managing Services Marketing: Text and Readings,* 3d ed. (Hinsdale, IL: Dryden Press, 1995).
5. See Theodore Levitt, "Marketing Intangible Products and Product Intangibles," *Harvard Business Review,* May–June 1981, pp. 94–102; and Berry, "Services Marketing Is Different."
6. See G. Lynn Shostack, "Service Positioning Through Structural Change," *Journal of Marketing,* January 1987, pp. 34–43.
7. See W. Earl Sasser, "Match Supply and Demand in Service Industries," *Harvard Business Review,* November–December 1976, pp. 133–40.
8. Christy Fisher, "Postal Service Looks to Stamp Out Woes," *Advertising Age,* September 12, 1994, p. 12.
9. See B. H. Booms and M. J. Bitner, "Marketing Strategies and Organizational Structures for Service Firms," in *Marketing of Services,* ed. J. Donnelly and W. R. George (Chicago: American Marketing Association, 1981), pp. 47–51.
10. Keaveny has identified more than 800 critical behaviors of service firms that cause customers to switch services. These behaviors fit into eight categories ranging from price, inconvenience, and core service failure to service encounter failure, failed employee response to service failures, and ethical problems. See Susan M. Keaveney, "Customer Switching Behavior in Service Industries: An Exploratory Study," *Journal of Marketing,* April 1995, pp. 71–82.
11. Christian Gronroos, "A Service Quality Model and Its Marketing Implications," *European Journal of Marketing,* 18, no. 4 (1984), 36–44. Gronroos's model is one of the most thoughtful contributions to service marketing strategy.
12. Leonard Berry, "Big Ideas in Services Marketing," *Journal of Consumer Marketing,* Spring 1986, pp. 47–51. See also Walter E. Greene, Gary D. Walls, and Larry J. Schrest, "Internal Marketing: The Key to External Marketing Success," *Journal of Services Marketing,* 8, no. 4 (1994), 5–13.
13. Gronroos, "Service Quality Model," pp. 38–39.
14. See Philip Kotler and Paul N. Bloom, *Marketing Professional Services* (Englewood Cliffs, NJ: Prentice Hall, 1984).
15. "'Gimme Shelter': Dissatisfied Investors Find a Safe Haven at Schwab," *Marketing Forum,* a supplement to *Management Review,* March 1995, pp. 1–2; and "The Schwab Revolution," *Business Week,* December 19, 1994, pp. 8 ff.
16. See Valarie A. Zeithaml, "How Consumer Evaluation Processes Differ between Goods and Services," in *Marketing of Services,* ed. Donnelly and George, pp. 186–90.
17. Amy Ostrom and Dawn Iacobucci, "Consumer Trade-Offs and the Evaluation of Services," *Journal of Marketing,* January 1995, pp. 17–28.
18. See "A New Course for Club Med," *Asian Business,* January

1991, pp. 96–98. For a look at Club Med's bid for total quality, see "Sun, Sea, Sand and Service," *International Journal of Health Care Quality Assurance,* 7, no. 4 (1994), 18–19.

19. A. Parasuraman, Valarie A. Zeithaml, and Leonard L. Berry, "A Conceptual Model of Service Quality and Its Implications for Future Research," *Journal of Marketing,* Fall 1985, pp. 41–50. See also Susan J. Devlin and H. K. Dong, "Service Quality from the Customers' Perspective," *Marketing Research: A Magazine of Management and Applications,* Winter 1994, pp. 4–13.

20. Leonard L. Berry and A. Parasuraman, *Marketing Services: Competing Through Quality* (New York: Free Press, 1991), p. 16.

21. See James L. Heskett, W. Earl Sasser, Jr., and Christopher W. L. Hart, *Service Breakthroughs* (New York: Free Press, 1990).

22. David Greising, "Quality: How to Make It Pay," *Business Week,* August 8, 1994, pp. 54–59.

23. John A. Martilla and John C. James, "Importance-Performance Analysis," *Journal of Marketing,* January 1977, pp. 77–79.

24. See John Goodman, Technical Assistance Research Program (TARP), U.S. Office of Consumer Affairs Study on Complaint Handling in America, 1986; Albrecht and Zemke, *Service America!;* Berry and Parasuraman, *Marketing Services;* and Roland T. Rust, Bala Subramanian, and Mark Wells, "Making Complaints a Management Tool," *Marketing Management,* 1, no. 3 (1992), 41–45.

25. Timothy W. Firnstahl, "My Employees Are My Service Guarantee," *Harvard Business Review,* July–August 1989, pp. 29–34.

26. See Hal F. Rosenbluth and Diane McFerrin Peters, *The Customer Comes Second* (New York: William Morrow, 1992).

27. Myron Magnet, "The Productivity Payoff Arrives," *Fortune,* June 27, 1994, pp. 79–84.

28. Theodore Levitt, "Production-Line Approach to Service," *Harvard Business Review,* September–October 1972, pp. 41–52; also see his "Industrialization of Service," *Harvard Business Review,* September–October 1976, pp. 63–74.

29. See William H. Davidow and Bro Uttal, *Total Customer Service: The Ultimate Weapon* (New York: Harper & Row, 1989).

30. Nilly Landau, "Are You Being Served?" *International Business,* March 1995, pp. 38–40.

31. See Milind M. Lele and Uday S. Karmarkar, "Good Product Support Is Smart Marketing," *Harvard Business Review,* November–December 1983, pp. 124–32.

32. For recent research on the effects of delays in service on service evaluations, see Shirley Taylor, "Waiting for Service: The Relationship Between Delays and Evaluations of Service," *Journal of Marketing,* April 1994, pp. 56–69.

33. See Ross M. Scovotti, "Customer Service . . . A Tool for Growing Increased Profits," *Teleprofessional,* September 1991, pp. 22–27.

34. Milind M. Lele, "How Service Needs Influence Product Strategy," *Sloan Management Review,* Fall 1986, pp. 63–70.

35. However, see Ellen Day and Richard J. Fox, "Extended Warranties, Service Contracts, and Maintenance Agreement—A Marketing Opportunity?" *Journal of Consumer Marketing,* Fall 1985, pp. 77–86.

DESIGNING

PRICING STRATEGIES

AND PROGRAMS

There ain't no brand loyalty that two-cents-off can't overcome.

ANONYMOUS

❖

The real issue is value, not price.

ROBERT T. LINDGREN

❖

All profit organizations and many nonprofit organizations set prices on their products or services. Price goes by many names:

> Price is all around us. You pay *rent* for your apartment, *tuition* for your education, and a *fee* to your physician or dentist. The airline, railway, taxi, and bus companies charge you a *fare;* the local utilities call their price a *rate;* and the local bank charges you *interest* for the money you borrow. The price for driving your car on Florida's Sunshine Parkway is a *toll,* and the company that insures your car charges you a *premium.* The guest lecturer charges an *honorarium* to tell you about a government official who took a *bribe* to help a shady character steal *dues* collected by a trade association. Clubs or societies to which you belong may make a special *assessment* to pay unusual expenses. Your regular lawyer may ask for a *retainer* to cover her services. The "price" of an executive is a *salary,* the price of a salesperson may be a *commission,* and the price of a worker is a *wage.* Finally, although economists would disagree, many of us feel that *income taxes* are the price we pay for the privilege of making money.[1]

Throughout most of history, prices were set by buyers and sellers negotiating with each other. Sellers would ask for a higher price than they expected to receive, and buyers would offer less than they expected to pay. Through bargaining, they would arrive at a mutually acceptable price.

Setting one price for all buyers is a relatively modern idea that arose with the development of large-scale retailing at the end of the nineteenth century. F. W. Woolworth, Tiffany and Co., John Wanamaker, and others advertised a "strictly one-price policy," because they carried so many items and supervised so many employees.

Traditionally, price has operated as the major determinant of buyer choice. This is still the case in poorer nations, among poorer groups, and with commodity-type products. And, although nonprice factors have become more important in buyer behavior in recent decades, price still remains one of the most important elements determining company market share and profitability. In fact, prices have been experiencing considerable downward pressure in recent years (Figure 17-1). As consumers' real incomes stagnate or decline and they experience diminishing expectations, they shop more carefully, forcing retailers to lower their prices. Retailers in turn put pressure on manufacturers to lower their prices. The result is a marketplace characterized by heavy discounting and sales promotion.

Price is the only element in the marketing mix that produces revenue; the other elements produce costs. Price is also one of the most flexible elements of the marketing mix, in that it can be changed quickly, unlike product features and channel commitments. At the same time, pricing and price competition are the number-one problems facing many marketing executives. Yet many companies do not handle pricing well. The most common mistakes are these: Pricing is too cost-oriented; price is not revised often enough to capitalize on market changes; price is set independent of the rest of the marketing mix rather than as an intrinsic element of market-positioning strategy; and price is not varied enough for different product items, market segments, and purchase occasions.

Companies handle pricing in a variety of ways. In small companies, prices are often set by top management rather than by marketing or salespeople. In large companies, pricing is typically handled by division and product-line managers. Even here, top management sets the general pricing objectives and policies and often approves the prices proposed by lower levels of management. In industries where pricing is a key factor (aerospace, railroads, oil companies), companies will

FIGURE 17-1

How Downward Price Pressure Is Transmitted

PART 4

Planning Marketing Programs

often establish a pricing department to set prices or assist others in determining appropriate prices. This department reports to either the marketing department, the finance department, or top management. Others who exert an influence on pricing include sales managers, production managers, finance managers, and accountants.

This chapter examines three questions:

♦ **How should a price be set on a product or service for the first time?**

♦ **How should the price be adapted over time and space to meet varying circumstances and opportunities?**

♦ **When should the company initiate a price change, and how should it respond to a competitor's price change?**

SETTING THE PRICE

A firm must set a price for the first time when the firm develops or acquires a new product, when it introduces its regular product into a new distribution channel or geographical area, and when it enters bids on new contract work.

The firm must decide where to position its product on quality and price. A company can position its product in the middle of the market, up three levels, or down three levels. The seven levels are as follows:

Segment	*Example (Automobiles)*
Ultimate	Mercedes-Benz
Luxury	Audi
Special Needs	Volvo
Middle	Buick
Ease/Convenience	Ford Escort
Me Too, but Cheaper	Hyundai
Price Alone	Daihatsu

Thus, in many markets, there is an ultimate brand (the *gold standard*), here the Mercedes-Benz automobile. Just below the ultimate are luxury brands, such as Audi, Lincoln, Lexus, Infiniti, and so on. Below them are brands that meet a special need: Volvo (safety) or Porsche (high performance). In the middle are a large number of brands, including Buick, Renault, Chevrolet, and so on. One step below the middle are brands that provide mainly the functional benefit sought—in this case, Ford Escort automobiles and cars like them. Below them are cheaper brands that nevertheless perform satisfactorily, such as the Hyundai. At the bottom are brands whose only appeal is price, such as the Yugo, a car that is not only cheap but also cheaply made.

This scheme suggests that the seven product positioning levels don't compete with each other but only compete within each group. Yet there can be competition between price-quality segments. Figure 17-2 on the next page shows nine possible price-quality strategies. The diagonal strategies 1, 5, and 9 can all coexist in the same market; that is, one firm offers a high-quality product at a high price, another firm offers an average-quality product at an average price, and still another firm offers a low-quality product at a low price. All three competitors can coexist as long as the market consists of three groups of buyers: those who insist on quality, those who insist on price, and those who balance the two considerations.

Positioning strategies 2, 3, and 6 represent ways to attack the diagonal positions. Strategy 2 says, "Our product has the same high quality as product 1 but we charge less." Strategy 3 says the same thing and offers an even greater saving. If

Designing Pricing Strategies and Programs

FIGURE 17-2

Nine Price-Quality
Strategies

		Price	
	High	Medium	Low
High	1. Premium strategy	2. High-value strategy	3. Super-value strategy
Medium	4. Overcharging strategy	5. Medium-value strategy	6. Good-value strategy
Low	7. Rip-off strategy	8. False economy strategy	9. Economy strategy

Product Quality (vertical axis label)

FIGURE 17-3

Setting Pricing Policy

1. Selecting the pricing objective
2. Determining demand
3. Estimating costs
4. Analyzing competitors' costs, prices, and offers
5. Selecting a pricing method
6. Selecting the final price

quality-sensitive customers believe these competitors, they will sensibly buy from them and save money (unless firm 1's product has acquired snob appeal).

Positioning strategies 4, 7, and 8 amount to overpricing the product in relation to its quality. The customers will feel "taken" and will probably complain or spread bad word of mouth about the company. Professional marketers should avoid these strategies.

The firm has to consider many factors in setting its pricing policy. In the following paragraphs, we will describe a six-step procedure for price setting: (1) selecting the pricing objective; (2) determining demand; (3) estimating costs; (4) analyzing competitors' costs, prices, and offers; (5) selecting a pricing method; and (6) selecting the final price (Figure 17-3).

Selecting the Pricing Objective

The company first has to decide what it wants to accomplish with its particular product offer. If the company has selected its target market and market positioning carefully, then its marketing-mix strategy—including price—will be fairly straightforward. For example, if a recreational vehicle company wants to produce a luxurious truck camper for affluent customers, it should probably charge a high price.

The clearer a firm's objectives, the easier it is to set price. A company can pursue any of six major objectives through its pricing: survival, maximum current profit, maximum current revenue, maximum sales growth, maximum market skimming, or product-quality leadership.

SURVIVAL. Companies pursue survival as their major objective if they are plagued with overcapacity, intense competition, or changing consumer wants. To keep the plant operating and the inventories turning over, they will cut prices. Profits are less important than survival. As long as prices cover variable costs and some fixed costs, the companies stay in business. However, survival is only a short-run objective. In the long run, the firm must learn how to add value or face extinction.

MAXIMUM CURRENT PROFIT. Many companies try to set the price that will maximize current profits. They estimate the demand and costs associated with alternative prices and choose the price that produces maximum current profit, cash flow, or rate of return on investment.

There are problems associated with current profit maximization. This strategy assumes that the firm has knowledge of its demand and cost functions; in reality, these are difficult to estimate. Also, by emphasizing current financial performance the company may sacrifice long-run performance, ignoring the effects of other marketing-mix variables, competitors' reactions, and legal restraints on price.

MAXIMUM CURRENT REVENUE. Some companies set a price that maximizes sales revenue. Revenue maximization requires estimating only the demand function. Many managers believe that revenue maximization will lead to long-run profit maximization and market share growth.

MAXIMUM SALES GROWTH. Some companies want to maximize unit sales. They believe that a higher sales volume will lead to lower unit costs and higher long-run profit. They set the lowest price, assuming the market is price sensitive. This practice is called *market-penetration pricing.* Texas Instruments (TI) practices market-penetration pricing. TI will build a large plant, set its price as low as possible, win a large market share, experience falling costs, and cut its price further as costs fall.

The following conditions favor setting a low price: (1) The market is highly price sensitive, and a low price stimulates market growth; (2) production and distribution costs fall with accumulated production experience; and (3) a low price discourages actual and potential competition.

MAXIMUM MARKET SKIMMING. Many companies favor setting high prices to "skim" the market. Du Pont is a prime practitioner of *market-skimming pricing.* With each innovation—cellophane, nylon, Teflon, and so on—it estimates the highest price it can charge, given the comparative benefits of its new product versus the available substitutes. The company sets a price that makes it just worthwhile for some segments of the market to adopt the new material. Each time sales slow down, Du Pont lowers the price to draw in the next price-sensitive layer of customers. In this way, Du Pont skims a maximum amount of revenue from the various market segments. Polaroid also practices market skimming. It first introduces an expensive version of a new camera, then gradually introduces simpler, lower-price models to draw in new price-sensitive segments.

Market skimming makes sense under the following conditions: (1) A sufficient number of buyers have a high current demand; (2) the unit costs of producing a small volume are not so high that they cancel the advantage of charging what the traffic will bear; (3) the high initial price does not attract more competitors to the market; (4) the high price communicates the image of a superior product.

PRODUCT-QUALITY LEADERSHIP. A company might aim to be the product-quality leader in the market. Maytag, a prime example, builds high-quality washing machines and prices them a few hundred dollars more than competitors' washing machines. (Maytag used the slogan "Built to last longer," and its ads featured "Ol' Lonely," the Maytag repairman, who is asleep at the phone because no one ever calls him for service. Maytag's premium quality/premium price strategy has earned it a consistently higher-than-average rate of return in its industry.)

OTHER PRICING OBJECTIVES. Nonprofit and public organizations may adopt a number of other pricing objectives. A university aims for *partial cost recovery,* knowing that it must rely on private gifts and public grants to cover the remaining costs. A nonprofit hospital may aim for *full cost recovery* in its pricing. A nonprofit theater company may price its productions to fill the maximum number of theater seats. A social service agency may set a *social price* geared to the varying income situations of different clients.

Determining Demand

Each price that the company might charge will lead to a different level of demand and will therefore have a different impact on its marketing objectives. The relation between alternative prices that might be charged in the current time period and

FIGURE 17-4

Inelastic and Elastic
Demand

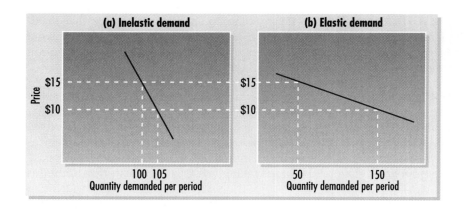

the resulting current demand is captured in a *demand curve* (Figure 17-4[a]). In the normal case, demand and price are inversely related. That is, the higher the price, the lower the demand, and the lower the price, the higher the demand.

In the case of prestige goods, the demand curve sometimes slopes upward. A perfume company found that by raising its price, it sold more perfume rather than less! Some consumers take the higher price to signify a better or more expensive perfume. However, if too high a price is charged, the level of demand will be lower.

FACTORS AFFECTING PRICE SENSITIVITY. The demand curve shows the market's purchase rate at alternative prices. It sums the reactions of many individuals who have different price sensitivities. The first step in estimating demand is thus understanding the factors that affect buyers' price sensitivity. Nagle has identified nine factors:

1. *Unique-value effect:* Buyers are less price sensitive when the product is more distinctive.
2. *Substitute-awareness effect:* Buyers are less price sensitive when they are less aware of substitutes.
3. *Difficult-comparison effect:* Buyers are less price sensitive when they cannot easily compare the quality of substitutes.
4. *Total-expenditure effect:* Buyers are less price sensitive the lower the expenditure is as a part of their total income.
5. *End-benefit effect:* Buyers are less price sensitive the smaller the expenditure is to the total cost of the end product.
6. *Shared-cost effect:* Buyers are less price sensitive when part of the cost is borne by another party.
7. *Sunk-investment effect:* Buyers are less price sensitive when the product is used in conjunction with assets previously bought.
8. *Price-quality effect:* Buyers are less price sensitive when the product is assumed to have more quality, prestige, or exclusiveness.
9. *Inventory effect:* Buyers are less price sensitive when they cannot store the product.[2]

METHODS OF ESTIMATING DEMAND CURVES. Most companies make some attempt to measure their demand curves. To do so, they can use several methods.

The first involves statistically analyzing existing data on past prices, quantities sold, and other factors to estimate their relationships. The data analyzed can either be longitudinal (over time) or cross-sectional (different locations at the same time). Building the appropriate model and fitting the data with the proper statistical techniques calls for considerable skill.

The second approach is to conduct price experiments. Bennett and Wilkinson used an in-store method of estimating the demand curve. They systematically varied the prices of several products sold in a discount store and observed the results.[3] An alternative approach is to charge different prices in similar territories to see how sales are affected.

The third approach is to ask buyers to state how many units they would buy at different proposed prices.[4] The major problem with this method is that buyers will tend to understate their purchase intentions at higher prices to discourage the company from setting higher prices.

In measuring the price/demand relationship, the market researcher must control for various factors that will influence demand. The competitor's response will make a difference: Does he react at all, and if so, does he respond by changing his prices or other marketing variables? Also, if the company changes other marketing-mix factors besides its price, the effect of the price change itself will be hard to isolate. Nagle has presented an excellent summary of the various methods for estimating price sensitivity and demand.[5]

PRICE ELASTICITY OF DEMAND. Marketers need to know how responsive, or elastic, demand would be to a change in price. Consider the two demand curves in Figure 17-4. In Figure 17-4(a), a price increase from $10 to $15 leads to a relatively small decline in demand from 105 to 100. In Figure 17-4(b), the same price increase leads to a substantial drop in demand from 150 to 50. If demand hardly changes with a small change in price, we say the demand is *inelastic*. If demand changes considerably, demand is *elastic*.

What determines the price elasticity of demand? Demand is likely to be less elastic under the following conditions: (1) There are few or no substitutes or competitors; (2) buyers do not readily notice the higher price; (3) buyers are slow to change their buying habits and search for lower prices; (4) buyers think the higher prices are justified by quality improvements, normal inflation, and so on.

If demand is elastic rather than inelastic, sellers will consider lowering the price. A lower price will produce more total revenue. This makes sense as long as the costs of producing and selling more units does not increase disproportionately.[6]

Price elasticity depends on the magnitude and direction of the contemplated price change. It may be negligible with a small price change and substantial with a large price change. It may differ for a price cut versus a price increase. Finally, long-run price elasticity may differ from short-run elasticity. Buyers may continue to buy from their current supplier after a price increase, because they do not notice the increase, or the increase is small, or they are distracted by other concerns, or they find choosing a new supplier takes time, but they may eventually switch suppliers. Here demand is more elastic in the long run than in the short run. Or the reverse may happen: Buyers drop a supplier after being notified of a price increase but return later. The distinction between short-run and long-run elasticity means that sellers will not know the total effect of their price change until time passes.

Estimating Costs

Demand sets a ceiling on the price that the company can charge for its product. And company costs set the floor. The company wants to charge a price that covers its cost of producing, distributing, and selling the product, including a fair return for its effort and risk.

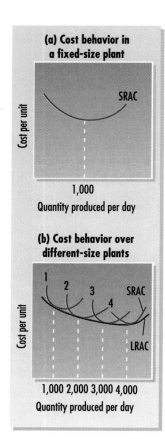

(a) Cost behavior in a fixed-size plant

Cost per unit

SRAC

1,000

Quantity produced per day

(b) Cost behavior over different-size plants

Cost per unit

1 2 3 SRAC
    4

LRAC

1,000 2,000 3,000 4,000

Quantity produced per day

FIGURE 17-5

Cost per Unit at Different Levels of Production per Period

TYPES OF COSTS. A company's costs take two forms, fixed and variable. *Fixed costs* (also known as *overhead*) are costs that do not vary with production or sales revenue. Thus a company must pay bills each month for rent, heat, interest, executive salaries, and so on, regardless of the company's output.

Variable costs vary directly with the level of production. For example, each hand calculator produced by Texas Instruments involves a cost of plastic, microprocessing chips, packaging, and the like. These costs tend to be constant per unit produced. They are called variable because their total varies with the number of units produced.

Total costs consist of the sum of the fixed and variable costs for any given level of production. *Average cost* is the cost per unit at that level of production; it is equal to total costs divided by production. Management wants to charge a price that will at least cover the total production costs at a given level of production.

COST BEHAVIOR AT DIFFERENT LEVELS OF PRODUCTION PER PERIOD. To price intelligently, management needs to know how its costs vary with different levels of production.

Take the case where a company such as TI has built a fixed-size plant to produce 1,000 hand calculators a day. The cost per unit is high if few units are produced per day. As production approaches 1,000 units per day, average cost falls. The reason is that the fixed costs are spread over more units, with each one bearing a smaller fixed cost. Average cost increases after 1,000 units, because the plant becomes inefficient: Workers have to queue for machines, machines break down more often, and workers get in each other's way (Figure 17-5[a]).

If TI believes that it could sell 2,000 units per day, it should consider building a larger plant. The plant will use more efficient machinery and work arrangements, and the unit cost of producing 2,000 units per day will be less than the unit cost of producing 1,000 units per day. This is shown in the long-run average cost curve in Figure 17-5(b). In fact, a 3,000-capacity plant would be even more efficient according to Figure 17-5(b). But a 4,000-daily production plant would be less efficient because of increasing diseconomies of scale: There are too many workers to manage, paperwork slows things down, and so on. Figure 17-5(b) indicates that a 3,000-daily production plant is the optimal size to build, if demand is strong enough to support this level of production.

COST BEHAVIOR AS A FUNCTION OF ACCUMULATED PRODUCTION. Suppose TI runs a plant that produces 3,000 hand calculators per day. As TI gains experience producing hand calculators its methods improve. The workers learn shortcuts, the flow of materials becomes smoother, procurement costs are cut, and so on. The result, as Figure 17-6 shows, is that average cost tends to fall with accumulated production experience. Thus the average cost of producing the

FIGURE 17-6

Cost per Unit as a Function of Accumulated Production: The Experience Curve

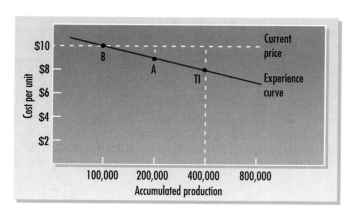

Cost per unit

$10 — — — — — B — — — — — — — — — — — Current price
$8 — — — — — — — A
$6 — — — — — — — — — — TI — — — — Experience curve
$4
$2

100,000 200,000 400,000 800,000

Accumulated production

Planning
Marketing
Programs

first 100,000 hand calculators is $10 per calculator. When the company has produced the first 200,000 calculators, the average cost has fallen to $9. After its accumulated production experience doubles again to 400,000, the average cost is $8. This decline in the average cost with accumulated production experience is called the *experience curve* or *learning curve*.

Now suppose three firms compete in this industry, TI, A, and B. TI is the lowest-cost producer at $8, having produced 400,000 units in the past. If all three firms sell the calculator for $10, TI makes $2 profit per unit, A makes $1 per unit, and B breaks even. The smart move for TI would be to lower its price to $9. This will drive B out of the market, and even A will consider leaving. TI will pick up the business that would have gone to B (and possibly A). Furthermore, price-sensitive customers will enter the market at the lower price. As production increases beyond 400,000 units, TI's costs will drop still further and faster and more than restore its profits, even at a price of $9. TI has used this aggressive pricing strategy repeatedly to gain market share and drive others out of the industry.

Experience-curve pricing nevertheless carries major risks. Aggressive pricing might give the product a cheap image. The strategy also assumes that the competitors are weak and not willing to fight it out, which may not be the case in reality. Finally, the strategy leads the company into building more plants to meet the demand while a competitor might innovate a lower-cost technology and obtain lower costs than the market leader, who is now stuck with the old technology.

Most experience-curve pricing has focused on manufacturing costs. But all costs, including marketing costs, are subject to learning improvements. Thus if three firms are each investing a large sum of money trying out telemarketing, the firm that has used it the longest might achieve the lowest telemarketing costs. This firm can charge a little less for its product and still earn the same return, all other costs being equal.[7]

COST BEHAVIOR AS A FUNCTION OF DIFFERENTIATED MARKETING OFFERS. Today's companies try to adapt their offers and terms to different buyers. Thus a manufacturer dealing with different retail chains will negotiate different terms. One retailer may want everyday delivery (to keep stock lower) while another retailer may accept twice-a-week delivery in order to get a lower price. As a result, the manufacturer's costs will differ with each retail chain, and its profits will differ too. To estimate the real profitability of dealing with different retailers, the manufacturer needs to use *activity-based cost (ABC) accounting* instead of *standard cost accounting*.[8]

ABC accounting tries to identify the real costs associated with serving each entity (the different customers). Both the variable costs and the overhead costs must be decomposed and tagged back to the entity. Companies that fail to measure their real costs correctly are not measuring their profit correctly. They are likely to misallocate their marketing and other efforts. Identifying the true costs arising in a customer relationship also enables a company to better explain its charges to the customer.

TARGET COSTING. We have seen that costs change with production scale and experience. They can also change as a result of a concentrated effort by the company's designers, engineers, and purchasing agents to reduce them. The Japanese in particular use a method called *target costing*.[9] They use market research to establish a new product's desired functions. Then they determine the price at which the product must sell given its appeal and competitors' prices. They deduct the desired profit margin from this price, and this leaves the target cost they must achieve. They then examine each cost element—design, engineering, manufacturing, sales, and so on—and break it down into further components.

They consider ways to reengineer components, eliminate functions, and bring down supplier costs. The whole objective is to bring the final cost projections into the target cost range. If they can't succeed, they may decide against developing the product because it couldn't sell for the target price and make the target profit. When they can succeed, profits are likely to follow. Consider one success story:

COMPAQ Target costing is the method Compaq used when it was battered by low-cost personal computer rivals in 1992. Here's how target pricing works at Compaq: A design team comes up with the specifications for a new computer. The designers sit down with marketing, manufacturing, customer service, purchasing, and other departments. Marketing gives the team a price target and management determines a profit-margin goal, and then the team determines what the costs will be. Achieving cost targets is tough and requires a new infusion of teamwork into the manufacturing process; engineers must design the product with fewer parts and work with other departments to reengineer factory processes to produce products cheaply and quickly. But, this hard work has paid off. The Prolinea personal computer and the Contura notebook computer were the first products manufactured under Compaq's new pricing system, and they set Compaq's sales volume skyrocketing to 64% and nearly doubled the company's profits.[10]

Target costing is an improvement over the usual method of developing new products, which is to design the product, estimate its costs, and then determine its price. Target costing focuses instead on taking costs out of the product during the planning and design stage, rather than trying to reengineer costs after the product has been introduced.

Analyzing Competitors' Costs, Prices, and Offers

Within the range of possible prices determined by market demand and costs, competitors' costs, prices, and possible price reactions help the firm establish where to set its prices. The company needs to benchmark its costs against its competitors' costs to learn whether it is operating at a cost advantage or disadvantage. The company also needs to learn the price and quality of competitors' offers. The firm can send out comparison shoppers to price and assess competitors' offers, acquire competitors' price lists, buy competitors' equipment and take it apart, and ask buyers how they perceive the price and quality of each competitor's offer.

Once the company is aware of competitors' prices and offers, it can use them as an orienting point for its own pricing. If the firm's offer is similar to a major competitor's offer, then the firm will have to price close to the competitor or lose sales. If the firm's offer is inferior, the firm will not be able to charge more than the competitor. If the firm's offer is superior, the firm can charge more than the competitor. The firm must be aware, however, that competitors might change their prices in response to the firm's price.

Selecting a Pricing Method

Given the three Cs—the customers' demand schedule, the cost function, and competitors' prices—the company is now ready to select a price. The price will be somewhere between one that is too low to produce a profit and one that is too high to produce enough demand. Figure 17-7 summarizes the three major considerations in price setting. Costs set a floor to the price. Competitors' prices and prices of substitutes provide an orienting point that the company has to consider in setting its price. Customers' assessment of unique product features in the company's offer establish the ceiling price.

Companies resolve the pricing issue by selecting a pricing method that includes one or more of these three considerations. The pricing method will then lead to a specific price. We will examine the following price-setting methods: markup pric-

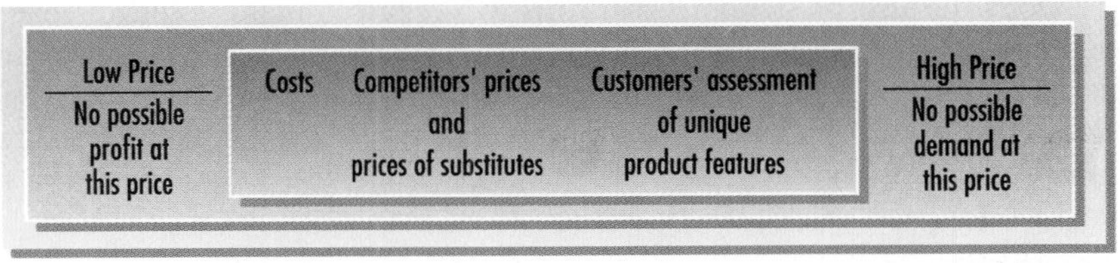

FIGURE 17-7

The Three Cs Model for
Price Setting

Low Price	Costs	Competitors' prices and prices of substitutes	Customers' assessment of unique product features	High Price
No possible profit at this price				No possible demand at this price

ing, target-return pricing, perceived-value pricing, value pricing, going-rate pricing, and sealed-bid pricing.

MARKUP PRICING. The most elementary pricing method is to add a standard markup to the product's cost. Construction companies submit job bids by estimating the total project cost and adding a standard markup for profit. Lawyers, accountants, and other professionals typically price by adding a standard markup to their costs. Some sellers tell their customers they will charge their cost plus a specified markup; for example, aerospace companies price this way to the government.

To illustrate markup pricing, suppose a toaster manufacturer has the following costs and sales expectations:

Variable cost per unit	$ 10
Fixed cost	$300,000
Expected unit sales	50,000

The manufacturer's unit cost is given by:

$$\text{Unit cost} = \text{variable cost} + \frac{\text{fixed costs}}{\text{unit sales}} = \$10 + \frac{\$300,000}{50,000} = \$16$$

Now assume the manufacturer wants to earn a 20% markup on sales. The manufacturer's markup price is given by:

$$\text{Markup price} = \frac{\text{unit cost}}{(1 - \text{desired return on sales})} = \frac{\$16}{1 - 0.2} = \$20$$

The manufacturer would charge dealers $20 per toaster and make a profit of $4 per unit. The dealers in turn will mark up the toaster. If dealers want to earn 50% on their selling price, they will mark up the toaster to $40. This is equivalent to a cost markup of 100 percent.

Markups vary considerably among different goods. Markups are generally higher on seasonal items (to cover the risk of not selling), specialty items, slower-moving items, items with high storage and handling costs, and demand-inelastic items. In addition, companies sometimes use higher markups when hidden or highly variable costs are involved. In fact, the markup of all markups seems to be that on compact discs (CDs), which retail for about $17:

> While most consumers already feel that CD prices are too high (particularly when compared with $8 or $9 for nearly obsolete vinyl records), they would be outraged to realize that the product has a markup of more than 2,000 percent. The actual manufacturing cost of a CD is about 75 cents, and the CDs are sold to record stores for $10 to $11. Executives at Time Warner, a major CD manufacturer, claim that the price is driven up by hidden costs in marketing, promotion, artists' fees, and royalties. Setting CD prices is "very arbitrary," says one executive at a major label. "It's a very speculative business that we're in. If a label can break one new band a year they're having a good year. The first 300,000 to 500,000 copies a record label sells of most CDs don't make money. That's 80 percent of all records that don't make money. The other 20 percent have to pay for the 80 percent."[11]

Does the use of standard markups to set prices make logical sense? Generally, no. Any pricing method that ignores current demand, perceived value, and competition is not likely to lead to the optimal price. Suppose the toaster manufacturer charged $20 but sold only 30,000 toasters instead of 50,000. Then the manufacturer's unit cost would have been higher, since the fixed costs are spread over fewer units, and its realized percentage markup on sales would have been lower. Markup pricing works only if the marked-up price actually brings in the expected level of sales.

Companies introducing a new product often price it high hoping to recover their costs as rapidly as possible. But a high-markup strategy could be fatal if a competitor is pricing low. This happened to Philips, the Dutch electronics manufacturer, in pricing its videodisc players. Philips wanted to make a profit on each videodisc player. Meanwhile, Japanese competitors priced low and succeeded in building their market share rapidly, which in turn pushed down their costs substantially.

Still, markup pricing remains popular for a number of reasons. First, sellers can determine costs much more easily than they can estimate demand. By tying the price to cost, sellers simplify their pricing task. Second, where all firms in the industry use this pricing method, their prices tend to be similar. Price competition is therefore minimized, which would not be the case if firms paid attention to demand variations when they priced. Third, many people feel that cost-plus pricing is fairer to both buyers and sellers. Sellers do not take advantage of buyers when the latter's demand becomes acute, and the sellers earn a fair return on their investment.

TARGET-RETURN PRICING. Another cost-pricing approach is *target-return pricing*. The firm determines the price that would yield its target rate of return on investment (ROI). Target pricing is used by General Motors, which prices its automobiles to achieve a 15 to 20% ROI. This pricing method is also used by public utilities, which need to make a fair return on their investment.

Suppose the toaster manufacturer has invested $1 million in the business and wants to set price to earn a 20% ROI, specifically $200,000. The target-return price is given by the following formula:

$$\text{Target-return price} = \text{unit cost} + \frac{\text{desired return} \times \text{invested capital}}{\text{unit sales}}$$

$$= \$16 + \frac{.20 \times \$1,000,000}{50,000} = \$20$$

The manufacturer will realize this 20% ROI provided its costs and estimated sales turn out to be accurate. But what if sales do not reach 50,000 units? The manufacturer can prepare a *break-even chart* to learn what would happen at other sales levels. Figure 17-8 shows the break-even chart. Fixed costs are $300,000 regardless of sales volume. Variable costs, not shown in the figure, rise with volume. Total costs equal the sum of fixed costs and variable costs. The total revenue curve starts at zero and rises with each unit sold.

The total revenue and total cost curves cross at 30,000 units. This is the *break-even volume*. It can be verified by the following formula:

$$\text{Break-even volume} = \frac{\text{fixed cost}}{\text{price} - \text{variable cost}} = \frac{\$300,000}{\$20 - \$10} = 30,000$$

The manufacturer, of course, is hoping that the market will buy 50,000 units at $20, in which case it earns $200,000 on its $1 million investment. But much depends on price elasticity and competitors' prices. Unfortunately, target-return pricing tends to ignore these considerations. The manufacturer needs to consider dif-

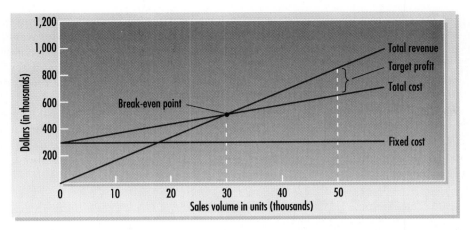

ferent prices and estimate their probable impacts on sales volume and profits. The manufacturer should also search for ways to lower its fixed and/or variable costs, because lower costs will decrease its required break-even volume.

PERCEIVED-VALUE PRICING. An increasing number of companies are basing their price on the product's *perceived value*. They see the buyers' perceptions of value, not the seller's cost, as the key to pricing. They use the nonprice variables in the marketing mix to build up perceived value in the buyers' minds. Price is set to capture the perceived value.[12]

Perceived-value pricing fits well with product-positioning thinking. A company develops a product concept for a particular target market with a planned quality and price. Then management estimates the volume it hopes to sell at this price. The estimate indicates the needed plant capacity, investment, and unit costs. Management then figures out whether the product will yield a satisfactory profit at the planned price and cost. If the answer is yes, the company goes ahead with product development. Otherwise, the company drops the idea.

Du Pont and Caterpillar are two major practitioners of perceived-value pricing. When Du Pont developed its new synthetic fiber for carpets, for example, it demonstrated to carpet manufacturers that they could afford to pay Du Pont as much as $1.40 per pound for the new fiber and still make their current profit. Du Pont calls the $1.40 the *value-in-use price*. Du Pont recognized, however, that pricing the new material at $1.40 per pound would leave the carpet manufacturers indifferent. So it set the price lower than $1.40 to provide a purchase inducement to adopt the new fiber. Du Pont did not use its manufacturing cost to set the price but only to judge whether there was enough profit to go ahead in the first place.

As another example of Du Pont pricing policy, consider the following: Du Pont will price a certain chemical at both a standard offer price and a premium offer price. Consider the following:

ATTRIBUTE	STANDARD OFFER	PREMIUM OFFER	ADDED VALUE
Quality	Impurities less than ten parts per million	Impurities less than one part per million	$1.40
Delivery	Within two weeks	Within one week	.15
System	Supply chemical only	Supply total system	.80
Innovation	Little R&D support	High-level R&D support	2.00
Retraining	Train initially	Retrain on request	.40
Service	Through home-office purchases	Locally available	.25
Price	$100/pound	$105/pound	$5.00

Du Pont has measured the perceived value of each added benefit at the premium level, and this amounts to a $5 premium per pound. The customer who wants the premium offer pays $105 instead of $100 a pound. This strategy is sometimes called *component-value pricing*. The customer may end up requesting a few but not all of the added values. If DuPont is willing to *unbundle* the premium offer, the customer will pay only for the chosen added values.

Caterpillar also uses perceived value to set prices on its construction equipment. It might price its tractor at $100,000, although a similar competitor's tractor might be priced at $90,000. And Caterpillar will sell more than the competitor does! When a prospective customer asks a Caterpillar dealer why he should pay $10,000 more for the Caterpillar tractor, the dealer answers:

$ 90,000	is the tractor's price if it is only equivalent to the competitor's tractor
$ 7,000	is the price premium for Caterpillar's superior durability
$ 6,000	is the price premium for Caterpillar's reliability
$ 5,000	is the price premium for Caterpillar's superior service
$ 2,000	is the price premium for Caterpillar's longer warranty on parts
$110,000	is the normal price to cover Caterpillar's superior value
−$ 10,000	discount
$100,000	final price

Thus, the Caterpillar dealer is able to show the customer why Caterpillar's tractor costs more than the competitor's tractor. The customer learns that although he is asked to pay a $10,000 premium for the Caterpillar tractor, he is actually getting $20,000 extra value! He ends up choosing the Caterpillar tractor because he is convinced that its lifetime operating costs will be lower.

The key to perceived-value pricing is to accurately determine the market's perception of the offer's value. Sellers with an inflated view of their offer's value will overprice their product. Sellers with an underestimated view will charge less than they could. Market research is needed to establish the market's perception of value as a guide to effective pricing.[13]

VALUE PRICING. In recent years, several companies have adopted *value pricing* in which they charge a fairly low price for a high-quality offering. Value pricing says that the price should represent a high-value offer to consumers. Lexus is a good example because Toyota could have priced Lexus, given its extraordinary quality, much closer to the Mercedes price.

Here are other examples of value-pricing marketers:[14]

SOUTHWEST AIRLINES Southwest Airlines charges about one third of what its competitors charge but provides a very comfortable flight and extremely friendly service, though one without frills. Southwest is one of the few U.S. airlines to post profits on a consistent basis.

TACO BELL In recent years Taco Bell reengineered its fast-food operations and lowered its prices significantly, to reintroduce the notion of value pricing to its fast-food customers.

NUCOR STEEL Nucor Steel, through running highly efficient mini-mill operations, has been able to offer steel customers high-quality steel at substantially lower prices than Bethlehem and other steel makers can charge.

Recently Procter & Gamble created quite a stir by changing its pricing policy for several of its products. Pampers and Luvs diapers, liquid Tide detergent, and Folger's coffee are now value priced rather than priced on perceived value. In the past, a brand-loyal family had to pay what amounted to a $725 premium for a year's worth of P&G products versus private-label or low-priced brands. P&G saw that, in these value-conscious times, this premium could spell trouble. To offer value prices, P&G underwent a major overhaul. It redesigned the way it develops, manufactures, distributes, prices, markets, and sells products to deliver better value at every point in the supply chain.[15] Hence, value pricing is not a matter of simply setting lower prices on one's products compared to competitors. It is a matter of reengineering the company's operations to truly become the low-cost producer without sacrificing quality, and lowering one's prices significantly to attract a large number of value-conscious customers.

An important type of value pricing is *everyday low pricing (EDLP),* which takes place at the retail level. A retailer who holds to an EDLP policy charges a constant, everyday low price with no temporary price discounts. These constant prices eliminate week-to-week price uncertainty and can be contrasted to the "high-low" pricing of promotion-oriented competitors. In *high-low pricing,* the retailer charges higher prices on an everyday basis but then runs frequent promotions in which prices are temporarily lowered below the EDLP level.[16]

The high-low strategy evolved during the early 1970s in the wake of rising inflation. When commodity prices began dropping, food manufacturers did not lower their inflated prices but instead offered deals to retailers on certain products. These discounts were then passed on as sales to consumers, who were able to comparison shop. But in recent years, high-low pricing has given way to EDLP at such widely different venues as General Motors' Saturn car dealerships and upscale department stores such as Nordstrom. But the king of EDLP is surely Wal-Mart, which practically defined the term. Except for a few sale items every month, Wal-Mart promises everyday prices on major brands. "It's not a short-term strategy," says one Wal-Mart executive. "You have to be willing to make a commitment to it, and you have to be able to operate with lower ratios of expense than everybody else."

Retailers adopt EDLP for a number of reasons, the most important of which is that constant sales and promotions are costly and have eroded consumer confidence in the credibility of everyday shelf prices. Consumers also have less time and patience for such time-honored traditions as watching for supermarket specials and clipping coupons to put into voluminous coupon files.

EDLP is not a guarantee of success, however. Sears' EDLP initiative failed when it was launched in 1989. The store didn't reduce costs to cushion it against the inevitable initial drop in business while consumers waited to see what was up. Wal-Mart has been able to stick to its EDLP policy because its expenses are only 15% of sales; Sears, in contrast, spends 29% of sales to cover administrative, occupancy, and other costs. Finally, Sears also failed to make sure its everyday low prices were actually lower than competitors', and it continued to advertise sales so that the low prices lost credibility with customers. The upshot: Sears now offers what the industry calls everyday *fair* pricing, a policy similar to Bloomingdale's under which the merchant tries to offer customers a consistent, fair price with fewer markdowns.[17]

GOING-RATE PRICING. In *going-rate pricing,* the firm pays less attention to its own costs or demand and bases its price largely on competitors' prices. The firm might charge the same, more, or less than its major competitor(s). In oligopolistic industries that sell a commodity such as steel, paper, or fertilizer, firms normally charge the same price. The smaller firms "follow the leader," changing their prices when the market leader's prices change rather than when their own demand or costs change. Some firms may charge a slight premium or slight discount, but they preserve the amount of difference. Thus minor gasoline retailers usually

Designing Pricing
Strategies and
Programs

charge a few cents less per gallon than the major oil companies, without letting the difference increase or decrease.

Going-rate pricing is quite popular. Where costs are difficult to measure or competitive response is uncertain, firms feel that the going price represents a good solution. The going price is thought to reflect the industry's collective wisdom as to the price that would yield a fair return and not jeopardize industrial harmony.

SEALED-BID PRICING. Competitive-oriented pricing is common where firms submit sealed bids for jobs. The firm bases its price on expectations of how competitors will price rather than on a rigid relation to the firm's costs or demand. The firm wants to win the contract, and winning normally requires submitting a lower price than competitors. At the same time, the firm cannot set its price below cost without worsening its position.

The net effect of these two opposite pulls can be described in terms of the bid's expected profit (Table 17-1). Suppose a bid of $9,500 would yield a high chance of getting the contract (say 81%) but only a low profit, say $100. The expected profit is calculated by multiplying the company's profit by the probability of having the bid accepted. Thus the expected profit of this bid is $81. If the firm bid $11,000, its profit would be $1,600, but its chance of getting the contract might be reduced, say to .01. The expected profit would thus be only $16. One logical bidding criterion would be to bid the price that would maximize the expected profit. According to Table 17-1, the best bid would be $10,000, for which the expected profit is $216.

Using expected profit as a criterion for setting price makes sense for the firm that makes many bids. In playing the odds, the firm will achieve maximum profits in the long run. The firm that bids only occasionally or that needs a particular contract badly will not find it advantageous to use the expected-profit criterion. This criterion, for example, does not distinguish between a $1,000 profit with a 0.10 probability and a $125 profit with an 0.80 probability. Yet the firm that wants to keep production going would prefer the second contract to the first.

Selecting the Final Price

Pricing methods narrow the price range from which the company must select its final price. In selecting the final price, the company must consider additional factors, including psychological pricing, the influence of other marketing-mix elements on price, company pricing policies, and the impact of price on other parties.

PSYCHOLOGICAL PRICING. Sellers should consider the psychology of prices in addition to their economics. Many consumers use price as an indicator of quality. When Fleischmann raised the price of its gin from $4.50 to $5.50 a bottle, its liquor sales went up, not down. Image pricing is especially effective with ego-sensitive products such as perfumes and expensive cars. A $100 bottle of perfume

TABLE 17-1	EFFECT OF DIFFERENT BIDS ON EXPECTED PROFIT		
COMPANY'S BID	COMPANY'S PROFIT	PROBABILITY OF GETTING AWARD WITH THIS BID (ASSUMED)	EXPECTED PROFIT
$ 9,500	$ 100	0.81	$ 81
10,000	600	0.36	216
10,500	1,100	0.09	99
11,000	1,600	0.01	16

might contain $10 worth of scent, but gift-givers pay $100 to communicate their high regard for the receiver.

A study of the relationship between price and quality perceptions of cars found the relationship to be operating in a reciprocal manner.[18] Higher-priced cars were perceived to possess (unwarranted) high quality. Higher-quality cars were likewise perceived to be higher priced than they actually were. When alternative information about true quality is available, price becomes a less significant indicator of quality. When this information is not available, price acts as a quality signal.

When looking at a particular product, buyers carry in their minds a *reference price* that might have been formed by noticing current prices, past prices, or the buying context. Sellers often manipulate these reference prices in pricing their product. For example, a seller can place its product among expensive products to imply that it belongs in the same class. Department stores will display women's apparel in separate departments differentiated by price; dresses found in the more expensive department are assumed to be of better quality. Reference-price thinking is also created by stating a high manufacturer's suggested price, or by indicating that the product was priced much higher originally, or by pointing to a competitor's high price.[19]

Many sellers believe that prices should end in an odd number. Newspaper ads are dominated by prices ending in odd numbers. Thus a stereo amplifier is priced at $299 instead of $300. Many customers see this as a price in the $200 range rather than $300 range. Another explanation is that odd endings convey the notion of a discount or bargain. But if a company wants a high-price image instead of a low-price image, it should avoid the odd-ending tactic.

THE INFLUENCE OF OTHER MARKETING-MIX ELEMENTS ON PRICE. The final price must take into account the brand's quality and advertising relative to competition. Farris and Reibstein examined the relationship among relative price, relative quality, and relative advertising for 227 consumer businesses and found the following:

1. Brands with average relative quality but high relative advertising budgets were able to charge premium prices. Consumers apparently were willing to pay higher prices for known products than for unknown products.

2. Brands with high relative quality and high relative advertising obtained the highest prices. Conversely, brands with low quality and low advertising charged the lowest prices.

3. The positive relationship between high prices and high advertising held most strongly in the later stages of the product life cycle, for market leaders, and for low-cost products.[20]

COMPANY PRICING POLICIES. The contemplated price must be consistent with company pricing policies. Many companies set up a pricing department to develop pricing policies and establish or approve pricing decisions. Their aim is to ensure that the salespeople quote prices that are reasonable to customers and profitable to the company.

IMPACT OF PRICE ON OTHER PARTIES. Management must also consider the reactions of other parties to the contemplated price. How will the distributors and dealers feel about it? Will the company sales force be willing to sell at that price or complain that the price is too high? How will competitors react to this price? Will suppliers raise the prices of their inputs when they see the company's price? Will the government intervene and prevent this price from being charged?

In the last case, marketers need to know the laws affecting price and make sure that their pricing policies are defensible. U.S. legislation states that sellers must set prices without talking to competitors; *price fixing* is illegal. In 1994 six

Designing Pricing
Strategies and
Programs

major airlines settled federal charges that they fixed ticket prices in a scheme that may have cost consumers nearly $2 billion between 1988 and 1992. In addition, many federal and state statutes protect consumers against deceptive pricing practices. For example, it is illegal for a company to set artificially high "regular" prices, then announce a "sale" at prices close to its previous everyday prices. For instance, the state of New York charged the Home Shopping Network with "deceptive reference pricing" of jewelry in 1994. New York's attorney general said that the network had inflated "suggested retail prices" quoted for jewelry and that these retail prices were often "a fantasy. A ring they were selling for $400 was probably worth about that—the trouble is, they were saying it would cost $1,200 elsewhere," he said.

Some forms of *price discrimination* (in which sellers offer different price terms to different people within the same trade group) are also illegal. However, price discrimination is legal if the seller can prove that its costs are different when selling to different retailers—for example, it costs less per unit to sell a large volume of bicycles to Sears than to sell a few bicycles to a local dealer. The seller can also discriminate in its pricing if it manufactures different qualities of the same product for different retailers, and to protect itself from competitors. However, *predatory pricing*—selling below cost with the intention of destroying competition—is against the law.[21]

ADAPTING THE PRICE

Companies usually do not set a single price but rather a pricing structure that reflects variations in geographical demand and costs, market-segment requirements, purchase timing, order levels, delivery frequency, guarantees, service contracts, and other factors. As a result of discounts, allowances, and promotional support, a company rarely realizes the same profit from each unit of a product that it sells. Here we will examine several price-adaptation strategies: geographical pricing, price discounts and allowances, promotional pricing, discriminatory pricing, and product-mix pricing.

Geographical Pricing (Cash, Countertrade, and Barter)

Geographical pricing involves the company in deciding how to price its products to different customers in different locations and countries. One issue is whether the company should charge higher prices to distant customers to cover the higher shipping costs and risk losing their business. Or should it charge a lower price, hoping that a lower price will generate higher sales volume?

Another issue is how to get paid. This issue is critical when buyers lack sufficient hard currency to pay for their purchases. Many times buyers want to offer other items in payment, and this practice has led to the rise of *countertrade*.

Many companies in the West are unfamiliar with countertrade and would prefer to make overseas sales in cash. Yet countertrade is used increasingly as a marketing strategy in Asia, the Middle East, and other areas of the world where sophisticated bargaining is part of the business culture. "[The United States] sit[s] in an isolated area where the dollar is king," says Dan West, chairman of the American Countertrade Association. "We don't bargain in this country, it's not part of our modus operandi." Yet American companies are often forced to engage in countertrade if they want the business. According to experts, countertrade already accounts for roughly 15% of world trade. Countertrade takes several forms:[22]

- *Barter:* Barter involves the direct exchange of goods, with no money and no third party involved. In 1993, Eminence S.A., one of France's major clothing makers, launched a five-year deal to barter $25 million worth of U.S.-produced underwear and sportswear to customers in Eastern Europe. In exchange, Eminence will receive a variety of goods and services, ranging from global transportation to advertising space in Eastern European magazines.

- *Compensation deal:* Here the seller receives some percentage of the payment in cash and the rest in products. A British aircraft manufacturer sold planes to Brazil for 70% cash and the rest in coffee.

- *Buyback arrangement:* The seller sells a plant, equipment, or technology to another country and agrees to accept as partial payment products manufactured with the equipment supplied. For example, a U.S. chemical company built a plant for an Indian company and accepted partial payment in cash and the remainder in chemicals to be manufactured at the plant.

- *Offset:* The seller receives full payment in cash but agrees to spend a substantial amount of that money in that country within a stated time period. For example, Pepsi-Cola sells its cola syrup to Russia for rubles and agrees to buy Russian vodka at a certain rate for sale in the United States.

More complex countertrade deals involve more than two parties. For example, Daimler-Benz agreed to sell 30 trucks to Romania and accept in exchange 150 Romanian-made jeeps, which it sold in Ecuador for bananas, which in turn were sold to a German supermarket chain for deutsche marks. Through this circuitous transaction, Daimler-Benz finally achieved payment in German currency.

In recent years the definition of countertrade has been expanding to include contractual agreements by exporters that provide some benefit or compensation to the buyer as a condition of sale. For instance, when U.S. aircraft maker McDonnell Douglas needed to clinch the sale of $250 million worth of Apache helicopters to the United Arab Emirates (UAE), it agreed to equip the Arab sheikdoms against a pesky airborne enemy: the whitefly. McDonnell Douglas is helping install an insect trap system in the UAE capital, Abu Dhabi, to fight a major infestation of the whitefly, which is destroying vegetable crops there.

Like many other large companies, McDonnell Douglas employs a substantial staff in a separate countertrade department. Some companies, however, rely on barter houses and countertrade specialists to assist in initiating and facilitating transactions. For instance, Eminence used the services of Atwood Richards Inc., one of the world's largest corporate barter firms.

Price Discounts and Allowances

Most companies will modify their basic price to reward customers for such acts as early payment, volume purchases, and off-season buying. Descriptions of these price adjustments—called *discounts* and *allowances*—follow. Before we begin, however, a word of warning is in order. Many companies are so ready to grant discounts, allowances, and special terms (e.g., co-op advertising, freight) to their dealers and customers that they may fail to realize how little profit may be left. Companies should measure the cost of granting each discount or allowance against its impact on making the sale. They should then establish better policies as to what should be granted to customers in bidding for their business.[23]

CASH DISCOUNTS. A *cash discount* is a price reduction to buyers who promptly pay their bills. A typical example is "2/10, net 30," which means that payment is due within 30 days and that the buyer can deduct 2% by paying the bill within 10 days. The discount must be granted to all buyers who meet these terms. Such discounts are customary in many industries and serve the purpose of improving the sellers' liquidity and reducing credit-collection costs and bad debts.

QUANTITY DISCOUNTS. A *quantity discount* is a price reduction to buyers who buy large volumes. A typical example is "$10 per unit for less than 100 units; $9 per unit for 100 or more units." Under the law, quantity discounts must be offered equally to all customers and must not exceed the cost savings to the seller associated with selling large quantities. These savings include reduced expenses of selling, inventory, and transportation. They can be offered on a noncumulative basis (on each order placed) or a cumulative basis (on the number of units ordered over a given period). Discounts provide an incentive to the customer to order more from a given seller rather than buy from multiple sources.

FUNCTIONAL DISCOUNTS. *Functional discounts* (also called *trade discounts*) are offered by the manufacturer to trade-channel members if they will perform certain functions, such as selling, storing, and record-keeping. Manufacturers may offer different functional discounts to different trade channels because of their varying functions, but under the law manufacturers must offer the same functional discounts within each trade channel.

SEASONAL DISCOUNTS. A *seasonal discount* is a price reduction to buyers who buy merchandise or services out of season. Seasonal discounts allow the seller to maintain steadier production during the year. Ski manufacturers will offer seasonal discounts to retailers in the spring and summer to encourage early ordering. Hotels, motels, and airlines will offer seasonal discounts in their slow selling periods.

ALLOWANCES. Allowances are other types of reductions from the list price. For example, *trade-in allowances* are price reductions granted for turning in an old item when buying a new one. Trade-in allowances are most common in the automobile industry and are also found in other durable-goods categories. *Promotional allowances* are payments or price reductions to reward dealers for participating in advertising and sales support programs.

PROMOTIONAL PRICING

Companies use several pricing techniques to stimulate early purchase. International companies must research these promotional pricing tools and make sure that they are lawful in the particular countries in which they do business.

♦ *Loss-leader pricing:* Here supermarkets and department stores drop the price on well-known brands to stimulate additional store traffic. But manufacturers typically disapprove of their brands being used as loss leaders because this practice can dilute the brand image as well as cause complaints from other retailers who charge the list price. Manufacturers have tried to restrain intermediaries from loss-leader pricing through lobbying for retail-price-maintenance laws, but these laws have been revoked.

♦ *Special-event pricing:* Sellers will establish special prices in certain seasons to draw in more customers. Thus linens are promotionally priced every January to attract shopping-weary customers into the stores.

♦ *Cash rebates:* Consumers are offered cash rebates to encourage their purchase of the manufacturer's product within a specified time period. The rebates can help the manufacturer clear inventories without cutting the list price. (Auto manufacturers have long offered rebates to stimulate sales, but the onset of value pricing has been eating away at rebates in recent years. The average rebates among the Detroit automakers dropped to about $700 per vehicle in the fourth quarter of 1993, down from $900 the previous quarter and about $1200 at the end of 1992.[24]) Rebates also appear in consumer-packaged-goods marketing. They stimulate sales without costing the company as much as it would cost to cut the price. The reason is that many buyers buy the product but fail to mail in the rebate coupon.

- *Low-interest financing:* Instead of decreasing its product's price, the company can offer customers low-interest financing. Automakers have announced 3% financing and in some cases 0% financing to attract customers. Since many auto buyers finance their auto purchases, low-interest financing is appealing.

- *Longer payment terms:* Sellers, especially mortgage banks and auto companies, stretch their loans over longer periods and thus lower monthly payments. Consumers often think less of the cost (i.e., the interest rate) of a loan and more about whether they can afford the monthly payment.

- *Warranties and service contracts:* The company can promote sales by adding a free warranty offer or service contract. Instead of charging for the warranty or service contract, it offers these free or at a reduced price.

- *Psychological discounting:* This strategy involves putting an artificially high price on a product and then offering it at substantial savings; for example, "Was $359, now $299." Illegitimate discount tactics are fought by the Federal Trade Commission and Better Business Bureaus. However, discounts from normal prices are a legitimate form of promotional pricing.

Promotional-pricing strategies are often a zero-sum game. If they work, competitors will copy them rapidly, and they will lose their effectiveness for the individual company. If they do not work, they waste company money that would have been put into longer-impact marketing tools, such as building up product quality and service and/or improving the product image through advertising.

Discriminatory Pricing

Companies often modify their basic price to accommodate differences in customers, products, locations, and so on. *Discriminatory pricing* (also called *price discrimination*) occurs when a company sells a product or service at two or more prices that do not reflect a proportional difference in costs. Discriminatory pricing takes several forms:

- *Customer-segment pricing:* Different customer groups are charged different prices for the same product or service. For example, museums often charge a lower admission fee to students and senior citizens.

- *Product-form pricing:* Different versions of the product are priced differently but not proportionately to their respective costs. Evian prices a 48-ounce bottle of its mineral water at $2. Evian takes the same water and packages 1.7 ounces in a moisturizer spray for $6. Through product-form pricing, Evian manages to charge $3 an ounce in one form and about four cents an ounce in another.

- *Image pricing:* Some companies price the same product at two different levels based on image differences. Thus a perfume manufacturer can put the perfume in one bottle, give it a name and image, and price it at $10 an ounce. It puts the same perfume in a fancier bottle with a different name and image and prices it at $30 an ounce.

- *Location pricing:* The same product is priced differently at different locations even though the cost of offering at each location is the same. A theater varies its seat prices according to audience preferences for different locations. Movie tickets cost more in New York City than in the New Jersey suburbs.

- *Time pricing:* Prices are varied by season, day, or hour. Public utilities vary their energy rates to commercial users by time of day and weekend versus weekday. It costs more to make a long-distance call during the week than it does on the weekend. A special form of time pricing is *yield pricing,* which is often used by hotels and airlines to ensure high occupancy. To ensure that all its berths are full, for example, a cruise ship may lower the price of the cruise two days before setting sail.

For price discrimination to work, certain conditions must exist. First, the market must be segmentable, and the segments must show different intensities of de-

Designing Pricing
Strategies and
Programs

mand. Second, members of the lower-price segment must not be able to resell the product to the higher-price segment. Third, competitors must not be able to undersell the firm in the higher-price segment. Fourth, the cost of segmenting and policing the market must not exceed the extra revenue derived from price discrimination. Fifth, the practice must not breed customer resentment and ill will. Sixth, the particular form of price discrimination must not be illegal.[25]

As a result of deregulation in several industries, competitors have increased their use of discriminatory pricing. Airlines, for example, charge different fares to passengers on the same flight depending on the seating class; the time of day (morning or night coach); the day of the week (workday or weekend); the season; the person's company, past business, or status (youth, military, senior citizen); and so on. This system, called *yield management,* is an exercise in trying to realize as much revenue as possible in filling the plane's seats.

Product-Mix Pricing

Price-setting logic must be modified when the product is part of a product mix. In this case, the firm searches for a set of prices that maximizes the profits on the total product mix. Pricing is difficult because the various products have demand and cost interrelationships and are subject to different degrees of competition. We can distinguish six situations involving product-mix pricing: product-line pricing, optional-feature pricing, capture-product pricing, two-part pricing, byproduct pricing, and product-bundling pricing.

PRODUCT-LINE PRICING. Companies normally develop product lines rather than single products. For example, Reebok International offers four different versions of its best-known sneaker, the Shaq Attaq. Starting with a stripped-down sneaker for $60, each successive sneaker offers additional features, permitting premium pricing for each more gadget-laden sneaker. The top-of-the line sneaker sells for $135. Management must decide on the *price steps* to establish from one sneaker to the next. The price steps should take into account cost differences between the sneakers, customer evaluations of the different features, and competitors' prices. If the price difference between two successive pairs of sneakers is small, buyers will often buy the fancier sneaker, and company profits will increase if the price difference is greater than the cost difference. If the price difference is large, customers will buy the simpler pair of sneakers.[26]

In many lines of trade, sellers use well-established price points for the products in their line. Thus a men's clothing store might carry men's suits at three price levels: $150, $250, and $350. The customers will associate low-, average-, and high-quality suits with the three price points. The seller's task is to establish perceived-quality differences that justify the price differences.

OPTIONAL-FEATURE PRICING. Many companies offer optional products or features along with their main product. The automobile buyer can order electric window controls, defoggers, and light dimmers. Pricing these options is a sticky problem, because automobile companies must decide which items to include in the sticker price and which to offer as options. For many years, U.S. auto companies' normal pricing strategy was to advertise a stripped-down model for $10,000 to pull people into the showrooms and devote most of the showroom space to feature-loaded cars at $13,000 and up. The economy model was stripped of so many comforts and features that most buyers rejected it. Yet now with the advent of value pricing, U.S. automakers are taking a cue from the Japanese and including a number of popular options in the sticker price. At General Motors and Ford, a value-priced or special edition car comes with a fixed set of popular options such as air conditioning, power window or door locks, and a rear window defroster, and it is advertised at a low (usually nonnegotiable) package price.[27]

Restaurants face a similar pricing problem. Restaurant customers can often order liquor in addition to the meal. Many restaurants price their liquor high and their food low. The food revenue covers the food and other restaurant costs, and the liquor produces the profit. This explains why servers often press hard to get customers to order drinks. Other restaurants price their liquor low and food high to draw in a drinking crowd.

CAPTIVE-PRODUCT PRICING. Some products require the use of ancillary, or *captive,* products. Examples of captive products are razor blades (razors are useless without them) and camera film (cameras are useless without film). Manufacturers of the main products (razors and cameras) often price them low and set high markups on the supplies. Thus Kodak prices its cameras low because it makes its money on selling film. Those camera makers who do not sell film have to price their cameras higher to make the same overall profit.

There is a danger in pricing the captive product too high in the *aftermarket* (i.e., the market for ancillary supplies to the main product). Caterpillar, for example, makes high profits in the aftermarket by pricing high its parts and service. It marks up its equipment by 30% and its parts sometimes by 200 percent. This practice has given rise to "pirates," who counterfeit these parts and sell them to "shady tree" mechanics who install them, sometimes without passing on the cost savings to the customers. Meanwhile Caterpillar loses sales. Caterpillar attempts to control this problem by exhorting equipment owners to use only authorized dealers if they want guaranteed performance. But clearly the problem is created by the high prices that manufacturers charge for their aftermarket products.[28]

TWO-PART PRICING. Service firms often engage in *two-part pricing*. That is, they charge a fixed fee plus a variable usage fee. Thus telephone users pay a minimum monthly fee plus charges for calls beyond a certain limit. Amusement parks charge an admission fee plus fees for rides over a certain minimum. The service firm faces a problem similar to captive-product pricing—namely, how much to charge for the basic service and how much for the variable usage. The fixed fee should be low enough to induce purchase of the service; the profit can then be made on the usage fees.

BYPRODUCT PRICING. The production of certain goods—meats, petroleum products, and other chemicals, for example—often results in byproducts. If the byproducts have value to a customer group, then they should be priced on their value. Any income earned on the byproducts will make it easier for the company to charge a lower price on its main product if competition forces it to do so.

Sometimes companies don't realize how valuable their byproducts are. For example, until Zoo-Doo Compost Company came along, many zoos did not realize that one of their byproducts—their occupants' manure—could be an excellent source of additional revenue:

ZOO-DOO COMPOST COMPANY Based in Memphis, Tennessee, Zoo-Doo Compost Company licenses its name to zoos and receives royalty on manure sales. Zoo-Doo has helped many zoos understand the costs and opportunities involved with their occupants' byproducts. "Many zoos don't even know how much manure they are producing or the cost of disposing of it," explains president and founder Pierce Ledbetter. According to Ledbetter, manure disposal costs are often lost in layers of city budgets, and when zoo management uncovers the actual amount, they are shocked. Zoos are often so pleased with any savings they can find on disposal that they don't think to move into active byproduct sales. They should, since sales of the smelly byproduct are substantial. So far novelty sales have been the largest with tiny containers of Zoo Doo (and even "Love Me Doo" valentines) available in 160 zoo stores and 700 additional retail outlets. For the long-term market, Zoo-Doo looks to organic gardeners who buy 15 to 70 pounds of manure at a time. Ledbetter is already planning a "Dung of the Month" club to reach this lucrative market.[29]

PRODUCT-BUNDLING PRICING. Sellers often bundle their products at a set price. Thus an auto manufacturer might offer an option package at less than the cost of buying all the options separately. A theater company will price a season subscription at less than the cost of buying all the performances separately. Since customers may not have planned to buy all of the components, the savings on the price bundle must be substantial enough to induce them to buy the bundle.[30]

Some customers will want less than the whole bundle. Suppose a medical equipment supplier's offer includes free delivery and training. A particular customer might ask to forgo the free delivery and training in order to get a lower price. The customer is asking the seller to "unbundle" its offer. The seller could actually increase its profit through unbundling if it saves more in cost than the price reduction that it offers to the customer for the items that are eliminated. Thus, if the supplier saves $100 by not supplying delivery and it reduces the customer's price by $80, the supplier has kept the customer happy while increasing its profit by $20.

INITIATING AND RESPONDING TO PRICE CHANGES

After developing their pricing strategies, companies will face situations where they may need to cut or raise prices.

Initiating Price Cuts

Several circumstances might lead a firm to cut its price. One circumstance is *excess plant capacity.* Here the firm needs additional business and cannot generate it through increased sales effort, product improvement, or other measures. To boost its sales, it may abandon follow-the-leader pricing and resort to aggressive pricing. But in initiating a price cut, the company might trigger a price war, as competitors try to hold on to their market shares.

Another circumstance that might lead to price cuts is a *declining market share.* Several American industries—automobiles, consumer electronics, musical instruments, watches, and steel—have been losing market share to Japanese competitors. To stem the losses, some have resorted to more aggressive pricing action. General Motors, for example, cut its subcompact car prices by 10% on the West Coast, where Japanese competition is strongest.

Companies will also initiate price cuts in a *drive to dominate the market through lower costs.* Either the company starts with lower costs than its competitors or it initiates price cuts in the hope of gaining market share, which would lead to falling costs through larger volume and more experience. The now-defunct People Express airline waged an aggressive low-price strategy and gained a large market share. But this strategy also involves high risks:

1. *Low-quality trap:* Consumers will assume that the quality is below that of the higher-priced competitors.

2. *Fragile-market-share trap:* A low price buys market share but not market loyalty. Customers will shift to another lower-price firm that comes along.

Analyzing Marketing-Mix Alternatives in an Economic Recession

Here we will describe an actual but disguised situation involving two competing appliance manufacturers. Company A's appliances are perceived to be more expensive and of higher quality than company B's appliances. Both companies are facing strong demand for their products.

An economic recession now occurs. There are fewer buyers and their preferences shift toward the cheaper appliance B. The number of buyers willing to buy the higher-price appliance diminishes. If company A does nothing about this, its market share will shrink.

Company A must identify its marketing alternatives and choose among them. At least eight marketing alternatives exist. ▼

The choice of a marketing strategy hinges on a number of considerations, including company A's current market share, current and planned capacity, market growth rate, customer price sensitivity and perceived-value sensitivity, market-share/profitability relationship, and competitors' probable strategic responses and initiatives. The company needs to forecast the impact of each marketing strategy on its sales, market share, costs, profit, and long-run investment.

STRATEGIC OPTIONS	REASONING	CONSEQUENCES
1. Maintain price and perceived quality. Engage in selective customer pruning.	Firm has high customer loyalty. It is willing to lose poorer customers to competitors.	Smaller market share. Lowered profitability.
2. Raise price and perceived quality.	Raise price to cover rising costs. Improve quality to justify higher prices.	Smaller market share. Maintained profitability.
3. Maintain price and raise perceived quality.	It is cheaper to maintain price and raise perceived quality.	Smaller market share. Short-term decline in profitability. Long-term increase in profitability.
4. Cut price partly and raise perceived quality.	Must give customers some price reduction but stress higher value of offer.	Maintained market share. Short-term decline in profitability. Long-term maintained profitability.
5. Cut price fully and maintain perceived quality.	Discipline and discourage price competition.	Maintained market share. Short-term decline in profitability.
6. Cut price fully and reduce perceived quality.	Discipline and discourage price competition and maintain profit margin.	Maintained market share. Maintained margin. Reduced long term profitability.
7. Maintain price and reduce perceived quality.	Cut marketing expense to combat rising costs.	Smaller market share. Maintained margin. Reduced long-term profitability
8. Introduce an economy model.	Give the market what it wants.	Some cannibalization but higher total volume.

3. *Shallow-pockets trap:* The higher-priced competitors may cut their prices and may have longer staying power because of deeper cash reserves.

People Express ultimately fell into these traps.

Companies may have to cut their prices in a period of *economic recession.* Fewer consumers are willing to buy higher-price versions of a product. The Marketing Insight titled "Analyzing Marketing-Mix Alternatives in an Economic Recession" discusses several ways in which a seller of a high-price product can adjust its price and/or marketing mix to counteract a declining demand situation.

Initiating Price Increases

A successful price increase can increase profits considerably. For example, if the company's profit margin is 3% of sales, a 1% price increase will increase profits by 33% if sales volume is unaffected. This situation is illustrated in Table 17-2, which

TABLE 17-2	PROFITS BEFORE AND AFTER A PRICE INCREASE	
	BEFORE	**AFTER**
Price	$ 10	$10.10 (a 1% price increase)
Units sold	100	100
Revenue	$1000	$ 1010
Costs	−970	−970
Profit	$ 30	$ 40 (a 33 1/3% profit increase)

assumes that a company charged $10 and sold 100 units and had costs of $970, leaving a profit of $30, or 3% on sales. By raising its price by 10¢ (1% price increase), it boosted its profits by 33%, assuming the same sales volume.

A major circumstance provoking price increases is *cost inflation*. Rising costs unmatched by productivity gains squeeze profit margins and lead companies to regular rounds of price increases. Companies often raise their prices by more than the cost increase in anticipation of further inflation or government price controls; this practice is called *anticipatory pricing*. Companies hesitate to make long-run price commitments to customers, fearing that cost inflation will erode their profit margins.

Another factor leading to price increases is *overdemand*. When a company cannot supply all of its customers, it can raise its prices, ration supplies to customers, or both. In this situation, the price can be increased in several ways, each with a different impact on buyers. The following price adjustments are common:

◆ *Adoption of delayed quotation pricing:* The company does not set its final price until the product is finished or delivered. Delayed quotation pricing is prevalent in industries with long production lead times, such as industrial construction and heavy equipment manufacture.

◆ *Use of escalator clauses:* The company requires the customer to pay today's price and all or part of any inflation increase that takes place before delivery. An escalator clause in the contract bases price increases on some specified price index, such as the cost-of-living index. Escalator clauses are found in many contracts involving industrial projects of long duration.

◆ *Unbundling of goods and services:* The company maintains its price but removes or prices separately one or more elements that were part of the former offer, such as free delivery or installation. IBM, for example, now offers training as a separately priced service. Many restaurants have shifted from total dinner pricing to à la carte pricing. A joke in Romania is that the current price of a car no longer includes the tires and steering wheel.

◆ *Reduction of discounts:* The company instructs its sales force not to offer its normal cash and quantity discounts.

A company might also have to decide whether to raise the price sharply on a one-time basis or to raise it by small amounts several times. For example, when costs rose for Supercuts stores (a franchised chain of hairdressers), management debated between raising the haircut price immediately from $6 to $8 or raising the price to $7 this year and $8 the following year. (Supercuts now charges $12.95 for a haircut.) Generally, consumers prefer small price increases on a regular basis to sharp price increases.

In passing price increases on to customers, the company needs to avoid the image of a price gouger. Customer memories are long, and they will turn against the price gougers when the market softens. For more details on how to avoid the image of price gouging, see the Marketing Memo titled "How *Not* to Raise Prices."

There are some ways that the company can respond to high costs or demand without raising prices. The possibilities include the following:

MARKETING MEMO

HOW *NOT* TO RAISE PRICES

Within 24 hours of the Iraqi invasion of Kuwait in 1990, gas prices in the United States increased substantially—the average retail price of unleaded gasoline went from $1.08 per gallon on August 1 to $1.20 on August 7. The U.S. public was furious. Granted, the gas companies are heavily dependent upon Iraqi and Kuwaiti oil. But the public at large didn't understand *why* that relationship would affect prices immediately. They wondered, "Why is this happening when oil supplies are supposedly pretty good?" While the oil companies' after-the-fact explanations made sense—heavy influences of futures-market trading added to the need to recover price increases already in the pipeline—the swiftness of the increase caused a public outcry and charges of war profiteering. The scenario provides some good don'ts (and two do's) for raising prices in the face of volatile cost run-ups:

- *DON'T forget that a sense of fairness must surround any price increase.* Increasing prices as war breaks out, for instance, doesn't seem fair. Consumers hate the thought of someone taking advantage of them.

- *DON'T violate the principles of "grandfathering" (that is, letting customers know ahead of time that things are going to change).* Customers expect some notification of a price increase so that they have a chance to take some precautions, such as forward buying or shopping around, in order to soften the blow.

- *DON'T patronize the customer by failing to explain the rationale behind sharp price increases.* Following the Iraqi invasion of Kuwait, the oil companies' blitz of price announcements carried a tone of, "You're going to pay more and there's nothing you can do about it." The best thing to do is explain in simple and understandable terms why prices are going to change and offer charts showing how prices move through the marketing pipeline.

- *DO exhaust your low-visibility price moves first.* Before sticking customers with highly visible product increases, use some indirect, low-visibility moves that are available to you—eliminating cash and quantity discounts, increasing minimum order sizes, curtailing production and sales of lower margin products, and charging for valuable services that you have customarily offered as free, to name a few.

- *DO employ escalator clauses in your contracts/bids.* This policy allows you to increase prices automatically across the board based on some previously stated formula. The objective is to pass the risks involved in cost increases along to the customer in a proactive, preidentified manner. To be deemed fair, the basis for escalations must include simple factors such as increases in recognized national price indexes. Published price increases from raw-material suppliers also serve as a good reference base for communicating a price increase.

Source: Adapted from: Eric Mitchell, "How Not to Raise Prices," *Small Business Reports*, November 1990, pp. 64–67.

- Shrinking the amount of product instead of raising the price. (Hershey Foods maintained its candy bar price but trimmed its size. Nestlé maintained its size but raised the price.)

- Substituting less-expensive materials or ingredients. (Many candy bar companies substituted synthetic chocolate for real chocolate to fight the price increases in cocoa.)

- Reducing or removing product features to reduce cost. (Sears engineered down a number of its appliances so they could be priced competitively with those sold in discount stores.)

- Removing or reducing product services, such as installation, free delivery, or long warranties.

- Using less expensive packaging material or promoting larger package sizes to keep down packaging cost.

Designing Pricing
Strategies and
Programs

- Reducing the number of sizes and models offered.
- Creating new economy brands. (The Jewel Food Stores introduced 170 generic items selling at 10% to 30% less than national brands.)

Reactions to Price Changes

Any price change can affect customers, competitors, distributors, and suppliers and may provoke government reaction as well.

CUSTOMERS' REACTIONS. Customers often question the motivation behind price changes.[31] A price cut can be interpreted in the following ways: The item is about to be replaced by a new model; the item is faulty and is not selling well; the firm is in financial trouble and may not stay in business to supply future parts; the price will come down even further, and it pays to wait; the quality has been reduced.

A price increase, which would normally deter sales, may carry some positive meanings to customers: The item is "hot" and might be unobtainable unless it is bought soon, or the item represents an unusually good value.

Customers are most price sensitive to products that cost a lot and/or are bought frequently, while they hardly notice higher prices on low-cost items that they buy infrequently. In addition, some buyers are less concerned with the product's price than they are with the total costs of obtaining, operating, and servicing the product over its lifetime. A seller can charge more than competitors and still get the business if the customer can be convinced that the product's total lifetime costs are lower.

COMPETITORS' REACTIONS. A firm contemplating a price change has to worry about competitors' as well as customers' reactions. Competitors are most likely to react where the number of firms in the industry is small, the product is homogeneous, and the buyers are highly informed.

How can the firm anticipate its competitors' likely reactions? Assume that the firm faces one large competitor. The firm can then estimate its competitor's reaction from two vantage points. One is to assume that the competitor reacts in a set way to price changes. The other is to assume that the competitor treats each price change as a fresh challenge and reacts according to self-interest at the time. In this case, the company will have to figure out what lies in the competitor's self-interest. It will need to research the competitor's current financial situation, along with recent sales and capacity, customer loyalty, and corporate objectives. If the competitor has a market share objective, it is likely to match the price change. If it has a profit-maximization objective, it may react on some other strategy front, such as increasing the advertising budget or improving the product quality. The challenge is to read the competitor's mind by using inside and outside sources of information.

The problem is complicated because the competitor can put different interpretations on a company price cut: The competitor can surmise that the company is trying to steal the market, that the company is doing poorly and trying to boost its sales, or that the company wants the whole industry to reduce prices to stimulate total demand.

When there are several competitors, the company must estimate each close competitor's likely reaction. If all competitors behave alike, this estimate amounts to an analysis of a typical competitor. If the competitors do not react uniformly because of differences in size, market shares, or policies, then separate analyses are necessary.

Responding to Competitors' Price Changes

How should a firm respond to a price change initiated by a competitor? In markets characterized by high product homogeneity, the firm has little choice but to meet a competitor's price cut. The firm should search for ways to enhance its augmented product, but if it cannot find any, it will have to meet the price reduction. (It will certainly lose market share if it does not, because people are not going to pay a higher price for what is essentially the same product as the lower-priced version.)

When a competitor raises its price in a homogeneous-product market, the other firms might not match it. They will comply if the price increase will benefit the industry as a whole. But if one firm does not think that it or the industry would gain, its noncompliance can make the leader (and the others who followed) rescind the price increases.

In nonhomogeneous-product markets, a firm has more latitude in reacting to a competitor's price change. Buyers choose the vendor on many considerations: service, quality, reliability, and other factors. These factors desensitize buyers to minor price differences.

Before reacting, the firm needs to consider the following issues: (1) Why did the competitor change the price? Is it to steal the market, to utilize excess capacity, to meet changing cost conditions, or to lead an industrywide price change? (2) Does the competitor plan to make the price change temporary or permanent? (3) What will happen to the company's market share and profits if it does not respond? Are other companies going to respond also? and (4) What are the competitor's and other firms' responses likely to be to each possible reaction?

Market leaders frequently face aggressive price cutting by smaller firms trying to build market share. Using price, Fuji attacks Kodak, Bic attacks Gillette, and Compaq attacks IBM. Brand leaders are also faced with a glut of lower-priced private store brands that appeal to today's budget-minded consumers. According to a recent survey, private labels grew by an average of 6% in 1995.[32] When the attacking firm's product is comparable to the leaders, its lower price will cut into the leader's share. The leader at this point has several options:

◆ *Maintain price:* The leader might maintain its price and profit margin, believing that (a) it would lose too much profit if it reduced its price, (b) it would not lose much market share, and (c) it could regain market share when necessary. The leader believes that it could hold on to good customers, giving up the poorer ones to the competitor. The argument against price maintenance is that the attacker gets more confident as its sales increase, the leader's sales force gets demoralized, and the leader loses more share than expected. The leader panics, lowers price to regain share, and finds that regaining its market position is more difficult and costly than expected.

◆ *Raise perceived quality:* The leader could maintain price but strengthen the value of its offer. It could improve its product, services, and communications. It could stress the relative quality of its product over that of the low-price competitor. The firm may find it cheaper to maintain price and spend money to improve its perceived quality than to cut price and operate at a lower margin.

◆ *Reduce price:* The leader might drop its price to the competitor's price. It might do so because (a) its costs fall with volume, (b) it would lose market share because the market is price sensitive, and (c) it would be hard to rebuild market share once it is lost. This action will cut profits in the short run. In response to the leader's price cut, some firms will reduce their product quality, services, and marketing communications to maintain profits, but this will ultimately hurt their long-run market share. The leader should try to maintain its quality as it cuts prices.

◆ *Increase price and improve quality:* The leader might raise its price and introduce new brands to bracket the attacking brand. Heublein, Inc. used this strategy when its Smirnoff vodka, which had 23% of the U.S. vodka market, was attacked by another brand, Wolfschmidt, priced at $1 less a bottle. Instead of lowering the price of Smirnoff

Designing Pricing
Strategies and
Programs

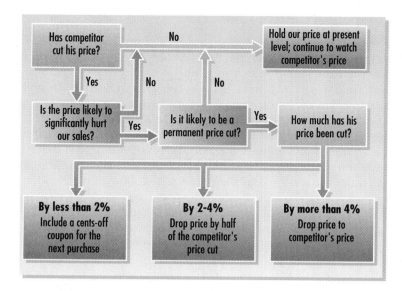

by $1, Heublein raised the price by $1 and put the increased revenue into its advertising. At the same time, Heublein introduced another brand, Relska, to compete with Wolfschmidt and still another, Popov, to sell for less than Wolfschmidt. This strategy effectively bracketed Wolfschmidt and gave Smirnoff an even more elite image.

◆ *Launch low-price fighter line:* One of the best responses is to add lower-price items to the line or to create a separate lower-price brand. This is necessary if the particular market segment being lost is price sensitive, since it will not respond to arguments of higher quality. This is what some major brands are doing to fight back against lower-priced store brands. Eastman Kodak is fighting off store brands with a new low-priced seasonal film called Funtime. Miller Beer started a new company called Plank Road Brewery, which launched a lower-priced beer brand called Red Dog.

The best response varies with situation. The company under attack has to consider the product's stage in the life cycle, its importance in the company's product portfolio, the competitor's intentions and resources, the market's price and quality sensitivity, the behavior of costs with volume, and the company's alternative opportunities.

An extended analysis of company alternatives is not always feasible when the attack occurs. The competitor might have spent considerable time in preparing this decision, but the company may have to react decisively within hours or days. About the only way to reduce price-reaction time is to anticipate possible competitors' price changes and to prepare contingent responses. Figure 17-9 shows a company *price-reaction program* to be used if a competitor cuts prices. Reaction programs for meeting price changes find their greatest application in industries where price changes occur with some frequency and where it is important to react quickly—for example, in the meatpacking, lumber, and oil industries.

SUMMARY

1. Despite the increased role of nonprice factors in the modern marketing process, price remains a critical element of the marketing mix. Price is the only one of the four Ps that produces revenue; the other three Ps produce costs.

2. In setting its pricing policy, a company follows a six-step procedure. First, it selects its pricing objective, what it wants to accomplish with its product offer (survival, maximum current profit, maximum current revenue, maximum sales growth, maximum market skimming, or product-quality leadership). Second, it estimates the demand curve, the

probable quantities that it will sell at each possible price. The more inelastic demand is, the higher the company can set its price. Third, it estimates how its costs vary at different levels of output, at different levels of accumulated production experience, and for differentiated marketing offers. Fourth, it examines competitors' costs, prices, and offers. Fifth, it selects one of the following pricing methods: markup pricing, target-return pricing, perceived-value pricing, value pricing, going-rate pricing, or sealed-bid pricing. Finally, it selects the final price, taking into account psychological pricing, the influence of other marketing-mix elements on price, company pricing policies, and the impact of price on other parties.

3. Companies do not usually set a single price, but rather a pricing structure that reflects variations in geographical demand and costs, market-segment requirements, purchase timing, order levels, and other factors. Several price-adaptation strategies are available: (1) geographical pricing, which often makes use of countertrade arrangements; (2) price discounts and allowances, including cash discounts, quantity discounts, functional discounts, seasonal discounts, and trade-in and promotional allowances; (3) promotional pricing, such as loss-leader pricing, special-event pricing, cash rebates, low-interest financing, longer payment terms, warranties and service contracts, and psychological discounting; (4) discriminatory pricing, in which the company sells a product at different prices to different market segments based on customer segment, product form, image, location, or time; and (5) product-mix pricing, which includes the setting of prices for product lines, optional features, captive products, two-part items, byproducts, and product bundles.

4. After developing their pricing strategies, firms often face situations where they need to change prices. A price decrease might be brought about by excess plant capacity, declining market share, a desire to dominate the market through lower costs, or economic recession. A price increase might be brought about by cost inflation or overdemand. These situations may call for anticipatory pricing, delayed quotation pricing, escalator clauses, unbundling of goods and services, and reduction or elimination of discounts. There are also several alternatives to increasing price, including shrinking the amount of product instead of raising the price, substituting less expensive materials or ingredients, and reducing or removing product features. It is often difficult to predict how customers and competitors will react to a price change.

5. The firm facing a competitor's price change must try to understand the competitor's intent and the likely duration of the change. The firm's strategy often depends on whether it is producing homogeneous or nonhomogeneous products. Market leaders who are attacked by lower-priced competitors can choose to maintain price, raise the perceived quality of their product, reduce price, increase price and improve quality, or launch a low-price fighter line. The best response depends on several factors.

CONCEPT APPLICATIONS

1. Many consumers around the world want and can afford an expensive car. In the past, many people were willing to buy a Mercedes for its performance but thought the luxury automobile was overpriced. This gave Toyota the idea of developing a new car that could be convincingly compared to a Mercedes but could be positioned as a better value. Buyers would get the feeling that they were "smart" buyers, not just throwing their money away to gain status.

   The result of Toyota's decision was the Lexus, with its sculptured look, attractive finish, and plush interior. In one of its first advertisements, Toyota pictured a Lexus next to a Mercedes and ran the headline: "The First Time in History that Trading a $73,000 Car for a $36,000 Car Could Be Considered Trading Up." Separate Lexus dealerships were set up featuring generous space, flowers, plants, free coffee, and professional salespeople and showrooms. Dealers developed a list of prospects and sent them a handsome package containing a 12-minute video dramatizing Lexus's performance features. For example, the videotape showed an engineer placing a glass of water on the engine blocks of a Mercedes and a Lexus. When the car engines were turned on, the water shook on the Mercedes' engine block, suggesting that the Lexus had a smoother engine and offered a smoother ride. Early Lexus buyers were not only satisfied, they were delighted and raved about their new car to their friends. They became the company's best (unpaid) salespeople.

What dilemma faces Mercedes and what are some of the possible actions it can take to respond to the challenges presented by Lexus?

2. Companies cannot always depend on their customers' recognizing the value of their offer against their competitors' offers. Each company's offer may differ not only in price but also in its impact on the customer's operating cost, working capital cost, ordering cost, setup costs, financing costs, and disposal costs. Sophisticated business-to-business companies use a tool called *economic value to the customer (EVC)* to build up their customer's perceptions of value. EVC is calculated by comparing the product's total costs to the customer against the benefits of the product that the customer is currently using (the *reference product*).

Figure 1 illustrates how one company determined EVC. Suppose McNally Manufacturing is developing two products, Y and Z, to compete with product X that a customer is currently using.

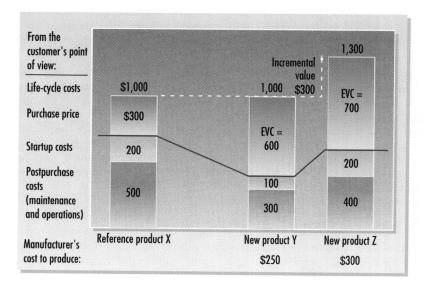

New product Y performs the same functions as reference product X, but its startup costs and postpurchase costs are only $400 (compared to $700 for product X), yielding a $300 savings for the customer. Because the customer's current product X has life-cycle costs of $1,000, the economic value that the new product Y offers the customer is $600 ($1,000 minus $400). It costs McNally $250 to produce one unit of product Y.

New product Z has more features or performance characteristics than product X or Y. These extra features of Z's have a perceived incremental value of $300 when compared with the reference product. So compared to the current product, Z saves $100 in postpurchase costs, resulting in an economic value to the customer of $700. Thus Z provides a higher EVC than Y despite its higher postpurchase costs because it provides additional customer value. It costs McNally $300 to produce one unit of Z.

Use Figure 1 to answer the following questions:

a. What is the highest amount that a firm would be willing to pay for product Y? For product Z?

b. The firm should set its price at a point between its costs and the EVC that is perceived by the customer. Assume that McNally adopts this practice for products Y and Z, and sets the price of each at $400 and $475, respectively. How much profit will McNally make on each unit of Y and Z sold?

c. How can McNally Manufacturing use EVC to determine the market segments it should enter with its new products?

3. Three companies A, B, and C produce rapid-relay switches. Industrial buyers are asked to examine and rate the respective companies' offers. To do so, they might use a *diagnostic method,* rating the three offers on a set of attributes. They allocate 100 points to the three companies with regard to each attribute. They also allocate 100 points to reflect the relative importance of the attributes. Suppose the results are as follows:

IMPORTANCE WEIGHT	ATTRIBUTE	PRODUCTS		
		A	B	C
25	Product durability	40	40	20
30	Product reliability	33	33	33
30	Delivery reliability	50	25	25
15	Service quality	45	35	20
100	(Average Perceived Value)	(41.65)	(32.65)	(24.9)

By multiplying the importance weights against each company's ratings, we find that company A's offer is perceived to be above average (at 42), company B's average (at 33), and company C's below average (at 25). (All figures are rounded to the nearest whole number.)

Figure 2 shows the result of Company A's lowering its price from $2.55 to $2.00.

FIGURE 2

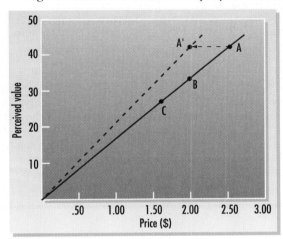

a. Assuming that buyers are willing to pay $2.00 for an average switch (that is, a switch with a perceived value of 33 points), how much could each company charge for its switch?
b. What strategies might Company A follow based on the results graphed in Figure 2? How might Company B respond to price changes by Company A?

4. Many companies are so ready to grant discounts, allowances, and special terms to their dealers and customers that they fail to realize how little profit may be left when they're done. Consider the following situation:

Dealer list price	$6.00
– Order size discount	.10
– Competitive discount	.12
= Invoice price	$5.78
– Payment terms discount	.30
– Annual volume discount	.37
– Off-invoice promotions	.35
– Co-op advertising	.20
– Freight	.19
= Pocket price	$4.37

Here the manufacturer quoted a $6.00 list price to a dealer but deducted an order size discount and a competitive discount, leaving an invoice price of $5.78. However, this number did not represent the manufacturer's pocket price (i.e., what is left in the manufacturer's pocket). Further costs result in the manufacturer's realizing a pocket price of only $4.37. Discuss the financial impact that these price reductions will have on the company's profitability. What percentage of the dealer's list price actually goes into the manufacturer's pocket in this example? What should a company consider before giving discounts?

5. A firm might set a low price on a product to discourage competitors from entering the market. Are there any situations in which a firm might deliberately want to attract competitors into a new market and set a high price?

6. Armco, a major steel company, has developed a new process for galvanizing steel sheets so that they can be painted and used in car-body parts to prevent rust (previously not possible). What factors should Armco consider in setting a price for this product?

7. Westinghouse is introducing a self-contained dishwasher that gets glasses and dishes "sparkling clean" in cold water. Westinghouse wants to evaluate the advantages and disadvantages of an introductory price-skimming approach versus a price-penetration approach. Discuss the pros and cons of each pricing strategy. On which factors will Westinghouse need to base its decision?

8. The purpose of this exercise is to demonstrate how retailers, such as grocery stores, use pricing in the development of marketing strategies. While comparing the pricing policies of different types of food stores, you will become aware of the wide variation in how much consumers pay for their "market basket."

Teams of four members should be formed. Each member of the team is assigned one store to examine. If possible, each member of the team should visit a different type of store (for example, convenience store, discount food store, national chain, local chain, independent, exclusive, neighborhood store, and so on). As an alternative, each team member could visit the same chain store but in different locations in the city or region.

Each member should record the prices of the following items using a form similar to the one below. (If necessary, product substitutions can be made.)

Name of store _____

Location _____

    1. Pound of Sizzlean bacon . . . . _____
    2. Dozen eggs (Grade A, large) . . . . _____
    3. Gallon milk (2%) . . . . _____
    4. Campbell's Chicken Noodle Soup (10 1/4 oz.) . . . . _____
    5. Baked Tostitos (13 1/2 oz.) . . . . _____
    6. Peter Pan Peanut Butter—Extra Crunchy (18 oz.) . _____
    7. Coke Classic (2 liter bottle) . . . . _____
    8. Total Cereal—Whole Grain (12 oz.) . . . . _____
    9. Kodak film (35 mm, 200 speed—24 exposures) . . . _____
 10. Energizer Batteries (2 pack, D-size) . . . . _____
 11. Quilted Northern Tissue (4 pack) . . . . _____
 12. Windex (22 oz.) . . . . _____
 13. Crest Toothpaste (6.3 oz. tube) . . . . _____
 14. Dry Idea Deodorant (2.5 oz.) . . . . _____
 15. Gillette Sensor Razor Blades (5 cartridges) . . . . . _____
                   Total . . . . _____

PART 4

Planning
Marketing
Programs

9. In principle, a reduction in price is tantamount to an increase in marketing effort. How can the price reduction be monetized into its equivalent in increased marketing effort?

NOTES

1. David J. Schwartz, *Marketing Today: A Basic Approach,* 3d ed. (New York: Harcourt Brace Jovanovich, 1981), p. 271.
2. Thomas T. Nagle and Reed K. Holden, *The Strategy and Tactics of Pricing,* 2d ed. (Englewood Cliffs, NJ: Prentice Hall, 1995), Chapter 4. This is an excellent reference book for making pricing decisions.
3. See Sidney Bennett and J. B. Wilkinson, "Price-Quantity Relationships and Price Elasticity Under In-Store Experimentation," *Journal of Business Research,* January 1974, pp. 30–34.
4. John R. Nevin, "Laboratory Experiments for Estimating Consumer Demand—A Validation Study," *Journal of Marketing Research,* August 1974, pp. 261–68; and Jonathan Weiner, "Forecasting Demand: Consumer Electronics Marketer Uses a Conjoint Approach to Configure Its New Product and Set the Right Price," *Marketing Research: A Magazine of Management and Applications,* Summer 1994, pp. 6–11.
5. Nagle and Holden, *Strategy and Tactics of Pricing,* Chapter 13.
6. For summary of elasticity studies, see Dominique M. Hanssens, Leonard J. Parsons, and Randall L. Schultz, *Market Response Models: Econometric and Time Series Analysis* (Boston: Kluwer Academic Publishers, 1990), pp. 187–91.
7. See William W. Alberts, "The Experience Curve Doctrine Reconsidered," *Journal of Marketing,* July 1989, pp. 36–49.
8. See Robin Cooper and Robert S. Kaplan, "Profit Priorities from Activity-Based Costing," *Harvard Business Review,* May–June 1991, pp. 130–35. For more on ABC, see Chapter 24 of this textbook.
9. See "Japan's Smart Secret Weapon," *Fortune,* August 12, 1991, p. 75.
10. Christopher Farrell, "Stuck! How Companies Cope When They Can't Raise Prices," *Business Week,* November 15, 1993, pp. 146–55.
11. Neil Strauss, "Pennies That Add Up to $16.98: Why CD's Cost So Much," *The New York Times,* July 5, 1995, C11:1.
12. Tung-Zong Chang and Albert R. Wildt, "Price, Product Information, and Purchase Intention: An Empirical Study," *Journal of the Academy of Marketing Science,* Winter 1994, pp. 16–27. See also G. Dean Kortge and Patrick A. Okonkwo, "Perceived Value Approach to Pricing," *Industrial Marketing Management,* May 1993, pp. 133–40.
13. For an empirical study of nine methods used by companies to assess customer value, see James C. Anderson, Dipak C. Jain, and Pradeep K. Chintagunta, "Customer Value Assessment in Business Markets: A State-of-Practice Study," *Journal of Business-to-Business Marketing,* 1, no. 1 (1993), 3–29.
14. See "Value Marketing," *Business Week,* November 11, 1991, pp. 54–60; and "What Intelligent Consumers Want," *Fortune,* December 28, 1992, pp. 56–60.
15. Bill Saporito, "Behind the Tumult at P&G," *Fortune,* March 7, 1994, pp. 74–82.
16. Stephen J. Hoch, Xavier Dreze, and Mary J. Purk, "EDLP, Hi-Lo, and Margin Arithmetic," *Journal of Marketing,* October 1994, pp. 16–27.
17. Adam Bryant, "Many Companies Try to Simplify Pricing," *The New York Times,* October 18, 1992, 4, 6:1; Stephanie Strom, "Retailers' Latest Tactic: If It Says $15, It Means $15," *The New York Times,* September 29, 1992, D1:3. See also Anne T. Coughlan and Naufel J. Vilcassim, "Retail Marketing Strategies: An Investigation of Everyday Low Pricing vs. Promotional Pricing Policies," working paper, Northwestern University, Kellogg Graduate School of Management, December 1989.
18. Gary M. Erickson and Johny K. Johansson, "The Role of Price in Multi-Attribute Product-Evaluations," *Journal of Consumer Research,* September 1985, pp. 195–99.
19. K. N. Rajendran and Gerard J. Tellis, "Contextual and Temporal Components of Reference Price," *Journal of Marketing,* January 1994, pp. 22–34.
20. Paul W. Farris and David J. Reibstein, "How Prices, Expenditures, and Profits Are Linked," *Harvard Business Review,* November–December 1979, pp. 173–84. See also Makoto Abe, "Price and Advertising Strategy of a National Brand Against Its Private-Label Clone: A Signaling Game Approach," *Journal of Business Research,* July 1995, pp. 241–50.
21. Henry Cheeseman, *Contemporary Business Law* (Englewood Cliffs, NJ: Prentice Hall, 1995).
22. See Michael Rowe, *Countertrade* (London: Euromoney Books, 1989); P. N. Agarwala, *Countertrade: A Global Perspective* (New Delhi: Vikas Publishing House, 1991); and Christopher M. Korth, ed., *International Countertrade* (New York: Quorum Books, 1987).
23. See Michael V. Marn and Robert L. Rosiello, "Managing Price, Gaining Profit," *Harvard Business Review,* September–October 1992, pp. 84–94.
24. Brian S. Moskal, "Consumer Age Begets Value Pricing," *Industry Week,* February 21, 1994, pp. 36, 38, 40.
25. Price discrimination laws in the United States are quite complex. For more information on the specific types of price discrimination that are illegal, see Cheeseman, *Contemporary Business Law.*
26. Farrell, "Stuck" pp. 146–55.
27. Moskal, "Consumer Age Begets Value Pricing," pp. 36, 38, 40.
28. See Robert E. Weigand, "Buy In–Follow On Strategies for Profit," *Sloan Management Review,* Spring 1991, pp. 29–37.
29. Susan Krafft, "Love, Love Me Doo," *American Demographics,* June 1994, pp. 15–16.
30. See Gerald J. Tellis, "Beyond the Many Faces of Price: An Integration of Pricing Strategies," *Journal of Marketing,* October 1986, pp. 146–60, here p. 155. This excellent article also analyzes and illustrates other pricing strategies.
31. For excellent review, see Kent B. Monroe, "Buyers' Subjective Perceptions of Price," *Journal of Marketing Research,* February 1973, pp. 70–80.
32. Jonathan Berry, "Attack of the Fighting Brands," *Business Week,* May 2, 1994, p. 125; Karen Benezra, "Mixed Messages," *Brandweek,* July 25, 1994, pp. 28–39.

SELECTING

AND MANAGING

MARKETING CHANNELS

*The middleman is not a hired link in a chain forged by a manufacturer,
but rather an independent market, the focus of a large group
of customers for whom he buys.*

PHILLIP McVEY

❖

*Adversarial power relationships work only if you never
have to see or work with the bastards again.*

PETER DRUCKER

Most producers do not sell their goods directly to the final users. Between producers and the final users stands a marketing channel, a host of marketing intermediaries performing a variety of functions and bearing a variety of names. Some intermediaries—such as wholesalers and retailers—buy, take title to, and resell the merchandise; they are called *merchants*. Others—such as brokers, manufacturers' representatives, and sales agents—search for customers and may negotiate on the producer's behalf but do not take title to the goods; they are called *agents*. Still others—such as transportation companies, independent warehouses, banks, and advertising agencies—assist in the distribution process but neither take title to goods nor negotiate purchases or sales; they are called *facilitators*.

Marketing-channel decisions are among the most critical decisions facing management. The company's chosen channels intimately affect all the other marketing decisions. The company's pricing depends on whether it uses mass merchandisers or high-quality boutiques. The firm's sales force and advertising decisions depend on how much training and motivation the dealers need. In addition, the company's channel decisions involve relatively long-term commitments to other firms. When an automaker signs up independent dealers to sell its automobiles, the automaker cannot buy them out the next day and replace them with company-owned outlets. Corey observed:

> A distribution system . . . is a key external resource. Normally it takes years to build, and it is not easily changed. It ranks in importance with key internal resources such as manufacturing, research, engineering, and field sales personnel and facilities. It represents a significant corporate commitment to large numbers of independent companies whose business is distribution—and to the particular markets they serve. It represents, as well, a commitment to a set of policies and practices that constitute the basic fabric on which is woven an extensive set of long-term relationships.[1]

Thus there is a powerful inertial tendency in channel arrangements. Therefore management must choose channels with an eye on tomorrow's likely selling environment as well as today's.

In this chapter, we address the following questions:

- **What are marketing channels?**
- **What decisions do companies face in designing, managing, evaluating, and modifying their channels?**
- **What trends are taking place in channel dynamics?**
- **How can channel conflict be managed?**

In the next chapter we will examine marketing-channel issues from the perspective of retailers, wholesalers, and physical-distribution agencies. Table 18-1 on page 530 provides a brief review of some marketing-channel terminology.

TABLE 18-1	MARKETING-CHANNEL TERMINOLOGY
Broker	An intermediary whose job is to bring together buyers and sellers, and who does not carry inventory, get involved in financing, or assume risk.
Facilitator	An intermediary who assists in the distribution process but neither takes title to goods nor negotiates purchases or sales.
Manufacturers' Representative	A company that represents and sells the goods of several manufacturers. Hired by companies instead of or in addition to an internal sales force.
Merchant	An intermediary who buys, takes title to, and resells merchandise.
Retailer	A business enterprise that sells goods or services directly to the final consumer for his or her personal, nonbusiness use.
(Sales) Agent	An intermediary who searches for customers and negotiates on a producer's behalf but does not take title to the goods.
Sales Force	A group of people hired directly by a company to sell its products and service its accounts.
Wholesaler (Distributor)	A business enterprise that sells goods or services to those who buy for resale or business use.

WHAT ARE MARKETING CHANNELS?

Most producers work with marketing intermediaries to bring their products to market. The marketing intermediaries make up a *marketing channel* (also called a *trade channel* or *distribution channel*). We will use Stern and El-Ansary's definition of marketing channels:

❖   **MARKETING CHANNELS** are sets of interdependent organizations involved in the process of making a product or service available for use or consumption.[2]

Why Are Marketing Intermediaries Used?

Why would a producer delegate some of the selling job to intermediaries? The delegation means relinquishing some control over how and to whom the products are sold. The producer appears to be placing the firm's destiny in the hands of intermediaries. But producers do gain several advantages by using intermediaries:

◆   Many producers lack the financial resources to carry out direct marketing. For example, General Motors sells its automobiles through more than 10,000 dealer outlets. Even General Motors would be hard pressed to raise the cash to buy out its dealers.

◆   In some cases direct marketing simply is not feasible. For example, the William Wrigley Jr. Company would not find it practical to establish small retail gum shops throughout the country or to sell gum by mail order. It would have to sell gum along with many other small products and would end up in the drugstore and grocery store business. Wrigley finds it easier to work through the extensive network of privately owned distribution organizations.

◆   Producers who do establish their own channels can often earn a greater return by increasing their investment in their main business. If a company earns a 20% rate of return on manufacturing and foresees only a 10% return on retailing, it will not want to undertake its own retailing.[3]

The use of intermediaries largely boils down to their superior efficiency in making goods widely available and accessible to target markets. Through their contacts, experience, specialization, and scale of operation, intermediaries usually

Planning
Marketing
Programs

offer the firm more than it can achieve on its own. According to Stern and El-Ansary:

> Intermediaries smooth the flow of goods and services. . . . This procedure is necessary in order to bridge the discrepancy between the assortment of goods and services generated by the producer and the assortment demanded by the consumer. The discrepancy results from the fact that manufacturers typically produce a large quantity of a limited variety of goods, whereas consumers usually desire only a limited quantity of a wide variety of goods.[4]

Figure 18-1 shows one major source of cost savings effected by using intermediaries. Part (a) shows three producers, each using direct marketing to reach three customers. This system requires nine different contacts. Part (b) shows the three producers working through one distributor, who contacts the three customers. This system requires only six contacts. In this way, intermediaries reduce the amount of work that must be done.

Channel Functions and Flows

A marketing channel performs the work of moving goods from producers to consumers. It overcomes the time, place, and possession gaps that separate goods and services from those who need or want them. Members of the marketing channel perform a number of key functions:

- *Information:* The collection and dissemination of marketing research information about potential and current customers, competitors, and other actors and forces in the marketing environment.
- *Promotion:* The development and dissemination of persuasive communications designed to attract customers to the offer.
- *Negotiation:* The attempt to reach final agreement on price and other terms so that transfer of ownership or possession can be effected.
- *Ordering:* Marketing-channel members' communication of intentions to buy to the manufacturer.
- *Financing:* The acquisition and allocation of funds required to finance inventories at different levels of the marketing channel.
- *Risk taking:* The assumption of risks connected with carrying out the channel work.
- *Physical possession:* The successive storage and movement of physical products from raw materials to the final customers.

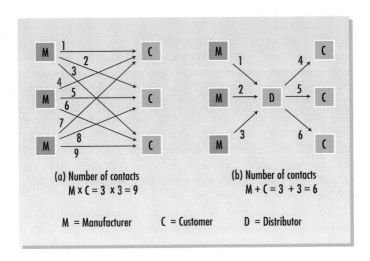

(a) Number of contacts
M x C = 3 x 3 = 9

(b) Number of contacts
M + C = 3 + 3 = 6

M = Manufacturer   C = Customer   D = Distributor

FIGURE 18-1

How a Distributor Effects an Economy of Effort

Selecting and Managing Marketing Channels

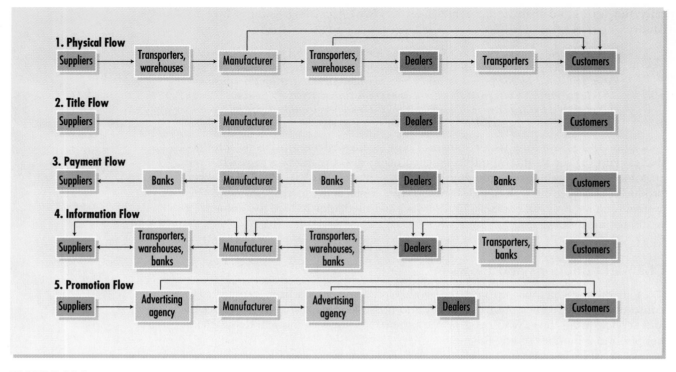

FIGURE 18-2

Five Different Marketing Flows in the Marketing Channel for Forklift Trucks

♦ *Payment:* Buyers' payment of their bills to the sellers through banks and other financial institutions.

♦ *Title:* The actual transfer of ownership from one organization or person to another.

Some functions (e.g., physical, title, promotion) take place in the *forward flow* of activity from the company to the customer; some functions (such as ordering and payment) occur in the *backward flow* of activity from customers to the company; and some functions (information, negotiation, financing, and risk taking) occur in both directions. Five of these flows are illustrated in Figure 18-2 for the marketing of forklift trucks. If all of these flows were superimposed in one diagram, the tremendous complexity of even simple marketing channels would be apparent.

A manufacturer that launches a physical product that might require service needs to set up at least three channels: a sales channel, a delivery channel, and a service channel. These channels need not be combined in one company. Thus Dell Computer uses the telephone as the sales channel, express mail services as the delivery channel, and local repair people as the service channel. Each of these channels is subject to further technological improvement. Over time, more companies will use their computer as the sales channel, as customers use online services (see Chapter 23) to search for the best buys. The computer can also be a delivery channel, as when a vendor downloads a software program to the customer's computer. Finally, repair service can be delivered via networked computers in the case of software failures, or over telephone lines by a physician dictating a treatment to a patient.

Thus the question is not *whether* various channel functions need to be performed—they must be—but rather *who* is to perform them. All of the functions have three things in common: They use up scarce resources; they can often be

Planning
Marketing
Programs

performed better through specialization; and they are shiftable among channel members. To the extent that the manufacturer performs the functions, the manufacturer's costs go up, and its prices must be higher. When some functions are shifted to intermediaries, the producer's costs and prices are lower, but the intermediary must add a charge to cover its work. If the intermediaries are more efficient than the manufacturer, the prices that consumers face should be lower. Consumers might decide to perform some of the functions themselves, in which case they should enjoy lower prices. The issue of who should perform various channel tasks is one of relative efficiency and effectiveness.

Marketing functions, then, are more basic than the institutions that perform them at any given time. Changes in channel institutions largely reflect the discovery of more efficient ways to combine or separate economic functions that must be carried on to provide meaningful assortments of goods to target customers.

Channel Levels

Each intermediary that performs work in bringing the product and its title closer to the final buyer constitutes a *channel level*. Since the producer and the final customer both perform work, they are part of every channel. We will use the number of intermediary levels to designate the *length* of a channel. Figure 18-3(a) on the next page illustrates several consumer-goods marketing channels of different lengths.

A *zero-level channel* (also called a *direct-marketing channel*) consists of a manufacturer selling directly to the final customer. The major zero-level channels are door-to-door sales, home parties, mail order, telemarketing, TV selling, and manufacturer-owned stores. Avon's sales representatives sell cosmetics to women on a door-to-door basis; Tupperware representatives sell kitchen goods through home parties; Franklin Mint sells collectible objects through mail order; Smith Barney brokers use the telephone to prospect for new customers; some manufacturers of exercise equipment sell through TV commercials or hour-long "infomercials"; and Singer sells its sewing machines through its own stores.

A *one-level channel* contains one selling intermediary, such as a retailer. A *two-level channel* contains two intermediaries. In consumer markets, they are typically a wholesaler and a retailer. A *three-level channel* contains three intermediaries. For example, in the meatpacking industry, wholesalers sell to jobbers, who sell to small retailers. (We examine the roles of wholesalers, retailers, and other intermediaries in detail in the next chapter.)

Longer marketing channels are also found. In Japan, for example, food distribution may involve as many as six levels. From the producer's point of view, the problem of obtaining information about the end users and exercising control increases with the number of channel levels.

Figure 18-3(b) shows channels commonly used in industrial marketing. An industrial-goods manufacturer can use its sales force to sell directly to industrial customers. Or it can sell to industrial distributors who sell to the industrial customers. Or it can sell through manufacturer's representatives or its own sales branches directly to industrial customers, or indirectly to industrial customers through industrial distributors. Thus zero-, one-, and two-level marketing channels are quite common in industrial marketing channels.

Channels normally describe a forward movement of products. One can also talk about *backward channels*. According to Zikmund and Stanton:

> The recycling of solid wastes is a major ecological goal. Although recycling is technologically feasible, reversing the flow of materials in the channel of distribution— marketing trash through a "backward" channel—presents a challenge. Existing backward channels are primitive, and financial incentives are inadequate. The

Selecting and
Managing
Marketing Channels

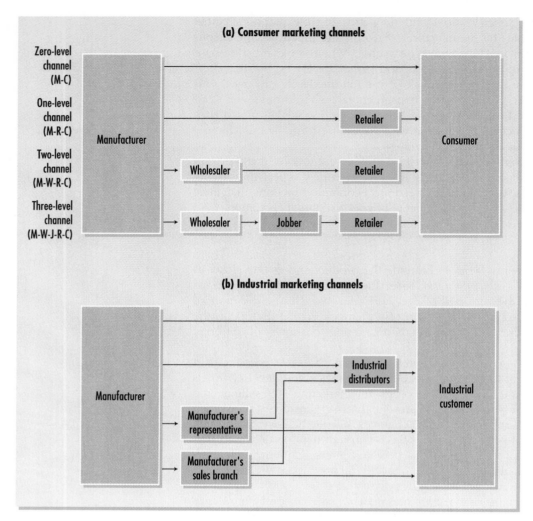

FIGURE 18-3

Consumer and Industrial Marketing Channels

consumer must be motivated to undergo a role change and become a producer— the initiating force in the reverse distribution process.[5]

Several intermediaries play a role in backward channels, including manufacturers' redemption centers, community groups, traditional intermediaries such as soft-drink intermediaries, trash-collection specialists, recycling centers, trash-recycling brokers, and central-processing warehousing.[6] Using various backward channels, Reynolds Metal Company received 11.8 billion used cans in 1994 and paid $155 million to consumers.

Channels in the Service Sector

The concept of marketing channels is not limited to the distribution of physical goods. Producers of services and ideas also face the problem of making their output available and accessible to target populations. For example, schools develop "educational-dissemination systems" and hospitals develop "health-delivery systems." These institutions must figure out agencies and locations for reaching a spatially distributed population:

Hospitals must be located in geographic space to serve the people with complete medical care, and we must build schools close to the children who have to learn. Fire stations must be located to give rapid access to potential conflagrations, and voting booths must be placed so that people can cast their ballots without expending unreasonable amounts of time, effort, or money to reach the polling stations. Many of our states face the problem of locating branch campuses to serve a burgeoning and increasingly well educated population. In the cities we must create and locate playgrounds for the children. Many overpopulated countries must assign birth control clinics to reach the people with contraceptive and family planning information.[7]

As technology advances, the delivery of certain services become easier for providers and more convenient for customers. For a look at how technology is changing the delivery of banking services, see the Vision 2000 feature on page 536 titled "Delivering Banking Services Online."

Marketing channels also are used in "person" marketing. Before 1940, professional comedians could reach audiences through seven channels: vaudeville houses, special events, nightclubs, radio, movies, carnivals, and theaters. Vaudeville houses have now vanished and been replaced with new channels such as comedy clubs and cable television performances on Home Box Office. Politicians also must find cost-effective channels—mass media, rallies, coffee hours, spot TV ads, faxes—for distributing their messages to voters.[8]

CHANNEL-DESIGN DECISIONS

In designing marketing channels, manufacturers have to decide what is ideal, what is feasible, and what is available. A new firm typically starts as a local operation selling in a limited market. Since it has limited capital, it usually uses existing intermediaries. The number of intermediaries in any local market is apt to be limited: a few manufacturers' sales agents, a few wholesalers, several established retailers, a few trucking companies, and a few warehouses. Deciding on the best channels might not be a problem. The problem might be to convince one or a few available intermediaries to handle the manufacturer's line.

If the new firm is successful, it might branch out to new markets. Again, the manufacturer will tend to work through the available intermediaries, although doing so might mean using different types of marketing channels in different areas. In the smaller markets, the firm might sell directly to retailers; in the larger markets, it might sell through distributors. In rural areas, it might work with general-goods merchants; in urban areas, with limited-line merchants. In one part of the country, it might grant exclusive franchises because the merchants normally work this way; in another, it might sell through all outlets willing to handle the merchandise. In one country it might use international sales agents; in another, it might partner with a local firm.[9] In short, the manufacturer's channel system evolves in response to local opportunities and conditions. Consider the case of one small soft-drink manufacturer that became world famous by carefully examining its marketing-channel opportunities:

SNAPPLE Snapple, a fruit-based beverage company founded in the early 1970s, began selling its product almost exclusively to health-food distributors in the New York City area. Then it gradually moved away from its original retail health-food distribution base into mom-and-pop delis and convenience stores. "At the beginning," says one Snapple executive, "chain stores were looking for companies that could pay a lot of money for slotting allowances [money paid to put products on store shelves]. We were a small company and didn't have the money to give at the time." Snapple's decision to pene-

Selecting and
Managing
Marketing Channels

Delivering Banking Services Online

In the banking industry, community branch banks have long been the marketing channels through which customers deposit money and make payments. But the bank branch may soon become a thing of the past. As a result of advances in bank automation—from automatic teller machines (ATMs) to telephone banking services—fewer than half of all bank customers (43%) now use bank branches. The upshot: Banks across the United States are preparing to close thousands of local branches. Half of the country's 52,000 branch offices may disappear within a decade.

Ultimately, the closing of branch offices comes down to one factor: costs. When compared to electronic banking, in which customers do their banking via a computer screen or voice-activated telephone service, the costs of brick-and-mortar banking are high. For instance, the cost of processing a teller transaction is more than double the cost of processing an ATM transaction. These savings are the main reason behind the ATM explosion: In 1994 there were 109,000 ATMs in the United States, up from 80,000 in 1990. And this is just the tip of the electronic iceberg. Banks are now gearing up for even higher-tech banking services, from PC-based home banking to banking that uses telephones with CRT screens and keyboards attached.

Also in development are a wide variety of financial services through the Internet. In 1995, First Union, a regional bank in Charlotte, North Carolina, launched the Internet's first bank-sponsored electronic marketplace called "Community Commerce." One of the reasons First Union launched the Community Commerce system was its fear of competition from nonbanks. First Union is convinced that if banks do not move quickly into electronic distribution, they risk having their business taken over by nonbank competitors. This strategy makes sense in a competitive marketplace, since an-

other reason for the demise of branch banking is that customers can increasingly go elsewhere for a wider range of services than banks currently offer. Billions of dollars in bank deposits have ended up in mutual funds; nonbank mortgage lenders have grown to dominate the market for home loans; and alternative sources of credit, investment advice, and other banking-type services are springing up everywhere.

The trump card that banks have always held is their protected monopoly over the payments system and their large measure of customer loyalty. But banks can't count on holding this trump card for long. Already a number of technological advances and innovative approaches to transaction processing are allowing nonbanks to enter the payments system and insert themselves between the customer and the bank. Companies such as Microsoft, Reuters, and the regional Bells want to control the interface between customer and bank. An access device—anything from a personal computer to an ATM or telephone—can now have the power of a mainframe and perform most, or all, of the customer's transaction processing electronically at the point of sale. This approach is called POPP, for point-of-purchase processing, and its ultimate goal is to allow customers to serve themselves anytime and anywhere. If POPP becomes widespread, then who will own the customer relationship? Microsoft? CompuServe? AT&T? Richard K. Crone of KPMG Peat Marwick says, "If banks do not control the distribution channels or PFM [personal financial management] faceplate, they may soon be competing for cyberspace the way packaged-goods companies compete for shelf space in supermarkets. . . . Banks need to recognize they are no longer geographically bound, and that this emerging electronic autobahn represents a whole new delivery channel for financial services."

Sources: Richard Crone, "Banking Without Banks," *United States Banker,* November 1994, p. 88; John W. Milligan, "Can Banking Regain Its Lost Market Share?" *United States Banker,* September 1994, pp. 28–87; Kelley Holland, "What Every Virtual Mall Needs: A Virtual Bank," *Business Week,* June 26, 1995, p. 101.

trate the often-neglected convenience store channel was well rewarded. While its national market share in this category is less than one percent at .9%, that number is very impressive when you consider that "C-stores" (as they're known in the trade) are a one-billion-plus-case market. In terms of product penetration, share of shelf space, and volume of bottles sold per week, Snapple has surpassed every brand but Coke in this market. By the time the company went national in 1992, it was able to leverage its performance in the All Other Market (AOM) channels—C-stores, mom-and-pop stores, health clubs, and small grocery stores—to gain shelf space in 80% of U.S. supermarket chains. As it has moved to this new level of distribution, Snapple is having to become much more involved with concepts such as couponing, pricing, and co-op advertising.[10]

Designing a channel system calls for analyzing customer needs, establishing channel objectives, and identifying and evaluating the major channel alternatives.

Analyzing Customers' Desired Service Output Levels

Understanding what, where, why, when, and how target customers buy is the first step in designing the marketing channel. The marketer must understand the *service output levels* desired by the target customers—the types and levels of services that people want and expect when they purchase a product. Channels produce five service outputs:

◆ *Lot size:* The lot size is the number of units that the marketing channel permits a typical customer to purchase on a purchase occasion. In buying cars for its fleet, Hertz prefers a channel from which it can buy a large lot size, and a household wants a channel that would permit buying a lot size of one. Obviously, different channels must be set up for fleet car buyers and household buyers. The smaller the lot size, the greater the service output level that the channel must provide.

◆ *Waiting time:* Waiting time is the average time that customers of that channel wait for receipt of the goods. Customers normally prefer fast delivery channels. Faster service often requires a greater service output level.

◆ *Spatial convenience:* Spatial convenience expresses the degree to which the marketing channel makes it easy for customers to purchase the product. Chevrolet, for example, offers greater spatial convenience than Cadillac, because there are more Chevrolet dealers than Cadillac dealers. Chevrolet's greater market decentralization helps customers save on transportation and search costs in buying and repairing an automobile. Spatial convenience is today being further augmented by the use of direct marketing.

◆ *Product variety:* Product variety represents the assortment breadth provided by the marketing channel. Normally customers prefer a greater assortment because more choices increase the customer's chance of finding what he needs. Thus car buyers would rather buy from a dealership carrying multiple manufacturer brands than only one manufacturer's brand.

◆ *Service backup:* Service backup represents the add-on services (credit, delivery, installation, repairs) provided by the channel. The greater the service backup, the greater the work provided by the channel.[11]

The marketing-channel designer must know the service outputs desired by the target customers. Providing increased levels of service outputs means increased costs for the channel and higher prices for customers. The success of discount stores indicates that many consumers are willing to accept lower-service outputs when this translates into lower prices.

Establishing the Channel Objectives and Constraints

The channel objectives should be stated in terms of targeted service output levels. According to Bucklin, under competitive conditions, channel institutions should arrange their functional tasks so as to minimize total channel costs with respect to desired levels of service outputs.[12] Usually, several market segments can be identified that desire differing service output levels. Effective channel planning requires determining which market segments to serve and the best channels to use in each case.

Channel objectives vary with product characteristics. Perishable products require more direct marketing because of the dangers associated with delays and repeated handling. Bulky products, such as building materials, require channels that minimize the shipping distance and the number of handlings in the movement from producer to consumers. Nonstandardized products, such as custom-built machinery and specialized business forms, are sold directly by company sales representatives. Products requiring installation and/or maintenance services such as heating and cooling systems are usually sold and maintained by the company or exclusively franchised dealers. High-unit-value products such as generators and turbines are often sold through a company sales force rather than through intermediaries.

Channel design must take into account the strengths and weaknesses of different types of intermediaries. (For example, manufacturers' reps are able to contact customers at a low cost per customer because the total cost is shared by several clients. But the selling effort per customer is less intense than if the company's sales reps did the selling. See Chapter 22.) Channel design is also influenced by the competitors' channels.

Channel design must also adapt to the larger environment. When economic conditions are depressed, producers want to move their goods to market using shorter channels and without nonessential services that add to the final price of the goods. Legal regulations and restrictions also affect channel design. U.S. law looks unfavorably upon channel arrangements that may tend to substantially lessen competition or tend to create a monopoly.

Identifying the Major Channel Alternatives

After a company has defined its target market and desired positioning, it should identify its channel alternatives. A channel alternative is described by three elements: the types of available business intermediaries, the number of intermediaries needed, and the terms and responsibilities of each channel participant.

TYPES OF INTERMEDIARIES. The firm needs to identify the types of intermediaries available to carry on its channel work. Here are two examples:

A test-equipment manufacturer developed an audio device for detecting poor mechanical connections in machines with moving parts. The company executives felt that this product would sell in all industries where electric, combustion, or steam engines were used, such as aviation, automobiles, railroads, food canning, construction, and oil. The company's sales force was small. The problem was how to reach these diverse industries effectively. The following channel alternatives were identified:

♦ *Company sales force:* Expand the company's direct sales force. Assign sales representatives to territories to contact all prospects in the area. Or develop separate sales forces for the different industries.

♦ *Manufacturers' agency:* Hire manufacturers' agents in different regions or end-use industries to sell the new test equipment.

♦ *Industrial distributors:* Find distributors in the different regions and/or end-use industries who will buy and carry the audio device. Give them exclusive distribution, adequate margins, product training, and promotional support.

* * *

A consumer electronics company produces cellular car phones. It identified the following channel alternatives:

♦ *OEM market:* The company could sell its car phones to automobile manufacturers to be installed as original equipment. OEM stands for *original equipment manufacture.*

Banks Work Feverishly to Develop a New Channel: Home Banking

Service banks in Great Britain are busily engaged in rolling out home banking. It all started in October 1989 when Midland Bank launched First Direct, a 24-hour telephone banking system. Today Midland has 500,000 customers and is adding 10,000 new customers every month. Not to be outdone, Lloyds launched its telephone service (called LloydsLine) a few years later and now has close to 100,000 customers. It also offers LloydsLink electronic banking by PC for its business customers.

These innovations have forced the nation's other banks to open home banking channels as well. Barclays is testing a PC-based home banking system using Microsoft software and Visa credit cards. Meanwhile, NatWest is testing a telephone banking system developed jointly with British Telecom. NatWest chose this option because telephone ownership is far more prevalent in Britain than PC ownership. Eventually, we can expect leading banks to offer both telephone-based and PC-based home banking.

Source: "Banks to Offer Customer Options," *Marketing Business*, September 1995, pp. 4–5.

◆ *Auto-dealer market:* The company could sell its car phones to auto dealers.

◆ *Retail automotive-equipment dealers:* The company could sell its car phones to retail automotive-equipment dealers through a direct sales force or through distributors.

◆ *Car phone specialist dealers:* The company could sell its car phones to car phone specialist dealers through a direct sales force or dealers.

◆ *Mail-order market:* The company could sell its car phones through mail-order catalogs.

Companies should search for innovative marketing channels. The Conn Organ Company merchandises organs through department stores and discount stores, thus drawing more attention to organs than it ever enjoyed in small music stores. The Book-of-the-Month Club merchandises books through the mail. Other sellers have followed with record-of-the-month clubs, candy-of-the-month clubs, flower-of-the-month clubs, fruit-of-the-month clubs, and dozens of others. (For more details on another innovative marketing channel, see the Marketing Insight titled "Banks Work Feverishly to Develop a New Channel: Home Banking.")

Sometimes a company chooses an unconventional channel because of the difficulty or cost of working with the dominant channel. The decision sometimes turns out extremely well. The advantage of the unconventional channel is that the company will encounter less competition during the initial move into this channel. Here are three examples:

TIMEX The U.S. Time Company originally tried to sell its inexpensive Timex watches through regular jewelry stores. But most jewelry stores refused to carry them. The company searched for other channels and placed its watches into mass-merchandise outlets. This turned out to be a great decision because of the rapid growth of mass merchandising.

AVON Avon chose door-to-door selling because it was not able to break into regular department stores. The company not only mastered door-to-door selling but also made more money than most cosmetics firms that sold through department stores.

CHIODO CANDY COMPANY

In the 1980s, Chiodo Candy Co. was getting clobbered by candy mega-company E. J. Brach in the war for supermarket shelf space. By 1988, the company began casting about for alternative distribution channels. It came up with a winner in club and warehouse stores, then new on the scene. The club stores didn't require any shelving fees and were receptive to new products. In keeping with these stores' demand for large packages, Chiodo developed a plastic tub that could hold up to two pounds of penny candy. Soon club buyers were ordering more than 8,000 tubs at a time.[13]

All said, the type of intermediary to use depends on the service outputs desired by the target market and the channel's transactions costs (for example, salaries and expenses, sunk investments, insurance, and so forth). The company must search for the channel alternative that promises the most long-run profitability.

NUMBER OF INTERMEDIARIES. Companies have to decide on the number of intermediaries to use at each channel level. Three strategies are available: exclusive distribution, selective distribution, and intensive distribution.

Exclusive Distribution. *Exclusive distribution* involves severely limiting the number of intermediaries handling the company's goods or services. It is used when the producer wants to maintain a great deal of control over the service level and service outputs offered by the resellers. Often it involves *exclusive dealing* arrangements, in which the resellers agree not to carry competing brands.

By granting exclusive distribution, the producer hopes to obtain more aggressive and knowledgeable selling. Exclusive distribution tends to enhance the product's image and allow higher markups. It requires greater partnership between the seller and the reseller and is found in the distribution of new automobiles, some major appliances, and some women's apparel brands.

Selective Distribution. *Selective distribution* involves the use of more than a few but less than all of the intermediaries who are willing to carry a particular product. It is used both by established companies and by new companies seeking to obtain distributors. The company does not have to dissipate its efforts over many outlets; rather, it can develop good working relations with its selected intermediaries and expect a better-than-average selling effort. Selective distribution enables the producer to gain adequate market coverage with more control and less cost than intensive distribution.

Intensive Distribution. In an *intensive distribution* strategy, the manufacturer places the goods or services in as many outlets as possible. When the consumer requires a great deal of location convenience, it is important to offer greater intensity of distribution. This strategy is generally used for convenience items such as tobacco products, soap, snack foods, and bubble gum.

Manufacturers are constantly tempted to move from exclusive or selective distribution to more intensive distribution to increase their coverage and sales. This strategy may help their short-term performance but often hurts their long-term performance. Suppose a fashion goods manufacturer such as Liz Claiborne were to drive for more intensive distribution. As the company expanded from its current high-end retailers to mass merchandisers, it would lose some control over the display arrangements, the accompanying service levels, and the pricing. As the product entered more retail outlets with differing overheads, some retailers would be in a position to undercut other retailers, resulting in a price war. Buyers would attach less prestige to Liz Claiborne apparel, and the manufacturer's ability to command premium prices would be reduced.

TERMS AND RESPONSIBILITIES OF CHANNEL MEMBERS. Relationship marketing is an important part of managing the marketing channel. The producer must determine the rights and responsibilities of the participating channel members, making sure that each channel member is treated respectfully and given the opportunity to be profitable.[14] The main elements in the "trade-relations mix" are price policies, conditions of sale, territorial rights, and specific services to be performed by each party.

Price policy calls for the producer to establish a price list and schedule of discounts that the intermediaries see as equitable and sufficient.

Conditions of sales refers to payment terms and producer guarantees. Most producers grant cash discounts to their distributors for early payment. Producers might also guarantee distributors against defective merchandise or price declines. A guarantee against price declines gives distributors an incentive to buy larger quantities.

Distributors' territorial rights are another element in the trade-relations mix. Distributors want to know where and under what terms the producer will enfranchise other distributors. They would also like to receive full credit for all sales taking place in their territory, whether or not they did the selling.

Mutual services and responsibilities must be carefully spelled out, especially in franchised and exclusive-agency channels. For example, McDonald's provides franchisees with a building, promotional support, a record-keeping system, training, and general administrative and technical assistance. In turn, franchisees are expected to satisfy company standards regarding physical facilities, cooperate with new promotional programs, furnish requested information, and buy specified food products.

Evaluating the Major Channel Alternatives

Suppose a producer has identified several channel alternatives and wants to determine the one best suited to its needs. Each alternative needs to be evaluated against *economic, control,* and *adaptive criteria.* We will discuss these criteria based on the following situation:

> A Memphis furniture manufacturer wants to sell its line to retailers on the West Coast. The manufacturer is trying to decide between two alternatives:
>
> 1. One alternative calls for hiring 10 new sales representatives, who would operate out of a sales office in San Francisco. They would receive a base salary plus commissions.
>
> 2. The other alternative would use a San Francisco manufacturers' sales agency that has extensive contacts with retailers. The agency has 30 sales representatives, who would receive a commission based on their sales.

ECONOMIC CRITERIA. Each channel alternative will produce a different level of sales and costs. The first step is to determine whether a company sales force or a sales agency will produce more sales. Most marketing managers believe that a company sales force will sell more. Company sales representatives concentrate entirely on the company's products; they are better trained to sell the company's products; they are more aggressive because their future depends on the company's success; and they are more successful because many customers prefer to deal directly with the company.

However, the sales agency could conceivably sell more than a company sales force. First, the sales agent has 30 sales representatives, not just 10. Second, the agency's sales force might be just as aggressive as a direct sales force. (This depends on how much commission the company offers.) Third, some customers prefer dealing with agents who represent several manufacturers rather than with salespersons from one company. Fourth, the agency has extensive contacts and marketplace knowledge, while a company sales force would need to build these from scratch. This would be a difficult, costly, and long-term process.

The next step is to estimate the costs of selling different volumes through each channel. The cost schedules are shown in Figure 18-4. The fixed costs of engaging a sales agency are lower than those of establishing a company sales office. But costs rise faster through a sales agency because sales agents get a larger commission than company salespeople.

The final step is comparing sales and costs. As Figure 18-4 shows, there is one sales level (S_B) at which selling costs are the same for the two channels. The sales agency is thus the better channel for any sales volume below S_B, and the company sales branch is better at any volume higher than S_B. Given this information, it is not surprising that sales agents tend to be used by smaller firms, or by large firms in their smaller territories (where the sales volume is too low to warrant a company sales force).

CONTROL CRITERIA. Channel evaluation must take into account control issues. Using a sales agency poses a control problem. A sales agency is an independent business firm seeking to maximize its profits. The agents may concentrate on the customers who buy the most, not necessarily of the manufacturer's goods. Furthermore, the agents might not master the technical details of the company's product or handle its promotion materials effectively.

ADAPTIVE CRITERIA. To develop a channel, the channel members must make some degree of commitment to each other for a specified period of time. Yet these commitments invariably lead to a decrease in the producer's ability to respond to a changing marketplace. In rapidly changing, volatile, or uncertain product markets, the producer needs to seek channel structures and policies that maximize control and ability to change marketing strategy swiftly.

CHANNEL-MANAGEMENT DECISIONS

After a company has chosen a channel alternative, individual intermediaries must be selected, motivated, and evaluated. Also, channel arrangements must be modified over time.

FIGURE 18-4

Break-Even Cost Chart for the Choice Between a Company Sales Force and a Manufacturer's Sales Agency

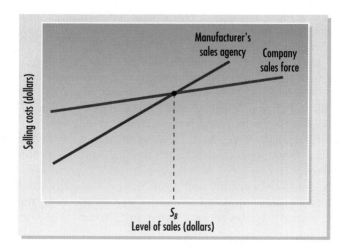

Planning
Marketing
Programs

Selecting Channel Members

Producers vary in their ability to attract qualified intermediaries within the chosen channel. Some producers have no trouble recruiting intermediaries. For example, Toyota was able to attract many new dealers for its new Lexus. In some cases, the promise of exclusive or selective distribution will draw a sufficient number of applicants.

At the other extreme are producers who have to work hard to get qualified intermediaries. When Polaroid started, it could not get photographic-equipment stores to carry its new cameras and was forced to use mass-merchandising outlets. Small food producers normally find it hard to get supermarket chains to carry their products. Equipment manufacturers often find it hard to locate qualified distributors and dealers. Consider what happened at Epson:

EPSON Japan's Epson Corporation, a leading manufacturer of computer printers, was preparing to add computers to its product line. Not happy with its current distributors nor trusting their ability to sell to new types of retail outlets, Epson's general manager, Jack Whalen, decided to quietly recruit new distributors to replace the existing ones. Whalen hired Hergenrather & Company, a recruiting company, and gave the following instructions:

- Search for applicants who have two-step distribution experience (factory to distributor to dealer) in either brown goods (TVs and so on) or white goods (refrigerators and so on).
- The applicants have to be CEO types who would be willing and able to set up their own distributorships.
- They will be offered $80,000 yearly salary plus bonus, and $375,000 to help them set up in business; each will add $25,000 of his or her own money, and each will get equity in the business.
- They will handle only Epson products but may stock other companies' software. Each distributor will hire a training manager and run a fully equipped service center.

The recruiting firm had a hard time finding qualified and motivated prospects. Their want ads in *The Wall Street Journal* (which did not mention the company's name) pulled almost 1,700 letters but mostly from unqualified people looking for jobs. Then the firm used the Yellow Pages to get the names of existing distributors and phoned the second-in-command managers. It arranged interviews and, after much work, produced a list of highly qualified individuals. Whalen interviewed them and chose the 12 most qualified candidates for his 12 distributor areas. The recruiting agency was paid $250,000 for its recruiting effort.

The final step called for terminating Epson's existing distributors. These distributors had no inkling of this development, since the recruitment was conducted in secrecy. Jack Whalen gave them a 90-day notice of the changeover. They were shocked, having worked with Epson as its first distributors. But they had no contracts. Whalen knew they lacked the ability to handle Epson's expanded computer product line and reach the target number of dealers. He saw no other solution.[15]

Whether producers find it easy or difficult to recruit intermediaries, they should at least determine what characteristics distinguish the better intermediaries. They will want to evaluate the intermediary's number of years in business, the other lines carried, growth and profit record, solvency, cooperativeness, and reputation. If the intermediaries are sales agents, producers will want to evaluate the number and character of other lines carried and the size and quality of the sales force. If the intermediaries are department stores that want exclusive distribution, the producer will want to evaluate the stores' locations, future growth potential, and type of clientele.

Motivating Channel Members

Intermediaries must be continuously motivated to do their best job. The terms that lead them to join the channel provide some motivation, but these must be supplemented by training, supervision, and encouragement. The producer must not only sell through the intermediaries but also to them. For example, dealer incentive programs can serve as a powerful motivator. When microbrewer Brewski Brewing Company launched its business, it offered attractive incentives to the large and small distributors who had signed on to sell its products. Once distributors began selling Brewski, they were rewarded with leather jackets valued at $300 for reaching distribution goals in a series of short-term incentive programs. In addition, the distributors are empowered to offer their top customers a solid wood, hand-carved, hand-painted tap handle that features the Brewski logo.[16]

Stimulating channel members to top performance must start with understanding of their needs and wants. McVey listed the following propositions to help understand intermediaries:

> [The intermediary often acts] as a purchasing agent for his customers and only secondarily as a selling agent for his suppliers. . . . He is interested in selling any product which these customers desire to buy from him. . . .

> The [intermediary] attempts to weld all of his offerings into a family of items which he can sell in combination, as a packaged assortment, to individual customers. His selling efforts are directed primarily at obtaining orders for the assortment, rather than for individual items. . . .

> Unless given incentive to do so, [intermediaries] will not maintain separate sales records by brands sold. . . . Information that could be used in product development, pricing, packaging, or promotion planning is buried in nonstandard records of [intermediaries], and sometimes purposely secreted from suppliers.[17]

Producers vary greatly in how they manage their distributors. They can draw on the following types of power to elicit cooperation:

♦ *Coercive power* is wielded by a manufacturer that threatens to withdraw a resource or terminate a relationship if intermediaries fail to cooperate. This power is quite effective if the intermediaries are highly dependent upon the manufacturer. But the exercise of coercive power produces resentment and can lead the intermediaries to organize countervailing power.

♦ *Reward power* occurs when the manufacturer offers intermediaries an extra benefit for performing specific acts or functions. Reward power typically produces better results than coercive power but can be overrated. The intermediaries are conforming to the manufacturer's wishes not out of conviction but because of an external benefit. They may come to expect a reward every time the manufacturer wants a certain behavior to occur. If the reward is later withdrawn, the intermediaries feel resentment.

♦ *Legitimate power* is wielded when the manufacturer requests a behavior that is warranted by the contract. Thus General Motors may insist that its dealers carry certain inventory levels as part of the franchise agreement. The manufacturer feels it has this right and the intermediaries have this obligation. As long as the intermediaries view the manufacturer as a legitimate leader, legitimate power works.

♦ *Expert power* can be applied when the manufacturer has special knowledge that the intermediaries value. For example, a manufacturer may have a sophisticated system for sales-lead generation or for distributor sales training. This is an effective form of power, if intermediaries would perform poorly without this help. Once the expertise is passed on to the intermediaries, however, this basis of power weakens. The manufacturer must continue to develop new expertise so that the intermediaries will want to continue cooperating.

♦ *Referent power* occurs when the manufacturer is so highly respected that intermediaries are proud to be identified with it. Companies such as IBM, Caterpillar, McDonald's, and Hewlett Packard have high referent power. To the extent possible, manufacturers will gain cooperation best if they would resort to referent power, expert power, legitimate power, and reward power, in that order, and generally avoid using coercive power.[18]

Intermediaries can aim for a relationship based on cooperation, partnership, or distribution programming.[19] Most producers see the main challenge as that of gaining intermediaries' *cooperation*. To do so, they often use positive motivators, such as higher margins, special deals, premiums, cooperative advertising allowances, display allowances, and sales contests. At times they will apply negative sanctions, such as threatening to reduce margins, slow down delivery, or terminate the relationship. The weakness of this approach is that the producer applies miscellaneous motivators based on crude stimulus-response thinking. McCammon notes that many manufacturer programs "consist of hastily improvised trade deals, uninspired dealer contests, and unexamined discount structures."[20]

More sophisticated companies try to forge a long-term *partnership* with their distributors. The manufacturer develops a clear sense of what it wants from its distributors in the way of market coverage, inventory levels, marketing development, account solicitation, technical advice and services, and marketing information. The manufacturer seeks distributor agreement with these policies and may introduce a functional compensation plan for adhering to the policies. For example, a dental supply company, instead of paying a straight 35% sales commission to its distributors, pays 20% for carrying out its basic sales work, another 5% for carrying a 60-day inventory, another 5% for paying its bills on time, and another 5% for reporting customer purchase information.

The most advanced supply/distributor arrangement is *distribution programming*, which McCammon defines as building a planned, professionally managed, vertical marketing system that incorporates the needs of both the manufacturer and the distributors.[21] The manufacturer establishes a department within the company called *distributor-relations planning*, and its job is to identify the distributors' needs and build up merchandising programs to help each distributor operate as efficiently as possible. This department and the distributors jointly plan the merchandising goals, inventory levels, space and visual merchandising plans, sales-training requirements, and advertising and promotion plans. The aim is to convert the distributors from thinking that they make their money primarily on the buying side (through tough negotiation with the manufacturer) to seeing that they make their money on the selling side (by being part of a sophisticated vertical marketing system). Kraft and Procter & Gamble are two companies with excellent distributor-relations planning (see the examples in Chapter 15).

Too many manufacturers think of their distributors and dealers as their customers rather than their working partners. The Marketing Insight on page 546 titled "Turning Industrial Distributors into Business Partners" describes the mechanisms progressive manufacturers can use to convert their distributors into partners.

Up to now, we have treated manufacturers and distributors as separate organizations. But many manufacturers are distributors of related products made by other manufacturers. Furthermore, some industrial distributors, such as Granger, also own or contract for the manufacturing of in-house brands. Such industrial firms therefore must master both the manufacturing and distribution functions.

Evaluating Channel Members

The producer must periodically evaluate intermediaries' performance against such standards as sales-quota attainment, average inventory levels, customer delivery time, treatment of damaged and lost goods, and cooperation in promotional and training programs.

Turning Industrial Distributors into Business Partners

Several manufacturers enjoy excellent working relations with their distributors. Here are some examples of successful partner-building practices:

1. *Timken Corporation* (roller bearings) has its sales representatives make multilevel calls on distributors, including their general managers, purchasing managers, and sales personnel.

2. *Square D* (circuit breakers, switchboards) has its sales representatives spend a day with each distributor, "working the counter" to understand the distributor's business.

3. *Du Pont* has established a distributor marketing steering committee, which meets regularly to discuss problems and trends.

4. *Dayco Corporation* (engineered plastics and rubber products) runs an annual week-long retreat with 20 young distributors' executives and 20 young Dayco executives interacting in seminars and outings.

5. *Parker Hannifin Corporation* (fluid-power products) sends out an annual mail survey asking its distributors to rate the corporation's performance on key dimensions. It also informs its distributors about new products and applications through newsletters and videotapes. It collects and analyzes photocopies of distributors' invoices and advises distributors on how to improve their sales.

6. *Cherry Electrical Products* (electrical switches and electronic keyboards) appointed a distributor marketing manager who works with distributors to produce formal distributor marketing plans. The company also operates a rapid response system to distributor calls by assigning two inside salespeople to each distributor.

7. *Vanity Fair, Levi Strauss, Hanes,* and other apparel manufacturers have formed "quick response" partnerships with both discounters and department stores. In these partnerships, retailers and suppliers work together to speed up the replenishment of inventories, improve customer service, reduce the need for markdowns, and cut the cost of bringing goods to the customer. By early 1993, Vanity Fair had some 300 partners in its flow-replenishment system and was promoting the partnership idea to other companies.

8. *Motorola* has formed a team that includes Motorola sales and logistics employees, a Motorola distributor, a customer named *Tellabs,* and managers from all three companies. Tellabs wanted Motorola to improve its on-time delivery to 100%, so the team came up with a solution to set up two Motorola stores on Tellabs' premises. Doing so has cut delivery times from 50 days to less than 24 hours.

9. *Loctite Corp.* acted on a distributor's query and rolled out a promotional campaign that featured six very different products, called the Survival Kit. The result: Loctite distributors earned more from the promotion over four months than from any other Loctite program.

10. *Rust-Oleum* sent to its distributors a letter that began "Hold the pickles, hold the lettuce, special orders don't upset us," to herald a new pull-through marketing program. And in response to distributors' requests for customized marketing programs, Rust-Oleum introduced a "menu" of marketing tools that varies each quarter; distributors choose from the menu those strategies that fit their marketing palate best.

Sources: The first six examples are found in James A. Narus and James C. Anderson, "Turn Your Industrial Distributors into Partners," *Harvard Business Review,* March–April 1986, pp. 66–71. The remaining examples come from John R. Johnson, "Promoting Profits Through Partnership," *Industrial Distribution,* March 1994, pp. 22–24; and Robert D. Buzzell and Gwen Ortmeyer, "Channel Partnerships Streamline Distribution," *Sloan Management Review,* Spring 1995, pp. 85–96.

The producer will discover on occasion that it is paying too much to particular intermediaries for what they are actually doing. One manufacturer discovered that he was compensating a distributor for holding inventories in his warehouse but that the inventories were actually being held in a public warehouse at the manufacturer's expense. Producers should set up functional discounts in which they pay specified amounts for the trade channel's performance of each agreed-upon service. Underperformers need to be counseled, retrained, or remotivated. If they do not shape up, it might be best to terminate their services.

Modifying Channel Arrangements

A producer must do more than design a good channel system and set it into motion. The system will require periodic modification to meet new conditions in the

Changing Marketing Channels over the Product Life Cycle

No marketing channel can be trusted to remain competitively dominant over the whole product life cycle. Early adopters might be willing to pay for high value-added channels, but later buyers will switch to lower-cost channels. Thus small office copiers were first sold by manufacturers' direct sales forces, later through office-equipment dealers, still later through mass merchandisers, and now by mail-order firms. Insurance companies that persist in using independent agents and auto companies that use independent dealers will face strong competition from new, lower-cost channels, and their reluctance to change might prove fatal in the long run.

Miland Lele developed the grid in Figure 1 to show how marketing channels have changed for PCs and designer apparel at different stages in the product life cycle:

- *Introductory stage:* Radically new products or fashions tend to enter the market through specialist channels (such as hobbyist shops, boutiques) that spot trends and attract early adopters.
- *Rapid growth stage:* As buyers' interest grows, higher-volume channels appear (dedicated chains, department stores) that offer services but not as many as the previous channels offered.
- *Maturity stage:* As growth slows down, some competitors move their product into lower-cost channels (mass merchandisers).
- *Decline stage:* As the decline begins, even lower-cost channels emerge (mail-order houses, off-price discounters).

The earliest channels face the challenge of market creation; they are high cost because they must search for and educate buyers. They are followed by channels that expand the market and offer sufficient services. In the maturity stage, many buyers want lower costs, and they patronize lower value-added channels. Finally, the remaining potential buyers can be reached only by creating very low prices in low, value-added channels.

Source: See Miland M. Lele, *Creating Strategic Leverage* (New York: John Wiley, 1992), pp. 249–51.

FIGURE 1
Channel Value-Added and Market Growth Rate

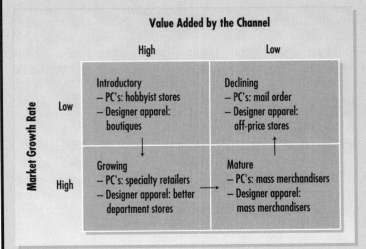

marketplace. Modification becomes necessary when the original distribution channel is not working as planned, consumer buying patterns change, the market expands, new competition arises, innovative distribution channels emerge, and the product moves into later stages in the product life cycle. (See the Marketing Insight titled "Changing Marketing Channels over the Product Life Cycle.")

This fact struck the manufacturer of the MicroFridge, a combination mini-refrigerator and microwave oven:

MICROFRIDGE When he kicked off his business, MicroFridge CEO Bob Bennett decided to sell his product through independent large appliance distributors. He lined up 170 sales representatives from 17 independent distributors to carry his new product. Bennett figured that the company had three quarters of the country covered this way, so he sat back to watch his sales take off. But after five months in business, 3,500 MicroFridge units were languishing in the mass-market distribution pipeline. The MicroFridge is designed for use in college dormitories, but Bennett's distributors had zero contacts on college campuses or army bases—which also boast a high dorm population. The distributors had foisted the appliances onto mass marketers who had no idea what to do with them. On the verge of going under, Bennett had to come up with an entirely new distribution channel. He hired four full-time sales reps to focus on college and army base housing directors. These new prospects quickly grasped the virtue of MicroFridge and in 1990 the company sold 11,000 units, with revenues climbing to $3.7 million.[22]

In competitive markets with low entry barriers, the optimal channel structure will inevitably change over time. The current channel structure will no longer produce the most efficient service outputs for the given costs. As a result, the current structure will necessarily change in the direction of the optimal structure. Three levels of channel adaptation can be distinguished. The change could involve adding or dropping individual channel members, adding or dropping particular market channels, or developing a totally new way to sell goods in all markets.

Adding or dropping specific intermediaries in the current channel requires an incremental analysis. What would the firm's profits look like with and without this intermediary? An automobile manufacturer's decision to drop a dealer would require subtracting the dealer's sales and estimating the possible sales loss or gain to the manufacturer's other dealers.

Sometimes a producer contemplates dropping all intermediaries whose sales are below a certain amount. For example, Navistar noted at one time that 5% of its dealers were selling fewer than three or four trucks a year. It cost the company more to service these dealers than their sales were worth. However, the decision to drop these dealers could have large repercussions on the system as a whole. The unit costs of producing trucks would be higher, since the overhead would be spread over fewer trucks; some employees and equipment would be idled; some business in these markets would go to competitors; and other dealers might become insecure. All of these factors would have to be taken into account. (Ultimately, Navistar dropped the marginal dealers.)

The most difficult decision involves revising the overall channel strategy.[23] Distribution channels clearly get outmoded with the passage of time. A gap arises between a seller's existing distribution system and the ideal system that would satisfy target customers' needs and desires. Examples of this abound: Avon's door-to-door system for selling cosmetics had to be modified as more women entered the work force, and IBM's exclusive reliance on a field sales force had to be modified with the introduction of low-priced personal computers.

Stern and Gemini Consulting have outlined an 14-step process for moving an obsolete distribution system closer to target customers' ideal system.[24]

- ◆ *Step 1.* Review existing materials and conduct research on channels.
- ◆ *Step 2.* Understand the current distribution system fully.
- ◆ *Step 3.* Conduct existing channel workshops and interviews.
- ◆ *Step 4.* Conduct competitor channel analysis.
- ◆ *Step 5.* Assess near-term opportunities in existing channels.
- ◆ *Step 6.* Develop a near-term plan of attack.

- ◆ *Step 7.* Conduct quantitative end-user analysis by way of focus groups and one-on-one interviews.
- ◆ *Step 8.* Conduct quantitative end-user needs analysis.
- ◆ *Step 9.* Analyze industry standards and systems currently in use.
- ◆ *Step 10.* Develop the "ideal" channel system.
- ◆ *Step 11.* Design a "management-bounded" system—that is, an ideal constrained by reality.
- ◆ *Step 12.* Conduct gap analysis—that is, determine the gaps that exist among the current system, the ideal system, and the management-bounded system.
- ◆ *Step 13.* Identify and develop strategic options.
- ◆ *Step 14.* Design optimal channels.

CHANNEL DYNAMICS

Distribution channels do not stand still. New wholesaling and retailing institutions emerge, and new channel systems evolve. In this section we will look at the recent growth of vertical, horizontal, and multichannel marketing systems and see how these systems cooperate, conflict, and compete.

Vertical Marketing Systems

One of the most significant recent channel developments is the rise of vertical marketing systems, which have emerged to challenge conventional marketing channels. A *conventional marketing channel* comprises an independent producer, wholesaler(s), and retailer(s). Each is a separate business entity seeking to maximize its own profits, even if this goal reduces profit for the system as a whole. No channel member has complete or substantial control over the other members. McCammon characterizes conventional channels as "highly fragmented networks in which loosely aligned manufacturers, wholesalers, and retailers have bargained with each other at arm's length, negotiated aggressively over terms of sale, and otherwise behaved autonomously."[25]

A *vertical marketing system* (VMS), by contrast, comprises the producer, wholesaler(s), and retailer(s) acting as a unified system. One channel member owns the others or franchises them or has so much power that they all cooperate. The vertical marketing system can be dominated by the producer, the wholesaler, or the retailer. McCammon characterizes VMSs as "professionally managed and centrally programmed networks, pre-engineered to achieve operating economies and maximum market impact."[26] VMSs arose as a result of strong channel members' attempts to control channel behavior and eliminate the conflict that results when independent channel members pursue their own objectives. They achieve economies through their size, bargaining power, and elimination of duplicated services. VMSs have become the dominant mode of distribution in the U.S. consumer marketplace, serving between 70% and 80% of the total market. There are three types of VMS: corporate, administered, and contractual.

CORPORATE VMS. A *corporate VMS* combines successive stages of production and distribution under single ownership. Vertical integration is favored by companies that desire a high level of control over their channels. For example, Sears obtains over 50% of the goods it sells from companies that it partly or wholly owns. Sherwin-Williams makes paint but also owns and operates 2,000 retail outlets. Giant Food Stores operates an ice-making facility, a soft-drink bottling operation, an ice-cream-making plant, and a bakery that supplies Giant stores with everything from bagels to birthday cakes.

ADMINISTERED VMS. An *administered VMS* coordinates successive stages of production and distribution not through common ownership but through the size and power of one of the members. Manufacturers of a dominant brand are able to secure strong trade cooperation and support from resellers. Thus Kodak, Gillette, Procter & Gamble, and Campbell's Soup are able to command high levels of cooperation from their resellers in connection with displays, shelf space, promotions, and price policies.

CONTRACTUAL VMS. A *contractual VMS* consists of independent firms at different levels of production and distribution integrating their programs on a contractual basis to obtain more economies and/or sales impact than they could achieve alone. Johnston and Lawrence have called them "value-adding partnerships" (VAPs).[27] Contractual VMSs have expanded greatly in recent years and constitute one of the most significant developments in the economy. Contractual VMSs are of three types:

◆ *Wholesaler-sponsored voluntary chains:* Wholesalers organize voluntary chains of independent retailers to help them compete with large chain organizations. The wholesaler develops a program in which independent retailers standardize their selling practices and achieve buying economies that enable the group to compete effectively with chain organizations.

◆ *Retailer cooperatives:* Retailers might take the initiative and organize a new business entity to carry on wholesaling and possibly some production. Members concentrate their purchases through the retailer co-op and plan their advertising jointly. Profits are passed back to members in proportion to their purchases. Nonmember retailers might also buy through the co-op but do not share in the profits.

◆ *Franchise organizations:* A channel member called a *franchisor* might link several successive stages in the production-distribution process. Franchising has been the fastest-growing retailing development in recent years. Although the basic idea is an old one, some forms of franchising are quite new.
  There are three forms of franchise. The first is the *manufacturer-sponsored retailer franchise system.* Ford, for example, licenses dealers to sell its cars. The dealers are independent businesspeople who agree to meet various conditions of sales and services. The second is the *manufacturer-sponsored wholesaler franchise system.* Coca-Cola, for example, licenses bottlers (wholesalers) in various markets who buy its syrup concentrate and then carbonate, bottle, and sell it to retailers in local markets. The third is the *service-firm-sponsored retailer franchise system.* Here a service firm organizes a whole system for bringing its service efficiently to consumers. Examples are found in the auto-rental business (Hertz, Avis), fast-food-service business (McDonald's, Burger King), and motel business (Howard Johnson, Ramada Inn).

THE NEW COMPETITION IN RETAILING. Many independent retailers that have not joined VMSs have developed specialty stores that serve market segments that are not attractive to the mass merchandisers. The result is a polarization in retailing between large vertical marketing organizations on the one hand, and independent specialty stores on the other. This development creates a problem for manufacturers. They are strongly tied to independent intermediaries, whom they cannot easily give up. But they must eventually realign themselves with the high-growth vertical marketing systems on less attractive terms. Vertical marketing systems constantly threaten to bypass large manufacturers and set up their own manufacturing. *The new competition in retailing is no longer between independent business units but between whole systems of centrally programmed networks (corpo-*

rate, administered, and contractual) competing against each other to achieve the best cost economies and customer response.

Horizontal Marketing Systems

Another channel development is the *horizontal marketing system,* in which two or more unrelated companies put together resources or programs to exploit an emerging marketing opportunity. Each company lacks the capital, know-how, production, or marketing resources to venture alone, or it is afraid of the risk. The companies might work with each other on a temporary or permanent basis or create a separate company. Adler calls this *symbiotic marketing.*[28] Here are some examples:

PILLSBURY AND KRAFT GENERAL FOODS   Pillsbury and Kraft General Foods have set up an arrangement where Pillsbury makes and advertises its line of refrigerated dough products, while Kraft uses its expertise to sell and distribute these products to the stores.

H&R BLOCK AND HYATT LEGAL SERVICES   H&R Block and Hyatt Legal Services formed a joint venture in which Hyatt's legal clinics are housed in H&R Block's tax-preparation offices. Hyatt pays a fee for office space, secretarial assistance, and office-equipment usage and enjoys a chance for accelerated market penetration through locating in H&R Block's nationwide office network. Meanwhile H&R Block benefits from renting its facilities, the traffic through which is highly seasonal.

LAMAR SAVINGS BANK AND SAFEWAY STORES   The Lamar Savings Bank of Texas arranged with Safeway Stores, Inc. to locate its savings offices and automated teller machines in Safeway stores. Lamar gained accelerated entry at a low cost, and Safeway was able to offer in-store banking convenience to its customers.

Multichannel Marketing Systems

In the past, many companies sold to a single market through a single channel. Today, with the proliferation of customer segments and channel possibilities, more companies have adopted multichannel marketing. *Multichannel marketing* occurs when a single firm uses two or more marketing channels to reach one or more customer segments. For example, Compaq sells its personal computers directly to corporate buyers as well as through mass electronics retailers, small computer specialist stores, and value-added resellers.

By adding more channels, companies can gain three important benefits. The first is increased market coverage—companies often add a channel to reach a customer segment that its current channels can't reach (e.g., adding rural agents to reach sparsely located farmer-customers). The second is lower channel cost—companies may add a new channel to lower their cost of selling to an existing customer group (e.g., selling by phone rather than personally visiting small customers). The third is more customized selling—companies may add a channel whose selling features fit customers' requirements better (e.g., adding a technical sales force to sell more complex equipment).

The gains from adding new channels come at a price, however. New channels typically introduce conflict and control problems. Conflict occurs when two or more company channels end up competing for the same customers. Control problems occur to the extent that the new channels are more independent and make cooperation more difficult.

FIGURE 18-5

The Hybrid Grid

Source: Rowland T. Moriarty and Ursula Moran, "Marketing Hybrid Marketing Systems," *Harvard Business Review,* November–December 1990, p. 150.

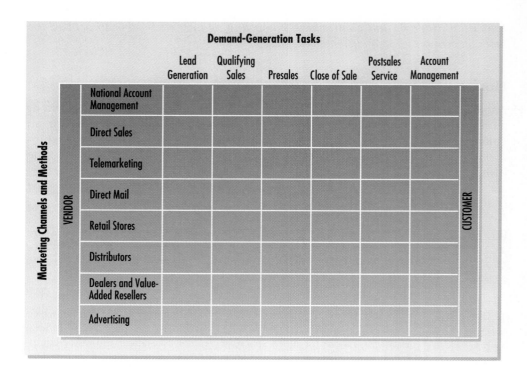

Clearly, companies need to think through their channel architecture in advance. Moriarty and Moran propose using a hybrid grid to plan the channel architecture (Figure 18-5).[29] The grid shows several marketing channels and several marketing tasks. One common practice is for companies to assign different channels to sell to different customer-size groups. For example, the company can use a direct sales force to sell to large customers, a telemarketing channel to sell to midsize customers, and distributors to sell to small customers and noncustomers. This looks like an attractive solution insofar as the company can serve more customers at an appropriate cost and customization level for each. But these gains may be offset by an increased level of conflict over who has *account ownership.* For example, the sales representatives may want credit for all sales in their territories, regardless of the size of the account or the marketing channel used.

Swartz and Moriarty believe that there is a better way to design and manage a hybrid marketing system.[30] They believe that marketing tasks, not marketing channels, are the fundamental building blocks for channel architecture. They would establish a centralized marketing database containing information about customers, prospects, products, marketing programs, and methods. They would generate prospect leads by ads, direct mail, and telemarketing. They would qualify the leads using telemarketing. They would pre-sell using advertising, direct mail, and telemarketing. They would turn the leads over to the sales force to close the sale. Service would be provided by distributors and dealers. Salespeople would handle account management. Eventually the expensive sales force would be used primarily for closing sales and managing the account for further sales. This hybrid channel architecture and management system optimizes coverage, customization, and control while minimizing cost and conflict.

Roles of Individual Firms in a Channel

Each firm in an industry has to define its role in the channel system. McCammon has distinguished five roles:[31]

- *Insiders* are members of the dominant channel. They enjoy access to preferred sources of supply and high respect in the industry. They want to perpetuate the existing channel arrangements and are the main enforcers of industry codes of conduct.

- *Strivers* are firms seeking to become insiders. They have less access to preferred sources of supply, which can handicap them in periods of short supply. They adhere to the industry code because of their desire to become insiders.

- *Complementers* are not part of the dominant channel. They perform functions not normally performed by others in the channel, serve smaller segments of the market, or handle smaller quantities of merchandise. They usually benefit from the present system and respect the industry code of conduct.

- *Transients* are outside the dominant channel and do not seek membership. They go in and out of the market and move around as opportunities arise. They have short-run expectations and little incentive to adhere to the industry code of conduct.

- *Outside innovators* are the real challengers and disrupters of the dominant channels. They develop a new system for carrying out the marketing work of the channel; if successful, they force major channel realignments. They are companies like McDonald's, Avon, and Dell Computer, which doggedly develop new systems to challenge the old.

Another important channel role is that of *channel captain*. The channel captain is the dominant member of a particular channel, the one who leads it. For example, General Motors is the channel captain of a system consisting of a huge number of suppliers, dealers, and facilitators. The channel captain is not always a manufacturer, as the examples of McDonald's and Sears indicate. Some channels do not have a channel captain; each firm simply proceeds on its own.

CHANNEL COOPERATION, CONFLICT, AND COMPETITION

No matter how well channels are designed and managed, there will be some conflict, if for no other reason than the interests of independent business entities don't always coincide. Here we examine three questions: What types of conflict arise in channels? What causes channel conflict? What can be done to resolve conflict situations?

Types of Conflict and Competition

Suppose a manufacturer sets up a vertical channel consisting of wholesalers and retailers. The manufacturer hopes for channel cooperation that will produce greater total channel profits than each channel member would generate if it acted only on self-interest. By cooperating, the channel members can more effectively sense, serve, and satisfy the target market.

Yet vertical, horizontal, and multichannel conflict can occur. *Vertical channel conflict* exists when there is conflict between different levels within the same channel. For example, General Motors came into conflict with its dealers years ago in trying to enforce policies on service, pricing, and advertising. Several automakers have run into conflict with their dealers, who resent the company's selling the same types of cars to auto-rental agencies—cars that eventually end up in the lucrative used-car market.[32] And Coca-Cola came into conflict with its bottlers who agreed to also bottle Dr. Pepper. (For more on this topic, see the Marketing Insight on pages 554–555 titled "Vertical Channel Conflict in the Consumer-Packaged-Goods Industry.")

Horizontal channel conflict exists when there is conflict between members at the same level within the channel. Some Ford car dealers in Chicago complained about other Chicago Ford dealers advertising and pricing too aggressively. Some

Selecting and
Managing
Marketing Channels

Vertical Channel Conflict in the Consumer-Packaged-Goods Industry

For many years, large consumer-packaged-goods manufacturers enjoyed high market power relative to retailers. Much of this power was based on pull strategies, where manufacturers spent huge amounts on advertising to build brand preference, and as a consequence retailers were obliged to carry their brands to meet consumer demand. But several developments have been shifting power to retailers relative to manufacturers:

1. The growth of giant retailers and their concentrated buying power. (In Switzerland, two retailers—Migros and the Coop—account for almost 70% of all retail food sales.)

2. Retailer development of well-regarded lower-price store brands to compete with manufacturers' brands.

3. The lack of sufficient shelf space to accommodate all the new brands being offered. (The average U.S. supermarket carries 24,000 items, and manufacturers offer 10,000 new items each year.)

4. Giant retailers' insistence on more trade-promotion money from manufacturers if they want their brands to enter or remain in the store and receive store support.

5. The reduced funds available to manufacturers to spend on advertising, and the erosion of mass audiences for advertising.

6. The retailers' growing marketing and information sophistication (for example, the use of bar codes, scanner data, electronic data interchange, and direct-product-profitability analyses.)

The growing power of retailers is manifested by their levying of *slotting fees* upon manufacturers wishing to get new products into the stores; *display fees* to cover space costs; *fines* for late deliveries and incomplete orders; and *exit fees* to cover the cost of returning terminated merchandise to the manufacturers.

Manufacturers are discovering that if their brand isn't one of the top two or three national brand leaders, they might as well drop out. Since the retailer may want to offer no more than four brands within a food category, and supplies two of its own, only the two top national brands will make money. The exiting minor brands will be driven to produce the store brands.

All of these developments have challenged manufacturers to figure out how they can regain or hold on to their power vis-à-vis retailers. Clearly, manufacturers can't set up their own retail outlets. Nor do manufacturers want to continue to spend so much money on trade promotion and thus weaken their brand-building spending ability. Market share leaders are resorting to the following strategies to maintain their power in the channel:

Pizza Inn franchisees complained about other Pizza Inn franchisees cheating on the ingredients, maintaining poor service, and hurting the overall Pizza Inn image. Benetton has been accused of franchising too many stores too close to one another, thus decreasing the profits of each individual store. In these cases, the channel captain must establish clear and enforceable policies and take quick action to control conflict.

Multichannel conflict exists when the manufacturer has established two or more channels that compete with each other in selling to the same market. When Levi Strauss agreed to distribute its jeans through Sears and J. C. Penney in addition to its normal specialty-store channel, it was highly resented by the specialty stores. When several clothing manufacturers—Ralph Lauren, Liz Claiborne, and Anne Klein—opened a set of their own stores, the department stores who carried their clothes were upset. When Goodyear began offering its popular tire brands for sale through mass-market retailers like Sears, Wal-Mart, and Discount Tire, it angered its independent dealers. (It eventually placated them by offering them exclusive tire models that would not be sold in other retail outlets.) Multichannel conflict is likely to be especially intense when the members of one channel either get a lower price (based on larger volume purchases) or are willing to work with a lower margin.

1. Focus on the brands that have a chance of being number one or two in their category and commit to continuous research to improve their quality, features, packaging, and so on.

2. Maintain an active program of line extensions and a careful program of brand extensions. As part of this program, develop fighter brands to compete with retailers' store brands.

3. Spend as much as possible on targeted advertising to build and maintain brand franchise.

4. Treat each major retail chain as a distinct target market, recognize their separate needs, and adjust offers and sales systems to serve each target retailer profitably. Treat them as strategic partners and be ready to customize products, packaging, services, benefits, electronic linkups, and cost savings.

5. Provide a high level of service quality and new services: on-time accurate delivery of complete orders, order-cycle time reduction, emergency delivery capability, merchandising advice, inventory management support, simplicity of order processing and billing, and access to information regarding order/shipment status.

6. Consider adopting everyday low pricing as an alternative to trade dealing, which leads to large forecasting errors, forward buying, and geographical diverting of merchandise.

7. Employ referent power, legitimate power, expert power, reward power, in that order, and avoid coercive power.

8. Support traditional retailers and aggressively expand into alternative retail outlets such as warehouse membership clubs, discount merchandisers, convenience stores, and some direct marketing.

Alert manufacturers who want to develop a strong position with their retail customers are implementing a system called *efficient consumer response (ECR)*. Four tools are involved. The first is activity-based cost accounting, which enables the manufacturer to measure and demonstrate to store chains the true costs of the resources consumed in meeting that chain's requirements (see Chapter 17). The second is electronic data interchange (EDI), which improves the manufacturer's ability to manage inventory, shipments, promotion announcements, and so on, to serve their own and retailers' interests (see Chapter 4). The third is a *continuous replenishment program (CPR),* which enables manufacturers to replenish products on the basis of actual and forecasted store demand. The final tool is *flow-through cross-dock replenishment,* which allows larger shipments to retailer distribution centers to be reloaded for shipment to individual stores, with little or no storage time lost at the distribution center. Manufacturers that master ECR will gain an edge over their competitors.

For additional reading, see "Not Everyone Loves a Supermarket Special: P&G Moves to Banish Wildly Fluctuating Prices That Boost Its Costs," *Business Week*, February 17, 1992, pp. 64–68; and Gary Davies, *Trade Marketing Strategies* (London: Paul Chapman Publishing, 1993).

Causes of Channel Conflict

It is important to identify the different causes of channel conflict. Some are easy to resolve, others more difficult.

A major cause is *goal incompatibility*. For example, the manufacturer may want to achieve rapid market growth through a low-price policy. The dealers, in contrast, may prefer to work with high margins and pursue short-run profitability. This is a difficult conflict to resolve.

Sometimes the conflict arises from *unclear roles and rights*. IBM sells personal computers to large accounts through its own sales force, and its licensed dealers are also trying to sell to large accounts. Territory boundaries, credit for sales, and so forth are grounds for conflict. (For more details, see the Marketing Insight on page 556 titled "The Downside of Multichannel Marketing: Channel Conflict at IBM.")

The conflict can also stem from *differences in perception*. The manufacturer may be optimistic about the short-term economic outlook and want dealers to carry higher inventory. But the dealers may be pessimistic about the short-term outlook.

The conflict might arise because of the intermediaries' *great dependence* on the manufacturer. The fortunes of exclusive dealers, such as auto dealers, are inti-

The Downside of Multichannel Marketing: Channel Conflict at IBM

When IBM added personal computers (PC's) to its product line in the late 1970s, it could not afford to sell them through its only existing channel, its high-cost field sales force. So, in less than 10 years, IBM added 18 new channels to reach PC customers, including dealers, catalog operations, direct mail, and telemarketing. IBM's aim was to utilize a range of the most cost-effective channels to reach different target buyer segments.

But by adding new channels, a company faces the possibility of channel conflict. In fact, the following three channel conflicts arose at IBM:

1. *Conflict between the national account managers and the field sales force:* To be effective, national account managers rely on field salespeople to make calls at the plants and offices of certain national account customers located in the salesperson's territory, sometimes on a moment's notice. The territory salesperson may receive requests from several national account managers to make such calls, and this can seriously disrupt the salesperson's normal call schedule and hurt his or her commissions. Salespeople may not cooperate with national account managers when doing so conflicts with their own interests.

2. *Conflict between the field sales force and the telemarketers:* Salespeople often resent their company setting up a telemarketing operation to sell to smaller customers. They want the right to call on small customers in their territory and earn commissions. They don't want the company to turn over these customers to an inside telemarketing operation. The company tells the salespeople that telemarketers free up the field staff's time to sell to larger accounts on which they can earn more commission, but the salespeople still object.

3. *Conflict between the field sales force and the dealers:* Dealers include value-added resellers, who buy computers from IBM and add specialized software needed by the target buyer, and computer retail stores, which are an excellent channel for selling small equipment to walk-in traffic and small business. In principle, these dealers are supposed to pursue only small customers, but many have chased larger accounts. They frequently can offer specialized software installation and training, better service, and even lower prices than IBM's direct sales force. The direct sales force becomes angry when these dealers go after their accounts and view them as "competition." They see these resellers as disrupting relationships with their accounts. They want IBM to refuse to sell through dealers who try to sell to large accounts against them. But IBM would lose a lot of business if it dropped these successful resellers. As an alternative, IBM decided to give credit to salespeople for business sold to their accounts by aggressive resellers.

When a company such as IBM finds that a significant percentage of its revenues are in conflict, it needs to establish clear *channel boundaries.* Boundaries can be established on the basis of customer characteristics, geography, or products. For example, IBM can require its value-added resellers who prepare software systems for hospitals to limit their selling to hospitals of under 200 beds (a customer boundary). It can use agents in rural areas and computer dealers in large cities. It could supply a modified personal computer to sell through dealerships as opposed to selling advanced PC's through its direct sales force. Clear channel boundaries will reduce some conflict, but there will remain debate over who should handle certain ambiguous account categories, such as small but fast-growing accounts and large accounts with decentralized purchasing units.

For further reading, see Frank V. Cespedes and E. Raymond Corey, "Managing Multiple Channels," *Business Horizons,* July–August 1990, pp. 67–77.

---

mately affected by the manufacturer's product design and pricing decisions. This situation creates a high potential for conflict.

Managing Channel Conflict

Some channel conflict can be constructive. It can lead to more dynamic adaptation to a changing environment. But too much conflict is dysfunctional. The challenge is not one of eliminating conflict but of managing it better. There are several mechanisms for effective conflict management.[33]

Perhaps the most important mechanism is the adoption of *superordinate goals.*

The channel members somehow come to an agreement on the fundamental goal they are jointly seeking, whether it is survival, market share, high quality, or customer satisfaction. They usually do this when the channel faces an outside threat, such as a more efficient competing channel, an adverse piece of legislation, or a shift in consumer desires. Working closely together might help them eliminate or neutralize the threat. There is also the chance that the intense cooperation might teach the parties a permanent lesson on the value of working toward the same end.

A useful conflict management device is the *exchange of persons* between two or more channel levels. For example, General Motors executives might agree to work in some dealerships, and some dealership owners might work at General Motors in GM's dealer policy department. Presumably, the participants will grow to appreciate the other's point of view and carry more understanding when returning to their original positions.

Cooptation is an effort by one organization to win the support of the leaders of another organization by including them in advisory councils, boards of directors, and the like. As long as the initiating organization treats the leaders of the other organization seriously and listens to their opinions, cooptation can reduce conflict. But the initiating organization also pays a price in that it may have to compromise its policies and plans in order to win the support of the other side.

Much can be accomplished by encouraging *joint membership in and between trade associations*. For example, there is good cooperation between the Grocery Manufacturers of America and the Food Marketing Institute, which represents most of the food chains; this cooperation led to the development of the universal product code (UPC). Presumably, the associations can consider issues between the food manufacturers and retailers and put them through an orderly process of resolution.

When conflict is chronic or acute, the parties may have to resort to diplomacy, mediation, or arbitration. *Diplomacy* takes place when each side sends a person or group to meet with a counterpart from the other side to resolve the conflict. It makes sense to assign diplomats to work more or less continuously with each other to avoid the flaring up of conflicts. *Mediation* means resorting to a neutral third party who brings skills in conciliating the two parties' interests. *Arbitration* occurs when the two parties agree to present their arguments to a third party (one or more arbitrators) and accept the arbitration decision.

Legal and Ethical Issues in Channel Relations

For the most part, companies are legally free to develop whatever channel arrangements suit them. In fact, the laws affecting channels seek to prevent the exclusionary tactics of companies that might keep other companies from using a desired channel. Most channel law deals with the mutual rights and duties of the channel members once they have formed a relationship. Here we briefly consider the legality of certain channel practices, including exclusive dealing, exclusive territories, tying agreements, and dealers' rights.

EXCLUSIVE DEALING. Many producers and wholesalers like to develop exclusive channels for their products. As we saw early in the chapter, a strategy in which the seller allows only certain outlets to carry its products is called *exclusive distribution*. When the seller requires that these dealers not handle competitors' products, its strategy is called *exclusive dealing*. Both parties benefit from exclusive arrangements: The seller obtains more loyal and dependable outlets, and the dealers obtain a steady source of supply and stronger seller support. But exclusive arrangements exclude other producers from selling to these dealers. They are legal

Selecting and
Managing
Marketing Channels

in the United States as long as they do not substantially lessen competition or tend to create a monopoly and as long as both parties enter into the agreement voluntarily.

EXCLUSIVE TERRITORIES. Exclusive dealing often includes exclusive territorial agreements. The producer may agree not to sell to other dealers in a given area, or the buyer may agree to sell only in its own territory. The first practice is normal under franchise systems as a way to increase dealer enthusiasm and commitment. It is also perfectly legal in the United States—a seller has no legal obligation to sell through more outlets than it wishes. The second practice, whereby the producer tries to keep a dealer from selling outside its territory, has become a major legal issue.

TYING AGREEMENTS. Producers of a strong brand sometimes sell it to dealers only if the dealers will take some or all of the rest of the line. This practice is called *full-line forcing.* Such tying agreements are not necessarily illegal, but they do violate U.S. law if they tend to lessen competition substantially. The practice may prevent consumers from freely choosing among competing suppliers of these other brands.

DEALERS' RIGHTS. Producers in the United States are free to select their dealers, but their right to terminate dealers is somewhat restricted. In general, sellers can drop dealers "for cause." But they cannot drop dealers if, for example, the dealers refuse to cooperate in a doubtful legal arrangement, such as exclusive dealing or tying agreements.

SUMMARY

1. Most producers do not sell their goods directly to the final users. Between producers and the final users stands one or more marketing channels, a host of marketing intermediaries performing a variety of functions. Marketing-channel decisions are among the most critical decisions facing management. The company's chosen channel(s) intimately affect all other marketing decisions.

2. Companies use intermediaries when they lack the financial resources to carry out direct marketing, when direct marketing is not feasible, and when they can earn more by doing so. The use of intermediaries largely boils down to their superior efficiency in making goods widely available and accessible to target markets. The most important functions performed by intermediaries are information, promotion, negotiation, ordering, financing, risk taking, physical possession, payment, and title. These marketing functions are more basic than the particular wholesale and retail institutions that may exist at any given time.

3. Manufacturers face many channel alternatives for reaching a market. They can sell direct or use one-, two-, or three-level channels. Deciding which type(s) of channel to use calls for (1) analyzing customer needs; (2) establishing channel objectives; and (3) identifying and evaluating the major channel alternatives, including the types and numbers of intermediaries that will be involved in the channel. The company must determine whether to distribute its product exclusively, selectively, or intensively, and it must clearly spell out the terms and responsibilities of each channel member.

4. Effective channel management calls for selecting intermediaries and motivating them. The goal is to build a long-term partnership that will be profitable for all channel members. Individual channel members must be periodically evaluated against pre-established

standards, and channel arrangements may need to be modified when market conditions change.

5. Marketing channels are characterized by continuous and sometimes dramatic change. Three of the most important trends are the growth of vertical marketing systems (in corporate, administered, and contractual forms), horizontal marketing systems, and multichannel marketing systems.

6. All marketing channels have the potential for channel conflict and competition resulting from such sources as goal incompatibility, poorly defined roles and rights, perceptual differences, and interdependent relationships. Companies can manage channel conflict by striving for superordinate goals, exchanging people among two or more channel levels, co-opting the support of leaders in different parts of the channel, and encouraging joint membership in and between trade associations.

CONCEPT APPLICATIONS

1. For many years, male employees in large Japanese firms were promised "lifetime employment." They began their career with a company, then retired from that company 30 or 40 years later. While lifetime employment is no longer guaranteed, the Japanese culture is still strongly family- and relationship-oriented. For example, Japanese salespeople work through the *jinmyaku,* a network of contacts that is a focal point in Japanese society.

   Amway, a company that sells detergents, vitamins, cosmetics, soap, and other consumer goods door to door in the United States, has entered the Japanese market. What channel(s) of distribution would you recommend for the company in the Japanese culture? How might Amway motivate its sales force, and how willing do you think the Japanese would be to work for Amway? What do you think Amway's chances of success are in Japan?

2. As cable TV systems become more competitive, cable companies will upgrade their service and offer hundreds of channels and (eventually) digital, interactive, and other not-yet-discovered technologies. Home shopping will grow and become even more sophisticated. Some envision a sort of video mall where shoppers will browse through channels as through individual stores, ask for information and advice, order, and pay—without ever leaving their La-Z-Boy. Even now, home shopping networks and infomercials are ringing up millions of dollars in sales and attracting the attention of Saks Fifth Avenue, Marshall Fields, and designer Diane von Furstenberg.

   The home shopping distribution channel offers a series of challenges to sellers. What advice would you offer Nordstrom (an upscale department store known for its elegance and customer service) as it begins to investigate how to market products and image through this distribution channel? How can Nordstrom offer the same intense level of personal service via TV or computer that it does in its stores?

3. Marketing channels can be viewed as a set of interdependent organizations with high potential for conflict. Then why would any business choose to become part of a channel system?

4. There is often conflict between manufacturers and retailers. In general, what does each party want from the other? Why might these expectations give rise to conflict?

5. Sears acquired Dean Witter Reynolds, the fifth largest stock brokerage firm in the United States, in order to capitalize on the growing demand for financial services. Sears has opened financial service centers in its stores, offering money market funds, casualty and life insurance, credit cards, auto and boat installment loans, and so forth. What forces are working for and against the success of such a venture?

6. Analyze the ad in Figure 1 on page 560. What does Pioneer want this ad to accomplish with regard to channel management? What channel members' actions is Pioneer trying to control?

Selecting and
Managing
Marketing Channels

7. "Middlemen are parasites" and "Eliminate the middleman and prices will come down" are charges that have been made for centuries. Assume that marketing intermediaries are legally banned. You now decide that you would like to have a loaf of whole wheat bread. Beginning with the wheat farmer, explain how the present distribution system works. In other words, how does the wheat get turned into a loaf of bread and into your hands? If this system were eliminated, what would a consumer have to do to get a loaf of bread? How much do you think a loaf of bread would cost?

8. Pizza Hut is contemplating introducing breakfast pizzas in order to tap a new market and increase its penetration of pizza in its current markets. The breakfast pizza would consist of sausage, eggs, bacon, and other familiar and traditional breakfast offerings. Also, the pizza would be in the shape of coffee cakes. Either individually or in small groups, brainstorm a number of new and alternative channels to the existing channels for pizza (i.e., retail stores and home delivery).

9. Experience in a wide variety of business-to-business, consumer, and service industries, is proving that the best distribution channel for a product changes over a product's life cycle. Some effective marketers advocate that producers move from one channel to another over the PLC—direct sales to dealers, to mass merchandisers, to discount warehouse clubs, and so forth—if they are to maintain a competitive edge. Design a channel strategy for a cordless power drill as it moves through each stage of the product life cycle.

    a. What should the company's strategic focus be in each stage?
    b. Which channels should be used in each stage?
    c. In which stages of the PLC will margins be the highest?
    d. Which stage(s) should use the most intermediaries, and which stage(s) should use the fewest?

10. Suggest some alternative channels for (a) a small firm that has developed a radically new harvesting machine, (b) a small plastics manufacturer that has developed a picnic pack for keeping bottles and food cold, and (c) a tankless instant water heater. What are the advantages and disadvantages of each channel alternative?

NOTES

1. E. Raymond Corey, *Industrial Marketing: Cases and Concepts,* 4th ed. (Englewood Cliffs, NJ: Prentice Hall, 1991), Chapter 5.

2. Louis W. Stern and Adel I. El-Ansary, *Marketing Channels,* 5th ed. (Upper Saddle River, NJ: Prentice Hall, 1996).

3. Some producers, however, will set up a partially owned distribution system. Thus McDonald's owns over one fifth of all its outlets. The advantages are that the company learns about managing retail outlets, can rapidly and flexibly test new products and ideas, provides a model for operator-owned outlets, and uses owned outlets to benchmark the performance of operator-owned outlets. The disadvantages are that operator-owners may resent the competition coming from company-owned outlets and fear that the company will eventually buy out the operators. Dual distribution often creates channel conflict.

4. Stern and El-Ansary, *Marketing Channels,* pp. 5–6.

5. William G. Zikmund and William J. Stanton, "Recycling Solid Wastes: A Channels-of-Distribution Problem," *Journal of Marketing,* July 1971, p. 34.

6. For additional information on backward channels, see Marianne Jahre, "Household Waste Collection as a Reverse Channel—A Theoretical Perspective," *International Journal of Physical Distribution and Logistics,* 25, no. 2 (1995), 39–55; and Terrance L. Pohlen and M. Theodore Farris II, "Reverse Logistics in Plastics Recycling," *International Journal of Physical Distribution and Logistics,* 22, no. 7 (1992), 35–37.

7. Ronald Abler, John S. Adams, and Peter Gould, *Spatial Organizations: The Geographer's View of the World* (Englewood Cliffs, NJ: Prentice Hall, 1971), pp. 531–32.

8. See Irving Rein, Philip Kotler, and Martin Stoller, *High Visibility* (New York: Dodd, Mead, 1987).

9. For a technical discussion of how service-oriented firms choose to enter international markets, see M. Krishna Erramilli, "Service Firms' International Entry-Mode Approach: A Modified Transaction-Cost Analysis Approach," *Journal of Marketing,* July 1993, pp. 19–38.

10. Kent Phillips, "Brand of the Year," *Beverage World,* May 1994, p. 140; Melissa Campanelli, "Profiles in Marketing: Arnold Greenberg," *Sales and Marketing Management,* August 1993, p. 12; Tim Stephens, "What Makes Snapple Pop?" *Beverage World,* October 1994, pp. 200, 202.

11. Louis P. Bucklin, *Competition and Evolution in the Distributive Trades* (Englewood Cliffs, NJ: Prentice-Hall, 1972). Also see Stern and El-Ansary, *Marketing Channels.*

12. Louis P. Bucklin, *A Theory of Distribution Channel Structure* (Berkeley: Institute of Business and Economic Research, University of California, 1966).

13. Teri Lammers Prior, "Channel Surfers," *Inc.,* February 1995, pp. 65–68.

14. For more on relationship marketing and the governance of marketing channels, see Jan B. Heide, "Interorganizational Governance in Marketing Channels," *Journal of Marketing,* January 1994, pp. 71–85.

15. Arthur Bragg, "Undercover Recruiting: Epson America's Sly Distributor Switch," *Sales and Marketing Management,* March 11, 1985, pp. 45–49.

16. Vincent Alonzo, "Brewski," *Incentive,* December 1994, pp. 32–33.

17. Philip McVey, "Are Channels of Distribution What the Textbooks Say?" *Journal of Marketing,* January 1960, pp. 61–64.

18. These bases of power were identified in John R. P. French and Bertram Raven, "The Bases of Social Power," in *Studies in Social Power,* ed. Dorwin Cartwright (Ann Arbor, MI: University of Michigan Press, 1959), pp. 150–67.

19. See Bert Rosenbloom, *Marketing Channels: A Management View,* 5th ed. (Hinsdale, IL: Dryden Press, 1995).

20. Bert C. McCammon, Jr., "Perspectives for Distribution Programming," in *Vertical Marketing Systems,* ed. Louis P. Bucklin (Glenview, IL: Scott, Foresman, 1970), p. 32.

21. McCammon, "Perspectives for Distribution Programming," p. 43.

22. McCammon, "Perspectives for Distribution Progamming," pp. 65–68.

23. For an excellent report on this issue, see Howard Sutton, *Rethinking the Company's Selling and Distribution Channels,* research report no. 885, Conference Board, 1986, 26 pp.

24. See Stern and El-Ansary, *Marketing Channels,* p. 189.

25. McCammon, "Perspectives for Distribution Programming," pp. 32–51.

26. McCammon, "Perspectives for Distribution Programming," pp. 32–51.

27. Russell Johnston and Paul R. Lawrence, "Beyond Vertical Integration—The Rise of the Value-Adding Partnership," *Harvard Business Review,* July–August 1988, pp. 94–101.

28. Lee Adler, "Symbiotic Marketing," *Harvard Business Review,* November–December 1966, pp. 59-71; and P. "Rajan" Varadarajan and Daniel Rajaratnam, "Symbiotic Marketing Revisited," *Journal of Marketing,* January 1986, pp. 7–17.

29. See Rowland T. Moriarty and Ursula Moran, "Marketing Hybrid Marketing Systems," *Harvard Business Review,* November–December 1990, pp. 146–55.

30. For more on MSP, see Gordon S. Swartz and Rowland T. Moriarty, "Marketing Automation Meets the Capital Budgeting Wall," *Marketing Management,* 1, no. 3, (1992).

31. Bert C. McCammon, Jr., "Alternative Explanations of Institutional Change and Channel Evolution," in *Toward Scientific Marketing,* ed. Stephen A. Greyser (Chicago: American Marketing Association, 1963), pp. 477–90.

32. See Devarat Purohit and Richard Staelin, "Rentals, Sales, and Buybacks: Managing Secondary Distribution Channels," *Journal of Marketing Research,* August 1994, pp. 325–38.

33. This section draws on Stern and El-Ansary, *Marketing Channels,* Chapter 6.

MANAGING RETAILING, WHOLESALING, AND MARKET LOGISTICS

When is a refrigerator not a refrigerator? . . . when it is in Pittsburgh at the time it is desired in Houston.

J. L. HESKETT, N. A. GLASKOWSKY, AND R. M. IVIE

❖

I n the previous chapter, we examined marketing intermediaries from the viewpoint of manufacturers who wanted to build and manage marketing channels. In this chapter, we view these intermediaries—retailers, wholesalers, and logistical organizations—as requiring and forging their own marketing strategies. Some of these intermediaries are so large and powerful that they dominate the manufacturers who deal with them. Many are using strategic planning, advanced information systems, and sophisticated marketing tools. They are measuring performance more on a return-on-investment basis than on a profit-margin basis. They are also segmenting their markets, improving their market targeting and positioning, and aggressively pursuing market expansion and diversification strategies.

In this chapter, we will answer the following questions about each sector (retailers, wholesalers, and physical-distribution firms):

♦ **What major types of organizations occupy this sector?**

♦ **What marketing decisions do organizations in this sector make?**

♦ **What are the major trends in this sector?**

RETAILING

❖   RETAILING includes all the activities involved in selling goods or services directly to final consumers for their personal, nonbusiness use. A RETAILER or RETAIL STORE is any business enterprise whose sales volume comes primarily from retailing.

Any organization that does this type of selling—whether a manufacturer, wholesaler, or retailer—is doing retailing. It does not matter *how* the goods or services are sold (by person, mail, telephone, or vending machine) or *where* they are sold (in a store, on the street, or in the consumer's home).

Types of Retailers

Retail organizations exhibit great variety and new forms keep emerging. Several classifications have been proposed. For our purposes, we will discuss store retailing, nonstore retailing, and retail organizations.

STORE RETAILING. Consumers today can shop for goods and services in a wide variety of stores. The most important retail-store types, many of which are found in most countries, fall into eight categories: specialty stores, department stores, supermarkets, convenience stores, discount stores, off-price retailers, superstores, and catalog showrooms (Table 19-1 on page 564). Perhaps the best-known type of retailer is the department store. Japanese department stores such as Takashimaya and Mitsukoshi attract millions of shoppers each year. These stores feature art galleries, cooking classes, and children's playgrounds. The El Cortes Ingles department store chain in Spain draws crowds of Spanish shoppers.

Like products, retail-store types pass through stages of growth and decline that can be described as the *retail life cycle*.[1] A retail-store type emerges, enjoys a pe-

Managing Retailing,
Wholesaling, and
Market Logistics

TABLE 19-1 | MAJOR RETAILER TYPES

TYPE	DESCRIPTION	EXAMPLES
SPECIALTY STORES	Carry a narrow product line with a deep assortment within that line: apparel stores, sporting-goods stores, furniture stores, florists, and bookstores. Specialty stores can be subclassified by the degree of narrowness in their product line. A clothing store would be a *single-line store;* a men's clothing store would be a *limited-line store;* and a men's custom-shirt store would be a *superspecialty store.* Some analysts contend that in the future, superspecialty stores will grow the fastest to take advantage of increasing opportunities for market segmentation, market targeting, and product specialization.	Athlete's Foot (sport shoes only); Tall Men (tall-men's clothing); The Limited (women's clothing); The Body Shop (cosmetics and bath supplies)
DEPARTMENT STORES	Carry several product lines—typically clothing, home furnishings, and household goods—with each line operated as a separate department managed by specialist buyers or merchandisers.	Sears, Saks Fifth Avenue, Marshall Fields, May's, J.C. Penney, Nordstrom, Bloomingdale's, Macy's
SUPERMARKETS	Relatively large, low-cost, low-margin, high-volume, self-service operations designed to serve the consumer's total needs for food, laundry, and household-maintenance products. Supermarkets earn an operating profit of only about 1% on their sales and 10% on their net worth. Despite strong competition from new and innovative competitors like superstores and discount stores, supermarkets remain the most frequently shopped type of retail store.	Grand Union, Kroger, Wilson's Supermarkets, Safeway, Food Lion, Waldbaums, A&P, Shop Rite
CONVENIENCE STORES	Relatively small stores that are located near residential areas, are open long hours seven days a week, and carry a limited line of high-turnover convenience products. Their long hours and their use by consumers mainly for "fill-in" purchases make them relatively high-price operations. Many have added sandwiches, coffee, and pastry for takeout. They fill an important consumer need, and people seem willing to pay for the convenience.	7-11, Circle K, Wawa
DISCOUNT STORES	Sell standard merchandise at lower prices by accepting lower margins and selling higher volumes. The use of occasional discounts or specials does not make a discount store. True discount stores *regularly* sell their merchandise at lower prices, offering mostly national brands, not inferior goods. Discount retailing has moved beyond general merchandise into specialty merchandise stores, such as discount sporting-goods stores, electronics stores, and bookstores.	*All-purpose discount stores:* Wal-Mart, Kmart *Specialty discount stores:* Circuit City (electronics), Crown Bookstores (books)
OFF-PRICE RETAILERS	Buy at less than regular wholesale prices and charge consumers less than retail. Tend to carry a changing and unstable collection of higher-quality merchandise, often leftover goods, overruns, and irregulars obtained at reduced prices from manufacturers or other retailers. There are three main types of off-price retailers: factory outlets, independent off-price retailers, and warehouse/wholesale clubs.	
Factory outlets	Owned and operated by manufacturers and normally carry the manufacturer's surplus, discontinued, or irregular goods. Such outlets increasingly group together in *factory outlet malls,* where dozens of outlet stores offer prices as much as 50% below retail on a broad range of items.	Mikasa (dinnerware), Dexter (shoes), Ralph Lauren and Liz Claiborne (upscale apparel)

riod of accelerated growth, reaches maturity, and then declines. Older retail forms took many years to reach maturity, but newer retail forms reach their maturity much earlier. The department store took 80 years to reach maturity, while warehouse retail outlets, a more modern form of retailing, reached their maturity in 10 years.

One reason that new store types emerge to challenge old store types is given by the *wheel-of-retailing* hypothesis.[2] Conventional retail-store types typically offer many services to their customers and price their merchandise to cover the cost.

TYPE	DESCRIPTION	EXAMPLES
OFF-PRICE RETAILERS (cont.) Independent off-price retailers	Owned and run either by entrepreneurs or by divisions of larger retail corporations.	Filene's Basement, Loehmann's, TJX Cos. (Hit or Miss and T. J. Maxx)
Warehouse clubs (or wholesale clubs)	Sell a limited selection of brand-name grocery items, appliances, clothing, and a hodgepodge of other goods at deep discounts to members who pay $25 to $50 annual membership fees. Warehouse clubs serve small businesses and group members coming from government agencies, nonprofit organizations, and some large corporations. The wholesale clubs operate in huge, low-overhead, ware-houselike facilities and offer few frills. Their costs are lower because they buy on deals and use less labor for stocking. Such clubs make no home deliveries and accept no credit cards. But they do offer rock-bottom prices—typically 20% to 40% below supermarket and discount-store prices.	Wal-Mart owned Sam's Club, Max Clubs, Price-Costco, BJ's Wholesale Club
SUPERSTORES	Average 35,000 square feet of selling space and have traditionally aimed at meeting consumers' total needs for routinely purchased food and nonfood items. Usually offer services such as laundry, dry cleaning, shoe repair, check cashing, and bill paying. Recent years have seen the advent of superstores that are actually giant specialty stores, the so-called "category killers" that carry a very deep assortment of a particular line and a knowledgeable staff. Variations on the superstore include the combination store and the hypermarket.	Borders Books and Music (books and records), Petsmart (pet supplies), Staples (office supplies), Home Depot (hardware and home decorating)
Combination stores	Represent a diversification of the supermarket store into the growing drug-and-prescription field. Combination food and drug stores average 55,000 square feet of selling space.	A&P combination stores that offer both a complete line of groceries and a full-service pharmacy
Hypermarkets	Range between 80,000 and 220,000 square feet and combine supermarket, discount, and warehouse retailing principles. Their product assortment goes beyond routinely purchased goods and includes furniture, large and small appliances, clothing items, and many other items. The basic approach is bulk display and minimum handling by store personnel, with discounts offered to customers who are willing to carry heavy appliances and furniture out of the store. The first hypermarket originated in France, and this form of retailing is still quite popular in Europe.	Carrefour and Casino (France); Pyrca, Continente, and Alcampo (Spain); Meijer's (Netherlands)
CATALOG SHOWROOMS	Sell a broad selection of high-markup, fast-moving, brand-name goods at discount prices. These include jewelry, power tools, cameras, luggage, small appliances, toys, and sporting goods. Customers order the goods from a catalog in the showroom, then pick these goods up from a merchandise pickup area in the store. Catalog showrooms made their money by cutting costs and margins to provide low prices that will attract a higher volume of sales.	Service Merchandise

Sources: For further reading, see Leah Rickard, "Supercenters Entice Shoppers," *Advertising Age*, March 29, 1995, pp. 1–10; Debra Chanil, "Wholesale Clubs: A New Era?" *Discount Merchandiser*, November 1994, pp. 38–51; Julie Nelson Forsyth, "Department Store Industry Restructures for the 90s," *Chain Store Age Executive*, August 1993, pp. 29A–30A; John Milton Fogg, "The Giant Awakens," *Success*, March 1995, p. 51; and J. Douglas Eldridge, "Non-store Retailing: Planning for a Big Future," *Chain Store Age Executive*, August 1993, pp. 34A–35A.

These higher costs provide an opportunity for new store forms to emerge—for example, discount stores, which offer lower prices, less service, and less status but have lower operating costs. A large number of shoppers use the conventional stores for deciding what to buy and then drive to the discount stores to make the actual purchase. As these discount stores increase their market share, they offer more services and upgrade their facilities. Their increased costs, however, force

FIGURE 19-1

Retail Positioning Map

Source: William T. Gregor and Eileen M. Friars, "Money Merchandising: Retail Revolution in Consumer Financial Service" (Cambridge, MA: The MAC Group, 1982).

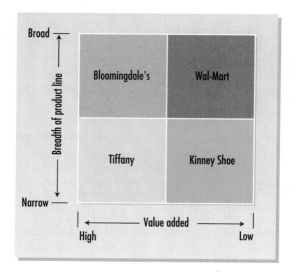

them to raise their prices until they start to resemble the conventional outlets they displaced. As a consequence, they become vulnerable to newer types of low-cost, low-margin operations. This wheel-of-retailing hypothesis partly explains the initial success and current troubles of U.S. department stores and, more recently, discount stores.

New store types emerge to meet widely different consumer preferences for service levels and specific services. Retailers in most product categories can position themselves as offering one of four levels of service:

◆ *Self-service retailing:* Used in many retailing operations, especially for obtaining convenience goods and, to some extent, shopping goods (see Chapter 15). Self-service is the cornerstone of all discount operations. Many customers are willing to carry out their own locate-compare-select process to save money.

◆ *Self-selection retailing:* Involves customers in finding their own goods, although they can ask for assistance. Customers complete their transactions by paying a salesperson for the item. Self-selection organizations have higher operating expenses than self-service operations because of the additional staff requirements.

◆ *Limited-service retailing:* Provides more sales assistance because these retailers carry more shopping goods, and customers need more information. Because the stores also offer services (such as credit and merchandise-return privileges) not normally found in less service-oriented stores, they have higher operating costs.

◆ *Full-service retailing:* Provides salespeople who are ready to assist in every phase of the locate-compare-select process. Customers who like to be waited on prefer this type of store. The high staffing cost—along with the higher proportion of specialty goods and slower-moving items (fashions, jewelry, cameras), the more liberal merchandise-return policies, various credit plans, free delivery, home servicing of durables, and customer facilities such as lounges and restaurants—results in high-cost retailing.

By combining these different service levels with different assortment breadths, we can distinguish the four broad positioning strategies available to retailers as shown in Figure 19-1:

1. Bloomingdale's typifies stores that feature a broad product assortment and high value added. Stores in this quadrant pay close attention to store design, product quality, service, and image. Their profit margin is high, and if they are fortunate enough to have high volume, they will be very profitable.

2. Tiffany typifies stores that feature a narrow product assortment and high value added. Such stores cultivate an exclusive image and tend to operate on a high margin and low volume.

3. Kinney Shoe typifies stores that feature a narrow line and low value added. Such stores appeal to price-conscious consumers. They keep their costs and prices low by designing similar stores and centralizing buying, merchandising, advertising, and distribution.

4. Wal-Mart typifies stores that feature a broad line and low value added. They focus on keeping prices low so that they have an image of being a place for good buys. They make up for their low margin by achieving a high volume.

NONSTORE RETAILING. Although the overwhelming majority of goods and services is sold through stores, *nonstore retailing* has been growing much faster than store retailing, amounting to more than 12% of all consumer purchases. Some observers predict that as much as half of all general merchandise will be sold through nonstore retailing by the end of the century. Nonstore retailing falls into four major categories: direct selling, direct marketing, automatic vending, and buying services (Table 19-2 on the next page). Some observers foresee as much as a third of all general-merchandise retailing being done through nonstore channels, such as mail-order shopping, TV shopping, and home computer shopping via the Internet, by the end of the century.

RETAIL ORGANIZATIONS. Although many retail stores are independently owned, an increasing number are falling under some form of corporate retailing. Retail organizations achieve many economies of scale, such as greater purchasing power, wider brand recognition, and better trained employees. The major types of corporate retailing—corporate chain stores, voluntary chains, retailer cooperatives, consumer cooperatives, franchise organizations, and merchandising conglomerates—are described in Table 19-3 on page 570. Franchising is described in detail in the Marketing Insight box titled "Franchise Fever" on pages 574–575.

Retailer Marketing Decisions

Retailers today are anxious to find new marketing strategies to attract and hold customers. In the past, they held customers by offering a convenient location, special or unique assortments of goods, greater or better services than competitors, and store credit cards to enable their buyers to buy on credit. All of this has changed. Today, many stores offer similar assortments: National brands such as Calvin Klein, Izod, and Levi are now found in most department stores, mass-merchandise outlets, and off-price discount stores. In their drive for volume, the national brand manufacturers placed their branded goods everywhere. The result has been that retail stores and other retailers have grown to look more and more alike.

Service differentiation also has eroded. Many department stores have trimmed their services, and many discounters have increased their services. Customers have become smarter, more price-sensitive shoppers. They do not see a reason to pay more for identical brands, especially when service differences are diminishing. Nor do they need to get credit from a particular store, as bank credit cards have become almost universally accepted by all stores.

For all these reasons, many retailers today are rethinking their marketing strategy.[3] For example, in the face of increased competition from discount houses and specialty stores, department stores are waging a comeback war. Historically located in the center of cities, many have opened branches in suburban shopping centers, where parking is plentiful and family incomes are higher. Others are running more frequent sales, remodeling their stores, and experimenting with mail order and telemarketing. Facing competition from superstores, supermarkets are opening larger stores, carrying a larger number and variety of items, and upgrading their facilities. Supermarkets have also increased their promotional budgets

TABLE 19-2	MAJOR TYPES OF NONSTORE RETAILING	
TYPE	**DESCRIPTION**	**EXAMPLES**
DIRECT SELLING	Started centuries ago with itinerant peddlers and has grown into a $9 billion industry, with over 600 companies selling door to door, office to office, or at home sales parties. (Direct selling as used here does not include business-to-business selling.) There are three types of direct selling: one-to-one selling, one-to-many (party) selling, and multilevel (network) marketing.	
One-to-one selling	A salesperson visits and tries to sell products to a single potential user.	Avon (personal-care products), Fuller Brush Company (cleaning products), Electrolux (vacuum cleaners), Southwestern Company of Nashville (Bibles), World Book (encyclopedias)
One-to-many (party) selling	A salesperson goes to the home of a host, who has invited friends and neighbors to the party. The salesperson then demonstrates the products and takes orders. Top-performing salespeople are often highly rewarded; for example, Mary Kay offers its top performers diamonds, minks, and the right to drive a pink Cadillac for an entire year.	Tupperware, Mary Kay Cosmetics
Multilevel (network) marketing	Pioneered by Amway, whose sales hit $5.3 billion in 1994 with half of its business taking place in Japan and the Asia Pacific region. A variant of direct selling in which companies recruit independent businesspeople who act as distributors for their products. These distributors in turn recruit and sell to subdistributors, who eventually recruit others to sell their products, usually in customer homes. A distributor's compensation includes a percentage of the sales to the entire sales group that the distributor recruited as well as earnings on any direct sales to retail customers.	Amway, Shaklee, NuSkin

and moved heavily into private brands to reduce their dependence on national brands and increase their profit margins.

We will now examine the marketing decisions faced by retailers in the areas of target market, product assortment and procurement, services and store atmosphere, price, promotion, and place.

TARGET-MARKET DECISION. A retailer's most important decision concerns the target market. Should the store focus on upscale, midscale, or downscale shoppers? Do the target shoppers want variety, assortment depth, or convenience? Until the target market is defined and profiled, the retailer cannot make consistent decisions on product assortment, store decor, advertising messages and media, price levels, and so on.

TYPE	DESCRIPTION	EXAMPLES
DIRECT MARKETING	Has roots in direct mail and catalog marketing but today includes reaching people in other ways, including telemarketing, television direct-response marketing (home shopping programs and infomercials), and electronic shopping (described in detail in Chapter 23).	Home Shopping Network and QVC Network (TV direct response); Lands' End, L. L. Bean, and Spiegel (catalog houses); 1-800-FLOWERS (telemarketing)
AUTOMATIC VENDING	Has been applied to a considerable variety of merchandise, including impulse goods with high convenience value (cigarettes, soft drinks, candy, newspapers, hot beverages) and other products (hosiery, cosmetics, food snacks, hot soups and food, paperbacks, record albums, film, T-shirts, insurance policies, and even fishing worms). In Japan, vending machines have advanced further and dispense jewelry, frozen beef, fresh flowers, whiskey, and even names of prospective dating partners. Vending machines are found in factories, offices, large retail stores, gasoline stations, hotels, restaurants, and many other venues. Vending machines offer customers the advantages of 24-hour selling, self-service, and unhandled merchandise.	Coca Cola machines, *The New York Times* newspaper boxes
BUYING SERVICE	A storeless retailer serving specific clienteles— usually the employees of large organizations, such as schools, hospitals, unions, and government agencies. The organization's members become members of the buying service and are entitled to buy from a selective list of retailers who have agreed to give discounts to buying service members. Thus a customer seeking a video camera would get a form from the buying service, take it to an approved retailer, and buy the appliance at a discount. The retailer would then pay a small fee to the buying service.	United Buying Service (offers its 900,000 members the opportunity to buy merchandise at "cost plus 8%")

Sources: For further reading, see J. Douglas Eldridge, "Nonstore Retailing: Planning for a Big Future, *Chain Store Age Executive,* August 1993, pp. 34 A–35 A; and Peter Clothier, *Multi-Level Marketing: A Practical Guide to Successful Network Selling* (London: Kogan Page, 1990).

Too many retailers have not clarified their target market. In trying to satisfy too many markets, they are satisfying none of them well. Even Sears, which serves so many different people, must define better which groups to make its major target customers so that it can fine-tune its product assortment, prices, locations, and promotions to these groups.

Some retailers have defined their target markets quite well. Here are two prime examples whose founders are among the richest men in the United States:

WAL-MART The late Sam Walton and his brother opened the first Wal-Mart discount store in Rogers, Arkansas, in 1962. It was a big, flat, warehouse-type store aimed at selling everything from apparel to automotive supplies to small appliances at the lowest possible prices to small-town America. More recently, Wal-Mart has been building

TABLE 19-3 | MAJOR TYPES OF RETAIL ORGANIZATIONS

TYPE	DESCRIPTION	EXAMPLES
CORPORATE CHAIN STORES	Two or more outlets that are commonly owned and controlled, employ central buying and merchandising, and sell similar lines of merchandise. Corporate chains appear in all types of retailing, but they are strongest in department stores, variety stores, food stores, drugstores, shoe stores, and women's clothing stores. Their size allows them to buy in large quantities at lower prices, and they can afford to hire corporate-level specialists to deal with such areas as pricing, promotion, merchandising, inventory control, and sales forecasting.	Tower Records, Fayva (shoes), Pottery Barn (dinnerware and home furnishings)
VOLUNTARY CHAIN	Consists of a wholesaler-sponsored group of independent retailers engaged in bulk buying and common merchandising.	Independent Grocers Alliance (IGA) in groceries, True Value in hardware
RETAILER COOPERATIVE	Consists of independent retailers who set up a central buying organization and conduct joint promotion efforts.	Associated Grocers (groceries), ACE (hardware)
CONSUMER COOPERATIVE	A retail firm owned by its customers. Consumer coops are started by community residents who feel that local retailers are not serving them well, either charging too-high prices or providing poor-quality products. The residents contribute money to open their own store, and they vote on its policies and elect a group to manage it. The store might set its prices low or, alternatively, set normal prices with members receiving a patronage dividend based on their individual level of purchases.	Various local consumer cooperatives across the country
FRANCHISE ORGANIZATION	Contractual association between a *franchiser* (a manufacturer, wholesaler, or service organization) and *franchisees* (independent businesspeople who buy the right to own and operate one or more units in the the franchise system). Franchise organizations are normally based on some unique product, service, or method of doing business, or on a trade name or patent, or on goodwill that the franchiser has developed. Franchising has been prominent in fast foods, video stores, health/fitness centers, hair cutting, auto rentals, motels, travel agencies, real estate, and dozens of other product and service areas.	McDonald's, Subway, Pizza Hut, Jiffy Lube, Meineke Mufflers, 7-Eleven
MERCHANDISING CONGLOMERATE	A free-form corporation that combines several diversified retailing lines and forms under central ownership, along with some integration of their distribution-and-management function.	F. W. Woolworth, in addition to its variety stores, operates Kinney Shoe Stores, Afterthoughts (costume jewelry and handbag specialty stores), Herald Square Stationers, Frame Scene, and Kids Mart

Sources: For further reading, see Rollie Tillman, "Rise of the Conglomerchant," *Havard Business Review,* November–December 1971, pp. 44–51. Also see *The Franchising Handbook,* Spring 1995 (1020 N. Broadway, Suite 111, Milwaukee, WI 53202).

stores in larger cities. Today, Wal-Mart operates 2,000 discount stores in the United States, 419 Sam's Clubs (its wholesale club), and 68 supercenters, and its annual sales exceed $67 billion, making it American's largest retailer. Wal-Mart's secret: Target small-town America, listen to the customers, treat the employees as partners, purchase carefully, and keep a tight rein on expenses. Signs reading "Satisfaction Guaranteed" and "We Sell for Less" hang prominently at each store's entrance, and customers are often welcomed by a "people greeter" eager to lend a helping hand. Wal-Mart spends considerably less than Sears and Kmart in advertising, and yet its sales are growing at the rate of 28% a year. In addition, Wal-Mart is frequently cited as a retailing pioneer. Its use of everyday low pricing (see Chapter 17) and EDI for speedy stock replenishment has been benchmarked by other retailers, and it was the first of the U.S. megamerchants to take the plunge into global retailing. Wal-Mart now operates 67 discount stores and Sam's Clubs in Mexico, as well as three stores in Brazil and two in Argentina. It also has three joint venture stores in Hong Kong and is planning to build in China.[4]

THE LIMITED Leslie H. Wexner borrowed $5,000 in 1963 to create *The Limited Inc.*, which started as a single store targeted to young, fashion-conscious women. All aspects of the store—clothing assortment, fixtures, music, colors, personnel— were orchestrated to match the target consumer. He continued to open more stores, but a decade later his original customers were no longer in the "young" group. To catch the new "youngs," he started the Limited Express. Over the years, he started or acquired other targeted store chains, including Lane Bryant, Victoria's Secret, Lerner's, Abercrombie & Fitch, Bath & Body Works, and so on. Today, The Limited operates 4,918 stores in 12 retailing divisions. Sales totaled $7.5 billion in 1994.

Despite its success, however, The Limited Inc. has faced some recent challenges. Sales of its flagship store, The Limited, began sagging in 1992 and dipped even lower for three consecutive years. The store's older thirty-something customers stopped frequenting the stores, noting that the clothes were too "young" and poorly made. Manufacturers said that The Limited lost its fashion direction when it began buying more of its merchandise from Asia several years ago. Ordering merchandise from overseas requires making decisions months in advance, which in turn makes it difficult to stock current fashions and keep track of quality. Now, in order to get the division back on track, The Limited Inc. is making a concerted effort to find creative and fresh merchandise for its 721 Limited stores.[5]

Given The Limited's experience, retailers should conduct periodic marketing research to ensure that they are reaching and satisfying their target customers— particularly in industries beset by fickle customers, such as apparel. Consider a store that seeks to attract affluent consumers but whose image is shown by the solid line in Figure 19-2 on the next page. The store's image does not appeal to its target market. The store has to either serve the mass market or redesign itself into a "classier store." Suppose it decides on the latter. Some time later, the store interviews customers again. The store image is now shown by the dashed line in Figure 19-2. The store has succeeded in realigning its image closer to its target market.

At the same time, a retailer's positioning must be somewhat flexible, especially if it manages outlets in locations with different socioeconomic patterns. A bank had located three branches in different parts of a city. It recognized that each branch needed to respond to a different customer expectation, as follows:

Branch	*Customer Expectation*
Branch A (high income, professional)	Timeliness
Branch B (middle income, homemakers)	Friendliness
Branch C (low income)	Competence

PRODUCT-ASSORTMENT-AND-PROCUREMENT DECISION. The retailer's *product assortment* must match the target market's shopping expectations. In fact, it becomes a key element in the competitive battle among similar retailers. The retailer has to decide on product-assortment *breadth* (narrow or wide) and

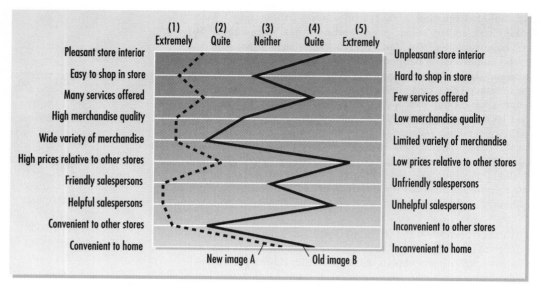

FIGURE 19-2

A Comparison Between the Old and the New Image of a Store Seeking to Appeal to a Class Market

Source: Adapted from David W. Cravens, Gerald E. Hills, and Robert B. Woodruff, *Marketing Decision Making: Concepts and Strategy* (Homewood, IL: Richard D. Irwin, 1976), p. 234. © 1976 by Richard D. Irwin, Inc.

depth (shallow or deep). Thus in the restaurant business, a restaurant can offer a narrow and shallow assortment (small lunch counters), a narrow and deep assortment (delicatessen), a broad and shallow assortment (cafeteria), or a broad and deep assortment (large restaurants). Another product-assortment dimension is the quality of the goods. The customer is interested in product quality as well as product range.

The retailer's real challenge begins after the store's product assortment and quality level have been defined. There will always be competitors with similar assortments and quality. The challenge is to develop a product-differentiation strategy. Wortzel suggests several product-differentiation strategies for retailers:

1. *Feature some exclusive national brands that are not available at competing retailers:* Thus Saks might get exclusive rights to carry the dresses of a well-known international designer.

2. *Feature mostly private branded merchandise:* Benetton and The Gap design most of the clothes carried in their respective stores. Many supermarket and drug chains are carrying an increasing percentage of private branded merchandise.

3. *Feature blockbuster distinctive merchandise events:* Bloomingdale's will run month-long shows featuring the goods of another country, such as India or China, throughout its store.

4. *Feature surprise or ever-changing merchandise:* Benetton changes some portion of its merchandise every month so that customers will want to drop in frequently. Loehmann's offers surprise assortments of distress merchandise (goods that the owner must sell immediately because it needs cash), overstocks, and close-outs.

5. *Feature the latest or newest merchandise first:* The Sharper Image will lead other retailers in introducing the newest electronic appliances from around the world.

6. *Offer merchandise customizing services:* Harrod's of London will make custom-tailored suits, shirts, and ties for customers, in addition to their ready-made men's wear.

7. *Offer a highly targeted assortment:* Lane Bryant carries goods for the larger woman. Brookstone offers unusual tools and gadgets for the person who wants to shop in an "adult toy store."[6]

Once the retailer decides on the product-assortment strategy, the retailer must decide on procurement sources, policies, and practices. In small businesses, the owner usually handles merchandise selection and buying. In large firms, buying is a specialized function and full-time job.

Consider supermarkets. In the corporate headquarters of a supermarket chain, specialist buyers (sometimes called *merchandise managers*) are responsible for developing brand assortments and listening to new-brand presentations by salespersons. In some chains, these buyers have the authority to accept or reject new items. In other chains, they are limited to screening "obvious rejects" and "obvious accepts"; they bring other items to the chain's buying committee for approval.

Even when an item is accepted by a chain-store buying committee, individual stores in the chain may not carry it. According to one supermarket chain executive: "No matter what the sales representatives sell or buyers buy, the person who has the greatest influence on the final sale of the new item is the store manager." In the nation's chain supermarkets, two thirds of the new items accepted at the warehouse are ordered on the store manager's own decision, and only one third represent required stocking by headquarters.

Manufacturers face a major challenge trying to get their new items onto store shelves. They offer the nation's supermarkets between 150 and 250 new items each week, of which store buyers reject over 70 percent. Store buyers also delete one item for every new item, since store space is at a premium. For this reason, manufacturers are very interested in knowing the acceptance criteria used by buyers, buying committees, and store managers. A. C. Nielsen Company asked store managers to rank on a three-point scale the importance of different elements in influencing their decision to accept a new item. They found that buyers are most influenced (in order of importance) by strong evidence of consumer acceptance, a well-designed advertising and sales-promotion plan, and generous financial incentives to the trade.

Retailers are rapidly improving their procurement skills. They are mastering the principles of demand forecasting, merchandise selection, stock control, space allocation, and display. They are using computers to track inventory, compute economic order quantities, prepare orders, and generate printouts of dollars spent on vendors and products. Supermarket chains are using scanner data to manage their merchandise mix better on a store-by-store basis. For example, Publix in Florida has installed larger floral departments in its stores in high-income areas than in low-income areas.

Stores are also learning to measure *direct product profitability* (DPP), which enables them to measure a product's handling costs from the time it reaches their warehouse until a customer buys it and takes it out of their retail store. DPP measures only the direct costs associated with handling the product—receiving, moving to storage, paperwork, selecting, checking, loading, and space cost. Resellers who have adopted DPP learn to their surprise that the gross margin on a product often has little correlation with the direct product profit. For example, some high-volume products may have such high handling costs that they are less profitable and deserve less shelf space than some low-volume products.

Clearly, manufacturers and vendors are facing increasingly sophisticated retail buyers. Vendors thus need to understand the retailers' changing requirements and to develop competitively attractive offers that help retailers serve their customers better. Table 19-4 lists several marketing tools used by vendors to improve their attractiveness to retailers. Here is an example of how one vendor, GE, took the initiative to establish higher service and profitability for its dealers:

Managing Retailing, Wholesaling, and Market Logistics

Franchise Fever

Once considered upstarts among independent business owners, franchises now command 35% of retail sales in the United States, and experts expect that number to increase to 50% by the turn of the century. This isn't hard to believe in a society where it's nearly impossible to stroll down a city block or drive on a suburban thoroughfare without seeing a Wendy's, a McDonald's, a Jiffy-Lube, or a 7-Eleven. One of the best-known and successful franchisers, McDonald's, now has 14,000 stores worldwide and racks up more than $23 billion in systemwide sales. Gaining fast is Subway Sandwiches and Salads, one of the fastest-growing franchises. With more than 8,500 shops in the United States, it even surpasses McDonald's 7,900 domestic units.

How does a franchising system work? The individual franchises are a tightly knit group of enterprises whose systematic operations are planned, directed, and controlled by the operation's innovator, called a *franchiser*. Generally, franchises are distinguished by three characteristics:

1. *The franchiser owns a trademark or service mark and licenses it to franchisees in return for royalty payments.*
2. *The franchisee is required to pay for the right to be a part of the system.* Yet this initial fee is only a small part of the total amount that franchisees invest when they sign a franchising contract. Startup costs include rental and lease of equipment and fixtures, and sometimes a regular license fee. McDonald's franchisees may invest as much as $600,000 in initial startup costs. The franchisee then pays the McDonald's franchiser a service fee and a rental charge that equal 11.5% of the franchisee's sales volume. Subway's success is partly due to its low startup cost of $45,000 to $70,000, which is lower than 70% of other franchise system startup costs.
3. *The franchiser provides its franchisees with a marketing and operations system for doing business.* McDonald's requires franchisees to attend its "Hamburger University" in Oak Brook, Illinois, for three weeks to learn how to manage the business, and the franchisees must adhere to certain procedures in buying materials. The most forward-looking franchisers also look to their franchisees for ideas. Quick printer Alpha-Graphics, for instance, makes a habit of consulting its franchisees for advice and ideas on how the business can be run better.

In the best cases, business format franchising is mutually beneficial to both franchiser and franchisee. Among the benefits reaped by franchisers are the ability to cover a territory in little more than the time it takes for a franchisee to sign a contract, the motivation and hard work of employees who are entrepreneurs rather than "hired hands," the franchisees' familiarity with local communities and conditions, and enormous purchasing power (consider the purchase order that Holiday Inn is likely to make for bed sheets, for instance). Franchisees benefit from buying into a proven

---

TABLE 19-4	VENDOR MARKETING TOOLS USED WITH RETAILERS

1. *Cooperative advertising,* where vendor agrees to pay a portion of the retailer's advertising costs for the vendor's product
2. *Preticketing,* where the vendor places a tag on each product listing its price, manufacturer, size, identification number, and color; these tags help the retailer reorder merchandise as it is sold
3. *Stockless purchasing,* where the vendor carries the inventory and delivers goods to the retailer on short notice
4. *Automatic reordering systems,* where the vendor supplies forms and computer links for the automatic reordering of merchandise by the retailer
5. *Advertising aids,* such as glossy photos and broadcast scripts
6. *Special prices* for storewide promotion
7. *Return and exchange privileges* for the retailer
8. *Allowances for merchandise markdowns* by the retailer
9. *Sponsorship of in-store demonstrations*

business with a well-known and accepted brand name. Franchisees also find it easier to borrow money from financial institutions and receive ongoing support in areas ranging from marketing and advertising to site selection and staffing.

As a result of the franchise explosion in recent years, many types of franchisers (such as fast-food franchisers) are looking at an increasingly saturated domestic market. One sign of this market saturation is the number of franchisee complaints filed with the Federal Trade Commission against parent companies, which has been growing by more than 50% annually since 1990. The most common complaint: Franchisers "encroach" on existing franchisees' territory by bringing in another store. Another complaint is higher-than-advertised failure rates. Subway, in particular, has been criticized for misleading its franchisees by telling them that it has only a 2% failure rate when the reality is much different. In addition, some franchisees feel that they've been misled by exaggerated claims of support, only to find poor or nonexistent support after the contract is signed and $100,000 is invested.

There will typically be a conflict between the franchisers, who benefit from growth, and the franchisees, who benefit only when they can earn a decent living. Some new directions that may deliver both franchiser growth and franchisee earnings are:

◆ *Strategic alliances with major outside corporations:* An example is that between film company Fuji USA and Moto Photo, a one-hour photo developer. Fuji won in-

stant market penetration through Moto Photo's 400 locations and Moto Photo franchisees enjoyed Fuji's brand-name recognition and advertising reach.

◆ *Expansion abroad:* Fast-food franchises have become very popular throughout the world. Today McDonald's has 4,700 overseas stores, including a 700-seat restaurant in Moscow. Domino's (pizza) has been brought to Japan by master franchisee Ernest Higa, who owns 106 stores in Japan with combined sales of $140 million. Part of Higa's success can be attributed to adapting Domino's product to the Japanese market, where presentation is everything. Higa meticulously charted the placement of pizza toppings and made cutmark perforations in the boxes for perfectly uniform slices.

◆ *Nontraditional site locations in the United States:* Franchises are opening in airports, sports stadiums, college campuses, hospitals, gambling casinos, theme parks, convention halls, and even river boats.

Franchising is even moving into new areas like education. LearnRight Corp. in State College, Pennsylvania, franchises its methods for teaching students thinking skills.

Sources: Norman D. Axelrad and Robert E. Weigand, "Franchising—A Marriage of System Members," in *Marketing Managers Handbook*, 3d ed., eds. Sidney Levy, George Frerichs, and Howard Gordon (Chicago: Dartnell, 1994), pp. 919–34; Meg Whittemore, "New Directions in Franchising," *Nation's Business*, January 1995, pp. 45–52; Andrew E. Serwer, "McDonald's Conquers the World," *Fortune*, October 17, 1994, pp. 103–16, and "Trouble in Franchise Nation," *Fortune*, March 6, 1995, pp. 115–29; Carol Steinberg, "Millionaire Franchisees," *Success*, March 1995, pp. 65–69; and Lawrence S. Welch, "Developments in International Franchising," *Journal of Global Marketing*, 6, nos. 1–2 (1992), 81–96.

GENERAL ELECTRIC

Before the late 1980s, GE operated a traditional system of trying to load its dealers with GE appliances. The underlying belief was that the dealer would have less space to carry other brands, and that its salespeople would therefore recommend GE appliances. But GE eventually realized that this approach created problems, especially for smaller independent appliance dealers who could ill afford to carry a large stock and who could not meet the price competition of the larger multi-brand dealers. So GE invented an alternative model called the Direct Connect system. Under this system, GE dealers carry only display models. They rely on a "virtual inventory" to fill orders. Dealers can access GE's order-processing system 24 hours a day, check on model availability, and place orders for next-day delivery. Furthermore, dealers get GE's best price, GE financing from GE credit, and no interest charge for the first 90 days. In exchange for these benefits, the dealers must commit to selling nine major GE product categories, generating 50% of their sales in GE products, opening their books to GE for review, and paying GE every month through electronic funds transfer. The result: GE dealers' profit margins have skyrocketed, and GE itself has dealers who are more committed to and dependent on GE. The new order entry system has saved GE substantial clerical costs. And GE now knows the actual sales of its goods at the retail level, which helps it to schedule its production more accurately.[7]

	TABLE 19-5	TYPICAL RETAIL SERVICES	

PREPURCHASE SERVICES	POSTPURCHASE SERVICES	ANCILLARY SERVICES
1. Accepting telephone orders	1. Delivery	1. Check cashing
2. Accepting mail orders	2. Shipping via U. S. mail or Federal Express	2. General information
3. Advertising	3. Gift wrapping	3. Free parking
4. Window display	4. Adjustments	4. Restaurants
5. Interior display	5. Returns	5. Repairs
6. Fitting rooms	6. Alterations	6. Interior decorating
7. Shopping hours	7. Tailoring	7. Credit
8. Fashion shows	8. Installations	8. Restrooms
9. Trade-ins	9. Engraving	9. Baby-attendant service

SERVICES-AND-STORE-ATMOSPHERE DECISION. Retailers must also decide on the *services mix* to offer customers. Table 19-5 lists some major services that full-service retailers can offer. The services mix is one of the key tools for differentiating one store from another.

The store's *atmosphere* is another element in its arsenal. Every store has a physical layout that makes it hard or easy to move around in. Every store has a "look"; one store is dirty, another is charming, a third is palatial, a fourth is somber. The store must embody a planned atmosphere that suits the target market and draws consumers toward purchase. A funeral parlor should be quiet, somber, and peaceful, and a dance club should be bright, loud, and vibrating. The Banana Republic Travel & Safari Clothing stores work on the concept of "retail theater"; customers feel they are shopping in an African bazaar or hunting lodge. Supermarkets have found that varying the tempo of music affects the average time spent in the store and the average expenditures; and supermarkets are exploring ways to release aromas through sticker displays on store shelves to stimulate hunger or thirst. (However, some commentators have pointed out ethical concerns with such subliminal influences.) Some fine department stores vaporize perfume fragrances in certain departments. The New Otani Hotel in Singapore features an $8 million waterfall that rises and falls to music. "Packaged environments" are designed by creative people who combine visual, aural, olfactory, and tactile stimuli aimed at achieving some customer objective.[8] For example:

CHICAGO RESTAURANTS Richard Melman is Chicago's preeminent restaurateur. Each of his 32 restaurants is thematic: Tucci Benucch resembles an outdoor Italian village café; Ed Debevic is a 1950s kitsch diner; R. J. Grunts is a burger-and-chili hangout; Ambria is an elegant crystal, tablecloth, and candle restaurant. According to food-industry consultant Ronald N. Paul, "Rich Melman is the Andrew Lloyd Webber of the restaurant industry. He doesn't just produce food, he produces theater."[9]

NIKE Chicago's four-story Niketown is now attracting more visitors than Chicago's famed Museum of Science and Industry. Niketown is the ultimate testimony to nichemanship: Every room is dedicated to a different sport where one can see and buy the appropriate outfits and shoes that belong to that sport. The teen-age would-be basketball star heads for the second floor, where he spots a giant picture of Michael Jordan, a whole array of basketball shoes and clothing, and even a basketball court where he can try on the shoes, shoot a few baskets, and sense how they help his performance.

MALL OF AMERICA The Mall of America near Minneapolis is a superregional mall plus theme park. Anchored by four major department stores—Nordstrom, Macy's, Bloomingdale's, and Sears—the giant complex contains another 800 specialty stores. One of the stores, Oshman Supersports USA, features a basketball court, a boxing gym, a baseball batting cage, a 50-foot archery range, and a simulated ski slope. The retail stores surround a seven-acre amusement park called Knott's Camp Snoopy, which consists of 26 rides, an ice skating rink, a miniature golf course on two levels, and a walk-through 1.2 million gallon aquarium featuring hundreds of marine specimens and a dolphin show.[10]

PRICE DECISION. The retailer's prices are a key positioning factor and must be decided in relation to the target market, the product-and-service-assortment mix, and competition. All retailers would like to charge high markups and achieve high volumes, but usually the two do not go together. Most retailers fall into the *high-markup, lower-volume group* (fine specialty stores) or the *low-markup, higher-volume group* (mass merchandisers and discount stores). Within each of these groups, there are further gradations. Thus X's on Rodeo Drive in Beverly Hills prices suits starting at $1,000 and shoes at $400, far in excess of the prices of fine department stores. At the other extreme, 47th Street Photo in New York City is a superdiscounter of well-known branded merchandise, pricing below even normal discounters and catalog houses. Some brands, such as the Maytag line of appliances (Figure 19-3 on page 578) both command a premium price *and* enjoy high sales volume.

Retailers must pay attention to pricing tactics. Most retailers will put low prices on some items to serve as traffic builders or loss leaders. They will run storewide sales on occasion. They will plan markdowns on slower-moving merchandise. For example, shoe retailers expect to sell 50% of their shoes at the normal markup, 25% at a 40% markup, and the remaining 25% at cost.

A growing number of retailers have abandoned "sales pricing" in favor of everyday low pricing (EDLP, see Chapter 17). EDLP could lead to lower advertising costs, greater pricing stability, a stronger store image of fairness and reliability, and higher retail profits. General Motors' Saturn division, for example, posts a low list price for its cars and its dealers refuse to bargain. One of Wal-Mart's major customer appeals is its everyday low prices. In 1989, Sears introduced EDLP, only to abandon it a year later because its costs couldn't support the EDLP initiative. Feather cites a study showing that supermarket chains practicing everyday low pricing are often more profitable than those practicing sales pricing.[11]

Coughlan and Vilcassim believe that in a duopolistic retail market with no retail differentiation, a sales price retailer will eventually be forced to become an EDLP retailer if it is facing an EDLP competitor.[12] Both firms would be unable to make above-normal profits because of competitive price pressures. Both firms will be tempted to run occasional sales in the hope of gaining a temporary advantage.

PROMOTION DECISION. Retailers use a wide range of promotion tools to generate traffic and purchases. They place ads, run special sales, issue money-saving coupons, and more recently have been adding frequent shopper programs, in-store food sampling, and coupons on shelves or at checkout points. Each retailer must use promotion tools that support and reinforce its image positioning. Fine stores will place tasteful full-page ads in magazines such as *Vogue* and *Harper's*. They will carefully train their salespeople in how to greet customers, interpret their needs, and handle complaints. Off-price retailers will arrange their merchandise to

Managing Retailing, Wholesaling, and Market Logistics

FIGURE 19-3
Maytag Advertisement

Even an engineer has trouble understanding how his Maytag washer keeps running.

Mr. Thomas Fisher of Newport News, Virginia is baffled. As a professional engineer, he's studied lots of machines before. In fact, he's got a pretty good sense how everything from a car to a computer operates. But he can't quite figure out how his Maytag washer keeps working. His family of five has had their machine for ten years now. In all those years of constant use, it's only needed a couple of minor repairs. And that's only half the story, because originally the Fishers got their washer from neighbors. And their family of five had used it for years before the Fishers even did a load. We can't promise every Maytag washer will last this long, but we build them all to last longer than any other brand. So take it from an expert like Mr. Fisher. He'll be the first to tell you a Maytag washer will keep running for years and years. Just don't ask him to explain it.

© 1994 Maytag Co.

MAYTAG
THE DEPENDABILITY PEOPLE™

promote the idea of bargains and large savings, while stinting on service and on-the-floor sales assistance.

PLACE DECISION. Like real estate agents, retailers are accustomed to saying that the three keys to success are "location, location, and location." For example, customers primarily choose the nearest bank and gas station. Department-store chains, oil companies, and fast-food franchisers must exercise great care in selecting locations. The problem breaks down into selecting regions of the country in which to open outlets, then particular cities, and then particular sites. A supermarket chain, for example, might decide to operate in the Midwest and Southeast; within the Midwest, in the cities and suburbs of Chicago, Milwaukee, and Indianapolis; and within the Chicago region, in 14 locations, mostly suburban. Two of the savviest location experts in recent years have been the off-price retailer T. J. Maxx and toy-store giant Toys "Я" Us. Both retailers put the majority of their new locations in areas with rapidly growing numbers of young families. The undisputed winner in the "place race" is Wal-Mart, whose strategy of being the first mass merchandiser to locate in small and rural markets has been one of the key factors in its phenomenal success.

Large retailers must wrestle with the problem of whether to locate several small stores in many locations or a few large stores in fewer locations. Generally speaking, the retailer should locate enough stores in each city or region to gain promotion and distribution economies. The larger the individual stores, the greater their trading area or reach.

Retailers have a choice of locating their stores in the central business district, a regional shopping center, a community shopping center, a shopping strip, or within a larger store.

- *Central business districts* represent the oldest and most heavily trafficked city area, often known as "downtown." Store and office rents are normally high. But a number of downtowns, such as Detroit's, have been hit by a flight to the suburbs. The result has been a deterioration of downtown retailing facilities, with the remaining retailers catering to a lower-income group of shoppers.

- *Regional shopping centers* are large suburban malls containing 40 to over 200 stores. They usually draw customers from a five-mile to twenty-mile radius. Typically, the malls feature one or two nationally known anchor stores, such as J. C. Penney or Lord & Taylor, and a great number of smaller stores, many under franchise operation. Malls are attractive because of generous parking, one-stop shopping, restaurants, and recreational facilities. Successful malls charge high rents and may get a share of the mall stores' profits.

- *Community shopping centers* are smaller malls with typically one anchor store and between 20 and 40 smaller stores.

- *Strip malls* (also called *shopping strips*) contain a cluster of stores, usually housed in one long building, serving a neighborhood's normal needs for groceries, hardware, laundry, and gasoline. They usually serve people within a five-minute to ten-minute driving range.

- *A location within a larger store* describes a growing phenomenon in which certain well-known retailers—McDonald's, Starbucks, Nathan's, Dunkin' Donuts—are locating new, smaller units as concession space within larger stores or operations, such as airports, schools, Wal-Marts, and Caldors.

In view of the relationship between high traffic and high rents, retailers must decide on the most advantageous locations for their outlets. They can use a variety of methods to assess locations, including traffic counts, surveys of consumer shopping habits, and analysis of competitive locations.[13] Several models for site location have also been formulated.[14]

Retailers can assess a particular store's sales effectiveness by looking at four indicators:

1. Number of people passing by on an average day
2. Percentage who enter the store
3. Percentage of those entering who buy
4. Average amount spent per sale

A store might be doing poorly for several reasons: It is in a poorly trafficked location, not enough passersby drop in, too many drop-ins browse but do not buy, or the buyers do not buy very much. Each problem can be remedied. Poor traffic is remedied by a better location; drop-ins are increased by better window displays and sales announcements; and the number buying and the amount purchased are largely a function of merchandise quality, prices, and personal selling.

Trends in Retailing

At this point, we can summarize the main developments that retailers need to take into account as they plan their competitive strategies:

NEW RETAIL FORMS. New retail forms constantly emerge to threaten established retail forms. A New York bank will deliver money to its important customers' offices or homes. Adelphi College offers "commuter train classroom education" in which businesspeople commuting between Long Island and Manhattan can earn credits toward an M.B.A. degree. American Bakeries started Hippopotamus Food Stores to allow customers to buy institutional-size packages at savings of 10 to 30 percent. One "new" and very lucrative form of retailing is actually a revival of the oldest form of retailing: pushcart peddlers:

PUSHCARTS AT THE MALL OF AMERICA In 1992 Shawna and Randy Heniger abandoned comfortable jobs with the Internal Revenue Service and moved from their home in Salt Lake City to sell refrigerator magnets and personalized key chains from peddler's carts at the Mall of America. Most of their friends thought the Henigers were crazy. Yet, it wasn't long before the Henigers' carts were grossing as much as $40,000 a month, and they moved from carts to a store in the mall. Looking for new ways to lure shoppers, malls have turned pushcarts into a multibillion-dollar retailing niche. Three fourths of the nation's major malls now have carts selling everything from casual ware to condoms, and the carts are also found in high-traffic urban areas such as New York's Grand Central Station. Successful carts average $30,000 to $40,000 a month in sales and can easily top $70,000 in December. With an average startup cost of only $3,000, pushcarts are a way for budding entrepreneurs to test their retailing dreams without a major cash investment. They are also providing a way for malls to bring in more mom-and-pop and trendy retailers, showcase seasonal merchandise, and prospect for permanent retailer tenants.

SHORTENING RETAIL LIFE CYCLES. New retail forms are facing a shortening life span. They are rapidly copied and quickly lose their novelty.

NONSTORE RETAILING. The electronic age has significantly increased the growth of nonstore retailing. Consumers receive sales offers over their televisions, computers, and telephones to which they can immediately respond by calling a toll-free number or via computer.

INCREASING INTERTYPE COMPETITION. Competition today is increasingly intertype, or between different types of outlets. Thus we see competition between store and nonstore retailers. Discount stores, catalog showrooms, and department stores all compete for the same consumers.

The competition between chain superstores and smaller independently owned stores has become particularly heated. Because of their bulk buying power, chains get more favorable terms than the independents, and the chain outlets' increased square footage allows them to put in such amenities as cafés and bathrooms for their customers. In many locations, the arrival of a superstore has forced nearby independents out of business. In the bookselling business, for example, Barnes and Noble superstores and Borders Books and Music have sometimes located within blocks of independent bookstores, resulting in struggles or eventually in closings for those smaller stores.

Yet the news is not all bad for smaller companies. Many small independent retailers are thriving. Independents are finding that sheer size and marketing muscle are often no match for the personal touch small stores can provide or the specialty niches that small stores can fill for a devoted customer base.

POLARITY OF RETAILING. Increasing intertype competition has produced retailers positioning themselves on extreme ends of the number of product lines carried. High profitability and growth have been achieved both by mass merchandisers like Kmart and specialty stores like Radio Shack.

GIANT RETAILERS. Superpower retailers are emerging. Through their superior information systems and buying power, these giant retailers are able to offer strong price savings to consumers.[15] (For more on this topic, see the Marketing Insight on page 582 titled "Superpower Retailers Are Riding High.")

CHANGING DEFINITION OF ONE-STOP SHOPPING. Department stores like Sears and Macy's used to be prized for their one-stop shopping convenience. Gradually, department stores gave way to malls, which feature a wide range of specialty stores and plenty of parking space. Now specialty stores within malls are becoming increasingly competitive with large department stores in offering one-stop shopping. In addition, supercenters that combine grocery items with a huge selection of nonfood merchandise (such as those owned by Kmart and Wal-Mart) may begin edging out malls as the one-stop shopper's dream.

GROWTH OF VERTICAL MARKETING SYSTEMS. Marketing channels are increasingly becoming professionally managed and programmed. As large corporations extend their control over marketing channels, independent small stores are being squeezed out. (See Chapter 18 for a review of vertical marketing systems and their advantages.)

PORTFOLIO APPROACH. Retail organizations are increasingly designing and launching new store formats targeted to different lifestyle groups. They are not sticking to one format, such as department stores, but are moving into a mix of businesses that appears promising.

GROWING IMPORTANCE OF RETAIL TECHNOLOGY. Retail technologies are becoming critically important as competitive tools. Progressive retailers are using computers to produce better forecasts, control inventory costs, order electronically from suppliers, send electronic mail between stores, and even sell to customers within stores. They are adopting checkout scanning systems,[16] electronic funds transfer, electronic data interchange,[17] in-store television, and improved merchandise-handling systems.

One innovative scanning system now in use is the shopper scanner, a radar-like system that counts store traffic. When a New Jersey Saks Fifth Avenue used one such system, ShopperTrak, it learned that there was a shopper surge between the hours of 11 A.M. and 3 P.M. To better handle the shopper flow, the store varied lunch hours for its counter clerks. Pier One Imports uses the same system to test, among other things, the impact of newspaper ads on store traffic. By combining traffic and sales data, retailers say they can find out how well the store converts browsers into buyers.[18]

GLOBAL EXPANSION OF MAJOR RETAILERS. Retailers with unique formats and strong brand positioning are increasingly moving into other countries.[19] Over the years, several giant U.S. retailers—McDonald's, The Limited, The Gap, Toys "Я" Us—have become globally prominent as a result of their great marketing prowess.

Due to mature and saturated markets at home, many more U.S. retailers are actively pursuing overseas markets to boost profits. However, retailers in the United States are still significantly behind Europe and the Far East when it comes to global expansion. Only 18% of the top U.S. retailers operate globally, compared to

Superpower Retailers Are Riding High

Retailers such as Wal-Mart, Toys "Я" Us, Circuit City Stores, Target Stores, Home Depot, and Costco are striking terror into the hearts of their competitors and their suppliers. These superpower retailers are using sophisticated marketing information and logistical systems to deliver good service and immense volumes of product at appealing prices to masses of consumers. They are crowding out smaller manufacturers and retailers in the process. Whereas total retailing is growing at about 5.25% annually, the sales of superpower retailers are growing at rates between 15 and 47 percent.

As a result of their size and sales volume, the superpower retailers believe they are in a better position than manufacturers to determine what customers want. Many of them are now telling even the most powerful manufacturers what to make, in what sizes, colors, and packaging; how to price and promote the goods; when and how to ship them; and even how to reorganize and improve their production and management. The manufacturers have little choice but to meet these demands. If they do not, they will cut themselves out of a possible 10% to 30% of the market. They know that their competitors are eagerly waiting in the wings to replace them. So they have to accept a much thinner profit margin for the sake of moving massive volumes through the super retailers.

And the manufacturers may also have to accommodate many other demands from the super retailers. Costco (a warehouse club giant) demands special package sizes. Home Depot (the giant home-improvement chain) requires lumber companies to place bar-code stickers on every piece of wood. Toys "Я" Us—the nation's largest toy retailer—gets exclusives such as a Barbie for President doll from Mattel. In addition, giant retailers often fine manufacturers for defective goods and late deliveries. They also demand special discounts for new store openings and other occasions.

All of these developments are revolutionizing the retail scene. Large manufacturers are now working more closely with the super retailers to meet their needs. For example, P&G now has a special liaison team of 70 employees working with Wal-Mart. In developing a new line of power tools, Black & Decker solicited Home Depot's advice on the name, color, and warranty to be sure that Home Depot found the line acceptable. Borden decided to collapse its eight sales organizations into one after Wal-Mart complained about having to deal with 28 different Borden people in ordering from Borden.

In addition, the number of small manufacturers is shrinking as a consequence of giant retailism. The giant retailers prefer to deal with fewer suppliers and prefer the larger ones. Small retailers don't have the budgets to meet demands for customized products and packages, to invest in electronic linkups, to make frequent delivery, or to advertise their brand names heavily. Those small manufacturers who do get into Wal-Marts and Kmarts make it big but find that they have to expand their investment and quality continuously and drop their prices. Many times so much of their business is dedicated to one retailer that they are extremely vulnerable. For example, Murray Becker Industries, which supplied 80% of its framed pictures to Kmart, sued Kmart for $2 million in damages on the grounds that it was wrongfully terminated.

Smaller retailers face particularly deadly competition from the superpowers. This is especially true of competition from "category killers," retailers that concentrate on a single product category—Toys "Я" Us (toys), Home Depot (home improvement), Circuit City Stores (electronics), Office Depot (business supplies). The category killers avoid large shopping centers and locate instead in accessible but less expensive facilities, offering low prices and wide selections. They end up grabbing a lion's share of retailing in the specific product category and force a reduction in the number of manufacturers. As a result of Toys "Я" Us controlling 20% of toy retailing, today six toy manufacturers dominate the industry, where ten years ago no toy manufacturer controlled more than 5 percent.

The consumers benefit from all of this, of course. The giant retailers' relentless drive for efficiency leads to savings passed on to consumers in the form of lower prices and better service. For example, Wal-Mart is able to price lower than Sears because its operating and selling expenses are 15% compared to 28% for Sears.

40% of European retailers and 31% of Far Eastern retailers. Among foreign retailers that have gone global are Britain's Marks and Spencer, Italy's Benetton, France's Carrefour hypermarkets, Sweden's Ikea home furnishings stores, and Japan's Yaohan supermarkets.[20] Marks and Spencer, which started out as a penny bazaar in 1884, grew into a chain of variety stores over the decades and now has a thriving string of 150 franchised stores around the world, which sell mainly its private-label clothes. It also runs a major food business. Benetton, often in the news due to its controversial and risqué advertising (see Chapter 21), remains one of the world's fastest expanding retailers with predicted sales of $2.5 billion in 1997. Ikea's well-constructed but fairly inexpensive furniture has proven very popular in the United States, where shoppers often spend an entire day in an Ikea store.

RETAIL STORES AS COMMUNITY CENTERS OR "HANGOUTS." With the rise in the number of people living alone, working at home, or living in isolated and sprawling suburbs, there has been a marked resurgence of establishments that, regardless of the product or service they offer, also provide a place for people to congregate. These places include cafés, tea shops, juice bars, bookshops, superstores, children's playspaces, brew pubs, and urban greenmarkets. Denver's two Tattered Covered Bookstores host more than 250 events annually, from folk dancing to women's meetings. Brew pubs such as New York's Zip City Brewing and Seattle's Trolleyman Pub (run by Red Hook Brewery) offer tastings and a place to pass the time. The Discovery Zone, a chain of children's play spaces, offers indoor spaces where kids can go wild without breaking anything and stressed-out parents can exchange stories. And, of course, there are the now-ubiquitous coffee houses and espresso bars, such as Starbucks, whose numbers have grown from 2,500 in 1989 to a forecasted 10,000 by 1999.[21]

WHOLESALING

❖ **WHOLESALING** includes all the activities involved in selling goods or services to those who buy for resale or business use. Wholesaling excludes manufacturers and farmers because they are engaged primarily in production, and it excludes retailers.

Wholesalers (also called *distributors*) differ from retailers in a number of ways. First, wholesalers pay less attention to promotion, atmosphere, and location because they are dealing with business customers rather than final consumers. Second, wholesale transactions are usually larger than retail transactions, and wholesalers usually cover a larger trade area than retailers. Third, the government deals with wholesalers and retailers differently in regard to legal regulations and taxes.

Why are wholesalers used at all? Manufacturers could bypass them and sell directly to retailers or final consumers. In general, wholesalers are used when they are more efficient in performing one or more of the following functions:

- *Selling and promoting:* Wholesalers provide a sales force that helps manufacturers reach many small business customers at a relatively low cost. Wholesalers have more contacts, and often buyers trust wholesalers more than they trust the distant manufacturer.

- *Buying and assortment building:* Wholesalers are able to select items and build the assortments their customers need, thus saving the customers considerable work.

- *Bulk breaking:* Wholesalers achieve savings for their customers through buying in large carload lots and breaking the bulk into smaller units.

- *Warehousing:* Wholesalers hold inventories, thereby reducing the inventory costs and risks to suppliers and customers.

- ◆ *Transportation:* Wholesalers can often provide quicker delivery to buyers because they are closer to the buyers than the manufacturer is.
- ◆ *Financing:* Wholesalers finance their customers by granting credit, and they finance their suppliers by ordering early and paying their bills on time.
- ◆ *Risk bearing:* Wholesalers absorb some risk by taking title and bearing the cost of theft, damage, spoilage, and obsolescence.
- ◆ *Market information:* Wholesalers supply information to their suppliers and customers regarding competitors' activities, new products, price developments, and so on.
- ◆ *Management services and counseling:* Wholesalers often help retailers improve their operations by training their sales clerks, helping with stores' layouts and displays, and setting up accounting and inventory-control systems. They may help their industrial customers by offering training and technical services.

The Growth and Types of Wholesaling

Wholesaling has grown in the United States at a compound growth rate of 5.8% over the past 10 years.[22] A number of factors have contributed to wholesaling's growth: the growth of larger factories located some distance from the principal buyers; the occurrence of production in advance of orders rather than in response to specific orders; an increase in the number of levels of intermediate producers and users; and the increasing need for adapting products to the needs of intermediate and final users in terms of quantities, packages, and forms. There are four types of wholesalers: *merchant wholesalers, brokers and agents, manufacturers' and retailers' branches and offices,* and *miscellaneous wholesalers.* Their functions are summarized in Table 19-6 on pages 586–587.

Wholesaler Marketing Decisions

Wholesaler-distributors have experienced mounting competitive pressures in recent years. They have faced new sources of competition, demanding customers, new technologies, and more direct-buying programs by large industrial, institutional, and retail buyers. As a result, they have had to develop appropriate strategic responses. One major drive has been to increase asset productivity by managing their inventories and receivables better. And they have had to improve their strategic decisions on target markets, product assortment and services, pricing, promotion, and place.

TARGET-MARKET DECISION. Wholesalers need to define their target markets and not try to serve everyone. They can choose a target group of customers according to size criteria (e.g., only large retailers), type of customer (e.g., convenience food stores only), need for service (e.g., customers who need credit), or other criteria. Within the target group, they can identify the most profitable customers and design stronger offers to build better relationships with them. They can propose automatic reordering systems, set up management-training and advisory systems, and even sponsor a voluntary chain. They can discourage less profitable customers by requiring larger orders or adding surcharges to smaller ones.

PRODUCT-ASSORTMENT-AND-SERVICES DECISION. The wholesalers' "product" is their assortment. Wholesalers are under great pressure to carry a full line and maintain sufficient stock for immediate delivery. But the costs of carrying huge inventories can kill profits. Wholesalers today are reexamining how many lines to carry and are choosing to carry only the more profitable ones. They are also examining which services count most in building strong customer relationships and which ones should be dropped or charged for. The key is to find a distinct mix of services valued by their customers.

PRICING DECISION. Wholesalers usually mark up the cost of goods by a conventional percentage, say 20%, to cover their expenses. Expenses may run 17% of the gross margin, leaving a profit margin of approximately 3 percent. In grocery wholesaling, the average profit margin is often less than 2 percent. Wholesalers are beginning to experiment with new approaches to pricing. They might cut their margin on some lines in order to win important new customers. They will ask suppliers for a special price break when they can turn it into an opportunity to increase the supplier's sales.

PROMOTION DECISION. Wholesalers rely primarily on their sales force to achieve promotional objectives. Even here, most wholesalers see selling as a single salesperson talking to a single customer instead of a team effort to sell, build, and service major accounts. However, wholesalers would benefit from adopting some of the image-making techniques used by retailers. They need to develop an overall promotion strategy involving trade advertising, sales promotion, and publicity. They also need to make greater use of supplier promotion materials and programs.

PLACE DECISION. In the past, wholesalers typically located in low-rent, low-tax areas and put little money into their physical setting and offices. Often the materials-handling systems and order-processing systems lagged behind the available technologies. Today progressive wholesalers have been improving materials-handling procedures and costs by developing *automated warehouses*. For example, McKesson, the world's largest pharmaceuticals distributor, has supplied independent pharmacies with computer terminals for ordering. Orders sent in by pharmacists are filled in five seconds. A blue plastic shipping box slips onto a conveyor system in one of McKesson's warehouses, and the computerized system automatically selects the right items, creates an itemized invoice, seals the box, and conveys it to a waiting truck, which then delivers the order overnight with 100% accuracy. The system also automatically orders replenishment stock from the drug manufacturers.[23] As another example, Grainger, a major industrial distributor, developed a local inventory-inquiry system to connect its 188 distribution branches. A Grainger branch can quickly determine whether items not in stock are available in another branch. This system has greatly reduced customer-response time and boosted sales.

Trends in Wholesaling

Manufacturers always have the option of bypassing wholesalers or of replacing inefficient wholesalers with better ones. Manufacturers' major complaints against wholesalers are as follows: They do not aggressively promote the manufacturer's product line, acting more like order takers; they do not carry enough inventory and therefore fail to fill customers' orders fast enough; they do not supply the manufacturer with up-to-date market, customer, and competitive information; they do not attract high-caliber managers and bring down their own costs; and they charge too much for their services.

The most successful wholesaler-distributors are those who adapt their services to meet their suppliers' and target customers' changing needs. They recognize that the rationale for their existence comes from adding value to the channel. They are constantly improving their services and/or reducing their operating costs by

TABLE 19-6	MAJOR WHOLESALER TYPES
TYPE	**DESCRIPTION**
MERCHANT WHOLESALERS	Independently owned businesses that take title to the merchandise they handle. In different trades they are called *jobbers, distributors,* or *mill supply houses.* They fall into two categories: full-service wholesalers and limited-service wholesalers.
FULL-SERVICE WHOLESALERS	Provide a full line of services: carrying stock, maintaining a sales force, offering credit, making deliveries, and providing management assistance. There are two types of full-service wholesalers: wholesale merchants and industrial distributors.
Wholesale merchants	Sell primarily to retailers and provide a full range of services. *General-merchandise wholesalers* carry several merchandise lines, while *general-line wholesalers* carry one or two lines in greater depth. *Specialty wholesalers* specialize in carrying only part of a line. (Example: health-food wholesalers, seafood wholesalers)
Industrial distributors	Sell to manufacturers rather than to retailers. Provide several services, such as carrying stock, offering credit, and providing delivery. May carry a broad range of merchandise, a general line, or a specialty line.
LIMITED-SERVICE WHOLESALERS	Offer fewer services to their suppliers and customers than full-service wholesalers. Limited-service wholesalers are of several types: cash-and-carry wholesalers, truck wholesalers, drop shippers, rack jobbers, producers' cooperatives, and mail-order wholesalers.
Cash-and-carry wholesalers	Have a limited line of fast moving goods and sell to small retailers for cash. Normally do not deliver.
Truck wholesalers	Perform primarily a selling and delivery function. Carry a limited line of semiperishable merchandise (such as milk, bread, snack foods), which they sell for cash as they make their rounds of supermarkets, small groceries, hospitals, restaurants, factory cafeterias, and hotels.
Drop shippers	Operate in bulk industries, such as coal, lumber, and heavy equipment. Do not carry inventory or handle the product. Upon receiving an order, they select a manufacturer, who ships the merchandise directly to the customer on the agreed-upon terms and time of delivery. The drop shipper assumes title and risk from the time the order is accepted to its delivery to the customer.
Rack jobbers	Serve grocery and drug retailers, mostly in the area of nonfood items. They send delivery trucks to stores, and the delivery people set up toys, paperbacks, hardware items, health and beauty aids, and so on. They price the goods, keep them fresh, set up point-of-purchase displays, and keep inventory records. Rack jobbers retain title to the goods and bill the retailers only for the goods sold to consumers. They do little promotion because they carry many branded items that are highly advertised.
Producers' cooperatives	Owned by farmer members and assemble farm produce to sell in local markets. The co-op's profits are distributed to members at the end of the year. They often attempt to improve product quality and promote a co-op brand name, such as Sun Maid raisins, Sunkist oranges, or Diamond walnuts.
Mail-order wholesalers	Send catalogs to retail, industrial, and institutional customers featuring jewelry, cosmetics, specialty foods, and other small items. Main customers are businesses in small outlying areas. No sales force is maintained to call on customers. Orders are filled and sent by mail, truck, or other efficient means of transportation.
BROKERS AND AGENTS	Do not take title to goods, and perform only a few functions. Main function is to facilitate buying and selling, for which they earn a commission of 2% to 6% of the selling price. Generally specialize by product line or customer types.

TYPE	DESCRIPTION
BROKERS	Their chief function is bringing buyers and sellers together and assisting in negotiation. They are paid by the party who hired them, and do not carry inventory, get involved in financing, or assume risk. The most familiar examples are food brokers, real-estate brokers, insurance brokers, and security brokers.
AGENTS	Represent either buyers or sellers on a more permanent basis than brokers do. There are several types: manufacturer's agents, selling agents, purchasing agents, and commission merchants.
Manufacturers' agents	Represent two or more manufacturers of complementary lines. They enter into a formal written agreement with each manufacturer covering pricing policy, territories, order-handling procedure, delivery service and warranties, and commission rates. They know each manufacturer's product line and use their wide contacts to sell the manufacturer's products. Often used in such lines as apparel, furniture, and electrical goods. Most manufacturers' agents are small businesses, with only a few employees, who are skilled salespeople. They are hired by small manufacturers who cannot afford to maintain their own field sales forces, and by large manufacturers who want to use agents to open new territories or to represent them in territories that cannot support full-time salespeople.
Selling agents	Have contractual authority to sell a manufacturer's entire output. The manufacturer either is not interested in the selling function or feels unqualified. The selling agent serves as a sales department and has significant influence over prices, terms, and conditions of sale. Selling agents normally have no territorial limits. They are found in such product areas as textiles, industrial machinery and equipment, coal and coke, chemicals, and metals.
Purchasing agents	Generally have a long-term relationship with buyers and make purchases for them, often receiving, inspecting, warehousing, and shipping the merchandise to the buyers. They provide helpful market information to clients and help them obtain the best goods and prices available.
Commission merchants	Take physical possession of products and negotiate sales. Normally, they are not employed on a long-term basis. They are used most often in agricultural marketing by farmers who do not want to sell their own output and do not belong to producers' cooperatives. A commission merchant takes a truckload of commodities to a central market, sells it for the best price, deducts a commission and expenses, and remits the balance to the producer.
MANUFACTURERS' AND RETAILERS' BRANCHES AND OFFICES	Wholesaling operations conducted by sellers or buyers themselves rather than through independent wholesalers. Separate branches and offices can be dedicated to either sales or purchasing.
SALES BRANCHES AND OFFICES	Sales branches and offices are set up by manufacturers to improve inventory control, selling, and promotion. *Sales branches* carry inventory and are found in such industries as lumber and automotive equipment and parts. *Sales offices* do not carry inventory and are most prominent in dry-goods and notions industries.
PURCHASING OFFICES	Perform a role similar to that of brokers or agents but are part of the buyer's organization. Many retailers set up purchasing offices in major market centers such as New York and Chicago.
MISCELLANEOUS WHOLESALERS	A few specialized types of wholesalers are found in certain sectors of the economy. These include agricultural assemblers (which buy the agricultural output of many farms), petroleum bulk plants and terminals (which consolidate the petroleum output of many wells), and auction companies (which auction cars, equipments, and so forth, to dealers and other businesses).

Managing Retailing,
Wholesaling, and
Market Logistics

investing in more advanced materials-handling technology and information systems. The Marketing Memo titled "Strategies of High-Performance Wholesaler-Distributors" outlines some of the strategies used by successful wholesale organizations.

Narus and Anderson interviewed leading industrial distributors and identified four ways they strengthened their relationships with manufacturers:

1. They sought a clear agreement with their manufacturers about their expected functions in the marketing channel.
2. They gained insight into the manufacturers' requirements by visiting their plants and attending manufacturer association conventions and trade shows.
3. They fulfilled their commitments to the manufacturer by meeting the volume targets, promptly paying their bills, and feeding back customer information to their manufacturers.
4. They identified and offered value-added services to help their suppliers.[24]

As the thriving wholesaling industry moves into the next century, it faces considerable challenges. The industry remains vulnerable to one of the most enduring trends of the 1990s—fierce resistance to price increases and the winnowing out of suppliers based on cost and quality. The trend toward vertical integration, in which manufacturers try to control their market share by owning the intermediaries that bring their goods to market, is still strong. In the health care sector, for instance, drug makers have purchased drug-distribution and pharmacy-management companies. This trend began in 1993 when drug-industry behemoth Merck acquired Medco Containment Services, a drug-benefits manager and mail-order distributor. The surviving wholesaler-distributors in this sector and in others will be bigger and will provide more services for their customers.[25]

MARKET LOGISTICS

The process of getting goods to customers has traditionally been called *physical distribution*. Physical distribution starts at the factory. Managers try to choose a set of warehouses (stocking points) and transportation carriers that will deliver produced goods to final destinations in the desired time and/or at the lowest total cost.

Recently, physical distribution has been expanded into the broader concept of *supply chain management*. Supply chain management starts earlier than physical distribution, attempting to procure the right inputs (raw materials, components, and capital equipment); convert them efficiently into finished products; and dispatch them to the final destinations. An even broader perspective calls for studying how the company's suppliers themselves obtain their inputs all the way back to the raw materials. The supply chain perspective can help a company identify superior suppliers and help them improve their productivity in the supply chain, which ultimately would bring down the company's costs.

Unfortunately, the supply chain view sees the markets as only a destination point. The company would be more effective by considering its target market's requirement first and then designing the supply chain backward from that point. This modern view is at the heart of today's *market logistics* systems, and it leads to an examination of the supply chain as the *demand chain*. Here are some examples of products that can benefit or have benefited from demand chain thinking:

MARKETING MEMO

STRATEGIES OF HIGH-PERFORMANCE WHOLESALER-DISTRIBUTORS

McCammon, Lusch, and their colleagues studied 97 high-performance wholesaler-distributors to uncover their core strategies for gaining a sustained competitive advantage. The study identified the following 12 core strategies:

1. *Mergers and acquisitions:* At least a third of the sampled wholesalers made new acquisitions aimed at entering new markets, strengthening their position in existing markets, and/or diversifying or vertically integrating.

2. *Asset redeployment:* At least 20 of the 97 wholesalers sold or liquidated one or more marginal operations in order to strengthen their core businesses.

3. *Corporate diversification:* Several wholesalers diversified their portfolio of businesses in order to reduce their firm's exposure to the business cycle.

4. *Vertical integration:* Several wholesalers increased their vertical integration in order to improve their margins.

5. *Proprietary brands:* A third of the companies increased their private-brand programs.

6. *Expansion into international markets:* At least 26 wholesalers operated on a multinational basis and planned to increase their penetration into Western Europe and East Asia.

7. *Value-added services:* Most wholesalers increased their value-added services, adding such services as emergency delivery, customized packaging operations, and computerized management information systems. McKesson, the large drug wholesaler, established direct computer links with 32 drug manufacturers, a computerized accounts-receivable program for pharmacists, and computer terminals for drugstores to be used for ordering inventories.

8. *Systems selling:* More wholesalers offered turnkey merchandising programs to their buyers, posing a threat to those wholesalers who remain off-the-shelf suppliers and provide fewer services. In a turnkey program, everything is set to make life easy for the dealer—in essence, all the dealer needs to do is "turn the key" and open his door for business.

9. *Strategies to attract new customers:* Some wholesalers spotted new customer groups and created new turnkey merchandising programs for them.

10. *Niche marketing:* To satisfy special markets neglected by larger competitors, some wholesalers have specialized in one or few product categories, carrying extensive inventories, maintaining high service, and promising rapid delivery.

11. *Multiplex marketing:* Multiplex marketing occurs when firms manage to simultaneously serve multiple market segments in a cost-effective and competitively superior way. Several wholesalers have added new market segments to their core segments, hoping to achieve larger economies of scale and competitive strength. For example, some drug wholesalers, in addition to serving hospitals, have created programs for doctor clinics, pharmacies, and health maintenance organizations.

12. *New distribution technologies:* High-performance wholesalers have improved their systems for computerized order entry, inventory control, and warehouse automation. In addition, they are making increased use of direct-response marketing and telemarketing.

Source: See Bert McCammon, Robert F. Lusch, Deborah S. Coykendall, and James M. Kenderdine, *Wholesaling in Transition* (Norman: University of Oklahoma, College of Business Administration, 1989).

◆ A software company normally sees its challenge as producing and packaging software disks and manuals, then shipping them to wholesalers—who ship them to retailers, who sell them to customers. The customers bring the software package to their home or office and spend time downloading the software onto their hard drive. Market logistics would raise the question of whether customers could be served better. There are at least two superior delivery systems. The first calls for customers to dial the software company's phone number to order and pay for the software, which will be downloaded over the telephone lines onto the customer's hard drive. Alternatively, popular software (such as Windows 95 or Lotus 1-2-3) could be loaded onto a computer at the computer factory when customers order a new computer. Both solutions eliminate the need for printing, packaging, shipping, and stocking millions of disks and manuals.

The same solutions are available for distributing music, newspapers, video games, films, and other products that deliver voice, text, data, and/or images. The consumer can phone and ask to listen to a sample of music and then order it downloaded. Today customers can order a customized version of *The Wall Street Journal* to arrive each morning on their computers, featuring only articles on topics in which they have specified an interest.

◆ At one time, German consumers purchased individual bottles of soft drinks. A soft-drink manufacturer surveyed German consumers about whether they would be willing to buy six bottles at a time in a six-pack. Consumers responded positively. Retailers also responded positively because the bottles could be loaded faster on the shelves, and more bottles would be purchased per occasion. The manufacturer designed the six-packs to fit on the store shelves. Then cases and pallets were designed for bringing these six-packs efficiently to the store's receiving rooms. Factory operations were redesigned to produce the new six-packs. The purchasing department let out bids for the new needed materials. Once the new six-packs hit the market, the manufacturer's market share rose substantially.

◆ Ingvar Kamprad, the founder of the Ikea furniture retailing chain, found a way to deliver good-quality furniture at a much lower cost than competitors'. Ikea's cost savings stem from several sources: (1) The company buys such large volumes of furniture that it gets lower prices, (2) the furniture is designed in "knockdown" form and therefore shipped flat at a much lower transportation cost, (3) the customer drives the furniture home, which saves delivery cost, (4) the customer rather than the store assembles the furniture, and (5) Ikea works on a low markup and high volume, in contrast to many of its competitors. Altogether, Ikea can charge 20% less than its competitors for comparable furniture.

Demand chain thinking can lead to ideas that raise productivity. Consider a company that manufactures washing machines, such as Whirlpool. In a traditional system, Whirlpool would forecast the retail demand for each washing machine in its line. It would set up a production schedule and produce enough washing machines each period to fill the pipeline (i.e., factory, warehouses, distribution centers, and retailers). Whirlpool would then hope that the expected demand occurs. If it does not, Whirlpool will bear a high inventory carrying cost.

A better approach—one centered on demand chain thinking—would consist of Whirlpool asking its dealers to carry only floor samples of its washing machines. The dealers would electronically report on a daily basis which machines and features have been ordered. Whirlpool would set its daily production schedule by the "demand pull" of these customer orders. Each washing machine would be produced within a few days and sent directly to the customer. This just-in-time system would greatly reduce the inventory costs that might result from poor forecasting. For this demand chain solution to work, the following ingredients are required:

1. Whirlpool is able to receive the latest information on orders placed at the retail level.

2. Whirlpool can produce and ship ordered washing machines within a few days. Here the key is for Whirlpool to produce the product in a modular fashion, leaving the customized features to be added last. The idea is to make 90% of the product in advance

and customize the last 10 percent. (For example, Benetton prepares its sweaters without color, and adds the colors last when it learns what colors are currently selling.)

3. The customer is willing to wait a few days for delivery.

Here, finally, is a definition of *market logistics:*

❖ **MARKET LOGISTICS** involves planning, implementing, and controlling the physical flows of materials and final goods from points of origin to points of use to meet customer requirements at a profit.

The task of companies managing value-added flows from suppliers to ultimate users involves coordinating the activities of suppliers, purchasing agents, manufacturers, marketers, channel members, and customers.

Information systems play a critical role in managing market logistics. Major gains in logistical efficiency have resulted from information technology advances, particularly computers, point-of-sale terminals, uniform product codes, satellite tracking, electronic data interchange (EDI), and electronic funds transfer (EFT). These developments have made it possible for companies to make or require promises such as "the product will be at dock 25 at 10 A.M. tomorrow," and controlling this promise through information. Wal-Mart was a pioneer in this area:

WAL-MART   Wal-Mart was one of the first retailers to make heavy investments in information technology. It equipped its stores with computerized scanning equipment for cash registers. This equipment enables Wal-Mart to know what customers are buying and therefore to tell manufacturers what to produce and where to ship the goods. Wal-Mart requires its suppliers to ship their goods tagged and hung, so that they can be moved directly into the store's selling space, thus reducing warehousing and data processing costs. As a result, Wal-Mart stores use only 10% of their space for goods storage, compared to the 25% average nonselling space in competitor stores. Another result of Wal-Mart's computerized ordering system is that Wal-Mart insists on linking its computers directly to its suppliers, bypassing brokers and other intermediaries. Suppliers such as Procter & Gamble, Kraft, and others are given the responsibility of making resupply decisions based on their access to Wal-Mart's information system. To discourage oversupply, Wal-Mart doesn't pay its suppliers until their products are sold.[26]

Another company that squeezes distribution costs is Benetton. The company operates only one distribution center in Castrette, Italy. Nicknamed "Big Charley," the huge center has enough robots to dispatch Benetton's latest fashions to any company store in 120 countries in 12 days—lightning speed in the apparel industry.[27]

Market logistics involves several activities (Figure 19-4 on the next page). The first is sales forecasting, on the basis of which the company schedules distribution, production, and inventory levels. The production plans indicate the materials that the purchasing department must order. These materials arrive through inbound transportation, enter the receiving area, and are stored in raw-material inventory. Raw materials are converted into finished goods. Finished-goods inventory is the link between the customers' orders and the company's manufacturing activity. Customers' orders draw down the finished-goods inventory level, and manufacturing activity builds it up. Finished goods flow off the assembly line and pass through packaging, in-plant warehousing, shipping-room processing, outbound transportation, field warehousing, and customer delivery and servicing.

Management has become concerned about the total cost of market logistics, which can amount to 30 to 40% of the product's cost. In 1993, for instance, U.S. companies spent $670 billion—10.5% of GDP—to wrap, bundle, load, unload, sort, reload, and transport goods. The grocery industry alone thinks it can decrease its annual operating costs by 10%, or $30 billion, by revamping its market logistics. A typical box of breakfast cereal spends 104 days getting from factory to supermarket, chugging through a labyrinth of wholesalers, distributors, brokers, and consolidators.[28] With expensive inefficiencies like these, it's no wonder that ex-

Managing Retailing,
Wholesaling, and
Market Logistics

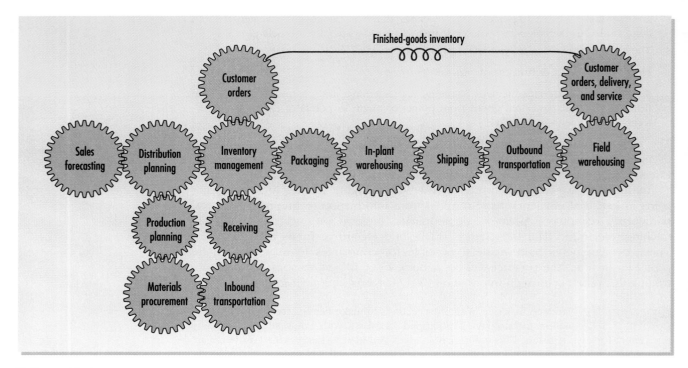

FIGURE 19-4

Major Activities Involved in Market Logistics

Source: Redrawn, with modifications, from Wendell M. Stewart, "Physical Distribution: Key to Improved Volume and Profits," *Journal of Marketing,* January 1965, p. 66.

perts call market logistics "the last frontier for cost economies." Lower market-logistics costs will permit lower prices, yield higher profit margins, or both.

Though the cost of market logistics can be high, a well-planned market-logistics program can be a potent tool in competitive marketing. Companies can attract additional customers by offering better service, faster cycle time, or lower prices through market-logistics improvements. Figure 19-5 shows an advertisement for Roadway Package System, which uses technology to add value to the customer at several stages of the delivery process.

What happens if a firm's market logistics are not set up properly? Companies lose customers when they fail to supply goods on time. Kodak made the mistake of launching its national advertising campaign for its new instant camera before it had delivered enough cameras to the stores. Customers found that it was not available and bought Polaroids instead. Laura Ashley found that it had to revamp its existing system, which was not getting its products to its Japanese stores quickly enough:

LAURA ASHLEY In the past, all the blouses made in Hong Kong for all the stores in the Laura Ashley chain were shipped to the company's distribution center in Wales. Then blouses ordered by a Tokyo store had to be located, repackaged, and sent all the way back to the Far East. Because of this roundabout supply chain, Laura Ashley often had full warehouses while its Japanese stores were sold out of 15 to 20% of the high-demand items. To reduce inefficiency and costs (and customer wrath), the company hired Federal Express to consult with Ashley's stores and determine how to structure, package, and ship orders. Now Laura Ashley's products go directly from the manufacturer to stores around the world, reducing distribution costs and speeding up the replenishment process.[29]

Market-Logistics Objectives

Many companies state their market-logistics objective as "getting the right goods to the right places at the right time for the least cost." Unfortunately, this objective provides little practical guidance. No market-logistics system can simultaneously maximize customer service and minimize distribution cost. Maximum customer service implies large inventories, premium transportation, and multiple warehouses, all of which raise market-logistics costs. Minimum market-logistics cost implies cheap transportation, low stocks, and few warehouses.

A company cannot achieve market-logistics efficiency by asking each market-logistics manager to minimize his or her own costs. Market-logistics costs interact and are often negatively related. For example:

> The traffic manager favors rail shipment over air shipment because rail reduces the company's freight bill. However, because the railroads are slower, rail shipment ties up working capital longer, delays customer payment, and might cause customers to buy from competitors who offer faster service.

> The shipping department uses cheap containers to minimize shipping costs. Cheaper containers lead to a high rate of damaged goods in transit and loss of customer goodwill.

> The inventory manager favors low inventories to reduce inventory cost. However, this policy increases stockouts, back orders, paperwork, special production runs, and high-cost fast-freight shipments.

Given that market-logistics activities involve strong trade-offs, decisions must be made on a total system basis.

The starting point for designing the market-logistics system is to study what the customers require and what competitors are offering. Customers are interested in on-time delivery, supplier willingness to meet emergency needs, careful handling of merchandise, the willingness of suppliers to take back defective goods and re-supply them quickly, and suppliers' willingness to carry inventory.

The company must then research the relative importance of these service out-puts. For example, service-repair time is very important to buyers of copying equipment. Xerox therefore developed a service-delivery standard that "can put a disabled machine anywhere in the continental United States back into operation within three hours after receiving the service request." Xerox then designed a service division of personnel, parts, and locations that would deliver on this promise.

The company must also take into account competitors' service standards. It will normally want to offer at least the same service level as competitors. But the objective is to maximize profits, not sales. The company has to look at the costs of providing higher levels of service. Some companies offer less service and charge a lower price. Other companies offer more service and charge a premium price.

The company ultimately has to establish market-logistics objectives to guide its planning. For example, Coca-Cola wants to "put Coke within an arm's length of desire." Some companies go even further, defining standards for each service factor.

> One appliance manufacturer has established the following service standards: to deliver at least 95% of the dealer's orders within seven days of order receipt, to fill the dealer's orders with 99% accuracy, to answer dealer inquiries on order status within three hours, and to ensure that damage to merchandise in transit does not exceed 1 percent.

Given the market-logistics objectives, the company must design a market-logistics system that will minimize the cost of achieving these objectives. Each possible market-logistics system will lead to the following cost:

$$M = T + FW + VW + S$$

where:

M = total market-logistics cost of proposed system
T = total freight cost of proposed system
FW = total fixed warehouse cost of proposed system
VW = total variable warehouse costs (including inventory) of proposed system
S = total cost of lost sales due to average delivery delay under proposed system

Choosing a market-logistics system calls for examining the total cost (M) associated with different proposed systems and selecting the system that minimizes it. If it is hard to measure S, the company should aim to minimize $T + FW + VW$ for a target level of customer service.

Market-Logistics Decisions

We will now examine the four major decisions that must be made with regard to market logistics: (1) How should orders be handled? (order processing); (2) Where should stocks be located? (warehousing); (3) How much stock should be held? (inventory); and (4) How should goods be shipped? (transportation).

ORDER PROCESSING. Market logistics begins with a customer order. Most companies today are trying to shorten the *order-to-remittance cycle*—that is, the elapsed time between the receipt of an order, delivery of the order, and payment for the order. This cycle involves many steps, including transmission of the order by the salesperson, order entry and customer credit check, inventory and production scheduling, order and invoice shipment, and receipt of payment. The longer this cycle takes, the lower the customer's satisfaction and the lower the company's profits.

Thanks to computers, companies are making great progress in speeding up order handling and payment cycles. For example:

GENERAL ELECTRIC General Electric operates an information system that checks the customer's credit standing upon receipt of an order, and determines whether and where the items are in stock. The computer issues an order to ship, bills the customer, updates the inventory records, sends a production order for new stock, and relays the message back to the sales representative that the customer's order is on its way—all in less than 15 seconds.

SARA LEE When Sara Lee developed sales teams (composed of sales managers, logistics managers, and marketing managers) to meet with one of its major retail customers, Target Stores, Target's managers made it clear how unhappy they were with Sara Lee's invoicing system. Invoices that should have been processed in one day were taking four to five days to process. As part of its "quick response" initiative, Sara Lee fixed the process so that Target can now process its invoices in six hours.[30]

WAREHOUSING. Every company has to store its finished goods until they are sold. A storage facility is necessary because production and consumption cycles rarely match. For example, many agricultural commodities are produced seasonally, but demand for them is continuous. The storage function helps to smooth discrepancies between desired quantities and timing to the market.

The company must decide on a desirable number of stocking locations. More stocking locations means that goods can be delivered to customers more quickly. But it also means higher warehousing costs. The number of stocking locations must strike a balance between customer service levels and distribution costs.

Some inventory is kept at or near the plant, and the rest is located in warehouses around the country. The company might own private warehouses and also rent space in public warehouses. *Storage warehouses* store goods for moderate-to-long periods of time. Sometimes companies can replace their storage warehouses with one central distribution warehouse. *Distribution warehouses* receive goods from various company plants and suppliers and move them out as soon as possible. For example, after National Semiconductor shut down its six storage warehouses and set up a central distribution warehouse in Singapore, its standard delivery time decreased by 47%, its distribution costs fell 2.5%, and its sales increased 34 percent.[31]

The older multistoried warehouses with slow elevators and inefficient materials-handling procedures are receiving competition from newer single-story *automated warehouses* with advanced materials-handling systems under the control of a central computer. The computer reads store orders and directs lift trucks and electric hoists to gather goods according to their bar codes, move them to loading docks, and issue invoices. These warehouses have reduced worker injuries, labor costs, pilferage, and breakage and have improved inventory control. When the Helene Curtis Company replaced its six antiquated warehouses with a new $32 million facility, it cut its distribution costs by 40 percent.[32]

Managing Retailing, Wholesaling, and Market Logistics

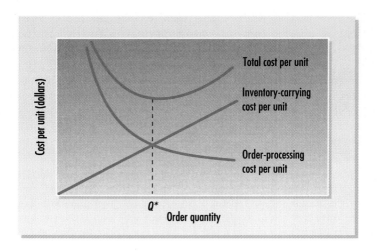

FIGURE 19-6
Determining Optimal Order Quantity

INVENTORY. Inventory levels represent a major market-logistics decision affecting customer satisfaction. Salespeople would like their companies to carry enough stock to fill all customer orders immediately. However, it is not cost effective for a company to carry this much inventory. *Inventory cost increases at an increasing rate as the customer service level approaches 100 percent.* Management would need to know by how much sales and profits would increase as a result of carrying larger inventories and promising faster order-fulfillment times, then make a decision accordingly.

Inventory decision making involves knowing when to order and how much to order. As inventory draws down, management must know at what stock level to place a new order. This stock level is called the *order (reorder) point.* An order point of 20 means reordering when the stock falls to 20 units. The order point should balance the risks of stockout against the costs of overstock.

The other decision is how much to order. The larger the quantity ordered, the less frequently an order has to be placed. The company needs to balance order-processing costs and inventory-carrying costs. *Order-processing* costs for a manufacturer consist of *setup costs* and *running costs* (operating costs when production is running) for the item. If setup costs are low, the manufacturer can produce the item often, and the average cost per item is stable and equal to the running costs. If setup costs are high, however, the manufacturer can reduce the average cost per unit by producing a long run and carrying more inventory.

Order-processing costs must be compared with *inventory-carrying costs.* The larger the average stock carried, the higher the inventory-carrying costs. These carrying costs include storage charges, cost of capital, taxes and insurance, and depreciation and obsolescence. Inventory-carrying costs might run as high as 30% of inventory value. This means that marketing managers who want their companies to carry larger inventories need to show that the larger inventories would produce incremental gross profit that would exceed incremental inventory-carrying costs.

The optimal order quantity can be determined by observing how order-processing costs and inventory-carrying costs sum up at different order levels. Figure 19-6 shows that the order-processing cost per unit decreases with the number of units ordered because the order costs are spread over more units. Inventory-carrying charges per unit increase with the number of units ordered because each unit remains longer in inventory. The two cost curves are summed vertically into a

596   PART 4

Planning
Marketing
Programs

total-cost curve. The lowest point on the total-cost curve is projected down on the horizontal axis to find the optimal order quantity, $Q*$.[33]

The growing interest in *just-in-time production methods* promises to change inventory-planning practices. Just-in-time production consists of arranging for supplies to come into the factory at the rate that they are needed. If the suppliers are dependable, then the manufacturer can carry much lower levels of inventory and still meet customer-order-fulfillment standards. Consider the following example:

TESCO   Tesco, the large British supermarket chain, has set up an innovative JIT market logistics system. Tesco's management wanted to greatly reduce costly backroom storage space. It accomplished this by arranging twice-a-day delivery of replenishment stock. Ordinarily it would have needed three separate trucks to deliver frozen goods, refrigerated goods, and regular goods on each trip. Instead, it designed new trucks with three compartments to carry the three types of goods.

For more on JIT, see Chapter 7.

TRANSPORTATION.   Marketers need to be concerned with their company's transportation decisions. Transportation choices will affect product pricing, on-time delivery performance, and the condition of the goods when they arrive, all of which will affect customer satisfaction.

In shipping goods to its warehouses, dealers, and customers, the company can choose among five transportation modes: rail, air, trucks, waterways, and pipelines. Shippers consider such criteria as speed, frequency, dependability, capability, availability, traceability, and cost. If a shipper seeks speed, air and truck are the prime contenders. If the goal is low cost, then water and pipeline are the prime contenders. Trucks stand high on most of the criteria.

Shippers are increasingly combining two or more transportation modes, thanks to containerization. *Containerization* consists of putting the goods in boxes or trailers that are easy to transfer between two transportation modes. *Piggyback* describes the use of rail and trucks; *fishyback*, water and trucks; *trainship*, water and rail; and *airtruck*, air and trucks. Each coordinated mode of transportation offers specific advantages to the shipper. For example, piggyback is cheaper than trucking alone, yet provides flexibility and convenience.

In deciding on transportation modes, shippers can choose from private, contract, and common carriers. If the shipper owns its own truck or air fleet, the shipper becomes a *private carrier*. A *contract carrier* is an independent organization selling transportation services to others on a contract basis. A *common carrier* provides services between predetermined points on a schedule basis and is available to all shippers at standard rates.

Transportation decisions must consider the complex trade-offs between various transportation modes and their implications for other distribution elements, such as warehousing and inventory. As transportation costs change over time, companies need to reanalyze their options in the search for optimal market-logistics arrangements.[34]

Organizational Lessons About Market Logistics

Experience with market logistics has taught executives several lessons. The first is that companies should appoint a senior vice-president to be the single point of contact for all logistical elements. This executive should be accountable for logistical performance on both cost criteria and customer-satisfaction criteria. The aim is to manage market logistics activities to create high customer satisfaction at a reasonable cost. Here are two examples:

Managing Retailing,
Wholesaling, and
Market Logistics

BURROUGHS The Burroughs Corporation organized the Distribution Services Department to centralize control over its market-logistics activities. This department reported to the marketing vice-president because of the great importance Burroughs attached to good customer service. Within two and one-half years following the reorganization, the company achieved savings of over $2 million annually (on $200 million of sales), plus a higher level of service to field branches and customers.

SEARS In 1993, Sears hired Lieutenant General William G. "Gus" Pagonis, the three-star general who managed the movement of troops and materials during Operation Desert Storm, as senior VP of market logistics. The hiring sent a clear signal that Sears views market logistics as critical in its fight to return to retailing success. Before this new leadership, Sears managed 50 regional distribution centers stocking inventory for home delivery of appliances and furniture. Today it carries its appliance inventory in only seven locations and has eliminated $300 million of inventory cost while also reducing stockouts by 70 percent.

Second, market logistics strategies must be derived from business strategies, rather than solely cost considerations. Third, the logistics system must be information intensive and establish electronic links among all the significant parties. Finally, the company should set its logistics goals to match or exceed competitors' service standards, and should involve members of all relevant teams in the logistical planning process.

SUMMARY

1. Retailing includes all the activities involved in selling goods or services directly to final consumers for their personal, nonbusiness use. Retailers can be classified in terms of store retailing, nonstore retailing, and retail organizations.

    Like products, retail-store types pass through stages of growth and decline. As existing stores offer more services to remain competitive, their costs and prices go up, which opens the door to new retail forms that offer a mix of merchandise and services at lower prices. The major types of retail stores are specialty stores; department stores; supermarkets; convenience stores; discount stores; off-price retailers (factory outlets, independent off-price retailers, and warehouse clubs); superstores (combination stores and hypermarkets); and catalog showrooms.

    Although the overwhelming majority of goods and services is sold through stores, nonstore retailing has been growing much faster than store retailing. The major types of nonstore retailing are direct selling (one-to-one selling, one-to-many/party selling, and multilevel/network marketing); direct marketing; automatic vending; and buying services.

    Although many retail stores are independently owned, an increasing number are falling under some form of corporate retailing. Retail organizations achieve many economies of scale, such as greater purchasing power, wider brand recognition, and better trained employees. The major types of corporate retailing are corporate chain stores, voluntary chains, retailer cooperatives, consumer cooperatives, franchise organizations, and merchandising conglomerates.

2. Like all marketers, retailers must prepare marketing plans that include decisions on target markets, product assortment and procurement, services and store atmosphere, price, promotion, and place. These decisions must take into account the major trends in retailing today: (1) the rise of new forms of retailing; (2) shortening retail life cycles; (3) the growth of nonstore retailing; (4) increasing competition among the different types of retailers; (5) the increased polarity of retailing, with retailers positioning themselves on extreme ends of the number of product lines carried; (6) the rise of superpower/giant retailers; (7) the changing definition of one-stop shopping; (8) the growth of vertical

marketing systems, with large corporations squeezing out independent smaller stores; (9) the tendency for large retailers to design and launch new store formats targeted to different lifestyle groups; (10) the rise of information technology as a competitive tool in managing all facets of the retailing process; (11) the expansion of many retailers past domestic borders into global markets; and (12) the rise of retail stores as community centers.

3. Wholesaling includes all the activities involved in selling goods or services to those who buy for resale or business use. Manufacturers use wholesalers because wholesalers can perform functions better and more cost effectively than the manufacturers can. These functions include, but are not limited to, selling and promoting, buying and assortment building, bulk breaking, warehousing, transportation, financing, risk bearing, dissemination of market information, and provision of management services and consulting.

There are four types of wholesalers: merchant wholesalers (full-service wholesalers like wholesale merchants and industrial distributors, and limited-service wholesalers like cash-and-carry wholesalers, truck wholesalers, drop shippers, rack jobbers, producers' cooperatives, and mail-order wholesalers); brokers and agents (including manufacturers' agents, selling agents, purchasing agents, and commission merchants); manufacturers' and retailers' sales branches, sales offices, and purchasing offices; and miscellaneous wholesalers such as agricultural assemblers and auction companies.

Like retailers, wholesalers must decide on target markets, product assortment and services, pricing, promotion, and place. The most successful wholesalers are those who adopt their services to meet their suppliers' and target customers' needs, recognizing that they exist to add value to the channel.

4. Producers of physical products and services must decide on market logistics—the best way to store and move their goods and services to their market destinations. The logistical task is to coordinate the activities of suppliers, purchasing agents, manufacturers, marketers, channel members, and customers. Major gains in logistical efficiency have come from advances in information technology. Though the cost of market logistics can be high, a well-planned market logistics program can be a potent tool in competitive marketing. The ultimate goal of market logistics is to meet customers' requirements in an efficient and profitable way.

Managers of market logistics must make four decisions: (1) How should orders be handled? (order processing); (2) Where should stocks be located? (warehousing); (3) How much stock should be held? (inventory); and (4) How should goods be shipped? (transportation). Many companies have set up a permanent committee composed of managers of the different market-logistics activities. The committee members meet periodically to develop policies for improving overall logistical efficiency.

CONCEPT APPLICATIONS

1. While major retail stores like Home Depot, Wal-Mart, and Toys "Я" Us have had strong sales in recent years, Kmart, The Gap, and The Limited have been struggling. Brainstorm some techniques that these retailers (and retailers in general) can use to keep customers coming into the stores.

2. Electronic data interchange (EDI) makes it possible for computers at two different locations to exchange business information in machine language. What are some of the implications of this technology for the retail industry?

3. Complete the following matrix of differing retail service levels. Identify a major retailer in each of these categories and indicate whether its product assortment is deep, broad, or scrambled. Discuss the broad positioning strategy used in each level.

SERVICE LEVEL	EXAMPLE	PRODUCT ASSORTMENT		
		DEEP	BROAD	SCRAMBLED
Store Retailers:				
Specialty store (Limited line)				
Department store				
Variety store				
Category killer				
Mass merchandiser				
Supermarket				
Combination store				
Hypermarket				
Discount store				
Off-price retailer				
Catalog showroom				
Nonstore Retailers:				
Direct selling				
Mail-order selling				
Home shopping				
Automatic vending				
Buying service				
Retail Organizations:				
Corporate chain				
Voluntary chain				
Retailer cooperative				
Consumer cooperative				
Franchise organization				
Merchandising chain				

4. Wholesalers typically do not invest much in the promotional part of their marketing mix. Why has this been a weak area for wholesalers?

5. A large consumer-goods manufacturer is having problems with its physical distribution systems. It realizes its solution lies in reorganizing its market-logistics system, but it is not sure how to proceed. Suggest a plan that will help the company identify and monitor its exact problems.

6. Apply the wheel-of-retailing concept to the brokerage business. How did this industry begin? How has it changed and evolved over the years? Where does the industry stand now?

7. Technology is becoming increasingly important in managing market logistics. One of the leaders in this area has been Federal Express. Prepare a brief report (two to five pages) summarizing FedEx's accomplishments in this area.

8. In two of its San Diego outlets, Montgomery Ward opened "Law Store" booths that provide a one-time consultation for a $10 fee. Customers are ushered to a telephone booth–like enclosure, where operators connect them to a central office of lawyers who respond to queries over the telephone.
   a. To whom is this service targeted? (Consider the demographics of the people who shop at Montgomery Ward.)
   b. What types of legal services are likely to be offered, simple or complex?
   c What types of atmospherics would you recommend for the Law Store?
   d. What is the Law Store's pricing strategy?
   e. What kinds of promotion is the Law Store likely to use?

9. For a number of years, computer manufacturer Gateway 2000 has been selling its computers through mail order. The company is now considering opening its own retail outlets. Discuss the factors involved in starting successful retail outlets. Where should Gateway locate its outlets? Once they are opened, how can Gateway assess the locations it

has chosen for its outlets? What other factors will be important to Gateway's success in the retail industry?

10. Hunt Midwest Mining mined limestone to be used in the construction of buildings, airport runways, and highways from 3,500 acres of land in an undeveloped state. As a result of removing approximately 25 acres of rock each year, Hunt created a huge underground cavern of 4 million square feet. The limestone was quarried by the room and pillar method, leaving pillars in an essentially regular alignment to support the cavern's roof (Figure 1). The lower 12 1/2 feet of the 22 1/2 foot limestone ledge was mined, leaving a smooth, natural ceiling that has a great deal of stability. Ceiling heights can be increased by simply lowering the floor level.

FIGURE I

Hunt has begun leasing out parts of SubTropolis, as the cavern is called. For example, it has leased part of the space to be used as a foreign trade zone where goods can be stored, manipulated, mixed with domestic and/or foreign materials, used in assembly or manufacturing process, and/or exhibited for sale. It has also begun leasing parts of the cavern as an underground storage facility. Why might a business want to lease an underground storage facility?

11. A company's inventory-carrying cost is 30 percent. A marketing manager wants her company to increase its inventory investment from $400,000 to $500,000, believing this would lead to increased sales of $120,000 because of greater customer loyalty and service. The gross profit on sales is 20 percent. Does it pay the company to increase its inventory investment?

NOTES

1. William R. Davidson, Albert D. Bates, and Stephen J. Bass, "Retail Life Cycle," *Harvard Business Review* (November–December 1976), pp. 89–96.

2. Stanley C. Hollander, "The Wheel of Retailing," *Journal of Marketing,* July 1960, pp. 37–42.

3. For a fuller discussion, see Lawrence H. Wortzel, "Retailing Strategies for Today's Marketplace," *Journal of Business Strategy,* Spring 1987, pp. 45–56; also see Roger D. Blackwell and W. Wayne Talarzyk, "Life-Style Retailing: Competitive Strategies for the 1980s," *Journal of Retailing,* Winter 1983, pp. 7–26.

4. Bill Saporito, "And the Winner Is Still . . . Wal-Mart," *Fortune,* May 2, 1994, pp. 62–70.

5. Margaret Webb Pressler, "Looking to Rack Up a Recovery: The Limited Struggles with a Sagging Image and Sagging Sales," *The Washington Post,* January 24, 1995, D1:2; Susan Caminiti, "The Limited: In Search of the 90's Consumer," *Fortune,* September 21, 1992, p. 100.

6. Wortzel, "Retailing Strategies."

7. See Michael Treacy and Fred Wiersema, "Customer Intimacy and Other Discipline Values," *Harvard Business Review,* January–February 1993, pp. 84–93.

8. For more discussion, see Philip Kotler, "Atmospherics as a Marketing Tool," *Journal of Retailing,* Winter 1973–1974, pp. 48–64; and Mary Jo Bitner, "Servicescapes: The Impact of Physical Surroundings on Customers and Employees," *Journal of Marketing,* April 1992, pp. 57–71.

9. See "Why Rich Melman Is Really Cooking," *Business Week,* November 2, 1992, pp. 127–28.

10. Howard Rudnitsky, "Battle of the Malls," *Forbes,* March 30, 1992.

11. Frank Feather, *The Future Consumer* (Toronto: Warwick Publishing, 1994), p. 171.

12. See Anne T. Coughlan and Naufel J. Vilcassim, "Retail Marketing Strategies: An Investigation of Everyday Low Pricing vs. Promotional Pricing Policies," working paper, Northwestern University, Kellogg Graduate School of Management, December 1989. Also see Stephen J. Hoch, Xavier Dreeze, and Mary E. Purk, "EDLP, Hi-Lo, and Margin Arithmetic," *Journal of Marketing,* October 1994, pp. 1–15.

13. R. L. Davies and D. S. Rogers, ed., *Store Location and Store Assessment Research* (New York: John Wiley, 1984).

14. See Sara L. McLafferty, *Location Strategies for Retail and Service Firms* (Lexington, MA: Lexington Books, 1987).

15. Jay L. Johnson, "Supercenters: An Evolving Saga," *Discount Merchandiser,* April 1995, pp. 26–30.

16. The electronic checkout systems known as "scanners," now common at grocery stores and nonfood retailers, have occasionally been found to misprice items—usually in the retailer's favor. Although the technology is capable of 100% accuracy, some stores average as low as 85 percent. A California survey of 9,000 items from 300 stores found overcharges on 2% of the products and undercharges on 1.3%, while a Michigan study uncovered a 4-to-1 ratio of overpricing to underpricing. Stores counter that the scanners are still more accurate than store clerks, who, they claim, punch in the wrong prices about 10% of the time. Because of the nationwide crackdown on scanner mispricing, many stores have launched programs to improve their systems. Sears, which says it has a 95% accuracy rate, rebates $5.00 or 5% off mispriced items, whichever is larger. And Wal-Mart offers a $3.00 refund per item to consumers who have been "scammed" while getting scanned. See Catherine Yang, "Maybe They Should Call Them 'Scammers,'" *Business Week,* January 16, 1995, pp. 32–33; Ronald C. Goodstein, "UPC Scanner Pricing Systems: Are They Accurate?" *Journal of Marketing,* April 1994, pp. 20–30.

17. For a listing of the key factors involved in success with an EDI system, see David T. Vlosky, Richard P. Smith, and Paul M. Wilson, "Electronic Data Interchange Implementation Strategies: A Case Study," *Journal of Business and Industrial Marketing,* 9, no. 4 (1994), pp. 5–18.

18. "Business Bulletin: Shopper Scanner," *The Wall Street Journal,* February 18, 1995, A1:5.

19. For further discussion of retail trends, see Louis W. Stern and Adel I. El-Ansary, *Marketing Channels,* 5th ed. (Upper Saddle River, NJ: Prentice Hall, 1996).

20. Shelley Donald Coolidge, "Facing Saturated Home Markets, Retailers Look to Rest of World," *Christian Science Monitor,* February 14, 1994, 7:1; Carla Rapoport with Justin Martin, "Retailers Go Global," *Fortune,* February 20, 1995, pp. 102–8.

21. Gherry Khermouch, "Third Places," *Brandweek,* March 13, 1995, pp. 36–40.

22. See Bert McCammon, Robert F. Lusch, Deborah S. Coykendall, and James M. Kenderdine, *Wholesaling in Transition* (Norman: University of Oklahoma, College of Business Administration, 1989).

23. See Feather p. 96.

24. James A. Narus and James C. Anderson, "Contributing as a Distributor to Partnerships with Manufacturers," *Business Horizons,* September–October 1987. Also see James D. Hlavecek and Tommy J. McCuistion, "Industrial Distributors—When, Who, and How," *Harvard Business Review,* March–April 1983, pp. 96–101.

25. Richard A. Melcher, "The Middlemen Stay on the March," *Business Week,* January 9, 1995, p. 87.

26. See Rita Koselka, "Distribution Revolution," *Forbes,* May 25, 1992, pp. 54–62.

27. Rapoport with Martin, "Retailers Go Global."

28. Ronald Henkoff, "Delivering the Goods," *Fortune,* November 28, 1994, pp. 64–78.

29. Stephanie Strom, "Logistics Steps onto Retail Battlefield," *The New York Times,* November 3, 1993, D1:2. See also Marita van Oldenborgh, "Power Logistics," *International Business,* October 1994, pp. 32–34, and James Aaron Cooke, "Will Logistics Be the Magic Bullet? Part 3," *Traffic Management,* May 1995, pp. 35–38.

30. E. J. Muller, "Faster, Faster, I Need It Now!" *Distribution,* February 1994, pp. 30–36.

31. Henkoff, "Delivering the Goods," pp. 64–78.

32. Koselka, "Distribution Revolution," pp. 54–62.

33. The optimal order quantity is given by the formula $Q^* = 2DS/IC$, where D = annual demand, S = cost to place one order, and I = annual carrying cost per unit. Known as the economic-order quantity formula, it assumes a constant ordering cost, a constant cost of carrying an additional unit in inventory, a known demand, and no quantity discounts. For further reading on this subject, see Richard J. Tersine, *Principles of Inventory and Materials Management,* 4th ed. (Englewood Cliffs, NJ: Prentice Hall, 1994).

34. For a study of the characteristics of 117 leading-edge logistics companies, see Donald J. Bowersox et al., *Leading Edge Logistics Competitive Positioning for the 1990's* (Oak Brook, IL: Council of Logistics Management, 1989). Also see Robert A. Novack, John Langley, Jr., and Lloyd M. Rinehart, *Creating Logistics Value* (Oak Brook, IL: Council on Logistics Management, 1995).

DESIGNING

AND MANAGING

INTEGRATED

MARKETING

COMMUNICATIONS

People no longer buy shoes to keep their feet warm and dry. They buy them because of the way the shoes make them feel— masculine, feminine, rugged, different, sophisticated, young, glamorous, "in." Buying shoes has become an emotional experience. Our business now is selling excitement rather than shoes.

FRANCIS C. ROONEY

❖

Modern marketing calls for more than developing a good product, pricing it attractively, and making it accessible to target customers. Companies must also communicate with their present and potential customers, retailers, suppliers, other stakeholders, and the general public. Every company is inevitably cast into the role of communicator and promoter. For most companies, the question is not whether to communicate but rather what to say, to whom, and how often.

The *marketing communications mix* (also called the *promotion mix*) consists of five major modes of communication:

◆ *Advertising:* Any paid form of nonpersonal presentation and promotion of ideas, goods, or services by an identified sponsor.

◆ *Sales promotion:* A variety of short-term incentives to encourage trial or purchase of a product or service.

◆ *Public relations and publicity:* A variety of programs designed to promote and/or protect a company's image or its individual products.

◆ *Personal selling:* Face-to-face interaction with one or more prospective purchasers for the purpose of making presentations, answering questions, and procuring orders.

◆ *Direct marketing:* Use of mail, telephone, fax, e-mail, and other nonpersonal contact tools to communicate directly with or solicit a direct response from specific customers and prospects.[1]

Table 20-1 lists numerous communication platforms. Thanks to technological breakthroughs, people can now communicate through traditional media (newspapers, radio, telephone, television), as well as through newer media forms (computers, fax machines, cellular phones, and pagers). By decreasing communication costs, the new technologies have encouraged more companies to move from mass communication to more targeted communication and one-to-one dialogue. As Marshall McLuhan observed, "The medium is the message"; that is, the media will affect the message's content.

But company communication goes beyond the specific communication platforms listed in Table 20-1. The product's styling and price, the package's shape and color, the salesperson's manner and dress, the place of business, the company's stationery—all communicate something to the buyers. The whole marketing mix, not just the promotional mix, must be orchestrated to deliver and establish the company's intended strategic positioning. We will discuss the movement toward integrated marketing communications later in the chapter.

This chapter examines three major questions:

◆ **How does communication work?**

◆ **What are the major steps in developing an effective marketing communications program?**

◆ **Who should be responsible for marketing communication planning?**

Chapter 21 deals with advertising, sales promotion, and public relations; Chapter 22, with the sales force and personal selling; and Chapter 23, with direct and online marketing.

Planning
Marketing
Programs

TABLE 20-1 | COMMON COMMUNICATION PLATFORMS

ADVERTISING	SALES PROMOTION	PUBLIC RELATIONS	PERSONAL SELLING	DIRECT MARKETING
Print and broadcast ads	Contests, games, sweep-stakes, lotteries	Press kits	Sales presentations	Catalogs
Packaging—outer	Premiums and gifts	Speeches	Sales meetings	Mailings
Packaging inserts	Sampling	Seminars	Incentive programs	Telemarketing
Motion pictures	Fairs and trade shows	Annual reports	Samples	Electronic shopping
Brochures and booklets	Exhibits	Charitable donations	Fairs and trade shows	TV shopping
Posters and leaflets	Demonstrations	Sponsorships		Fax mail
Directories	Coupons	Publications		E-mail
Reprints of ads	Rebates	Community relations		Voice mail
Billboards	Low-interest financing	Lobbying		
Display signs	Entertainment	Identity media		
Point-of-purchase displays	Trade-in allowances	Company magazine		
Audio-visual material	Continuity programs	Events		
Symbols and logos	Tie-ins			
Videotapes				

A VIEW OF THE COMMUNICATION PROCESS

Too often, marketing communications focus on overcoming an awareness, an image, or a preference gap in the target market. But this approach to communication has several limitations: It is too short-term and too costly, and most messages of this type fall on deaf ears.

Today there is a movement toward viewing communications as the *management of the customer buying process over time,* during the preselling, selling, consuming, and postconsuming stages. And because customers differ, communications programs need to be developed for specific segments, niches, and even individuals. Given the new electronic technologies, companies must ask not only "How can we reach our customers?" but also "How can we find ways to let our customers reach us?"

The starting point in the communications process is thus an audit of all the potential interactions target customers may have with the product and company. For example, someone purchasing a new computer would talk to others, see television ads, read articles in newspapers and magazines, and observe computers in a store. The marketer needs to assess which of these experiences and impressions will have the most influence at the different stages of the buying process. This understanding will help marketers allocate their communication dollars more efficiently.

To communicate effectively, marketers need to understand the fundamental elements underlying effective communication. Figure 20-1 on the next page shows a communication model with nine elements. Two elements represent the major parties in a communication—*sender* and *receiver.* Two represent the major communication tools—*message* and *media.* Four represent major communication functions—*encoding, decoding, response,* and *feedback.* The last element in the system is *noise* (i.e., random and competing messages that may interfere with the intended communication).[2]

The model underscores the key factors in effective communication. Senders must know what audiences they want to reach and what responses they want. They must encode their messages in a way that takes into account how the target audience usually decodes messages. They must also transmit the message through efficient media that reach the target audience and develop feedback channels to monitor the receiver's response to the message.

FIGURE 20-1
Elements in the Communication Process

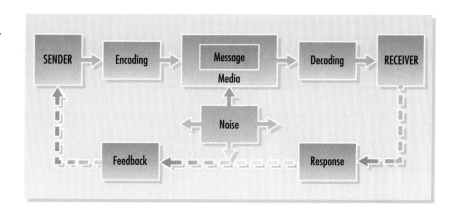

For a message to be effective, the sender's encoding process must mesh with the receiver's decoding process. Thus the best messages are essentially signs that are familiar to the receiver. The more the sender's field of experience overlaps with that of the receiver, the more effective the message is likely to be. This requirement puts a burden on communicators from one social stratum (such as advertising people) who want to communicate effectively with another stratum (such as factory workers).

The sender's task is to get his or her message through to the receiver. The target audience may not receive the intended message for any of three reasons:

◆ *Selective attention:* People are bombarded by 1,600 commercial messages a day, of which 80 are consciously noticed and about 12 provoke some reaction. Thus the communicator must design the message to win attention in spite of surrounding distractions. Selective attention explains why ads with bold headlines promising something, such as "How to Make a Million," along with an arresting illustration and little copy, have a high likelihood of grabbing attention. For very little effort, the receiver might gain a great reward.

◆ *Selective distortion:* People may twist the message to hear what they want to hear. Receivers have set attitudes, which lead to expectations about what they will hear or see. They will hear what fits into their belief system. As a result, receivers often add things to the message that are not there (*amplification*) and do not notice other things that are there (*leveling*). The communicator's task is to strive for message simplicity, clarity, interest, and repetition to get the main points across to the audience.

◆ *Selective recall:* People will retain in long-term memory only a small fraction of the messages that reach them. Whether a message passes from the receiver's short-term memory to his or her long-term memory depends on the amount and type of *message rehearsal* by the receiver. Rehearsal is not simply message repetition; rather, it is a process by which the receiver elaborates on the meaning of the information in a way that brings related thoughts from the receiver's long-term memory into his or her short-term memory. If the receiver's initial attitude toward the object is positive and he or she rehearses support arguments, the message is likely to be accepted and have high recall. If the receiver's initial attitude is negative and the person rehearses counter-arguments, the message is likely to be rejected but to stay in long-term memory. Counter-arguing inhibits persuasion by making an opposing message available. Because much of persuasion requires the receiver's rehearsal of his or her own thoughts, much of what is called persuasion is actually self-persuasion.[3]

The communicator should look for audience traits that correlate with persuasibility and use them to guide message and media development. People of high education and/or intelligence are thought to be less persuasible, but the evidence is inconclusive. Persons who accept external standards to guide their behavior and who have a weak self-concept appear to be more persuasible, as are people who are low in self-confidence. However, research by Cox and Bauer showed a curvilinear relation between self-confidence and persuasibility, with those moderate in self-confidence being the most persuasible.[4]

Communicators also need to think about their audienceís awareness that the communicator is attempting to persuade them. People who have been exposed to previous persuasion attempts have a different response to persuasion than those who have not been exposed to such attempts.[5] Fiske and Hartley have outlined some general factors that influence the effectiveness of a communication:

1. The greater the monopoly of the communication source over the recipient, the greater the recipient's change or effect in favor of the source.

2. Communication effects are greatest where the message is in line with the receiver's existing opinions, beliefs, and dispositions.

3. Communication can produce the most effective shifts on unfamiliar, lightly felt, peripheral issues, which do not lie at the center of the recipient's value system.

4. Communication is more likely to be effective where the source is believed to have expertise, high status, objectivity, or likability, but particularly where the source has power and can be identified with.

5. The social context, group, or reference group will mediate the communication and influence whether or not the communication is accepted.[6]

DEVELOPING EFFECTIVE COMMUNICATIONS

We will now examine the eight steps in developing an effective total communication and promotion program. The marketing communicator must (1) identify the target audience, (2) determine the communication objectives, (3) design the message, (4) select the communication channels, (5) establish the total promotion budget, (6) decide on the promotion mix, (7) measure the promotion's results, and (8) manage and coordinate the integrated marketing communication process.

Identifying the Target Audience

A marketing communicator must start with a clear target audience in mind. The audience could be potential buyers of the company's products, current users, deciders, or influencers. The audience could be individuals, groups, particular publics, or the general public. The target audience will critically influence the communicator's decisions on what to say, how to say it, when to say it, where to say it, and to whom to say it.

IMAGE ANALYSIS. A major part of audience analysis entails assessing the audience's current image of the company, its products, and its competitors.

❖ **IMAGE** is the set of beliefs, ideas, and impressions that a person holds regarding an object. People's attitudes and actions toward an object are highly conditioned by that object's image.

The first step is to measure the target audience's knowledge of the object, using the following *familiarity scale:*

Never Heard of	Heard of Only	Know a Little Bit	Know a Fair Amount	Know Very Well

If most respondents circle only the first two categories, then the company's challenge is to build greater awareness.

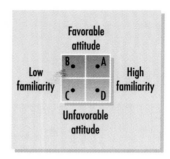

FIGURE 20-2
Familiarity-Favorability Analysis

Respondents who are familiar with the product can be asked how they feel toward it, using the following *favorability scale:*

Very Unfavorable	Somewhat Unfavorable	Indifferent	Somewhat Favorable	Very Favorable

If most respondents check the first two categories, then the organization must overcome a negative image problem.

The two scales can be combined to develop insight into the nature of the communication challenge. To illustrate, suppose area residents are asked about their familiarity with and attitudes toward four local hospitals, A, B, C, and D. Their responses are averaged and shown in Figure 20-2. Hospital A has the most positive image: Most people know it and like it. Hospital B is less familiar to most people, but those who know it like it. Hospital C is viewed negatively by those who know it, but (fortunately for the hospital) not too many people know it. Hospital D is seen as a poor hospital, and everyone knows it!

Clearly, each hospital faces a different communication task. Hospital A must work at maintaining its good reputation and high community awareness. Hospital B must gain the attention of more people, since those who know it consider it a good hospital. Hospital C must find out why people dislike it and take steps to improve its performance while keeping a low profile. Hospital D should lower its profile (avoid news), improve its quality, and then seek public attention again.

To meet its challenges, each hospital needs to research the specific content of its image. The most popular tool for this research is the *semantic differential*.[7] It involves the following steps:

1. *Developing a set of relevant dimensions:* The researcher asks people to identify the dimensions they would use in thinking about the object. People could be asked, "What things do you think of when you consider a hospital?" If someone suggests "quality of medical care," this dimension would be turned into a five- or seven-point bipolar adjective scale, with "inferior medical care" at one end and "superior medical care" at the other. A set of additional dimensions for a hospital is shown in Figure 20-3.

2. *Reducing the set of relevant dimensions:* The number of dimensions should be kept small to avoid respondent fatigue. There are three types of scales:

   ◆ Evaluation scales (good-bad qualities)
   ◆ Potency scales (strong-weak qualities)
   ◆ Activity scales (active-passive qualities)

FIGURE 20-3
Images of Three Hospitals (Semantic Differential)

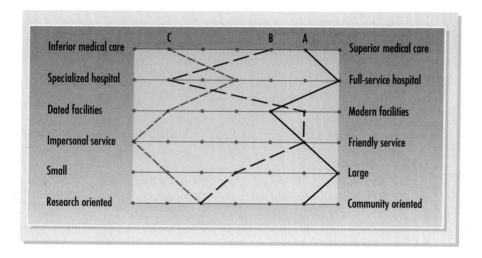

Using these scales as a guide, the researcher can remove redundant scales that fail to provide much information.

3. *Administering the instrument to a sample of respondents:* The respondents are asked to rate one object at a time. The bipolar adjectives should be randomly arranged so that all of the unfavorable adjectives are not listed on one side.

4. *Averaging the results:* Figure 20-3 shows the results of averaging the respondents' pictures of hospitals A, B, and C (hospital D is left out). Each hospital's image is represented by a vertical "line of means" that summarizes people's average perception of that hospital. Thus hospital A is seen as a large, modern, friendly, and superior hospital. Hospital C, in contrast, is seen as a small, dated, impersonal, and inferior hospital.

5. *Checking on the image variance:* Since each image profile is a line of means (that is, averages), it does not reveal how variable the image is. Did everyone see hospital B as shown, or was there considerable variation? In the first case, we would say that the image is highly *specific*; and in the second case, highly *diffused*. An organization might not want a very specific image. Some organizations prefer a diffused image so that different groups will see the organization in different ways.

The management should now propose a desired image in contrast to the current image. Suppose hospital C would like the public to view more favorably the quality of the hospital's medical care, facilities, friendliness, and so on. Management must decide which image gaps it wants to close first. Is it more desirable to improve the hospital's friendliness (through staff training programs) or the quality of its facilities (through renovation)? Each image dimension should be reviewed in terms of the following questions:

◆ What contribution to the organization's overall favorable image would be made by closing that particular image gap?

◆ What strategy (combination of real changes and communication changes) would help close that particular image gap?

◆ What would be the cost of closing that image gap?

◆ How long would it take to close that image gap?

Basically, management must decide what position it wants to occupy in the marketplace. The aim is not to close every gap but to be distinctly better at that which its target market values.

An organization seeking to improve its image must have great patience. Images are "sticky"; they persist long after the organization has changed. Thus a famous hospital's medical care might have deteriorated, and yet it continues to be highly regarded in the public mind. Image persistence is explained by the fact that once people have a certain image of an object, they selectively perceive further data. They perceive what is consistent with their image. It will take highly disconfirming information to raise doubts and open their minds to new information. Thus an image has a life of its own, especially when people do not have continuous or new firsthand experiences with the changed object. This was the case with Thom McAn, the once-popular shoe company that is staging a comeback:

THOM McAN During its heyday in the 1930s through the 1960s, Thom McAn sold good but inexpensive shoes and was the best-selling shoe brand in the United States. Yet in focus groups held for 1990s consumers, the words used to describe Thom McAn shoes were "boring," "ugly," and "nerdy." While people still expressed a liking of the brand, they were going elsewhere for their shoes. With sales at only $275 million, down from $440 million in 1981, clearly an image makeover was in order.

The company went about changing its image in an unusual way: It poked fun at its own stodgy image. "Please excuse some of our shoe styles of the past," read the first line in a series of New York City subway ads designed to draw attention to the company's new, hipper shoes. Over a photo of a speeding truck, the copy read, "For years our new and updated shoes were rerouted by a disgruntled postal worker and abandoned under a bridge near Chicago." Another ad read, "Through a fluke computer error, the office supply store sent us the wrong desk calendar and we still thought it was 1976."[8]

Determining the Communication Objectives

Once the target market and its characteristics are identified, the marketing communicator must decide on the desired audience response. The desired ultimate responses are purchase, high satisfaction, and favorable word-of-mouth. But purchase behavior is the end result of a long process of consumer decision making. The marketing communicator needs to know how to move the target audience to higher states of readiness to buy.

The marketer can be seeking a *cognitive, affective,* or *behavioral* response from the target audience. That is, the marketer might want to put something into the consumer's mind, change the consumer's attitude, or get the consumer to act. Even here, there are different models of consumer-response stages. Figure 20-4 summarizes the four best-known *response hierarchy models.*

All of these models assume that the buyer passes through a cognitive, affective, and behavioral stage, in that order. This sequence is the "learn-feel-do" sequence and is appropriate when the audience has high involvement with a product category perceived to have high differentiation, as is the case in purchasing an automobile. An alternative sequence is the "do-feel-learn" sequence, which is relevant when the audience has high involvement but perceives little or no differentiation within the product category, as in purchasing aluminum siding. A third sequence is the "learn-do-feel" sequence, which is relevant when the audience has low involvement and perceives little differentiation within the product category, as is the case in purchasing salt. By understanding the appropriate sequence, the marketer can do a better job of planning communications.[9]

Here we will assume that the buyer has high involvement with the product category and perceives high differentiation within the category. Therefore we will work with the *hierarchy-of-effects* model (learn, feel, do—see the second column of Figure 20-4) and describe how marketers should behave in each of the six buyer-readiness states—awareness, knowledge, liking, preference, conviction, and purchase:

♦ *Awareness:* If most of the target audience is unaware of the object, the communicator's task is to build awareness, perhaps just name recognition. This task can be accomplished with simple messages repeating the product's name. But building awareness takes time. Suppose a small Iowa college named Pottsville seeks applicants from Nebraska but has no name recognition in Nebraska. And suppose there are 30,000 high school juniors and seniors in Nebraska who may potentially be interested in Pottsville College. The college might set the objective of making 70% of these students aware of Pottsville's name within one year.

♦ *Knowledge:* The target audience might have company or product awareness but not know much more. Pottsville may want its target audience to know that it is a private four-year college with excellent programs in English, foreign languages, and history. It thus needs to learn how many people in the target audience have little, some, or much knowledge about Pottsville. Based on this information, the college may then decide to select product knowledge as its first communication objective.

♦ *Liking:* If target members know the product, how do they feel about it? If the audience looks unfavorably on Pottsville College, the communicator has to find out why and then develop a communication campaign to shore up favorable feelings. If the unfavorable view is based on real problems of the college, then a communication campaign alone cannot do the job. Pottsville will have to fix its problems and then communicate its renewed quality. Good public relations call for "good deeds followed by good words."

Planning
Marketing
Programs

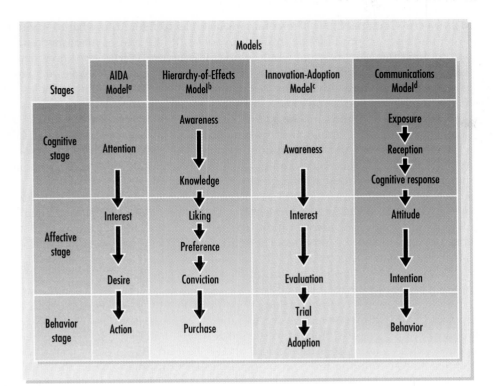

FIGURE 20-4

Response Hierarchy Models

Sources: (a) E. K. Strong, *The Psychology of Selling* (New York: McGraw-Hill, 1925), p. 9; (b) Robert J. Lavidge and Gary A. Steiner, "A Model for Predictive Measurements of Advertising Effectiveness," *Journal of Marketing,* October 1961, p. 61; (c) Everett M. Rogers, *Diffusion of Innovation* (New York: Free Press, 1962), pp. 79–86; (d) various sources.

The figure content (reproduced from the image):

Models

Stages	AIDA Model[a]	Hierarchy-of-Effects Model[b]	Innovation-Adoption Model[c]	Communications Model[d]
Cognitive stage	Attention	Awareness → Knowledge	Awareness	Exposure → Reception → Cognitive response
Affective stage	Interest → Desire	Liking → Preference → Conviction	Interest → Evaluation	Attitude → Intention
Behavior stage	Action	Purchase	Trial → Adoption	Behavior

- ◆ *Preference:* The target audience might like the product but not prefer it to others. In this case, the communicator must try to build consumer preference. The communicator will promote the product's quality, value, performance, and other features. The communicator can check on the campaign's success by measuring audience preferences again after the campaign.

- ◆ *Conviction:* A target audience might prefer a particular product but not develop a conviction about buying it. The communicator's job is to build conviction among interested students that Pottsville College is their best choice.

- ◆ *Purchase:* Finally, some members of the target audience might have conviction but not quite get around to making the purchase. They may wait for more information or plan to act later. The communicator must lead these consumers to take the final step. Actions might include offering the product at a low price, offering a premium, or letting consumers try it on a limited basis. Thus Pottsville might invite selected high school students to visit the campus and attend some classes. Or it might offer partial scholarships to deserving students.

Designing the Message

Having defined the desired audience response, the communicator moves to developing an effective message. Ideally, the message should gain *attention*, hold *interest*, arouse *desire*, and elicit *action* (*AIDA model*—see the first column of Figure 20-4). In practice, few messages take the consumer all the way from awareness through purchase, but the AIDA framework suggests the desirable qualities of any communication.

Formulating the message will require solving four problems: what to say (message content), how to say it logically (message structure), how to say it symbolically (message format), and who should say it (message source).

MESSAGE CONTENT. The communicator has to figure out what to say to the target audience to produce the desired response. In the age of mass marketing, it was thought that one message would work for everyone. Today we know that different people seek different benefits from the same product. People are paying less attention to mass advertising because of time pressure and their belief that many brands are the same. They are channel surfing through TV stations and pressing scanner buttons on the radio. The challenge is therefore to create messages that will get the attention of specific target groups. For example, Coca-Cola's ad agency, Creative Artists, has produced a pool of different commercials for different market segments. Local and global Coca-Cola managers decide which commercials would work best with each target segment.

In determining the best message content, management searches for an *appeal, theme, idea,* or *unique selling proposition.* This amounts to formulating some kind of benefit, motivation, identification, or reason why the audience should think about or investigate the product. There are three types of appeals: rational, emotional, and moral.

Rational appeals appeal to the audience's self-interest. They show that the product will produce the claimed benefits. Examples are messages demonstrating a product's quality, economy, value, or performance. It is widely believed that industrial buyers are most responsive to rational appeals. They are knowledgeable about the product class, trained to recognize value, and accountable to others for their choices. (Figure 20-5 reproduces a U.S. West ad that appeals to the buyer's rational side by offering free consulting services.) Consumers, when they buy certain big-ticket items, also tend to gather information and compare alternatives. Like business buyers, they will respond to quality, economy, value, and performance appeals.

Emotional appeals attempt to stir up negative or positive emotions that will motivate purchase. Marketers search for the right *emotional selling proposition (ESP).* The product may be similar to the competition but have unique associations for consumers (examples are Rolls Royce, Harley Davidson, and Rolex); communications should appeal to these associations. In addition, communicators have worked with negative appeals such as fear, guilt, and shame to get people to do things they should (e.g., brush their teeth, have an annual health checkup) or stop doing things they shouldn't (e.g., smoking, alcohol or abuse, overeating). Fear appeals are effective up to a point, but they work best when they are not too strong. Research findings indicate that neither extremely strong nor extremely weak fear appeals are as effective as moderate ones in producing adherence to a recommendation. Furthermore, fear appeals work better when source credibility is high. The fear appeal is also more effective when the communication promises to relieve, in a believable and efficient way, the fear it arouses.[10]

Communicators also use positive emotional appeals such as humor, love, pride, and joy. However, evidence has not established that a humorous message is necessarily more effective than a straight version of the same message. Advocates for humorous messages claim that they attract more attention and create more liking and belief in the sponsor. Cliff Freeman, the adman responsible for Little Caesars' humorous "Pizza, Pizza" ad and the venerable "Where's the beef?" campaign for Wendy's, contends that "Humor is a great way to bound out of the starting gate. When you make people laugh, and they feel good after seeing the commercial, they like the association with the product." But others maintain that humor can detract from comprehension, wear out its welcome fast, and overshadow the product.[11]

Moral appeals are directed to the audience's sense of what is right and proper. They are often used to exhort people to support social causes, such as a cleaner environment, better race relations, equal rights for women, and aid to the disad-

Planning
Marketing
Programs

FIGURE 20-5
U.S. West Home Office
Rational-Appeal
Advertisement

Call now for our free guide to the home office.

Ditto.

Introducing the U S WEST Home Office Consultant.
A specially trained expert who knows phones as well as you know your home business. So you can get the simple answers you need to work from home more efficiently.

For instance, your consultant can tell you about the latest innovations in phone products and services. Such as the news about how you can now choose to get an additional residential line for your home office without paying a business rate.

Your consultant can also suggest simple, practical ideas that solve big problems with little added expense. Such as using Custom Ringing. That way you'll always know which calls are for the household and which are strictly business.

And the fee is right. Every call to a U S WEST Home Office Consultant is free. No phone charge. No consultation charge. And there's no obligation to buy whatsoever.

In fact, call today, and you'll also receive our complete Home Office Resource Guide *free*.

This exclusive book is loaded with 36 pages of ideas and information. From how to set up an office at home to information on the latest business equipment.

So call 1-800-898-WORK for a U S WEST Home Office Consultant today. And get the two best guides for the home office.

1 8 0 0 8 9 8 W O R K
Call Today And Get Our Home Office Resource Guide *Free*.

USWEST ®

© 1994 U S WEST Communications. Not available in all areas. Some restrictions may apply.

---

vantaged. An example is the March of Dimes appeal: "God made you whole. Give to help those He didn't." Moral appeals are less often used in connection with everyday products.

Some advertisers believe that messages are most persuasive when they are moderately discrepant with what the audience believes. Messages that state only what the audience already believes attract less attention and at best only reinforce audience beliefs. If the messages are too discrepant with the audience's beliefs, however, they will be counter-argued in the audience's mind and be disbelieved.

Some Forces at Work in Global Advertising and Promotion

Multinational companies wrestle with a number of challenges in developing their global communications programs. First they must decide whether ads should be created at headquarters or locally. For example, Nike favors a standard global ad program designed at corporate headquarters, with some slight adjustments in each market. In contrast, Reebok favors different, localized commercials using different themes. Gillette chose a standard global advertising campaign when it launched its Sensor Shaver in 19 countries ("Gillette: the best a man can get"). Meanwhile, Hewlett Packard delegates most advertising decisions to its local companies, subject to certain companywide identity and design standards and budgets.

Even if a company favors strong corporate standardization, legal restrictions may force adaptation. Italy and the Republic of Ireland restrict or ban TV ads for certain pharmaceutical products. The Netherlands and the United Kingdom ban cigarette advertising in broad-

cast media, and Italy bans it in all media. The use of premiums is completely banned in Austria and Germany.

In addition, because media availability varies from country to country, advertising media mixes must often be modified. Commercial television is not available in Norway, Denmark, Sweden, and Saudi Arabia. In Germany, commercial ad time is limited to 40 minutes daily, and appears in blocks that do not interrupt programs; the result is that broadcast ad viewership is very low.

However, satellite TV channels make governments less able to restrict broadcast ad viewing. Sky and Super Channel reach tens of millions of people, carry different languages, and count among their advertisers such firms as Nike, Coca-Cola, and Gillette. The fact that satellite TV can reach wide audiences has led more advertisers to favor Eurobrands and global brands over standardized campaigns. Campbell's launched a new Eurobrand, Biscuits Maison, simultaneously in France, Germany, Belgium, and the Netherlands. Johnson & Johnson launched Dolormin, an ibuprofen analgesic, as a Eurobrand. Revlon is moving toward developing a global name for all its products.

The challenge is to design a message that is moderately discrepant and avoids the two extremes.

Companies that sell their products in different countries must be prepared to vary their message. In advertising its hair care products in different countries, for example, Helene Curtis adjusts its messages. Middle-class British women, for example, wash their hair frequently, while the opposite is true among Spanish women. Japanese women also avoid overwashing their hair for fear of removing its protective oils. For more details on developing communications for global markets, see the Marketing Insight titled "Some Forces at Work in Global Advertising and Promotion."

MESSAGE STRUCTURE. A message's effectiveness depends on its structure as well as its content. Hovland's research at Yale has shed much light on message content and its relation to conclusion drawing, one- versus two-sided arguments, and order of presentation.

Some early experiments supported stating conclusions for the audience rather than allowing the audience to reach its own conclusions. Recent research, however, indicates that the best ads ask questions and allow readers and viewers to form their own conclusions.[12] Conclusion drawing might cause negative reactions in the following situations:

♦ If the communicator is seen as untrustworthy, the audience members might resent the attempt to influence them.

♦ If the issue is simple or the audience is intelligent, the audience might be annoyed at the attempt to explain the obvious.

◆ If the issue is highly personal, the audience might resent the communicator's attempt to draw a conclusion.

Drawing too explicit a conclusion can also limit a product's appeal or acceptance. If Ford had hammered away on the point that the Mustang was for young people, this strong definition might have blocked other age groups who were attracted to it. Thus *stimulus ambiguity* can lead to a broader market definition and more spontaneous uses of certain products. Conclusion drawing seems better suited for complex or specialized products where a single and clear use is intended.

One would think that *one-sided presentations* that praise a product would be more effective than *two-sided arguments* that also mention the product's shortcomings. Yet two-sided messages may be more appropriate in certain situations, especially when some negative association must be overcome. In this spirit, Heinz ran the message "Heinz Ketchup is slow good" and Listerine ran the message "Listerine tastes bad twice a day."[13] Here are some findings:[14]

◆ One-sided messages work best with audiences that are initially predisposed to the communicator's position, and two-sided arguments work best with audiences who are opposed.

◆ Two-sided messages tend to be more effective with better-educated audiences.

◆ Two-sided messages tend to be more effective with audiences that are likely to be exposed to counterpropaganda.

Finally, the order in which arguments are presented is important.[15] In the case of a one-sided message, presenting the strongest argument first has the advantage of establishing attention and interest. This is important in newspapers and other media where the audience often does not attend to the whole message. However, it means an anticlimactic conclusion. With a captive audience, a climactic presentation might be more effective. In the case of a two-sided message, the issue is whether to present the positive argument first or last. If the audience is initially opposed, the communicator might start with the other side's argument and conclude with his or her strongest argument.[16]

MESSAGE FORMAT. The communicator must develop a strong format for the message. In a print ad, the communicator has to decide on the headline, copy, illustration, and color. If the message is to be carried over the radio, the communicator has to carefully choose words, voice qualities (speech rate, rhythm, pitch, articulation), and vocalizations (pauses, sighs, yawns). The "sound" of an announcer promoting a used automobile has to be different from one promoting a new Cadillac. If the message is to be carried on television or in person, then all of these elements plus body language (nonverbal clues) have to be planned. Presenters have to pay attention to their facial expressions, gestures, dress, posture, and hair style. If the message is carried by the product or its packaging, the communicator has to pay attention to color, texture, scent, size, and shape.

Color plays an important communication role in food preferences. When women sampled four cups of coffee that had been placed next to brown, blue, red, and yellow containers (all the coffee was identical, though the women did not know this), 75% felt that the coffee next to the brown container tasted too strong and nearly 85% judged the coffee next to the red container to be the richest. Nearly everyone felt that the coffee next to the blue container was mild and that the coffee next to the yellow container was weak.

MESSAGE SOURCE. Messages delivered by attractive or popular sources achieve higher attention and recall. Advertisers often use celebrities as spokespeople, such as Michael Jordan for Nike, Candice Bergen for Sprint, and Cindy Crawford for Revlon. Celebrities are likely to be effective when they personify a key product attribute. But what is equally important in the spokesperson is credibility. Messages delivered by highly credible sources are more persuasive. Pharmaceutical companies want doctors to testify about their products' benefits because doctors have high credibility. Antidrug crusaders will use ex-drug addicts to warn high school students against drugs because ex-addicts have higher credibility than teachers.

What factors underlie source credibility? The three factors most often identified are expertise, trustworthiness, and likability.[17] *Expertise* is the specialized knowledge the communicator possesses to back the claim. Doctors, scientists, and professors rank high on expertise in their respective fields. *Trustworthiness* is related to how objective and honest the source is perceived to be. Friends are trusted more than strangers or salespeople, and people who are not paid to endorse a product are often considered more trustworthy than people who are paid.[18] *Likability* describes the source's attractiveness to the audience. Such qualities as candor, humor, and naturalness make a source more likable. The most highly credible source would be a person who scores high on all three dimensions.

If a person has a positive attitude toward a source and a message, or a negative attitude toward both, a state of *congruity* is said to exist. What happens if the person holds one attitude toward the source and the opposite toward the message? Suppose a homemaker hears a likable celebrity praise a brand that she dislikes. Osgood and Tannenbaum posit that *attitude change will take place in the direction of increasing the amount of congruity between the two evaluations.*[19] The homemaker will end up respecting the celebrity somewhat less or respecting the brand somewhat more. If she encounters the same celebrity praising other disliked brands, she will eventually develop a negative view of the celebrity and maintain her negative attitudes toward the brands. The *principle of congruity* says that communicators can use their good image to reduce some negative feelings toward a brand but in the process might lose some esteem with the audience.

Selecting the Communication Channels

The communicator must select efficient channels of communication to carry the message. In many cases, many different channels must be used. For example, pharmaceutical companies' salespeople can rarely wrest more than 10 minutes' time from a busy physician. Their presentation must be crisp, quick, and convincing. This makes pharmaceutical sales calls extremely expensive and the industry has had to amplify its battery of communication channels. These include placing journal ads, sending direct mail (including audio and videotapes), passing out free samples, and even telemarketing. Pharmaceutical companies sponsor clinical conferences to which they invite and pay for a large number of physicians to spend a weekend listening in the morning to leading physicians extol certain drugs, followed by an afternoon of golf or tennis. Salespeople will arrange evening teleconferences where physicians are invited to be at their phone to discuss a common problem with an expert. And salespeople will sponsor small group lunches and dinners with physicians. All of these approaches are undertaken in the hope of building physician preference for a branded therapeutic agent that may not differ much from its generic counterpart.

Communication channels are of two broad types, *personal* and *nonpersonal*. Within each are found many subchannels:

PERSONAL COMMUNICATION CHANNELS. Personal communication channels involve two or more persons communicating directly with each other. They might communicate face to face, person to audience, over the telephone, or through the mails. Personal communication channels derive their effectiveness through the opportunities for individualizing the presentation and feedback.

A further distinction can be drawn among advocate, expert, and social channels of personal communication. *Advocate channels* consist of company salespeople contacting buyers in the target market. *Expert channels* consist of independent experts making statements to target buyers. *Social channels* consist of neighbors, friends, family members, and associates talking to target buyers. In a study of 7,000 consumers in seven European countries, 60% said they were influenced to use a new brand by family and friends.[20]

Many companies are becoming acutely aware of the power of the "talk factor" or "word-of-mouth" coming from expert and social channels in generating new business. They are seeking ways to stimulate these channels to provide recommendations for their products and services. For example, Regis McKenna advises a software company launching a new product to initially promote it to the trade press, opinion luminaries, financial analysts, and others who can supply favorable word-of-mouth; then to dealers; and finally to customers.[21] MCI has attracted customers by launching its Friends and Family program, which encourages MCI users to ask their friends and family members to use MCI so that both parties will benefit from lower telephone rates. Some companies have even begun to use a word-of-mouth theme in their advertising campaigns (Figure 20-6, page 618). For more on this topic, see the Marketing Insight on page 619 titled "Developing Word-of-Mouth Referral Channels to Build Business."

Personal influence carries especially great weight in two situations. One is with products that are expensive, risky, or purchased infrequently. Here buyers are likely to be strong information seekers and go beyond mass-media information to seek the recommendations of experts and social acquaintances. The other situation is where the product suggests something about the user's status or taste. Here buyers will consult others to avoid embarrassment.

Companies can take several steps to stimulate personal influence channels to work on their behalf:

- *Identify influential individuals and companies and devote extra effort to them.*[22] In industrial selling, the entire industry might follow the market leader in adopting innovations. Early sales efforts should thus focus on the market leader.

- *Create opinion leaders by supplying certain people with the product on attractive terms.* A new tennis racket might be offered initially to members of high school tennis teams at a special low price to "talk up" their new racket to other students. Or Toyota could offer its more satisfied customers a small gift if they are willing to take calls from prospective buyers.

- *Work through community influentials such as local disk jockeys, class presidents, and presidents of women's organizations.* When Ford introduced the Thunderbird, it sent invitations to executives offering them a free car to drive for the day. Of the 15,000 who took advantage of the offer, 10% indicated that they would become buyers, while 84% said they would recommend it to a friend.

- *Use influential or believable people in testimonial advertising.* Quaker Oats pays Michael Jordan several million dollars to make Gatorade commercials. Jordan is viewed as the world's premiere athlete, so his association with a sports drink is a credible connection, as is his extraordinary ability to connect with consumers, particularly children. Interestingly enough, the same company also has a spokesperson who was a back-office employee until ads for Snapple catapulted her into the public limelight. Wendy Kaufman, better known as "The Snapple Lady," was originally hired to answer the company's voluminous mail, but when some innovative ads let her answer mail on TV, she became a hit with viewers who identified with her warmth and accessibility.[23]

- *Develop advertising that has high "conversation value."* Ads with high conversation value often have a slogan that becomes part of the national vernacular. In the mid-

Designing and Managing Integrated Marketing Communication

FIGURE 20-6
British Airways Word-of-Mouth Advertisement

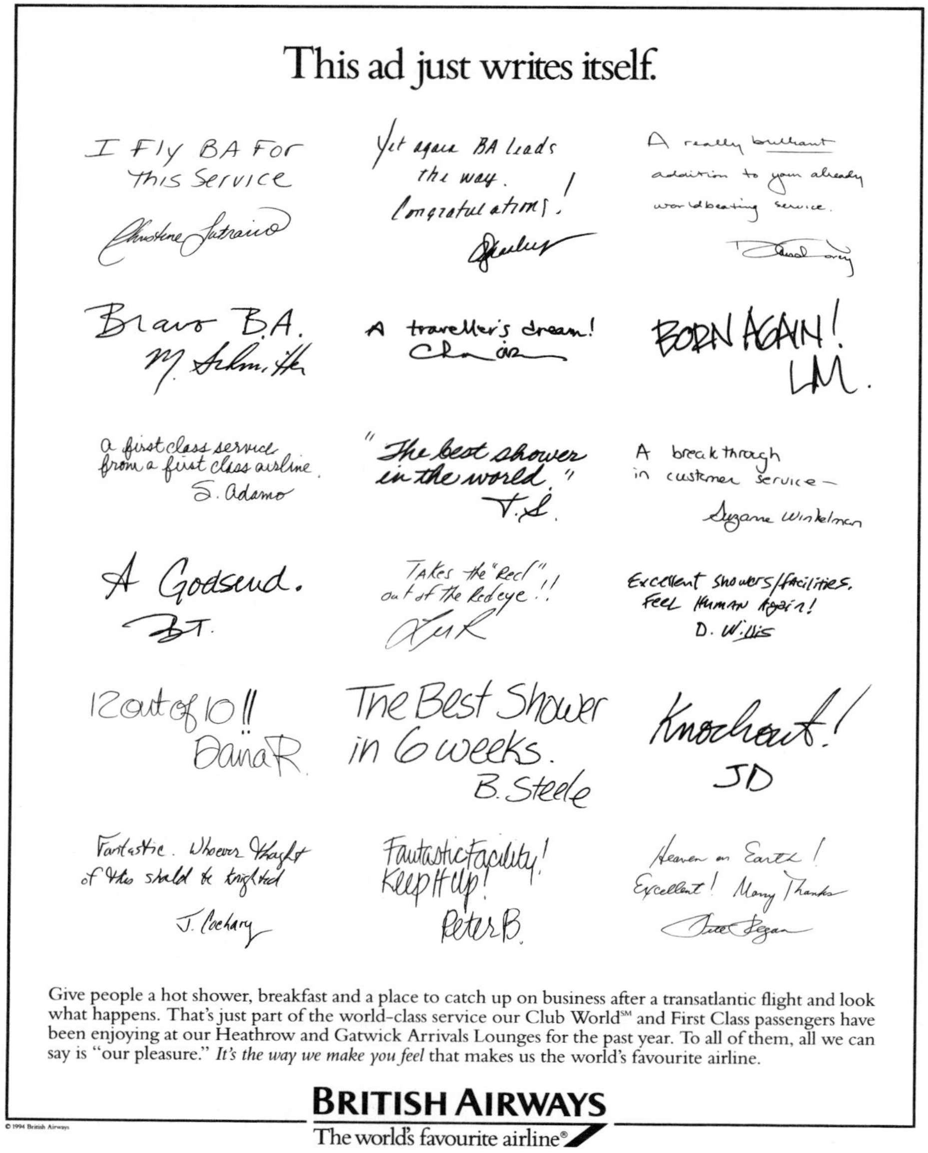

1980s, Wendy's "Where's the Beef?" campaign (showing an elderly lady named Clara questioning where the hamburger was hidden in all that bread) created high conversation value. More recently, people are talking about Energizer bunny's battery, which "keeps going and going and going." In addition, Nike's "Just do it" ads have created a popular command for those unable to make up their minds or take some action, as in "Whaddaya sitting there for? JUST DO IT."

♦ *Develop word-of-mouth referral channels to build business*. Professionals will often encourage their clients to recommend their services to others. Dentists, for example, can ask satisfied patients to recommend friends and acquaintances and subsequently thank them for their recommendations.

♦ *Establish an electronic forum*. Toyota owners who use an online service like Prodigy or America Online can hold online discussions to share their experiences. Toyota personnel can monitor the discussion and respond when appropriate.

Developing Word-of-Mouth Referral Channels to Build Business

There are hundreds of occasions when people will ask others—friends, acquaintances, professionals—for a recommendation. These include times when someone is seeking a physician, electrician, hotel, hospital, lawyer, management consultant, insurance agent, architect, interior decorator, and so on. If we have confidence in the recommender, we will normally act on the referral. In such cases, the recommender has potentially benefited the service provider as well as the service seeker.

The recommender, of course, must be prudent in making the recommendation. If the service seeker acts on the recommendation and is dissatisfied, he or she could lose confidence in the recommender. He or she may even stop patronizing the recommender or in extreme cases, start bad-mouthing or suing the recommender.

Given these risks, why would anyone take the responsibility of recommending anyone? There are three potential benefits. First, the recommender may feel good about having helped the client or friend. Second, the client or friend may now be bonded even more strongly to the recommender. Third, the recommender may receive some tangible benefit from the service provider.

In the last case, the benefit may take one of four forms. First, the service provider might reciprocate by referring business to the recommender. Second, the service provider might give the recommender enhanced service, a discounted price, or on-premise ad-

vertising. Third, the service provider, in gratitude, may send small gifts to the recommender, such as tickets to sporting events, subscriptions, or holiday gifts. Last, the service provider may pay a commission, kickback, or finder's fee. This is clearly illegal or unethical in some professions but occurs in other cases; for example, car dealers can accept commissions on the loans they send to banks.

Service providers clearly have a strong interest in building *referral channels*. Service providers not only promote their organization directly to potential customers but also to potential *referral sources*. Thus, architects know that they might get recommendations from lawyers, accountants, building contractors, banks, and interior decorators. Child psychiatrists know that they might get recommendations from school counselors, clergy, social workers, and physicians. The challenge is to locate high-yield referral sources and take active measures to cultivate their support. Service providers build relationships with referral sources by sending them newsletters, taking them to lunch, offering free consultation, and so on. When service providers get new clients on recommendations, they should send an acknowledging note appreciating the referral; and after serving the client, they should notify the recommender of the service outcome. All said, service providers must view potential referral sources as another target market requiring a specific marketing plan for cultivating their support.

Sources: For additional reading, see Scott R. Herriott, "Identifying and Developing Referral Channels," *Management Decision,* 30, no. 1 (1992), 4–9; Peter H. Reingen and Jerome B. Kernan, "Analysis of Referral Networks in Marketing: Methods and Illustration," *Journal of Marketing Research,* November 1986, pp. 370–78; Jerry R. Wilson, *Word-of-Mouth Marketing* (New York: John Wiley, 1991); and Michael E. Cafferky, *Let Your Customers Do the Talking* (Chicago: Dearborn Financial Publishing, 1995).

NONPERSONAL COMMUNICATION CHANNELS. Nonpersonal communication channels carry messages without personal contact or interaction. They include media, atmospheres, and events.

Media consist of print media (newspapers, magazines, direct mail), broadcast media (radio, television), electronic media (audio tape, videotape, videodisk, CD-ROM), and display media (billboards, signs, posters). Most nonpersonal messages come through paid media.

Atmospheres are "packaged environments" that create or reinforce the buyer's leanings toward product purchase. Thus law offices are decorated with Oriental rugs and oak furniture to communicate "stability" and "success."[24] A luxury hotel will incorporate elegant chandeliers, marble columns, and other tangible signs of luxury.

CHAPTER 20   **619**

Designing and Managing
Integrated Marketing
Communication

Events are occurrences designed to communicate particular messages to target audiences. Public-relations departments arrange news conferences, grand openings, and sport sponsorships to achieve specific communication effects with a target audience.

Although personal communication is often more effective than mass communication, mass media might be the major means of stimulating personal communication. Mass communications affect personal attitudes and behavior through a two-step flow-of-communication process. Ideas often flow from radio, television, and print to *opinion leaders* and from these to the less active population groups.

This two-step communication flow has several implications. First, the influence of mass media on public opinion is not as direct, powerful, and automatic as supposed. It is mediated by opinion leaders, people whose opinions are sought in one or more product areas. Opinion leaders are more exposed to mass media than those they influence. They carry messages to people who are less exposed to media, thus extending the influence of the mass media. They may carry altered messages or none at all, thus acting as gatekeepers.

Second, the two-step communication flow challenges the notion that people's consumption styles are primarily influenced by a "trickle-down" effect from higher-status classes. On the contrary, people interact primarily within their own social class and acquire their fashion and other ideas from people like themselves who are opinion leaders.

Third, two-step communication means that mass communicators would be more efficient by directing their messages specifically to opinion leaders and letting them carry the message to others. Thus pharmaceutical firms try to promote their new drugs to the most influential physicians first. Recent research indicates that both opinion leaders and the general public are affected by mass communication. Opinion leaders are prompted by the mass media to spread information, while the general public seeks information from the opinion leaders.

Communication researchers are moving toward a social-structure view of interpersonal communication.[25] They see society as consisting of *cliques*, small social groups whose members interact with each other more frequently than with others. Clique members are similar, and their closeness facilitates effective communication but also insulates the clique from new ideas. The challenge is to create more system openness whereby cliques exchange more information with others in the society. This openness is helped by people who function as liaisons and bridges. A *liaison* is a person who connects two or more cliques without belonging to either. A *bridge* is a person who belongs to one clique and is linked to a person in another clique.

Establishing the Total Promotion Budget

One of the most difficult marketing decisions facing companies is how much to spend on promotion. John Wanamaker, the department-store magnate, said, "I know that half of my advertising is wasted, but I don't know which half."

Thus it is not surprising that industries and companies vary considerably in how much they spend on promotion. Promotional expenditures might amount to 30 to 50% of sales in the cosmetics industry and only 10 to 20% in the industrial equipment industry. Within a given industry, low- and high-spending companies can be found. Philip Morris is a high spender. When it acquired the Miller Brewing Company, and later the Seven-Up Company, it substantially increased total promotion spending. The additional spending at Miller raised its market share from 4% to 19% within a few years.

How do companies decide on their promotion budget? We will describe four common methods used to set a promotion budget: the affordable method,

620 PART 4

Planning
Marketing
Programs

percentage-of-sales method, competitive-parity method, and objective-and-task method.

AFFORDABLE METHOD. Many companies set the promotion budget at what they think the company can afford. One executive explained this method as follows: "Why, it's simple. First, I go upstairs to the controller and ask how much they can afford to give us this year. He says a million and a half. Later, the boss comes to me and asks how much we should spend and I say 'Oh, about a million and a half.'"[26]

The affordable method of setting budgets completely ignores the role of promotion as an investment and the immediate impact of promotion on sales volume. It leads to an uncertain annual promotion budget, which makes long-range market communication planning difficult.

PERCENTAGE-OF-SALES METHOD. Many companies set their promotion expenditures at a specified percentage of sales (either current or anticipated) or of the sales price. A railroad company executive said: "We set our appropriation for each year on December 1 of the preceding year. On that date we add our passenger revenue for the next month, and then take 2% of the total for our advertising appropriation for the new year."[27] Automobile companies typically budget a fixed percentage for promotion based on the planned car price. Oil companies set the appropriation at a fraction of a cent for each gallon of gasoline sold under their own label.

Supporters of the percentage-of-sales method claim a number of advantages for it. First, its use means that promotion expenditures vary with what the company can "afford." This satisfies the financial managers, who believe that expenses should be closely related to the movement of corporate sales over the business cycle. Second, it encourages management to think in terms of the relationship among promotion cost, selling price, and profit per unit. Third, it encourages competitive stability to the extent that competing firms spend approximately the same percentage of their sales on promotion.

In spite of these advantages, the percentage-of-sales method has little to justify it. Its reasoning is circular: It views sales as the determiner of promotion rather than as the result. It leads to a budget set by the availability of funds rather than by market opportunities. It discourages experimenting with countercyclical promotion or aggressive spending. The promotion budget's dependence on year-to-year sales fluctuations interferes with long-range planning. The method does not provide a logical basis for choosing the specific percentage, except what has been done in the past or what competitors are doing. Finally, it does not encourage building up the promotion budget by determining what each product and territory deserves.

COMPETITIVE-PARITY METHOD. Some companies set their promotion budget to achieve share-of-voice parity with their competitors. This thinking is illustrated by the executive who asked a trade source, "Do you have any figures which other companies in the builders' specialties field have used which would indicate what proportion of gross sales should be given over to advertising?"[28] This executive believes that by spending the same percentage of his sales on advertising as his competitors, he will maintain his market share.

Two arguments are made in support of the competitive-parity method. One is that the competitors' expenditures represent the collective wisdom of the industry. The other is that maintaining a competitive parity helps prevent promotion wars.

Neither argument is valid. There are no grounds for believing that competition knows better what should be spent on promotion. Company reputations, re-

Designing and Managing
Integrated Marketing
Communication

sources, opportunities, and objectives differ so much that their promotion budgets are hardly a guide. Furthermore, there is no evidence that budgets based on competitive parity discourage promotional wars from breaking out.

OBJECTIVE-AND-TASK METHOD. The objective-and-task method calls upon marketers to develop their promotion budgets by defining their specific objectives, determining the tasks that must be performed to achieve these objectives, and estimating the costs of performing these tasks. The sum of these costs is the proposed promotion budget.

Ule showed how the objective-and-task method could be used to establish an advertising budget. Suppose Helene Curtis wants to launch a new woman's anti-dandruff shampoo, Clear.[29] The steps are as follows:

1. *Establish the market-share goal.* The company estimates that there are 50 million potential users and sets a target of attracting 8% of the market—that is, 4 million users.

2. *Determine the percentage of the market that should be reached by Clear advertising.* The advertiser hopes to reach 80% (40 million prospects) with the advertising message.

3. *Determine the percentage of aware prospects that should be persuaded to try the brand.* The advertiser would be pleased if 25% of aware prospects (10 million) tried Clear. This is because it estimates that 40% of all triers, or 4 million people, would become loyal users. This is the market goal.

4. *Determine the number of advertising impressions per 1% trial rate.* The advertiser estimates that 40 advertising impressions (exposures) for every 1% of the population would bring about a 25% trial rate.

5. *Determine the number of gross rating points that would have to be purchased.* A *gross rating point* is one exposure to 1% of the target population. Since the company wants to achieve 40 exposures to 80% of the population, it will want to buy 3,200 gross rating points.

6. *Determine the necessary advertising budget on the basis of the average cost of buying a gross rating point.* To expose 1% of the target population to one impression costs an average of $3,277. Therefore, 3,200 gross rating points would cost $10,486,400 (= $3,277 × 3,200) in the introductory year.

The objective-and-task method has the advantage of requiring management to spell out its assumptions about the relationship among dollars spent, exposure levels, trial rates, and regular usage.

A major question is how much weight promotion should receive in the total marketing mix (as opposed to product improvement, lower prices, more services, and so on). The answer depends on where the company's products are in their life cycles, whether they are commodities or highly differentiable products, whether they are routinely needed or have to be "sold," and other considerations. In theory, the total promotional budget should be established where the marginal profit from the last promotional dollar just equals the marginal profit from the last dollar in the best nonpromotional use. Implementing this principle, however, is not easy.

Deciding on the Promotion Mix

Companies face the task of distributing the total promotion budget over the five promotional tools—advertising, sales promotion, public relations and publicity, sales force, and direct marketing. Within the same industry, companies can differ considerably in how they allocate their promotional budget. It is possible to achieve a given sales level with varying promotional mixes. Avon concentrates its promotional funds on personal selling, while Revlon spends heavily on advertising. In selling vacuum cleaners, Electrolux spends heavily on a door-to-door sales force, while Hoover relies more on advertising.

Companies are always searching for ways to gain efficiency by substituting one promotional tool for another. Many companies have replaced some field sales activity with ads, direct mail, and telemarketing. Other companies have increased their sales-promotion expenditures in relation to advertising. The substitutability among promotional tools explains why marketing functions need to be coordinated in a single marketing department. For more details on promotion budgets, see the Marketing Insight on page 624 titled "How Do Companies Set Their Promotion Budgets?"

Many factors influence the marketer's choice and mix of promotional tools. We will examine these factors in the following sections, and in more detail in Chapters 22 and 23.

THE PROMOTIONAL TOOLS. Each promotional tool has its own unique characteristics and costs. Marketers have to understand these characteristics.[30]

Advertising. Because of the many forms and uses of advertising, it is difficult to make all-embracing generalizations about its distinctive qualities as a component of the promotion mix.[31] Yet the following qualities can be noted:

- *Public presentation:* Advertising is a highly public mode of communication. Its public nature confers a kind of legitimacy on the product and also suggests a standardized offering. Because many persons receive the same message, buyers know that their motives for purchasing the product will be publicly understood.

- *Pervasiveness:* Advertising is a pervasive medium that permits the seller to repeat a message many times. It also allows the buyer to receive and compare the messages of various competitors. Large-scale advertising by a seller says something positive about the seller's size, power, and success.

- *Amplified expressiveness:* Advertising provides opportunities for dramatizing the company and its products through the artful use of print, sound, and color. Sometimes, however, the tool's very success at expressiveness may dilute or distract from the message.

- *Impersonality:* Advertising cannot be as compelling as a company sales representative. The audience does not feel obligated to pay attention or respond. Advertising is able to carry on only a monologue in front of, not a dialogue with, the audience.

On the one hand, advertising can be used to build up a long-term image for a product (Coca-Cola ads), and on the other, to trigger quick sales (a Sears ad for a weekend sale). Advertising is an efficient way to reach numerous geographically dispersed buyers at a low cost per exposure. Certain forms of advertising (such as TV advertising) can require a large budget while other forms (such as newspaper advertising) can be done on a small budget. Advertising might have an effect on sales simply through its presence. Consumers might believe that a heavily advertised brand must offer "good value"; otherwise, why would advertisers spend so much money touting the product?

Blurring the advertising category are two relatively new additions to the promotion mix. *Advertorials* are print ads that offer editorial content and are designed in a way that makes it difficult to distinguish them from a newspaper's or magazine's contents. *Infomercials* are TV commercials that appear to be 30-minute television shows, but are really advertisements for products or sales-lead generators. Infomercials usually ask viewers to call in to order the product and, hence, produce directly measurable results. Gross sales of products generated by infomercial programs grew from about $350 million in 1988 to about $900 million in 1993. Fortune 1000 advertisers are now looking at infomercials as part of their marketing mix because they produce measurable results and because they can help to educate consumers about products with uses that aren't very clear at first glance.

How Do Companies Set Their Promotion Budgets?

Although companies can benefit by using marketing theories and models to set their marketing budgets—and some do—most companies go through a process that is partly rational, partly political, and partly expedient. Low and Mohr carried out in-depth interviews with 21 managers at consumer-products firms to learn how they set and allocated marketing communication budgets. At issue was how brand managers set the total promotion budget and its allocation to advertising, consumer promotion, and trade promotion. They found that all the companies developed their budgets through a "brand team" approach. The teams included managers from sales, trade marketing, manufacturing, accounting, and marketing research, as well as the brand manager, brand assistants, and a category manager (if this position exists).

As the first step in the budgeting process, the brand team does an extensive situation analysis in the course of developing the annual marketing plan. Based on this analysis, the team establishes marketing objectives and a broad strategy. Then the brand manager forecasts the brand sales and profits based on the broad strategy. Second, the team develops an initial allocation of the budget to advertising, consumer promotion, and trade promotion. Some companies treat trade promotion as a given, and then allocate the balance to advertising and consumer promotion, based on historical precedent. The allocation is then adjusted further in the light of competitors' promotional activity and other factors. For example, if the competitor is expected to increase trade promotion, the brand manager would switch more money to trade promotion.

Third, the brand plan is presented to senior management—the company president, marketing vice president, group managers, sales vice president, and a senior financial manager. At this stage, senior managers

may require or advise changes, partly reflecting what they think this brand deserves in relation to the other brands under review. The revised plan is then implemented.

During the year, the brand manager will adjust the allocations in response to competitive and economic developments. Toward the end of the period, brand managers will often cut advertising when the brand is not meeting its profit objectives, since this money falls to the bottom line without hurting short-term sales. At the end of the year, companies should—though many don't—do a post-mortem to evaluate the previous year's spending in order to improve the managers' ability to use marketing tools more effectively in the future.

In sum: The budget-setting process is a rational sequence of steps that involves political negotiation, the use of traditional promotion allocation rules, and reactive last-minute adjustments to marketplace events.

Low and Mohr also examined the factors that influence the relative allocation of funds to the different promotional tools. Here are some of their findings:

1. More money is put into advertising—compared to sales promotion—in the introduction and growth stages of the product life cycle, especially if the market growth rate is strong. Companies with the largest market share, profit margin, and/or product differentiation also spend relatively more on advertising.

2. More money is put into sales promotion the greater the competition, the more the short-term focus of management, the more the political influence of the firm's sales force, and the more the retailers' strength.

3. Advertising tends to have a positive effect on consumer attitudes and long-term market share but little effect on short-term market share.

4. Consumer and trade promotion tend to have a stronger effect on consumer attitudes and market share in the short run.

Source: See George S. Low and Jakki J. Mohr, "The Advertising Sales Promotion Trade-Off: Theory and Practice" (Cambridge, MA: Marketing Science Institute, Report Number 92-127, October 1992).

Sales Promotion. Although sales-promotion tools—coupons, contests, premiums, and the like—are highly diverse, they all offer three distinctive benefits:

- *Communication:* They gain attention and usually provide information that may lead the consumer to the product.

- *Incentive:* They incorporate some concession, inducement, or contribution that gives value to the consumer.

- *Invitation:* They include a distinct invitation to engage in the transaction now.

Companies use sales-promotion tools to create a stronger and quicker response. Sales promotion can be used to dramatize product offers and to boost sagging sales. Sales-promotion effects are usually short run, however, and not effective in building long-run brand preference.

Public Relations and Publicity. The appeal of public relations and publicity is based on their three distinctive qualities:

- *High credibility:* News stories and features are more authentic and credible to readers than ads.
- *Ability to catch buyers off guard:* Public relations can reach many prospects who prefer to avoid salespeople and advertisements. The message gets to the buyers as news rather than as a sales-directed communication.
- *Dramatization:* Like advertising, public relations has the potential for dramatizing a company or product.

Marketers tend to underuse public relations and publicity or use them as an afterthought. Yet a well-thought-out public-relations program coordinated with the other promotion-mix elements can be extremely effective.

Personal Selling. Personal selling is the most cost-effective tool at later stages of the buying process, particularly in building up buyers' preference, conviction, and action. The reason is that personal selling, when compared with advertising, has three distinctive benefits:

- *Personal confrontation:* Personal selling involves an alive, immediate, and interactive relationship between two or more persons. Each party is able to observe the other's needs and characteristics at close hand and make immediate adjustments.
- *Cultivation:* Personal selling permits all kinds of relationships to spring up, ranging from a matter-of-fact selling relationship to a deep personal friendship. Effective sales representatives will normally keep their customers' best interests at heart if they want to maintain long-run relationships.
- *Response:* Personal selling makes the buyer feel under some obligation for having listened to the sales talk. The buyer has a greater need to attend and respond, even if the response is a polite "thank you."

These distinctive qualities come at a cost. A sales force represents a greater long-term cost commitment than advertising. Advertising can be turned on and off, but the size of a sales force is more difficult to alter.

Direct Marketing. Although there are many forms of direct marketing—direct mail, telemarketing, electronic marketing, and so on—they all share four distinctive characteristics. Direct marketing is:

- *Nonpublic:* The message is normally addressed to a specific person.
- *Customized:* The message can be customized to appeal to the addressed individual.
- *Up-to-date:* A message can be prepared very quickly for delivery to an individual.
- *Interactive:* The message can be altered depending on the person's response.

FACTORS IN SETTING THE PROMOTION MIX. Companies must consider several factors in developing their promotion mix: the type of product market in which they are selling, whether to use a push or pull strategy, how ready consumers are to make a purchase, the product's stage in the product life cycle, and the company's market rank.

Type of Product Market. Promotional tool utilization varies between consumer and business markets (see Figure 20-7). Consumer-goods companies spend on sales

Designing and Managing
Integrated Marketing
Communication

Consumer goods

Sales promotion

Advertising

Personal selling

Public relations

Relative spending

Industrial goods

Personal selling

Sales promotion

Advertising

Public relations

Relative spending

FIGURE 20-7
Relative Spending on Promotional Tools in Consumer versus Business Markets

promotion, advertising, personal selling, and public relations in that order. Business-goods companies spend on personal selling, sales promotion, advertising, and public relations in that order. In general, personal selling is more heavily used with complex, expensive, and risky goods and in markets with fewer and larger sellers (hence, business markets).

While advertising is used less than sales calls in business markets, it still plays a significant role. Advertising can perform the following functions in business markets:

- *Awareness building:* Prospects who are not aware of the company or product might refuse to see the sales representative. Advertising can be an introduction to the company and its products.
- *Comprehension building:* If the product embodies new features, some of the burden of explaining them can be effectively undertaken by advertising.
- *Efficient reminding:* If prospects know about the product but are not ready to buy, reminder advertising would be more economical than sales calls.
- *Lead generation:* Advertisements offering brochures and carrying the company's phone number are an effective way to generate leads for sales representatives.
- *Legitimization:* Sales representatives can use tear sheets of the company's ads in leading magazines to legitimize their company and products.
- *Reassurance:* Advertising can remind customers how to use the product and reassure them about their purchase.

A number of studies have underscored advertising's important role in business-to-business marketing. Morrill showed in his study of industrial-commodity marketing that advertising combined with personal selling increased sales 23% over what they had been with no advertising. The total promotional cost as a percentage of sales was reduced by 20 percent.[32] Freeman developed a formal model for dividing promotional funds between advertising and personal selling on the basis of the selling tasks that each performs more economically.[33] Levitt's research also showed the important role that advertising can play in business marketing. Specifically, Levitt found that:

1. A company's reputation improves its sales force's chances of getting a favorable first hearing and an early adoption of the product. Therefore, corporate advertising that can build up the company's reputation (other factors also shape its reputation) will help the company's sales representatives.
2. Sales representatives from well-known companies have an edge in getting the sale if their sales presentations are adequate. But a sales representative from a lesser-known company who makes a highly effective sales presentation can overcome the disadvantage. Smaller companies should use their limited funds to select and train good sales representatives rather than spend the money on advertising.
3. Company reputations help most where the product is complex, the risk is high, and the purchasing agent is less professionally trained.[34]

Lilien researched business marketing practices in a major project called ADVISOR and reported the following:[35]

- The average industrial company set its marketing budget at 7% of its sales. It spent only 10% of its marketing budget on advertising. Companies spent the remainder on sales force, trade shows, sales promotion, and direct mail.
- Industrial companies spent a higher-than-average amount on advertising, where their products had higher quality, uniqueness, or purchase frequency, or where more customer growth was occurring.
- Industrial companies set a higher-than-average marketing budget when their customers were more dispersed or where the customer growth rate was higher.

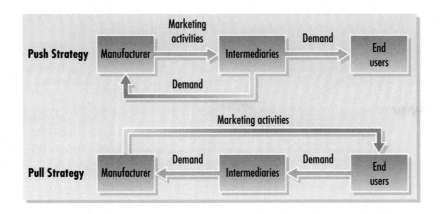

FIGURE 20-8
Push versus Pull Strategy

Personal selling can also make a strong contribution in consumer-goods marketing. Some consumer marketers play down the role of the sales force, using them mainly to collect weekly orders from dealers and to see that sufficient stock is on the shelf. The common feeling is that "salespeople put products on shelves and advertising takes them off." Yet even here an effectively trained sales force can make three important contributions:

◆ *Increased stock position:* Sales representatives can persuade dealers to take more stock and devote more shelf space to the company's brand.

◆ *Enthusiasm building:* Sales representatives can build dealer enthusiasm for a new product by dramatizing the planned advertising and sales-promotion backup.

◆ *Missionary selling:* Sales representatives can sign up more dealers to carry the company's brands.

Push Versus Pull Strategy. The promotional mix is heavily influenced by whether the company chooses a push or pull strategy to create sales. The two strategies are contrasted in Figure 20-8. A *push strategy* involves manufacturer marketing activities (primarily sales force and trade promotion) directed at channel intermediaries. The goal is to induce the intermediaries to order and carry the product and promote it to end users. Push strategy is especially appropriate where there is low brand loyalty in a category, brand choice is made in the store, the product is an impulse item, and product benefits are well understood. A *pull strategy* involves marketing activities (primarily advertising and consumer promotion) directed at end users. The purpose is to induce them to ask intermediaries for the product and thus induce the intermediaries to order the product from the manufacturer. Pull strategy is especially appropriate when there is high brand loyalty and high involvement in the category, people perceive differences between brands, and people choose the brand before they go to the store. Companies in the same industry may differ in their emphasis on push or pull. For example, Lever Brothers relies more heavily on push, Procter & Gamble more heavily on pull.

Buyer-Readiness Stage. Promotional tools vary in their cost effectiveness at different stages of buyer readiness. Figure 20-9 on the next page shows the relative cost effectiveness of four promotional tools. Advertising and publicity play the most important roles in the awareness stage, much more important than the roles played by "cold calls" from sales representatives or by sales promotion. Customer comprehension is primarily affected by advertising and personal selling. Customer conviction is influenced mostly by personal selling and less by advertising and sales promotion. Closing the sale (ordering) is influenced mostly by personal selling and sales promotion. Reordering is also affected mostly by personal selling and sales promotion, and somewhat by reminder advertising. Clearly, advertising and

Designing and Managing
Integrated Marketing
Communication

FIGURE 20-9

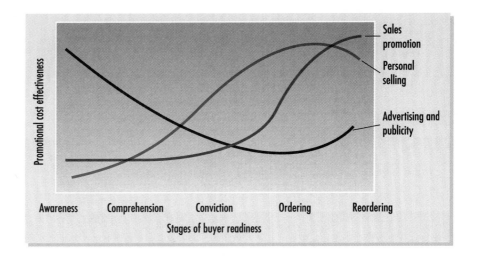

publicity are most cost effective at the early stages of the buyer decision process, and personal selling and sales promotion are most effective at the later stages.

Product-Life-Cycle Stage. Promotional tools also vary in their cost effectiveness at different stages of the product life cycle. Figure 20-10 offers a speculative view of their relative effectiveness.

♦ In the introduction stage, advertising and publicity have the highest cost effectiveness, followed by personal selling to gain distribution coverage and sales promotion to induce trial.

♦ In the growth stage, all the tools can be toned down because demand has its own momentum through word-of-mouth.

♦ In the maturity stage, sales promotion, advertising, and personal selling all grow more important, in that order.

♦ In the decline stage, sales promotion continues strong, advertising and publicity are reduced, and salespeople give the product only minimal attention.

FIGURE 20-10

**Cost Effectiveness of
Different Promotional Tools
at Different Stages of the
Product Life Cycle**

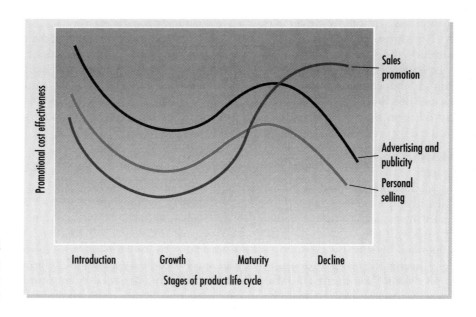

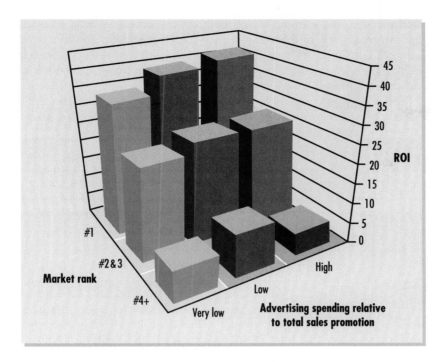

FIGURE 20-11
How Market Rank and the Advertising/Profitability Ratio Affects Profitability

Source: Bradley T. Gale, "Power Brands: The Essentials," an unpublished paper, November 1991, p. 2.

Company Market Rank. As Figure 20-11 shows, top-ranking brands derive more benefit from advertising than sales promotions. For the top three brands, return on investment (ROI) rises with a rising ratio of advertising spending to sales promotion. For brands ranked fourth or worse, profitability decreases in moving from low to high advertising.

Measuring the Promotion's Results

After implementing the promotional plan, the communicator must measure its impact on the target audience. This involves asking the target audience whether they recognize or recall the message, how many times they saw it, what points they recall, how they felt about the message, and their previous and current attitudes toward the product and company. The communicator should also collect behavioral measures of audience response, such as how many people bought the product, liked it, and talked to others about it.

Figure 20-12 provides an example of good feedback measurement. Looking at brand A, we find that 80% of the consumers in the total market are aware of brand A, 60% have tried it, and only 20% who have tried it are satisfied. This indicates that the communication program is effective in creating awareness, but the product fails to meet consumer expectations. In contrast, only 40% of the consumers in the total market are aware of brand B, and only 30% have tried it, but 80% of those who have tried it are satisfied. In this case, the communication program needs to be strengthened to take advantage of the brand's satisfaction-generating power.

Managing and Coordinating Integrated Marketing Communications

Many companies still rely primarily on one or two communication tools to achieve their communication aims. This practice persists in spite of the disintegration of

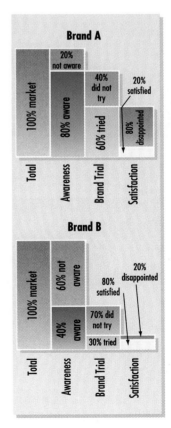

FIGURE 20-12
Current Consumer States for Two Brands

mass markets into a multitude of minimarkets, each requiring its own communication approach; the proliferation of new types of media; and the growing sophistication of consumers. The wide range of communication tools, messages, and audiences makes it imperative that companies give thought to a fresher and fuller use and orchestration of communication tools.

Today, a growing number of companies are adopting the concept of *integrated marketing communications (IMC)*. As defined by the American Association of Advertising Agencies (4 As), IMC is:

> . . . *a concept of marketing communications planning that recognizes the added value of a comprehensive plan that evaluates the strategic roles of a variety of communications disciplines—for example, general advertising, direct response, sales promotion and public relations—and combines these disciplines to provide clarity, consistency, and maximum communications' impact through the seamless integration of discrete messages.*

Here is a creative example of integrated marketing communications:

WARNER-WELLCOME Warner-Wellcome, maker of Benadryl, wanted to promote the antihistamine to allergy sufferers. The company used advertising and public relations to increase brand awareness, and to promote a toll-free number that provided people with the pollen count in their area. People who called the number more than once received free product samples, coupons, and in-depth materials describing the product's benefits. These people also received an ongoing newsletter that includes advice on how to cope with allergy problems.[36]

A 1991 study of top management and marketing executives in large consumer products companies indicated that over 70% favored the concept of integrated marketing communications as a way to improve their communications impact. At that time several large advertising agencies—Ogilvy & Mather, Young & Rubicam, Saatchi and Saatchi—acquired major agencies specializing in sales promotion, public relations, and direct marketing in order to provide one-stop shopping. But to their disappointment, most clients have not bought their integrated marketing communications package, preferring to deal with separate agencies instead.

Why the resistance? In part, large companies employ different communication specialists to work with the company's brand managers. Each communication specialist will fight for more budget. The sales manager will want to hire two extra sales representatives for $80,000, while the advertising manager will want to spend the same money on a prime-time TV commercial. The public-relations manager sincerely believes that a publicity program will work wonders, while telemarketing and direct-mail program specialists believe they have the answer.

Brand managers themselves are often poorly trained in the various forms of marketing communications. Many times they have only traditional experience in media advertising. They know very little about direct marketing, sales promotion, or public relations. The head of each functional communication tool knows little about the other communication tools. Furthermore, the communication heads usually have favorite outside specialist agencies and oppose turning over all communication responsibilities to one superadvertising agency. They argue that the company should choose the best specialist agency for each purpose, not second- and third-rate agencies just because they belong to the superadvertising agency. They are convinced that the advertising agency doesn't have its act together either, with each department in the agency operating as a separate profit center. They believe that the ad agency will still put most of the advertiser's money into the advertising budget.

Integrated marketing communications will produce more message consistency and greater sales impact. It gives someone responsibility—where none existed be-

PART 4

Planning
Marketing
Programs

MARKETING MEMO

CHECKLIST FOR INTEGRATING MARKETING COMMUNICATIONS

Marketers who have gained the ear of management can take the lead in putting together a proposal for achieving integrated marketing communications. Such proposals often include the following recommendations:

- *Audit the pockets of communications-related spending throughout the organization.* Itemize the budgets and tasks and consolidate these into a single budgeting process. Reassess all communications expenditures by product, promotional tool, stage of the life cycle, and observed effect. Use this as a basis for improving further use of these tools.

- *Create shared performance measures.* Develop systems to evaluate communications activities. Since IMC attempts to change consumer purchase behavior, this behavior must be measured to ultimately demonstrate communications' impact on the bottom line. ROI can be measured either by tracking a company's own communications efforts or through syndicated customer data.

- *Use database development and issues management to understand your stakeholders.* Include customers, employees, investors, vendors, and all other stakeholders at every stage of your communications plan.

- *Identify all contact points for the company and its products.* Use this audit to determine where communications can best be used to reinforce the company's messages. Measure communications' ability to do so at each contact point, whether it be your product packaging, retail display, shareholder meeting or spokesperson, and so forth. Work to ensure your communications efforts are occurring when, where, and how your *customers* want them.

- *Analyze trends—internal and external—that can affect your company's ability to do business.* Look for areas where communications can help the most. Determine the strengths and weaknesses of each communications function. Develop a combination of promotional tactics based on these strengths and weaknesses. Use this mix to meet marketing goals.

- *Create business and communication plans for each local market.* Integrate these into a global communications strategy.

- *Appoint a director responsible for the company's persuasive communications efforts.* This move encourages efficiency by centralizing planning and creating shared performance measures.

- *Create compatible themes, tones, and quality across all communications media.* This consistency achieves greater impact and prevents the unnecessary duplication of work across functions. When creating materials, consider how they can be used for a range of audiences. Make sure each carries your unique primary messages and selling points.

- *Hire only team players.* Employees trained in this new, integrated way of thinking will not be locked into functional silos. Rather, they thrive on group accountability and are open to any new responsibility that enables them to better meet the needs of customers.

- *Link IMC with management processes, such as participatory management.* This produces a fully integrated management effort aimed at meeting corporate goals. An integrated strategy should permit efficiency in each communication function contributing to the success of the corporate mission.

Source: Reprinted from Matthew P. Gonring, "Putting Integrated Marketing Communications to Work Today," *Public Relations Quarterly,* Fall 1994, pp. 45–48.

fore—to unify the company's brand images and messages as they come through thousands of company activities. IMC will improve the company's ability to reach the right customers with the right messages at the right time and in the right place.[37] Duke Power, the North Carolina utility, found out how useful IMC can be when its top management chartered an Integrated Communications Project Team (ICPT) in 1993:

DUKE POWER To develop an approach to integrated marketing communications, Duke Power conducted lengthy interviews with company officers, customer surveys, literature reviews, and "best practice" interviews with other companies. Out of this process, the ICPT made four recommendations: (1) that Duke manage its reputation as a corporate asset; (2) that the company develop and implement an integrated communications process to manage all aspects of its communications; (3) that the company train all its employees in how to communicate, since Duke's customers responded more to employees' actions than to specific planned programs; and (4) that the company develop and enhance a strategic database to help it anticipate customer interests and improve customer satisfaction and retention. Based on these recommendations, the ICPT developed integrated communications processes that are directly tied to the company's business processes.[38]

Advocates of integrated marketing communications describe it as a new way of looking at the whole marketing process instead of focusing on only individual parts of it. For a list of some specific steps that companies can take to create an integrated whole out of the marketing communication parts, see the Marketing Memo on page 631 titled "Checklist for Integrating Marketing Communications."

SUMMARY

1. Modern marketing calls for more than developing a good product, pricing it attractively, and making it accessible to target customers. Companies must also communicate with their present and potential customers, retailers, suppliers, other stakeholders, and the general public. The marketing communications mix consists of five major modes of communication: advertising, sales promotion, public relations and publicity, personal selling, and direct marketing.

2. The communication process consists of nine elements: sender, receiver, message, media, encoding, decoding, response, feedback, and noise. To get their messages through, marketers must encode their messages in a way that takes into account how the target audience usually decodes messages. They must also transmit the message through efficient media that reach the target audience and develop feedback channels to monitor the receivers' response to the message. The audience may not receive the message due to selective attention, selective distortion, or selective recall.

3. Developing effective communications involves eight steps: (1) identify the target audience, (2) determine the communication objectives, (3) design the message, (4) select the communications channels, (5) establish the total promotion budget, (6) decide on the promotion mix, (7) measure the promotion's results, and (8) manage and coordinate the integrated marketing communication process.

   In identifying the target audience, the marketer needs to perform familiarity and favorability analyses, then seek to close any gap that exists between current public perception and the ideal sought. The communications objectives may be cognitive, affective, or behavioral—that is, the company might want to put something into the consumer's mind, change the consumer's attitude, or get the consumer to act. In designing the message, marketers must carefully consider message content (which may include rational, emotional, and/or moral appeals), message structure (one-sided versus two-sided arguments, order of presentation), message format (print versus spoken), and source (including the source's degree of expertise, trustworthiness, and likability). Communication channels may be personal (advocate, expert, and social channels) or nonpersonal (media, atmospheres, and events). While there are many methods used to set the promotion budget, the objective-and-task method, which calls upon marketers to develop their budgets by defining their specific objectives, is the most desirable. In deciding on the promotion mix, marketers must examine the distinct advantages and costs of each promotional tool. They must also consider the type of product market in which they are selling, whether to use a push or a pull strategy, how ready consumers are to make a purchase, the product's stage in the product life cycle, and the company's market rank. Measuring the promotion mix's effectiveness involves asking the target audience whether they recognize or recall the message, how many times they saw it, what points they recall, how they felt about the message, and their previous and current attitudes toward the product and company. Managing and coordinating the entire communications process calls for integrated marketing communications (IMC).

CONCEPT APPLICATIONS

1. Reflect back on a major decision you made concerning a potential purchase, such as a car, college, and the like. Using the model of elements in the communication process (Figure 20-1), determine how each of these elements affected your decision. Which element had the greatest influence on your final decision? What additional information would have been helpful? What did you decide?

2. When determining an ad's message content, the communicator must determine what type of message will have the desired effect on the target audience. Bring to class examples of print ads making the following rational or emotional appeals:

   a. quality   e. guilt
   b. economy   f. humor
   c. performance   g. pride
   d. fear   h. sympathy

   Explain why you think the advertiser selected this appeal. Do you agree or disagree with the communicator's decision?

3. Bring to class five print ads that make use of celebrity endorsements. Is the endorser chosen for expertise, trustworthiness, or likability? How effective do you think these ads are? Are the ads believable? What is your feeling toward each of the celebrities in the ads? Do you think these ads are targeted toward you? What are some issues facing companies that use celebrity endorsers?

4. Respond to the following marketing challenges:
   a. The target audience for your product (an upscale women's fragrance sold only in exclusive department stores) has reservations about it. What personal qualities would you recommend that the spokesperson for your message possess? Whom would you recommend as a spokesperson? Why?
   b. Explain what kinds of appeal marketers would find most effective in marketing the following products or services: disposable diapers, laundry detergent, a quit smoking program, the United Way, seat belts, and life insurance.

5. The major mass media—newspapers, magazines, radio, television, and outdoor media—show striking differences in their capacity for dramatization, credibility, attention getting, and other valued aspects of communication. Describe the special characteristics of each media type, along with its advantages and disadvantages.

6. What factors are critical to the success of an integrated marketing communications (IMC) program? How can organization structure act as a barrier to IMC?

7. The American Cancer Society has hired you to develop an integrated marketing communications plan that will inform and persuade people of the risks of skin cancer due to overexposure to the sun. Additionally, the campaign would inform "sunners" how to prevent the disease. In teams of five, develop an integrated marketing communications plan for the American Cancer Society. Use the following grid to help you organize your thoughts.

	ADVERTISING	PUBLIC RELATIONS	SALES PROMOTION	DIRECT RESPONSE
a. Health objective b. Target c. Purpose d. Promise e. Support f. Personality g. Aperture h. Consumer contact points				

Definitions:

  a. *Health objective:* Goal of the communication in terms of the person's health

  b. *Target:* Audience to whom the communication is targeted

  c. *Purpose:* A "solution" for helping the target audience meet the health objective

  d. *Promise:* What the target audience will receive in return for meeting the health objective

  e. *Support:* Sources of credible support for the claims made in the communications

  f. *Personality:* The "flavor" of the communication—serious, humorous, and so forth

  g. *Aperture:* Time frame in which to appeal to the target audience

  h. *Consumer contact points:* Places at which the target audience can be reached, and the forms of media best suited to target audience members

8. Lite Beer commercials by Miller were the most often noticed, remembered, and liked ads on TV. The same year, Oscar Meyer commercials ranked twelfth on the list of most remembered commercials. Can we claim that Miller ads were considerably more successful than Oscar Meyer ads? Why or why not?

9. Assume that at Wilson Sporting Goods, Inc., the sales managers and communications managers report directly to the director of marketing. How can the marketing director keep both the sales department and the communications department (two departments that are often at odds) operating on the same wavelength? Furthermore, how can she get extra mileage from her communication program so that advertising is designed to inform and motivate the target audience as well as to sell Wilson's own distributors and salespeople?

10. What kind of consumer responses should marketers aim for when communicating about the following products: legal services, frozen pizza, veterinary services, sewing machines, pianos, telephone answering machines, hammers? You may find it useful to divide these products into two or three categories, then base your answer on those categories.

NOTES

1. The definitions are adapted from Peter D. Bennett, *Dictionary of Marketing Terms* (Chicago: American Marketing Association, 1995).

2. For an alternate communication model developed specifically for advertising communications, see Barbara B. Stern, "A Revised Communication Model for Advertising: Multiple Dimensions of the Source, the Message, and the Recipient," *Journal of Advertising,* June 1994, pp. 5–15.

3. See Brian Sternthal and C. Samuel Craig, *Consumer Behavior: An Information Processing Perspective* (Englewood Cliffs, NJ: Prentice Hall, 1982), pp. 97–102.

4. Donald F. Cox and Raymond A. Bauer, "Self-Confidence and Persuasibility in Women," *Public Opinion Quarterly,* Fall 1964, pp. 453–66; and Raymond L. Horton, "Some Relationships between Personality and Consumer Decision-Making," *Journal of Marketing Research,* May 1979, pp. 233–46.

5. Marian Friestad and Peter Wright, "The Persuasion Knowledge Model: How People Cope with Persuasion Attempts," *Journal of Consumer Research,* June 1994, pp. 1–31.

6. See John Fiske and John Hartley, *Reading Television* (London: Methuen, 1980), p. 79. For the effects of expertise on persuasion, see also Elizabeth J. Wilson and Daniel L. Sherrell, "Source

Effects in Communication and Persuasion Research: A Meta-Analysis of Effect Size," *Journal of the Academy of Marketing Science,* Spring 1993, pp. 101–12.

7. The semantic differential was developed by C. E. Osgood, C. J. Suci, and P. H. Tannenbaum, *The Measurement of Meaning* (Urbana: University of Illinois Press, 1957).

8. Joshua Levine, "Please Excuse Our Shoe Styles of the Past," *Forbes,* January 2, 1995, p. 64.

9. See Michael L. Ray, *Advertising and Communications Management* (Englewood Cliffs, NJ: Prentice Hall, 1982).

10. See Michael R. Solomon, *Consumer Behavior,* 3d ed. (Upper Saddle River, NJ: Prentice Hall, 1996), pp. 208–10 for references to research articles on fear appeals.

11. Kevin Goldman, "Advertising: Knock, Knock. Who's There? The Same Old Funny Ad Again," *The Wall Street Journal,* November 2, 1993, B10:4. See also Marc G. Weinberger, Harlan Spotts, Leland Campbell, and Amy L. Parsons, "The Use and Effect of Humor in Different Advertising Media," *Journal of Advertising Research,* May–June 1995, pp. 44–55.

12. See James F. Engel, Roger D. Blackwell, and Paul W. Minard, *Consumer Behavior,* 8th ed. (Fort Worth, TX: Dryden, 1994).

13. See Ayn E. Crowley and Wayne D. Hoyer, "An Integrative Framework for Understanding Two-Sided Persuasion," *Journal of Consumer Research,* March 1994, pp. 561–74.

14. See C. I. Hovland, A. A. Lumsdaine, and F. D. Sheffield, *Experiments on Mass Communication,* Vol. 3 (Princeton, NJ: Princeton University Press, 1948), Chapter 8; and Crowley and Hoyer, "An Integrative Framework for Understanding Two-sided Persuasion." For an alternative viewpoint, see George E. Belch, "The Effects of Message Modality on One- and Two-Sided Advertising Messages," in *Advances in Consumer Research,* ed. Richard P. Bagozzi and Alice M. Tybout (Ann Arbor, MI: Association for Consumer Research, 1983), pp. 21–26.

15. Curtis P. Haugtvedt and Duane T. Wegener, "Message Order Effects in Persuasion: An Attitude Strength Perspective," *Journal of Consumer Research,* June 1994, pp. 205–18; H. Rao Unnava, Robert E. Burnkrant, and Sunil Erevelles, "Effects of Presentation Order and Communication Modality on Recall and Attitude," *Journal of Consumer Research,* December 1994, pp. 481–90.

16. See Sternthal and Craig, *Consumer Behavior,* pp. 282–84.

17. Herbert C. Kelman and Carl I. Hovland, "Reinstatement of the Communication in Delayed Measurement of Opinion Change," *Journal of Abnormal and Social Psychology,* 48 (1953), 327–35.

18. David J. Moore, John C. Mowen, and Richard Reardon, "Multiple Sources in Advertising Appeals: When Product Endorsers Are Paid by the Advertising Sponsor," *Journal of the Academy of Marketing Science,* Summer 1994, pp. 234–43.

19. C. E. Osgood and P. H. Tannenbaum, "The Principles of Congruity in the Prediction of Attitude Change," *Psychological Review,* 62 (1955), 42–55.

20. Michael Kiely, "Word-of-Mouth Marketing," *Marketing,* September 1993, p. 6.

21. See Regis McKenna, *The Regis Touch* (Reading, MA: Addison-Wesley, 1985); and Regis McKenna, *Relationship Marketing* (Reading, MA: Addison-Wesley, 1991).

22. Michael Cafferky has identified four kinds of people that companies try to reach to stimulate word-of-mouth referrals: opinion leaders, marketing mavens, influentials, and product enthusiasts. *Opinion leaders* are people who are widely respected within defined social groups, such as fashion leaders. They have a large relevant social network, high source credibility, and a high propensity to talk. *Marketing mavens* are people who spend a lot of time learning the best buys (values) in the marketplace. *Influentials* are people who are socially and politically active; they try to know what is going on and influence the course of events. *Product enthusiasts* are people who are known experts in a product category, such as art connoisseurs, audiophiles, and computer wizards. See *Let Your Customers Do the Talking* (Chicago: Dearborn Financial Publishing, 1995), pp. 30–33.

23. Greg W. Prince, "A Tale of Two Spokestars," *Beverage World,* January 1995, p. 35.

24. See Philip Kotler, "Atmospherics as a Marketing Tool," *Journal of Retailing,* Winter 1973–1974, pp. 48–64.

25. See Everett M. Rogers, *Diffusion of Innovations,* 4th ed. (New York: Free Press, 1995).

26. Quoted in Daniel Seligman, "How Much for Advertising?" *Fortune,* December 1956, p. 123. For a good discussion of setting promotion budgets, see Michael L. Rothschild, *Advertising* (Lexington, MA: D. C. Heath, 1987), Chapter 20.

27. Albert Wesley Frey, *How Many Dollars for Advertising?* (New York: Ronald Press, 1955), p. 65.

28. Frey, *How Many Dollars,* p. 49.

29. Adapted from G. Maxwell Ule, "A Media Plan for 'Sputnik' Cigarettes," *How to Plan Media Strategy* (American Association of Advertising Agencies, 1957 Regional Convention), pp. 41–52.

30. See Sidney J. Levy, *Promotional Behavior* (Glenview, IL: Scott, Foresman, 1971), Chapter 4.

31. Relatively little research has been done on the effectiveness of business-to-business advertising. For a survey, see Wesley J. Johnson, "The Importance of Advertising and the Relative Lack of Research," *Journal of Business and Industrial Marketing,* 9, no. 2 (1994), 3–4.

32. *How Advertising Works in Today's Marketplace: The Morrill Study* (New York: McGraw-Hill, 1971), p. 4.

33. Cyril Freeman, "How to Evaluate Advertising's Contribution," *Harvard Business Review,* July–August 1962, pp. 137–48.

34. Theodore Levitt, *Industrial Purchasing Behavior: A Study in Communication Effects* (Boston: Division of Research, Harvard Business School, 1965).

35. See Gary L. Lilien and John D. C. Little, "The ADVISOR Project: A Study of Industrial Marketing Budgets," *Sloan Management Review,* Spring 1976, pp. 17–31; and Gary L. Lilien, "ADVISOR 2: Modeling the Marketing Mix Decision for Industrial Products," *Management Science,* February 1979, pp. 191–204.29.

36. Paul Wang and Lisa Petrison, "Integrated Marketing Communications and Its Potential Effects on Media Planning," *Journal of Media Planning,* 6, no. 2 (1991), 11–18.

37. See Don E. Shultz, Stanley I. Tannenbaum, and Robert F. Lauterborn, *Integrated Marketing Communications: Putting It Together and Making It Work* (Lincolnwood, IL: NTC Business Books, 1992); Ernan Roman, *Integrated Direct Marketing: The Cutting-Edge Strategy for Synchronizing Advertising, Direct Mail, Telemarketing, and Field Sales* (Lincolnwood, IL: NTC Business Books, 1995); and Mary L. Koelle, "Integrated Marketing Communications: Barriers to the Dream," *Integrated Marketing Communications,* June 19, 1991, pp. 7–9.

38. Don E. Schultz, "The Next Step in IMC?" *Marketing News,* August 15, 1994, pp. 8–9.

MANAGING ADVERTISING, SALES PROMOTION, AND PUBLIC RELATIONS

If you think advertising doesn't pay—we understand there are twenty-five mountains in Colorado higher than Pike's Peak. Can you name one?

THE AMERICAN SALESMAN

❖

Gifts are like hooks.

MARTIAL (A.D. 86)

❖

We despise no source that can pay us a pleasing attention.

MARK TWAIN

n this chapter, we describe the nature and use of three promotional tools—advertising, sales promotion, and public relations. Although their effectiveness is not always easy to gauge, they can contribute strongly to marketing performance. We will consider the following questions:

- **What is advertising, and what steps are involved in developing an advertising program?**

- **What explains the growing use of sales promotion, and how are sales-promotion decisions made?**

- **How can companies best exploit the potentials of public relations and publicity in their marketing mix?**

DEVELOPING AND MANAGING AN ADVERTISING PROGRAM

Advertising is one of the most common tools companies use to direct persuasive communications to target buyers and publics. We define advertising as follows:

❖   **ADVERTISING** is any paid form of nonpersonal presentation and promotion of ideas, goods, or services by an identified sponsor.

Advertisers include not only business firms but also museums, charitable organizations, and government agencies that advertise to various target publics. Ads are a cost-effective way to disseminate messages, whether to build brand preference for Coca-Cola or to educate a nation's people to avoid hard drugs.

Organizations handle their advertising in different ways. In small companies, advertising is handled by someone in the sales or marketing department, who works with an advertising agency. A large company will often set up its own advertising department, whose manager reports to the vice-president of marketing. The advertising department's job is to develop the total budget; help develop advertising strategy; approve ads and campaigns; and handle direct-mail advertising, dealer displays, and other forms of advertising not ordinarily performed by the agency. Most companies use an outside advertising agency to help them create advertising campaigns and to select and purchase media.

In developing an advertising program, marketing managers must always start by identifying the target market and buyer motives. Then they can proceed to make the five major decisions in developing an advertising program, known as the five Ms:

- *Mission:* What are the advertising objectives?
- *Money:* How much can be spent?
- *Message:* What message should be sent?
- *Media:* What media should be used?
- *Measurement:* How should the results be evaluated?

These decisions are further summarized in Figure 21-1 on page 638 and described in the following sections.

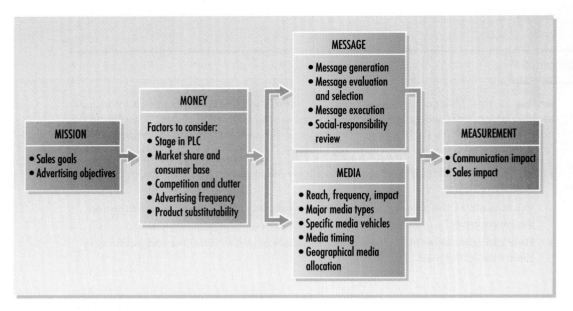

FIGURE 21-1
The Five Ms of Advertising

Setting the Advertising Objectives

The first step in developing an advertising program is to set the advertising objectives. These objectives must flow from prior decisions on the target market, market positioning, and marketing mix. The marketing-positioning and marketing-mix strategies define the job that advertising must do in the total marketing program.

Many specific communication and sales objectives can be assigned to advertising. Colley lists 52 possible advertising objectives in his well-known *Defining Advertising Goals for Measured Advertising Results*.[1] He outlines a method called DAGMAR (after the book's title) for turning advertising objectives into specific measurable goals. An *advertising goal* (or *objective*) is a specific communication task and achievement level to be accomplished with a specific audience in a specific period of time. Colley provides an example:

> To increase among 30 million homemakers who own automatic washers the number who identify brand X as a low-sudsing detergent and who are persuaded that it gets clothes cleaner—from 10% to 40% in one year.

Advertising objectives can be classified according to whether their aim is to inform, persuade, or remind. Table 21-1 lists examples of these objectives.

♦ *Informative advertising* figures heavily in the pioneering stage of a product category, where the objective is to build primary demand. Thus the yogurt industry initially had to inform consumers of yogurt's nutritional benefits and many uses.

♦ *Persuasive advertising* becomes important in the competitive stage, where a company's objective is to build selective demand for a particular brand. Most advertising falls into this category. For example, Chivas Regal attempts to persuade consumers that it delivers more status than any other brand of Scotch whisky. Some persuasive advertising has moved into the category of *comparative advertising,* which seeks to establish the superiority of one brand through specific comparison of one or more attributes with one or more other brands in the product class.[2] Comparative advertising has been used in such product categories as deodorants, fast food, toothpastes, tires, and automobiles. The Burger King Corporation has developed comparitive advertising for its product against McDonald's (Burger King's burgers are flame-broiled; McDonald's are fried). Schering-

TABLE 21-1 POSSIBLE ADVERTISING OBJECTIVES

TO INFORM

Telling the market about a new product	Describing available services
Suggesting new uses for a product	Correcting false impressions
Informing the market of a price change	Reducing buyers' fears
Explaining how the product works	Building a company image

TO PERSUADE

Building brand preference	Persuading buyers to purchase now
Encouraging switching to the brand	Persuading buyers to receive a sales call
Changing buyers' perception of product attributes	

TO REMIND

Reminding buyers that the product may be needed in the near future	Keeping it in buyers' minds during off-seasons
Reminding buyers where to buy it	Maintaining its top-of-mind awareness

Plough claimed that "New OcuClear relieves three times longer than Visine." In using comparative advertising, a company should make sure that it can prove its claim of superiority and that it cannot be counterattacked in an area where the other brand is stronger. Comparative advertising works best when it elicits cognitive and affective motivations simultaneously.[3]

◆ *Reminder advertising* is highly important with mature products. Expensive four-color Coca-Cola ads in magazines have the purpose not of informing or persuading but of reminding people to purchase Coca-Cola. A related form of advertising is *reinforcement advertising,* which seeks to assure current purchasers that they have made the right choice. Automobile ads often depict satisfied customers enjoying special features of their new car.

The choice of the advertising objective should be based on a thorough analysis of the current marketing situation. For example, if the product class is mature, the company is the market leader, and brand usage is low, the proper objective should be to stimulate more brand usage. If the product class is new, the company is not the market leader, but the brand is superior to the leader, then the proper objective is to convince the market of the brand's superiority.

Deciding on the Advertising Budget

After determining advertising objectives, the company can proceed to establish its advertising budget for each product. The role of advertising is to increase demand for the product. The company wants to spend the amount required to achieve the sales goal. But how does a company know if it is spending the right amount? If the company spends too little, the effect will be insignificant. If the company spends too much on advertising, then some of the money could have been put to better use. Some critics charge that large consumer-packaged-goods firms tend to overspend on advertising as a form of insurance against not spending enough, and that industrial companies underestimate the power of company and product image and therefore generally underspend on advertising.[4]

A counterargument to the charge that consumer-packaged-goods companies spend too much is that advertising has a carryover effect that lasts beyond the current period. Although advertising is treated as a current expense, part of it is really an investment that builds up an intangible value called *goodwill* (or *brand equity*). When $5 million is spent on capital equipment, the equipment may be treated as a five-year depreciable asset and only one fifth of the cost is written off in the first year. When $5 million is spent on advertising to launch a new product, the entire cost must be written off in the first year. This treatment of advertising as a complete expense reduces the company's reported profit and therefore limits the number of new-product launches that a company can undertake in any one year.

There are five specific factors to consider when setting the advertising budget:[5]

- *Stage in the product life cycle:* New products typically receive large advertising budgets to build awareness and to gain consumer trial. Established brands usually are supported with lower advertising budgets as a ratio to sales.

- *Market share and consumer base:* High-market-share brands usually require less advertising expenditure as a percentage of sales to maintain their share. To build share by increasing market size requires larger advertising expenditures. Additionally, on a cost-per-impression basis, it is less expensive to reach consumers of a widely used brand than to reach consumers of low-share brands.

- *Competition and clutter:* In a market with a large number of competitors and high advertising spending, a brand must advertise more heavily to be heard above the noise in the market. Even simple clutter from advertisements not directly competitive to the brand creates a need for heavier advertising.

- *Advertising frequency:* The number of repetitions needed to put across the brand's message to consumers has an important impact on the advertising budget.

- *Product substitutability:* Brands in a commodity class (e.g., cigarettes, beer, soft drinks) require heavy advertising to establish a differential image. Advertising is also important when a brand can offer unique physical benefits or features.

Marketing scientists have built a number of advertising-expenditure models that take into account these and other factors. One of the best early models was developed by Vidale and Wolfe.[6] Essentially, the model called for a larger advertising budget, the higher the sales-response rate, the higher the sales-decay rate (i.e., the rate at which customers forget the advertising and brand), and the higher the untapped sales potential. Unfortunately, this model leaves out other important factors, such as the rate of competitive advertising and the effectiveness of the company's ads.

Professor John Little proposed an adaptive-control method for setting the advertising budget.[7] Suppose the company has set an advertising-expenditure rate based on its most current information on the sales-response function. It spends this rate in all markets except in a subset of $2n$ markets randomly drawn. In n test markets the company spends at a lower rate, and in the other n it spends at a higher rate. This procedure will yield information on the average sales created by low, medium, and high rates of advertising that can be used to update the parameters of the sales-response function. The updated function is used to determine the best advertising-expenditure rate for the next period. If this experiment is conducted each period, advertising expenditures will closely track optimal advertising expenditures.[8]

Choosing the Advertising Message

Advertising campaigns differ in their creativity. As William Bernbach observed: "The facts are not enough. . . . Don't forget that Shakespeare used some pretty hackneyed plots, yet his message came through with great execution." Consider the following example:

In 1987, the television commercial featuring claymation California raisins dancing to Marvin Gaye's "I Heard It Through the Grapevine" was one of the top-ranking spots in the United States, while the advertising budget that produced it was only 1% of that spent on the spot that ranked fifth.[9]

Clearly, the effect of the creativity factor in a campaign can be more important than the number of dollars spent. Only after gaining attention can a commercial help to increase the brand's sales. The advertising adage is, "Until it's compelling, it isn't selling."

However, a warning is in order. All the creative advertising in the world cannot boost market share for a flawed product. This was the case for Miles Inc.'s Alka-Seltzer tablets:

ALKA-SELTZER For the past 30 years, Alka-Seltzer antacid tablets have been the beneficiary of some of the most creative advertising in history: In 1969, the company began airing the classic "prison spot" in which 260 jailbirds, led by actor George Raft, rebelled against prison food by banging tin cups on tables while chanting "Alka-Seltzer." Later that same year, the company aired two more classic Alka-Seltzer TV spots: "Honeymoon," in which the tablets saved a bridegroom after his bride cooked up such meals as poached oysters and marshmallow meatballs, and ads that are remembered for the line "That's a spicy meatball." Through the 1970s and into the 80s, the company pushed out more classic TV commercials for Alka-Seltzer, utilizing such lines as "Try it. You'll like it," "I can't believe I ate the whole thing," and "Plop-plop, fizz-fizz, oh, what a relief it is." Yet Alka-Seltzer's market share, which was 25% of the antacid market in 1968, had dwindled to just under 10% by 1993. Despite some of the bubbliest ad campaigns ever aired, Alka-Seltzer lost its fizz.[10]

Advertisers go through four steps to develop a creative strategy: message generation, message evaluation and selection, message execution, and message social-responsibility review.

MESSAGE GENERATION. In principle, the product's message—the major benefit that the brand offers—should be decided as part of developing the product concept. Yet even within this concept, there may be latitude for a number of possible messages. And over time, the marketer might want to change the message without changing the product, especially if consumers are seeking new or different benefits from the product.

Creative people use several methods to generate possible advertising appeals. Many creative people proceed *inductively* by talking to consumers, dealers, experts, and competitors. Consumers are the major source of good ideas. Their feelings about the strengths and shortcomings of existing brands provide important clues to creative strategy. Leo Burnett advocates "in-depth interviewing where I come realistically face to face with the people I am trying to sell. I try to get a picture in my mind of the kind of people they are—how they use this product and what it is."[11]

Some creative people use a *deductive* framework for generating advertising messages. Maloney proposed one framework (Table 21-2, on page 642).[12] He saw buyers as expecting one of four types of reward from a product: rational, sensory, social, or ego satisfaction. Buyers might visualize these rewards from results-of-use experience, product-in-use experience, or incidental-to-use experience. Crossing the four types of rewards with the three types of experience generates twelve types of advertising messages.

The advertiser can generate a theme for each of the 12 cells as possible messages for the product. For example, the appeal "gets clothes cleaner" is a rational-reward promise following results-of-use experience. The phrase "real gusto in a great light beer" is a sensory-reward promise connected with product-in-use experience.

How many alternative ad themes should the advertiser create before making a choice? The more ads that are independently created, the higher the probability of finding an excellent one. Yet the more time spent on creating ads, the higher the

TABLE 21-2 | EXAMPLES OF 12 TYPES OF APPEALS

TYPES OF POTENTIALLY REWARDING EXPERIENCE WITH A PRODUCT	POTENTIAL TYPE OF REWARD			
	RATIONAL	**SENSORY**	**SOCIAL**	**EGO SATISFACTION**
Results-of-Use Experience	1. Gets clothes cleaner	2. Settles stomach upset completely	3. When you care enough to serve the best	4. For the skin you deserve to have
Product-in-Use Experience	5. The flour that needs no sifting	6. Real gusto in a great light beer	7. A deodorant to guarantee social acceptance	8. The store for the young executive
Incidental-to-Use Experience	9. The plastic pack keeps the cigarette fresh	10. The portable television that's lighter in weight, easier to lift	11. The furniture that identifies the home of modern people	12. Stereo for the man with discriminating taste

Source: Adapted from John C. Maloney, "Marketing Decisions and Attitude Research," in *Effective Marketing Coordination,* ed. George L. Baker, Jr. (Chicago: American Marketing Association, 1961), pp. 595–618.

costs. There must be an optimal number of alternative ads that an agency should create and test for the client. Under the present commission system, typically 15%, the agency does not like to go to the expense of creating and pretesting many ads. (For more on how commissions work, see the Marketing Insight titled "How Does an Advertising Agency Work?") Fortunately, the expense of creating rough ads is rapidly falling with the advance of computer desktop publishing techniques. An ad agency's creative department can compose many alternative ads in a short time by drawing from computer files containing different still and video images, type sets, and so on.

MESSAGE EVALUATION AND SELECTION.   The advertiser needs to evaluate the alternative messages. A good ad normally focuses on one core selling proposition. Twedt suggested that messages be rated on *desirability, exclusiveness,* and *believability.*[13] The message must first say something desirable or interesting about the product. The message must also say something exclusive or distinctive that does not apply to every brand in the product category. Finally, the message must be believable or provable. For example:

THE MARCH OF DIMES The March of Dimes searched for an advertising theme to raise money for its fight against birth defects. Several messages came out of a brainstorming session. A group of young parents was asked to rate each message for interest, distinctiveness, and believability, assigning up to 100 points for each. For example, "700 children are born each day with a birth defect" scored 70, 62, and 80 on interest, distinctiveness, and believability, while "Your next baby could be born with a birth defect" scored 58, 51, and 70. The first message outperformed the second on all accounts.[14]

The advertiser should conduct market analysis and research to determine which appeal is most likely to succeed with its target audience:

SCHOTT Schott is a German manufacturer of glass for industrial and consumer products. The technical glass division of its U.S. subsidiary, Schott America, makes 50,000 products, but in 1989 it appealed to NYC ad agency Hammond Farrell for help with one of its products, Ceran. This glass-ceramic material is used to cover the cooking surface of electric ranges, and it was in high demand in Europe. Yet when Schott's U.S. rep tried to sell Ceran to its target market of 14 U.S. appliance manufacturers, the compa-

How Does an Advertising Agency Work?

Madison Avenue is a familiar name to most Americans. It is a street in New York City where several major advertising agency headquarters are located. But most of the nation's 10,000 agencies are found outside New York, and almost every city has at least one agency, even if it is a one-person shop. Some ad agencies are huge—the largest U.S. agency, Omnicom Group, New York, has annual worldwide billings of $16 billion. WWP Group out of London is the world's largest agency, with worldwide billings of $20 billion.

Agencies employ specialists who generally can perform advertising tasks better than a company's own staff. Agencies also bring an outside point of view to solving a company's problems, along with years of experience from working with different clients and situations. And because the firm can dismiss its agency, an agency works hard to do a good job.

Advertising agencies usually have four departments: *creative*, which develops and produces ads; *media*, which selects media and places ads; *research*, which studies audience characteristics and wants; and *business*, which handles the agency's business activities. Each account is supervised by an account executive, and people in each department are usually assigned to work on one or more accounts.

Agencies often attract new business through their reputation or size. Generally, a client invites a few agencies to make a presentation for its business and then selects one of them.

Ad agencies have traditionally been paid through commissions and some fees. Under this system, the agency usually receives 15% of the purchased media cost as a rebate. Suppose the agency buys $60,000 of magazine space for a client. The magazine bills the ad-

vertising agency for $51,000 ($60,000 less 15%), and the agency bills the client for $60,000, keeping the $9,000 commission. If the client bought space directly from the magazine, it would have paid $60,000 because commissions are paid only to recognized advertising agencies.

However, both advertisers and agencies have become increasingly unhappy with the commission system. Large advertisers complain that they pay more for the same services received by small advertisers, simply because large companies place more advertising. Advertisers also believe that the commission system drives agencies away from low-cost media and short advertising campaigns. Agencies are unhappy because they provide many extra services for an account without earning more. As a result, the trend is now toward paying either a straight fee or a combination commission and fee. And some large advertisers are tying agency compensation to the performance of the agency's advertising campaigns. Campbell's is happy to pay a 15% commission if the advertising campaign is excellent; if the campaign is only good, the agency gets 13%; and if the campaign is poor, the agency gets 13% and a warning. Philip Morris prefers to pay its agencies 15% and then add a bonus if the campaign is especially effective. The key problem with these pay-for-performance schemes is how to judge whether the campaign is excellent, good, fair, or poor. Sales and communication measures can both be misleading.

Another trend: In recent years, as growth in advertising spending has slowed, many agencies have tried to keep growing by buying other agencies, thus creating huge agency holding companies. One of the largest agency "megagroups" is Omnicom, which includes DDB-Needham, BBDO, Goodby Silverstein, and TBWA/Chiat Day.

Source: For further reading, see "World's Top 50 Advertising Organizations," *Advertising Age,* April 10, 1995, p. S-18.

---

nies ordered sample quantities of each available color and never called Schott again. Hammond Farrell's market analysis and research confirmed that the product was virtually unknown, not just among consumers but also among all the important intermediaries such as dealers, designers, and architects. The research also revealed a significant surprise: When selecting a range-top to buy or include in their designs, none of these people cared at all about the sophisticated engineering that Schott's sales reps were touting: Ceran's long-lasting, nonporous surface and its ability to keep heat from spreading across the range. Rather, the market's biggest question was, "How does it look?" That's when Hammond Farrell came up with an ingenious—and very successful—ad campaign based on the slogans "Formal-wear for your kitchen," and "More than a rangetop, a means of expression."[15]

MESSAGE EXECUTION. The message's impact depends not only upon what is said but also on how it is said. Some ads aim for *rational positioning* and others for *emotional positioning*. U.S. ads typically present an explicit feature or benefit designed to appeal to the rational mind: "Gets clothes cleaner," "Brings relief faster," and so on. Japanese ads (i.e., those used in Japan) tend to be more indirect and appeal to the emotions: An example was Nissan's Infiniti car ad, which showed not the car but beautiful scenes from nature aimed at producing an emotional association and response.

The choice of headlines, copy, and so on, can make a difference in the ad's impact. Lalita Manrai reported a study in which she created two ads for the same car. The first ad carried the headline "A New Car"; the second, the headline "Is This Car for You?" The second headline utilized an advertising strategy called *labeling,* in which the consumer is labeled as the type of person who is interested in that type of product. The two ads also differed in that the first ad described the car's features and the second described the car's benefits. In the test, the second ad far outperformed the first ad in terms of overall impression of the product, reader interest in buying the product, and likelihood of recommending it to a friend.[16]

Message execution can be decisive for products that are highly similar, such as detergents, cigarettes, coffee, and vodka. Consider the success of Absolut Vodka:

ABSOLUT VODKA　Vodka is generally viewed as a commodity product. Yet the amount of brand preference and loyalty in the vodka market is astonishing. Most of it is based on selling an image, not the product. When the Swedish brand Absolut entered the U.S. market in 1979, the company sold a disappointing 7,000 cases that year. By 1991, sales had soared to over 2 million cases. Absolut became the largest selling imported vodka in the United States, with 65% of the market. Its sales are also skyrocketing globally. Its secret weapon: a targeting, packaging, and advertising strategy. Absolut aims for sophisticated, upwardly mobile, affluent drinkers. The vodka is in a distinctive odd-shaped bottle suggestive of Swedish austerity. The bottle has become an icon and is used as the centerpiece of every ad, accompanied by puns such as "Absolut Magic" or "Absolut Larceny." Well-known artists—including Warhol, Haring, Scharf—have designed many Absolut ads, and the bottle image always figures in a clever way in the ad. Absolut has won more industry awards than any advertising campaign in history.

In preparing an ad campaign, the advertiser usually prepares a *copy strategy statement* describing the objective, content, support, and tone of the desired ad. Here is the strategy statement for a Pillsbury product called 1869 Brand Biscuits:

PILLSBURY　The *objective* of the advertising is to convince biscuit users that now they can buy a canned biscuit that's as good as homemade—Pillsbury's 1869 Brand Biscuits. The *content* consists of emphasizing the following product characteristics: They look like homemade biscuits; they have the same texture as homemade biscuits; and they taste like homemade biscuits. *Support* for the "good as homemade" promise will be twofold: (1) 1869 Brand Biscuits are made from a special kind of flour (soft wheat flour) used to make homemade biscuits but never before used in making canned biscuits, and (2) the use of traditional American biscuit recipes. The *tone* of the advertising will be a news announcement, tempered by a warm, reflective mood emanating from a look back at traditional American baking quality.

Creative people must also find a *style, tone, words,* and *format* for executing the message. All of these elements must deliver a cohesive image and message.

Style. Any message can be presented in any of the following different execution styles, or a combination of them:

- *Slice of life:* Shows one or more persons using the product in a normal setting. A family seated at the dinner table might express satisfaction with a new biscuit brand.

- *Lifestyle:* Emphasizes how a product fits in with a lifestyle. A Scotch whisky ad shows a handsome middle-aged man holding a glass of Scotch whisky in one hand and steering his yacht with the other.

- *Fantasy:* Creates a fantasy around the product or its use. Perfume ads commonly use fantasy to appeal to consumers, such as Chanel No. 5's "Share the Fantasy" campaign. In one of the Chanel No. 5 ads, a moviegoer watching Marilyn Monroe onscreen finds herself suddenly transformed into the movie star icon, and her popcorn barrel has become a two-quart bottle of Chanel No. 5. With digital technology at their command, advertising creatives can now produce seamless fantasy sequences such as the Chanel spots.[17]

- *Mood or image:* Evokes a mood or image around the product, such as beauty, love, or serenity. No claim is made about the product except through suggestion. While advertisers of cars and cigarettes are well known for their attempts to evoke a mood or create an image (Philip Morris's "macho" Marlboro Man and R. J. Reynolds' "cool" Joe Camel), other product categories are getting into the act, particularly those seeking an image change. Recently computer companies have begun relying more on ads that present "hip" and "global" images. A television ad for IBM even features subtitles as a French senior citizen strolls along the Seine complaining to his friend that his hard drive is "maxed out."

- *Musical:* Uses background music or shows one or more persons or cartoon characters singing a song involving the product. Many cola ads have used this format. The most famous is probably the Coca-Cola ad featuring a song titled "I'd Like to Teach the World to Sing."

- *Personality symbol:* Creates a character that personifies the product. The character might be animated (Jolly Green Giant, Pillsbury Doughboy, Mr. Clean) or real (Marlboro man, Morris the Cat).

- *Technical expertise:* Shows the company's expertise, experience, and pride in making the product. For instance, ads for cars made by GM's Saturn division gained kudos for taking consumers behind the scenes to the Spring Hill, Tennessee, plant where the cars are made.

- *Scientific evidence:* Presents survey or scientific evidence that the brand is preferred over or outperforms other brands. This style is common in the over-the-counter drug category. A print ad for Whitehall Robins' Dimetapp cold and allergy medicines shows a pediatrician and her daughter above the headline, "I doctor my daughter's allergies with great tasting Dimetapp." The tagline reads: "Dimetapp, the cold and allergy medicine pediatricians recommend most."

- *Testimonial evidence:* This features a highly credible, likable, or expert source endorsing the product. It could be a celebrity like Ed McMahon or ordinary people saying how much they like the product. (For more on this topic, see the Marketing Insight on page 646 titled "Celebrity Endorsements as a Strategy.")

Tone. The communicator must also choose an appropriate tone for the ad. Procter & Gamble is consistently positive in its tone—its ads say something superlatively positive about the product, and humor is almost always avoided so as not to take attention away from the message. In contrast, ads for Staples office-supply superstores, while advertising equally mundane products, focus on a humorous situation rather than on the products themselves. Other companies use emotions to set the tone—particularly film, telephone, and insurance companies, which stress human connections and milestones.

Words. Memorable and attention-getting words must be found. The following themes listed on the left would have had much less impact without the creative phrasing on the right:[18]

Celebrity Endorsements as a Strategy

Marketers have used celebrities from time immemorial to endorse their products. A well-chosen celebrity can at the very least draw attention to a product or brand, as when comedian Jerry Seinfeld appears in American Express ads or when tennis star Gabriela Sabatini sports a little milk mustache in ads that proclaim "Milk. What a surprise!" Or the celebrity's mystique can transfer over to the brand—supermodel Cindy Crawford in an ad for Revlon's Outrageous Daily Beautifying Shampoo. Or the celebrity's expertise and authority transfers to the brand—Michael Jordan endorsing Nike's Air Jordan basketball shoes.

The choice of the right celebrity is critical. The celebrity should have high recognition, high positive affect (that is, a high positive emotional effect on the target audience), and high appropriateness to the product. The late Howard Cosell had high recognition but negative affect among many groups. Sylvester Stallone has high recognition and high positive affect but might not be appropriate for advertising a World Peace Conference. Paul Newman, Candice Bergen, and Bill Cosby could successfully advertise a large number of products because they have extremely high ratings for well-knownness and likability (known as the *Q factor* in the entertainment industry).

Athletes are a particularly effective endorsing group, especially for athletic products, beverages, and apparel. Michael Jordan, star of the Chicago Bulls, earns about $4 million a year endorsing Nike, Wilson, Coca-Cola, Johnson Products, and McDonald's. Not only does the celebrity's image appear in ads but the message is multiplied in the sales of T-shirts, toys, and games, and hundreds of additional merchandise items.

One of advertisers' main worries is that their celebrity endorsers will get mixed up in a scandal or embarrassing situation. Football hero O. J. Simpson pitched Hertz rental cars for 20 years until he was charged with murdering his wife in 1994. Then there was Michael Jackson, whom Pepsi dropped in the wake of child-molestation charges. When actor James Garner encountered well-publicized heart problems, his illness did not reflect well on the beef industry, which he had been promoting. And spokesperson Cybill Shepherd embarrassed the Beef Council when she admitted she had stopped eating beef.

Perhaps due to the frequency of celebrity scandals, insurers are now offering to protect advertisers against such risks. One insurance company has begun offering advertisers "death, disablement, and disgrace" insurance to cover the failings and foibles of their celebrity endorsers. The policies—with coverage limits up to $5 million—protect corporations "against losses associated with the cancellation of celebrity promotions or endorsements due to events that are beyond the insured's control." Alternatively, advertisers can choose not to use real, live fallible humans to endorse their products but opt for "spokescharacters" instead. For example, Owens-Corning has used the Pink Panther for nearly 15 years to endorse its pink-colored insulation products, and Metropolitan Life has used the Peanuts Gang to promote its insurance products. Images projected by a specific cartoon or animated character don't deviate dramatically from one moment to the next, and companies have more control over them.

Sources: See Irving Rein, Philip Kotler, and Martin Stoller, *High Visibility: How Executives, Politicians, Entertainers, Athletes, and Other Professionals Create, Market, and Achieve Successful Images* (New York: Dodd, Mead, 1987); Willy Stern, "Rebel with a Cachet," *Business Week,* July 17, 1995, pp. 74, 76; and Christine Unruh, "Snap Crackle Pop," *Journal of Business Strategy,* March–April 1995, pp. 39–43.

Theme	*Creative Copy*
7-Up is not a cola.	"The Un-Cola."
Let us drive you in our bus instead of driving your car.	"Take the bus, and leave the driving to us."
Shop by turning the pages of the telephone directory.	"Let your fingers do the walking."
We don't rent as many cars, so we have to do more for our customers.	"We try harder."
Red Roof Inns offer inexpensive lodging.	"Sleep cheap at Red Roof Inns."

Creativity is especially required for headlines. There are six basic types of headlines: *news* ("New Boom and More Inflation Ahead . . . and What You Can Do About It"); *question* ("Have You Had It Lately?"); *narrative* ("They Laughed When I Sat Down at the Piano, but When I Started to Play!"); *command* ("Don't Buy Until You Try All Three"); *1-2-3 ways* ("12 Ways to Save on Your Income Tax"); and *how-what-why* ("Why They Can't Stop Buying").

Format. Format elements such as ad size, color, and illustration will make a difference in an ad's impact as well as its cost. A minor rearrangement of mechanical elements within the ad can improve its attention-getting power. Larger-size ads gain more attention, though not necessarily by as much as their difference in cost. Four-color illustrations instead of black and white increase ad effectiveness and ad cost. By planning the relative dominance of different elements of the ad, optimal delivery can be achieved. New electronic eye movement studies show that consumers can be led through an ad by strategic placement of the ad's dominant elements.

A number of researchers into print advertisements report that the *picture, headline,* and *copy* are important, in that order. The reader first notices the picture, and it must be strong enough to draw attention. Then the headline must propel the person to read the copy. The copy itself must be well composed. Even then, a really outstanding ad will be noted by less than 50% of the exposed audience. About 30% of the exposed audience might recall the headline's main point; about 25% might remember the advertiser's name; and less than 10% will read most of the body copy. Ordinary ads do not achieve even these results.

An industry study listed the following characteristics for ads that scored above average in recall and recognition: innovation (new product or new uses), "story appeal" (as an attention-getting device), before-and-after illustration, demonstrations, problem solution, and the inclusion of relevant characters that become emblematic of the brand (these may be cartoon figures or actual people, including celebrities).[19]

In recent years critics both inside and outside the advertising industry have bemoaned a spate of bland ads and slogans and, in particular, the frequent use of the nonreferential "it," as in "Coke is it"; Nike's popular "Just do it"; and the most egregious offender, Miller Lite's short-lived ad proclaiming, "It's it and that's that."[20] The questions are often raised: Why do so many ads look or sound alike? Why aren't advertising agencies more creative? Norman W. Brown, former head of the advertising agency of Foote, Cone & Belding, answers that in many cases the advertisers, and not their agencies, are to blame. When his agency develops a highly creative campaign, the brand manager or higher management levels worry about the risk and either reject it or ask for so many modifications that it loses its force. Brown's conclusion: "Many ads aren't creative because many companies want comfort, not creativity."

SOCIAL-RESPONSIBILITY REVIEW. Advertisers and their agencies must make sure that their "creative" advertising doesn't overstep social and legal norms. Most marketers work hard to communicate openly and honestly with consumers. Still, abuses may occur, and public policy makers have developed a substantial body of laws and regulations to govern advertising.

Under U.S. law, companies must avoid false or deceptive advertising. Advertisers must not make false claims, such as stating that a product cures something when it does not. They must avoid false demonstrations, such as using sand-covered plexiglass instead of sandpaper in a commercial to demonstrate that a razor blade can shave sandpaper.

It is also illegal in the United States to create ads that have the capacity to deceive, even though no one may actually be deceived. For example, a floor wax cannot be advertised as giving six months' protection unless it does so under typical conditions, and a diet bread cannot be advertised as having fewer calories simply because its slices are thinner. The problem is how to tell the difference between deception and "puffery"—simple acceptable exaggerations not intended to be believed.

In addition, sellers in the United States are legally obligated to avoid bait-and-switch advertising that attracts buyers under false pretenses. For example, suppose a seller advertises a sewing machine at $149. When consumers try to buy the advertised machine, the seller cannot then refuse to sell it, downplay its features, show a faulty one, or promise unreasonable delivery dates in order to switch the buyer to a more expensive machine.[21]

To be socially responsible, advertisers must also be careful not to offend any ethnic groups, racial minorities, or special-interest groups. Consider the following examples:[22]

- A Nynex spot was criticized by animal-rights activists because it showed a rabbit colored with a blue dye.
- A commercial for Black Flag insecticide was altered after a veterans group protested the playing of Taps over dead bugs.
- Ads for Calvin Klein apparel, featuring the waifish model Kate Moss, have come under attack from Boycott Anorexic Marketing.

Some companies have begun to build ad campaigns on a platform of social responsibility. The Body Shop, which we discussed in Chapter 1, is one such company. Another company that has done so is the Benetton Group, the Italian manufacturer and retailer of stylish apparel:

BENETTON Benetton's controversial billboard and print ads feature such dramatic photos as a dying AIDS patient with the words "HIV Positive" stamped on his body, a Mafia hit victim with a relative's face reflected in a pool of blood, and a blood-soaked uniform of a soldier in the former Yugoslavia. The only copy in each ad is enclosed in a tiny box and reads simply "United Colors of Benetton." Oliviero Toscani, the company's in-house creative director and photographer of the ad campaign, has said that the point of the campaign was to raise social awareness and that ". . . everyone uses emotion to sell a product. The difference here is that we are not selling a product. We want to show . . . human realities that we are aware of."

However well-intentioned and attention-grabbing the Benetton ads are, they have recently received more condemnation than praise. In 1995 a German court ruled that three images in the Benetton campaign, including that of child labor in Latin America, are exploitative and illegal. The German court's decision followed an earlier ruling by a French court, which ordered Benetton to pay $32,000 in damages for its "HIV positive" ad to French people infected with the virus that causes AIDS.[23]

Deciding on the Media

After choosing the advertising message, the advertiser's next task is to choose advertising media to carry it. The steps here are deciding on desired reach, frequency, and impact; choosing among major media types; selecting specific media vehicles; deciding on media timing; and deciding on geographical media allocation.

DECIDING ON REACH, FREQUENCY, AND IMPACT

- ❖ **MEDIA SELECTION** involves finding the most cost-effective media to deliver the desired number of exposures to the target audience.

What do we mean by the desired number of exposures? Presumably, the advertiser is seeking a certain response from the target audience—for example, a certain level of product trial. The rate of product trial will depend, among other things, on the level of audience brand awareness. Suppose the rate of product trial increases at a diminishing rate with the level of audience awareness, as shown in Figure 21-2(a). If the advertiser seeks a product trial rate of (say) T^*, it will be necessary to achieve a brand awareness level of A^*.

The next task is to find out how many exposures, E^*, will produce a level of audience awareness of A^*. The effect of exposures on audience awareness depends on the exposures' reach, frequency, and impact:

- *Reach (R):* The number of different persons or households exposed to a particular media schedule at least once during a specified time period.
- *Frequency (F):* The number of times within the specified time period that an average person or household is exposed to the message.
- *Impact (I):* The qualitative value of an exposure through a given medium (thus a food ad in *Good Housekeeping* would have a higher impact than in the *Police Gazette*).

Figure 21-2(b) shows the relationship between audience awareness and reach. Audience awareness will be greater, the higher the exposures' reach, frequency, and impact. The media planner recognizes important trade-offs among reach, frequency, and impact. Suppose the media planner has an advertising budget of $1,000,000 and the cost per thousand exposures of average quality is $5. This means that the advertiser can buy 200,000,000 exposures (= $1,000,000 ÷ [$5/1,000]). If the advertiser seeks an average exposure frequency of 10, then the advertiser can reach 20,000,000 people (= 200,000,000 ÷ 10) with the given budget. But if the advertiser wants higher-quality media costing $10 per thousand exposures, the advertiser will be able to reach only 10,000,000 people unless it is willing to lower the desired exposure frequency.

The relationship among reach, frequency, and impact is captured in the following concepts:

- *Total number of exposures (E):* This is the reach times the average frequency; that is, $E = R \times F$. This measure is referred to as the *gross rating points* (GRP). If a given media schedule reaches 80% of the homes with an average exposure frequency of 3, the media schedule is said to have a GRP of 240 (= 80 × 3). If another media schedule has a GRP of 300, it is said to have more weight, but we cannot tell how this weight breaks down into reach and frequency.

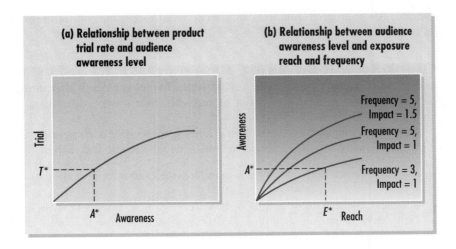

FIGURE 21-2

Relationship Among Trial, Awareness, and the Exposure Function

Managing Advertising, Sales Promotion, and Public Relations

- *Weighted number of exposures (WE):* This is the reach times average frequency times average impact, that is $WE = R \times F \times I$.

The media planning trade-off is as follows. With a given budget, what is the most cost-effective combination of reach, frequency, and impact? Reach is most important when launching new products, flanker brands, extensions of well-known brands, or infrequently purchased brands, or when going after an undefined target market. Frequency is most important where there are strong competitors, a complex story to tell, high consumer resistance, or a frequent-purchase cycle.[24]

Many advertisers believe that a target audience needs a large number of exposures for the advertising to work. Too few repetitions can be a waste, since they will hardly be noticed. Others doubt the value of high ad frequency. They believe that after people see the same ad a few times, they either act on it, get irritated by it, or stop noticing it. Krugman asserted that three exposures to an advertisement might be enough:

> The first exposure is by definition unique. As with the initial exposure to anything, a "What is it?" type of cognitive response dominates the reaction. The second exposure to a stimulus . . . produces several effects. One may be the cognitive reaction that characterized the first exposure, if the audience missed much of the message the first time around. . . . More often, an evaluative "What of it?" response replaces the "What is it?" response. . . . The third exposure constitutes a reminder, if a decision to buy based on the evaluations has not been acted on. The third exposure is also the beginning of disengagement and withdrawal of attention from a completed episode.[25]

Krugman's thesis favoring three exposures has to be qualified. He means three actual *advertising exposures*—i.e., the person sees the ad three times. These exposures should not be confused with *vehicle exposures*. If only half the magazine readers look at magazine ads, or if the readers look at ads only every other issue, then the advertising exposure is only half of the vehicle exposures. Most research services estimate vehicle exposures, not ad exposures. A media strategist would have to buy more vehicle exposures than three to achieve Krugman's three "hits."[26]

Another factor arguing for advertising repetition is that of forgetting. The job of advertising repetition is partly to put the message back into memory. The higher the forgetting rate associated with a brand, product category, or message, the higher the warranted level of repetition.

But repetition is not enough. Ads wear out and viewers tune out. Advertisers should not coast on a tired ad but insist on fresh executions by their advertising agency. For example, Duracell can choose from more than 40 different versions of its basic ad.

CHOOSING AMONG MAJOR MEDIA TYPES. The media planner has to know the capacity of the major media types to deliver reach, frequency, and impact. The major advertising media along with their costs, advantages, and limitations are profiled in Table 21-3.

Media planners make their choice among these media categories by considering several variables, the most important of which are the following:

- *Target-audience media habits:* For example, radio and television are the most effective media for reaching teenagers.
- *Product:* Women's dresses are best shown in color magazines, and Polaroid cameras are best demonstrated on television. Media types have different potentials for demonstration, visualization, explanation, believability, and color.

TABLE 21-3 PROFILES OF MAJOR MEDIA TYPES

MEDIUM	VOLUME IN BILLIONS	PERCENTAGE	EXAMPLE OF COST	ADVANTAGES	LIMITATIONS
Newspapers	32.0	23.2	$45,900 for one page, weekday *Chicago Tribune*	Flexibility; timeliness; good local market coverage; broad acceptance; high believability	Short life; poor reproduction quality; small "pass-along" audience
Television	30.6	22.2	$1,900 for 30 seconds of prime time in Chicago	Combines sight, sound, and motion; appealing to the senses; high attention; high reach	High absolute cost; high clutter; fleeting exposure; less audience selectivity
Direct mail	27.3	19.8	$1,520 for the names and addresses of 40,000 veterinarians	Audience selectivity; flexibility; no ad competition within the same medium; personalization	Relatively high cost; "junk mail" image
Radio	9.6	6.9	$400 for one minute of drive time (during commuting hours, A.M. and P.M.) in Chicago	Mass use; high geographic and demographic selectivity; low cost	Audio presentation only; lower attention than television; non-standardized rate structures; fleeting exposure
Magazines	7.4	5.3	$126,755 for one page, four-color in *Newsweek*	High geographic and demographic selectivity; credibility and prestige; high-quality reproduction; long life; good pass-along readership	Long ad purchase lead time; some waste circulation; no guarantee of position
Outdoor	1.1	0.8	$25.500 per month for 71 billboards in metropolitan Chicago	Flexibility; high repeat exposure; low cost; low competition	No audience selectivity; creative limitations
Other	30.1	21.8			
Total	138.1	100.0			

Source: Columns 2 and 3 are from Robert J. Coen, "Ad Gain of 5.2% in '93 Marks Downturn's End," *Advertising Age*, May 2, 1994, p. 4.

◆ *Message:* A message announcing a major sale tomorrow will require radio or newspaper. A message containing a great deal of technical data might require specialized magazines or mailings.

◆ *Cost:* Television is very expensive, while newspaper advertising is relatively inexpensive. What counts is the cost-per-thousand exposures rather than the total cost.

Ideas about media impact and cost must be reexamined regularly. For a long time, television enjoyed the dominant position in the media mix, and other media were neglected. Then media researchers began to notice television's reduced effectiveness, which was due to increased commercial clutter (advertisers beamed shorter and more numerous commercials at the television audience, resulting in poorer audience attention and impact), increased "zipping and zapping" of commercials, and lowered commercial TV viewing owing to the growth in cable TV and VCRs. Furthermore, television advertising costs rose faster than other media costs. Several companies found that a combination of print ads and television commercials often did a better job than television commercials alone.

Another reason for review is the continuous emergence of *new media*. For example, advertisers have increased their spending on outdoor media substantially

CHAPTER 21   **651**

Managing Advertising, Sales Promotion, and Public Relations

Keeping Up with the New Advertising Media

Forty years ago, U.S. advertisers trying to reach mass audience had to buy only 30 seconds of time on one of the three network TV stations. Today, as new forms of media and communication emerge, the mass market has fragmented into millions of minimarkets. To target these micromarkets effectively, advertisers going beyond network TV, radio, print, and billboard advertising to shout their messages from buses and subways, sports stadiums, movie screens, clothing, and supermarket shelves. They are also sending their messages to our mailboxes, telephones, computer screens, and fax machines.

The advent of the new electronic media is simply the latest stage in a natural sequence of events. From the time the ancient Egyptian bricklayers "branded" their bricks, media, like other products and services, have passed through clearly identified life-cycle stages. Each new medium has a period of dominance followed by decline. The other media don't die but petrify at some level, experiencing new surges of interest from time to time. Forty years ago the three major TV networks had 100% share of the viewing audience, but by 1980 that share was down to 87% and by 1990, to 62 percent. This share decline is related directly to the increasing penetration of cable and pay-per-view television. In print media, where advertisers once relied on a handful of national publications such as *Life* and the now defunct *Look* and *Saturday Evening Post,* they now have several thousand special-interest magazines to choose from. These magazines have made it increasingly difficult for large-scale, general-interest magazines to compete.

Marketers who wish to advertise in print face several constraints, the most important of which is the limited amount of space in each publication. To solve this problem, some advertisers have proposed huge space billboards that would display corporate logos in the sky. Fortunately for advertisers, however, the combination of telecommunications, computer, and video technology is opening up a seemingly infinite amount of cyberspace. Here's a sampling of the new electronic media that advertisers have begun to explore:

Digizines (or e-zines)
With names like *Blender, Trouble & Attitude,* and *Launch,* the latest magazines are not on the newsstand but are accessible only on computer via online services or the Internet. Digizines are much cheaper to start up and operate than are print magazines. For instance, starting a glossy publication for men aged 18 to 34

over the last decade. Outdoor advertising provides an excellent way to reach important local consumer segments. Cable television now reaches a majority of U.S. households and produces billions of dollars in advertising revenue a year. Cable systems allow narrow programming formats such as all sports, all news, nutrition programs, and arts programs—all of which are appealing to marketers who target select groups.

Another promising new media site is the store itself. Older promotional in-store vehicles, such as end-aisle displays and special price tags, are being supplemented by a flurry of new media vehicles. Some supermarkets are selling space on their tiled floors for company logos. They are experimenting with talking shelves, where shoppers get information as they pass certain food sections. One company has introduced the "videocart," which contains a computerized screen that carries consumer-benefit information ("cauliflower is rich in vitamin C") 70% of the time and advertiser promotions ("20¢ off on White Star Tuna this week") 30% of the time.

Ads have also begun appearing in best-selling paperback books, in movie theaters, and in movie videotapes. Written material such as annual reports, data sheets, catalogs, and newsletters are increasingly carrying ads. Many companies sending out monthly bills (credit-card companies, department stores, oil companies, airlines, and the like) are including inserts in the envelope that advertise

today would require at least $10 million, while digizine startup costs are between $200,000 and $500,000. Still to be worked out, however, is the ad equation. Most digizines are charging by the megabyte, although some appear to be experimenting with numbers just to determine what the market will bear.

Interactive TV

Combined computer, telephone, and TV hookups have now made it possible for people to participate in two-way communication with programs or information services via their television sets. While home shopping networks allow customers to call in their orders after seeing merchandise on their TV screens, *interactive TV* goes a step further by allowing consumers to use a computer keyboard and modem to communicate directly with sellers on their TV screen. So far interactive TV technology is only in the testing phase, with tests (or partial rollouts) being readied by Time-Warner, U.S. West, Bell Atlantic, Viacom, AT&T, and BellSouth.

Fax-on-demand

Used most by business marketers, fax-on-demand technology allows businesses to store information in a fax technology program. Customers who need information call a toll-free number, and the fax program automatically faxes the information to them

within five minutes. Customers can access the information 24 hours a day, seven days a week. The service can be set up for as little as $1,000, and business marketers feel that the cost savings in postage alone are worth the investment. Another benefit is that the technology allows businesses to track ad placements and see where they are most effective. By adding different three-digit extensions to the toll-free fax numbers placed in different print ads, the business can see which extension is getting the most calls and eliminate ads that don't bring a return.

What do all the new electronic media mean for the future of advertising? Rust and Oliver have said that the proliferation of new media means the death of traditional mass-media advertising as we know it. It also means a greater amount of direct producer-consumer interaction, with benefits to both parties. Producers, who gain more information about their customers, can customize their products and messages better; customers gain greater control because they can choose whether to receive an advertising message or not.

Sources: Roland T. Rust and Richard W. Oliver, "Notes and Comments: The Death of Advertising," *Journal of Advertising,* December 1994, pp. 71–77; Lorien Golaski, "Product Ads Are Just a Call Away," *Business Marketing,* September 1994, p. 26; Dennis Donlin, "Scaling New-Media Mountains," *Advertising Age,* March 27, 1995, p. 22; and Steve Yahn, "Advertising's Brave New World," *Advertising Age,* May 16, 1994, pp. 1, 53.

products. And some companies mail audio tapes or videotapes that advertise their products to prospects. For more details on some of the newest electronic advertising media, see the Vision 2000 feature titled "Keeping Up with the New Advertising Media" and Chapter 23.

Given the abundant media and their characteristics, the media planner must first decide on how to allocate the budget to the major media types. For example, in launching its new biscuit, Pillsbury might decide to allocate $3 million to daytime network television, $2 million to women's magazines, $1 million to daily newspapers in 20 major markets, and $50,000 to maintaining its home page on the Internet.

SELECTING SPECIFIC MEDIA VEHICLES. The media planner must next search for the most cost-effective media vehicles within each chosen media type. For example, the advertiser who decides to buy 30 seconds of advertising on network television can pay $100,000 for a popular prime-time TV program, $380,000 for an especially popular program like *Roseanne* or *Seinfeld,* or $1,000,000 for an event like the Super Bowl. How does the media planner make choices among the rich array of media? The media planner relies on media-measurement services that provide estimates of audience size, composition, and media cost. Audience size has several possible measures:

Managing Advertising,
Sales Promotion, and
Public Relations

- *Circulation:* The number of physical units carrying the advertising.

- *Audience:* The number of people who are exposed to the vehicle. (If the vehicle has pass-on readership, then the audience is larger than circulation.)

- *Effective audience:* The number of people with the target audience's characteristics who are exposed to the vehicle.

- *Effective ad-exposed audience:* The number of people with the target audience's characteristics who actually saw the ad.

The Cost-Per-Thousand Criterion. Media planners calculate the *cost per thousand persons reached* by a vehicle. If a full-page, four-color ad in *Newsweek* costs $84,000 and *Newsweek's* estimated readership is three million people, the cost of exposing the ad to 1,000 persons is approximately $28. The same ad in *Business Week* may cost $30,000 but reach only 775,000 persons—at a cost per thousand of $39. The media planner would rank each magazine by cost per thousand and favor those magazines with the lowest cost per thousand for reaching target consumers. The magazines themselves often put together a "reader profile" for their advertisers, summarizing the characteristics of the magazine's typical reader with such data as age, income range, residence, marital status, and leisure activities.

Several adjustments have to be applied to the initial cost-per-thousand measure. First, the measure should be adjusted for *audience quality.* For a baby lotion advertisement, a magazine read by one million young mothers would have an exposure value of one million, but if read by one million old men it would have almost a zero exposure value. Second, the exposure value should be adjusted for the *audience-attention probability.* Readers of *Vogue,* for example, pay more attention to ads than do readers of *Newsweek.* Third, the exposure value should be adjusted for the *editorial quality* (prestige and believability) that one magazine might have over another. Fourth, the exposure value should be adjusted for the magazine's ad placement policies and extra services (such as regional or occupational editions and lead-time requirements).

Media planners are increasingly using more sophisticated measures of media effectiveness and employing them in mathematical models for arriving at the best media mix. Many advertising agencies use a computer program to select the initial media and then make further improvements based on subjective factors omitted in the model.[27]

DECIDING ON MEDIA TIMING. In deciding which types of media to use, the advertiser faces a macroscheduling problem and a microscheduling problem.

Macroscheduling Problem. The macroscheduling problem calls for deciding how to schedule the advertising in relation to seasonal and business-cycle trends. Suppose 70% of a product's sales occur between June and September. The firm has three options. It can vary its advertising expenditures to follow the seasonal pattern, to oppose the seasonal pattern, or to be constant throughout the year. Most firms pursue a policy of seasonal advertising. Yet consider this example:

> Some years ago, one of the soft-drink manufacturers put more money into off-season advertising. This resulted in increased nonseasonal consumption of its brand, while not hurting the brand's seasonal consumption. Other soft-drink manufacturers started to do the same, with the net result that a more-balanced consumption pattern occurred. The previous seasonal concentration of advertising had created a self-fulfilling prophecy.

Forrester has proposed using his "industrial dynamics" methodology to test cyclical advertising policies.[28] He believes that advertising has a delayed impact on consumer awareness; awareness has a delayed impact on factory sales; and factory sales have a delayed impact on advertising expenditures. These time relationships can be studied and formulated mathematically into a computer-simulation model.

The model could then simulate alternative timing strategies to assess their varying impacts on company sales, costs, and profits. Rao and Miller also developed a lag (delay) model to relate a brand's share to advertising and promotional expenditures on a market-by-market basis. They tested their model successfully with five Lever brands in fifteen districts, relating market share to dollars spent on TV, print, price-off, and trade promotions.[29]

Kuehn developed a model to explore how advertising should be timed for frequently purchased, highly seasonal, low-cost grocery products.[30] He showed that the appropriate timing pattern depends on the degree of advertising carryover and the amount of habitual behavior in customer brand choice. *Carryover* refers to the rate at which the effect of an advertising expenditure wears out with the passage of time. A carryover of 0.75 per month means that the current effect of a past advertising expenditure is 75% of its level in the previous month. *Habitual behavior* indicates how much brand holdover occurs independent of the level of advertising. High habitual purchasing, say 0.90, means that 90% of the buyers repeat their brand choice in the next period.

Kuehn found that when there is no advertising carryover or habitual purchasing, the decision maker is justified in using a percentage-of-sales rule to budget advertising. The optimal timing pattern for advertising expenditures coincides with the expected seasonal pattern of industry sales. But if there is advertising carryover and/or habitual purchasing, the percentage-of-sales budgeting method is not optimal. It would be better to time advertising to lead sales. Advertising expenditures should peak before sales peak. Lead time should be greater, the higher the carryover. Furthermore, the advertising expenditures should be steadier, the greater the habitual purchasing.

Microscheduling Problem. The microscheduling problem calls for allocating advertising expenditures within a short period to obtain the maximum impact.

Suppose the firm decides to buy 30 radio spots in the month of September. Figure 21-3 shows several possible patterns. The left side shows that advertising messages for the month can be concentrated in a small part of the month ("burst" advertising), dispersed continuously throughout the month, or dispersed intermit-

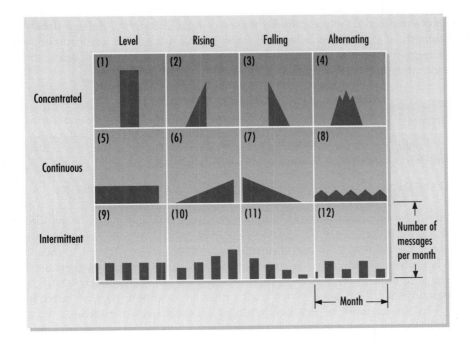

FIGURE 21-3
Classification of Advertising Timing Patterns

Managing Advertising, Sales Promotion, and Public Relations

tently throughout the month. The top side shows that the advertising messages can be beamed with a level, rising, falling, or alternating frequency.

The most effective pattern depends upon the communication objectives in relation to the nature of the product, target customers, distribution channels, and other marketing factors. Consider the following cases:

A retailer wants to announce a preseason sale of ski equipment. She recognizes that only certain people are interested in skis. She thinks that the target buyers need to hear the message only once or twice. Her objective is to maximize reach, not frequency. She decides to concentrate the messages on sale days at a level rate but to vary the time of day to avoid the same audiences. She uses pattern (1).

A muffler manufacturer-distributor wants to keep his name before the public. Yet he does not want his advertising to be too continuous because only 3% to 5% of the cars on the road need a new muffler at any given time. He chooses to use intermittent advertising. Furthermore, he recognizes that Fridays are paydays, so he sponsors a few messages on a midweek day and more messages on Friday. He uses pattern (12).

The timing pattern should consider three factors. *Buyer turnover* expresses the rate at which new buyers enter the market; the higher this rate, the more continuous the advertising should be. *Purchase frequency* is the number of times during the period that the average buyer buys the product; the higher the purchase frequency, the more continuous the advertising should be. The *forgetting rate* is the rate at which the buyer forgets the brand; the higher the forgetting rate, the more continuous the advertising should be.

In launching a new product, the advertiser has to choose among ad continuity, concentration, flighting, and pulsing. *Continuity* is achieved by scheduling exposures evenly throughout a given period. But high advertising costs and seasonal variations in sales discourage continuous advertising. Generally, advertisers use continuous advertising in expanding market situations, with frequently purchased items, and in tightly defined buyer categories. *Concentration* calls for spending all the advertising dollars in a single period. This makes sense for products with only one selling season or holiday. *Flighting* calls for advertising for some period, followed by a hiatus with no advertising, followed by a second flight of advertising activity. It is used when funding is limited, the purchase cycle is relatively infrequent, and with seasonal items. *Pulsing* is continuous advertising at low-weight levels reinforced periodically by waves of heavier activity. Pulsing draws upon the strength of continuous advertising and flights to create a compromise scheduling strategy.[31] Those who favor pulsing feel that the audience will learn the message more thoroughly, and money can be saved.

ANHEUSER-BUSCH Anheuser-Busch's research indicated that Budweiser could substantially reduce advertising in a particular market and experience no adverse sales effect for at least a year and a half. Then the company could introduce a six-month burst of advertising and restore the previous growth rate. This analysis led Budweiser to adopt a pulsing advertising strategy.

DECIDING ON GEOGRAPHICAL MEDIA ALLOCATION. A company has to decide how to allocate its advertising budget over space as well as over time. The company makes "national buys" when it places ads on national TV networks or in nationally circulated magazines. It makes "spot buys" when it buys TV time in just a few TV markets or regional editions of magazines. In these cases, the ads reach a market 40 to 60 miles from a city center. These markets are called *areas of dominant influence (ADIs)* or *designated marketing areas (DMAs)*. The company makes "local buys" when it advertises in local newspapers, radio, or outdoor.

As an example of the geographical allocation issues that arise in advertising planning, consider the following example:

PIZZA HUT   Pizza Hut levies a 4% advertising fee on its franchisees. It spends 2% of its budget on national media and 2% on regional and local media. Some of the national advertising is wasted because of Pizza Hut's low penetration in certain areas. Thus, even though Pizza Hut may have a 30% share of the franchised pizza market nationally, this share may vary from 5% in some cities to 70% in other cities. The franchisees in the higher market share cities want much more advertising money spent in these areas. But if Pizza Hut spent its whole budget on regional media, there would only be enough money to cover half of the nation. Regional spending involves greater production costs and a larger number of creative executions to match local situations, instead of only one creative execution for the national market. Thus, national advertising offers efficiency but fails to effectively address the different local situations.

Evaluating Advertising Effectiveness

Good planning and control of advertising depend critically on measures of advertising effectiveness. Yet the amount of fundamental research on advertising effectiveness is appallingly small. According to Forrester, "Probably no more than 1/5 of 1% of total advertising expenditure is used to achieve an enduring understanding of how to spend the other 99.8%."[32]

Most measurement of advertising effectiveness is of an applied nature, dealing with specific ads and campaigns. Most of the money is spent by agencies on pretesting ads, and much less is spent on postevaluating their effects. Many companies develop an advertising campaign, put it into the national market, and then evaluate its effectiveness. It would be better to limit the campaign to one or a few cities first and evaluate its impact before rolling a campaign throughout the country with a very large budget. One company tested its new campaign first in Phoenix. The campaign bombed, and the company saved all the money that it would have spent going national.

Most advertisers try to measure the communication effect of an ad—that is, its potential effect on awareness, knowledge, or preference. They would also like to measure the ad's sales effect but often feel it is too difficult to measure. Yet both can and should be researched.

COMMUNICATION-EFFECT RESEARCH.   *Communication-effect research* seeks to determine whether an ad is communicating effectively. Also called *copy testing*, it can be done before an ad is put into media and after it is printed or broadcast.

There are three major methods of advertising pretesting. The *direct rating method* asks consumers to rate alternative ads. These ratings are used to evaluate an ad's attention, read-through, cognitive, affective, and behavior strengths (Figure 21-4 on the next page). Although an imperfect measure of an ad's actual impact, a high rating indicates a potentially more effective ad. *Portfolio tests* ask consumers to view and/or listen to a portfolio of advertisements, taking as much time as they need. Consumers are then asked to recall all the ads and their content, aided or unaided by the interviewer. Their recall level indicates an ad's ability to stand out and to have its message understood and remembered. *Laboratory tests* use equipment to measure consumers' physiological reactions—heartbeat, blood pressure, pupil dilation, perspiration—to an ad. These tests measure an ad's attention-getting power but reveal nothing about its impact on beliefs, attitudes, or intentions. Table 21-4 (page 658) describes some specific advertising research techniques.

Haley, Stafforoni, and Fox argue that current copy-testing methods have become so familiar and well-established that it is easy to overlook their sizable limitations. Specifically, these methods tend to be excessively rational and verbal, and tend to rely primarily on respondents' playback in one form or another. They ar-

FIGURE 21-4

Simplified Rating Sheet for Ads

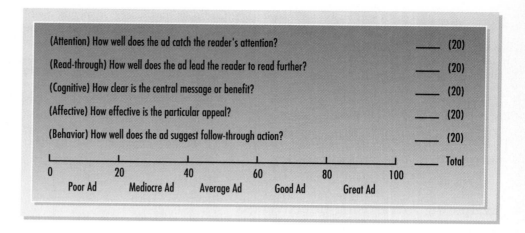

(Attention) How well does the ad catch the reader's attention?	____ (20)
(Read-through) How well does the ad lead the reader to read further?	____ (20)
(Cognitive) How clear is the central message or benefit?	____ (20)
(Affective) How effective is the particular appeal?	____ (20)
(Behavior) How well does the ad suggest follow-through action?	____ (20)
	____ Total

0	20	40	60	80	100
Poor Ad	Mediocre Ad	Average Ad	Good Ad	Great Ad	

gue that marketers need to take more account of ads' nonverbal elements, which can be very strong influences on behavior.[33]

Advertisers are also interested in posttesting the overall communication impact of a completed advertising campaign. To what extent did the ad campaign increase brand awareness, brand comprehension, stated brand preference, and so on? Assuming that the advertiser measured these levels before the campaign, the

TABLE 21-4	ADVERTISING RESEARCH TECHNIQUES
Print Ads	Starch and Gallup & Robinson, Inc. are two widely used print pretesting services in which test ads are placed into magazines. The magazines are then circulated to consumers. These consumers are contacted later and interviewed concerning the magazines and their advertising. Recall and recognition tests are used to determine advertising effectiveness. In Starch's case, three readership scores are prepared: (a) *noted*, the percentage of readers who recall seeing the ad in the magazine; (b) *seen/associated*, the percentage who correctly identify the product and advertiser with the ad; and (c) *read most*, the percentage who say they read more than half of the written material in the ad. Starch also furnishes data showing the average "read" scores for each product class for the year, and separately for men and women for each magazine, to enable advertisers to compare their ads to competitors' ads.
Broadcast Ads *In-home tests*	A small-screen projector is taken into the homes of target consumers. These consumers then view the commercials. The technique gains a subject's complete attention but creates an unnatural viewing situation.
Trailer tests	To get closer to the consumers' actual decision point, pretesting is conducted in a trailer in a shopping center. Shoppers are shown the test products and given an opportunity to select a series of brands in a simulated shopping situation. Consumers then view a series of commercials and are given coupons to be used in the shopping center. By evaluating redemption, advertisers can estimate the commercial's influence on purchase behavior.
Theater tests	Consumers are invited to a theater to view a potential new television series along with some commercials. Before the show begins, the consumers indicate their preferred brands in different categories. After the viewing, consumers are again asked to choose their preferred brands in various categories. Preference changes are assumed to measure the commercials' persuasive power.
On-air tests	These tests are conducted on a regular TV channel. Respondents are recruited to watch the program during the test commercial or are selected based on their having viewed the program. They are asked questions about their commercial recall. This technique creates a real-world atmosphere in which to evaluate commercials.

advertiser can draw a random sample of consumers after the campaign to assess the communication effects. If a company hoped to increase brand awareness from 20% to 50% and succeeded in increasing it to only 30%, then something is wrong: The company is not spending enough, its ads are poor, or some other factor is missing.

SALES-EFFECT RESEARCH. Communication-effect advertising research helps advertisers assess advertising's communication effects but reveals little about its sales impact. What sales are generated by an ad that increases brand awareness by 20% and brand preference by 10 percent?

Advertising's sales effect is generally harder to measure than its communication effect. Sales are influenced by many factors besides advertising, such as the product's features, price, availability and competitors' actions. The fewer or more controllable these other factors are, the easier it is to measure advertising's effect on sales. The sales impact is easiest to measure in direct-marketing situations and hardest to measure in brand or corporate-image-building advertising.

Companies are generally interested in finding out whether they are overspending or underspending on advertising. One approach to answering this question is to work with the following formulation:

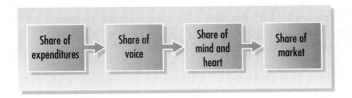

In other words, a company's share of advertising expenditures produces a share of voice that earns a share of minds and hearts and ultimately a share of market. Peckham studied the relationship between share of voice and share of market for several consumer products over a number of years and found a 1-to-1 ratio for established products and a 1.5–2.0 to 1.0 ratio for new products.[34] Using this information, suppose we observed the following data for three well-established firms selling an almost identical product at an identical price:

	(1) ADVERTISING EXPENDITURE	(2) SHARE OF VOICE	(3) SHARE OF MARKET	(4) ADVERTISING EFFECTIVENESS (COLUMN 3/COLUMN 2)*
A	$2,000,000	57.1	40.0	70
B	1,000,000	28.6	28.6	100
C	500,000	14.3	31.4	220

*Note:** An advertising effectiveness rating of 100 means an effective level of advertising expenditure. A rating below 100 means a relatively ineffective advertising level; a level above 100 indicates a very effective advertising level.

Firm A spends $2,000,000 of the industry's total expenditures of $3,500,000, so its share of voice is 57.1%. Yet its share of market is only 40 percent. By dividing its share of market by its share of voice, we get an advertising-effectiveness ratio of 70, suggesting that firm A is either overspending or misspending. Firm B is spending 28.6% of total advertising expenditures and has a 28.6 market share; the conclusion is that it is spending its money efficiently. Firm C is spending only 14.3% of the total and yet achieving a market share of 31.4%; the conclusion is that it is spending its money superefficiently and should probably increase its expenditures.

Researchers try to measure the sales impact through analyzing either historical or experimental data. The *historical approach* involves correlating past sales to past advertising expenditures using advanced statistical techniques. Palda studied the effect of advertising expenditures on the sales of Lydia Pinkham's Vegetable Compound between 1908 and 1960.[35] He calculated the short-term and long-term marginal sales effects of advertising. The marginal advertising dollars increased sales by only 50 cents in the short term, suggesting that Pinkham spent too much on advertising. But the long-term marginal sales effect was three times as large. Palda calculated a post-tax marginal rate of return on company advertising of 37% over the whole period.

Montgomery and Silk estimated the sales effectiveness of three communication tools used in the pharmaceutical industry.[36] A drug company spent 38% of its communication budget on direct mail, 32% on samples and literature, and 29% on journal advertising. Yet the sales-effects research indicated that journal advertising, the least-used communication tool, had the highest long-run advertising effectiveness, followed by samples and literature, and lastly by direct mail. Montgomery and Silk concluded that the company spent too much on direct mail and too little on journal advertising.

Other researchers use *experimental design* to measure advertising's sales impact. Instead of spending the normal percentage of advertising to sales in all territories, the company spends more in some territories and less in others. If the high-spending tests produce substantial sales increases, it appears that the company has been underspending. If they fail to produce more sales and if low-spending tests do not lead to sales decreases, then the company has been overspending. These tests, of course, must be accompanied by good experimental controls and last sufficiently long to capture delayed effects of changed advertising-expenditure levels.

DU PONT   Du Pont was one of the first companies to design advertising experiments. Du Pont's paint division divided 56 sales territories into high, average, and low market share territories. Du Pont spent the normal amount for advertising in one third of the group; in another third, two and one-half times the normal amount; and in the remaining third, four times the normal amount. At the end of the experiment, Du Pont estimated how much in extra sales was created by higher levels of advertising expenditure. Du Pont found that higher advertising expenditure increased sales at a diminishing rate, and that the sales increase was weaker in Du Pont's high market share territories.[37]

Another approach to allocating an advertising budget geographically is to use a model that considers the differences between geographic areas in terms of their market size, advertising response, media efficiency, competition, and profit margins. Urban developed a media allocation model that relies upon these geographic variables to allocate the advertising budget.[38]

In general, a growing number of companies are striving to measure the sales effect of advertising expenditures instead of settling only for communication-effect measures. For example, Millward Brown International has conducted tracking studies in the United Kingdom for many years. A key objective of these studies is to provide information to help advertising decision makers decide whether their advertising is working to benefit their brand.[39]

Advertising Effectiveness: A Summary of Current Research.

Although companies need to do more research into advertising effectiveness, professional researchers have drawn some general conclusions that are useful to marketers.[40]

- *The impact of advertising on brand switching:* Tellis analyzed household purchases of 12 key brands of a frequently purchased consumer product and concluded that advertising appears effective in increasing the volume purchased by loyal buyers but less effective in winning new buyers. For loyal buyers, high levels of exposure per week may be unproductive because of a leveling off of ad effectiveness. Advertising appears unlikely to have some cumulative effect that leads to loyalty; rather, features, displays, and especially price have a stronger impact on response than does advertising.[41] These findings did not sit well with the advertising community, and several people attacked Tellis' data and methodology. A set of controlled experiments by the research firm IRI found advertising-produced sales gains during the test year that lasted two to three years later. Thus, IRI concluded, advertising's impact is grossly underestimated when only a one-year perspective is employed.

- *The effect of surroundings:* Ads may be more effective when their message is congruent with their surroundings. For example, a "happy" commercial placed within an upbeat television show is more likely to be effective than a downbeat commercial in the same place. Similarly, a "serious" commercial usually works best when placed within a serious program.[42] In addition, people are more likely to believe a TV or radio advertisement, and to become more positively disposed toward the brand it supports, when the ad is placed within a program that they like or with which they are heavily involved.[43]

- *The effect of positive versus negative messages:* Consumers may sometimes respond more to negative messages than to positive messages. For example, one credit-card company contacted customers who did not use the card for three months. To one group of the nonusers it sent a message explaining the benefits of using the card. To another group of nonusers it sent a message explaining the losses they could suffer by not using the card. The impact of the loss-oriented message was much stronger than the impact of the gain-oriented message. The percentage of customers who started to use the card in the loss conditions was more than double the percentage in the gain conditions, and the charges of the former customers were more than twice as much as the charges of the latter customers.[44]

- *Advertising versus sales promotions:* In a recent study, John Philip Jones used data provided by Nielsen, a market-research firm, to study the effects of advertising. Jones found that 70% of the ad campaigns in his sample boosted sales immediately, but that the effect was strong only in 30% of the cases. Only 46% of the campaigns appeared to result in a long-term sales boost. Jones also asserts that increased sales can come from a single advertisement, that blitz campaigns suffer diminishing returns, and that ads that do not generate extra sales on their first airing should be pulled.[45]

SALES PROMOTION

Sales promotion is a key ingredient in marketing campaigns. We define it as follows:

❖ **SALES PROMOTION** consists of a diverse collection of incentive tools, mostly short term, designed to stimulate quicker and/or greater purchase of particular products/services by consumers or the trade.[46]

Where advertising offers a *reason* to buy, sales promotion offers an *incentive* to buy. Sales promotion includes tools for *consumer promotion* (samples, coupons, cash refund offers, prices off, premiums, prizes, patronage rewards, free trials, warranties, tie-in promotions, cross-promotions, point-of-purchase displays, and demonstrations); *trade promotion* (prices off, advertising and display allowances, and free goods); and *business and sales force promotion* (trade shows and conventions, contests for sales reps, and specialty advertising).

Sales-promotion tools are used by most organizations, including manufacturers, distributors, retailers, trade associations, and nonprofit organizations. As examples of the last, churches often sponsor bingo games, theater parties, testimonial dinners, and raffles.

The Rapid Growth of Sales Promotion

A decade ago, the advertising-to-sales-promotion ratio was about 60:40. Today, in many consumer-packaged-goods companies, sales promotion accounts for 65% to 75% of the combined budget. Sales-promotion expenditures have been increasing as a percentage of budget expenditure annually for the last two decades,[47] and the fast growth rate is expected to continue. McDonald's heavy use of sales promos tied to popular Hollywood movies boosted its sales 7.1% to $14.2 billion in 1993, compared to only a 6.6% increase for the entire fast-food industry. MasterCard's shift to a promotional strategy stressing rebates and discounts has helped it end a five-year share slide and rebound two points, to 28.9 percent.[48]

Several factors contributed to the rapid growth of sales promotion, particularly in consumer markets.[49] Internal factors include the following: Promotion is now more accepted by top management as an effective sales tool; more product managers are qualified to use sales-promotion tools; and product managers are under greater pressure to increase their current sales. External factors include the following: The number of brands has increased; competitors use promotions frequently; many brands are seen as similar; consumers are more price-oriented; the trade has demanded more deals from manufacturers; and advertising efficiency has declined because of rising costs, media clutter, and legal restraints.

The rapid growth of sales-promotion media (coupons, contests, and the like) has created a situation of *promotion clutter,* similar to advertising clutter. There is a danger that consumers will start tuning out, in which case coupons and other forms of promotion will weaken in their ability to trigger purchase. Manufacturers will have to find ways to rise above the clutter—for instance, by offering larger coupon-redemption values or using more dramatic point-of-purchase displays or demonstrations.

Purpose of Sales Promotion

Sales-promotion tools vary in their specific objectives. A free sample stimulates consumer trial, while a free management-advisory service aims at cementing a long-term relationship with a retailer.

Sellers use incentive-type promotions to attract new triers, to reward loyal customers, and to increase the repurchase rates of occasional users. New triers are of three types—users of another brand in the same category, users in other categories, and frequent brand switchers. Sales promotions often attract the brand switchers, because users of other brands and categories do not always notice or act on a promotion. Brand switchers are primarily looking for low price, good value, or premiums. Sales promotions are unlikely to turn them into loyal brand users. Sales promotions used in markets of high brand similarity produce a high sales response in the short run but little permanent gain in market share. In markets of high brand dissimilarity, sales promotions can alter market shares permanently.

Today, many marketing managers first estimate what they need to spend in trade promotion, then what they need to spend in consumer promotion. Whatever is left they will budget for advertising. There is a danger, however, in letting advertising take a back seat to sales promotion. Advertising typically acts to build brand loyalty, while sales promotion aims to weaken brand loyalty. When a brand is price promoted too much of the time, the consumer begins to think less of it and buy it mainly when it goes on sale. There is risk in putting a well-known brand leader on promotion more than 30% of the time.[50] Dominant brands offer deals less frequently, since most deals would only subsidize current users. Brown's study of 2,500 instant coffee buyers concluded that:

◆ Sales promotions yield faster and more measurable responses in sales than advertising does.

◆ Sales promotions do not tend to yield new, long-term buyers in mature markets because they attract mainly deal-prone consumers who switch among brands as deals become available.

◆ Loyal brand buyers tend not to change their buying patterns as a result of competitive promotion.

◆ Advertising appears to be capable of deepening brand loyalty.[51]

There is also evidence that price promotions do not permanently build total category volume. They usually build short-term volume that is not maintained.

Small-share competitors find it advantageous to use sales promotion, because they cannot afford to match the market leaders' large advertising budgets. Nor can they obtain shelf space without offering trade allowances or stimulate consumer trial without offering consumer incentives. Price competition is often used by a small brand seeking to enlarge its share, but it is less effective for a category leader whose growth lies in expanding the entire category.[52]

The upshot is that many consumer-packaged-goods companies feel that they are forced to use more sales promotion than they want to. Kellogg, Kraft, and other market leaders have announced that they will put a growing emphasis on the pull side of the business and increase their advertising budgets. They blame the heavy use of sales promotion for causing decreasing brand loyalty, increasing consumer price sensitivity, brand-quality-image dilution, and a focus on short-run marketing planning.

Farris and Quelch, however, dispute this conclusion.[53] They counter that sales promotion provides a number of benefits that are important to manufacturers as well as consumers. Sales promotions enable manufacturers to adjust to short-term variations in supply and demand. They enable manufacturers to test how high a list price they can charge, because they can always discount it. They induce consumers to try new products instead of never straying from their current ones. They lead to more varied retail formats, such as the everyday-low-price store and the promotional-pricing store, giving consumers more choices. They promote greater consumer awareness of prices. They permit manufacturers to sell more than they would normally sell at the list price. They help the manufacturer adapt programs to different consumer segments. Consumers themselves enjoy some satisfaction from being smart shoppers when they take advantage of price specials.

Major Decisions in Sales Promotion

In using sales promotion, a company must establish its objectives, select the tools, develop the program, pretest the program, implement and control it, and evaluate the results.

ESTABLISHING THE SALES-PROMOTION OBJECTIVES. Sales-promotion objectives are derived from broader promotion objectives, which are derived

TABLE 21-5   MAJOR CONSUMER-PROMOTION TOOLS

TOOL	DESCRIPTION	EXAMPLE
Samples	Offer of a free amount of a product or service. The sample might be delivered door to door, sent in the mail, picked up in a store, found attached to another product, or featured in an advertising offer. Sampling is the most effective and most expensive way to introduce a new product.	Lever Brothers had so much confidence in its new Surf detergent that it distributed free samples to four out of five U.S. households at a cost of $43 million.
Coupons	Certificates entitling the bearer to a stated saving on the purchase of a specific product. Coupons can be mailed, enclosed in other products or attached to them, or inserted in magazine and newspaper ads. The redemption rate varies with the mode of distribution. About 2% of newspaper coupons are redeemed; about 8% of direct-mail-distributed coupons; and about 17% of pack-distributed coupons. Coupons can be effective in stimulating sales of a mature brand and inducing early trial of a new brand. Experts believe that coupons should provide a 15% to 20% saving to be effective.	P&G broke into the Pittsburgh market with its Folger's brand of coffee by offering a 35¢ discount coupon on a one-pound can mailed to area homes and a coupon in the coffee can for 10¢ off.
Cash Refund Offers (rebates)	Provide a price reduction after the purchase rather than at the retail shop. The consumer sends a specified "proof of purchase" to the, manufacturer, who "refunds" part of the purchase price by mail.	Toro ran a clever preseason promotion on specific snowblower models, offering a rebate if the snowfall in the buyer's market area was below average. Competitors were not able to match this offer on such short notice.
Price Packs (cents-off deals)	Offers to consumers of savings off the regular price of a product, flagged on the label or package. They can take the form of a *reduced-price pack,* which is a single package sold at a reduced price (such as two for the price of one), or a *banded pack,* which is two related products banded together (such as a toothbrush and toothpaste). Price packs are very effective in stimulating short-term sales, even more so than coupons.	Air freshener companies sometimes specially package several types of air fresheners together: for example, a spray mist, carpet deodorizer, and solid air freshener.
Premiums (gifts)	Merchandise offered at a relatively low cost or free as an incentive to purchase a particular product. A *with-pack premium* accompanies the product inside (in-pack) or on (on-pack) the package. The package itself, if a reusable container, can serve as a premium. A *free in-the-mail premium* is an item mailed to consumers who send in a proof of purchase, such as a box top or UPC code. A *self-liquidating premium* is an item sold below its normal retail price to consumers who request it. Manufacturers now offer consumers all kinds of premiums bearing the company's name.	Quaker Oats ran a promotion where it inserted $5 million in gold and silver coins in bags of Ken-L Ration dog food. The Budweiser consumer can order T-shirts, hot-air balloons, and hundreds of other items with Bud's name on them.

from more basic marketing objectives developed for the product. The specific objectives set for sales promotion vary with the target market. For consumers, objectives include encouraging purchase of larger-size units, building trial among nonusers, and attracting switchers away from competitors' brands. For retailers, objectives include persuading retailers to carry new items and higher levels of inventory, encouraging off-season buying, encouraging stocking of related items, offsetting competitive promotions, building brand loyalty, and gaining entry into new retail outlets. For the sales force, objectives include encouraging support of a new product or model, encouraging more prospecting, and stimulating off-season sales.[54]

TOOL	DESCRIPTION	EXAMPLE
Prizes (contests, sweepstakes, games)	*Prizes* are offers of the chance to win cash, trips, or merchandise as a result of purchasing something. A *contest* calls for consumers to submit an entry—a jingle, estimate, suggestion—to be examined by a panel of judges who will select the best entries. A *sweepstake* asks consumers to submit their names in a drawing. A *game* presents consumers with something every time they buy—bingo numbers, missing letters—which might help them win a prize. All of these tend to gain more attention than do coupons or small premiums.	A British cigarette company included a lottery ticket in each pack providing the chance to win up to $10,000 if the lottery ticket won. Sometimes the prize is a person, as when Canada Dry offered the winner either $1 million or dinner with actress Joan Collins (cash won out in this case).
Patronage Awards	Values in cash or in other forms that are proportional to one's patronage of a certain vendor or group of vendors. Trading stamps also represent patronage rewards in that customers receive stamps when they buy from certain merchants. They can redeem the stamps for merchandise at stamp redemption centers or through mail-order catalogs.	Most airlines offer frequent-flyer plans, providing points for miles traveled that can be turned in for free airline trips. Marriott Hotels have adopted an honored guest plan that awards points for users of their hotels. Cooperatives pay their members dividends according to their annual patronage.
Free Trials	Invite prospective purchasers to try the product without cost in the hope that they will buy the product.	Auto dealers encourage free test drives to stimulate purchase interest.
Product Warranties	Explicit or implicit promises by sellers that the product will perform as specified or that the seller will fix it or refund the customer's money during a specified period.	When Chrysler offered a five-year car warranty, substantially longer than GM's or Ford's, customers took notice. And Sears's offer of a lifetime warranty on its auto batteries certainly screams quality to the buyers.
Tie-in Promotions	Involve two or more brands or companies that team up on coupons, refunds, and contests to increase their pulling power. Companies pool funds with the hope of broader exposure, and multiple sales forces push these promotions to retailers, giving them a better shot at extra display and ad space.	MCI has offered 10 minutes of free long-distance service on cans of Crystal Light powdered soft drinks and Taster's Choice coffee, and boxes of Keebler cookies and crackers.
Cross-Promotions	Involve using one brand to advertise another noncompeting brand.	Nabisco cookies might advertise that they contain Hershey chocolate chips and the box may even contain a coupon to buy a Hershey product.
Point-of-Purchase (POP) Displays and Demonstrations	MPOP displays and demonstrations take place at the point of purchase or sale. Unfortunately, many retailers do not like to handle the hundreds of displays, signs, and posters they receive from manufacturers. Manufacturers are responding by creating better POP materials, tying them in with television or print messages, and offering to set them up.	The L'eggs pantyhose display is one of the most creative in the history of POP materials and has been a major factor in the success of this brand.

Sources: For more information, see "Consumer Incentive Strategy Guide." *Incentive*, May 1995, pp. 58–63; William Urseth, "Promos 101." *Incentive*, January 1994, pp. 53–55; William Urseth, "Promos 101, Part II," *Incentive*, February 1994, pp. 43–45; and Jonathan Berry, "Wilma! What Happened to the Plain Old Ad?" *Business Week*, June 6, 1994, pp. 54–58.

SELECTING THE SALES-PROMOTION TOOLS. Many sales-promotion tools are available. The promotion planner should take into account the type of market, sales-promotion objectives, competitive conditions, and each tool's cost effectiveness.

Consumer-Promotion Tools. The main consumer-promotion tools are summarized in Table 21-5. We can distinguish between *manufacturer promotions* and *retailer promotions* to consumers. The former are illustrated by the auto industry's frequent use of rebates, gifts to motivate test drives and purchases, and high-value trade-in credit. The latter include price cuts, feature advertising, retailer coupons, and retailer contests/premiums. We can also distinguish between sales-promotion tools that are "consumer-franchise building," which reinforce the consumer's brand understanding, and those that are not. The former impart a selling message along with the deal, as in the case of free samples, coupons when they include a selling message, and premiums when they are related to the product. Sales-promotion tools that are not consumer-franchise building include price-off packs, consumer premiums not related to a product, contests and sweepstakes, consumer refund offers, and trade allowances.

Sales promotion seems most effective when used together with advertising. In one study, a price promotion alone produced only a 15% increase in sales volume. When combined with feature advertising, sales volume increased 19%; when combined with feature advertising and a point-of-purchase display, sales volume increased 24 percent.[55]

Many large companies have a sales-promotion manager whose job is to help brand managers choose the right promotional tool. The following example shows how one firm determined the appropriate tool:

> A firm launched a new product and achieved a 20% market share within six months. Its penetration rate (i.e., the percentage of the target market that purchased the brand at least once) is 40 percent. Its repurchase rate (the percentage of the first-time triers who repurchased the brand one or more times) is 10 percent. This firm needs to create more loyal users. An in-pack coupon would be appropriate to build more repeat purchases. But if the repurchase rate had been high, say 50%, then the company should try to attract more new triers. Here a mailed coupon might be appropriate.

Trade-Promotion Tools. Manufacturers use a number of trade-promotion tools (Table 21-6). Surprisingly, a higher proportion of the promotion pie is devoted to trade-promotion tools (46.9%) than to consumer promotion (27.9%), with media advertising capturing the remaining 25.2 percent. Manufacturers award money to the trade for four reasons:

1. *Trade promotion can persuade the retailer or wholesaler to carry the brand.* Shelf space is so scarce that manufacturers often have to offer price-offs, allowances, buyback guar-

TABLE 21-6	MAJOR TRADE-PROMOTION TOOLS
TOOL	**DESCRIPTION**
Price-Off (off-invoice or off-list)	A straight discount off the list price on each case purchased during a stated time period. The offer encourages dealers to buy a quantity or carry a new item that they might not ordinarily buy. The dealers can use the buying allowance for immediate profit, advertising, or price reductions.
Allowance	An amount offered in return for the retailer's agreeing to feature the manufacturer's products in some way. An *advertising allowance* compensates retailers for advertising the manufacturer's product. A *display allowance* compensates them for carrying a special product display.
Free goods	Offers of extra cases of merchandise to intermediaries who buy a certain quantity or who feature a certain flavor or size. Manufacturers might offer push money or free specialty advertising items to the retailers that carry the company's name, such as pens, pencils, calendars, paperweights, memo pads, and ashtrays.

Source: **For more information, see Betsy Spethman, "Trade Promotion Redefined,"** *Brandweek,* **March 13, 1995, pp. 25–32.**

antees, free goods, or outright payments (called *slotting allowances*) to get on the shelf, and once there, to stay on the shelf.

2. *Trade promotion can persuade the retailer or wholesaler to carry more units than the normal amount.* Manufacturers will offer volume allowances to get the trade to carry more in their warehouses and stores. Manufacturers believe that the trade will work harder when they are "loaded" with the manufacturer's product.

3. *Trade promotion can induce the retailers to promote the brand by featuring, display, and price reductions.* Manufacturers might seek an end-of-aisle display, increased shelf facings, or price reduction stickers and obtain them by offering the retailers allowances paid on "proof of performance."

4. *Trade promotion can stimulate retailers and their sales clerks to push the product.* Manufacturers compete for retailer sales effort by offering push money, sales aids, recognition programs, premiums, and sales contests.

Manufacturers probably spend more on trade promotion than they would want to spend. The increased concentration of buying power in the hands of fewer and larger retailers has increased the trade's ability to demand manufacturers' financial support at the expense of consumer promotion and advertising.[56] The trade has come to depend on promotion money from the manufacturers. No manufacturer could unilaterally stop offering trade allowances without losing retailer support. In some countries, the retailers have become the major advertisers, using mostly the promotional allowances extracted from their suppliers to pay for the advertising.

The company's sales force and its brand managers are often at odds over trade promotion. The sales force says that the local retailers will not keep the company's products on the shelf unless they receive more trade-promotion money, while the brand managers want to spend the limited funds on consumer promotion and advertising. Since the sales force knows the local market better than a brand manager sitting at headquarters, some companies have given a substantial part of the sales-promotion budget to the sales force to handle.

Manufacturers face several challenges with trade promotions. First, they often find it difficult to police retailers to make sure that they are doing what they agreed to do. Retailers do not always convert buying allowances into reduced prices for consumers, and they might not provide extra shelving or display even after receiving merchandise or display allowances. In the wake of several highly publicized cases of retailers billing manufacturers for nonexistent retail promotions, manufacturers are increasingly insisting on proof of performance before paying any allowances. Second, more retailers are doing *forward buying*—that is, buying a greater quantity of the brand during the deal period than they can sell during the deal period. Retailers might respond to a 10% off-case allowance by buying a 12-week or longer supply. The manufacturer finds that it has to schedule more production than planned and bear the costs of extra work shifts and overtime. Third, retailers are doing more *diverting,* buying more cases than needed in a region in which the manufacturer offered a deal and shipping the surplus to nondeal regions. Manufacturers are trying to handle forward buying and dealing by limiting the amount they will sell at a discount, or producing and delivering less than the full order in an effort to smooth production.[57]

All said, manufacturers feel that trade promotion has become a nightmare. It contains layers of deals, is complex to administer, and often leads to lost revenues. Kevin Price describes trade promotion in the following way:

> *A decade ago, the retailer was a chihuahua nipping at the manufacturer's heels— a nuisance, yes, but only a minor irritant; you fed it and it went away. Today it's a pit bull and it wants to rip your arms and legs off. You'd like to see it roll over, but you're too busy defending yourself to even try . . . Today management of trade promotions is a president-level issue.*[58]

Business- And Sales Force Promotion Tools. Companies spend billions of dollars on business- and sales force promotion tools (Table 21-7). These tools are used to gather business leads, impress and reward customers, and motivate the sales force to greater effort. Companies typically develop budgets for each business-promotion tool that remain fairly constant from year to year.

DEVELOPING THE SALES-PROMOTION PROGRAM.

In planning sales-promotion programs, marketers are increasingly blending several media into a total campaign concept. Kerry E. Smith describes a complete sales-promotion program:

> *A sports trivia game to create pull-through at taverns for a premium beer brand would use TV to reach consumers, direct mail to incentivize distributors, point-of-purchase for retail support, telephones for consumer call-ins, a service bureau for call processing, live operators for data entry, and computer software and hardware to tie it all together. . . . Companies use telepromotions not only to pull product through at retail but also to identify customers, generate leads, build databases and deliver coupons, product samples and rebate offers.*[59]

In deciding to use a particular incentive, marketers have several factors to consider. First, they must determine the *size* of the incentive. A certain minimum in-

TABLE 21-7	**MAJOR BUSINESS- AND SALES FORCE PROMOTION TOOLS**
TOOL	**DESCRIPTION**
Trade Shows and Conventions	Industry associations organize annual trade shows and conventions. Firms selling products and services to the particular industry buy space and set up booths and displays to demonstrate their products at the trade show. Over 5,600 trade shows take place every year, drawing approximately 80 million attendees. Trade show attendance can range from a few thousand people to over 70,000 for large shows held by the restaurant or hotel-motel industries. The participating vendors expect several benefits, including generating new sales leads, maintaining customer contacts, introducing new products, meeting new customers, selling more to present customers, and educating customers with publications, videos, and other audiovisual materials. Business marketers may spend as much as 35% of their annual promotion budget on trade shows. They face a number of decisions, including which trade shoes to participate in, how much to spend on each trade show, how to build dramatic exhibits that attract attention, and how to effectively follow up on sales leads.
Sales Contests	A *sales contest* is a contest involving the sales force or dealers, aimed at inducing them to increase their sales results over a stated period, with prizes going to those who succeed. A majority of companies sponsor annual or more frequent sales contests for their sales force. The top performers may receive trips, cash prizes, or gifts. Some companies award points for performance, which the receiver can turn into any of a variety of prizes. An unusual though not very expensive prize may often work better than much more costly prizes. Incentives work best when they are tied to measurable and achievable sales objectives (such as finding new accounts or reviving old accounts) where employees feel they have an equal chance.
Specialty Advertising	Specialty advertising consists of useful. low-cost items bearing the company's name and address, and sometimes an advertising message. Salespeople give these items to prospects and customers without obligation. Common items are ball-point pens, calendars, cigarette lighters, and memo pads. The item keeps the company's name before the prospect and creates goodwill because of the item's utility. One survey indicated that over 86% of manufacturers supply their salespeople with specialty items.

centive is necessary if the promotion is to succeed. A higher incentive level will produce more sales response but at a diminishing rate.

Second, the marketing manager must establish *conditions* for participation. Incentives might be offered to everyone or to select groups. A premium might be offered only to those who turn in proof-of-purchase seals or UPC codes. Sweepstakes might not be offered in certain states or to families of company personnel or to persons under a certain age.

Third, the marketer has to decide on the *duration* of promotion. If the sales-promotion period is too short, many prospects will not be able to take advantage of it, since they might not be repurchasing at the time. If the promotion runs too long, the deal will lose some of its "act now" force. According to one researcher, the optimal frequency is about three weeks per quarter, and optimal duration is the length of the average purchase cycle.[60] Of course, the optimal promotion cycle varies by product category and even by specific product.

Fourth, the marketer must choose a *distribution vehicle*. A fifteen-cents-off coupon can be distributed in the package, store, mail, or advertising media. Each distribution method involves a different level of reach, cost, and impact.

Fifth, the marketing manager must establish the *timing* of promotion. For example, brand managers develop calendar dates for their annual promotions. These dates are used by the production, sales, and distribution departments.

Finally, the marketer must determine the *total sales-promotion budget*. The sales-promotion budget can be developed in two ways. It can be built from the ground up, with the marketer choosing the individual promotions and estimating their total cost. The cost of a particular promotion consists of the administrative cost (printing, mailing, and promoting the deal) and the incentive cost (cost of premium or cents-off, including redemption costs), multiplied by the expected number of units that will be sold on the deal. In the case of a coupon deal, the cost would take into account the fact that only a fraction of the consumers will redeem the coupons. For an in-pack premium, the deal cost must include the procurement cost and packaging of the premium, offset by any price increase on the package.

The more common way to develop the sales-promotion budget is to use a conventional percentage of the total promotion budget. For example, toothpaste might get a sales-promotion budget of 30% of the total promotion budget, while shampoo might get 50%. These percentages vary for different brands in different markets and are influenced by the stages of the product life cycle and competitive expenditures on promotion.

PRETESTING THE SALES-PROMOTION PROGRAM. Although most sales-promotion programs are designed on the basis of experience, pretests should be conducted to determine if the tools are appropriate, the incentive size optimal, and the presentation method efficient. Unfortunately, a large percentage of premium offers are not pretested. Strang maintains that promotions can usually be tested quickly and inexpensively and that large companies should test alternative strategies in selected market areas with each national promotion.[61] Consumers can be asked to rate or rank different possible deals, or trial tests can be run in limited geographical areas.

IMPLEMENTING AND CONTROLLING THE SALES-PROMOTION PROGRAM. Marketing managers must prepare implementation and control plans for each individual promotion. Implementation planning must cover lead time and sell-in time. *Lead time* is the time necessary to prepare the program prior to launching it. Lead time covers initial planning, design, and approval of package modifications or material to be mailed or distributed; preparation of advertising

Managing Advertising,
Sales Promotion, and
Public Relations

and point-of-sale materials; notification of field sales personnel; establishment of allocations for individual distributors; purchasing and printing of special premiums or packaging materials; production of advance inventories in preparation for release at a specific date; and, finally, the distribution to the retailer.[62]

Sell-in time begins with the promotional launch and ends when approximately 95% of the deal merchandise is in the hands of consumers. This time frame can last one to several months, depending on the deal duration.

EVALUATING THE SALES-PROMOTION RESULTS. Evaluation of the promotion's results is crucial. Manufacturers can use three methods to measure sales-promotion effectiveness: sales data, consumer surveys, and experiments.

The first method involves using scanner sales data, which are available from companies such as Information Resources Inc. and Nielsen. Marketers can analyze the types of people who took advantage of the promotion, what their behavior was before the promotion, and how consumers who purchased the promoted brand behaved later toward the brand and other brands. Suppose a company has a 6% market share in the prepromotion period. The share jumps to 10% during the promotion, falls to 5% immediately after the promotion, and rises to 7% in the postpromotion period (Figure 21-5). The promotion evidently attracted new triers and also stimulated more purchasing by existing customers. After the promotion, sales fell as consumers worked down their inventories. The long-run rise to 7% indicates that the company gained some new users. In general, sales promotions work best when they attract competitors' customers to try a superior product and these customers permanently switch as a result. If the company's product is not superior, the brand's share is likely to return to its prepromotion level. The sales promotion altered only the time pattern of demand rather than the total demand. The promotion may have covered its costs, but more likely did not. One recent study of more than 1,000 promotions concluded that only 16% paid off.[63]

If more information is needed, *consumer surveys* can be conducted to learn how many recall the promotion, what they thought of it, how many took advantage of it, and how the promotion affected subsequent brand-choice behavior.[64] Sales promotions can also be evaluated through *experiments* that vary such attributes as incentive value, duration, and distribution media. For example, coupons can be sent to half of the households in a consumer panel. Scanner data can be used to track whether the coupons led more people to buy the product immedi-

FIGURE 21-5
Effect of Consumer Deal on Brand Share

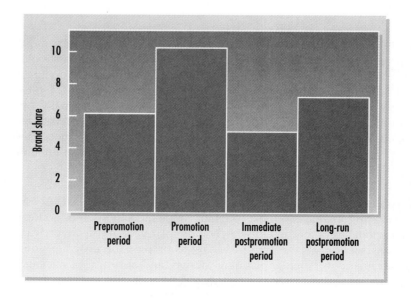

Planning
Marketing
Programs

ately and in the future. This information can then be used to calculate the increase in revenues that stemmed from the promotion.

Beyond these methods of evaluating the results of specific promotions, management must recognize other potential costs and problems. First, promotions might decrease long-run brand loyalty by making more consumers deal prone rather than advertising prone. Second, promotions can be more expensive than they appear. Some are inevitably distributed to the wrong consumers (specifically: nonswitchers; always switchers; and the company's own customers, who get a free subsidy). Third, there are the costs of special production runs, extra sales force effort, and handling requirements. Finally, certain promotions irritate retailers, who may demand extra trade allowances or refuse to cooperate in the promotion.[65]

PUBLIC RELATIONS

Like advertising and sales promotion, public relations is an important marketing tool. Not only must the company relate constructively to its customers, suppliers, and dealers, but it must also relate to a large set of interested publics. We define a public as follows:

> ❖ A PUBLIC is any group that has an actual or potential interest in or impact on a company's ability to achieve its objectives. PUBLIC RELATIONS (PR) involves a variety of programs designed to promote and/or protect a company's image or its individual products.

A public can facilitate or impede a company's ability to achieve its objectives. PR has often been treated as a marketing stepchild, an afterthought to more serious promotion planning. But the wise company takes concrete steps to manage successful relations with its key publics. Most companies operate a public relations department to plan these relations. The PR department monitors the attitudes of the organization's publics and distributes information and communications to build goodwill. When negative publicity breaks out, the PR department acts as a troubleshooter. The best PR departments spend time counseling top management to adopt positive programs and to eliminate questionable practices so that negative publicity does not arise in the first place.

PR departments perform the following five activities, not all of which support marketing objectives:

- *Press relations:* Presenting news and information about organization in the most positive light.
- *Product publicity:* Sponsoring various efforts to publicize specific products.
- *Corporate communication:* Promoting understanding of the organization with internal and external communications.
- *Lobbying:* Dealing with legislators and government officials to promote or defeat legislation and regulation.
- *Counseling:* Advising management about public issues and company positions and image. This includes advising in the event of a product mishap when the public confidence in a product is shaken.[66]

Marketing managers and PR specialists do not always talk the same language. One major difference is that marketing managers are much more bottom-line oriented, while PR practitioners see their job as preparing and disseminating communications. But these differences are disappearing. Many companies are turning to *marketing public relations (MPR)* to directly support corporate/product promotion and image making. Thus MPR, like financial PR and community PR, would serve a special constituency, namely the marketing department.[67]

The old name for MPR was *publicity,* which was seen as the task of securing editorial space—as opposed to paid space—in print and broadcast media to promote or "hype" a product, place, or person. But MPR goes beyond simple publicity and plays an important role in the following tasks:

◆ *Assisting in the launch of new products:* The amazing commercial success of toys such as Teenage Mutant Ninja Turtles, Mighty Morphin' Power Rangers, and Barney (the annoying purple dinosaur) owe a great deal to clever publicity.

◆ *Assisting in repositioning a mature product:* New York City had extremely bad press in the 1970s until the "I Love New York" campaign began, bringing millions of additional tourists to the city.

◆ *Building interest in a product category:* Companies and trade associations have used MPR to rebuild interest in declining commodities like eggs, milk, and potatoes and to expand consumption of such products as tea, pork, and orange juice.

◆ *Influencing specific target groups:* McDonald's sponsors special neighborhood events in Latino and African-American communities and in turn builds up a good company image.

◆ *Defending products that have encountered public problems:* Johnson & Johnson's masterly use of MPR was a major factor in saving Tylenol from extinction following two incidents in which poison-tainted Tylenol capsules were found.

◆ *Building the corporate image in a way that projects favorably on its products:* Iacocca's speeches and his autobiography created a whole new winning image for the Chrysler Corporation.

As the power of mass advertising weakens, marketing managers are turning more to MPR. In a survey of 286 U.S. marketing managers, three fourths reported that their companies were using MPR. They found it particularly effective in building awareness and brand knowledge for both new and established products. MPR is particularly effective in blanketing local communities and reaching specific ethnic and other groups. In several cases, MPR proved more cost effective than advertising. Nevertheless, it must be planned jointly with advertising. MPR needs a larger budget, and the money might have to come from advertising.[68] In addition, marketing managers need to acquire more skill in using PR resources. The Gillette company is a trend setter here: Each brand manager is required to have a budget line for MPR and to justify *not* using it if he or she does not.

Clearly, public relations can potentially impact public awareness at a fraction of the cost of advertising. The company does not pay for the space or time obtained in the media. It pays for a staff to develop and circulate the stories and manage certain events. If the company develops an interesting story, it could be picked up by the news media and be worth millions of dollars in equivalent advertising. The Body Shop, for example, has spent very little money on advertising; its success has been almost entirely due to publicity. And, in general, MPR carries more credibility than advertising. Some experts say that consumers are five times more likely to be influenced by editorial copy than by advertising.

A recent success story in MPR is provided by Intel, which turned a potentially disastrous situation to its advantage with PR:

INTEL AND THE PENTIUM CHIP When users of Intel's Pentium computer chip began to notice a problem with it in 1994, the company refused to replace the chip unless the computer users could prove that they needed their computers for complex mathematical operations (the only operations affected by the flaw). Following an uproar of consumer dissatisfaction, Intel's MPR people came to the rescue by using a "one-two punch," following up intense one-on-one marketing to corporate and retail Pentium users with the introduction of a worldwide network of Pentium-replacement service centers (offering free replacements on request). Rather than just focusing on the media or large customers, Intel tried to reach customers one-on-one, whether they were large cus-

A PR Blitz: Microsoft Launches Windows 95

From time to time, a company will spend an inordinate amount of money to bring a new product to the public's attention. One of the most recent blitz campaigns came when Microsoft spent $220 million hyping its new operating system. Windows 95 represented not so much a new product as one that would make Windows as easy to use as it's rival, the Macintosh system.

The campaign was a marketing public relations success story. No paid ads for Windows 95 had appeared by August 24, 1995, the product's launch day. Yet everyone knew about it! *The Wall Street Journal* estimated 3,000 headlines, 6,852 stories, and over 3 million words dedicated to Windows 95 from July 1 through August 24. Microsoft teams around the world developed attention-grabbing publicity stunts. Microsoft hung a 600-foot Windows 95 banner from Toronto's CN Tower. The Empire State Building in New York was bathed in the red, yellow and green colors of the Windows 95 logo. Microsoft paid *The London Times* to distribute free its entire daily run of 1.5 million copies to the public. When Windows finally went on sale, crowds of thousands lined up to buy it. By the end of the first week, U.S. sales alone were $108 million, not bad for a $90 product. The lesson is clear: Good advance product PR can be much more effective than millions of dollars spent on an ad campaign.

Why did Microsoft's Bill Gates think it necessary to spend this much on PR? Here are two possible reasons. (1) Worrying about bugs in early versions of the new operating system, computer users might hesitate to buy it. Microsoft wanted to overcome this hesitancy. (2) Apple Computer was rapidly cutting its computer prices in the hope of selling more Macintosh computers before the look-alike Windows 95 went on sale. Thus Microsoft wanted to stem the tide of Macintosh sales by selling as many Windows 95 packages as soon as possible.

tomers or individual users. The company did this by mobilizing huge numbers of people inside the company, putting them on phone lines to talk to anybody concerned, and by flying marketing teams all over the country to visit corporate accounts and replace Pentium chips. To reach individual consumers, Intel even placed its own employees inside retail stores in the weeks before Christmas of 1994. As a result of the intense MPR campaign, Intel was able to rescue its reputation, which had been seriously jeopardized just a few weeks earlier.[69]

For another example of a successful MPR campaign, see the Marketing Insight titled "A PR Blitz: Microsoft Launches Windows 95."

Major Decisions in Marketing PR

In considering when and how to use MPR, management must establish the marketing objectives, choose the PR messages and vehicles, implement the plan carefully, and evaluate the results. The main tools of MPR are described in Table 21-8 on page 674.

ESTABLISHING THE MARKETING OBJECTIVES. MPR can contribute to the following objectives:

- *Build awareness:* MPR can place stories in the media to bring attention to a product, service, person, organization, or idea.
- *Build credibility:* MPR can add credibility by communicating the message in an editorial context.
- *Stimulate the sales force and dealers:* MPR can help boost sales force and dealer enthusiasm. Stories about a new product before it is launched will help the sales force sell it to retailers.

TABLE 21-8	MAJOR TOOLS IN MARKETING PR
TOOL	**DESCRIPTION**
Publications	Companies rely extensively on published materials to reach and influence their target markets. These include annual reports, brochures, articles, company newsletters and magazines, and audio-visual materials. Chrysler's *annual report* almost serves as a sales brochure, promoting each new car to the stockholder. *Brochures* can play an important role in informing target customers about what a product is, how it works, and how it is to be assembled. Thoughtful *articles* written by company executives can draw attention to the company and its products. Company *newsletters* and *magazines* can help build up the company's image and convey important news to target markets. *Audio-visual and multimedia material,* such as films, slides-and-sound, and video and audiocassettes, are coming into increasing use as promotion tools. The cost of audio-visual and multimedia materials is usually greater than the cost of printed material, but so is the impact. Today, it is common for colleges to hire a professional firm to prepare an attractive video to be shown on recruiting trips or sent to applicants to encourage their choosing the college.
Events	Companies can draw attention to new products or other company activities by arranging special events. These include news conferences, seminars, outings, exhibits, contests and competitions, anniversaries, and sport and cultural sponsorships that will reach the target publics. Sponsoring a popular sports event, such as the Coors International Bicycle Class or the Volvo International Tennis Tournament, gives these companies high visibility among their suppliers, distributors, and customers.
News	One of the major tasks of PR professionals is to find or create favorable news about the company, its products, and its people. News generation requires skill in developing a story concept, researching it, and writing a press release. But the PR person's skill must go beyond preparing news stories. Getting the media to accept press releases and attend press conferences calls for marketing and interpersonal skills. A good PR media director understands the press's needs for stories that are interesting and timely and for press releases that are well written and attention getting. The media director needs to build favorable relations with editors and reporters. The more the press is cultivated, the more likely it is to give more and better coverage to the company.
Speeches	Speeches are another tool for creating product and company publicity. Lee Iacocca's charismatic talks before large audiences helped Chrysler sell its cars. Increasingly, company executives must field questions from the media or give talks at trade associations or sales meetings, and these appearances can build the company's image. Companies are choosing their spokespersons carefully and using speechwriters and coaches to help improve their spokesperson's public-speaking abilities.
Public-Service Activities	Companies can improve public goodwill by contributing money and time to good causes. Large companies typically will ask executives to support community affairs where their offices and plants are located. In other instances, companies will donate an amount of money (usually in relation to now much consumers buy of their brand) to a specified cause. Such *cause-related marketing* is used by a growing number of companies to build public goodwill. Procter & Gamble and Publishers' Clearing House jointly coordinated a promotion to aid the Special Olympics. Product coupons were included in the Publishers' Clearing House mailing, and Procter & Gamble donated 10¢ per redeemed coupon to the Special Olympics program.
Identity media	In a society marked by sensory overload, companies have to compete for attention. They should strive to create a visual identity that the public immediately recognizes. The visual identity is carried by the company's logos, stationery, brochures, signs, business forms, business cards, buildings, and dress codes.

Source: For further reading on cause-related marketing, see P. Rajan Varadarajan and Anil Menon, "Cause-Related Marketing: A Co-Alignment of Marketing Strategy and Corporate Philanthropy," *Journal of Marketing,* July 1988, pp. 58–74.

◆ *Hold down promotion costs:* MPR costs less than direct mail and media advertising. The smaller the company's promotion budget, the stronger the case for using PR to gain share of mind.

Specific objectives should be set for every MPR campaign. The Wine Growers of California hired the public-relations firm of Daniel J. Edelman, Inc., to develop a publicity campaign to convince Americans that wine drinking is a pleasurable part of good living and to improve the image and market share of California wines. The following publicity objectives were established: (1) Develop magazine stories about wine and get them placed in top magazines (*Time, House Beautiful*) and in newspapers (food columns, feature sections); (2) develop stories about wine's many health values and direct them to the medical profession; and (3) develop specific publicity for the young adult market, college market, governmental bodies, and various ethnic communities. These objectives were refined into specific goals so that final results could be evaluated.

CHOOSING THE PR MESSAGES AND VEHICLES.

After establishing the MPR objectives, the manager must identify or develop interesting stories to tell about the product. Suppose a relatively unknown college wants more visibility. The MPR practitioner will search for possible stories. Do any faculty members have unusual backgrounds, or are any working on unusual projects? Are any new and unusual courses being taught? Are any interesting events taking place on campus?

If the number of interesting stories is insufficient, the MPR practitioner should propose newsworthy events that the college could sponsor. Here the challenge is to create news rather than find news. PR ideas include hosting major academic conventions, inviting expert or celebrity speakers, and developing news conferences. Each event is an opportunity to develop a multitude of stories directed at different audiences.

Event creation is a particularly important skill in publicizing fund-raising drives for nonprofit organizations. Fund-raisers have developed a large repertoire of special events, including anniversary celebrations, art exhibits, auctions, benefit evenings, bingo games, book sales, cake sales, contests, dances, dinners, fairs, fashion shows, parties in unusual places, phonathons, rummage sales, tours, and walkathons. No sooner is one type of event created, such as a walkathon, than competitors spawn new versions, such as readathons, bikeathons, and jogathons.[70]

For-profit organizations also use various events to call attention to their products and services. Fuji Photo Film Company flew its blimp over the renovated Statue of Liberty during its massive celebration, outdoing its rival Kodak, which had mounted a permanent photo exhibit at the site. Anheuser-Busch sponsored a Black World Championship Rodeo in Brooklyn, attracting more than 5,000 spectators. Of course, a company must choose events that will interest the target market and create positive feeling toward the sponsor. P&G, for example, chose to sponsor a Barry Manilow concert tour under the names of some of its detergent products, because it wanted to attract the middle-aged women who were Barry Manilow fans and who were the target market for the detergents.

The best MPR practitioners are able to find or create stories on behalf of even mundane products such as pork ("the other white meat"), garlic, and potatoes. Here is an example for cat food:

9-LIVES CAT FOOD   One of the top brands of cat food is Star-Kist Foods' 9-Lives. Its brand image revolves around Morris the Cat. The Leo Burnett advertising agency wanted to make Morris more of a living, breathing, real-life feline to whom cat owners and cat lovers could relate. It worked with a public-relations firm that proposed and carried out the following ideas: (1) Launch a Morris "look-alike" contest in nine major markets; (2) write a book called *Morris, an Intimate Biography;* (3) establish a coveted award called The Morris, a bronze statuette given to the owners of award-winning cats at local cat shows; (4) sponsor an "Adopt-a-Cat Month," with Morris as the official "spokescat"; and (5) distribute a booklet called "The Morris Method" on cat care. These publicity steps strengthened the brand's market share in the cat-food market.

IMPLEMENTING THE MPR PLAN. Implementing public relations requires care. Consider the matter of placing stories in the media. A great story is easy to place. But most stories are less than great and might not get past busy editors. One of the chief assets of publicists is their personal relationship with media editors. Public-relations practitioners are often ex-journalists who know many media editors and know what they want. PR people look at media editors as a market to satisfy so that these editors will continue to use their stories.

Publicity requires extra care when it involves staging special events, such as testimonial dinners, news conferences, and national contests. PR practitioners need a good head for detail and for coming up with quick solutions when things go wrong.

EVALUATING THE MPR RESULTS. MPR's contribution to the bottom line is difficult to measure, because it is used along with other promotional tools. If it is used before the other tools come into action, its contribution is easier to evaluate. The three most commonly used measures of MPR effectiveness are number of exposures, awareness/comprehension/attitude change; and contribution to sale and profits.

Exposures. The easiest measure of MPR effectiveness is the number of *exposures* carried by the media. Publicists supply the client with a clippings book showing all the media that carried news about the product and a summary statement such as the following:

> Media coverage included 3,500 column inches of news and photographs in 350 publications with a combined circulation of 79.4 million; 2,500 minutes of air time of 290 radio stations and an estimated audience of 65 million; and 660 minutes of air time on 160 television stations with an estimated audience of 91 million. If this time and space had been purchased at advertising rates, it would have amounted to $1,047,000.[71]

The exposure measure is not very satisfying because it contains no indication of how many people actually read, heard, or recalled the message and what they thought afterward. Nor does it contain information on the net audience reached, since publications overlap in readership. Because publicity's goal is reach, not frequency, it would be more useful to know the number of unduplicated exposures.

Awareness/Comprehension/Attitude Change. A better measure is the change in product *awareness/comprehension/attitude* resulting from the MPR campaign (after allowing for the effect of other promotional tools). For example, how many people recall hearing the news item? How many told others about it (a measure of word-of-mouth)? How many changed their minds after hearing it? In a Potato Board campaign, the Board found that the number of people who agreed with the statement "Potatoes are rich in vitamins and minerals" went from 36% before the campaign to 67% after the campaign, a significant improvement in product comprehension.

Sales-And-Profit Contribution. Sales-and-profit impact is the most satisfactory measure, if obtainable. For example, 9-Lives sales had increased 43% by the end of the Morris the Cat PR campaign. However, advertising and sales promotion had also been stepped up, and their contribution has to be allowed for. Suppose total sales have increased $1,500,000, and management estimates that MPR contributed 15% of the total sales increase. Then the return on MPR investment is calculated as follows:

MARKETING MEMO

DM + PR = AN INTEGRATED MARKETING SUCCESS STORY

While PR practitioners will continue to reach their target publics through the mass media, MPR is increasingly borrowing the techniques and technology of direct-response marketing to reach target audience members one-to-one. Thomas L. Harris, PR expert and author of *The Marketer's Guide to Public Relations,* offers five suggestions for how PR and direct-response marketing can work together to achieve specific marketing objectives.

1. *Build marketplace excitement before media advertising breaks.* The announcement of a new product offers a unique opportunity for obtaining publicity and for dramatizing the product. Hence, marketers should disseminate news of the new product's introduction before advertising begins. To get its new LH sedans off to a quick start, for example, Chrysler's marketing and PR departments joined forces on a program targeted to a high-profile, high-exposure potential audience across the United States. Chrysler identified VIPs in key markets and offered them the opportunity to test drive a car for two or three days, with the cars delivered and picked up from them when they were through. In addition, as part of the national press previews in New York and Los Angeles, Chrysler invited a select list of VIPs to receptions and invited them to sign up for test drives.

2. *Build a core consumer base.* Marketers are increasingly recognizing the value of maintaining consumer loyalty, since it costs far less to keep a consumer than to get a new one. For Pepperidge Farm, PR firm Langdon Starr created the Pepperidge Farm No Fuss Pastry Club. The club communicates directly with known users of Pepperidge Farm's products, showing them how to make delicious easy-to-prepare meals with frozen puff pastry. The club, which was launched in 1992, now has over 30,000 members, who were made aware of the club's existence through magazine mail-in offers, an offer on the package, point-of-sale displays, and other publicity tools. In the pharmaceuticals industry, SmithKline Beecham now sends a quarterly newsletter called "Gut Reactions" to a list of 200,000 over-the-counter antacid users. The newsletter consists of health-care-related articles and includes coupons for SmithKline's Gaviscon OTC antacid. The newsletter was created by a PR firm, Gilbert & Christopher Associates, and is mailed to a database of names generated by a Carol Wright direct-mail consumer survey.

3. *Build a person-to-person relationship with consumers.* For instance, the Butterball Turkey Talkline, a PR initiative created in the mid-1980s, has become the brand's principal marketing tool. The Talkline is promoted primarily by publicity. In 1992 alone the Talkline handled 25,000 calls during the November to December peak turkey sales season, and this number translated into 25,000 names added to Butterball's turkey lover database. All callers received advice on how to prepare their holiday turkey from a Butterball home economist. The company keeps in touch with callers by sending them recipe booklets, Butterball calendars, and coupon offers for Butterball turkeys that keep Butterball on their mind throughout the year.

4. *Turn satisfied customers into advocates.* Upjohn Company used its database of Rogaine users to attack a PR problem. Only two years after the product was introduced as the first drug effective for growing hair, Rogaine was old news and articles on hair loss categorized it as expensive and sometimes ineffective. Yet research indicated that users who had success with Rogaine were universally enthusiastic about it. Upjohn's PR firm, Manning Selvage & Lee, compiled an extensive profile of Rogaine users by conducting a database search. These users then sent 5,000 completed questionnaires to Rogaine. Based on the responses and follow-up phone and personal interviews, Rogaine identified role models in 19 selected markets and started the Rogaine Recognition program for Personal Achievement. These satisfied users-turned-spokespeople were booked for extensive media interviews in their markets, and the interviews focused on messages about Rogaine's effectiveness.

5. *Influence the influentials.* The influencer may be an authority figure like a teacher, a doctor, or a pharmacist, but it could also be someone who has a different kind of one-to-one relationship with the consumer, such as a beautician or a bartender. Wonder Bread targeted U.S. dietitians to counter the notion that white bread is unhealthy. Continental Baking Company, the bakers of Wonder Bread, financed a study that dispelled the myth that bread is fattening and even suggested that adding bread improves the daily diet. The company mailed invitations to 4,500 members of the American Dietetic Association who were preregistered for the annual ADA meeting in Washington, DC, inviting them to a seminar where the results of the study were to be announced. They were also invited to a "thumbs up for white bread rally" devised by Continental's public relations firm, Porter-Novelli. The day of the event, a special newspaper called "The Washington Toast," detailing the research findings, was delivered under hotel-room doors of all conference attendees. The rally was covered on network TV and made newspaper headlines; the message that white bread was "O.K." was delivered to those most influential on U.S. diets; and Wonder Bread sales experienced a spurt.

Source: Adapted from Thomas L. Harris, "PR Gets Personal," *Direct Marketing,* April 1994, pp. 29–32.

Total sales increase	$1,500,000
Estimated sales increase due to PR (15%)	225,000
Contribution margin on product sales (10%)	22,500
Total direct cost of MPR program	−10,000
Contribution margin added by PR investment	$ 12,500
Return on MPR investment ($12,500/$10,000)	125%

In the years ahead, we can expect marketing public relations to play a larger role in the company's communication efforts. We can also expect MPR to join forces with other parts of the promotion mix, including direct mail. For more on this topic, see the Marketing Memo on page 677 titled "DM + PR = An Integrated Marketing Success Story."

SUMMARY

1. *Advertising* is any paid form of nonpersonal presentation and promotion of ideas, goods, or services by an identified sponsor. Advertisers include not only business firms but also charitable, nonprofit, and government agencies that advertise to various publics.

    Developing an advertising program involves a five-step process. First, marketers must set advertising objectives; they must decide whether they want their advertising to inform, persuade, or remind/reinforce. Second, they must establish a budget that takes into account the stage in the product life cycle, market share and consumer base, competition and clutter, advertising frequency, and product substitutability. Third, they must choose the advertising message, determining how the message will be generated; evaluating alternative messages for desirability, exclusiveness, and believability; and executing the message with the most appropriate style, tone, words, and format and in a socially responsible manner. Fourth, they must decide on the media they will use. This decision involves choosing the ad's desired reach, frequency, and impact, then choosing the media that will deliver the desired results in terms of circulation, audience, effective audience, and effective ad-exposed audience. Finally, marketers must take steps to evaluate the communication and sales effects of advertising.

2. *Sales promotion* consists of a diverse collection of incentive tools, mostly short term, designed to stimulate quicker and/or greater purchase of particular products/services by consumers or the trade. Where advertising offers a reason to buy, sales promotion offers an incentive to buy. Sales promotion includes tools for consumer promotion (samples, coupons, cash refund offers, prices off, premiums, prizes, patronage rewards, free trials, warranties, tie-in promotions, cross-promotions, point-of-purchase displays, and demonstrations); trade promotion (prices off, advertising and display allowances, and free goods); and business and sales force promotion (trade shows and conventions, contests for sales reps, and specialty advertising). Sales-promotion expenditures have been increasing as a percentage of budget expenditure annually for the last two decades, and the rate of growth is likely to continue.

    In using sales promotion, a company must establish its objectives, select the tools, develop the program, pretest the program, implement and control it, and evaluate the results. Most people agree that sales promotion works to increase sales and market share in the short run, but does not have much effect in the long run. In addition, marketers face a series of challenges in most forms of sales promotion, especially the high costs of supporting them.

3. A *public* is any group that has an actual or potential interest in or impact on a company's ability to achieve its objectives. *Public relations (PR)* involves a variety of programs designed to promote and/or protect a company's image or its individual products. Many companies today use marketing public relations (MPR) to support their marketing departments in corporate/product promotion and image making. MPR can potentially impact public awareness at a fraction of the cost of advertising, and is often

much more credible. The main tools of PR are publications, events, news, speeches, public-service activities, and identity media.

In considering when and how to use MPR, management must establish the marketing objectives, choose the PR messages and vehicles, implement the plan carefully, and evaluate the results. Results are usually evaluated in terms of number of exposures and cost savings, awareness/comprehension/attitude change, and sales-and-profit contribution.

CONCEPT APPLICATIONS

1. Bring to class an example of your company's advertising and an ad from one of your competitors. Which ad do you think is more effective? What is the most striking part of the ad? What do you like most about each ad? What changes would you suggest to make your company's advertisement better? (*Note:* If you are not presently employed, bring in advertisements from two competing companies in the same industry.)

2. Bring to class a sample of one of your company's sales promotions. What is this sales promotion's objective? Do you think that it will accomplish its objective? What do you think is the most interesting or intriguing part about the sales promotion? Should it be continued? Why or why not? What are some of the negatives associated with this sales promotion, and with sales promotions in general? (*Note:* If you are not presently employed, bring in a sales-promotion sample from any company and analyze it using the questions above.)

3. Your company knows that bad publicity could have a lasting negative effect on its future, yet it wants all levels of management to feel comfortable meeting the press with both good news and bad news. Individually or with a group, assist the public relations staff in developing a 10-point media interview checklist. This checklist will used by all managers who might possibly questioned by either the print or electronic media.

Here are two points to get you started:

- If a reporter calls, determine the reason for the call and the information sought. If you can't talk at the time or if you need additional information, promise to call the reporter back before his or her deadline. Then make sure you do it.

- Don't expect the news story to be exactly the way you would have reported it or written it. Expect some confusion in the facts, but if the mistakes aren't major, don't ask for a correction.

4. The following is an excerpt from Motel 6's successful radio campaign featuring spokesman Tom Bodett:

> *Hi, Tom Bodett for Motel 6 with a plan for anyone whose kids are on their own now. Take a drive, see some of the country and visit a few relatives. Like your sister Helen and her husband Bob. They're wonderful folks always happy to pull the hide-a-bed out for you, but somehow the smell of mothballs just isn't conducive to gettin' a good night's sleep. And since Bob gets up at 5:30, well that means you do, too. So here's the plan. Check into Motel 6. 'Cause for around 22 bucks, the lowest price of any national chain, you'll get a clean, comfortable room and Helen and Bob'll think you're mighty considerate. Well, you are, but maybe more important, you can sleep late and not have to wonder if the towels in their bathroom are just for decoration. My rule of thumb is, if they match the tank and seat cover, you better leave 'em alone. . . . Give my best to Helen and Bob and we'll leave the light on for you.*

For its first 24 years in business, Motel 6 never advertised. Instead, it let price and the power of word-of-mouth bring in guests. This was a successful strategy against independents and small regional chains, but when low-priced national chains emerged, price was no longer a sufficient point of differentiation. In 1985 Motel 6 still did not offer rooms with telephones, it cost $1.49 to turn on the TV, and the price of a room was

Managing Advertising,
Sales Promotion, and
Public Relations

$17.95 systemwide. Guests paid cash in advance; credit cards were not accepted; there was a charge for children; and guests had to write to individual motels for reservations. All the national chains provided free TV and rooms with telephones, allowed children to stay for free, and accepted credit cards. The Motel 6 chain's occupancy rate dropped from 81% in 1981 to 69.5% in 1985.

In the mid-1980s, consumer research showed that changes in the marketing mix were necessary. To whom is Motel 6's advertising campaign using Tom Bodett targeted? Why do you think it has been so successful? What other changes might you suggest in Motel 6's marketing mix?

5. What is a "public"? Explain why most organizations serve more than one public. Name at least 15 publics that a hospital serves. How might a public-relations program be influenced by the existence of several publics?

6. Analyze the two ads in Figure 1. What is the objective of each ad? Which of the twelve types of appeals in Table 21-2 does each ad make use of? How would you describe the style and tone of each ad?

7. Suppose a brand of after-shave lotion will be marked down $.09 for a limited period. (In other words, the manufacturer will sell the item to retailers and/or wholesalers for 9 cents less than its normal price.) The item sells regularly for $1.09, of which $.40 represents a contribution to the manufacturers' profits before marketing expenses. The brand manager expects a million bottles to be sold under this deal. The administrative costs of the promotion are estimated at $10,000.
   a. Determine the total cost of this promotion.
   b. Assume that the company expected to sell 800,000 bottles of the lotion without the promotion. Is the promotion worth undertaking?

8. Black and Decker recently acquired the small-household-appliances division of General Electric, which manufactures toasters, portable mixers, can openers, electric knives, irons, toaster ovens, and so forth. One of the decisions it now has to make is in the area of promotion. The small-household-appliances industry traditionally has been characterized by a push strategy, with trade promotions representing the largest proportion of the promotional mix. However, Black and Decker is considering a pull strategy as a dominant part of its promotional mix.

Planning Marketing Programs

Individually or in small teams, brainstorm whether B&D should use trade or consumer promotions to launch its newly acquired product line. Would you recommend a push strategy or a pull strategy? What specific types of promotions would you use, and why?

9. For years, baseball was considered "The American Pastime"—America's favorite sport. However, in recent years fans have become disenchanted with the game because of its slow pace (nine innings take a long time to play), lockouts, strikes, high salaries, and apparent disregard for the fans. Each time a work stoppage took place, fans would say that they were through with baseball—but they always came back. Things seem to have changed in 1995. Fans appeared to strongly resent the cancellation of the World Series in 1994, and attendance during the 1995 season decreased substantially. Even as the season got into full swing, there was still no labor agreement—which meant that the World Series could be canceled again.

Players and management must now work together to rekindle interest in this mature product. In groups of four, discuss the problems facing baseball and offer some suggestions regarding how baseball can use promotion to get fans back in the stadiums.

10. A canned-dog-food manufacturer is trying to choose between medium A and medium B. Medium A has 10,000,000 readers and charges $20,000 for a full-page ad ($2 per 1,000). Medium B has 15,000,000 readers and charges $25,000 for a full-page ad ($1.67 per 1,000). What other information does the dog-food manufacturer need before deciding which is the better medium?

11. Review three recent crises in which an organization's credibility was threatened (other than those mentioned in the text). In each case, how was the damage to the product's or organization's image managed from a PR perspective? Can you suggest a strategy for damage control from these experiences?

NOTES

1. See Russell H. Colley, *Defining Advertising Goals for Measured Advertising Results* (New York: Association of National Advertisers, 1961).

2. See William L. Wilkie and Paul W. Farris, "Comparison Advertising: Problem and Potential," *Journal of Marketing,* October 1975, pp. 7–15.

3. See Randall L. Rose, Paul W. Miniard, Michael J. Barone, Kenneth C. Manning, and Brian D. Till, "When Persuasion Goes Undetected: The Case of Comparative Advertising," *Journal of Marketing Research,* August 1993, pp. 315–30; and Sanjay Putrevu and Kenneth R. Lord, "Comparative and Noncomparative Advertising: Attitudinal Effects under Cognitive and Affective Involvement Conditions," *Journal of Advertising,* June 1994, pp. 77–91.

4. For a good discussion, see David A. Aaker and James M. Carman, "Are You Overadvertising?" *Journal of Advertising Research,* August–September 1982, pp. 57–70.

5. See Donald E. Schultz, Dennis Martin, and William P. Brown, *Strategic Advertising Campaigns* (Chicago: Crain Books, 1984), pp. 192–97.

6. M. L. Vidale and H. R. Wolfe, "An Operations-Research Study of Sales Response to Advertising," *Operations Research,* June 1957, pp. 370–81.

7. John D. C. Little, "A Model of Adaptive Control of Promotional Spending," *Operations Research,* November 1966, pp. 1075–97.

8. For additional models for setting the advertising budget, see Gary L. Lilien, Philip Kotler, and K. Sridhar Moorthy, *Marketing Models* (Englewood Cliffs, NJ: Prentice Hall, 1992), Chapter 6.

9. David N. Martin, *Romancing the Brand: The Power of Advertising and How to Use It* (New York: Amacom, 1989), pp. 73, 106–7.

10. Joshua Levine, "Fizz, Fizz . . . Plop, Plop," *Forbes,* June 21, 1993, p. 139; "Mission Impossible," *Advertising Age,* March 8, 1993, p. 18.

11. See "Keep Listening to That Wee, Small Voice," in *Communications of an Advertising Man* (Chicago: Leo Burnett Co., 1961), p. 61.

12. John C. Maloney, "Marketing Decisions and Attitude Research," in *Effective Marketing Coordination,* ed. George L. Baker, Jr. (Chicago: American Marketing Association, 1961), pp. 595–618.

13. Dik Warren Twedt, "How to Plan New Products, Improve Old Ones, and Create Better Advertising," *Journal of Marketing,* January 1969, pp. 53–57.

14. See William A. Mindak and H. Malcolm Bybee, "Marketing Application to Fund Raising," *Journal of Marketing,* July 1971, pp. 13–18.

15. For a look at how some business-to-business ad agencies are using strategic thinking, see Nancy Arnott, "Getting the Picture," *Sales and Marketing Management,* June 1994, pp. 74–82.

16. Lalita Manrai, "Effect of Labeling Strategy in Advertising: Self-Referencing versus Psychological Reactance," Ph.D. dissertation, Northwestern University, 1987.

17. Bob Garfield, "Wondrous Chanel No. 5 Spot Deftly Nurtures the Product," *Advertising Age,* December 12, 1994, p. 3.

18. L. Greenland, "Is This the Era of Positioning?" *Advertising Age,* May 29, 1972.

19. David Ogilvy and Joel Raphaelson, "Research on Advertising Techniques That Work—And Don't Work," *Harvard Business Review,* July–August 1982, pp. 14–18.

20. Joanne Lipman, "It's It and That's a Shame: Why Are Some Slogans Losers?" *The Wall Street Journal,* July 16, 1993, A1:4; Paul Farhi, "The Wrong One Baby, Uh-Uh: Has Madison Avenue Lost It?" *The Washington Post,* February 28, 1993, C5:1.

21. For further reading, see Dorothy Cohen, *Legal Issues in Marketing Decision Making* (Cincinnati, OH: South-Western, 1995).

22. Kevin Goldman, "Advertising: From Witches to Anorexics: Critical Eyes Scrutinize Ads for Political Correctness," *The Wall Street Journal,* May 19, 1994, B1:3.

23. Nathaniel C. Nash, "Advertising: A German Court Rules that Images in a Benetton Campaign Are Exploitative and Illegal," *The New York Times,* July 7, 1995, D6: 1; Kevin J. Clancy and Robert S. Shulman, *Marketing Myths That Are Killing Business* (New York: McGraw-Hill, 1994), pp. 148–49.

24. Schultz et al., *Strategic Advertising Campaigns,* p. 340.

25. See Herbert E. Krugman, "What Makes Advertising Effective?" *Harvard Business Review,* March–April 1975, pp. 96–103, here p. 98.

26. See Peggy J. Kreshel, Kent M. Lancaster, and Margaret A. Toomey, "Advertising Media Planning: How Leading Advertising Agencies Estimate Effective Reach and Frequency" (Urbana: University of Illinois, Department of Advertising, paper no. 20, January 1985). Also see Jack Z. Sissors and Lincoln Bumba, *Advertising Media Planning,* 3d ed. (Lincolnwood, IL: NTC Business Books, 1988), Chapter 9.

27. See Roland T. Rust, *Advertising Media Models: A Practical Guide* (Lexington, MA: Lexington Books, 1986).

28. See Jay W. Forrester, "Advertising: A Problem in Industrial Dynamics," *Harvard Business Review,* March–April 1959, pp. 100–10.

29. See Amber G. Rao and Peter B. Miller, "Advertising/Sales Response Functions," *Journal of Advertising Research,* April 1975, pp. 7–15.

30. See Alfred A. Kuehn, "How Advertising Performance Depends on Other Marketing Factors," *Journal of Advertising Research,* March 1962, pp. 2–10.

31. See also Hani I. Mesak, "An Aggregate Advertising Pulsing Model with Wearout Effects," *Marketing Science,* Summer 1992, pp. 310–26; and Fred M. Feinberg, "Pulsing Policies for Aggregate Advertising Models," *Marketing Science,* Summer 1992, pp. 221–34.

32. Forrester, "Advertising," p. 102.

33. Russell I. Haley, James Stafforoni, and Arthur Fox, "The Missing Measures of Copy Testing," *Journal of Advertising Research,* May–June 1994, pp. 46–56. (Also see this May–June 1994 issue of the *Journal of Advertising Research* for more articles on copy testing.)

34. See J. O. Peckham, *The Wheel of Marketing* (Scarsdale, NY: privately printed, 1975), pp. 73–77.

35. Kristian S. Palda, *The Measurement of Cumulative Advertising Effect* (Englewood Cliffs, NJ: Prentice Hall, 1964), p. 87.

36. David B. Montgomery and Alvin J. Silk, "Estimating Dynamic Effects of Market Communications Expenditures," *Management Science,* June 1972, pp. 485–501.

37. See Robert D. Buzzell, "E. I. Du Pont de Nemours & Co.: Measurement of Effects of Advertising," in his *Mathematical Models and Marketing Management* (Boston: Division of Research, Graduate School of Business Administration, Harvard University, 1964), pp. 157–79.

38. See Glen L. Urban, "Allocating Ad Budgets Geographically," *Journal of Advertising Research,* December 1975, pp. 7–16.

39. See Nigel Hollis, "The Link Between TV Ad Awareness and Sales: New Evidence from Sales Response Modelling," *Journal of the Market Research Society,* January 1994, pp. 41–55.

40. In addition to the sources cited below, see David Walker and Tony M. Dubitsky, "Why Liking Matters," *Journal of Advertising Research,* May–June 1994, pp. 9–18, Abhilasha Mehta, "How Advertising Response Modeling (ARM) Can Increase Ad Effectiveness," *Journal of Advertising Research,* May–June 1994, pp. 62–74, and Karin Holstius, "Sales Response to Advertising," *International Journal of Advertising,* 9, no. 1 (1990), 38–56.

41. Gerald J. Tellis, "Advertising Exposure, Loyalty, and Brand Purchase: A Two-Stage Model of Choice," *Journal of Marketing Research,* May 1988, pp. 134–44.

42. See Michael A. Kamins, Lawrence J. Marks, and Deborah Skinner, "Television Commercial Evaluation in the Context of Program Induced Mood: Congruency versus Consistency Effects," *Journal of Advertising,* June 1991, pp. 1–14.

43. See Kenneth R. Lord and Robert E. Burnkrant, "Attention versus Distraction: The Interactive Effect of Program Involvement and Attentional Devices on Commercial Processing," *Journal of Advertising,* March 1993, pp. 47–60; Kenneth R. Lord, Myung-Soo Lee, and Paul L. Sauer, "Program Context Antecedents of Attitude Toward Radio Commercials," *Journal of the Academy of Marketing Science,* Winter 1994, pp. 3–15.

44. See Yoav Ganzach and Nili Karashi, "Message Framing and Buying Behavior: A Field Experiment," *Journal of Business Research,* January 1995, pp. 11–17.

45. "It's Official: Some Ads Work," *The Economist,* April 1, 1995, p. 52.

46. From Robert C. Blattberg and Scott A. Neslin, *Sales Promotion: Concepts, Methods, and Strategies* (Englewood Cliffs, NJ: Prentice Hall, 1990). This text provides the most comprehensive and analytical treatment of sales promotion to date.

47. "It's Official: Some Ads Work," p. 52.

48. Jonathan Berry, "Wilma! What Happened to the Plain Old Ad?" *Business Week,* June 6, 1994, pp. 54–58.

49. Roger A. Strang, "Sales Promotion—Fast Growth, Faulty Management," *Harvard Business Review,* July–August 1976, pp. 115–24, here pp. 116–19.

50. For a good summary of the research on whether promotion erodes the consumer franchise of leading brands, see Blattberg and Neslin, *Sales Promotion.*

51. Robert George Brown, "Sales Response to Promotions and Advertising," *Journal of Advertising Research,* August 1974, pp. 33–39, here pp. 36–37.

52. F. Kent Mitchel, "Advertising/Promotion Budgets: How Did We Get Here, and What Do We Do Now?" *Journal of Consumer Marketing,* Fall 1985, pp. 405–47.

53. See Paul W. Farris and John A. Quelch, "In Defense of Price Promotion," *Sloan Management Review,* Fall 1987, pp. 63–69.

54. For a model for setting sales promotions objectives, see David B. Jones, "Setting Promotional Goals: A Communications Relationship Model," *Journal of Consumer Marketing,* 11, no. 1 (1994), pp. 38–49.

55. See John C. Totten and Martin P. Block, *Analyzing Sales Promotion,* 2d ed. (Chicago: Dartnell, 1994), pp. 69–70.

56. See Paul W. Farris and Kusum L. Ailawadi, "Retail Power: Monster or Mouse?" *Journal of Retailing,* Winter 1992, pp. 351–69.

57. See "Retailers Buy Far in Advance to Exploit Trade Promotions," *The Wall Street Journal,* October 9, 1986, p. 35.

58. "Trade Promotion: Much Ado About Something," *PROMO,* October 1991, pp. 15, 37, 40.

59. Quoted from Kerry E. Smith, "Media Fusion," *PROMO,* May 1992, p. 29.

60. Arthur Stern, "Measuring the Effectiveness of Package Goods

Promotion Strategies," paper presented to the Association of National Advertisers, Glen Cove, NY, February 1978.

61. Strang, "Sales Promotion," p. 120.

62. Kurt H. Schaffir and H. George Trenten, *Marketing Information Systems* (New York: Amacom, 1973), p. 81.

63. See Magid M. Abraham and Leonard M. Lodish, "Getting the Most Out of Advertising and Promotion," *Harvard Business Review,* May–June 1990, pp. 50–60.

64. See Joe A. Dodson, Alice M. Tybout, and Brian Sternthal, "Impact of Deals and Deal Retraction on Brand Switching," *Journal of Marketing Research,* February 1978, pp. 72–81. They found that deals generally increase brand switching, the rate depending on the type of deal. Media-distributed coupons induce substantial switching, cents-off deals induce somewhat less switching, and package coupons hardly affect brand switching. Furthermore, consumers generally return to the preferred brands after the deal.

65. Books on sales promotion include John C. Totten and Martin P. Block, *Analyzing Sales Promotion: Text and Cases,* 2d ed. (Chicago: Dartnell, 1994); Don E. Schultz, William A. Robinson, and Lisa A. Petrison, *Sales Promotion Essentials,* 2d ed. (Lincolnwood, IL: NTC Business Books, 1994); John Wilmshurst, *Below-the-Line Promotion* (Oxford, England: Butterworth/Heinemann, 1993); and Robert C. Blattberg and Scott A. Neslin, *Sales Promotion: Concepts, Methods, and Strategies* (Englewood Cliffs, NJ: Prentice Hall, 1990). For an expert systems approach to sales promotion, see John W. Keon and Judy

Bayer, "An Expert Approach to Sales Promotion Management," *Journal of Advertising Research,* June–July 1986, pp. 19–26.

66. Adapted from Scott M. Cutlip, Allen H. Center, and Glen M. Broom, *Effective Public Relations,* 8th ed. (Englewood Cliffs, NJ: Prentice Hall, 1997).

67. For an excellent account, see Thomas L. Harris, *The Marketer's Guide to Public Relations* (New York: John Wiley, 1991).

68. Tom Duncan, *A Study of How Manufacturers and Service Companies Perceive and Use Marketing Public Relations* (Muncie, IN: Ball State University, December 1985). For more on how to contrast the effectiveness of advertising with the effectiveness of PR, see Kenneth R. Lord and Sanjay Putrevu, "Advertising and Publicity: An Information Processing Perspective," *Journal of Economic Psychology,* March 1993, pp. 57–84.

69. Kate Bertrand, "Intel Starts to Rebuild," *Business Marketing,* February 1995, pp. 1, 32; John Markoff, "In About-face, Intel Will Swap Its Flawed Chip," *The New York Times,* December 21, 1994, A1:1; T. R. Reid, "It's a Dangerous Precedent to Make the Pentium Promise," *The Washington Post,* December 26, 1994, WBIZ 14:1.

70. See Dwight W. Catherwood and Richard L. Van Kirk, *The Complete Guide to Special Event Management* (New York: John Wiley, 1992).

71. Arthur M. Merims, "Marketing's Stepchild: Product Publicity," *Harvard Business Review,* November–December 1972, pp. 111–12. Also see Katerine D. Paine, "There Is a Method for Measuring PR," *Marketing News,* November 6, 1987, p. 5.

MANAGING

THE SALES FORCE

I don't know who you are.
I don't know your company.
I don't know your company's product.
I don't know what your company stands for.
I don't know your company's customers.
I don't know your company's record.
I don't know your company's reputation.
Now—what was it you wanted to sell me?

MCGRAW-HILL PUBLICATIONS

❖

oktober Louis Stevenson observed that "everyone lives by selling something." U.S. firms spend over $140 billion annually on personal selling—more than they spend on any other promotional method. Over 11 million Americans are employed in sales and related occupations.[1] Different companies have different objectives for their sales forces. IBM's sales representatives are responsible for selling, installing, and upgrading customer computer equipment, as well as helping their customers solve problems. AT&T sales representatives are responsible for developing, selling, and protecting accounts.

Sales forces are found in nonprofit as well as for-profit organizations. College recruiters are the university's sales force arm for attracting new students. Churches use membership committees to attract new members. The U.S. Agricultural Extension Service sends agricultural specialists to sell farmers on new farming methods. Hospitals and museums use fund-raisers to contact donors and ask them for money.

The term *sales representative* covers a broad range of positions. McMurry devised the following classification of sales positions:[2]

1. *Deliverer:* A salesperson whose major task is the delivery of a product (e.g., milk, bread, fuel, oil)

2. *Order taker:* A salesperson who acts predominantly as an inside order taker (e.g., the haberdashery salesperson standing behind the counter) or outside order taker (e.g., the soap salesperson calling on the supermarket manager)

3. *Missionary:* A salesperson who is not expected or permitted to take an order but whose major task is to build goodwill or to educate the actual or potential user (e.g., the medical "detailer" representing an ethical pharmaceutical house)

4. *Technician:* A salesperson with a high level of technical knowledge (e.g., the engineering salesperson who is primarily a consultant to the client companies)

5. *Demand creator:* A salesperson who relies on creative methods for selling tangible products (e.g., vacuum cleaners, refrigerators, siding, encyclopedias) or intangibles (e.g., insurance, advertising services, or education)

6. *Solution vendor:* A salesperson whose expertise is in the solving of a customer's problem, often with a system of the company's products and services (for example, computer and communications systems)

These positions range from the least to the most creative types of selling. The least creative call for servicing accounts and taking new orders, while the most creative require seeking prospects and influencing them to buy. Our discussion will focus on the more creative types of selling.

No one debates the importance of the sales force in the marketing mix, especially for big-ticket items. However, companies are highly sensitive to the high and rising costs (salaries, commissions, bonuses, travel expenses, and benefits) of maintaining a sales force. Because the average cost of a personal sales call ranges from $250 to $500, and closing a sale typically requires four calls, the total cost to close a sale ranges from $1,000 to $2,000.[3] Thus companies need to carefully consider when and how to use sales representatives. Not surprisingly, companies are seeking to substitute inside mail- and phone-based selling units to reduce field sales expenses. And they are trying to increase the productivity of the remaining sales force through better selection, training, motivation, and compensation.

This chapter examines three major questions related to the sales force:

Managing
the Sales
Force

DESIGNING THE SALES FORCE

Sales personnel serve as the company's personal link to the customers. The sales representative *is* the company to many of its customers, and it is the sales rep who brings back to the company much-needed information about the customer. Therefore, the company needs to give its deepest thought to issues in sales force design—namely, the development of sales force objectives, strategy, structure, size, and compensation.

Sales Force Objectives

Companies must carefully define the specific objectives they expect their sales force to achieve. The old idea was that the sales force should "sell, sell, and sell." At IBM, salespeople would "push metal" and at Xerox they would "sell boxes." Salespeople had sales quotas, and the better salespeople met or exceeded their quotas. Later, the idea arose that sales representatives should be skilled in customer problem solving, that they should know how to diagnose a customer's problem and propose a solution. More recently, some industries have begun to insist that the sales force engage in "commitment selling." Under this concept, salespeople do not initially try to sell a specific product or solve a specific problem. Rather, they show a customer-prospect how their company can help the customer improve its profitability. They seek to join their company with the customer's company as "partners for profit."

Regardless of the selling context, salespeople will have one or more of the following specific tasks to perform:

♦ *Prospecting:* Sales representatives search for prospects, or leads.

♦ *Targeting:* Sales representatives decide how to allocate their time among prospects and customers.

♦ *Communicating:* Sales representatives skillfully communicate information about the company's products and services.

♦ *Selling:* Sales representatives know the art of sales—approaching, presenting, answering objections, and closing sales.

♦ *Servicing:* Sales representatives provide various services to the customers—consulting on their problems, rendering technical assistance, arranging financing, and expediting delivery.

♦ *Information gathering:* Sales representatives conduct market research and intelligence work and fill in call reports.

♦ *Allocating:* Sales representatives decide which customers will get scarce products during product shortages.

Companies typically define the specific objectives they want their sales force to achieve. For example, the company might want its sales representatives to spend

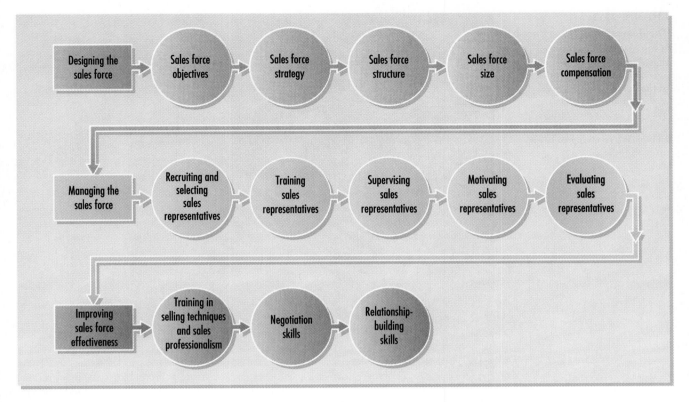

FIGURE 22-1

Steps in Designing and Managing the Sales Force

80% of their time with current customers and 20% with prospects, and 85% of their time on established products and 15% on new products. If norms are not established, sales representatives might spend most of their time selling established products to current accounts and neglect new products and new prospects.

The sales representative's mix of tasks varies with the state of the economy. During product shortages, sales representatives have no problem selling. Some companies jump to the conclusion that fewer sales representatives are needed during such periods. But this thinking overlooks the salesperson's other roles—allocating the product, counseling unhappy customers, communicating company plans on remedying shortages, and selling the company's other products that are not in short supply.

As companies compete harder for customers, they are increasingly judging their sales reps on their ability to create customer satisfaction and company profits. Here are two examples:

GENERAL MOTORS' SATURN DIVISION Harassment and manipulation used to be the hallmark of the U.S. car salesman—that is, until GM's Saturn division came up with its no-haggle sticker price and a commitment to customer satisfaction. All new salespeople are trained in the art of customer service at off-site three-day sessions. The goal: To get salespeople, and every other Saturn employee, to turn competitive energy into cooperative spirit by referring customers to each other and working together to exceed customer expectations. Customers see this team effort when they pick up their new Saturn car: An entire team gathers around them, including representatives from service, sales, parts, and reception. They cheer, snap your picture, and hand you the keys. It may be corny, but Saturn scored third in a J. D. Power customer satisfaction study in 1993, just behind Lexus and Infiniti, whose cars cost up to five times as much.

FIGURE 22-2

The James River Sales Force

"Our customers demanded that we change," says a manager at James River, speaking of the company's new sales approach and methods. "They're looking to reduce costs and increase their efficiency. We're trying to team up with them."

JAMES RIVER CORP James River, which sells paper products such as toilet tissue and Dixie cups (Figure 22-2), has reorganized to help its retailer customers reduce costs and increase efficiency. James River sales reps now share proprietary marketing information with their customers to help them sell more paper products. In one instance, it told its West Coast client, Lucky Stores, how often shoppers generally buy paper goods and which items they tend to buy together. Lucky has since reshelved all of its paper products and has consequently won market share in the category from competing stores. James River also no longer has separate salespeople approach a customer like Lucky stores, each selling a different product. If each rep secured an order, the customer was obliged to buy full truckloads of each product to get the lowest price from James River. Now a unified team from James River will sell a store one truckload with a mix of paper products at the lowest price.[4]

To maintain a market focus, salespeople should know how to analyze sales data, measure market potential, gather market intelligence, and develop marketing strategies and plans. Sales representatives need analytical marketing skills, and these skills become especially important at the higher levels of sales management. Marketers believe that sales forces will be more effective in the long run if they understand marketing as well as selling.

Sales Force Strategy

Companies compete with other companies to get orders from customers. They must therefore deploy their sales forces strategically so that they call on the right customers at the right time and in the right way. Sales representatives work with customers in several ways:

◆ *Sales representative to buyer:* A sales representative discusses issues with a prospect or customer in person or over the phone.

◆ *Sales representative to buyer group:* A sales representative gets to know as many members of the buyer group as possible.

◆ *Sales team to buyer group:* A company sales team works closely with the members of the customer's buying group.

- *Conference selling:* The sales representative brings company resource people to discuss a major problem or opportunity.
- *Seminar selling:* A company team conducts an educational seminar for the customer company about state-of-the-art developments.

Thus today's sales representatives often act as "account managers" who arrange contact between various people in the buying and selling organizations. Selling increasingly calls for teamwork requiring the support of other personnel, such as top management, who are increasingly involved in the sales process, especially when national accounts or major sales are at stake; technical people, who supply technical information and service to the customer before, during, or after product purchase; customer service representatives, who provide installation, maintenance, and other services to the customer; and an office staff, consisting of sales analysts, order expediters, and secretaries. An example of a successful sales-team orientation is provided by Du Pont:

DU PONT   Du Pont spent the 1980s cultivating flexible sales teams recruited from all company ranks to develop and sell new products. In 1990, a team of chemists, sales and marketing executives, and regulatory specialists noted that corn growers needed a herbicide they could apply less often. In response, they created a product that topped $57 million in sales its first year.[5]

Once the company decides on a desirable selling approach, it can use either a direct or a contractual sales force. A *direct (company) sales force* consists of full- or part-time paid employees who work exclusively for the company. This sales force includes *inside sales personnel,* who conduct business from their office using the telephone and receive visits from prospective buyers, and *field sales personnel,* who travel and visit customers. A *contractual sales force* consists of manufacturers' reps, sales agents, and/or brokers, who are paid a commission based on their sales.

Sales Force Structure

The sales force strategy has implications for the sales force's structure. If the company sells one product line to one end-using industry with customers in many locations, the company would use a territorial sales force structure. If the company sells many products to many types of customers, it might need a product or market sales force structure. Table 22-1 on page 690 summarizes the most common sales force structures. The Marketing Insight on page 691 titled "Major Account Management—What It Is and How It Works" discusses major account management, a specialized form of sales force structure.

Established companies need to revise their sales force structure as market and economic conditions change. IBM is an excellent example:[6]

IBM   IBM lost market share in the computing industry for two reasons. First, it failed to see that PCs were the wave of the future. Second, it was burdened by a bureaucratic and monolithic marketing and sales organization that had lost touch with its customers. The company's worldwide marketing and sales head count was 150,000 at its peak in 1990 and was organized geographically, with teams of sales reps devoted to customers in a wide range of industries. Since the company's inception, IBM reps had gained a reputation for educating their customers about computer technology—and when IBM was the biggest game in town, that meant educating them solely about IBM products. But gradually the company's "one-size-fits-all presentations" began to turn its increasingly computer-savvy customers off. A case in point: IBM reps tried to talk GTE out of moving from mainframes to networks of inexpensive computers and pushed its own main-

| **TABLE 22-1** | ALTERNATIVE STRUCTURES FOR THE SALES FORCE |

Territorial-Structured Sales Force	Each sales representative is assigned an exclusive territory in which to represent the company's full line. This sales structure has a number of advantages. First, it results in a clear definition of the salesperson's responsibilities. As the only salesperson working the territory, he or she bears the credit or blame for area sales to the extent that personal selling effort makes a difference. Second, territorial responsibility increases the sales rep's incentive to cultivate local business and personal ties. These ties contribute to the sales rep's selling effectiveness and personal life. Third, travel expenses are relatively small, since each sales rep travels within a small geographical area. **Territory Size.** Territories can be designed to provide either equal sales potential or equal workload. Territories of *equal potential* provide each sales representative with the same income opportunities and provide the company with a means to evaluate performance. Persistent differences in sales yield by territory may reflect differences in salespersons' abilities or efforts. However, because customer density varies by territory, territories with equal potential can vary widely in size. Alternatively, territories could be designed to *equalize the sales workload* so that each sales rep can cover his or her territory adequately. **Territory Shape.** Territories are formed by combining smaller units, such as counties or states, until they add up to a territory of a given sales potential or workload. Territorial design must take into account the location of natural barriers, the compatibility of adjacent areas, the adequacy of transportation, and so forth. Territory shape can influence the cost and ease of coverage and the sales reps' job satisfaction. Today, companies can use computer programs to design sales territories that optimize such criteria as compactness, equalization of workload or sales potential, and minimal travel time.
Product-Structured Sales Force	The importance of sales reps' knowing their products, together with the development of product divisions and product management, has led many companies to structure their sales forces along product lines. Product specialization is particularly warranted where the products are technically complex, highly unrelated, or very numerous. For example, Kodak uses one sales force for its film products that are intensively distributed, and another sales force selling complex products that require technical understanding.
Market-Structured Sales Force	Companies often specialize their sales forces along industry or customer lines. Separate sales forces can be set up for different industries and even different customers. For example, IBM set up a sales office for finance and brokerage customers in New York, another for GM in Detroit, and still another for Ford in nearby Dearborn. The most obvious advantage of market specialization is that each sales force can become knowledgeable about specific customer needs. The major disadvantage arises when the customers are scattered throughtout the country, thus requiring extensive travel by each sales force.
Complex Sales Force Structures	When a company sells a wide variety of products to many types of customers over a broad geographical area, it often combines several principles of sales force structure. Sales representatives can be specialized by territory-product, territory-market, product-market, and so on. A sales representative might then report to one or more line and staff managers.

frames instead of listening to GTE's concerns. GTE left IBM and moved to Hewlett Packard. Ultimately, lost market share and the huge cost of maintaining its sales force made IBM rethink and reorganize its entire sales and marketing operation in the following ways:

♦ By 1994 the sales and marketing head count was reduced from 150,000 to 70,000. Not only did IBM reduce its sales staff, but it moved them out of their plush offices into no-frills warehouse buildings.

Major Account Management—What It Is and How It Works

When a company sells to many small accounts, it uses a territory-based sales force. However, major accounts (also called key accounts, national accounts, global accounts, or house accounts) are often singled out for special attention and handling. If the account is a large company with many divisions operating in many parts of the country or world and subject to many buying influences (such as General Electric or General Motors), it is likely to be handled as a *major account* and assigned to a specific major account manager (MAM) or sales team. If the company has several such accounts, it is likely to organize a *major account management division*. The company will then sell to these larger customers through this division. A company such as Xerox handles about 250 major accounts.

Major account management is growing for a number of reasons. As buyer concentration increases through mergers and acquisitions, fewer buyers account for a larger share of a company's sales. Thus the largest 20% of accounts might account for more than 80% of a company's sales. Another factor is that many buyers are centralizing their purchases of certain items instead of leaving those purchases to the local units. This gives them more bargaining power with the sellers. The sellers in turn need to devote more attention to these major buyers. Still another factor is that as products become more complex, more groups in the buyer's organization become involved in the purchase process, and the typical salesperson might not have the skill, authority, or coverage to be effective in selling to the large buyer.

In organizing a major account program, a company faces a number of issues, including how to select major accounts; how to manage them; how to select, manage, and evaluate major account managers; how to organize a structure for major account managers; and where to locate major account management in the organization.

Companies use a number of criteria in selecting major accounts. They look for accounts that purchase a high volume (especially of the company's more profitable products), purchase centrally, require a high level of service in several geographical locations, may be price-sensitive, and may want a long-term partnering relationship with the company. In turn, these major accounts have certain expectations of their suppliers. They expect the account manager to understand their business, industry, competitive environment, marketplace, technologies, products, and services. Companies must therefore appoint MAMs who are able to understand, oversee, and grow these accounts. MAMs must be able to research and reach the various buying influences in the customer organization. They must know how to add value and do long-term account planning. They must be able to mobilize groups within their own organization—salespeople, R&D staff, manufacturing people—to meet the customer's requirements. MAMs are the company's relationship managers, linking all the people in their company with all the relevant people in the customer's company.

Companies often make the mistake of selecting their most productive salespeople as MAMs. But different sets of skills are required for the two jobs. One MAM said, "My position must not be as a salesman, but as a 'marketing consultant' to our customers and a salesman of my company's capabilities as opposed to my company's products."

Major accounts normally receive more favorable pricing based on their purchase volume. But companies often point out that major accounts receive a lot of added value, including a single point of dedicated contact, single billing, special warranties, EDI links, priority shipping, early information releases, and so on. Not surprisingly, some major accounts appreciate these added services and don't press too hard for favorable pricing.

Sources: For further reading, see John F. Martin and Gary S. Tubridy, "Major Account Management," in *AMA Management Handbook*, 3d ed., John J. Hampton, (New York: Amacom, 1994), pp. 3-27 to 3-25. More information can be obtained from NAMA (National Account Management Association), 150 N. Wacker Dr., Suite 1760, Chicago, IL 60606.

♦ Salespeople who formerly reported to regional managers—who were responsible for all of the industries in their geographical region—now report to regional executives within specific industries. The company has reorganized vertically along 14 industry-specific lines such as finance, petroleum, and retail.

♦ The sales force retains a mix of industry and product specialists. For instance, if an executive calls on Bank of America in San Francisco and discovers that the bank needs a software solution, she can call a software specialist in the region to sell the product.

- Sales reps have taken on an active role as consultant rather than mere order taker or product pusher. Their mission is to seek customer solutions, even if doing so means recommending a competitor's technology.

- Customers choose how they want to deal with IBM. For some customers, this means tapping IBM business consultants, product specialists, or systems integrators to tie products into corporate information systems. At the other end of the spectrum are customers who never see a sales representative in person but rely exclusively on IBM telephone sales reps.

Sales Force Size

Once the company clarifies its sales force strategy and structure, it is ready to consider sales force size. Sales representatives are one of the company's most productive and expensive assets. Increasing their number will increase both sales and costs.

Once the company establishes the number of customers it wants to reach, it can use a *workload approach* to establish sales force size. This method consists of the following steps:

1. Customers are grouped into size classes according to their annual sales volume.
2. The desirable call frequencies (number of sales calls on an account per year) are established for each class.
3. The number of accounts in each size class is multiplied by the corresponding call frequency to arrive at the total workload for the country, in sales calls per year.
4. The average number of calls a sales representative can make per year is determined.
5. The number of sales representatives needed is determined by dividing the total annual calls required by the average annual calls made by a sales representative.

Suppose the company estimates that there are 1,000 A accounts and 2,000 B accounts required in the nation. A accounts require 36 calls a year and B accounts require 12 calls a year. This means the company needs a sales force that can make 60,000 sales calls a year. Suppose the average sales representative can make 1,000 calls a year. The company would need 60 full-time sales representatives.

Facing tremendous pressure to cut costs, many companies are shrinking their sales forces because the sales department is one of the costliest to maintain. Consider the case of Coca Cola Amatil, the Australian Coke franchisee:

COCA COLA AMATIL Amatil used to maintain an army of reps to call on small milk bar (corner store) accounts. The milk bar reps would often make up to 30 sales calls per day, giving them just enough time to take an order and maybe show one new product. When Amatil looked at the costs of putting these reps in front of milk bar customers—salary, car, phone, office support, and so forth—it saw a good deal of wasted time and money. Now Amatil contacts these small accounts through its new telemarketing department, and the field reps make few milk bar calls and concentrate their efforts on larger accounts. Each milk bar has a day of the week when it will be contacted or when it can phone in. This move has resulted in a much lower cost per order and made small accounts financially feasible.

Sales Force Compensation

To attract top-quality sales reps, the company has to develop an attractive compensation package. Sales reps would like income regularity, extra reward for above-average performance, and fair payment for experience and longevity. Management would like to achieve control, economy, and simplicity. Some of management's objectives, such as economy, will conflict with sales reps' objectives, such as financial security. No wonder that compensation plans exhibit a tremendous variety from industry to industry and even within the same industry.

Management must determine the level and components of an effective compensation plan. The level of compensation must bear some relation to the "going market price" for the type of sales job and required abilities. For example, the average earnings of a typical U.S. sales representative in 1992 was $50,000.[7] If the market price for salespeople is well defined, the individual firm has little choice but to pay the going rate. Paying less would bring forth less than the desired quantity or quality of applicants, and paying more would be unnecessary. However, the market price for salespeople is seldom well defined. Published data on industry sales force compensation levels are infrequent and generally lack sufficient detail.

The company must next determine the four components of its sales force's compensation—a fixed amount, a variable amount, expense allowances, and benefits. The *fixed amount,* a salary, is intended to satisfy the sales reps' need for income stability. The *variable amount,* which might be commissions, bonus, or profit sharing, is intended to stimulate and reward greater effort. *Expense allowances* enable the sales reps to meet the expenses involved in travel, lodging, dining, and entertaining. *Benefits,* such as paid vacations, sickness or accident benefits, pensions, and life insurance, are intended to provide security and job satisfaction.

Sales management must decide on the relative importance of these components in the compensation plan. A popular rule favors making about 70% of the salesperson's total income fixed and allocating the remaining 30% among the other elements. But the variations around this average are so pronounced that it can hardly serve as a guide. Fixed compensation receives more emphasis in jobs with a high ratio of nonselling to selling duties and in jobs where the selling task is technically complex and involves teamwork. Variable compensation receives more emphasis in jobs where sales are cyclical or depend on individual initiative.

Fixed and variable compensation give rise to three basic types of sales force compensation plans—straight salary, straight commission, and combination salary and commission. Only one fourth of all firms use either a straight-salary or straight-commission method. Three quarters use a combination of the two, though the relative proportion of salary versus incentives varies widely across firms.[8]

Straight-salary plans have several advantages. They provide sales reps with a secure income, make them more willing to perform nonselling activities, and give them less incentive to overstock customers. From the company's perspective, they provide administrative simplicity and lower sales force turnover. The advantages of straight-commission plans are as follows: They attract higher sales performers, provide more motivation, require less supervision, and control selling costs. Combination plans feature the benefits of both plans while reducing their disadvantages.

With compensation plans that combine fixed and variable pay, companies may link the variable portion of a salesperson's pay to a wide variety of strategic goals. Some see a new trend toward de-emphasizing volume measures as a factor in determining sales compensation in favor of factors related to achieving strategic priorities and managing territories for improved profitability. A recent study found that increasing numbers of companies are recognizing business-unit and/or small-team performance for incentive purposes; the percentage of companies considering rewards for business-unit performance rose from 13% in 1991 to 22% in 1994. Also, as more and more companies emphasize customer satisfaction as part of an overall quality improvement initiative, they are tying pay to customer satisfaction measures. In 1992 GE began testing the use of customer satisfaction surveys as a

Managing
the Sales
Force

factor in sales compensation. AT&T's Universal credit-card unit has an in-house staff monitor customer satisfaction in order to set bonuses for everyone from 800-line operators to the division president.   And a crucial part of IBM's sales force reorganization is that IBM now rewards salespeople on the basis of customer satisfaction as measured by customer surveys (in addition to rewarding for profitability).[9]

MANAGING THE SALES FORCE

Once the company has established the sales force's objectives, strategy, structure, size, and compensation, it has to move to recruiting, selecting, training, supervising, motivating, and evaluating sales representatives. Various policies and procedures guide these decisions.

Recruiting and Selecting Sales Representatives

At the heart of a successful sales force is the selection of effective sales representatives. The performance difference between an average and a top sales representative can be considerable. One survey revealed that the top 27% of the sales force brought in over 52% of the sales. Beyond the differences in sales productivity are the great wastes in hiring the wrong people. The average annual sales force turnover rate for all industries is almost 20 percent. When a salesperson quits, the costs of finding and training a new salesperson—plus the cost of lost sales—can run as high as $50,000 to $75,000. And a sales force with many new people is less productive.[10]

The financial loss due to turnover is only part of the total cost. If a new sales representative receives $30,000 a year, another $30,000 goes into fringe benefits, expenses, supervision, office space, supplies, and secretarial assistance. Consequently, the new sales representative needs to produce sales on which the gross margin at least covers the selling expenses of $60,000. If the gross margin is 10%, the new salesperson will have to sell at least $600,000 for the company to break even.

WHAT MAKES A GOOD SALES REPRESENTATIVE?   Selecting sales reps would be simple if one knew what traits to look for. One good starting point is to ask customers what traits they like and prefer in salespeople. Most customers say they want the sales rep to be honest, reliable, knowledgeable, and helpful. The company should look for these traits when selecting candidates.

Another approach is to look for traits common to the most successful salespeople in the company. Charles Garfield, in his study of superachievers, concluded that supersales performers exhibit the following traits: risk taking, powerful sense of mission, problem-solving bent, care for the customer, and careful call planners.[11] Robert McMurry wrote: "It is my conviction that the possessor of an effective sales personality is a habitual 'wooer,' an individual who has a compulsive need to win and hold the affection of others."[12] He listed five additional traits of the supersalesperson: "A high level of energy, abounding self-confidence, a chronic hunger for money, a well-established habit of industry, and a state of mind that regards each objection, resistance, or obstacle as a challenge."[13] Mayer and Greenberg offered one of the shortest lists of traits. They concluded that the effective salesperson has two basic qualities: *empathy,* the ability to feel as the customer does; and *ego drive,* a strong personal need to make the sale.[14]

In defining the profile of a desirable sales rep, the company must consider the characteristics of the specific sales job. Is there a lot of paperwork? Does the job call for much travel? Will the salesperson confront a high proportion of rejections?

RECRUITMENT PROCEDURES. After management develops its selection criteria, it must recruit. The human resources department seeks applicants by various means, including soliciting names from current sales representatives, using employment agencies, placing job ads, and contacting college students. Unfortunately, few students decide to go into selling as a career. Reasons include "Selling is a job and not a profession," and "There is insecurity and too much travel." To counter these objections, company recruiters emphasize starting salaries, income opportunities, and the fact that one fourth of the presidents of large U.S. corporations started out in marketing and sales.

APPLICANT-RATING PROCEDURES. Recruitment procedures, if successful, will attract many applicants, and the company will need to select the best ones. The selection procedures can vary from a single informal interview to prolonged testing and interviewing, not only of the applicant but of the applicant's spouse.[15] If the spouse is not ready to support the "away from home" lifestyle of the salesperson, the hire will not be a good one.

Many companies give formal tests to sales applicants. Although test scores are only one information element in a set that includes personal characteristics, references, past employment history, and interviewer reactions, they are weighted quite heavily by such companies as IBM, Prudential, Procter & Gamble, and Gillette. Gillette claims that tests have reduced turnover by 42% and have correlated well with the subsequent progress of new reps in the sales organization.

Training Sales Representatives

Many companies send their new sales representatives into the field almost immediately after hiring them. They are supplied with samples, order books, and a description of their territory. And much of their selling is ineffective. A vice-president of a major food company spent one week watching 50 sales presentations to a busy buyer for a major supermarket chain. Here is what he observed:

> The majority of salesmen were ill prepared, unable to answer basic questions, uncertain as to what they wanted to accomplish during the call. They did not think of the call as a studied professional presentation. They didn't have a real idea of the busy retailer's needs and wants.[16]

Today's customers, who are more demanding and deal with many suppliers, cannot put up with inept salespeople. Customers expect salespeople to have deep product knowledge, to add ideas to improve the customer's operations, and to be efficient and reliable. These demands have required companies to make a much higher investment in sales training.

Today's new sales rep may spend a few weeks to several months in training. The median training period is 28 weeks in industrial-products companies, 12 in service companies, and four in consumer-products companies. Training time varies with the complexity of the selling task and the type of person recruited into the sales organization. At IBM, new sales reps receive extensive initial training and may spend 15% of their time each year in additional training.

Sales training programs have several goals:

- *Sales representatives need to know and identify with the company:* Most companies devote the first part of the training program to describing the company's history and objectives, organization and lines of authority, chief officers, financial structure and facilities, and chief products and sales volumes.

- ◆ *Sales representatives need to know the company's products:* Sales trainees are shown how the products are produced and how they function in various uses.

- ◆ *Sales representatives need to know customers' and competitors' characteristics:* Sales reps learn about the different types of customers and their needs, buying motives, and buying habits. They learn about the company's and competitors' strategies and policies.

- ◆ *Sales representatives need to know how to make effective sales presentations:* Sales reps receive training in the principles of selling. In addition, the company outlines the major sales arguments for each product and may provide a sales script.

- ◆ *Sales representatives need to understand field procedures and responsibilities:* Sales reps learn how to divide time between active and potential accounts and how to use the expense account, prepare reports, and route effectively.

New methods of training are continually emerging. Among the instructional approaches are role playing, sensitivity training, cassette tapes, videotapes, CD-ROMs, programmed learning, and films on selling and on company products. IBM uses a self-study system called Info-Window that combines a personal computer and a laser videodisc. A sales trainee can practice sales calls with an on-screen actor who portrays a buying executive in a particular industry. The actor-buyer responds differently depending on what the sales trainee says.

As sales-automation technology has freed reps from the office and put them on the road, it has become more costly to train them by traditional in-house methods. Reps simply are not in the office enough, and they are often overwhelmed with paperwork and information whether they're in-house or on the road. But technology promises to help reps increase their efficiency and productivity. Many companies are now embracing CD-ROM-based interactive training. For instance, reps at Tandem Computers used to complain that they could not keep up with the printed information and training materials the company sent them. Now field reps carry their own miniature training rooms with them—they simply slip a CD-ROM disc (complete with presentation modules and a resource library) into their laptop computers. The cost for mastering, duplicating, and mailing the CD-ROMs (which include more than 1,000 documents and presentations) is equal to the previous cost of printing and mailing just one data sheet. Overall, the company says it saves about $2 million per year using the technology.[17]

Training departments need to collect evidence of the effect of different training approaches on sales performance. There should be a measurable impact on sales force turnover, sales volume, absenteeism, average sale size, calls-to-close ratio, customer complaints and compliments, new accounts per time unit, and volume of returned merchandise.

Supervising Sales Representatives

New sales representatives are given more than a territory, a compensation package, and training—they are also given supervision. Supervision is the fate of everyone who works for someone else. It is the expression of their employers' natural and continuous interest in their employees' activities.

Companies vary in how closely they supervise their sales reps. Sales reps who are paid mostly on commission generally receive less supervision. Those who are salaried and must cover definite accounts are likely to receive substantial supervision.

DEVELOPING NORMS FOR CUSTOMER CALLS. In 1989, the average salesperson made 4.2 sales calls a day.[18] This was down from five daily sales calls in the early 1980s. The downward trend is due to the increased use of the phone and fax machines, the increased reliance on automatic ordering systems, and the drop-in cold calls owing to better market research information for pinpointing prospects.

The real issue is how much sales volume can be expected from a particular account as a function of the annual number of calls. Magee described an experiment where similar accounts were randomly split into three sets.[19] Sales representatives were asked to spend less than five hours a month with accounts in the first set, five to nine hours a month with those in the second set, and more than nine hours a month with those in the third set. The results demonstrated that additional calls produced more sales, leaving only the question of whether the magnitude of sales increase justified the additional cost. Some later research has suggested that today's sales reps are spending too much time selling to smaller, less profitable accounts when they should be focusing more of their efforts on selling to larger, more profitable accounts.[20]

DEVELOPING NORMS FOR PROSPECT CALLS. Companies often specify how much time their sales forces should spend prospecting for new accounts. Spector Freight wants its sales representatives to spend 25% of their time prospecting and to stop calling on a prospect after three unsuccessful calls.

Companies set up prospecting standards for a number of reasons. If left to their own devices, many sales reps will spend most of their time with current customers. Current customers are better-known quantities. Sales reps can depend upon them for some business, while a prospect might never deliver any business. Unless sales reps are rewarded for opening new accounts, they might avoid new-account development. Some companies rely on a missionary sales force to open new accounts.

USING SALES TIME EFFICIENTLY. Studies have shown that the best sales reps are those who manage their time effectively.[21] One effective planning tool is the *annual call schedule* showing which customers and prospects to call on in which months and which activities to carry out. For example:

THE BELL TELEPHONE COMPANIES Sales representatives of Bell Telephone companies plan their calls and activities around three concepts. The first is market development—various efforts to educate customers, cultivate new business, and gain greater visibility in the buying community. The second is sales-generating activities—direct efforts to sell particular products to customers on particular calls. The third is market-protection activities—various efforts to learn what competition is doing and to protect relations with existing customers. The sales force aims for balance among these activities, so that the company does not achieve high current sales at the expense of long-run market development.

Another tool is *time-and-duty analysis,* which helps reps understand how they spend their time and ways that they might increase their productivity. For example, the sales rep spends time in the following ways:

- *Preparation:* The time salespeople spend in getting information and planning their call strategy.
- *Travel:* In some jobs, travel time amounts to over 50% of total time. Travel time can be cut down by using faster means of transportation—recognizing, of course, that such methods will increase costs. Companies encourage air travel for their sales force, to increase their ratio of selling to total time.
- *Food and breaks:* Some portion of the sales force's workday is spent in eating and taking breaks. These breaks should be timed to coincide with the times that clients are unavailable.

- *Waiting:* Waiting consists of time spent in the buyer's outer office. This is dead time unless the sales representative uses it to plan or to fill out reports.

- *Selling:* Selling is the time spent with the buyer in person or on the phone. It breaks down into "social talk" and "selling talk." Sales reps must maintain balance here.

- *Administration:* Administration is time spent in report writing and billing, attending sales meetings, and talking to others in the company about production, delivery, billing, sales performance, and other matters. Reps should spend time on administration early in the morning and later in the evening, when it is less likely that sales prospects will be available for meetings.

With sales reps having so many duties, it is no wonder that actual face-to-face selling time can amount to as little as 25% of total working time![22] Companies are constantly seeking ways to improve sales force productivity. Their methods take the form of training sales representatives in the use of "phone power," simplifying record-keeping forms, and using the computer to develop call and routing plans and to supply customer and competitive information.

To reduce time demands on their outside sales force, many companies have increased the size and responsibilities of their inside sales force. In a survey of 135 electronics distributors, Narus and Anderson found that an average of 57% of the sales force's members were inside salespeople.[23] As reasons for the growth of the internal sales force, managers cited the escalating cost of outside sales calls and the growing use of computers and innovative telecommunications equipment.

Inside salespeople are of three types. There are *technical support people,* who provide technical information and answers to customers' questions. There are *sales assistants,* who provide clerical backup for the outside salespersons. They call ahead and confirm appointments, carry out credit checks, follow up on deliveries, and answer customers' questions when they cannot reach the outside sales rep. And there are *telemarketers,* who use the phone to find new leads, qualify them, and sell to them. A telemarketer can call up to 50 customers a day compared to the four that an outside salesperson can contact. They can be effective in the following ways: cross-selling the company's other products; upgrading orders; introducing new company products; opening new accounts and reactivating former accounts; giving more attention to neglected accounts; and following up and qualifying direct-mail leads. (We discuss telemarketing in detail in the next chapter.)

The inside sales force frees the outside sales reps to spend more time selling to major accounts, identifying and converting new major prospects, placing electronic ordering systems in customers' facilities, and obtaining more blanket orders and systems contracts. Meanwhile, the inside salespeople spend more time in checking inventory, following up orders, phoning smaller accounts, and so on. The outside sales reps are paid largely on an incentive compensation basis, and the inside reps on a salary or salary plus bonus pay.

Another dramatic breakthrough in improving sales force productivity is provided by new technological equipment—desktop and laptop computers, videocassette recorders, videodiscs, automatic dialers, electronic mail, fax machines, teleconferencing. The salesperson has truly gone "electronic." Not only is sales and inventory information transferred much faster, but specific computer-based decision support systems have been created for sales managers and sales representatives. For more on this topic, see the Vision 2000 feature titled "Salespeople's Productivity Rises Sharply with Sales Automation."

Motivating Sales Representatives

Some sales representatives will put forth their best effort without any special coaching from management. To them, selling is the most fascinating job in the

Salespeople's Productivity Rises Sharply with Sales Automation

The buzz in sales today is *sales automation*. Companies are equipping their salespeople with computers, software, printers, modems, fax/copier machines, and pagers, all in the hope of increasing sales productivity. Companies want their sales reps to spend less time doing paperwork and more time selling. Some companies have seen 5% to 10% increases in their sales reps' selling time as a result of sales automation. National Life Insurance believes that as much as 50% of its recent sales gain may be attributable to its sales force's use of a laptop-based sales support system.

What is included in a complete sales force automation system? Shell Chemical Company's sales automation package consists of several applications: (1) an automatic-expense-statement program that easily and accurately records expenses and allows for faster reimbursement; (2) a sales-inquiry function that allows sales reps to retrieve the latest account-specific information, including phone numbers, addresses, recent developments, and prices; (3) electronic mail, which allows reps to send and receive messages rapidly; (4) business forms, such as territory work plans and sales call reports, which can be filled out quickly and sent electronically; (5) an appointment calendar; (6) a to-do list; (7) a spreadsheet; and (8) a graphics software package, which helps salespeople prepare charts and graphs for customer presentations.

Other companies include different elements in their systems. For example, salespeople from Nordstrom Valve have a software program that allows them to instantly determine the appropriate valve for a customer's project. The customer can check the accuracy of the calculations, discuss purchase terms, and sign a contract coming out of the salesperson's printer.

Sales reps must be won over to using the new technologies. Objections such as "I'm not a typist" and "I'm going to spend so much time entering and reading information that I won't have time to make sales calls" have to be answered. Some salespeople also feel uneasy about sharing customer information with the home office, preferring to keep valuable information to themselves. Companies need to allay these fears and involve salespeople in the development of the sales automation program. "It's vital to first understand what problems your salespeople are having, and then design an automation system that solves those problems," says the president of the Sales Automation Association in Dearborn, Michigan.

Sales automation has progressed to the point that several companies have even eliminated their sales offices. Compaq, for example, helped its 220-plus salespeople set up offices in their homes, with Compaq furnishing a laptop computer, docking bay, laser printer, fax/copier, and two phone lines. Each morning, the Compaq salesperson logs into Compaq's network to retrieve marketing material, technical reports, press releases, and e-mail. The salesperson then travels to his or her accounts (no need to waste time traveling back and forth to the office). At night, the sales rep writes and prints letters, responds to e-mail, and prepares for the next day. All said, the company has saved a lot of rented space expense and the salesperson has saved travel time, leaving more time for selling.

Sources: "Computer-Based Sales Support: Shell Chemical's System" (New York: Conference Board, Management Briefing: Marketing, April–May, 1989), pp. 4–5; R. Lee Sullivan, "The Office That Never Closes," *Forbes*, May 23, 1994, pp. 212–13; John W. Verity. "Taking a Laptop on a Call," *Business Week*, October 25, 1993, pp. 124–25; Jack Falvey, "Manager's Journal: The Hottest Thing in Sales Since the Electric Fork," *The Wall Street Journal*, January 10, 1994, A12:3; Louis A. Wallis, *Computer-Based Sales Force Support* (New York: The Conference Board, Report No. 953, 1990); Robert Shaw, *Computer-Aided Marketing and Selling: Information Asset Management* (Oxford, England: Butterworth-Heinemann, 1993); and George W. Columbo, *Sales Force Automation* (New York: McGraw-Hill, 1994).

world. They are ambitious self-starters. But the majority of sales reps require encouragement and special incentives to work at their best level. This is especially true of field selling, for the following reasons:

♦ *The nature of the job:* The selling job is one of frequent frustration. Sales reps usually work alone, their hours are irregular, and they are often away from home. They confront aggressive, competing sales reps; they have an inferior status relative to the buyer; they often do not have the authority to do what is necessary to win an account; and they sometimes lose large orders that they have worked hard to obtain.

- *Human nature:* Most people operate below capacity in the absence of special incentives, such as financial gain or social recognition.
- *Personal problems:* Sales reps are occasionally preoccupied with personal problems, such as sickness in the family, marital discord, or debt.

The problem of motivating sales representatives has been studied by Churchill, Ford, and Walker.[24] Their basic model is as follows:

$$Motivation \longrightarrow Effort \longrightarrow Performance \longrightarrow Rewards \longrightarrow Satisfaction$$

This model says that the higher the salesperson's motivation, the greater his or her effort. Greater effort will lead to greater performance; greater performance will lead to greater rewards; greater rewards will lead to greater satisfaction; and greater satisfaction will reinforce motivation. The model thus implies the following:

1. *Sales managers must be able to convince salespeople that they can sell more by working harder or by being trained to work smarter.* But if sales are determined largely by economic conditions or competitive actions, this linkage is undermined.

2. *Sales managers must be able to convince salespeople that the rewards for better performance are worth the extra effort.* But if the rewards seem to be set arbitrarily or are too small or of the wrong kind, this linkage is undermined.

The researchers went on to measure the importance of different possible rewards. The reward with the highest value was pay, followed by promotion, personal growth, and sense of accomplishment. The least-valued rewards were liking and respect, security, and recognition. In other words, salespeople are highly motivated by pay and the chance to get ahead and satisfy their intrinsic needs, and less motivated by compliments and security. But the researchers also found that the importance of motivators varied with the salespersons' demographic characteristics:

1. Financial rewards were mostly valued by older, longer-tenured salespeople and those who had large families.

2. Higher-order rewards (recognition, liking and respect, sense of accomplishment) were more valued by young salespeople who were unmarried or had small families and usually more formal education.

Motivators also vary across countries. A 1992 survey of 2,800 sales professional in six countries revealed that while money is the number-one motivator of 37% of U.S. salespeople, only 20% of salespeople in Canada feel the same way. Salespeople in Australia and New Zealand were the least motivated by a fat paycheck.[25]

We discussed compensation as a motivator earlier. Here we will examine sales quotas and supplementary motivators.

SALES QUOTAS. Many companies set sales quotas prescribing what their sales reps should sell during the year. Quotas can be set on dollar sales, unit volume, margin, selling effort or activity, and product type. Compensation is often tied to the degree of quota fulfillment.

Sales quotas are developed from the annual marketing plan. The company first prepares a sales forecast. This forecast becomes the basis for planning production, work-force size, and financial requirements. Management then establishes sales quotas for its regions and territories, which typically add up to more than the sales forecast. Sales quotas are set higher than the sales forecast to encourage sales managers and salespeople to perform at their best level. If they fail to make their quotas, the company nevertheless might make its sales forecast.

Each area sales manager divides the area's quota among the area's sales reps. There are three schools of thought on quota setting. The *high-quota school* sets quotas higher than what most sales reps will achieve but that are attainable. Its adherents believe that high quotas spur extra effort. The *modest-quota school* sets quotas that a majority of the sales force can achieve. Its adherents feel that the sales force will accept the quotas as fair, attain them, and gain confidence. The *variable-quota school* thinks that individual differences among sales reps warrant high quotas for some, modest quotas for others.

One general view is that a salesperson's quota should be at least equal to the person's last year's sales plus some fraction of the difference between territory sales potential and last year's sales. The more the salesperson reacts favorably to pressure, the higher the fraction should be.

SUPPLEMENTARY MOTIVATORS. Companies use additional motivators to stimulate sales force effort. Periodic *sales meetings* provide a social occasion, a break from routine, a chance to meet and talk with "company brass," and a chance to air feelings and to identify with a larger group. Sales meetings are an important communication and motivational tool.

Companies also sponsor *sales contests* to spur the sales force to a special selling effort above what is normally expected. The awards could be cars, vacations, cash, or recognition. The contest should present a reasonable opportunity for enough salespeople to win. At IBM, about 70% of the sales force qualifies for the 100% Club. Their reward is a three-day trip that includes a recognition dinner and a blue and gold pin. If only a few salespersons can win or almost everyone can win, the contest will fail to spur additional effort. The sales contest period should not be announced in advance. If it is, some salespersons will defer sales and others pad their sales during the period with customer promises to buy that do not materialize after the contest period ends.

Some companies are reaching for less conventional rewards to motivate their sales personnel and having great success:

> Ann Machado, founder and owner of Creative Staffing (an employment services firm), rewards both sales and nonsales employees with expensive dinners, parties, chauffeured shopping sprees, flowers, spa sessions, cooking lessons, and extra vacation time. One might think that her company would need an entire department just to develop and deliver rewards, but Machado's secret is letting people pick the reward they want and outline what they'll do to earn it. Then all she has to do is approve it. "Letting people choose their own rewards and goals empowers them," says Machado.[26]

Evaluating Sales Representatives

We have been describing the *feed-forward* aspects of sales supervision—how management communicates what the sales reps should be doing and motivates them to do it. But good feed-forward requires good *feedback*. And good feedback means getting regular information from sales reps to evaluate their performance.

SOURCES OF INFORMATION. Management obtains information about its sales representatives in several ways. The most important source is sales reports. Additional information comes through personal observation, customers' letters and complaints, customer surveys, and conversations with other sales representatives.

Sales reports are divided between *activity plans* and *write-ups of activity results*. The best example of the former is the *salesperson's work plan,* which sales reps submit a week or month in advance. The plan describes intended calls and routing. This report forces the members of the sales force to plan and schedule their activities, informs management of their whereabouts, and provides a basis for comparing their plans and accomplishments. Sales reps can be evaluated on their ability to "plan their work and work their plan."

Many companies require their sales representatives to develop an annual *territory marketing plan* in which they outline their program for developing new accounts and increasing business from existing accounts. This type of report casts sales reps into the role of market managers and profit centers. Their sales managers study these plans, make suggestions, and use them to develop sales quotas.

Sales reps write up their completed activities on *call reports*. Call reports inform sales management of the salesperson's activities, indicate the status of specific customer accounts, and provide useful information for subsequent calls. Sales representatives also submit expense reports, new-business reports, lost-business reports, and reports on local business and economic conditions.

These reports provide raw data from which sales managers can extract key indicators of sales performance. The key indicators are (1) average number of sales calls per salesperson per day, (2) average sales call time per contact, (3) average revenue per sales call, (4) average cost per sales call, (5) entertainment cost per sales call, (6) percentage of orders per hundred sales calls, (7) number of new customers per period, (8) number of lost customers per period, and (9) sales force cost as a percentage of total sales. These indicators answer several useful questions: Are sales representatives making too few calls per day? Are they spending too much time per call? Are they spending too much on entertainment? Are they closing enough orders per hundred calls? Are they producing enough new customers and holding on to the old customers?

FORMAL EVALUATION OF PERFORMANCE. The sales force's reports along with other observations supply the raw materials for evaluating members of the sales force. Formal evaluation procedures lead to at least three benefits. First, they allow management to communicate their standards for judging sales performance. Second, they force managers to gather comprehensive information about each salesperson. Third, the knowledge that they will be evaluated motivates sales reps to achieve their quotas.

There are several approaches to conducting evaluations.

Current-to-Past Sales Comparisons. One type of evaluation compares a sales representative's current performance to past performance. An example is shown in Table 22-2.

The sales manager can learn many things about John Smith from this table. Smith's total sales increased every year (line 3). This does not necessarily mean that Smith is doing a better job. The product breakdown shows that he has been able to push the sales of product B further than the sales of product A (lines 1 and 2). According to his quotas for the two products (lines 4 and 5), his success in increasing product B sales could be at the expense of product A sales. According to gross profits (lines 6 and 7), the company earns more selling A than B. Smith might be pushing the higher-volume, lower-margin product at the expense of the more profitable product. Although he increased total sales by $1,100 between 1995 and 1996 (line 3), the gross profits on his total sales actually decreased by $580 (line 8).

Sales expense (line 9) shows a steady increase, although total expense as a percentage of total sales seems to be under control (line 10). The upward trend in Smith's total dollar expense does not seem to be explained by any increase in the number of calls (line 11), although it might be related to his success in acquiring new customers (line 14). There is a possibility that in prospecting for new customers, he is neglecting present customers, as indicated by an upward trend in the annual number of lost customers (line 15).

TERRITORY: MIDLAND

SALES REPRESENTATIVE: JOHN SMITH

	1993	1994	1995	1996
1. Net sales product A	$251,300	$253,200	$270,000	$263,100
2. Net sales product B	423,200	439,200	553,900	561,900
3. Net sales total	674,500	692,400	823,900	825,000
4. Percent of quota product A	95.6	92.0	88.0	84.7
5. Percent of quota product B	120.4	122.3	134.9	130.8
6. Gross profits product A	$ 50,260	$ 50,640	$ 54,000	$ 52,620
7. Gross profits product B	42,320	43,920	55,390	56,190
8. Gross profits total	92,580	94,560	109,390	108,810
9. Sales expense	$ 10,200	$ 11,100	$ 11,600	$ 13,200
10. Sales expense to total sales (%)	1.5	1.6	1.4	1.6
11. Number of calls	1,675	1,700	1,680	1,660
12. Cost per call	$ 6.09	$ 6.53	$ 6.90	$ 7.95
13. Average number of customers	320	324	328	334
14. Number of new customers	13	14	15	20
15. Number of lost customers	8	10	11	14
16. Average sales per customer	$ 2,108	$ 2,137	$ 2,512	$ 2,470
17. Average gross profit per customer	$ 289	$ 292	$ 334	$ 326

The last two lines show the level and trend in Smith's sales and gross profits per customer. These figures become more meaningful when they are compared with overall company averages. If Smith's average gross profit per customer is lower than the company's average, he could be concentrating on the wrong customers or not spending enough time with each customer. A review of his annual number of calls (line 11) shows that Smith might be making fewer annual calls than the average salesperson. If distances in his territory are similar to other territories, this could mean that he is not putting in a full workday, he is poor at sales planning and routing, and/or he spends too much time with certain accounts.

Customer Satisfaction Evaluation. John Smith might be quite effective in producing sales but not rate high with his customers. Perhaps he is slightly better than the competitors' salespeople, or his product is better, or he keeps finding new customers to replace others who don't like to deal with him. An increasing number of companies are measuring customer satisfaction not only with their product and customer support service but also with their salespeople. The customers' opinion of the salesperson, product, and service can be measured by mail questionnaires or telephone calls. Company salespeople who score high on satisfying their customers can be given special recognition, awards, or bonuses.

Qualitative Evaluation of Sales Representatives. Evaluations can also assess the salesperson's knowledge of the company, products, customers, competitors, territory, and responsibilities. Personality characteristics can be rated, such as general manner, appearance, speech, and temperament. The sales manager can review any problems in motivation or compliance.[27]

The sales manager can also check that the sales representative knows and observes the law. For example, it is illegal for salespeople to lie to consumers or mislead them about the advantages of buying a product. Under U.S. law, salespeople's statements must match advertising claims. In selling to businesses, salespeople may not offer bribes to purchasing agents or others influencing a sale.

They may not obtain or use competitors' technical or trade secrets through bribery or industrial espionage. Finally, salespeople must not disparage competitors or competing products by suggesting things that are not true.[28]

Each company must decide what would be most useful to know. It needs to communicate these criteria to the sales reps so that they know how their performance is judged and can make an effort to improve it.

PRINCIPLES OF PERSONAL SELLING

We turn now from designing and managing a sales force to the principles of personal selling. Personal selling is an ancient art. It has spawned a large literature and many principles. Effective salespersons have more than instinct; they are trained in methods of analysis and customer management. We will examine three major aspects of personal selling: sales professionalism, negotiation, and relationship marketing.[29]

Sales Professionalism

Today's companies spend hundreds of millions of dollars each year to train their salespeople in the art of selling. Over a million copies of books, cassettes, and videotapes on selling are purchased annually, with such tantalizing titles as *Questions That Make the Sale; Green Light Selling: Your Secret Edge to Winning Sales and Avoiding Dead Ends; You'll Never Get No for an Answer; Secrets of Power Persuasion; What They Don't Teach You in Sales 101; Close! Close! Close! How to Make the Sale; How to Make Money Tomorrow Morning; Samurai Selling;* and *World Class Selling.* One of the most enduring books is Dale Carnegie's *How to Win Friends and Influence People.*

All sales-training approaches try to convert a salesperson from a passive order taker into an active order getter. *Order takers* operate on the following assumptions: Customers know their own needs, resent attempts to influence them, and prefer courteous and self-effacing salespersons. An example of an order-taking mentality would be a Fuller Brush salesperson who knocks on dozens of doors each day, simply asking consumers if they need any brushes.

There are two basic approaches in training salespersons to be *order getters,* a sales-oriented approach and a customer-oriented approach. The *sales-oriented approach* trains the salesperson in high-pressure selling techniques such as those used in selling encyclopedias or automobiles. The techniques include exaggerating the product's merits, criticizing competitive products, using a slick presentation, selling yourself, and offering some price concession to get the order on the spot. This form of selling assumes that the customers are not likely to buy except under pressure, that they are influenced by a slick presentation, and that they will not be sorry after signing the order—or, if they are, that it doesn't matter.

The *customer-oriented approach* trains salespeople in customer problem solving. The salesperson learns how to listen and question in order to identify customer needs and come up with sound product solutions. Presentation skills are secondary to customer-need analysis skills. This approach assumes that customers have latent needs that constitute opportunities, that they appreciate constructive suggestions, and that they will be loyal to sales reps who have their long-term interests at heart. The problem solver is a much more congruent concept for the salesperson under the marketing concept than the hard seller or order taker.

No sales approach works best in all circumstances. Yet most sales-training programs agree on the major steps involved in any effective sales process. These steps are shown in Figure 22-3 and discussed next.[30]

PROSPECTING AND QUALIFYING.
The first step in the selling process is to identify prospects. Although the company will try to supply leads, sales representatives need skill in developing their own leads. Leads can be developed in the following ways:

- Asking current customers for the names of prospects
- Cultivating other referral sources, such as suppliers, dealers, noncompeting sales representatives, bankers, and trade association executives
- Joining organizations to which prospects belong
- Engaging in speaking and writing activities that will draw attention
- Examining data sources (newspapers, directories, CD-ROMs) in search of names
- Using the telephone and mail to find leads
- Dropping in unannounced on various offices (called *cold canvassing*)

Sales reps need to know how to screen out poor leads. The salesperson might phone or write to prospects before deciding whether to visit them. Prospects can be qualified by examining their financial ability, volume of business, special requirements, location, and likelihood of continuous business. The leads can be categorized as cool leads, warm leads, and hot leads, with the hot leads contacted first.

Sometimes companies let employees other than sales representatives do the prospecting. One of the most original recent sales prospecting strategies has come from a rather old-line manufacturing company, John Deere:

JOHN DEERE In 1993 the dwindling demand for farm equipment and the aggressive actions of competitors pushed Deere's managers to create a strategy that involved its hourly assembly workers in finding and approaching sales prospects. Deere sent some of its more experienced and knowledgeable workers to regional trade exhibits across North America to pitch the company's equipment to dealers and farmers. The workers also made unscheduled visits to local farmers to discuss their special problems. Customers perceived these new "reps" as presenting an honest, grass-roots account of what goes into making Deere products. Once the new reps had wooed potential customers with their expertise in advanced manufacturing methods and total quality programs, the company could then decide how to skillfully introduce sales reps at the optimum time to make further presentations or close the sale.[31]

PREAPPROACH.
The salesperson needs to learn as much as possible about the prospect company (what it needs, who is involved in the purchase decision) and its buyers (their personal characteristics and buying styles). The salesperson can consult standard sources (*Moody's, Standard and Poor's, Dun and Bradstreet*), acquaintances, and others to learn about the company. The salesperson should set call objectives, which might be to qualify the prospect, gather information, or make an immediate sale. Another task is to decide on the best *approach,* which might be a personal visit, a phone call, or a letter. The best timing should also be considered because many prospects are busy at certain times. Finally, the salesperson should plan an overall sales strategy for the account.

APPROACH.
The salesperson should know how to greet the buyer to get the relationship off to a good start. The salesperson might consider wearing clothes similar to what buyers wear (for instance, in Texas the men wear open shirts and no ties); show courtesy and attention to the buyer; and avoid distracting manner-

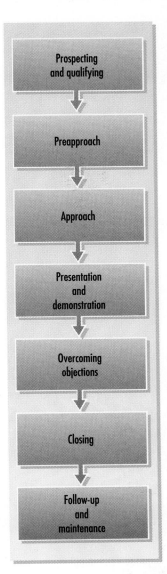

FIGURE 22-3
Major Steps in Effective Selling

Managing
the Sales
Force

isms, such as pacing the floor or staring at the customer. The opening line should be positive; for example, "Mr. Smith, I am Alice Jones from the ABC Company. My company and I appreciate your willingness to see me. I will do my best to make this visit profitable and worthwhile for you and your company." This opening line might be followed by key questions and active listening to understand the buyer and his or her needs better.

PRESENTATION AND DEMONSTRATION. The salesperson now tells the product "story" to the buyer, following the AIDA formula of gaining *attention,* holding *interest,* arousing *desire,* and obtaining *action.* Throughout the presentation, the salesperson emphasizes customer benefits, calling attention to product features as evidence of these benefits. A *benefit* is any advantage, such as lower cost, less work, or more profit for the buyer. A *feature* is a product characteristic, such as weight or size. A common selling mistake is to dwell on product features (a product orientation) instead of customer benefits (a market orientation).

Companies have developed three different styles of sales presentation. The oldest is the *canned approach,* which is a memorized sales talk covering the main points. It is based on stimulus-response thinking; that is, the buyer is passive and can be moved to purchase by the use of the right stimulus words, pictures, terms, and actions. Canned presentations are used primarily in door-to-door and telephone selling. The *formulated approach* is also based on stimulus-response thinking but identifies early the buyer's needs and buying style and then uses a formulated approach to this type of buyer. The salesperson initially draws the buyer into the discussion in a way that reveals the buyer's needs and attitudes. Then the salesperson moves into a formulated presentation that shows how the product will satisfy the buyer's needs. It is not canned but follows a general plan.

The *need-satisfaction approach* starts with a search for the customer's real needs by encouraging the customer to do most of the talking. This approach calls for good listening and problem-solving skills. The salesperson takes on the role of a knowledgeable business consultant hoping to help the customer save money or make more money. IBM's new sales organization uses this approach.

Sales presentations can be improved with demonstration aids such as booklets, flip charts, slides, movies, audio and videocassettes, product samples, and computer-based simulations. Toshiba uses the most advanced technology to demonstrate its CAT and MRI scanners to medical professionals:

TOSHIBA Toshiba's CAT and MRI scanners are extremely large and expensive. A typical installation would fill the average living room; the products are highly technical; and operation specs are changing constantly. To convey information on such complex products, Toshiba's reps introduce customers to the product by way of a sophisticated laptop-based interactive presentation. In it the customer sees elaborate 3-D animations, high-resolution scans, and video clips of the product in operation, as well as narrated testimonials from satisfied customers. The presentation program even features an architectural schematic showing the space requirements needed.[32]

To the extent that the buyer can see or handle the product, he or she will better remember its features and benefits. During the demonstration, the salesperson can draw on five influence strategies:[33]

- ◆ *Legitimacy:* The salesperson emphasizes the reputation and experience of his or her company.
- ◆ *Expertise:* The salesperson shows deep knowledge of the buyer's situation and company's products.
- ◆ *Referent power:* The salesperson builds on any shared characteristics, interests, and acquaintances.

- *Ingratiation:* The salesperson provides personal favors (a free lunch, promotional gratuities) to strengthen affiliation and reciprocity feelings.
- *Impression management:* The salesperson tries to convey favorable impressions of himself or herself.

OVERCOMING OBJECTIONS. Customers almost always pose objections during the presentation or when asked for the order. Their resistance can be psychological or logical. *Psychological resistance* includes resistance to interference, preference for established supply sources or brands, apathy, reluctance to giving up something, unpleasant associations created by the sales rep, predetermined ideas, dislike of making decisions, and neurotic attitude toward money. *Logical resistance* might consist of objections to the price, delivery schedule, or certain product or company characteristics. To handle these objections, the salesperson maintains a positive approach, asks the buyer to clarify the objection, questions the buyer in a way that the buyer has to answer his or her own objection, denies the validity of the objection, or turns the objection into a reason for buying. The salesperson needs training in the broader skills of negotiation, of which handling and overcoming objections is a part.

CLOSING. Now the salesperson attempts to close the sale. Some salespeople do not get to this stage or do not do it well. They lack confidence or feel uncomfortable about asking for the order or do not recognize the right psychological moment to close the sale. Salespersons need to know how to recognize closing signs from the buyer, including physical actions, statements or comments, and questions. Salespersons can use one of several closing techniques. They can ask for the order, recapitulate the points of agreement, offer to help the secretary write up the order, ask whether the buyer wants A or B, get the buyer to make minor choices such as the color or size, or indicate what the buyer will lose if the order is not placed now. The salesperson might offer the buyer specific inducements to close, such as a special price, an extra quantity at no charge, or a token gift.

FOLLOW-UP AND MAINTENANCE. Follow-up and maintenance are necessary if the salesperson wants to ensure customer satisfaction and repeat business. Immediately after closing, the salesperson should cement any necessary details on delivery time, purchase terms, and other matters that are important to the customer. The salesperson should schedule a follow-up call when the initial order is received to make sure there is proper installation, instruction, and servicing. This visit will detect any problems, assure the buyer of the salesperson's interest, and reduce any cognitive dissonance that might have arisen. The salesperson should also develop an account maintenance plan to make sure that the customer is not forgotten or lost.

Negotiation

Much of business-to-business selling involves negotiating skills. The two parties need to reach agreement on the price and the other terms of sale. Salespersons need to win the order without making deep concessions that will hurt profitability.

NEGOTIATION DEFINED. Marketing is concerned with exchange activities and the manner in which the terms of exchange are established. In *routinized exchange,* the terms are established by administered programs of pricing and distribution. In *negotiated exchange,* price and other terms are set via bargaining behavior, in which two or more parties negotiate long-term binding agreements (e.g., joint ventures, franchises, subcontracts, vertical integration).

Although price is the most frequently negotiated issue, other issues include contract completion time; quality of goods and service offered; purchase volume; responsibility for financing, risk taking, promotion, and title; and product safety. The number of negotiation issues is virtually unlimited.

Marketers who find themselves in bargaining situations need certain traits and skills to be effective. The most important traits are preparation and planning skill, knowledge of subject matter being negotiated, ability to think clearly and rapidly under pressure and uncertainty, ability to express thoughts verbally, listening skill, judgment and general intelligence, integrity, ability to persuade others, and patience. These will help the marketer in knowing when to negotiate and how to negotiate.[34]

WHEN TO NEGOTIATE. Lee and Dobler have listed the following circumstances where negotiation is an appropriate procedure for concluding a sale:

1. When many factors bear not only on price, but also on quality and service
2. When business risks cannot be accurately predetermined
3. When a long period of time is required to produce the items purchased
4. When production is interrupted frequently because of numerous change orders[35]

Negotiation is appropriate whenever a *zone of agreement* exists.[36] A zone of agreement exists when there are simultaneously overlapping acceptable outcomes for the parties. This concept is illustrated in Figure 22-4. Suppose two parties are negotiating a price. The seller has a *reservation price, s,* which is the *minimum* he will accept. Any final contract value, *x,* that is below *s* is worse than not reaching an agreement at all. For any $x > s$, the seller receives a surplus. Obviously, the seller desires as large a surplus as possible while maintaining good relations with the buyer. Likewise, the buyer has a reservation price, *b,* that is the *maximum* he will pay; any *x* above *b* is worse than no agreement. For any $x < b$, the buyer receives a surplus. If the seller's reservation price is below the buyer's—that is, $s < b$—then a zone of agreement exists, and the final price will be determined through bargaining.

There is an obvious advantage in knowing the other party's reservation price and in making one's own reservation price seem higher (for a seller) or lower (for a buyer) than it really is. However, the openness with which buyers and sellers reveal their reservation prices depends upon the bargainers' personalities, the negotiation circumstances, and the expectation about future relations.

FIGURE 22-4

The Zone of Agreement

Source: Reprinted by permission of the publishers from The *Art and Science of Negotiation,* by Howard Raiffa, Cambridge, MA: The Belknap Press of Harvard University Press, copyright 1982 by the President and Fellows of Harvard College.

Planning
Marketing
Programs

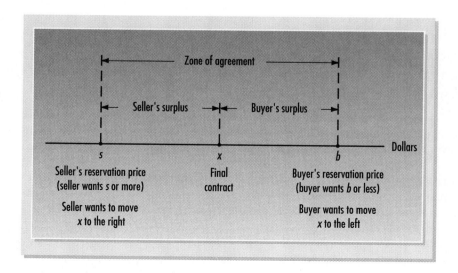

Zone of agreement

Seller's surplus   Buyer's surplus

Dollars

s   x   b

Seller's reservation price   Final   Buyer's reservation price
(seller wants s or more)   contract   (buyer wants b or less)

Seller wants to move   Buyer wants to move
x to the right   x to the left

The Principled-Negotiation Approach to Bargaining

In a research program known as the Harvard Negotiation Project, Roger Fisher and William Ury arrived at four points for conducting "principled negotiations."

1. *Separate the people from the problem*. Because people are involved in the bargaining, it is easy for emotions to become entangled with the objective merits of the issue being negotiated. Framing negotiation issues in terms of the personalities involved rather than the interests of the parties can lead to ineffective bargaining. Negotiation deteriorates when it becomes a test of wills instead of a joint problem-solving activity.

   Separating the people from the problem first involves making accurate perceptions. Each party must understand empathetically the opponents' viewpoint and try to feel the level of emotion with which they hold it. Second, emotions brought into or evolving out of negotiations should be made explicit and acknowledged as legitimate. Openly discussing both parties' emotions while not reacting to an emotional outburst helps keep negotiations from degenerating into unproductive name-calling sessions. Third, clear communications must exist between parties. Listening actively, acknowledging what is being said, communicating about problems rather than the opponent's shortcomings, and directly addressing interests will improve the chances of reaching a satisfactory solution.

2. *Focus on interests, not positions*. The difference between positions and interests is that one's position is something one decided upon, while one's interests are what caused one to adopt the position. Thus a bargaining *position* may be that a contract must include a stiff penalty for late shipment; but the party's *interest* is to maintain an unbroken flow of raw materials. Reconciling interests works better because for every interest there usually exist several possible positions that could satisfy that interest.

3. *Invent options for mutual gain*. Inventing options for mutual gain involves searching for a larger pie rather than arguing over the size of each slice. Looking for options that offer mutual gain helps identify shared interests.

4. *Insist on objective criteria*. When an opposing negotiator is intransigent and argues his position rather than his interests, a good strategy is to insist that the agreement must reflect fair objective criteria independent of either side's position. By discussing objective criteria instead of stubbornly held positions, neither party is yielding to the other; both are yielding to a fair solution. Such objective criteria may be market value, depreciated book value, competing prices, replacement costs, wholesale price index, and so on.

Source: Adapted from Roger Fisher and William Ury, *Getting to Yes: Negotiating Agreement Without Giving In*, rev. ed. (Boston: Houghton Mifflin, 1992), p. 57.

FORMULATING A NEGOTIATION STRATEGY. Negotiation involves preparing a strategic plan before meeting the other party and making good tactical decisions during the negotiation sessions.

❖ A **NEGOTIATION STRATEGY** is a commitment to an overall negotiation approach that has a good chance of achieving the negotiator's objectives.

For example, some negotiators pursue a "hard" strategy with opponents, while others maintain that a "soft" strategy yields more favorable results. Fisher and Ury propose another strategy, that of "principled negotiation." (For more on this topic, see the Marketing Insight titled "The Principled-Negotiation Approach to Bargaining.")[37]

BARGAINING TACTICS DURING NEGOTIATIONS. Negotiators use a variety of tactics when bargaining. Bargaining tactics can be defined as maneuvers to be made at specific points in the bargaining process. Threats, bluffs, last-chance offers, hard initial offers, and other tactics occur in bargaining. Several other classic bargaining tactics are listed in Table 22-3 on the next page.

Fisher and Ury have offered tactical advice that is consistent with their strategy of principled negotiation. Their first piece of tactical advice concerns what should be done if the other party is more powerful. The best tactic is to

TABLE 22-3 CLASSIC BARGAINING TACTICS

Acting Crazy	Put on a good show by visibly demonstrating your emotional commitment to your position. This increases your credibility and may give the opponent a justification to settle on your terms.
Big Pot	Leave yourself a lot of room to negotiate. Make high demands at the beginning. After making concessions, you'll still end up with a larger payoff than if you started too low.
Get a Prestigious Ally	The ally can be a person or a project that is prestigious. You try to get the opponent to accept less because the person/object he or she will be involved with is prestigious.
The Well Is Dry	Take a stand and tell the opponent you have no more concessions to make.
Limited Authority	You negotiate in good faith with the opponent, and when you're ready to sign the deal, you say, "I have to check with my boss."
Whipsaw/Auction	You let several competitors know you're negotiating with them at the same time. Schedule competitors' appointments with you for the same time and keep them all waiting to see you.
Divide and Conquer	If you're negotiating with the opponent's team, sell one member of the team on your proposals. That person will help you sell the other members of the team.
Get Lost/Stall for Time	Leave the negotiation completely for a while. Come back when things are getting better and try to renegotiate then. Time period can be long (say you're going out of town) or short (go to the bathroom to think).
Wet Noodle	Give no emotional or verbal response to the opponent. Don't respond to his or her force or pressure. Sit there like a wet noodle and keep a "poker face."
Be Patient	If you can afford to outwait the opponent, you'll probably win big.
Let's Split the Difference	The person who first suggests this has the least to lose.
Trial Balloon	You release your possible/contemplated decision through a so-called reliable source before the decision is actually made. This enables you to test reactions to your descision.
Surprises	Keep the opponent off balance by a drastic, dramatic, sudden shift in your tactics. Never be predictable—keep the opponent from anticipating your moves.

Source: From a list of over 200 tactics prepared by Professor Donald W. Hendon of the University of North Alabama in his seminar "How to Negotiate and Win."

know one's BATNA—Best Alternative to a Negotiated Agreement. By identifying one's alternatives if a settlement is not reached, the company sets a standard against which any offer can be measured. Knowing its BATNA protects the company from being pressured into accepting unfavorable terms from a more powerful opponent.

Another set of bargaining tactics are responses to opposition tactics that are intended to deceive, distort, or otherwise influence the bargaining. What tactic should be used when the other side uses a threat or a take-it-or-leave-it tactic, or seats the other party on the side of the table with the sun in his eyes? A negotiator should recognize the tactic, raise the issue explicitly, and question the tactic's legitimacy and desirability—in other words, negotiate over it. If negotiating fails, the company should resort to its BATNA and terminate the negotiation until the other side ceases to employ these tactics. Meeting such tactics with defending principles is more productive than counterattacking with tricky tactics.

Relationship Marketing

The principles of personal selling and negotiation as described are *transaction-oriented* because they aim to help salespeople close a specific sale with a customer. But in many cases, the company is not seeking simply a sale but rather has targeted a major customer account that it would like to win and serve. The company would like to demonstrate to the account that it has the capabilities to serve the account's needs in a superior way, particularly if the two parties can form a committed relationship. The type of selling to establish a long-term collaborative relationship is more complex than that described earlier in this chapter. Neil Rackham has developed a method that he calls *SPIN selling* (Situation/Problem/Implication/Need-Payoff). Companies can use SPIN selling when they are seeking not an immediate sale to the customer but rather a long-term, mutually beneficial relationship. A long-term commitment to working together requires the development of a whole set of agreements. Thus, according to Rackham, the selling process moves from preliminaries to investigating the prospect's problems and needs, then demonstrating the supplier's capabilities, and finally obtaining a long-term commitment.[38]

More companies today are moving their emphasis from transaction marketing to *relationship marketing* (see Chapter 2). The days of the "lone salesperson" working his or her territory and being guided only by a sales quota and a compensation plan are numbered. Today's customers are large and often global. They prefer suppliers who can sell and deliver a coordinated set of products and services to many locations; who can quickly solve problems that arise in different locations; and who can work closely with customer teams to improve products and processes. Unfortunately, most companies are not set up to meet these requirements. Their products are sold by separate sales forces that don't work together easily. The company's technical people may not be willing to spend time to educate a customer.

Companies recognize that sales teamwork will increasingly be the key to winning and maintaining accounts. Yet they recognize that asking their people for teamwork doesn't produce it. They need to revise their compensation system to give credit for work on shared accounts. They must set up better goals and measures for their sales force. And they must emphasize the importance of teamwork in their training programs, while at the same time honoring the importance of individual initiative.[39]

Relationship marketing is based on the premise that important accounts need focused and continuous attention. Salespeople working with key customers must do more than call when they think customers might be ready to place orders. They should call or visit at other times, taking customers to dinner, making useful suggestions about their business, and so on. They should monitor these key accounts, know their problems, and be ready to serve them in a number of ways.

Here are the main steps in establishing a relationship marketing program in a company:

- *Identify the key customers meriting relationship marketing.* The company can choose the five or ten largest customers and designate them for relationship marketing. Additional customers who show exceptional growth can be added to the list later on.
- *Assign a skilled relationship manager to each key customer.* The salesperson servicing the customer should receive training in relationship marketing.

Managing
the Sales
Force

When—and How—to Use Relationship Marketing

Barbara Jackson argues that relationship marketing is not effective in all situations but is extremely effective in the right situations. She sees transaction marketing as more appropriate with customers who have a short time horizon and low switching costs, such as buyers of commodities. A customer buying steel can buy from one of several steel suppliers and choose the one offering the best terms. The fact that one steel supplier has been particularly attentive or responsive does not automatically earn it the next sale; its terms have to be competitive.

In contrast, relationship marketing investments pay off handsomely with customers who have long time horizons and high switching costs, such as buyers of office automation systems. Presumably, the customer for a major system carefully researches the competing suppliers and chooses one from whom it can expect good long-term service and state-of-the-art technology. Both the customer and the supplier invest a lot of money and time in the relationship. The customer would find it costly and risky to switch to another vendor, and the seller would find that losing this customer would be a major loss. Relationship marketing has the greatest payoff with these customers, whom Jackson calls "lost-for-good customers."

In lost-for-good situations, the challenge is different for the in-supplier versus out-supplier. The in-supplier's strategy is to make switching difficult for the customer. The in-supplier will develop product systems that are incompatible with competitive products and will install proprietary ordering systems that facilitate inventory management and delivery. The out-supplier will design product systems that are compatible with the customer's system, are easy to install and learn, save the customer a lot of money, and promise to improve through time.

Anderson and Narus believe that transaction versus relationship marketing is not so much an issue of the type of industry as it is an issue of the particular customer's wishes. Some customers value a high service bundle and will stay with that supplier for a long time. Other customers want to cut their costs and will switch suppliers for lower costs. In this case, the company can still try to retain the customer by agreeing to reduce the price, provided the customer is willing to accept fewer services. For example, the customer may forego free delivery, some training, and so on. This customer would be treated on a transaction basis rather than on a relationship-building basis. As long as the company cuts its own costs by as much or more than its price reduction, the transaction-oriented customer will still be profitable.

Sources: Barbara Bund Jackson, *Winning and Keeping Industrial Customers: The Dynamics of Customer Relationships* (Lexington, MA: D. C. Heath, 1985); and James C. Anderson and James A. Narus, "Partnering as a Focused Market Strategy," *California Management Review*, Spring 1991, pp. 95–113.

♦ *Develop a clear job description for relationship managers.* The job description should describe the relationship managers' reporting relationships, objectives, responsibilities, and evaluation criteria. The relationship manager is responsible for the client, is the focal point for all information about the client, and is the mobilizer of company services for the client. Each relationship manager will have only one or a few relationships to manage.

♦ *Appoint an overall manager to supervise the relationship managers.* This person will develop job descriptions, evaluation criteria, and resource support to increase relationship managers' effectiveness.

♦ *Each relationship manager must develop long-range and annual customer-relationship plans.* The annual relationship plan will state objectives, strategies, specific actions, and required resources.

When a relationship management program is properly implemented, the organization will begin to focus as much on managing its customers as on managing its products. At the same time, companies should realize that while there is a strong and warranted move toward relationship marketing, it is not effective in all situations. Ultimately, companies must judge which segments and which specific customers will respond profitably to relationship management. (For some guidelines, see the Marketing Insight on page 712 titled "When—and How—to Use Relationship Marketing.")

SUMMARY

1. Sales personnel serve as a company's link to its customers. The sales rep *is* the company to many of its customers, and it is the rep who brings back to the company much-needed information about the customer.

2. Designing the sales force requires decisions regarding sales force objectives, strategy, structure, size, and compensation. The sales force's objectives may include prospecting, targeting, communicating, selling, servicing, information gathering, and allocating. Determining the sales force strategy requires choosing the mix of selling approaches that are most effective (solo selling, team selling, conference selling, and/or seminar selling). Choosing the sales force structure entails dividing territories by geography, product, or market (or some combination of these). Estimating how large the sales force needs to be involves estimating the total workload and how many sales hours (and hence salespeople) will be needed. Compensating the sales force entails determining what types of salaries, commissions, bonuses, expense accounts, and benefits to give, and how much weight customer satisfaction should have in determining a sales rep's total compensation.

3. There are five steps involved in managing the sales force: (1) recruiting and selecting sales representatives; (2) training the representatives in sales techniques and in the company's products, policies, and customer satisfaction orientation; (3) supervising the sales force, helping them to plan their time efficiently; (4) motivating the sales force, balancing quotas, monetary rewards, and supplementary motivators; and (5) evaluating sales reps' individual and group performance.

4. Effective salespeople are trained in the methods of analysis and customer management, as well as the art of sales professionalism. No sales approach works best in all circumstances, but most sales-training programs agree that selling is a seven-step process: prospecting and qualifying customers; preapproach; approach; presentation and demonstration; overcoming objections; closing; and follow-up and maintenance. Another aspect of selling is negotiation, the art of arriving at transaction terms that satisfy both parties. A third aspect is relationship marketing, which focuses on developing long-term, mutually beneficial relationships between two parties.

CONCEPT APPLICATIONS

1. It has been said that there are two parts to every sale—the part performed by the salesperson and the part performed for the salesperson by his or her organization. What should the company provide for the salesperson to help increase total sales? How does the sales manager's job differ from the sales rep's job?

2. Organizations that achieve good sales and profits year after year—like Dell Computer, Nordstrom, Merck, Four Seasons (hotel chain), Vanguard Group, Wal-Mart, Midwest Express, Hertz, Home Depot, UPS, and Du Pont—do so in part because they have good sales management. For example:

   ◆ *Dell Computer* keeps track of customers through the use of computer technology. Dell offers warranties, upgrades, and lifetime technical support for users. The computers arrive already loaded with an operating system. The company also conducts intense training programs that help the company's marketers sell computers and advanced technology via telemarketing and direct mail.

♦ *Nordstrom* gives intense, personalized attention to customers and maintains a database on previous purchases so that its sales associates can better assist customers with future purchases. Customers remain very loyal to Nordstrom.

Choose any three of the remaining companies and prepare a brief report (three to five pages) on how good sales management contributes to their overall success.

3. A packaged-goods company is putting together a training program for its sales representatives. The company has established the program's design and objectives and is currently working on the evaluation part of the program. The team is aware of at least two errors that may affect evaluations:

♦ *Halo effect:* Occurs when trainees (or trainers or evaluators) are overly impressed by one or two major features of the session and lose their critical objectivity about other factors

♦ *Boomerang effect:* Sometimes results when trainees purposefully give opposite impressions of what they really feel just to influence or sabotage the evaluation process

What other kinds of errors should the team be aware of? How can it design its evaluation program to avoid these kinds of errors?

4. Suppose a salesperson can make 1,600 calls a year. If he or she has been closing $420,000 worth of business a year, how many calls can the sales rep make to a $10,000-a-year account without diluting the total business closed during the year?

5. A district sales manager voiced the following complaint at a sales meeting: "The average salesperson costs our company $40,000 in compensation and expenses. Why can't we buy a few less $40,000 full-page ads in *Time* magazine and use the money to hire more people? Surely one individual working a full year can sell more products than a one-page ad in one issue of *Time*" Evaluate this argument.

6. Should sales representatives participate in the establishment of a sales quota for their territories? What are the advantages and disadvantages of their participation?

7. An industrial company has recently switched its sales force structure. Previously, it used manufacturers' representatives; now it has hired and is developing its own sales force. In groups of five, develop a compensation plan for the sales force.

8. Pharmaceutical companies provide a valuable service for physicians and the health care community. They provide the capital used to discover new and advanced drugs to increase the quality of life and the quality of health care. Without funding from the private sector and the competitive forces of a free-market society, we would not have many of the drugs available today. However, pharmaceutical companies' marketing practices and selling techniques do affect physicians' prescribing habits and, ultimately, the cost of health care. These pharmaceutical concerns are also struggling to meet the profit demands of stockholders while seeking to develop quality products.

Individually or in small groups, brainstorm some ways in which sales representatives can meet the financial goals established by management while maintaining high ethical standards. What ethical sales promotions should sales reps in this industry use? What could the pharmaceutical industry do to keep the present marketing and sales system from coming under greater government regulation and control?

9. Being a successful sales manager is often a function of having the right sales reps to manage. Imagine that you are a sales manager, and write three "yes" or "no" questions that you could ask yourself about the person you have just interviewed for a business-to-business sales position. Make sure your questions focus on qualities that you expect to find in your sales force. After composing your three questions, get together in your teams of five and make a list of about ten questions that will help you identify good job candidates.

10. For each situation, indicate whether the sales force should be compensated more on a straight-salary plan or more on a commission plan.

a. Nonselling duties (e.g., providing technical services, giving time to public relations, setting up displays) are most important.
b. The selling task is complex and involves a sales team, such as in the selling of data processing equipment or heavy machinery.
c. The key objective is the generation of greater sales volume through new accounts.
d. The company desires highly entrepreneurial sales reps who will not need much supervision.
e. Sales show a marked seasonal pattern, with sales very high in some periods and very low in others.
f. The company's major goal is increased sales coming from one-time transactions.
g. The company actively seeks long-term relationships with its customers and excellence in customer service.
h. The selling task is so routine that it amounts to order taking, such as in wholesaling and the selling of staple consumer goods.

NOTES

1. See Rolph Anderson, *Essentials of Personal Selling: The New Professionalism* (Englewood Cliffs, NJ: Prentice Hall, 1995); and Douglas J. Dalrymple, *Sales Management: Concepts and Cases,* 5th ed. (New York: John Wiley, 1994).
2. Adapted from Robert N. McMurry, "The Mystique of Super-Salesmanship," *Harvard Business Review,* March–April 1961, p. 114. Also see William C. Moncrief, III, "Selling Activity and Sales Position Taxonomies for Industrial Salesforces," *Journal of Marketing Research,* August 1986, pp. 261–70.
3. For estimates of the cost of sales calls, see *Sales Force Compensation* (Chicago: Dartnell's 27th Survey, 1992), and *Sales and Marketing Management's* 1993 sales manager's budget planner (June 28, 1993), pp. 3–75.
4. Jaclyn Fierman, "The Death and Rebirth of the Salesman," *Fortune,* July 25, 1994, pp. 80–91.
5. Christopher Power, "Smart Selling: How Companies Are Winning Over Today's Tougher Customer," *Business Week,* August 3, 1992, pp. 46–48.
6. Ira Sager, "The Few, the True, the Blue," *Business Week,* May 30, 1994, pp. 124–26; Geoffrey Brewer, "IBM Gets User-Friendly," *Sales and Marketing Management,* July 1994, p. 13.
7. For estimates of sales reps' salaries, see *Sales and Marketing Management,* "What Salespeople Are Paid," February 1995, pp. 30–31.
8. Luis R. Gomez-Mejia, David B. Balkin, and Robert L. Cardy, *Managing Human Resources* (Englewood Cliffs, NJ: Prentice Hall, 1995), pp. 416–18.
9. "What Salespeople Are Paid," *Sales and Marketing Management,* February 1995, pp. 30–31; Power, "Smart Selling" pp. 46–48; William Keenan, Jr., ed., *The Sales and Marketing Management Guide to Sales Compensation Planning: Commissions, Bonuses and Beyond* (Chicago: Probus Publishing, 1994).
10. George H. Lucas, Jr., A. Parasuraman, Robert A. Davis, and Ben M. Enis, "An Empirical Study of Sales Force Turnover," *Journal of Marketing,* July 1987, pp. 34–59.
11. See Charles Garfield, *Peak Performers: The New Heroes of American Business* (New York: Avon Books, 1986); "What Makes a Supersalesperson?" *Sales and Marketing Management,* August 23, 1984, p. 86; "What Makes a Top Performer?" *Sales and Marketing Management,* May 1989; and Timothy J. Trow, "The Secret of a Good Hire: Profiling," *Sales and Marketing Management,* May 1990, pp. 44–55.
12. McMurry, "Super-Salesmanship," p. 117.
13. McMurry, "Super-Salesmanship," p. 118.
14. David Mayer and Herbert M. Greenberg, "What Makes a Good Salesman?" *Harvard Business Review,* July-August 1964, pp. 119–25.
15. James M. Comer and Alan J. Dubinsky, *Managing the Successful Sales Force* (Lexington, MA: Lexington Books, 1985), pp. 5–25.
16. From an address given by Donald R. Keough at the 27th Annual Conference of the Super-Market Institute, Chicago, April 26–29, 1964.
17. Robert L. Lindstrom, "Training Hits the Road," *Sales and Marketing Management,* June 1995, pp. 10–14.
18. *Sales Force Compensation* (Chicago: Dartnell's 25th Survey, 1989) p. 13.
19. See John F. Magee, "Determining the Optimum Allocation of Expenditures for Promotional Effort with Operations Research Methods," in *The Frontiers of Marketing Thought and Science,* ed. Frank M. Bass (Chicago: American Marketing Association, 1958), pp. 140–56.
20. Michael R. W. Bommer, Brian F. O'Neil, and Beheruz N. Sethna, "A Methodology for Optimizing Selling Time of Salespersons," *Journal of Marketing Theory and Practice,* Spring 1994, pp. 61–75.
21. See Thomas Blackshear and Richard E. Plank, "The Impact of Adaptive Selling on Sales Effectiveness Within the Pharmaceutical Industry," *Journal of Marketing Theory and Practice,* Summer 1994, pp. 106–25.
22. "Are Salespeople Gaining More Selling Time?" *Sales and Marketing Management,* July 1986, p. 29.
23. James A. Narus and James C. Anderson, "Industrial Distributor Selling: The Roles of Outside and Inside Sales," *Industrial Marketing Management,* 15 (1986), 55–62.
24. See Gilbert A. Churchill, Jr., Neil M. Ford, and Orville C. Walker, Jr., *Sales Force Management: Planning, Implementation and Control,* 4th ed. (Homewood, IL: Irwin, 1993).
25. "What Motivates U.S. Salespeople?" *American Salesman,* February 1994, pp. 25, 30.
26. "A Gift for Rewards," *Sales and Marketing Management,* March 1995, pp. 35–36.
27. See Philip M. Posdakoff and Scott B. MacKenzie, "Organizational Citizenship Behaviors and Sales Unit Effectiveness," *Journal of Marketing Research,* August 1994, pp. 351–63.

28. For further reading, see Dorothy Cohen, *Legal Issues in Marketing Decision Making* (Cincinnati, OH: South-Western, 1995).

29. For an excellent summary of the skills needed today by sales representatives and sales managers, see Rolph Anderson and Bert Rosenbloom, "The World Class Sales Manager: Adapting to Global Megatrends," *Journal of Global Marketing,* 5, no. 4 (1992), 11–22.

30. Some of the following discussion is based on W. J. E. Crissy, William H. Cunningham, and Isabella C. M. Cunningham, *Selling: The Personal Force in Marketing* (New York: John Wiley, 1977), pp. 119–29.

31. Norton Paley, "Cultivating Customers," *Sales and Marketing Management,* September 1994, pp. 31–32.

32. Lindstrom, "Training Hits the Road," pp. 10–14.

33. See Rosann L. Spiro and William D. Perreault, Jr., "Influence Use by Industrial Salesmen: Influence Strategy Mixes and Situational Determinants," paper, Graduate School of Business Administration, University of North Carolina, 1976.

34. For additional reading, see Howard Raiffa, *The Art and Science of Negotiation* (Cambridge, MA: Harvard University Press, 1982); Max H. Bazerman and Margaret A. Neale, *Negotiating Rationally* (New York: Free Press, 1992); James C. Freund, *Smart Negotiating* (New York: Simon & Schuster, 1992); and Frank L. Acuff, *How to Negotiate Anything with Anyone Anywhere Around the World* (New York: American Management Association, 1993).

35. See Donald W. Dobler, *Purchasing and Materials Management,* 5th ed. (New York: McGraw-Hill, 1990).

36. This discussion of zone of agreement is fully developed in Raiffa, *The Art and Science of Negotiation.*

37. Roger Fisher and William Ury, *Getting to Yes: Negotiating Agreement Without Giving In,* rev. ed. (Boston: Houghton Mifflin, 1992).

38. Neil Rackham, *SPIN Selling* (New York: McGraw-Hill, 1988).

39. See Frank V. Cespedes, Stephen X. Doyle, and Robert J. Freedman, "Teamwork for Today's Selling," *Harvard Business Review,* March–April 1989, pp. 44–54, 58. Also see Cespedes, *Concurrent Marketing: Integrating Product, Sales, and Service* (Boston: Harvard Business School Press, 1995).

MANAGING DIRECT AND ONLINE MARKETING

Mass marketing is obsolete. This is due to changing households, complex technology-based products, new ways to shop and pay, intense competition, additional channels, and declining advertising effectiveness. Personal marketing is what the customers want.

JEFF SNEDDEN, MCCAW CELLULAR

❖

The emergence of 1:1 media will produce a totally new kind of business competition— 1:1 marketing. In the 1:1 future, you will find yourself competing for business one customer at a time. . . . You will not be trying to sell a single product to as many customers as possible. Instead, you'll be trying to sell a single customer as many products as possible— over a long period of time, and across different product lines.

DON PEPPERS AND MARTHA ROGERS, *THE ONE-TO-ONE FUTURE*

❖

Many of the promotional tools we examined in Chapters 21 and 22 were developed in the context of *mass marketing:* Companies sought to reach thousands or even millions of buyers with a single product and a standard message. Thus, Procter & Gamble originally launched Crest toothpaste in one version with a single message ("Crest fights cavities"), hoping that 250 million Americans would learn the message and buy the brand. P&G did not need to know its customers' names or anything else about them, only that they wanted to take good care of their teeth.

Of course, Crest competed against other brands in the market, but each brand used the same mass-marketing strategy of a single brand and a single message. After some years, competition forced each mass marketer to add brand line extensions (tartar-control toothpaste, teeth-whitening toothpaste, fresh-breath toothpaste, and so forth) and different ads for different age and lifestyle groups. Some competitors spotted niche opportunities and created niche brands. Still, most marketers did not know their individual customers' names. Most marketing communications consisted of monologue directed at, not dialogue with, customers.

Yet not all companies were mass marketers. Among the businesses that gathered customer names and sold direct were catalog companies, direct mailers, and telemarketers. Their selling tools were mainly the mail and the telephone. Today, new media—computers, modems, fax machines, e-mail, the Internet, and online services—permit more sophisticated direct marketing. Their arrival and reasonable costs have substantially enlarged direct marketing opportunities. Companies can now talk directly with customers and customize their products to meet their customers' needs.

In this chapter, we examine the nature, role, and growing applications of direct marketing and online marketing. We address the following questions:

- **What are the benefits of direct marketing?**
- **How do customer databases support direct marketing?**
- **What channels do direct marketers use to reach individual prospects and customers?**
- **What marketing opportunities do online channels provide?**
- **How can companies use integrated direct marketing for competitive advantage?**
- **What public and ethical issues do direct and online marketing raise?**

THE GROWTH AND BENEFITS OF DIRECT MARKETING

The Direct Marketing Association (DMA) defines *direct marketing* as follows:

> ❖ **DIRECT MARKETING** is an interactive marketing system that uses one or more advertising media to effect a measurable response and/or transaction at any location.

This definition emphasizes a measurable response, typically a customer order. Thus direct marketing is sometimes called *direct-order marketing*.

Today, many direct marketers see direct marketing as playing a broader role, that of building a long-term relationship with the customer (*direct relationship marketing*).[1] Direct marketers occasionally send birthday cards, informational materials, or small premiums to select members in their customer base. Airlines, hotels, and other businesses are building strong customer relationships through frequency award programs (for example, frequent-flier miles) and other programs.

The Growth of Direct Marketing and Electronic Shopping

Sales produced through traditional direct-marketing channels (catalogs, direct mail, and telemarketing) have been growing rapidly. While U.S. retail sales grow around 3% annually, catalog/direct-mail sales are growing at around 7 percent. These sales include sales to the consumer market (50%), business-to-business sales (29%), and fund-raising by charitable institutions (21%). Sales through catalog/direct mail are estimated at over $252 billion annually. Per capita annual direct sales are $461.[2]

The extraordinary growth of direct marketing in the consumer market is a response to the marketing reality of the 1990s. Market "demassification" has resulted in an ever-increasing number of market niches with distinct preferences. Higher costs of driving, traffic congestion, parking headaches, lack of time, a shortage of retail sales help, and queues at checkout counters all encourage at-home shopping. Consumers are responding favorably to direct marketers' toll-free phone numbers, their willingness to accept telephone orders at night and on weekends, and their commitment to customer service. The growth of 24-hour and 48-hour delivery via Federal Express, Airborne, DHL, and other express carriers has made ordering fast and easy. In addition, many chain stores have dropped slower-moving specialty items (for example, back scratchers), thus creating an opportunity for direct marketers to promote these items directly to interested buyers. Finally, the growth of affordable computer power and customer databases has enabled direct marketers to single out the best prospects for any product they wish to sell.

Direct mail and telemarketing have also grown rapidly in business-to-business marketing, partly in response to the high and increasing costs of reaching business markets through the sales force. Table 23-1 shows the typical cost per contact of reaching business markets with different media. Clearly, when out-of-town field sales calls cost $250 per contact, they should be made only to high-potential customers and prospects. Lower cost-per-contact media—such as telemarketing, direct mail, and the newer electronic media—will prove more cost effective in reaching and selling to more prospects and customers.

Electronic communication and advertising media are showing rapid growth indeed. The creation of the "information superhighway" promises to revolutionize commerce. *Electronic commerce* is the general term for a buying and selling

Personal sales calls	$250	(out of town)	**TABLE 23-1**
	52	(local)	
Seminars, trade show exhibits	40		**TYPICAL COST PER CONTACT**
Salesperson writes a single letter	25		**OF REACHING BUSINESS**
Showroom or counter selling	16		**MARKETS WITH DIFFERENT**
Yellow Pages large display ad	16		**MEDIA VEHICLES**
Telephone order desk	9	(toll-free number)	
	6	(local)	
Mass phoning program	8	(national)	
	4	(local)	
Direct mail	.30		
Selective media	.15	(ad in trade publication)	
Mass media	.01–.05	(radio, newspaper, TV)	

Source: John Klein & Associates, Inc., Cleveland, OH, 1988.

process that is supported by electronic means. *Electronic markets* are sponsored information utilities that (1) describe the products and services offered by sellers and (2) allow buyers to search for information, identify what they need or want, and place orders using a credit card. The product is then delivered physically (to the customer's house or office) or electronically (for example, software can be sent directly to a customer's computer).

The electronic shopping explosion is all around us.[3] Here are some examples:

A reporter wants to buy a 35 mm camera. She turns on her computer and clicks on "Shopper's Advantage," then clicks on cameras, then on 35 mm cameras. A list of all the major brands appears, along with information about each brand. She can retrieve a photo of each camera and reviews by experts. Finding the camera she wants, she places the order by typing in her credit-card number, address, and preferred shipping mode.

An affluent investor decides to do his own banking and investing. He signs onto an on-line stock sales and information service that displays current stock prices. He then retrieves relevant company reports and places buy and sell orders.

An executive is planning a trip to London and wants to locate a hotel that meets her needs. She signs onto the Easy SABRE program and inputs her criteria (rate, location, amenities, safety). The computer produces a list of appropriate hotels, and she can book a room once she has made her choice. Eventually, videos giving a "guided tour" of each hotel will be included in the program.

An elderly man with high blood pressure needs to locate a specialist. Turning on his computer, he visits an electronic market listing various physicians, their education, years of experience, and their rates. He chooses a doctor, then phones the physician's office for an appointment.

It is too early to tell exactly how many consumers will turn to electronic shopping, but the prospects are encouraging. Today over 30% of the 97 million U.S. households have a PC. McKinsey & Company estimates that sales from electronic shopping in the United States will reach $4 billion to $5 billion a year by 2003. What are the implications of electronic commerce for marketing theory and practice? Here are some predictions:[4]

- Electronic markets will permit prices to change faster. Hotels and airlines can change their prices daily as a function of demand and supply, a practice known as *yield management pricing*. Electronic marketers can customize their price for different buyers depending on the buyer's purchases to date and other factors. Consumers will be more aware of what an item costs throughout the world at any particular time, thus tending to narrow price differences.

- Electronic shopping will change the role of "place" in marketing, in that consumers can order clothing, electronics, flowers, and other items from anywhere and at any time, without going to a store. Electronic markets will result in the need for fewer intermediaries between manufacturers and consumers, a process known as *retail disintermediation*.

- Shoppers will have instant access to information about competitive products, as well as to electronic communities that exchange information and experiences about product categories. As a result, advertising will be designed more to inform and less to persuade than is currently the case.

The Benefits of Direct Marketing

Direct marketing benefits customers in a number of ways. Consumers report that home shopping is fun, convenient, and hassle-free. It saves time and introduces them to a larger selection of merchandise. They can do comparative shopping by browsing through mail catalogs and online shopping services, and can order goods for themselves or others. Industrial customers also cite a number of advantages; they particularly like learning about available products and services without tying up time in meeting salespeople.

Sellers also benefit. Direct marketers can buy a mailing list containing the names of almost any group: left-handed people, overweight people, millionaires, and so on. They can then personalize and customize their messages. According to Pierre Passavant: "We will store hundreds . . . of messages in memory. We will select ten thousand families with twelve or twenty or fifty specific characteristics and send them very individualized laser-printed letters."[5] Furthermore, direct marketers can build a continuous relationship with each customer. The parents of the newborn baby will receive periodic mailings describing new clothes, toys, and other goods as the child grows. (For example, Nestlé's baby food division continuously builds a database of new mothers and mails six personalized packages of gifts and advice at key stages in the baby's life.) Direct marketing can be timed to reach prospects at the right moment, and direct-marketing material receives higher readership because it is sent to more interested prospects. Direct marketing permits the testing of alternative media and messages in search of the most cost-effective approach. Direct marketing also makes the direct marketer's offer and strategy less visible to competitors. Finally, direct marketers can measure responses to their campaigns to decide which have been the most profitable.

CUSTOMER DATABASES AND DIRECT MARKETING

Don Peppers and Martha Rogers recently listed the main differences between mass marketing and what they call *one-to-one marketing* (Table 23-2).[6] Companies that know their individual customers can customize their product, offer, message, shipment method, and payment method to maximize customer appeal. And today's companies have a very powerful tool to gather the names, addresses, and other pertinent information about individual customers and prospects: the customer database.

❖ A **CUSTOMER DATABASE** is an organized collection of comprehensive data about individual customers or prospects that is current, accessible, and actionable for such marketing purposes as lead generation, lead qualification, sale of a product or service, or maintenance of customer relationships. **DATABASE MARKETING** is the process of building, maintaining, and using customer databases and other databases (products, suppliers, resellers) for the purpose of contacting and transacting.

TABLE 23-2	MASS MARKETING VERSUS ONE-TO-ONE MARKETING

MASS MARKETING	ONE-TO-ONE MARKETING
Average customer	Individual customer
Customer anonymity	Customer profile
Standard product	Customized market offering
Mass production	Customized production
Mass distribution	Individualized distribution
Mass advertising	Individualized message
Mass promotion	Individualized incentives
One-way message	Two-way messages
Economies of scale	Economies of scope
Share of market	Share of customer
All customers	Profitable customers
Customer attraction	Customer retention

Source: Adapted from Don Peppers and Martha Rogers, *The One-to-One Future* (New York: Doubleday/Currency, 1993).

Managing
Direct and
Online Marketing

Many companies confuse a customer mailing list with a customer database. A *customer mailing list* is simply a set of names, addresses, and telephone numbers. A customer database contains much more information. In business-to-business marketing, the salesperson's customer profile contains the products and services the customer has bought; past volumes and prices; key contacts (and their ages, birthdays, hobbies, and favorite foods); competitive suppliers; status of current contracts; estimated customer expenditures for the next few years; and qualitative assessment of competitive strengths and weaknesses in selling and servicing the account. In consumer marketing, the customer database contains an individual's demographics (age, income, family members, birthdays), psychographics (activities, interests, and opinions), past purchases, and other relevant information. For example, the catalog company Fingerhut possesses some 1,400 pieces of information about each of the 30 million households in its massive customer database.

Database marketing is frequently used by business-to-business marketers and service retailers (hotels, banks, and airlines). It is used less often by packaged-goods retailers (Wal-Mart, Waldenbooks) and consumer-packaged-goods companies, though some (Quaker Oats, Ralston Purina, and Nabisco among them) have been experimenting in this area. A well-developed customer database is a proprietary asset that can give the company a competitive edge.

Armed with the information in its customer database, a company can achieve much more target-market precision than it can under mass marketing, segment marketing, or niche marketing. The company can identify small groups of customers to receive fine-tuned marketing offers and communications. Lands' End, for example, uses a technique known as "data mining" to identify different groups of catalog clothing purchasers; at last count, it had identified 5,200 different segments! According to Donnelley Marketing Inc.'s annual survey of promotional practices, 56% of manufacturers and retailers currently have or are building a database, an additional 10% plan to do so, and 85% believe they'll need database marketing to be competitive past the year 2000.[7]

Companies use their databases in four ways:

1. *Identifying prospects:* Many companies generate sales leads by advertising their product or offer. The ad generally has some sort of response feature, such as a business reply card or toll-free phone number. The database is built from these responses. (For more on this topic, see the Marketing Insight titled "Where Do the Data in a Database Come From?") The company sorts through the database to identify the best prospects, then reaches them by mail, phone, or personal calls in an attempt to convert them into customers.

2. *Deciding which customers should receive a particular offer:* Companies set up criteria describing the ideal target customer for an offer. Then they search their customer databases for those most closely resembling the ideal type. By noting the contacts' response rates, the company can improve its target precision over time. Following a sale, it can set up an automatic sequence of activities: One week later, send a thank-you note; five weeks later, send a new offer; ten weeks later (if customer has not responded), phone the customer and offer a special discount.

3. *Deepening customer loyalty:* Companies can build customers' interest and enthusiasm by remembering their preferences; by sending appropriate gifts, discount coupons, and interesting reading material; and so on. Here are some examples:

INTER-CONTINENTAL HOTELS For members of its frequent business traveler program, Inter-Continental Hotels record information that will allow them to automatically assign the perfect room to each customer. The hotels' database includes the customer's preferences for room type (smoking, nonsmoking), bed type (king, queen, double, single), and floor (high or low), as well as other details, such as a specific kind of soap or a desire for extra pillows.

Planning
Marketing
Programs

Where Do the Data in a Database Come From?

How do marketers get the data they need to create a database, and then how do they combine and categorize those data? First, marketers must decide what types of information they need and develop ways to get it. Many simply collect information as sales are rung up; charge cards and catalog companies collect information this way. Packaged-goods and appliance companies get consumers to send in information by way of coupons, sweepstakes, warranty cards, and surveys. In addition, data are available in public records—for example, driver's licenses, auto registrations, and mortgage-tax rolls are all valuable sources of data.

Using sophisticated statistical programs, a computer merges different sets of data into a coherent, consolidated database. By making use of powerful *neural-networking software,* a brand manager can "drill down"

into the data to any level of detail. For example, American Express uses massively parallel computers to sort through individual card members' transactions, then helps its clients base their future promotions on these transactions. At a secret location in Phoenix, security guards watch over American Express's 500 billion bytes of data on how customers have used its 35 million green, gold, and platinum charge cards. Every month since the program began in 1993, AmEx has been using this information to send out precisely targeted offers. The offers go out in millions of customized monthly bills that the company says amount to "individualized newsletters." For instance, in Britain, a purchase at Harrod's one month will trigger a notice of a special sale at the store next month. In Belgium, AmEx's European division is testing a system that makes offers based on a combination of the card holders' past spending and postal code data. If a new restaurant opens, card holders who live within walking distance and are known to eat out often might receive a special discount.

MARS   Mars is a market leader not only in candy but also in pet food. In Germany, Mars has compiled the names of virtually every German family that owns a cat. Mars obtained these names by contacting veterinarians and also by offering the public a free booklet titled "How to Take Care of Your Cat." Those who requested the booklet filled out a questionnaire. As a result, Mars knows (among other things) the cat's name, age, and birthday. Mars now sends a birthday card to each cat in Germany each year, along with a new cat food sample and/or money-saving coupons for Mars brands. Do the cat owners appreciate this? You bet!

4. *Reactivating customer purchases:* Companies can install automatic mailing programs (*automatic marketing*) that send out birthday or anniversary cards, Christmas shopping reminders, or off-season promotions to the customers in their database. The database can help the company make attractive offers of product replacement or upgrades just when customers might be ready to act. Consider the following example:

GENERAL ELECTRIC   A General Electric customer database indicates each customer's geodemographics, psychographics, mediagraphics, appliance purchasing history, and so on. GE's direct marketers can determine which past customers might be ready to replace their washing machines—for instance, those who bought their GE washing machines six years ago and have large families. They can determine which customers would be interested in a new GE videorecorder based on their purchase history of other GE consumer electronic products. They can identify the heaviest past GE purchasers and send them gift certificates to apply against their next purchase of a major GE appliance.

Like many other marketing tools, database marketing requires a special investment. Companies must invest in computer hardware, database software, analytical programs, communication links, and skilled personnel. The database system must be user friendly and available to various marketing groups, including those in product and brand management, new-product development, advertising and promotion, direct mail, telemarketing, field sales, order fulfillment, and customer service. A well-managed database should lead to sales gains that will more than cover its costs. Miami-based Royal Caribbean cruises has had success in this area. Database marketing allows it to offer spur-of-the-moment cruise packages that help to fill all the berths on its ships. Fewer unbooked rooms means maximized profits for the cruise line.

The above examples notwithstanding, many things can go wrong if database marketing is not done carefully and strategically. For instance, at CNA Insurance, five programmers worked for nine months loading five years of claims data into a computer, only to discover that the data had been miscoded. For a list of mistakes to avoid when setting up and using a marketing database, see the Marketing Memo titled "Six Mistakes Database Marketers Make."

As more companies move into database marketing, the marketing paradigm will change. Mass marketing and mass retailing will continue, but their prevalence and power may diminish as more buyers turn to nonretail shopping. More consumers will use electronic shopping to search for the information and products they need. Online services will provide more objective information about the comparative merits of different brands. Marketers will need to think of new ways to create effective online messages, as well as new channels for delivering products and services efficiently.

Major Channels for Direct Marketing

Direct marketers can use a large number of channels for reaching prospects and customers. These include face-to-face selling, direct-mail marketing, catalog marketing, telemarketing, TV and other direct-response media, kiosk marketing, and online channels.

Face-to-Face Selling

The original and oldest form of direct marketing is the sales call, which we examined in the previous chapter. Today most industrial companies rely heavily on a professional sales force to locate prospects, develop them into customers, and grow the business. Or they hire manufacturers' representatives and agents to carry out the direct selling task. In addition, many consumer companies use a direct selling force: insurance agents, stockbrokers, and those working part- or full-time for direct-sales organizations such as Avon, Amway, Mary Kay, and Tupperware.

Direct-Mail Marketing

Direct-mail marketing involves sending an offer, announcement, reminder, or other item to a person at a particular address. Using highly selective mailing lists, direct marketers send out millions of mail pieces each year—letters, flyers, foldouts, and other "salespeople with wings." Some direct marketers mail audio tapes, videotapes, and even computer diskettes to prospects and customers. For example, the company that produces the Nordic Track Cardiovascular Exerciser advertises a free videotape showing the equipment's uses and health advantages. Ford sends a computer diskette called "Disk Drive Test Drive" to consumers responding to its ads in computer publications. The diskette's menu provides technical specifications and attractive graphics about Ford cars, and answers frequently asked questions.

Direct mail is a popular medium because it permits high target-market selectivity, can be personalized, is flexible, and allows early testing and response measurement. Although the cost per thousand people reached is higher than with mass media, the people reached are much better prospects. Over 45% of Americans purchased something through direct mail in 1993. The same year, charities raised over $50 billion via direct mail.

Until recently, all mail was paper-based and handled by the U.S. Post Office, telegraphic services, or for-profit mail carriers such as Federal Express, DHL, or Airborne Express. Then three new forms of mail delivery appeared in the 1980s:

- *Fax mail:* Fax machines enable one party to send a paper-based message to another party over telephone lines. Today's computers can also serve as fax machines. Fax mail has one major advantage over regular mail: The contents can be sent and received almost instantaneously. Marketers have begun to send fax mail announcing offers, sales, and events to prospects and customers with fax machines. Fax numbers of companies and individuals are now available through published directories. However, some prospects and customers resent receiving unsolicited fax mail, which clutters their machines and consumes their paper.

- *E-mail:* E-mail (short for *electronic mail*) allows users to send a message or file from one computer directly to another. The message arrives almost instantly but might be stored until the receiving person goes to his computer, inputs his password, and retrieves his messages (though some e-mail programs do offer a "notification" feature that announces the arrival of new messages). Marketers are beginning to send sales announcements, offers, and other messages to e-mail addresses—sometimes to a few indi-

Managing
Direct and
Online Marketing

viduals, sometimes to large groups. As people begin to receive more e-mail messages, including unimportant ones, they may look for an "agent" software program to sort out the more important messages from those than can be ignored or discarded.

◆ *Voice mail:* Voice mail is a system for receiving and storing oral messages at a telephone address. Telephone companies sell this service as a substitute for answering machines. The person with a voice mail account can check messages by dialing into the voice mail system and punching in a personal code. Some marketers have set up programs that will dial a large number of telephone numbers and leave the selling message in the recipients' voice mailboxes.

These three new forms deliver pieces of mail at incredible speed, compared to the post office's "snail mail" pace. Yet, much like mail delivered through traditional channels, they may be viewed as "junk mail" if they are sent to people who have no interest in them. For this reason, marketers must carefully identify appropriate prospects and customers and not waste their time or the addressees' time.

How can direct-mail marketers construct an effective direct-mail campaign? Direct marketers must decide on their objectives, target markets and prospects, offer elements, means of testing the elements, and measures of campaign success. We examine each of these in the paragraphs that follow. Much of what we say here applies to catalog, telephone, and online marketing as well.

OBJECTIVES. Most direct marketers aim to receive an order from prospects. The campaign's success is judged by the response rate. An order-response rate of 2% is normally considered good, although this number varies with product category and price.

Direct mail has other objectives as well. One is to produce prospect leads for the sales force. Another is to strengthen customer relationships. Some direct marketers run campaigns to inform and educate customers to prepare them for later purchase; thus Ford mailed booklets to prospects on "How to Take Good Care of Your Car."

TARGET MARKETS AND PROSPECTS. Direct marketers need to identify the characteristics of prospects and customers who are most able, willing, and ready to buy. Bob Stone, a major writer on direct marketing, recommends applying the R-F-M formula (recency, frequency, monetary amount) for rating and selecting customers: The best customer targets are those who bought most recently, who buy frequently, and who spend the most. Points are established for varying R-F-M levels, and each customer is scored. The higher the score, the more attractive the customer.[8]

Direct marketers use further segmentation criteria in targeting prospects. Prospects can be identified on the basis of such variables as age, sex, income, education, previous mail-order purchases, and so forth. Occasions provide a good departure point for segmentation. New parents will be in the market for baby clothes and baby toys; college freshmen will buy computers and small television sets; and newlyweds will be looking for housing, furniture, appliances, and bank loans. Another useful segmentation variable is consumer lifestyle groups, such as computer buffs, cooking buffs, and outdoor buffs. For business markets, Dun & Bradstreet runs an information service that provides a wealth of data (Figure 23-1).

Once the target market is defined, the direct marketer needs to obtain specific names. Here is where mailing-list acquisition and mailing-list/database building come into play. The company's best prospects are customers who have bought the company's products in the past. Additional names can be obtained by advertising some free offer. The direct marketer can also buy lists of names from list brokers. But these lists often have problems, including name duplication, incomplete data, obsolete addresses, and so on. The better lists include overlays of demographic and psychographic information. Direct marketers typically buy and test a sample of names on the list before buying further names from the same list.

OFFER ELEMENTS.   Direct marketers must construct an effective offer. Nash sees the offer strategy as consisting of five elements—the product, the offer, the medium, the distribution method, and the creative strategy.[9] Fortunately, all of these elements can be tested.

In addition to planning the product and distribution elements of the direct-mail campaign, the direct-mail marketer has to decide on five components of the mailing itself: the outside envelope, sales letter, circular, reply form, and reply envelope. Here are some findings:

♦   The outside envelope will be more effective if it contains an illustration, preferably in color, and/or a catchy reason to open the envelope, such as the announcement of a contest, premium, or benefit to the recipient. Envelopes are more effective—but more costly—when they contain a colorful commemorative stamp, when the address is hand-typed or handwritten, and when the envelope differs in size or shape from standard envelopes.

♦   The sales letter should use a personal salutation and start with a headline in bold type in the form of a news lead, a how/what/why statement, a narrative, or a question to gain attention. The letter should be printed on good-quality paper and be brief, with some indented paragraphs and underlining of pertinent phrases and sentences. A computer-type letter usually outperforms a printed letter, and the presence of a pithy P.S. at the letter's end increases the response rate, as does the signature of someone whose title is important.

♦   In most cases, a colorful circular accompanying the letter will increase the response rate by more than its cost.

♦   Better results are obtained when the reply form features a toll-free number and contains a perforated receipt stub and guarantee of satisfaction.

- The inclusion of a postage-free reply envelope will dramatically increase the response rate.

TESTING DIRECT-MARKETING ELEMENTS. One of the great advantages of direct marketing is the ability to test, under real marketplace conditions, the efficacy of different elements of an offer strategy—product features, copy, prices, media, mailing lists, and the like. Testing the campaign's key components can add substantially to its overall response rate and the company's profitability.

Direct marketers must remember that response rates typically understate a campaign's long-term impact. Suppose only 2% of the recipients who receive a direct-mail piece advertising Samsonite luggage place an order. A much larger percentage became aware of the product (direct mail has high readership), and some percentage may have formed an intention to buy at a later date (either by mail or at a retail outlet). Furthermore, some of them may mention Samsonite luggage to others as a result of the direct-mail piece. To derive a more comprehensive estimate of the promotion's impact, some companies are measuring direct marketing's impact on awareness, intention to buy, and word-of-mouth.

MEASURING THE CAMPAIGN'S SUCCESS. By adding up the planned campaign costs, the direct marketer can figure out in advance the needed break-even response rate. This rate must be net of returned merchandise and bad debts. Returned merchandise can kill an otherwise effective campaign. The direct marketer needs to analyze the main causes of returned merchandise (late shipment, defective merchandise, damage in transit, not as advertised, incorrect order fulfillment, and so forth).

By carefully analyzing past campaigns, direct marketers can steadily improve their performance. Even when a specific campaign fails to break even, it might still be profitable. Consider the following situation:

> Suppose a membership organization spends $10,000 on a new-member campaign and attracts 100 new members, each paying annual dues of $70. It appears that the campaign has lost $3,000 (= $10,000 − $7,000). But if 80% of the new members renew their membership in the second year, the organization gets another $5,600 without any effort. It has now received $12,600 (= $7,000 + $5,600) for its investment of $10,000. To figure out the long-term break-even rate, one needs to know the percentage who renew each year and for how many years they renew.

This example illustrates the concept of customer *lifetime value,* which we first examined in Chapter 2.[10] A customer's ultimate value is not revealed by his or her purchase response to a particular mailing. Rather, the customer's lifetime value is the expected profit made on all of his/her future purchases net of customer acquisition and maintenance costs. For an average customer, one would calculate the average customer longevity, average customer annual expenditure, and average gross margin (properly discounted for the opportunity cost of money), minus the average cost of customer acquisition and maintenance. This formula would be adjusted for nonaverage customers. Data Consult claims that it is able to estimate the expected lifetime value of a customer from as few as three or four transactions. This information enables marketers to adjust the nature and frequency of communications to match the customer's lifetime value.

After assessing customer lifetime values, the company can focus its communication efforts on the more attractive customers. These efforts include sending communications that do not "sell" the customer anything but rather maintain the customer's interest in the company and its products. Such communications may include free newsletters, booklets, and brochures, all of which serve to build a stronger customer relationship.

Catalog Marketing

Catalog marketing occurs when companies mail one or more product catalogs to selected addressees who have a high likelihood of placing an order. Catalogs are a huge business—catalog marketers mail annually over 12.4 billion copies of more than 8,500 different catalogs. The average household receives at least 50 catalogs per year. Some of the catalogs are sent by the major general-merchandise retailers—J. C. Penney and Spiegel, for example. Others are sent by specialty department stores, such as Neiman-Marcus and Saks Fifth Avenue, which send catalogs to cultivate an upper-middle-class market for high-priced, sometimes exotic merchandise. Using catalogs, Avon sells cosmetics, W. R. Grace sells cheese, and General Mills sells sports shirts. Several major corporations have acquired or developed mail-order divisions, but there are also thousands of smaller enterprises in the mail catalog business, typically issuing catalogs in specialty-goods areas, such as consumer electronics, lawn and garden equipment, women's wear, household wares, and so on. An increasing number of business-to-business marketers are sending their catalogs on CD-ROM to prospects and customers.

The success of a catalog business depends greatly on the company's ability to manage its customer lists so carefully that there is little duplication or bad debts, to control its inventory carefully, to offer quality merchandise so that returns are low, and to project a distinctive customer-benefiting image. Some catalog companies distinguish their catalogs by adding literary or information features, sending swatches of materials, operating a special hotline to answer questions, sending gifts to their best customers, and donating a percentage of their profits to good causes. In addition, some catalog houses (Neiman-Marcus, Spiegel) are experimenting with video catalogs that they mail to their best customers and prospects; and some have put their catalog on the Internet, in which case they have saved considerable money in printing and mailing costs.[11] Eventually, global consumers will be ordering from catalogs issued in other countries; today many Japanese consumers are saving money by ordering items from U.S. catalogs.[12]

Telemarketing

Telemarketing has become a major direct-marketing tool. In 1991, marketers spent an estimated $234 billion in telephone charges to sell their products and services. The average household receives 19 telemarketing calls each year and makes 16 calls to place orders.

Some telemarketing systems are fully automated. For example, automatic-dialing and recorded-message players (ADRMPs) can dial numbers, play a voice-activated advertising message, and take orders from interested customers on an answering-machine device or by forwarding the call to an operator. Telemarketing is increasingly used in business marketing as well as consumer marketing. For example, Raleigh Bicycles used telemarketing to reduce the amount of personal selling needed for contacting its dealers. In the first year, sales force travel costs were reduced by 50%, and sales in a single quarter went up 34 percent.

Effective telemarketing depends on choosing the right telemarketers, training them well, and providing incentives to perform. Telemarketers should have pleasant voices and project enthusiasm. Women are more effective than men for many products. The telemarketers should initially train with a script and eventually move toward more improvisation. The opening lines are critical: They should be brief and lead with a good question that catches the listener's interest. The telemarketer needs to know how to end the conversation if the prospect seems to be a poor one. The call should be made at the right time, which is late morning and afternoon to reach business prospects, and evening hours between 7 and 9 to reach households. The telemarketing supervisor can build up telemarketers' enthusiasm by offering prizes to the first one who gets an order or to the top performer. Given privacy issues and the higher cost per contact for telemarketing contacts, precise list selection is critical.

Television and Other Major Media Direct-Response Marketing

Television is used in three ways to market products directly to consumers. The first is through *direct-response advertising.* Direct-response marketers air television spots, often 60 or 120 seconds long, that persuasively describe a product and provide customers with a toll-free number for ordering. One of the best examples is Dial Media's ads for Ginsu knives, which ran for seven years and sold almost 3 million sets of knives worth over $40 million in sales. Recently, some companies have prepared 30- and 60-minute *infomercials,* which resemble documentaries (on quitting smoking, curing baldness, or losing weight), carry testimony from satisfied users of the product or service, and include a toll-free number for ordering or getting further information.

A second television marketing approach is *at-home shopping channels,* which are entire television channels dedicated to selling goods and services. The largest is the Home Shopping Network (HSN), which broadcasts 24 hours a day. The program's hosts offer bargain prices on products ranging from jewelry, lamps, collectible dolls, and clothing to power tools and consumer electronics—usually obtained by HSN at closeout prices. Viewers call a toll-free number to order goods. Orders are shipped within 48 hours. A second, more upscale channel, QVC, also sells 24 hours a day. In 1993 more than 22 million adults watched home shopping programs, and close to 13 million bought merchandise from a home shopping program.

A third approach is *videotext,* in which the consumer's TV set is linked with a seller's computer databanks by cable or telephone lines. The videotext service consists of a computerized catalog of products offered by producers, retailers, banks, travel organizations, and others. Consumers place orders via a special keyboard device connected to the system by two-way cable. Much research is now going on to perfect interactive TV as the next step after videotext.

Magazines, newspapers, and radio can also be used in direct-response selling channels. The person hears or reads about an offer and dials a toll-free number to place an order.

Kiosk Marketing

Some companies have designed "customer-order-placing machines" called *kiosks* (in contrast to vending machines, which dispense actual products) and placed them in stores, airports, and other locations. For example, the Florsheim Shoe Company includes a machine in several of its stores in which the customer indicates the type of shoe he wants (dress, sport), along with the color and size. Pictures of Florsheim shoes appear on the screen that meet his criteria. If the particular shoes are not available in the store, the customer can dial an attached phone and type in his credit-card number and where the shoes should be delivered.

Online Channels

The most recent channel for direct marketing is composed of online channels. We describe these in detail in the next section.

MARKETING IN THE TWENTY-FIRST CENTURY: ONLINE MARKETING

An *online marketing channel* is one that a person can reach via computer and modem. A modem connects the computer to a telephone line so that the computer user can reach various online information services. There are two types of online channels:

- *Commercial online channels:* Various companies have set up online information and marketing services that can be accessed by those who have signed up for the service and pay a monthly fee. The best-known online services are CompuServe, America Online, and Prodigy, with more than 3,200,000, 3,000,000, and 1,600,000 subscribers respectively. These online channels provide subscribers with five main services: information (news, libraries, education, travel, sports, reference), entertainment (fun and games), shopping services, dialogue opportunities (bulletin boards, forums, chat boxes), and e-mail.

- *The Internet:* The Internet is a global web of some 45,000 computer networks that has made instantaneous and decentralized global communication possible. Originally established to facilitate research and scholarly exchanges, the Internet is now available to a much broader audience, some 25 million people. Users can send e-mail, exchange views, shop for products, and access news, food recipes, art, and business information. The Internet itself is free, though individual users may need to pay a commercial service to be hooked up to it.

The Benefits of Online Marketing

Why have online services become so popular? First, they provide three major benefits to potential buyers:[13]

- *Convenience:* Customers can order products 24 hours a day wherever they are. They don't have to sit in traffic, find a parking space, and walk through countless aisles to find and examine goods. And they don't have to drive all the way to a store, only to find out that the desired product is out of stock.

- *Information:* Customers can find reams of comparative information about companies, products, and competitors without leaving their office or home. They can focus on objective criteria such as prices, quality, performance, and availability.

- *Fewer hassles:* With online services, customers don't have to face salespeople or open themselves up to persuasion and emotional factors.

Second, online services also provide a number of benefits to marketers:

- *Quick adjustments to market conditions:* Companies can quickly add products to their offering and change prices and descriptions.

- *Lower costs:* Online marketers avoid the expense of maintaining a store and the accompanying costs of rent, insurance, and utilities. They can produce digital catalogs for much less than the cost of printing and mailing paper catalogs.

- *Relationship building:* Online marketers can talk with consumers and learn much from them. Marketers can also upload useful reports, or a free demo of their software, or a free sample of their newsletter, onto the system. Consumers can then download these items into their electronic mailboxes.

- *Audience sizing:* Marketers can learn how many people visited their online site and how many stopped at particular places on the site. This information can help the marketers improve their offers and ads.

Clearly, marketers will want to consider using online services to find, reach, communicate, and sell. Online marketing has at least four great advantages. First, both small and large firms can afford it. Second, there is no real limit on advertising space, in contrast to print and broadcast media. Third, information access and retrieval are fast, compared to overnight mail and even fax. And fourth, shopping can be done privately and swiftly. However, online marketing is not for every company nor for every product; thought has to be given to if, when, and how it should be done.

Online Marketing Channels

Marketers can conduct online marketing in four ways: by creating an electronic storefront; participating in forums, newsgroups, and bulletin boards; placing ads online; and using e-mail.

CREATING AN ELECTRONIC STOREFRONT. Thousands of businesses have established a *home page* on the Internet—an opening menu screen. Many home pages serve as electronic storefronts that offer users a wide variety of information:

1. Descriptions of the company and its products, in both text and pictorial form. The browser simply clicks on any text or icon to bring up more detail about a particular product.
2. A company catalog describing products' features, availability, and prices.
3. Company news, including reports on financial results, current events, new products and upgrades, dates of training seminars, and so on.
4. Technical information and product brochures.
5. Information about company employment opportunities.
6. Opportunities to speak to staff members.
7. The ability to place an order before leaving the site.

For example, when a person types in Sun Microsystems' site code, http://www.sun.com/, Sun's home page appears in full color and several options are shown. The user can choose to see descriptions of Sun's products and solutions, request sales and service, or talk to staff members. GE Plastics has placed more than 1,500 pages of information on its Internet site, and customers can get answers and information about its products any time and from anywhere in the world.

It is estimated that product sales on commercial online services are somewhere between $50 million and $200 million per year. Hundreds of companies now offer merchandise online. One can order clothing from Lands' End or J. C. Penney, books from Simon & Schuster, or flowers from Grant's Flowers to be sent anywhere in the world. Suppose an Internet subscriber wants to buy a turtleneck. He goes to Lands' End's home page (http://www.landsend.com/) and clicks on "The Goods." A menu of articles appears: men's products, women's products, luggage. He clicks on men's products, and a listing of different types of apparel appears: tops, bottoms, activewear, and so forth. By going further and further into the menus, he can find the turtleneck he wants and see a color picture and full description of it. He likes the sweater, and clicks to place an order. Figure 23-2 on pages 734–735 shows the Internet screen at each stage in this process.

Given these online marketing opportunities, each company has to decide whether and how to go online, with what products, for what audiences, with what copy and budget. If a company decides to open an electronic storefront, it has two choices:[14]

◆ The company can open its own store on the Internet. There are several ways to do this. A World Wide Web server is the preferred choice, since it permits the company to display graphics, sounds, and video, as well as text. Renting a Web server can cost $250 and up per month, depending on the desired speed, number of pages, and so on. One major cost is designing the store's front door, graphics, and navigational system. Most companies hire the services of an online agency to help them get started.

◆ The company can buy a location on a commercial online service. It can either rent storage space on the online service's own computer or establish a link or gateway from its computer to the online service's shopping mall. J. C. Penney, for example, has gateways to CompuServe and Prodigy and therefore has access to millions of subscribers to these commercial online services. The online services will typically design the electronic storefront for the company and advertise its addition to the shopping mall for a limited period of time. For these services, the company may have to pay the online service provider $20,000 and up per year, plus 2% of the company's online sales. This is costly considering that only about 4% of CompuServe electronic mall browsers actually buy something.

Having an online location is one thing; getting people to visit the location is another. Companies with home pages try to attract prospects to their address through e-mail, mailing lists, newspaper and magazine ads, advertising on online billboard space, and newsgroups (described below). Various companies use sweepstakes, questionnaires, games, and other devices that require users to give their names and addresses to participate. The key is to use information and entertainment to entice browsers to visit the company's home page frequently. This means that companies must constantly update their home pages to keep them fresh and exciting. Doing so involves time and expense, but it would be worse not to update the information.

PARTICIPATING IN FORUMS, NEWSGROUPS, AND BULLETIN BOARDS.
Companies may decide to participate in various groups that are not organized specifically for commercial purposes. Their participation may increase their company's visibility and credibility. The three groups with the highest visibility are forums, newsgroups, and bulletin boards:

◆ *Forums* are discussion groups located on commercial online services. A forum may operate a library, a conference room for real-time chatting, and even a classified ad directory. To participate, a person subscribes to the forum at a nominal cost or no cost. The forum's home page will show icons for newsflashes, libraries, messages, and conference rooms. Most forums are sponsored by general or interest groups. Thus Yamaha might start a forum on classical music partly because of its role as a major musical instruments manufacturer.

◆ *Newsgroups* are the Internet's version of forums, but newsgroups are limited to people posting and reading messages on a particular topic, rather than managing libraries or conferencing. Internet users can participate in newsgroups without subscribing. There are thousands of newsgroups, most of which are listed in *The Internet Yellow Pages* (Table 23-3 on page 736 lists a sample).

◆ *Bulletin board systems (BBSs)* are specialized online services that center on a specific topic or group. BBS subscribers tend to be loyal and active, and resent blatant marketing efforts. There are over 60,000 BBSs in the United States, dealing with such topics as vacations, health, computer games, real estate, and so on. Marketers might want to identify a few BBSs that have the type of subscribers who fit their target market, and then participate in the BBS subtly.

PLACING ADS ONLINE.
Companies and individuals can place ads on commercial online services in three ways. First, the major commercial online services offer an ad section for listing classified ads; the ads are listed according to when they arrived, with the latest ones heading the list. Second, ads can be placed in certain newsgroups that are set up for commercial purposes. Finally, ads can be put on online billboards; they pop up while subscribers are using the service, even

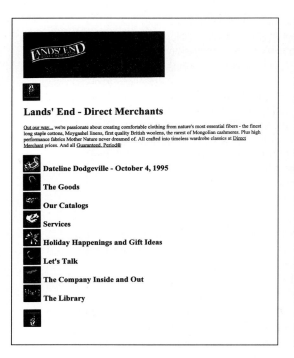

(a) From Lands' End's home page, the user clicks on "Our Catalogs."

(b) The customer chooses "Men's Products."

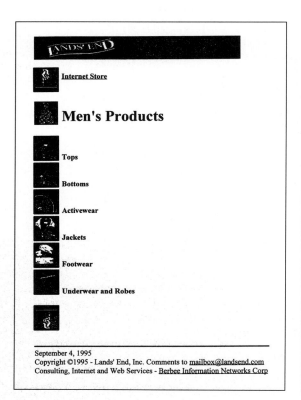

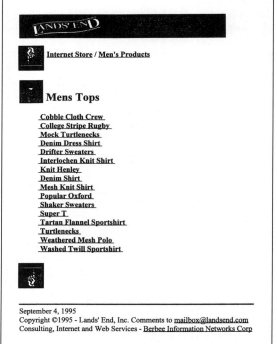

(c) The customer receives a listing of Lands' End's Men's products.

(d) The customer selects "Mens Tops" and is given a detailed listing of the products available.

FIGURE 23-2
Lands' End Internet Store-front

Internet Store / Men's Products / Tops

Men's and Women's Mock Turtlenecks

$16.00

74 kb

We figured out a way to escape the choke-hold.

You're gasping for air. That turtleneck has you in a choke-hold. You tug, yank, pull, twist hoping to loosen it up a bit. (UGH! Some aerobic classes are easier than this, not that you men would know.) Granted not everyone feels this way about them, but that's they way some people describe turtlenecks.

That's why a lot of people prefer mocks. No need for tug-of-war skills. The neck is shorter and much looser. We add just enough Lycra® spandex to hold its shape, but never choke you. And since sleeves are constantly being yanked, pulled on or pushed up, we put some in the cuffs too.

Where do we stand on shoulder abuse? We put elasticized tape along the shoulder seams. Even after some pretty tough stretches, they'll bounce back. Helps prevent the shoulders from sagging to your elbows, too.

What makes our cotton interlock mock so soft? Come closer and I'll let you in on the secret. It's an extra layer of yarn (one more than jersey or mesh) that acts like springs inside your shirt. Lifts the fabric.

How come we know so much about this stuff? We modeled our mock after one of the best in the business, our famous turtleneck. We set-up the same tough standards. Fortunately, the only thing that came up short was the neck. As you might expect our mock has a traditional fit, same as our regular turtle. Machine wash. Made in USA.

Men's Regular 100% Cotton Mock Turtleneck in *Black, Classic Navy, Cranberry, Dark Teal Blue, Dark Wine, Fawn, Light Terracotta, Straw, White* M L XL **0238-0A50** $16.00

Women's Regular 100% Cotton Mock Turtleneck in *Black, Classic Navy, Cranberry, Dark Teal Blue, Dark Wine, Fawn, Light Terracotta, Straw, White* S M L XL **1585-5A52** $16.00

Women's Regular 50/50 Cotton/Polyester Solid Mock Turtleneck in *Black, Classic Navy, Cranberry, Dark Teal Blue, Dark Wine, Fawn, Light Terracotta, Straw, White* S M L XL **1957-0A54** $16.00

Men's Regular 50/50 Cotton/Polyester Solid Mock Turtleneck in *Black, Classic Navy, Cranberry, Dark Teal Blue, Dark Wine, Fawn, Light Terracotta, Straw, White* M L XL **1956-9A59** $16.00

 How to order

(e) The customer is interested in "Mock Turtlenecks" and selects that option to receive more information about the product.

 HOW TO ORDER:

We offer four convenient ways for you to order: Online, using our Electronic Order Blank; or by fax, phone or mail. For all orders, please include a daytime and evening phone number, e-mail address or fax number where you can be reached - and let us know your preferred method of contacting you.

By Electronic Order Blank: Download this simple program and you can fill in your information and e-mail it directly via the Internet, or save it to attach to your America OnLine, CompuServe, or other gateway service e-mail message. In either case, all the information you enter will be encrypted for security.

    Note: You can fill in the Electronic Order Blank as you select items for purchase, save it and add more items later.

By Fax: Fill in the Electronic Order Blank and print it out, fill in. Please SIGN the order form where indicated and enter your credit card number and expiration date. Fax to 1-800-332-0103. (Fax orders can be placed with a credit card only.)

By Phone: Call 1-800-963-4816.

By Mail:
Lands' End Direct Merchants
1 Lands' End Lane
Dodgeville, WI 53595

(f) The customer can then place an order by phone, fax, mail, or Internet.

TABLE 23-3 INTERNET NEWSGROUPS

NEWSGROUP NAME	DESCRIPTION
comp.databases	Database and data management issues and theory
comp.internet.library	Electronic libraries—administration and creation
comp.multimedia	Interactive multimedia technologies of all kinds
misc.consumers	Consumer interests, product reviews, and the like
misc.health.alternative	Alternative, complementary, and holistic health care
misc. invest	Investments and the handling of money
rec.arts.books	Books of all genres, and the publishing industry
rec.arts.movies	Discussion of movies and movie making
rec.audio.car	Discussions of automobile audio systems
rec.bicycles.racing	Bicycle racing techniques, rules, and results
rec.food.cooking	Food, cooking, cookbooks, and recipes
rec.music.cd	CDs—availability and other discussion
rec.music.country.western	Country and Western music, performers, performances, and so on
rec.pets.dogs	Any and all subjects relating to dogs as pets
rec.scuba	Hobbyists interested in scuba diving
rec.sport.golf	Discussions about all aspects of golfing
sci.environment	Discussion about the environment and ecology
sci.virtual-worlds.apps	Current and future uses of virtual-worlds technology
soc.culture.brazil	Talk about the people and culture of Brazil
soc.religion.islam	Discussion of the Islamic faith
talk.politics.guns	The politics of firearms ownership and (mis)use

though they did not request an ad. In this case, a subscriber may be looking up movie ratings on Prodigy and suddenly an ad for Alamo Rent-A-Car might appear with a statement: "Rent a car from Alamo and get up to 2 days free!"

Advertising on the free-access Internet is frowned upon by many. Two lawyers who advertised their services on the Net were "flamed" for doing so; they received more than 20,000 nasty messages via e-mail.

USING E-MAIL. A company can encourage prospects and customers to send questions, suggestions, and even complaints to the company, using the company's e-mail address. Customer service representatives can respond to the customers in a short time via e-mail.

The company may also gather the names of prospects or customers and send periodic or special information to their e-mail address. The group may be a fan club, a set of people who want to receive a regular newsletter or a company annual report, and so on. Companies can use the list to send reminders to car owners to bring their cars in for service, or to cat owners to bring their cats in for annual rabies shots, or to managers to attend new seminars.

Planning
Marketing
Programs

THE GROWING USE OF INTEGRATED DIRECT MARKETING

Although direct marketing and online marketing have boomed in recent years, a large number of companies still relegate them to minor roles in their communication/promotion mix. The company's advertising and sales-promotion departments receive most of its communication dollars and jealously guard their budgets. The sales force may also see direct marketing as a threat to its turf. Sales reps often perceive a loss of territorial sales control when they are forced to turn over their smaller customers and prospects to direct mailers and telemarketers.

However, companies are increasingly recognizing the importance of applying a full-systems perspective in using their communication tools. Some companies are appointing a Chief Communications Officer (CCO) in addition to a CIO (Chief Information Officer). Reporting to the CCO are specialists in advertising, sales promotion, public relations, and direct/online marketing. The aim is to set the right overall communication budget and the right allocation of funds to each communication tool. This movement toward integrated communications has been called by different names: Schultz calls it *integrated marketing communications* (IMC), Roman calls it *integrated direct marketing* (IDM), and Rapp and Collins call it *maximarketing*.[15]

How can different communication tools be integrated in campaign planning? Imagine a marketer using a single communication tool in a "one-shot" effort to reach and sell a prospect. An example of a *single vehicle, single-stage campaign* would involve a one-time mailing offering a cookware item. A *single vehicle, multiple-stage campaign* would involve successive mailings to the same prospect. Magazine publishers, for example, send about four renewal notices to a household before giving up.

A more powerful approach is the *multiple vehicle, multiple-stage campaign.* Consider the following sequence:

News campaign about a new product → *Paid ad with a response mechanism* → *Direct mail* → *Outbound telemarketing* → *Face-to-face sales call* → *Ongoing communication*

For example, Compaq might launch a new laptop computer by first arranging news stories to stir interest. Then Compaq might place full-page ads offering a free booklet on "How to Buy a Computer." Compaq would then mail the booklet to those who responded, along with an offer to sell the new computer at a special discount before it arrives in retail stores. Suppose 4% of those who receive the booklet order the computer. Compaq telemarketers then phone the 96% who did not buy the computer, to remind them of the offer. Suppose another 6% now order the computer. Those who do not place an order are offered a face-to-face sales call or demonstration in a local retail store. Even if the prospect is not ready to buy, there is ongoing communication.

Roman says that the use of *response compression,* whereby multiple media are deployed within a tightly defined time frame, increases message reach and impact. The underlying idea is to deploy a sequence of multimedia messages with precise timing intervals in the hope of generating incremental sales and profits that exceed the costs involved. As an example, Roman cites a Citicorp campaign to market home equity loans. Instead of using only "mail plus an 800 number," Citicorp used "mail plus coupon plus 800 number plus outbound telemarketing plus print advertising." Although the second campaign was more expensive, it resulted in a 15% increase in the number of new accounts compared with direct mail alone. Roman concluded:

When a mailing piece which might generate a 2% response on its own is supplemented by a toll-free 800-number ordering channel, we regularly see response rise

Managing
Direct and
Online Marketing

The "Maximarketing" Model for Integrated Marketing

Rapp and Collins's maximarketing model consists of nine steps:

1. *Maximized targeting* calls upon the marketer to define and identify the best target prospects for the offer. The marketer either buys appropriate mailing lists or searches the customer database for characteristics that point to high interest, ability to pay, and readiness to buy. "Best customers" include those who buy with some frequency, don't return many orders, don't complain, and pay on time. Mass marketers can go "fishing" for prospects with direct-response advertising in such mass media as television, newspaper supplements, and magazine insert cards.

2. *Maximized media* leads the direct marketer to examine the exploding variety of media and choose those that allow for convenient two-way communication and measurement of results.

3. *Maximized accountability* calls for evaluating campaigns on the basis of cost per prospect response rather than on the cost per thousand exposure (as used in mass advertising).

4. *Maximized awareness* involves searching for messages that will break through the clutter and reach the prospects' hearts and minds by means of "whole brain" advertising that appeals to a person's rational and emotional sides.

5. *Maximized activation* emphasizes that advertising must trigger purchase or at least advance prospects to a mea-

surably higher stage of buying readiness. Activation devices include statements like "Send for more information" and "Reply coupon must be returned by September 30."

6. *Maximized synergy* involves finding ways of doing double duty with the advertising—for instance, combining awareness building with direct response, promoting other distribution channels, and sharing costs with other advertisers.

7. *Maximized linkage* calls for linking the advertising to the sale by concentrating on the better prospects and spending more of the total budget to convert them, rather than spending money simply to send an awareness message to the world at large.

8. *Maximized sales* through database building calls on the marketer to continue to market directly to known customers by cross-selling, upgrading, and introducing new products. The marketer keeps enhancing the customer database with more customer information and ends up with a rich private advertising medium. With the aim of maximizing customer lifetime value, many marketers today are as interested in the loyalty-building process as they are in the customer-acquisition process.

9. *Maximized distribution* involves the marketer in building additional channels to reach prospects and customers—for instance, when a direct marketer opens retail stores or obtains shelf space in existing retail stores, or when a manufacturer such as General Foods decides to sell a premium brand of coffee directly to the consumer.

Sources: Summarized from Stan Rapp and Thomas L. Collins, *Maximarketing* (New York: McGraw-Hill, 1987). Also see their *Beyond Maximarketing: The New Power of Caring and Daring* (New York: McGraw-Hill, 1994) for specific companies and cases of successful maximarketing.

by 50–125%. A skillfully integrated outbound telemarketing effort can add another 500% lift in response. Suddenly our 2% response has grown to 13% or more by adding interactive marketing channels to a "business as usual" mailing. The dollars and cents involved in adding media to the integrated media mix is normally marginal on a cost-per-order basis because of the high level of responses generated . . . Adding media to a marketing program will raise total response . . . because different people are inclined to respond to different stimuli.[16]

Rapp and Collins's maximarketing model makes direct-marketing techniques the driving force in the general marketing process.[17] This model recommends the creation of a customer database and advocates making direct marketing a full partner in the marketing process. Maximarketing consists of a comprehensive set of steps for reaching the prospect, making the sale, and developing the relationship. For more details, see the Marketing Insight titled "The 'Maximarketing' Model for Integrated Marketing."

Citicorp, AT&T, IBM, Ford, and American Airlines have used integrated direct marketing to build profitable relations with customers over the years. Retailers such as Saks Fifth Avenue, Bloomingdale's, and Frederick's of Hollywood regularly send out catalogs to supplement their in-store sales. Direct-marketing companies such as L. L. Bean, Eddie Bauer, Franklin Mint, and Sharper Image made fortunes in the direct-marketing mail-order and phone-order business, then opened retail stores after establishing strong brand names as direct marketers.

PUBLIC AND ETHICAL ISSUES IN THE USE OF DIRECT MARKETING

Direct marketers and their customers usually enjoy mutually rewarding relationships. Occasionally, however, a darker side emerges. Concerns include excesses that irritate consumers, instances of unfairness, cases of outright deception and fraud, and invasion-of-privacy issues.

- *Irritation:* Many people find the increasing number of hard-sell and direct-marketing solicitations to be a nuisance. They dislike direct-response TV commercials that are too loud, too long, and too insistent. Especially bothersome are dinner-time or late-night phone calls, poorly trained callers, and computerized calls placed by an auto-dial recorded message player.

- *Unfairness:* Some direct marketers take advantage of impulsive or less sophisticated buyers. TV shopping shows and infomercials may be the worst culprits. They feature smooth-talking hosts, elaborately staged demonstrations, claims of drastic price reductions, "while they last" time limitations, and unexcelled ease of purchase to capture buyers who have low sales resistance.

- *Deception and fraud:* Some direct marketers design mailers and write copy intended to mislead buyers. They may exaggerate product size, performance claims, or the "retail price." Political fund-raisers sometimes use gimmicks such as "lookalike" envelopes that resemble official documents, simulated newspaper clippings, and fake honors and awards. Some nonprofit organizations pretend to be conducting research surveys when they are actually asking leading questions to screen or persuade consumers. The Federal Trade Commission receives thousands of complaints each year about fraudulent investment scams or phony charities. By the time the buyers realize that they have been bilked and alert the authorities, the thieves are usually somewhere else plotting new schemes.

- *Invasion of privacy:* Invasion of privacy is perhaps the toughest public-policy issue now confronting the direct-marketing industry. It seems that almost every time consumers order products by mail or telephone, enter a sweepstakes, apply for a credit card, or take out a magazine subscription, their names, addresses, and purchasing behavior are entered into some company's already bulging database. Consumers often benefit from such database marketing—they receive more offers that are closely matched to their interests. However, direct marketers sometimes find it difficult to walk the fine line between their desires to reach carefully targeted audiences and consumers' rights to privacy. Many critics worry that marketers may know *too* much about consumers' lives, and that they may use this knowledge to take unfair advantage of consumers. They ask: Should AT&T be allowed to sell marketers the names of consumers who frequently call catalog companies' 800 numbers? Is it right for credit bureaus to compile and sell lists of people who have recently applied for credit cards—people who are considered prime direct-marketing targets because of their spending behavior? Is it right for states to sell the names and addresses of driver's license holders, along with height, weight, and gender information, allowing apparel retailers to target tall or overweight people with special clothing offers?

People in the direct-marketing industry are attempting to address these issues. They know that left untended, such problems will lead to increasingly negative consumer attitudes, lower response rates, and calls for greater state and federal legislation to restrict direct-marketing practices. In the final analysis, most direct marketers want the same thing that consumers want: honest and well-designed marketing offers targeted only toward consumers who will appreciate and respond to them.

SUMMARY

1. *Direct marketing* is an interactive marketing system that uses one or more advertising media to effect a measurable response and/or transaction at any location. Direct marketing is now widely used in consumer markets, business-to-business markets, and the markets for charitable contributions. One of the most valuable direct-marketing tools is the *customer database,* which is an organized collection of comprehensive data about individual prospects or customers. Companies use their databases to identify prospects, decide which customers should receive a particular offer, deepen customer loyalty, and reactivate customer purchases.

2. Direct marketers use a wide variety of channels to reach prospects and customers. The oldest form of direct marketing is the sales call. Direct-mail marketing involves sending an offer, announcement, reminder, or other item to a person at a particular address. Catalog marketing and telemarketing are very popular forms of direct marketing. Growing in importance are television direct-response marketing and infomercials, as well as home shopping channels and videotext/interactive TV marketing. Other forms of media, such as magazines, newspapers, and radio are also used in direct marketing, as are kiosks and online services.

   To be successful, direct marketers must plan their campaigns carefully. They must decide on their objectives, target their markets and prospects precisely, design the offer's elements, test the elements, and establish measures to determine the campaign's success.

3. There are two types of online marketing channels: commercial online services and the Internet. Online advertising offers convenience to buyers and lower costs to sellers. Companies can choose to go online by creating electronic storefronts; participating in forums, newsgroups, and bulletin boards; placing ads online; and using e-mail. However, not all companies should go online; each company must determine whether the revenues gained from going online will exceed the costs of doing so.

4. Although some companies still relegate direct and online marketing to a subsidiary role in the marketing/communications mix, many companies have begun practicing *integrated marketing communications,* also called *integrated direct marketing (IDM).* IDM programs, which focus on a multimedia approach to advertising, are generally much more effective than single communications programs.

5. Direct marketers and their customers usually enjoy mutually rewarding relationships. However, marketers must be careful to avoid campaigns that irritate consumers, are perceived as unfair, are deceptive or fraudulent, and/or invade their customers' privacy.

CONCEPT APPLICATIONS

1. As the electronic marketing revolution gains steam, corporations are discovering that it is not enough to simply employ marketers with high levels of technical competence. These same personnel must also be able to anticipate technological changes and use them to the company's advantage. Smaller companies, which may not be able to support a heavy payroll, may need to team up with larger companies to move onto the information superhighway. For example, AT&T recently agreed to sell Bolt Beranek and Newman's (BBN) Internet-access services to businesses, thus giving the small technology company a major boost onto the global computer network. Commenting on this partnership, one industry analyst said, "This is a huge coup for BBN because the com-

pany has never understood how to market its technology and now they have 12,000 feet on the street who can recommend them." Why do you think AT&T chose to partner with such a small organization?

2. While the Internet itself is not a business, its growth has spawned a large number of Internet-related services and businesses. There are now companies that specialize in designing home pages for the Internet, and others that make their living by selling advertising space on the Net. In addition, a variety of organizations are offering Internet seminars and workshops to businesses, consumers, and educational institutions (Figure 1). What benefits can corporations receive from participating in the Internet? What should organizations learn about the Internet before getting involved? How do the Internet's capabilities affect an organization's marketing plans?

3. Don E. Schultz, an expert on integrated marketing from Northwestern University, says that he receives calls from marketing practitioners who say, "We heard you speak (or read your book, or talked to some of your clients, or something else), and we're ready to get into integrated marketing communications. We know a database is the heart of the process you are developing." They go on to say what their product is and ask, "How big should the computer be, and what type of software should we buy?" Why are these the wrong questions for companies just beginning to use database marketing? What questions should they ask first? What precautions should the company take once its database is up and running?

4. Describe the marketing objectives and target markets of the following companies. What benefits might each company receive from an online shopping service?

a. Sears   e. Hallmark

b. Saks Fifth Avenue   f. Merrill Lynch

c. Williams-Sonoma   g. ComputerLand

d. Ticketmaster   h. TWA

FIGURE I
Courtesy of National Seminars Group.

Managing
Direct and
Online Marketing

5. Retail catalogs were one of the first forms of direct marketing as we know it today. Some retail stores are now using catalogs, delivered through the mail or with newspapers, to increase in-store sales. Why would retail stores decide to issue catalogs? Why might an established retail store decide to enter the mail-order business and produce a catalog?

6. You are developing a business to sell personal computers. Because of limited resources, you have been advised to use a direct-marketing approach. Using the five-step direct-marketing decision framework explained on pages 726–728, describe the major decisions you need to make at each step. Which direct-marketing media do you think will be most successful in helping you achieve your goals?

7. Suppose that Jamestown, New Jersey, has two florists. Florist A uses a traditional mass-marketing approach to attract customers, while Florist B uses a "one-to-one" approach. Which florist is more likely to use each of the following marketing campaigns?

   a. Mother's Day and Valentine's Day specials, supported by radio commercials the week before each holiday.

   b. Notes to children reminding them when their mother's birthday is coming up.

   c. Color brochures of wedding flowers sent to women registered on Bergdorf-Goodman's bridal registry (the florist obtains this list through Bergdorf's marketing department).

   d. An ad in the Yellow Pages that reads "Flowers for all occasions."

   e. A small bouquet of flowers sent to newlyweds on their first anniversary.

   f. A billboard that says, "Did you send flowers to someone you love today?"

8. As more of an organization's employees gain access to the Internet and can begin to bypass the traditional communication channels, organizations may face new challenges. Identify some of the problems that organizations might face if employees begin communicating with other Internet members or contacting suppliers directly without going through normal organizational channels or public-relations departments. Also identify some guidelines that a company should put in place to prevent these problems from occurring.

9. Spend a week monitoring the goings-on in one of the Internet newsgroups listed in Table 23-3. Prepare a brief report for the class summarizing the things discussed in each newsgroup, along with their marketing implications.

10. You are planning to publish a new magazine targeted toward middle-class African-Americans. You are also planning to launch a huge telemarketing campaign in which you will contact more than 500,000 African-American families by telephone and ask them to take out a charter subscription. Your telemarketers need a catchy opening line that will get the attention of the target market. Individually or with a small group, come up with a brief script that your telemarketers will use.

NOTES

1. The terms *direct-order marketing* and *direct relationship marketing* were suggested as subsets of direct marketing by Stan Rapp and Tom Collins in *The Great Marketing Turnaround* (Englewood Cliffs, NJ: Prentice Hall, 1990).

2. See Arnold Fishman's *1994 Guide to Mail Order Sales* (Highland Park, IL: Market Logistics. Tel: [708] 831-1575); and "1994 Mail Order Overview," *Direct Marketing,* August 1994, pp. 26–28.

3. See the interesting discussion in Arvind Rangaswamy and Jerry Wind, "Don't Walk In, Just Log In! Electronic Markets and What They Mean for Marketing" (Wharton School, University of Pennsylvania: October 1994).

4. Rangaswamy and Wind, "Don't Walk In."

5. Pierre A. Passavant, "Where Is Direct Marketing Headed in the 1990s?" an address in Philadelphia, May 4, 1989.

6. See Don Peppers and Martha Rogers, *The One-to-One Future* (New York: Doubleday/Currency, 1993).

7. Jonathan Berry, "A Potent New Tool for Selling: Database Marketing," *Business Week,* September 5, 1994, pp. 56–62; Vincent Alonzo, "'Til Death Do Us Part," *Incentive,* April 1994, pp. 37–41.

8. Bob Stone, *Successful Direct Marketing Methods,* 5th ed. (Lincolnwood, IL: NTC Business Books, 1994).

9. Edward L. Nash, *Direct Marketing: Strategy, Planning, Execution,* 3d ed. (New York: McGraw-Hill, 1995).

10. Also see Richard J. Courtheoux, "Calculating the Lifetime Value of a Customer," in *Integrated Direct Marketing: The Cutting-Edge Strategy for Synchronizing Advertising, Direct Mail, Telemarketing, and Field Sales,* ed. Ernan Roman (Lincolnwood, IL: NTC Business Books, 1995), pp. 198–202. Also see Rob Jackson and Paul Wang, *Strategic Database Marketing* (Lincolnwood, IL: NTC Business Books, 1994), pp. 188–201.

11. For more reading, see Janice Steinberg, "Cacophony of Catalogs Fill All Niches," *Advertising Age,* October 26, 1987, pp. S1-2.

12. "Japan Is Dialing 1 800 BuyAmerica: U.S. Catalogers Offer Bargains Shoppers Can't Find at Home," *Business Week,* June 12, 1995.

13. See Daniel S. Janal, *Online Marketing Handbook* (New York: Van Nostrand Reinhold, 1995).

14. Jay Conrad Levinson and Charles Rubin, *Guerrilla Marketing Online: The Entrepreneur's Guide to Earning Profits on the Internet* (Boston: Houghton Mifflin, 1995), Chapter 5.

15. Don E. Schultz, Stanley I. Tannenbaum, and Robert F. Lauterborn, *Integrated Marketing Communications* (Lincolnwood, IL: NTC Business Books, 1993); Ernan Roman, *Integrated Direct Marketing: The Cutting Edge Strategy for Synchronizing Advertising, Direct Mail, Telemarketing, and Field Sales* (Lincolnwood, IL: NTC Business Books, 1995); Stan Rapp and Thomas L. Collins, *Maximarketing* (New York: McGraw-Hill, 1987), and *Beyond Maximarketing: The New Power of Caring and Daring* (New York: McGraw-Hill, 1994).

16. Roman, *Integrated Direct Marketing,* p. 3.

17. Rapp and Collins, *Maximarketing.*

Managing
Direct and
Online Marketing

ORGANIZING, IMPLEMENTING, EVALUATING, AND CONTROLLING MARKETING ACTIVITIES

Vision without action is a daydream. Action without vision is a nightmare.

JAPANESE PROVERB

Having lost sight of our objective, we redoubled our efforts.

OLD ADAGE

We now turn from the strategic and tactical side of marketing to the *administrative* side of marketing. Our goal is to examine how firms organize, implement, evaluate, and control their marketing activities. In this chapter, we will answer the following questions:

◆ **What trends are occurring in company organization?**

◆ **How are marketing and sales organized in various companies?**

◆ **What is the marketing department's relation to each of the company's other departments?**

◆ **What steps can a company take to build a stronger companywide market-focused orientation?**

◆ **How can a company improve its marketing-implementation skills?**

◆ **What tools are available to help companies evaluate, control, and improve their marketing activities?**

COMPANY ORGANIZATION

Companies often need to reorganize their business and marketing in response to significant changes in the business environment. These changes include globalization, deregulation, advances in computer technology and telecommunications, market fragmentation, and other developments mentioned throughout the book.

To keep up with these changes, companies are increasingly focusing on developing their core businesses and core competences.[1] This is a change from the 1960s and 1970s, when many companies diversified into totally unrelated industries. Although the industries looked promising, the companies lacked the appropriate skills and knowledge to compete. Prime examples are Mobil's purchase of Montgomery Ward and Exxon's venture into the office-equipment business.

Large companies have also realized that while they are good at scaling up existing businesses, they are less effective in starting new businesses. Small entrepreneurs do the latter much better. But some large companies are beginning to cultivate "intrapreneurship" by giving their managers more freedom to produce ideas and take some risks.

Companies have also "downsized" and "delayered": They have reduced the number of organizational levels to get closer to the customer.[2] At one time, AT&T had nineteen organizational levels. Clearly, top management was too far removed from customers to fully understand their changing needs. One corrective action was to advise managers at all levels to do more "managing by walking around." But a more basic corrective was to flatten the organization. Tom Peters proposed that no well-managed organization needed more than five hierarchical levels. The key to a flatter organization was figuring out how each manager could manage more people, say thirty instead of eight. This could be accomplished by empowering employees to excel at self-management.

As a result of this trend, hierarchy has been giving way to *networking*. With more companies using computers, electronic mail, and fax machines, messages increasingly pass between people at different levels of the organization. Companies encourage more teamwork centered around core business processes, trying to break down departmental walls. Companies are also trying to break down walls between themselves and their suppliers and distributors by treating them as business partners and including them in the information flow. Calyx and Corolla (C&C), a tremendously successful business that sells fresh flowers by catalog, is a good example of a company that uses information technology to create a network organization:

CALYX & COROLLA C&C customers select an order from an impressive array of flower arrangements in the catalog and phone their order into C&C. The order is then transmitted to one of 25 or more growers in C&C's network who cuts and packages the arrangement using materials and guidelines provided by C&C. Federal Express picks up the order and delivers the fresh flowers to the designated office or house. The FedEx information system also links the network members. C&C's management credits the use of this information technology as a key factor fueling its double-digit growth.[3]

In this context, we will now look at how the organization of marketing departments is changing.

MARKETING ORGANIZATION

Over the years, marketing has grown from a simple sales department into a complex group of activities. Here we will examine how marketing departments have evolved in companies, how they are organized, and how they interact with other company departments.

The Evolution of the Marketing Department

Marketing departments have evolved through six stages, and today companies can be found in each stage.

STAGE 1: SIMPLE SALES DEPARTMENT. Small companies typically appoint a sales vice-president, who manages a sales force and also does some selling. When the company needs marketing research or advertising, the sales vice-president hires help from the outside (Figure 24-1[a]).

STAGE 2: SALES DEPARTMENT WITH ANCILLARY MARKETING FUNCTIONS. As the company expands, it needs to add or enlarge certain marketing functions. For example, an East Coast firm that plans to open in the West will need to conduct marketing research to learn about customer needs and market potential. Afterward, it will have to advertise its name and products in the area. The sales vice-president will need to hire specialists—such as a marketing research manager and an advertising manager—to handle these marketing activities. The sales vice-president might hire a *marketing director* to manage these and other marketing functions (Figure 24-1[b]).

STAGE 3: SEPARATE MARKETING DEPARTMENT. The continued growth of the company will warrant additional investment in marketing research, new-product development, advertising and sales promotion, and customer service. Yet the sales vice-president normally focuses time and resources on the sales force. The marketing director will plead for a large budget but will usually get less than needed.

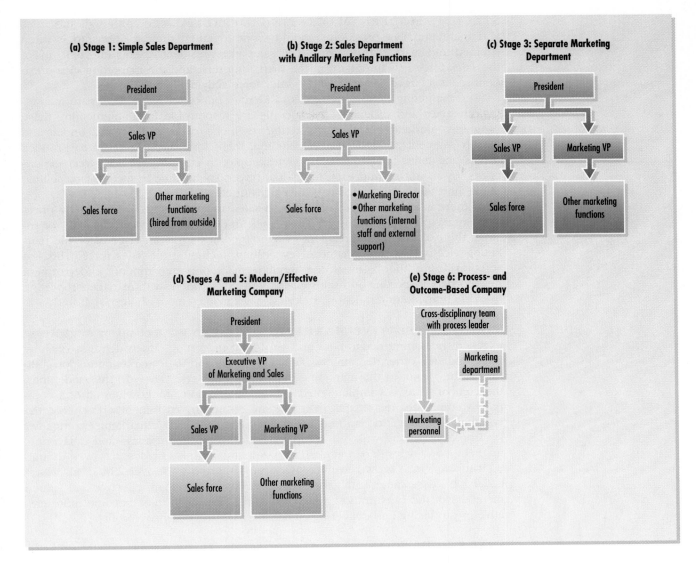

FIGURE 24-1

Stages in the Evolution of the Marketing Department

Eventually the company president will see the advantage of establishing a separate marketing department headed by a marketing vice-president, who reports, along with the sales vice-president, to the president or executive vice-president (Figure 24-1[c]). At this stage, sales and marketing are separate functions that are expected to work closely together.

This arrangement permits the company president to obtain a more balanced view of company opportunities and problems. Suppose sales start slipping and the company president asks for solutions. The sales vice-president might recommend hiring more salespeople, raising sales compensation, running a sales contest, providing more sales training, or cutting the price so that the product will be easier to sell. The marketing vice-president will want to analyze the forces affecting the marketplace. Is the company going after the right segments and customers? Do the target customers have a changing view of the company's and competitors' products? Are changes in product features, styling, packaging, services, distribution, or promotion warranted?

STAGE 4: MODERN MARKETING DEPARTMENT.

Although the sales and marketing vice-presidents should work together, their relationship is often strained and marked by distrust. The sales vice-president resents efforts to make the sales force less important in the marketing mix, and the marketing vice-president seeks a larger budget for non–sales force activities.

The marketing manager's task is to identify opportunities and prepare marketing strategies and programs. Salespeople are responsible for implementing these programs. Marketers rely on marketing research, try to identify and understand market segments, spend time in planning, think long term, and aim to produce profits and gains in market share. Salespeople, in contrast, rely on street experiences, try to understand each individual buyer, spend time in face-to-face selling, think short term, and try to meet their sales quotas.

If there is too much friction between sales and marketing, the company president might place marketing activities back under the sales vice-president, or instruct the executive vice-president to handle conflicts that arise, or place the marketing vice-president in charge of everything, including the sales force. This last solution forms the basis of the modern marketing department, a department headed by a marketing and sales executive vice-president with managers reporting from every marketing function, including sales management (Figure 24-1[d]).

STAGE 5: EFFECTIVE MARKETING COMPANY.

A company can have an excellent marketing department and yet fail at marketing. Much depends on how the company's other departments view customers and their marketing responsibilities. If they point to the marketing department and say, "They do the marketing," the company has not implemented effective marketing. Only when all of a company's employees realize that their jobs are created by customers who choose the company's products does the company become an effective marketing company.[4]

Ironically, in the wake of company cost cutting, downsizing, and delayering, marketing and sales departments have been among those hardest hit, even though their mission is to grow revenue. Between 1992 and 1994 over 28% of all white-collar job losses came from sales and marketing.[5] To remain effective and valued members of the organization, marketers and salespeople must become more creative in producing and delivering customer value and company profits.

STAGE 6: PROCESS- AND OUTCOME-BASED COMPANY.

Many companies are now refocusing their organizational structure on key processes rather than departments. Departmental organization is increasingly viewed as a barrier to the smooth performance of fundamental business processes such as new-product development, customer acquisition and retention, order fulfillment, and customer service. In the interest of achieving certain process outcomes, companies are now appointing process leaders who manage cross-disciplinary teams. Marketing people and salespeople are consequently spending an increasing percentage of their time as process team members. As a result, marketing personnel may have a solid line responsibility to their teams, and a dotted line responsibility to the marketing department (Figure 24-1 [e]). Each team sends periodic evaluations of the marketing member's performance to the marketing department. The marketing department is also responsible for planning more training for its marketing personnel, assigning them to new teams, and evaluating their overall performance.

Ways of Organizing the Marketing Department

Modern marketing departments can take numerous forms. The marketing department may be organized by function, geographical area, products or brands, and/or customer markets.

FUNCTIONAL ORGANIZATION. The most common form of marketing organization consists of functional-marketing specialists reporting to a marketing vice-president, who coordinates their activities. Figure 24-2 shows five specialists. Additional specialists might include a customer service manager, a marketing planning manager, and a market-logistics manager.

It is quite a challenge to develop smooth working relations within the marketing department, let alone between marketing and other departments. Cespedes has urged companies to improve the critical interfaces among field sales, customer service, and product management groups, since they collectively have a major impact on customer service. He has proposed several ways to form tighter linkages among these three key marketing groups.[6]

The main advantage of a functional-marketing organization is its administrative simplicity. However, this form loses effectiveness as the company's products and markets increase. First, a functional organization often leads to inadequate planning for specific products and markets, since no one has full responsibility for any product or market. Products that are not favored by anyone are neglected. Second, each functional group competes with the other functions for budget and status. The marketing vice-president constantly has to weigh the claims of competing functional specialists and faces a difficult coordination problem.

GEOGRAPHICAL ORGANIZATION. A company selling in a national market often organizes its sales force (and sometimes other functions, including marketing) along geographical lines. The national sales manager may supervise four regional sales managers, who each supervise six zone managers, who in turn supervise eight district sales managers, who supervise ten salespeople.

Several companies are now adding *area market specialists* (regional or local marketing managers) to support the sales efforts in high-volume, distinctive markets. One such market might be Miami, which has a Latino population of 56%, as compared to neighboring Fort Lauderdale, with a Latino population of only 4 percent. The local market specialist for Miami, for example, would know Miami's customer and trade makeup in great detail; help headquarters marketing managers adjust their marketing mix for Miami; prepare local annual and long-range plans for selling all the company's products in Miami; and help sell their field salespeople on the new programs.

Several factors have fueled the move toward regionalization and localization. First, the U.S. mass market for most products has slowly subdivided into a profusion of minimarkets: baby boomers, senior citizens, African-Americans, single mothers—the list goes on. Today, marketers find it difficult to create a single product or program that appeals to all of these diverse groups. Just consider these demographic figures and you can see why marketers cannot look at the United States as one homogenous country:[7]

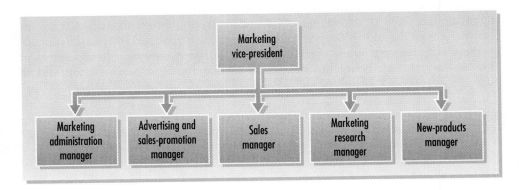

FIGURE 24-2
Functional Organization

CHAPTER 24   **749**

Organizing, Implementing,
Evaluating, and Controlling
Marketing Activities

- About the same number of people live in New England as in the Mountain Region. Yet the Mountain Region is growing at a much faster rate and the population's median age is lower.

- The South has gained almost 20 million jobs over the last decade, while another area of the country was dubbed the "Rust Belt."

- Portland, Maine, is almost totally white while Washington, DC, is predominantly black.

Second, improved information and marketing research technologies have also spurred regionalization. For example, data from retail-store scanners allow instant tracking of product sales from store to store, helping companies pinpoint local problems and opportunities that might call for localized marketing actions. A third important factor is the increasing power of retailers. Scanners give retailers mountains of market information, and this information gives them power over manufacturers. Retailers are often lukewarm about large, national marketing campaigns aimed at masses of consumers. They strongly prefer local programs tied to their own promotion efforts and aimed at consumers in their own cities and neighborhoods. Thus, to keep retailers happy and to get shelf space for their products, manufacturers must now allot more of their marketing budgets to local, store-by-store promotions.

Campbell's Soup has jumped into regionalization with both feet:

CAMPBELL'S SOUP Campbell's has created many successful regional brands. It sells its spicy Ranchero beans in the Southwest, Creole soup in the South, and red bean soup in Latino areas. For northwesterners, who like their pickles very sour, it created Zesty pickles. These and other brands appealing to regional tastes add substantially to Campbell's annual sales. In addition, Campbell's has divided its market into 22 regions, each responsible for planning local marketing programs. The company has allocated 15% to 20% of its total marketing budget to support local marketing.

Within each region, Campbell's sales managers and salespeople create advertising and promotions geared to local market needs and conditions. They choose whatever local advertising media work best in their areas. They work closely with local retailers on displays, coupon offers, price specials, and local promotional events.[8]

Other companies that have shifted to regional marketing are McDonald's, which now spends about 50% of its total advertising budget regionally; American Airlines, which realized that the travel needs of Chicagoans and southwesterners are very different during the winter months; and Anheuser-Busch, which has subdivided its regional markets into ethnic and demographic segments with different ad campaigns for each.

Regionalization may be accompanied by a move toward branchising. *Branchising* means empowering the company's districts or local offices to operate more like franchises. IBM recently told its branch managers to "make it your business." Thus, the branches resemble profit centers and local managers have more strategy latitude and incentive.

Regionalization need not be limited to regions within a country. In fact, large multinationals often structure their sales and marketing efforts to market more effectively across the globe. Several multinationals have replaced international headquarters with regional ones. Quaker Oats has set up a European headquarters in Brussels, and British Petroleum has based its operations in Asia and the Middle East in Singapore.[9] Citibank has also innovated here:

CITIBANK As a global bank, Citibank has had to figure out how to service its major global accounts in different parts of the world. Its solution: A parent account manager (PAM) is appointed for each global account and sits in the company's New York headquarters. Each PAM has built a network of field account managers (FAMs) in the various countries and calls upon them when the specific account needs service.

PRODUCT- OR BRAND-MANAGEMENT ORGANIZATION. Companies

producing a variety of products and brands often establish a product- (or brand-) management organization. The product-management organization does not replace the functional-management organization but rather serves as another layer of management. The product-management organization is headed by a products manager who supervises product category managers, who in turn supervise specific product and brand managers. A product-management organization makes sense if the company's products are quite different, or if the sheer number of products is beyond the ability of a functional-marketing organization to handle.

Product management first appeared in the Procter & Gamble Company in 1927. A new company soap, Camay, was not doing well, and one of the young executives, Neil H. McElroy (later president of P&G), was assigned to give his exclusive attention to developing and promoting this product. He did it successfully, and the company soon added other product managers.

Since then, many firms have established product-management organizations. Kraft General Foods, for example, uses a product-management organization in its Post Division. There are separate product category managers in charge of cereals, pet food, and beverages. Within the cereal product group, there are separate product managers for nutritional cereals, children's presweetened cereals, family cereals, and miscellaneous cereals.

The product manager's role is to develop product plans, implement them, monitor the results, and take corrective action when necessary. This responsibility breaks down into six tasks:

- Developing a long-range and competitive strategy for the product
- Preparing an annual marketing plan and sales forecast
- Working with advertising and merchandising agencies to develop copy, programs, and campaigns
- Stimulating support of the product among the sales force and distributors
- Gathering continuous intelligence on the product's performance, customer and dealer attitudes, and new problems and opportunities
- Initiating product improvements to meet changing market needs

These basic functions are common to both consumer- and industrial-product managers. However, consumer-product managers typically manage fewer products than industrial-product managers. They also spend more time on advertising, sales promotion, and working with others in the company and various agencies. They are often younger and MBA-educated. Industrial-product managers, in contrast, spend more time with customers and laboratory and engineering personnel, think more about the technical aspects of their product and possible design improvements, and work more closely with the sales force and key buyers. They pay less attention to advertising, sales promotion, and promotional pricing. They emphasize rational product factors over emotional ones.

The product-management organization introduces several advantages. First, the product manager can concentrate on developing a cost-effective marketing mix for the product. Second, the product manager can react more quickly to problems in the marketplace than a committee of functional specialists can. Third, the company's smaller brands are less neglected, because they have a product advocate. Fourth, product management is an excellent training ground for young executives, for it involves them in almost every area of company operations (Figure 24-3, on page 752).

But a product-management organization is not without its disadvantages. First, product management creates some conflict and frustration. Typically, product managers are not given enough authority to carry out their responsibilities effec-

Organizing, Implementing,
Evaluating, and Controlling
Marketing Activities

FIGURE 24-3
The Product Manager's Interactions

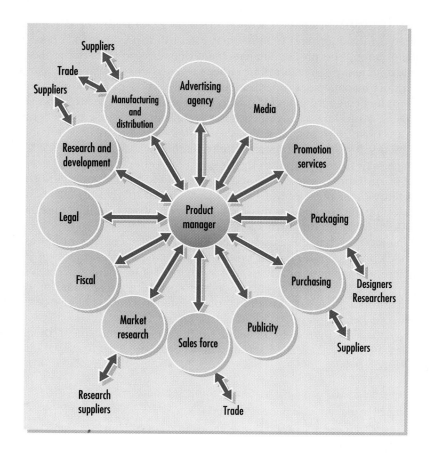

tively. They have to rely on persuasion to get the cooperation of advertising, sales, manufacturing, and other departments. They are told they are "minipresidents" but are often treated as low-level coordinators. They are burdened with a great amount of "housekeeping" paperwork. They often have to go over the heads of others to get something done.

Second, product managers become experts in their product but rarely become experts in any of the functions. They vacillate between posing as experts and being cowed by real experts. This is unfortunate when the product depends on a specific type of expertise, such as advertising.

Third, the product-management system often turns out to be costlier than anticipated. Originally, one person is appointed to manage each major product. Soon product managers are appointed to manage even minor products. Each product manager, usually overworked, pleads for and gets an associate brand manager. Later, both overworked, they persuade management to give them an assistant brand manager. With all these people, payroll costs climb. In the meantime, the company continues to increase its functional specialists in copy, packaging, media, sales promotion, market surveys, statistical analysis, and so on. The company becomes saddled with a costly structure of product-management people and functional specialists.

Fourth, brand managers normally manage their brand for only a short time. Either product managers move up in a few years to another brand or product, or they transfer to another company, or they leave product management altogether. Their short-term involvement with the brand leads to short-term marketing planning and plays havoc with building up the brand's long-term strengths.

Fifth, the fragmentation of markets means that it gets harder to develop a national strategy from headquarters. Brand managers must please more regional-based trade groups and rely more on the local sales force and on local sales promotion.

Pearson and Wilson have suggested five steps to make the product-management system work better:[10]

- *Clearly delineate the limits of the product manager's role and responsibility for the product.* At too many companies, product managers are essentially proposers, not deciders.
- *Build a strategy-development-and-review process to provide an agreed-to framework for the product manager's operations.* Too many companies allow product managers to get away with shallow marketing plans featuring a lot of statistics but little strategic rationale.
- *Take into account areas of potential conflict between product managers and functional specialists when defining their respective roles.* Clarify which decisions are to be made by the product manager, which by the expert, and which will be shared.
- *Set up a formal process that forces to the top all conflict-of-interest situations between product management and functional line management.* Both parties should put the issues in writing and forward them to general management for settlement.
- *Establish a system for measuring results consistent with the product manager's responsibilities.* If product managers are accountable for profit, they should be given more control over the factors that affect profitability.

A second alternative is to switch from a product-manager to a product-team approach. There are three types of product-team structures in product management (Figure 24-4):

- *Vertical product team:* Consists of a product manager, associate product manager, and product assistant (Figure 24-4[a]). The product manager is the leader and primarily deals with other managers to gain their cooperation. The associate product manager assists in these tasks and also does some paperwork. The product assistant carries out most of the paperwork and routine analysis.
- *Triangular product team:* Consists of a product manager and two specialized product assistants, one who takes care of (say) marketing research and the other, marketing communications (Figure 24-4[b]). This design is used at the Illinois Central Railroad, where three-person teams manage different commodities. Also, the Hallmark Company uses a "marketing team" consisting of a market manager (the leader), a marketing manager, and a distribution manager.
- *Horizontal product team:* Consists of a product manager and several specialists from marketing and other functions (Figure 24-4[c]). 3M has teams consisting of a team leader and representatives from sales, marketing, laboratory, engineering, accounting, and marketing research. Dow Corning sets up teams of five to eight people; each team manages a product, market, or process. For example, one team manages the process of manufacturing and selling silicone to companies making shampoos, and another team manages coatings for printed circuit boards sold to computer companies.

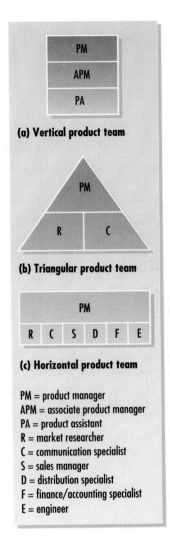

(a) Vertical product team

(b) Triangular product team

(c) Horizontal product team

PM = product manager
APM = associate product manager
PA = product assistant
R = market researcher
C = communication specialist
S = sales manager
D = distribution specialist
F = finance/accounting specialist
E = engineer

FIGURE 24-4
Three Types of Product Teams

A third alternative is to eliminate product-manager positions for minor products and assign two or more products to each remaining product manager. This is especially feasible where two or more products appeal to a similar set of needs. Thus a cosmetics company does not need separate product managers for each cosmetic product because cosmetics serve one major need—beauty—whereas a toiletries company needs different managers for headache remedies, toothpaste, soap, and shampoo, because these products differ in their use and appeal.

A fourth alternative is to introduce *category management,* in which a company focuses on product categories to manage its brands. For example, P&G found too much internal competition among its brands in each category: Puritan and Crisco were both fighting for a budget increase, and Cheer started to copy the same claim as Tide, thus diluting Tide's positioning. P&G's answer: Brand managers are now accountable to a new corps of category managers, who resolve conflicts, protect

Organizing, Implementing, Evaluating, and Controlling Marketing Activities

positionings, allocate budgets, and develop new brands for the category. Category management is also a response to the fact that supermarkets are reorganizing along category buying lines. Kraft General Foods has moved in the category direction:

KRAFT GENERAL FOODS Kraft has changed from a classic brand-management structure, in which each brand competed for organizational resources and market share, to a category-based structure in which category business directors (or "product integrators") lead cross-functional teams composed of representatives from marketing, R&D, consumer promotion, and finance. The category business directors have both broad responsibility and bottom-line accountability. No longer viewed solely as marketers, they are as responsible for identifying opportunities to improve the efficiency of the supply chain as they are for developing the next advertisement. Kraft's category teams work in conjunction with process teams dedicated to each product category, and with customer teams dedicated to each major customer (Figure 24-5). After years of declining real growth, escalating trade promotion spending, and increasingly demanding customers, Kraft's new team structure is spurring strong sales.[11]

Category management is not a panacea, for a simple reason. It is still a product-driven, not a customer-driven, system. Colgate recently moved from brand management (Colgate toothpaste) to category management (toothpaste category), to a new stage called "customer-need management" (mouth care). This last step finally focuses the organization on basic customer needs.[12]

MARKET-MANAGEMENT ORGANIZATION. Many companies sell their products to a diverse set of markets. For example, Canon sells its fax machines to consumer, business, and government markets. U.S. Steel sells its steel to the railroad, construction, and public-utility industries. When customers fall into different user groups with distinct buying preferences and practices, a market-management organization is desirable. A *markets manager* supervises several *market managers* (also called *market development managers, market specialists,* or *industry specialists*). The market managers draw upon functional services as needed. Market managers of important markets might even have functional specialists reporting to them.

Market managers are staff (not line) people, with duties similar to those of product managers. Market managers develop long-range and annual plans for their markets. They must analyze where their market is going and what new products

FIGURE 24-5

Managing Through Teams at Kraft

Source: Michael George, Anthony Freeling, and David Court, "Reinventing the Marketing Organization," *The McKinsey Quarterly,* No. 4 (1994), 43–62.

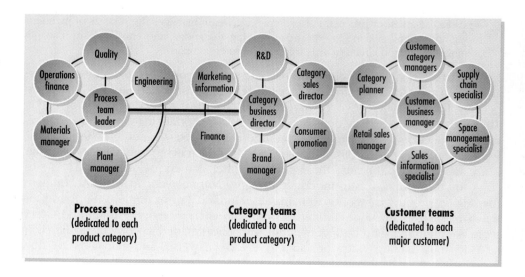

their company should offer to this market. Their performance is judged by their contribution to market share growth as well as their market's current profitability. This system carries many of the same advantages and disadvantages of product-management systems. Its strongest advantage is that the marketing activity is organized to meet the needs of distinct customer groups rather than focused on marketing functions, regions, or products per se.

Many companies are reorganizing along market lines. Hanan calls these companies *market-centered organizations* and argues that "the only way to ensure being market oriented is to put a company's organizational structure together so that its major markets become the centers around which its divisions are built."[13] Xerox has converted from geographical selling to selling by industry, as has IBM, which recently reorganized its 235,000 employees into 14 customer-focused divisions. Hewlett Packard has also moved away from a regional sales approach and set up a structure in which salespeople concentrate on businesses within individual industries. But market-centered reorganization has not been confined to manufacturing or packaged-goods companies; Chemical Bank recently reorganized its retail marketing function around income-based consumer segments, in an attempt to do away with the product silos that had long prevented it from effectively cross-selling products that appeal to the same markets.

Several studies have confirmed the value of a market-based organization. Narver and Slater created a measure of market orientation and then analyzed its effect on business profitability. Using a sample of 140 business units consisting of commodity-products businesses and noncommodity businesses, they found a substantial positive effect of market orientation on both types of businesses.[14]

PRODUCT-MANAGEMENT/MARKET-MANAGEMENT ORGANIZATION. Companies that produce many products flowing into many markets face a dilemma. They could use a product-management system, which requires product managers to be familiar with highly divergent markets. Or they could use a market-management system, which means that market managers would have to be familiar with highly divergent products bought by their markets. Or they could install both product and market managers—that is, a *matrix organization*.

Du Pont was a pioneer in developing the matrix structure (Figure 24-6). Its textile fibers department consists of separate product managers for rayon, acetate, nylon, orlon, and dacron; and separate market managers for men's wear, women's wear, home furnishings, and industrial markets. The product managers plan the sales and profits of their respective fibers. Their aim is to expand the use of their fiber. They ask market managers to estimate how much of their fiber they can sell

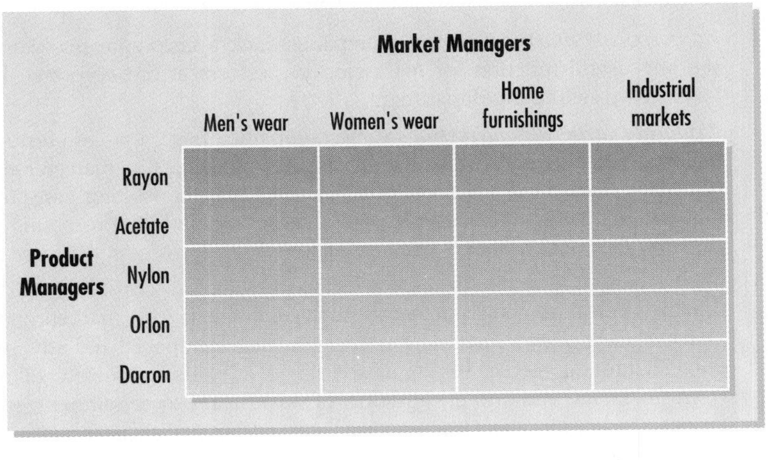

FIGURE 24-6
Product-/Market-Management Matrix System

Organizing, Implementing, Evaluating, and Controlling Marketing Activities

in each market at a proposed price. The market managers are more interested in meeting their market's needs rather than pushing a particular fiber. In preparing their market plans, they ask each product manager about different fibers' planned prices and availabilities. The final sales forecasts of the market managers and the product managers should add to the same grand total.

Companies like Du Pont can go one step further and view their market managers as the main marketers, and their product managers as suppliers. The men's wear market manager, for example, would be empowered to buy textile fibers either from Du Pont's product managers, or, if Du Pont's price is too high, from outside suppliers. This system would force Du Pont product managers to become more efficient. If a Du Pont product manager fails to match the "arm's length pricing" levels of competitive suppliers, then it is questionable whether Du Pont should continue to produce that fiber.

A matrix organization would seem desirable in a multiproduct, multimarket company. The rub is that this system is costly and often creates conflicts. There is the cost of supporting all the managers. There are also questions about where authority and responsibility should reside. Here are two of many dilemmas:

- *How should the sales force be organized?* Should there be separate sales forces for rayon, nylon, and the other fibers? Or should the sales forces be organized according to men's wear, women's wear, and other markets? Or should the sales force not be specialized? (The marketing concept favors organizing the sales force by markets, not product.)

- *Who should set the prices for a particular product/market?* Should the nylon product manager have final authority for setting nylon prices in all markets? What happens if the men's wear market manager feels that nylon will lose out in this market unless special price concessions are made on nylon? (Product managers, nevertheless, should retain the ultimate authority over pricing, in the author's opinion.)

By the early 1980s a number of companies had abandoned matrix management. But matrix management has resurfaced and is flourishing today in the form of "business teams" staffed with full-time specialists reporting to one team boss. The major difference is that companies today provide the right context in which a matrix can thrive—an emphasis on flat, lean team organizations focused around business processes that cut horizontally across functions.[15]

CORPORATE/DIVISIONAL ORGANIZATION. As multiproduct/multimarket companies grow, they often convert their larger product and/or market groups into separate divisions. The divisions set up their own departments and services. This raises the question of what marketing services and activities should be retained at corporate headquarters.

Divisionalized companies have reached different answers to this question. Corporate marketing staffs follow one of three models:

- *No corporate marketing:* Some companies lack a corporate marketing staff. They don't see any useful function for marketing to perform at the corporate level. Each division has its own marketing department.

- *Moderate corporate marketing:* Some companies have a small corporate marketing staff that performs a few functions, primarily (1) assisting top management with overall opportunity evaluation, (2) providing divisions with consulting assistance on request, (3) helping divisions that have little or no marketing, and (4) promoting the marketing concept to other departments of the company.

- *Strong corporate marketing:* Some companies have a corporate marketing staff that, in addition to the preceding activities, also provides various marketing services to the divisions. The corporate marketing staff might provide specialized advertising services (e.g., coordination of media buying, institutional advertising, review of division advertising from an image standpoint, auditing of advertising expenditures), sales-promotion services (e.g., companywide promotions, central buying of promotional materials), marketing research services (e.g., advanced mathematical analysis, research on marketing development cutting across divisional lines), sales-administration services (e.g., counsel on sales organization and sales policies, development of common sales-reporting systems, management of sales forces selling to common customers), and miscellaneous services (e.g., counseling on marketing planning, hiring and training of marketing personnel).

Do companies tend to favor one of these models? The answer is no. Some companies have recently installed a corporate marketing staff for the first time; others have expanded their corporate marketing department; others have reduced its size and scope; and still others have eliminated it altogether.

The potential contribution of a corporate marketing staff varies in different stages of the company's evolution. Most companies begin with weak marketing in their divisions and often establish a corporate marketing staff to bring stronger marketing into the divisions through training and other services. Some members of the corporate marketing staff might be transferred to head divisional marketing departments. As the divisions become strong in their marketing, corporate marketing has less to offer them. Some companies might decide that corporate marketing has done its job and proceed to eliminate the department.[16]

Marketing's Relations with Other Departments

In principle, all the functions of a business should interact harmoniously to pursue the firm's overall objectives. In practice, however, interdepartmental relations are often characterized by deep rivalries and distrust. Some interdepartmental conflict stems from differences of opinion as to what is in the company's best interests, some from real trade-offs between departmental well-being and company well-being, and some from unfortunate departmental stereotypes and prejudices.

In the typical organization, each business function has a potential impact on customer satisfaction. Under the marketing concept, all departments need to "think customer" and work together to satisfy customer needs and expectations. The marketing department must drive this point home. The marketing vice-president has two tasks: (1) to coordinate the company's internal marketing activities and to (2) coordinate marketing with finance, operations, and other company functions to serve the customer.

Yet there is little agreement on how much influence and authority marketing should have over other departments to bring about coordinated marketing. Typically, the marketing vice-president must work through persuasion rather than authority. This situation is well illustrated in the case of the marketing vice-president of a major European airline. His mandate is to build up his airline's market share. Yet he has no authority over other functions that affect customer satisfaction: He can't hire or train the cabin crew (personnel department). He can't determine the type or quality of food (catering department). He can't enforce cleanliness standards on the plane (maintenance department). He can't determine schedules (operations department). He can't establish the fares (finance department). What does he control? He controls marketing research, the sales force, advertising, and promotion. But he must work through the other departments to shape key determinants of customer satisfaction.

Other departments often resist bending their efforts to meet the customers' interests. Just as marketing stresses the customer's point of view, other departments stress the importance of their tasks. Inevitably, departments define company problems and goals from their point of view. As a result, conflicts of interest are unavoidable. Table 24-1 on the next page summarizes the main differences in orientation between marketing and other departments. We will briefly examine the typical concerns of each department.

TABLE 24-1

DEPARTMENT	DEPARTMENT EMPHASIS	MARKETING'S EMPHASIS
R&D	Basic research Intrinsic quality Functional features	Applied research Perceived quality Sales features
Engineering	Long design lead time Few models Standard components	Short design lead time Many models Custom components

Purchasing	Narrow product line
	Standard parts
	Price of material
	Economical lot sizes
	Purchasing at infrequent
	   intervals
		Broad product line
		Nonstandard parts
		Quality of material
		Large lot sizes to avoid stockouts
		Immediate purchasing for customer
		   needs

Manufacturing	Long production lead time Long runs with few models No model changes Standard orders Ease of fabrication Average quality control	Short production lead time Short runs with many models Frequent model changes Custom orders Aesthetic appearance Tight quality control
Operations	Staff convenience Normal disposition Ordinary service	Customer convenience Pleasant disposition Extraordinary service

Finance	Strict rationales for spending
	Pricing to cover costs
	Hard and fast budgets
		Intuitive arguments for spending
		Pricing to further market develop-
		   ment
		Flexible budgets to meet changing
		   needs

Accounting	Standard transactions Few reports	Special terms and discounts Many reports

Credit	Full financial disclosures by
	   customers
	No credit risk
	Tough credit terms
	Tough collection procedures
		Minimum credit examination of
		   customers
		Some credit risk
		Easy credit terms
		Easy collection procedures

R&D. The company's drive for successful new products is often thwarted by weak working relations between R&D and marketing. In many ways, these groups represent different cultures in the organization.[17] The R&D department is staffed with scientists and technicians who pride themselves on scientific curiosity and detachment, like to work on challenging technical problems without much concern for immediate sales payoffs, and prefer to work without much supervision or accountability for research costs. The marketing/sales department is staffed with business-oriented people who pride themselves on a practical understanding of the marketplace, like to see many new products with sales features that can be promoted to customers, and feel compelled to pay attention to costs. Each group often carries negative stereotypes of the other. Marketers see the R&D people as seeking to discover or maximize technical qualities rather than design for customer requirements, while R&D people see marketers as gimmick-oriented hucksters who are more interested in sales than in the product's technical features. These stereotypes get in the way of productive teamwork.

A balanced company is one in which R&D and marketing share responsibility for successful market-oriented innovation. The R&D staff takes responsibility not for innovation alone but for a successful product launch. The marketing staff takes responsibility not for new sales features alone but also for helping identify new ways to satisfy needs.

Gupta, Raj, and Wilemon concluded that a balanced R&D-marketing coordination is strongly correlated with innovation success.[18] R&D-marketing cooperation can be facilitated in several ways:[19]

- Sponsor joint seminars to build understanding and respect for each other's goals, working styles, and problems.

- Assign each new project to functional teams including an R&D person and a marketing person, who work together through the life of the project. R&D and marketing jointly establish the development goals and marketing plan.

- Allow for R&D's continued participation into the selling period, including involvement in preparing technical manuals, participating in trade shows, carrying out postintroductory marketing research with customers, and even doing some selling.

- Work out conflicts by going to higher management, following a clear procedure. In one company, R&D and marketing both report to the same vice-president.

ENGINEERING.   Engineering is responsible for finding practical ways to design new products and new production processes. Engineers are interested in achieving technical quality, cost economy, and manufacturing simplicity. They come into conflict with marketing executives when the latter want several models to be produced, often with product features requiring custom rather than standard components. Engineers see marketers as wanting "bells and whistles" on the products rather than intrinsic quality. They often think of marketing people as inept technically, as continually changing priorities, and as not fully credible or trustworthy. These problems are less pronounced in companies where marketing executives have engineering backgrounds and can communicate effectively with engineers.

PURCHASING.   Purchasing executives are responsible for obtaining materials and components in the right quantities and quality at the lowest possible cost. They see marketing executives pushing for several models in a product line, which requires purchasing small quantities of many items rather than large quantities of a few items. They think that marketing insists on too high a quality of ordered materials and components. They also dislike marketing's forecasting inaccuracy, which causes them to place rush orders at unfavorable prices and to carry excessive inventories.

MANUFACTURING.   Manufacturing people are responsible for the smooth running of the factory to produce the right products in the right quantities at the right time for the right cost. They have spent their lives in the factory, with its attendant problems of machine breakdowns, inventory stockouts, and labor disputes. They see marketers as having little understanding of factory economics or politics. Marketers will complain about insufficient plant capacity, delays in production, poor quality control, and poor customer service. Yet marketers often turn in inaccurate sales forecasts, recommend product features that are difficult to manufacture, and promise more factory service than is reasonable.

Marketers do not see the factory's problems, but rather the problems of their customers, who need the goods quickly, who receive defective merchandise, and who cannot get factory service. Marketers often don't show enough concern for the extra factory costs involved in helping a customer. The problem is not only poor communication but an actual conflict of interest.

Companies settle these conflicts in different ways. In *manufacturing-driven companies,* everything is done to ensure smooth production and low costs. The

Organizing, Implementing, Evaluating, and Controlling Marketing Activities

company prefers simple products, narrow product lines, and high-volume production. Sales campaigns calling for a hasty production buildup are kept to a minimum. Customers on back order have to wait.

Other companies are *marketing driven,* in that the company goes out of its way to satisfy customers. In one large toiletries company, the marketing personnel call the shots, and the manufacturing people have to fall in line, regardless of overtime costs, short runs, and so on. The result is high and fluctuating manufacturing costs, as well as variable product quality.

Companies need to develop a balanced orientation in which manufacturing and marketing jointly determine what is in the company's best interests. Solutions include joint seminars to understand each other's viewpoint, joint committees and liaison personnel, personnel exchange programs, and analytical methods to determine the most profitable course of action.[20]

Company profitability is greatly dependent on achieving effective manufacturing-marketing working relations. Marketers need to understand the marketing potentials of new manufacturing strategies—the flexible factory, automation and robotization, just-in-time production, total quality management, and so on. Manufacturing strategy depends upon whether the company wants to win through low cost, high quality, high variety, or fast service. Manufacturing is also a marketing tool insofar as buyers often want to visit the factory to assess how well it is managed.

OPERATIONS. The term "manufacturing" is used for industries making physical products. The term "operations" is used for industries that create and provide services. In the case of a hotel, for example, the operations department includes front desk people, doormen, waiters and waitresses, and so on. Because marketing makes promises about the company's service levels, it is extremely important that marketing and operations work well together. If operations personnel lack a customer orientation and motivation, negative word-of-mouth will eventually destroy the business. The operations staff member may be inclined to focus on his or her own convenience, exhibit a normal attitude, and give ordinary service, while marketers want the staff to focus on customer convenience, show a positive and friendly disposition, and provide extraordinary service. Marketing people must fully understand the capabilities and mind-set of those delivering the service and continuously try to improve their attitudes and capabilities.

FINANCE. Financial executives pride themselves on being able to evaluate the profit implications of different business actions. When it comes to marketing expenditures, they feel frustrated. Marketing executives ask for substantial budgets for advertising, sales promotions, and sales force, without being able to prove how much sales revenue these expenditures will produce. Financial executives suspect that the marketers' forecasts are self-serving. They think that marketing people do not spend enough time relating marketing expenditures to results. They think that marketers are too quick to slash prices to win orders, instead of pricing to make a profit.

On the other side of the coin, marketing executives often see financial people as controlling the purse strings too tightly and refusing to invest funds in long-term market development. They think that financial people see all marketing expenditures as expenses rather than investments and are overly conservative and risk averse, causing many opportunities to be lost. The solution lies in giving marketing people more financial training and giving financial people more marketing training. Financial executives need to adapt their financial tools and theories to support strategic marketing.

ACCOUNTING. Accountants see marketing people as lax in providing their sales reports on time. They dislike the special deals that salespeople make with customers because these require special accounting procedures. Marketers dislike the way accountants allocate fixed-cost burdens to different products in the line. Brand managers may feel that their brand is more profitable than it looks, the problem being that it was assigned too high an overhead burden. They would also like accounting to prepare special reports on sales and profitability by channels, territories, order sizes, and so on.

CREDIT. Credit officers evaluate potential customers' credit standing and deny or limit credit to the more doubtful ones. They think that marketers will sell to anyone, including those from whom payment is doubtful. Marketers, in contrast, often feel that credit standards are too high. They think that "zero bad debts" really means that the company lost a lot of sales and profits. They feel they work too hard to find customers to hear that they are not good enough to sell to.

Strategies for Building a Companywide Marketing Orientation

Many companies are beginning to realize that they are not really market and customer driven—they are product or sales driven. These companies—such as Baxter, Ameritech, Ford, Shell, and J. P. Morgan—are attempting to reorganize themselves into true market-driven companies. The task is not easy. It won't happen as a result of the CEO making speeches and urging every employee to "think customer." The change *will* require a change in job and department definitions, responsibilities, incentives, and relationships. The Marketing Memo on page 762 shows an audit instrument that can be used to evaluate which of the company departments are truly customer driven.

What steps must a CEO take if he or she hopes to create a market- and customer-focused company? Here are the main steps:

1. *Convince the management team of the need to become customer focused.* The CEO must convince the company's top managers that becoming more market focused and customer centered will pay off. The CEO must give frequent speeches to employees, suppliers, and distributors about the importance of delivering quality and value to customers. The CEO must personally exemplify strong customer commitment and reward those in the organization who do likewise.

2. *Appoint a top marketing officer and a marketing task force.* The company should hire a top marketing officer and establish a marketing task force to assist in bringing modern marketing thinking and practices into the company. The task force should include the CEO; the vice-presidents of sales, R&D, purchasing, manufacturing, finance, and human resources; and a few other key individuals.

3. *Get outside help and guidance:* The marketing task force would benefit from outside consulting expertise in building a company marketing culture. Consulting firms have considerable experience in helping companies move toward a marketing orientation.

4. *Change the reward structures in the company.* The company will have to change department reward structures if it expects departmental behavior to change. As long as purchasing and manufacturing are rewarded for keeping costs low, they will resist accepting some costs required to serve customers better. As long as the finance department focuses on short-term profit performance, it will oppose major marketing investments designed to build more satisfied and loyal customers.

5. *Hire strong marketing talent.* The company should hire well-trained marketing talent from outside, preferably from leading marketing companies. When Citibank got serious about marketing, it hired away several marketing managers from General Foods. The company will need a strong marketing vice-president who not only manages the marketing department but also gains respect and influence with the other vice-presidents. A

MARKETING MEMO

AUDIT: CHARACTERISTICS OF COMPANY DEPARTMENTS THAT ARE TRULY CUSTOMER DRIVEN

R&D
- ____ They spend time meeting customers and listening to their problems.
- ____ They welcome the involvement of marketing, manufacturing, and other departments on each new project.
- ____ They benchmark competitors' products and seek "best of class" solutions.
- ____ They solicit customer reactions and suggestions as the project progresses.
- ____ They continuously improve and refine the product on the basis of market feedback.

Purchasing
- ____ They proactively search for the best suppliers rather than choose only from those who solicit their business.
- ____ They build long-term relations with fewer but more reliable high-quality suppliers.
- ____ They don't compromise quality for price savings.

Manufacturing
- ____ They invite customers to visit and tour their plants.
- ____ They visit customer factories to see how customers use the company's products.
- ____ They willingly work overtime when it is important to meet promised delivery schedules.
- ____ They continuously search for ways to produce goods faster and/or at lower costs.
- ____ They continuously improve product quality, aiming for zero defects.
- ____ They meet customer requirements for "customization" where this can be done profitably.

Marketing
- ____ They study customer needs and wants in well-defined market segments.
- ____ They allocate marketing effort in relation to the long-run profit potential of the targeted segments.
- ____ They develop winning offerings for each target segment.
- ____ They measure company image and customer satisfaction on a continuous basis.
- ____ They continuously gather and evaluate ideas for new products, product improvements, and services to meet customers' needs.
- ____ They influence all company departments and employees to be customer centered in their thinking and practice.

Sales
- ____ They have specialized knowledge of the customer's industry.
- ____ They strive to give the customer "the best solution."
- ____ They make only promises that they can keep.
- ____ They feed back customers' needs and ideas to those in charge of product development.
- ____ They serve the same customers for a long period of time.

Logistics
- ____ They set a high standard for service delivery time and they meet this standard consistently.
- ____ They operate a knowledgeable and friendly customer service department that can answer questions, handle complaints, and resolve problems in a satisfactory and timely manner.

Accounting
- ____ They prepare periodic "profitability" reports by product, market segment, geographic areas (regions, sales territories), order sizes, and individual customers.
- ____ They prepare invoices tailored to customer needs and answer customer queries courteously and quickly.

Finance
- ____ They understand and support marketing expenditures (e.g., image advertising) that represent marketing investments that produce long-term customer preference and loyalty.
- ____ They tailor the financial package to the customers' financial requirements.
- ____ They make quick decisions on customer credit worthiness.

Public Relations
- ____ They disseminate favorable news about the company and they "damage control" unfavorable news.
- ____ They act as an internal customer and public advocate for better company policies and practices.

Other Customer Contact Personnel
- ____ They are competent, courteous, cheerful, credible, reliable, and responsive.

multidivisional company would benefit from establishing a strong corporate marketing department to consult and strengthen divisional marketing programs.

6. *Develop strong in-house marketing training programs.* The company should design well-crafted marketing training programs for top corporate management, divisional general managers, marketing and sales personnel, manufacturing personnel, R&D personnel, and so on. These programs should deliver marketing knowledge, skills, and attitudes to both managers and employees.

7. *Install a modern marketing planning system.* An excellent way to train managers in marketing thinking is to install a modern market-oriented planning system. The planning format will require managers to think about the market environment, marketing opportunities, competitive trends, and other forces. These managers would then prepare marketing strategies and sales and profit forecasts for specific products and segments and be accountable for performance.

8. *Establish an annual marketing excellence recognition program.* The company should encourage business units that believe they have developed exemplary marketing plans to submit a description of their plans and results. A special committee would review these plans, select the best plans, and reward the winning teams at a special ceremony. These plans would be disseminated to the other business units as "models of marketing thinking." Such programs are carried on by Arthur Andersen, Becton-Dickinson, and Du Pont.

9. *Consider reorganizing from a product-centered company to a market-centered company.* Many companies consist of product divisions, with each product division selling in many markets. Becoming market centered means setting up an organization that will focus on the needs of specific markets and coordinate the planning and providing of the company products that are needed by each segment.

10. *Shift from a department focus to a process/outcome focus.* The company should define the fundamental business processes that determine its success. It should appoint process leaders and cross-disciplinary teams to reengineer and implement these processes, and make sure that marketing people spend more time on these teams than in their own department.

Du Pont exemplifies a company that successfully made the transition from an inward-looking to an outward-looking orientation. Under CEO Richard Heckert's leadership, Du Pont undertook a number of initiatives to build a "marketing community." Several divisions were reorganized along market lines. Du Pont held a series of marketing management training seminars, which were ultimately attended by 300 senior people, 2,000 middle managers, and 14,000 employees. Du Pont established a corporate marketing excellence recognition program and honored 32 Du Pont employees from around the world who had developed innovative marketing strategies, service improvements, and so on.[21]

Hewlett Packard, SAS, British Airways, Ford, and other major companies have also shown that achieving a marketing culture is both possible and profitable. It takes a great amount of planning and patience to get managers to accept the fact that customers are the foundation of the company's business and future. But it can be done.

MARKETING IMPLEMENTATION

We now turn to the question of how marketing managers can effectively implement marketing plans. We define marketing implementation as follows:[22]

❖ **MARKETING IMPLEMENTATION** is the process that turns marketing plans into action assignments and ensures that such assignments are executed in a manner that accomplishes the plan's stated objectives.

A brilliant strategic marketing plan counts for little if it is not implemented properly. Consider the following example:

> A chemical company decided that customers were not getting good service from any of the competitors. The company decided that it would make customer service its strategic thrust. When this strategy failed, a postmortem revealed a number of implementation failures. The customer service department continued to be held in low regard by top management; it was understaffed; and it was used as a dumping ground for weak managers. Furthermore, the company's reward system continued to focus on cost containment and current profitability. The company had failed to make the changes required to carry out its strategy.

Whereas strategy addresses the *what* and *why* of marketing activities, implementation addresses the *who, where, when,* and *how.* Strategy and implementation are closely related in that one layer of strategy implies certain tactical implementation assignments at a lower level. For example, top management's strategic decision to "harvest" a product must be translated into specific actions and assignments.

Bonoma identified four skills related to the effective implementation of marketing programs:

- Skills in recognizing and diagnosing a problem
- Skills in assessing the company level where the problem exists
- Skills in implementing plans
- Skills in evaluating implementation results[23]

We examine these skills in the following paragraphs.

DIAGNOSTIC SKILLS. The close interrelationship between strategy and implementation can pose difficult diagnostic problems when marketing programs do not fulfill their expectations. Was the low sales rate the result of poor strategy or poor implementation? Moreover, is the issue to determine what the problem *is* (diagnosis) or what should be *done* about it (action)? Each problem calls for specific management tools and solutions.

COMPANY LEVELS. Marketing implementation problems can occur at three levels. One level is that of carrying out a *marketing function* successfully. For example, how can the company get more creative advertising from its advertising agency? Another level is that of implementing a *marketing program* that has to blend marketing functions into a coherent whole. This problem arises in launching a new product into the marketplace. A third level is that of implementing a *marketing policy.* For example, the company might want every employee to treat the customer as number one.

MARKETING IMPLEMENTATION AND EVALUATION SKILLS. Marketers must possess a set of skills to achieve effective implementation of any marketing program or policy. The four skills are allocating, monitoring, organizing, and interacting.

Marketing managers use *allocating skills* in budgeting resources (time, money, and personnel) to functions, programs, and policies. They use *monitoring skills* to evaluate the results of marketing actions. They use *organizing skills* to develop an effective working organization. Understanding the informal as well as formal marketing organization is important to carrying out effective implementation. Finally, they use *interacting skills* to get things done by influencing others. Marketers not only must motivate the company's own people but also must motivate outsiders—marketing research firms, ad agencies, dealers, wholesalers, agents—whose objectives might differ from the company's.

CONTROLLING MARKETING ACTIVITY

Because many surprises occur during the implementation of marketing plans, the marketing department has to continuously monitor and control marketing activities. In spite of this need, many companies have inadequate control procedures. This conclusion was reached in a study of 75 companies of varying sizes in different industries. The main findings were these:

- Smaller companies do a poorer job of setting clear objectives and establishing systems to measure performance.

- Fewer than half of the companies studied knew their individual products' profitability. About one third of the companies had no regular review procedures for spotting and deleting weak products.

- Almost half of the companies failed to compare their prices with competition, to analyze their warehousing and distribution costs, to analyze the causes of returned merchandise, to conduct formal evaluations of advertising effectiveness, and to review their sales force's call reports.

- Many companies take four to eight weeks to develop control reports, which are occasionally inaccurate.

As summarized in Table 24-2, there are four types of marketing control: annual-plan control, profitability control, efficiency control, and strategic control. We discuss each of these in the following paragraphs.

TABLE 24-2	TYPES OF MARKETING CONTROL		
TYPE OF CONTROL	**PRIME RESPONSIBILITY**	**PURPOSE OF CONTROL**	**APPROACHES**
I. Annual-plan control	Top management Middle management	To examine whether the planned results are being achieved	• Sales analysis • Market share analysis • Expense-to-sales analysis • Financial analysis • Market-based scorecard analysis
II. Profitability control	Marketing controller	To examine where the company is making and losing money	Profitability by: • product • territory • customer • segment • trade channel • order size
III. Efficiency control	Line and staff management Marketing controller	To evaluate and improve the spending efficiency and impact of marketing expenditures	Efficiency of: • sales force • advertising • sales promotion • distribution
IV. Strategic control	Top management Marketing auditor	To examine whether the company is pursuing its best opportunities with respect to markets, products, and channels	• Marketing-effectiveness rating instrument • Marketing audit • Marketing excellence review • Company ethical and social responsibility review

Organizing, Implementing, Evaluating, and Controlling Marketing Activities

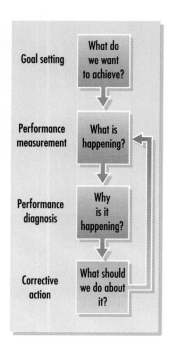

Goal setting	What do we want to achieve?
Performance measurement	What is happening?
Performance diagnosis	Why is it happening?
Corrective action	What should we do about it?

FIGURE 24-7
The Control Process

Annual-Plan Control

The purpose of annual-plan control is to ensure that the company achieves the sales, profits, and other goals established in its annual plan. The heart of annual-plan control is *management by objectives*. Four steps are involved (Figure 24-7). First, management sets monthly or quarterly goals. Second, management monitors its performance in the marketplace. Third, management determines the causes of serious performance deviations. Fourth, management takes corrective action to close the gaps between its goals and performance. This could require changing the action programs or even changing the goals.

This control model applies to all levels of the organization. Top management sets sales and profit goals for the year. These goals are elaborated into specific goals for each lower level of management. Thus each product manager is committed to attaining specified levels of sales and costs. Each regional and district sales manager and each sales representative is also committed to specific goals. Each period, top management reviews and interprets the results and ascertains whether any corrective action is needed.

Managers use five tools to check on plan performance: sales analysis, market share analysis, marketing expense–to–sales analysis, financial analysis, and market-based scorecard analysis.

SALES ANALYSIS. *Sales analysis* consists of measuring and evaluating actual sales in relation to sales goals. Two specific tools are used in sales analysis.

Sales-variance analysis measures the relative contribution of different factors to a gap in sales performance. Suppose the annual plan called for selling 4,000 widgets in the first quarter at $1 per widget, for total revenue of $4,000. At quarter's end, only 3,000 widgets were sold at $.80 per widget, for total revenue of $2,400. The sales performance variance is $1,600, or 40% of expected sales. How much of this underperformance is due to the price decline and how much to the volume decline? The following calculation answers this question:

Variance due to price decline	= ($1.00 − $.80)(3,000)	= $ 600	37.5%
Variance due to volume decline	= ($1.00)(4,000 − 3,000)	= $1,000	62.5%
		$1,600	100.0%

Almost two thirds of the sales variance is due to a failure to achieve the volume target. The company should look closely at why it failed to achieve its expected sales volume.

Microsales analysis may provide the answer. *Microsales analysis* looks at specific products, territories, and so forth that failed to produce expected sales. Suppose the company sells in three territories and expected sales were 1,500 units, 500 units, and 2,000 units, respectively. The actual sales volume was 1,400 units, 525 units, and 1,075 units, respectively. Thus territory 1 showed a 7% shortfall in terms of expected sales; territory 2, a 5% surplus; and territory 3, a 46% shortfall! Territory 3 is causing most of the trouble. The sales vice-president can check into territory 3 to see which hypothesis explains the poor performance: Territory 3's sales representative is loafing or has a personal problem; a major competitor has entered this territory; or GDP is depressed in this territory.

Managing
the Marketing
Effort

MARKET SHARE ANALYSIS. Company sales do not reveal how well the company is performing relative to competitors. For this purpose, management needs to track its market share. Table 24-3 summarizes the four measures of mar-

| **TABLE 24-3** | DEFINING AND MEASURING MARKET SHARE |

Overall Market Share	The company's overall market share is its sales expressed as a percentage of total market sales. Two decisions are necessary to use this measure. The first is whether to use unit sales or dollar sales to express market share. The other decision is how to define the total market. For example, Harley Davidson's share of the U.S. motorcycle market depends on whether motor scooters and motorized bikes are included in the market definition. If they are, then Harley Davidson's share will be smaller.
Served Market Share	The company's served market share is its sales expressed as a percentage of the total sales to its served market. Its *served market* is all the buyers who are able and willing to buy its product. If Harley Davidson produces and sells expensive motorcycles only on the East Coast, its served market share would be its sales as a percentage of the total sales of expensive motorcycles sold on the East Coast. A company's served market share is always larger than its overall market share. A company could capture 100% of its served market and yet have a relatively small share of the total market. A company's first task is to win the lion's share of its served market. As it approaches this goal, it should add new served markets.
Relative Market Share (to top three competitors)	The company's relative market share to its top competitor expresses its sales as a percentage of the three largest competitors' combined sales. If the company has 30% of the market, and the next two largest competitors have 20% and 10%, then this company's relative market share is 50% = 30/60. Relative market shares above 33% are considered strong.
Relative Market Share (to leading competitor)	Some companies track their shares as a percentage of their leading competitor's sales. A relative market share greater than 100% indicates a market leader. A relative market share of exactly 100% means that the company is tied for the lead. A rise in the company's relative market share means that it is gaining on its leading competitor.

ket share. If the company's market share goes up, the company is gaining on competitors; if it goes down, the company is losing relative to competitors.

These conclusions from market share analysis, however, are subject to certain qualifications:

- *The assumption that outside forces affect all companies in the same way is often not true.* The U.S. Surgeon General's Report on the harmful consequences of cigarette smoking caused total cigarette sales to falter, but not equally for all companies. Companies whose cigarettes had better filters were hurt less.

- *The assumption that a company's performance should be judged against the average performance of all companies is not always valid.* A company's performance should be judged against the performance of its closest competitors.

- *If a new firm enters the industry, then every existing firm's market share might fall.* A decline in a company's market share might not mean that the company is performing any worse than other companies. A company's share loss depends on the degree to which the new firm hits the company's specific markets.

- *Sometimes a market share decline is deliberately engineered by a company to improve profits.* For example, management might drop unprofitable customers or products to improve its profits.

- *Market share can fluctuate for many minor reasons.* For example, market share can be affected by whether a large sale occurs on the last day of the month or at the beginning of the next month. Not all shifts in market share have marketing significance.[24]

Managers must carefully interpret market share movements by product line, customer type, region, and other breakdowns. A useful way to analyze market share movements is in terms of four components:

$$\begin{matrix} Overall \\ market = Customer & \times & Customer \times & Customer \times & Price \\ share & penetration & loyalty & selectivity & selectivity \end{matrix}$$

where:

- *Customer penetration* is the percentage of all customers who buy from the company.
- *Customer loyalty* is the purchases from the company by its customers expressed as a percentage of their total purchases from all suppliers of the same products.
- *Customer selectivity* is the size of the average customer purchase from the company expressed as a percentage of the size of the average customer purchase from an average company.
- *Price selectivity* is the average price charged by the company expressed as a percentage of the average price charged by all companies.

Now suppose the company's dollar market share falls during the period. The overall market share equation provides four possible explanations: The company lost some of its customers (lower customer penetration); existing customers are buying a smaller share of their total supplies from the company (lower customer loyalty); the company's remaining customers are smaller in size (lower customer selectivity); and/or the company's price has slipped relative to competition (lower price selectivity).

MARKETING EXPENSE–TO–SALES ANALYSIS. Annual-plan control requires making sure that the company is not overspending to achieve its sales goals. The key ratio to watch is *marketing expense–to–sales*. In one company, this ratio was 30% and consisted of five component expense–to–sales ratios: sales force–to–sales (15%); advertising–to–sales (5%); sales promotion–to–sales (6%); marketing research–to–sales (1%); and sales administration–to–sales (3%).

Management needs to monitor these marketing-expense ratios, which will normally exhibit small fluctuations that can be ignored. But fluctuations outside of the normal range are a cause for concern. The period-to-period fluctuations in each ratio can be tracked on a *control chart* (Figure 24-8). This chart shows that the advertising expense–to–sales ratio normally fluctuates between 8% and 12%, say 99 out of 100 times. In the fifteenth period, however, the ratio exceeded the upper control limit. One of two hypotheses can explain this occurrence:

- *Hypothesis A:* The company still has good expense control, and this situation represents one of those rare chance events.
- *Hypothesis B:* The company has lost control over this expense and should find the cause.

If hypothesis A is accepted, no investigation is made to determine whether the environment has changed. The risk in not investigating is that some real change might have occurred, and the company will fall behind. If hypothesis B is accepted, the environment is investigated. Here the risk is that the investigation will uncover nothing and be a waste of time and effort.

The behavior of successive observations even within the upper and lower control limits should be watched. Note in Figure 24-8 that the level of the expense-to-sales ratio rose steadily from the ninth period onward. The probability of encountering six successive increases in what should be independent events is only 1 in 64.[25] This unusual pattern should have led to an investigation sometime before the fifteenth observation.

FINANCIAL ANALYSIS. The expense-to-sales ratios should be analyzed in an overall financial framework to determine how and where the company is mak-

FIGURE 24-8
The Control Chart Model

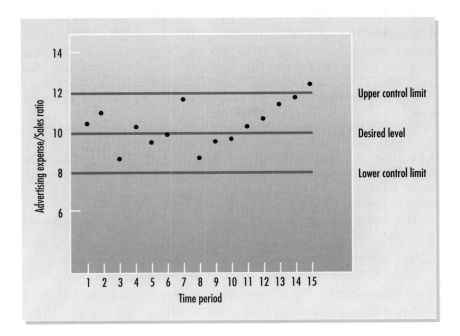

ing its money. Marketers are increasingly using financial analysis to find profitable strategies beyond sales-building strategies.

Management uses financial analysis to identify the factors that affect the company's *rate of return on net worth*.[26] The main factors are shown in Figure 24-9, along with illustrative numbers for a large chain-store retailer. The retailer is earning a 12.5% rate of return on net worth. The rate of return on net worth is the product of two ratios, the company's *return on assets* and its *financial leverage*. To improve its rate of return on net worth, the company must either increase the ratio of its net profits to its assets or increase the ratio of its assets to its net worth. The company should analyze the composition of its assets (i.e., cash, accounts receivable, inventory, and plant and equipment) and see if it can improve its asset management.

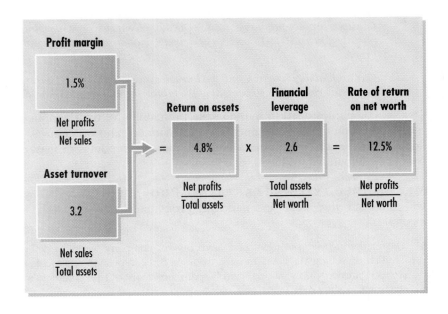

FIGURE 24-9
Financial Model of Return on Net Worth

Organizing, Implementing, Evaluating, and Controlling Marketing Activities

The return on assets is the product of two ratios, the *profit margin* and the *asset turnover*. The profit margin in Figure 24-9 seems low, while the asset turnover is more normal for retailing. The marketing executive can seek to improve performance in two ways: (1) Increase the profit margin by increasing sales or cutting costs; and (2) increase the asset turnover by increasing sales or reducing the assets (e.g., inventory, receivables) that are held against a given level of sales.[27]

MARKET-BASED SCORECARD ANALYSIS. The preceding control measures are largely financial. Most company measurement systems amount to preparing a financial-performance scorecard at the expense of more qualitative measures showing the company's health. Companies would do well to prepare two market-based scorecards that reflect company performance and provide possible early warning signals.

The first, a *customer-performance scorecard,* records how well the company is doing year after year on such customer-based measures as:

- New customers
- Dissatisfied customers
- Lost customers
- Target market awareness

- Target market preference
- Relative product quality
- Relative service quality

Norms should be set for each measure, and management should take action when current results get out of bounds.

The second is called a *stakeholder-performance scorecard.* Companies need to track the satisfaction of various constituencies who have a critical interest in and impact on the company's performance: employees, suppliers, banks, distributors, retailers, stockholders. Again, norms should be set for each group and management should take action when one or more stakeholder groups register increased levels of dissatisfaction.[28]

Profitability Control

Here are some disconcerting findings from a bank profitability study:

> We have found that anywhere from 20 to 40 percent of an individual institution's products are unprofitable, and up to 60 percent of their accounts generate losses.

> Our research has shown that, in most firms, more than half of all customer relationships are not profitable, and 30 to 40 percent are only marginally so. It is frequently a mere 10 to 15 percent of a firm's relationships that generate the bulk of its profits.

> Our profitability research into the branch system of a regional bank produced some surprising results . . . 30 percent of the bank's branches were unprofitable.[29]

Clearly, companies need to measure the profitability of their various products, territories, customer groups, segments, trade channels, and order sizes. This information will help management determine whether any products or marketing activities should be expanded, reduced, or eliminated.

METHODOLOGY OF MARKETING-PROFITABILITY ANALYSIS. We will illustrate the steps in marketing-profitability analysis with the following example:

> The marketing vice-president of a lawn mower company wants to determine the profitability of selling its lawn mower through three types of retail channels: hardware stores, garden supply shops, and department stores. The company's profit-and-loss statement is shown in Table 24-4.

TABLE 24-4

TABLE 24-4 | **A SIMPLIFIED PROFIT-AND-LOSS STATEMENT**

Sales		$60,000
Cost of goods sold		39,000
Gross margin		$21,000
Expenses		
Salaries	$9,300	
Rent	3,000	
Supplies	3,500	
		15,800
Net profit		$ 5,200

Step 1: Identifying The Functional Expenses.

Assume that the expenses listed in Table 24-4 are incurred to sell the product, advertise it, pack and deliver it, and bill and collect for it. The first task is to measure how much of each expense was incurred in each activity.

Suppose that most salary expense went to sales representatives and the rest went to an advertising manager, packing and delivery help, and an office accountant. Let the breakdown of the $9,300 be $5,100, $1,200, $1,400, and $1,600, respectively. Table 24-5 shows the allocation of the salary expense to these four activities.

Table 24-5 also shows the rent account of $3,000 as allocated to the four activities. Since the sales representatives work away from the office, none of the building's rent expense is assigned to selling. Most of the expenses for floor space and rented equipment are in connection with packing and delivery. A small portion of the floor space is used by the advertising manager and office accountant.

Finally, the supplies account covers promotional materials, packing materials, fuel purchases for delivery, and home-office stationery. The $3,500 in this account is reassigned to the functional uses made of the supplies.

Step 2: Assigning The Functional Expenses To The Marketing Entities.

The next task is to measure how much functional expense was associated with selling through each type of channel. Consider the selling effort. The selling effort is indicated by the number of sales made in each channel. This number is found in the selling column of Table 24-6 on page 772. Altogether, 275 sales calls were made during the period. Since the total selling expense amounted to $5,500 (see Table 24-5), the selling expense per call averaged $20.

Advertising expense can be allocated according to the number of ads addressed to the different channels. Since there were 100 ads altogether, the average ad cost $31.

The packing and delivery expense is allocated according to the number of orders placed by each type of channel. This same basis was used for allocating billing and collection expense.

TABLE 24-5 | **MAPPING NATURAL EXPENSES INTO FUNCTIONAL EXPENSES**

NATURAL ACCOUNTS	TOTAL	SELLING	ADVERTISING	PACKING AND DELIVERY	BILLING AND COLLECTING
Salaries	$ 9,300	$5,100	$1,200	$1,400	$1,600
Rent	3,000	—	400	2,000	600
Supplies	3,500	400	1,500	1,400	200
	$15,800	$5,500	$3,100	$4,800	$2,400

TABLE 24-6 BASES FOR ALLOCATING FUNCTIONAL EXPENSES TO CHANNELS

CHANNEL TYPE	SELLING	ADVERTISING	PACKING AND DELIVERY	BILLING AND COLLECTING
Hardware	200	50	50	50
Garden supply	65	20	21	21
Department stores	10	30	9	9
	275	100	80	80
Functional expense	$5,500	$3,100	$4,800	$2,400
÷ No. of units	275	100	80	80
Equals	$ 20	$ 31	$ 60	$ 30

Step 3: Preparing A Profit-And-Loss Statement For Each Marketing Entity. A profit-and-loss statement can now be prepared for each type of channel. The results are shown in Table 24-7. Since hardware stores accounted for one half of total sales ($30,000 out of $60,000), this channel is charged with half the cost of goods sold ($19,500 out of $39,000). This leaves a gross margin from hardware stores of $10,500. From this must be deducted the proportions of the functional expenses that hardware stores consumed. According to Table 24-6, hardware stores received 200 out of 275 total sales calls. At an imputed value of $20 a call, hardware stores have to be charged with a $4,000 selling expense. Table 24-6 also shows that hardware stores were the target of 50 ads. At $31 an ad, the hardware stores are charged with $1,550 of advertising. The same reasoning applies in computing the share of the other functional expenses to charge to hardware stores. The result is that hardware stores gave rise to $10,050 of the total expenses. Subtracting this from the gross margin, the profit of selling through hardware stores is only $450.

This analysis is repeated for the other channels. The company is losing money in selling through garden supply shops and makes virtually all of its profits in selling through department stores. Notice that the gross sales through each channel are not a reliable indicator of the net profits being made in each channel.

DETERMINING THE BEST CORRECTIVE ACTION. It would be naive to conclude that the company should drop garden supply shops and possibly hardware stores so that it can concentrate on department stores. The following questions would need to be answered first:

◆ To what extent do buyers buy on the basis of the type of retail outlet versus the brand? Would they seek out the brand in those channels that are not eliminated?

TABLE 24-7 PROFIT-AND-LOSS STATEMENTS FOR CHANNELS

	HARDWARE	GARDEN SUPPLY	DEPT. STORES	WHOLE COMPANY
Sales	$30,000	$10,000	$20,000	$60,000
Cost of goods sold	19,500	6,500	13,000	39,000
Gross margin	$10,500	$ 3,500	$ 7,000	$21,000
Expenses				
Selling ($20 per call)	$ 4,000	$ 1,300	$ 200	$ 5,500
Advertising ($31 per advertisement)	1,550	620	930	3,100
Packing and delivery ($60 per order)	3,000	1,260	540	4,800
Billing ($30 per order)	1,500	630	270	2,400
Total Expenses	$10,050	$ 3,810	$ 1,940	$15,800
Net profit or loss	$ 450	$ (310)	$ 5,060	$ 5,200

- What are the trends with respect to the importance of these three channels?
- Have company marketing strategies directed at the three channels been optimal?

On the basis of the answers, marketing management can evaluate a number of alternative actions:

- *Establish a special charge for handling smaller orders.* This move assumes that small orders are a cause of the relative unprofitability of dealing with garden supply shops and hardware stores.

- *Give more promotional aid to garden supply shops and hardware stores.* This strategy assumes that the store managers could increase their sales with more training or promotional materials.

- *Reduce the number of sales calls and the amount of advertising going to garden supply shops and hardware stores.* This action assumes that some costs can be saved without seriously hurting sales in these channels.

- *Do nothing.* This lack of action assumes that current marketing efforts are optimal and either that marketing trends point to an imminent profit improvement in the weaker channels or that dropping any channel would reduce profits because of repercussions on production costs or on demand.

- *Do not abandon any channel as a whole but only the weakest retail units in each channel.* This strategy assumes that a detailed cost study would reveal many profitable garden shops and hardware stores whose profits are concealed by the poor performance of other stores in these categories.

In general, marketing-profitability analysis indicates the relative profitability of different channels, products, territories, or other marketing entities. It does not prove that the best course of action is to drop the unprofitable marketing entities, nor does it capture the likely profit improvement if these marginal marketing entities are dropped.

DIRECT VERSUS FULL COSTING. Like all information tools, marketing profitability analysis can lead or mislead marketing executives, depending on the degree of their understanding of its methods and limitations. The lawn mower company showed some arbitrariness in its choice of bases for allocating the functional expenses to its marketing entities. Thus the "number of sales calls" was used to allocate selling expenses, when in principle "number of sales working-hours" is a more accurate indicator of cost. The former base was used because it involves less record-keeping and computation. These approximations may not involve too much inaccuracy, but marketing executives should acknowledge the ramifications of their choices.

Far more serious is another judgmental element affecting profitability analysis. The issue is whether to allocate *full costs* or only *direct and traceable costs* in evaluating a marketing entity's performance. The lawn mower company sidestepped this problem by assuming only simple costs that fit in with marketing activities. But the question cannot be avoided in real-world analyses of profitability. Three types of costs have to be distinguished:

- *Direct costs:* These are costs that can be assigned directly to the proper marketing entities. For example, sales commissions are a direct cost in a profitability analysis of sales territories, sales representatives, or customers. Advertising expenditures are a direct cost in a profitability analysis of products to the extent that each advertisement promotes only one company product. Other direct costs for specific purposes are sales force salaries and traveling expenses.

- *Traceable common costs:* These are costs that can be assigned only indirectly, but on a plausible basis, to the marketing entities. In the example we used, rent was analyzed in this way. The company's floor space was needed for three different marketing activities, and an estimate was made of how much floor space supported each activity.

Organizing, Implementing, Evaluating, and Controlling Marketing Activities

◆ *Nontraceable common costs:* These are costs whose allocation to the marketing entities is highly arbitrary. Consider "corporate image" expenditures. To allocate them equally to all products would be arbitrary, because all products do not benefit equally from corporate image making. To allocate them proportionately to the sales of the various products would be arbitrary because relative product sales reflect many factors besides corporate image making. Other examples of difficult-to-assign common costs are top management salaries, taxes, interest, and other types of overhead.

No one disputes including direct costs in marketing cost analysis. There is a small amount of controversy about including traceable common costs, which lump together costs that would change with the scale of marketing activity and costs that would not change. If the lawn mower company drops garden supply shops, it will probably continue to pay the same rent for contractual reasons. In this event, its profits would not rise immediately by the amount of the present loss in selling to garden supply shops ($310).

The major controversy concerns whether the nontraceable common costs should be allocated to the marketing entities. Such allocation is called the *full-cost approach,* and its advocates argue that all costs must ultimately be imputed in order to determine the company's true profitability. But this argument confuses the use of accounting for financial reporting with its use for managerial decision making. Full costing has three major weaknesses:

◆ The relative profitability of different marketing entities can shift radically when one arbitrary way to allocate nontraceable common costs is replaced by another.

◆ The arbitrariness demoralizes managers, who feel that their performance is judged adversely.

◆ The inclusion of nontraceable common costs could weaken efforts at real cost control. Operating management is most effective in controlling direct costs and traceable common costs. Arbitrary assignments of nontraceable common costs can lead them to spend their time fighting the arbitrary cost allocations rather than managing their controllable costs well.

Companies are showing a growing interest in using marketing profitability analysis or its broader version, *activity-based cost accounting* (ABC), to quantify the true profitability of different activities. According to Cooper and Kaplan, ABC "can give managers a clear picture of how products, brands, customers, facilities, regions, or distribution channels both generate revenues and consume resources."[30] To improve profitability, the managers can then examine ways to reduce the resources required to perform various activities, or make the resources more productive or acquire them at a lower cost. Alternatively, management may raise prices on products that consume heavy amounts of support resources. The contribution of ABC is to refocus management's attention away from using only labor or material standard costs to allocate full cost, and toward capturing the actual costs of supporting individual products, customers, and other entities.

Efficiency Control

Suppose a profitability analysis reveals that the company is earning poor profits in connection with certain products, territories, or markets. The question is whether there are more efficient ways to manage the sales force, advertising, sales promotion, and distribution in connection with these poorer-performing marketing entities.

Some companies have established a *marketing controller* position to assist marketing personnel in improving marketing efficiency. Marketing controllers work out of the controller's office but specialize in the marketing side of the business. At companies such as General Foods, Du Pont, and Johnson & Johnson, they perform a sophisticated financial analysis of marketing expenditures and results. Specifically, they examine adherence to profit plans, help prepare brand managers' budgets, measure the efficiency of promotions, analyze media production costs, evaluate customer and geographic profitability, and educate marketing personnel on the financial implications of marketing decisions.[31]

SALES FORCE EFFICIENCY. Sales managers need to monitor the following key indicators of sales force efficiency in their territory:

- Average number of sales calls per salesperson per day
- Average sales-call time per contact
- Average revenue per sales call
- Average cost per sales call
- Entertainment cost per sales call
- Percentage of orders per 100 sales calls
- Number of new customers per period
- Number of lost customers per period
- Sales force cost as a percentage of total sales

When a company starts investigating sales force efficiency, it often finds areas for improvement. General Electric reduced the size of one of its divisional sales forces after discovering that its salespeople were calling on customers too often. When a large airline found that its salespeople were both selling and servicing, they transferred the servicing function to lower-paid clerks. Another company conducted time-and-duty studies and found ways to reduce the ratio of idle-to-productive time.

ADVERTISING EFFICIENCY. Many managers believe that it is almost impossible to measure what they are getting for their advertising dollars. But they should try to keep track of at least the following statistics:

- Advertising cost per thousand target buyers reached by media vehicle
- Percentage of audience who noted, saw/associated, and read most of each print ad
- Consumer opinions on the ad's content and effectiveness
- Before-after measures of attitude toward the product
- Number of inquiries stimulated by the ad
- Cost per inquiry

Management can undertake a number of steps to improve advertising efficiency, including doing a better job of positioning the product, defining advertising objectives, pretesting messages, using computer technology to guide the selection of advertising media, looking for better media buys, and doing advertising posttesting.

SALES-PROMOTION EFFICIENCY. Sales promotion includes dozens of devices for stimulating buyer interest and product trial. To improve sales-promotion efficiency, management should record the costs and sales impact of each sales promotion. Management should watch the following statistics:

- Percentage of sales sold on deal
- Display costs per sales dollar
- Percentage of coupons redeemed
- Number of inquiries resulting from a demonstration

If a sales-promotion manager is appointed, that manager can analyze the results of different sales promotions and advise product managers on the most cost-effective promotions to use.

Organizing, Implementing, Evaluating, and Controlling Marketing Activities

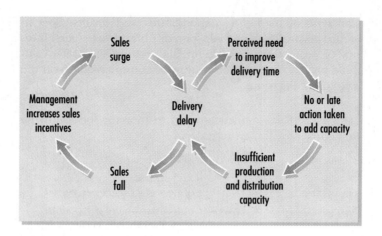

DISTRIBUTION EFFICIENCY. Management needs to search for distribution economies. Several tools are available for improving inventory control, warehouse locations, and transportation modes. One problem that frequently arises is that distribution efficiency declines when the company experiences strong sales increases. Peter Senge describes a situation in which a strong sales surge causes the company to fall behind in meeting its promised delivery dates.[32] This leads customers to bad-mouth the company and eventually sales fall. Management responds by increasing sales force incentives to secure more orders. The sales force succeeds but once again the company slips in meeting its promised delivery dates. Management needs to identify the real bottleneck and invest in more production and distribution capacity. The situation is mapped in Figure 24-10. The left loop shows how sales surges are transformed into sales declines because of delivery delays. The right loop shows the fundamental problem, which is management's failure to invest in additional production and distribution capacity to meet substantial sales increases.

Strategic Control

From time to time, companies need to undertake a critical review of their overall marketing goals and effectiveness. Each company should periodically reassess its strategic approach to the marketplace. Two tools are available: marketing-effectiveness reviews and marketing audits. Companies can also perform marketing excellence reviews and ethical/social responsibility reviews.

THE MARKETING-EFFECTIVENESS REVIEW. Here is an actual situation.

The president of a major industrial-equipment company reviewed the annual business plans of various divisions and found several division plans lacking in marketing substance. He called in the corporate vice-president of marketing and said:

> *I am not happy with the quality of marketing in our divisions. It is very uneven. I want you to find out which of our divisions are strong, average, and weak in marketing. I want to know if they understand and are practicing customer-oriented marketing. I want a marketing score for each division. For each marketing-deficient division, I want a plan for improving its marketing effectiveness over the next several years. I want evidence next year that each marketing-deficient division is improving its market capabilities.*

The corporate marketing vice-president agreed, recognizing his task as formidable. His first inclination was to base the evaluation of marketing effectiveness on each division's performance in sales growth, market share, and profitability. His thinking was that high-performing divisions had good marketing leadership and poor-performing divisions had poor marketing leadership.

However, marketing effectiveness is not necessarily revealed by current sales and profit performance. Good results could be due to a division's being in the right place at the right time, rather than having effective marketing management. Improvements in that division's marketing might boost results from good to excellent. Another division might have poor results in spite of excellent marketing planning. Replacing the present marketing managers might only make things worse.

A company's or division's marketing effectiveness is reflected in the degree to which it exhibits the five major attributes of a marketing orientation: *customer philosophy, integrated marketing organization, adequate marketing information, strategic orientation,* and *operational efficiency*. Each of these attributes can be measured. The Marketing Memo on page 778 presents a *marketing-effectiveness review instrument* based on these five attributes. This instrument is filled out by marketing and other managers in the division. The scores are then summarized.

The instrument has been tested in a number of companies, and very few achieve scores within the superior range of 26 to 30 points. The few include well-known master marketers such as Procter & Gamble, McDonald's, Rubbermaid, and Nike. Most companies and divisions receive scores in the fair-to-good range, indicating that their own managers see room for marketing improvement. Low attribute scores indicate that the attribute needs attention. Divisional management can then establish a plan for correcting its major marketing weaknesses.[33]

THE MARKETING AUDIT.   Those companies that discover marketing weaknesses through applying the marketing-effectiveness rating review should undertake a more thorough study known as a marketing audit.[34]

❖   A **MARKETING AUDIT** is a comprehensive, systematic, independent, and periodic examination of a company's—or business unit's—marketing environment, objectives, strategies, and activities with a view to determining problem areas and opportunities and recommending a plan of action to improve the company's marketing performance.

Let us examine the marketing audit's four characteristics:

◆ *Comprehensive:* The marketing audit covers all the major marketing activities of a business, not just a few trouble spots. It would be called a *functional audit* if it covered only the sales force, pricing, or some other marketing activity. Although functional audits are useful, they sometimes mislead management. Excessive sales force turnover, for example, could be a symptom not of poor sales force training or compensation but of weak company products and promotion. A comprehensive marketing audit usually is more effective in locating the real source of the company's marketing problems.

◆ *Systematic:* The marketing audit involves an orderly examination of the organization's macro- and micromarketing environment, marketing objectives and strategies, marketing systems, and specific marketing activities. The audit indicates the most needed improvements, which are then incorporated into a corrective-action plan involving both short-run and long-run steps to improve the organization's overall marketing effectiveness.

◆ *Independent:* A marketing audit can be conducted in six ways: self-audit, audit from across, audit from above, company auditing office, company task-force audit, and outsider audit. Self-audits, in which managers use a checklist to rate their own operations, can be useful, but most experts agree that self-audits lack objectivity and independence.[35] The 3M Company has made good use of a corporate auditing office, which provides marketing audit services to divisions on request.[36] Generally speaking, however, the best audits are likely to come from outside consultants who have the necessary objectivity, broad experience in a number of industries, some familiarity with the industry being audited, and the undivided time and attention to give to the audit.

◆ *Periodic:* Typically, marketing audits are initiated only after sales have turned down, sales force morale has fallen, and other company problems have occurred. Ironically, companies are thrown into a crisis partly because they failed to review their marketing

Organizing, Implementing, Evaluating, and Controlling Marketing Activities

MARKETING MEMO

MARKETING-EFFECTIVENESS REVIEW INSTRUMENT
(CHECK ONE ANSWER TO EACH QUESTION)

CUSTOMER PHILOSOPHY

A. *Does management recognize the importance of designing the company to serve the needs and wants of chosen markets?*
   0   Management primarily thinks in terms of selling current and new products to whoever will buy them.
   1   Management thinks in terms of serving a wide range of markets and needs with equal effectiveness.
   2   Management thinks in terms of serving the needs and wants of well-defined markets and market segments chosen for their long-run growth and profit potential for the company.

B. *Does management develop different offerings and marketing plans for different segments of the market?*
   0   No.   1   Somewhat.   2   To a large extent.

C. *Does management take a whole marketing system view (suppliers, channels, competitors, customers, environment) in planning its business?*
   0   No. Management concentrates on selling and servicing its immediate customers.
   1   Somewhat. Management takes a long view of its channels although the bulk of its effort goes to selling and servicing the immediate customers.
   2   Yes. Management takes a whole marketing systems view, recognizing the threats and opportunities created for the company by changes in any part of the system.

INTEGRATED MARKETING ORGANIZATION

D. *Is there high-level marketing integration and control of the major marketing functions?*
   0   No. Sales and other marketing functions are not integrated at the top and there is some unproductive conflict.
   1   Somewhat. There is formal integration and control of the major marketing functions but less than satisfactory coordination and cooperation.
   2   Yes. The major marketing functions are effectively integrated.

E. *Does marketing management work well with management in research, manufacturing, purchasing, logistics, and finance?*
   0   No. There are complaints that marketing is unreasonable in the demands and costs it places on other departments.
   1   Somewhat. The relations are amicable although each department pretty much acts to serve its own interests.
   2   Yes. The departments cooperate effectively and resolve issues in the best interest of the company as a whole.

F. *How well organized is the new-product development process?*
   0   The system is ill-defined and poorly handled.
   1   The system formally exists but lacks sophistication.
   2   The system is well-structured and operates on teamwork principles.

ADEQUATE MARKETING INFORMATION

G. *When were the latest marketing research studies of customers, buying influences, channels, and competitors conducted?*
   0   Several years ago.   1   A few years ago.   2   Recently.

H. *How well does management know the sales potential and profitability of different market segments, customers, territories, products, channels, and order sizes?*
   0   Not at all.   1   Somewhat.   2   Very well.

I. *What effort is expended to measure and improve the cost effectiveness of different marketing expenditures?*
   0   Little or no effort.   1   Some effort.   2   Substantial effort.

STRATEGIC ORIENTATION

J. *What is the extent of formal marketing planning?*
  0   Management conducts little or no formal marketing planning.
  1   Management develops an annual marketing plan.
  2   Management develops a detailed annual marketing plan and a strategic long-range plan that is updated annually.

K. *How impressive is the current marketing strategy?*
  0   The current strategy is not clear.
  1   The current strategy is clear and represents a continuation of traditional strategy.
  2   The current strategy is clear, innovative, data based, and well reasoned.

L. *What is the extent of contingency thinking and planning?*
  0   Management does little or no contingency thinking.
  1   Management does some contingency thinking but little formal contingency planning.
  2   Management formally identifies the most important contingencies and develops contingency plans.

OPERATIONAL EFFICIENCY

M. *How well is the marketing strategy communicated and implemented?*
  0   Poorly.   1   Fairly.   2   Successfully.

N. *Is management doing an effective job with its marketing resources?*
  0   No. The marketing resources are inadequate for the job to be done.
  1   Somewhat. The marketing resources are adequate but they are not employed optimally.
  2   Yes. The marketing resources are adequate and are employed efficiently.

O. *Does management show a good capacity to react quickly and effectively to on-the-spot developments?*
  0   No. Sales and market information are not very current and management reaction time is slow.
  1   Somewhat. Management receives fairly up-to-date sales and market information; management reaction time varies.
  2   Yes. Management has installed systems yielding highly current information and fast reaction time.

TOTAL SCORE

The instrument is used in the following way. The appropriate answer is checked for each question. The scores are added—the total will be somewhere between 0 and 30. The following scale shows the level of marketing effectiveness:

0–5 = None	11–15 = Fair	21–25 = Very good
6–10 = Poor	16–20 = Good	26–30 = Superior

operations during good times. A periodic marketing audit can benefit companies in good health as well as those in trouble.

A marketing audit starts with a meeting between the company officer(s) and the marketing auditor(s) to work out an agreement on the audit's objectives, coverage, depth, data sources, report format, and time frame. A detailed plan as to who is to be interviewed, the questions to be asked, the time and place of contact, and so on is carefully prepared so that auditing time and cost are kept to a minimum. The cardinal rule in marketing auditing is: Don't rely solely on the company's managers for data and opinion. Customers, dealers, and other outside groups must also be interviewed. Many companies do not really know how their customers and dealers see them, nor do they fully understand customer needs and value judgments.

The marketing audit examines six major components of the company's marketing situation. The major auditing questions are listed in Table 24-8 (pages 780–781).

Organizing, Implementing, Evaluating, and Controlling Marketing Activities

TABLE 24-8 COMPONENTS OF A MARKETING AUDIT

PART I. MARKETING ENVIRONMENT AUDIT

MACROENVIRONMENT

A. Demographic	What major demographic developments and trends pose opportunities or threats to this company? What actions has the company taken in response to these developments and trends?
B. Economic	What major developments in income, prices, savings, and credit will affect the company? What actions has the company been taking in response to these developments and trends?
C. Environmental	What is the outlook for the cost and availability of natural resources and energy needed by the company? What concerns have been expressed about the company's role in pollution and conservation, and what steps has the company taken?
D. Technological	What major changes are occurring in product and process technology? What is the company's position in these technologies? What major generic substitutes might replace this product?
E. Political	What changes in laws and regulations might affect marketing strategy and tactics? What is happening in the areas of pollution control, equal employment opportunity, product safety, advertising, price control, and so forth, that affects marketing strategy?
F. Cultural	What is the public's attitude toward business and toward the company's products? What changes in customer lifestyles and values might affect the company?

TASK ENVIRONMENT

A. Markets	What is happening to market size, growth, geographical distribution, and profits? What are the major market segments?
B. Customers	What are the customers' needs and buying processes? How do customers and prospects rate the company and its competitors on reputation, product quality, service, sales force, and price? How do different customer segments make their buying decisions?
C. Competitors	Who are the major competitors? What are their objectives, strategies, strengths, weaknesses, sizes, and market shares? What trends will affect future competition and substitutes for the company's products?
D. Distribution and Dealers	What are the main trade channels for bringing products to customers? What are the efficiency levels and growth potentials of the different trade channels?
E. Suppliers	What is the outlook for the availability of key resources used in production? What trends are occurring among suppliers?
F. Facilitators and Marketing Firms	What is the cost and availability outlook for transportation services, warehousing facilities, and financial resources? How effective are the company's advertising agencies and marketing research firms?
G. Publics	Which publics represent particular opportunities or problems for the company? What steps has the company taken to deal effectively with each public?

PART II. MARKETING STRATEGY AUDIT

A. Business Mission	Is the business mission clearly stated in market-oriented terms? Is it feasible?
B. Marketing Objectives and Goals	Are the company and marketing objectives and goals stated clearly enough to guide marketing planning and performance measurement? Are the marketing objectives appropriate, given the company's competitive position, resources, and opportunities?
C. Strategy	Has the management articulated a clear marketing strategy for achieving its marketing objectives? Is the strategy convincing? Is the strategy appropriate to the stage of the product life cycle, competitors' strategies, and the state of the economy? Is the company using the best basis for market segmentation? Does it have clear criteria for rating the segments and choosing the best ones? Has it developed accurate profiles of each target segment? Has the company developed an effective positioning and marketing mix for each target segment? Are marketing resources allocated optimally to the major elements of the marketing mix? Are enough resources or too many resources budgeted to accomplish the marketing objectives?

PART III. MARKETING ORGANIZATION AUDIT

A. Formal Structure	Does the marketing vice-president have adequate authority and responsibility for company activities that affect customers' satisfaction? Are the marketing activities optimally structured along functional, product, segment, end-user, and geographical lines?

B. Functional Efficiency	Are there good communication and working relations between marketing and sales? Is the product management system working effectively? Are product managers able to plan profits or only sales volume? Are there any groups in marketing that need more training, motivation, supervision, or evaluation?
C. Interface Efficiency	Are there any problems between marketing and manufacturing, R&D, purchasing, finance, accounting, and/or legal that need attention?

PART IV. MARKETING SYSTEMS AUDIT

A. Marketing Information System	Is the marketing intelligence system producing accurate, sufficient, and timely information about marketplace developments with respect to customers, prospects, distributors and dealers, competitors, suppliers, and various publics? Are company decision makers asking for enough marketing research, and are they using the results? Is the company employing the best methods for market measurement and sales forecasting?
B. Marketing Planning Systems	Is the marketing planning system well conceived and effectively used? Do marketers have decision support systems available? Does the planning system result in acceptable sales targets and quotas?
C. Marketing Control System	Are the control procedures adequate to ensure that the annual-plan objectives are being achieved? Does management periodically analyze the profitability of products, markets, territories, and channels of distribution? Are marketing costs and productivity periodically examined?
D. New-Product Development System	Is the company well organized to gather, generate, and screen new-product ideas? Does the company do adequate concept research and business analysis before investing in new ideas? Does the company carry out adequate product and market testing before launching new products?

PART V. MARKETING PRODUCTIVITY AUDIT

A. Profitability Analysis	What is the profitability of the company's different products, markets, territories, and channels of distribution? Should the company enter, expand, contract, or withdraw from any business segments?
B. Cost-Effectiveness Analysis	Do any marketing activities seem to have excessive costs? Can cost-reducing steps be taken?

PART VI. MARKETING FUNCTION AUDITS

A. Products	What are the company's product-line objectives? Are they sound? Is the current product line meeting the objectives? Should the product line be stretched or contracted upward, downward, or both ways? Which products should be phased out? Which products should be added? What are the buyers' knowledge and attitudes toward the company's and competitors' product quality, features, styling, brand names, and so on? What areas of product and brand strategy need improvement?
B. Price	What are the company's pricing objectives, policies, strategies, and procedures? To what extent are prices set on cost, demand, and competitive criteria? Do the customers see the company's prices as being in line with the value of its offer? What does management know about the price elasticity of demand, experience-curve effects, and competitors' prices and pricing policies? To what extent are price policies compatible with the needs of distributors and dealers, suppliers, and government regulation?
C. Distribution	What are the company's distribution objectives and strategies? Is there adequate market coverage and service? How effective are distributors, dealers, manufacturers' representatives, brokers, agents, and others? Should the company consider changing its distribution channels?
D. Advertising, Sales Promotion, Publicity, and Direct Marketing	What are the organization's advertising objectives? Are they sound? Is the right amount being spent on advertising? Are the ad themes and copy effective? What do customers and the public think about the advertising? Are the advertising media well chosen? Is the internal advertising staff adequate? Is the sales-promotion budget adequate? Is there effective and sufficient use of sales-promotion tools such as samples, coupons, displays, and sales contests? Is the public-relations staff competent and creative? Is the company making enough use of direct, online, and database marketing?
E. Sales Force	What are the sales force's objectives? Is the sales force large enough to accomplish the company's objectives? Is the sales force organized along the proper principles of specialization (territory, market, product)? Are there enough (or too many) sales managers to guide the field sales representatives? Do the sales-compensation level and structure provide adequate incentive and reward? Does the sales force show high morale, ability, and effort? Are the procedures adequate for setting quotas and evaluating performance? How does the company's sales force compare to competitors' sales forces?

Source: Author.

TABLE 24-9		THE MARKETING EXCELLENCE REVIEW: BEST PRACTICES	
POOR		**GOOD**	**EXCELLENT**
Product driven		Market driven	Market driving
Mass-market oriented		Segment oriented	Niche oriented and customer-oriented
Product offer		Augmented product offer	Customer solutions offer
Average product quality		Better than average	Legendary
Average service quality		Better than average	Legendary
End-product oriented		Core-product oriented	Core-competency-oriented
Function oriented		Process oriented	Outcome-oriented
Reacting to competitors		Benchmarking competitors	Leapfrogging competitors
Supplier exploitation		Supplier preference	Supplier partnership
Dealer exploitation		Dealer support	Dealer partnership
Price driven		Quality driven	Value driven
Average speed		Better than average	Legendary
Hierarchy		Network	Teamwork
Vertically integrated		Flattened organization	Strategic alliances
Stockholder driven		Stakeholder driven	Societally driven

Source: Author.

THE MARKETING EXCELLENCE REVIEW. Companies can use another instrument to rate their performance in relation to the best practices of high-performing businesses. The three columns in Table 24-9 distinguish among poor, good, and excellent business and marketing practices. Management can place a check on each line as to their perception of where the business stands. The resulting profile exposes the business's weaknesses and strengths, highlighting where the company might move to become a truly outstanding player in the marketplace.

THE ETHICAL AND SOCIAL RESPONSIBILITY REVIEW. Companies need to evaluate whether they are truly practicing ethical and socially responsible marketing. Business success and continually satisfying the customer and other stakeholders are intimately tied to adoption and implementation of high standards of business and marketing conduct. The most admired companies in the world abide by a code of serving people's interests, not only their own.

The practices of business are often under attack because business situations routinely pose tough ethical dilemmas. One can go back to Howard Bowen's classic questions about the responsibilities of businesspeople:

> Should he conduct selling in ways that intrude on the privacy of people, for example, by door-to-door selling. . . ? Should he use methods involving ballyhoo, chances, prizes, hawking, and other tactics which are at least of doubtful good taste? Should he employ "high pressure" tactics in persuading people to buy? Should he try to hasten the obsolescence of goods by bringing out an endless succession of new models and new styles? Should he appeal to and attempt to strengthen the motives of materialism, invidious consumption, and "keeping up with the Joneses"?[37]

Other ethical issues, many of which we reviewed in earlier chapters, are listed in Figure 24-11. Clearly the company's bottom line cannot be the sole measure of corporate performance.

Raising the level of socially responsible marketing calls for a three-pronged attack. First, society must use the law to define, as clearly as possible, those practices that are illegal, antisocial, or anticompetitive. Second, companies must adopt and disseminate a written code of ethics, build a company tradition of ethical behavior, and hold their people fully responsible for observing the ethical and legal guidelines. (Figure 24-12 reproduces the American Marketing Association's Code of

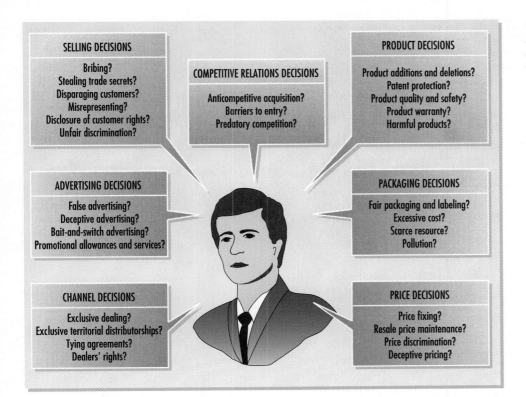

SELLING DECISIONS

Bribing?
Stealing trade secrets?
Disparaging customers?
Misrepresenting?
Disclosure of customer rights?
Unfair discrimination?

COMPETITIVE RELATIONS DECISIONS

Anticompetitive acquisition?
Barriers to entry?
Predatory competition?

PRODUCT DECISIONS

Product additions and deletions?
Patent protection?
Product quality and safety?
Product warranty?
Harmful products?

ADVERTISING DECISIONS

False advertising?
Deceptive advertising?
Bait-and-switch advertising?
Promotional allowances and services?

PACKAGING DECISIONS

Fair packaging and labeling?
Excessive cost?
Scarce resource?
Pollution?

CHANNEL DECISIONS

Exclusive dealing?
Exclusive territorial distributorships?
Tying agreements?
Dealers' rights?

PRICE DECISIONS

Price fixing?
Resale price maintenance?
Price discrimination?
Deceptive pricing?

Ethics.) Third, individual marketers must practice a "social conscience" in their specific dealings with customers and various stakeholders.

The future holds a wealth of opportunities for companies as they move into the twenty-first century. Technological advances in solar energy, online computer networks, cable and satellite television, genetic engineering, and telecommunications promise to change the world as we know it. At the same time, forces in the socioeconomic, cultural, and natural environments will impose new limits on marketing and business practice. Companies that are able to innovate new solutions and values in a socially responsible way are the most likely to succeed.

Members of the American Marketing Association are committed to ethical, professional conduct. They have joined together in subscribing to this Code of Ethics embracing the following topics:

Responsibilities of the Marketer

Marketers must accept responsibility for the consequences of their activities and make every effort to ensure that their decisions, recommendations, and actions function to identify, serve, and satisfy all relevant publics: customers, organizations and society.

Marketers' professional conduct must be guided by:

1. The basic rule of professional ethics: not knowingly to do harm;
2. The adherence to all applicable laws and regulations;
3. The accurate representation of their education, training and experience; and
4. The active support, practice and promotion of this Code of Ethics.

Honesty and Fairness

Marketers shall uphold and advance the integrity, honor, and dignity of the marketing profession by:

1. Being honest in serving consumers, clients, employees, suppliers, distributors, and the public;
2. Not knowingly participating in conflict of interest without prior notice to all parties involved; and
3. Establishing equitable fee schedules including the payment or receipt of usual, customary and/or legal compensation for marketing exchanges.

(cont'd)

Rights and Duties of Parties in the Marketing Exchange Process

Participants in the marketing exchange process should be able to expect that:

1. Products and services offered are safe and fit for their intended uses;
2. Communications about offered products and services are not deceptive;
3. All parties intend to discharge their obligations, financial and otherwise, in good faith; and
4. Appropriate internal methods exist for equitable adjustment and/or redress of grievances concerning purchases.

It is understood that the above would include, but is not limited to, the following responsibilities of the marketer:

In the area of product development and management,

* disclosure of all substantial risks associated with product or service usage;
* identification of any product component substitution that might materially change the product or impact on the buyer's purchase decision;
* identification of extra cost-added features.

In the area of promotions,

* avoidance of false and misleading advertising;
* rejection of high pressure manipulations, or misleading sales tactics;
* avoidance of sales promotions that use deception or manipulation.

In the area of distribution,

* not manipulating the availability of a product for purpose of exploitation;
* not using coercion in the marketing channel;
* not exerting undue influence over the resellers' choice to handle a product.

In the area of pricing,

* not engaging in price fixing;
* not practicing predatory pricing;
* disclosing the full price associated with any purchase.

In the area of marketing research,

* prohibiting selling or fundraising under the guise of conducting research;
* maintaining research integrity by avoiding misrepresentation and omission of pertinent research data;
* treating outside clients and suppliers fairly.

Organizational Relationships

Marketers should be aware of how their behavior may influence or impact on the behavior of others in organizational relationships. They should not demand, encourage or apply coercion to obtain unethical behavior in their relationships with others, such as employees, suppliers, or customers.

1. Apply confidentiality and anonymity in professional relationships with regard to privileged information;
2. Meet their obligations and responsibilities in contracts and mutual agreements in a timely manner;
3. Avoid taking the work of others, in whole, or in part, and represent this work as their own or directly benefit from it without compensation or consent of the originator or owner;
4. Avoid manipulation to take advantage of situations to maximize personal welfare in a way that unfairly deprives or damages the organization of others.

Any AMA member found to be in violation of any provision of this Code of Ethics may have his or her Association membership suspended or revoked.

FIGURE 24-12
American Marketing Association Code of Ethics

SUMMARY

1. The modern marketing department evolved through six stages, and today companies can be found in each stage. In the first stage, companies simply start out with a sales department. In the second stage, they add ancillary marketing functions, such as advertising and marketing research. In the third stage, a separate marketing department is created to handle the increased number of ancillary marketing functions. In the fourth stage, both sales and marketing report to a marketing and sales vice-president. In the fifth stage, all of a company's employees are market and customer centered. In the sixth stage, marketing personnel work mainly on cross-disciplinary teams.

2. Modern marketing departments can be organized in a number of ways. Some companies are organized by functional specialization, while others focus on geography and regionalization. Still others emphasize product and brand management or market-segment

management. Some companies establish a matrix organization consisting of both product and market managers. Finally, some companies have strong corporate marketing, others have limited corporate marketing, and still others place marketing only in the divisions.

3. Effective modern marketing organizations are marked by a strong cooperation and customer focus among the company's departments: marketing, R&D, engineering, purchasing, manufacturing, operations, finance, accounting, and credit.

4. A brilliant strategic marketing plan counts for little if it is not implemented properly. Implementing marketing plans calls for skills in recognizing and diagnosing a problem, assessing the company level where the problem exists, implementation skills, and skills in evaluating the implementation results.

5. Because many surprises occur during the implementation of marketing plans, the marketing department has to continuously monitor and control marketing activities. The purpose of *annual-plan control* is to ensure that the company achieves the sales, profits, and other goals established in its annual plan. The main tools of annual-plan control are sales analysis, market share analysis, marketing expense–to–sales analysis, financial analysis, and market-based scorecard analysis. *Profitability control* seeks to measure and control the profitability of various products, territories, customer groups, segments, trade channels, and order sizes. An important part of controlling for profitability is assigning costs and generating profit-and-loss statements. *Efficiency control* focuses on finding ways to increase the efficiency of the sales force, advertising, sales promotion, and distribution. *Strategic control* entails a periodic reassessment of the company and its strategic approach to the marketplace, using the tools of the marketing-effectiveness review and the marketing audit. Companies should also undertake marketing excellence reviews and ethical/social responsibility reviews.

CONCEPT APPLICATIONS

1. Rewrite the questions in the Components of a Marketing Audit (Table 24-8) in such a way that they reflect the individual problems and terminology associated with your industry. Be as specific and as detailed as you can when writing the questions. If you are not presently employed, rewrite the questions for either a company you have worked for or one for which you would like to work in the future.

2. Take one part of the Components of a Marketing Audit (Table 24-8) and conduct a mini-audit at your organization. You may need to rewrite the questions in such a way that they use terminology that is more understandable to others in your industry. If you are not presently employed, you might want to contact a religious, charitable, or educational institution in your area and see if its directors would like you to perform a mini-audit for them.

3. As society has become more litigious, companies have stepped up their search for ways to control their employees' activities and their products' safety features to minimize the risk of loss. For example, since the Exxon *Valdez* oil spill in Alaska, some groups have begun to call for double-hulled tankers. These vessels lower the probability of oil leakage, but cost about 8% more than the tankers presently in use and can carry only about 60% of the current tankers' capacity. To maintain the present flow of oil, two additional tankers would be required for every five single-hull ships currently in use—and the new ships would create more traffic on the seas and require more docks to be built. In addition, the chance of human error will increase because the industry would need to hire more crews to operate these ships.

Do you think the potential problems are great enough for the industry to go to this additional expense? Should mandatory drug testing be required of people in this industry? If yes, should any industries be exempt from employee drug testing? What lessons can industries that have an effect on the environment learn from the *Valdez* oil spill?

4. A sales manager examined her company's sales by region and noted that East Coast sales were about 2% below the quota. To probe further, the sales manager examined district sales figures. She discovered that the Boston sales district within the East Coast region was responsible for most of the underachievement. She then examined the individual sales of the four salespeople in the Boston sales district. This examination revealed that the top salesman, Roberts, had filled only 60% of his quota for the period. Is it safe to conclude that Roberts is loafing or having personal problems?

5. A large manufacturer of industrial equipment has a salesperson assigned to each major city. Regional sales managers supervise the sales representatives in several cities. The chief marketing officer wants to evaluate the profit contribution of the different cities. How might each of the following costs be allocated to each of the cities: (a) the aggregate costs of sending bills to customers; (b) district sales manager's expenses; (c) national magazine advertising; and (d) marketing research?

6. NAPLCO (North American Phillips Lighting Corporation) wanted to put Norelco bulbs on supermarket shelves as a third national brand (GE had 60% of the market and Westinghouse had 20% of the market). Light bulb purchases had been slowly declining over the last five years. Light bulbs were the grocer's most profitable store item per linear foot of goods stocked. NAPLCO concluded that the strong Norelco name, proven capability at making quality light bulbs, and profits for supermarkets would make this project very successful. After conducting consumer research, it created a new and clever gravity-fed display and novel transparent and protective package for the bulbs themselves. The display held 12 of the most popular light bulb types. (Most supermarkets carried 50 types of light bulbs, and double that number constituted a full line.) Norelco decided not to do any consumer advertising but to rely more heavily on push money. It also decided to use a broker rather than hire its own sales force. After two and a half years, gross sales of Norelco's bulbs were $1.1 million against a projected $7.5 million. Why do you think the project failed from an implementation standpoint?

7. A new vice-president at a major telecommunications company was hired and given the freedom to innovate and develop an entrepreneurial spirit within the organization. He replaced endless memos, interminable meetings, and strict chains of command; discarded planning manuals; threw out employee tests; put salespeople on the highest commission-based compensation plans in the company's history; and fired those who could not meet his tough quotas. Twelve months later he was removed from his job. Why do you suppose he was fired?

8. What reasons can you offer to justify doing a marketing audit for a very successful manufacturer and distributor of power boats designed for the upscale end of the market?

9. As the readership and prestige of automobile magazines like *Road and Track, Car and Driver,* and *Motor Trend* have increased over the years, automobile manufacturers have been trying to find more ways to receive favorable mention in these kinds of magazines. Automobile manufacturers have invited reporters (and their spouses) on all-expense-paid press trips to exclusive vacation spots. They've also given reporters gifts of luggage, CD players, and binoculars. To protect the integrity of his magazine, the editor of *Car and Driver* has told his writers to stop accepting consulting fees from the auto industry and has asked car manufacturers to limit gifts to souvenirs and mementos.

   Most journalists agree that reporters should not be accepting consulting fees from players in the industry that the writer is covering. However, some in the automobile magazine field contend that they are not influenced by trips and gifts because they objectively evaluate all cars that they inspect, and use a standard checklist when test driving cars. Nissan has said that it will respect the *Car and Driver's* new policy, but that it will continue to have showings of its cars in exotic locations because it wants to put the car in the best light for the reviewers.

   Do you think that all-expense-paid press trips are a legitimate and ethical part of the automobile product-review process? Is there a difference between receiving sales promotions from a manufacturer and receiving consulting fees from them? What applications does this incident have to other industries?

10. Consider the following data for product X:

	PERIOD 1	PERIOD 2
Customer penetration	60%	55%
Customer loyalty	50%	50%
Customer selectivity	80%	75%
Price selectivity	125%	130%
Market share	?	?

Complete the last row of the table. Did market share increase or decrease from period 1 to period 2? What were the main causes of this change?

11. O'Brien Candy Company is a hypothetical medium-size candy company located in the Midwest. In the past two years, its sales and profits have barely held their own. Top management feels that the trouble lies with the sales force, that they don't "work hard or smart enough." To correct the problem, management plans to introduce a new incentive-compensation system and hire a trainer to train the sales force in modern merchandising and selling techniques. Before doing this, however, they decide to hire a marketing consultant to carry out a marketing audit. The auditor interviews managers, customers, sales representatives, and dealers and examines various sets of data. The auditor's findings are as follows:

a. The company's product line consists primarily of 18 products, mostly candy bars. Its two leading brands are mature and account for 76% of the company's total sales. The company has looked at the fast-developing markets of chocolate snacks but has not made any moves yet.

b. The company recently researched its customer profile. Its products appeal especially to lower-income and older people. Respondents who were asked to assess O'Brien's chocolate products in relation to competitors' products described them as "average quality and old-fashioned."

c. O'Brien sells its products to candy jobbers and large supermarkets. Its sales force calls on many of the small retailers reached by the candy jobbers, to fortify displays and provide ideas; its sales force also calls on many small retailers not covered by jobbers. O'Brien enjoys good penetration of small retailing, though not in all segments, such as the fast-growing restaurant areas. Its major approach to intermediaries is a "sell-in" strategy: discounts, exclusive contracts, and stock financing. At the same time, O'Brien has not adequately penetrated the mass-merchandise chains. Its competitors rely more heavily on mass-consumer advertising and in-store merchandising and are more successful with the mass merchandisers.

d. O'Brien's marketing budget is set at 15% of its total sales, compared with competitors' budgets of close to 20 percent. Most of the marketing budget supports the sales force, and the remainder supports advertising. Consumer promotions are very limited. The advertising budget is spent primarily in reminder advertising for the company's two leading products. New products are not developed often, and when they are, they are introduced to retailers via a push strategy.

e. The marketing organization is headed by a sales vice-president. Reporting to the sales VP is the sales manager, the market research manager, and the advertising manager. Having come up from the ranks, the sales VP is partial to sales force activities and pays less attention to the other marketing functions. The sales force is assigned to territories headed by area managers.

The marketing auditor concluded that O'Brien's problems would not be solved by actions taken to improve its sales force. If you were the auditor, what short-term and long-term recommendations would you make to O'Brien's top management?

Organizing, Implementing, Evaluating, and Controlling Marketing Activities

1. See C. K. Prahalad and Gary Hamel, "The Core Competence of the Corporation," *Harvard Business Review,* May–June 1990, pp. 79–91.

2. See Rahul Jacob, "The Struggle to Create an Organization for the 21st Century," *Fortune,* April 3, 1995, pp. 90–99.

3. David W. Cravens, Shannon H. Shipp, and Karen S. Cravens, "Reforming the Traditional Organization: The Mandate for Developing Networks," *Business Horizons,* July–August 1994, pp. 19–26.

4. See Frederick E. Webster, Jr., "The Changing Role of Marketing in the Corporation," *Journal of Marketing,* October 1992, pp. 1–17.

5. Alan Mitchell, "Top Brass Fall for False Economies," *Marketing Week,* September 9, 1994, pp. 28–29.

6. See Frank V. Cespedes, *Concurrent Marketing: Integrating Product, Sales, and Service* (Boston: Harvard Business School Press, 1995); and *Managing Marketing Linkages: Text, Cases, and Readings* (Upper Saddle River, NJ: Prentice Hall, 1996).

7. Robert E. Lineman and John L. Stanton, Jr., "A Game Plan for Regional Marketing," *Journal of Business Strategy,* November–December 1992, pp. 19–25.

8. See Scott Hume, "Execs Favor Regional Approach," *Advertising Age,* November 2, 1987, p. 36; "National Firms Find That Selling to Local Tastes Is Costly, Complex," *The Wall Street Journal,* February 9, 1987, B1; and Shawn McKenna, *The Complete Guide to Regional Marketing* (Homewood, IL: Business One Irwin, 1992).

9. ". . . and Other Ways to Peel the Onion," *The Economist,* January 7, 1995, pp. 52–53.

10. Andrall E. Pearson and Thomas W. Wilson, Jr., *Making Your Organization Work* (New York: Association of National Advertisers, 1967), pp. 8–13.

11. Michael George, Anthony Freeling, and David Court, "Reinventing the Marketing Organization," *The McKinsey Quarterly,* No. 4 (1994), 43–62.

12. For further reading, see Robert Dewar and Don Schultz, "The Product Manager, an Idea Whose Time Has Gone," *Marketing Communications,* May 1989, pp. 28–35; "The Marketing Revolution at Procter & Gamble," *Business Week,* July 25, 1988, pp. 72–76; and Kevin T. Higgins, "Category Management: New Tools Changing Life for Manufacturers, Retailers," *Marketing News,* September 25, 1989, pp. 2, 19.

13. Mack Hanan, "Reorganize Your Company Around Its Markets," *Harvard Business Review,* November–December 1974, pp. 63–74.

14. Stanley F. Slater and John C. Narver, "Market Orientation, Customer Value, and Superior Performance," *Business Horizons,* March–April 1994, pp. 22–28. See also Frederick E. Webster, *Market-Driven Management: Using the New Marketing Concept to Create a Customer-Oriented Company* (New York: John Wiley, 1994); and John C. Narver and Stanley F. Slater, "The Effect of a Market Orientation on Business Profitability," *Journal of Marketing,* October 1990, pp. 20–35.

15. Richard E. Anderson, "Matrix Redux," *Business Horizons,* November–December 1994, pp. 6–10.

16. For further reading on marketing organization, see Nigel Piercy, *Marketing Organization: An Analysis of Information Processing, Power and Politics* (London: George Allen & Unwin, 1985); Robert W. Ruekert, Orville C. Walker, and Kenneth J. Roering, "The Organization of Marketing Activities: A Contingency Theory of Structure and Performance," *Journal of Marketing,* Winter 1985, pp. 13–25; and Tyzoon T. Tyebjee, Albert V. Bruno, and Shelby H. McIntyre, "Growing Ventures Can Anticipate Marketing Stages," *Harvard Business Review,* January–February 1983, pp. 2–4.

17. Gary L. Frankwick, Beth A. Walker, and James C. Ward, "Belief Structures in Conflict: Mapping a Strategic Marketing Decision," *Journal of Business Research,* October–November 1994, pp. 183–95.

18. Askok K. Gupta, S. P. Raj, and David Wilemon, "A Model for Studying R&D-Marketing Interface in the Product Innovation Process," *Journal of Marketing,* April 1986, pp. 7–17.

19. See William E. Souder, *Managing New Product Innovations* (Lexington, MA: D. C. Heath, 1987), Chapters 10 and 11; and William L. Shanklin and John K. Ryans, Jr., "Organizing for High-Tech Marketing," *Harvard Business Review,* November–December 1984, pp. 164–71.

20. See Benson P. Shapiro, "Can Marketing and Manufacturing Coexist?" *Harvard Business Review,* September–October 1977, pp. 104–14. Also see Robert W. Ruekert and Orville C. Walker, Jr., "Marketing's Interaction with Other Functional Units: A Conceptual Framework and Empirical Evidence," *Journal of Marketing,* January 1987, pp. 1–19.

21. Edward E. Messikomer, "Du Pont's 'Marketing Community,'" *Business Marketing,* October 1987, pp. 90–94.

22. For more on developing and implementing marketing plans, see H. W. Goetsch, *Developing, Implementing and Managing an Effective Marketing Plan* (Chicago: American Marketing Association; Lincolnwood, IL: NTC Business Books, 1993).

23. Thomas V. Bonoma, *The Marketing Edge: Making Strategies Work* (New York: Free Press, 1985). Much of this section is based on Bonoma's work.

24. See Alfred R. Oxenfeldt, "How to Use Market-Share Measurement," *Harvard Business Review,* January–February 1969, pp. 59–68.

25. There is a one-half chance that a successive observation will be higher or lower. Therefore, the probability of finding six successively higher values is given by $(1/2)^6 = 1/64$.

26. Alternatively, companies need to focus on the factors affecting *shareholder value.* The goal of marketing planning is to take the steps that will increase shareholder value. Shareholder value is the *present value* of the future income stream created by the company's present actions. *Rate-of-return analysis* usually focuses on only one year's results. See Alfred Rapport, *Creating Shareholder Value* (New York: Free Press, 1986), pp. 125–30.

27. For additional reading on financial analysis, see Peter L. Mullins, *Measuring Customer and Product Line Profitability* (Washington, DC: Distribution Research and Education Foundation, 1984).

28. See Robert S. Kaplan and David P. Norton, "Putting the Balanced Scorecard to Work," *Harvard Business Review,* September 1993, pp. 134–42.

29. The MAC Group, *Distribution: A Competitive Weapon* (Cambridge, MA: MAC Group, 1985), p. 20.

30. See Robin Cooper and Robert S. Kaplan, "Profit Priorities from Activity-Based Costing," *Harvard Business Review,* May–June 1991, pp. 130–35.

31. Sam R. Goodman, *Increasing Corporate Profitability* (New York: Ronald Press, 1982), Chapter 1. Also see Bernard J. Jaworski,

Vlasis Stathakopoulos, and H. Shanker Krishnan, "Control Combinations in Marketing: Conceptual Framework and Empirical Evidence," *Journal of Marketing,* January 1993, pp. 57–69.

32. See Peter M. Senge, *The Fifth Discipline: The Art and Practice of the Learning Organization* (New York: Doubleday/Currency, 1990), Chapter 7.

33. For further discussion of this instrument, see Philip Kotler, "From Sales Obsession to Marketing Effectiveness," *Harvard Business Review,* November–December 1977, pp. 67–75.

34. See Philip Kotler, William Gregor, and William Rodgers, "The Marketing Audit Comes of Age," *Sloan Management Review,* Winter 1989, pp. 49–62.

35. However, useful checklists for a marketing self-audit can be found in Aubrey Wilson, *Aubrey Wilson's Marketing Audit Checklists* (London: McGraw-Hill, 1982); and Mike Wilson, *The Management of Marketing* (Westmead, England: Gower Publishing, 1980). Also a marketing audit software program is described in Ben M. Enis and Stephen J. Garfein, "The Computer-Driven Marketing Audit," *Journal of Management Inquiry,* December 1992, pp. 306–18.

36. Kotler, Gregor, and Rodgers, "The Marketing Audit."

37. Howard R. Bowen, *Social Responsibilities of the Businessman* (New York: Harper & Row, 1953), p. 215. "Invidious consumption" is ostentatious consumption that produces envy in others.

Organizing, Implementing, Evaluating, and Controlling Marketing Activities

THE THEORY OF EFFECTIVE MARKETING-RESOURCE ALLOCATION

Marketing managers at a growing number of companies are using computers to develop and estimate the revenue and cost of different marketing strategies. These computer programs utilize equations that describe how sales and profits respond to different marketing-mix expenditures. This appendix illustrates the types of equations and other tools used to determine the profitability of marketing expenditures.

THE PROFIT EQUATION

Every marketing-mix strategy will lead to a certain level of profit. The profit can be estimated through a profit equation. A product's profits (Z) by definition are equal to the product's revenue (R) minus its costs (C):

$$Z = R - C \tag{A1-1}$$

Revenue is equal to the product's net price (P') times its unit sales (Q):

$$R = P'Q \tag{A1-2}$$

The product's net price (P') is equal to its list price (P) minus any allowance per unit (k) representing freight allowances, commissions, and discounts:

$$P' = P - k \tag{A1-3}$$

The product's total costs can be conveniently classified into unit variable nonmarketing costs (c), fixed costs (F), and marketing costs (M):

$$C = cQ + F + M \tag{A1-4}$$

Substituting equations (A1-2), (A1-3), and (A1-4) into (A1-1) and simplifying,

$$Z = Q[(P - k) - c] - F - M \tag{A1-5}$$

where:

Z = total profits
P = list price
k = allowance per unit (such as freight allowances, commissions, discounts)
c = production and distribution variable cost (such as labor costs, delivery costs)
Q = number of units sold
F = fixed costs (such as salaries, rent, electricity)
M = discretionary marketing costs (such as advertising, sales promotion)

The expression $[(P - k) - c]$ is *the gross contribution margin per unit*—the amount the company realizes on the average unit after deducting allowances and the variable costs of producing and distributing the average unit. The expression $Q[(P - k) - c]$ is the *gross contribution margin*—the net revenue available to cover the fixed costs, profits, and discretionary marketing expenditures.

THE SALES EQUATION

To use the profit equation for planning purposes, the product manager needs to develop a model of the variables affecting sales volume (Q). The relation of sales volume to these variables is specified in a sales equation:

$$Q = f(X_1, X_2 \ldots, X_n, Y_1, Y_2, \ldots, Y_m) \tag{A1-6}$$

where:

$(X_1, X_2, \ldots, X_n)$ = sales variables under the firm's control
$(Y_1, Y_2, \ldots, Y_m)$ = sales variables not under the firm's control

Y variables include the size of the target market, its income, competitors' prices, and so on. As these variables change, so does the market's buying rate. The manager has no influence over the Y variables but needs to estimate them for forecasting purposes. We will assume that the manager has estimated Y variables and their effect on sales volume, which is conveyed by

$$Q = f(X_1, X_2, \ldots, X_n \mid Y_1, Y_2, \ldots, Y_m) \tag{A1-7}$$

This equation says that sales volume is a function of the X variables, for given levels of the Y variables.

The X variables are the variables that the manager can set to influence the sales level. The X variables include the list price (P), allowances (k), variable cost (c) (to the extent that high variable costs reflect improved product quality, delivery time, and customer service), and marketing expenditures (M). Thus sales, as a function of the manager's controllable variables, are described by

$$Q = f(P, k, c, M) \tag{A1-8}$$

We can make one additional refinement. The marketing budget, M, can be spent in several ways, such as advertising (A), sales promotion (S), sales force (D), and marketing research (R).

The sales equation is now

$$Q = f(P, k, c, A, S, D, R) \tag{A1-9}$$

where the elements in the parentheses represent the *marketing mix*.

FORECASTING SALES-RESPONSE FUNCTIONS

Suppose the manager wants to find a marketing mix that will maximize profits in the coming year. This requires having an idea of how each element in the marketing mix will affect sales. The term *sales-response function* is used to describe the relationship between sales volume and a particular element of the marketing mix. Specifically:

❖ The **SALES-RESPONSE FUNCTION** forecasts the likely sales volume during a specified time period associated with different possible levels of a marketing-mix element, holding constant the other marketing-mix elements.

It should not be thought of as describing a relationship over time between the two variables. To the extent that managers have a good intuition for the relevant sales-response functions, they are in a position to formulate more effective marketing plans.

What are the possible shapes of sales-response functions? Figure A1-1 shows several possibilities. Figure A1-1(a) shows the well-known relationship between price and sales volume known as the *law of demand*. The relationship states that, other things being equal, more sales will occur at lower prices. The illustration shows a curvilinear relationship, although a linear relationship is also possible.

Figure A1-1(b) shows four possible functional relationships between sales volume and marketing expenditures. Marketing expenditure function (*A*) is the least plausible: It states that sales volume is not affected by the level of marketing expenditures. Function (*A*) would mean that the number of customers and their purchasing rates are not affected by sales calls, advertising, sales promotion, or marketing research. Marketing expenditure function (*B*) states that sales volume grows linearly with marketing expenditures. In the illustration, the *y*-intercept (the point at which the function crosses the *y*-axis) is 0, but the *y*-intercept would be above zero if some sales take place even in the absence of marketing expenditures.

Marketing expenditure function (*C*) is a concave function showing sales volume increasing at a decreasing rate. It is a plausible description of sales response to increases in sales force size. The rationale is as follows: If a field sales force consisted of one sales representative, that representative would call on the best

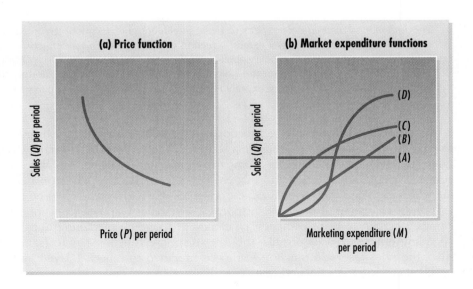

(a) Price function

Sales (*Q*) per period

Price (*P*) per period

(b) Market expenditure functions

Sales (*Q*) per period

(*D*)
(*C*)
(*B*)
(*A*)

Marketing expenditure (*M*) per period

FIGURE A1-1
Sales-Response Functions

The Theory of Effective Marketing-Resource Allocation

prospects, and the marginal rate of sales response (that is, the rate at which sales increase with each additional sales representative) would be highest. A second sales rep would call on the next best prospects, and the marginal rate of sales response would be somewhat less. Successively hired sales reps would call on successively less responsive prospects, resulting in a diminishing rate of sales increase.

Marketing expenditure function (D) is an **S**-shaped function showing sales volume initially increasing at an increasing rate and then increasing at a decreasing rate. It is a plausible description of sales response to increasing levels of advertising expenditure. The rationale is as follows: Small advertising budgets do not buy enough advertising to create more than minimal brand awareness. Larger budgets can produce high brand awareness, interest, and preference, all of which might lead to increased purchase response. Very large budgets, however, may not produce much additional response because the target market becomes highly familiar with the brand.

The relation of eventually diminishing returns to increases in marketing expenditures is plausible for the following reasons. First, there is an upper limit to the total potential demand for any particular product. The easier sales prospects buy almost immediately, leaving behind the more recalcitrant sales prospects. As the upper limit is approached, it becomes increasingly expensive to attract the remaining buyers. Second, as a company steps up its marketing effort, its competitors are likely to do the same, with the net result that each company experiences increasing sales resistance. Third, if sales were to increase at an increasing rate as marketing expenditures increase, *natural monopolies* would result. A single firm would take over each industry. Yet we do not see this happening.

How can marketing managers estimate the sales-response functions that apply to their business? Three methods are available:

♦ The *statistical method* asks the manager to gather data on past sales and levels of marketing-mix variables and then estimate the sales-response functions through statistical techniques. Several researchers have used this method with varying degrees of success, depending on the quantity and quality of available data and the stability of the underlying relationships.[1]

♦ The *experimental method* calls for varying the marketing expenditure and mix levels in matched samples of geographical or other units and noting the resulting sales volume.[2] The experimental method produces the most reliable results but is not used extensively because of its complex requirements, high cost, and inordinate level of management resistance.

♦ The *judgmental method* asks experts to make intelligent guesses about the needed magnitudes. This method requires a careful selection of the experts and a defined procedure for gathering and combining their estimates, such as the Delphi method (see Chapter 4). The judgmental method is often the only feasible one and can be quite useful. We believe that using the estimates of experts is better than foregoing formal analysis of profit optimization.

In estimating sales-response functions, some cautions must be observed. The sales-response function assumes that other variables remain constant over the range of the function. Thus the company's price and competitors' prices are assumed to remain unchanged no matter what the company spends on marketing. Since this assumption is unrealistic, the sales-response function has to be modified to reflect competitors' probable responses. The sales-response function also assumes a certain level of company efficiency in spending marketing dollars. If the spending efficiency rises or falls, the sales-response function has to be modified. Also, the sales-response function has to be modified to reflect delayed impacts of expenditures on sales beyond one year.[3]

The Theory of Effective
Marketing-Resource
Allocation

PROFIT OPTIMIZATION

Once the sales-response functions are estimated, how are they used in profit optimization? Here we will present a numerical example that makes use of two marketing-mix variables, advertising and sales promotion.

Jane Melody, a product manager, handles a small battery testing device that sells for $16. For some years, she has been using a low-price, low-promotion strategy. Last year she spent $10,000 on advertising and another $10,000 on sales promotion. Sales were 12,000 units and profits were $14,000. Her boss thinks more profits could be made on this item. Ms. Melody is anxious to find a strategy to increase profits.

Her first step is to visualize some alternative marketing-mix strategies. She imagines the eight strategies shown in the first four columns of Table A1-1 (the first strategy is the current one). These strategies were formed by assuming a high and a low level for each of three marketing variables and elaborating all the combinations ($2^3 = 8$).

Her next step is to estimate the likely sales that would be attained with each marketing mix. She feels that these estimates are unlikely to be found in historical data or through conducting experiments. She decides to ask the sales manager for his estimates, since he has shown an uncanny ability to be on target. He provides the sales estimates shown in the next-to-last column in Table A1-1.

The final step calls for determining which marketing mix maximizes profits, assuming the sales estimates are reliable. This step calls for using a profit equation and inserting the different marketing mixes into this equation to see which one maximizes profits.

Suppose fixed costs, F, are $38,000; unit variable costs, c, are $10; and the contemplated allowance off list price, k, is $0. The two components of M here are advertising (A) and promotion (S). Substituting these values into the profit equation (A1-5) gives:

$$Z = Q[(P - k) - c] - F - M$$
$$Z = Q[(P - 0) - 10] - 38,000 - A - S \tag{A1-10}$$

Thus profits (Z) are a function of the number of units sold (Q), chosen price (P), advertising budget (A), and sales-promotion budget (S). Marketing mix #5, calling for a price of $24, advertising of $10,000, and promotion of $10,000, yields the highest expected profits ($19,000).

Melody can take one more step. Some marketing mix not shown might yield a still higher profit. To check that possibility, she can create a sales equation that will fit the data shown in Table A1-1. The sales estimates in that table can be viewed as a sample from a larger universe of expert judgments concerning the

TABLE A1-1	MARKETING MIXES AND ESTIMATED SALES				
MARKETING MIX NO.	PRICE (P)	ADVERTISING (A)	PROMOTION (S)	UNIT SALES (Q)	PROFITS (Z)
1	$16	$10,000	$10,000	12,400	$16,400
2	16	10,000	50,000	18,500	13,000
3	16	50,000	10,000	15,100	− 7,400
4	16	50,000	50,000	22,600	− 2,400
5	24	10,000	10,000	5,500	19,000
6	24	10,000	50,000	8,200	16,800
7	24	50,000	10,000	6,700	− 4,200
8	24	50,000	50,000	10,000	2,000

The Theory of Effective
Marketing-Resource
Allocation

sales equation $Q = f(P, A, S)$. A plausible mathematical form for the sales equation is the multiple exponential:

$$Q = bP^p A^a S^s \qquad \text{(A1-11)}$$

where:

b = a scale factor
p, a, s = elasticity of price, advertising, and promotion, respectively

Using least-squares regression estimation (not shown), Melody finds the fitted sales equation to be

$$Q = 100,000 P^{-2} A^{1/8} S^{1/4} \qquad \text{(A1-12)}$$

This equation fits the sales estimates in Table A1-1 extremely well. Price has an elasticity of -2; that is, a 1% reduction in price, other things being equal, tends to increase unit sales by 2 percent. Advertising has an elasticity of 1/8, and promotion has an elasticity of 1/4. The coefficient 100,000 is a scale factor that translates the dollar magnitudes into sales-volume units.

Melody now substitutes this sales equation for Q in the profit equation (A1-10). Doing so yields, when simplified:

$$Z = 100,000 \, A^{1/8} S^{1/4} [P^{-1} - 10 P^{-2}] - 38,000 - A - S \qquad \text{(A1-13)}$$

Profits are shown to be strictly a function of the chosen marketing mix. Melody can insert any marketing mix (including those not shown in Table A1-1) and derive an estimate of profits. To find the profit-maximizing marketing mix, she applies standard calculus (not shown here). The optimal marketing mix (P, A, S) is ($20; $12,947; $25,894). Twice as much is spent on promotion as on advertising because its elasticity is twice as great. In this case, Melody would forecast a sales volume of 10,358 units and profits of $26,735. While other marketing mixes can produce higher sales, no other marketing mix can produce higher profits. Using this equation, Melody has solved not only the optimum marketing mix but also the optimum marketing budget ($A + S = \$38,841$).

The preceding analysis neglected to take into account effects between two or more marketing-mix variables. Here are some interaction effects to consider:

◆ Higher advertising expenditures reduce buyers' price sensitivity. Thus a company wishing to charge a higher price should spend more on advertising.

◆ Advertising expenditures have a greater sales impact on low-priced products than on high-priced products.

◆ Higher advertising expenditures reduce the total cost of selling. The advertising expenditures presell the customer, and sales representatives can concentrate their time on answering objections and closing the sale.

◆ Higher perceived product quality allows the company to charge a disproportionately higher price.

◆ Higher quality does not cost more to produce and often costs less than lower quality.

◆ Higher prices lead buyers to impute higher product quality.

◆ Tighter credit terms require greater selling and advertising effort to move the same volume of goods.

One final note on the limitations of the preceding analysis. The analysis assumed that the firm set its marketing mix with full knowledge of its' competitors planned marketing mixes. Some analysts prefer to recast the analysis in terms of explaining the company's market share, not sales. The company's market share would then be treated as a function of the company's price, advertising, sales promotion, and so on, relative to the competition. For example, if the company spent

The Theory of Effective
Marketing-Resource
Allocation

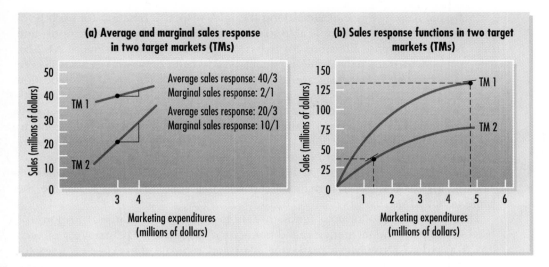

FIGURE A1-2
Sales-Reponse Functions in Two Target Markets (TMs)

20% of total industry advertising expenditures, it should normally enjoy a 20% market share, providing that its advertising is effective and other variables are equivalent. The other limitation in the analysis is that marketing competition should be viewed dynamically, not statically. Every company marketing move is likely to be met by competitive responses. Marketing is like a tennis game, with competitors responding to each stroke.

MARKETING-ALLOCATION OPTIMIZATION

How should a given marketing budget be allocated to the company's various target markets (TMs)? The TMs could be different sales territories, customer groups, or other market segments. Even with a given marketing budget and mix, it may be possible to increase sales and profits by shifting funds among different markets.

Most marketing managers allocate their marketing budgets to the various TMs on the basis of some percentage of actual or expected sales. Unfortunately, size rules for allocating funds lead to inefficient allocations because such rules confuse "average" and "marginal" sales response. Figure A1-2(a) illustrates the difference between the two and indicates that there is no reason to assume they are correlated. The two dots in the figure show current marketing expenditures and company sales in two TMs. The company spends $3 million on marketing in both TMs. Company sales are $40 million in TM 1 and $20 million in TM 2. The average sales response to a dollar of marketing effort is thus greater in TM 1 than in TM 2; it is 40/3 as opposed to 20/3, respectively. It might seem desirable to shift funds from TM 2 to TM 1, where the average response is greater. Yet the real issue is one of the *marginal* response—the *additional* sales generated by *additional* spending over the current level. The marginal response is represented by the *slope* of the sales function through the points. TM 2 has a higher slope than TM 1. The respective slopes show that another $1 million in marketing expenditure would produce a $10 million sales increase in TM 2 and only a $2 million sales increase in TM 1. Clearly, marginal response, not average response, should guide the allocation of marketing funds.

Marginal response is indicated along the sales-response function for each territory. Assume that a company is able to estimate TM sales-response functions, and that the sales-response functions for two TMs are those shown in Figure A1-2(b). The company wishes to allocate a budget of B dollars between the two TMs to maximize profits. When costs are identical for the two TMs, then the allocation that will maximize profits is the one that will maximize sales. The funds are optimally allocated when they exhaust the budget and the marginal sales response is the same in both TMs. Geometrically, this means that the slopes of the tangents to the two sales-response functions at the optimal allocations will be equal. Figure A1-2(b) shows that a budget of $6 million would be allocated in the amounts of approximately $4.6 million to TM 1 and $1.4 million to TM 2 to produce maximum sales of approximately $180 million. The marginal sales response would be the same in both TMs.

The principle of allocating funds to TMs to equalize the marginal response is used in the planning technique called *zero-based budgeting*.[4] The manager of each TM is asked to formulate a marketing plan and estimate the expected sales for (say) three levels of marketing expenditure, such as 30% below the normal level, the normal level, and 30% above the normal level. An example is shown in Table A1-2, outlining what a marketing manager would do with each budget level and the manager's estimate of the resulting sales volume. Then higher management reviews this response function against those of other product managers and gives serious consideration to shifting funds from TMs with low marginal responses to TMs with higher marginal responses.

Measuring sales-response functions can lead to substantial shifts in company marketing strategy. A major oil company had located its service stations in every large U.S. city.[5] In many markets, it operated only a small percentage of the total stations. Company management began to question this broad location strategy. It decided to estimate how the company's market share in each city varied with its percentage share of marketing expenditures in each city (as measured by the share of outlets). A curve was fitted showing the share of outlets and share of markets in different cities. The resulting curve was **S** shaped (see Figure A1-3 on the next page). This curve showed that having a low percentage of stations in a city yielded an even lower percentage of market volume. The practical implication was clear: The company should either withdraw from its weak markets or build them up to, say, 15% of the competitive outlets (the point at which share of outlets = share of

TABLE A1-2	ILLUSTRATION OF ZERO-BASED MARKETING BUDGETING	
BUDGET (M)	**MARKETING PLAN**	**SALES FORECAST (Q)**
$1,400,000	Maintain sales and market share in the short term by concentrating sales effort on largest chain stores, advertising only on TV, sponsoring two promotions a year, and carrying on only limited marketing research.	60,000 units
$2,000,000	Implement a coordinated effort to expand market share by contracting 80% of all retailers, adding magazine advertising, adding point-of-purchase displays, and sponsoring three promotions during the year.	70,000 units
$2,600,000	Seek to expand market size and share by adding two new product sizes, enlarging the sales force, increasing market research, and expanding the advertising budget.	90,000 units

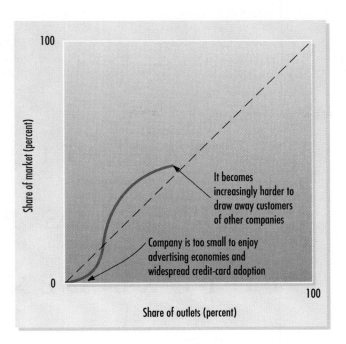

FIGURE A1-3
**Share of Market as a
Function of Share of
Outlets**

It becomes
increasingly harder to
draw away customers
of other companies

Company is too small to enjoy
advertising economies and
widespread credit-card adoption

Share of market (percent)

Share of outlets (percent)

market). Instead of establishing a few outlets in each of many cities, the oil company should establish a large number of outlets in a smaller number of cities. In fact, most major oil companies today are concentrating geographically and trying to be the regional leader.

NOTES

1. For references to empirical studies using fitted sales-response functions, see Dominique M. Hanssens, Leonard J. Parsons, and Randall L. Schultz, *Market Response Models: Econometric and Time Series Analysis* (Boston: Kluwer Academic Publishers, 1990), Chapter 6.
2. See Russell Ackoff and James R. Emshoff, "Advertising Research at Anheuser-Busch," *Sloan Management Review,* Winter 1975, pp. 1–15.
3. See Gary L. Lilien, Philip Kotler and K. Sridhar Moorthy, *Marketing Models* (Englewood Cliffs, NJ: Prentice Hall, 1992).
4. See Paul J. Stonich, *Zero-Base Planning and Budgeting: Improved Cost Control and Resource Allocation* (Homewood, IL: Dow Jones-Irwin, 1977).
5. See John J. Cardwell, "Marketing and Management Science—A Marriage on the Rocks?" *California Management Review,* Summer 1968, pp. 3–12.

APPENDIX

2

STATISTICAL METHODS FOR FUTURE DEMAND PROJECTION

The key to organizational survival and growth is the firm's ability to adapt its strategies to a rapidly changing environment. This puts a large burden on management to anticipate future events correctly. The damage can be enormous when a mistake is made. For example, Montgomery Ward lost its leadership in the department store field after World War II because its chairman, Sewell Avery, bet on a stagnant economy while its major competitor, Sears, bet on an expanding economy.

How do firms develop macroenvironmental forecasts? Large firms have planning departments that develop long-run forecasts of key environmental factors affecting their markets. General Electric, for example, has a forecasting staff who study worldwide forces that affect its operations. GE makes its forecasts available to GE divisions and also sells certain forecasts to other firms.

The following is a list of some statistical methodologies for producing macroenvironmental forecasts.

EXPERT OPINION. Knowledgeable people are selected and asked to assign importance and probability ratings to possible future developments. The most refined version, the Delphi method (see Chapter 4), puts experts through several rounds of event assessment, in which they keep refining their assumptions and judgments.

TREND EXTRAPOLATION. Researchers fit best-fitting curves (linear, quadratic, or S-shaped growth curves) through past time series and extrapolate from these curves. This method can be very unreliable in that new developments can completely alter future directions.

TREND CORRELATION. Researchers correlate various time series in the hope of identifying leading and lagging indicators that can be used for forecasting. The

National Bureau of Economic Research has identified 12 of the best leading economic indicators and publishes their values monthly in the *Survey of Current Business*.

ECONOMETRIC MODELING. Researchers build sets of equations that describe the underlying economic system. The coefficients in the equations are fitted statistically. Econometric models containing more than 300 equations, for example, are used to forecast changes in the U.S. economy.

CROSS-IMPACT ANALYSIS. Researchers identify a set of key trends (those high in importance and/or probability). The question is then put: "If event A occurs, what will be its impact on other trends?" The results are then used to build sets of "domino chains," with one event triggering others.

MULTIPLE SCENARIOS. Researchers build pictures of alternative futures, each internally consistent and having a certain probability of occurring. The major purpose of the scenarios is to stimulate management to think about and plan for contingencies.

DEMAND/HAZARD FORECASTING. Researchers identify major events that would greatly affect the firm. Each event is rated for its convergence with several major trends taking place in society. It is also rated for its appeal to each major public in the society. The higher the event's convergence and appeal, the higher its probability of occurring. The highest-scoring events are then researched further.

TIME-SERIES ANALYSIS. Many firms prepare their forecasts on the basis of past sales. Past sales (Q) are broken down into four major components.

- The first component, *trend* (T), is the result of basic developments in population, capital formation, and technology. The trend is found by fitting a straight or curved line through past sales.
- The second component, *cycle* (C), captures the up-and-down movements in sales. Many sales are affected by periodic swings in general economic activity. The cyclical component can be useful in intermediate-range forecasting.
- The third component, *season* (S), refers to a consistent pattern of sales movements within the year. The term "season" broadly describes any recurrent hourly, weekly, monthly, or quarterly sales pattern. The seasonal component may be related to weather factors, holidays, and trade customs. The seasonal pattern provides a norm for forecasting short-range sales.
- The fourth component, *erratic events* (E), includes strikes, blizzards, fads, riots, fires, war scares, and other unpredictable disturbances. Because erratic components are unpredictable, they should be removed from past data to discern the more normal behavior of sales.

After the past sales series, Q, is decomposed into the components, T, C, S, and E, these components are recombined to produce the sales forecast. Here is an example:

> An insurance company sold $12,000 in new ordinary life-insurance policies this year. It would like to predict next year's December sales. The long-term trend shows a 5% sales growth rate per year. This suggests sales next year of $12,600 (= $12,000 × 1.05). However, a business recession is expected next year and will probably result in total sales achieving only 90% of the expected trend-adjusted sales. Sales next year will more likely be $11,340 (= $12,600 × 0.90). If sales were the same each month, monthly sales would be $945 (= $11,340/12). However, December is an above-average month for insurance-policy sales, with a seasonal index standing at 1.2. Therefore December sales may be as high as $1,134 (= $945 × 1.2). No erratic events, such as strikes or new in-

surance regulations, are expected. Therefore the best estimate of the number of new policy sales next December is $1,134.

For a company that has hundreds of items in its product line and wants to produce efficient and economical short-run forecasts, a time-series technique called *exponential smoothing* is available. In its simplest form, exponential smoothing requires only three pieces of information: this period's actual sales, Q_t; this period's smoothed sales, $\overline{Q}_t$; and a smoothing parameter, α. The sales forecast for next period's sales is given by

$$\overline{Q}_{t+1} = \alpha Q_t + (1 - \alpha) \overline{Q}_t \qquad \text{(A2-1)}$$

where:

$\overline{Q}_{t+1}$ = sales forecast for next period
α = the smoothing constant, where α is between 0 and 1
Q_t = current sales in period t
$\overline{Q}_t$ = smoothed sales in period t

Suppose the smoothing constant is 0.4, current sales are $50,000, and smoothed sales are $40,000. Then the sales forecast is

$$\overline{Q}_{t+1} = 0.4 (\$50,000) + 0.6 (\$40,000) = \$44,000$$

In this method, the sales forecast will always be between current sales and smoothed sales. The relative influence of current and smoothed sales depends on the smoothing constant, here 0.4. Thus the sales forecast "tracks" actual sales. The method can be refined to reflect seasonal and trend factors by adding two more constants, one to represent season and one to represent trend.[1]

STATISTICAL-DEMAND ANALYSIS. Time-series analysis treats past and future sales as a function of time rather than a function of any real demand factors. Yet numerous real factors affect the sales of any product. *Statistical-demand analysis* is a set of statistical procedures designed to discover the most important real factors affecting sales and their relative influence.

Statistical-demand analysis consists of expressing sales (Q) as a variable that is dependent on a number of independent demand variables ($X_1, X_2, \ldots, X_n$). That is:

$$Q = f(X_1, X_2, \ldots, X_n)$$

The independent variables most commonly analyzed are price, income, population, and promotion. Using multiple-regression analysis, various equation forms can be statistically fitted to the data in search of the best predicting variables and equation.

For example, Jain and Vilcassim found that the following demand equation explained well the market share of brand 1 in a three-brand market of instant decaffeinated freeze-dried coffee:[2]

$$MS_1 = .76 - 1.27P_1 + .59P_2 + 34P_3 = .14A_1 - .03A_2 = .03A_3$$

where:

MS_1 = weekly market share of brand 1
P_i = weekly price of brand i
A_i = a dummy variable (0 or 1) depending on whether brand i was featured in newspaper advertising that week

Note that brand 1's market share will be negatively affected if its price rises and positively affected if it advertises that week. Furthermore, Brand 1's market share will rise if brands 2 and 3 raise their prices. Finally, Brand 1's market share will fall if Brand 2 and/or 3 place ads that week. All of these conclusions are consistent with normal theory of how a brand's market share will be affected by its own and competitors' ads.

Computers have rendered statistical-demand analysis increasingly easy to perform. The user, however, should be aware of several difficulties that might diminish the validity or usefulness of a statistical-demand equation: too few observations, too much correlation among the independent variables, violation of normal curve assumptions, two-way causation, and emergence of new variables not accounted for.

NOTES

1. See S. Makridakis and S. C. Wheelwright, *Forecasting Methods for Management,* 5th ed. (New York: John Wiley, 1989). Also see George Kress and John Snyder, *Forecasting and Market Analysis Techniques: A Practical Approach* (Westport, CT: Quorum Books, 1994).

2. Dipak C. Jain and Naufel J. Vilcassim, "Testing Functional Forms of Market Share Models Using the Box-Cox Transformation and the Lagrange Multiplier Approach," *International Journal of Research in Marketing,* No.6 (1989), 95–107, here pp. 101–2.

PHOTO/AD CREDITS

Chapter 1 **6** Adapted from Alistair Ping, "Social Conscience for Sales," *Marketing,* September 1993, pp. 22, 23–24. Reprinted with permission of the American Marketing Association.

Chapter 2 **42** Courtesy of Unisys Corp. **59** Courtesy of Hewlett Packard Company.

Chapter 3 **104** Courtesy of Lands' End. **105** Courtesy A. T. Cross Company.

Chapter 4 **119** Bob Daemmrich, The Image Works.

Chapter 5 **151** *Brandweek,* October 31, 1994. **155** Courtesy of Sears Roebuck & Company and Mendoza, Dillon & Asociados, Inc. **160** Paul Howell, Gamma-Liaison, Inc./Dan Lamont, Matrix International. **168** NordicTrack, Inc.

Chapter 6 **189** Courtesy of the National Pork Producers Council.

Chapter 7 **207** SPS Technologies, Inc. **224** Used by permission of the American Iron and Steel Institute.

Chapter 9 **253** Louis Psihoyos/Matrix International.

Chapter 10 **293** Rahul Jacob, "Corporate Reputations," *Fortune,* March 6, 1995. The Intel Inside Logo and Pentium are registered trademarks of Intel Corporation. Reprinted with permission. Reprinted with permission of 3M. Courtesy of Hewlett Packard. Courtesy of Coca-Cola. Courtesy of Microsoft. Courtesy of Rubbermaid. UPS and UPS in shield design are registered trademarks of United Parcel Service of America, Inc. Used by permission. Courtesy of Proctor & Gamble. Motorola, Inc. Reprinted with permission of Motorola. Courtesy of The Home Depot. **304** Michael Dwyer, Stock Boston.

Chapter 12 **369** Reprinted by permission of The Andrew Jergens Company.

Chapter 13 **380** Courtesy of AT&T Archives. **394** Rob Doyle, *Business Week,* June 26, 1995.

Chapter 14 **415** Wayne Simpson, *Brandweek,* March 27, 1995, p. 32.

Chapter 15 **453** Sara Lee Company. **462** © Celestial Seasonings, Inc., Boulder, Colorado.

Chapter 18 **560** Advertisement reprinted with the permission of Pioneer Electronics (USA) Inc.

Chapter 19 **578** Courtesy of Maytag and the EFFIE Awards. **593** Courtesy of Roadway Package System. **601** Hunt MidWest Enterprises, Inc.

Chapter 20 **613** Courtesy of U.S. West and the EFFIE Awards. **618** Courtesy of British Airways.

Chapter 21 **680** Courtesy of Yoplait and the EFFIE Awards. Courtesy of Waterford and the EFFIE Awards.

Chapter 22 **688** David Graham.

Chapter 23 **727** Courtesy of Dun & Bradstreet Information Services. **734–735** Courtesy of Lands' End. **741** Courtesy of National Seminars Group.

AUTHOR INDEX

E

Economist, The, 294*n*13, 661*n*45, 662*n*47, 750*n*9
Eiglier, P., 466*n*2, 472
Eisman, R., 175
El-Ansary, A. I., 530*n*2, 531*n*4, 548*n*24, 556*n*33, 581*n*19
Eldridge, J. D., 565, 569
Eliashberg, J., 128*n*31
Elliott, G. R., 27*n*33
Elliott, S., 181*n*11
Ellis, J. E., 219
Embley, L. L., 28*n*35
Emshoff, J. R., A-3*n*2
Engel, J. F., 192*n*27, 612*n*12
Enis, B. M., 433*n*5, 694*n*10, 777*n*35
Erevelles, S., 615*n*15
Erickson, G. M., 509*n*18
Erickson, T. J., 65*n*2
Erramilli, M. K., 535*n*9
Ettore, B., 487
Evans, F. B., 260*n*23
Evans, P., 84*n*23
Evirgen, M., 127*n*24a

F

Fahey, A., 376*n*4
Fair, R. C., 205*n*3
Falvey, J., 699
Farhi, P., 647*n*20
Faris, C. W., 206*n*7, 214*n*22, 216
Farnham, 57
Farquhar, P. H., 444*n*11
Farrell, C., 502*n*10, 514*n*26
Farris, M. T., II, 534*n*6
Farris, P. W., 509*n*20, 638*n*2, 663*n*53, 667*n*56
Fawcett, A. E., 140*n*38
Feather, F., 259*n*19, 577*n*11, 585*n*23
Fefer, M. D., 271*n*41
Feinberg, F. M., 656*n*31
Feinstein, S., 123*n*18
Feldman, D., 187*n*19
Feldman, L. P., 360*n*30
Ferrero, M. J., 66*n*5
Field, M., 316
Fierman, J., 688*n*4
Finkbeiner, C., 268*n*35
Firnstahl, T. W., 482*n*25
Fishbein, M., 195*n*31, 196*n*35
Fisher, C., 407, 472*n*8
Fisher, R., 709*n*37
Fishman, A., 719*n*2
Fiske, J., 607*n*6
Fitzgerald, K., 448
Fitzgerald, M., 212*n*18
Flax, S., 240*n*13
Flynn, L. R., 261–62*n*25
Fogg, J. M., 565
Forbes, C., 219
Ford, H., 315, 377*n*6

Ford, J. B., 177*n*5
Ford, N. M., 700*n*24
Fornell, C., 352*n*15
Forrester, J. W., 654*n*28, 657*n*32
Forsyth, J. N., 565
Fortune, 67*n*9, 331*n*35, 501*n*9
Foster, D., 390
Fox, A., 657–58*n*33
Fox, K., 31*n*39
Fox, R. J., 487*n*35
Franchising Handbook, The, 570
Frankwick, G. L., 758*n*17
Freedman, R. J., 711*n*39
Freeling, A., 754*n*11
Freeman, C., 612, 626*n*33
Freeman, L., 156*n*13
French, J. R. P., 545*n*18
Freund, J. C., 708*n*34
Frey, A. W., 92*n*33, 621*n*27, 621*n*28
Frey, J. B., 352-53*n*22
Friars, D. M., 566
Friestad, M., 196*n*33, 607*n*5
Fryzell, D. A., 241
Fuchsberg, G., 70*n*15
Fuld, L. M., 229*n*3, 241*n*14

G

Gaiter, D. J., 273*n*46
Galagan, P., 301*n*25
Gale, B. T., 55*n*20, 382*n*11, 382*n*12, 484, 629
Gannes, S., 396*n*32
Ganzach, Y., 661*n*44
Gardner, B., 271*n*40
Garfein, S. J., 777*n*35
Garfield, B., 645*n*17
Garfield, C., 694*n*11
Garner, J., 646
Garrett, E. M., 66–67*n*6
Garvin, D. A., 284*n*3
Gaskin, S. P., 378
Gates, B., 673
Gatignon, H., 336–37*n*45, 352–53
Gentile, A., 313
Gentile, J., 313
George, M., 754*n*11
Ghoshal, S., 424*n*17
Gilly, M. C., 198*n*42
Glazer, R., 295*n*16
Glines, D., 66*n*4
Goerne, C., 161*n*18
Goetsch, H. W., 763*n*22
Golanty, J., 324*n*24
Golask, L., 652–53
Golder, P. N., 352*n*20
Goldman, A., 348
Goldman, K., 612*n*11, 648*n*22
Goldsmith, R. E., 261–62*n*25
Goll, S. D., 152
Gomez-Mejia, L. R., 693*n*8
Gonik, J., 141*n*40
Gonring, M. P., 631

Goodman, J., 481*n*24
Goodman, S. R., 775*n*31
Goodstein, R. C., 581*n*16
Gordon, W. J. J., 315
Gould, P., 534–35*n*7
Greenbaum, T. L., 119*n*14
Greenberg, H. M., 694*n*14
Greene, W. E., 473*n*12
Greenfield, J., 28
Greenland, L., 645*n*18
Green, P. E., 109*n*1, 194*n*30, 195*n*31, 320*n*23
Gregor, W. R., 566, 777*n*31, 777*n*36
Greising, D., 478*n*22
Griffin, J., 48
Gronroos, C., 473*n*11, 473*n*13
Grossman, J., 349*n*10, 362*n*32
Grover, R., 295*n*15
Gubar, G., 180
Guinta, L. R., 319*n*22
Gummesson, E., 15*n*15
Gupta, A. K., 759*n*18
Gutman, J., 184*n*14

H

Hakansson, H., 12–13*n*13
Hakuta, K., 349
Haley, R. I., 261, 331*n*35, 331*n*36, 657–58*n*33
Hamel, G., 21–22*n*24, 66–67*n*, 745*n*1
Hamermesh, R. G., 382*n*13
Hammer, M., 66*n*3
Hammonds, K. H., 376*n*4
Hanan, M., 316*n*19, 468, 755*n*13
Han, J. Y., 444*n*11
Hansen, R. W., 198*n*42
Hanssens, D. M., 499*n*6, A-3*n*1
Hardle, B. G. S., 452*n*22, 454
Harkavay, M. D., 291*n*9
Harrell, S., 63*n*1
Harrigan, K. R., 232*n*5, 360*n*28
Harris, B. F., 446*n*14
Harris, J. E., 382*n*13
Harris, T. L., 671*n*67, 677
Hart, C. W. L., 478*n*21
Harte, S., 213*n*21
Hartley, J., 607*n*6
Hartley, W. D., 420*n*15
Harvey, M. G., 325*n*25
Haugtvedt, C. P., 615*n*15
Hauser, J., 319*n*22
Hauser, J. T., 378
Hayes, L. O., 52–53*n*15
Heany, D. F., 382*n*11, 382*n*12
Heckert, R., 763
Heide, J. B., 216*n*23, 541*n*14
Heil, O. P., 161*n*18
Helliker, K., 113*n*7
Helmer, O., 141*n*41

COMPANY/BRAND INDEX

SUBJECT INDEX

A

Access Russia, 241

Accountable marketing, meaning of, 49

Accounting, activity-based cost accounting, 501, 774

Achiever lifestyle, 182

A.C. Nielson Company, as data source, 118

Activities, interests, and opinions (AIO) classification, lifestyles, 182

Activity-based cost accounting, 501, 774

Actualizer lifestyle, 182

Adaptation, by market-follower, 394

Adapted marketing: international marketing, 413, 414–15; promotional aspects, 418–19

ADCAD, marketing decision support system (MDSS), 128

Administered vertical marketing systems, 550

Adoption: consumer-adoption process, 335–37; meaning of, 335

Advertising, 623; advertorials, 623; as attack by market challenger, 393; budget for, 639–40; in business markets, 626; celebrity endorsements, 646; characteristics of, 623; communication media in, 605; comparative advertising, 638; definition of, 604, 637; effectiveness, research on, 661; efficiency monitoring of, 775; global businesses, 614; and image differentiation, 293; infomercials, 623; informative advertising, 638; international, 418; major decisions in, 637–38; objectives of, 638–39; persuasive advertising, 638–39; and pricing, 509; reminder advertising, 639; on World Wide Web, 8. *See also* Marketing communications

Advertising agency, operation of, 643

Advertising media, 648–57; choosing media type, 650–53; cost-per-thousand criteria, 654; costs of, 651, 653, 654; geographic allocation issues, 656; macroscheduling problem,

654–55; media selection, 648–50; microscheduling problem, 655–56; new media, 651–53; reach/frequency/impact exposures, 649–50

Advertising message, 640–48; appeals in, 643, 644; copy strategy statement, 644; format of, 647; generation of, 641–42; inductive and deductive framework, 641; rational and emotional positioning, 644; selection of message, 642–43; social-responsibility review, 647–48; style of, 644–45; tone of, 645; words in, 645–47

Advertising research, 657–60; broadcast ad testing, 658; communication-effect research, 657–59; print ad testing, 658; sales-effect research, 659–60

Advertorials, nature of, 623

ADVISOR, 626

Advocate channels, of communication, 617

Advocates, customers as, 49

Affinity groups, 50

Affordable method, promotion budget, 621

African Americans, marketing to, 174–75

Aftermarket, definition of, 515

Age: and consumer behavior, 179; and demographic market segmentation, 258

Age mix: acronyms for age groups, 153; and marketing, 155; of population, 152–53

Agents: meaning of, 529; in wholesaling, 586–87

Airtruck, 597

Allowances: as sales promotion, 666; types of, 512

Alpha testing, 332

Alternatives, in buying decision process, 194–96

American Marketing Association Code of Ethics, 784

Annual call scheduling, by sales force, 697

Annual-plan control, 766–70; financial analysis, 768–70; as marketing control, 94; marketing

expense-to-sales analysis, 768; market share analysis, 766–68; sales analysis, 766; scorecard analysis, 770

"Annual Survey of Buying Power," 137

Antimerger Act, 162

Appeals, 612–13; in advertising message, 643, 644; emotional appeals, 612; moral appeals, 612–13; rational appeals, 612

Application positioning, meaning of, 300

Arbitron, 118

Area market potential, 135–38; calculation of, 135–38; computation of, 135–38

Area market specialists, 749

Areas of dominant influence (ADIs), for advertising, 656

Arranged interviews, 123

Aspirational groups, 177

Asset turnover, 770

Association tests, brand name testing, 451

At-home shopping channels, 730

Atmosphere: as communication channel, 619; and image differentiation, 293; of retail stores, 576

Attitudes, 188; attitude groups, types of, 263, 264; and behavioral market segmentation, 263–64; and buying decisions, 196; and consumer behavior, 188; definition of, 188

Attribute listing, idea-generation method, 313–14

Attribute positioning, meaning of, 299

Audience analysis, in marketing communications program, 607–10

Audit Bureau of Circulation, as data source, 118

Audits and Surveys, 118

Automated warehouses, 595

Automatic vending, characteristics of, 569

Automobile Information Disclosure Act, 162

Available market, 131

Average costs, meaning of, 500

B

Backfire effect, and research questionnaires, 120
Backward channels, marketing channels, 533–34
Backward integration, 79
Banking services: home banking, 539; online services, 536
Bank marketing, stages in, 30
Barter transactions, 11; nature of, 511
Basic marketing, meaning of, 49
Behavioral market segmentation, 260–64; and attitude, 263–64; benefit segmentation, 260–61; buyer-readiness stage, 263; and loyalty status, 262–63; occassion segmentation, 260; and user rate, 261–62; and user status, 261
Behavioral response, and marketing, 11–12
Beliefs, 187–88; brand beliefs, 194–95; and consumer behavior, 187–88; definition of, 187; societal, 165–66
Believer lifestyle, 182
Benchmarking: in firm evaluation, 45; goals of, 238; to improve competitive performance, 237–38; steps in, 238
Benefit market segmentation, 260–61
Benefit positioning, meaning of, 299
BERI, 404
Beta testing, 332
Bird dogging, 137
Blanket contract, 220
Blanket family name, for brand, 450
Border changes, and global business, 404
Brainstorming: guidelines for, 315; idea-generation method, 314–15
Branchising, 750
BRANDAID, marketing decision support system (MDSS), 127
Brand beliefs, 194–95
Brand competition, 230
Brand concept, 318
Brand development, 445–57; brand extensions, 454–55; brand-name, 450–52; brand-repositioning decision, 457; brand-sponsor decision, 447; brand strategy, 452, 454–57; cobranding, 456–57; global branding, 453; initial decision, 445–47; line extensions, 452, 454, 455; manufacturer's versus store brands, 447–50; multibrands, 456; new brands, 456
Brand development index (BDI), 137–38

Brand dilution, 454–55
Brand-dominant hierarchy, 256
Branded variants, 452
Brand familiarity, 191
Brand image, 194
Brand ladder, 449
Brand name, 450–52; desirable qualities for, 451; licensing of, 447, 448; naming strategies, 450; testing of, 451
Brand parity, 449
Brand personalities, 260
Brand-positioning map, 318
Brand-repositioning decision, 457
Brands, 442–57; brand equity, measurement of, 444–45; branding, advantages of, 446–47; brand loyalty, 263, 444; brand meaning, levels of, 443–44; brand portfolios, 444; deep and shallow, 443; definition of, 432, 443; versus generics, 446; product life cycle of, 345, 346; weakened position of, 449; world's most valuable brands, 445
Break-even chart, 504
Breakeven volume, 504
Bridge generation, 155
British, lifestyle classification, 181
Brokers, in wholesaling, 586–87
Budget: for advertising, 639–40; promotion budget, 620–22; for sales promotion, 669; zero-based budgeting, A-7
Bulletin boards, online, 733
Bundling: product-bundling pricing, 516; unbundling and pricing, 518
Business analysis: cost and profit estimation, 324–25; for new products, 323–25; total sales estimation, 323–24
Business International's (BI) Country Assessment Service, 404
Business market, 91, 204–6; advertising in, 626; business segments, types of, 267–68; characteristics of, 205–6; industries in, 204; segmentation of, 266–68. *See also* Organizational buying
Business mission, example of, 80
Business Periodicals Index, 118
Business sector: bank marketing, 30; components of, 466; marketing management in, 31
Business services, types of, 435
Business strength, of strategic business units, 74–77
Business success, McKinsey 7-S framework, 87
Business units: monitoring areas for, 81. *See also* Strategic business units
Business unit strategic planning, 80–88; feedback/control, 87–88; goal formulation, 84; implemen-

tation of plan, 87; internal environment analysis, 82–84; opportunity and threat analysis, 81–82; program formulation, 87; strategic plan, goals of, 64; strategy formulation, 84–86
Buyback arrangement, nature of, 511
Buyer surveys, test market, 330
Buyflow maps, for business buying, 220, 221
Buygrid model, organizational buying process, 216
Buying behavior. *See* Consumer behavior
Buying center, business buying, 209, 210
Buying decision process, 192–99; evaluation of alternatives, 194–96; information search, 193; marketing methods in determination of, 193; postpurchase behavior, 197–98; problem recognition, 192–93; purchase decision, 196–97; stage model, 192
Buying-power index, 137
Buying process: business buying. *See* Organizational buying process; and buying roles, 189–90; complex buying behavior, 190–91; decision making in. *See* Buying decision process; dissonance-reducing buyer behavior, 191; habitual buying behavior, 191–92; variety-seeking buying behavior, 192
Buying service, characteristics of, 569
Bypass attack, by market challenger, 390
Byproduct pricing, 515–16

C

Cable television, as advertising media, 652
CALLPLAN, marketing decision support system (MDSS), 127
Call reports, 702
Cannibalized income, 325
Capital items, definition of, 435
Captive-product pricing, 515
Carryover effect, and research questionnaires, 120
Cash-and-carry wholesalers, role of, 586
Cash cows, of growth-share matrix, 74
Cash discounts, 511
Cashing out, as economic trend, 148
Cash rebates, meaning of, 512
Cash refund offers, as sales promotion, 664
Catalog marketing, nature of, 729
Catalog showrooms, characteristics of, 565
Category concept, 318

Caterpillar, as market leader, 386–87
Cause-related marketing, 28–29
Celebrity endorsements, advertising, 646
Census of Manufacturers, 136
Central business districts, characteristics of, 579
Centralized purchasing, business buying, 212
Chain-ratio method, total market potential computation, 135
Channel boundaries, 556
Channel captain, 553
Channel differentiation, nature of, 291
Cheaper-goods strategy, by market challenger, 392
Chernobyl, 405
Child Protection Act, 163
Children, as consumers, 178
China, multinationals in, 406
City version, of product in foreign country, 416
Clayton Act, 162
Clients, meaning of, 49
Cliques, and communication, 620
Cloning, by market-follower, 394
Closed-end questions, 120
Club marketing programs, 50–51; affinity groups, 50; examples of, 50–51
Cluster analysis, in marketing decision support system (MDSS), 128
Clustered preferences, in market, 255
Cobranding, 456–57; forms of, 456
Cocooning, as economic trend, 148
Coercive power, definition of, 544
Combination stores, characteristics of, 565
Commercialization of new products, 332–35; critical path scheduling, 334–35; geographic factors, 333–34; introductory market strategy, 334–35; target-market prospects, 334; timing factors, 333
Commission merchants, role of, 587
Committees: idea committee, 315; marketing information system (MIS) committee, 112; new-product committees, 311; new-product departments, 311; new-product venture teams, 311
Common carrier, 597
Common costs: nontraceable, 774; traceable, 773
Communication channels, 616–20; nonpersonal channels, 619–20; personal channels, 616–19
Communication-effect research, in advertising, 657–59
Communication process, 605–7; communication channels in, 616–20; effective communication, elements of, 607; elements of, 605–6; non-receptive audience,

reasons for, 606. *See also* Marketing communications
Community shopping centers, characteristics of, 579
Companies, 8; networking in, 745–46; organization of, 745–46
Company demand: definition of, 133; meaning of, 133–34
Company sales forecast, 134
Company sales potential, 134
Company trade name, for brand, 450
Comparative advertising, nature of, 638–39
Compensation deal, nature of, 511
Competition: and benchmarking, 237–38; brand competition, 230; capabilities-based competition, 84; competitive positions of firms, 373; competitor-centered company, 244; competitor mind-set, types of, 239; examining for market research, 114; form competition, 230; generic competition, 230; in global economy, 232–33; ideas for new products from, 313; industry competition, 230; industry concept of, 230–33; market concept of, 233; and pricing, 502, 520–22; in retailing, 550–51, 567, 580, 582
Competition analysis: assessment of competitor reaction patterns, 238–40; assessment of competitor strengths/weaknesses, 236–37; determination of competitor objectives, 235–36; identification of competition, 229–32; market research areas, 242; strategic group identification, 233–35
Competitive advantage: meaning of, 53–54; and positioning, 300–301
Competitive cycle: in product life cycle, 353–54; stages of, 353–54
Competitive differentiation, of service businesses, 474–76
Competitive intelligence system, 240–44; close versus distant competitors, 243; and customer value analysis, 241–43; good versus bad competitors, 243–44; steps in system design, 240; strong versus weak competitors, 243
Competitive-parity method, promotion budget, 621–22
Competitive scopes, in mission statement, 69–70
Competitive situation, in marketing plan, 97
Competitor-centered company, nature of, 244
Competitor positioning, meaning of, 300
Complaints. *See* Customer complaints
Complex buying behavior, nature of, 190–91

Component cobranding, 456
Component materials, meaning of, 434
Component parts, meaning of, 434
Component-value pricing, 506
Computer-aided design (CAD), and new product development, 327
Computer-aided manufacturing (CAM), and new product development, 327
Concentric diversification strategy, 79
Concept development. *See* Product concept development
Concurrent new-product development, 308–9
Conditions of sales, meaning of, 541
Conflict, and marketing channels, 553–57
Conformance quality, 55; definition of, 285; product differentiation by, 285
Conglomerate diversification strategy, 79
Congruity, and credibility, 616
Conjoint analysis: concept testing, 320–22; in marketing decision support system (MDSS), 128
Consumer-adoption process, 335–37; approaches to, 335; influencing factors, 336–37; stages in, 335–36
Consumer behavior: and age, 179; and beliefs/attitudes, 187–88; and economic circumstances, 179–80; and family, 177–79; and learning, 186–87; and life-cycle stage, 179, 180; and lifestyle, 180–81; and motivation, 181, 184–85; and occupation, 179; and perception, 185–86; and personality, 181; and reference groups, 175, 177; and roles/statuses, 179; and self-concept, 181; and social class, 173–76; stimulus-response model, 171–72; study of, 171; and subculture, 173
Consumer cooperative, characteristics of, 570
Consumer goods, 433–34; promotion tools, 664–65; types of, 433–34
Consumer Goods Pricing Act, 163
Consumerist movement, 164
Consumer markets, 91
Consumer panels, test market, 330
Consumer preferences, measurement of, 328
Consumer Product Safety Act, 163
Consumers: business, types of, 268; categories of, 264; characteristics of, 8